ROUTLEDGE HANDBOOK OF JEWISH RITUAL AND PRACTICE

Ritual and practice are some of the most defining features of religion, linked with its central beliefs. Discussing the wide range of Jewish ritual and practice, this volume provides a contemporary guide to this significant aspect of religious life and experience.

Drawing on a wide range of disciplines, this volume describes not only what takes place, but the reasons behind this and the implications both the theory and practice have for our understanding of Judaism. Organized in terms of texts, periods, practices, languages and relationships with the other, the book includes accounts of prayer, food, history, synagogues and the various legal and ideological debates that exist within Judaism with the focus on how they influence practice. Coming at a time of renewed interest in the role of the body in religion, this book aims to bring the theoretical and scriptural issues which arise in this area of Jewish life and culture up to date.

This volume is aimed at students and researchers working in Jewish studies specifically, and religious studies in general. Designed to be helpful to those on courses in relevant areas, especially in the United States, this book includes substantial bibliographical material.

Oliver Leaman teaches at the University of Kentucky and his books include *Evil and Suffering in Jewish Philosophy* (1995); *History of Jewish Philosophy*, ed. D. Frank & O. Leaman (Routledge, 1996); *Moses Maimonides* (Routledge, 1997); *A Reader in Jewish Philosophy*, ed. D. Frank, O. Leaman & C. Manekin (Routledge, 2000); *Cambridge Companion to Medieval Jewish Philosophy*, ed. D. Frank & O. Leaman; *Lost in Translation: Essays in Islamic and Jewish Philosophy* (2004); *Jewish Thought: An Introduction* (Routledge, 2006); *Judaism: An Introduction* (2011). He is editor of the Routledge Jewish Studies Series.

ROUTLEDGE HANDBOOK OF JEWISH RITUAL AND PRACTICE

Edited by Oliver Leaman

ADVISORY BOARD

YULIA EGOROVA (UNIVERSITY OF DURHAM),
VANESSA OCHS (UNIVERSITY OF VIRGINIA)

LONDON AND NEW YORK

Cover image: © Getty Images

First published 2023
by Routledge
4 Park Square, Milton Park, Abingdon, Oxon OX14 4RN

and by Routledge
605 Third Avenue, New York, NY 10158

Routledge is an imprint of the Taylor & Francis Group, an informa business

© 2023 Oliver Leaman

The right of Oliver Leaman to be identified as the author of the editorial material, and of the authors for their individual chapters, has been asserted in accordance with sections 77 and 78 of the Copyright, Designs and Patents Act 1988.

All rights reserved. No part of this book may be reprinted or reproduced or utilised in any form or by any electronic, mechanical, or other means, now known or hereafter invented, including photocopying and recording, or in any information storage or retrieval system, without permission in writing from the publishers.

Trademark notice: Product or corporate names may be trademarks or registered trademarks, and are used only for identification and explanation without intent to infringe.

British Library Cataloguing-in-Publication Data
A catalogue record for this book is available from the British Library

Library of Congress Cataloging-in-Publication Data
A catalog record has been requested for this book

ISBN: 978-0-367-47012-8 (hbk)
ISBN: 978-1-032-27199-6 (pbk)
ISBN: 978-1-003-03282-3 (ebk)

DOI: 10.4324/9781003032823

Typeset in Bembo
by Newgen Publishing UK

For Max Moshe
טוֹבִים הַשְּׁנַיִם, מִן-הָאֶחָד
Ecclesiastes 4.9

CONTENTS

List of Figures	*xi*
Notes on Contributors	*xiii*
Acknowledgments	*xviii*
Introduction	*xix*

PART I
Texts   **1**

1   The Jewish Bible   3
     Oliver Leaman

2   Midrash   12
     Rachel S. Mikva

3   Talmud   25
     Gail Labovitz

4   Ambiguity and Notation: Jewish Law and Legal Pluralism   46
     Adam Seligman

PART II
Periods   **57**

5   Archaeology   59
     Benjamin D. Gordon

6	See and Sanctify: Ceremonies and Ceremonial Art in Medieval Ashkenaz and Italy *Shalom Sabar*	71
7	Visualizations of Ritual in Medieval Book Culture *Katrin Kogman-Appel*	93
8	Material Culture in the Jewish Medieval World of Islam: Books, Clothing and Houses *Miriam Frenkel*	125
9	The Ritual Turn in the Early Modern Period *Roni Weinstein*	137
10	Jewish Material Culture in the Modern Age *Jeffrey Shandler*	150

PART III
Groups   161

11	A Study of Two Traditions: Sephardi and Ashkenazi *Yamin Levy*	163
12	Karaite Judaism: An Introduction to its Theology and Practices *Shawn Lichaa*	179
13	The Modern Orthodox in America *Samuel Heilman*	193
14	Haskalah: Jewish Practice and Romantic Religion *Olga Litvak*	203
15	Ritual and Practice in Hasidism *Gadi Sagiv*	215
16	Conservative Judaism *David Golinkin*	229
17	Reform *Oliver Leaman*	248
18	Jewish Ritual and Social Justice in America *Eric Caplan*	257

19	The American Jewish Family *David C. Dollahite, Trevan G. Hatch, and Loren D. Marks*	275
20	A Jewish Family on TV: Reflections on Ritual *Oliver Leaman*	294

PART IV
Practices — **303**

21	Circumcision *Oliver Leaman*	305
22	Body Image and Jewish Rituals and Practices *Jonathan E. Handelzalts and Shulamit Geller*	314
23	Hair *Amy K. Milligan*	327
24	Clothes *Oliver Leaman*	335
25	Food *Maria Diemling*	345
26	Sanctuary in Time: Shabbat as the Soul of Modern Jewry and the Essence of "Doing" Judaism *Trevan G. Hatch and Loren D. Marks*	361
27	Sometimes God Sneaks Back In: Jewish Secular Rituals *Avner Dinur*	371
28	"For the Amen Meal, You Don't Have to Keep the Religious Duties": Amen Meals as a New Age Phenomenon *Rivka Neriya-Ben Shahar*	385
29	Models of Sexuality (and Marriage) in the Jewish Tradition *Michael J. Broyde*	400
30	Music and the Experience of Jewish Ritual and Practice *Gordon Dale*	414
31	The Theological Implications of the State of Israel *Vernon H. Kurtz*	427

32	Death and Dying *Simcha Paull Raphael*	436
33	Between Tradition and Innovation: Alternative Funeral Rites in Israel *Anna Prashizky*	446

PART V
Languages — 461

34	The Hebrew Language as a Source of Ritual and Practice *Stefan Reif*	463
35	The Role of Judezmo/Ladino in 'Ottoman Sephardic' Jewish Religious Ritual and Practice *David M. Bunis*	472
36	Yiddish *Jan Schwarz*	501

PART VI
Others — 509

37	Jewish Magical Practices *Ortal-Paz Saar*	511
38	Disabilities and Inclusion *Abigail Uhrman*	526
39	The Early Christian Reception of Jewish Rituals During the "Parting of the Ways" *Paul A. Hartog*	540
40	Christianity *Ruth Langer*	558
41	Samaritans *Reinhard Pummer*	568
42	Interfaith Rituals *Jonathan Romain*	579

Index — *590*

FIGURES

5.1	One of the roads identified as an ancient Jewish pilgrimage route near Maale Akrabim in southern Israel	60
5.2	An artistic reconstruction of the southwestern corner of Herod's Temple enclosure	61
5.3	A private domestic *mikveh* of the Early Roman period from a Jewish residential area of Sepphoris in the Galilee	63
5.4	An assemblage of stone vessels of the Early Roman period from the Jewish Quarter in Jerusalem	64
5.5	Three Galilean synagogues of late antiquity—Meiron, Baram, and Nabratein—as reconstructed based on the archaeological remains	66
5.6	A seven-branched marble menorah from the late antique synagogue at Maon in the Hebron hills	67
7.1	The Initiation of Sacrifice: mural from the Synagogue of Dura-Europos, Syria, 244–45, western wall	94
7.2	Prophet Reading from a Scroll: mural from the Synagogue of Dura-Europos, Syria, 244–45, western wall	95
7.3	Worms, Synagogue, 1175 (destroyed in 1938 and rebuilt in 1960), interior of the men's section	97
7.4	Albrecht Altdorfer, Entrance to the Synagogue of Regensburg, Regensburg 1519, etching	98
7.5	Beginning of the Liturgy	99
7.6	Synagogue Service	101
7.7	Binding of Isaac; Circumcision of Isaac	103
7.8	Circumcision	104
7.9	Shavuot	105
7.10	Moses' Wedding	108
7.11	Search for Leaven	110
7.12	Clearing the House of Leaven	111

7.13	Search for Leaven	112
7.14	*Seder* Table	113
7.15	*Seder* Table	114
7.16	*Seder* Table	115
7.17	Breaking of *Matsah* and Dipping of Vegetables	116
7.18	Beginning of Haggadah Recitation: This Is the Bread of Distress	117
7.19	Beginning of Haggadah Recitation: This Is the Bread of Distress	118
7.20	Returning the *'afiqoman*	119
7.21	Search for Leaven	119
7.22	New Year Service in the Synagogue	120
30.1	High Holiday Maariv, Adolph Katchko, Volume 3	420
30.2	Shacharit Shalosh Regalim, Adolph Katchko, Volume 2	421
30.3	Shabbat Maariv, Adolph Katchko, Volume 1	421
30.4	Shabbat Schacharit, Adolph Katchko, Volume 1	421
30.5	*Sha'm'a V'Tismach Tzion*, Adolph Katchko, Volume 3	423
37.1	Bronze amulet for Esther, daughter of Tatis	515
37.2	An incantation bowl in Jewish Aramaic, for the protection of 'Ummu-l-ḥubāb	516
37.3	Child's linen shirt with "knots" on the margins, before and after unfolding	517
37.4	Bronze bracelets with bells from a tomb in Beit Shemesh, Israel	518
37.5	Bronze ring with roaring lion from a tomb in Sajur, Israel	519

NOTES ON CONTRIBUTORS

Michael J. Broyde is Professor of Law at Emory University School of Law and the Berman Projects Director of its Center for the Study of Law and Religion. He was for many years a member of the Beth Din of America and has served in various rabbinic roles from synagogue rabbi to *Rosh Kollel*.

David M. Bunis is a professor in the Center for Jewish Languages and the Department of Hebrew, The Hebrew University of Jerusalem. He has published extensively on the Judezmo (Ladino, Judeo-Spanish) language and the literature created in it.

Eric Caplan is Associate Professor of Contemporary Judaism and Jewish Education at McGill University (Montreal, Canada). He is co-founder and vice president of the Mordecai M. Kaplan Center for Jewish Peoplehood.

Gordon Dale is Visiting Assistant Professor of Ethnomusicology in The Debbie Friedman School of Sacred Music of HUC-JIR, and the executive director of The Jewish Music Forum.

Maria Diemling (D.Phil., Vienna 1999) is Reader in Jewish-Christian Relations at Canterbury Christ Church University (UK). She has published on early modern Jewish identities, conversion, perceptions of the 'Jewish body' and Jewish food practices.

Avner Dinur is a lecturer of Jewish studies at Sapir College, Israel. He has published papers on the myth of Jewish male menstruation, on the conflicting identities of Palestinians and Israelis, and his research focuses on "secular theology" through the works of Hans Jonas, Emanuel Levinas and Martin Buber.

David C. Dollahite is Camilla Eyring Kimball Professor of Family Life at Brigham Young University where he is co-director of the American Families of Faith Project and his current research focuses on the relational effects of religious transitions. He is co-editor of *Strengths in Diverse Families of Faith: Exploring Religious Differences* (2020, Routledge).

Notes on Contributors

Miriam Frenkel teaches Jewish history and culture in the medieval lands of Islam in the Department for Jewish History at the Hebrew University of Jerusalem. She is Menahem Ben-Sasson chair in Judaism & Islam Through the Ages, and head of The Institute for History at the Hebrew University.

Shulamit Geller, Ph.D., is a senior lecturer and chair of the clinical psychology graduate program, at the Academic College of Tel-Aviv-Yaffo, Israel. She is a supervising clinical psychologist, a member of the Israeli Institute of Group Analysis, a research fellow at the international institute for counter terrorism (ICT) Herzliya, and in private practice.

David Golinkin is the president of the Schechter Institutes, Inc. and a professor of Talmud and Halakhah at the Schechter Institute of Jewish Studies in Jerusalem. He is the author or editor of 60 books in the fields of Halakhah, Midrash and other areas of Jewish Studies.

Benjamin D. Gordon is Assistant Professor of Religious Studies and the Rosenberg-Perlow Fellow in Classical Judaism at the University of Pittsburgh. He is the author of the book *Land and Temple: Field Sacralization and the Agrarian Priesthood of Second Temple Judaism* (2020).

Jonathan E. Handelzalts, Ph.D., is a supervising clinical psychologist. He is a senior lecturer in the graduate program of clinical psychology at the Academic college of Tel-Aviv Yaffo, Israel, and an adjunct associate professor in the Psychiatry Department of the University of Michigan, USA.

Paul A. Hartog (Ph.D., Loyola University Chicago), is Professor of Theology at Faith Baptist Theological Seminary. His primary research field is the history of second-century Christianity, and he has authored several books, as well as numerous journal articles and collected-volume essays.

Trevan G. Hatch is the Anthropology, Bible & Ancient Near East, Middle East, and Religious Studies specialist in the Lee Library at Brigham Young University. His current research interests are on the Jewish context of the Gospels and Jesus traditions, Messianic expectations of Jews and Christians, and pilgrimage and religious tourism in Israel-Palestine.

Samuel Heilman was, until his retirement in August 2020, Emeritus Distinguished Professor of Sociology at Queens College CUNY, where he held the *Harold Proshansky Chair* in Jewish Studies at the Graduate Center. He has authored 15 books, some of which have been translated into Spanish and Hebrew, and is the winner of three National Jewish Book Awards. He was awarded the Marshall Sklare Lifetime Achievement Award in Jewish Studies.

Katrin Kogman-Appel holds a chair in Jewish Studies at the University of Münster, Germany. She has published work on medieval Jewish art and is particularly interested in Hebrew manuscript illumination and its cultural and social contexts.

Vernon H. Kurtz is Rabbi Emeritus of North Suburban Synagogue Beth El in Highland Park, Illinois and Adjunct Professor of Rabbinics at Spertus Institute for Jewish Learning and Leadership. He is the author of *Encountering Torah: Reflections on the Weekly Portion* (2013). He currently resides in Jerusalem.

Notes on Contributors

Gail Labovitz is Professor of Rabbinic Literature at the American Jewish University, where she teaches for the Ziegler School of Rabbinic Studies. Her teaching specialties include rabbinic literature, Jewish law and gender theory. She is the author of *Marriage and Metaphor: Constructions of Gender in Rabbinic Literature* (2009) and the volume on tractate *Moed Qatan* for the Feminist Commentary on the Babylonian Talmud (2021), as well as numerous articles, chapters and reviews.

Ruth Langer is Professor of Jewish Studies in the Theology Department of Boston College and interim director of its Center for Christian-Jewish Learning. Her research focuses on the history of Jewish liturgy and on Christian-Jewish relations from a liturgical perspective.

Yamin Levy is the spiritual leader of a Sephardic Community in Great Neck, Long Island and is the founder and international director of the Maimonides Heritage Center. He spent several years as the Director of Sephardic Studies at Yeshiva University before dedicating his time and energies to helping build Sephardic communities in the United States, Canada and Israel.

Shawn Lichaa is the founder of The Karaite Press (TheKaraitePress.com), which aims to drive deeper discussion about Karaite approaches to Jewish law and philosophy.

Olga Litvak holds the Roth Chair in Modern European Jewish History at Cornell University. Her most recent book, *Haskalah: The Romantic Movement in Judaism* (2012), addresses the problem of "enlightenment" in the making of Jewish modernity.

Loren D. Marks is Professor of Family Life at Brigham Young University where he is director of the graduate program and his current research focuses on religion in couples in interfaith marriages and religiously unaffiliated couples. He is co-director of the American Families of Faith Project and co-author of *Religion and Families: An Introduction* (2017, Routledge).

Rachel S. Mikva is the Rabbi Herman Schaalman Professor in Jewish Studies and Senior Faculty Fellow for the InterReligious Institute at Chicago Theological Seminary. Her most recent book is *Dangerous Religious Ideas: The Deep Roots of Self-Critical Faith in Judaism, Christianity, and Islam* (2020).

Amy K. Milligan is the Batten Endowed Assistant Professor of Jewish Studies and Women's, Gender, and Sexuality Studies at Old Dominion University, where she also directs the Institute for Jewish Studies and Interfaith Understanding. Her research concentrates on Jewish embodiment with special attention to hair and head covering.

Rivka Neriya-Ben Shahar is a senior lecturer at Sapir Academic College in Sderot, Israel, teaching courses in research methods, communication, religion, and gender. She researches the mass media from the perspectives of religion and gender, most recently the tension between religious values and new technologies among Old Order Amish women and Jewish ultra-Orthodox women.

Anna Prashizky is a senior lecturer in the Sociology and Anthropology Department of Western Galilee College. Her research interests are in the area of the anthropology of Judaism and the immigration from the Former Soviet Union to Israel.

Reinhard Pummer is Professor Emeritus, Department of Classics and Religious Studies, University of Ottawa, Canada. His research focuses on Samaritanism and among his publications are the books *The Samaritans in Flavius Josephus* (2009) and *The Samaritans: A Profile* (2016).

Simcha Paull Raphael, Ph.D., is founding director of the DA'AT Institute for Death Awareness, Advocacy and Training, and works as a psychotherapist and spiritual director in Philadelphia. A Fellow of the Rabbis Without Borders Network, he is author of numerous publications including the groundbreaking *Jewish Views of the Afterlife* (2019), and co-editor of *Jewish End-of-Life Care in a Virtual Age: Our Traditions Reimagined* (2021).

Stefan Reif is Emeritus Professor of Medieval Hebrew and Fellow of St John's College, University of Cambridge, and holds senior research posts at Haifa and Tel Aviv universities. He founded and directed the Genizah Research Unit at Cambridge University Library (1973–2006) and is known internationally as author and lecturer.

Jonathan Romain is minister of Maidenhead synagogue. He is the author of several books including *Till Faith Us Do Part: Couples Who Fall in Love Across the Religious Divide* (1996).

Ortal-Paz Saar (Utrecht University, Netherlands) is a cultural historian of Judaism in Late Antiquity and the medieval period. She researches magic and funerary culture, and is particularly interested in portraying the interaction between different religious traditions.

Shalom Sabar is Professor Emeritus of Jewish Art and Folklore at the Hebrew University of Jerusalem. His research and publications concentrate on the history of Jewish art, ceremonies and rituals, objects in the life and year cycles, visual folklore, and material culture of Jewish communities in Christian Europe and the Islamic East. He has published more than 230 essays and several books on these topics.

Gadi Sagiv is a faculty member at the Open University of Israel. Sagiv is the author of *Dynasty: The Chernobyl Hasidic Dynasty and Its Place in the History of Hasidism* (2014; in Hebrew); co-editor of *Habad: History, Theology, Image* (2016; in Hebrew and English); co-author of *Hasidism: A New History* (2017).

Adam Seligman is Professor of Religion at Boston University and Founding Director of CEDAR – *Communities Engaging with Difference and Religion*. Winner of the Leopold Lucas Prize in 2020, he has a long record of writing about – and of trying to find concrete ways of – living with difference.

Jan Schwarz has been Associate Professor of Yiddish Studies at Lund University, Sweden since 2011. He is the author of *Survivors and Exiles: Yiddish after the Holocaust* (2015) and is working on a major scholarly project about Isaac Bashevis Singer.

Jeffrey Shandler is Distinguished Professor of Jewish Studies at Rutgers University.

Abigail Uhrman is Assistant Professor of Jewish Education in the William Davidson Graduate School of Jewish Education at the Jewish Theological Seminary. Her research is focused on diversity, equity and inclusion in the Jewish community.

Roni Weinstein teaches at the Hebrew University (Jerusalem). In recent years he has been working on Jewish religious history in the Mediterranean during the early modern period, especially in the context of Jewish-Islamicate encounters.

ACKNOWLEDGMENTS

Oliver Leaman

In the past when I have edited books such as this I have sought to establish a common system of transliteration and style. I have not done so with this book, since it seems to me that there are a variety of styles to be found in the literature, and readers might be better off seeing something of that variety here. I have of course sought to correct errors and done my best to produce a readable text, but readers will find varieties of spelling of Hebrew and other terms here. Readers will also find a wide variety of views and approaches, and that is all to the good in a book like this. The study of ritual and practice is often controversial and different authors have taken different approaches. Some are writing from a social scientific perspective, others more theologically or philosophically. Some have been rather combative in the presentation of their views, others more descriptive. This reproduces something of the variety of approaches and techniques that those writing in the field pursue. No author should be assumed to agree with what any other author has written, and there has been no attempt here at producing a party line.

I have encouraged authors to produce useful bibliographical information so that readers can follow up the accounts provided here with further study and inquiry. There are many issues in Islamic ritual and practice which have not been covered, to discuss everything is more a task for an encyclopedia than a handbook, but we have here what is, I hope, a reasonable survey of the area. Readers will find a variety of arguments, facts and assessments that present the topic in much of its richness and complexity.

I am grateful to the authors and the rest of my colleagues during the publishing process for their hard work on the project. 2020 was not the easiest year to work on such a project although, given the ways that religious ritual, like everything else, had to adapt and change, it did serve to focus minds on the topic rather more than is sometimes the case.

August 2021/Elul 5781
London

INTRODUCTION

Oliver Leaman

One of the first concepts one thinks of when religion is mentioned is ritual. Religions not only use ritual as part of their activity but they often spend a good deal of time and space talking about it, insisting on it, defining it and challenging other rituals. Many religious spaces are based on ritual and would not exist in the form they do without it, or were it to be different. Differences between religious practitioners on the subject of ritual frequently result in violence, so important is the topic taken to be. The opposite is also true, people come together through ritual and it obviously plays a significant role in producing and cementing solidarity within what it comes to define as a community. This point should not be over-emphasized since societies can also welcome a variety of rituals, and this may occur within a religious group itself, where the concept of community is widened to take account of difference. Some believers may find this difficult to do, although they feel it is something they ought to make an effort to accomplish, and others impossible. This brings out something very important about ritual in religion, it is what philosophers sometimes call an essentially contested concept. How it is carried out within the religion is often a subject of debate and controversy, and whether it should be carried out at all is also an issue.

There has been a long and exciting debate in social science and religious studies about what ritual is and how it operates in religion and there is no intention here of establishing a party line for the volume and obliging all our authors to obey it. That would, in itself, be to try to establish a ritual and require practitioners to accept it. Readers should be aware that individual authors have their own views of the role of ritual in religion and they will discuss their particular topic on the basis of those views. That is entirely as it ought to be and in this way the variety of views on the topic are accurately reflected in the book. It is worth emphasizing here though that much more is involved when it comes to ritual than just description. Rituals are described but within that description values also appear. Rituals themselves embody values, and we all have opinions of how significant they are and where they should be taking us. Within religions themselves there are controversies about what the point of the ritual itself is, where it comes from and how rigorously it has to be stuck to. There are also personal reactions to ritual, and these of course are highly subjective and individual. We all have our own responses and attitudes to ritual in religion; there is a wide continuum of those who are intent on following every jot and tittle of the law, at one end, to those who do everything they can to break the law. Along the continuum there are those who are intent on adapting the religion to local conditions in a variety of ways, while others are equally intent on avoiding all such suggestions. This is being written during the COVID-19 pandemic in 2020, and in the run up to Passover some advocated the use of modern technology such as computers and Zoom to broadcast the seder, so that those who would otherwise attend can still at least virtually participate. Yet this involves the use of electricity on a holiday when such a use is something that many Jews regard as legally unacceptable. It is worth mentioning here that were it not for the pandemic, those who are prepared to use electricity would not in many cases have tolerated its use. In exceptional conditions though, exceptional changes in ritual can be contemplated for some, not at all by others.

One can only imagine the flood of books and articles that will appear after the pandemic, if the pandemic actually ever ends or largely dissipates, on how ritual and practice has changed during its height. It is difficult to think of anything very new arising from these studies. There will be religious groups who adapt, some who do not, and some who do a little but less than other groups. There will be speculation on why these different reactions took place, and no doubt controversies will arise about different explanatory frameworks, and many of the studies will go into exhaustive detail on precisely what people did and why they said they did it. Even if the pandemic does not really end, the reactions of the religious communities will be studied and we will be told that they changed in particular ways during this period, or that they resisted change but nonetheless could not ignore it completely. Religion often portrays itself as being based on eternal truths, and will be shown to respond to transient emergencies, as though this is a novel finding and totally unexpected.

It is worth pointing out that there are, indeed, personal reactions to ritual, but there are also arguments that lead to different practitioners taking up different positions. Cynics might say that the use of arguments is no more objective than anything else since we can choose which arguments (and authorities) to accept and which to reject. For example, the *haredim* (often labelled Ultra-Orthodox) tend to be organized in different groups, each headed by a rabbi or groups of rabbis, and they tell their followers who is an authority on ritual. So the arguments they get to study are part of a circle of approved authorities, and although the details of each argument may exhibit some variety, the principles on which they rest will not. They will define the particular group and support that definition by the arguments that are studied within the group. This should not be pushed too far, since it often happens that someone in a group becomes aware of the deficiencies in the rational underpinning of the group and comes to challenge the group, or leave it. They may also stay within it and do what they are expected to do without having any real emotional or rational commitment to it, perhaps a description of the majority of people in such groups. They just do what they are expected to do or what they have been brought up to do and do not stand aside and consider whether they ought to carry on in that way. It is like speaking the language you were brought up in, it is just there and you operate with it. Those critical of religious ritual often point to how elaborate it can be and what a commitment of time and effort is involved. Of course, that provides a plausible motive for those carrying out those rituals to avoid seeing them critically. They are so busy acting they have little time to think about what they are doing and why.

It is the aim of these essays to describe, analyze and evaluate Jewish ritual and practice from a wide variety of often competing and contrasting points of view. The treatment is very far from exhaustive but indicates a range of intriguing ways of understanding religious life, along with those who live on the periphery of such a life. Both kinds of people are marked by their proximity or distance from religious ritual and practice, and they are given a voice in this volume.

PART I

Texts

1
THE JEWISH BIBLE

Oliver Leaman

There is a great deal in the Jewish Bible that discusses rituals and practice. The Five Books of Moses, the first five books of the Jewish Bible, have a great deal of information in these areas. Some of these references are direct and are about laws and regulations, and one of the books itself in the familiar translation of its name, Leviticus, refers to the role of the priests and their responsibility for monitoring and regulating the carrying out of the religious rites. There are often said to be 613 commandments or *mitzvot* in the *Chumash*, the Five Books of Moses, although there are probably more, and from each of these more can be derived. Along with these direct rules come indirect ones that can be extracted, or have been extracted, from the more discursive parts of the text. People we are supposed to regard as exemplars often appear to act badly and we should then wonder how this is possible. For example, Jacob cheats Esau out of his birthright, does that mean that it is acceptable to cheat someone, even a brother? Abraham, when he was merely Abram, was told by God to sacrifice his son Isaac and unquestioningly proceeds to carry out the task. Earlier he had pleaded on behalf of the cities in the plain who were about to be destroyed by God, saying quite rudely to God that it would be unjust. Is it right to act in accordance with what God tells us or should we always be prepared to question Him? These and similar issues have come in for a lot of discussion by commentators, as one would expect, and this is because the special status of the Bible gives rise to the view that everything in it is of significance and deserves analysis. As Ben Bag Bag comments: "Turn it and turn it, for everything is in it. Reflect on it and grow old and gray with it. Don't turn from it, for nothing is better than it" (*Pirke Avot* 5:24).

Rituals and Morality

As a source of moral practice, the Jewish Bible is often problematic. Many of the main characters in it cheat, steal, lie, run away, dissimulate, and disobey God. Sometimes they are feeble minded and confused, often cynical and exploitative, and the situation only gets worse when we move on from the Five Books of Moses to later books. David, for example, conspires to get someone killed while fighting in his army so that he can sleep with his wife. Many of the prophets, such as Jeremiah and Isaiah, were enthusiastic about their role but apparently rather ineffective, while Jonah, who ran away when he was told to go to Nineveh and prophesy, was the most successful of them all, he just had to wander around the city mumbling that they had 40 days to repent and we are told that everyone heeded his advice, that they acted accordingly and avoided the punishment. Jonah seems to have been very unhappy about this result, yet this thoroughly reluctant prophet produced much better results than any of his peers. Even Moses, after whom the Five Books are, after all, named, is denied entry to the Promised Land since he is taken to have erred on his retrieval of the Jews from Egypt in a number of what look like rather minor ways. His brother Aaron's sons were killed by God (Lev. 10: 1–7) since we are told they carried out a ritual but with "strange fire", and that led to their death sentence. These people do not seem to be exemplars but quite the reverse, just rather ordinary people who often behave poorly.

We are told at Deuteronomy 32: 51–52 why Moses was not permitted to enter the Promised Land:

> This is because … you broke faith with me in the presence of the Israelites at the waters of Meribah Kadesh in the Desert of Zin and because you did not uphold my holiness among the Israelites. Therefore, you will only see the land from afar, you will not enter the land I am giving to the people of Israel.

That might be regarded as a very harsh punishment indeed. Moses' whole mission is to get the Israelites to the Land they were promised, and he is to be denied this due to his actions described in Numbers 20. There was no water and the community turned against Moses and his brother, and God told them to gather the people together and speak to the rock. Water would emerge. Moses organized the people and apparently he impatiently hit the rock with his staff (Num. 20: 10–11) and water did emerge. In the very next verse, though, God accuses them of failing to trust him. Moses made it look like *he* got the water to appear, and not God, and he was told to speak to the rock, not hit it. As with Aaron's sons, God decides on a ritual and if it is not performed in exactly the right way there are consequences. It is worth noticing that though Moses got it wrong here he merely did what he had done in the past at Exodus 17 when he struck the rock to produce water in a very similar situation, where people were moaning and threatening his leadership. The difference is, though, that on that occasion he was told to strike the rock, not on the later occasion. Moses had got the ritual wrong and punishment was soon to follow.

Even the lives of ordinary people can serve as useful indications of how we should, and should not, behave, of course, and perhaps that is what the more historical parts of the Five Books are meant to suggest. When it comes to the actual legislation, we can distinguish between two types of rules. Some have an obvious point, while others do not and we are not told what their point is. We are often told to be nice to strangers, and this is linked to the experience that Jews had of being strangers in Egypt, although it is not clear how this serves as a reason since presumably the rule of being nice to strangers does not only apply to Jews, or to groups who in the past had themselves been strangers somewhere else. Some rules are fairly obvious, any community that did not have a rule against murder would be a difficult place to live, and indeed we see today that there are parts of the world that are largely in the power of criminal gangs, sometimes unofficial and sometimes not, and life there is nasty, brutish and short for many of the unfortunate inhabitants. But the dietary laws do not have an obvious reason, except to separate the community from other communities, which is also often given as a reason for establishing rituals. Some other rules which are to do, for example, with the cloth covering the ark of the covenant are entirely arbitrary, or so it seems, as are the later rules about how to conduct sacrifices in the Temple.

Reasons for Rules

Distinguishing between rules with rationales and those without has been a popular activity among commentators. It is a little surprising that this should be the case since presumably God could establish rules just because He wanted to establish them, to help us understand that we should do what we are told to do even if we do not understand why. That is itself a rationale of course, but even if it was not, we might think that God knew the reason for the rule and we do not. The dietary rules are good examples here, they are complex and quite specific, yet there is no notion that Jews are asked to eat things that are good for them and avoid those things that are the opposite. Or we could take the example of the fringes that Jews are supposed to wear, and their colors and shape, what they are made of, all these things could easily have been different. Perhaps they have some transcendental meaning that only God knows, although it is not easy to see why a pork sausage is in any way worse in itself than a beef sausage, where the meat comes from the approved part of the cow and is slaughtered in the right sort of way. If there are going to be rules, then often they are arbitrary and we obey them because we respect or fear, or both, whoever establishes the rules. It would not have to be the case that we thought that there was a reason for it and God knew what it was and we do not. Rather, there needed to be a rule not because that particular rule is important but because we need to accept the idea that someone sets the rules and we should obey them, whatever they are. The reason for the rule is then that there is no reason, it is established by divine fiat.

There are advantages to such an approach, since if we think that the reasons for the rules are available to us, it becomes plausible to change them in certain circumstances. That might seem to be an advantage since in changing circumstances the rules can then adapt to those changes. For example, it is a rule that ten men are required for many important prayers and they need to be physically present in the same place where the prayers are recited. During the COVID-19 emergency it became very difficult and unsafe to gather ten people together, let alone men, and yet prayers needed to be said. Was it possible to create a virtual *minyan* where the right number of people are available online but not actually present in the same space? During the pandemic some Jewish groups refused to distance themselves because they wished to continue with their traditional communal practices, including rules of prayer, and they then suffered major casualties as a result. For them the rigorous application and preservation of rules is of primary significance. Of course, in Judaism the preservation of life is also of primary significance, so there is scope for a discussion here even among the haredi community about how adaptations might be made in certain compelling circumstances. From their point of view there is a determination to try to avoid the slippery slope. Once a rule is set aside or changed then perhaps everything will gradually be changed or the attitude of respect for rules in general will be weakened. That is a very real question and although those hostile to traditional lifestyles may accuse them of unthinking conformism, the desire to maintain rules is an important part of many religions, including Judaism. One of the entertaining aspects of the haredi lifestyle is that the rules they follow actually are not that traditional, they often go back to some community in Eastern Europe from a few centuries ago, and to the religious authorities and their successors who organized that community. They do not extend much further into the medieval or biblical past. It has often been pointed out that there is nothing as modern as tradition and anyone who seeks to stick to a traditional lifestyle has nonetheless to constantly make choices about what to do, and other choices about whom he or she follows in making those choices.

Obeying the Rules

The Five Books does also take a firm line on behavior. Toward the end of the last book (Deuteronomy 4) Moses draws up the Israelites and warns them of what will happen if they misbehave in the future. Even in the period of the exodus his community were hardly obedient, they seem to have constantly complained and looked back nostalgically at their time in Egypt. When he was delayed at Mount Sinai and did not come down for a period, they built the Golden Calf and worshipped that. Like many of the main biblical characters, the Israelites were far from perfect, and perhaps as the Qur'an suggests they were given such extensive legislation because they were so unwilling to follow even simpler rules. The second and longest sura, al-Baqarah (The Cow), criticizes the ways in which the Israelites argued about how to carry out the sacrifices that God ordered. To punish them God gave them the rather harsh ritual laws that we have been familiar with ever since. This seems a bit implausible; after all, if someone is bad at following rules, why punish him by giving him even harder rules? He will be unlikely to carry them out, even more unlikely to carry them out than the earlier and more lenient rules, surely? If there are sanctions then perhaps not and we do tend to punish rule breakers by giving them harsher rules to observe. We may imprison people who break the law, and while in prison they have to follow tougher rules than when they were free. When in prison, rule breakers may have even more stringent regulations to obey, such as solitary confinement, restricted exercise and so on.

When we think of punishing people, we come across two ways of justifying what we do, one based on the consequences and one entirely focused on what people deserve. This dichotomy represents nicely two different approaches to justifying the rules we find in the Bible. They often seem to be there in order to differentiate one community from others. One community has been chosen and has a covenantal relationship with God, while the others do not, and some way must be found to distinguish them from each other. Hence the very specific rules for the Israelites, they might be important not because of what they are inherently but due to their power to distinguish between people. It is a bit like a country's flag, it is in itself of little significance, merely a piece of cloth with a design on it, yet what it symbolizes is immensely important in the eyes of those who live in a particular country, and who either are attached to that symbol or may have a variety of negative emotions about it. This is not a very good example since flags do have some sort of rationale about them, in the sense that different colors and images often are taken to represent something about a country. Take the stripes that represent different ranks in the army, they have an entirely arbitrary meaning, they are allocated to different ranks just so that everyone knows the status of everyone else by just looking at their uniform or cap.

Rituals as Expressive

We can ask what the role of a ritual is in a practice, and we can also ask what it expresses. The obvious questions are what is it for, what does it do, but rituals have non-instrumental features also. We might like to do something just because someone has asked us to do it, we do it to express an attitude to that person. We do it to validate a relationship we have or think we have with that person. There is a well-known example in moral philosophy of two people living by themselves on a desert island, having been shipwrecked presumably, and one is very pragmatic and grows things to eat while the other likes flowers and decorative plants and concentrates on them. Presumably there is enough food for them both to survive. The flower enthusiast falls ill and in his dying words asks the other person to look after his plants when he has died.

The promise is made and death follows soon after. As soon as he can the vegetable grower digs up the flowers and plants more vegetables. The fact that they live on a desert island means that a promise broken has no effects on anyone else, such as a general decline in making and respecting promises, for example, and he is perhaps entitled to think that since he likes potatoes and not tulips, and there is no one left who likes tulips, he might as well grow potatoes and not tulips. What would be the point of tulips since there is no one around who likes tulips? The only inhabitant who liked tulips died happy in the belief that his tulips would be looked after into the future.

What makes this story rather shocking is that we can see the logic of it but wonder what it means about the relationship between the individuals concerned. The survivor might have felt that he would have liked to preserve the flowers in memory of his departed companion, or at least some flowers. We do on the whole respect the wishes of the dead, although we limit what they can ask us to do in a number of ways. This has a point in that people who feel that their wishes will be respected after they are dead may be more motivated to create wealth. That has wider social benefits, but none of this applies to the island, of course. The flower lover is happy if he thinks that his flowers will carry on after his death, but once he is dead what do his wishes mean? We do tend to memorialize people after they are dead by doing things like keeping their rooms as they were when they were alive, or looking after their clothes, or their plants, and often there is a stage in the grieving process where we stop doing this. Our way of thinking about them has moved on, we say, and what we did in the past no longer seems appropriate or necessary.

This brings out the expressive nature of what we do, which is often very different or even in conflict with its instrumental value. There was a significant discussion in China about the value of elaborate funerals and all that they entailed, including music and priests and so on. Confucius defended them on the grounds that it is important that society marks the importance of our ancestors and when they did the appropriate ritual should be followed, whatever the expense and the effect that paying for it would have on the lives of the survivors. His opponents argued that dead bodies are just trash and we should spend no more time on them or with them than we do with ordinary rubbish, we should just dispose of them and get on with things. Some critics of this latter view asked if people would be upset if they came home and saw foxes chewing at their parent's body, it having been thrown out with the rubbish. Disgust is, of course, an expressive rather than an instrumental value, many of the things that disgust us are perfectly safe, and many things that we appreciate are rather questionable.

A ritual is often seen as linking us with the past and the future in ways that cannot be accomplished otherwise. There is a well-known story about the Baal Shem Tov, the founder of Hasidism. When he saw that the Jewish people were threatened by tragedy, he would go to a particular place in the forest where he lit a fire, recited a particular prayer, and asked for a miracle to save the Jews from the threat. The holy fire and the prayer led to a miracle, averting the tragedy. Later, when the Baal Shem Tov's disciple, the Maggid of Mezrich, had to intervene with heaven for the same reason, he went to the same place in the forest where he admitted that he did not know how to light the fire, but he could still recite the prayer, and again, the miracle was accomplished. Later still, Rabbi Moshe Leib of Sasov, in turn a disciple of the Maggid of Mezrich, went into the forest to save his people, not knowing how to light the fire or the words of the prayer, but at least he knew the right place to go to, and the miracle occurred.

When it was the turn of Rabbi Israel of Rizhyn, the great grandson of the Maggid of Mezrich, to avert the threat, he sat in his armchair, holding his head in his hands, and said to God: "I am unable to light the fire, I do not know the prayer, and I cannot even find the place in the forest. All I can do is to tell the story. That must be enough." We are not told if the tragedy was averted as a result of the final effort. Was there enough of the ritual there to accomplish the task? This brings out a feature of rituals, the issue of whether they decline over time and lose their efficacy. The Five Books ends with the idea that the rituals performed by the priests were very important, and their significance was to continue in the days of the Temples, they are intermediaries between the community and God and the correct carrying out of the rituals expresses that relationship. Later on in the Bible, though, many of the prophets criticize the following of rules because it went on at the same time as widespread immorality. Amos is vocal on the wrongness of the keeping of the religious laws while at the same time not helping the poor, which he says God hates (5: 21) and will end in disaster. He very much sets himself up against the high priest Amaziah who is more concerned with the rituals than with the widespread hypocrisy and oppression of the poor that was prevalent at the time.

We may eat something on a particular occasion to remember someone who used to eat it, we may wear a sweater to remember someone who used to wear it in the past, or who said they liked it. We may not especially like the sweater, or what we eat, but we do it because of what we think it shows about our relationship with that person. It would be easy to transfer the same logic in religion to our relationship with God, and that is how religions often describe rituals, but it need not be about a relationship with God but with the religion as an idea, or with a community, or with a particular culture. In the Five Books, the covenant is often referred to as the basis of the relationship God has with a particular people, and the rituals that develop around that point celebrate and commemorate that relationship. Yet over time rituals change and are forgotten and replaced by others, as the Hasidic story suggests, yet some think that the core of the ritual, its essential meaning, remains and can be expressed in a variety of new and different ways.

Changing Rituals

This is the basis of the idea that religions can be reformed and changed, and indeed, need to be over time. There is not much scope for such a view in the Five Books, since the sons of Aaron were punished with death for apparently wandering away from the precise terms of the ritual they were engaged on (although some commentators suggest they were drunk). We do often think that unless a ritual is followed completely and exactly it will not work, as it were, like a password that has to be exact. It is worth recalling that the group of people who left Egypt are often described as an *erev rav*, a great number of people (Ex. 12: 38), and that is often taken to mean that there were many there who were not Israelites, but wives, children, servants and so on, and this fairly diverse group needed to be molded into a community of some sort, and ritual plays a large role in such a socialization process. One should think about groups like army recruits, for instance, who come from all over the country and indeed the world, and who need to be made to feel a loyalty to each other and to those in authority over them, and it is often through the acceptance and imposition of rituals that this is made possible. Having brightly polished boots is probably not much of a help when fighting, in fact the reverse, but the discipline involved in polishing boots is presumably supposed to be helpful in instilling attitudes of discipline and obedience in soldiers. We are back here with giving an instrumental value to ritual, and this can be misleading when thinking of religion. The idea that we practice ritual in order to bring something about, perhaps to please God or cement a community, is to give an incomplete picture of what rituals are about.

This is because often we carry out a ritual because we want to mark something in our lives that we think is important but has no other motive. For example, we might do something in a certain way because in the past someone we admire did it, or some group of people did it. The dietary laws are a good example of this. Because they were presumably carried out in the past and because we want to link ourselves up with those people, we might decide to obey the same laws they were supposed to obey. Whether they did obey them of course we do not know, and that hardly matters, since our observance of them is expressive of our perceived link with those earlier communities. Muslims often follow what they take the behavior of the Prophet to have been even in very minor issues such as how they brush their teeth or shake hands, we do not of course know precisely how he acted, although there is an extensive literature of what he is supposed to have done, and this is done to a certain extent in order to express an attitude to him. He is an exemplar and even in very small matters his followers might wish to copy him. Charismatic figures often have this sort of impact on their followers. The fashion industry is built on this sort of idea. When we see a beautiful person dressed in particular clothes we might think that if we wear those clothes we will also be beautiful, or we may wish to show that to at least a degree we are like that person. We too can wear the clothes and think about what it would be like to be beautiful.

Ever since Paul produced his famous critique of Judaism for its apparent obsession with rules, this has become very much of a theme among many observers. We should not over-emphasize the role of Paul here since there is little doubt that it was discussed even before him. There are resonances in the Jewish Bible that make one wonder how the rituals should be regarded. This is a normal feature of religion; what rituals one should observe, how important they are to the religion, how we can tell we are following the right rituals, these issues arise all the time. When the Israelites revolted against monotheism in the desert they presumably had had enough of the existing rituals, and in later books in the Bible the people are often referred to as abandoning their religious practices and adopting new ones. Rituals go along with society, there were no rituals in the Garden of Eden, not even dealing with clothing, and the implication of what is said when Adam and Eve are expelled is that from that time on things will be difficult. Hence presumably the need for rituals to assuage the harshness of mortal life in society. Yet it is worth noting that rituals do seem to be presented quite negatively, as the consequence of original wrongdoing. By contrast with the Qur'an which claims that nothing hard will be demanded of human beings by their religion, the Five Books does not make such an observation. Can we take it then that the implication is that the rituals will be demanding?

Since it is difficult to see most of the biblical characters as exemplars, the Israelites did not have much in the way of a paradigm to follow in past or present leaders. The main characters are often very human and although there is much admirable in their character, they are far from perfect. Hence even Moses passes priestly authority to his brother Aaron, and it is the priests who are to carry out the appropriate rituals. They are not the arbiters in matters of morality, this is something we should be able to do ourselves given the teachings of the Bible (it is not in heaven) or seek the help of the rabbis and commentators on the Bible in later Jewish history. The rituals though are complex and require training and precision, and should be left to those professionally qualified to carry them out. We recall the fate of Aaron's sons who got them wrong.

Rituals and Their Point

It is an interesting question to wonder what the significance of rituals in the Five Books is. They are often not moral, but deal with pollution and acquiring forgiveness for others. Such rules seem to be superfluous, since if people know in general what they ought to do morally why do they need additional rules dealing with such apparently minor issues? It is a question that often arises within any sort of organization; do we need the hierarchy and the bureaucracy which gets built up over the ordinary things that people do? Many of us work in organizations such as universities where people carry out the actual work of the organization – teaching, researching and so on – while other people run the organization and do not seem to do very much at all, apart from earn very large salaries. This latter group are actually the important people in the institution, in the sense that they have high status and power, and they no doubt see themselves as the preservers of the "mission" of the institution and the facilitators of its work. Religions are very bureaucratic institutions on the whole, and change often takes place when one bureaucracy overthrows a previous bureaucracy, and even in the desert we are told there needed to be a system for delegating ritual tasks to a specific group of specialists. This graduated later of course into the service of the Temples, and a priestly class developed who no doubt acquired considerable political and financial power, along with their religious role. It is sometimes suggested that the account in the Five Books may have been constructed later on with an eye to justifying the Temple hierarchy and privileges, by arguing that even in the desert it was important to make a separation between one group of people, the community at large, and those who were responsible for that community's ritual status.

It is worth reminding ourselves of the importance of the theme in the Five Books of the idea of separation. The laws are often presented as there to separate one group from another group – the Israelites from everyone else – something that came to be made much of by later commentators who often argued for the need to build a fence around the Torah. Men need to be separated from women, blood from what is eaten, one tribe from another tribe, animals from human beings, ordinary life from rituals, clean food from the unclean, normal days from special days, the married from the unmarried, sanctuary cities from other cities, and so on. Basically, the idea is to stress the difference between an us and a them, and this needs to be monitored and policed in some way. There is a great deal of capital punishment in the Five Books, although this was surely more of a threat than an actuality. Separation requires rituals to mark them since in themselves the things that are separated are entirely arbitrary. There is nothing wrong with eating pigs, in the sense that if you eat meat pigs are no different from other types of meat in general. There is nothing different between the Sabbath and other days of the week, they are all just days, a measure we mark to do with our calculation of time and our perception of how the earth relates to the sun. There is nothing special about the priests, they are just members of the community, no taller or wiser and nicer than anyone else. If a separation is to be instituted between things which really are rather similar then this has to be based on something taken to be authoritative and powerful, obedient to higher levels of sanction and even spirituality. This is the magic of rules, that even when they are obviously irrelevant and inappropriate people will obey them, or be tempted to obey them, since they are taken to have acquired the aura of something transcendental.

We return to the expressive aspects of rituals. I have on my mantelpiece a pair of pince-nez that no one in my household wears. They gather dust and look out of place. They serve no useful function at all. What they do is remind me of my father (z"l) who used to wear them. I find it a more personal object than a photograph since something that someone has handled so frequently becomes very much of a symbol of them, especially if it is rather unusual and distinctive. We do often keep things like that because we use them as links with the past, a past which is after all past and so no longer pressing in on us, yet it is something we may seek to commemorate in some way. After a bereavement, the time often comes when we throw everything out that someone has left behind, and that does not mean that we no longer think of them, it is just that we think of them in a different way. Initially though we may be reluctant to make any changes, and this is a useful way of seeing our relationship with rituals. Rituals change all the time, and an effective ritual may have an end date for some people and so require replacing with something else. For others, nothing need ever change, they just continue to do what they started off doing. It is because of this vast variety of reaction that saying anything general about rituals is so difficult. The Bible wants the Jews to follow the rules precisely and in tandem, and constantly reports on their inability to do so. This is yet another example of how realistic the text is. We often find it difficult to do what we are told to do. Our ideas about what we ought to do may change over time. God may punish us for what we do but there is no evidence from either the Bible or the world in general that the reality of punishment alters behavior very much. People will carry on working out their own attitude to the rituals and practices of religion. That is what we see in the Jewish Bible and that is what we find to be the case subsequently.

Bibliography

Leaman, Oliver. 2006. *Jewish Thought: An Introduction*. Abingdon: Routledge.
Maimonides. 1948. *ShemonahPeraqim*. Ed. M.D. Rabinowitz. Tel Aviv: Rishonim, chapter 5.
Pedaya, Haviva. 2003. *Nahmanides: Elevation: Cyclical Time and Sacred Ritual* [Hebrew]. Tel Aviv: Am Oved Publishers.
Pedaya, Haviva. 2011. *Walking Through Trauma: Rituals of Movement in Jewish Myth, Mysticism, and History* [Hebrew]. Tel Aviv: Resling.

2
MIDRASH

Rachel S. Mikva

It would be useful at the start to define midrash—but this is always a challenging proposition. As James Kugel quips after reviewing a number of flawed attempts to do so, "Since these studies have already not defined midrash in ample detail, there is little purpose in our not defining it again here" (1983, 144). Perhaps it is more appropriate to describe the ways in which midrash is understood for purposes of this study. It is a body of rabbinic literature, with many classic texts redacted during the tannaitic and amoraic periods (1st–5th c.) but continuing in diverse forms through the Middle Ages and into the contemporary era. Within these texts, one finds straightforward and more imaginative exegesis—frequently offering multiple interpretations—as well as passages rooted in folklore, history, homily, mysticism, liturgy, theology, and other genres. They treat praxis (*midrash halakhah*) and extralegal ideas (*midrash aggadah*). Although it is not possible in this brief chapter to provide in-depth analysis of different midrashic works and their historical contexts, it is important to recognize that each has its own character, perspective, and redaction process—and that the literature continues to develop over time, repurposing themes and interpretive traditions along the way.

Midrash is also a way of reading, purposefully elastic as it searches out possibilities of meaning in the Hebrew Bible. As such, it is embedded in a broad range of Jewish literatures and practices. Advancing the importance of midrash in the development of religious tradition, Ithamar Gruenwald calls it "a form of cognition that supplies terms of reference and channels of perception for people who organize their lives in accordance with a scriptural world of ideas" (1993, 6). His expansive definition connects midrash as a way of reading to midrash as Jewish praxis in its own right.

Delineating Practice, Elucidating Meaning, Justifying Observance

Mira Balberg notes that "ritualization (of the law and of everyday life) is a key characteristic of the rabbinic project at large, and that ritually-oriented discourse is pervasive in rabbinic texts" (2017, 90). Some of the earliest redacted collections of midrash are frequently referred to as *midrash halakhah* because they contain substantial discussion of Jewish praxis. A third-century midrash on the Book of Exodus entitled *Mekhilta de-Rabbi Ishmael*, for example, repeatedly seeks to ground rabbinically prescribed rituals in scriptural instruction—even or especially when it is not evident. Broad elaborations of dietary restrictions are excavated from the terse biblical mention of not boiling a kid in its mother's milk, transforming what was most likely a cultic concern into a dietary one (Ex. 23:19). With their gift for close reading and conviction that no word in the Hebrew Bible is superfluous, the rabbis extrapolated from the repetition of this instruction (Ex. 34:26, Deut. 14:21) to preclude cooking, eating, or benefiting from any mixture of meat and milk. The discussion does not establish this aspect of *kashrut*, which was already practiced by rabbinic Jews, but substantiates its authority by binding it to the Written Torah (*Mekhilta Kaspa 5*).

Similarly, the sages legitimated their radical rereading of "an eye for an eye" (Ex. 21:24) to require monetary compensation in the case of physical injury. Using established hermeneutical principles like reasoning from minor to major (*kal vaḥomer*), general and specific (*klal ufrat*), and linguistic analogy (*gezerah shavah*), the text builds an argument that Torah could not have intended retaliatory wounding (*Mekhilta Nezikin 8-9*). Again, the midrash is authenticating an already familiar rendering of the law rather than creating it (cf. *m. Baba Kamma 8:1*).

David Weiss Halivni asserts that rabbinic Judaism consistently demonstrates such predilection for justified law, often accomplished by locating prooftexts within the Hebrew Bible. He sees the apodictic nature of the Mishnah as an exception that proves the rule, since it was subsequently buttressed with the Gemara that also sought to ground rabbinic praxis in Scripture (1986, 5). Jane Kanarek complicates this picture somewhat by demonstrating that the sages frequently reached far afield to secure their biblical authorization, bypassing more obvious verses. While it may have been motivated by a desire to demonstrate the sages' textual dexterity, the pattern ultimately conveys the idea that *rabbinic reading of* Scripture (rather than Scripture itself) is what constitutes authority (2014, 135). Whether obvious or far-fetched, midrashic efforts to delineate and explicate Jewish praxis help establish parameters for belief, behavior, and belonging. This process prompts considerations of power, an analytical framework that has been part of ritual studies at least since Durkheim. Ritualized action is a strategy for negotiating social control (Bell 1992, 171), and midrash served to advance rabbinic Judaism's claims of normativity for Jewish practice.

Often midrash brings precedent as its prooftext, attaching holiday, liturgy, and life cycle praxis to biblical figures. An 8–9th-century narrative midrash called *Pirqe de-Rabbi Eliezer* (*PRE*), for example, teaches that women's special observance of the New Moon is reward for their faithful wisdom during the wilderness wandering. Noticing that Aaron instructed the men to take jewelry from their wives to help build the golden calf (Ex. 32:2) but the women brought it on their own to build the tabernacle (Ex. 35:22), the text concludes that the women were unwilling to support idolatry and attributes it to their merit (*PRE 45*). The "Chair of Elijah" that is designated at a *brit milah* (covenant of circumcision) ceremony provides another example. Elijah's accusation that the Israelites were abandoning the covenant is cited in midrash as the reason that he is required to be "present" at every *brit*, to witness the people's continued fidelity (see 1Kings 19, *PRE 29*, *Zohar Gen. 93a*).

Occasionally such passages read not only as etiologies of Jewish practice, but also as Jewish renderings of common mythological themes. Adam observed *havdalah*—the ceremony marking the end of the Sabbath—according to the Talmud redacted in the Land of Israel (*y. Berakhot 8:6 (12b)*), midrashic collections on Genesis and Psalms (*Gen. Rab. 11:2, Mid. Ps. 92:4*), and *Pirqe de-Rabbi Eliezer* (*PRE 20*). As darkness descends, Adam is terrified—so God gives him the gift of fire. (In *PRE*, God provides a pillar of fire; in the other texts, God teaches Adam to make fire by striking stones together.) In response, Adam blesses God for creating the lights of fire. Thus, at the close of the Sabbath, Jewish practice is to light a candle as part of *havdalah* and repeat this act of blessing. There is no exegetical support for such a tale but, from the perspective of Jewish praxis, it represents a virtuous cycle: the midrash sanctions the ritual and the ritual reinforces the ideology of the text. In fact, the passage in *Pirqe de-Rabbi Eliezer* goes on to provide additional details regarding customs of *havdalah*. Some of them (e.g. looking at the light reflected on one's fingernails) appear to be of recent origin, highlighting the fact that midrash helps make room for innovation with its dynamic and multivocal nature.

There were a number of scholars in anthropology and religion who emphasized correspondence between myth and ritual, identifying them as phenomena that find their origins or meanings within one another (e.g. Frazer 2013; Eliade 1963). Midrashic traditions like the one about Adam suggest this kind of relationship, weaving his imagined experience into a classic fire motif to attach cosmic significance to *havdalah*. It would seem simple to discern here Eliade's conception of myth as a form of knowledge that is absorbed ritually—a Jewish way to reenact primordial events and thus slip into the realm of eternal return (1954; 1963, 18–19). Yet, as Rachel Adelman points out, "the assumption that linear time is somehow transcended through ritual, that history is 'abolished' in mythic, cyclical time … is fundamentally at odds with the significance of the ceremony" (2009, 155). Instead, Jewish ritual embeds the eternal within time and history. It is less about the etiology of fire and more about the continuing distinction between Sabbath (when halakhically observant Jews do not light fire) and other days of the week.

Consequently, it is useful to add the perspective of later theorists (e.g. Mary Douglas, Claude Levi-Strauss, Clifford Geertz) who concentrated on symbolic meaning. Ritual is like a text to be interpreted and midrash can provide a hermeneutical key. Sabbath, with its sanctified rest and service to the Most High, is a foretaste of the World-to-Come. Midrashic association with Adam establishes Eden as its analogue, and the darkness that envelops him as night falls after his expulsion from the Garden reflects the Jewish realities of exile. Yet God provides adaptation for the loss of creation's pristine light. Through midrashic explication of the *havdalah* ritual, "the transition from Eden to Exile is translated into temporal terms within the real world" (Adelman 2009, 161). Reentering the world-as-it-is at Sabbath's conclusion, Jews may experience the same sense of existential dread that Adam felt in literal and metaphysical darkness, but the ritual provides reassurance that they have been given tools to manifest God's light in the world through the work of the week.

Ritual significance is sometimes embedded in rabbinic hagiography. *Midrash Tanḥuma* (Buber) relates a presumably fictional story of the Roman governor of Judea, Turnus Rufus, in conversation with the first-century sage Rabbi Akiba. Always seeking to provoke, the governor asks whether the works of God or of humans are more beautiful. Rabbi Akiba surprisingly responds, "The works of human beings are more beautiful than those of the Holy One." As evidence, he points to the way humans turn grain into sumptuous breads and weave flax into elegant garments. Rufus ultimately challenges him to explain why Jewish boys are circumcised, and Akiba claims that he knew where this discussion was heading. Jews circumcise their sons, he explains, because God has given all the commandments as means of refinement—even to "improve" on God's own handiwork (*Tanḥuma Buber Tazria* 7). In this European recension of a Geonic-era text, we see a different dimension of power relations in regard to ritual. Roman society reviled circumcision and European Christian culture perpetuated the hostility; this invented conversation subverts the dominant culture's presumption to define the boundaries of legitimate practice. More than an *apologia* for the ritual of circumcision, however, the story also conveys the theological conviction that we play a critical role in advancing God's purposes for creation.

Catherine Bell (1992) and Ronald L. Grimes (2013) appropriately caution not to lose sight of the fact that rituals are embodied actions rather than ideas, a perspective that is particularly important for Jewish practice. The purposeful act of *doing* is what counts in Jewish conceptions of *mitzvah*; as Rabbi Shimon ben Gamliel taught, "Explication (midrash) is not the most important thing—rather, action is" (*m. Avot 1:17*). In actuality, they are linked: an essential role of midrashic exposition is to inspire observance of Jewish ritual. The practice of reciting the *Sh'ma*, for instance, is readily "justified" by pointing to the biblical instruction in Deuteronomy 6:7 to speak these words when you lie down and when you rise up; Jews recite the passage before going to bed and it is included in the evening and morning liturgy. So what does *Genesis Rabbah 98:3* come to teach in tracing the tradition back to Jacob? This 4–5th-century midrashic collection is commenting on the verse that begins Jacob's address to his children at the end of his life: "Assemble and hearken, O children of Jacob; Listen to Israel your father" (Gen. 49:2). It plays with his two names, Jacob and Israel, the second of which was bestowed on him after wrestling with the angel in Genesis 32.

> Rabbi Eleazar ben Aḥvei said: From here [the people of] Israel received the privilege to recite *Sh'ma*. When our father Jacob was departing this world, he called his twelve sons and said to them, "Listen, is the God of Israel who is in the heavens your father? Perhaps your heart is divided about the Holy One of Blessing." They said to him, "Listen, Israel (*sh'ma Yisrael*, Deut 6:4), our father. Just as your heart is not divided in regard to the Holy One of Blessing, so there is no division in our hearts. Rather, *Adonai is our God, Adonai alone*" (ibid). So Jacob parted his lips and uttered, "Blessed is God's glorious name forever." Rabbi Berachiah and R. Ḥelbo said in Rabbi Samuel's name: This is why [the people of] Israel recite each morning and evening, *Hear O Israel (sh'ma Yisrael)*—our ancestor who lies buried in the Cave of Machpelah—what you charged us we still practice: *Adonai is our God, Adonai alone*.

Jacob's response in the story is the whispered line of the liturgy that follows recitation of Deuteronomy 6:4. Connecting the *Sh'ma* prayer to his deathbed scene does not appear to unlock symbolic meaning. Rather, it augments the affective power of the action—embodying the *mitzvah* and affirming the faith of our ancestors.

Interestingly, the tension between thinking about ritual as actions versus ideas plays out within rabbinic literature. Sages periodically expressed hesitation about providing rationales for the *mitzvot*, concerned that giving reasons might mislead people or invite disobedience regarding those that had no ready explanation (see, e.g., *b. San. 21b*). Ultimately, the rabbis privileged obedience to God as an overriding purpose. Using the examples of *kashrut* and forbidden sexual relations, for instance, *Leviticus Rabba 20:22* cites Rabbi Eleazar ben Azariah as saying that Jews should avoid violating *halakhah*—not because they do not want to (that is, for their own reasons), but rather because "our Father in Heaven" forbids it.

Yet midrash is littered with explanations of praxis, displaying diverse ideas about the logic of specific *mitzvot* (Heinemann 2008, 15–33). Some motivations are symbolic, as with the multiple possibilities of meaning for gathering the four species during Sukkot—to recognize aspects of the Holy One, or the matriarchs and patriarchs, or the community of leaders and scholars, or how differing strengths and weaknesses of the people Israel can compensate for each other in service to God (*Lev. Rab. 30:9–12*). Others address theo-ethical considerations, like raising your enemy's pack animal who has fallen in order to promote social harmony (*Tanḥuma Mishpatim 1*), or explaining why a thief is punished more severely than a robber. In the latter case, one might expect the opposite since a robber threatens both person and property, but a thief is clearly more afraid of human beings than of God and believes it is possible to conceal the crime (*Mekhilta Nezikin 15*). We also find summative reasons, such as the idea that the default purpose of all the commandments is to refine human beings (*Gen. Rab. 44:1*).

By the medieval period, Jews were composing systematic treatises about *ta'amei hamitzvot* (reasons for the commandments), adding philosophical, mystical, and utilitarian layers of meaning. Midrash expanded explanations as well. A medieval anthology called *Lekaḥ Tov*, for instance, roots the practice of lighting Sabbath candles in the period of wilderness wandering and also provides more practical, "contemporary" reasons: to preserve *shalom* in the home, to prevent desecrating Sabbath if one needs light for an ill person or an animal, and to prevent accidental violation of *kashrut* if something crawls into your food (*Lekaḥ Tov Ex. 35:3*). Yet the dialectical tension related to idea versus action remained. Maimonides, the great medieval Jewish philosopher, believed that all the commandments had a rational purpose—and still he felt obliged to offer a cautionary note:

> It is appropriate that one meditate, according to one's intellectual ability, regarding the laws of the Torah to penetrate their deeper meaning. Those laws for which one finds no reason and knows no purpose, however, should not be treated lightly.
> *Mishneh Torah Meilah 8:8*

Sincere intent and deep understanding are valuable, but the general halakhic principle that doing is primary abides.

Midrashic Texts and Themes as Part of Ritual

Sometimes midrash is part of the doing. An early and important example is telling the Passover story as part of the seder. The Mishnah gives various instructions for the ritual meal, including foods and wine, statements of thanksgiving and praise, and the requirement to share the story (*m. Pes. 10:4*). The text says to teach one's children according to their capacity and to expound (*doresh*) on Deuteronomy 26:5–10, which relates the Exodus narrative in succinct fashion. Medieval manuscripts of *haggadot* include various midrashic explications of this biblical passage, intended to be read and discussed at the seder (Rovner 2000; Bokser 1984).

Other familiar parts of the Passover *haggadah* also incorporate midrash; the tradition of the Four Children, for example (found in the Babylonian rite), is similar to a passage in *Mekhilta de-Rabbi Ishmael* (*Pisḥa 18*). As participants recite these passages and invest themselves in interpretation, they write themselves into the story—fulfilling the teaching that everyone should feel as if they themselves went forth out of slavery from Egypt, and making every Jewish home a site of liberation. The ritual and the narrative of the Exodus are combined in the midrashic act itself. According to the *haggadah*, even if each person at the seder is wise and knowledgeable in Torah, it is a *mitzvah* to engage in the telling, and whoever talks about it at length is praiseworthy.

Contemporary innovations are similarly incorporated into the Passover seder through midrash. There is an aggadic tradition that a miraculous well of water followed the Israelites in the wilderness, attributed to the merit of Miriam (*b. Taanit 9a, Num. Rab. 1:2*). It stems from the juxtaposition of her death in Numbers 20:1 and the subsequent crisis that the community was without water—a problem one might expect more often given the challenge of sustaining a multitude in an arid region. Many modern Jews searching for usable symbols to acknowledge the contributions of women to the Exodus narrative—the midwives, Moses' mother, Miriam, Pharaoh's daughter—have chosen to include "Miriam's cup" in their seder, filled with water. Sharing the midrashic narrative of the well, they root this new practice in tradition in order to secure its place at the table. In recent decades artists have begun to craft "Miriam cups," giving midrash a visual expression as well (Women of Reform Judaism 2003).

The very notion of religious art, perhaps suspect given the restriction in the Ten Commandments about carving images (Ex. 20:4), is authorized midrashically. In the Babylonian Talmud (*b. Shab. 133b*), the sages explore the meaning of a verse from the Song at the Sea, "This is my God and I will adorn Him" (Ex. 15:2). How is it possible to add glory to the Divine? Adorn oneself by making a beautiful *sukkah*, a beautiful *lulav*, a beautiful *shofar*, a beautiful Torah scroll and then wrap it in fine silks. Thus, artistic expression has a long-standing relationship with Jewish ritual and midrash is sometimes a part of it. We see it embedded in prayer practices through synagogue decoration, as at the third-century synagogue in Dura Europos (present-day Syria), excavated in the 1920s and 30s. The synagogue's walls are covered with frescos depicting biblical and midrashic themes. One image portrays the dramatic showdown between Elijah and the priests of Baal (1Kings 18). They each prepare an altar but agree not to light a fire on it; the true god will be discovered by which offering is set aflame. In the midrash, the priests of Baal know that their god does not have such power, so they set a person under the altar platform to light it from inside. Subverting their desire to mislead people, God sends a poisonous snake to kill the hidden figure—and this moment is captured in the fresco (*Ex. Rab. 15:14, Yalkut Shimoni 1Kings 214, Pesiqta Rabbati 4*). Kära Schenk discusses additional midrashic associations of the frescos, focused primarily around images related to the Temple and prayer. "The crucial and unchanging function of the images," she concludes, "is the way in which they draw the congregation itself into the sacred narrative, designating them as Israel at worship before the sanctuary" (2010, 229).

Midrash has numerous links to liturgical practices throughout the year. Some texts are included verbatim as part of prayer rituals, such as the material that follows the morning blessing to occupy oneself with the study of Torah (Tabory 1997, 125). In the Sephardic rite, the passages include the "Baraita of Rabbi Ishmael"—a list of hermeneutical principles appended to the beginning of the midrash on Leviticus (*Sifra*). Midrashic interpretations are also woven into synagogue *piyyut*, liturgical poetry composed from late antiquity to the Middle Ages, some of which is still incorporated into prayerbooks and services. A *qedushta* written by Simon ben Isaac (11th c. Germany) for Rosh haShanah, for example, speaks of angels created anew each day and then extinguished like flax—burning at the touch of God's finger. Incorporating a motif found in *Genesis Rabbah 78:1* and *Lamentations Rabbah 3:8*, it is emblematic of the way that *piyyutim* reimagine midrashic motifs in poetic language (Hollander 2008, 105).

Scholars have long tried to determine how midrash might relate to synagogue preaching and teaching in late antiquity. Motifs that appear in midrash were likely performed as part of Targum, live Aramaic translation of the Torah reading; texts like Targum Pseudo-Jonathan record a good deal of midrashic-style elaboration. Some midrashic literature bears markers of oral presentation, and collections such as *Pesiqta de-Rav Kahana* and *Pesiqta Rabbati* are organized around the liturgical calendar of feasts and special sabbaths. These characteristics hint at a connection to synagogue observance but it is not definitive.

In reviewing the debate between scholars who view the midrashic teachings as products of the rabbinic academy (*beit midrash*) versus those who see traces of oral homilies from the synagogue, Rachel Anisfeld recognizes the importance of treating each text separately. She focuses on the 5th-century *Pesiqta de-Rav Kahana* (PRK) and states:

> We do not know exactly how PRK was used, whether as a pre-sermon sourcebook or a post-sermon record or simply as a midrashic work created and edited by those involved in some way in homiletical work. What we do know is that some rabbinic preaching was taking place during this period. Jerome, who flourished in the fourth and early fifth centuries, speaks of a popular preaching done by rabbis to great

> applause and appreciation. Certain rabbinic statements also indicate that people would come in masses to hear well-known rabbinic preachers, that there was a preference for aggadic topics over halakhic ones.
>
> Anisfeld 2009, 18–19

The sages recognized that aggadic midrash could not only sustain the relevance of Bible and tradition, but also entice listeners, provide solace in adversity, and move people's hearts. In *Sifre Deuteronomy 11:22* they noted, "If you want to know the Creator of the World, study aggadah, for through it you will come to know God and cleave to God's ways."

As we move a bit later in history, clearer links between midrash and synagogue teaching or preaching begin to emerge. The *Sheiltot de-Rav Aḥa*, composed in the Geonic era, collects multiple four-part lectures. Although the extant text is incomplete, the third part of the lectures includes a good deal of homiletical midrash. Most scholars believe that this work reflects literary redactions of lectures presented in the synagogue of the yeshiva for the beginning of the academic term, public assemblies (*kallot*), and other sabbaths.

Several of the "minor midrashim" reflect a connection to synagogue ritual as an outgrowth of targumic-exegetical practice; they appear to have been integrated into live Torah interpretation on the festivals—at least for several centuries (c. 1250–1500) in Ashkenaz and Italy. *Midrash vaYosha*, for instance, explicates the Song at the Sea which is read on the seventh day of Passover, the day on which the Israelites crossed through the waters to freedom according to rabbinic tradition. The midrash is copied into prayerbook manuscripts and there are instructions for how to incorporate it into the Torah reading. It is also likely that *Midrash on the Ten Commandments* had some association with the reading of the Ten Commandments on Shavuot, even though printed recensions appear to be more similar to short story collections than to standard rabbinic exegesis (Mikva 2011).

As the sermon grew more regular and more prominent within Jewish synagogue ritual, midrash continued to have a place. A number of preachers were well-known for creative and compelling integration of midrash within their sermonic teaching. Rabbi Adolph Jellinek (c. 1820–1893), for instance, was a celebrated orator in Vienna with a gift for using midrash aggadah to bring Jewish tradition into conversation with contemporary issues. It inspired many imitators, not always to good effect in his view. He complained in a letter to a friend:

> Because … I utilize the aggadah on a larger scale, all the text jugglers who puff and blow under an excessive load of the aggadah in their sermons believe that they are disciples of my school … . These persons are like poor cooks who use pepper not as a spice but as a food.
>
> Mayer 1921, 166

Integration of midrashic passages and motifs within Jewish practice illuminates an important dynamic. Scholars of rabbinic literature have noted the cyclical nature of oral traditions redacted as written texts, which then circulated for reoralization in diverse contexts. Themes evolve, with changes large and small as they appear in texts from different times and places. We cannot know the precise relationship between the oral and written forms, but midrash highlights a fluidity that exists within the ostensible fixity of ritual observance. Drawing on terminology used by Dell Hymes, performance is repeatable because it follows a script, but it also represents the emergent because the actualization of the script can vary and then help to determine future scripts and performances (Brown 2003, 6, 8). Performance theory has been drawn into ritual theory because of obvious overlaps. Midrash similarly can be stored, transmitted, and adapted; its transformations both reflect historical context and shape it.

Midrash as a Practice

Utilizing an interdisciplinary approach to performance theory, Richard Schechner coined the term "transformance." It is intended to communicate the power of performance (including ritual performance) to effect social, psychological and spiritual transformation (2003, 130). In the examples above, the contributions of midrash to the meaning, execution, and substance of ritual can surely augment their transformative power. Yet there is also a way in which midrash is itself a practice, effecting transformation by organizing Jewish lives through its scriptural world of ideas. In a maxim taught by the tannaitic figure Ben Bag Bag, interpretation of Torah is the crux of Jewish life: "Turn it over and over, for everything is within it. Look deeply into it, grow old and gray with it—for you have no better portion" (*m. Avot 5:22*).

As the practice of interpretation becomes multilayered, with study of both Hebrew Bible and rabbinic literature (Written and Oral Torah) seen as essential, it gets ever more thickly woven into the fabric of Jewish history. George Steiner (1989, 40) comments,

> Hermeneutic unendingness and survival in exile are, I believe, kindred. The text of the Torah, of the biblical canon, and the concentric spheres of texts about these texts, replace the destroyed Temple. ... The commentary underwrites—a key idiom—the continued authority and survival of the primary discourse. It liberates the life of meaning from that of historical-geographical contingency. In dispersion, the text is homeland.

He is not speaking specifically about the teachings within midrashic literature, but rather about the midrashic act—the act of interpretation. It is a foundational Jewish practice with intellectual, spiritual, behavioral, and social import.

It is not only a practice of reading, but also one of ongoing creation. Let us consider a range of examples. Some projects use drama, woven into ancient Jewish interpretive traditions. Storahtelling, for instance, sees its approach as an extension of live Targum.

> Its signature pedagogy ... draws from the ancient tradition of Torah reading alternating with an interpretive translation in the local language. [Facilitators] transform Scripture into scripts, making ancient stories and traditions accessible for new generations, advancing Judaic literacy, and raising modern social consciousness with meaningful conversations.
>
> *https://labshul.org/storahtelling*

Bibliodrama, as taught by Peter Pitzele and others, uses improvisational theater, inviting participants to step into the role of a character or an object in the text and give it voice.

> Deriving from the Jewish tradition of midrash, Bibliodrama explores the unspoken in the lives of the characters, the "back story" or "subtext" in the written narrative, even the spaces between the words, to bring the Bible alive. ... It becomes a window into the Bible and at the same time becomes a mirror in which participants can recognize parts of themselves.
>
> *www.bibliodrama.com/what-is-bibliodrama/*

Jewish music is also viewed at times through a midrashic lens, with composition and performance standing as interpretations of biblical and rabbinic texts. Debbie Friedman, an American singer-songwriter who helped to popularize folk aesthetics within Jewish music, taught a course at Hebrew Union College-Jewish Institute of Religion called "Music as Midrash." She described the process as one of responding to the text; her creative English expansions and musical expression certainly gave new life and meaning to the words, advancing her goal to involve people more deeply in the experience of Jewish prayer and practice. While her impact is most significant within the Reform movement, it extends across the Jewish spectrum (Bordowitz 2002). Other contemporary Jewish musicians, such as the multi-genre artist Alicia Jo Rabins and rapper Matt Bar, similarly see their work "as part of an unbroken chain of Jewish textual interpretation," creating modern midrash (Salzberg nd). On occasion, it explicitly incorporates a traditional midrash, as with Rabins' song "River So Wide" that envisages Satan playing a role in the binding of Isaac and Sarah's subsequent death (*Gen. Rab. 56:4, PRE 32*). Generally, however, such midrashic practices adapt interpretive modalities rather than content.

One familiar strategy in midrashic practice is to build a story around people and events in our own time, like ancient hagiography. The modern custom of adding an orange to the seder plate falls into this category. Some Jews who have incorporated the symbol see it as a feminist statement; they tell a story about a man who announced to a visiting female rabbi that women belong on the *bimah* about as much as oranges belong on the seder plate (i.e. not at all). The origin of the addition more likely traces back to a group of lesbians who placed bread crusts on the seder plate to protest their marginalization—changed to an orange by those who did not want to subvert Passover's food restrictions but wanted to express solidarity (Alpert 1997, 2–3). Since part of the ritual of the seder is to explain the significance of the ceremonial foods, these interpretive acts feel like authentic expansions of midrashic tradition. (And true to tradition, the story is rarely told the same way twice.) The orange innovation has led to a host of ideas for new foods on the seder plate, each with a tale of its own: an olive to protest the fact that many Palestinian farmers are unable to access their groves safely, a tomato to demonstrate concern for farmworkers, Skittles to make a statement against systemic racism, etc. The practice is not widespread but it does feel midrashic: it ties implicitly to scriptural concern for the marginalized, and explication accompanies the ritual as part of its performance.

The most obvious extension of midrash as practice is the ongoing production of textual interpretation, e.g. *Modern Midrash: The Retelling of Traditional Jewish Narratives by Twentieth-Century Hebrew Writers* (Jacobson 1987), *Dirshuni: Israeli Women Writing Midrash* (Weingarten-Mintz and Biala 2009), or the periodical of the Institute for Contemporary Midrash titled *Living Text* (1995–2004). They demonstrate the continuing organization of thought and behavior around a scriptural world of ideas. While some contemporary material challenges traditional Jewish theology or perspectives, the practice of midrash locates these efforts within a Jewish universe of discourse. As Judith Plaskow notes, "Invention is permitted and even encouraged. Midrash is not a violation of historical canons but an enactment of commitment to the fruitfulness and relevance of biblical texts" (Plaskow 1991, 56).

It has been a particularly generative mode of exploration for Jewish women in modernity. Plaskow continues,

> The discovery of women in our history can feed the impulse to create midrash; midrash can seize on history and make it religiously meaningful. Remembering and inventing together help recover the hidden half of Torah, reshaping Jewish memory to let women speak.
>
> *ibid.*

As an aspirational project, it embraces Victor Turner's conviction that performance (in this case, of women's voices in textual interpretation and women's bodies in ritual) can not only reflect culture but also impact its development (1986, 24). This approach was clearly manifest during second-wave Jewish feminism in the 1980s; one popular trend built on the traditional midrashic teaching that Rosh Chodesh was a special women's holiday, and resources were created for women who gathered together at the new moon to study Jewish texts and to claim their voice within Judaism. See, for example, Penina Adelman's *Miriam's Well: Rituals for Jewish Women Around the Year* (1990), originally published in 1986. There have also been efforts to mine biblical and midrashic literature more thoroughly for women's experiences that *are* present in traditional texts.

Feminist scholars offer several useful cautions about these endeavors. Although some classic midrash passages may partially subvert patriarchal assumptions, many still portray women in ways that advance androcentric power structures. Texts that appear to celebrate women's agency, for example, frequently are honoring their commitment to giving birth and producing male leaders (Fonrobert 2006, 270–73). Biblical interpretation cannot entirely escape the character of its foundational text, or the social and cultural processes that continue to shape both men's and women's voices. There are also questions about which women's perspectives are represented—a challenge that intersects with race, class, sexuality, and other aspects of Jewish identity—and about how to avoid universalizing assumptions regarding women's experience (Peskowitz 1995, 28–29). Further, there are concerns that the ongoing practice and production of midrash cannot effectively challenge historical marginalization because Jewish tradition has treated this discourse as less significant than halakha. As seen in the first section, midrash was often framed to support and enhance the halakhic system (Peskowitz 1995, 26; Fonrobert 2006, 247).

Nonetheless, the allure of midrash as a means to excavate unheard perspectives within sacred texts is so strong that it extends beyond Jewish efforts. An Episcopal priest and scholar of the Hebrew Bible and rabbinics, Wilda Gafney, authored a collection entitled *Womanist Midrash*. She describes it as embodying "a set of interpretive practices, including translation, exegesis, and biblical narratives, that attends to marginalized characters in biblical narratives, especially women and girls, intentionally including non-Israelite peoples and enslaved persons" (2017, 3). The multivocality and ongoing exploration of meaning in midrash are similarly attractive across religious boundaries. Ellen Davis at Duke Divinity School lifts up the teaching of Ben Bag Bag mentioned above:

> The ancient rabbis had another image for what it is to read Scripture critically, a saying I especially like: *"Hafokh bah wehafokh bah ... .* Turn it over and over; everything is in it—and in it [or, through it] you will see something." *Hafokh*—it is a verb one might use of turning a crystal over and over to examine its different facets, or of turning compost until it is ready for the soil. That latter nuance is especially suggestive of what it is to live productively with Scripture and out of its richness. Reading Scripture well is like being a master gardener, and the Bible is like soil; the thoughts of those who study it deeply grow in that medium.
>
> Davis 2007, 37

Within Judaism, midrash as a practice serves not only to cultivate relevance for modern readers of Scripture, but also to sustain a vital relationship with Jewish ritual. Especially for non-halakhic Jews, the claim that *mitzvot* have is in the way that they endow people's actions with significance and abiding value. As Robert Cover argues, "no set of legal institutions or prescriptions exists apart from the narratives that locate it and give it meaning" (1983, 4). Midrash creates the environment that makes ritual possible.

Bibliography

Adelman, Penina V. 1990. *Miriam's Well: Rituals for Jewish Women Around the Year*, 2nd edition. New York: Biblio Press.
Adelman, Rachel. 2009. *Return of the Repressed: Pirqe de-Rabbi Eliezer and the Pseudepigrapha*. Leiden: Brill.
Alpert, Rebecca. 1997. *Like Bread on a Seder Plate: Jewish Lesbians and the Transformation of Tradition*. New York: Columbia University Press.
Anisfeld, Rachel. 2009. *Sustain Me with Raisin-Cakes: Pesikta deRav Kahana and the Popularization of Rabbinic Judaism*. Leiden: Brill.
Balberg, Mira. 2017. "Ritual Studies and the Study of Rabbinic Literature," *Currents in Biblical Research* 16, no. 1 (October): 71–98.
Bell, Catherine. 1992. *Ritual Theory, Ritual Practice*. New York: Oxford University Press.
Bokser, Baruch. 1984. *The Origins of the Seder*. Berkeley: University of California Press.
Bordowitz, Hank. 2002. "Debbie Friedman: Singing Unto God," *Reform Judaism Magazine* 30, no. 4 (Summer), www.myjewishlearning.com/article/debbie-friedman-singing-unto-god/.
Boyarin, Daniel. 1990. *Intertextuality and the Reading of Midrash*. Bloomington: Indiana University Press.
Brown, Gavin. 2003. "Theorizing Ritual as Performance: Explorations of Ritual Indeterminacy," *Journal of Ritual Studies* 17, no. 1: 3–18.
Cover, Robert M. 1983. "The Supreme Court, 1982 Term—Forward: Nomos and Narrative," *Harvard Law Review* 97, no. 4: 4–68.
Davis, Ellen F. 2007. "The Soil that Is Scripture," in *Engaging Biblical Authority: Perspectives on the Bible as Scripture*. Ed. William P. Brown. Louisville, KY: Westminster John Knox, 36–44.
Eisen, Arnold. 1998. *Rethinking Modern Judaism: Ritual, Commandment, Community*. Chicago, IL: University of Chicago Press.
Eliade, Mircea. 1954. *The Myth of the Eternal Return: Or, Cosmos and History*. Trans. William R. Trask. Princeton, NJ: Princeton University Press.
——— 1963. *Myth and Reality*. New York: Harper & Row.
Fonrobert, Charlotte Elisheva. 2006. "The Handmaid, the Trickster, and the Birth of the Messiah: A Critical Appraisal of the Feminist Valorization of Midrash Aggadah," in *Current Trends in the Study of Midrash*. Ed. Carol Bakhos. Leiden: Brill, 245–75.
Fraade, Steven D. 2011. *Legal Fictions: Studies of Law and Narrative in the Discursive Worlds of Ancient Jewish Sectarians and Sages*. Leiden: Brill.
Frazer, James. 2013. *The Golden Bough* (originally published in 1890). Oxford: Oxford University Press.
Gafney, Wilda C. 2017. *Womanist Midrash: A Reintroduction to the Women of the Torah and the Throne*. Louisville, KY: Westminster John Knox.
Grimes, Ronald L. 2013. *The Craft of Ritual Studies*. New York: Oxford University Press.
Gruenwald, Ithamar. 1993. "Midrash and the 'Midrashic Condition': Preliminary Considerations," in *The Midrashic Imagination: Jewish Exegesis, Thought, and History*. Ed. Michael Fishbane. Albany: State University of New York Press, 6–22.
Halivni, David Weiss. 1986. *Midrash, Mishnah, and Gemara: The Jewish Predilection for Justified Law*. Cambridge, MA: Harvard University Press.
Heinemann, Isaac. 2008. *The Reasons for the Commandments in Jewish Thought: From the Bible to the Renaissance* (originally published in 1942), trans. Leonard Levin. Boston, MA: Academic Studies Press.
Hollander, Elizabeth. 2008. *Piyyut Commentary in Medieval Ashkenaz*. Berlin: Walter de Gruyter.
Homolka, Walter. 1997. "'God is Thy Rescue' as the Central Message of the *Seder* Ritual: The Midrash on Devarim 26 in its Biblical Context," *European Judaism: A Journal for the New Europe* 30, no. 2 (Autumn): 72–85.
Irshai, Ronit. 2017. "'And I Find a Wife More Bitter Than Death' (Eccl. 7:26): Feminist Hermeneutics, Women's Midrashim, and the Boundaries of Acceptance in Modern Orthodox Judaism," *Journal of Feminist Studies in Religion* 33, no. 1: 69–86.

Jacobson, David C. 1987. *Modern Midrash: The Retelling of Traditional Jewish Narratives by Twentieth-Century Hebrew Writers*. Albany, NY: State University of New York Press.

Kanarek, Jane. 2014. *Biblical Narrative and the Formation of Rabbinic Law*. New York: Cambridge University Press.

Kugel, James. 1983. "Two Introductions to Midrash," *Prooftexts* 3, no. 2 (May): 133–55.

Mayer, Harry H. 1921. "The History of Jewish Preaching," *Yearbook of the Central Conference of American Rabbis* 31: 158–85.

Mikva, Rachel S. 2011. "Midrash in the Synagogue and the Attenuation of Targum," *Jewish Studies Quarterly* 18, no. 4: 319–42.

——— 2021. "Medieval Biblical Commentary and Aggadic Literature," in *Judaism*, Vol. 2. Eds. Burton Visotzky and Michael Tilly. Stuttgart: W. Kohlhammer Verlag, 205–36.

Myers, Jody. 2000. "The Midrashic Enterprise of Contemporary Jewish Women," in *Jews and Gender: The Challenge of Hierarchy*. Ed. Jonathan Frankel. New York: Oxford University Press, 119–42.

Peskowitz, Miriam. 1995. "Engendering Jewish Religious History," Shofar: An Interdisciplinary *Journal of Jewish Studies* 14, no. 1 (Fall): 8–34.

Pitzele, Peter A. 1997. *Scripture Windows: Toward a Practice of Bibliodrama*. Los Angeles, CA: Alef Design Group.

Plaskow, Judith. 1991. *Standing Again at Sinai: Judaism from a Feminist Perspective*. New York: HarperCollins.

Rabins, Alicia Jo. Undated. "River So Wide: Explanation of a Musical Midrash," Jewish Women's Archive, https://jwa.org/article/river-so-wide-explanation-of-musical-midrash.

Rovner, Jay. 2000. "An Early Passover Haggadah According to the Palestinian Rite," *Jewish Quarterly Review* 90, no. 3/4 (Jan.–Apr.): 337–96.

Rubin, Nissan. 2008. *Time and Life Cycle in Talmud and Midrash: Socio-Anthropological Perspectives*. Brookline, MA: Academic Studies Press.

Safrai, Shmuel, Zeev Safrai, Joshua Schwartz, and Peter J. Tomson, eds. 2006. The Literature of the Sages, Second Part: Midrash and Targum, Liturgy, Poetry, Mysticism, Contracts, Inscriptions, Ancient Science and the Languages of Rabbinic Literature. Minneapolis: Royal van Gorcum and Fortress Press.

Salzberg, Alieza. Undated. "Modern Midrash," www.myjewishlearning.com/article/modern-midrash/.

Schechner, Richard. 2003. *Performance Theory* (originally published in 1977). New York: Routledge.

Schenk, Kära L. 2010. "Synagogue, Community, and the Sacred Narrative in the Duro-Europos Synagogue," *AJS Review* 34, no. 2 (November): 195–229.

Stein, Dina. 2005. *Maxims, Magic, Myth: A Folkloristic Perspective of Pirkei deRabbi Eliezer* (Hebrew). Jerusalem: Magnes Press.

Steiner, George. 1989. *Real Presences: Is There Anything in What We Say?* London: Faber and Faber.

Tabory, Joseph. 1997. "The Prayer Book (Siddur) as an Anthology of Judaism," *Prooftexts* 17, no. 2 (May): 115–32.

Turner, Victor. 1986. *The Anthropology of Performance*. New York: Performing Arts Journal.

Weingarten-Mintz, Neḥamah and Tamar Biala, eds. 2009. *Dirshuni: Israeli Women Writing Midrash* (Hebrew). Tel Aviv: Yediot Aḥronot.

Women of Reform Judaism. 2003. *Visiting Miriam's Well: A Study Guide*. New York.

Primary midrashic texts mentioned in the article that are available in English (of varying quality)

Berman, Samuel A. trans. and ed. 1996. *Midrash Tanhuma-Yelammedenu: An English Translation of Genesis and Exodus*. Hoboken, NJ: Ktav.

Braude, William G. trans. and ed. 1959. *Midrash on Psalms*. New Haven, CT: Yale University Press.

——— 1968. *Pesikta Rabbati*. New Haven, CT: Yale University Press.

Finkelstein, Louis. trans. and ed. 2014. *Sifra: A Commentary on the Book of Leviticus,* 5 vols. Philadelphia, PA: Jewish Publication Society.

Freedman, Harry and Maurice Simon. trans. and eds. 1983. *Midrash Rabbah*, 10 vols. London: Soncino Press.

Friedlander, Gerald. trans. and ed. 2004. *Pirkê de Rabbi Eliezer*. Skokie, IL: Varda Books.

Hammer, Reuven. trans. and ed. 1987. *Sifre: A Tannaitic Commentary on the Book of Deuteronomy*. New Haven, CT: Yale University Press.

Lauterbach, Jacob Z. trans. and ed. 2010. *Mekhilta de-Rabbi Ishmael*, 2 vols. Philadelphia, PA: Jewish Publication Society.
Mandelbaum, Bernard. trans. and ed. 1962. *Pesikta de-Rav Kahana: A Critical Edition*. New York: Jewish Theological Seminary of America.
Mikva, Rachel S. trans. and ed. 2012. *Midrash vaYosha: Translation, Annotation and Commentary*. Tübingen: Mohr Siebeck.
Townsend, John T. trans. and ed. 1997. *Midrash Tanhuma* (Buber recension), Vol. 2: Exodus and Leviticus. Hoboken, NJ: Ktav.

3
TALMUD

Gail Labovitz

The two Talmuds – of Roman Palestine (Yerushalmi) and Sassanian Babylonia (Bavli) are, on the surface, structured as a commentary on the Mishnah, a text redacted in Roman Palestine at about the turn of the 3rd century CE. Thus, in one sense, what either Talmud has to say about Jewish ritual is already guided to a significant degree by the agenda of that text. On the other hand, the Talmuds regularly further define, elaborate on, or even contest the information on ritual inherited from their predecessor. This, of course, should not be surprising given both the passage of time and that the Bavli is composed in a different geographical and political climate. Moreover, as will be seen repeatedly below, although the Bavli in particular would later become a foundational document for subsequent Jewish practice at the very end of Late Antiquity and early medieval period, at this time there was still a great deal of fluidity in Jewish ritual and liturgy, including regional differences in practice.

Another important point to note at the outset is that rabbinic Judaism (across all its strata) is a highly gendered system. Thus ritual practices relating to daily life and/or the annual cycle of holidays and other occasions that were expected (or not) of those gendered male and those gendered female often differed significantly. Most notably, m. Kid. 1:7 states:

> All positive commandments [literally: "do" commandments, that is, things the Torah states that a person must affirmatively do] that are caused by time, men are obligated and women are exempted, but all positive commandments that are not caused by time, men and women are similarly obligated; and all negative [literally: "you shall not do"] commandments, whether caused by time or not caused by time, men and women are similarly obligated.

However, as Elizabeth Shanks Alexander (2013) has demonstrated, this does not appear to be (yet) a prescriptive principle in the period of the Mishnah (and related tannaitic texts). Even into the Talmudic period, examples exist of positive, time-bound commandments (that is, acts that are meant to be performed at specific times of the day or on specific days of the year) to which women *are* obligated, and/or texts that find other justifications for exempting women. This theme will be threaded throughout the discussion below; similarly, as will be seen, life cycle events are marked differently (or not at all) depending on gender.

Life Cycle Rituals
Birth

Rites and rituals for a newborn child in rabbinic literature are very much a male-coded enterprise. Going back into the fundamental biblical texts, the birth of a male child necessitates the circumcision *(milah)* of the baby on his eighth day of life (Gen. 17:10–14 and 21:4; Lev. 12:3). Moreover, the responsibility to circumcise the child is placed first and foremost on the father biblically and rabbinically and is one of a father's primary responsibilities toward his son (see m. Kid. 1:7 and b. Kid. 29a); secondarily responsibility falls on the man himself or male rabbinic authorities. The Talmud also makes explicit that no such responsibility devolves on the mother (b. Kid. 29a). That is, as Lawrence A. Hoffman has observed,

> Circumcision was no life-cycle ceremony for a newborn; it was a ritualization of male status within Judaism ... a rite of masculine status bestowal in which one man, the father, initiates a man-to-be, his son, into the covenant with God.
>
> *Hoffman 1996, 80*

Shaye J. D. Cohen further notes that during this period circumcision takes on religious/ritual trappings, so that, for example, it must be performed with intent and by a Jewish *mohel*/circumciser (in place of the father himself), and is accompanied by blessings and related prayers (Cohen 2005, 21–22). Similarly, Talmudic and other rabbinic texts delineate technical details of the procedure, such as its essential surgical procedures (see m. Shab 19:2, and 6; also b. Yev 71b), or how and when the ceremony may need to be postponed for various reasons related to the health of the infant or calendrical considerations (such as when it is uncertain if the child was born on the Sabbath or not; see, for example, m. Shab. 19:5). As for the liturgy surrounding the ritual, much of the circumcision ceremony even as it is practiced to this day is rabbinic, both tannaitic and amoraic, in its origins (though it now includes a number of later accretions; Hoffman 1996, 74). The operation itself is preceded by a blessing said by the *mohel* and another said by the father, each acknowledging that a commandment is being fulfilled in this process; though the formula may have been somewhat variable still at this time (Hoffman 1996, 74), both the Yerushalmi (Ber 9:3, 14a) and Bavli (Shab. 137b) specify that both blessings use the introductory formula typical of the short blessings said to precede/accompany the performance of a commanded act. After the father's blessing, a short response is offered by those present. After the circumcision is completed, another blessing of praise is said; in current practice it is said by the *mohel*, over a cup of wine; however, in the Talmudic period, no mention is made of the wine, and the one saying it is designated simply as "the blesser," suggesting this may be someone other than the *mohel* or father (Rubin 1995, 107; see also Hoffman 1996, 83–89 and Cohen 2005, 34–36). Naming the child at the *milah* ceremony also does not appear yet in rabbinic sources; Nissan Rubin considers it likely this would have occurred at the *milah* at least as of the late rabbinic period (post-Talmudic), but obviously cannot say when in the ceremony this might have taken place (Rubin 1995, 112; see also Hoffman 1996, 90, 92–95). The circumcision ceremony was likely shared with others in the community (as evidenced by the communal response discussed above) and followed by a celebratory meal. At least one source, b. Ket. 8a, mentions a rabbi attending a "house of circumcision," while another, b. BQ 80a, states that several rabbis together went to a celebration of either a *"shavu'ah haben"* (the week of a son, presumably a circumcision ceremony; on this phrase see also t. Meg. 3:15, y. Ket. 1:5, 25c, b. BB 60b and b. San. 32b, and Rubin 1995, 114–17) or a *"y'shu'ah haben"* (redemption of the son; see the next item below).

How and when a newborn girl was named is not mentioned at all in rabbinic sources, nor is there any ritual prescribed to mark her birth or welcome her into the Jewish covenant. It may be noted that Lev. 12 prescribes a period of ritual impurity for the woman who has just given birth, and that indeed the length of the impurity is doubled (two weeks versus one) if the newborn is female. During a subsequent period of time (again doubled for the birth of a girl over that for a boy) any vaginal bleeding the mother experiences is deemed pure. While the biblical text describes a ritual of sacrifice to restore the mother to full purity, in rabbinically prescribed practice, the mother must immerse in a ritual bath (*mikvah*) at the end of the week/two weeks of initial impurity, while the need for a subsequent immersion is debated in m. Nid. 10:7. At least one amora, cited in y. Hag. 3:3, 79b, rules according to the more stringent position requiring the immersion, though as a protective measure rather than as an interpretation of biblical law.

Pidyon ha-ben (Redemption of the First Born Son)

Biblically, first born sons were dedicated to God in commemoration of the Israelite first borns having been spared in the final plague in Egypt, while after the sin of the Golden Calf first born sons were supplanted by the Levites (see Num. 3:40–51 and 18:13–19); in either case multiple passages dictate that they be "redeemed" (even in just Ex, see 13:15, 22: 28, 34:20). The question of which sons must be redeemed, however, is still somewhat open in the Talmudic period. If both parents are Israelites and the mother has had no prior miscarriages, still-births, or non-vaginal births, then if her first child is male, he must be redeemed. The Mishnah (m. Bekh. 1:1) presumes that sons of male priests and Levites are exempt, but it is left to later authorities to provide an explanation of why this is so (b. Bekh. 4a and 5a; see Rubin 1995, 126–27). It is also an open question among the amoraim as to whether the first born son of a woman who comes from a priestly or levitical family is exempt (though at least one tannaitic source, m. Bekh. 8:1, also suggests he is; in the Talmud, see b. Bekh. 4a and 47a). For those to whom it does apply, rabbinic tradition dictates that the obligation begins once the child has survived thirty days. Moreover, if the redemption did not take place on the thirty first day, the obligation remained, though there was no penalty imposed for the delay (see Rubin 1995, 128–29).

As with circumcision, the obligation of redemption falls primarily on the father of the newborn, but on a man himself if his father did not redeem him; despite the obligation coming into being because of the mother, she has no binding role in this process (b. Kid. 29a-b). Similarly, b. Pes. 121b presumes that the rite was accompanied by blessings, as was typical in rabbinic practice for the performance of a commanded act, and b. Kid. 8a further hints at a formula of intent stated by the father. However, there is no clear description of the ceremony or who (the father or the priest) says exactly what, and it is likely that practices varied over time and place during this period (Rubin 1995, 136). There are hints that the rite may have been conducted publicly or with guests, accompanied by a celebratory meal. In part, this depends on differing versions of a tradition referring either to "the week (*shavuah*)" (i.e., the circumcision, as already mentioned above) or "the redemption (*yeshua*)" of a son (b. BQ 80a, and see also b. BB 60b and Pes. 121b; Rubin 1995, 117–19).

Marriage

Marriage in rabbinic literature is described as a two-step process of betrothal (*erusin* being the term derived from biblical literature, while the rabbis add the term *kiddushin*; see particularly

Satlow 2001, 76–77; Labovitz 2009, 63–95) and nuptials (most commonly termed *nissu'in*, but see also further discussion below). The former creates a form of "inchoate" marriage, that is, a legal bond between the bride and groom that can only be severed by a formal divorce or the death of one of the parties; the latter initiates the consummation of the marriage and cohabitation. Although both are incorporated into one ceremony in the current day ritual, in the rabbinic era a significant period of time might separate the two (see, for example, m. Ket. 5:2), based on such factors as the age of the bride and whether this was her first marriage or not.

Betrothal

M. Kid. 1:1 states that "a woman is acquired in three ways … by money, by document, and by sexual intercourse"; t. Kid. 1:1–3 further specifies how each method is enacted and clarifies that the outcome is betrothal (see Labovitz 2009, 69–70). Susan Marks (2013, 11–69), however, makes a cogent argument that while the rabbis, beginning in the tannaitic period, delineated the legal methods and requirements for performing a valid and binding betrothal, they were far less concerned with representing this act as a ritual: "most, if not all, rabbinic explanations of betrothal deserve rather to be understood as licensing" (12). That said, at least a few tannaitic sources make mention of a "betrothal feast" (m. Pes. 3:7, t. Pes. 3:12, t. Meg. 3–14 and 15; m. BB 9:5 also mentions a "groom's meal" that a man might attend at the home of his future father-in-law), and similarly several Talmudic sources also mention such feasts (*yBet* 5:2, 63a, *yTaan* 1:8, 64d and 4:6, 69b, *yKet* 1:1, 24d, b. MQ 18b); b. Git. 89a also describes certain signs of a celebration that could indicate that a betrothal had taken place (moreover, it may be noted that this text includes the presence of women at the celebration). A "groom's/ grooms' blessing" is mentioned in both m. Meg. 4:3 and t. Meg. 3:14; the latter states that this blessing is recited at both a betrothal and wedding meal, but no text for the blessing is given. A later Talmudic text (b. Ket. 7b–8a, which will be discussed at greater length below) instead debates the possibility of distinct blessings for betrothal vs. the nuptials (while also noting that some rabbis preserved the practice of saying the same blessings at a betrothal as at a wedding), and provides a text for the former that continues to be used (with some minor emendations) before the act of betrothal at many Jewish weddings to this day. During the betrothal period, gifts might be exchanged between the families. At some point, a marriage contract (*ketubah*) was drafted and signed, including a pledge of a monetary settlement that would be due to the woman if widowed or divorced, and delineating property that she brought into the marriage from her family.

Weddings

Rabbinic texts are also reticent to provide a clear outline of wedding rituals, and thus it may be questioned to what extent a fixed ritual was observed in this period: "rabbis leave weddings relatively 'unritualized' … they rarely script or prescribe what needs to be done or said at a wedding" (Satlow 2010, 357). In the descriptions and discussions that do appear in the literature, however, certain consistent components of the process appear regularly. These include a procession taking the bride from her paternal/familial home to that of the groom and his paternal family, a feast, and the "*huppah*." As already hinted above, blessings accompanied the feast; the liturgy for these blessings seems to be in the early process of becoming standardized though not yet fully fixed.

Procession

Many different ethnic and religious groups in this time period shared the practice of initiating a wedding with a procession, conveying the bride from her paternal home to that of her husband-to-be and his family. Various rabbinic sources describe a variety of elements that might be part of such a procession. Several Babylonian Talmudic sources in particular (though often claiming to be citing earlier sources) refer to this part of the ritual as "*hakhnasat (ha) kallah*" – bringing in the bride (to the groom's home) – and clearly designate it as a public display (Suk. 49b, Meg. 3b and 29a, Ket. 17a, Mak. 24a). The bride would likely be dressed and adorned with cosmetics and jewelry, by her mother or other women, to the best of her family's ability, and sources describe her as being carried in a litter. Bride, and groom as well, could be decked in garlands or crowns. Various foods or other items might be paraded or scattered before the bride (m. Ket. 2:1, y. Ket. 2:1, 26b, b. Ket. 16b, b. Git. 57a); the procession might be accompanied by musicians, with participants dancing, singing, or otherwise praising and celebrating the bride/couple (m. Sotah 9:14, y. Pe 1:1, 15d and AZ 3:1, 42c, b. Ket. 16b–17a). Moreover, some of these customs and practices could attest to the bride's status as never previously married (and presumably a virgin) or as widow/divorcee. All told, however, our rabbinic evidence is fragmentary at best, and rabbis did not devote a great deal of attention to fixing the rituals of this event (except, perhaps, to prohibit some practices; see particularly Marks (2013, 107–33) on this point). It could, however, still carry legal import, as, for example, to establish whether the bride was previously never married, for the purposes of her marital settlement; also among the functions of a procession enumerated by Satlow (2001, 170) is that "it provides public 'proof' that a legitimate marriage occurred." In Satlow's understanding, the elements of the procession,, such as adorning the bride, garlands and the litter, "imply a link between marriage and royal coronation: the couple becomes 'royalty for a day'" (2001, 172). Rubin, on the other hand, suggests that the underlying purpose was "that the bride's family presented itself to the family of the groom by the bride and the rich rituals accompanying her," and as such "the bride was not important in her own right," but rather "served merely as a symbol representing her family's honor" (Rubin 2008, 114). The symbolism of removing the bride from her family of origin to that of her husband (and transferring her from the jurisdiction of her father to that of her husband) is also readily apparent; it is particularly her status and her personal and familial identity that is altered in the course of the wedding rituals (Satlow 2001, 172; Rubin 2008, 105).

Huppah

While in current Jewish practice, the term "*huppah*" signifies a public and open-sided canopy under which the wedding takes place, this is a post-Talmudic development. The rabbinic *huppah*, rather, is a chamber of some sort – either free-standing or a prepared room in the household of the groom and his paternal family (Büchler 1927), intended as a space for the sexual consummation of the union between bride and groom. Nor is such a chamber unique to Jewish weddings at this time period (Satlow 2001, 173–75; Marks 2013, 154–59 and 164–67). As noted, the wedding procession led from the home of the bride to that of the groom, and hence Satlow suggests that "it would end at the *ḥuppah*, a private place prepared by the groom or his family," but also notes that at this point in the proceedings a feast (see below) took place and thus only that "at some point—we do not know exactly when—the new couple would retire to their chamber" (Satlow 2001, 172 and 175). It may be that the bride was escorted to the chamber, perhaps with her mother or another woman to help her prepare, before the arrival of the groom. The *huppah* is paradoxically both a private space out of the sight of others (see, for example, b. Suk. 25b and Ket. 8b; and see Marks 2013, 159 and Satlow 2001, 175), and yet proximate to the public celebration; indeed, as Marks observes, it is the very presence of the *huppah* nearby that sets the character of a wedding feast and distinguishes it from other feasts (Marks 2013, 154).

Regardless of exactly when in the course of the proceedings either the bride or the groom entered the chamber, however, it was this moment in the ritual that seems to seal the status of the couple as married, such that "*k'nissa l'huppah*," entering into the *huppah*, becomes another rabbinic term for the nuptials stage of marriage already in tannaitic passages. Moreover, these tannaitic rulings (such as m. Yev. 3:10 and Ket. 5:3) indicate this legal point by noting certain obligations and rights between the spouses that only commence once entry to the *huppah* has occurred (see particularly Schremer 2003, 326–33, especially 327, and 342–44). That said, since the purpose of the *huppah* was as a space for consummation of the marriage, a failure of successful sexual initiation between the couple could result in a conundrum as to whether the marriage was indeed now binding, with all the attendant consequences (see, for example, m. Edu. 8:2 or t. Yev. 10:1–2, Ket. 4:3, Edu. 3:2; see Satlow 2001, 175). Finally, both Satlow and Marks note that there is no clear evidence that displaying evidence of hymeneal blood occurred at the wedding of a previously unmarried woman (Marks 2013, 160; Satlow 2001, 177).

Feast and Blessings

Feasts were a common part of celebrations in the ancient world, both rabbinic and beyond, and so just as with the circumcision ritual, a wedding was accompanied by feasting. Moreover, there is ample evidence that the wedding celebration consisted not of a single feast, but (at least for a first-time bride or groom) of a seven-day celebration marked by additional communal meals (see, for example, m. Neg. 3:2, y. Ket. 1:1, 25a, b. Ket. 4a and 7b). Since the wedding procession ended at the groom's paternal home, and this was the location of the *huppah*, this was almost certainly where at least the initial wedding feast took place. Thus, there is evidence that it was the task of the father to arrange the wedding celebrations on behalf of his son (Satlow 2001, 178; see also Schremer 2003, 99), while Tal Ilan notes that the term "*mishteh*"/feast "in rabbinic literature, beginning with the Mishnah, … is almost exclusively tied up with the word 'his son' … and understood as referring to wedding feasts" (Ilan 2017, 415, and see also the top of 416; see also the commentary to b. MQ 8b–9a in Labovitz 2021b, 166–68). Indeed, since the bride likely entered the *huppah* some time before being joined by the groom, it is an open question if the bride was present at all for most of the feast.

The feast is also the site of the most obvious and significant Talmudic addition to wedding rites, *birkat hatanim*, the grooms' blessing(s), the precursor to what would become the "*Shevah Berakhot*" (Seven Blessings) that remain part of the wedding liturgy down to the present. As discussed above, t. Meg. 3:14 mentions a blessing by this name that is recited at *both* a betrothal and wedding feast, but gives no further indication of the content of the blessing. The only text of such a blessing that comes down to us from rabbinic literature appears in b. Ket. 7b–8a in the name of Rav Yehudah, a Babylonian rabbi, who in fact lists six distinct blessings (though several have common themes and even repetitive language with each other; in subsequent practice, the seventh is for the wine over which the other blessings are said). The passage in which his blessings appear moreover opens (on 7b) by proposing language for a distinct betrothal blessing unique to that occasion, and presumably *different* from the grooms' blessing said at the nuptials. Thus there is a vigorous scholarly debate as to whether Rav Yehudah's blessings represent a

Babylonian innovation, or a passed down tradition (in part or whole) of the grooms' blessing mentioned in earlier sources. On the one hand, Satlow argues that at least the first three display themes more strongly associated with Palestinian amoraic thought and therefore "suggest a Palestinian origin for the motifs contained in these blessings" (Satlow 2001, 65 and see also 179; see also Katz and Sabato 2007). Others, however, suggest that this text should be read as Babylonian in both origin and outlook (Schremer 2003, 340–41; Marks 2013, 135–52; Ilan 2017, 135–43). Even this latter view is not to say, of course, that there were not earlier or other versions of blessings (since as already noted, blessings are already mentioned in earlier and/or Palestinian texts). In fact, if anything, the passage suggests that practice and liturgy were in flux throughout this time period; it reports multiple different practices (six blessings, five blessings, longer or shorter blessings, a blessing to be said after the initial seven days throughout the first year of the marriage, the practice of saying the same blessings at betrothal and the wedding, and so on; see also Hoffman 1996, 88). Of these scholars, Marks makes the most emphatic claim that the blessings are an amoraic ritual innovation, and describes this new practice as "a new Judaization of weddings," by which "[r]itual and ritual actors *particularized* wedding feasts in the Amoraic period" (Marks 2013, 140). Relatedly, Satlow observes that while rabbinic sources do not yet indicate the necessity for a rabbi to oversee a wedding, nonetheless "they do indicate the beginnings of a rabbinic desire to intrude into these proceedings" (Satlow 2001, 179).

In any case, Marks in particular also convincingly establishes that blessings were recited at the feast, and not to the couple in the *huppah* (that is, not as in current practice, where they are recited under the wedding canopy; Marks 2013, 162–63). Indeed, multiple scholars raise significant questions as to whether the blessings were said to the couple at all, or rather whether the name of *grooms'* blessings should be considered telling. The blessings are said only in the presence of a quorum of ten men, a number in which the groom is counted (y. Kid. 1:1, 25a, and b. Ket. 8a; similarly m. Meg. 4:3, t. Meg. 3:14 regarding tannaitic practice), suggesting that at least his presence is expected/required. If in fact the bride entered the *huppah* prior to the groom, and did not attend some or all of the feast (note an episode in b. Shab. 156b in which only the bride at the wedding is able to hear a beggar at the door, while *everyone else* is engaged in the feast), then the blessings might be directed at the groom alone, prior to joining the bride in the marital chamber (Buchler 1927, 129). The Yerushalmi, in Ket. 1:1, 25a, distinctly dismisses any need for the bride to be present, at least at subsequent feasts during the week of celebration (on this topic, see also Marks 2013, 145–46; similarly Ilan 2017, 143–44).

Death

Funeral and Burial

While tannaitic texts presume that close relatives of a person who has died undertake mourning rituals (see, for example, m. MQ 3:7), it is the Yerushalmi and Bavli which specify (albeit based on sources presented as tannaitic) the circle of those obligated. All agree that relatives of one degree – parents, children, siblings, and spouses – are obligated to each other, while some debate ensues about secondary relatives (such as grandparents or parents-in-law; y. MQ 35, 82d and b. MQ 20b). Prior to burial, the mourner is known as an *onen* (or "one whose dead lies before him") and is exempt from many other usual daily rituals (such as prayer) and is considered to be engaged primarily in seeing to the burial of the deceased (see m. Ber. 3:1 and b. Ber. 17b–18a).

The Mishnah in several places describes a process of *hesped* which took place as a person was escorted to burial. Though the term is often translated as "eulogy," it more accurately encompasses the entire funeral process, including a public procession, musicians, and loud lament. The body might be placed down along the way for words of praise and grief. Whereas the Mishnah suggests that this last element was observed only for men (m. MQ 3:8–9; see Labovitz 2021a, 26–28; Labovitz 2021b, 109–11), amoraic commentary reopens the possibility that the limitation did not apply to all women, and the Bavli may reflect differing customs in different parts of the Babylonian rabbinic community (b. MQ 27b–28a; see Labovitz 2021b, 444–49).

It is largely in the Talmud that the figure of the professional "eulogizer" (*sapdan/a*) comes to prominence, and in the Talmud that we find examples of rabbinic eulogies. A collection of several such orations appears in b. MQ 25b, while others are scattered elsewhere in the Talmud, but it is not clear from the small corpus available to us if these represent most particularly rabbinic eulogies (that is, eulogies given either for and/or by rabbis) or indicate a broad practice. The texts we do have are typically poetic and figurative, constructed from biblical citations and allusions, and enigmatic in meaning (on rabbinic eulogies, see Feldman 1972, Sysling 2007, Mandel 2005, Kraemer 2000, 99–102, Rubin 1997, 206–11). Similarly, while female (likely professional) wailing women are already an expected part of a funeral in tannaitic texts, it is again the Talmud that includes our only sample of words used by women (in the Babylonian town of Shehantziv) as part of such laments (b. MQ 28b). That these laments are representative of broader practices in the Babylonian Jewish community is certain possible, but we cannot be certain. If this was a typical part of funeral ritual, however, rabbinic Jewish practice, in Babylonia as well as Roman Palestine, would be similar to that of (upper class) Romans in the early common era, which included both speeches given by men (typically relatives, in the Roman case) known as the *laudatio funebris*, and chants known as *nenia* by professional female lamenters. The purpose of these eulogies and laments would be to increase crying and other expressions of grief among those assembled (see Labovitz 2021b, 469–81, and also 145–49). Mention may also be made here of a passage in b. MQ 27a–b; building upon m. MQ 3:7, the Talmud presents a series of sources attributed to the tannaitic period (and see t. Nid. 9:17), which limited ostentation and shows of wealth in practices of both the funeral procession carrying the body to rest and in caring for the mourners afterwards, as a kind of rabbinic sumptuary law.

Regarding burial, one additional significant concern must be noted. As already hinted, rabbinic (and quite likely other) Jews of Roman Palestine in this period followed funerary and burial practices that were largely in concord with (or even highly influenced by) the practices of their pagan and Christian neighbors (see Labovitz 2021a, 24–26, 30–32) – with the one likely exception that Romans often practiced cremation, while rabbinic tradition insisted on interment in the ground or burial caves (see Kraemer 2000, 97–98). Babylonian (rabbinic) Jews, however, found fundamental and problematic differences between their own preferred practices and those of the surrounding, primarily Zoroastrian, culture (see, for example, Kraemer 2000, 95–96), most notably in that Zoroastrians' beliefs dictated that the purity of the earth must be protected from the impurity of the corpse; hence burial was deemed sinful and corpses were instead to be exposed. That said, Talmudic sources are reticent on this topic and what little material there is remains difficult to interpret.

Mourning/Comforting the Mourner

The formal mourning period begins immediately after burial (or when the body leaves the local boundaries, if being taken to be buried in another town or the Land of Israel; b. MQ 22a), with what rabbinic texts sometimes call "the closing with the stone," i.e., the closing of the entrance to the burial cave. Already tannaitic sources (m. Ber. 3:2 and MQ 3:7, t. Ber. 2:11) presume that following the burial, participants in the funeral formed "lines" to comfort the mourners. Amoraic texts add only a small amount of detail, such as a requirement for ten men, not including the mourners, to perform this ritual, and noting changes in practice over time and place as to whether the lines passed before the mourners or the mourners passed through the lines (y. Pes. 8:8, 36c, and San. 2:1, 20a; b. San. 19a). There is little to no information in the sources on what the comforters said, or if indeed there were specific ritualized statements prescribed (Rubin 1997, 220–23; Kraemer 2000, 30, 40–41, 126–27).

Upon arriving home, the mourners were served a meal (known as *se'udat havra'ah*) prepared/brought by members of the community (see Rubin 1997, 235–39; Kraemer 2000, 32). Again, this custom is already present in tannaitic texts such as m. MQ 3:7 and San. 2:3 (see also t. BB 6:13). M. MQ 3:7 and t. Nid. 9:17 place limitations on what sorts of vessels were used to transport food brought to the mourner(s), which the latter explicitly explains as a measure so that the ostentation of the more wealthy should not embarrass those of lesser means; b. MQ 27a follows in this vein regarding the use of vessels in the household of the mourners themselves. Otherwise the amoraic tradition has little to add on this practice other than to continue to presume that it should be done; y. Ber. 3:1, 6a describes lentils being served at such a meal, while b. BB 16b provides a homiletical reason for such a custom.

Mourners were also ritually comforted by the mourners' blessing(s). According to some sources these were said throughout the week of initial mourning, not unlike the grooms' blessings of the wedding feast and week of celebrations, although there are varying accounts as to both the context in which the blessings were said and the number and content of the blessings. Several sources require that a quorum of ten men is required (similar to the groom's blessing), but the mourner(s) is not counted (in contrast to the groom). At least one early source (m. MQ 3:7; see Mandel 2005, 394) suggests the blessings were said immediately following the burial (perhaps as part of making the lines of comforters), but another (t. Ber. 3:23–24) situates them at a meal, presumably in the home of the mourner, along with ten cups of wine drunk at various points in the meal (Rubin 1997; Kraemer 2000; Katz and Sabato 2007). The ten cups are also mentioned briefly in both Yerushalmi (Ber. 3:1, 6a) and Bavli (Ket. 8a–b, Pes. 110a), with some differences as to how they are distributed through the meal, but both also suggest alternative sites at which the blessings might be recited, such as the synagogue (y. Pes. 8:8, 36b) and "the plaza" (meaning perhaps an open area in the burial grounds or a town square; b. Meg. 23b and Ket. 8a). T. Ber. 3:23 also notes that there is not a single custom, but rather variant practices of saying one, two, or three blessings, and provides themes but not full texts for a ritual of three blessings, apparently incorporated into the Grace after meals. Only one version of what seems to be a full text appears in the sources (b. Ket. 8a), but it is impossible to know if this is representative of common practice (see also b. Ber. 46b). As with other blessings that accompanied other life cycle rituals, it is likely that the exact text(s) of the blessings remained fluid (see Rubin 2008, 186). Rubin also argues that at a later period in Babylonian amoraic practice, only one blessing was said over a cup of wine after the meal (Rubin 2008, 188), and the rite fell out of common practice sometime not long after the Talmudic period.

Similarly, it is in the Talmud that many customs of mourning are most thoroughly described, though these are often attributed to earlier sources. Already in m. MQ 3:5 we read of mourning periods of seven and thirty days, but little of what mourning practices apply during those days, although subsequent paragraphs note tearing one's clothing, baring the shoulder (on this practice, see Rubin 1997, 167–70 and Labovitz 2021b, 374–76), and eating at least the original mourner's meal seated on an overturned couch. The first two paragraphs of the previous chapter, m. MQ 2:1–2, also hint that mourners refrained from labor, and m. Ber. 2:6 includes a ban on bathing. The Tosefta (t. Taan. 1:6) adds the obligation to refrain from wearing shoes, and (depending on how it is read; see Kraemer 2000, 41) several other restrictions such as bathing, work, and sexual intercourse; t. MQ 2:1–2 restricts hair cutting, laundering, and cutting one's nails, and 2:9 specifies that the mourner sits on an overturned couch for the entire first week of mourning (see also t. Pes. 3:16 on greeting mourners). Thus it falls to the two Talmuds to provide extended lists and discussion of mourning practices and restrictions. They add details to already known customs (for example, determining how long a tear must be and on which garment, and when/whether it may be mended), and provide more thorough and systematized lists of mourning practices for both seven and thirty days (and their reasons); these come to include, during the first seven days, restrictions on washing and anointing oneself with oil, sexual relations, wearing leather shoes, laundering clothes, and performing labor, and until the thirtieth day cutting one's hair or shaving, and attending joyous social events. If one is mourning a parent in particular, prohibitions may be extended throughout the first year. The most extended amoraic treatments on this topic appear in the commentaries to m. MQ 3:1 and 5–9, particularly y. MQ 3:5, 82a–83a and b. MQ 14b–16a and 19a–24a (and see Rubin 1997, 163–88 and Kraemer 2000, 84–87 and 117–20).

Calendrical Rituals

In the rabbinic conceptualization of the calendar, the Sabbath is Divinely set and built into the ontological nature of creation (Gen. 2:1–3); it occurs every seventh day (from sunset to sunset, as is the case for all days in the Jewish calculation) whether recognized by human beings or not (see Tabory 2006, 560). On the other hand, humans are instrumental in monitoring the cycles of both the lunar month and solar year so as to establish the beginning of each new month and hence the days on which holidays will occur. The most prominent feature both linking and distinguishing the Sabbath and major festivals (the Pilgrimage festivals and High Holydays), however, is the command to abstain from labor, one which is repeated numerous times in the Torah (and is included in the Ten Commandments as regards the Sabbath: Ex. 20:8–11, Deut. 5:12–15; see also Lev. 23 and Num. 28–29 regarding the festivals). While there is evidence that this prohibition, variously understood, was well-associated with the Sabbath in Jewish sources prior to the rabbinic period, much rabbinic energy was engaged in defining and delineating what activities were forbidden and how one came to violate the prohibition (see, for example, Cohen 2007, 134–38; Doering 2010, 570–71; Hidary 2015). The primary distinction between the Sabbath and the festivals is in the permission to cook and prepare food on the holidays (with certain limitations) and related acts that become permitted more generally on those days (see m. Meg. 1:5 and Beitzah 5:2; see also Tabory 1995, 63–70). An additional set of activities that were not considered to be labor as specified in Torah, but still antithetical to the prohibitions of Shabbat and holidays (either because of their "everyday" nature and/or that they might lead to a prohibited activity) were forbidden under the rubric of "*shevut*," restfulness (Tabory 1995, 70–71; Hidary 2015).

The Sabbath

Aryeh Cohen goes so far as to make an argument that refraining from the forbidden labors is *the* defining feature of the rabbinic Sabbath, and hence becomes a ritual in its own right and/or lends a ritual cast to any (including otherwise ordinary) activities that do occur on that day: "Shabbat is a space which is constructed by an absence of activity. … Everything that happens on this blank canvas – from walking to eating to praying – is a Shabbat ritual" (A. Cohen 2012, 114). That said, there are ritual acts that mark both the onset and conclusion of the Sabbath and festivals, and liturgical features that mark both occasions. Tannaitic law, for example, presumes that lamps, which cannot be kindled, extinguished, or even adjusted during the Sabbath, should be lit prior to sunset so as to provide consistent light in the household (see m. Shab. 2), although the ritualization of this act through an accompanying blessing is post-Talmudic. A blessing over wine to acknowledge the holiness of the in-coming day – *Kiddush*, from the root *k.d.sh* meaning holy and/or set aside – should be recited at the start of the Sabbath or holiday, and certainly before eating. Similarly at the conclusion of the day, the *Havdalah* – from the root *b.d.l/* to separate or distinguish – is a series of blessings recited over wine, a lit lamp (to symbolize that it is permissible again to ignite a flame), and fragrant spices. Into the amoraic period, however, the exact text of these blessings (and their order) was likely fluid (as with much of the liturgy; see, for example, b. Pes. 102b–105a regarding *Havdalah*), and women's obligation to participate was an open question (see b. Ber. 20b regarding *Kiddush*). The Sabbath is intended to be, both in rabbinic law and in records known to us of practices in Jewish communities during this time period (from both Jewish and non-Jewish sources), a day of joy and physical pleasure; there should be three meals during the course of the day (in contrast to the usual expectation of two) and marital sex is encouraged (S. Cohen 2012; Doering 2010, 572–73; Tabory 2006, 561–62). Additionally, the Sabbath is marked liturgically by the addition of the "*Musaf*" service, a prayer meant to represent the additional sacrificial offerings of the Sabbath and other holy days in biblical law/Temple practice, and by communal readings of the Torah; this latter practice likely well-preceded the rabbinic period.

Pilgrimage Festivals (Passover, Sukkot, the Feast of Weeks)

The very terms used collectively for these three festivals in the Torah, *regalim* and *hagim*, both derive from roots that identify these occasions as pilgrimage festivals. They were marked by seasonal agricultural offerings and animal sacrifice, and also celebrated stages in the agricultural cycle of the Land of Israel. In the wake of the destruction of the Temple in Jerusalem, the rabbis adapted and developed existing rituals of the holidays (particularly for Passover and Sukkot) that could be practiced by individuals, family groups, and communities, and perhaps even created new rituals. Much of this process already occurs in the tannaitic period in the Mishnah and related documents: instructions for removing leavened products from the home and the seder ritual for Passover (m. Pes. chaps 1–3 and 10), and for building and dwelling in a *sukkah* (a temporary hut) and gathering the four species (palm, willow, myrtle, and *etrog*/citron) on Sukkot. Reciting the Hallel, a collection of Psalms, on these days is also noted already in multiple locations in the Mishnah and cognate literature, as is the *Musaf* (additional) service.

The Talmud(s), therefore, does little to add new ritual elements, but rather considers questions that follow from tannaitic texts and prescriptions, and adds explanations, details, and clarifications to the tannaitic rituals. On occasion, differences between Palestinian and Roman influenced practice and that of Sassanian Babylonia may be noted (see, for example, b. Pes. 116a, in which Babylonian rabbis are unfamiliar with the Palestinian practice of dipping vegetables at the start of a meal, and hence the way in which this practice is incorporated into the Passover seder). Amoraic texts do also suggest that the question of women's obligation to and/or participation in holiday rituals remained open into/during this period. On the one hand, holiday rituals would seem to represent very clearly "time-bound commandments," given that they are to be performed on specific dates (and some at specific times of the day as well), and hence women ought to be exempt, especially as the principle of m. Kid. 1:7 (discussed in the Introduction) came to be increasingly understood as prescriptive rather than descriptive (see Alexander 2013). Yet women come to be obligated to drinking four cups of wine on the basis that "they too took part in the miracle" (b. Pes. 108b), and consuming matzah and bitter herbs on the first night of Passover (y. Pes. 8:1, 35d, b. Pes. 43b, 91b); they are (generally) exempted from reclining at the meal (b. Pes. 108a; the brief passage in y. Pes. 10:1, 37b is unclear and thus Hezser (2007, 103) and Hauptman (2007, 111), draw diametrically opposed conclusions), but nonetheless seem to have been expected to be present and could even have been participants in the ritual (on this point and women's roles in Passover rituals more generally, see Lehman 2003, Hezser 2007, and Hauptman 2007). Women were formally exempted from the central rituals of Sukkot – taking the four species and dwelling in the *sukkah* (see Lehman 2006) – but in this case there is some evidence for women's presence in the *sukkah* nonetheless in the amoraic period, as documented by Shulamit Valler (see Valler 2007 and Valler 2009, particularly 10–11).

A few words are also in order specifically regarding Shavuot, known as Atzeret in rabbinic literature. Biblically, this holiday is entirely agricultural in emphasis and has no historical associations (as Passover does with the Exodus or Sukkot with the time of the Israelites' wanderings in the wilderness); it is the occasion on which first fruits are brought to the Temple. It thus had little ritual associated with it after the destruction of the Temple, and has no tractate dedicated to it in the Mishnah as do Passover and Sukkot. It is most particularly in the Talmud that a rationale is offered for the preservation of this holiday nonetheless, by setting it as the anniversary of the date on which the Revelation at Sinai occurred. This is done through the combination of two related calculations: (a) determining the date of Revelation on either the sixth or seventh of the month of Sivan based on the account in Ex. 19 (see particularly b. Shab. 86b–88a), and (b) fixing of the date for the biblical holiday through a (somewhat tendentious) interpretation of Lev. 23:15–16 such that the counting of seven weeks (a practice known as counting the Omer, which continues to the current day) begins on the second day of Passover (the sixteenth of Nissan), with the result that the fiftieth day will be the sixth of Sivan (see particularly b. Men. 65a–66a, and also b. RH 6b; Tabory 1995, 151–54). This connection is stated at least once, in b. Pes. 68b, while a subtle hint that this association became normative in the Talmudic period may be found in b. Meg. 31a (and see also y. Meg. 3:7, 74b): while the Mishnah (m. Meg. 3:5) proposes that the reading from the Torah on the holiday be one about the holiday itself (encompassing the passage beginning at Deut. 16:9), the Talmud offers an additional tannaitic source that "some say (the reading should begin with) 'In the third month'" (Ex. 19:1) – that is, the account of Revelation – and adds that "now that there are two days [see just below], we read both" (with the Revelation read on the first day; see Tabory 1995, 153–54 and Doering 2010, 577–78). Other ritual elaborations of this connection, however, would develop only after the Talmudic period.

One of the most far-reaching innovations recorded in the Talmudic period (but see also the single tannaitic reference in t. Eruv. 4:3), however, is that of the second day of the festivals. Biblically, Passover and Sukkot are marked by a single festival day at the beginning and end of the week-long holiday, and the Feast of Weeks is celebrated for a single day. According to the Talmudic account (m. RH 2:2–4 and b. RH 21a), the calendar and hence the days of the festivals were originally set by a religious court based on observation of the new moon – which might occur on either the twenty-ninth or thirtieth day after the previous new moon – and the news of a new month was spread by a system of signal fires. When these were disrupted, messengers were sent out, but it would not have always been possible for the messengers to reach far-flung diaspora communities before the date of a holiday. Unsure of the length of the prior month, these communities developed a practice of observing holidays for two days, performing all the rituals of the holiday on each day, such that one or the other would be the correct date (the first if the prior month were shorter, the second if it had been extended). This prompted a number of questions such as which communities were subject to the practice and how a person traveling between locations with different practices (one day or two) was to act (b. Pes. 51b–52a, RH 21a), and whether the two days were to be understood as one "long day" or two distinct days (b. Bets. 4b; see also Tabory 1995, 81–82 for additional examples). Moreover, during this period of time (and beyond), rabbinic culture moved toward the creation of a fixed calendar (see, for example, Stern 1993), such that dates for the holidays could be known with confidence to all Jewish communities, thereby potentially obviating the stated reason for the custom. Hence each of the texts already cited here also notes contention on whether the custom must be observed, but b. Bets. 4b (and see also y. Eruv. 3:9, 21c; but also Katz 1988, 385–86, n. 2) records that "they sent from there [that is, from the Land of Israel to Babylonia], 'be careful of the practice of your ancestors (that is) in your hand; sometimes (the government) issues decrees of persecution (against the Jews) and it (the setting of the calendar) will come to be disrupted'" (see Tabory 1995, 80; Stern 1993, 51; Katz 1988, 386–87). The practice thus persisted, and is observed in many communities outside of Israel to this day.

High Holydays (Rosh haShanah and Yom Kippur)

Torah declares the first of Tishrei to be "a day when the horn is sounded" (Num. 29:1) or "a sacred occasion commemorated with loud blasts" (Lev. 23:24), but gives little if any additional information on the nature or purpose of the holiday. Although both Nisan and Tishrei function at different places in Scripture as the transition time between years, the establishment of this day as Rosh haShanah (the beginning of the year) – the very name by which this holiday is known to this day – is a rabbinic innovation (see m. RH 1:1). The rabbis further associated Rosh haShanah with a day of judgment (m. RH 1:2; y. RH 1:3, 57a; b. RH 8a–b and 27a; see Tabory 1995, 217–20) and, according to some, Tishrei as the month in which the world was created (b. RH 8a, 10b–11a).

In keeping with the biblical accounts of the holiday, however, rabbinic texts center the blowing of a *shofar* (a hollowed out horn of a ram or similar animal) as the primary ritual of the day, as can be seen particularly in chapter 3 of m. RH, but also other tannaitic texts. Debate continued into the amoraic period, in both Palestine and Babylonia, however, as to the required number, sounds, and sequence of the blasts (see, for example, y. RH 4:10, 59c, and b. RH 33b–34a, and discussion in Tabory 1995, 242–45). While men are required to either blow the *shofar* or hear it blown by someone else similarly obligated, both tannaitic and amoraic texts exempt women on the grounds that the obligation is "time bound" (t. RH 2:5, y. Ber. 3:3, 6b and Kid. 1:7, 61c, b. RH 30a – but see also 33a – and Kid. 33b). *Shofar* blasts were also connected to the other prominent liturgical element of the day, the sections of the Musaf prayer known as "*Malkhuyot*" ("Divine Sovereignty"), "*Zikhronot*" ("Remembrances"), and "*Shofarot*" ("*Shofar* blasts"), each of which includes a recitation of Scriptural verses and a concluding blessing related to its theme (see m. RH 4:5–6 and t. RH 1:12 and 2:12–14). Talmudic texts add some guidelines for selecting (or excluding) verses but it appears that the liturgy was somewhat fluid throughout the rabbinic period and subject to the knowledge and creativity of the person leading the recitation (see y. RH 4:7, 59c and b. RH 32a–b; y. RH 1:3, 57a also records a piece of a personal prayer attributed to the amora Rav for the day). The *shofar* was blown at the conclusion of each section (as is still the case in traditional liturgy).

Having given Rosh haShanah an identity as a day of judgment, it is also not surprising that the rabbis then deemed the days between Rosh haShanah and Yom Kippur, the Day of Atonement (see just below) a particularly propitious time for repentance (though the name

"Days of Repentance" appears only once in y. RH 1:3, 57a, but not in the Bavli). Thus, in one instance (b. Ber. 12b; see also y. RH 4:6, 59c and Tabory 1995, 232), Babylonian amoraim discuss whether certain minor emendations emphasizing Divine sovereignty and justice should be included in the daily liturgy, a practice which many communities still preserve.

Yom Kippur, the tenth of Tishrei, was easier for the rabbis to assimilate into a system without a temple or sacrifices. Although a significant part of the holiday as described biblically focuses on an annual ritual of purification of the sanctuary (Lev. 16:1–28), the final verses of the chapter and other references to the occasion provided seeds for a reworking of the meaning of the day (an occasion of atonement for sins both religious and interpersonal; Lev. 16:30 and 34; Lev. 23:27–28) and its rituals. Multiple passages specify that the day is one of "self-denial" (Lev. 16:29 and 31; Lev. 23:27–29 and 32; Num. 29:7) and likely this was established to mean a fast well prior to the beginnings of the rabbinic movement (see Tabory 1995, 274). Rabbinic literature, however, provides additional proscriptions: "Yom Kippur is prohibited in eating and drinking, washing and anointing (with oil), wearing shoes and sexual relations" (m. Yoma 8:1) – though Talmudic sources continue to consider fasting from food and drink as the most central and critical prohibition relative to the others (see particularly y. Yoma 8:1, 44d and b. Yoma 74b; Tabory 1995, 278–79 and Rosenthal 2000). Talmudic sources also attempt to find biblical sources for or allusions to these restrictions, further define their limits and violations (y. Yoma 8:3, 45a, b. Yoma 74b and 76a–79a, 80a–81a), and consider to whom they apply: women – including those who are pregnant – are expected to fast (m. Yoma 8:5, b. Yoma 82a), children may be educated to fast prior to reaching full majority (m. Yoma 8:4, t. Yoma 4:2, b. Yoma 82a), the sick may be exempted (m. Yoma 8:6, t. Yoma 4:4, b. Yoma 83a).

The other most notable rituals of Yom Kippur are in the prayers for the day. As for any day on which Scripture prescribes an additional offering, there is a Musaf service. Yom Kippur, however, is unique in being the only day in the holiday cycle on which a fifth service is added to the day (as already noted in m. Taanit 4:1). This service is known as *Neilah* (the closing; or "*Neilat haShe'arim*," the closing of the gates) and occurs in the evening near the end of the day. As is common, amoraim further discuss the nature of this service (are the closing gates those of the Temple or of Heaven?) with further implications for exactly when it takes place (y. Ber. 4:1, 7c and Taanit 4:1, 67c), and in the Bavli dispute even if it includes a separate recitation of the *Amidah* prayer (b. Yoma 87b; see also Tabory 1995, 283–84). In addition, every *Amidah* prayer of every service of Yom Kippur includes "*vidui*," a statement confessing sins, a requirement introduced in t. Yoma 4:14–15. Once again, amoraim took up the task of discussion exactly where in one's prayer this should be said, and suggested language to be said (b. Yoma 87b; see the discussion in Tabory 1995, 285–90).

Minor Festivals, New Moon, Fasts

As already discussed above, one of the main developments of the amoraic period in regard to the Jewish calendar was the move toward a system of intercalation. Thus, although the Talmud continues to discuss the process of taking testimony to the appearance of the new moon, this was not the practice at this time. The main ritual additions for the date determined to be the New Moon are the Musaf prayer (which corresponds to an additional offering that was to be made on this day; Num. 28: 11–15), a mention of the occasion in other daily prayers and the blessing after eating, and reading from the Torah; these are already established by the tannaim. The main addition of the Talmud in this regard is to determine the exact starting and end point of the reading, and how it should be divided among those called to the Torah (b. Meg. 21b–22a). A single source, b. Taan. 28b, hints at the recitation of Hallel (in a slightly reduced form) on this day in Babylonia, as a custom rather than an obligation, but this continued to be a point of debate and controversy for some time after the Talmudic period, before becoming normative Jewish practice (on the rituals of Rosh Hodesh, see Tabory 1995, 37–39).

Although the holiday of Hanukah has its roots in the books of the Maccabees and the events recorded there (see I Macc. 4:52–59, II Macc. 10:5–8) and is mentioned in other early sources such as Josephus (who refers to it as the "Holiday of Lights," *Antiquities*, 12, 7, 7), it gets very little attention from the rabbis of the tannaitic period. Only one mishnaic (and parallel toseftan) source makes even peripheral reference to Hanukah lamps (m. BQ 6:6 and t. BQ 6:28), while one toseftan passage mentions reciting Hallel all eight days of the holiday (t. Sukkah 3:2) and m. Meg. 3:6 assigns a reading from the Torah; neither is there any sustained cohesive discussion of the rites of the holidays in the Yerushalmi (though see y. Trumah 11:5, 48b, Orlah 1:1, 60d, Shabbat 2:1, 4c and Sukkah 3:4, 53d, each very brief references to lighting a Hanukah lamp). Rather, it is the Babylonian Talmud, over several pages in tractate Shabbat (21a–24a), that gathers together information and provides the outlines of the holiday as it came to be known in subsequent Jewish practice, giving a reason for the custom of lighting lamps (the miracle of the oil that lasted for eight days, an account not found in Maccabees) and delineating relevant details of how this ritual is to be performed. This leads Geoffrey Herman to conclude that "the Babylonian contribution would appear to have been quite decisive in shaping the holiday observances in the direction of emphasizing the kindling of light(s)" (2014, 266), while others continue to see roots in tannaitic and Palestinian practice (see, for example, Tabory 1995, 376–78, Aminoah 1998, and Friedman 2006; for a somewhat intermediary position, see Benovitz 2007). Be that as it may, the central ritual of Hanukah becomes the lighting of a lamp at nightfall to "publicize the miracle," the minimal requirement being one lamp each night for the entire household (while only the most dedicated light multiple lamps on varying nights of the holiday; b. Shabbat 21b), which should then be placed at the doorway of the house (b. Shabbat 22b–23a), with a blessing accompanying the lighting (b. Shab. 23b; for a discussion and summary of these practices, see Tabory 1995, 376–86). Women are, according to Rabbi Yehoshua ben Levi, obligated to light (as they are obligated to wine at seder and hearing the book of Esther) because "they too were part of [that is, saved by] the miracle" (b. Shabbat 23a).

The primary ritual obligation of the holiday of Purim is the reading of the biblical book of Esther, which recounts the events the holiday subsequently celebrates – the genocidal degree of Haman against the Jews in the kingdom of Persia, and actions of Esther (wife of King Ahashueros) and her cousin (and foster father) Mordechai to avert it. As with many other rituals discussed here, the Mishnah, in tractate Megillah, provides the outlines of this practice (when it is to take place, from what sort of scroll, and so on), while the Talmuds add nuance and detail, including that women are obligated to hear the scroll read (b. Meg. 4a). Hallel is not recited on Purim, and several amoraim propose reasons for why this is (not) so, including that the reading of Esther fulfills the same purpose (b. Meg. 14a and Arakhin 10b). The only other ritual mentioned in the Mishnah even in passing is the giving of gifts to the poor (m. Meg. 1:4), based on Esther 9:22 (and see also 18–19): "They were to observe them as days of feasting and merrymaking, and as an occasion for sending gifts to one another and presents to the poor." A short passage in b. Meg. 7a–b (and see also y. Meg. 1:4, 90d) expounds on and sets rules for this charitable practice (and see Tabory 1995, 357–60), while also doing the same for the other elements of the verse – sending gifts between friends and engaging in a festive meal (on feasting, see also y. Meg. 1:1, 70a, and 1:7, 70b, and Tabory 1995, 354–55). One rabbi of this period also declared that the feasting should include drinking until "one does not know how to distinguish between 'cursed be Haman' and 'blessed be Mordechai'" (b. Meg. 7b), a ruling that engendered much commentary and controversy in later sources and practices (see Tabory 1995, 355–56).

Tannaitic literature (m. Taan. 4:5–7 and RH 1:3; t. Taan. 3:6, 10–14) records one particularly significant annual day of communal fasting and mourning, the ninth of Av, commemorating the destruction of both the first and second Jerusalem Temples (both said to have occurred on this date), and it appears that this fast in particular was also observed in the amoraic period (see b. RH 18b and Taan. 12b; Tabory 1995, 403). In truth, similar to the case with dating the Revelation at Sinai, ambiguities and inconsistencies in the biblical record led to rabbinic discussion and disagreement as to the exact date of the destruction of the first Temple (see, for example, t. Taan. 3:10), and some considered it obligatory to fast on some or all of the tenth as well (y. Taan. 4:6, 69b–c and Meg. 1:4, 70c). On the other hand, there are also indications that some sought to abolish the fast, generally or at least on the occasion when it fell on the Sabbath and had to be deferred (y. Taan 4:6, 69c and Meg. 1:4, 70c, b. Meg. 5b). The procedures for fasting and other restrictions of the day are both similar to those of the fast on Yom Kippur and to restrictions placed on those in mourning (see, for example, t. Taan, 3:12, b. Taan 29b–30a and Pes. 54b); there is a reading from the Torah and the book of Lamentations is read, and some say laments composed for the occasion (on the rituals of this day, see also Tabory 1995, 402–04).

Rituals of Daily Life

The mishnaic tractate of Berakhot/Blessings, broadly considers three, or perhaps four primary topics: the recitation of the biblical verses that comprise the "*Shema*" (named after the first word of the first verse recited, Deut. 6:4) and several blessings that precede and follow it, the daily "Prayer" that was to be said (at least by men) at several set times of the day, and blessings – which might be further subdivided into blessings said before and after food consumption, and blessings over other events (such as receiving good or bad news, building a new house, using new vessels) and/or phenomena (lightning and thunder, earthquakes, encountering the ocean). A number of ritual acts, such as those relating to holidays related above (for example, eating matzah on Passover or taking the *lulav* and *etrog* on Sukkot) or to daily observances were also typically expected to be accompanied by a blessing. As in many areas of Jewish law, the starting point of Talmudic ritual and practice, then, is these rulings of the tannaitic period. That said, it is also in the amoraic period that elaborate rules for the composition and organization of liturgy develop, as detailed at length by Ruth Langer (Langer 1998, 19–36, and see particularly 25–29; see also Heinemann 1977, 53–55 and 233–40); this includes setting the basic structure of blessings, which are in turn the building blocks of much of rabbinic liturgy.

Food Blessings

Scholars widely agree that the concept of blessing food (either before or after partaking) is pre-rabbinic, even biblical (see Deut. 26:15, I Sam. 9:13; and particularly the discussion and examples in Benovitz 2010). The rabbis, however, put their own distinctive stamp on the practice; indeed, this ritual practice became a means of distinguishing and shaping rabbinic Jews through the seemingly mundane act of eating (a point emphasized by Brumberg-Kraus 2005, 305–06, Kraemer 2007, 73, and Marks 2014, 73, for example). Rabbinic texts, beginning with the Mishnah (most particularly Ber. chapters 6 and 7), attempt to develop a specific rabbinic language and formulation for food blessings, and protocols for which blessing should be said when and how.

The rabbinic system of food blessings encompasses several components. First, there are blessings to be made both prior and subsequent to eating (indeed, rabbinic sources, both tannaitic and amoraic, debate whether one or both is the primary, biblical obligation, or whether either is a rabbinic enactment; see Benovitz 2010). As regards a blessing prior to eating, the underlying theology of the ritual gestures toward the Divine source and ultimate ownership of all that exists in the world (an idea frequently linked to Psalm 24:1 by the rabbis), such that partaking without an acknowledgment of that source is equivalent to stealing from God or (in the language of the Temple system) misusing sanctified property (see b. Ber. 35a–b for an example using both analogies). "Blessings are thus a desacralizing vehicle" that "render sacred food 'profane,' ... making it fit for everyday human consumption" (Hoffman 1996, 160; similarly Bokser 1981, Kraemer 2007, 75–77, Benovitz 2010). David Kraemer further notes that rabbinic formulations "speak of God as the creator of the food to be consumed and *they all do so in the present tense*," the intended theological message being that "God is actively and continually the creator of the earth and its fruits" (2007, 76–77, emphasis in the original; see also Brumberg-Kraus 2005, 305).

Thus, blessings also entail distinguishing between particular types of food (see m. Ber. chapter 6). In the words of Kraemer (2007, 78), the "system outlined here clearly prefers greater specificity," and agricultural products in particular are distinguished by how they grow (tree fruits and grains being distinguished from other plants); the system also "privileges certain specific kinds of foods" (notably bread/grain products, wine, and items considered particularly typical of the Land of Israel). He therefore suggests that one particular contribution of the amoraim to this ritual is further discussion of these distinctions and the process of determining which is the "correct" blessing, as for example, when multiple food items are being consumed on a single occasion (85). As with other areas of liturgy, there is evidence to suggest that while the rabbis were moving to standardize blessings, formulas remained somewhat fluid and subject to debate (a good example may be seen at b. Ber. 40b).

The blessings after eating, meanwhile, express gratitude and, when said for something considered of sufficient significance to potentially constitute a meal, may be understood in rabbinic thought as demanded by and fulfilling the commandment of Deut. 26:15. Thus, blessings after eating become more extended and complex if the food eaten was in a more significant category (bread, grains, and produce of the Land) or of sufficient quantity to constitute a meal. Multiple rabbinic sources claim that the most extended version of the after meal blessing liturgy, said after eating bread in particular (or possibly a full meal even if bread was not an essential component) and known as *Birkat haMazon*, has three core blessings but also includes a fourth that was added at a later time, though there is reason to question which is the additional blessing and why it was added (b. Ber. 48b; on these questions see Shemesh 1995); foods of the "seven species" of the Land other than bread are followed by a blessing that encompasses the themes of the *Birkat haMazon* blessings into one. *Birkat haMazon*, moreover, might also require a communal call and response (*zimmun*) to initiate the blessing if a group of three or more have eaten together or in proximity, and in the rabbinic period was said over a cup of wine. Susan Marks further suggests that this ritual, by virtue of posing questions as to what constitutes a group and who is to be included or excluded, thereby "stands at the very core of shaping the [rabbinic] movement" (2014, 73; but see also Heinemann 1962 and Brumberg-Kraus 2005 who connect this practice to pre-rabbinic Pharisaic table fellowships). Also along these lines, the amoraic discussion takes up the question of women's obligation particularly to the blessing following meals; this encompasses both whether women have an obligation – or rather, since women have an obligation (see m. Ber. 3:3), is it biblical or rabbinic in origins – and (perhaps as a result of how one answers the previous question), may women be part of the communal blessing process (may they be counted for a quorum for a *zimmun*, may they lead the call to bless; see m. Ber. 7:2) and/or say the blessing on behalf of another person. That said, the Talmudic texts on these questions and the relationship of the questions to each other are sparse (b. Ber. 20b and 45b, and Arakh. 3a), somewhat contradictory internally and to each other, and inconclusive (see Cahan 2014 and Tucker and Rosenberg 2017, 172–84).

Daily Prayer

Rabbinic sources presume that the (adult, male) Jew will pray on a regular, daily basis. Moreover, already according to the Mishnah (Ber., chaps 1–5), that prayer has two core, obligatory components: (a) the twice daily (once in the morning and once after nightfall) recitation of the "*Shema*," a collection of verses (named for the first word of the first verse recited, Deut. 6:4) and a surrounding set of blessings; (b) a liturgical composition known as "the Prayer," or "the eighteen blessings" (for its weekday version), or "*Amidah*"/the "Standing Prayer," because it is said standing (this name is hinted at but not used directly in Talmud: see y. Ber. 4:1, 7a, and b. Ber. 6b and 26b), to be said two or three times daily (morning, afternoon, and possibly evening). However, the composition of each of these – that is, whether there was an original more or less fixed composition (or structure) and how such a composition might have come about – remains a matter of much modern scholarly debate and contention. It is clear that the rabbis (or many of the rabbis) attempted to create a more fixed, and (more significantly, in terms of distinguishing rabbinic prayer ritual from its predecessors) obligatory prayer practice (as suggested by the rulings of the Mishnah; see Fleischer 1990). Less clear is to what extent they drew on earlier practices/customs, or created a distinct liturgy of their own, and concomitantly, to what extent (or how early) rabbinic literature had set forms versus allowing for personal innovation from the person praying or leading a communal prayer. The poles of the debate may be broadly identified with two scholars, Ezra Fleischer and Joseph Heinemann. Heinemann (1977) rejects the idea that there is an "original" version of Jewish prayers, but rather argues that there was a variety of diverse popular or personal forms of pre-rabbinic prayer and that "the task of the rabbis was to systematize and to impose order on this multiplicity of forms, patterns and structures" (Heinemann 1977, 37 and see also Chap. 9; also Elbogen 1993 [1913], 209); this process remained on-going throughout the rabbinic period. Fleischer, by contrast, takes as reliably historical the rabbinic account that an early rabbinic figure – Shimon haPakuli, on behalf of the leader of the rabbinic community at Yavne, Rabban Gamliel – drafted a fully formed liturgy for the eighteen daily blessings (see m. Ber. 4:3 and b. Ber. 28b and Meg. 17b) shortly after the destruction of the Temple (though not without resistance from some other rabbis); indeed, he further argues that a requirement to pray on a regular basis makes little sense without such a liturgy (Fleischer 1990 and 1993).

Certainly, Talmudic sources follow the tannaitic assumption that there are required prayers, and what is left to add (as in so many instances already discussed in this essay) are matters of detail and expansion on tannaitic sources and practices. For example, at the time of the Mishnah, the two elements of *Shema* (and its blessings) and *Amidah* do not appear to be intrinsically linked as part of a single service of either the morning or evening, and it is in the amoraic period that rabbis begin to debate as to whether they should be connected (with the blessing following the *Shema* leading into the *Amidah*; see y. Ber. 1:1, 2d, b. Ber 4b, 9b, 42a, similarly 26a; see also Kimelman 1997, 108 and 117, Langer 1998, 17–18). The evening service comes to be understood as obligatory (see, for example, y. Ber. 4:1, 7c–d and b. Ber. 27b). Prayer is commonly explained and structured as a (temporary) substitute for Temple worship and sacrifices (see, for example, the discussion in Langer 1998, 5–14, Kimelman 2006, 580–93), and becomes increasing located in communal settings/the synagogue, with a leader reciting liturgy on behalf of those present and certain prayers said only in the presence of a quorum of ten adult males (see Elbogen 1993 [1913], 205–06, Kimelman 2006, 573–80 and 598–99). While women are deemed obligated for prayer (though it is not clear if this means at regular times of day, as for men), yet exempted from the recitation of *Shema* (m. Ber. 3:3), Talmudic sources further consider (and problematize) the reasons for and implications of the mishnaic ruling (see particularly b. Ber. 20b and the analyses in Kraemer 1996, 86–95 and Alexander 2013, 111–15).

The Talmud, similarly to the Mishnah, provides only snippets of liturgical texts. Thus, both the Yerushalmi and Bavli are aware of the contents and order of the blessings of the *Amidah*, and attempt to explain their logical sequence (y. Ber. 2:4, 4d and 4:3, 8a; b. Meg. 17b–18a; compare also the earlier text of t. Ber. 3:25). As Langer notes, however, what fragments we do have of actual texts of rabbinic prayer tend to be included "where there was a matter of dispute or where some particular problem required discussion" (Langer 2003, 133). Another way of putting this would be that where Talmudic texts discuss the content of blessings and prayers, it is often in a context in which there is disagreement, or at least multiple suggestions, as to what the text ought to be (see, for example, the discussion in Elbogen 1993 [1913], 207–08). The on-going tension between fixity and fluidity in prayer language in this period manifests on multiple occasions in Talmudic literature. Note, for example, the multiple interpretations and responses presented in both the Yerushalmi and Bavli (y. Ber. 4:4 8a; b. Ber. 29b) to Rabbi Eliezer's view in m. Ber. 4:4 that "fixed" prayer (that is, the *Amidah*) is *not* to be considered valid petitioning of the Divine: these include calls for continuing innovation in liturgy, but also attempts to redefine "fixed" as reference to concentration and intent with which one prays (rather than as opposition to a fixed liturgy) and concerns that innovation will lead to errors. So too rabbinic stories tell of incidents in which a prayer leader innovated language in a manner that a rabbi in attendance found problematic (y. Ber. 9:1, 12d; Ber. 33b/Meg. 25a, Ber. 34a; see Heinemann 1977, 45–47, Langer 1998, 31–32 and 2003, 136–38). Similar discussion regarding the blessings surrounding the *Shema* appear in b Ber. 11a–12a; while the amoraim broadly agree on themes of each blessing, they present variant texts and consider assigning different versions of the blessings for day and nighttime recitation. Indeed, in response to all these competing trends, the 4th-century Babylonian amora Rav Papa would offer the "solution" that allowed "for the combination of variant liturgical texts into single, ultimately universal norm" (Langer 1998, 35; similarly Elbogen 1993 [1913], 208).

References

Alexander, Elizabeth Shanks. 2013. *Gender and Timebound Commandments in Judaism*. Cambridge: Cambridge University Press.

Aminoah, Noah. 1998. "The Arrangement of the Laws of Hanukka in Tractate Shabbat" [Heb.], *Sidra: A Journal for the Study of Rabbinic Literature* 14: 59–76.

Benovitz, Moshe. 2007 "'Until the Feet of the *Tarmoda'i* are Gone': The Hannukah Light in Palestine during the Tannaitic and Amoraic Periods" [Heb.], in *Torah Lishma: Essays in Honor of Professor Shamma Friedman*. Eds. David Golinken, Moshe Benovitz, Mordechai Akiva Friedman, Menahem Schmelzer, and Daniel Sperber. Jerusalem: Schechter Institute of Jewish Studies, The Jewish Theological Seminary of America, Bar Ilan University Press, 39–78.

Benovitz, Moshe. 2010. "Blessings before the Meal in Second Temple Period and Tannaitic Literature" [Heb.], *Meghillot: Studies in the Dead Sea Scrolls* 8/9: 81–96.

Bokser, Baruch. 1981. "*Ma'al* and Blessings Over Food: Rabbinic Transformation of Cultic Terminology and Alternative Modes of Piety," *Journal of Biblical Literature* 100:4: 557–74.

Brumberg-Kraus, Jonathan D. 2005. "Meals as Midrash: A Survey of Ancient Meals in Jewish Studies Scholarship," *Food and Judaism: A Special Issue of Studies in Jewish Civilization* 15: 297–317.

Buchler, A. 1927. "The Induction of the Bride and the Bridegroom in the Huppah in the First and Second Centuries in Palestine." in *Livre D'hommage a La Memoire Du Dr. Samuel Poznanski (1864-1921)*. Warsaw: Comité de la Grande Synagogue, 82–132.

Cahan, Joshua. 2014. "Women's Disputed Level of Obligation in Birkat Hamazon," *Jewish Studies Quarterly* 21:2: 116–35.

Cohen, Aryeh. 2012. "The Gender of Shabbat," in *Introduction to Seder Qodashim: A Feminist Commentary on the Babylonian Talmud V.* Eds. Tal Ilan, Monika Brockhaus, and Tanja Hidde. Tübingen: Mohr Siebeck, 109–26.

Cohen, Shaye J. D. 2005. *Why Aren't Jewish Women Circumcised? Gender and Covenant in Judaism.* Berkeley: University of California Press.

Cohen, Shaye J. D. 2007. "The Judaean Legal Tradition and the Halakhah of the Mishnah," in *The Cambridge Companion to the Talmud and Rabbinic Literature.* Eds. Charlotte Elisheva Fonrobert and Martin S. Jaffee. Cambridge: Cambridge University Press, 121–43.

Doering, Lutz. 2010. "Sabbath and Festivals," in *The Oxford Handbook of Daily Life in Roman Palestine.* Ed. Catherine Hezser. Oxford: Oxford University Press, 566–86.

Elbogen, Ismar. 1993 [1913]. *Jewish Liturgy: A Comprehensive History.* Trans. Raymond P. Scheindlin. Philadelphia, Jerusalem: The Jewish Publication Society.

Feldman, Emanuel. 1972. "The Rabbinic Lament," *The Jewish Quarterly Review* 63:1: 51–75.

Fleischer, Ezra. 1990. "On the Beginnings of Obligatory Jewish Prayer" [Heb.], *Tarbiz* 59:3/4: 397–441.

Fleischer, Ezra. 1993. "The Shemone Esre – Its Character, Internal Order, Content and Goals" [Heb.], *Tarbiz* 62:2: 179–223.

Friedman, Shamma. 2006. "Hanukkah in the Scholion of Megillat Ta'anit" [Heb.], *Zion* 71:1: 5–40.

Hauptman, Judith. 2007. "From the Kitchen to the Dining-Room: Women and Ritual Activities in Tractate *Pesahim*," in *A Feminist Commentary on the Babylonian Talmud: Introduction and Studies.* Eds. Tal Ilan, Tamara Or, Dorothea M. Salzer, Christiane Steuer, and Irina Wandrey. Tübingen: Mohr Siebeck, 109–26.

Heinemann, Joseph. 1962. "Birkath Ha-Zimmun and Havurah Meals," *Journal of Jewish Studies* 13, 23–29.

Heinemann, Joseph. 1977. *Prayer in the Talmud.* Berlin, New York: Walter de Gruyter.

Herman, Geoffrey. 2014. "Religious Transformation Between East and West: Hanukkah in the Babylonian Talmud and Zoroastrianism," in *Religions and Trade: Religious Formation, Transformation and Cross-Cultural Exchange between East and West.* Eds. Peter Wick and Volker Rabens. Leiden, Boston: Brill, 261–81.

Hezser, Catherine. 2007. "Passover and Social Equality: Women, Slaves and Minors in *Bavli Pesahim*," in *A Feminist Commentary on the Babylonian Talmud: Introduction and Studies.* Eds. Tal Ilan, Tamara Or, Dorothea M. Salzer, Christiane Steuer, and Irina Wandrey. Tübingen: Mohr Siebeck, 91–107.

Hidary, Richard. 2015. "'One May Come to Repair Musical Instruments': Rabbinic Authority and the History of the *Shevut* Laws," *Jewish Studies, an Internet Journal*, 13: 1–26.

Hoffman, Lawrence A. 1996. *Covenant of Blood: Circumcision and Gender in Rabbinic Judaism.* Chicago, IL: University of Chicago Press.

Ilan, Tal. 2017. *Massekht Hullin: Text, Translation, and Commentary, A Feminist Commentary on the Babylonian Talmud V/3.* Tübingen: Mohr Siebeck.

Katz, Jacob. 1988. "The Orthodox Defense of the Second Day of the Festivals" [Hebrew], *Tarbiz* 57:3: 385–434.

Katz, Menahem and Mordechai Sabato. 2007. "The Groom's Blessing and the Mourners' Blessing," *Kenishta: Studies in the Synagogue World* 3: 155–86.

Kimelman, Reuven. 1997. "The Shema and the Amidah: Rabbinic Prayer," in *Prayer from Alexander to Constantine: A Critical Anthology.* Ed. Mark Kiley. London and New York: Routledge, 108–20.

Kimelman, Reuven. 2006. "Rabbinic Prayer in Late Antiquity," in *The Cambridge History of Judaism, Volume IV.* Ed. Steven T. Katz. Cambridge: Cambridge University Press, 573–611.

Kraemer, David. 1996. *Rereading the Rabbis: the Talmud as Literature.* Oxford: Oxford University Press.

Kraemer, David. 2000. *The Meanings of Death in Rabbinic Judaism.* London and New York: Routledge.

Kraemer, David. 2007. *Jewish Eating and Identity Through the Ages.* New York, London: Routledge.

Labovitz, Gail. 2009. *Marriage and Metaphor: Constructions of Gender in Rabbinic Literature.* Lanham, MD: Lexington Books.

Labovitz, Gail. 2021a. "'Teach Your Daughters Wailing': M. Mo'ed Katan 3:8–9 and the Gendering of Tannaitic Funeral Practice," *Shofar* 39:1: 21–44.

Labovitz, Gail. 2021b. *Massekhet Moed Qatan: Text, Translation, and Commentary, A Feminist Commentary on the Babylonian Talmud II/11.* Tübingen, Germany: Mohr Siebeck.

Langer, Ruth. 1998. *To Worship God Properly: Tensions between Liturgical Custom and halakhah in Judaism.* Cincinnati, OH: Hebrew Union College Press.

Langer, Ruth. 2003. "The 'Amidah as Formative Rabbinic Prayer," in *Identität durch Gebet: Zur gemeinschaftsbildende Funktion institutionalisierten Betens in Judentum und Christentum*. Ed. Stephan Wahle. Paderborn, Munich, Wien, Zürich: Ferdinand Schöningh, 127–56.

Lehman, Marjorie. 2003. "Women and Passover Observance: Reconsidering Gender in the Study of Rabbinic Texts," *Women and Judaism: Studies in Jewish Civilization* 14: 45–66.

Lehman, Marjorie. 2006. "The Gendered Rhetoric of Sukkah Observance," *Jewish Quarterly Review* 96:3: 309–35.

Mandel, Pinhas. 2005. "'And a Living One Should Take It to Heart': On Funeral and Condolences Practices in Babylonia and the Land of Israel in the Talmudic Period" [Heb.], in *Studies in Talmudic and Midrashic Literature in Memory of Tirzah Lifshitz*. Eds. M. Bar-Asher, J. Levinson, and B. Lifshitz. Jerusalem: The Bialik Institute, 385–410.

Marks, Susan. 2013. *First Came Marriage: The Rabbinic Appropriation of Early Jewish Wedding Ritual*. Piscataway, NJ: Gorgias Press.

Marks, Susan. 2014. "In the Place of Libation: *Birkat Hamazon* Navigates New Ground," in *Meal in Early Judaism: Social Formation at the Table*. Eds. Susan Marks and Hal Taussig. New York: Palgrave Macmillan, 71–97.

Rosenthal, Leah. 2000. "'Inui Nefesh' (Self-Affliction) on Yom Kippur: A Literary and Conceptual Analysis of a Talmudic Discussion," in *Torah of the Mothers: Contemporary Jewish Women Read Classical Jewish Texts*. Eds. Ora Wiskind Elper and Susan Handelman. Jerusalem and New York: Urim Publications and Lambda Publishers, Inc., 338–54.

Rubin, Nissan. 1995. *The Beginning of Life [Reshit HaHayim]: Rites of Birth, Circumcision, and Redemption of the Son in Rabbinic Sources* [Heb.]. Tel Aviv: ha-Ḳibuts ha-me'uḥad.

Rubin, Nissan. 1997. *The End of Life [Ketz HaHayim]: Rites of Burial and Mourning in the Talmud and Midrash* [Heb.]. Tel Aviv: Hakibbutz Hameuchad.

Rubin, Nissan. 2008. *Time and Life Cycle in Talmud and Midrash: Socio-anthropological Perspectives*. Boston, MA: Academic Studies Press.

Satlow, Michael L. 2001. *Jewish Marriage in Antiquity*. Princeton and Oxford: Princeton University Press.

Satlow, Michael L. 2010. "Marriage and Divorce," in *The Oxford Handbook of Daily Life in Roman Palestine*. Ed. Catherine Hezser. Oxford: Oxford University Press, 344–61.

Schremer, Adiel. 2003. *Male and Female He Created Them: Jewish Marriage in the Late Second Temple, Mishnah, and Talmud Periods [Heb.]*. Jerusalem: The Zalman Shazar Center.

Shemesh, Aaron. 1995. "The Grace After Meals – Three Blessings or Four?" [Heb.], *Sidra* 11: 153–66.

Stern, Sacha. 1993. "The Second Day of Yom Tov in the Talmudic and Geonic Literature," *Proceedings of the World Congress of Jewish Studies*, C1: 49–55.

Sysling, Harry. 2007. "Laments at the Departure of a Sage: Funeral Songs for Great Scholars as Recorded in Rabbinic Literature," in *Studies in Hebrew Literature and Jewish Culture: Presented to Albert van der Heide on the Occasion of his Sixty-Fifth Birthday*. Eds. Martin F. J. Baasten and Reiner Munk. Dordrecht, the Netherlands: Springer, 81–102.

Tabory, Joseph. 1995. *Jewish Festivals in the Time of the Mishnah and Talmud* [Heb.]. Jerusalem: Magnes Press.

Tabory, Joseph. 2006. "Jewish Festivals in Late Antiquity," in *Cambridge History of Judaism: Volume 4, The Late Roman-Rabbinic Period*. Eds. Steven T. Katz, William David Davies, and Louis FinklesteinCambridge: Cambridge University Press, 556–72.

Tucker, Ethan and Micha'el Rosenberg. 2017. *Gender Equality and Prayer in Jewish Law*. New York: KTAV Publishing.

Valler, Shulamit. 2007. "Women and Dwelling in the *Sukkah* in the *Bavli*," in *A Feminist Commentary on the Babylonian Talmud: Introduction and Studies*. Eds. Tal Ilan, Tamara Or, Dorothea M. Salzer, Christiane Steuer, and Irina Wandrey. Tübingen: Mohr Siebeck, 151–67.

Valler, Shulamit. 2009. *Massekhet Sukkah: Text, Translation, and Commentary. A Feminist Commentary on the Babylonian Talmud* II/6. Tübingen: Mohr Siebeck.

4
AMBIGUITY AND NOTATION
Jewish Law and Legal Pluralism

Adam Seligman

In this chapter,[1] I would like to explore what I take to be a consistent strain of ambiguity that inheres in many facets of Jewish law and normative order. One of my reasons for exploring this theme is the feeling that in this ambiguity there is much to be learned when approaching some of the challenges facing societies and legal orders in the twenty-first century. In the following I will explore three discrete realms of Jewish law where this sense of ambiguity can be felt. First, I will look, briefly, at the tensions between truth and trust, justice and peace – as they manifest themselves in certain legal texts. Then I will move to consider the attitude taken toward non-Jewish courts and juridical processes. Finally, I will explore some meta-legal themes as they pertain to the statutes of the Torah and our understanding of God's commandments.

I begin by simply reviewing some of the very different attitudes toward justice that one can find in the rabbinic corpus. On the one hand, we are, of course, enjoined to seek justice and learn that the judge who judges truthfully is compared to one who stands together with the Creator at the creation of the world. Contra wise, the judge who does not judge truthfully causes the Holy countenance to depart from Israel (Tur, 1861, 14a). Indeed, the calls to justice are as frequent as one would suppose in a religious system as "legalistic" as the Jewish one is often purported to be. But, on the other hand, one can for example turn to the *Tosefta* on *Sanhedrim* and find the claim that wherever there is true justice there is no peace and wherever there is peace there is no true justice. So, yes, in fact true justice is so strong as to split mountains, and so mighty as to bring the Lord down from the heavens – but it is not at all sure that this is a good thing. For at the end of the day, social peace and, with it, social existence, is founded not on true or absolute justice, but in fact on compromise. And when we turn from the abstract and hortatory to the practical and this-worldly, it is to the values of peace and compromise that we find the system leaning. Indeed, a good deal of time is spent in exploring how far into a case can judges still seek compromise between two litigants: for if they reach a point where they definitively know who is guilty and who innocent, then to compromise would in fact be to perpetrate an injustice. Yet, even in these later cases, if a verdict has not been explicitly and verbally rendered, compromise should still be sought (Tur, 1861,18a–b). Indeed, the final ending of a litigation in court can be understood to be pushed back again and again, in an almost endless regress and clear reticence to actually come to finality and thus close the door to compromise. Similarly in the matter of bringing additional witnesses (not available at the time of the hearing), every effort is made to keep the proceedings "open" and free from that type of closure that would make compromise impossible.

The concern to maintain the bonds of society, I almost said of solidarity, between litigants and, one senses, between litigants and the social whole (via the role of the judges, who are of course taken from the community), pervades much of the first twenty-six chapters of the *Hoshen Mishpat* – those dedicated to the laws of the judiciary. The *Hoshen Mishpat* of Yaakov ben Asher, I should note, was composed in the first half of the fourteenth century in Spain and provides us with the first practical digest of halachic laws, and was destined to be the model for the more normative compilation Joseph Karo in the sixteenth century.

One way to frame the tension evinced in these texts is as that between truth and trust. All legal systems are, in fact, forced to serve these two masters – or perhaps to mediate between them. The demand for truth and understanding of justice in terms of ascertaining the "facts" of the case, does not always correlate with the need to maintain the bonds of solidarity and community. These later desiderata do not always square with a straightforward demand for truth, especially when understood with a capital "T".

In Jewish law, I am arguing, there is a clear recognition that justice, without the quality of – what I have just termed – trust, is a dangerous entity; not only can it "destroy mountains"; it can be most destructive of human wellbeing (Zuckermandel, 1881/2004: 415). Justice, must in fact be continually mediated with peace – a mediation that is achieved through compromise, which is always the preferred mode of resolution of differences, rather than any appeal to "pure" justice. Peace in this context means social peace – that is the maintenance of the bonds of mutual wellbeing and solidarity that make human society possible. Justice – abstract, cold, avenging justice – is a quality of God and as such not always advisable for mere mortals to dabble in. If we think in terms of the more commonplace distinction between justice and mercy – we can see that it is somewhat of a subset of our own distinction; one form among many that the contradiction and tension between truth and trust works itself out. What is intriguing to me is the ability of the tradition to, as it were, glory in the contradiction, rather than obsess in it.

The ability of the tradition to "sit astride" this tension is matched, I would claim, with a parallel capacity to recognize and even perhaps partially legitimize, that which it at the very same time excoriates. This seems to me of great significance to what is one of the most pressing challenges of social and legal ordering in the world today. Here, I am referring to the problem of legal pluralism and the existence of multiple and competing legal systems claiming jurisdiction and challenging the legitimacy of one another's moral codes and claims.

What we now term, multicultural jurisprudence has emerged out of the growing recognition that the centrism characterizing the legal order of the State is not as unproblematic as it was once thought to be (Foblets and Renteln, 2009). With the growth of the nation-state during the nineteenth century, and with the extension of its power and hegemony over ever more arenas of human action and interaction, the law of the State came to be seen as the only source of legally valid normative orders. The legal system of the State attained its apogee in the formulations of positivistic legal thought, procedural in nature, which made nary a claim to transcendent, revelatory or otherwise other-worldly or ultimate sources of their authority.

This picture began to change about a quarter of a century ago. The publication of Robert Cover's (1992) "Nomos and Narrative" made clear the existence of very different "interpretive communities" within the boundaries of the nation-state that did not necessarily share the same "narrative" of meaning-giving order which was represented in and through the legal codes of the state. At roughly the same time the idea of legal pluralism had begun to take root. It argued for the existence within one country of multiple legal orders and normative frameworks; that is, of communities that regulated their lives according to different (often hierarchically ordered) sets of legal criteria, not all of which could be subsumed within the logic of the law of the State. Today of course the challenge of Muslim communities in Europe and increasing issues of multiple legal systems interacting within the confines of the nation-state worldwide has pushed this issue of legal pluralism to the top of the agenda of all sociologists, anthropologists, philosophers and legal scholars working in the field (Foblets et al., 2010).

In my judgment, a potentially rich resource for tackling these issues is to be found in Jewish legal texts dealing with the legitimacy and illegitimacy of gentile courts *(arka'ot shel goyiim)*. Moreover, and as I shall try to argue, Jewish legal attitudes toward these gentile courts are characterized by the type of ambiguity or duality, of principled exhortation and more pragmatic application, noted above.

While Jewish law, from the Amoraic period onward, has included the dictum of *dina d'malkhuta dina* (the law of the State is the law), the understanding, circumscription, interpretation and enactment of this legal principle has, as shown in the monumental work by Shmuel Shilo, varied considerably in different periods (Shilo, 1974). How, for example, to accept its principal implications but not, at the same time, lose the specificity of one's own legal system has been much debated over the generations of legal theorists from the seventh century until today. Does the law pertain only to matters between the king and his subjects (and not for example in matters of torts or family law)? Is it restricted to matters of taxation, punishment, or eminent domain? Do such laws apply to returned property, and if so, when and in which circumstance?

Further complications arise in matters of contracts. Contracts drawn up in gentile courts are valid, with the exception of divorce decrees and the manumission of slaves. Yet the scope of these exceptions and their meaning has been given to very different understandings at different times and in different places of the Jewish diaspora. All these matters and more were thus the subject of continual debate and contestation within circles of Jewish legal decisors from early medieval into modern times. Here, the dictum of *dina d'malkhuta dina*, the local law is the law, will be taken as the broad context within which the more specific problems of gentile courts, *arka'ot shel goyim*, can be studied. The generally accepted view – as evinced clearly in the legal codes of Moses Maimonides (*Mishneh Torah*), Jacob b. Asher (*Arba Turim*), Joseph Karo (*Shulchan Arukh*) and others – is that recourse to gentile courts is prohibited in the strictest of fashions. Yet a closer reading of texts and commentaries tends to mediate this harsh view and the very different sets of extenuating circumstances, exceptions to the rule and principled recognition of non-Jewish courts add a complexity to the binary view that has dominated much of medieval and modern understandings.

So, for example, in matters of damages it is, in the general run of things, strictly forbidden to have recourse to a gentile court (such recourse is likened to a revolt against and desecration of the Law of Moses). Yet, despite this rhetoric it appears that this prohibition is based more on an incongruity of procedure between gentile and Jewish courts than – what is so often assumed – a categorical condemnation of gentile judicial systems. For, whereas in Jewish courts two witnesses are needed to effect the transfer of property from defendant to claimant, in gentile courts one witness is sufficient. In those situations where Jewish law admits the evidence of one witness only (as in the case of a witness for the defense), a Jew is permitted to give testimony in a gentile court because in such a case the requirements of Jewish law are satisfied (Tur, 1861, 40a). Accordingly, parsing the problem in procedural terms forces us to rethink our understanding of the broader rhetorical tropes and condemnations. It also raises interesting possibilities for how different legal systems may accommodate one another.

In a similar manner, a close and comparative reading of rules incident to contracts that specify their possible adjudication by gentile courts – which, while rejecting such clauses – do so in subtly different ways, and with different emphases, raise very probing questions as to how the halakhic system viewed the system of gentile courts and their potential role in disputes between Jews.

Moreover, and somewhat surprisingly, at certain points and among certain decisors there seems to be a willingness to adopt (or accede to) discrete non-Jewish practices, such as the swearing in of witnesses which, according to the *Beit Yosef* of Caro was a Christian practice that certain Jewish communities, knowing no better, accepted as the law and in such circumstances could be practiced in Jewish courts.

All such features of the law, as well as the exceptions to the blanket prohibition on gentile courts (the most important being the permission to go to gentile courts when dealing with a man of known violent inclinations) lead me to believe that we are looking at a system that can both accommodate and even (partially) legitimate alternative normative orders. If we were to invoke more contemporary anthropological and linguistic theory, we would say that the relevant juridical "performatives" must be carried out in a Jewish court but the praxis of legal ordering can indeed by shared by both Jewish and gentile juridical systems. If the symbolic enactment must be reserved for Jewish courts according to its own liturgical orders, the practical enactment could be shared with non-Jewish courts.

To support this claim, however, much further study is necessary. More detailed exploration of the position of Jewish law on these matters is needed, as is a wider, comparative perspective that will help highlight the uniquely singular and the more broadly shared components – and potentialities – of different systems. We would need, for example, to integrate three important types of legal source: responsa literature, rabbinic court records, and communal legislation (*takkanot ha-kahal*). The cases treated in rabbinic responsa offer entrée into the thinking of jurists actively engaged in legal decision-making, while communal legislation would offer the perspective of public law and public policy. Records of the *beit din* (rabbinic court) would, on the other hand, provide evidence of the reality on the ground and shed light on the strategies used by rabbinic courts in defining their relationship to the gentile courts. In the late eighteenth century, for example, in a departure from the late medieval period, this relationship tended to be cooperative. The historian, Jay Berkovitz (2010, 271–94) for example, has done important work on the records of the Metz rabbinic court in this period and uncovered not only the pervasive integration of French legal terms and concepts into halachic rulings; but the repeated validation of contractual relations established first in gentile courts. In yet other cases, rabbinic courts acceded to rulings of the French civil court in assigning priority to different creditors of a deceased's estate – and in so doing, overruled the marriage contract, *ketuba*. What he found was nothing less than a powerful impulse to coordinate with the French legal system. Something then, very different from the normatively accepted notion that recourse to gentile courts was tantamount to: "overturning the laws of Moses".

The work of other historians has in fact substantiated this close working of Jewish courts and individuals with gentile courts in other times and other climes as well. Francesca Trivellato (2009) has explored the successful recourse of North African Jewish merchants to non-Jewish courts in both Livorno and Genoa, even going so far as to impugn the authority of halachic decrees made in North African Jewish courts. Matt Goldish (2008) has analyzed in fascinating detail the use made of non-Jewish (mostly Muslim) courts by Jews in the early modern period. Among his examples are the use made by rabbis of Muslim courts in Egypt in order to force an unwilling Jewish husband to grant a divorce (*get*) to his wife. While most of these cases do of course rest on very practical concerns of tort law, and of the social relations so regulated, it is at least arguable that this ability to develop everyday practices that would seem to contradict the very core injunctions of the law, is not limited to this realm alone: but does perhaps speak to some more fundamental aspect of the tradition.

To anyone who is familiar with what the *Tur* or the *Shulchan Arukh* has to say about gentile courts – at least on the level of hortatory proclamations, if not always in the details of the many extenuating circumstances – the work of these historians must stand out as a challenge. For while the *Beit Yosef* and the *Ramah* may tell us that even the enabler of one who seeks judgment in a gentile court should be excommunicated, and this is so even if both sides to the dispute agree to pursue their suit in a gentile court, and even if the procedures are the same as in a Jewish court – here we see rabbis using Muslim courts to trick a husband into granting a divorce or, with Berkovitz, of relying on the rulings of the French civil court system or the advice of its *avocats* in order to rule on a case.

Appeal to gentile courts may have been a challenge and desecration of the Law of Moses – especially if used as a form of coercion on a fellow Jew. But at the very same time, it may also point to a recognition of a shared universe and of the public good provided by this very coercive apparatus, as indeed we are enjoined to make use of such courts in the case of a violent man, who rejects the decisions of the rabbinic court. What makes a State a State, as Max Weber has taught us, is its monopoly on the legitimate use of force. This too is a crucial aspect of governance, without which there is no social order. It provides a public good, no less than the construction of bridges, roads, city walls and defensive ramparts, the digging of wells or provisions for orphans and widows. And just as Jews and non-Jews, Christians and/or Muslims share the use of wells, roads, bridges and so on – they also share in the benefits of good (indeed of any) governance and the public space that this allows for the pursuit of one's own interests, both material and ideal. Many different publics, with different understandings of their interests – whether individual interests tied to bills of exchange, inheritance or divorce, or collective interests in the maintenance of their common heritage, familial, communal and corporate entities – are all dependent on that public good, which is, crucially, a shared good among different communities and, in the pre-nation-state era, not seen as residing on any Rousseauvian general will (an idea which, through the thought of Malebranche was still seen as residing in the realm of the Divine) but on a rich fabric and network of transactions and exchanges (Riley, 1988).

In a totally different context, when discussing the laws of witnesses and how unlike a regular partnership, residents of a city cannot "buy out" of their benefits from public goods (roads, wells, bridges, etc.), the *Beit Yosef* ends up comparing public baths to a *Sefer Torah*: as essentially similar in terms of being a public good from which the beneficiaries (a city's residents) cannot opt out (*Tur*, 1861, 62b). I would like to suggest that we adopt a similar temerity when approaching Jewish use of gentile legal structures and see in this practice a recognition of some essentially shared component of a public life, that even if ad hoc and pragmatic, has no less import as a model of behavior than more normative coordinates on the evils of gentile places and practices. By granting such normative orders the status of a legitimate public good toward which one can have recourse – even if on an ad hoc basis – the agents and authorities in the histories studied by Berkovitz, Goldish and Trivellato are recognizing the shared nature of our world: a recognition all too often denied by their descendants in the worlds we inhabit today.

Let me now change gear and move from the quotidian realm of contract law to what is perhaps the most significant aspect of ancient Jewish ritual practice – the laws of purity – upon which the whole Temple system rested and which were dissolved with the destruction of the Temple, except for those laws pertaining to women's menstrual purity. I will quote a story referring to the ritual of the Red Heifer, but which goes to the very core of any understanding of the normative order and which is therefore of great relevance to our work here.

As recorded in the *Pesikta d'Rav Khana* (a sixth-century Palestinian collection of Aggadic material):

> A heathen said to Raban Yochanan ben Zakai: "The things you Jews do appear to be a kind of sorcery. A heifer is brought, is burned up and is pounded [into ashes] and its ashes are gathered up. Then, when one of you gets defiled by contact with a corpse, two or three drops of water mixed with these ashes are sprinkled upon him, and he is told, 'You are now cleansed!'"
>
> Rabban Yochanan asked the heathen, "Has the spirit of madness ever possessed you?" He replied, "No." "Have you ever seen anyone possessed by the spirit of madness? The heathen replied, "Yes." "And have you seen what you people do to the man?" "Roots are brought, they are made to smoke under him, and water is splashed on him, until the spirit flees."
>
> Rabban Yochanan then said, "Do not your ears hear what your mouth is saying? A man defiled is like a man possessed by a spirit. This spirit is a spirit of uncleanness. When water of lustration is splashed on it, it flees."
>
> After the heathen left, Rabban Yochanan's disciples said, "Our master, you thrust off the heathen with a mere reed of an answer, but what reply will you give us?"
>
> Rabban Yochanan answered, "As you live, the corpse does not defile, nor does the [mixture of ashes and] water cleanse. The truth is that the rite of the Red Heifer is a decree of the King who is King of kings. The Holy One said: I have set down a statute, I have issued a decree. You are not permitted to transgress my decree. 'This is a statute of the Torah.'" [Num. 19.2]
>
> *Bialik and Ravnitzky, 1992, 459–460*

Now think for a moment what is means to say: "Corpses do not defile!" This is perhaps the most significant statement in the whole narrative. After all, in the world of ancient Judaism of the period the greatest source of impurity was death. Nothing else approached the degree of impurity caused by contact with the dead. Death is, after all, negation. It is a perennial threat to all aspects of humanly constructed order, indeed to human existence itself. Yet, corpses do not defile! There is nothing inherent in the corpse, or even in death itself, which defiles. We are not – we are told – dealing with natural phenomena, with things as they are, with the world as it presents itself to our senses and intelligence. We are, rather, dealing with the nominal world as constituted by the Almighty.

This understanding of rite and ritual laws opens a whole additional layer of meanings. In Judaism things, objects in themselves in their natural state, do not transfer impurity. (Even the dead themselves are not impure – though those who come in contact with them are.) Only after the object has been fashioned by human hands, will, intention and labor, after the material has actually become implicated in the human world, can impurity be transferred (and of course there are myriad debates in the Talmud over defining that stage in the construction of an artifact that impurity can inhere to it). This is true whether it is a matter of clay utensils, wrought iron, already harvested crops (as opposed to those still in the ground), and so on. Thus the very constitutive terms of impurity are dual. Impurity is both an aspect of an object (as, at some point, things do transfer impurity) as well as being a relationship, a status. There is moreover a continual tension between both understandings of impurity. The one is never fully transformed into the other. The answer to the Roman must now come to be seen in a more subtle light than our first reading. R. Yochanan's assertion that corpses do not defile and the Red Heifer does not purify would not have its tremendous force if it were not contrasted to the commonly accepted view that corpses do in fact defile and the red heifer does indeed render pure (and to this day Jewish people wash their hands upon leaving a cemetery). R. Yochanan is engaging in high theology, arguing a position which interrogates a view, shared by both Roman magic and less-than-critical Jewish ritual practice wherein the general, accepted view of Jewish ritual acts is something not far from Roman magic!

This is what is in fact so striking. Earlier we saw how specific legal practices were developed that quite contravened both the letter and spirit of the law. Here we see how the very reality that the law is to address, that is the reality of impurity, as well as the purported salutary effects of the law, the attained state of purity, have actually no basis in reality. The Law of the Red Heifer is a statute handed down by God, and the rest – the whole complicated system of human conceptions regarding purity and impurity – are but rationalizations, no more or less meaningful (or efficacious one senses) than Roman magic.

There are different levels of relevance here that are worth parsing out. On the one hand, the story is yet another example of a certain built-in ambiguity in the very rabbinic construction of the normative order. There is an ultimately unknowable will of God at the basis of the commandments and everything else, the very skein of meaning and ordering and so human actions, are seen to be not much more valuable than those of the Romans.

In fact the gentile plays a critical role in this story, as embodiment of one pole of the rabbinic tension between realist and transcendent understandings of religious action. The gentile, that is the Roman, understands religious action in a way consistent with the shared, uncritical nature of most religious practice (of prayer, for example) which sees it in terms of an empirical efficacy (natural or supernatural). This common understanding then allows the leap to the much more radical transcendence of R. Yochanan, which subsumes such understanding in the principle of a transcendent a priori.

This idea of radical transcendence – relativizing and trivializing the words, orders and notations of the world in light of that which is beyond all human ordering – was a position illustrated close to a millennium later, in another work that also rests on the interaction between Jews and gentiles – R. Yehuda HaLevi's *Al Khazari* (Book 3, para. 53) which argues that: "the approach to God is only possible through the medium of God's command, and there is no road to knowledge of the commands of God except by way of prophesy, but not by means of speculation and reasoning." Again, radical transcendence, beyond reason and reasoning – made accessible only through the "opening" of prophesy.

In essence, R. Yochanan is declaring that the very system of religious meanings cannot express itself in its own terms. Or perhaps, phrased differently, it can only express itself in its own terms, but these are not the terms of true meaning, which are forever beyond us. The system's terms (here of religious ritual – corpses defile, Red Heifer purifies) are by nature human terms – and as such, incomplete, fragile, limited. The rabbinic system may privilege them; rabbis may have the last word, but they do not have the only word. Even more importantly in its very incomplete, fragmented and limited nature, the rabbinic system is somehow akin to the Roman's own understanding. The Roman's view then, expressed by his cure for spirit possession, still captures a truth of our shared, embodied humanity – and so also of both the necessity and limits of any system of rules and regulations. The radical transcendence that is at the heart of Jewish monotheism would thus seem not only to relativize the Jewish practice of such rules, vis à vis the divine, but also in its relation to alternative practices of different peoples.

And it is here I believe that this story takes us beyond its own boundaries and helps to throw some light on the broader issue of rules and regulations – be they of ritual contact in the face of impurity, or the laws of torts, swearing in of witnesses and validity of contracts – for what this story points to is precisely a questioning of all forms of human notation and categorization. By notation I mean the process of rule making, or category production through which we impose order on the inherent chaos of unordered reality. Its primary exemplar is the law which attempts to reduce ambiguity and keep chaos at bay, in the relations between human actors, and – in the ritual sphere – in relations between human actors and external realities. Laws are, in a sense, the way we notate social life. And while we must categorize in order to live, we should not forget that every category pulls us away from the shifting and complex experience of reality. Every category thus leaves an ambiguous zone at its edges. Human existence and our need to interact with one another and the natural world force on us both ambiguity and categorization. The very production of categories to deal with those interactions inevitably generates additional ambiguities and forces us to face the problem of how to deal with them. As the evolutionary biologists joke: every time they find a missing link, it produces two new missing links.

Notation then, and with it law, cannot in itself solve the problem of ambiguity – indeed it goes a long way toward producing more ambiguity at the boundaries of its own categories. This is perhaps the paradox at the heart of the legal endeavor. What seems so fascinating in the Jewish attitude toward law however is its ability – at one and the same time – to both recognize and validate the law as the highest of human endeavor even as it relativizes it vis à vis transcendent realities. At one and the same time, everything is the law, and it is even much debated if there is an autonomous realm of the moral or the ethical beyond the law, and yet the law itself is nothing but the fragile and human attempt to make sense of transcendent reality.

One cannot but help wonder if this duality, as expressed so well in the story of the Rabbi Yochanan, the Roman matron and the Red Heifer, is not at some place also at work in permitting the more quotidian – and historically verified – attitudes toward gentile courts and contracts with which we began. If the whole notational framework is but an approximation, and a shadow of what is beyond its categories, then surely the practical realities of any given existential situation can – in certain situations – trump what John Henry Newman termed mere "notational assents" (Newman, 1978[1874]). To judge truthfully may indeed be likened to participating in creation – but the social needs of solidarity and maintaining community and interaction following the trial trump even such majesty. To have recourse to gentile courts may indeed be compared to the utter repudiation of the laws of Moses, but if the defendant is a violent man, then such recourse is permitted without question – which of course means that at some fundamental level Jewish law recognizes the legitimacy of gentile systems and their role in the governance and maintenance of social order.

While rabbis fulminated against their coreligionists for bringing disputes to gentile courts, there is no doubt that use of plural jurisdictions was not uncommon, and was often, in the end, accepted by rabbinic decisors and, as we have seen above, in certain circumstances, even recognized before the fact, as legitimate modes of arbitrating disputes. As Jay Berkovitz (2010, 283, 286) claims: "respect for the legal procedures of the civil court system was a consistent theme of the beit din rulings". And legal integration and acculturation could go hand in hand with what he terms an "ethos of religious and social distinctiveness, even chauvinism". We are thus not dealing with communities who make little of their boundaries or are particularly liberal in their dealings with and attitudes toward their gentile neighbors. The ability of Jewish community members to move in a world of plural jurisdictions is not, Berkovitz is arguing derivative of some sociological liberalism or fuzzy identities. It is at least worth arguing then that it must have much to do with attitudes toward the law itself, to its normative cast when thrust against the exigencies of daily life. One doubts that the doctor or householder or widow in Metz studied *the Pesikta d'Rav Kahana* and formed their legal attitudes from such study. But I am asking if the attitude toward the law embodied in that homiletic work did not manifest itself in their actions, as well as in the normative pronouncements that one can find in *Tur*, the *Shulchan Aruch* or in the *Ramah*.

In this context we may recall Isidore Twersky's seminal distinction between code and commentary in Jewish law and how, despite the continual push toward notation and codification, there has been, over the centuries, an equally strong counter push toward commentary, that is – toward greater and greater contextualization of the code, and its mediation by the citation of alternative rulings, divergent explanations, minority decisions, and an expansive amplification of possibilities beyond those codified. In Twersky's own words:

> Attempts to compress the Halachah by formal codification alternate with counter-attempts to preserve the fullness and richness of both the method and substance of the Halacha by engaging in interpretation, analogy, logical inference, and only then formulating the resultant normative conclusion. Any student who follows the course of rabbinic literature from Geonic works of the eighth century through the Mishneh Torah and Turim and on down to the Shulhan 'Aruk cannot ignore this see-saw tendency. The tension is ever present and usually catalytic. No sooner is the need for codification met than a wave of non-codificatory work rises. A code could provide guidance and certitude for a while but not finality. … A code, even in the eyes of its admirers, required vigilant explanation and judicious application.
>
> *Twersky, 1967, 149*

While codes, such as that of Maimonides, sought to eliminate divergent rulings and interpretations, commentary thrived on the never-ending addition of context, detail and the plethora of conflicting explanations and interpretations. Indeed, Maimonides sought in his code to abstract purely formulated behavioral norms from the Talmud. This attempt, however, failed perhaps to realize that these can become a shared world only by being embedded in their contexts, which was precisely those parts of the Talmud that Maimonides sought to excise from the "curricula" of study (Halbertal, 1997, 100–119). This was the point made a millennium later by Cover (1992). In just the same way, the utility of major codes such as Joseph Karo's *Shulchan Arukh*, which to this day remains normative, did not prevent them from being questioned and seen by many others as giving too short a shrift to the immutable and often "incommunicable values and aspirations of religious experience and spiritual existence" (Twersky, 1967, 15). What made this debate possible and prevented it from ultimately leading to the growth of communal schism – to what is termed "two toroth" (literally, two laws)? I would suggest that as radically divergent as were the understandings of the role of a code in the practice of Judaism, all parties to the dispute were united in the practice of ritual. This itself mediates the purely abstract nature of any code, or body of law. Ritual is in fact an integral part of that particularly Jewish communal narrative within which the nomos is grounded. The thick bonds of shared ritual are themselves an interpretation of code, even as the continuing and collective study of commentary provides both armature and ornament for both. Here too, then, we see the constitution of the normative order via an infinite skein of practices that, in their very nature, belie the idea of any unambiguous understanding or interpretation of tradition or even, of the law.

Note

1 This chapter appeared first in German as, "Ambiguitat und Notation: Jüdisches Recht und Rechtpluralismus", pp. 197–212 in K.-H. Ladeur and I. Augsberg (eds) *Talmudische Tradition und modernne Rechtstheorie*. Tubingen: Mohr Siebeck, 2013. It is reproduced here with the permission of the publisher.

References

Ben Asher, Yaakov. 1861. *Tur Hosen Mishpat*, Section 1, (Warsaw) reprinted, Jerusalem: Vegshel, 1990.
Berkovitz, Jay. 2010. "Acculturation and Integration in Eighteenth-Century Metz," *Jewish History* 24: 271–94.
Bialik, H. N. and Y. H. Ravnitzky. 1992. *The Book of Legends*, trans. William Braude. New York: Schocken Press.
Cover, Robert. 1992. *Narrative, Violence and the Law: The Essays of Robert Cover*. Ann Arbor: University of Michigan Press.
Foblets, Marie-Claire and Alison Dundes Renteln. eds. 2009. *Multicultural Jurisprudence: Comparative Perspectives on the Cultural Defense*. Oxford: Hart Publishing.
Foblets, Marie-Claire, Jean-François Gaudreault-DesBiens and Alison Dundes Renteln. eds. 2010. *Cultural Diversity and the Law: State Responses from Around the World*. Brussels: Bruylant.
Goldish, Matt. 2008. *Jewish Questions: Responsa on Sephardic Life in the Early Modern Period*. Princeton, NJ: Princeton University Press.
Halbertal, Moshe. 1997. *People of the Book: Canon, Meaning and Authority*. Cambridge, MA: Harvard University Press.
HaLevy Yehusha. 1140. *Sefer Hakuzari*, Part III, section 53, Sefaria: www.sefaria.org/Sefer_Kuzari.3.53?lang=bi&with=all&lang2=en (accessed 8 March 2020).
Newman, John Henry. 1978[1874]. *An Essay in Aid of a Grammar of Assent*. Notre Dame, IL: University of Notre Dame Press.
Riley, Patrick. 1988. *The General Will Before Rousseau: The Transformation of the Divine into the Civic*. Princeton, NJ: Princeton University Press.
Shilo, Shmuel. 1974. *Dina De-Malkhuta Dina* (The Law of the State is the Law). Jerusalem: Jerusalem Academic Press [Hebrew].
Trivellato, Francesca. 2009. "Sephardic Merchants Between State and Rabbinic Courts: Malfeasance, Property Rights and Religious Authority in the Eighteenth Century Mediterranean," in *From Florence to the Mediterranean and Beyond: Essays in Honor of Anthony Molho*, vol. 2. Eds. Diogo Ramada Curto, Eric R Dursteler, Julius Kirshner, and Francesca Trivellato. Florence: Leo Olschki.
Twersky, Isadore. 1967. "The Shulkan Aruk: Enduring Code of Jewish Law," *Judaism* 16, no. 2 (Spring): 141–58.
Zuckermandel, M. S. Ed. 1881/2004. *Tosefta*. Trier: Linz'schen Buchhandlung [Hebrew].

PART II

Periods

5
ARCHAEOLOGY

Benjamin D. Gordon

Introduction

Early Jewish texts such as the sectarian works of the Dead Sea Scrolls, the histories of Josephus, and the writings of the rabbis, as revealing as they may be, still provide an incomplete picture of the diverse range of Jewish practices in antiquity. Archaeology can improve our understanding of that diversity, and scholars working at the intersection of religious studies and material culture have done just that in studies of the archaeology of Israel-Palestine in classical antiquity (Magness 2011; Meyers and Chancey 2012). Moreover, the turn in religious studies toward materiality, with its attention to the body, the senses, objects, and spaces, can enhance our understanding of ritual and practice too. The approach has been applied to Israelite religion in the Iron Age (e.g., Mandell and Smoak 2019) and to assorted religious groups of the ancient Mediterranean in antiquity (e.g., Raja and Rüpke 2015). This is a shift of focus away from religious doctrine and toward the lived experiences of the practitioners of religion. There has been a similar shift in the framing of ritual studies (Mitchell 2017). Yet we await a comprehensive study devoted to the archaeology of ancient Jewish ritual and practice. The present chapter discusses some of the potential avenues of inquiry into the subject by drawing on the insights of material religion and ritual studies and concentrating on three areas: the archaeology of Jewish pilgrimage; the archaeology of bodily practice, including purification, eating practices, and mortuary customs; and the archaeology of the communal gathering at the synagogue. Its emphasis is primarily, though not exclusively, on material remains from Israel-Palestine in the Roman and Byzantine periods, namely the first century BCE through the sixth century CE. These are the centuries for which we have the most archaeological evidence on ancient Jewish ritual and practice.

The Archaeology of Pilgrimage

The holiest space in Judaism, the Western Wall, is a site of ritualized lament in the modern day. In antiquity, it enclosed the massive sacred precinct of Herod's Temple to the God of Israel (late first century BCE), the largest sacred complex in the Roman world at the time and probably a source of pride for Jews throughout the Mediterranean world. Pilgrims to the Temple would have encountered a building whose size was awe-inspiring, a visual stimulus that may have heightened the spiritual response by lifting one up from the mundane experiences of the everyday (Gordon 2018). As with any pilgrimage festival, there were performative components to the ritual, which was an opportunity for Jews to put their piety on display. In fact, one might view the Temple as a material expression of ancient Jewish piety, whether it be that of the local leaders who helped fund it, the craftsmen who built it, or the pilgrims who glorified it by journeying to the place with offerings in tow.

Herod's Temple was effectively the Third Temple because so much of the Second Temple, which had been in operation since 516 BCE, had to be disassembled to accommodate it. The sacred enclosure was also considerably larger, now measuring up to 488 × 315 meters (Meyers and Chancey 2012, 55). Though the cult of sacrifice at the Temple was in operation year-round, the major events were the three great pilgrimage festivals of Passover, Shavuot, and Sukkot, which were marked by throngs of visitors to the city, some coming from abroad (Hezser 2011, 374–381). These events would have been far greater than pilgrimages to the Jewish temple at Leontopolis in Egypt, the other functioning site of a cult of sacrifice to the God of Israel in this period, but one that has left no conclusive archaeological evidence of its whereabouts or its design (Wardle 2010, 129–131).

International pilgrimage to Jerusalem from the Jewish diaspora began on a massive scale only in the first century BCE, due in no small part to the potential of Herod's new temple to attract visitors from afar (Goodman 1999). There are traces on archaeological record of the infrastructure required to accommodate the ritualized movement of Jews on foot for the three annual festivals. An extensive network of pilgrimage roads has been identified, particularly in the lowlands leading up from the coastal plain to Jerusalem from the west (Figure 5.1; Tepper and Tepper 2013).

The roads climb slopes not with switchbacks but with steps, indicating their primary use for foot traffic; they also tend to be located near sources of water or pools for immersion (Tepper

Figure 5.1 One of the roads identified as an ancient Jewish pilgrimage route near Maale Akrabim in southern Israel. Photo courtesy of Yotam Tepper (see Tepper and Tepper 2013, Fig. 7).

and Tepper 2013, 194–195, 202–209). Pilgrims coming by sea in this period would typically have disembarked at Caesarea-Maritima, the main port for Herod's kingdom. The port underwent a major upgrade under the king's auspices, precisely to accommodate increased traffic into Judea (Patrich 2018, 130–139).

Within the holy city, processional routes connected the pilgrim encampments outside the city walls to the north, west, and south (Maoz 1985, 48, 50–51). The southern of these processional routes has been exposed, quite controversially, in excavations in a tunnel recently dug under Palestinian homes within the Silwan neighborhood, the so-called "City of David." Others formed the armature of the Roman city plan of the second century CE onward, marking the lines of the main decumanus and eastern cardo. The processional routes terminated at the major entrance points to the Temple, including the Hulda Gate tunnels, the monumental stairway at Robinson's Arch (Figure 5.2), and the pedestrian bridge over Wilson's Arch. Remnants of these infrastructural components have been documented archaeologically and the latter two can be visited by the public. Remarkably, the Hulda Gate tunnels partially survive too—some of their ornamental domes still in situ—but they are off-limits to visitors (Peleg-Barkat 2017, 162–163).

The Romanizing elements of Herod's Temple could have reminded pilgrims of the cultural change Judea was experiencing as it came to be integrated into the Roman Empire. Excavations immediately following the Six Day War revealed extensive rubble from the Temple complex, including hundreds of decorative architectural fragments, which allow for a reconstruction of the decorative program of Herod's Temple. As Orit Peleg-Barkat has shown (2017), the program drew heavily on Roman styles of architectural décor, innovative for its day, with ample use of the Corinthian capital and of the modillion cornice, among others, all adopted by the local Judean craftsmen responsible for executing the design. Meanwhile, the plan of the

Figure 5.2 An artistic reconstruction of the southwestern corner of Herod's Temple enclosure, looking north along the ancient street under Robinson's Arch. Image by Balage Balogh.

complex is itself indebted to the Roman imperial cult building known as a Caesareum, with a central esplanade surrounded by porticoes and a large basilica on one end (Peleg-Barkat 2017, 112–113). This allowed for the complex to serve as the city forum, its outer esplanade accessible by all and utilized for various municipal and legal activities.

There were traditions to uphold in the pilgrimage event, of course, and rules to follow. The main specialists responsible for preserving the traditions of the Temple were the priests (*kohanim*). This was a much-esteemed group of thousands of men, whose privileges were inherited and whose periods of service were organized by clan (Schaper 2020). The lower-ranking Levites were also involved in the festivities. Perhaps the most startling material evidence of the rule-governance of these classes of holy men is an inscription in Greek on a low parapet delineating the Temple's inner courts, which were off-limits to non-Jews (Cotton et al. 2010, 42–45). The inscription, two copies of which survive, threatens death to those who trespass. Another material reflection of rule-governance within the Temple is an inscription in Hebrew, found among the rubble at the foot of the southwestern corner of the enclosure, which labels the place where trumpeters stood (49–50). Those trumpeters presumably announced the start of the Sabbath at sundown (Josephus, *War* 4.582).

Religious festivals were events of local economic significance. They were an opportunity for commercial exchange in city markets, the consumption of a large quantity of meat and other agricultural products, and the redistribution of such goods among entitled families, namely those of priests and Levites (Keddie 2019, 161–176). Hayim Lapin (2017) has employed a consumption model to quantify the economic demand created by the pilgrimage event. He estimates, among other things, that an average Passover festival in the first century CE would have called for the slaughter of an impressive number of 27,500 lambs and 15,500 pairs of birds (246). Indeed, large quantities of animal bones have been uncovered in an area of Jerusalem used as a city dump in the period; they include the typical mix of kosher species (Bar-Oz et al. 2007, 5–6). There were everyday products to buy in the Jerusalem markets too. A distinctive class of stone weights, for use with a weighing scale, was in use in the markets in the Early Roman period (Reich 2015). They are made of Jerusalem limestone instead of metal, an unusual feature that may have provided a local flavor or even an air of traditionalism to the market proceedings; limestone had also been used for weights in the Kingdom of Judah in the late Iron Age (235–240). Finally, the water consumption demands on the city would have been considerable during the festivals and numerous open-air pools dated to this period are understood as having stored water for these needs (Gurevich 2017).

With the destruction of the Jerusalem Temple in 70 CE and that at Leontopolis in 73 CE, pilgrimage to holy space shifted to other locations. Fine cult objects taken by the Romans from Jerusalem were put on display at the newly built Temple of Peace in Rome, and Jews appear to have visited Rome to pay homage to them. They may even have offered prayers to their deity from within the Temple of Peace, turning an otherwise pagan space into an opportunity for continued spiritual connection in a Jewish vein (Chapman 2009, 113–117). Jews also made pilgrimages in late antiquity to the burial sites of the prophets of Israel (Satran 1995, 105–110) and to places commemorating miraculous biblical events (Bar-Ilan 1996).

The Archaeology of Bodily Practice

The ancient Judean *mikveh* offers a glimpse into an extraordinary moment in the history of Jewish bodily practice. This type of bathing installation (Figure 5.3), which usually consist of steps leading down to an immersion basin, appears on archaeological record throughout Jewish sites of Israel-Palestine somewhat abruptly in the first century BCE and then just as suddenly

Figure 5.3 A private domestic *mikveh* of the Early Roman period from a Jewish residential area of Sepphoris in the Galilee. Image and photo courtesy of Eric Meyers and Carol Meyers, Duke University.

recedes from view in the second century CE. Hundreds of them have been catalogued in a landmark study by Ronny Reich (2013).

They were supplied by harvested rainwater that utilized rooftop or surface-catchment hydraulic systems. And they are understood to have been used in observance of biblical purity laws, which call for the skin to be washed after exposure to defiling agents such as menstrual blood, semen, corpses, and infected skin. The context of these installations, however, suggests Jews were immersing themselves in water for other reasons too, such as before entering the Temple precinct or a synagogue, or even as part of agricultural work (Zissu and Amit 2008).

In fact, precisely how and why the ancient Judean *mikvehs* were used remains unclear. Their regular appearance in private domestic contexts implies a need for daily use if not also for privacy, and one might connect this phenomenon with the ancient Jewish custom of post-coital and post-ejaculatory immersion, as described by Josephus (*Jewish Antiquities* 3.263; *Against Apion* 2.203). The custom would seem to be yet another manifestation of a deep-seated societal belief that sex is a defiling act that should be regulated (Feinstein 2014, 26–27). Interestingly, in later antiquity rabbinic authorities no longer required men to ritually immerse after ejaculation, though they upheld the requirement for post-menstrual immersion among women (Kiperwasser 2012, 311–338). We might therefore surmise that the practice of Jewish ritual immersion was once more common among men than women.

The *mikvehs* may also have had some basic hygienic use, as they only rarely appear alongside bathtubs and other washing installations. The very introduction of immersion baths in observance of biblical law in the second and first centuries BCE appears to be correlated with the rise in popularity in the Greco-Roman world of immersion bathing for health and leisure (Gordon 2020). Prior to that point, purification was carried out by a cleansing bath using jugs and basins. Moreover, the swift decline of Judean *mikvehs* on the archaeological record by the second century CE can be linked with the growing popularity in that era of the public bathhouse. By that point in time, Jews feeling obliged to purify themselves by immersion could simply visit the local bathhouse to do so, precluding the need to maintain stepped pools in the home, and providing the added benefit of a cleansing bath in a public facility with fresher water (Gordon 2020, 448–449).

Figure 5.4 An assemblage of stone vessels of the Early Roman period from the Jewish Quarter in Jerusalem. Photo courtesy of Zev Radovan.

Rituals surrounding food consumption have left their mark on the archaeological record too. A few hundred cooking pots from sites of the Early Roman period (37 BCE–70 CE) in Judea, particularly from Jerusalem, have been discovered with a curious feature: each was intentionally punctured in antiquity, leaving a small roundish hole about the size of a coin. Perhaps the holes were meant to render the vessels immune to defilement, or to purify them after contact with a defiling agent, or to signal their previous use for cooking sacrifices, or even to subject them to punishment as if they were endowed with spirit despite their inanimateness (Stern and Noam 2015, 346–348). What unites these explanations is an awareness of the extent to which ancient Jews were concerned with warding off contaminating agents in their eating practices.

A similar awareness has guided the modern interpretation of stone vessels, another distinctive class of artifact from Early Roman Judea (Figure 5.4).

Lathe-turned or hand-carved out of the local chalkstone, these vessels are very common alongside regular ceramic wares in the local pottery assemblages of the first centuries BCE and CE in the region (Magen 2002). Their popularity may be due to the fact that many Jews saw stone as impervious to defilement by contact with a contaminating agent. The "measuring cup" and "*kalal*" types of stone vessels may have been used for the ritual washing of the hands before meals (Berlin 2005, 430–431). The handwashing ritual would have thus had its own accoutrement, and like immersion in *mikvehs*, the ritual reflects an ancient Jewish interest in protecting the body from contamination. Interestingly, the ritual also appears to have been inspired by a Greco-Roman custom that was reframed to suit Jewish purity concerns (Furstenberg 2016, 100–106).

The ancient Jewish sect called the Essenes were particularly fastidious in their bodily practice. If we accept the widely held theory that the archaeological site of Qumran in the Judean Desert was an Essene settlement (Meyers and Chancey 2012, 92–100), then the remains there can provide some material evidence of their everyday lives. Several phenomena on the site are worthy of note, each attesting to a distinctive ancient Jewish practice pertaining to the body.

One involves the need for full immersion after defecation—an Essene practice described by Josephus (*War* 2.149) and reflected at Qumran in the placement of a toilet next to a *mikveh* (Magness 2011, 135). A second involves numerous deposits of animal bones within pottery vessels placed around the settlement. These may have been the vestiges of a cult of sacrifice run at the settlement itself (Magness 2016), or the remnants of communal meals discarded in a manner resembling priestly practice at the Temple (Mizzi 2016). Either explanation is rooted in the assumption that the Essenes saw their communities as holy spaces akin to the Temple in Jerusalem but improving upon it, given their perception that the Temple had become corrupt.

Another material reflection of Essene bodily practice involves food consumption, which is described in the ancient source material as having been carried out in large communal meals in a state of ritual purity, after immersion in a *mikveh* (e.g., Josephus, *War* 2.129–131). The site of Qumran indeed has several very large *mikvehs*, one of which is adjacent to the space identified as the communal dining hall. Even more extraordinary are the over 1,000 small bowls excavated in a pantry next to the dining hall; each bowl was just big enough for an individual portion of food (Berlin 2005, 447). Perhaps the bowls were preferred to the more common casserole dishes or cooking pots, both usable for shared dishes, because they minimized risk of contamination by a defiling agent. In any case, the bowls offer yet another manifestation of the patterned daily existence of the Qumran sectarians, as well as the large numbers of participants in their communal meals. Taken together with the other material remains of their everyday lives, we can reconstruct a community where ritualized behaviors were a kind of social drama marked by displays of piety and obedience.

The archaeology of death and burial also provides a window into bodily practice. Maintaining the integrity of the body after death appears to have been particularly important to Jews from the Early Roman period onward, as shown by the remains of copious tombs of elite families that survive in the vicinity of Jerusalem (Kloner and Zissu 2007). Bodies were interred in the tombs in individual burial niches (loculi or *kokhim*), where they decomposed in isolation before the bones were transferred to stone ossuaries. Prior to the adoption of ossuaries in the first century BCE, the custom was to deposit bones into a communal charnel pit. The change may reflect new ideas about resurrection or concerns about fragmentation of the body after death (Meyers and Chancey 2012, 79–80). The individuation of burial remains into niches and ossuaries also allowed for mourners to direct their attention toward a specific set of bodily remains during visits to the tomb. Attending to the dead in an otherworld may have been practiced as well, given the presence in the Jerusalem tombs of burial goods including common ceramic vessels, cosmetic items, and personal possessions (Kloner and Zissu 2007, 123–125). While the family unit is the central organizing principle behind these tombs, the sprawling catacombs at Beit Shearim in the Lower Galilee, which were an active burial site through the Roman and Byzantine periods, appear to have been run by burial societies (Weiss 2010, 218–225). In some cases, bones of the dead were brought to Beit Shearim from diasporic lands, perhaps so they could lie forever near the remains of the sages interred there.

The Archaeology of the Synagogue Gathering

While temples were centralized organizations responsible for cults of sacrifice, synagogues were more diffuse institutions whose social functions included the maintenance of a healthy relationship with the deity through the reading of scripture and communal prayer. The earliest group of synagogues surviving on archaeological record, from the Early Roman period, consist of fairly generic spaces for communal gatherings. A stone block bearing Temple imagery in relief, from the Jewish village of Magdala on the Sea of Galilee, may have been used as a Torah-reading table (Hachlili 2013, 40–41), while side rooms next to a number of the main assembly halls may have been for the safekeeping of the scrolls. The Theodotus inscription indicates that synagogues in Jerusalem were functioning while the Temple was still in operation, and that such synagogues could have served as hostels for pilgrims (Levine 2005, 57–58).

The Early Roman synagogues contrast with the synagogues of late antiquity (third–sixth c. CE), whose visual programs seem more explicitly meant to elicit a sense of wonder among the congregants, or to create a sacred aura, as holy spaces often do. The walls of the Dura Europos synagogue in Syria (third c. CE), for example, were covered in portraits of biblical figures and scenes from the Hebrew Bible—a visual reminder for congregants of the rootedness of their identity in scripture. This would have been particularly important in an environment such as Dura Europos, where Christians were laying claim in their own religious practice to the same body of holy texts (Fine 2005. 172–183). It would also have enhanced the ritualized reading of scripture by drawing further attention to the stories, legends, and characters contained within it. The late antique synagogues in the Galilee and Golan tend to be basilica spaces oriented toward Jerusalem, with a Torah shrine consisting of an aedicula, apse, or niche on the Jerusalem-oriented wall. The mosaic floors of these spaces, which have been richly studied (Fine 2005; Levine 2012; Talgam 2014), are adorned with scenes from the Hebrew Bible, images of cultic objects from the Temple, and a Zodiac motif that might be interpreted as a visual manifestation of the deity's supremacy over the cosmos—with its allotment of time into seasons, months, and festival days. Moreover, the synagogue exteriors can illuminate how these early Jewish communities saw themselves fitting into society. Many of the buildings are marked by monumental facades drawing elements from the religious architecture of the ancient world. The Galilean synagogues in particular are known for their classicizing exterior décor, with lavish doorways, window treatments, and entablatures (Figure 5.5). These elements signaled sanctity, wealth, proud participation in the broader milieu, and a heritage of fine distinction.

Most of these synagogues would have allowed for the gathering of about 150–300 persons, based on their size and sporadic evidence for the existence of second-floor galleries, though some were considerably larger (Spigel 2012). Columns supported the roofs and stone benches surrounded the perimeter, with movable wooden benches or rugs possibly used in the

Figure 5.5 Three Galilean synagogues of late antiquity—Meiron, Baram, and Nabratein—as reconstructed based on the archaeological remains. Image courtesy of Eric Meyers and Carol Meyers, Duke University.

middle to accommodate more seating. The rigid frontal orientation of the basilica form, as well as the placement of the Torah shrine at front, implies harmonized body positioning toward both Jerusalem and the Torah. Archaeological evidence can do little to address the question of whether there was separate seating for women and men (Hachlili 2013, 579–580), though the remains do suggest that prominent individuals sat apart from the rest. A throne-like seat built of stone—a so-called "seat of Moses"—has been found among some synagogue remains; among others is evidence for special seating on benches or chairs facing the congregation (Zangenberg 2019, 105–106; Levine 2005, 339–340). The continued reverence of priests within these spaces is evidenced materially through a few inscriptions listing the names and villages in the Galilee of the 24 priestly courses (*mishmarot*) from the Temple (Hachlili 2013, 670–671).

Finally, to better appreciate the sensory experience of attending synagogue in the ancient world, one must attend to the accoutrement. Windows would have provided natural light and oil lamps could have been suspended from the ceilings by metal chains to illuminate the spaces too. Glass bowl lamps connected to a metal chain bearing a menorah decoration have been discovered at Khirbet Wadi Hamam, for example (Jackson-Tal 2018, 471; Farhi 2018, 498). The Torah shrine may have been lit up by an eternal lamp (*ner tamid*). A hole in the center of a decorative stone pediment from the synagogue ruins at Nabratein seems to have been used for one (Meyers and Meyers 2009, 75, 85). Remains of the seven-branched Temple menorah, carved out of stone or marble, have been found among synagogue ruins (Figure 5.6), while depictions of them are commonplace on the floor mosaics, suggesting that they were placed on either side of the Torah shrine (Fine 2016, 42–76).

Indeed, the Temple menorah had become by late antiquity a common identifier of Jewish space and a counterpart to the ubiquitous Christian cross. On the mosaics they appear with other cult objects, such as the *shofar*, *lulav*, and incense shovel, all of which evoke the Temple while also finding a place in synagogue ritual. The *shofar* and *lulav* would have been central to Rosh Hashanah and Sukkot rites, respectively, while incense may have been used during

Figure 5.6 A seven-branched marble menorah from the late antique synagogue at Maon in the Hebron hills. Photo courtesy of Zev Radovan.

services too. A bronze incense burner was recovered from among synagogue ruins at Beit Shean (Shemesh 2017, 2–3) and ceramic incense shovels that are similar in appearance to those depicted on synagogue mosaics have been found in a Jewish residential area of Sepphoris (Meyers 2018).

Conclusion

A focus on the materiality of ancient Jewish ritual and practice can shed light on the embodied, sensory, and experiential elements of early Judaism. Archaeological remains can give us a sense of the drama of the action of pilgrimage to Jerusalem in antiquity, with its multisensory experiences and its copious visual stimuli, including the Temple. They can also teach us about the social and economic mechanics of pilgrimage—the foot-traffic infrastructure, the market practices, and the policing of behavior by religious authorities, among others. Furthermore, the archaeology of bodily practice can enhance our understanding of ancient Jewish attitudes toward the clean and the unclean. Attention to the purity of the body finds material expression most conspicuously in *mikvehs* from Jewish sites of Israel-Palestine in the Early Roman period, but also in stone vessel assemblages and in the idiosyncratic remains at Qumran. Evolving burial customs emerge from the material record too, with evidence for the careful individuation of burial remains by the Early Roman period, including the secondary burial of bones in ossuaries. Finally, the archaeology of the synagogue can provide a window into sacred Jewish place-making for the purposes of communal rituals at the village level. Synagogue ruins are extant at dozens of sites throughout the ancient world but are most common in the Jewish centers of settlement in the Galilee and Golan of the fourth–sixth centuries CE. The ruins allow for an understanding of the sensory elements of the synagogue environment. The visual elements within these sacred spaces draw on biblical stories, Temple imagery, and pagan motifs, grounding synagogue practices and enhancing them.

References

Bar-Ilan, Meir. 1996. "Fabulous Places in the Land of Israel in Antiquity," *Judea and Samaria Research Studies* 5: 229–239 [in Hebrew].
Bar-Oz, Guy, Ram Bouchnik, Ehud Weiss, Lior Weissbrod, Daniella E. Bar-Yosef Mayer, and Ronny Reich. 2007. "'Holy Garbage': A Quantitative Study of the City-Dump of Early Roman Jerusalem," *Levant* 39: 1–12.
Berlin, Andrea M. 2005. "Jewish Life Before the Revolt: The Archaeological Evidence," *Journal for the Study of Judaism* 36, no. 4: 417–470.
Chapman, Honora Howell. 2009. "What Josephus Sees: The Temple of Peace and the Jerusalem Temple as Spectacle in Text and Art," *Phoenix* 63, no. 1: 107–130.
Cotton, Hannah M., Leah Di Segni, Werner Eck, Benjamin Isaac, Alla Kushnir-Stein, Haggai Misgav, et al. eds. 2010. *Corpus Inscriptionum Iudaeae/Palaestinae. Volume I: Jerusalem,* Part 1. Berlin: De Gruyter.
Farhi, Yoav. 2018. "Metal Artifacts from Khirbet Wadi Ḥamam and Mount Nitai," in *Khirbet Wadi Ḥamam: A Roman-Period Village and Synagogue in the Lower Galilee.* Ed. Uzi Leibner. Jerusalem: Institute of Archaeology, The Hebrew University of Jerusalem, 495–512.
Feinstein, Eve Levavi. 2014. *Sexual Pollution in the Hebrew Bible.* Oxford: Oxford University Press.
Fine, Steven. 2005. *Art and Judaism in the Greco-Roman World: Toward a New Jewish Archaeology.* Cambridge; New York: Cambridge University Press.
Fine, Steven. 2016. *The Menorah: From the Bible to Modern Israel.* Cambridge, MA; London: Harvard University Press.
Furstenberg, Yair. 2016. *Purity and Community in Antiquity: Traditions of the Law from Second Temple Judaism to the Mishnah.* Jerusalem: Magnes Press [in Hebrew].

Goodman, Martin. 1999. "The Pilgrimage Economy of Jerusalem in the Second Temple Period," in *Jerusalem: Its Sanctity and Centrality to Judaism, Christianity, and Islam*. Ed. Lee I. Levine. New York: Continuum, 69–76.

Gordon, Benjamin D. 2018. "Sightseeing and Spectacle at the Jewish Temple," *AJS Review* 43: 271–292.

Gordon, Benjamin D. 2020. "Health and the Origins of the Miqveh," *Journal of Ancient Judaism* 11: 418–459.

Gurevich, David. 2017. "The Water Pools and the Pilgrimage to Jerusalem in the Late Second Temple Period," *Palestine Exploration Quarterly* 149, no. 2: 103–134.

Hachlili, Rachel. 2013. *Ancient Synagogues—Archaeology and Art: New Discoveries and Current Research*. Boston, MA: Brill.

Hezser, Catherine. 2011. *Jewish Travel in Antiquity*. Tübingen: Mohr-Siebeck.

Jackson-Tal, Ruth E. 2018. "Glass Finds," in *Khirbet Wadi Ḥamam: A Roman-Period Village and Synagogue in the Lower Galilee*. Ed. Uzi Leibner. Jerusalem: Institute of Archaeology, The Hebrew University of Jerusalem, 465–477.

Keddie, Anthony. 2019. *Class and Power in Roman Palestine: The Socioeconomic Setting of Judaism and Christian Origins*. Cambridge: Cambridge University Press.

Kiperwasser, Reuven. 2012. "The Immersion of *Baallei Qerain*," *Jewish Studies Quarterly* 19: 311–338.

Kloner, Amos, and Boaz Zissu. 2007. *The Necropolis of Jerusalem in the Second Temple Period*. Leuven; Dudley, MA: Peeters.

Lapin, Hayim. 2017. "Temple, Cult, and Consumption in Second Temple Jerusalem," in *Expressions of Cult in the Southern Levant in the Greco-Roman Period. Manifestations in Text and Material Culture*. Eds. Oren Tal and Zeev Weiss. Turnhout: Brepols, 241–253.

Levine, Lee I. 2005. *The Ancient Synagogue: The First Thousand Years*, 2nd ed. New Haven, CT; London: Yale University Press.

Levine, Lee I. 2012. *Visual Judaism in Late Antiquity: Historical Contexts of Jewish Art*. New Haven, CT; London: Yale University Press.

Magen, Yitzhak. 2002. *The Stone Vessel Industry in the Second Temple Period: Excavations at Hizma and the Jerusalem Temple Mount*. Jerusalem: Israel Exploration Society.

Magness, Jodi. 2011. *Stone and Dung, Oil and Spit: Jewish Daily Life in the Time of Jesus*. Grand Rapids, MI: William B. Eerdmans.

Magness, Jodi. 2016. "Were Sacrifices Offered at Qumran? The Animal Bone Deposits Reconsidered," *Journal of Ancient Judaism* 7: 5–34.

Mandell, Alice, and Jeremy Smoak. 2019. "The Material Turn in the Study of Israelite Religions: Spaces, Things, and the Body," *Journal of Hebrew Scriptures* 19: 1–42.

Maoz, Zvi Uri. 1985. "On the Hasmonean and Herodian Town-Plan of Jerusalem," *Eretz-Israel* 18: 46–57 [in Hebrew].

Meyers, Eric M. 2018. "Ceramic Incense Shovels," in *The Architecture, Stratigraphy, and Artifacts of the Western Summit of Sepphoris*. Eric M. Meyers, Carol L. Meyers and Benjamin D. GordonUniversity Park, PA: Eisenbrauns, 644–652.

Meyers, Eric M., and Mark A. Chancey. 2012. *Alexander to Constantine: Archaeology of the Land of the Bible*, Vol. 3. New Haven, CT: Yale University Press.

Meyers, Eric M., and Carol L. Meyers. 2009. *Excavations at Ancient Nabratein: Synagogue and Environs*. Winona Lake, IN: Eisenbrauns.

Mitchell, Jon P. 2017. "From Ritual to Ritualization," in *Religion, Theory, Critique: Classic and Contemporary Approaches and Methodologies*. Ed. Richard King. New York: Columbia University Press, 377–391.

Mizzi, Dennis. 2016. "The Animal Bone Deposits at Qumran: An Unresolvable Riddle," *Journal of Ancient Judaism* 7: 51–70.

Patrich, Joseph. 2018. *A Walk to Caesarea: A Historical-Archaeological Perspective*. Jerusalem: Israel Exploration Society, Yad Itzhak Ben-Zvi.

Peleg-Barkat, Orit. 2017. *The Temple Mount Excavations in Jerusalem, 1968–1978, Directed by Benjamin Mazar, Final Reports, Vol. V: Herodian Architectural Decoration and King Herod's Royal Portico*. Jerusalem: Institute of Archaeology, Hebrew University of Jerusalem.

Raja, Rubina, and Jörg Rüpke, eds. 2015. *A Companion to the Archaeology of Religion in the Ancient World*. Malden, MA; Oxford: Wiley Blackwell.

Reich, Ronny. 2013. *Miqwa'ot (Jewish Ritual Baths) in the Second Temple, Mishnaic and Talmudic Periods*. Jerusalem: Yad Ben-Zvi, Israel Exploration Society [in Hebrew].

Reich, Ronny. 2015. *Stone Scale-Weights of the Late Second Temple Period*. Jerusalem: Zinman Institute of Archaeology, University of Haifa; Israel Exploration Society.

Satran, David. 1995. *Biblical Prophets in Byzantine Palestine: Reassessing the Lives of the Prophets*. Leiden; New York: E.J. Brill.

Schaper, Joachim. 2020. "Priesthood," in *T&T Clark Encyclopedia of Second Temple Judaism*. Eds. Daniel Gurtner and Loren T. Stuckenbruck. London: T&T Clark, 622–624.

Shemesh, Abraham O. 2017. "Those Who Require '[…] The Burning of Incense in Synagogues Are the Rabbinic Jews': Burning Incense in Synagogues in Commemoration of the Temple," *HTS Theological Studies* 73, no. 3: 1–6.

Spigel, Chad S. 2012. *Ancient Synagogue Seating Capacities: Methodology, Analysis and Limits*. Tübingen: Mohr Siebeck.

Stern, Ian, and Vered Noam. 2015. "Holey Vessels of Maresha," *Aram* 27: 343–364.

Talgam, Rina. 2014. *Mosaics of Faith: Floors of Pagans, Jews, Samaritans, Christians, and Muslims in the Holy Land*. Jerusalem; University Park, PA: Yad Ben-Zvi; Pennsylvania State University Press.

Tepper, Yigal, and Yotam Tepper. 2013. *The Road that Bears the People: Pilgrimage Roads to Jerusalem in the Second Temple Period*. Jerusalem; Tel Aviv: Hakibbutz Hameuchad [in Hebrew].

Wardle, Timothy. 2010. *The Jerusalem Temple and Early Christian Identity*. Tübingen: Mohr Siebeck.

Weiss, Zeev. 2010. "Burial Practices in Beth She'arim and the Question of Dating the Patriarchal Necropolis," in *'Follow the Wise': Studies in Jewish History and Culture in Honor of Lee I. Levine*. Eds. Zeev Weiss, Oded Irshai, Jodi Magness, and Seth Schwartz. Winona Lake, IN: Eisenbrauns, 207–231.

Zangenberg, Jürgen K. 2019. "Will the Real Women Please Sit Down. Interior Space, Seating Arrangements, and Female Presence in the Byzantine Synagogue of Horvat Kur in Galilee," in *Gender and Social Norms in Ancient Israel, Early Judaism and Early Christianity: Texts and Material Culture*. Eds. Michaela Bauks, Katharina Galor, and Judith Hartenstein. Göttingen: Vandenhoeck & Ruprecht, 91–117.

Zissu, Boaz, and David Amit. 2008. "Common Judaism, Common Purity, and the Second Temple Period Judean *Miqwa'ot* (Ritual Immersion Baths)," in *Common Judaism: Explorations in Second-Temple Judaism*. Eds. Wayne O. McCready and Adele Reinhartz. Minneapolis: Fortress Press, 47–62.

6
SEE AND SANCTIFY
Ceremonies and Ceremonial Art in Medieval Ashkenaz and Italy

Shalom Sabar

Notwithstanding the importance and advantages of material culture, the number of extant Judaic artifacts that can be dated to the Middle Ages is very small. Many factors contribute to this absence, that is even more pronounced in the realm of the ceremonial objects that concern us here. Life as a religious minority and the vicissitudes of the Jewish people in medieval Europe – often subject to pogroms, deportations and expulsions – resulted in the forced abandonment of material possessions, the destruction of synagogues and their contents, the confiscation or melting down of costly items – a familiar phenomenon that is unfortunately not limited to medieval Jewish society but practiced even more harshly in Europe of the modern period. The medieval circumstances were coupled by the Jewish tradition that does not encourage the preservation or the veneration of ritual objects, recommending the replacement of worn-out books and items that can no longer be used regularly for the performance of the commandments for which they were created. And though timeworn ritual objects that are considered sacred may not be thrown out, they need to go to a special storage called a *genizah*, which is subsequently put away or buried.

Notwithstanding the scarcity of material objects, the situation with respect to a leading branch of the visual arts in medieval Europe, namely the illuminated manuscript, is much better. A relatively large number of Hebrew illuminated codices survived from the leading Jewish communities of Germany (Ashkenazi), Spain and Portugal (Sephardi), and Italy. The Hebrew book as a cultural object occupied a central place in medieval Jewish life, East and West, reflecting the veneration for the written word and love of the sacred Hebrew texts, whether the classics of the past, prayer books, Passover Haggadot, or works by medieval authorities.[1] The treasured books, commonly made of durable and costly parchment sheets, were protected by their owners even in difficult times, and often carried with them from one place to another in times of forced deportations. While some remained with the descendants of their families generation after generation, many others were later acquired by Hebraists, book collectors, libraries and museums. As a result the number of extant copies exceeds by far any other category of the Jewish visual arts that survived from the Middle Ages.

The miniatures in the manuscripts supplement the three-dimensional objects, allowing glimpses into the material culture and daily reality of the time. Even when the artists depicted biblical scenes, they commonly referred indirectly to the familiar realm of their time.[2]

Accordingly the figures of the past are dressed often as contemporaries, the settings, architecture, or landscapes are those the artists encountered and knew. In addition, many illustrations deal directly with rituals of the life and year cycles – a central topic of traditional Jewish art. The illuminations, however, should be dealt with cautiously for a number of reasons. The artists were at times non-Jews and not well versed with the Jewish rituals. In addition, whether Jewish or Christian, the artists of the time often employed symbolic, ideal or stereotyped motifs that testify to their makers and their abilities as well as their ambitions and hopes more than actual practices or the daily ambience.

The two categories – Judaic ritual objects and Hebrew manuscript illumination – have another distinctive feature. The place of figurative representations or "graven images" has its limitations in Jewish culture because of the "Second Commandment" and its rabbinic interpretation over the ages.[3] In medieval Ashkenaz its most pronounced expression is in the illumination of 13th–14th-century sacred texts that was frowned upon by some authorities, and human figures were often depicted by animal heads, thereby avoiding full figurative imagery. By contrast, lavish ceremonial artifacts were not only permitted by the rabbis but highly recommended and even encouraged. This favorable attitude is embodied in the rabbinic concept of *hiddur mitzvah* – "beautification of the commandment", which developed in the Talmudic period.[4] This concept calls for the production and usage of costlier and rather attractive objects for the performance of the commandments. In a large part this rabbinic endorsement contributed to the development of the chief field of traditional Jewish art. In the process of creating and "beautifying" ceremonial items, their design and enrichment reflect diverse modes of expression and styles of decoration, whether among the communities residing in Europe or the lands of Islam. Traditional Jewish art, ceremonial in particular, developed accordingly around three basic categories:

- Ritual art for the synagogue
- Ceremonial objects for the life cycle
- Ceremonial objects for the annual cycle.

The Synagogue and its Contents

Of the numerous synagogues that existed in medieval Ashkenaz and Italy, at least one in every community, only one original structure stands almost intact today. This is the Altneuschul in Prague – the oldest synagogue of Europe, that since its completion in 1270 is still in use today.[5] The nearly miraculous continuous survival of the building has been accompanied by many stories and legends, which undoubtedly added much to its fame and made it a celebrated prototype of the medieval Ashkenazi synagogue, created in Gothic style. A Romanesque synagogue, the earliest known from Germany, was in use in Worms as late as 1938, when it was destroyed during Kristallnacht.[6] First built in 1034, the Worms synagogue "witnessed" the vicissitudes of Jewish life in the Rhineland – in 1096 it was demolished during the First Crusade, rebuilt in 1175, damaged again in the pogroms of 1349 and 1615, and in 1961 this well-documented building was reconstructed fully, using the original bricks that survived the 1938 destruction.

Other medieval synagogues were generally reduced to rubble, never to be built again. Archeological remains of a few, dated from Roman times on, survived – e.g., in Italy, the 1st-century synagogue of Ostia Antica near Rome was still in use in the 5th century. Some other relevant synagogues, not necessarily free-standing structures, including sites outside Germany and Italy, have been significantly altered and/or their identification is conjectural; a notable example is the Romanesque house in Lincoln, England that is identified by some as a former synagogue. Aside from actual structures or remains, evidence comes also from written documents and travelogues. In the case of Italy, where magnificent synagogues survive only from the 16th century on, there are significant but short accounts of the impressive and spacious Sicilian synagogues that existed in Palermo and Messina before the Expulsion (1493), described by the noted Mishnah commentator, Rabbi Obadiah of Bertinoro ("The Bartenura," ca. 1445–1515).[7] There are, in addition, some pictorial depictions of destroyed synagogues by Christian artists – notably the leading German painter Albrecht Altdorfer (1480–1538), who made two arresting etchings of the porch and interior view of the early 13th-century synagogue of Regensburg just before it was demolished on February 22, 1519 and the Jews expelled from the town.[8]

The Altneuschul and Worms synagogues, along with partially known related others, reflect the dominant architectural styles of the Romanesque and Gothic periods in Western Europe, adapted to Jewish usage. Commonly divided into two parallel naves by typical columns and piers of the time, the reader's platform or *bimah* from which the Torah is recited and services led, stood in the center between two columns, while the Torah ark, containing the Torah scrolls, is at the eastern end in the direction of Jerusalem. Called by medieval Ashkenazi Jews *almemor* (or *almemar, almembra; almenbre* by Rashi) – a term derived from the Muslim *minbar* (*al-minbar*), the raised pulpit in the mosque[9] – the *bimah* is an imposing rectangular enclosure in Gothic style, often elevated by a few steps, and in the case of the Altneuschul it is a stone platform upon which stands a wrought iron grille with ogee arches. Stone is used also for the framework of the Torah ark, surmounted by an ornate gable carved with vine leaves and fruits (both *bimah* and ark are later repairs). Raised above the floor by steps, the massive ark is covered by interchangeable attractively embroidered *parokhet* (Torah ark curtain) and *kapporet* (valance), typical of Ashkenazi synagogues – though none survived from the Middle Ages.[10] From Italy, on the other hand, survived free-standing wooden Torah arks created in the second half of the 15th century from Modena (dated 1472) and Urbino (ca. 1500). The construction and design of the earlier Modena ark conforms to miniatures in Italian Hebrew codices of the preceding period, reflecting Gothic style of decoration, while the Urbino ark that was modified in 1624 exemplifies the transition to the decorative modes of the Renaissance.[11]

The most sacred object in the synagogue, or in Judaism is general, is the Torah scroll (*Sefer Torah* in Hebrew), containing the Pentateuch or five books of Moses, written by a proficient and pious scribe on parchment sheets produced from the skin of kosher animals.[12] The Torah scroll is likened in the Jewish tradition to a princess or bride and since the Talmudic period it is accordingly majestically "dressed," adorned and protected from possible damages. In order to handle the long and heavy scroll and protect its sheets from being mutilated, since Late Antiquity it was rolled on a rod or a roller. While some medieval miniatures from Ashkenaz and Italy show at times a single roller as well, it became more widespread to use a pair of rollers or wooden staves, symbolically called in Hebrew *atzei hayyim* or "trees of life" (based on Prov. 3:18). It is possible that the term *tzipui zahav* ("gold plating"), mentioned by the 11th-century Rabbi Judah Cohen of Mainz in connection with the Torah scroll refers to the gilding of the staves.[13] This form of adornment is corroborated by a miniature in the Ulm Mahzor, dated 1459/60, showing Torah scrolls with silver-colored staves.[14] Other Ashkenazi as well as Italian miniatures depicting Torah scrolls, show colored wooden staves, at times topped by a bulbous section to aid carrying and rolling them.[15] The importance of the wooden *atzei hayyim* in rabbinic literature and the visual arts is strengthened by a single pair of splendid boxwood staves that survived from medieval Europe (Tel Aviv, Gross Family Collection).[16] Produced in the Emilia region of Italy during the second half of the 15th century, the staves bear, in monumental Hebrew letters, the name of Nathaniel Trabot, a well-known rabbi and scribe whose family immigrated to Italy from France. Each of the staves resembles a towering structure, delicately carved with late Gothic designs comprised of round and pointed arches containing typical lancet windows.

The "dressing" of the scroll in medieval Ashkenaz and Italy, as well as the Iberian Peninsula, is markedly different from that of the lands of Islam, where the tradition in this respect harks back to Roman times. Thus, while in Islamic lands the Torah scroll is enshrined permanently in a wooden case called *tik* (derived from the Greek term *theke* – case or chest), in Europe it is covered by expensive embroidered textile garments, which are removed from the scroll to be read while lying flat on the desk, a tradition that is followed to this day among these communities.[17] This tradition involves tying the Torah scroll tightly and securely by a binder when not in use. Made of a long narrow strip of cloth, the Torah binder was referred to in medieval Germany by the Hebrew term *mappah* (later in German, *Wimpel*), while in Italy it was commonly called in Italian *fascia*. Though in the Middle Ages the *mappah* was apparently a simple and undecorated piece of linen or cotton, a new tradition was introduced around 1500. The custom that emerged in Germany was to make the *Wimpel* from the swaddling cloth that covered the male newborn during his circumcision. Embroidered and decorated with a personal inscription, it was given to the synagogue to tie the scroll the first time the baby was taken to visit there.[18] In Italy, on the other hand, the binders were often made of weave pattern silk, and donated to the synagogue by women whose names they record, at times accompanied by their families' coats of arms.[19]

The rolled and tied scroll is draped with a garment or mantle, called by Ashkenazi Jews *me'il* ("robe" in Hebrew), intentionally following the term for the vestment of the High Priest in biblical times (Exodus 28:4). None survived from the Middle Ages, either from Germany or Italy, but miniatures, especially in Italian codices, show scrolls covered by embroidered silks or elaborate brocade fabrics, richly decorated with gold threads.[20] Though none survived, at the top of the protruding rollers are placed silver ornaments called *rimmonim* ("pomegranates") or Torah finials. On festive occasions, the finials are replaced by a sumptuous crown called *keter Torah* ("Torah crown") or, in Italy, *atarah* ("crown").[21] Extant Ashkenazi Torah crowns date only from the 17th century and they were often modeled on the actual royal crowns of Europe. Other Torah ornaments, such as the highly ornamental silver Torah shields, used to mark the place where the scroll is open, developed only in the late Middle Ages, and the evidence for their existence in the 15th century is mainly found in rabbinical writings.

Objects and Images in the Life Cycle

The life cycle of the traditional Jew from cradle to burial is accompanied by many ceremonies and rites of passage, for many of which appropriate ritual objects are produced. And though medieval compilations of the Halakha, that is the corpus of Jewish laws and ordinances, along with many other rabbinic writings of the time, deal with diverse aspects of the rituals and their performance, the material culture related to them is secondary in these works. This problem is more acute in the light of the scarcity of extant items whose attribution and provenance are certain.[22]

The visual reality of childbirth and childhood ceremonies is mostly recorded in miniatures. These are mostly biblical and/or Midrashic miniatures depicting the early childhood of biblical heroes such as Isaac, Rebecca's twins, or Moses – often modeled on contemporary rituals and daily life. In the so-called Second Nuremberg Haggadah from Germany, ca. 1460–70, for example, there is a cycle of images related to the childhood of Jacob and Esau.[23] It starts with Isaac and Rebecca praying to God for children, and continues on the same page with pregnant

Rebecca visiting sages in their study to consult about the fate of her unborn twins – which they apparently do by a randomly chosen passage from a book (bibliomancy) (fol. 32v); the next page shows her lying in bed before delivering her babies, assisted by two midwives, and then she leads her little sons to school (33r). In the "Regensburg Bible" (Bavaria, Germany, ca. 1300), the medieval Ashkenazi circumcision ceremony is shown through the story of Isaac being circumcised by Abraham.[24] The scene takes place in the interior of a structure with Gothic arches – implying a synagogue, and stepping out of the right arch are four women, the first one of whom carries a baby, who is shown again in the hands of a seated man while another one kneels in front of him to perform the circumcision. In accordance with the custom of Ashkenazi Jewry in the 14th–15th centuries a respectable woman, commonly the wife of the *sandek* ("companion of child" or "godfather"), called in the sources *ba'alat ha-brit* ("mistress of the circumcision" or simply *sandeket*) receives the baby from his mother and conveys him at the door, commonly to the *sandek*, who then sits in the "Elijah chair" with the baby on his knees, while the *mohel* ("circumciser") performs the ritual.[25] The door through which the newborn is brought to the sacred space of the synagogue, where women could not enter, is called in later sources *Jüdisch-Tür* ("circumcision door").[26] In circumcision miniatures from Italy more implements of the circumcision ritual are shown, placing emphasis on the high and ornamental Elijah chairs, at times provided with a convenient stool[27] – as is known from centuries later Italian Elijah chairs.[28] But, again, none of these items survived from the medieval period from any of these communities.

The circumcision ceremony gave rise to many other customs and objects, such as the transformation of the swaddling cloth into the decorative and highly popular Torah binder (*Wimpel*) mentioned above, which emerged due to the custom to perform the ritual in the synagogue.[29] Evidence for other items and rituals comes in most cases from written sources of the time and the preserved items are of a later period, though evidently they are imbued with centuries-old traditions. The high mortality rate of infants during childbirth in the Middle Ages (and subsequent centuries), entailed, for example, the production of amulets which were hung around the room of the woman in confinement.[30] Special measures were taken on the eve of circumcision, believed to be the most dangerous and the final opportunity for the evil spirits and the demon Lilith to attack the mother and child. It became common, therefore, for men and women to gather in the home of the newborn throughout this night, called *Wachnacht* ("watchnight") in Germany, or commonly *Veglia* ("vigil") in Italy, in order to safeguard the mother and against these evil forces.[31]

The subsequent significant rite of passage in the Jewish life cycle, namely the requirement to redeem the firstborn (*Pidyon ha-Ben*), based on the biblical commandment (Exodus 13:12–15), for which a price of five *shekalim* (ancient coins) was set by the lawgiver (Numbers 18:15–16).[32] And although some ceremonial objects were created specifically for this ritual,[33] none survived from the medieval period. Moreover, even in the miniatures it rarely appears[34] – perhaps because this ceremony is by far less common than circumcision and is performed only in the special cases where the firstborn who "opens the womb" is male born by natural means (for example, not following a miscarriage). Even less common visually, though extremely popular to this day, is the Bar Mitzvah ceremony – a relative latecomer in the Jewish life cycle.[35] It developed and matured in medieval Germany, but as an established full-fledged ritual was not practiced widely before the 14th–15th centuries, mainly in the Rhineland, reaching Italy only about a century later.[36] The early stages in the development of this ceremony, marking the Jewish coming of age and accountability of the boy for his actions when he turns 13 years old, left no explicit material evidence or even an image in the Hebrew manuscripts of the time.[37]

The situation is different with the important rite of passage in the life of both males and females, i.e. the wedding ceremony. Extant materials include miniatures, an illustrated marriage contract, and jewelry. The earliest known image of a Jewish wedding appears in the Worms Mahzor, dated 1272, and subsequently in several other Mahzor codices and Passover Haggadah manuscripts.[38] The Mahzorim actually depict the allegorical marriage between God and Israel, which the artists generally modeled on the wedding ritual as celebrated in Ashkenaz at the time, while the 15th-century Haggadot, generally refer to the wedding of Moses and Zipporah.[39] The wedding is performed with an officiant holding a cup of wine, while the couple is shown standing under a piece of textile (*sudar*) – symbolic of the bridal chamber (*huppah*) of Talmudic times.[40]

The only extant illustrated marriage contract from medieval Ashkenaz, depicting a bridal couple as well, commemorates a wedding in Krems (Lower Austria), 1391/92.[41] The groom wears a typical pointed Jewish hat, *Judenhut*, and holds a wedding ring set with a reddish gem, while his bride at left, donned with a high crown, stretches her right hand to accept it. The images of both the ring and crown may be based on actual precious jewelry used in the Jewish wedding. In 1997, a gold ring was discovered in a Jewish treasure trove hidden during the Black Death in Erfurt, which, therefore, must be dated before 1349, as is also clearly evident from its Gothic style. Despite the halakhic requirement that the band of the wedding ring be plain, the bezel is shaped as an elaborate Gothic tracery surrounding an hexagonal tent roof, each side of which is engraved with a Hebrew letter, spelling out *mazal tov* – the typical Ashkenazi wedding blessing meaning "good luck."[42] The same blessing appears on another golden ring discovered in 1863 in a treasure trove at Colmar, decorated likewise with a six-sided pointed roof.[43]

Though crowns in the Jewish wedding are mentioned already in the Bible (Song of Songs 3:11), they were restricted in the Talmudic period (Mishnah, Sotah, 9, 15), but most likely resurfaced in the case of brides in medieval Ashkenaz, influenced by the common practice among the elite in particular in the surrounding society. An elaborate medieval golden crown was found in 1988 among the precious items of an abundant hoard discovered during renovations in the area of the old medieval Jewish quarter of Neumarkt in Silesia (now part of the Polish town of Środa Śląska).[44] Though this bejeweled fleuron crown (National Museum, Wrocław) was intended for a royal woman, it is not unlikely that while it was pawned to a wealthy Jewish pawnbroker, it was used to crown brides of the family during their weddings. Likewise, another 14th-century piece of elaborate jewelry that was discovered in the Erfurt treasure, namely a sumptuous girdle, elaborately decorated with mythical creatures and inscribed with the Latin-German inscription AMOR VINCIT OMNIA MIT LIB ("love conquers all – with love"), may have been an item used in the Jewish wedding.[45]

Lavish wedding scenes appear also in miniatures of Hebrew manuscripts of 15th-century Italy. Unlike Germany, they depict the placing of the ring being performed not under the *huppah* but in the preceding betrothal ceremony, which was extravagantly celebrated among the Jewish elite of the time. The bridal couple is generally dressed in luxuriant garments in accordance with the high fashion of the Italian Renaissance, and the officiant is shown uniting their right hands[46] – a gesture of concord known in Italy since Roman times, called in Latin *dextrarum iunctio*. Adding to the splendor of the scene in the Mantuan miniature is a small wind orchestra playing on the tribune while the couple is dancing at the opening of the ball. Mixed dancing that was generally forbidden among other European Jews was tolerated by some rabbis in Italy.[47] They did, however, try to forbid the extravagance of such ceremonies, convening synods, notably the one held in Forlì 1418, issuing enactments (*takkanot*) spelling out in detail the measures as to what is permitted (e.g., the maximum number of guests that could be invited to a wedding).[48]

Despite the centrality of the ring ceremony in the Italian wedding miniatures, no rings survived from the early period. Later wedding rings from Italy (17th–18th century) are made of gold and set with precious stones.[49] Documentary evidence shows that Jews were likewise involved in the production of majolica plates – a favorite craft in the Italian Renaissance – at times intended as wedding souvenirs and decorated and inscribed accordingly. Here again early Jewish wedding plates did not survive, though a few late imitations or copies are known. Similarly, no illustrated Italian *ketubbot* are known prior to the 16th century, and this artistic practice flourished in Baroque Italy only after the arrival of Sephardi exiles brought it from the Iberian Peninsula.[50] A unique three-dimensional wedding item that did survive, is a *cofanetto* – a small silver box that was presented to an unknown Jewish bride, apparently of Ashkenazi descent, in northern Italy during the second half of the 15th century.[51] The front side of the bridal box is engraved in niello with the three commandments incumbent on the Jewish woman: separating the *hallah*, immersing in a ritual bath, and lighting the Sabbath candles, while the lid has eight dials, each labeled in a Judeo-Italian dialect (inscribed in Hebrew letters) with the names of the assorted clothing items of the household.[52] The dials helped the young bride to keep track of the quantity of each item, while the keys to the cassone or clothes sheets were kept in the box, which the *halakha* forbids carrying on the Sabbath, but she could wear the silver key of the box attached to a pin.[53] The style of the decorations, especially of the central figure with the daring frontal nude woman standing in the knee-high tub, exquisitely reflects the attitude to the human figure in the spirit of the Renaissance and its significant influence on Jewish culture.

Images of death and burial are far less common than any of the other central rites of passage. It is only the "Rothschild Miscellany" that presents a series of scenes pertaining to this topic.[54] In the first, a couple dressed in black from bottom to top – except for the white veil of the woman – is shown in gestures of prayer, lamenting over a wooden coffin fully covered by a black garment. Influenced by the surrounding society, the use of coffins was by and large more customary in Ashkenaz than the Sephardi world, though at times also the Ashkenazim used it only to transport the body to the cemetery. But even when a wooden coffin is used, Jewish law requires it be plain wood, hammered by wooden pegs instead of iron nails, have holes at the bottom (so that the body comes into direct contact with the earth), and contain no metal parts or jewelry. In both cases, the body of the deceased, no matter the gender, age, or class, is to be covered by a plain cloth shroud made of pure linen (*tachrichim*). The other miniature in the Miscellany depicts two pairs of an old and a young man participating in a meal – the first one eaten on returning from the funeral (called *seudat havra'ah* or "a meal of consolation"). One pair, dressed in colored clothes, is shown seated behind a regular table set with silverware, representing those who traditionally come to console two mourners, while the latter are dressed in black, showing the required tear (in Hebrew *keri'ah*) in the case of the old man, and seat at a low table on cushions placed on the ground, as is the custom throughout the seven-day period of grief and mourning (*shiva'a*).[55]

An important source of material for customs connected to death among medieval Ashkenazi Jewry is provided by extant cemeteries. Few survived from the Middle Ages, the oldest being that of Worms, known as *Heiliger Sand*, which has tombstones dating from the 11th century to 1911, when the community established a new cemetery.[56] As in other Ashkenazi cemeteries down to the modern era, and in contradistinction with their Sephardi counterparts, the tombstone slabs are placed vertically or in an upright position. Also characteristic is the usage of sandstone of rectangular shape with a decorative upper part, and the prominence of the epitaphs and the inscription. The letters are engraved, deep-sunk, in the slabs in typical square Ashkenazi lettering. In Worms, the early tombstones erected prior to the pogroms of the Black Death are often given a decorative three-foil (or more) top – resembling a Gothic stained-glass window. Notwithstanding the lengthy inscriptions, some tombstones bear engraved decorative designs, prominently the lily – a popular design at the time that was most likely given Jewish interpretation, based on the symbolic meaning of the lily or *shushan* in Hebrew according to rabbinic tradition in several biblical texts, in particular Song of Songs (2:16, 4:5, 5:13, 6:2–3, 7:3).[57] The lengthy epitaphs contain invaluable information, whether on unknown individuals or prominent rabbinic figures and leaders of medieval Ashkenazi Jewry who are buried in Worms, such as Rabbi Meir of Rothenberg (1215–1293) or Yaakov ben Moshe Levi Moelin (the Maharal; 1365–1427), whose graves have been visited as holy sites from the Middle Ages to this day.[58] The epitaphs open a window, in addition, to issues of daily life not always dealt with in the written sources, such as that of the realm of the woman: common female names and nicknames used at the time, ideals of Jewish womanhood and the women's commandments, cleanliness and righteousness, sufferings, and messianic hopes.[59]

Objects and Images for the Sabbath and Holidays

The observance of Jewish time, determined by scriptures dating back to biblical times, required a lot of attention, special arrangements, and necessary, often difficult, adjustments to life in a Christian-dominated environment. Yet great attention was given to strict adherence to the laws of the Sabbath and holidays as they were first delineated in the Torah and other books of the Bible and later modified and formulated by rabbinic authorities, who imbued them with many meanings and symbols. Nearly all the festivals throughout the Hebrew calendar require the preparation of special foods and implements for their traditional and proper celebration. Some of these were prescribed already in biblical and Talmudic sources, others develop in the Middle Ages and later periods; some of the holidays called for the production of many implements (e.g., Sabbath, Passover), others only a single or a few items (for example, Hanukkah, Shavuot).[60] Also in the case of this category of Judaic ritual art, very few items survived from medieval Ashkenaz or Italy, and the images in the Hebrew manuscripts of the time help to complement the story.

Only a single miniature from medieval Germany depicts one of the most central commandments of the Sabbath – kindling the Sabbath lights at home on Friday afternoon before sunset, marking the "entry" or beginning of the holy day (as the day in Jewish tradition is counted from sunset to sunset).[61] This rabbinically mandated law was adopted for practical reasons – so that the festive Sabbath meal is not eaten in the dark (as fire is not permitted on the Sabbath). The miniature illustrates the fourth commandment, "Remember the Sabbath day, to keep it holy" (Exodus 20:7), showing two scenes taking place in the interior of a Jewish home on the Eve of Sabbath: an elegantly dressed woman kindling the Sabbath lamp hanging from the ceiling (left), and the husband and wife seated at the Sabbath table, beneath the Sabbath lamp, while they drink the *kiddush* wine from large typical medieval goblets (right). The special Sabbath lamp consists of a central shaft attached to a decorative oil container, with three protruding lighted spouts, and at the bottom a catch receptacle for the overflow oil. Known as *lampa* in rabbinic writings, at least one such lamp that can be reliably identified as Jewish survived from medieval Germany (New York, Jewish Museum). This characteristic 14th-century lamp, made of cast and engraved bronze (16.8 × 17.8 cm) in Gothic style, was excavated in the medieval Jewish quarter of Deutz, today part of Cologne.[62] The attribution of other medieval star-shaped lamps as Jewish – for example, the bronze lamp in the Erfurt cathedral, engraved with biblical scenes, and dated to the 12th century – is uncertain.[63] This type of star-shaped hanging lamp was actually commonly used for lighting houses throughout Germany and elsewhere in medieval Europe, but when it fell into disuse among the surrounding society, German Jews continued to utilize it down to the modern era, and thus since the 16th century it became known as *Judenstern* ("Jews' star").[64]

Evidence from other illuminated Hebrew manuscripts of the Middle Ages, shows that the hanging lamp was widely used in Germany not only for the Sabbath but also for other festivals. It particularly appears in Ashkenazi Haggadot, hanging over the Seder table.[65] Miniatures of synagogue interiors show it as well. It is possible that Ashkenazi immigrants brought this type of lamp to northern Italy, where it was modified in slightly different ways, emphasizing at times a bowl-shaped oil container. This type of lamp actually appears also in the Sabbath scene which is engraved on the 15th-century *cofanetto* mentioned above. However, other miniatures show another type of lamp that is placed on the festive table – a brass candlestick with two branches, each lighted with a candle (Rothschild Miscellany, fols. 156r–166r). And although this candlestick accompanies solely the text of the Passover Haggadah, the first miniature in the series (fol. 156r) is dedicated to the *kiddush* when the Seder night falls on the eve of the Sabbath. Similarly, the large footed gold cup upon which the man is reciting the blessing was apparently shaped to be used for Sabbath, Passover, and the other holidays.

Despite the centrality of the *kiddush* in Jewish ritual – whether for the Sabbath or the other festivals in the Jewish year, as well as events in the life cycles, and in spite of the frequent appearance of *kiddush* cups in medieval miniatures, rabbinic literature hardly discusses the form of the various goblets and beakers used in the rituals – concentrating its discussion on the ritualistic function of these vessels. Two sets of silver beakers dated to the first half of the 14th century were discovered in Bohemia and Germany, which scholars associate with Jewish ownership.[66] Five nested hexagonal beakers (8.2 to 9.2 cm in height), shaped as typical drinking vessels of the time as cups – some embossed with imperial coats of arms – were found in a Gothic house in the central Bohemian silver town of Kutná Hora (Kuttenberg).[67] A second set is part of another Jewish treasure trove found in 1969 in Lingenfeld, southwest Speyer, containing numerous coins, an elaborate double-cup, rings, clothing ornaments, and six silver vessels, three of which are attractively designed beakers.[68] It stands to reason that these luxurious beakers at the hand of Jewish patrons were used for the Sabbath and other rituals, as illustrated profusely in several German Haggadot.

The most important home ritual at the conclusion of the Sabbath is called *havdalah* – literally "distinction" or "separation" (that is, between the holy Sabbath and the "profane" weekdays). The ceremony, which may be conducted publicly in the synagogue following the evening service (*ma'ariv*), is commonly performed also at home so that women can participate as well. The master of the house recites the blessings over a cup overflowing with wine (symbol of fertility), spices, and fire or a burning candle. A rare, simply delineated, image of the ceremony appears in a late 14th-century siddur of Ashkenazi rite, which depicts a bearded man reciting the blessing from a written page over a lighted candle.[69]

While none of the rich ceremonial objects for this ritual survived from the medieval period, the most ornate ritual implement of the ceremony as it developed in Ashkenaz, and one of the most divergent Jewish ceremonial artifacts, is a special container designed to hold the required spices that were a rare commodity in the West at the time. Though mentioned in the rabbinic literature of the 15th century, no spice box (*hadas* in Hebrew or *Besamimbüchse* in German) survives from before the 16th century. Created by Christian silversmiths, the design of the early extant spice boxes (and those of the subsequent centuries), often portrays medieval patterns.

The most widespread form of the spice boxes, certainly characteristic of the early examples, is a tower-shaped silver container, probably inspired by the Christian monstrances and reliquaries the silversmiths apparently commonly produced.[70]

Aside from images and objects for the Sabbath's domestic rituals, the medieval Ashkenazi Mahzorim depict scenes for special Sabbaths in the Jewish year, especially the four falling in the month of Adar, between the end of winter and the beginning of spring. In most cases, the images in these are symbolic or refer to the events of the past, only occasionally referring to a contemporary ritual, its performance, and ceremonial objects.[71]

The autumn festivals open with the Jewish New Year, or Rosh ha-Shanah, falling on the first two days of the month of Tishrei. Several miniatures are dedicated to this festival in the Ashkenazi and Italian Hebrew manuscripts. However, most of them relate to the narrative and ideas of the holiday, referring to the liturgical poems or biblical passages recited in the synagogue, in particular the scene of the Binding of Isaac whose story is recited, with accompanying *piyyutim*, on the second day of Rosh ha-Shanah. The Binding of Isaac, nonetheless, is related to the most characteristic ritual object of the holiday – the *shofar* – an ancient musical horn, used to fulfill the biblical commandment "to sound the trumpets" (Num. 29:1) on this sacred day that is "commemorated with trumpet blasts" (Lev. 23:24). Following the Talmudic association of this commandment with the Binding story (e.g., BT, *Rosh ha-Shanah* 16a), the horn is made of ram's horn – a concept reiterated by medieval authorities. In the Leipzig Mahzor, for example, a piyyut for Rosh ha-Shanah is flanked by the ram caught in the thicket, his gilt horns emphasized, while the initial panel with a crowned word *melekh* ("King" – referring to God) depicts a medieval Jew with the conical hat blowing the *shofar*.[72] Parallel scenes are found in Italian manuscripts, such as a colorful one showing a man wrapped in a prayer shawl (*tallit*), blowing the *shofar* before the congregants on Rosh ha-Shanah (Rothschild Miscellany, fol. 137v).[73] In both Ashkenaz and Italy the ram's horn was treated carefully on both the outer and inner surfaces, so that the outer surface became shiny and smooth to touch (unlike some other communities – e.g., the Yemenite). In addition, in Ashkenaz, a small horn was commonly used, straightened and the wide end from which the sound emerges is curved – symbol of the heart that should be curved or bent before God on this day of judgment. No *shofar* however survived from the Middle Ages. A related "ceremonial object" is a three-legged stool shown in some miniatures, upon which the *ba'al tokeah* (lit. "master of the blast") places his right foot while he blows the *shofar* in order, according to folk belief, to ward off demons and evil forces coming from under the ground during the sounding of the *shofar*.[74]

Closely linked to Rosh ha-Shanah, is the holiest day of the Jewish year, Yom Kippur ("Day of Atonement"), completing the cycle of ten days known as *Yamim Nora'im* ("Days of Awe") that begins with the New Year. In spite of the fact that there are many rituals that are practiced on the eve of the day in particular, some miniatures depict bygone practices (e.g., the biblical ritual of the scapegoat, based on Lev. 16:21–22) rather than contemporary ones. Also common are symbolic images for the day, such as widely opened gates of the Torah ark or a massive structure – illustrating the supplication to God to "open the gates of mercy".[75] Blowing the *shofar* on this day, a topic shown in relevant miniatures, depicts the same type of ram's horn as that for Rosh ha-Shana.

Popular Yom Kippur folk customs, at times criticized by some authorities, are commonly not shown as well, perhaps not accidentally. A typical example is the central *Kapparot* ritual (substitutive immolation performed by passing a chicken over one's head and then slaughtering it),[76] which in spite of its considerable popularity, is not depicted in any known Ashkenazi manuscript. The same is true with other rituals celebrated on the eve of Yom Kippur, which perhaps were seen to be worthy or representative and actually start to appear in the visual arts only from the 16th century on in books by Christian Hebraists wishing to ridicule Jewish "superstitious customs" – including the *Kapparot* or the symbolic practice involving flagellation of 39 lashes by a leather whip.[77]

In contrast to the two High Holidays, the one which begins four days after Yom Kippur ends, namely Sukkot ("Feast of Tabernacles"), is richer with the visual references to the rituals of the holiday. This tradition is partly carried on from Late Antiquity where the items associated with and reminiscent of the holiday as one of the Three Pilgrimage Festivals (*shalosh regalim*) before the destruction of Jerusalem Temple (70 CE), became major symbols of ancient Jewish art. These are the Four Species of the holiday, prescribed in the Pentateuch (Lev. 23:40), and are identified by the Talmudic rabbis as *etrog* (citron fruit), *lulav* (a date palm branch), *hadas* (leaves of myrtle tree), and *arava* (willow tree branches).[78] Medieval illuminators, especially in Ashkenaz of the 13th–14th centuries and Italy of the late 14th–15th centuries depicted contemporary Jews holding the Four Species while reciting the blessings or chanting the hymns and special prayers of the festivals. Moreover, since halakhic authorities put great emphasis on the physical shape and appearance of the Species, and reiterate that one should aspire to obtain a beautiful and the best in each species,[79] illuminators attempted at times to depict them with more naturalistic details than other "ordinary" plants, and especially the more exotic *lulav* and *etrog* get particular attention.[80]

The main feature of Sukkot is the construction of a temporary, hut-like dwelling, or *sukkah*, in which Jews spend time, including eating and sleeping, during the seven days of the festival (cf. Lev. 23: 42). Images of the *sukkah* appear especially in Italian manuscripts of the 14th and 15th centuries. They allow us to see the varieties of how the *sukkot* looked like in this period. In one miniature,[81] the entire *sukkah*, walls and roof, are comprised of leafy green branches, intertwining with each other. Other miniatures depict the construction of the *sukkah* by a busy group of young Jews in the region of Emilia, while another shows four people seated in the middle of the *sukkah* around a set table, apparently on the festive eve of the holiday, while one of them recites the blessing over the *kiddush* wine.[82] Aside from actual *sukkah* structures, some miniatures in Ashkenazi codices depict the Midrashic fierce battle at the end of days between three beasts called Behemoth, Leviathan, and the Ziz, at the end of which the righteous shall celebrate a messianic banquet in a *sukkah* made from the skin of Leviathan.[83]

The two subsequent holidays, Hanukkah and Purim – the first is post-Biblical and the second post-Pentateuchal – were added to the cycle of Jewish festivals by the Talmudic rabbis. Both are thus considered less significant, or minor, in comparison to those mentioned in the Torah. Their place in the field of medieval Hebrew book illumination as well as material culture is therefore lesser as well. Instead of showing the heroic deeds of the Maccabees, which were apparently belittled already by the rabbis of old, a preferred heroine was the apocryphal figure of the pious Judith, who was linked in Midrashic sources with the Hasmonean dynasty, although there is no historical basis for this association.[84] Moreover, in one Ashkenazi manuscript the patrons and artist preferred to depict the persecutions and martyrdom of the Jews in the times of the Maccabees rather than their victories.[85]

The most important ritual of the festival, as regulated by the rabbis of old, consists of lighting the Hanukkah lamp – a symbol of the miracle of the one-day oil cruse that miraculously lasted for eight days. Only a single miniature of this ritual survived – depicting a 14th-century Italian Jew lighting a Hanukkah lamp, apparently made of yellow metal, with a row of light pointed oil receptacles, and an attached backplate in the form of a crenellated wall.[86] This type of "bench type" Hanukkah lamp (that is, placed on the window sill or table, rather than hung on the wall) and its decoration is known from later Italian Hanukkah lamps, first created in the Renaissance and later recast in bronze, whose crenellated back panel imitates public Italian palaces, such as the Palazzo Pubblico of Siena.[87] No such miniature is known from Ashkenaz and only one lamp has been attributed by some scholars to 14th-century Germany or Italy. This is the so-called "Lehman/Figdor Lamp" that has a triangular back panel (hanging lamp) decorated with three medallions depicting animals, the central one of which, set in a Gothic quatrefoil frame, shows a mythical animal (phoenix or a salamander – symbol of light). Below the medallions appears an inscription in monumental Ashkenazi square script: "For the commandment is a lamp and Torah is light" (Prov. 6:23) – associated by medieval commentators with Hanukkah (New York, Temple Emanu-El).[88] The authenticity of this lamp, however, has been questioned, with the suggestion that it is a 19th-century product.[89]

The Book of Esther and its liturgical public reading on the holiday gave rise to miniatures depicting selected events from the book, highlighting the triumph of Mordechai and Esther, the heroes of the Megillah (scroll [of Esther]), and the defeat of their enemies in Shushan (Susa), the capital of ancient Persia. These topics are either based on the narrative of the text (e.g., the hanging of Haman together with the hanging of his ten sons on the same tall tree – based on Esther 7:9 and 9:13–14), or on Midrashic accounts (e.g., during the parade of triumphant Mordechai, Haman's daughter, shown as a young woman with blond hair, throws out the contents of a chamber pot onto her father, who leads the horse, and then, having realized her mistake, jumps to her death from the tower).[90] The same is true about Italy, though miniatures are from the 15th century. In Italy, however, more attention was given to contemporary Purim rituals and customs. It is here that the first image ever of masquerades and dressing up on Purim appears – predating the rabbinical discussion of the topic. The miniature in question, from the Maimonides manuscript of *Mishneh Torah* shows next to the open *sukkah* a Purim ball with a typical Italian buffoon dressed in yellow, leaping around and gesturing with his hands.[91] Moreover, in front of him are two elegantly dressed couples involved in fashionable mixed dancing – commonly frowned upon by rabbinical authorities, though some rabbis in Italy allowed it for married couples on special occasions, including weddings and Purim.[92] It was also in Italy that the liturgical Esther scroll, used in the synagogue to follow the reader during the Purim service, was first enriched by captivating illustrations, whether architectural and decorative or small miniatures with biblical and ritual scenes.[93] But the earliest extant illustrated Esther scrolls do not date prior to the 16th century and grew in popularity only in the 17th and 18th centuries.

The holiday whose rituals received the most varied and extensive attention from the point of view of the visual arts is undoubtedly the spring festival of Passover. The wealth of material concerning this festival, whether from Germany, Italy, Spain, Greece, or other European countries, is closely associated with the popularity of the liturgical book of the holiday, the Passover Haggadah. From around 1300, when the first illustrated Haggadah known to us was created in south Germany (Birds Heads Haggadah, Jerusalem, Israel Museum), and from the 14th and 15th centuries to the present day, many illustrated Haggadot were produced, making this book the most frequently illustrated book in Jewish history. Since the Passover holiday, and by extension the Haggadah, put great emphasis on the rituals, their order, meaning, and significance, the depiction of the long and detailed preparations and subsequent ceremonies of Passover constitute a central topic. Thus, for example, the basic biblical commandment prohibiting any type of leavened bread (*chametz*) during Passover led to numerous images depicting the search for breadcrumbs on the evening before the holiday. Called *bedikat chametz* ("search for leaven"), the images depicting this ritual, as well as the other preparations for Passover, open a wide window to the realia of the time – the interior of the houses, process of baking and ovens, cleansing the utensils by immersing them in boiling water (*haga'lah*) so that they become suitable for use on

Passover, etc. The same is true for the rituals during the holiday – in particular the symbolic meal on Passover eve, called *leil ha-seder*. The festive Seder meals reveal many customs particular to this night, as well as foods and utensils. In fact, a full discussion of the rituals and the objects that accompany them, even in one selected Haggadah, demands detailed research or a full chapter, as some scholars have done, and can be also seen in the text volumes accompanying the facsimile editions of the Haggadot.[94]

Seven weeks after the first day of Passover, the holiday of Shavuot ("Feast of Weeks") is celebrated – always falling on the sixth day of the month of Sivan. It was originally an agricultural holiday, marking the wheat harvest in ancient Israel, following exactly the 49-day period called *Sefirat ha-Omer* or counting verbally the sheaf offering (in Hebrew *korban ha-omer*) in Temple times (cf. Lev. 23:15–16). Talmudic rabbis identified the date of the holiday with the Giving of the Law on Mount Sinai, so associating the holiday with the dramatic moment in the biblical history of Israel, and with Passover and the Exodus from Egypt. Most Mahzorim, indeed, refer to the narrative historical story, depicting the solemn event whose hero is Moses, receiving the Tablets of the Law and delivering them to the Israelites waiting at the bottom of Mount Sinai.[95] These images commonly accompany the medieval Ashkenazi piyyut *Adon imnani* ("The Lord has taught [or trained] me"), that is recited during the morning prayers on the first day of Shavuot as if it is "sung" by the Torah itself, glorifying its gift to the people of Israel.

While no ordinary specific Shavuot rituals seemed worthy of visual enhancement, one prominent exception is the Leipzig Mahzor. As in the other codices, *Adon imnani* is also here illustrated with the Giving of the Law, although its iconography slightly deviates from the other Mahzorim.[96] More important is that in this manuscript the facing page remarkably exhibits an unique episode that skillfully and meaningfully associates the historical event with a contemporary ritual – the initiation of the Jewish child to school for the study of Torah.[97] The illustration at the bottom of the page is divided into three scenes, showing various stages of the ceremony. The first phase is actually the central scene, depicting the father or a pious figure (teacher or a rabbi), wearing the typical *Judenhut*, and who is carrying the child wrapped in his cloak so that he cannot see anything impure on the way, so protecting him from the evil eye. The child holds in his hands two objects that were prepared for him in advance before the holiday: a honey cake and a hard-boiled egg (more prominently visible in the subsequent episodes). The next stage, shown at left, takes place after the two have reached the synagogue or the school room, indicated by a school bench upon which is seated the teacher (*melamed*). In his lap is one child who holds high the boiled egg and cake, while two other boys wait for their turn, holding likewise the eggs and cakes. The teacher has in his right hand a slate upon which, according to the custom, are written verses in Hebrew letters covered by honey, like his honey cake. The teacher reads the letters and verses and the child repeats after him, licking off the honey and eating parts of the symbolic foods – so that the first time of learning is remembered by him as something pleasant and sweet (Is. 50:4–5; Ezek. 3:3). In the final episode, at right, the teacher leads the boys to a river filled with fish – a symbol of the Torah in rabbinic teachings, based on verses such as: "Let your fountains [=teachings] be dispersed abroad, and rivers of waters in the streets" (Prov. 5:16).[98]

In conclusion, this initiation ritual is indicative of the significance attached to the ceremonies in the life of medieval Jewry. The first day of school, a seemingly common event in the development of a child, is given meanings far beyond an introduction to educational instruction. The event became a veritable and carefully set up "rite of passage" imbued with many symbolic acts. Not only is every item and move meticulously planned and enacted, but the contemporary ritual is juxtaposed with the Sinai experience of the ancient Israelites, showing how even little children can fulfill the role of inheritors of the traditions passed from one generation to the next. The multiple meanings attached to the rituals, their careful setting and proper performance, and the great attention given to an effective design and shape of the specific objects created for each, all illustrate the significance and importance of the ritual in the life of medieval Jewry.

Notes

1 See David Stern. 2017. *The Jewish Bible: A Material History*, Seattle: University of Washington Press; and cf. Shalom Sabar. 2018. *The Sarajevo Haggadah: History & Art*. Sarajevo: National Museum of Bosnia and Herzegovina, text volume, pp. 5–18.
2 In the context of this chapter, a helpful compendium of miniatures from Hebrew manuscripts, arranged by aspects of religious, social, economic and other facets of Jewish life in mediaeval Europe, is Thérèse and Mendel Metzger. 1982. *Jewish Life in the Middle Ages: Illuminated Hebrew Manuscripts of the Thirteenth to the Sixteenth Centuries*. New York: Alpine Fine Arts Collection.
3 For a wide collection of rabbinic (and other) opinions in English translation on the visual in Jewish life throughout history, see, Vivian B. Mann. 2000. *Jewish Texts on the Visual Arts*. Cambridge: Cambridge University Press; and for a deep analysis of the medieval and modern attitudes of Jewish thinkers, see Kalman P. Bland. 2000. *The Artless Jew: Medieval and Modern Affirmations and Denials of the Visual*. Princeton, NJ: Princeton University Press.
4 The idea is mentioned in several Talmudic discussions – in particular, BT, Bava Kamma, 9b, and Shabbat, 133b (also in Nazir, 2b). Cf. Shalom Sabar, 2022. "*Hadar* and *Hiddur*: The Etrog in Jewish Art and Artifacts," in *Be Fruitful! The Etrog in Jewish Art, Culture, and History*, exhibition catalog, eds. Warren Klein, Sharon Liberman Mintz, and Joshua Teplitsky. New York: Herbert & Eileen Bernard Museum of Judaica, Temple Emanu-El, New York. Jerusalem: Mineged Press (in press).
5 Of the vast literature on the synagogue, see for example, Carol Herselle Krinsky. 1985. *Synagogues of Europe: Architecture, History, Meaning*. New York: Architectural History Foundation, 169–75 (with extensive bibliography, 176–77).
6 Ibid., 319–24. For an overview of the medieval Ashkenazi synagogue, see Ena Giurescu Heller. 2020. "Western Ashkenazi Synagogues in Medieval and Early Modern Europe," in Steven Fine (ed.) *Jewish Religious Architecture: From Biblical Israel to Modern Judaism*. Leiden, Boston: Brill, 169–83.
7 Cf. David Cassuto and Nicolò Bucaria. 2011. "The Synagogue and the Ritual Baths in Palermo in Light of Textual and Archaeological Evidence," in Elisheva Baumgarten, Amnon Raz-Krakotzkin, and Roni Weinstein (eds) *Tov Elem: Memory, Community and Gender in Medieval and Early Modern Jewish Societies. Essays in Honor of Robert Bonfil*. Jerusalem: Mossad Bialik, 241–81 (in Hebrew).
8 Ashley D. West. 2017. "Preserving Destruction: Albrecht Altdorfer's Etchings of the Regensburg Synagogue as Material Performances of the Past and Future," in Debra Cashion, Henry Luttikhuizen, and Ashley West (eds) *The Primacy of The Image in Northern European Art, 1400-1700. Essays in Honor of Larry Silver*. Leiden, Boston: Brill, 284–300.
9 Rashi on BT, Sukkah 51b, Sotah 41a, Avodah Zarah 16a (spelling in Hebrew אלמינבר"א). Cf. Rachel Wischnitzer. 1964. *The Architecture of the European Synagogue*. Philadelphia: Jewish Publication Society of America, 48.
10 For a vast collection of Torah ark curtains and valances from Bohemia and Moravia, see Ludmila Kybalova, Eva Kosakova, and Alexandr Putik, eds. 2003. *Textiles from Bohemian and Moravian Synagogues: From the Collections of the Jewish Museum in Prague*. Prague: Jewish Museum.
11 See Vivian B. Mann. 1986–7. "The Recovery of a Known Work," *Jewish Art* 12–13: 269–78; and cf. Dora Liescia Bemporad. 2019. "A Late Gothic Carved Pair of Torah Staves from Italy," in Shalom Sabar, Emile Schrijver, and Falk Wiesemann (eds) *Windows on Jewish Worlds: Essays in Honor of William Gross*. Zutphen: Walburg Pers bv, 22–33 (esp. 27–29); Ilia Rodov. 2010. "Tower-Like Torah Arks: The Tower of Strength and the Architecture of the Messianic Temple," *Journal of the Warburg and Courtauld Institutes*, 73: 65–98 (esp. 72–79).
12 For the process of making, inscribing, and "dressing" the Torah scroll, see Joseph Gutmann. 1983. *The Jewish Sanctuary* ("Iconography of Religions," Section 23, Judaism, fasc. 1), Leiden: E.J. Brill, 4–12.
13 Cf. Vivian B. Mann. 1996. "Torah Ornaments before 1600," in Rafi Grafman, *Crowning Glory: Silver Torah Ornaments of the Jewish Museum*. New York: Jewish Museum, and Boston: David R. Godine, 1–15 (esp. p. 9).

14 Munich, Bayerische Staaatsbibliothek, Cod. hebr. 3/I, fol. 48r; reproduced in Metzger, *Jewish Life in the Middle Ages*, 69 fig. 98.
15 E.g., "The Rothschild Miscellany," Northern Italy, ca. 1470; Jerusalem, Israel Museum, Ms. 180/051, fol. 105v; reproduced in ibid., 69 fig. 97.
16 See on them, Bemporad, "Late Gothic Carved Pair of Torah Staves," 22–33.
17 For a comprehensive study of the development of the Torah textiles among the different communities, see Bracha Yaniv. 2019. *Ceremonial Synagogue Textiles: From Ashkenazi, Sephardi, and Italian Communities*. London: Littman Library of Jewish Civilization & Liverpool University Press.
18 For the custom and wide selection of examples, see Annette Weber, Evelyn Friedlander, and Fritz Armbruster, eds. 1997. *Mappot – Blessed Be Who Comes: The Band of Jewish Tradition*. Osnabrück: Secolo Verlag (in English and German); and see also the essays cited in notes 29 [Gutmann] and 37 [Feuchtwanger].
19 Cf. Cissy Grossman. 1980. "Womanly Arts: A Study of Italian Torah Binders in the New York Jewish Museum Collection," *Journal of Jewish Art* 7: 35–43.
20 Cf. the miniature in the Rothschild Miscellany cited in note 15, above.
21 For the silver implements for the Torah from Ashkenaz and Italy, see Grafman, *Crowning Glory* (arranged by type and chronology; and see the "Index of Places and Origin", 385–86).
22 For an introductory discussion of the most common objects in the Jewish life cycle, see Joseph Gutmann. 1987. *The Jewish Life Cycle* ("Iconography of Religions," Section 23, Judaism, fasc. 4), Leiden: E.J. Brill.
23 London, David Sofer Coll. (formerly, Jerusalem, Schocken Library), fols. 32v–33r. For this Haggadah and its biblical miniatures, see Katrin Kogman-Appel. 1999. *Die zweite Nürnberger und die Jehuda Haggada: jüdische Illustratoren zwischen Tradition und Fortschritt*. Frankfurt am Main: P. Lang (for the cycle of Rebecca and her sons, see pp. 74–79).
24 Jerusalem, Israel Museum, Ms. 180/052, fol. 18v; Metzger, *Jewish Life in the Middle Ages*, 226 fig. 359.
25 Cf. Elisheva Baumgarten. 2004. *Mothers and Children Jewish Family Life in Medieval Europe*. Princeton, NJ: Princeton University Press, 70–77, and 73–74 figs 3–4.
26 Cf. Gutmann, *Jewish Life Cycle*, 5.
27 E.g., a manuscript with the books of Psalms, Job, and Proverbs, from north Italy, ca. 1450; Parma, Biblioteca Palatina, Ms. Parm. 3596, fol. 267r; Metzger, *Jewish Life in the Middle Ages*, 222 fig. 332.
28 Cf. Shalom Sabar. 2005. "Prophet Elijah Visits Venice: A Rare Italian Elijah Chair from Early Nineteenth Century Venice," in Emanuela Lodi and Silvia Guastalla (eds) *La nascita nella tradizione ebraica / Birth in Jewish Tradition*. Livorno: S. Belforte, 98–123 (in English and Italian). For these and other objects in the life cycle of the Italian Jews in the early modern period, see also Shalom Sabar. 2020. "Objects Reveal: The Life and its Rituals," 2020. in Andreina Contessa, Simonetta Della Seta, Carlotta Ferrara degli Uberti, and Sharon Reichel (eds) *Beyond the Ghetto: Inside & Out*, exhibition catalog, National Museum of Italian Judaism and the Shoah, Ferrara. Milan: SilvanaEditoriale S.p.A., 36–47.
29 For the custom, see Joseph Gutmann. 1983. "*Die Mappe Schuletragen*: An Unusual Judeo-German Custom," *Visible Religion – Annual for Religious Iconography* 2: 167–73.
30 For medieval Jewish magic, see Gideon Bohak. 2015. "Jewish Magic in the Middle Ages," in David J. Collins (ed.) *The Cambridge History of Magic and Witchcraft in the West: From Antiquity to the Present*. Cambridge: Cambridge University Press, 268–300; for the child mortality and the contents of the amulets in Germany, Italy, and other countries (in later periods), see Shalom Sabar. 2002. "Childbirth and Magic: Jewish Folklore and Material Culture," in David Biale (ed.) *Cultures of the Jews: A New History*. New York: Schocken Books, 670–722.
31 On the development of the *Wachnacht* and *Veglia* customs from Medieval to later periods, see Elliott S. Horowitz. 1989. "The Eve of the Circumcision," *Journal of Social History* 23: 45–69.
32 For the ritual, cf. Ivan G. Marcus. 2004. *The Jewish Life Cycle: Rites of Passage from Biblical to Modern Times*. Seattle: University of Washington Press, 66–68.
33 Cf. Gutmann, *Jewish Life Cycle*, 8–9, and pls XVI–XVII.
34 One of the surviving examples, in an Italian manuscript of life cycle rituals, produced in the late 15th century (Princeton, University Library, MS Garrett 26, fol. 8r), is illustrated in Metzger, *Jewish Life in the Middle Ages*, 227 fig. 341. On the "adventures" of this codex and its miniatures, see Elliott S. Horowitz. 1993–4. "Giotto in Avignon, Adler in London, Panofsky in Princeton: On the Odyssey of an Illustrated Hebrew Manuscript from Italy and on its Meaning," *Jewish Art* 19–20: 98–111.

35 "Skipped" here is another important post-biblical ritual of childhood, created specifically for the child's entry to school. As the ritual took place on the holiday of Shavuot, it is discussed herewith in the context of the year cycle (last part of the chapter).
36 There are, to be sure, some antecedents known in particular from the lands of Islam – but not in the form of the ritual that crystalized and became familiar later. Cf. Marcus, "Bar Mitzvah, Bat Mitzvah, Confirmation," in *The Jewish Life Cycle*, 82–123; Gutmann, *Jewish Life Cycle*, 9–10.
37 In later periods, aspects of the Bar Mitzvah are depicted on the *Wimpeln* mentioned above. See Naomi Feuchtwanger-Sarig. 2005. "'May he grow to the Torah…': The Iconography of Torah Reading and *Bar Mitzvah* on Ashkenazi Torah Binders," in Ruth Langer and Steven Fine (eds) *Liturgy in the Life of the Synagogue; Studies in the History of Jewish Prayer*. Winona Lake, IN: Eisenbrauns, 161–76.
38 Worms Mahzor, Jerusalem, National Library of Israel, 781/I, fol. 34v. On this episode in the Worms Mahzor and parallel manuscripts, see Sarit Shalev-Eyni. 2005. "Iconography of Love: Illustrations of Bride and Bridegroom in Ashkenazi Prayerbooks of the Thirteenth and Fourteenth Century," *Studies in Iconography* 26: 27–57.
39 Second Nuremberg Haggadah, fol. 12v; and a parallel scene in the so-called Yahuda Haggadah (Franconia, Southern Germany, 1470–80) – Jerusalem, Israel Museum, 180/050, fol. 11v.
40 For the Medieval Ashkenazi *huppah*, see Joseph Gutmann. 1989. "Jewish Medieval Marriage Customs in Art: Creativity and Adaptation," in David Kraemer (ed.) *The Jewish Family: Metaphor and Memory*. New York: Oxford University Press, 47–62 (esp. 48–50).
41 Vienna, Österreichischen Nationalbibliothek, Cod. Hebr. 218. For the *ketubbah* and its art in Medieval Ashkenaz and later centuries, see Shalom Sabar. 1990. *Ketubbah: Jewish Marriage Contracts of the Hebrew Union College Skirball Museum and Klau Library*. Philadelphia and New York: Jewish Publication Society, esp. 8–9, 287–99; and cf. note 50, below (on the relationships between the Ashkenazi *ketubbah* and the beginning of this art form in Italy).
42 See Maria Stürzebecher. 2020. "The Medieval Jewish Wedding Ring from the Erfurt Treasure: Ceremonial Object or Bride Price?" *Ritual Objects in Ritual Contexts* ("Erfurter Schriften zur Jüdischen Geschichte") 6: 72–79.
43 See Barbara Drake Boehm. 2019. *The Colmar Treasure: A Medieval Jewish Legacy*, exhibition catalog, New York: Scala Publishers & The Metropolitan Museum of Art, New York, 44–45.
44 For this crown and its association with medieval Ashkenazi wedding, see Ido Noy. 2016. "The Fleuron Crown from Neumarkt in Silesia (Środa Śląska): Christian Material Culture in Jewish Context," *Ars Judaica* 12: 23–38.
45 A long belt with gold bejeweled items appears in the wedding scene of Moses and Zipporah mentioned above (Second Nuremberg Haggadah). See Ido Noy. 2018. "Love Conquers All: The Erfurt Girdle as a Source for Understanding Medieval Jewish Love and Romance," *Images: Journal of Jewish Art & Visual Culture* 11: 227–246.
46 A notable example is a manuscript of Arba'ah Turim – the halakhic code by Jacob ben Asher, copied in Mantua 1435 (Vatican, Biblioteca Apostolica, Ms. Ross. 555, fol. 220r); for this page, see Joseph Gutmann. 1978. *Hebrew Manuscript Painting*. New York: George Braziller, 106–07 pl. 34.
47 Cf. Shalom Sabar. 1999. "Bride, Heroine and Courtesan: Images of the Jewish Woman in Hebrew Manuscripts of the Renaissance in Italy," *Proceedings of the Tenth World Congress of Jewish Studies*, Division D/II: Art, Folklore and Music. Jerusalem: World Union of Jewish Studies, 63–70.
48 For the Forlì *takkanot* of the years 1416–18, see Louis Finkelstein. 1924. *Jewish Self-Government in the Middle Ages*. New York: Jewish Theological Seminary of America, 280–95.
49 On the ornamental rings of this period, see Gertrud Seidman. 1981. "Marriage Rings, Jewish Style," *Connoisseur*, 206: 48–61.
50 See Shalom Sabar. 1987. "The Beginnings of Ketubbah Decoration in Italy: Venice in the Late Sixteenth to the Early Seventeenth Centuries," *Jewish Art* 12–13: 96–110.
51 Jerusalem, The Israel Museum, 131/030. For the story and analysis of the *cofanetto*, see Mordechai Narkiss. 1958. "An Italian Niello Casket of the Fifteenth Century," *Journal of the Warburg and Courtauld Institutes* 21: 288–95.
52 Ibid., 289. Note that the words beneath the bottom left dial are not the name of the artist, as Narkiss suggests, but another category of linen. For this, and for the three womanly commandments in Jewish art of Italy and Germany, see Shalom Sabar. 2013. "Mitzvot Hannah: Visual Depictions of the 'Three Women's Commandments' among the Jews of Europe from the Middle Ages to Late Nineteenth Century," in Hagar Salamon and Avigdor Shinan (eds) *Textures – Culture, Literature, Folklore for Galit Hasan-Rokem*. Jerusalem: Magnes Press, 2: 383–413 (Hebrew; English summary), esp. 388–90 and n. 15.

53 The *cofanetto*'s silver key is lost; however, silver and silver-plated keys discovered in the Colmar and Erfurt treasures have been identified as possibly created for use as pieces of jewelry for the Sabbath. See Merav Schnitzer. 2020. "The Silver Key from the Erfurt Treasure: Suggesting a Context," *Ritual Objects in Ritual Contexts* ("Erfurter Schriften zur Jüdischen Geschichte") 6: 94–103.
54 Fols. 121v, 122v – reproduced in Metzger, *Jewish Life in the Middle Ages*, 231–32 fig. 346–47. Other rituals concerning the last phase of life, including "instructional in the matter of mourning," a "confessional prayer," and a "funeral procession," appear in the Italian liturgical manuscript in Princeton (note 34, above) – see Horowitz, "Giotto in Avignon," 103–109, figs 3–5, respectively.
55 For the Jewish death and burial customs in historical perspective, see Marcus. 2003. "Aging, Dying, Remembering," *The Jewish Life Cycle*, 193–248; and cf. Harvey E. Goldberg, *Jewish Passages: Cycles of Jewish Life*. Berkeley: University of California Press, 196–227.
56 For the medieval tombstones, see Michael Brocke. 2013. "Der jüdische Friedhof Worms im Mittelalter – 1059 bis 1519: Beobachtungen an einem singulären Ort," in Pia Heberer and Ursula Reuter (eds) *Die SchUM-Gemeinden Speyer – Worms – Mainz; auf dem Weg zum Welterbe*. Regensburg: Schnell & Steiner, 111–54.
57 Cf. Michael Brocke. 2011. "The Lilies of Worms," *Zutot: Perspective on Jewish Culture* 8: 3–13.
58 Cf. Ephraim Shoham-Steiner. 2006. "'For a Prayer in That Place Would Be Most Welcome': Jews, Holy Shrines, and Miracles—A New Approach," *Viator* 37: 369–95.
59 For transcription of the Worms tombstones and of other early Jewish cemeteries in Germany, see the Internet site of Epidat – Research Platform for Jewish Epigraphy (the epigraphs are arranged chronologically from the earliest to the latest).
60 For a general survey, based on the customs and ritual objects, see Isaiah Shachar. 1975. *The Jewish Year* ("Iconography of Religions," Section 23, Judaism, fasc. 3). Leiden: E.J. Brill.
61 The miniature appears in a collection of liturgical texts, South Germany, ca. 1300; New York, JTS, MS Mic 8972, fol. 119v. See on it, Sabar, "Mitzvot Hannah: Visual Depictions of the 'Three Women's Commandments'," 385–87 and fig. 1.
62 See Norman L. Kleeblatt and Vivian B. Mann. 1986. *Treasures of the Jewish Museum*. New York: Jewish Museum & Universe Books, 30–31.
63 Hans Gerhard Meyer. 1982. "Eine Sabbatlampe im Erfurter Dom," *Studien zur Kunstgeschichte* 16: 7–10.
64 See on them, Adi Blumberg. 2001. *Hanging Sabbath Lamps*. Jerusalem: Adi Foundation.
65 E.g., in the Second Nuremberg Haggadah, fol. 4v – reproduced in Metzger, *Jewish Life in the Middle Ages*, 105 fig. 152.
66 See on them, Vivian B. Mann. 1988. "'New' Examples of Jewish Ceremonial Art from Medieval Ashkenaz," *Artibus et Historiae* 17: 13–24 (esp. 17–18).
67 Nuremberg, Germanisches Nationalmuseum, HG 11628 a–e; reproduced ibid., 17 figs 7–8.
68 Speyer, Historisches Museum der Pfalz; reproduced ibid., 18 fig. 9.
69 Vatican, Biblioteca Apostolica, Ms. ebr. 324, fol. 41v – reproduced in Metzger, *Jewish Life in the Middle Ages*, 242 fig. 357.
70 See Mordechai Narkiss. 1981. "Origins of the Spice Box," *Journal of Jewish Art* 8: 28–41. For a wide selection of examples, see Marilyn Gold Koolik. 1982. *Towers of Spice: The Tower-shape Tradition in Havdalah Spiceboxes*, exhibition catalog, Jerusalem: Israel Museum.
71 On the iconography of the special Sabbaths in the Mahzorim, see Gabrielle Sed-Rajna. 1983. *Le mahzor enluminé: Les voies de formation d'un programme iconographique*. Leiden: E.J. Brill (a comparative list of the visual topics in the various codices, arranged by the liturgical year, appears on pp. 58–61). An example for one referring to an event of the past are the illustrations accompanying *Shabbat Zachor* ("Sabbath of Remembrance") that falls immediately before Purim, when an additional portion of the Torah is recited (Deut. 25:17–19), calling the Israelites to remember the Amalekite plot against them and their descendants, which is compared in the liturgy to the plot of Haman. The illustrations depict a medieval combat or a scribe shown writing, recording the story for the future (ibid. pl. 10 figs 19–20). The liturgical episodes are those of the wedding in medieval Germany, that illustrate *Shabbat ha-Gadol* ("The Great Sabbath") – the Sabbath that immediately precedes Passover (ibid., pls 7–8 figs 13–16, and pl. 34 fig. 71). Though the images refer to the symbolic wedding between God and Israel (based on the commentary of Song of Songs which is read in Ashkenazi synagogues on the Sabbath that falls during Passover), they are modeled on the contemporary Ashkenazi wedding, as referred to above.
72 Leipzig Mahzor, southwest Germany, ca. 1310; Leipzig, Universitätsbibliothek, Ms V 1102, Vol. 2, fol. 26v. For the illustration of this Mahzor, see Bezalel Narkiss. 1964. "Introduction to the Mahzor Lipsiae," in Elias Katz (ed.) *Machsor Lipsiae: 68 Facsimile Plates of the Mediaeval, Illuminated Hebrew Manuscript in*

the Possession of the Leipzig University Library. Vaduz: Société pour le Commerce Intercontinental Trust Reg, 85–110 (the *shofar* miniature, p. 97; and for additional examples with the ram, see Sed-Rajna, *Le mahzor enluminé*, pl. 22 figs 42, 44). A more recent study of the Leipzig Mahzor is Katrin Kogman-Appel. 2012. *A Mahzor from Worms: Art and Religion in a Medieval Jewish Community*. Cambridge, MA: Harvard University Press (for the miniature on fol. 26v, see pp. 31, 33 and Figure 3).

73 Reproduced in color in Filip Vukosavovic, ed. 2011. *Sound the Shofar: A Witness to History*, exhibition catalog, Jerusalem: Bible Lands Museum, 43.

74 Cf. Shalom Sabar, "The Shofar in Medieval Jewish Thought and Art / The Shofar in the Modern Period – 18th–20th Centuries," in ibid., 40–46.

75 E.g., the Wroclaw Mahzor (Germany, ca. 1290; Wroclaw, Poland, University Library, Ms. Or. I/1, fol. 89v) – see Sed-Rajna, *Le mahzor enluminé*, pl. 27 fig. 53. And cf. another symbolic scene of "opening the gates" accompanying the closing services (*Tefilat ne'ilah*) of Yom Kippur, where two men appear in the Gothic turrets of the elaborate gate, each blowing a large *shofar* (Leipzig Mahzor, Vol. 2, fol. 176r; Narkiss, "Mahsor Lipsiae," 99).

76 For the possible origins of the custom in ancient and medieval sources, see Jacob Z. Lauterbach. 1970. "The Ritual for the Kapparot Ceremony," in *Studies in Jewish Law, Custom and Folklore*. New York: Ktav Pub. House, 133–42.

77 For these two practices in post-medieval visual materials, see Shalom Sabar. 2003. "Between Poland and Germany: Jewish Religious Practices in Illustrated Postcards of the Early Twentieth Century," *Polin: Studies in Polish Jewry*, 16: 137–166 (esp. 148–57).

78 Cf. Rivka Ben-Sasson. 2012. "Botanics and Iconography: Images of the 'Lulav' and the 'Etrog'," *Ars Judaica* 8: 7–22.

79 As mentioned specifically in the Talmudic concept of *hiddur mitzvah* discussed in the beginning of this essay. And cf. Shalom Sabar, "Hadar and Hiddur: The Etrog in Jewish Art and Artifacts".

80 An example from an Ashkenazi manuscript: the Leipzig Mahzor, Vol. 2, fol. 181v (Narkiss, "Mahsor Lipsiae," 99); and an Italian: Rothschild Miscellany, fol. 147r. For a study of these and other relevant miniatures, see Evelyn M. Cohen, "The Four Species in Medieval and Renaissance Illuminated Hebrew Manuscripts," in *Be Fruitful! The Etrog in Jewish Art, Culture, and History*, exhibition catalog, eds. Warren Klein, Sharon Liberman Mintz, and Joshua Teplitsky. New York: Herbert & Eileen Bernard Museum of Judaica, Temple Emanu-El, New York. Jerusalem: Mineged Press (in press)

81 Decisions of R. Isaiah of Trani the Younger, probably Rimini or Perugia, Italy, 1374; London, British Library, MS Or. 5024, fol. 70v. Reproduced in Metzger, *Jewish Life in the Middle Ages*, 251 fig. 369.

82 Mahzor of Italian rite, Emilia, ca. 1465–75 – Jerusalem, Georges Weill Collection, p. 505; and Maimonides, *Mishneh Torah* – copied in North Italy, ca. 1457 – Vatican, Biblioteca Apostolica, Ms. Ross. 498, fol. 85v; both reproduced in Metzger, *Jewish Life in the Middle Ages*, 251–52, figs 368 and 372, respectively.

83 Notable is the full-page miniature in the Ambrosian Bible, Germany, 1236–38 – Milan, Bibl. Ambrosiana MS B 32 INF, fol. 136r. Of the vast literature on the topic, see Joseph Gutmann. 1968. "Leviathan, Behemoth and Ziz: Jewish Messianic Symbols in Art," *Hebrew Union College Annual* 39: 219–30, and more recently, Eva Frojmovic. 2015. "Feasting at the Lord's Table," *Images: Journal of Jewish Art & Visual Culture*, 7: 5–21.

84 See Mira Friedman. 1987. "The Metamorphoses of Judith," *Jewish Art* 12–13: 225–46; Shalom Sabar. 1995. "The Heroism of the Maccabees in Jewish Art of the Middle Ages and the Renaissance," in David Amit and Hanan Eshel (eds) *In the Time of the Hasmoneans: Sources and Studies*. Jerusalem: Ben-Zvi Institute, 277–90 (in Hebrew).

85 "Hamburg Miscellany," Hamburg, Die Staats- und Universitätsbibliothek, Cod. Hebr. 37, fols. 78r–81r. See Sabar "The Heroism of the Maccabees," esp. pp. 280–83; Sarit Shalev-Eyni. 2014. "Martyrdom and Sexuality: The Case of an Eleventh-century 'Piyyut' for Hanukkah and its Visual Interpretation in the Fifteenth Century," in Israel J. Yuval and Ram Ben-Shalom (eds) *Conflict and Religious Conversation in Latin Christendom. Studies in Honour of Ora Limor*. Turnhout: Brepols, 133–65.

86 Decisions of R. Isaiah of Trani (see note 81, above), fol. 19r; reproduced in Ilana Tahan. 2007. *Hebrew Manuscripts: The Power of Script and Image*. London: British Library, 110 fig. 97.

87 For examples, see Chaya Benjamin. 1987. *The Stieglitz Collection: Masterpieces of Jewish Art*. Jerusalem: Israel Museum, 146–47, 152–75, pls 113–14, 117–132.

88 See Cissy Grossman. 1989. *A Temple Treasury: The Judaica Collection of Congregation Emanu-El of the City of New York*. New York: Hudson Hills Press, 144–47.

89 Cf. Joseph Gutmann. 1999. "On Medieval Hanukkah Lamps," *Artibus et Historiae* 20: 187–90.

90 Both topics appear on the same page in the Leipzig Mahzor, Vol. 1, fol. 51v. Cf. Gutmann, *Hebrew Manuscript Painting*, 88–89 pl. 25.
91 The Vatican *Mishneh Torah* (note 82, above), fol. 85v – reproduced in Metzger, *Jewish Life in the Middle Ages*, 252 fig. 372.
92 Cf. Sabar, "Bride, Heroine and Courtesan," (note 47, above), 63–70.
93 For a succinct survey of the development of the art of the Esther scroll, see Shalom Sabar. 2013. "Esther Scroll," in Raphael Patai and Haya Bar-Itzhak (eds) *Encyclopedia of Jewish Folklore and Traditions*. Armonk, NY/London: M.E. Sharpe, Vol. 1, 144–47.
94 For an early example, see Bruno Italiener, Aron Freimann, August L. Mayer, and Adolf Schmidt, eds. 1927–28. *Die Darmstädter Pessach-Haggadah: Codex orientalis 8 der Landesbibliothek zu Darmstadt aus dem Vierzehnten Jahrhundert*, 2 vols. Leipzig: K. W. Hiersemann; and another important edition: Moshe Spitzer, ed. 1965–67. *The Birds' Head Haggada of the Bezalel National Art Museum in Jerusalem*, 2 vols. Jerusalem: Tarshish Books. For a comparative iconographical study of the medieval Haggadot, including discussions of each of the rituals, foods, preparations, etc., see Mendel Metzger. 1973. *La Haggada enluminée*. Leiden: E. J. Brill; Metzger, *Jewish Life*, 258–66, figs 378–80.
95 Cf. Sed-Rajna, *Le mahzor enluminé*, 25–26, pls 19–21 figs 37–40. Cf. Gutmann, *Hebrew Manuscript Painting*, 92–93 pl. 27; Bezalel Narkiss. 1969. *Hebrew Illuminated Manuscripts*. Jerusalem: Encyclopaedia Judaica, 94–95 pl. 27, 108–09 pl. 34.
96 Leipzig Mahzor, Vol. 1, fol. 130v; Narkiss, "Mahsor Lipsiae," 96.
97 Leipzig Mahzor, Vol. 1, fol. 131r; Narkiss, "Mahsor Lipsiae," 96–97; Kogman-Appel, *A Mahzor from Worms*, 98–108 and fig. 15.
98 For a detailed analysis of the initiation ritual in Ashkenaz and its origins in rabbinic Judaism, see Ivan G. Marcus. 1996. *Rituals of Childhood: Jewish Acculturation in Medieval Europe*, New Haven, CT: Yale University Press (and cf. Kogman-Appel, *A Mahzor from Worms*, 98–108). For other "rituals of education" in later periods among various Jewish communities, including in the lands of Islam, see Goldberg, *Jewish Passages*, 77–113.

References

Baumgarten, Elisheva. 2004. *Mothers and Children: Jewish Family Life in Medieval Europe*, Princeton, NJ: Princeton University Press.
Bemporad, Dora Liescia. 2019. "A Late Gothic Carved Pair of Torah Staves from Italy," in *Windows on Jewish Worlds: Essays in Honor of William Gross*, eds. Shalom Sabar, Emile Schrijver, and Falk Wiesemann, Zutphen: Walburg Persbv, 22–33.
Benjamin, Chaya. 1987. *The Stieglitz Collection: Masterpieces of Jewish Art*, Jerusalem: Israel Museum.
Ben-Sasson, Rivka. 2012. "Botanics and Iconography: Images of the 'Lulav' and the 'Etrog'," *Ars Judaica* 8: 7–22.
Bland, Kalman P. 2000. *The Artless Jew: Medieval and Modern Affirmations and Denials of the Visual*, Princeton, NJ: Princeton University Press.
Blumberg, Adi. 2001. *Hanging Sabbath Lamps*, Jerusalem: Adi Foundation.
Boehm, Barbara Drake. 2019. *The Colmar Treasure: A Medieval Jewish Legacy*, exhibition catalog, New York: Scala Publishers & The Metropolitan Museum of Art.
Bohak, Gideon. 2015. "Jewish Magic in the Middle Ages," in *The Cambridge History of Magic and Witchcraft in the West: From Antiquity to the Present*, ed. David J. Collins, Cambridge: Cambridge University Press, 268–300.
Brocke, Michael. 2011. "The Lilies of Worms," *Zutot: Perspective on Jewish Culture* 8: 3–13.
Brocke, Michael. 2013. "Der jüdische Friedhof Worms im Mittelalter – 1059 bis 1519: Beobachtungen an einem singulären Ort," in *Die SchUM-Gemeinden Speyer – Worms – Mainz; auf dem Weg zum Welterbe*, eds. Pia Heberer and Ursula Reuter, Regensburg: Schnell & Steiner, 111–54.
Cassuto, David, and Nicolò Bucaria. 2011. "The Synagogue and the Ritual Baths in Palermo in Light of Textual and Archaeological Evidence," in *Tov Elem: Memory, Community and Gender in Medieval and Early Modern Jewish Societies. Essays in Honor of Robert Bonfil*, eds. Elisheva Baumgarten, Amnon Raz-Krakotzkin, and Roni Weinstein, Jerusalem: Mossad Bialik (in Hebrew), 241–81.
Cohen, Evelyn M. Forthcoming. "The Four Species in Medieval and Renaissance Illuminated Hebrew Manuscripts," in *Be Fruitful! The Etrog in Jewish Art, Culture, and History*, exhibition catalog, eds. Warren Klein, Sharon Liberman Mintz, and Joshua Teplitsky. New York: Herbert & Eileen Bernard Museum of Judaica, Temple Emanu-El, New York. Jerusalem: Mineged Press (in press).

Feuchtwanger-Sarig, Naomi. 2005. "'May He Grow to the Torah…': The Iconography of Torah Reading and *Bar Mitzvah* on Ashkenazi Torah Binders," in *Liturgy in the Life of the Synagogue; Studies in the History of Jewish Prayer*, eds. Ruth Langer and Steven Fine, Winona Lake, IN: Eisenbrauns, 161–76.

Finkelstein, Louis. 1924. *Jewish Self-Government in the Middle Ages*, New York: Jewish Theological Seminary of America.

Friedman, Mira. 1987. "The Metamorphoses of Judith," *Jewish Art* 12–13: 225–46.

Frojmovic, Eva. 2015. "Feasting at the Lord's Table," *Images: Journal of Jewish Art & Visual Culture*, 7: 5–21.

Goldberg, Harvey E. 2003. *Jewish Passages: Cycles of Jewish Life*, Berkeley: University of California Press.

Grafman, Rafi. 1996. *Crowning Glory: Silver Torah Ornaments of the Jewish Museum*, New York: Jewish Museum, and Boston: David R. Godine.

Grossman, Cissy. 1980. "Womanly Arts: A Study of Italian Torah Binders in the New York Jewish Museum Collection," *Journal of Jewish Art* 7: 35–43.

Grossman, Cissy. 1989. *A Temple Treasury: The Judaica Collection of Congregation Emanu-El of the City of New York*, New York: Hudson Hills Press.

Gutmann, Joseph. 1968. "Leviathan, Behemoth and Ziz: Jewish Messianic Symbols in Art," *Hebrew Union College Annual* 39: 219–30.

Gutmann, Joseph. 1978. *Hebrew Manuscript Painting*, New York: George Braziller.

Gutmann, Joseph. 1983. "*Die Mappe Schuletragen*: An Unusual Judeo-German Custom," *Visible Religion – Annual for Religious Iconography* 2: 167–73.

Gutmann, Joseph. 1983. *The Jewish Sanctuary* ("Iconography of Religions," Section 23, Judaism, fasc. 1), Leiden: E.J. Brill.

Gutmann, Joseph. 1987. *The Jewish Life Cycle* ("Iconography of Religions," Section 23, Judaism, fasc. 4), Leiden: E.J. Brill.

Gutmann, Joseph. 1989. "Jewish Medieval Marriage Customs in Art: Creativity and Adaptation," in *The Jewish Family: Metaphor and Memory*, ed. David Kraemer, New York: Oxford University Press, 47–62.

Gutmann, Joseph. 1999. "On Medieval Hanukkah Lamps," *Artibus et Historiae* 20: 187–90.

Heller, Ena Giurescu. 2020. "Western Ashkenazi Synagogues in Medieval and Early Modern Europe," in *Jewish Religious Architecture: From Biblical Israel to Modern Judaism*, ed. Steven Fine, Leiden; Boston, MA: Brill.

Horowitz, Elliott S. 1989. "The Eve of the Circumcision," *Journal of Social History* 23: 45–69.

Horowitz, Elliott S. 1993–94. "Giotto in Avignon, Adler in London, Panofsky in Princeton: On the Odyssey of an Illustrated Hebrew Manuscript from Italy and on its Meaning," *Jewish Art* 19–20: 98–111.

Italiener, Bruno, Aron Freimann, August L. Mayer, and Adolf Schmidt, eds. 1927–28. *Die Darmstädter Pessach-Haggadah: Codex orientalis 8 der Landesbibliothek zu Darmstadt aus dem Vierzehnten Jahrhundert*, 2 vols. Leipzig: K. W. Hiersemann.

Kleeblatt, Norman L., and Mann, Vivian B. 1986. *Treasures of the Jewish Museum*, New York: Jewish Museum & Universe Books.

Kogman-Appel, Katrin. 1999. *Die zweite Nürnberger und die Jehuda Haggada: jüdische Illustratoren zwischen Tradition und Fortschritt*, Frankfurt am Main: P. Lang.

Kogman-Appel, Katrin. 2012. *A Mahzor from Worms: Art and Religion in a Medieval Jewish Community*, Cambridge, MA: Harvard University Press.

Koolik, Marilyn Gold. 1982. *Towers of Spice: The Tower-shape Tradition in Havdalah Spiceboxes*, exhibition catalog, Jerusalem: Israel Museum.

Krinsky, Carol Herselle. 1985. *Synagogues of Europe: Architecture, History, Meaning*, New York: Architectural History Foundation.

Kybalova, Ludmila, Eva Kosakova, and Alexandr Putik, eds. 2003. *Textiles from Bohemian and Moravian Synagogues: From the Collections of the Jewish Museum in Prague*, Prague: Jewish Museum.

Lauterbach, Jacob Z. 1970. "The Ritual for the Kapparot Ceremony," in *Studies in Jewish Law, Custom and Folklore*, New York: Ktav Pub. House, 133–42.

Mann, Vivian B. 1986–87. "The Recovery of a Known Work," *Jewish Art* 12–13: 269–78.

Mann, Vivian B. 1988. "'New' Examples of Jewish Ceremonial Art from Medieval Ashkenaz," *Artibus et Historiae* 17: 13–24.

Mann, Vivian B. 1996. "Torah Ornaments before 1600," in Grafman, Rafi, *Crowning Glory: Silver Torah Ornaments of the Jewish Museum*, New York: Jewish Museum, and Boston: David R. Godine, 1–15.

Mann, Vivian B. 2000. *Jewish Texts on the Visual Arts*, Cambridge, UK: Cambridge University Press.

Marcus, Ivan G. 1996. *Rituals of Childhood: Jewish Acculturation in Medieval Europe*, New Haven, CT: Yale University Press.

Marcus, Ivan G. 2004. *The Jewish Life Cycle: Rites of Passage from Biblical to Modern Times*, Seattle: University of Washington Press.

Metzger, Mendel. 1973. *La Haggada enluminée*, Leiden: E. J. Brill.

Metzger, Thérèse and Metzger Mendel. 1982. *Jewish Life in the Middle Ages: Illuminated Hebrew Manuscripts of the Thirteenth to the Sixteenth Centuries*, New York: Alpine Fine Arts Collection.

Meyer, Hans Gerhard. 1982. "Eine Sabbatlampe im Erfurter Dom," *Studien zur Kunstgeschichte* 16: 7–10.

Narkiss, Bezalel. 1964. "Introduction to the Mahzor Lipsiae," in *Machsor Lipsiae: 68 Facsimile Plates of the Mediaeval, Illuminated Hebrew Manuscript in the Possession of the Leipzig University Library*, ed. Elias Katz, Vaduz: Société pour le Commerce Intercontinental Trust Reg, 85–110.

Narkiss, Bezalel. 1969. *Hebrew Illuminated Manuscripts*, Jerusalem: Encyclopaedia Judaica.

Narkiss, Mordechai. 1958. "An Italian Niello Casket of the Fifteenth Century," *Journal of the Warburg and Courtauld Institutes* 21: 288–95.

Narkiss, Mordechai. 1981. "Origins of the Spice Box," *Journal of Jewish Art* 8: 28–41.

Noy, Ido. 2016. "The Fleuron Crown from Neumarkt in Silesia (Środa Śląska): Christian Material Culture in Jewish Context," *Ars Judaica* 12: 23–38.

Noy, Ido. 2018. "Love Conquers All: The Erfurt Girdle as a Source for Understanding Medieval Jewish Love and Romance," *Images: Journal of Jewish Art & Visual Culture* 11: 227–46.

Rodov, Ilia. 2010. "Tower-Like Torah Arks: The Tower of Strength and the Architecture of the Messianic Temple," *Journal of the Warburg and Courtauld Institutes* 73: 65–98.

Sabar, Shalom. 1987. "The Beginnings of Ketubbah Decoration in Italy: Venice in the Late Sixteenth to the Early Seventeenth Centuries," *Jewish Art* 12–13: 96–110.

Sabar, Shalom. 1990. *Ketubbah: Jewish Marriage Contracts of the Hebrew Union College Skirball Museum and Klau Library*, Philadelphia, PA; New York: Jewish Publication Society.

Sabar, Shalom. 1995. "The Heroism of the Maccabees in Jewish Art of the Middle Ages and the Renaissance," in *In the Time of the Hasmoneans: Sources and Studies*, eds. David Amit and Hanan Eshel, Jerusalem: Ben-Zvi Institute, 277–90 (in Hebrew).

Sabar, Shalom. 1999. "Bride, Heroine and Courtesan: Images of the Jewish Woman in Hebrew Manuscripts of the Renaissance in Italy," *Proceedings of the Tenth World Congress of Jewish Studies*, Division D/II: *Art, Folklore and Music*, Jerusalem: World Union of Jewish Studies, 63–70.

Sabar, Shalom. 2002. "Childbirth and Magic: Jewish Folklore and Material Culture," *Cultures of the Jews: A New History*, ed. David Biale, New York: Schocken Books, 670–722.

Sabar, Shalom. 2003. "Between Poland and Germany: Jewish Religious Practices in Illustrated Postcards of the Early Twentieth Century," *Polin: Studies in Polish Jewry*, 16: 137–66.

Sabar, Shalom. 2005. "Prophet Elijah Visits Venice: A Rare Italian Elijah Chair from Early Nineteenth Century Venice," in *La nascita nella tradizione ebraica / Birth in Jewish Tradition*, eds. Emanuela Lodi and Silvia Guastalla, Livorno: S. Belforte, 98–123 (in English and Italian).

Sabar, Shalom. 2011. "The Shofar in Medieval Jewish Thought and Art / The Shofar in the Modern Period – 18th–20th Centuries," in *Sound the Shofar: A Witness to History*, ed. Filip Vukosavovic, exhibition catalog, Jerusalem: Bible Lands Museum, 40–46.

Sabar, Shalom. 2013. "Mitzvot Hannah: Visual Depictions of the 'Three Women's Commandments' among the Jews of Europe from the Middle Ages to Late Nineteenth Century," in *Textures – Culture, Literature, Folklore for Galit Hasan-Rokem*, eds. Hagar Salamon and Avigdor Shinan, Jerusalem: Magnes Press, 2: 383–413 (in Hebrew; English summary).

Sabar, Shalom. 2013. "Esther Scroll," in *Encyclopedia of Jewish Folklore and Traditions*, eds. Raphael Patai and Haya Bar-Itzhak, Armonk, NY; London: M. E. Sharpe, 1: 144–47.

Sabar, Shalom. 2018. *The Sarajevo Haggadah: History & Art*, Sarajevo: National Museum of Bosnia and Herzegovina.

Sabar, Shalom. 2020. "Objects Reveal: The Life and its Rituals," in *Beyond the Ghetto: Inside & Out*, eds. Andreina Contessa, Simonetta Della Seta, Carlotta Ferrara degli Uberti, and Sharon Reichel, exhibition catalog, National Museum of Italian Judaism and the Shoah, Ferrara. Milan: SilvanaEditoriale S.p.A., 36–47.

Sabar, Shalom. 2022. "*Hadar* and *Hiddur*: The Etrog in Jewish Art," in *Be Fruitful! The Etrog in Jewish Art, Culture, and History*, exhibition catalog, eds. Warren Klein, Sharon Liberman Mintz, and Joshua Teplitsky. New York: Herbert & Eileen Bernard Museum of Judaica, Temple Emanu-El, New York. Jerusalem: Mineged Press (in press).

Schnitzer, Merav. 2020. "The Silver Key from the Erfurt Treasure: Suggesting a Context," *Ritual Objects in Ritual Contexts* ("Erfurter Schriften zur Jüdischen Geschichte") 6: 94–103.

Sed-Rajna, Gabrielle. 1983. *Le mahzor enluminé: Les voies de formation d'un programme iconographique*, Leiden: E. J. Brill.
Seidman, Gertrud. 1981. "Marriage Rings, Jewish Style," *Connoisseur*, 206: 48–61.
Shachar, Isaiah. 1975. *The Jewish Year* ("Iconography of Religions," Section 23, Judaism, fasc. 3), Leiden: E. J. Brill.
Shalev-Eyni, Sarit. 2005. "Iconography of Love: Illustrations of Bride and Bridegroom in Ashkenazi Prayerbooks of the Thirteenth and Fourteenth Century," *Studies in Iconography* 26: 27–57.
Shalev-Eyni, Sarit. 2014. "Martyrdom and Sexuality: The Case of an Eleventh-century 'Piyyut' for Hanukkah and its Visual Interpretation in the Fifteenth Century," in *Conflict and Religious Conversation in Latin Christendom. Studies in Honour of Ora Limor*, eds. Israel J. Yuval and Ram Ben-Shalom, Turnhout: Brepols, 133–65.
Shoham-Steiner, Ephraim. 2006. "For a Prayer in that Place Would Be Most Welcome': Jews, Holy Shrines, and Miracles — A New Approach," *Viator* 37: 369–95.
Spitzer, Moshe, ed. 1965–67. *The Birds' Head Haggada of the Bezalel National Art Museum in Jerusalem*, 2 vols. Jerusalem: Tarshish Books.
Stern, David. 2017. *The Jewish Bible: A Material History*, Seattle: University of Washington Press.
Stürzebecher, Maria. 2020. "The Medieval Jewish Wedding Ring from the Erfurt Treasure: Ceremonial Object or Bride Price?" *Ritual Objects in Ritual Contexts* ("Erfurter Schriften zur Jüdischen Geschichte") 6: 72–79.
Tahan, Ilana. 2007. *Hebrew Manuscripts: The Power of Script and Image*, London: British Library.
Vukosavovic, Filip, ed. 2011. *Sound the Shofar: A Witness to History*, exhibition catalog, Jerusalem: Bible Lands Museum.
Weber, Annette, Evelyn Friedlander, and Fritz Armbruster, eds. 1997. *Mappot – Blessed Be Who Comes: The Band of Jewish Tradition*, Osnabrück: Secolo Verlag (in English and German).
West, Ashley D. 2017. "Preserving Destruction: Albrecht Altdorfer's Etchings of the Regensburg Synagogue as Material Performances of the Past and Future," in *The Primacy of The Image in Northern European Art, 1400–1700. Essays in Honor of Larry Silver*, eds. Debra Cashion, Henry Luttikhuizen, and Ashley West, Leiden; Boston, MA: Brill.
Wischnitzer, Rachel. 1964. *The Architecture of the European Synagogue*, Philadelphia: Jewish Publication Society of America.
Yaniv, Bracha. 2019. *Ceremonial Synagogue Textiles: From Ashkenazi, Sephardi, and Italian Communities*, London: Littman Library of Jewish Civilization & Liverpool University Press.

7
VISUALIZATIONS OF RITUAL IN MEDIEVAL BOOK CULTURE

Katrin Kogman-Appel

Introduction

A central question in any attempt to evaluate the contribution of medieval book art to our understanding of the performance of ritual concerns the degree to which illustrations in medieval manuscripts "document" religious life or were meant to do so.[1] Medieval book art served as a medium of visual communication between the patrons and the artists they employed, on the one hand, and the users of the books, on the other. The rituals depicted were performed within groups so they also had a social dimension, but no such illustration was ever created to serve as a historical document. By and large, medieval art was not designed to depict life realistically; moreover, there were no genre images. Medieval representations of rituals embrace a whole range of symbolic and mythical elements together with visualized performative acts, and they tend to enhance the former at the expense of the latter. The selection of certain pictorial elements and the incorporation of other means of emphasis underscore certain aspects of the patron's or the artist's message and guide the viewer through the reception process. The modern eye approaching these images has to take careful note of the function of such elements in the pictorial language.

In the present chapter, I offer a brief survey of premodern visualizations of Jewish rituals with a focus on performance and, thus, filter out and neglect some of the symbolic and mythical aspects of the images. For example, my discussion of an image showing the circumcision of Isaac in a medieval Pentateuch does not approach it as a case study of biblical imagery with all its implications, such as the role this scene may have played in contemporaneous exegesis or its potential for teaching us something about Jewish-Christian entanglement. Rather, I focus on how the artist's (or patron's) life experience might have shaped their perception of a circumcision scene.

The following sections are structured roughly along communal ritual, on the one hand, and the private arena, on the other, even though we shall see that these two spheres occasionally interfaced or overlapped. I start with a brief discussion of visual references to synagogal ritual as it emerged in late antiquity, a time when the memory of sacrificial worship still dominated the visual language. An analysis of images showing public prayer with a focus on the role of the prayer leader and his attire is at the core of the section I call "Communal Ritual in the Middle Ages." That is followed by a look at the role of the communal arena in preparations for Passover.

DOI: 10.4324/9781003032823-9

The third section addresses life cycle events that were celebrated in the public sphere. The succeeding discussion of the private sphere focuses on Passover; I first describe the ritualization of the cleaning processes that were carried out in the home and then move on to a selection of *seder* rituals, wherein I explain how they changed over time. Thus, I move between two poles: fixity and flexibility. The chapter ends with a brief look at the early modern period and some observations on contemporaneous social change and its effects on book culture.

Late Antiquity: From Sacrificial Worship to Synagogal Liturgy

Several mosaic pavements in late antique synagogues in Israel depict a set of Sanctuary vessels abstractly spread on flat surfaces without any spatial relationship to one another. Most often interpreted as references to the Third (messianic) Temple (Revel-Neher, 1984), it has also been suggested that these arrays were meant to recall a Pharisean custom of displaying the vessels publicly during pilgrim rituals (Fraade, 2009).

Actual ritual performances were only rarely visualized. There are two known representations of priestly worship: one, a mural on the western wall of the Dura Europos synagogue in eastern Syria (c. 244–245; Figure 7.1) and the other, a floor mosaic in the fifth-century synagogue at Sepphoris in the Galilee (Weiss, 2005). The mural shows the Temple in the background, Aaron prominently figured as the high priest, a small altar, and several priests attending to sacrificial animals. It is not quite clear if this image depicts the initiation of sacrificial services (see, e.g., Laderman, 1997) or simply reflects daily practice in the Temple (Schenk, 2010). The

Figure 7.1 The Initiation of Sacrifice: mural from the Synagogue of Dura-Europos, Syria, 244–45, western wall.

Source: After Goodenough, *Jewish Symbols*

very poorly preserved mosaic in Sepphoris shows the remains of an altar, a corner of a priestly garment, and some animals.

Although it is possible to approach these images as "visual texts" and interpret them as narrative pictorials of history or the messianic future (Weiss, 2005, chapter 3 on Sepphoris), some scholars link them to the synagogue as a functioning liturgical space, with the congregation as its audience. Two fragments of a liturgical text on parchment found near the Durene synagogue are instrumental in approaches to this, and other prayer halls, from the point of view of their ritual functions. Given that synagogal liturgy in many ways parallels the pre-70 CE sacrificial services, the depiction of sacrifices can be interpreted in conjunction with both the memory of Temple worship (Laderman, 1997) and later liturgical performances. Indeed, further observations made at Dura relate to the ritual context: a male figure holding a scroll near the Torah shrine addresses the practice of ritualized recitations from the Bible (Figure 7.2). Aramaic inscriptions adjacent to some of the biblical scenes are written in a language that is close to the Aramaic *targumim* and may suggest that these (in an oral form) were also recited in the Durene synagogue. Other figures are imaged in the Roman-style prayer gesture (*orans*), and the themes of several biblical narratives can be read as echoes of the concerns mentioned in the principal prayer of the rabbinic liturgy. Moreover, the biblical pictorials can also be understood as references to sermonizing in the synagogue (Fine, 2005).

A similar approach to imageries in synagogues as expressions of their liturgical settings was also employed toward interpreting the program in Sepphoris, relying on late antique *piyyutim* (liturgical hymns) that mention many of the elements figured on the panels (Fine, 1999).

Figure 7.2 Prophet Reading from a Scroll: mural from the Synagogue of Dura-Europos, Syria, 244–45, western wall

Source: After Goodenough, *Jewish Symbols*

Communal Ritual in the Middle Ages
Public Prayer

Beyond a space properly designed to fulfill its ritual functions (the synagogue), the enactment of communal ceremonies implies a ritual expert or agent (the *hazan* [cantor] or *sheliach tsibur* [prayer leader, lit. "the messenger of the community"]) to guide the community through prayer or other performative acts, and various items such as vessels, attire, and/or books.

Synagogal liturgies emerged in parallel with the development of the synagogue as a ritual space. Although not much is known about the liturgy that was common in late antique synagogues, scholars have discussed the role of prayer in its relationship to teaching. We have more information about the Geonic period as several contemporaneous liturgical fragments were discovered in the Cairo Genizah and there is an extant prayer book, which was composed by Saadia Gaon (d. 942). As early as in the late antique period, the core elements of the statutory prayer service – the recitation of *sh'ma Israel* ("Hear, Oh Israel") and the *'amidah*, a set of seven (on Saturdays) or nineteen benedictions (on weekdays) – was occasionally embellished with optional *piyyutim* (liturgical hymns). The tradition of chanting *piyyutim* developed further in the Middle Ages, despite the fact that some halakhic authorities criticized the practice. It was particularly in the Ashkenazi communities that the recitation of *piyyutim* became a core element of local *minhag* (custom) and eventually acquired quasi halakhic status. Whereas the statutory prayers were (and still are) spelled out in siddurim (lit. "order," the order of prayers), optional liturgical hymns were collected in mahzorim.[2] During the course of the thirteenth century, the Ashkenazi mahzor developed into a particularly lavish book genre. Mahzorim were large-scale codices, most commonly in two volumes with elaborate page layouts in large square letters to facilitate public recitation and luxurious illustrations. Commissioned by wealthy private patrons, who kept them in their homes, they served as communal ritual objects during holyday services. In many ways their layout and adornments were utilized to visualize the structure of the liturgy (Shalev-Eyni, 2010).

The following discussion is an attempt to reconstruct some aspects of the ritual performances that took place in the medieval synagogue of Worms, a city in the Middle Rhine region in what we now call Germany (Kogman-Appel, 2012). Destroyed during the Nazi riots on the night of November 9, 1938, the synagogue was reconstructed during the 1960s, so that it is possible to appreciate the nature of the ritual space as it existed in the fourteenth century (Figure 7.3). Around the year 1310, a wealthy member of the Worms community commissioned a mahzor in two volumes, still extant and kept today in the University Library of Leipzig (MS Voller 1102/I–II).

On every holiday between c. 1310 and c. 1615 (when a pogrom disrupted communal life in Jewish Worms and the communal mahzor was apparently taken to Poland), the synagogue attendant would have carried one of the enormous volumes of the Leipzig Mahzor into the synagogue. An engraving by Albrecht Altdorfer captures that very moment in the medieval synagogue of Regensburg in 1519, showing a man in the narthex carrying a huge volume and walking toward the main hall (Figure 7.4).[3] The congregation is assembled, the men in the main hall and the women in an adjacent section (built in Worms as a separate wing in 1213).

After the attendant had placed the volume on a lectern near the Torah shrine, the *sheliach tsibur*, accompanied by two prominent members of the congregation, would take his place near the lectern. He would have wrapped himself in his *talit*, covering his head, with two of the *talit*'s corners thrown over his shoulders, opened the book and begun to recite the texts designated

Visualizations in Medieval Book Culture

Figure 7.3 Worms, Synagogue, 1175 (destroyed in 1938 and rebuilt in 1960), interior of the men's section
Source: Image in the public domain

for the particular service. According to the fifteenth-century scholar Jacob Moelin (Maharil, d. 1427), the community's reverence for its prayer book guaranteed the acceptance of its prayers in the divine spheres (*Sefer Maharil, Hilkhot yom kippur* 11).

An image at the beginning of the Leipzig Mahzor captures these actions (Figure 7.5).

It shows the *sheliach tsibur* wrapping himself in a large *talit*, which covers his head, with two of the fringed corners prominently displayed. He seems to be actually in the act of wrapping, as his right hand is arranging the *talit* around his head. One of the corners is lying on his back, apparently having been thrown over his shoulder. The illustration was placed at the beginning of the liturgical section after the short *shokhen 'ad merom* (He who dwells on high), which is part of the daily statutory liturgy and is, in fact, the only one of the statutory prayers that was occasionally included in the Ashkenazi mahzorim; it marked the beginning of the communal service, which requires a quorum of ten men.

The image combines several aspects of the successful performance of medieval communal prayer: it delineates a ritual space (by the rather abstract means of the colorful zig-zag frame and the dark background), it shows a ritual agent in ritual attire, and a ritual object, the mahzor itself. Whereas the synagogue had established itself as a well-defined ritual space as early as in late antiquity, the *sheliach tsibur*, the *talit* as ritual attire, and the mahzor as a ritual object all evolved and changed significantly during the Middle Ages, and in a way the image in the Leipzig Mahzor documents these processes.

Figure 7.4 Albrecht Altdorfer, Entrance to the Synagogue of Regensburg, Regensburg 1519, etching
Source: New York, Metropolitan Museum (© bpk-Bildagentur, Berlin)

The *sheliach tsibur* has been the agent through whom the community observes the precept of prayer since late antiquity. He goes "down before the Torah shrine to fulfill the obligation of many" (*Tosefta, Rosh Hashanah* 2:18). Although Talmudic sources do not attach any sacramental aura to the *sheliach tsibur*, who is simply a knowledgeable member of the community worthy of representing it before God, in the medieval Rhineland, likely owing to the influence of Ashkenazi Pietism, he eventually acquired the special status that is reflected in our image. He was not only a "mediator," who facilitated the participation of the congregation in prayer, but he also had a major influence on the development of liturgical rites (Grossman, 1988; Ta-Shma, 2003; Fishman, 2004).

The Ashkenazi Pietists (whose precise nature as a movement or a small, somewhat eccentric group is still discussed by scholars) flourished in the late twelfth and early thirteenth centuries. Ashkenazi Pietism and Rhineland custom, including that of *piyyut* recitation, had their roots in late antique Palestinian *'aggadah* and liturgical tradition (Ta-Shma, 1999), which reached the Rhineland in the early Middle Ages via Byzantium and Italy. In certain aggadic contexts in the Palestinian tradition, the *sheliach tsibur* might, for example, have had the ability to overcome satanic powers (Ta-Shma, 2003). A midrashic work likely compiled in southern Italy conveys the image of "the *hazan* of the congregation […] standing there like an angel of God and the Book of Torah in his arms, and the congregation encircles him as if he were an altar" (*Midrash*

Figure 7.5 Beginning of the Liturgy
Source: Leipzig, Universitätsbibliothek, MS Voller 1102/I, Mahzor, Worms c. 1310, fol. 27r (image in the public domain)

Tehillim 17:5; Geula, 2007). The image of the *sheliach tsibur* who appears like an angel of God returns later in almost identical wording in several sources from the Rhineland.

The special status of the *sheliach tsibur* is emphasized in our image by his large and striking *talit*. This attire went through crucial evolutions within the context of the Ashkenazi tradition, where the act of wrapping would eventually be fully ritualized. Late antique rabbinic sources frequently refer to the *talit* as part of a man's everyday costume, a pallium-like mantle, a rectangular piece of cloth worn as an upper garment fit for various mundane purposes (see, e.g., *Mishnah Pe'ah* 4:3). As a rectangular garment with four corners, the *talit* had to have the set of halakhic fringes as a daily reminder of the divine precepts (Deut. 22:12). Since prayer and teaching require that one's body be appropriately covered, the *talit* fulfilled that purpose as well. In some paintings in the synagogue at Dura Europos, men are wearing pallia, and one can see the fringes at the corners (Figure 7.2). Although these pallia were used to cover oneself during prayer (this being only one of their many purposes), these fringed *talitot* can in no way be interpreted as ritual garments, as implied in the Leipzig Mahzor or as we know them from modern ritual practice.

Pallia went out of fashion during the course of the Middle Ages and were replaced in Europe by tailored mantles. The disappearance of the *talit* from the everyday wardrobe naturally caused some concern from the point of view of the halakhic consequences. The attachment of fringes as a biblical precept could not simply be given up and, in fact, this development opened the way to the evolution of the *talit* as a ritual object. It was again in the vicinity of the Rhineland Pietists where this change was most apparent. Some post-Talmudic sources assign the *talit* to the sphere of ritual and prayer and mark a shift in its status from a mere reminder of the precepts to a garment carrying its own ritual significance and occasionally even an aura of sanctity. Several text references somewhat similar to the one quoted above led the way toward this view. For example: " 'And the Lord passed by before him [on Mount Sinai] and proclaimed.' Rabbi Yohanan said: [...] this verse teaches us that the Holy one blessed be He, wrapped Himself like a *sheliach tsibur* and showed Moses the order of prayer" (*Rosh Hashanah* 17b).

The motif of God wrapping himself and its variations frequently appear in Palestinian midrashim and, later, in Pietist traditions. The image of the *sheliach tsibur* wrapped in a *talit*, together with the distinct ritual significance he enjoys in texts such as this one, created a notion of the *talit* that was very different from the late antique mundane piece of cloth as a mere reminder of halakhic precepts. In its association with God and in the meaning that it attaches to the *talit*, this type of clothing eventually became an item of ritual attire. The *sheliach tsibur* in our image was clearly purposefully drawn in the actual act of wrapping himself. Moreover, the custom of throwing two of the *talit*'s four fringes over one's back during wrapping is yet another motif found in the same string of tradition from the Palestinian midrash via southern Italian references up to the writings of Ashkenazi Pietists (Geula, 2007).

A look at some representations of worshippers in other illuminated manuscripts discloses the specificity of the different elements of the Ashkenazi ritual of wrapping in a *talit*. Several images of men, mostly prayer leaders, covered or wrapped in *talitot* can be found in French, German, Italian, and Iberian manuscripts. In Italy, France, and Iberia the *talit* simply drapes from the head with its four corners touching the shoulders and covers the upper body. Occasionally, when the worshipper is shown holding a Torah scroll, the *talit* covers his hands. In images from the German lands, however, men with *talitot* are almost always shown with the end of the *talit* "thrown" over the shoulder with the fringes clearly visible on their backs (Figure 7.6).

Other visual links to the liturgy performed within the public space of the synagogue are rare. In another mahzor, copied and illustrated in Würzburg in 1272, but kept for centuries in Worms and, hence, called the Worms Mahzor (Jerusalem, National Library of Israel, cod. 4°781, vol. 1, fol. 111r), we find a visualization of the Transmission of the Law. The Sinai narrative in the Book of Exodus (Chap. 19) implies that God himself announced the Ten Commandments. Since the Giving of the Law is commemorated on the Shavuot festival, the illustration that decorates the first *piyyut* for Shavuot often images this event. The liturgy on that day includes a recitation of the Ten Commandments in a special cantillation reserved for this occasion. The image in the Worms Mahzor shows ten men holding banderoles inscribed with the Ten Commandments and it is likely that it was meant to visualize this recitation ritual (Shalev-Eyni, 2018).

Figure 7.6 Synagogue Service
Source: Hamburg, Staats –und Universitätsbibliothek, cod. Heb. 37, Miscellany, Mainz (?), c. 1425, fol. 114r (with permission of the Staats -und Universitätsbibliothek, Hamburg)

Passover Preparations in the Public Sphere

The Leipzig Mahzor also visualizes an initiation rite common among Ashkenazi Jews in the Middle Ages, which I discuss in the next section, and two acts of preparation for the Passover week, and especially for the *seder* on the eve of the holiday. Both these acts went through processes of ritualization during the Middle Ages, and even though the *seder* itself takes place in the private sphere, both were performed in public spaces. Every year on the Sabbath before Passover, known as the Great Sabbath, Eleazar ben Judah of Worms (d. 1232) delivered a sermon, one, he said, that he had received from his teacher, which dealt with the rules that ensured a kosher Passover week (*Derashah Lepesah*). It was apparently intended to turn into some sort of tradition to be "recited" by later authorities and eventually evolved into a ritual in its own right. On the same day, the *piyyut adir dar metuchim* (The Mighty One dwells on high), which is recited as part of the *musaf* service, tells about the precepts to be fulfilled during the upcoming week. At the core of these rules are the ritual cleansing and scalding of vessels and the baking of *matsot*, and both of these acts are depicted in the Mahzor's margins adjacent to the liturgy of the Great Sabbath.

The marginal image adorning the first page of the *piyyut* shows two women standing beside an enormous cauldron set over a fire (vol. 1, fol. 68v), which features images of various metal dishes, all rendered in gold, which indicate its contents. The *piyyut* gives precise instructions about what kinds of dishes and implements have to be scorched or scalded in order to become ritually clean,[4] and our image, which shows a variety of utensils, some of them clearly made of metal, seems to be referencing these guidelines. Apart from discussing the halakhic issue, Eleazar's sermon (as well as his halakhic work *Ma'aseh Haroqeah*, par. 4) emphasizes that the scalding was to be undertaken publicly in a large cauldron for the entire community, rather than privately in one's own home. The enormous size of the cauldron depicted in the marginal image clearly suggests that it refers to the practice of communal scalding.

The second act of preparation for Passover depicted in the Leipzig Mahzor is the baking of *matsot* (vol. 1, fol. 70v). The image shows two women and a man preparing the unleavened breads. The meticulous instructions to guarantee minimal contact between the flour and the water to avoid leavening are extremely detailed in medieval halakhic sources. The large stove shown in the image indicates that this procedure, too, was carried out in a communal bakery rather than at home. Contemporary Jewish bakeries, and specifically the one in Worms, are known from medieval sources (Barzen, 2002).

The shift of both these acts from the private into the communal sphere is noteworthy. The dishes are used within the framework of a private household, but the process of making them ritually clean was undertaken within the public arena. The same is true of the unleavened breads: they are consumed during private meals at home but were produced in the public sphere. Relevant scholarship has proposed two possible reasons. On the one hand, rabbinic supervision was particularly dominant at the time and aimed at enhancing communal cohesion (Kogman-Appel, 2012). On the other hand, Christian reports of murder libels claimed that Jews celebrated Passover to re-enact the crucifixion and thus used blood for the preparation of the unleavened dough. Occasionally such libels also included an element of scalding, either of the victim when still alive or the corpse. It is possible that the scalding of the dishes and the baking of the *matsot* were moved into the public sphere in an effort to counter such libels (Yuval, 2006, chaps 4 and 5).

Life Cycle Events in the Public Arena

Circumcision

The question posed in the introduction about the degree to which the illustrations under discussion reflect actual ritual performance takes on extra weight when we consider depictions of circumcisions. Hebrew manuscripts portray several images of biblical circumcisions but most of them are in no way indicative of the actual performance of the circumcision ritual in the Middle Ages. Rather, they serve various other functions: they tell biblical stories, such as the tale of Zipporah circumcising her son, a story of obedience to divine precepts, and one of the circumcision being likened to sacrifice and martyrdom, but they do not reveal anything about the authentic enactment of one of the central rituals in the Jewish life cycle.

However, an image in the Regensburg Pentateuch (Jerusalem, Israel Museum, MS 180/52) from c. 1300 that shows Isaac's circumcision stands out as an exception in that regard and was, indeed, interpreted as a projection of the biblical event onto medieval ritual practice (Figure 7.7; Baumgarten, 2004, 70–76; Frojmovic, 2005).

Whereas in the earlier Middle Ages, circumcisions were commonly performed in the private sphere of the family home (as became common again in the modern period), the Regensburg circumcision is set in the communal space of the synagogue. Even though the image is shown within one unifying frame, it actually depicts two stages of a narrative flow. To the right we see the entrance to the main hall of the synagogue and three women, two of them in particularly lavish costumes. One of them is carrying the child and bringing him into the prayer hall. The child is shown a second time in the center of the composition on the lap of his godfather (*ba'al brit*), who is seated on an elaborate chair, with the circumciser kneeling in front of him performing the circumcision. The image conveys a message of gender separation and female marginalization. From Ashkenazi texts, we know that until the late thirteenth century women acted as godmothers (*ba'alat brit*) and even as circumcisers, a custom that was sharply criticized by Meir ben Barukh of Rothenburg (d. 1293), who, in fact, managed to stop it within his

Visualizations in Medieval Book Culture

Figure 7.7 Binding of Isaac; Circumcision of Isaac
Source: Jerusalem, Israel Museum, MS 180/52, Pentateuch with Megillot ("Regensburg Pentateuch"), Regensburg, 1300, fol. 18v (with permission of the Israel Museum, Jerusalem)

sphere of influence. It is notable in this context that it was around the same time that women were consigned to a separate space in the synagogue. We do find the notion of godmother in later sources, but they do not refer to a woman who held the baby but, rather, to the wife of the godfather, whose function was to bring the child to the entrance of the main prayer hall, where only the men were assembled. That is the moment that is shown on the right-hand section of the Regensburg miniature.

The separation of genders that followed Meir ben Barukh's ruling is also observable in later renderings of the ritual. In an image of a circumcision in the Rothschild Miscellany (Israel Museum, MS 180/51), produced in late fifteenth-century Ferrara for a male patron of Ashkenazi origin, women are completely absent from the composition; the ritual is taking place in an area where only men are present (fol. 118v, discussed in Elhadad-Aroshas, 2014, 38–39).

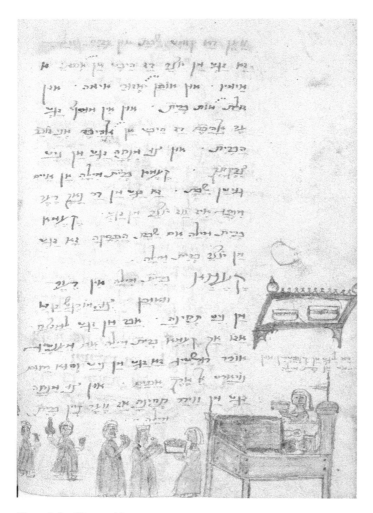

Figure 7.8 Circumcision
Source: Paris, Bibliothèque nationale de France, cod. hébr. 586, *Minhagim* Book in Yiddish, Northern Italy, 1503, fol. 115v (image in the public domain)

In contrast, in a *minhagim* (customs) book in Yiddish from the sixteenth century (more below) produced for a varied (both male and female) readership, we see another circumcision scene, one that focuses on the role of women before and after the ritual itself (Figure 7.8; Wolfthal, 2004, 72).

Initiation

The Leipzig Mahzor includes yet another illustration of a ritual. One of a kind, this depiction is of particular interest in that it shows a rite of passage – young boys at their transition from early childhood in the private sphere to schooling in the public arena (Figure 7.9).

Visualizations in Medieval Book Culture

Figure 7.9 Shavuot
Source: Leipzig, Universitätsbibliothek, MS Voller 1102/I, Mahzor, Worms, c. 1310, fol. 131r–132v (image in the public domain)

A double-page opening with marginal images illustrating the Shavuot festival shows the Giving of the Law on the right-hand page (which addresses the mythical background of the initiation ritual) faced on the left-hand page by a visualization of a customary initiation rite of young schoolboys in several Ashkenazi communities during the late Middle Ages. A teacher is seated to the left with a young boy on his lap; two other children are approaching him. A man, apparently a father, is carrying a fourth child wrapped in his mantle. To the far right, another man is walking toward a river with two more youngsters, who have cakes and eggs in their hands.

Ivan Marcus studied this ritual in depth several years ago from a historical-anthropological point of view, considering, on the one hand, issues of the acculturation of Ashkenazi Jews to Christian society and, on the other, anthropological concepts about rites of passage (Marcus,

Figure 7.9 Continued

1996). Descriptions of the introduction of young boys to Torah study have come down to us in several sources, the earliest record appearing in a section in the thirteenth-century *Sefer Haroqeah* by Eleazar ben Judah (d. c. 1232), the communal rabbi of Worms, the same community that produced the Leipzig Mahzor several decades later. The text reads that study begins "on Shavuot because that is when the Torah was given." It also notes that on the way to the teacher the boy should be covered "so that he will not see a Gentile or a dog on the day he is instructed in the holy letters." The child is given a tablet with letters inscribed and after he recites them with the help of the teacher, the tablet is covered with honey for the boy to lick. He is also given honey cakes and a boiled egg, both inscribed with biblical verses (*Sefer Haroqeah, Hilkhot Shavuot*, par. 296; Marcus 2001). In Marcus' interpretation, the custom ritualizes Ezekiel's metaphoric vision of eating God's sweet words of Torah (Ezek. 3:3). Another text, by a student of Eleazar, also describes how the children are taken to the riverbank, "according to the Torah's being compared to water" (*Sefer Ha'asufot*, fol. 67r).

These sources together with the image in the Leipzig Mahzor indicate that this custom developed in the Rhineland; somewhat later it was also mentioned in sources from northern and southern France. Marcus suggests that it appeared in reaction to French Tosafists promoting new types of learning that emphasized the study of Talmud and higher education. In terms of its function, this ritual was a classic rite of passage from early childhood to a stage of formal education, helping the child cope with the social change he is about to experience. But there is more to this illustration: it marks the boys' transition from the private sphere into the public arena, and from a realm that was primarily female into an environment that was predominantly male.

Marriage

Several marriage scenes are known from Hebrew book art. Many Ashkenazi mahzorim visualize the principal *piyyut* of the liturgy on the Great Shabbat with a marriage ceremony. The *piyyut* "Come with me from Lebanon, my bride" is based on the Song of Songs and allegorizes the biblical love poem as the love of God for his people. These images feature several elements of real-life marriage ceremonials (such as a *talit* spread over the couple, a predecessor of the later baldachin; a ring; and/or a goblet filled with wine), but they are not particularly realistic and the allegorical language governs the imagery.

An exception is seen in the depiction of a biblical marriage – Moses' wedding to Zipporah – in a pair of fifteenth-century Passover haggadot from Franconia, in the southern German lands (Jerusalem, Israel Museum, MS 180/50, Figure 7.10).

The couple is standing under a cloth and is shown at the moment that the groom gives his bride the ring. The couple is accompanied by a mature woman, a man who conducts the ceremony, and some merrymakers. Although we know from halakhic sources that it was customary to use a *talit* as a *huppah*, this portrayal reflects a local custom, as described by Moses Minz, who was active around the same time in various locations in Franconia. The most common male headgear in the German lands was the *gugel*, a hood of sorts with a long tail made of cloth, which was useful in various ways, for example, as protection in bad weather. In a description of a marriage ceremonial Minz noted that the groom was wearing a *gugel* and that its tail served as the *huppah* (Kogman-Appel, 1999, 91–95).

The Private Sphere

The late thirteenth century saw the emergence of a new book genre – the stand-alone Passover haggadah. Originally the haggadah, the liturgical text recited during the *seder* meal, which is a ceremony that takes place within the family and is, thus, enacted without the guidance of a ritual agent, was part of the general prayer book. The Passover festival commemorates the departure of the Children of Israel from Egypt, and the recitation is designed to transmit the liberation narrative from one generation to the next. The ceremony entails various kinds of foodstuff, all with symbolic meanings, and is, thus, relatively rich in performative acts. The independent haggadah, which might well have been developed as some sort of ritual guide, was generally abundantly illustrated. Marginal miniatures seem to have served as bookmarks to guide the one who conducts the *seder* through the various steps of the ceremony (Kogman-Appel, 2020).

Rituals of Cleaning before Passover

According to Exodus 13:3, no leaven is to be eaten or kept in one's home during the entire Passover week. This requirement entails certain preparatory activities: the house is to be cleaned and searched for leaven – remaining leaven has to be nullified and burned – and dishes have

Figure 7.10 Moses' Wedding
Source: Jerusalem, Israel Museum, MS 180/50, Haggadah ("Yahuda Haggadah"), Franconia, c. 1460–65, fol. 11v (with permission of the Israel Museum, Jerusalem)

to be made ritually clean for use during the Passover week, as described above. The cleaning of the house (Mishna, *Pesahim* 1:1–4) takes us into the private sphere. It can be observed that the basically simple acts of cleaning were gradually ritualized during the Middle Ages and various illustration programs, especially from Ashkenaz, seem to manifest this process. First of all, it is noteworthy that medieval haggadot introduced texts that explained how to prepare for the holiday, including instructions for the necessary cleaning. These texts were occasionally written in the square script used for the main liturgy, as if they were part of that text. In some haggadot, most often those of Italian origin, we find a lengthy tract describing the procedures in yet greater detail.

The cleaning of the house was first visualized in three fourteenth-century Iberian haggadah manuscripts, but their visual language did not emphasize the ritualization of the search as we find in the Ashkenazi haggadot. Several Iberian haggadot feature extensive biblical image cycles and the preparation scenes immediately follow these pictorials, which have a focus on Israelite history (see, e.g., the Golden Haggadah, London, British Library, Add. MS 27210, fol. 15r). These preparation scenes were designed to bridge the gap between past and present and create a direct link following a historiosophical concept often found in Iberian Jewish scholarship (Kogman-Appel, 2006). Their contribution to our understanding of the cleaning procedures as rituals is thus limited.

In Ashkenaz and northern Italy the context of cleaning scenes was different. The Bodmer Haggadah (Cologny, Fondation Martin Bodmer, cod. 81), copied around 1450 in northern Italy by Joel ben Simeon, a scribe and illustrator originally from the Rhineland, contains several pages of halakhic instructions (and not just the brief paragraph mentioned above). It is also the earliest extant Ashkenazi haggadah to include an image of the cleaning ritual (Figure 7.11).

A small drawing accompanying the instructions shows a young man near a cupboard holding a bowl and a feather with which to wipe its upper section. An adjacent banderole bears the inscription: "The Burning of Leaven." The inclusion of a lengthy text with halakhic instructions, all entitled *seder*, delineates them as a fixed order of acts accompanied by blessings. The addition of an image indicates that by 1450 this process of the ritualization of the preparatory acts, which began with the inclusion of the above-mentioned *piyyutim* in the liturgy of the Great Sabbath, had reached a high point. It is likely that the instructions were added at the patron's request, and they may very well have led to the introduction of an image, the first of its kind in an Ashkenazi haggadah.

The Passover haggadot from Franconia (c. 1460–65) mentioned above feature the most extensive cycle of illustrations related to the cleaning ritual. Composed as a set of unframed drawings, it spans the margins of two pages (Figures 7.12 and 7.13).

As in all the pictures in these books, the preparation scenes are accompanied by rhymed explanatory captions. The images depict these preparations action by action, while the captions point to the different halakhic precepts, recommendations, and restrictions. They go well beyond the mere genre of illustration and the viewer could follow them as a set of detailed visualized instructions (Kogman-Appel, 2019).

Seder Rituals

From the consumption of a publicly slaughtered sacrificial animal in the biblical context, in antiquity the Passover *seder* had evolved into a meal embracing various rituals that involve consuming foodstuffs that are designed to enhance the commemorative act. Thus, throughout that period the nature of both the ritual meal and the ritual act of narration changed. This process remained dynamic throughout the medieval years, as the ritualistic aspect of many actions was enhanced and new rites were added.

Given the limited scope of this chapter, in the following I focus on the visualization of one specific ritual, the recitation of the opening section of the haggadah: "This Bread of Distress" (*h'a lahm'a*). As the primary purpose of the haggadah is instruction, these ritual acts are designed to capture the interest of the children. The opening section tells of the distress of bondage and contrasts it with the notion of liberty. It presents the *matsah*, the focus of the recitation of this paragraph and the related actions, as a symbol of distress. The *seder* leader takes the middle *matsah* out of a pile of three imaged in a large bowl (in Ashkenazi communities) or a basket (in Iberia) and breaks it in two. One of the pieces (the *'afiqoman*) is put aside and kept for the end of the meal.

Figure 7.11 Search for Leaven
Source: Cologny, Fondation Martin Bodmer MS 81, Haggadah (Joel ben Simeon), Italy, c. 1450, fol. 1r (image in the public domain)

Illustrated haggadot figure this ritual in various ways. In a Catalan haggadah dated to c. 1325, this passage is adorned with a small image of a man raising half a *matsah* (London, British Library, MS Or. 2884, fol. 32v), but the figure is simply a marker to suggest the ritual and does not feature any performative act. In general, as I noted earlier, the visualization of rituals only plays a minor role in Iberian haggadot. An extensive cycle of ritual imagery is found in only

Figure 7.12 Clearing the House of Leaven
Source: Jerusalem, Israel Museum, MS 180/50, Haggadah ("Yahuda Haggadah"), Franconia, c. 1460–65, fol. 2v (with permission of the Israel Museum, Jerusalem)

one such manuscript (London, British Library, Add. MS 14761, Schonfield, 1992), which is datable to the 1340s and may have been produced in southern France (Kogman-Appel, 2016). The very first illustration in this book shows a large family gathered around a richly set table with a large basket covered with a napkin that hides its contents (Figure 7.14).

A few pages further on, the *seder* leader, who is imaged on the left, has the basket in front of him, which is now uncovered so that we can see the symbolic foods within it. He is about to break the *matsah*, while a younger man to the right is busying himself with wrapping the *'afiqoman* in a napkin (as if the bread has already been broken; Figure 7.16).

These two miniatures illustrate not the ritual itself, but the instructions that precede the liturgical text. Finally, during the recitation of "The Bread of Distress," the *seder* leader lifts

Figure 7.13 Search for Leaven
Source: Jerusalem, Israel Museum, MS 180/50, Haggadah ("Yahuda Haggadah"), Franconia, c. 1460–65, fol. 3r (with permission of the Israel Museum, Jerusalem)

the basket and places it on the head of one of the youngsters to encourage the children to ask questions (an act perhaps reminiscent of the practice of carrying loads on one's head). The basket's contents are again covered to enhance curiosity.

The earliest extant Ashkenazi illuminated haggadah manuscript – the Bird's Head Haggadah (Jerusalem, Israel Museum, MS 180/57) – includes an image of a small *seder* table with two men. One of them breaks the *matsah* and passes half of it to his friend for the *'afiqoman*, who puts it underneath the tablecloth. To the left we see another table with two men dipping the vegetables (Figure 7.17).

The bowl always seems to be uncovered, and we read nothing about raising it; it simply remains on the table. The fact that two separate tables are shown indicates that it was the artist's

Figure 7.14 *Seder* Table
Source: London, British Library, Add. MS 14761, Haggadah, Southern France (?), c. 1340–45, fol. 17v
(© The British Library Board)

or patron's intention to show as many ritual acts as possible and to visualize them at different stages.

Several new elements were introduced into the ceremony during the fifteenth century, all designed to keep the children awake and interested. A haggadah included in a miscellany from the 1420s, now in Hamburg (Staats- und Universitätsbibliothek, cod. heb. 37), instructs the *seder* leader to remove the vegetables and other foods from the bowl at some stage and to display them on the table. The bowl is raised so it can be seen by all and then passed to the other end of the table. A miniature incorporated in an initial panel shows the *seder* leader and his wife with their hands on the uncovered bowl in front of them, perhaps about to pass it to the other end of the table (Figure 7.18).

The other participants are pointing toward the couple, gesturing in a very expressive manner. We are apparently witnessing a new custom here, "invented" during those years, again, in order to enhance the teaching, and this image seems somehow to underscore the innovation.

Figure 7.15 *Seder* Table
Source: London, British Library, Add. MS 14761, Haggadah, Southern France (?), c. 1340–45, fol. 19v
(© The British Library Board)

The aforementioned Franconian haggadot are yet more explicit in their visual language. The opening section about the *matsah* features a large family around the table and the *seder* leader raising the napkin-covered bowl as he passes it to his wife (Figure 7.19).

We also find a small marginal drawing of a table with a man and three boys around it. The man is holding a large *matsah* and is apparently instructing the boys, whose expressive gestures indicate interest. The captions explain that the boys are about to receive the *'afiqoman* from their father. Many pages later, the meal is finished and the *'afiqoman* about to be eaten at that point is returned by one of the boys, who had hidden it (Figure 7.20).

The now popular custom of stealing the *'afiqoman* did not exist in the Middle Ages, and our images seem to offer the first evidence of that rite, which is not mentioned in the contemporaneous sources.

Figure 7.16 Seder Table
Source: London, British Library, Add. MS 14761, Haggadah, Southern France (?), c. 1340–45, fol. 20v
(© The British Library Board)

The opening passage is also illustrated in Italian prayerbooks, both haggadot and mahzorim. There is a particular focus in these manuscripts on the visual representation of the contents of the bowl or the basket (both kinds of holders were common in Italy). In most of the images, the bowl or basket is shown uncovered, while being raised. Whereas Ashkenazi patrons thought that removing the various ritual foods from the bowl would serve to awaken the children's interests, Italian patrons and artists focused on the bowl's particularly rich contents, which they showed in great detail (Figure 7.21).

In the fourteenth and fifteenth centuries, European Jews, especially in Ashkenaz and Italy, developed a whole range of customs to whet the children's curiosity and in that way ensure the successful fulfillment of the precept of teaching the young the story of the liberation. Several of the contemporaneous halakhic works are particularly concerned with a careful differentiation between law and custom, and the late medieval period saw the publication of several "Books of Customs," generally designed to offer concise guidelines regarding customary ritual actions.

Figure 7.17 Breaking of *Matsah* and Dipping of Vegetables
Source: Jerusalem, Israel Museum, MS 180/57 ("Bird's Head Haggadah"), Mainz (?), c. 1300, fol. 6v (with permission of the Israel Museum, Jerusalem)

Books of this genre often dealt with the different minor acts that accompany the ritual of *h'a lahm'a*. In contrast to their approach to the actual ritual law, the rabbinic authorities exhibited a great deal of flexibility in dealing with the customs, and as the goal was to keep the children awake and interested, these were dynamic and ever changing (Kogman-Appel, 2018).

Social Change on the Threshold to Early Modernity: An Illustrated Minhagim Book for the Middle Class

For the most part, Books of Customs addressed lay groups, and some were produced for the middle class, which began to emerge in the late Middle Ages. One such book, in Yiddish, now in Paris (Bibliothèque nationale de France, cod. hébr. 586), written for a member of the

Figure 7.18 Beginning of Haggadah Recitation: This Is the Bread of Distress
Source: Hamburg, Staats –und Universitätsbibliothek, cod. Heb. 37, Miscellany, Mainz (?), c. 1425, fol. 24r (with permission of the Staats -und Universitätsbibliothek, Hamburg)

Ashkenazi community in northern Italy, where Yiddish had been in use for some generations after its migration from the German lands (Raspe, 2018), was compiled around 1503. Richly illustrated, it describes Ashkenazi rites for the entire year in both the communal and the private spheres. It explains how to light candles before Shabbat, how to perform the *havdalah* service (a ceremony to "separate" Shabbat from the following weekday), numerous Passover customs, and various holiday and life cycle rituals.

Most likely the images were drawn by the manuscript's scribe, who apparently was not a professional artist. One of them shows the synagogue service during the New Year and the blowing of the *shofar*. Even though the scribe was unable to render a complex synagogue interior in perspective, he took great pains to convey a feeling of spatial extension crowded with people and a sense of communal worship (Figure 7.22).

The illustration covers a full opening, an arrangement that appears only rarely in this book. To the far right, we see an elevated, large, and richly decorated Torah shrine standing at the

Figure 7.19 Beginning of Haggadah Recitation: This Is the Bread of Distress
Source: Jerusalem, Israel Museum, MS 180/50 ("Yahuda Haggadah"), Franconia, c. 1460–65, fol. 6r (with permission of the Israel Museum, Jerusalem)

eastern wall of the building. The male members of the community, all wearing *talitot*, are seated in a row beneath the shrine and facing the interior. One of them holds a Torah scroll. Moving toward the left we discern a *bimah* (table for the reading of Torah scrolls) adorned with two lighted candles, and a man in front of it blowing the *shofar*. On the facing page we find the women, most of whom are holding prayer books (as the men do). The image captures the most important moment of the ritual and the halakhic requirement to hear the *shofar*.

Even though this book of customs focuses primarily on enactments in public, several images also depict the intimacy of the private home. Some of the Passover rituals discussed above are shown, their renderings being clearly reminiscent of earlier haggadah illustration: fetching water for the preparation of *matsot*, the cleaning ritual, a *seder* table, drinking a cup of wine, raising the *matsah* and the *maror*, and more.

Some of the images seem to address the role of women. This does not mean that the book was intended for women or that it was designed to imbue women with a special ritual role. It

Visualizations in Medieval Book Culture

Figure 7.20 Returning the 'afiqoman
Source: Jerusalem, Israel Museum, MS 180/50 ("Yahuda Haggadah"), Franconia, c. 1460–65, fol. 25v (with permission of the Israel Museum, Jerusalem)

Figure 7.21 Search for Leaven
Source: Cologny, Fondation Martin Bodmer MS 81, Haggadah (Joel ben Simeon), Italy, c. 1450, fol. 5r (image in the public domain)

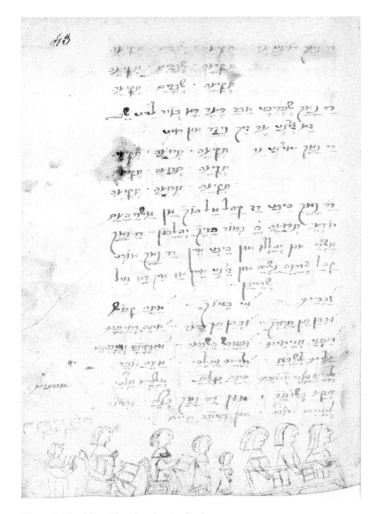

Figure 7.22 New Year Service in the Synagogue
Source: Paris, Bibliothèque nationale de France, cod. hébr. 586, *Minhagim* Book in Yiddish, Northern Italy, 1503, fol. 42v–43r (image in the public domain)

seemed rather to have been the patron's intention to confine women to their traditional roles (Wolfthal, 2004). One of the pages shows a woman kindling a star-shaped Shabbat lamp with a candle (fol. 7r). Although released from the fulfillment of time-bound commands, women are still obliged to observe three active precepts, the kindling of the Shabbat lights being one of them. Recent scholarship elaborates on this norm and has elucidated the various ways in which medieval Jewish women expressed their piety by observing a whole range of other precepts (Baumgarten, 2014) and the image of the women listening to the *shofar* being blown described above demonstrates their, albeit passive, involvement. In a way, then, this Yiddish book, naive as its style may be, seems to offer subtle and accurate images of ritual acts and reflect what actually took place in Ashkenazi societies in Italy during their transition to the early modern period.

Figure 7.22 Continued

Conclusion

Despite the reservations I noted in the introduction, the foregoing brief survey demonstrates that while engaging the necessary interpretive filters, we are still able to extract fruitful information about rituals, ritualization processes, and various elements of ritual performance from medieval illustrations. What rites were depicted in a particular context or at a particular time depended on various factors and often had to do with the topical issues of the day and ritual change. The image of the prayer leader in the Leipzig Mahzor was not designed simply to show a prayer leader but was intended to underscore the centrality of *piyyut* recitation, which was considered one of the cornerstones of Ashkenazi religious life. The depictions of the public scalding of dishes and/or the baking of unleavened bread document the transition of these actions into the public sphere as an outcome of efforts to counter Christian libels. The image of the circumcision of Isaac emphasizes rabbinic approaches to gender roles in the public space of the synagogue. Thus, in a way, these polemic and rabbinic discourses might have determined what rituals were actually visualized.

The case of the illustrated haggadah was somewhat different. The haggadah only began to emerge as an independent book in the thirteenth century, apparently as a by-product of social and cultural changes that affected the way the *seder* ceremony was conducted. The haggadah was not simply a liturgical text, but, rather, it developed into a ritual guidebook and as such was often illustrated. The many images would have helped the patron – often not a scholar – to conduct the *seder* ritual, which was (and still is) particularly rich in terms of performative acts.

Notes

1 An attempt to take medieval Jewish art at face value and to reconstruct "Jewish life in the Middle Ages," by Metzger and Metzger, 1982, was heavily criticized by several scholars for its methodology: see Horowitz, 1986; Kogman-Appel, 1999, 91–95; Frojmovic, 2005, 221; recently Sabar, 2018, chapter 6, who suggests looking at ritual images from the fourteenth-century with an "ethnographic eye" and to approach them as depicting reality.
2 In the modern usage, a *mahzor* is a festival prayer book, mostly for the high holidays of autumn. This was not true in the Middle Ages. Whereas the delineation of the medieval Ashkenazi *mahzor* is clearcut, i.e., a book limited to *piyyutim*, in other communities it was more flexible; Italian and Iberian manuscripts often include both statutory prayers and optional hymns and their denomination in catalogues or other publications is interchangeable.
3 The engraving documents the synagogue prior to its destruction in the same year that the city council, which numbered Altdorfer among its members, decided to expel the Jews and destroy the synagogue (Angerstorfer, 2012).
4 Ritually clean for Passover implies that the dishes are freed from any previous contact with leaven.

References

Primary Sources

Midrash Tehillim. 1891. Ed. Solomon Buber. Vilnius: Romm, 1891.
Tosefta Qifshuta. 1955-88. Ed. Saul Liebermann. New York: Jewish Theological Seminary Press.
Sefer Ha'asufot. Private collection of D. H. Feinberg. New York, formerly Jews' College, MS Montefiori 134.
Eleazar ben Judah. 1993. *Sefer Ma'ase Roqeah Hashalem*, ed. Hayyim Y. Waldman. Jerusalem: Makhon Torah mitsiyon.
Eleazar ben Judah. 2006. *Derashah Lepesah*, ed. Simha Emanuel. Jerusalem: Meqitse nirdamim.
Eleazar ben Judah. 1967. *Sefer Haroqeah*, ed. Barukh S. Shneurson. Jerusalem: 'Otsar haposqim.
Jacob ben Moshe Halevi Moelin. 1965. *Sefer Maharil*, ed. Shlomo Y. Spitzer. Jerusalem: Makhon Yerushalayim.

Secondary Literature

Angerstorfer, Andreas. 2012. "Die Rolle Altdorfers beim Judenpogrom 1519 und bei der Wallfahrt zur Schönen Maria," in *Albrecht Altdorfer. Kunst als zweite Natur*, eds. Christoph Wagner and Oliver Jehle. Regensburg: Schnell & Steiner, 161–70.
Barzen, Rainer. 2002. "Zur Siedlungsgeschichte der Juden im mittleren Rheingebiet bis zum Beginn des 16. Jahrhunderts," in *Geschichte der Juden im Mittelalter von der Nordsee bis zu den Südalpen – Kommentiertes Kartenwerk*, ed. Alfred Haverkamp. Hannover: Hahnsche Buchhandlung, vol. 1: *Kommentarband*, 7, 55–73.
Baumgarten, Elisheva. 2004. *Mothers and Children: Jewish Family Life in Medieval Europe*. Princeton, NJ: Princeton University Press.
———. 2014. *Practicing Piety in Medieval Ashkenaz: Men, Women, and Everyday Religious Observance*. Philadelphia, University of Pennsylvania Press.

Elhadad-Aroshas, Deborah. 2014. "Gazing through the Window: Depictions of Women in the *Rothschild Miscellany* manuscript [in Hebrew]," MA thesis, Beer Sheva, Ben-Gurion University of the Negev.

Fine, Steven. 1999. "Art and Liturgical Context of the Sepphoris Synagogue Mosaic," in *Galilee Through the Centuries. Confluence of Cultures*, ed. Eric M. Meyers. Winona Lake, IN: Eisenbrauns, 227–37.

———. 2005. "Liturgy and the Art of the Dura Europos Synagogue," in *Liturgy in the Life of the Synagogue: Studies in the History of Jewish Prayer*, eds. Ruth Langer and Steven Fine. Winona Lake: Eisenbrauns, 41–72.

Fishman, Talya. 2004. "Rhineland Pietist Approaches to Prayer and the Textualization of Rabbinic Culture in Medieval Northern Europe," *Jewish Studies Quarterly* 11: 313–31.

Fraade, Steven. 2009. "The Temple as Marker of Jewish Identity Before and After 70 CE: The Role of the Holy Vessels in Rabbinic Memory and Imagination," in *Jewish Identities in Antiquity: Studies in Memory of Menahem Stern*, eds. Lee I. Levine and Daniel R. Schwartz. Tübingen: Mohr Siebeck, 237–62.

Frojmovic, Eva. 2005. "Reframing Gender in Medieval Jewish Images of Circumcision," in *Framing the Family: Narrative and Representation in the Medieval and Early Modern Periods*, eds. Rosalynn Voaden and Diane Wolfthal. Temple: Arizona Center for Medieval and Renaissance Studies, 22–43.

Geula, Amos. 2007. "Lost Aggadic Midrashim Known Only from Ashkenazi Sources: Avkir, Asefa, and Deuteronomy Zutta [in Hebrew]," PhD dissertation. The Hebrew University, Jerusalem.

Goodenough, Erwin. 1953–1968. *Jewish Symbols in the Greco–Roman Period*. Vol. 10. New York: Patheon Books.

Grossman, Abraham. 1988. *The Early Sages of Ashkenaz* [in Hebrew]. Jerusalem: Magnes Press.

Horowitz, Elliott E. 1986. "The Way We Were: Jewish Life in the Middle Ages," *Jewish History* 1: 75–90.

Kogman-Appel, Katrin. 1999. *Die Zweite Nürnberger und die Jehuda Haggada: Jüdische Künstler zwischen Tradition und Fortschritt*. Frankfurt/Main-Berlin-New York-Paris-Wien: Peter Lang, Europäischer Verlag für Wissenschaft.

———. 2006. *Illuminated Haggadot from Medieval Spain: Biblical Imagery and the Passover Holiday*. University Park: Pennsylvania State University Press.

———. 2012. *A Mahzor from Worms: Art and Religion in a Medieval Jewish Community*. Cambridge, MA: Harvard University Press.

———. 2016. "Une Haggada de Pâques provenant du Midi de la France: Le programme des images dans le manuscrit de Londres MS Add. 14761," in *Culture religieuse méridionale: les manuscrits et leur contexte artistique – 51ᵉ Colloque de Fanjeaux*, ed. Alison Stones, Cahiers de Fanjeaux 51, 325–44.

———. 2018. "Books for Communal Liturgy and Domestic Worship: Structure, Function, and Illustration of the Mahzor and the Haggadah," in *Liturgische Bücher in der Kulturgeschichte Europas (Bibliothek und Wissenschaft, vol. 51)*, ed. Hanns-Peter Neuheuser. Wiesbaden: Harrassowitz Verlag, 101–37.

———. 2019. "Ritualizing the Cleaning of the House before Passover in Medieval Ashkenaz: Image and Text in Illuminated Haggadot," *Ritual Dynamics in Jewish and Christian Contexts*, eds. Benedikt Kranemann and Claudia D. Bergmann. Leiden and Boston, MA: Brill, 28–55.

———. 2020. "'And You Shall Tell Your Son on this Day': Visual Didactics in Medieval Illustrated Haggadot," in *Prodesse et delectare: Case Studies on Didactic Literature in the European Middle Ages / Fallstudien zur didaktischen Literatur des europäischen Mittelalters*, eds. Norbert Kössinger and Claudia Wittig (Beihefte Das Mittelalter. Perspektiven mediävistischer Forschung). Berlin: de Gruyter, 138–73.

Laderman, Shula. 1997. "A New Look at the Second Register of the West Wall in Dura Europos," *Cahier Archéologiques* 45: 5–18.

Marcus, Ivan G. 1996. *Rituals of Childhood: Jewish Acculturation in Medieval Europe*. New Haven, CT: Yale University Press.

———. 2001. "Honey Cakes and Torah: A Jewish Boy Learns His Letters," in *Judaism in Practice: From the Middle Ages through the Early Modern Period*, ed. Lawrence Fine. Princeton, NJ: Princeton University Press, 115–30.

Metzger, Mendel and Thérèse Metzger. 1982. *Jewish Life in the Middle Ages: Illuminated Hebrew Manuscripts of the Thirteenth to the Sixteenth Century*. New York: Alpine Fine Arts Collection.

Raspe, Lucia. 2018. "The Migration of German Jews into Italy and the Emergence of Local Rites of *Slihot* Recitation," in *The Jews of Europe around 1400. Disruption, Crisis, and Resilience*. eds. Lukas Clemens and Christoph Cluse. Wiesbaden: Harrassowitz Verlag, 173–94.

Revel-Neher, Elisabeth. 1984. *L'Arche d'Alliance dans l'art juif et chrétien du second au dixième siècles: Le signe de la rencontre*. Paris: Association des amis des études archéologiques byzantine-slaves et du christianisme oriental.

Sabar, Shalom. 2018. *The Sarajevo Haggadah – History and Art* (commentary volume attached to Mirsad Sijarić, ed., *The Sarajevo Haggadah*. Sarajevo: The National Museum of Bosnia and Herzegovina.

Schenk, Kära. 2010. "Temple, Community, and Sacred Narrative in the Dura-Europos Synagogue," *Association of Jewish Studies Review* 34/2: 195–229.

Schonfield, Jeremy, ed. 1992. *The Barcelona Haggadah. An Illuminated Passover Compendium from Fourteenth-Century Catalonia in Facsimile*. MS British Library Add. 14761. London: Facsimile Editions.

Shalev-Eyni, Sarit. 2010. *Jews Among Christians: Hebrew Book Illumination from Lake Constance*. Turnhout: Brepols and London: Harvey Miller.

———. 2018. "Aural-Visual and Performing Aspects of Illuminated Manuscripts for Liturgical and Ritual Use," in *Clothing Sacred Scriptures: Book Art and Book Religion in Christian, Islamic, and Jewish* Cultures, eds. David Ganz and Barbara Schellewald. Berlin: de Gruyter, 283–96.

Ta-Shma, Israel M. 1999. *Early Ashkenazi Custom* [in Hebrew]. Jerusalem: Magnes Press.

———. 2003. *The Early Ashkenazic Prayer: Literary and Historical Aspects* [in Hebrew]. Jerusalem: Magnes Press.

Weiss, Zeev. 2005. *The Sepphoris Synagogue: Deciphering an Ancient Message through Its Archaeological and Socio-Historical Contexts*. Jerusalem: Israel Exploration Society and Institute of Archaeology, The Hebrew University of Jerusalem.

Wolfthal, Diane. 2004. *Picturing Yiddish: Gender, Identity, and Memory in the Illustrated Yiddish Books of Renaissance Italy*. Leiden and Boston, MA: Brill.

Yuval, Israel Y. 2006. *Two Nations in Your Womb: Perceptions of Jews and Christians in Late Antiquity and the Middle Ages*, transl. Barbara Harshav and Jonathan Chipman. Berkeley: University of California Press.

8
MATERIAL CULTURE IN THE JEWISH MEDIEVAL WORLD OF ISLAM

Books, Clothing and Houses

Miriam Frenkel

The materiality of medieval Jewish life in the lands of Islam is mainly manifested in the documents preserved in the Cairo Geniza. The many letters, bills and lists preserved in the Geniza contain a plethora of information about the ordinary, everyday and even trivial objects that surrounded people's lives at this time. When read analytically, they may not only provide us with a nomenclature of objects but also illustrate the lived experience of contemporary people and even yield significant insights about the minds and beliefs of people in this civilization.

This chapter deals with three categories of material life: books, clothing and houses. All three categories bear witness to a long process of historical change. Paper books in the form of the codex generated a cultural and sociological revolution that enhanced literacy and created a reading society. Reading sharpened people's ability to differentiate and observe, which resulted in higher degrees of sensitivity and self-awareness and generated a new code of dressing, according to which people ought to conceal the natural contour of their bodies as much as possible. With their tremendously variegated fabrics and colors, textiles became the major industry of these times. But it was not only the human body that ought to be fully covered: the house too was mainly furnished by textiles: alongside carpets, cushions and draperies, almost every piece of furniture, jars, stools, wall niches, mattresses and large trays, were "dressed" by some kind of textile. Textiles of all kinds replaced the wood furniture of antiquity and totally changed the concept of furnishing a house. Books, clothing and houses were related to each other also in contemporary imagination, each serving as a metaphor for the other. Books were metaphorically conceived as edifices, with their chapters called *gates* (*bab*, pl. *abwab*) and indexes *keys* (*miftah*, pl. *mafatih*). The house was perceived as a dress: the main living room imagined as a wide robe with the small chambers its "sleeves" (*qumm*, pl. *aqmam*).

Books

Perhaps the most salient feature of material life in the Geniza society was the appearance of books and the dominant role they began to play in people's lives. During the long period from the late Second Temple time, in which the rich Jewish writings found in the Judean desert were composed, and until the 9th century, when the earliest surviving Jewish codices were written, no Hebrew book has survived. This lack of surviving Hebrew books in any form from Late Antiquity to the High Middle Ages can be attributed to their destruction by conquerors and persecutors. But one should also consider the possibility that until the Islamic period, Jewish tradition, the Talmudic and midrashic literature, was mainly transmitted orally. From the 9th century on, hundreds of Hebrew books originating from the lands of Islam have been found, many if not most of them in the Cairo Geniza.

The 300 years between the 10th and the 12th centuries, usually termed "the classical Genizah period," were actually the era of the book itself. Books spread in the world of Islam among Muslims, Christians and Jews alike, bringing about a profound cultural revolution. The first stirrings of this revolution began already in the 9th century. The prominent Muslim writer, al-Jaḥiẓ (d. 869), writing in the 9th century, could dedicate page upon page praising the excellence of certain books,[1] while in 10th-century Baghdad, the bibliographer Ibn al-Nadim (d. 965) could already cite thousands of titles.[2] But though this revolution had started already in the 9th century, it is from the 11th century onwards that the diffusion of the written word in the form of books caused a distinctive transformation of cultural practices in the Jewish world as well. It was a profound and widespread revolution. From the point of view of the volume of production and dissemination of books, as well as of their quality and variegation, it can be safely compared to the revolution of print. The full social and cultural meaning of this revolution is best attested by the Geniza, specifically by the 250,000 leaves with literary contents, which originally formed parts of books composed, produced and consumed by Jews in the lands of Islam during this period, and also by letters and other documents from the Geniza that expose the cultural and social implications of this revolution.

It is the physicality of the books and the ways they were produced, transmitted and consumed that testify to this tremendous change. As Malachi Beit Arie has pointed out, the sheer volume of books found in the Geniza not only reflects a large production of books, but being a trash bin, a depository of used books that have lost all value to their possessors, the Geniza also proves the intensive use made by books, their intensive consumption.[3] The revolution of the book involved a significant morphological change: the traditional form of a parchment or papyrus roll was gradually abandoned and replaced by a paper codex, which became the predominant book form. The codex replaced the old form of the roll (either the horizontal scroll or the vertical rotulus) in a gradual process that had far-reaching cultural, functional, material, historical, ideological and social implications. In the innovative form of the codex, a number of sheets are folded into quires and stitched together at the center to form a series of opening pages, easily carried, stored and used. The codex format has clear advantages over the scroll. It is more comfortable for reading, since it can be browsed, which makes it much easier to find in it a particular reference. Its leaves can be written on both sides, which is more economical than the one-sided scroll, and finally it can be better preserved by a compact binding.

This new, practical book form was not invented by the Muslims. It was first adopted and promoted either by the early Christians, for copying the Bible, or by the Byzantine jurists, who used it for recording their legal texts.[4] In any case, by the 4th century the codex and the roll were employed equally, and by the 6th century the roll was used only for documentary and liturgical purposes. But the Jews of the Roman and Byzantine empires did not participate in this progressive replacement of the roll format by the codex. They continued to use the scroll format for all their books, both sacred and profane. They did so much longer than their neighbors and indeed became associated with the scroll format. When the 9th-century Muslim writer ʿAbd al-Masīḥ ibn Isḥaq al Kindi (801–873, Iraq) tried to show that the very first Quran manuscripts were written on leaves or on rolls, he clarified: "rolls like those used by the Jews." In fact, the few preserved fragments of Hebrew texts dating from the late Byzantine and early Islamic periods are all remnants of horizontal scrolls.

The earliest evidence of Jews using the codex format date from after the Muslim conquest. It may then be safely assumed that the Jews adopted the codex from the Muslims. Indeed, the very term for 'codex' in medieval Hebrew is *mișḥaf*, an Arabic loanword. The appearance, or the reappearance, of the Jewish book brought about deep social consequences. The Jewish ruling elite adopted the new world of the book and turned it into its cultural epithet. The production of books, their distribution through copying, selling, buying, lending and pawning, as well as their consumption through learning and reading, became central activities for the elite members of the Jewish community.[5] News about books – written, copied, borrowed, sold, lost or captured – occupies a central place in the Geniza correspondence. Books were a central issue about which one commonly wrote to friends and partners, since they constituted a major role in life. The passion for books is reflected in the correspondence of 'Amram ben Isaac, who left in the Geniza numerous letters he wrote to Ḥalfōn ben Nethanel. Written in his last years when he was terminally ill, lonely and preoccupied with a very sick wife, he still keeps begging his addressee, in letter after letter, to send him some books to read:

> I have already asked you several times to send your poor, sick brother the exegesis on Isaiah so that he will be able to read it as long as he is still alive. I hereby beg you once again; please send it to me as soon as possible with whomever you find.[6]

On the other end of the age spectrum are the secret letters written by young Nathaniel ben Moses, who had been grounded by his father so that he might concentrate on his learning. Young Nathaniel, secretly and against his father's explicit orders, corresponded with some of his close friends. But strikingly enough, what occupies these young restless adolescents are books, which they exchange and read with great enthusiasm. Nathaniel even asks his friends to clandestinely smuggle some books into his home prison.[7]

The high cost of books and the intensive labor that their production required, made them a very sensitive product. Even their exchange required much credence and became a major way to express trust and intimacy. The most famous illustration of this are the words of Moses ibn Tibbon (d. 1283) in his introduction to the Hebrew translation of Maimonides' Book of Commandments:

> I asked one of the learned people (*maskilīm*) of our country who frequents Alexandria to look for it (for the original version of the Judeo Arabic book) over there and that if he could not find it, to write a letter on my behalf to the great Nagid, the son of the Rav, the composer (i.e., Abraham, Maimonides' son) and ask him to order one of the copyists of his country to copy it and send it to him. The Geat Nagid, being so kind and benevolent and in honor of our long lasting love and friendship, sent him his own personal book to copy.[8]

The lending of the private copy is, thus, perceived as a symbolic act of grace and love, which brings to mind the custom of *khil'ah*, which originated in the granting of the king's used robes as a sign of favor and friendship.

The elite members who were the main consumers of books, were also their producers. They used to copy books for themselves and for their friends, edit them, punctuate them, cut and straighten their paper, and finally also bind them with their own hands. The deep involvement of the elite in the field of books is illustrated by the profile of Solomon ben Elijah, the youngest son of judge Eliah ben Zachariah of 13th-century Fustat. Solomon earned his living by teaching young children, hence his title (*kunyah*): *ha-Melammed*, the teacher. He served as secondary judge in Cairo and was involved in a wide range of communal activities: he was a professional witness at the communal court, ran the communal slaughterhouse (quite a powerful position), fulfilled the function of trustee of the court, and for some time occupied the post of the cantor of Bilbais (in the Nile delta). In addition, he was a merchant of wine and cheese, two very sensitive products, which required high credibility and integrity because of the strict laws of "*kashrut*" applied to them. On top of all this, Solomon was very much involved in books. He sold and bought books independently and also served as a broker (*simsar*) in book transactions. Being known in the business, people used to deposit books in his hands hoping that he would succeed in selling them. Solomon also initiated the copying and producing of books in order to sell them. Thus, he actually acted as a kind of book-entrepreneur.

Solomon also acted as a pawnbroker, lending cash against books, which were pawned to him.[9] In addition, he dealt with writing materials and appliances: he bought and sold paper. In one very worried letter, Abu al-Majd of Alexandria asks him why the *mistarah* (a professional tool for marking lines on writing paper) that he had ordered, and for which he had already paid, had not yet been delivered. The production and the exchange of books became the cohesive glue of the elite. The shared occupation with books served as a central axis around which the links and affinities of its members were consolidated and served to strengthen the ties of friendship. The mutual exchange of books was interpreted as a symbolic gesture of love, intimacy and belonging to the same social milieu.

A clear illustration of the way in which dealing with books strengthened the ties of friendship is found in the correspondence between the same Nahray ben Nissim, who was a well-known public figure in Fustat, and Yeshuʻah ben Joseph, the leader of the community of Alexandria. Their correspondence touches on many communal issues, such as a ransom to be paid for Jewish captives and reciprocal help for the poor. They also both ran textile businesses – another factor strengthening their commercial relationship. But what makes their ties personal and binding is undoubtedly their shared intellectual and practical interest in books. Yeshuʻah invests Nahray with the task of supervising the manufacture of ten books in different formats, which he had ordered in Alexandria. Their correspondence also includes practical advice concerning their mutual interest. In one letter Nahray asks Yeshuʻah to send him reed pens made of reeds from lake Mariut (near Alexandria), and Yeshuʻah answers:

> As for the Maryūt reeds you have asked for, I have to warn you that at this time of the year they are still wet. They won't be cut before August at the time of vintage. I shall order them then and bring them and cut them for you into fine pens that will suit you best, and then I shall send them to you.[10]

The reed pens, then, both served these two intellectuals as their working tools but were also another – clearly related – subject for general discussion. In today's terms these two men could be university teachers discussing the pros and cons of some new software.

Gradually, the consumption of books descended to lower social classes too. Books are found in many property-lists of people of quite modest means. Judith Olszowy Schlanger found books in the form of improvised small sized rotuli, written on low-quality writing material and with no pricking or ruling of the sheets. Although Olszowy Schlanger assumes they were used by the intellectual elite for their personal devotion, study and work, they could also provide a cheap solution for the lower echelons to obtain a book.[11]

Books, then, were part of the large repertoire of inanimate things that surrounded people's lives and loaded them with meaning. As such, they had the ability to signify things for them, to establish social meanings on behalf of them, to carry personal and emotional meanings and to facilitate interpersonal interactions and group attachments.

Clothing

With books occupying such a central place in life, reading sharpened people's aptitude to differentiate and to observe. This resulted in an incredible sensitivity to colors and shades. This is how S. D. Goitein described what he called "the color intoxication" of the Geniza people:

> While men today are normally satisfied with various shade of gray, brown, blue, black and white, the medieval man, like tropical singing birds, liked in addition to these colors, green, red, and intense yellow, and, above all, intricate nuances with all kinds of "glitter", "gloss", iridescence, stripes, waves, and patterns. ... The Geniza people were by no means barbarians running riot with colors. The careful description with the exact hues desired ... betray taste.[12]

This new degree of sensitivity made people also more aware of others and more conscious of their own visibility in the eyes of others. To use Roland Barthes' terminology, it raised their threshold of embarrassment. It was not only religious commandments but also this new self-awareness that generated a new code of dressing, according to which the body is expected to be entirely covered by many layers of clothing. The dressed body turned into an expression of civilized humanity.

Clothing made the difference between animals and humans. The more a person was dressed, the more respectable he was. Nakedness, on the other hand, was a disgrace. A decent person's robe had to hide his entire body, and the robe itself had to be entirely covered by the outwear. In this way, the complete opposite of nakedness was obtained: the body's natural contours became totally invisible. This was the proper way civilized persons could show themselves respectfully in public. The Jews in the medieval lands of Islam shared this perception of clothing as signifiers of civility with their Muslim and Christian contemporaries. They too put much effort into ensuring that they were properly and well dressed. Here for instance is a letter written by a Jewish merchant from Fustat to his cousin in Alexandria:

> When the Sicilian boats arrive please buy me two narrow robes of excellent quality, costing about 2½ dinars, and two attractive robes worth about 1½ dinars, and bring them with you. And if you, my lord, depart before the arrival of the Sicilian boats, bring me two attractive robes, which have some elegance, and give 2½ dinars to Joseph for the purchase and forwarding of two robes, for I do not have anything to wear on weekdays.[13]

Concern for clothing was manifested in the desire to be well dressed even in death. Thus, for example, in a deathbed will found in the Cairo Geniza, a man wishes to have a "simple" burial:

> no wailing women, please: and of garments in which I shall be buried I wish to have no more than these: two cloaks, three robes, a washed turban of fine linen – it is already wound up – new underpants of mine, and a new waist band of mine.[14]

It was not only the perception of clothing that Jews shared with their Muslim contemporaries, but also the apparel itself. Although they were legally supposed to wear distinctive clothing, the Geniza documents show that Jews, male and female, high and low, shared with their Muslim contemporaries the same wardrobe. Except for infrequent times of crises, when the discriminatory clothing was imposed on them, Jews dressed like other people in their non-Jewish environment and could not be distinguished by their attire.

The most important part of the outfit was the head cover. It was an indispensable part of the wardrobe, worn by everybody – men, women and children. It was usually composed of long pieces of fabric wound around the head, sometimes embedded with precious stones and golden threads. Goitein calculated that the cost of the headgear of middle-class women and men in the 12th century was worth five times as much as their finest costumes.[15] The other parts of the attire were composed of numerous sheets of fabric of various sizes that were wrapped around the body, one layer upon the other. To these pieces of textile, very wide sleeves (*kumm*, pl. *akmam*) were attached by a decorated strip of material of a different color (*tiraz*). A long piece of material was inserted inside the sleeve (*mandil kumm*), in which coins and other small objects could be carried, thus fulfilling the function of pockets. The bulbous sleeves created an impression of the upper part of the body as a single unit, as if the arms and chest were one, thus further blurring the body's natural form.

Footwear received much attention, as manifested in the many orders for expensive and extravagant shoes preserved among the Geniza letters. On the other hand, shoes implied profanity and had to be taken off upon entering a synagogue. Male and female clothing did not differ much. Husband and wife could use the same outwear. As in the case of Sitt al-Dar, Nathan ben Samuel ha-Nezer's second wife, a rich and childless woman who bequeathed all her clothing to her husband, except a few dresses that she willed to her two slave girls. Standard clothing – such as: *thawb* (robe), *ḥulla* (gala costume), *malḥafa* (cloak), *jubba* (gown with sleeves), *jukanniyya* (short robe for daily use), *ghilala* (undershirt) – were common to both sexes and had the same form.[16]

Still, some garments were considered exclusively female. The *'Aqbiyya*, for example, which appears in trousseau lists of rich women, is a long robe covering the heels (*'aqb*), unlike the usual dress, which exposed the lower end of the pants. This long dress presented the woman wearing it as a noble lady, restricted in her movements, and thus exempted from any physical work. Clothing was expensive and could function as a means of payment. It was capital and it could guarantee its proprietor in time of need. When the Spanish Hebrew poet Judah ha-Levi (1075–1141) was about to set sail from Egypt to the Holy Land, he received a letter from a young relative announcing his intention to travel to Egypt. Ha-Levi sent him, through the mailman, a turban, which was supposed to be sold in order to finance the young man's intended travel.[17]

Since clothing was considered capital, dowries, which were meant to guarantee the wife's economic security, included mainly garments of all kinds. As such, clothes had to be durable, and their owners invested many efforts to protect them. They refrained from washing them too frequently in order to preserve their color and general form. Washed clothes (*ghasil*) lost much of their value. Nevertheless, washed garments do appear in trousseau lists and were even traded overseas. Just like books, clothes too were a way to express friendship. The habit of bestowing a personal used garment as a sign of friendship was rooted in the royal rite of *khil'a*. Caliphs and other Muslim rulers used to honor their subjects by adorning them with their own discarded dress, which became a robe of honor. The custom dripped down the social scale and was imitated by members of the Jewish elite merchant class. Giving one's personal dress to a friend was conceived as giving him the more sublime and civilized part of your own self. By giving a discarded dress to a friend, an intimate alliance was created between giver and receiver.

Dressing was also a major metaphor. Poetry itself was perceived as dressed up language, language clothed and decorated by tropes and metaphors. The dress was the additional layer that exalted the carnal body and made it human, just as tropes and poetic devices turned prosaic writing into elevated poetry.

The House

Not only human bodies were dressed, but houses as well. The objects furnishing the interior of a house were all "dressed" by many kinds of textiles, while the house's various quarters were imagined as dressing garments. The basic form of urban dwelling documented in the Geniza was the *dar*, a multi-unit building, which normally contained several apartments, but could also contain only one living area. Most *dar*s belonged to several owners, who were not necessarily kin, nor even coreligionists. Jews, Muslims and Christians habitually shared possession of one and the same *dar*. A *dar* would frequently change its internal division, as attested by many property transactions from the Geniza. It could be divided into smaller units, or extended by joining several units together. This points at the elusiveness of houses, which could frequently change their shapes, their dimensions and their destinies.

The following biography of a house in Alexandria illustrates the versatility of these houses. When the celebrated Spanish philosopher and poet Judah ha-Levi approached his 50s, he decided to abandon what seemed to him his previous hedonistic and bohemian way of life. As part of his repentance, he chose to perform the pilgrimage to the Holy Land. Around 1140 he embarked upon a long journey across the Mediterranean from Spain to Palestine. When his ship arrived at the port of Alexandria in Egypt for an interim stopover, he was received by the local Jewish community with great enthusiasm. The warm hospitality he encountered in Alexandria and Cairo convinced him to remain in Egypt for the year before continuing his pilgrimage to the Holy Land. In this way, many of his letters and other writings of this year reached the Cairo Geniza, where they were preserved until discovered by Goitein in the 1970s.[18] Judah ha-Levi's main host while in Alexandria was R. Aaron ibn al-ʿAmmāni, a rich court physician, a local judge (*dayyan*) and one of the prominent leaders of the Jewish community. Judah ha-Levi thanked him for his very generous hospitality by composing several poems in his praise. In these poems, as well as in some prose letters, ha-Levi admitted that the lavishness of Ibn al-ʿAmmāni's house tempted him to postpone the pilgrimage and to extend his stay in these luxurious surroundings. In the laudatory poems ha-Levi wrote in honor of his host, he described the extravagance he indulged in as a guest of Aaron. His luxurious house with its beautiful garden and the fountain in its midst received in these poems special attention and were depicted in minute detail.

> The most fragrant oils and balsam / the choicest spices and delicacies / a sculpted garden with a fountain in its midst / in a gentle valley and by a flowing brook / a mosaic floor in an enchanted glade / tiled in gold / the waters of the vale empty upwards / above a canopy of myrtle / And birds and doves / companions and lovers / And roses and spices old and new / The soul shall indulge in all delicacy / on beautiful dishes and from overflowing jugs.

And also:

> I came to twelve springs / in Noa Amon[=Alexandria], and to seventy date palms / to a house of delicacy, of cinnamon and spice / and to an orchard of henna and nard.[19]

And more prosaically, in a letter to R. Samuel ha-Nagid, head of the Jewish communities of Egypt:

> He met me with grace, and delicate generosity/ with gifts and a house of repose, a sanctuary with a spacious alcove / a tabernacle and a domicile, a table and a candelabra, I indulged in the comforts he afforded me / I was surrounded by his exquisite foods. Low beds, and strewn pillows, let us dine on delicacies, and become intoxicated in his pleasures.[20]

We see, then, how Ibn al-'Ammāni's house acted as an agent that triggered ha-Levi's emotions and influenced his decisions and actions.

Magnificent houses were a popular theme in contemporary Arabic poetry. The stately mansions owned by the upper echelons of Cairo and Alexandria, with their enormous sizes and splendid gardens inspired works by contemporary Muslim poets and writers. Ibn Qalaqis, for example, an Alexandrian Muslim poet of the Fatimid era, wrote a laudatory poem about the palace of Bani Khulaif, an enormously wealthy family of qadis,[21] and the magnificent palace by the sea owned by the Alexandrian Qadi Abu al-Makram ibn al-Habbab (1201) was commemorated in several contemporary Muslim chronicles.[22] One might then suspect that the descriptions of the splendid house in ha-Levi's poems are but conventional literary formulae. But since the detailed verses describing the pomp and splendor of his host's house are unique to Ibn al-'Ammāni's house, and are not used in other laudatory poems dedicated to other people who accommodated him during his stay in Egypt, we may assume that they accurately reflect an actual mansion.

Moreover, we have the opportunity to follow the biography of Ibn al-'Ammāni's house, as this very house is described in a later, very different historical source. In a halakhic query presented to Maimonides in 1195, over 50 years later, Maimonides was asked about the validity of a leasing bill of a house in Alexandria known as the house (*dar*) of R. Aaron ibn al-'Ammāni, or the Judge's house (*dar al-dayyan*). The huge mansion was now divided between several heirs and parts of it were rented. There was a dispute between the heirs concerning their relative shares in the house, and it was decided that an evaluation of the income received from the lease of the various sections of the house would be carried out. The assessment provided describes a five-story mansion: a ground floor [*sufl*] with the women's quarters [*ḥurumiyya*] and another large room; above were another three floors of living quarters and a top floor [*'alw*] with a hidden door [*bab al-sirr*] and a kitchen [*maṭbaḥ*].[23] Unfortunately, the document is torn and we have only a partial description of the house, but even this incomplete description indicates the stately dimensions of this residence.

This functional and informative description differs significantly from the poetically emotional depiction of the same house in Judah ha-Levi's poems. The two descriptions represent two very different ways to conceive of houses. We see how perceptions of houses, in different situations and over time, may change. They can turn from a powerful emotional agent, closely connected, almost identified with, a person, into a commodity that can be split, divided and assessed through its economic value. In both cases, the house acts as a powerful agent that triggers humans' actions and emotions.

The informative description in the responsum reflects the modularity of Geniza houses and suits well the general outline of typical houses of middle- to high-class dwellers, as is known from other Geniza documents. Such a house, as described by Goitein on the basis of Geniza documents,[24] would have at least two floors: a ground floor [*sufl*] and a top floor [*'alw*]. The entrance was normally an arched gateway with two door leaves. Above the doorway, extending out of the wall there was a bay window, a kind of alcove allowing the inhabitants to observe what is going on in the street. It was usually called *Rawshan* or *Gezoztra*. Beside this window balcony, a house had regular windows also made of glass. A curved vestibule (*Dihliz*) led into the inner parts of the house. It had to be curved in order to prevent a visitor seeing into the interior. On its two sides were built benches of stone (*mastaba*), on which big water jars were situated. In Fustat, the water was brought from the Nile by water carriers who would dispose of their load at the doorway. From the corridor one entered the ground floor, which included the courtyard and the living room (*majlis*). The women's quarters (*ḥurumiyya*), mentioned in the responsum is exceptional and can be found only in Alexandrian houses. The courtyard was open to the sky and sometimes contained a garden.

The *majlis*, literally "sitting room," was the one very large social room (or "living room") where the social life of the family took place. This central reception hall together with the central courtyard connected the various parts of the house. The spacious *majlis* was imagined as a large robe, and the two adjacent small rooms it normally had on its two sides were accordingly called "sleeves" (*aqmam*). Just as the untailored sheets of textiles of various sizes and shapes bound together by a central belt could make an elegant and civilized dress, so was the spacious, seemingly unconstructed house connected by the *majlis*.

A wooden door separated the corridor from the *majlis*. It was usually of carved wood, a craft for which the Fatimid artists were known as specialists. Carvings adorned the ceilings and doors of palaces and mosques, as well as of residential houses, and synagogues. The *majlis'* walls were decorated with textile wall hangings. A *majlis* would contain a wind catcher (*malqaf; bahdhanj*). This device was intended to carry fresh air from the roof above into the inner parts of a house. It must have been large, since people used to sleep in it to enjoy the cool night breeze. Other cooling devices were the *fisqiyya* and the *shadhirwan*. The *fisqiyya* was a basin with a fountain situated in the *majlis*, and sometimes in the courtyard. The *shadhirwan*, was an inclined slab, over which water flowed into a basin.

The *majlis* was lighted by many devices, mainly by candlewax situated in candle holders or candelions, some of which, as found in archeological excavations, are works of real metal art. The *'alwu*, or upper floor was intended for habitation. It contained the wash room and the kitchen [*maṭbaḥ*]. The upper floor consisted, as a rule, of different levels. This was intentional and planned in advance and not a result of haphazard building during several periods. It was meant to enable the division of the space into smaller units and to secure the privacy of the inhabitants. Some typical components, which are not mentioned in the responsum are: the *mashraqa*, a terrace on an upper, east-facing floor where the wheat was kept to protect it from dampness; the *mafrash*, a place to hang laundry; and the *maṭmura*, which functioned as a kind of treasure room and could have contained books, papers, coins and other valuables.

Roofs were flat. Domed roofs were constructed only above public buildings, including synagogues. The typical house was void of furniture in the western sense of the word. Instead of chairs and armchairs it had built-in sofas or benches placed along the walls and instead of cupboards and armoires it had recesses in the walls. This furnishing conception made the house spacious and adaptable. Unlike the tightly constructed western domicile, the typical Geniza house was dynamic and modular. This is how it was portrayed by Goitein:

> Despite the rich architectural nomenclature of the Geniza and contemporary Muslim documents we would look there in vain for such terms as dining room, or bedroom. In winter one slept in a small closet, which could easily be warmed by a brazier; in summer one sought relief from the heat in the spacious living room with its ventilation shaft, which brought the cool north wind from the roof into the interior of the

various floors. The meals were taken where it was appropriate in accordance with the circumstances. There were no fixed tables surrounded by chairs; food was brought in from the kitchen on trays and put on movable low stools. Thus, whether resting or being with other people one could enjoy either roominess or intimacy. But the emphasis was on space.[25]

This spacious house, void of tables, chairs and cupboards, was apt to accommodate textiles of all kinds.

Textiles actually furnished the whole house. They served as divisions between rooms, were hung on the walls for decoration, spread on the floor as carpets, served in the form of cushions instead of chairs and in the form of mattresses instead of couches. This displays a totally new architectural perception, significantly different from the ancient Egyptian, Israelite, Greek or Roman architecture. It is closely related to the great development of textiles with their precious fabrics and spectacular colors, which served not only for clothing, but also for seating, bedding, carpets and hangings.

Conclusion

The material culture of the Geniza society is marked by the introduction of new abilities to discern and to differentiate. These are fundamental abilities for a reading society, in which books and reading occupy a central place. These propensities went hand in hand with self-awareness toward one's body and with particular conceptions about the way it should be presented in public. The prevailing dress code dictated many layers of fabrics, which totally concealed the outline of the human body. Textiles was the main industry of the time and produced a plethora of variegated fabrics that served not only for dressing but also for furnishing the houses, which were accordingly spacious and modular. Jewish medieval society in the lands of Islam was, in many ways, a society of books and textiles.

Notes

1 James E. Montgomery, *Al Jahiz in Praise of Books*, Edinburgh 2013, pp. 3–9. Montgomery called it "The Knowledge Revolution."
2 Devin Stewart, "The Structure of the Fihrist: Ibn al-Nadim as Historian of Islamic Legal and Theological Schools," *International Journal of Middle East Studies*, 39/3 (August, 2007). The bibliography itself: Ibn al-Nadīm, *al-Fihrist*, ed. I. Ramaḍān, Beirut: Dār al-maʿrifa, 1994.
3 Malachi Beit-Arié, "The Cairo Geniza's Contribution to Hebrew Paleography," *Peʿamim* 41 (1989): 32–40 [Hebrew].
4 Robert Resnick and others argue that the change was made by the early Christians for ideological reasons, as a way to manifest their self-identity. C. C. McCowan argued that the early Christians were motivated by practical reasons, aiming to get their "New Covenant" into a cheap and convenient form for constant use. Serena Ammirati maintains that the first to use the codex were the Byzantine jurists, as it proved to be the ideal format for a corpus of founding texts that accumulated over time and shaped into a normative system – such were the Byzantine imperial constitutions that began to be formalized from the 3rd century until Justinian's initiatives.
5 Miriam Frenkel, *"The Compassionate and Benevolent": Jewish Ruling Elites in the Medieval Islamicate World. Alexandria as a Case Study*, Berlin: De Gruyter, 2020.
6 TS 13 J 19.23, Frenkel, *The Compassionate*, no. 70, pp. 216–217.
7 S. D. Goitein, *A Mediterranean Society: The Jewish Communities of the Arab World as Portrayed in the Documents of the Cairo Geniza*, vols. I–V, Berkeley and Los Angeles, 1967–1988, vol. 5, pp. 426–432.
8 Moses Maimonides, *Book of Commandments*, ed. C. Heller, Jerusalem, 1946, introduction, p. 19.

9 TS 13 J 22.9, published in: Aryeh L. Motzkin, *The Arabic Correspondence of Judge Elijah and His Family (Papers from the Cairo Geniza): A Chapter in the Social History of 13th Century Egypt*, 1–2, Ph.D. dissertation (University of Pennsylvania, 1965), vol. 2, p. 145.
10 Bodl. MS Heb. C13.20, published in: Moshe Gil, *In The Kingdom of Ishmael; Studies in Jewish History in Islamic Lands in the Early Middle Ages*, Tel Aviv and Jerusalem, 1997 [Hebrew], vol. 4, no. 673; Miriam Frenkel, *"The Compassionate and Benevolent": The Leading Elite in the Jewish Community of Alexandria in the Middle Ages*, Jerusalem, 2006 [Hebrew], p. 217.
11 Olszowy Schlanger, "Cheap books in medieval Egypt; rotuli from the Cairo Geniza," *Intellectual History of the Islamicate World* 4 (2016), 82–101.
12 Goitein, vol. I, p. 106.
13 TS 13 J 18.8.
14 TS NS J 284 ll.2–4. Translated by Goitein, *Mediterranean*, vol. IV, p. 160.
15 Ibid., p. 158.
16 Ibid., pp. 153–155.
17 Moshe Gil and Ezra Fleischer, *Yehuda Ha-Levi and his Circle; 55 Geniza Documents*, Jerusalem 2001, pp. 245–250.
18 The research on Judah ha-Levi's biography is summed up in Gil and Fleischer's book.
19 Samuel b. Judah ha-Levi, *Diwan des abu-l-Hasan Jehuda ha-Levi*, 4 vols, ed. Ḥayyim Brody, Berlin: Mekize Nirdamim, 1894–1930, vol. II, p. 258.
20 Ibid., vol. I, p. 212.
21 al-Maqqarī, Aḥmad ibn Muḥammad, *Nafḥ al-ṭīb fī ghuṣn al-Andalus al-raṭīb*, Cairo: Maṭbaʿat al-Bābī al-Ḥalabī, 1949, vol. IV, p. 24; Sālim, ʿAbd al-ʿAzīz. *Tārīkh al-Iskandariyya wa-ḥaḍāratihā fī al-ʿaṣr al-Islāmī*, Alexandria: Dār al-Maʿārif, 1982, p. 215.
22 al-Maqrīzī, Taqī al-Dīn, *Ittiʿāẓ al-ḥunafāʾ bi-akhbār al-āʾimma al-fāṭimiyyīn al-khulafāʾ*, Cairo: al-Majlis al-Aʿlā lil-shuʾūn al-islāmiyya, 1967, vol. II, p. 381, vol. III, p. 91.
23 Moses Maimonides, *Responsa*, ed. J. Blau, Jerusalem: Reuven Mass, 2014, vol. 1, no. 2, pp. 2–3.
24 S. D. Goitein, *A Mediterranean Society; The Jewish Communities of the Arab World as Portrayed in the Documents of the Cairo Geniza*, vol. IV, Berkeley, Los Angeles, and London: University of California Press, 1983, pp. 47–149.
25 Goitein, MS, vol. IV, p. 48.

References

Beit-Arié, Malachi. 1989. "The Cairo Geniza's Contribution to Hebrew Paleography," *Peʿamim* 41: 32–40 [Hebrew].
Frenkel, Miriam. 2020. *"The Compassionate and Benevolent": Jewish Ruling Elites in the Medieval Islamicate World. Alexandria as a Case Study.* Berlin: De Gruyter.
Gil, Moshe. 1997. *In the Kingdom of Ishmael: Studies in Jewish History in Islamic Lands in the Early Middle Ages.* Tel Aviv and Jerusalem: Tel Aviv University and The Bialik Institute. [Hebrew].
Gil, Moshe and Ezra Fleischer. 2001. *Yehuda Ha-Levi and his Circle; 55 Geniza Documents.* Jerusalem: World Union of Jewish Studies.
Goitein, S. D. 1967–88. *A Mediterranean Society: The Jewish Communities of the Arab World as Portrayed in the Documents of the Cairo Geniza*, vols I–V. Berkeley and Los Angeles: University of California Press.
ha-Levi, Samuel b. Judah. 1894–1930. *Diwan des abu-l-Hasan Jehuda ha-Levi*, 4 vols, ed. Ḥayyim Brody. Berlin: Mekize Nirdamim.
Ibn al-Nadim. 1994. *al-Fihrist*, ed. I. Ramaḍan. Beirut: Dar al-maʿrifa.
Maimonides, Moses. 1946. *Book of Commandments*, ed. Chaim Heller. Jerusalem and New York: Mosad Ha-Rav Kook.
Maimonides, Moses. 2014. *Responsa*, ed. Joshua Blau. Jerusalem: Reuven Mass.
al-Maqqari, Aḥmad ibn Muḥammad. 1949. *Nafḥ al-ṭīb fī ghuṣn al-Andalus al-raṭīb*. Cairo: Maṭbaʿat al-Babi al-Ḥalabi.
al-Maqrizi, Taqi al-Din. 1967. *Ittiʿāẓ al-ḥunafāʾ bi-akhbār al-aʾimma al-fāṭimiyyīn al-khulafāʾ*. Cairo: al-Majlis al-Aʿla lil-shuʾun al-islamiyya.
Montgomery, James E. 2013. *Al Jahiz in Praise of Books*. Edinburgh: Edinburgh University Press, 3–9.

Motzkin, Arie L. 1965. *The Arabic Correspondence of Judge Elijah and His Family (Papers from the Cairo Geniza): A Chapter in the Social History of 13th Century Egypt*, 1–2. Ph.D. dissertation, University of Pennsylvania.

Olszowy, Schlanger. 2016. "Cheap Books in Medieval Egypt: Rotuli from the Cairo Geniza," *Intellectual History of the Islamicate World* 4: 82–101.

Sālim, ʿAbd al-ʿAzīz. 1982. *Tarikh al-Iskandariyya wa-ḥaḍaratiha fi al-ʿaṣr al-Islami*. Alexandria: Dar al-Maʿarif.

Stewart, Devin. 2007. "The Structure of the Fihrist: Ibn al-Nadim as Historian of Islamic Legal and Theological Schools," *International Journal of Middle East Studies* 39/3 (Aug): 369–387.

9
THE RITUAL TURN IN THE EARLY MODERN PERIOD

Roni Weinstein

In the year 1533 the eminent Talmudic scholar R. Joseph Karo (1488–1575) and the Kabbalist Solomon/Shelomo Alkabetz (1505–1584) convened with their mystical confraternity at Salonica during the eve of Pentecost (*Shavuot* in Hebrew) to recite verses from the Jewish Canon, especially the 'Book of Splendor' (*Sefer HaZohar* in Hebrew).[1] This somewhat esoteric event is paradigmatic to what I term 'The Ritual Turn' of Jewish culture during the sixteenth and seventeenth centuries. It was initiated and inspired by dominant persons, such as Karo and Alkabetz, heading a new religious institution – a mystical confraternity (*Havurah* in Hebrew). Both of them represent the rise of new heroes in the Jewish cultural arena, and their deep imprint on Jewish religiosity. Not by coincidence, it brought to the forefront the encounter between Law and Legality – the Jewish *Halakhah* – and active mysticism of Jewish Kabbalah. Within the rich repertoire of Jewish mysticism, a new corpus of writings was becoming ever more dominant, which is *Sefer HaZohar*, at the expense of previous medieval currents. The divine Zoharic spheres were the destination in this event, especially the last one, the feminine divine presence – the *Shechinah* – speaking through the mouth of R. Karo. The messages were put into writing, and served the members of this elite confraternity, but it pointed at a new current of addressing wider circles within the Jewish public and the intention to disseminate the Kabbalistic lore. 'Classical' components of Jewish heritage – such as the feast of *Shavuot* – were put to new use, and charged with new meanings. The time and place are no less significant; the persons participating in this event and in its later ramifications lived in the Mediterranean basin under the rule of Ottoman civilization and Muslim tradition. The end-result was the invention of a new ritual pattern – the Pentecost Emendation (*Tikkun Leil Shavuto* in Hebrew) – becoming an exciting component of Pentecost celebration and current until the present day in Jewish tradition. The early modern period witnessed a fermentation of ritualistic life within the Jewish context in various domains, charging old ritualistic patterns with new energy, and a shift of their role in religious life.

Two parameters accompanied Jewish religious culture and life, and seem fundamental though not related to specific content, positions, or to theological perspective. They endow Jewish traditions with a large degree of internal freedom in matters of beliefs. The first one is the centrality of texts and textuality, as a kind of encounter zone between various generations.[2] Any innovation or a turn in religious patterns needed a justification by reference to and re-reading of

DOI: 10.4324/9781003032823-11

the classical textual canon. The second parameter is the fundamental role of religious practice, rather than a statement of religious beliefs or definition of a religious credo. Appertaining to the Jewish collective – until the secularization process from late eighteenth century – implied some kind of adherence to patterns of Jewish life and rituals, rather than any other component. Both these elements point to the role of the rabbinic elite as the bearer and embodiment of Jewish culture, in shaping Jewish praxis (*Mitzvot* or *Kium Mitzvot* in Hebrew) and providing them with institutional and cultural legitimacy.

Due to their eminent role in shaping the identity of the Jewish collective, religious rituals reflect well the constancy and turns in Jewish cultural religious.[3] They further expose the variations and differences between Jewish diasporas under Islam or Catholic (and later Protestant) Europe, the shared elements next to deep variations, the economic and material aspects of religious tradition, the interstice between orality and written culture, the authority (or lack) of the cultural elite in relation to popular patterns not necessarily derived from Halakhic or post-Talmudic discussions, or crisis in the ritualistic domain (as in Sabbatian movement, or later in West European Enlightenment).

Ritual changes were part of religious dynamics along the centuries, yet in most cases the changes were unnoticeable and accumulative and did not effect a sense of sharp turn or a crisis. They were progressively absorbed into the ritual repertoire, and shortly after considered as flesh and blood of habitual tradition. This process is testified by anthropological works, as common among oral societies, tending to present various aspects of the common heritage as leaning on past tradition, including new elements.

The accumulative process entered a new phase in the early modern period, roughly from the sixteen until the mid-seventeenth century, in the city of Safed. From the early sixteenth century, Safed turned into a hub of Jewish life in the Holy Land, due to immigration waves and economic prosperity under the Ottomans.[4] It harbored the most important and influential scholars of Jewish tradition in its various domains: Halakhah, Kabbalah, Ethical Literature (*Sifrut Musar* in Hebrew), Biblical Exegesis, Pietistic Practice, and Liturgy. It included some of the leading intellectuals and mystics, such as R. Jacob Beirav, Joseph Karo, Isaac Luria known as *HaAri*, Chayim Vital, and Moses Cordovero. Some of them expressed implicitly their sense and commitment to reform and renovate major aspects of Jewish tradition and life. Contrary to Jewish rabbinic ethos – to be found in other Mediterranean traditions – of 'Decline of Generations' (*Yeridat HaDorot* in Hebrew), and the inferiority of contemporary scholars in regard to past figures, some of them considered themselves as better than all previous generations, including eponymous figures such as Moses or past scholars of the Mishnah and Talmud periods. This self-constructed image empowered them, indeed even constrained them, to reconsider all the fundamental elements of Jewish heritage and charge them with new meaning or even expand the borders of ancient lore. The ritual domain was certainly one of objects of reconsideration and re-structuring.

One of the major changes initiated especially in early modern Safed was the Kabbalistic shift from esotericism and secrecy toward a policy of disseminating some elements of Kabbalah in public. Along the late antiquity and later, in the Middle Ages, Jewish mysticism was maintained in utter secrecy, among tight circles of master and his few disciples, and mostly passed down orally. The main channels of disseminating Jewish tradition to the public at large – ethical literature, Halakhic-legal rulings, Torah hermeneutic, and liturgical modes – were hardly colored by any Kabbalistic-mystical content. This shift toward publicity, then, was a radical turn in Jewish tradition. It connected directly to the religious Renaissance taking place in contemporary Safed, and the missionary zeal of its sages. Jewish communities all along the Mediterranean basin, and even beyond, as a second wave in Western, East and Central Europe, were inspired by the writings and standards set by Safed scholars.

Was it by coincidence that the Ritual Turn took place in the Ottoman context and within the Muslim-Sunni tradition? The Islamicate world offered a welcoming ground as both Jewish and Muslim traditions shared important and fundamental elements; both read the Sacred Canon (Bible, Qur'an) in its original language (Hebrew, Arabic). Language itself was considered sacred and delivered by God or his messengers, either prophets or archangels. These texts set the basis for further elaboration and hermeneutics to expand the domain of religious normative life. It culminated in the mystical level, considered as relevant in all aspects of religious tradition, including the ritual practices. In both traditions, legal discourse and its specialists (rabbis, *ulama*) were considered as essential continuation of divine revelation, and initiated a long tradition of legal scholarship, extended along various legal schools. Relevant to this chapter is the importance of religious practice as an axial component in shaping the identity of the religious community, and the individual commitment of each believer to God.

Relating to the early modern period, it is not Islam or Islamicate civilization in general that needs to be taken into consideration but, more concretely, the Ottoman Empire. Along the fifteenth and sixteenth centuries it expanded into immense territories, stretching from north Africa, the Balkans, Anatolia, the Arab lands – including the two holy cities – and further east close to India. A major civilization was established, encompassing cultural elements from Turkish origins, Sunni Islam, Balkan Christian traditions, and Persian culture. No less important is the direct and later mediated presence of Ottoman politics and culture in Eastern Europe, following military conquests over major parts of contemporary Ukraine and Poland, through local Muslim communities, intensive trade, and the Tatar Khanate in the Crimea.[5] In short, the Ottoman Empire was the focal point of encounter of the major Jewish diasporas in the early modern period, and in position to affect the entire Jewish Ecumene.

Following recurring expulsions of Jews in Western Europe, especially from German cities toward the end of the Middle Ages, and ensuing waves of immigration eastward, a new Jewish diaspora was being constructed in Eastern Europe, mainly in contemporary Poland and Ukraine.[6] The dramatic demographic rise and the concurrent construction of major centers of rabbinic schools (*Yeshivot* in Hebrew), turned this diaspora into the leading center of Jewish life from the late seventeenth century onwards, until the Second World War. The Polish Jewry soon evolved its own religious patterns of scholarship and rituality, yet remained connected with the religious messages arriving from Safed.

Other thriving and dynamic centers of Jewish life were the local communities in Italy.[7] These communities had the longest history in Europe, dating back to late antiquity and even earlier. Being entirely urban in their locations they were deeply immersed in Italian cities and in their political and cultural life. The Renaissance and later the Catholic Reformation left a deep imprint on Jewish-Italian religiosity. In the late Middle Ages it was the largest and most prosperous diaspora in Western Europe; it served as the mediating bridge between Jewish communities living under Islamic-Ottoman rule and the Jewish diasporas in Western Europe and its extension in Eastern Europe. During the early modern period Jewish-Italian communities hosted the leading printing presses that served the entire Jewish Ecumene. Most of the fundamental books of the Jewish Canon were first printed on Italian printing presses – mostly owned by non-Jews – and later circulated in the international market.

Added to this was the important center of Jewish life in Northern Africa, with its own long history and particular course of Halakhic, Kabbalistic and ritual patterns.[8] The co-existence of the four major centers mentioned thus far – the Ottoman and especially the city of Safed with its reverberating spirit, Italy, North Africa especially Morocco, and Eastern Europe – would lead us to become attentive to Moshe Idel's important observation that Jewish religious history during the early modern period should *not* be considered as revolving around one dominant center – not even the Safedian, but as a multi-focal network, where these four centers of Jewish life interacted and affected the entire religious scene.[9]

In this multi-centered dynamics there was still a dominant player, which was the Sephardi diaspora, following the expulsion of the Iberian Jews from Spain (1492) and Portugal (1497).[10] These refugees had unquestionable advantages over the Jewish communities of the new destinations in northern Europe, and especially along the Mediterranean communities: They had the sense of superiority and distinct identity in regard to other Jewish diasporas, which they insisted of maintaining in their community patterns, charity policy and internal marriage strategies. At their disposal stood their long political experience, their direct links with Spanish kings (prior to the expulsion) and later the Ottoman sultans, international spies, and involvement in long-distance trade. They carried a distinct Talmudic heritage, prospering to an unprecedented degree in the sixteenth century in the new religious schools (*Yeshivot* or *Batei-Midrash* in Hebrew) in the Ottoman Empire under the leadership of renowned rabbis and Talmudic scholars. The encounter of Sephardi exiles with local Jewish communities was rarely peaceful, as the newcomers intended to impose their own religious heritage upon the local Jews and, due to their political and economic power, succeeded in many cases. The fate of the major Kabbalistic corpus of 'Book of Splendor' (*Sefer HaZohar* or simply *HaZohar* in Hebrew) was emblematic of this cultural change over the early modern period.

The story behind the composition and dissemination of *Sefer HaZohar* integrates, to a large degree, with the passage of Kabbalistic traditions from the Middle Ages to the early modern period.[11] The Zoharic corpus was composed (the traditional medieval position stated was: 'discovered') during the thirteenth century by R. Moses di Leon in Spain and by some affiliated mystics, and it included several parts of different literary genres of writing. As a collective work, the Zoharic corpus was never clearly defined and the medieval manuscripts could vary in their length and content. Put differently, it was not considered as a well-defined and finished text. The main copying areas of this grand mystical corpus were found in Italy and among Byzantine Jews along the fourteenth and fifteenth centuries. Yet the main occupation and citations of the Zoharic tradition definitely related to the Sephardi tradition. The rabbinic elite in Ashkenaz, Italy or North Africa showed little interest in discussing, interpreting or clarifying its position in relation to other aspects of Jewish tradition prior to the sixteenth century.

Following the dispersion of Jewish-Iberian communities along the Mediterranean communities the Zohar exerted an unprecedented impact on Jewish religiosity. It was considered by the Sephardi exiles as an important component in their particular heritage, and its increasing role demonstrated once more their dominant lead in relation to other Jewish diasporas. The hundred and fifty years prior to the general expulsion from Spain witnessed a decrease in Kabbalistic vitality among Spanish Kabbalists, and the declining interest in composing new tracts. This void was filled by a parallel expansion of the Zoharic traditions and turning it into a major representative of Spanish Kabbalistic tradition. Some of the leading rabbis of the pre-expulsion period – such as R. Isaac Canpanton 'The Erudite of Castile' (*Geon Castiliya* in Hebrew) – started to occupy themselves with the Zohar alongside their Talmudic-legalistic studies. The main body of the Zohar revolves around the historical figure of R. Simeon/Shimon bar-Yochai, a sage of the Mishnaic period (roughly second and third centuries AD). Bar-Yochai was presented as towering in his mystical comprehensions above the great eponymous figures of the Jewish past, even of Moses. These utterly unusual positions in rabbinical context already herald the intention of the Zoharic group to position an alternative authority of inspirational character next to the rabbinic one, and to compete in the domain of guiding Jewish life and practices. Indeed, the Zohar dedicated long discussions to Jewish rituals, their secretive-mystical meaning, in relation to previous Talmudic discussions, as well as to suggesting new ritual patterns – though to a lesser extent.

The Zohar was put to print twice during the sixteenth century in Italy, the center of contemporary Jewish book printing. The Zoharic corpus became a well-defined book, available to all potential buyers, beyond the mystical esoteric circles. This act, joining the printing of the major books of the Jewish Canon at this period, intensified the shift of Jewish Kabbalah from a restricted esoteric milieu to the public domain. The battle over its role in Jewish religiosity concentrated now not on holding the secretive text but on its interpretation. Again, most of the hermeneutical battles over the printed Zohar were waged among Sephardi scholars, who composed long books and super-commentaries throughout the sixteenth and seventeenth centuries. Safed staged some of the leading Kabbalists of this period, most eminent among them were R. Moses Cordovero (1522–1570), and R. Isaac Luria 'The Lion' (*HaAri* in Hebrew) (153–-1572). Luria became, in later years, the dominant figure of early modern Kabbalah, basing his authority on the sanctified aura of the Zohar. He claimed that only those of spiritual level equal to that of bar-Yochai and his mystical confraternity could provide a correct reading of their inspired text, thus maintaining the monopoly of the Kabbalistic elite over the Zohar, at least over its theosophical aspects, beyond the reach of the general public.

Yet the Book of Splendor contained other less secretive aspects, which turned it into an ever more popular composition in the Jewish Ecumene in the coming centuries. The claim of R. Luria and his followers for interpretive monopoly could not stop the interest of other aspects of the Zohar, such as his biblical readings, the ethical guidance, and its ritual suggestions. Throughout the sixteenth and seventeenth centuries, bibliographical tools helped to expand its presence in Jewish culture. It added to the publication of shortened and popularized versions of books, composed in Hebrew or in 'vulgar' Jewish languages such as Yiddish and Ladino. The aim of such books, as stated explicitly by their composers and publishers, was to reach as large a reading public as possible. Wide ethical literature was composed under its inspiration and became increasingly popular.[12] It is no mere accident that such books preceded the publication and printing of books discussing the theosophical and secretive aspects of the Zoharic world. The Zohar was often cited in contemporary literature, and its ascribed author worshipped in dedicatory liturgy. What the protagonists of the Zohar, and later its exegetes, had to say about the Jewish way of life concerned directly the major source of normative Jewish life, the Halakhah.

The Talmudic-legal tradition evolving in rabbinic scholarship was considered as the main and most legitimate (in the Weberian sense) channel of the Jewish way of life and regulative factor of religious practice since the Gaonic period in early Islam. During the Middle Ages a potential competitor to this normative source arose, the philosophical school inspired by Aristotelian philosophy and its elaboration in the Islamicate world. The 'Jewish Philosophers' were not interested in discussing the Jewish ritual tradition, considered by most of them to be the primary level on the road toward eternal truth, and suitable to the ignorant people rather than for the philosophical elite. They certainly showed no interest in expanding or changing the ritual domain, or giving their opinions on the elaborate details of each act. Not so the Kabbalistic domain.

The interest of Kabbalists in Mitzvot had a long history in the Middle Ages.[13] Starting from the late thirteenth century, the Kabbalistic sources, those considered as reliable, infiltrated the Halakhic writing in Spanish tradition. This fusion of Halakhic and mystic writing intensified during the fourteenth and fifteenth centuries, mainly in Sephardi communities prior to the general expulsion, and later in Jewish communities along the Mediterranean basin with Jewish-Iberian presence, such as Provence, Italy, the core land of the Ottoman Empire (Rumelia and Anatolia), the Holy Land and Egypt. It was a current substantiated predominantly by Sephardi Talmudic scholars, and by some major local scholars who considered the use of Kabbalistic assertions in Talmudic discourse as legitimate. The deep interest of R. Isaac Canpanton in the Zohar was mentioned previously, adding to his revelations of mystical secrets of the Torah by a divine angelic-like figure. Yet this fusion encountered decisive opposition from most of Ashkenazi, Italian, Romaniote (Byzantine prior to the Ottoman conquest) rabbis and Halakhic decisors (*Poskei Halakhah* in Hebrew).

As much as the Zoharic corpus was considered an authentic source from the classical rabbinic period, sanctified as an ultimate mystical reading of the entire Jewish heritage, and turned into further component in the traditional Jewish Canon along the sixteenth century, a need to regulate the two competing sources became ever more urgent. A 'Regulative Rule' was pronounced by R. Isaac Karo (the uncle of R. Joseph Karo, and probably his first master in Talmudic studies, 1458–1535) and R. David ben-Zimrah (known under the acronym *HaRidbaz*, 1479–1473)[14] that whenever an issue is not discussed in the Talmud, or when the issue at stake did not reach a resolution among Talmudic scholars, the matter could be decided according to Kabbalistic sources. It implied that the mystical assertions could not overcome a direct and lucid saying by Talmudic scholars. This rule implied that Halakhah could not be decided according to abstract theosophical perspectives, but could be determined in such a way only when the issue was not resolved by Talmudic-legalistic discourse. Innovations in ritual practice based predominantly on mystical knowledge of the divine domains generally encountered fierce opposition by the rabbinic establishment in Safed and beyond the Holy Land. The position of rabbis, their inclusion in community life and tight interaction with Jewish political leadership, provided them with a clear advantage over the rising Kabbalistic current. Added to this, most of the distinguished Jewish mystics in the early modern period and before were deeply immersed in Talmudic scholarship, so that their reading of Jewish rituality substantiated the traditional perspective in the first place.

This regulative tenet reflected the rabbinic perspective, aiming to control the changes in the sixteenth century, but to no avail. The rise of popularity in Kabbalistic traditions could not be contained by rabbinic instructions. The sanctification of the Zohar – or 'The Sacred Zohar' as it increasingly became known – made it harder on Talmudic and rabbinic authorities to oppose its ritualistic readings and suggestions. The sixteenth and seventeenth centuries witnessed an increasing osmosis of Kabbalistic arguments into Halakhic traditions and ruling. A similar trend was taking place in the varied Responsa literature (*Sifrut HaShut* or *Sifrut HaShe'elot veHatshuvot* in Hebrew), discussing concrete cases in Jewish life.[15] An important element in the rise of Kabbalistic presence in Jewish was R. Isaac Luria, certainly one of the most impressive figures in the history of Jewish mysticism. The remarkable spread of Hagiographical literature around him as a saintly figure, interacting with sacred persons of the Jewish past and endowed with quasi-divine capabilities, intensified the role of Kabbalistic adjudication in Halakhic and ritual matters on theosophical grounds, due to direct and divine inspiration, and disregarding the legalistic reasoning. During the late sixteenth century and especially the seventeenth century, rabbinical authorities expressed their apprehension to confront or oppose the sayings and instructions attributed to R. Luria. The centrality of the Zohar was another front in establishing the Sephardi hegemony in the entire Jewish Ecumene, and especially in the early modern Mediterranean basin. To a large extent it marginalized other mystical schools of the medieval period, and became the major focus of Kabbalistic creativity and innovation in the ritual domain as well. It also enhanced the importance of the city of Safed, as the local Kabbalists lived in geographical vicinity to the grave of bar-Yochai, where the Zoharic events of this mystical confraternity were supposed to have taken place. The Kabbalistic messages were disseminated by books molded in imitation of Halakhic patterns; For instance, following the publication and popularity of R. Joseph Karo's codes of law – especially his *Shulchan 'Aruch* – scholars with Kabbalistic affiliations composed the *Shulchan 'Aruch HaAri* and *Shulchan 'Aruch HaZohar*. Maran Joseph Karo contributed greatly to this change when he inserted Kabbalistic – mainly Zoharic – instructions in his important codes of law. He even did not justify it according to the regulative rule mentioned previously, as if the mystical assertions were part of the entire Jewish heritage and Talmudic tradition. Even more significant were the publications of popular books addressing the public at large, in which the Kabbalistic lore played a dominant role:

> While adhering to maximalist stands in the metaphysical domain, Kabbalah infiltrated the daily rituals, ethos, and moral virtues. The human world is elevated and as if immerged into the world of divine emanations. ... The active world does not stand by itself, but "pulled" by the spiritual-ideational-mystical world. ... The symbolical thinking and the ecstatic experience require man's total devotion, posing final and elevated goals, so that the entire religious life is illuminated by the mystical world.[16]

Putting the Zohar into print certainly enlarged the circle of its potential readers, and it found echo in 'Books of Customs' (*Sifrei Minhagim* in Hebrew), literature addressed specifically to women, popular guidance tracts and folkloristic stories. Anthologies of different parts of the Zohar corpus addressed the general public during the seventeenth century. Yet its theosophical and more elaborate aspects were still retained among the intellectual and mystical Jewish elite even through the seventeenth century, while exposing the narrative parts and the sections devoted to rituals' derivatives. This restricted monopoly over the mystical reading of the Zohar was enhanced by the claim of R. Luria and his followers that the book is sealed to regular human understanding, and is accessible only to those who reached the same spiritual-mystical degrees as the book's composers.

Once addressing the public at large, putting the immanent innovative element of the Kabbalah into concrete reality was unavoidable – especially the Zoharic corpus, now in print, and considered henceforward as an essential element of the Jewish Sacred Canon.[17] The casuistic patterns of Talmudic discussions, where every issue is examined separately without any meta-instructions or overall rules for deciding Halakhah, was substituted by a concept characterized by Moshe Hallamish as 'total'. It is interested primarily in the distinct divine domains, and consequently in its projection on the human life. The four fundamental books of Jewish sacred and canonical traditions – Bible, Mishnah, Talmud, and Kabbalah – reflected according the mystical perspective the four divine domains or worlds that stand in between God and the created world, of *Atzilut*, *Briya*, *Yetzirah*, and *'Asiya* (known in Kabbalistic parlance as the *Avi'ah* system). In a similar manner every ritualistic act or Mitzvah is rooted in and linked to some aspect of the divine domain. The metaphysical and theosophical perspectives of Sephirotic Kabbalah – especially following the Zoharic tradition – had concrete repercussions on religious life. It caused the innovation of new rituals, in domains 'uncovered' by the classical Halakhah. The weight of these concepts related to the strong theurgical aspect of early modern Kabbalah, and the sense of significant dialogue between the human and the divine. It played a decisive role in the process leading to salvation and the coming messianic time. Some Kabbalistic-oriented writers claimed that in future time the entire Halakhah would follow the instructions of bar-Yochai, the main Zoharic protagonist, as the realization of a higher level of Torah and religious life. The totality-oriented character of early modern Kabbalah did not consider positively any leniency in Halakhic and ritual matters and inclined to strictness in Halakhic ruling. As every detail of ritual activity reflected some component in the divine, it necessitated a meticulous course of action. It expressed the ultimate commitment to God and to his service, using no legalistic stratagem as an excuse for leniency. It also related to the pietistic atmosphere in the city of Safed, inspired by the leading figures and mystical confraternities, and later projecting to Jewish communities in the Mediterranean and East Europe.

The result was an impressive occupation with the ritualistic domain, both charging it with new sense and widening it to new spheres, casting the entire religious life in a new light. It showed in the following aspects:

- The arena most affected by Kabbalistic innovation was Prayer. It turned Jewish liturgy – an event of clear public nature, conducted in synagogue in the presence of at least a ten-person quorum, and on a daily basis by the entire male group of the community – into a process of meditation and direct interaction with God through *Kavanot*. It meant addressing the prayers' intentions toward the precise aspects within divinity. Prayer was conceived as one of the essential means of theurgy and affecting the processes within the divine spheres, according to Kabbalistic knowledge. Leading Kabbalists during the sixteenth and seventeenth centuries were divided regarding the question to what extent these *Kavanot* were to be practiced by the public or maintained within the confined circles of those knowledgeable of these meditative practices, requiring a pre-prayer process of purification and internal concentration. The Kabbalistic mode of prayer was increasingly presented as the common liturgical foundation for the various versions of Jewish prayer of different diasporas. It later inspired the composition of the 'Prayer-Book according to R. Luria' (*Siddur HaAri* in Hebrew). In this, the leading Kabbalist of the seventeenth century composed prayers to serve beyond the frame of synagogue regular service.
- The celebration of the Sabbath was another important front in spreading the Kabbalistic influence, as it was a regular weekly event, involving the entire community, families and individuals.[18] It expressed very clearly the tendency to follow the regular ritual patterns of Jewish traditions – as evolved by the rabbinic elite and the Jewish public – and charge them with entirely new meaning. The Sabbath as discussed in Talmudic and post-Talmudic scholars was basically a reflection of the divine rhythm of creation: six days of activity and one day of rest. Kabbalists turned it into a reflection and resonance of processes taking place within divinity, and a special liminal time of encountering God, or at least the sphere of the feminine *Shechinah* (the divine presence).
- The Tikkunim were short prayers composed by Kabbalistic persons of authority to serve beyond the synagogue regular and normative prayers.[19] They were comprised of readings from all parts of the Jewish Canon, including mystical tracts, especially the Zohar. They became very popular in Jewish-Italian communities, later spreading to Polish communities where they reached a wide audience of users. It enabled the uninitiated to take part in the Kabbalistic world and relate to the tendency to adhere more intimately to divine worlds. They served the general public, groups with pietistic practices and Kabbalists. The occasions for their use were varied, but some of them – such as the Tikkun of Pentecost, mentioned previously – added mystical dimensions to the regular festivity, and turned them into especially sacred moments. Another famous and increasingly popular Tikkun served those performing night vigils, and was practiced around midnight, under the title of *Tikkun Chatzot*.

- Mystical confraternities offered an important institutional channel of innovation and dissemination of the Kabbalistic perspective to the public at large.[20] There were two models of these confraternities, inspired by similar traditions in Islam and Catholicism: The confraternities (*Chavurot Mitzvah* in Hebrew) prospered in Safed and later in the seventeenth century inspired communities along the Mediterranean basin under the Ottoman Empire. Like the Sufi brotherhoods they revolved around a figure of a dominant mystical master. The Jewish-Italian communities supplied a fertile ground for confraternities inspired by the Catholic tradition, of lay people grouped for pietistic devotion beyond the regular religious service, not necessarily guided by churchmen. Common to Jewish confraternities under both Ottoman-Islam and Catholic Europe, were regulation of conduct among their members and their own ritual and liturgical practices. Various confraternities followed their own religious patterns and self-regulation, and commonly objected to any external guidance. In Italy they initiated the composition of various prayers and ritual patterns, to serve their particular needs and religious inclinations.
- The supervision of the body and sexuality became an important issue in early modern Jewish society, and Kabbalistic traditions played a major role in this respect.[21] Every aspect of bodily functions was discussed and regulated in Kabbalistic writings, even those considered as neutral from the formalistic-Halakhic perspective – such as eating, table manners, clothes, or sleep. Jewish Kabbalah played a similar role in increasing control over people's behavior, even in the private domain and intimate moments, which reflected the increasing intervention of political regimes in their subjects' lives. This process, described by historians of both European and Islamicate civilizations as 'Confessionalization', showed clearly in the instructions of Kabbalists regarding the conjugal moments of intimacy – unprecedented in Halakhic literature – regarding the acts and the consciousness of the actors.
- Ritual reading of the Zohar became ever more popular during the seventeenth century. It symbolized the canonization of the Zoharic corpus and its insertion into regular religious activity of regular persons and their devotion to the Kabbalistic tradition. It also reflected the sanctification of the figure of its ascribed composer, bar-Yochai. Songs and hymns were composed to honor him, and addressing him for assistance or beseeching his intercession to achieve greater spiritual levels.
- Pilgrimages to holy graves, hosting the remnants of saintly figures – especially of Kabbalistic affiliation – became extremely popular from the late sixteenth century onward. They reflected a popular religiosity shared by all monotheistic religions in the Mediterranean, and were often shared by the believers of Jewish, Muslim and Christian traditions. They were inspired by the will to stay in direct contact with the buried person and achieve spiritual elevation.
- Especially in relation to the grave of bar-Yochai a new ritual pattern of Lag ba'Omer evolved during the sixteenth century to mark the mystical death of this enigmatic figure. It was supported by eminent figures in Safed, including R. Luria. It was celebrated 33 days after Passover and became a popular festival among Galilee Jews. The feast disseminated later in Eastern Europe and is still highly popular in Jewish life to the present day.
- Small gestures – bodily and verbal – were elaborated to attract the attention prior to ritual acts. One of them was the saying that the ritual act about to be committed is 'done to unify the almighty God and the Shechinah.' It aimed to contextualize the entire ritual-corporeal performance as a reflection of divine aspects within the Godhead. The self-commitment of religious practice was expressed by another verbal act of saying, 'I undertake upon myself to love the other as myself' before entering the synagogue precinct. Further and similar acts were meant to escort the daily routine of religious activity.

- Charity acquired another mystical meaning beyond its social role. It was meant to amend the wounds within the human world and not less so in the divine domain. Generosity was to be reflected in the Godhead, especially to symbolize the need to show solidarity with the *Shechinah* wandering in exile, like the people of Israel. For that purpose, some Safed Kabbalists instructed the giving of charity at specific moments during prayer.
- The sequence between all the words, as a continuous chain of being, showed in the intimate interaction between the living and the dead. Conceptions of reincarnation, impregnations ('*Ibbur* in Hebrew, that is being temporarily pervaded) by dead Kabbalists' souls, possession, and direct contact with the souls of the dead Righteous (*Tzaddik* in Hebrew) became ever more popular and present in Jewish early modern religiosity. In such a religious context the increasing interest in death and death rituals was unavoidable. Several major books were composed – mainly in Italy and later in Ashkenazi tradition – to guide persons at the moment of death, so as to provide the dying person with assistance in the afterlife. Other instructions aimed at the living, guiding them in their period of mourning, or regarding the interaction between the living and the dead in general. It also showed in the rising interest with demonic powers and magic practices. For example, moments of prayer and concentration set the arena of battle between righteous and demonic thought, and the powers in charge of them. The sacred power of the Hebrew language was another channel of magical activity.
- The aspiration for purity as a precondition to contact with the divine gave rise to practices of Confession. It reflected the impact of counter-Reformation religiosity on Jewish tradition, alongside Sufi practices. During the early modern period they were practiced among members of some confraternities in Safed, while in Italy it was considered as a condition of a proper death.
- Mystical techniques were practiced among those devoted to Kabbalistic traditions. These included the visual practice of imagining the letters of God's name, especially the Tetragrammaton, or reading parts of the Jewish Canon – Bible, Mishnah – in a certain musical mode in order to achieve closeness and unity (*Devekut* in Hebrew) with God.
- The examples of the eminent Kabbalists in Safed – especially R. Isaac Luria – later served as inspiration for new ritual practices. They were labeled Hanhagot (literally: concrete practices) and concerned various aspects in religious life. His prestige made it difficult for Halakhic authorities to oppose him.
- Early modern Kabbalah inspired an impressive rise of Jewish liturgy, in both poetical and musical forms. Leading in this respect was Israel Najara (1555–1625) whose liturgies (*Piyyutim* in Hebrew) became popular in and beyond the Mediterranean context. Beside being a gifted poet, he was sensitive to musical traditions of Balkan, Arabic, Ottoman and Persian origins. His poetical work enriched the Jewish annual liturgical circle and expanded it to musical events beyond the synagogue regular prayers.

The early modern Jewish world went through dramatic changes regarding demography, expulsions and the establishment of new centers of Jewish life (Poland, Ottoman Empire), encounters among the various Jewish traditions, and the impact of the printing press. No less important regarding its impact on Jewish communities and religious traditions was the establishment of grand political states and empires and the religious and cultural changes they were undergoing. It reflected directly in the role of rabbinic elite, the codification of Halakhah by R. Joseph Karo, and the rise of Jewish mysticism as a public phenomenon. The Ritual Turn joined as another element in this overall change:

> Early modern Jewish society underwent a process of what may be termed a 'ritualization of life'. Among the many new customs created during this period, we can note,

for example, the midnight vigil, fresh ways to celebrate the new moon, and new rituals for the sick and the dying. The religious creativity of sixteenth and seventeenth century Jewry can be compared in its formative power to that of the second century, when rabbinic Judaism defined itself after the destruction of the temple against the background of paganism and especially against the new religion undergoing formation, Christianity. The early modern period, characterized by a particularly significant burgeoning of the formulation and establishment of rituals, was a time of exuberance in the practical shaping of religious life within Judaism.[22]

Innovation continued later in the messianic movement of Sabbetai Zvi. Beyond its bold theological innovations, its deep resonance on Jewish life continued even after the conversion of Sabbetai Zvi to Islam, in shaping and intensifying penitential patterns and shaping new rituals, such a *Tu BiShvat*, or the celebration of vegetal new-year's eve by readings and by eating certain fruits.[23] Starting from the late seventeenth century this feast became ever popular in Jewish communities in spite of its Sabbatian origins. Again, the ritual Sabbatian turn was indicative of deep changes within the Jewish religious tradition.

Notes

1. Altshuler 2016, Ch. 8 – 'Tikkun Leil Shavuot', 139–159. See also Bar-Ilan 1997; Wilhelm 1948–1952.
2. Halbertal 1997.
3. Weinstein 2003, regarding Jewish marriage rituals in early modern Italy. They integrate with other important components of Jewish life among Italian Jews during the Renaissance and early modern period. As rituals shared and practiced by the entire Jewish population – and not only by men, or the cultural elite – they illuminated important components of local mentality. No less so they echo the deep sensitivity to non-Jewish surroundings in Italian urban settings.
4. Weinstein 2016, passim.
5. On the deep involvement of the Ottomans and Tatars in Eastern Europe, see Kołodziejczyk 2011.
6. Reiner, 2006; Kalik 2009, Rosman 1990.
7. Bonfil 1994.
8. Hallamish 2001.
9. Idel 1998.
10. Weinstein 2016, Weinstein 2021; Beinart 1992.
11. Huss 2016.
12. Gries 1990.
13. Alongside the important works of Hallamish mentioned above, see also Pely 2012, 2014, 2015; Katz 1983; Kadosh 2004.
14. Pely 2012.
15. Kadosh 2004, passim.
16. Hallamish 2019, 35, 45–46, 48. See also Gries 1990.
17. The following analysis owes much to the important works of Hallamish 2000, 2019.
18. See for instance Ginsburg 1989.
19. Navarro 2006.
20. Weinstein 2012; Andreatta 2007.
21. Weinstein 2008. On the theosophical motivations, see Idel 2005.
22. Bar-Levav 2002; citation from ibid., p. 69.
23. Huss 2009.

References

Altshuler, Mor. 2016. *The Life of Rabbi Yosef Karo* [in Hebrew]. Tel-Aviv: Tel-Aviv University Press.
Andreatta, Michela. 2007. *Poesia religiosa ebraica di età barocca. L'innario della confraternità Šomerim La-Boqer (Mantova 1612)*. Padua: Studio Editoriale Gordini.

Bar-Ilan, Meir. 1997. "Tikkun Leil Shavuot: Its Formation and Precedents" [in Hebrew], *Mechkari Hag* 8: 28–48.
Bar-Levav, Avriel. 2002. "Ritualisation of Jewish Life and Death in the Early Modern Period," *Leo Baeck Institute Year Book* 47: 69–82.
Beinart, Haim. Ed. 1992. *Moreshet Sepharad: The Sephardi Legacy*. Jerusalem: Magnes Press.
Bonfil, Robert. 1994. *Jewish Life in Renaissance Italy*, trans. Anthony Oldcorn. Berkeley: University of California Press.
Ginsburg, Elliot K. 1989. *The Sabbath in the Classical Kabbalah*. Albany: State University of New York Press.
Gries, Zeev. 1990. *Conduct Literature (Regimen Vitae): Its History and Place in the Life of Beshtian Hasidim* [in Hebrew]. Jerusalem: Mosad Bialik.
Halbertal, Moshe. 1997. *People of the Book: Canon, Meaning, and Authority*. Cambridge, MA and London: Harvard University Press.
Hallamish, Moshe. 2000. *Kabbalah in Liturgy, Halakhah and Customs* [in Hebrew]. Ramat-Gan: Bar-Ilan University Press.
Hallamish, Moshe. 2001. *The Kabbalah in North Africa: A Historical and Cultural Survey* [in Hebrew]. Tel-Aviv: HaKibbutz HaMeuchad.
Hallamish, Moshe. 2019. *Kabbalistic Ritual: The Integration of Theory and Practice* [in Hebrew]. Tel-Aviv: Idra.
Huss, Boaz. 2009. "'The Pleasant Tree Ben Yishai Lives on the Earth:' On the Sabbatean Origins of the *Tu BiShvat* Seder," in *Meir Benayahu Memorial Volume*, Vol. 2, eds. Moshe Bar-Asher, Yehuda Liebes, Moshe Asis and Yosef Kaplan.. Jerusalem: Carmel, 909–19.
Huss, Boaz. 2016. *The Zohar: Reception and Impact*, trans. Yudith Nave. Oxford and Portland, OR: Littman Library of Jewish Civilization.
Idel, Moshe. 1998. "On Mobility, Individuals and Groups: Prolegomenon for a Sociological Approach to Sixteenth-Century Kabbalah," *Kabbalah: Journal for the Study of Jewish Mystical Texts* 3, 145–73.
Idel, Moshe. 2005. *Kabbalah and Eros*. New Haven, CT: Yale University Press.
Kadosh, Meir. 2004. "Kabbalistic Jewish Laws in Responsa from the 13th Century to the Early Years of the 17th Century" [in Hebrew], Ph.D. submitted at Bar-Ilan University, Ramat-Gan.
Kalik, Yehudit. 2009. *The Scepter of Judah: The Jewish Autonomy in the Eighteenth-Century Crown Poland*. Leiden: Brill.
Katz, Jacob. 1983. "Post-Zoharic Relations between Halakhah and Kabbalah," in *Jewish Thought in the Sixteenth Century*, ed. Bernard D. Cooperman. Cambridge, MA: Harvard University Press, 283–307.
Kołodziejczyk, Dariusz. 2011. *The Crimean Khanate and Poland-Lithuania International Diplomacy on the European Periphery (15th–18th Century): A Study of Peace Treaties Followed by Annotated Documents*. Leiden: Brill.
Navarro, Assaf. 2006. "'Tikkun': From Lurianic Kabbalah to Popular Culture" [in Hebrew], Ph.D. submitted at the Ben-Gurion University of the Negev, Be'er Sheva.
Pely, Hagai. 2012. "Kabbalah in R. Karo's Halakhic Decisions: A Chapter in the Genealogy of Castilian Halakhic-Ruling until the Sixteenth Century" [in Hebrew], *Kabbalah: Journal for the Study of Jewish Mystical Texts* 26: 243–72.
Pely, Hagai. 2014. "The Lurianic Kabbalah: Halakhic and Meta-Halakhic Aspects" [in Hebrew], Ph.D. submitted at Ben-Gurion University of the Negev, Be'er Sheva.
Pely, Hagai. 2015. "Halakhah, Pietism, Kabbalah and Revelation in Sixteenth Century Safed: A Study in R. Yosef Karo's Works" [in Hebrew], *Jerusalem Studies in Jewish Thought* 24: 201–34.
Reiner, Elchanan. 2006. "On the Roots of the Urban Jewish Community in Poland in the Early Modern Period" [in Hebrew], *Gal-Ed: On the History and Culture of Polish Jewry* 20: 13–37.
Rosman, Marry Jay. 1990. *The Lords' Jews: Magnate-Jewish Relations in the Polish-Lithuanian Commonwealth during the Eighteenth Century*. Cambridge, MA: Harvard University Press.
Weinstein, Roni. 2003. *Marriage Rituals Italian Style: A Historical Anthropological Perspective on Early Modern Italian Jews*. Leiden: Brill.
Weinstein, Roni, 2008. *Juvenile Sexuality, Kabbalah, and Catholic Religiosity among Jewish Italian Communities: "Glory of Youth" by Pinhas Baruch b. Pelatya Monselice (Ferrara, XVII Century)*. Boston, MA and Leiden: E. J. Brill.

Weinstein, Roni. 2012. "Kabbalistic Innovation in Jewish Confraternities in the Early Modern Mediterranean," in *Faith's Boundaries: Laity and Clergy in Early Modern Confraternities*, eds. Nicholas Terpstra, Adriano Prosperi, and Stefania Pastore. Turnhout: Brepols, 234–47.

Weinstein, Roni. 2016. *Kabbalah and Jewish Modernity*. London: Littman Library of Jewish Culture.

Weinstein, Roni. 2021. *R. Joseph Karo: Early Modern Jewish Legality in a Global Age*. London, Boston, New Delhi: forthcoming in Anthem Press.

Wilhelm, Y. D. 1948–1952. "Sidrei Tikunim" [Protocols of Kabbalistic Emendations – in Hebrew], *'Alei 'Ayin: Homage to Shlomo Zalman Schocken for his Seventieth Birthday*. Jerusalem: n.p., 125–46.

10
JEWISH MATERIAL CULTURE IN THE MODERN AGE

Jeffrey Shandler

Among the many innovations in Jewish life during the modern period, the burgeoning of material culture is perhaps the most wide-ranging; so much so that its significance can easily be overlooked. This phenomenon includes a vast number and variety of ritual objects for home and synagogue as well as the creation of new items that reflect the expansion of modern Jewish culture beyond traditional devotional practices. Noteworthy in addition to the great abundance and diversity of these things is the advent of new social practices involving material culture, such as collecting, marketing, preserving, and exhibiting. These developments have sometimes been characterized as inimical to traditional Jewish values. To cite one example, in 1887 Rabbi Moses Weinberger groused that, rather than "investigating and enriching scholarship, language, and literature," immigrant Jews in New York "delve relentlessly into the practical world. … They sink up to their necks in a torrent of present-day banalities and material possessions" (Sarna 1982, 61). But it is also possible to view these objects and activities as situating material culture at the center of a number of innovative ways of realizing Jewishness, whether individually or communally, as an extension of commitments to traditional devotion or diverging from it.

By the beginning of the modern period, marked by the advent of Enlightenment in western Europe, Jewish communities throughout the world had well-established inventories of ceremonial objects. These items pertained to ritual activity in the home (e.g., Hanukkah lamps; candle holders, wine goblets, and spice boxes for Sabbath rituals; Passover seder plates and covers for matzoh) and the synagogue (e.g., crowns, breastplates, pointers, and mantles or cases for torah scrolls; curtains for the arks in which these scrolls were kept), as well as items of personal attire, such as those traditionally worn by adult Jewish males during worship: a prayer shawl, phylacteries, and skull cap or other head covering. Jewish homes also contained the materials of what may be termed "folk religion," some of them ephemeral—for example, amulets, written on paper, to protect newborn infants from evil spirits; candles, made with wicks that measure the height of deceased relatives' tombs, which were then burned on Yom Kippur to implore the deceased to protect the living; or breads baked in special shapes, such as birds or ladders, for holidays.

The form, material, and ornamentation of these objects could vary considerably from one locale to another and often reflected regional styles of decoration beyond the Jewish community. In addition, the production of ritual objects evinced local socioeconomic circumstances.

For example, ceremonial items made of silver in German lands were usually the work of Christian craftsmen, as Jews were not admitted to the guilds that controlled silversmithing. By contrast, in Arab lands similar objects were produced by Jewish artisans, who prevailed in the metalwork trades (Braunstein 2004, 12). The choice of material used to create ritual objects—such as gold or silver versus pewter or brass—and their means of production—individually hand-chased works versus multiples cast from a mold—also reflected differences in the wealth of the items' owners. Gifts of ceremonial objects to a synagogue, such as ornaments for a torah scroll, could provide elite members of a local Jewish community with the opportunity to materialize publicly their patronage of the congregation and prestige within the community generally, especially when these objects bore inscriptions identifying the donors' names (Cohen 1998, 71). Other ritual objects reflect the gendering of traditional Jewish life. Thus, women in western Ashkenaz embroidered torah binders, made from the cloths used during the circumcision of infant boys, for presentation during their sons' first visit to the synagogue (Kirshenblatt-Gimblett 1982). Similarly, women in a number of diaspora Jewish communities made curtains for arks and sacks for phylacteries and prayer shawls as means of enhancing male-centered worship and manifesting women's support of men's devotional practices.

While the types of ritual objects made during the modern era have generally continued this established inventory, the period is distinguished by the development of new practices involving Jewish material culture, beginning with its collection. The first collectors of Judaica were prosperous Jews living in western or central Europe, such as the court Jews David Oppenheim (1664–1736) and Alexander David (1687–1785), the composer Isaac Strauss (1796–1888), and the merchant Lesser Gieldziński (1830–1910). Their accumulation of books, manuscripts, and ceremonial objects resembled, in part, the creation of a *Wunderkammer*, or cabinet of curiosities, found in the homes of Christian members of the political and economic elite in western Europe. These assemblages of a wide range of items, including natural specimens and exotic artifacts, were a manifestation of Enlightenment interests in learning about the world expansively through the direct scrutiny of phenomena. This attention by members of the Christian elite extended to the study of rituals and beliefs of other peoples, including Jews, whose material culture was also depicted and described in publications by Bernard Picart (*Cérémonies et coutumes religieuses de tous les peoples du monde*, 1723) and Johan Bodenschatz (*Kirchliche Verfassung der heutigen deutschen Juden*, 1748/9), among others (Cohen 1998, 10–67).

In contrast to the practices of Christians at this time, early collectors of Judaica were motivated at least as well, if not primarily, by a desire to enhance engagement in their own traditions. Thus, David's collection of ceremonial objects was originally intended for use in his private synagogue in Braunschweig (Cohen 1998, 190), and Oppenheim kept his books in a family library in Hanover, granting limited access to visitors (Teplitsky 2019). By the second half of the nineteenth century, these personal interests were directed outward, as the items amassed by some Judaica collectors formed the basis of the first public displays of Jewish ceremonial objects. In particular, Isaac Strauss's collection, which he assembled in the course of his travels in western Europe, was shown at landmark presentations in Paris, at the Exposition Universelle of 1878, and London, at the Anglo-Jewish Exhibition of 1887 (Kirshenblatt-Gimblett 1998, 79–128).

Eventually, these collections found their way into public museums and libraries. Strauss's Judaica, purchased by the Baroness Nathaniel de Rothschild and donated to the Musée de Cluny in 1890, is now in the Musée d'art et d'histoire du Judaïsme, which opened in Paris in 1998 (Klagsbald 1981). David's collection is now housed in the Jewish department of the Braunschweig Landesmuseum, and Oppenheim's books and manuscripts were eventually acquired by the Bodleian Library at Oxford. Gieldziński displayed his Judaica collection, as well as an extensive assemblage of art and antiques, in his home in Danzig to invited guests. Then, in 1904, he donated his Jewish ceremonial objects to Danzig's Great Synagogue, where he stipulated that they were to be "exhibited in a separate and appropriate room, carefully preserved and open free to all" (Mann and Gutman 1980, 44). The same year, a gift from jurist Mayer Sulzberger of a small number of ritual objects, along with a much larger collection of books and manuscripts, to the library of the Jewish Theological Seminary, inaugurated what would eventually become the Jewish Museum of New York (Miller and Cohen 1997).

The establishment of Jewish museums, beginning with the Jüdisches Museum Wien in 1895, constitutes the most elaborate innovation in Jewish public life involving material culture. By the eve of World War II, Jewish museums had opened in more than a dozen cities in Europe, Palestine, the Soviet Union, and the United States. The displays in these museums consisted primarily of Jewish ritual objects, books, and manuscripts. These institutions were founded with distinct concerns for their internal audiences versus the general public. At a time when growing numbers of Jews were abandoning traditional study and worship, the creators of these museums sought new ways for Jews to engage with their history and culture as sources of inspiration and pride. As a result, the turn to this new kind of institution engendered innovative practices for Jews, both as individuals and as communities, to realize their Jewishness. Centered on the museums' displays of material culture, these practices involved instructive observing, rather than devotional observance; reading in the vernacular, rather than sacred languages; attending on an occasional basis, rather than daily, weekly, or seasonally, and in a venue where non-Jews were equally welcome participants. Indeed, at the same time that these museums addressed the particular concerns of the Jewish visitor, they also sought to educate the general public about Jewish beliefs and observances, as well as their contributions to Western civilization, in order to counteract new forms of anti-Semitic rhetoric and action (Grossman 2003).

Whereas the first Jewish museums in western Europe and the United States often drew on the preexisting collections of ceremonial objects assembled by elite individuals or prosperous communities, concomitant efforts to create Jewish museums in eastern Europe turned to different sources by other means. These undertakings focused on the material culture of "ordinary" Jews, as part of a larger interest in folkways and popular culture as constituting a Jewish national patrimony. The first major project of its kind was the work of folklorist S. An-sky (the penname of Shloyme Zanvl Rapoport, 1863–1920), who gathered an extensive array of materials from Jewish communities in the southwestern provinces of the Russian Empire as part of the landmark ethnographic expedition he organized during the years 1912–1914. While much of the collecting was centered on recording oral folklore—folktales, songs, legends, traditional remedies, and the like—An-sky and his team of researchers also sought out examples of material folkways, including ritual objects, clothing, artworks, and domestic implements. He also commissioned photographs documenting synagogues, including their decorated interiors, and the work of traditional artisans, such as tombstone carvers and weavers of prayer shawls. An-sky envisioned his collections as providing the basis for works of modern Jewish culture in literature, theater, music, and visual art. His plans also included creating a network of ethnographic and art museums throughout the western provinces of Russia. Some of the expedition's collections were displayed briefly in 1914 at the Jewish Ethnographic and Historical Society in St. Petersburg and again in 1917, after which material from the collection was displayed periodically in different venues in the Soviet Union until 1941 (Avrutin et al. 2009, 189–212). During the interwar years, the YIVO Institute for Jewish Research, then based in Vilna, oversaw a collection of different Jewish objects—the scripts, playbills, posters, and other ephemera that were originally housed in the Ester-Rokhl Kaminska Theater Museum—reflecting YIVO's focus on Yiddish language and culture as well as the institute's secular orientation (Quint 2018).

Jewish material culture was also acquired by institutions with broader, and sometimes shifting, collection agendas. A remarkable case in point is the United States National Museum (now the Smithsonian Institution). Beginning in 1888, the museum began acquiring Jewish ceremonial objects as part of its Section of Oriental Antiquities. The initiative was led by Cyrus Adler, a scholar of Semitics and leading figure in the establishment or administration of multiple American Jewish institutions. Like others undertaking similar collections for public display at the turn of the twentieth century, Adler envisioned the effort as a "first step toward his ultimate goal of countering anti-Semitic stereotypes and gaining acceptance for Jews as truly equal partners in American society" (Grossman and Ahlborn 1997, 1). The Smithsonian's Judaica collection was largely assembled over the next forty years. Subsequently, as the institution's acquisition and collection management policies changed, its efforts to acquire Judaica languished, and the existing objects, as well as its holdings of ceremonial objects of other religions, were distributed among other divisions within the museum's vast inventory. Interest in the Jewish items was renewed beginning in 1969, as part of the Smithsonian's increased attention to the material culture of American regional and minority groups, and an effort to locate and catalog the dispersed Judaica collection was undertaken in the 1980s (Grossman and Ahlborn 1997, 52).

While the types of Jewish ceremonial objects largely remained fixed, the twentieth century witnessed a widening range of their styles and means of production. Some objects were mass-produced, such as a pressed-tin Hanukkah lamp, first manufactured in the United States in 1909 (Braunstein 2004, 190). Versions of this inexpensive object are still made, facilitating widespread observance of the ritual of lighting candles on the eight days of this holiday. At the same time, artists undertook efforts to create ritual objects with a distinct Jewish national aesthetic, exemplified by the Bezalel School. Inaugurated by Boris Schatz in Jerusalem in 1906, Bezalel evolved a style of ritual objects and works of decorative art that integrated orientalist Jewish motifs and techniques, such as Yemenite metalwork, with aesthetic idioms of art nouveau.

After World War II, this range of production extended further—on one hand, with the advent of hand-crafted ritual objects, exemplified by the "do-it-yourself" ethos of *The Jewish Catalogue*, first published in the United States in 1973, which explains how to make a skull cap, prayer shawl, and *shofar* ("ram's horn"), among other objects (Siegel et al. 1973). On the other hand, collectors and museums commissioned artists to create unique artworks that sometimes deliberately tested the limits of ritual objects' form and function. For example, in 1961 the Albert A. List family asked American artist Ben Shahn to create a *ketubah* ("wedding contract"). This artwork, never intended for use in an actual marriage, was eventually donated to the Jewish Museum in New York. From 1957 to 1989 the museum ran a workshop, under the directorship of goldsmith Ludwig Wolpert, dedicated to creating modernist designs for ritual objects (Perten 2019).

The history of the *ketubah* exemplifies the transformation of ritual objects in the modern period, evolving from a traditional legal document, decorated and displayed at weddings, to a collectible, along with other manuscripts, then a museum artifact and, eventually, a work of home décor. Collectors and museums have brought together *ketubot* created in a wide range of styles, most of them highly localized. Museums not only have presented the public with the diversity of *ketubah* decoration; they also have assigned *ketubot* new significance through curatorial commentary, juxtaposition with other artifacts, and the rubrics of display. In the decades since World War II, elaborately ornamented *ketubot*, often hand-crafted, have become popular among Jews in North America and elsewhere in the Western diaspora. As most of them are Ashkenazim, who traditionally did not decorate the *ketubah*, this attraction to ornamented *ketubot* likely emerged from encountering the decorative practices of other Jewish communities through exhibitions and publications, such as museum catalogs. This postwar development imbued the *ketubah* with a new significance and a new function. Rather than being filed away with birth certificates, wills, and other legal papers, the *ketubah* became a domestic work of art, framed and displayed on a wall in the couple's home, further reflecting the influence of the museum on Jewish domestic material culture. In a remarkable reflexive response to this development, some Jewish museums have received donations of *ketubot* from divorcing couples. Doing so might be understood as a gesture of rendering these documents—and, perhaps, the marriages they represent—as artifacts of communal history and culture. Moreover, donating *ketubot* to a museum following divorce may also evince desires to validate Jewish continuity through participation in a public form of Jewish culture, in which the museum is understood as a keeper of communal relics (Shandler 2010).

Jewish life in postwar America has witnessed a burgeoning of new forms of material culture, including recent examples that transform adventitious objects associated with life-cycle rituals into customized works of craft. Couples can not only purchase a special glass for the one traditionally broken during the Jewish wedding ceremony; they can also order objects, such as a mezuzah or picture frame, created from the glass's shards (National Museum of American Jewish History 2021). At cemeteries, people now leave decorated stones, some painted with messages, at the graves of their loved ones, thereby elaborating the longstanding practice of simply picking up a small rock nearby to place it on the tombstone as a sign of one's visit (Blomquist 2020). Other new objects reflect contemporary religious innovations. These include feminist ritual objects, such as the Miriam's cup, which is displayed at the Passover seder to recall the role of Moses' sister during the Exodus. This cup, filled with water, complements the traditional goblet of wine set on the seder table for the prophet Elijah (Ochs 2007, 87–111). The Jewish renewal movement has produced a wealth of new items used in its group rituals (e.g., meditation cushions, drums) as well as innovations to traditional ritual objects, such as hand-woven prayer shawls in different colors that evoke the ten *sefirot* ("emanations of divinity") in Jewish mysticism. By characterizing these objects as works of "handmade midrash [commentary]," they are imbued with the same value of spiritual interpretation as venerable commentaries and interpretations of canonical texts of rabbinic Judaism (Weissler 2007, 361). Innovations in Jewish material culture of the period extend to folkways that elaborate holiday practices and, at times, test the limits of what constitutes Jewish observance. The expansive material culture of Hanukkah, inspired in considerable measure by its seasonal proximity to Christmas, includes objects that seek to offer a Jewish parallel to Christmas decorations (Joselit 1994, 229–243). In addition, the integration of observing these two holidays, especially by mixed-faith families, has inspired holiday cards that merge emblems of Judaism with Christmas imagery, such as a reindeer whose antlers form a menorah or a six-pointed Star of David wrought out of candy canes (Shandler and Weintraub 2007).

At the same time, other Jews have created new items that enhance traditional observances, such as kiddush fountains, which distribute wine from one large goblet into a set of smaller cups—so that guests at a holiday meal can share the same cup of wine, over which a blessing has been recited, without using the same drinking vessel—or Sabbath lamps, which have movable parts that block or reveal their light, so that they can be used without violating the traditional prohibition against work, which includes turning on lamps. The domestic display of Judaica constitutes a material practice in its own right, including not only ceremonial objects placed in cabinets or *étagères* designed especially for this purpose, but also bookshelves arrayed with sacred tomes, sometimes purchased especially for their deluxe leather bindings (Stolow 2010, 167–170). American Hasidim have created a rich material culture for children, ranging from Yiddish board games to collectible cards of famous sages, thereby adopting the forms of mainstream popular culture while imbuing them with pious content (Shandler 2020). And the increased stringency of observance among some segments of Orthodox Jewry has engendered objects that not only help enforce regulations but also materialize the regulation of daily life. A case in point is a "*tzniut* [modesty] ruler," used to measure the length of skirts to ensure that they properly cover a girl's or woman's knees at all times.

Concomitant with this elaboration of the material culture of traditional Jewish observance has been a flourishing of objects and practices of a decidedly secular nature. Many of these items are concerned with materializing Jewish heritage. They include commemorative items, such as collectible medals honoring famous Jews, figurines of Jewish types in traditional garb, and souvenirs brought home by tourists from their visits to Israel or venerable sites in the Jewish diaspora. Beyond material remembrances of actual places where Jews have lived are objects that reify an imagined Jewish past, exemplified by a wide array of collectibles based on the 1964 Broadway musical *Fiddler on the Roof* (Solomon 2013, 312–313). Other examples straddle the divide between the secular and the religious, such as hundreds of "Jewish hearts"—six-pointed stars with a heart at their center—made by crafters in a variety of materials, as a response to the mass shooting at the Tree of Life Synagogue in Pittsburgh, Pennsylvania, in 2018. The creating, collecting, and displaying of these hearts throughout the city materialized expressions of solidarity with the congregation and protest against anti-Semitism (Eichler-Levine 2020, 136–146).

As collecting Judaica in the post-World War II era has come to embrace an ever greater range of items, including items manufactured for collection as well as objects of daily life, the intent of collecting has also evolved, responsive to the upheavals wrought by war, genocide, and mass immigration. For example, Peter Schweitzer, an avid collector of American Jewish ephemera, characterizes his extensive holdings as a form of cultural salvage:

> I regard the stray pieces I have discovered in the market as symbolic of the scattered Jewish people, unprotected, bereft of their homeland, up against the elements and the forces of time. … By rescuing them from their wayward journeys, by collecting them, I and other collectors perform symbolic acts of redemption and revitalization.
>
> *Schweitzer 2007, x*

Schweitzer eventually donated the bulk of his collection to the National Museum of American Jewish History, located in Philadelphia, consolidating his commitment to collecting as a form of cultural protection by securing it in an institutional home.

Projects of public memory can also center on the symbolic gathering of objects, such as the Yiddish Book Center, which houses hundreds of thousands of abandoned Yiddish books in its Amherst, Massachusetts, headquarters. Its many shelves of books are meant as much for the visitor's contemplation in their mass display as they are for providing readers with copies of out-of-print works of Yiddish literature, if not more so. Indeed, the Yiddish Book Center complements its vast holdings of vintage volumes with digitized versions of thousands of these titles, which are made available as reprints on high quality paper. Yiddish has also been materialized in a wide array of objects: T-shirts, coffee mugs, refrigerator magnets, and other collectibles, all bearing one or more Yiddish words. Despite their modest, low-brow form, these items can offer powerfully, if tacitly, ambivalent statements about Jewish culture through language play and the play between language and materiality. In particular, these objects reinforce associations of Yiddish with the vulgar in its multiple meanings, especially when the vitality of Jewish vulgarity appears to be both endangered and attractive (Shandler 2005, 155–176).

Complementing objects of retrospection is the forward-looking material culture of Jewish philanthropy, especially support for the *yishuv* ("the Jewish settlement in Palestine") and, as of 1948, the State of Israel. In addition to iconic blue-and-white tins for collecting funds for the Jewish National Fund, Zionist fundraising organizations produced an array of items that materialize support for the Jewish State: certificates, badges, pins, trophies, plaques, as well as fundraising cards that simulate building a wall of bricks or growing leaves on a tree through the accumulation of incremental donations. American support for the *yishuv* extended to championing the purchase of Jewish products from Palestine—wine, almonds, even cigarettes—as an act of Zionist patriotism (Shandler and Wenger 1997, 32–36).

Acquiring all these items has engendered new institutions and practices of consumption, including Jewish book stores, museum and synagogue gift shops, community book fairs, plus catalogues and, more recently, online sites for ordering Judaica (Heilman 1988). These developments build on earlier institutions, such as nineteenth-century charity fairs. Created largely by German Jewish women in the United States to raise funds for various causes, these events established new material and social practices that enacted Jewishness through the production and circulation of goods. Thus, charity fairs were coordinated with the Jewish holiday calendar, associating these new consumer rites with the sacred (Kirshenblatt-Gimblett 2006). All these institutions and events contribute to an ongoing practice of buying as an act of what has been termed "symbolic consumption" (McCracken 1988).

Consumer practices invested with symbolic value can include boycotts, such as American Jews' refusal to buy Ford automobiles during the 1920s, in protest of Henry Ford's anti-Jewish policies, including his support of the anti-Semitic newspaper *The Dearborn Independent*. More recently, boycotting Israeli products has become a divisive issue among Jews who variously support or condemn Israel's occupation of Palestine. Concerns about anti-Semitism also redound to collecting. Both individuals and institutions have collected examples of anti-Semitic items—most in the form of caricatures, figurines, and other ephemera—whether to document discrimination against Jews or to keep these items out of public circulation (Wiesemann 2005).

The fate of Jewish material culture during the Holocaust serves as a measure of the destruction of European Jewry and looms large in the genocide's remembrance. On the eve of World War II, the leaders of the Great Synagogue in Danzig attempted to rescue its Judaica collection—and thereby raise funds for their beleaguered community—by selling these ritual objects to the American Jewish Joint Distribution Committee (Mann and Gutman 1980). A wide range of everyday objects serve as metonyms for the enormity of the genocide's human toll through their display in Holocaust exhibitions. These include individual items—such as the Bundist leader Szmul Zygielbojm's broken eyeglasses, displayed in the original core exhibition of New York's Museum of Jewish Heritage—as well as heaps of objects: shoes, suitcases, toothbrushes, and the like, all confiscated from concentration camp prisoners. In addition to being exhibited in museums established on former campgrounds of Auschwitz and Majdanek, where masses of these objects were found at the end of the war, they have also been loaned from these sites to Holocaust museums situated far from these locations, such the United States Holocaust Memorial Museum in Washington, DC.

The presence of these objects in museums also serves as a reminder of how ordinary material goods acquired new values of unprecedented urgency and consequence during the Holocaust. The extensive imbrication of human lives with the stuff of daily life—articles of clothing, household goods, tools—came apart as the social contract in Nazi-controlled lands was breached.

Nazi Germany persecuted its victims by confiscating their property, by replacing their basic material needs with inferior goods (such as wooden clogs instead of shoes for concentration camp inmates, their uniforms made of coarse cloth woven from nettles), by scavenging their bodies for hidden treasures (gold, jewelry), and ultimately by reducing human beings to raw material for commodities (turning hair into cloth, attempting to use fat for soap). The scarcity of paper, pens, and pencils figured in the extraordinary challenges inherent in the act of writing during the Holocaust (Shallcross 2011).

The charged meaning of ordinary goods continued after the war. The discovery of Nazi Germany's large-scale looting of property from Jewish individuals and communities during the Holocaust—works of art, books, ritual objects, home furnishings, personal effects—prompted efforts by the Western Allies to identify the former owners of these items and return them. This undertaking largely proved unfeasible for a variety of reasons, including the tragic extent to which the people to whom these objects once belonged had been murdered, as well as the widespread relocation of the genocide's survivors. Moreover, these things acquired new significance as reminders of the destruction of vibrant Jewish communities that had flourished in Europe for centuries. Each item's provenance became a narrative of rupture and displacement, leaving the object bereft of its prewar use and ownership. The "restitution" of the looted material culture of vanquished Jewish communities, including their archival records, to other venues, especially institutions in Israel and the United States, implicitly acknowledged the Jews in these places as the successors of European Jewry (Gallas et al. 2020; Lustig 2017).

Many Holocaust survivors have maintained personal collections of artifacts of their wartime experience. These include both items specific to the genocide, such as concentration camp uniforms, yellow six-pointed star Jewish badges, or ghetto currency, and things that are ordinary in their appearance—photographs, articles of clothing, jewelry, religious objects, tools, musical instruments, and the like—but which materialize narratives of survivors' extraordinary experiences. Survivors can be seen displaying these objects and explaining their significance in some of the video interviews that have been recorded of their life histories, in which the interviewees assume the role of curator and docent, arranging and explaining items that provide material evidence of their experiences during the Holocaust and that testify to survivors' postwar endurance as well as their "sense of history, whether personal or on a grand scale" (Shandler 2017, 154).

Postwar efforts to recall Jewish life in Europe before the Holocaust often involve material culture, sometimes in ways that concretize the profound ambivalence and fraught emotions that these efforts can evoke. A case in point are small wooden carvings of Jews, part of a larger repertoire of figurines made by Polish artisans that are popular talismans for Poles—especially figures of Jews holding coins or sacks of money, said to bring good luck—and are sold as souvenirs to tourists in Poland. These Jewish figurines, which are now more numerous than Jews living in the country, materialize both the absence of a once extensive Jewish population and the wide-ranging sentiments about the Polish Jewish past harbored by both Jews and Poles (Lehrer 2014).

Searching the landscape for material traces of prewar Jewish life in eastern Europe regularly centers on what is fragmented or absent, exemplified by discovering the empty recesses in the doorways of buildings, once inhabited by Jews, that held mezuzahs before the Holocaust. In the case of Mi Polin's "Mezuzah From This Home," this "first Polish Judaica company since World War II" transforms these empty spaces into ritual objects by making bronze castings of the voids to fashion new mezuzahs, as part of a commitment to "make Judaism tangible" in contemporary Poland. The creators of these objects explain that the project commemorates Jewish life of prewar Poland by not only recalling the Jews who once lived in the homes where these voids are found but also "giv[ing] a new life to those long gone and fulfill[ing] their holy function. ... Every mezuzah is a story of a given house, family and person. Touching the mezuzah activates a link between past and present" (Mi Polin 2020). Here, the physical filling of a void materializes the rebuilding of Jewish life, bridging former sites of Jewish residence with new places that Jews call home.

Throughout much of Europe, the presence of former Jewish communities is manifest through material traces, primarily cemeteries and former synagogue buildings. Now bereft of local Jewish communities, these structures haunt their landscapes as reminders of former neighbors and of their expulsion or annihilation. Increasingly, sites in Europe have become the focus of memory projects, variously involving Jewish communities abroad as well as local non-Jewish populations. These projects include preserving neglected or vandalized Jewish cemeteries and recovering tombstones that had been used to pave sidewalks or for other sacrilegious purposes. Synagogue buildings, which once may have been used as warehouses, shops, gyms, or cinemas, are being restored and transformed into cultural venues—art galleries, concert halls, libraries, or museums. In the process, these buildings are identified as sites of the local Jewish past. Much of this work is reported by Jewish Heritage Europe, a website and newsletter established in 2009, following an international convening of representatives of Jewish communities and experts in Jewish heritage (Jewish Heritage Europe 2020).

Finally, scholarly activity on Jewish material culture may be considered a new practice in its own right. While much of this is a relatively recent development, research on material culture in Jewish Studies has an extensive history among scholars of antiquity, for whom archeological finds have long played a central role in understanding the ancient period, complementing textual evidence. The study of material culture has more recently become a key development in Jewish Studies for later periods. In addition to scholars researching the modern and contemporary periods in the fields of anthropology, art history, folkloristics, history, literature, museum studies, religion studies, and sociology, such as those whose works are cited in this essay, other academics have addressed Jewish material culture in the medieval (e.g., Shatzmiller 2013) and early modern eras (e.g., Leibman 2012). Though the material culture of Jewish life varies greatly over time and place, as does the available evidence from earlier epochs, it has become a subject of attention for growing numbers of Jewish Studies scholars, in tandem with research on embodiment, topography, and other aspects of Jews' physical existence.

References

Avrutin, Eugene M., Valerii Dymshits, Alexander Lvov, Harriet Murav, and Alla Sokolova, eds. 2009. *Photographing the Jewish Nation: Pictures from S. An-sky's Ethnographic Expeditions*. Waltham, MA: Brandeis University Press.

Blomquist, Mala. 2020. "The Mystery of the Libe Shteyn," *Oregon Jewish Life* (April 21). https://orjewishlife.com/the-mystery-of-the-libe-shteyn/ (accessed June 18, 2021).

Braunstein, Susan. 2004. *Luminous Art: Hanukkah Menorahs of The Jewish Museum*. New Haven, CT: Yale University Press.

Cohen, Richard I. 1998. *Jewish Icons: Art and Society on Modern Europe*. Berkeley: University of California Press.

Eichler-Levine, Jodi. 2020. *Painted Pomegranates and Needlepoint Rabbis: How Jews Craft Resilience and Create Community*. Chapel Hill: University of North Carolina Press.

Gallas, Elisabeth, Anna Holzer-Kawalko, Caroline Jessen, and Yfaat Weiss, eds. 2020. *Contested Heritage: Jewish Cultural Property after 1945*. Göttingen: Vandenhoeck & Ruprecht.

Grossman, Grace Cohen. 2003. *Jewish Museums of the World*. New York: Hugh Lauter Levin Associates, Inc.

Grossman, Grace Cohen and Richard Eighme Ahlborn. 1997. *Judaica at the Smithsonian: Cultural Politics as Cultural Model*. Washington, DC: Smithsonian Institution Press.

Heilman, Samuel. 1988. "Jews and Judaica: Who Owns and Buys What?" in *Persistence and Flexibility: Anthropological Perspectives on the American Jewish Experience*. Ed. Walter P. Zenner. Albany: State University of New York Press, 260–279.
Jewish Heritage Europe. 2020. "Jewish Heritage Europe." https://jewish-heritage-europe.eu (accessed March 19, 2020).
Joselit, Jenna Weissman. 1994. *The Wonders of America: Reinventing Jewish Culture, 1880–1950*. New York: Hill and Wang.
Kirshenblatt-Gimblett, Barbara. 1982. "The Cut That Binds: The Western Ashkenazic Torah Binder as Nexus between Circumcision and Torah," *Celebration: Studies in Festivity and Ritual*. Ed. Victor Turner. Washington, DC: Smithsonian Institution Press, 136–146.
Kirshenblatt-Gimblett, Barbara. 1998. *Destination Culture: Tourism, Museums, and Heritage*. Berkeley: University of California Press.
Kirshenblatt-Gimblett, Barbara. 2006. "The Moral Sublime: Jewish Women and Philanthropy in Nineteenth-Century America," in *Writing a Modern Jewish History: Essays in Honor of Salo W. Baron*. Ed. Barbara Kirshenblatt-Gimblett. New Haven, CT: Yale University Press, 36–54.
Klagsbald, Victor. 1981. *Catalogue raisonné de la collection juive du musée de Cluny*. Paris: Ministère de la Culture, Éditions de la Réunion des musées nationaux.
Lehrer, Erica. 2014. *Na szczęście to Żyd: Polskie figurki Żydów / Lucky Jews: Poland's Jewish Figurines*. Kraków: Korporacja Ha!art.
Leibman, Laura Arnold. 2012. *Messianism, Secrecy and Mysticism: A New Interpretation of Early American Jewish Life*. Portland, OR: Vallentine Mitchell.
Lustig, Jason. 2017. "Who Are to Be the Successors of European Jewry? The Restitution of German Jewish Communal and Cultural Property," *Journal of Contemporary History* 52, no. 3: 519–545.
Mann, Vivian and Joseph Gutman. 1980. *Danzig 1939: Treasures of a Destroyed Community*. New York: The Jewish Museum / Detroit: Wayne State University Press.
McCracken, Grant. 1988. *Culture and Consumption: New Approaches to the Symbolic Character of Consumer Goods and Activities*. Bloomington: Indiana University Press.
Mi Polin. 2020. "Mezuzah from This Home." www.mipolin.pl/products/mezuzah-from-this-home/ (accessed March 15, 2020).
Miller, Julie, and Richard I. Cohen. 1997. "A Collision of Cultures: The Jewish Museum and JTS, 1904–1971," in *Tradition Renewed: A History of the Jewish Theological Seminary*. Ed. Jack Wertheimer. New York: Jewish Theological Seminary, 309–361.
National Museum of American Jewish History (2021) "Wedding Season Is Here." http://nmajh.activehosted.com/index.php?action=social&chash=9a1158154dfa42caddbd0694a4e9bdc8.81&s=8aff28bd56708d9ffac41dc29efe834e (accessed June 18, 2020).
Ochs, Vanessa. 2007. *Inventing Jewish Ritual*. Philadelphia: Jewish Publication Society.
Perten, Rebecca Sandler. 2019. "Postwar American Jewish Religious Identity, Ritual Objects, and Modern Design: Ludwig Y. Wolpert, the Tobe Pascher Workshop, and the Joint Committee on Ceremonies of the Union of American Hebrew Congregations/Central Conference of American Rabbis." Doctoral dissertation, Bard Graduate Center: Decorative Arts, Design History, Material Culture, Bard College.
Quint, Alyssa. 2018. "Visual Artists and Yiddish Avant-garde Theatre in Poland," Digital Yiddish Theatre Project (June 20). https://web.uwm.edu/yiddish-stage/avant-garde-yiddish-theater-in-interwar-pol and (accessed February 4, 2020).
Sarna, Jonathan ed. and trans. 1982. *People Walk on Their Heads: Moses Weinberger's Jews and Judaism in New York*. New York: Holmes and Meier.
Schweitzer, Peter H. 2007. "The Making of a Collection," in *Collections: Celebrating the Cultural Heritage of the Jewish People in America*. Philadelphia: National Museum of American Jewish History.
Shallcross, Bożen. 2011. *The Holocaust Object in Polish and Polish-Jewish Culture*. Bloomington: Indiana University Press.
Shandler, Jeffrey. 2005. *Adventures in Yiddishland: Postvernacular Language and Culture*. Berkeley: University of California Press.
Shandler, Jeffrey. 2010. "Transformations of the *Ketubbah*: Or, the Gallery of Broken Marriages," *Images: A Journal for Jewish Art and Visual Culture* 4, no. 1: 25–45.
Shandler, Jeffrey. 2017. *Holocaust Memory in the Digital Age: Survivors' Stories and New Media Practices*. Stanford, CA: Stanford University Press.
Shandler, Jeffrey. 2020. "Looking for Yiddish in Boro Park," in *How Yiddish Changed America and How America Changed Yiddish*. Eds. Ilan Stavans and Josh Lambert. Brooklyn, NY: Restless Books, 97–105.

Shandler, Jeffrey, and Aviva Weintraub. 2007. "'Santa, Shmanta': Greeting Cards for the December Dilemma," *Material Religion* 3, no. 3 (November): 380–403.

Shandler, Jeffrey, and Beth S. Wenger, eds. 1997. *Encounters with the "Holy Land": Place, Past and Future in American Jewish Culture*. Waltham, MA: Brandeis University Press / Philadelphia: Center for Judaic Studies, University of Pennsylvania / Philadelphia: National Museum of American Jewish History.

Shatzmiller, Joseph. 2013. *Cultural Exchange: Jews, Christians, and Art in the Medieval Marketplace*. Princeton, NJ: Princeton University Press.

Siegel, Richard, Michael Strassfeld, and Sharon Strassfeld, eds. 1973. *The First Jewish Catalog: A Do-it-yourself Kit*. Philadelphia, PA: Jewish Publication Society.

Solomon, Alisa. 2013. *Wonder of Wonders: A Cultural History of "Fiddler on the Roof"*. New York: Metropolitan Books.

Stolow, Jeremy. 2010. *Orthodox by Design: Judaism, Print Politics, and the ArtScroll Revolution*. Berkeley: University of California Press.

Teplitsky, Joshua. 2019. *Prince of the Press: How One Collector Built History's Most Enduring and Remarkable Jewish Library*. New Haven, CT: Yale University Press.

Weissler, Chava. 2007. "Art *Is* Spirituality: Practice, Play, and Experiential Learning in the Jewish Renewal Movement," *Material Religion* 3, no. 3 (November): 354–379.

Wiesemann, Falk. 2005. *Antijüdischer Nippes und populäre "Judenbilder": Die Sammlung Finkelstein*. Essen: Klartext Verlag.

PART III
Groups

11
A STUDY OF TWO TRADITIONS
Sephardi and Ashkenazi

Yamin Levy

Sephardic Jews, the term *Sepharadi* notwithstanding, do not necessarily come from Spain. The reality is that the overwhelming majority of Sephardic Jews do not originate from Spain. This was understood early on when Abraham the son of Maimonides (1186–1237) referred to Rabbis Nissim (990–1062) and Hananel (990–1053) – both of whom were from Kairouan in North Africa – as Sepharadim. Similarly, Rabbi Saadia Gaon (882–942), who lived his entire life in Egypt, is often referred to as *HaSepharadi*. A more accurate definition of Sephardi is a Jew whose diaspora experience took place in non-Christian environments post-destruction of the Second Temple (68 CE). Ashkenazi Jewry, on the other hand, includes all of Jewry whose diaspora experience took place in Christian lands. This working definition explains the Sephardi attribution to all Jews from Syria, Persia, Yemen, Egypt, and Libya – none of whose ancestors originated from Spain (Faur, 1992a).

While this qualification is accurate, it is not precise. Sephardic Jewry includes Jews whose ancestors emerged from Northern Christian Spain, who may share common customs with Sephardic Jewry, but whose philosophic underpinnings are more aligned epistemologically with Ashkenazi Jewry. For example, one cannot place Ramban (1194–1270), also known as Rabbi Moses Ben Nachman or Nachmanides, and Rambam (1138–1204) Rabbi Moses Ben Maimon or Maimonides, in the same school of philosophical thought. Nachmanides believed in spirits and ghosts while Maimonides thought that they were a figment of people's imagination. Nachmanides and Maimonides both emerge from Spain but are heir to two vastly different philosophic traditions. Nachmanides' creative output is influenced by medieval Christian theology and the mysticism of Northern Spain, with little or no access to the philosophical and scientific works of the day. On the other hand, Maimonides' creative and philosophic output is influenced by early medieval Islam's openness to Greek philosophy and sciences from southern Spain (known as Andalusia) (Faur, 1992a). Additionally, one must note that the Jewish community of northern Spain was further influenced, to a certain extent, by the presence and rulings of Rabbi Asher ben Yechiel (1256–1327), who emigrated from Cologne Germany around 1286 due to renewed persecution of the Jews in those parts of Europe. His presence was so commanding that his rulings were considered authoritative in Castille and in Toledo for over a dozen years. Rabbi Yosef Caro (1488–1575), citing Rabbi Levi ben Habib, writes that the Sepharadim accepted Rabbi Asher ben Yechiel as their master for purposes of *halakhic* decision making (*Orach Chayyim* no. 215).

Following the destruction of the Second Temple around 68 CE, and certainly after the failed rebellion of Bar Kochba around 135 CE, the Jewish settlements in Israel began dispersing. Many joined their coreligionists in Iraq (Babel), Persia, Egypt, and North Africa while a significant sector of the Jewish population emigrated to Italy and Europe. Judaism, at this point, ceased being a national religion tied to a land. Instead, both Jewry and Judaism became synonymous with the study of Torah, the observance of Jewish law, and the development of *minhag* (customs). The study of Torah flourished in Christian Europe in an environment that limited their practitioners' access to secular texts, philosophy, and science. This resulted in Torah scholars concentrating on rabbinic texts but not on the Bible, Hebrew grammar, literature, secular philosophy, and sciences. In its place, Ashkenazi Jewry developed a limited conception of Jewish thought influenced by medieval Christian mysticism with the expected trappings of superstition, demonology, necromancy, and magic. This attitude survived the Middle Ages right through modern-day rabbinic rulings of Ashkenazi authorities. Rabbi Moshe Feinstein (1895–1986) was raised and trained in Eastern Europe, emigrated to New York, and continues to be recognized as a significant rabbinic authority for modern-day Ashkenazi Jewry. For Feinstein, the study of secular subjects is at best a concession to the laws of the host country (*Iggerot Moshe, Yoreh De'ah* 3:73). He forbids the study of scientific texts that deny God created the world. A teacher of science, rules Rabbi Feinstein, "must rip those pages out of the textbooks" (*Iggerot Moshe, Yoreh De'ah* 3:73). In traditional Ashkenazi schools one is forbidden to read Greek philosophy which Rabbi Feinstein considered "foolish and empty" (*Iggerot Moshe, Yoreh De'ah* 2:52). This attitude is what gave rise to what became the reform and conservative movements, which do not exist in the Sephardic communities.

In the early medieval period in Andalusia, Sephardic Jewry had access to the latest advances in the study of science and logic as well as to translations of Greek philosophy. They mastered Hebrew grammar as their Islamic counterparts mastered Arabic grammar. What emerged was a Jewish philosophy that was grounded, to a certain extent, in neo-Aristotelian thinking. The creative output of the Golden Age of southern Spain produced works in biblical grammar, biblical exegesis, works in philosophy, and codes of Jewish law organized and accessible to the non-expert. A welcoming of secular studies can still be found among Sephardic rabbinic authorities. Rabbi Haim David Halevy (1924–1996), one of the leading *halakhic* authorities of modern-day Sephardic Jewry, had a vastly different attitude to secular studies including Greek philosophy, than that of Rabbi Moshe Feinstein. Rabbi Halevy permitted the study of secular studies on Shabbat to prepare for exams if "it is for the sake of heaven" (*Aseh Lecha Rav* 1:36).

The Maimonidean controversy, which took place from 1180 to 1240 and peaked with the infamous ban on the study of Maimonides' philosophic works is an example of a clash between two models of religious thinking: one developed in Moorish Spain and the other in Christendom. The Maimonidean tradition was heir to a pluralistic worldview developed in Andalus and Islamic lands while the anti-Maimonidean movement emerged in the authoritarian societies of France, Germany, and Christian Spain. The Sephardi scholar Jose Faur argues that a primary element of the conflict between the Maimonideans and their opposition was a fundamental principle about religion and Jewish law. The Sephardic communities adopted the Geonic premise that Judaism is driven by a legal system based on an immutable covenant with God, while European Jewry introduced an element of fervor and zeal that at times supersedes the legal principles set forth by *halakha* (Faur, 1992b). A prevailing value that characterizes Ashkenazi European attitudes toward Jewish law is the idea that piety superseded *halakha* and is the noblest expression of Jewish practice (Heschel, 1949; Faur, 1992b). For European *halakhic* authorities, *humra* (stringencies) became a standard pattern in religious rulings. The religious outlook and ideals of Sephardic Jewry found their clearest and possibly most sophisticated expression in the writings of Maimonides (1138–1204). His *Mishneh Torah*, the first and only complete legal code, is both precise in formulation and scientifically organized comprising the entire gamut of Jewish law (Twersky, 1980). His *Guide for the Perplexed* is an exquisite work on Judaism's esoteric tradition based on rational principles tracing the qualities of the individual and communal aspects of the human being's relationship with God. His countless *teshuvoth* (responsa) attest to his absolute commitment to *halakha* and rabbinic tradition.

The Vision that Never Came About

Rabbi Joseph Caro, born in Toledo, Spain 1488–1575, author of the *Bet Yosef* and *Shulchan Arukh*, sought to unify Sephardic and Ashkenazi Jewry together under one law, merging the Sephardic with the Ashkenazi practices. Initially, Rabbi Caro's *Bet Yosef* was to present the Talmudic sources for the *halakhic* decisions and explain the basis of the disputes cited in Rabbi Yaacob Ben Asher's *Arbah Turim* (referred to as *Tur*). Rabbi Caro expanded the scope of the *Tur*, enriching it with diverse material from earlier authorities, both Sephardic and Ashkenazi.

The scope of this work is indeed remarkable. In Rabbi Caro's *Shulchan Arukh*, his code of Jewish law, he sought to resolve fundamental disputes and to create a unified code by arbitrating between the three most prominent codifiers: Rabbi Isaac Alfasi (1003–1103), Maimonides and Rabbi Asher ben Yechiel (1259–1327). Rabbi Caro's ambition was clearly stated in his noteworthy mystical diary, *Maggid Mesharim*. In this document, which contains relatively few surviving pages, Caro depicts his vision and desire to complete his compositions, including the *Bet Yosef* where he renders universal *halakhic* guideposts for all Jews. This theme appears several times both in sections composed in Turkey, before Rabbi Caro emigrated to the Holy Land, as well as after, when he settled in Safed. Caro went public with this ambition after the publication of the *Bet Yosef*. In his introduction to the *Bet Yosef*, Rabbi Caro suggested that on the whole Maimonides, al-Fasi and Asher would be regarded as the major legal authorities. When two of them agreed, that was the law. Caro employed democratic principles in legislation, something he believed would resonate with all Jewry and all rabbinic authorities.

Alas, it did not. Ashkenazi Jewry did not employ democratic principles in legislative matters. Rather, they ruled authoritatively. Rabbi Moshe Isserles, better known as Rema (or Rama) was born in Krakow around 1530. He assumed his rabbinic leadership role as head of the community around the time that Rabbi Yosef Caro was completing his *Bet Yosef* and *Shulchan Arukh*. Despite the broad sources Caro utilized to cast a net over the European Jewish community's traditions, Rema published glosses to Caro's *Shulchan Arukh*, thereby supplanting his rulings with that of Ashkenazi Jewry's customs and rulings. Rema deprived Caro's oeuvre of its categorical universal authoritative quality and applicability, writing in the introduction of his glosses that he added to the text details of where its statements should be challenged.

So Rema undid the latter's lifework. As a result, Rabbi Caro's *Shulchan Arukh* is no longer a pure Sephardic legal code even though it has been given such designation. Rema, who died an untimely death at age 42, achieved notoriety by glossing over another scholar's work.

Minhag

Minhag (custom) comprises a formidable body of rabbinic law. There are three different types of *minhag*. First is *minhag* that emerges from *halakhah* (Jewish law) and is rooted in *halakhic* practice, possibly surfacing because of multiple valid yet conflicting views. Alternatively, there are *minhagim* that have no *halakhic* source but are established by the practice of the Jewish people and ratified by the *Sanhedrin* (supreme court of Israel). Regarding these two types of *minhag*, Maimonides writes:

> Whoever goes against any one of the regulations of the rabbis is transgressing a negative commandment, since it says in the Torah "You must follow according to all that they teach you." This includes amendments, decrees, and *minhag* (customs) that they teach the multitudes to strengthen their minds and improve the world.
>
> *Mishneh Torah Mamrim 1:2*

A third type of *minhag* emerges locally – within a community or even a family – and is often based on local culture and customs of the host society. The first two types of *minhagim* are extremely hard to differentiate from rabbinically ordained *mitzvot*. The third, while still called *minhag*, is significantly less binding.

Halakhah, and the first two categories of *minhag*, expose Judaism's core values while the third kind of *minhag* reflects the community's fears and aspiration. How a community dresses a particular lifecycle moment with joy or navigates ceremonies through moments of sadness is often based on the customs of the host culture. The purpose of this kind of *minhag* is to transform ritual into a culturally relevant aesthetic experience. European legalists did not distinguish between the first two types of *minhag* and the third. They spoke of the local *minhag* with the same authoritative voice as they did when codifying *halakha* while Sephardic authorities clearly distinguish between *halakha* and *minhag*.

Practical Differences Between Sephardic and Ashkenazi *Minhag*
Law and Custom: The Sephardic and Ashkenazi Wedding Ceremony

The wedding ceremony offers a unique vantagepoint on the intersection between law and custom and the differences on how Sephardic Jews and Ashkenazi Jews celebrate this important lifecycle event. Take, for example, the first part of the traditional wedding ceremony called *erusin* (or *kiddushin*). Here, the groom places a ring that is worth at least a *peruta* (a coin of minimum value) on the bride's finger. The ring ratifies the *kinyan* (agreement). That it is of minimum value suggests the symbolic nature of the transaction (Biale, 1995). *Halakhically*, this transaction can be accomplished by giving the bride anything of minimum value and declaring that the exchange is for purposes of *erusin*. The use of a ring is indeed a *minhag* – one can use a coin, jewelry, or anything else of value to complete the *erusin* ceremony. The preferred choice for Sephardic Jews has always been a ring, a coin, or a piece of jewelry. Ashkenazi Jewry, on the other hand, only permits the use of a simple gold ring band with no aesthetic value. European *halakhic* authorities not only transformed this custom into binding *halakhah*, but introduced a good amount of details about this custom, including: which hand the groom must hold the ring, which finger the ring must be placed on, what happens if the groom is left handed, and why a round ring is chosen. The simple act of giving the ring becomes infused with theological and kabbalistic meaning. An entire genre of literature was created to validate the authority of this *minhag*.

A certain sector of Ashkenazi Jewry will not perform a marriage ceremony in a synagogue because of *Ma'aseh Goyim* (mimicking the Church). This idea does not exist in Sephardic circles. Here as well, a local custom generated a substantive amount of literature that discusses the metaphysical symbolism to the *chupah* such as Mount Sinai and the giving of the Torah, the *mishkan*, *Bet HaMikdash*, creation and the garden of Eden. This entire body of literature was created in order to make the case that a *chupah* is best performed outdoors or in a non-sanctuary setting. The *erusin* is introduced with a blessing over wine, as is the *nisu'in*, the second part of the wedding ceremony. Here as well Sephardic custom differs from Ashkenazi practice. Ashkenazi tradition dictates that a second, unused, cup of wine be utilized for the *nisu'in*, while Sephardic Jews simply refill the first cup. The European tradition has nothing to do with *yayin pagum* (disqualified wine), which halakhically can be easily rectified by adding "non-*pagum*" wine into the existing cup.[1] This Ashkenazi custom is explained in two fascinating ways. Some suggest that the two cups represent the distinction between the two ceremonies that in previous times were held apart. A second argument states that the bride or groom may be Shabbath violators and by drinking from the wine they make it impure and disqualify it from being blessed again. Each of the two explanations is intriguing in its own way. The first suggests such a strong lingering and nostalgic commitment to the way ceremonies were once observed that they are prepared to forgo *halakha* in order to create a new custom. The second explanation is a window into how the European clergy viewed the masses. Contact with people was filled with spiritual pitfalls (a recurring theme) and therefore *halakhic* strictures had to be put in place.

The *chupah* itself is understood by Sephardic Jews differently than it is understood by Ashkenazi Jewry. For Sephardic Jews, the *chupah* completes the act of marriage because it is an unambiguous public demonstration that this couple is now married. The groom, in a Sephardic ceremony, drapes himself and the bride with a newly purchased *talit* (prayer shawl) as a further public act of matrimony. Ashkenazi Jewry do not consider the ceremony complete until the couple spends a minimum of nine minutes in a secluded place witnessed by two men who fit the *halakhic* criteria of legal witnesses. They call this part of the ceremony *yichud*. Here again we see the creation of a new legal category, adding a new layer to the marriage ceremony.

Another noteworthy difference between Sephardic and Ashkenazi Jewry is the legal origin of the *ketubah* (*halakhic* marriage contract). The Talmud discusses whether the *ketubah* is biblically commanded or not. The opinion of Rabbi Shimon ben Gamliel is that the *ketubah* is biblical while the majority opinion of the sages is that it is a rabbinic concept. Sephardic Jews follow the majority opinion of the sages and therefore write in their *ketubah* that "the 200 *zuz* that are entitled to you per rabbinic decree." Ashkenazi Jewry, in their *ketubah*, state that "the 200 *zuz* that are entitled to you per Biblical mandate." I argue in a previously published article (Levy, 2015) that the reason Ashkenazi authorities imputed a biblical origin to the *ketubah*, disregarding the conclusion of the Talmud, was to emphasize the importance of the marriage contract to the masses. Again, we find evidence that the legal authorities in Europe deviated from legislative protocol and amplified the significance of a law or custom because of their distrust of the people's moral or religious fiber. This may also explain why in Ashkenazi wedding ceremonies the entire *ketubah* is read out loud while in Sephardic wedding ceremonies the *ketubah* is only partially read.

The *tena'im* contract is also something the Sephardic community does not include in its wedding celebration. *Tena'im* is an agreement between the two families to set the wedding date and stipulate certain prenuptial conditions. Rabbi Yaakov Tzvi Hirsch Eisenstadt, author of the *Pitchei Teshuva*, writes that duly signed *tena'im* will assure the bride will not have a menstrual cycle on the night of her wedding. It is unclear if he meant that the family of the bride will appropriately schedule the wedding night or miraculously in the merit of the *tena'im* such an occurrence will not happen. The *tena'im* ceremony is completed with the breaking of an earthenware dish by the two future mothers-in-law.

There was a time when the Sephardic communities did sign such contracts but since the document contained no religious significance and did not involve any blessing, it was discarded. In Ashkenazi tradition, the *tena'im* ceremony is infused with religious meaning and thus was ensured a longer lifespan. The difference in attitude toward the *tena'im* may have to do with their respective attitudes toward the cancellation of engagements. In Sephardic lands, the cancellation of an engagement did not cast aspersions or shame on the family and Sephardic rabbis did not impose financial penalties. On the other hand, the Ashkenazi Jewish community penalized families who broke engagements. Ze'ev Falk attributed the strict rules about canceling engagements to the influence of the surrounding Christian society in Europe (Falk, 1966).

The pattern that emerges is this strong attachment Ashkenazi Jewry has to non-*halakhic* custom, which is often influenced by the rabbinic leadership's desire to create reverence and practice of the ritual. The starkest difference between the two marriage traditions is their respective attitude toward sexuality. A common practice among Ashkenazi Jewry is having the bride and groom fast on the day of their wedding. At the *mincha* service on the day of their wedding the bride and groom recite *aneinu* in the *amidah*, a prayer recited on days of mourning for the destruction of the Temple. In some Chabad circles, the father of the bride also fasts on the day of his daughter's wedding. Rabbi Levi Yitzchak Schneerson (1878–1944), in his *Likutim*, writes: "Whoever increases and intensifies his tears on the day his daughter marries, a day likened to Yom Kippur, is praiseworthy." The Yom Kippur theme is further amplified by having the bride and groom recite prayers reserved for the eve of Yom Kippur such as *al chet* (the penitential prayers) and *vidui* (confessional prayers). The accepted Ashkenazi practice is for the groom to wear a *kittel* under the *chupah*. The *kittel* is a white cotton robe without pockets that one wears on various occasions, including one's own burial. The *kittel* worn on Yom Kippur and Rosh Hashanah is a clear evocation of death. In Frankfurt Germany it was customary for the groom to cover his head like a mourner. In some Ashkenazi communities the groom places ashes on his forehead as a sign of mourning for Jerusalem. The *chupah* in Ashkenazi tradition evokes the motif of repentance, sobriety, solemnity, mourning and death.

In Sephardic circles, any association with death or tragedy at an auspicious moment like a wedding ceremony would be frowned upon and regarded as a bad omen. Such customs would be contrary to the celebratory and festive quality infused in every aspect of the day. The Talmud states clearly: "Any man who has no wife lives without joy, without blessing and without goodness" (Babylonian Talmud *Yevamoth* 62b). This and other such statements in the Talmud clearly reflect a positive attitude toward marriage. Furthermore, the Talmud takes very seriously the *mitzvah* to rejoice with the bride and groom on the day of their wedding. It is therefore not surprising that Rabbi Ovadia Yoseph and earlier Sephardic *halakhic* authorities took serious exception against those who fasted on their wedding day. In contrast to the *kittel*, the Sephardic groom wears a newly purchased *talit* – usually gifted from the bride. The new *talit* gives the groom an opportunity to recite the *shehecheyanu* blessing under the *chupah*. The festive blessing is intended for both the *talit* and the *mitzvah* of marriage.

One can only speculate as to the origins of the marriage customs introduced by European Jewry. Numerous suggestions have been put forward in an attempt at understanding the differences between Sephardic and Ashkenazi attitudes toward marriage. While the general attitude toward marriage in Judaism is favorable, one cannot escape the tension between the permissibility of sexuality within marriage and the value of ascetic denial of the libidinal drive. This tension is exquisitely expressed in the following rabbinic statement: "Let us be thankful to our fathers for had they not sinned (by having sexual intercourse) we would not have come into this world" (Babylonian Talmud *Avodah Zara* 5a). It appears that Sephardic customs and Ashkenazi customs through the Middle Ages and into contemporary practice have each emphasized different dimensions of sexuality.

In Muslim and Middle Eastern countries sexuality, while scrutinized, was celebrated in literature, poetry, and art. On the verse in Exodus 21:11 the Torah lists the obligations a man has toward his spouse – Nachmanides suggests that these obligations all refer to sexual intimacy. Shemuel HaNagid's well-known erotic poetry could only emerge in a society that is comfortable with sexuality. One does not find this kind of ease with sexuality in Christian Europe. As a result, Ashkenazi customs reflect a very different attitude toward sexual intimacy and eroticism even in the context of marriage.

Women Reciting Blessings

Jewish law exempts women from the obligation of observing time-bound *mitzvot*, such as the *mitzvah* of Lulav, Sukkah, and Tefillin. The Talmud records a difference of opinion as to whether women can voluntarily observe *mitzvot* they are not commanded to perform. The Talmud concludes that women can indeed observe the *mitzvot* because of the spiritual lift the *mitzvot* provide (Babylonian Talmud *Chagiga* 16b). The question is: do the women who choose to observe time-bound *mitzvot* have an obligation to recite a blessing prior to observing the commandment?

Maimonides rules in accordance with the Talmud that women are permitted to perform *mitzvot* from which they are exempt (Mishneh Torah *Zizit* 3:9) however, he rules that the blessing should not be recited. According to Maimonides, reciting an unnecessary blessing is equivalent to the biblical violation of reciting God's name in vain. The Tosafot (*Chagiga* 16b), based on the opinion of Rabbenu Tam (1100–1171), rules that women may recite a blessing when performing a *mitzvah* they are normally exempt from observing. The Tosafot argue that all blessings are rabbinic in nature and so the rabbis have the authority to rule who may and may not recite blessings. The difference between the Sephardi practice and the Ashkenazi practice finds expression in Rabbi Caro's *Shulchan Arukh* who rules in accordance with the view of Rambam (*Orach Chayyim* 17:2 and 589:6) while Rema rules in accordance with the ruling of the Tosafot and Rabbenu Tam. While some contemporary Sephardi *poskim* (legal authorities) rule in accordance with the Ashkenazi position (Rabbi Chaim David Azulai (Chida) and Rabbi Chaim David HaLevy volume 2:33), Rabbi Ovadia Yosef strongly encourages Sephardic women to follow the ruling of Rabbi Yosef Caro and Rambam.

Birkat Kohanim, the Priestly Blessing

Birkat kohanim, the priestly blessing, is often referred to as *nesiat kapayim* (the raising of the hands) and is associated with the daily service in the *Bet HaMikdash* (the Temple). The Talmud (Babylonian Talmud *Sota* 38a) concludes that *birkat kohanim* was to also be observed outside the *Beth HaMikdash*. Since it is associated with the Temple service, it is placed immediately following the *Rezeh* prayer in the *Amida*, which petitions for the restoration of the Temple Service. Based on the Talmud (Palestinian Talmud *Nazir* 7:1) Rambam (*Mitzvat Aseh* 26), Ramban (*Bemidbar* 8:2), and later rabbinic authorities such as the author of *Peri Megadim*, Rabbi Yoseph Ben Meir Teomim (1727–1792), argue that *birkat kohanim* is biblically ordained outside the *Beth HaMikdash* even after the Temple was destroyed in 68 CE and must be recited on a daily basis.

Ashkenazi communities, since the early 15th century, eliminated the *birkat kohanim* from their daily service for the following reasons:

> Since the custom of the Kohanim is to immerse in the Mikveh before reciting the *birkat kohanim* and it is difficult to do so in the winter and also because it delays people from going to work, and if the *Kohen* is not called upon to ascend he does not violate a positive Mitzvah.
> *Maharil Rabbi Yaakov ben Moshe Moelin cited by the Bet Yoseph 128*

Rabbi Yoseph Caro criticizes this practice, suggesting there is no excuse to eliminate a positive commandment from the daily service.

Rema (*Orach Chayyim* 128:48), in his glosses to the *Shulchan Arukh*, notes that the practice in Ashkenazi lands is to not recite *birkat kohanim* except during the *musaf* service on holy days. He introduces a third reason: the holy days are festive times and because the *Kohanim* are joyous, they fulfill their commandment with greater intention. While the practice in Europe to eliminate *birkat kohanim* received strong criticism from prominent Ashkenazi *halakhic* authorities, the practice was never changed. One of the most famous proponents among Ashkenazi authorities to reinstitute *birkat kohanim* was the illustrious Gaon of Vilna. It is believed that the practice in Jerusalem, where even the Ashkenazi recite *birkat kohanim* on a daily basis, is attributed to the many students of the Gaon of Vilna who emigrated to Jerusalem in the late 18th century.

Noteworthy is the comment by Netziv (1816–1893; full name Naftali Tzvi Yehuda Berlin) regarding this matter:

> I remember hearing from my father-in-law, the Gaon Rav Yitzchak of Volozhin, that once our teacher the Vilna Gaon agreed to recite the *Birkat Kohanim* each day in the Beit Midrash but he was prevented to do so by heaven and taken to prison during the great controversy in Vilna. At one point, the Gaon and Rav Chaim of Volozhin agreed that the next day he would tell the Kohanim to recite the *Birkat Kohanim*. That night half the city was burnt, including the city's Synagogue. They saw this as a message from heaven and concluded that there must be a secret effect of the blessing bestowed by the Kohanim in the Diaspora.
> *Meshiv Davar 2:104*

This ruling was ratified by *Arukh HaShulchan* (126:68) who suggests that these incidents were messages from God that *birkat kohanim* should not be recited daily. This is yet another excellent example of the difference between the way Sephardic and Ashkenazi Jewry understand the legislative process of *halakhah*. Jewish law, for Sephardic Jews, is determined by the Talmudic tradition and post Talmudic codifiers. European *halakhic* authorities permitted themselves greater latitude in the legal process.

Counting a Minor for *Birkat HaMazon* and *Minyan*

Birkat HaMazon (grace after a meal that includes bread), is a biblically ordained blessing according to both Sephardic and Ashkenazi authorities. The Talmud, regarding *Birkat HaMazon*, states as follows: "If three people have eaten together, it is their duty to invite one another to say grace [together]" (*Mishnah TB Berachot* 45a).

The same passage in the Talmud provides two biblical sources for this practice:

> From where is this derived? Rabbi Assi says: "Magnify the Lord with me and let us exalt His name together (Psalm 34:4)." Rabbi Abbahu derives it from the verse: "When I proclaim the name of the Lord, ascribe [plural] greatness unto our God."
> *Deuteronomy 32:3*

This invitation to recite the *Birkat HaMazon* is called *zimun* and is performed if at least three people recite the blessing together. Sephardic and Ashkenazi scholars disagree as to the nature of *zimun*. European rabbinic authorities, consistent with their belief that there are blessings other than *Birkat HaMazon* biblically ordained (*DeOrayta*), list *zimun* as a biblical obligation (see Rashi Berachot 45a; Ra'avad in Rif pages 44b). Sephardic authorities, notwithstanding the above Talmudic passage, assume *zimun* is rabbinic in nature (see Rambam *Berakhot* 5:2; Rashba *Berachot* 50a, Ritva and others).

The Talmud states that "Women, slaves and minors cannot be counted among those who complete a quorum for *zimun*." The Talmud nevertheless cites numerous opinions suggesting a minor can indeed participate in a *zimun* (TB Berakhot 47b–48a). Based on this reading of the Talmud, Ashkenazi authorities will only allow a minor to participate in *zimun* if he has reached puberty (which is understood to mean thirteen years old and one day). Additionally, the thirteen-year-old must understand "to who he prays" (Rosh, *Mordeakhai Berakhot* 172), while Sephardic authorities rely on the narrative in the Talmud and permit a minor to participate in *zimun* before puberty, even if he does not know "to whom we pray" (see Ramban *Milchamot Hashem* 35b and Rambam *Hilkhot Berakhot* 5:7). The *Shulchan Arukh* (199:10) rules in accordance with the Rif and Rambam. This is indeed the practice of Sephardic Jews.

A Minor in a *Minyan*

While Ashkenazi authorities do not count a minor for a *zimun*, they do count a minor in a *minyan* (quorum of ten men). Some authorities even permit multiple children to be counted. This position is based on a Gaonic tradition that suggests the *Shekhinah* (Divine presence) is present in a gathering of ten regardless of age. This belief is based on the verse: "And I will be sanctified among the children of Israel." Rosh (*Berakhot* 7:20, Rabbenu *Tam Berakhot* 48a) applied this Geonic teaching to rule that a minor who has not yet reached puberty may be counted in a *minyan*. The author of *Ba'al HaMa'or*, Zechariah HaLevi of Gerona (1115–1186; *Berakhot* 35b) adds that one may count up to four minors in a *minyan*.

Rambam (*Tefilah* 8:4) and *Shulchan Arukh* (55:4) reject this idea and refuse to base a *halakhic* ruling on a Gaonic *haggadic* (legend or anecdote) statement. Rema agrees with Rabbi Caro but adds that Ashkenazi Jews are lenient under extenuating circumstances. Rabbi Mordechai Joffe (author of *Levush*, 16th century) introduces the idea that one may give a minor a *chumash* to hold in order to be counted in the *minyan*. While Rabbi Yisrael Meir Kagan, the author of *Mishna Berura* (1838–1933; 55:240), as well as Rabbi Michal Epstein, the author of *Arukh HaShulchan* (1829–1908; 55:10) discourage Rabbi Joffe's idea, they do, however, concede that under extenuating circumstances, it is permitted.

Sitting or Standing for *Kaddish*

Popular belief notwithstanding, *kaddish* has little to do with death and is a central part of the prayer services. It praises God and affirms life without making mention of death. There are five variations of the *kaddish*[2] that are recited during the prayer service, assuming there is a *minyan*. The *Hatzi Kaddish*, the earliest text of *kaddish*, first appears in the liturgy compiled by Rav Amram ben Sheshna Gaon, head of the Sura Academy in Babylonia, circa 856–874.[3] The *kaddish* text varies slightly between Sephardic Jews and Ashkenazi Jews – a development that requires further research (Levy, 2003). The *kaddish* is constructed around the words "*Yehei Shemei Rabba Mevorach*" – "May Your great name be blessed" (*Babylonian Talmud Berakhot* 3a). It is not surprising that there are variant versions of *kaddish* because *kaddish* was a flexible text often customized by various communities to include names of deceased scholars and leaders. What is surprising is the variant custom of sitting or standing while *kaddish* is being recited. In an Ashkenazi prayer service, the entire congregation stands while the reader recites *kaddish*. In a Sephardic prayer service, only the reader stands while reciting *kaddish* – everyone else remains sitting. The emergence of the Ashkenazi custom to stand during the recitation of *kaddish* is based on Rema's ruling where he quotes a problematic version of the Talmud Yerushalmi (Palestinian Talmud). The proof-text in question suggests that Eglon, the evil king of Moab (Judges 3:20), stood when he heard God's name. The Gemara concludes one should stand for all sacred prayers.

The problem with this source is that it is a misquotation of the Talmudic text (Rabbi Haim Vital 1542–1620, *Sha'ar HaKavanot, Derush HaKadish* page 16; also *Hatam Sofer* 2:35) making the entire premise and conclusion faulty. The verses quoted in the Talmud Yerushalmi are incorrect, as is the recorded narrative of the incident between Ehud and Eglon. The entire proof-text of Rema is thrown into question.

All Sephardi *halakhic* authorities support the custom of sitting during the recitation of *kaddish*.[4] Despite the recognition of the faulty evidence, *Mishna Berura* encourages Ashkenazi worshippers to stand during the recitation of *kaddish* simply because it is their custom.

A Sephardic Jew in an Ashkenazi Service and Vice Versa

May a Sephardic worshipper recite the Sephardic *kaddish* in an Ashkenazi service? May an Ashkenazi worshipper recite the Ashkenazi *kaddish* in a Sephardic service? The answer to these questions is a source of dispute between Sephardic and Ashkenazi *halakhic* authorities. Rabbi Moshe Feinstein (*Iggerot Moshe* OC 3:89) rules that an Ashkenazi worshipper may not deviate from the customs of the service they are attending. In other words, in a Sephardi service, one must recite the Sephardi *kaddish*. On the other hand, a Sephardi praying in an Ashkenazi service is instructed to recite the Sephardi *kaddish* (*Or LeTzion* volume 3 5:11) in accordance with his tradition, despite the surroundings.

Over Le'Asiyatan

There is a Talmudic principle called *over le'asiyatan*, which requires one to recite a blessing before performing the action of a *mitzvah* (*TB Pesachim* 7b). Rabbi Yom Tov Assivili, better known as Ritba, (1260–1320) explains that reciting the blessing prior to the act associated with the *mitzvah* ensures a spiritual preparedness that otherwise would be missing. Maimonides offers an alternate understanding by introducing a Talmudic passage (*TB Berakhot* 35a) which teaches that one may not benefit from this world without first reciting a blessing. The idea being that one may not perform a *mitzvah* without first acknowledging God: "Just as we recite blessings for benefit which we derive from this world, we should also recite blessings for each Mitzvah before we fulfill it" (*Mishneh Torah Berakhot* 1:3). The significance of this principle for Maimonides is reflected in his ruling that if one does not recite a blessing prior to the fulfillment of a *mitzvah*, one loses the opportunity to recite the blessing (*Mishneh Torah Hilkhot Berakhot* 11:5).[5] The Talmud, as explained by Rabbenu Hananel, mentions only one exception to the rule of *over le'asiyatan* – immersion in the *mikveh* by one converting to Judaism. Reciting a blessing is only relevant after the would-be convert is immersed and thus has the status of a Jew.

Shabat Candles

Ashkenazi rabbinic authorities introduced several other exceptions to this principle such as the lighting of Shabat candles. Rabbi Avraham Gombiner (17th century), also known as Magen Avraham, expressed concern that once women recite the blessing, they assume all of the Shabat restrictions and therefore are forbidden to light the candles. Because of this concern, he suggests that the women forgo the principle of *over le'asiyatan* and light the candles before they recite the blessing. This suggestion was adopted by all Ashkenazi rabbinic authorities (Rema and Mishnah Berura OC 263:27). Sephardi authorities not only insist that the Magen Avraham's concerns are unfounded but insist that reciting the blessing after the lighting of the candles is actually a serious transgression of reciting an unnecessary blessing, and a violation of stating God's name in vain. Rabbi Ovadia Yoseph goes to great lengths encouraging Sephardic women to light their Shabat candles in accordance with their tradition (*Yabia Omer* Volume 2 OC 16; *Yechaveh Da'at* Volume 2 chapter 33; *Yalkut Yoseph* page 42 and *Leviat Chen* page 3).

Mikveh

Similarly, Ashkenazi authorities rule that women recite their blessing on the *mitzvah* of *mikveh* after they have already immersed in the water. Sephardic authorities follow the *Shulchan Aruch* which rules women must recite their blessing prior to entering the *mikveh* (YD 200, see Rema).

Morning Blessing

Talmudic rabbinic authorities (*TB Berachot* 60b) instituted blessings to be recited upon waking up in the morning. These blessings include those recited for hearing the sound of the rooster, getting out of bed, getting dressed, opening one's eyes, and standing upright. There is a total of eighteen such blessings. The Talmud clearly associates each of these blessing with a specific action – the intent being that when one opens the eyes, the blessing is recited; when one stands upright, the blessing is recited. The blessing, according to the Talmud, should be directly linked to the expression of gratitude for God's abundant gifts.

Ashkenazi rabbinic authorities compiled the eighteen blessings into one unit to be recited as an introduction to the morning prayers, dissociating the blessing from the action completely. This exception was created by Ashkenazi authorities because they believe most people are ignorant and do not know how to recite their prayers independently in the earlier part of the morning. Maimonides disagrees with this custom and rules that all the blessings must be recited exactly as intended by the Talmud: each blessing at its appropriate time upon rising in the morning. Maimonides writes:

> These eighteen blessings do not have a particular order. Rather, one recites each of them in response to the condition for which the blessing was instituted, at the appropriate time. In other words, when one fastens his belt while still in bed he recites the blessing "who girds Israel with strength." When one hears the sound of the rooster one recites the blessing "who gives understanding to the rooster." Any blessing in

which one is not obligated should not be recited. If one sleeps in his outer garment he should not recite the blessing "who clothes the naked." One who walks barefoot does not recite the blessing, "For You have provided me with all my needs."

It has become customary for people in the majority of our cities to recite these blessings one after the other in the synagogue, whether they are obligated to do so or not: This practice is mistaken, and it is not proper to follow. One should not recite a blessing unless he is obligated to do so

Mishneh Torah Tefilah 7:7

It is quite unusual for Maimonides to disqualify or prohibit a practice that "has become customary for people in the majority of our cities." This suggests that Maimonides considered the practice of Ashkenazi Jewry a blatant error (Levy, 2002). The *Shulchan Arukh* rules like Maimonides, and Sephardic Jewry accepts their stance. Rema rules like Ashkenazi authorities, a practice followed today in Ashkenazi synagogues. The pattern is clear, Ashkenazi rabbinic authorities felt the need to guide the masses who could not be trusted to know and practice the ritual correctly at home.

Rosh Hashanah, Yom Kippur and the Prayer Experience

J. D. Eisenstein, in his *Ozar Masaot* includes a story of an Ashkenazi rabbi named Simha Ben Yehoshua. This rabbi was traveling to the land of Israel on a ship in the late summer of 1774. Most of the travelers on the ship were Sephardic Jews. The voyage took place before Rosh Hashanah and Yom Kippur, when Sephardic Jews rise early to recite their *Selichot* (penitential prayers). Rabbi Simha made the following observation:

On the entire voyage, we prayed with the Sepharadim. The Sepharadim awoke prior to daybreak to recite their penitential prayers with a quorum, as is their custom during the month of Ellul. During the day, they eat and rejoice and are happy of heart and they pray in that manner as well. Some of them spend their entire day in the study of Torah.

Eisenstein, 1969, 241

Rabbi Simha was reacting to an aesthetic and experiential difference in the way Sephardic and Ashkenazi Jews pray. In a Sephardic prayer service, the liturgy is recited out loud in its entirety. It is either chanted by the entire congregation in unison, or responsively with the *Hazan* (Cantor) or sung by the *Hazan* alone. Melodies and tunes are assigned to various prayers often specific to a season, holy day, or forthcoming holy day. The prayer experience is always upbeat and designed for maximum participation. The Ashkenazi European prayer experience is quite different. The liturgy is primarily recited silently, the *Hazan* chanting first and last verses or clauses. In an Ashkenazi service where a professional *Hazan* leads the prayers, certain parts of the liturgy are selected to be sung solely by the *Hazan*, often in an operatic manner.

While this distinction is evident all year round, including in daily prayers, it is alarmingly poignant on the High Holy Days. In a Sephardic Rosh Hashanah or Yom Kippur service, while reflecting the tone of judgment, the music is not at all tearful or somber. In fact, the tunes and melodies are uplifting and festive, even when petitioning God for mercy. One of the *piyyutim* (Jewish poem) sung on Yom Kippur, which has the following refrain: *hatanu lefanekha rahem aleinu* ("we have sinned before you, have mercy on us") is sung responsively by the congregation with the *Hazan* in an upbeat, festive melody. Even the most contrite confessional moments of the liturgy are expressed with joy and fervor.

The Ashkenazi European High Holy Day experience is radically different. Men attend synagogue wearing a *kittel* as a reminder of their mortality. The tunes are somber and tearful. The highpoint of the Rosh Hashanah and Yom Kippur service is a poem called *Unetanu Tokef* which is recited in a weeping and tearful fashion. It tells the explicit story of a man tortured by the Church because he refused to convert to Christianity. The poem is his last will and testament to the community.

Conclusion

It is only natural that time and geography, over a period of 1,400 years, have caused diverging approaches between Sephardi and Ashkenazi Jewry. The differences can be seen in Jewish law and the attitude toward Jewish law, differences in customs and practices, and even basic assumptions on tenets of Jewish philosophy and the authority of *halakha*. While the 18th and 19th centuries hailed rights of citizenship and entry into universities for European Jewry, Jews continued to struggle for basic civil rights. Anti-Jewish attitudes climaxed in the early 20th century leading up to the Holocaust. And yet, Ashkenazi Jewry today represents a large majority of world Jewry. Ashkenazi Jewry's response to the Holocaust was to double-down on the creation of *yeshivot* (Jewish schools) mirroring the *yeshivot* in Europe, *kollelim* (full-time Torah study), uniformity in preservation of European dress code, mainstreaming Yiddish language, and safeguarding attitudes toward study, Jewish law, and European customs.

Sephardi Jewry endured its share of oppression, and yet, as Andre Chouraqui, a scholar on North African Jewry noted: "The Judaism of the most conservative of Maghreb's Jews was marked by a flexibility, a hospitality, a tolerance" (Chouraqui, 2001, 61). In an attempt to characterize the differences between Sephardi Jewry and Ashkenazi Jewry, Rabbi Hayyim David Azulai (1724–1806) suggested that in matters of *halakha*, Sephardi sages clung to the quality of *hesed* (kindness) and, as a result, sought ways of being lenient while Ashkenazi sages manifested the quality of *gevurah* (heroism) and, as a result, tend to be strict in *halakhic* matters. Rabbi Azulai's characterization was primarily an apologetic indication of his own approach to Jewish law. He and his Sephardi colleagues saw themselves as voices for a welcoming and pleasant *halakhic* outlook.

H. J. Zimmels, in his seminal work *Ashkenazim and Sepharadim* (1996), notes how Ashkenazi Jews impose upon themselves greater stringencies beyond what *halakha* demands and, in time, many of their observances became normative. Rabbi Benzion Uziel offers his own perspective on the differences between Sephardi and Ashkenazi attitudes and customs: "Sephardic rabbis allowed themselves the authority to annul customs that stem from host cultures not rooted in Jewish law, while European rabbis sought to strengthen such customs" (introduction to *Mishpetei Uziel*). Rabbi Abraham Joshua Heschel, in his book *The Earth is The Lord's* (1949) – a presentation of what he refers to as "the inner world of the Jew in Eastern Europe" – devotes an entire chapter to contrasting the "Two Great Traditions": Sepharadi and Ashkenazi. He argues that "the intellectual life of the Sephardic Jew was deeply influenced by the surrounding world," while in Ashkenazi Jewry, "the spiritual life of the Jew … was lived in isolation." He adds that the culture of the Sepharadim "was shaped by the elite … and drew inspiration from classical philosophy and science," while that of Ashkenaz was "archaic simplicity, imaginative naiveté and unaffected naturalness of the humble mass." He notes that the Ashkenazim did not write poetry or *piyyutim* as the Sepharadim did. They wrote mostly *selichot* – simple penitential prayers and elegies. Heschel continues by pointing out that Sephardic Jewry produced classical intellectual works "distinguished by their strict logical arrangement. Composed according to a clear plan, every one of their details has it's assigned place, and the transition from one subject to the next is clear and simple." Ashkenazi authors, writes Heschel, were "irregular, vague, and often perplexingly entangled; their content restless."

For Heschel, the Sephardic world is born out of the classic tradition while the Ashkenazi world is based on a more romantic tradition. To that end he writes:

> What distinguishes Sephardic from Ashkenazic culture is, however, primarily a difference of form rather than a divergence of content. It is a difference that cannot be characterized by categories of rationalism versus mysticism, or the speculative versus the intuitive mentality. The difference goes beyond this and might be more accurately expressed as a distinction between a static form, in which the spontaneous is subjected to strictness and abstract order, and a dynamic form which does not compel the content to conform to what is already established. … Room is left for the outburst, for the surprise, for the instantaneous.
>
> *Heschel, 1948*

He ends his apology with a defense of Ashkenazi custom and attitude: "the inward counts infinitely more than the outward," suggesting that the Sephardic tradition is inferior because it is external.

Differences exist within the Sephardic community itself. Similar to the differences between Ashkenazi subgroups such as the Litvaks, Galazianers, German Jews, Polish Jews, and Chassidic Jews, there exist differences between Moroccan, Iraqi, Spanish, and Portuguese Jews. Even within the Syrian community, differences in custom exist between the Jews of Aleppo, Aram Tzoba, and northern Syria. In the 20th century the Ashkenazi community became more centrally integrated, publishing uniform siddurim and creating *yeshivoth* that serve all their various subgroups. There is a trend to cast a net over all Sephardic communities and refer to them as *Eidot Mizrah* or *Mizrachim* (easterners). As a result of affluence, however, and easy access to publishing houses, Sephardic communities are dodging the trend of uniformity.

Throughout the 20th century, the ultra-Orthodox European leadership sought to strengthen its hold by gaining influence over the community of Jews who observe Jewish law. Successful and well-funded outreach movements were created by Lithuanian-trained rabbis, as well as Chabad (which launched a world-wide outreach movement). All these initiatives infiltrated Sephardic communities throughout the world. In 1984, the ultra-Orthodox community successfully gained influence over the Mizrachi/Sephardic communities throughout Israel by creating a political party called Shas. Shas, which means "guardian of the Sepharadim," was the Sephardic Jew's solution to the continuing economic hardships and identity crisis in the early years of the State of Israel. In the first decade of its existence, Shas was under the influence of the Ashkenazi ultra-Orthodox community. This resulted in a new leadership of Sephardic rabbis trained in the Ashkenazi Lithuanian ultra-Orthodox model. Rabbi Ovadia Yoseph's indisputable mastery of Jewish law and rabbinic texts made him a credible leader in both the Ashkenazi and Sephardic worlds. Though he himself was ultra-Orthodox, he successfully weaned the Shas party away from the Lithuanian influence.

A survey of the contemporary landscape of Sephardic and Ashkenazi Jewry finds that the only sector in which either of the traditions remain as a creative force is in the religious liberal to modern Orthodox communities, while the Sephardic and Ashkenazic Jews who identify with the ultra-Orthodox have assimilated into an eastern European mode of religious and cultural expression.

Notes

1. Disqualified from being blessed upon because someone drank from it.
2. For a more elaborate discussion see my *Journey Through Grief: A Sephardic Manual for the Bereaved and Their Community*, Ktav Publishing House, 2003 pages 105–108.
3. See David Telsner, *The Kaddish: Its History and Significance*, Jerusalem: Tal Orot Institute, 1995.
4. Hida, Tov Ayin 18:32; Rabbi Haim Pelaggi, Kaf HaChaim 13:7; Ben Ish Hai, Veyehi 8; Rabbi Yaacov Haim Sofer Kaf Hachayim 56:20; Rabbi Ovadia Yoseph, Yehave Da'at 3:4.
5. Isaac Ben Moshe, author of *Or Zarua Hilkhot Kerita* Shema 1:25 (Vienna, thirteenth century) disagrees.

Bibliography

Angel, Marc. 1988. "A Study of the Halakhic Approaches of Two Modern Posekim," *Tradition* 23(3) Spring: 41–52.
Angel, Marc. 1999. *Loving Truth and Peace: The Grand Religious Worldview of Rabbi Benzion Uziel*. Northvale, NJ: Jason Aronson.
Angel, Marc D. 2006. *Foundations of Sephardic Spirituality: The Inner Life of the Jews of the Ottoman Empire*. Woodstock, VT: Jewish Lights.
Angel, Marc D. 2015. *The Rhythms of Jewish Living: A Sephardic Exploration of Judaism's Spirituality*. Woodstock, VT: Jewish Lights.
Biale, Rachel. 1995. *Women and Jewish Law: The Essential Texts, Their History, and Their Relevance for Today*. New York: Schocken Books.
Caro, Yosef. https://torah.org/series/shulchan-aruch/
Caro, Yosef. www.sefaria.org/Beit_Yosef
Chouraqui, Andre, 2001. *Between East and West: A History of the Jews of North Africa*. Trans. Michael M. Bernet. Skokie, IL: Varda Books.
Eisenstein, J. D. 1969. *Ozar Masaot*. Tel Aviv.
Elazar, Daniel J. 1988. *The Other Jews: The Sepharadim Today*. New York: Basic Books.
Falk, W. Ze'ev. 1966. *Jewish Matrimonial Law in the Middle Ages*. Oxford: Oxford University Press.
Faur, Jose. 1992a. *In The Shadow of History: Jews and Conversos at the Dawn of Modernity*. New York: State University of New York Press.
Faur, Jose. 1992b. "Two Models of Jewish Spirituality," *Shofar*(10): 5–46.
Feinstein, Moshe. 1988. *Iggerot Moshe, Yoreh De'ah*. Jerusalem: Beth Medrash L'Torah V'Horaah.
Grossman, Avraham. 2004. *Pious and Rebellious: Jewish Women in Medieval Europe*. Waltham, MA: Brandeis University Press.
Heschel, Abraham J. 1948. "The Two Great Traditions". *Commentary*. May. www.commentary.org/articles/abraham-heschel/the-two-great-traditionsthe-sephardim-and-the-ashkenazim/
Heschel, Abraham J. 1949. *The Earth is The Lord's: The Inner World of The Jew in Eastern Europe*. New York: Jewish Lights.
Johnson, Paul. 1988. *A History of The Jews*. New York: Harper and Row.
Kanerfogel, Ephraim. 2017. "Rabbinic Conceptions of Marriage and Matchmaking in Christian Europe," in Elisheva Baumgarten, Ruth Mazo Karras, and Katelyn Mesler eds. *Entangled Histories: Knowledge, Authority, and Jewish Culture in the Thirteenth Century*. Philadelphia, PA: Penn Press, 23–37, 267–77.
Levy, Yamin. 2002. "רחשה וינעב וכרב תורעה" [Bet Yitzchak]. Yeshiva University, 369–80.
Levy, Yamin. 2003. *Journey Through Grief: A Sephardic Manual for the Bereaved and Their Community*. New York: Ktav.
Levy, Yamin. 2015. "Comparative Study of the Sephardic and Ashkenazic Wedding Ceremony," *Conversations*, September, www.jewishideas.org/article/comparative-study-sephardic-and-ashkenazic-wedding-ceremony
Maimonides, Moses. 2000. *Mishneh Torah*. Ed. Shabse Frankel. Jerusalem: Hotzaat Shabse Frankel.
Maimonides Mishneh Torah www.sefaria.org/texts/Halakhah/Mishneh%20Torah

Netziv. 1894. *Meshiv Davar*. Warsaw: Halter and Eisentadt.
Raphael, Chaim. 1991. *The Sephardi Story: A Celebration of Jewish History*. London: Valentine Mitchell.
Sachar, Howard M. 1994. *Farewell Espana: The World of the Sepharadim Remembered*. New York: Alfred A. Knopf.
Twersky, Isadore. 1980. *Introduction to The Code of Maimonides*. New Haven, CT: Yale University Press.
Yoseph, Rabbi Ovadia. Nd. *Yabia Omer, Yechaveh Da'at, Yalkut Yoseph Levyat Chen*. Jerusalem: Meor Yisrael.
Zimmels, H. J. 1996. *Ashkenazim and Sephardim: Their Relations, Differences, and Problems as Reflected in the Rabbinical Responsa*. Hoboken, NJ: Ktav.

12
KARAITE JUDAISM
An Introduction to its Theology and Practices

Shawn Lichaa

Introduction

Karaite Judaism is a historical Jewish movement[1] that derives its rules from three main sources: (i) the written biblical text (Hebrew: *katuv*), (ii) logical inference (Hebrew: *hekesh*), and (iii) what Karaites refer to as "the burden of the inheritance" (Hebrew: *sevel hayerusha*).[2] The main theological difference between Karaite Judaism and Rabbinic Judaism is that in traditional Rabbinic thought, God gave Moses two sets of laws: one oral and one written. In contrast, Karaite Jews maintain that God gave Moses one law: the written Torah. This different theological approach yields an entirely distinct paradigm through which to view Jewish law, and to put a fine point on it, Karaite Jews do not accept the Talmud as having a divine basis, and therefore do not derive their laws from it.[3]

The primary focus of this chapter is to provide an overview of the foundational elements of Karaite Judaism and provide a framework for understanding how those elements empowered Karaite Jews to develop practices that are different from those found in Rabbinic Judaism. Before delving into these topics, we would be remiss not to mention that Karaites are an extremely diverse set of Jews. Karaites spanned large geographic regions and time frames, and even exist to this day. As such, the breadth of their views, theology, and practices cannot be fully captured herein. Rather, we have intentionally chosen to paint with broad strokes so that the reader might come away with a meaningful understanding of the concept of Karaite Judaism; inevitably, this is at the expense of conveying all of the contours of various Karaite communities and interpretations.[4]

The Fundamental Tenet and Its Relation to the Sources of Karaite Law

The fundamental tenet of Karaite Judaism has been encapsulated by the maxim, "Search the Scripture well, and do not rely on my opinion." This statement has been attributed to 'Anan ben David, who lived in the eighth century and who many believe to be the founder of the Karaite movement.[5] In order to understand the statement fully, it needs to be dissected into its two components: (i) Search the Scripture well; and (ii) do not rely on my opinion.

"Search the Scripture Well"

The phrase "search the Scripture well" relates directly to the three aforementioned sources of Karaite law (that is: (i) the written text, (ii) logical inference, and (iii) the burden of the inheritance) and the Karaite methods of interpretation.

The Three Sources of Karaite Law:

The Written Text

Karaites and Rabbanites[6] have the same *Tanakh*, and the distinction between the Karaites and Rabbanites is one of interpretation. We must here address the threshold question of how much of the written text do Karaites derive their religious obligations from. Do Karaites derive obligations only from the five books of the Torah? Or do they derive them from the entire *Tanakh*? Karaite sages, up until recent times, derived at least some of their obligations from the entire *Tanakh*. An example of this is that Karaite literature deemed Purim (a post-Torah holiday) to be obligatory. Moshe Firrouz, the current Chief Hakham of the Karaite community, believes that Purim is non-binding and that the prophets and writings (i.e., the *Tanakh*) impose no new obligations on the Jewish people, but merely serve to clarify the commandments in the Torah.[7]

Logical Inference

Logical inference is the process by which Karaites (and other exegetes) seek to determine how to apply the laws of the Torah beyond the specific words in the text. Each Karaite may reach a different conclusion as to the proper inference in a particular verse; however, once an individual Karaite has derived an understanding of the text, this inference is treated *as if it were* written into the text. We bring two examples of logical inference, both of which are oft-cited by Karaites.

Example 1 – Plowing with an ox and a donkey: In the book of Deuteronomy, we find the commandment, *Thou shalt not plow with an ox and a donkey together* (Deuteronomy 22:10). Without using logical inference, it is impossible to know how to apply this commandment. For example, does the commandment apply only to "plowing" (the verb in the written text) or does it apply to all types of work? Does it apply only to an "ox and a donkey" (the animals in the written text) or does it apply to other species of animals as well? And if it does apply to other species, what is the underlying principle to determine how to extend this commandment to other species?

Various Karaites, as did various Rabbanites, understood this prohibition in different ways. 'Anan ben David, in his book of commandments, understood the ox and the donkey, respectively, to be representative of pure and impure animals. 'Anan further understood the word "plow" to have both the literal meaning of plowing a field, but also the secondary meaning of "intercourse."[8] In contrast, Aaron ben Elijah, who lived in fourteenth-century Byzantium, understood the ox and the donkey, respectively, to be representative of strong and weak animals, and expressly rejects the opinion that the word plow conveys a secondary meaning of intercourse.[9] The seventeenth-century Karaite Solomon ben Aaron set forth his opinion as follows:

> for from the word "plowing" an analogy and similarity is established to all kinds of work; and from the words *with an ox and a donkey*, to any two species, that is, a pure species with an impure species, or a strong one with a weak one.[10]

Example 2 – Uncovering the nakedness of your father's sister: As another example, in the book of Leviticus we find the commandment, *You shall not uncover the nakedness of your father's sister, she is your father's kin* (Leviticus 18:12). The words of the text alone prohibit relationships between a nephew and his aunt, but say nothing about the relationship between a niece and her uncle. Are these forbidden as well? The difficulty here (as with the example concerning the ox and the donkey in the previous example) is that the Torah does not tell us why the nephew–aunt relationship is forbidden, aside from the fact that an aunt is kin to the nephew's father. If direct kinship is all that matters, then extending the prohibition to niece–uncle relationships may seem reasonable. In fact, the traditional Karaite Jewish view is that niece–uncle relationships are strictly forbidden.[11] In contrast, Rabbanites permit niece–uncle relationships.[12]

Burden of the Inheritance

The final source of Karaite law is the "burden of the inheritance." In its most narrow explication, the burden of the inheritance refers to legally binding information that is entrenched in Jewish practice from the time of Moses, even though this information is not explicitly stated in the Torah. In this narrow view, this information was passed down orally from generation to generation and has support in the *Tanakh*. This oral information is different from the Oral Law of the Rabbanites, because Karaites do not believe that the oral information that forms the basis of the burden of the inheritance came from God; rather, this information was already known to the Israelites receiving the Torah.

This point is made by the thirteenth-century, Byzantium-based Karaite exegete Aaron ben Joseph in his biblical commentary, *Sefer Ha-mivchar*:

> Now, this commandment [of setting the month] is not elaborated upon [in the written Torah] as is the custom for most of the commandments, [for which] it [generally] states: Speak to the Israelites, that they should do such and such ... for Scripture does not give details regarding matters that the patriarchs [already] practiced, such as [kosher] slaughter, for the commandment to act according to these teachings relies on the burden of inheritance.[13]

Karaites, thus, acknowledge that the Torah does not instruct the people of Israel on how to set the start of the month or how to perform ritual slaughter. This poses a conundrum for Karaites, who believe that there is indeed a proper way to set the month and a proper way to perform slaughter, but also believe that the Torah requires no oral accompaniment. We next analyze the Karaite arguments for the burden of the inheritance with respect to the setting of the month and ritual slaughter.[14]

Example 1 – Setting of the Month: Karaites generally advance linguistic and historical arguments that ancient Israelites knew that the new moon signals the beginning of the month – despite the lack of an explicit statement in the *Tanakh*. First, Karaites observe that the Hebrew word for month, *ḥodesh*, is linguistically related to the word "new" or "renewal." This suggests that something is renewing itself every month. Karaites explain that ancient Israel was a society that relied on physical signs – such as the setting and rising of the sun, the crescent moon and the full moon. The sign that renews itself on a monthly basis is the moon. The moon, further, literally looks new on the first day of the month, because this is the day that the moon reappears after being invisible to the human eye for a period of time. Second, Karaites explain that the word *ḥodesh* itself also had the meaning of moon in biblical times. For example, the word *ḥodesh* is used in parallel with the word *yeraḥ*, which is another biblical word for moon (See 1

Kings 6:1, 1 Kings 8:2). In totality, Karaites argue that these verses show that the moon (and its newness) is inextricably linked to the setting of the month, and this was obvious to ancient Israelites receiving the Torah.

Example 2 – Ritual Slaughter: Both Karaites and Rabbanites believe that ritual slaughter, *sheḥita* in Hebrew, is properly performed at the neck of an animal – again, even without an express commandment in the (written) Torah in this regard. Here, too, Karaites bring biblical proof that the ancient Israelites understood how to slaughter *prior to receiving the Torah*. For example, in Genesis 37:29, we see that when Joseph's brothers attempted to convince their father that Joseph had died, they slaughtered a goat and put the goat's blood on Joseph's coat. Significantly for present purposes, the Torah describes this act of slaughtering the goat as "*vayyishḥatu*" (literally, "they slaughtered"; from the same root as *sheḥita*). This verse only suggests that *a method* of slaughter was known prior to the Torah; but the verse does not prove that slaughter was performed at *the animal's neck*.[15] Yet, this is the crux of the burden of the inheritance; Karaites bind themselves by practices that were passed down and taught from generation to generation, provided there is some biblical basis for them.

To be clear, Karaites assert that these linguistic, historical and biblical arguments *add support* for the requirement to set the month by the new moon and for slaughtering by the neck. But these arguments and proof-texts are *not the source* of the practice. The source of the practice is the burden of the inheritance. As set forth in *Aderet Eliyahu* (the "Mantle of Elijah") by the fifteenth-century Karaite Elijah Bashyachi, the last great codifier of Karaite law:

> Our sages have said that all tradition that does not stand in opposition to the written [Torah] and does not add to what is said in the written [Torah] and all Israel acknowledges [to be correct][16] and there is support in the written [Torah] we shall call the "transmission" and we shall receive it upon ourselves [as binding].[17]

Now that we have looked at the three sources of Karaite law, we turn our attention to the second part of the fundamental tenet.

"Do Not Rely on My Opinion"

The second part of the maxim attributed to 'Anan is "do not rely on my opinion."[18] This phrase emphasizes that each person has the obligation to search the Scripture well, and this concept is woven throughout Karaite literature. For example, the ninth-century Jerusalem-based Karaite Daniel al-Kumisi wrote a letter to the Karaites of the diaspora urging them to pronounce God's name (i.e., the Tetragrammaton) as "Adonai," as opposed to pronouncing it as it is written.[19] After offering biblical texts to support his view that saying the Name is forbidden, Kumisi directs them to research the matter for themselves: "I have written for you my opinion regarding speaking God's name. But *you*, you shall examine the matter according to *your* wisdom, lest you act according to *my* wisdom [and] in reliance on *my* opinion."[20]

Similarly, in the preface to his commentary *Sefer Ha-Michvar*, Aaron ben Joseph explains that he does not always follow the edicts of previous Karaite leaders, because the correct interpretation is intrinsic to the interpretation itself and not to the speaker.[21] Likewise, even the general members of a community may disagree with a sage and refuse to follow the sage's edicts: "All that which any individual sage (*ḥakham*) prohibits or permits in his time, it is not obligatory that the entire community act in accordance with that prohibition or permission."[22] The same concept serves as the underpinning in the letters from the Karaites of the Crimea to the Karaites of

Egypt. By way of background, the Karaites of Crimea held a conference in Eupatoria in 1910 to discuss relaxing certain marital restrictions, including the relaxation of the Karaite prohibition of two brothers marrying two sisters (see *supra* fn. 11). The Crimean Karaites then sent correspondence to the Egyptian Karaites:

> Let the Cairene Karaites now form their own opinion, "without feeling bound by us or obliged to defer to us, just as it is not necessary to defer to our past scholars, for there is no deference (to persons) in matters of law."[23]

Karaite Interpretive Methods

In general, Karaites seek the plain meaning (*peshat*) of the text. The plain meaning may be literal or it may be metaphorical. The same word may be literal in one context and metaphorical in another context. For example, the plain meaning of the command to circumcise one's son in Genesis 17:10–14 is literal; whereas the plain meaning of the directive to circumcise the foreskin of one's heart in Deuteronomy 10:16 is metaphorical. As noted *supra*, 'Anan believed that the plain meaning of the word 'plow' was both literal and metaphorical in the same verse (Deuteronomy 22:10).

Practical Distinctions between Karaites and Rabbanites

Karaite literature (and thus Karaite exegesis) generally falls into three main time frames:

1. Pre-thirteenth century: These Karaites were willing to engage meaningfully with the text *and* were willing to reach conclusions that differ from the Rabbanites.
2. Thirteenth through fifteenth century: These Karaites were willing to engage meaningfully with the text *but* were not as willing to reach conclusions that differ from the Rabbanites.
3. Sixteenth century through the twentieth century: These Karaites were mostly summarizing the Karaite practices of their day, even where they diverged from previous Karaite interpretations.[24]

Against this background, the following examples may provide additional context with respect to how Karaites interpret the *Tanakh* differently from the Rabbanites. They also shed light on intra-Karaite debates over the proper interpretation of verses. The trends typified by these three timeframes of Karaite literature are reflected in many of the examples below.

Fires on Shabbat

One of the fiercest polemics between the Karaites and Rabbanites of the Middle Ages concerned the permissibility of fire on Shabbat. The debate centers on the proper interpretation of Exodus 35:3, which is commonly translated as "You shall kindle no fire (*lo teva'aru esh*) throughout all your habitations on the Sabbath Day." Early Karaites believed that a plain reading of the text forbade any fire burning on Shabbat – even those flames kindled before Shabbat. As a result, these Karaites strictly objected to the Rabbinic practice of lighting Shabbat candles. In response to this debate, it became customary among Rabbanites to say a blessing while lighting candles:

But afterwards [from the eighth century onward], in order to combat the hostility of the Karaite Jewish community, which forbade the use of all light on the Sabbath, it became mandatory to light candles and to recite a blessing, thus making it a holy act.[25]

Later Karaites, such as Elijah Bashyachi (fifteenth century) and Solomon ben Aaron (seventeenth century)[26] sided with the Rabbanites in this debate, and permitted flames that were lit prior to the Sabbath. Yet Solomon ben Aaron's contemporary, Mordecai ben Nisan, held that such flames were prohibited.[27] The majority view today among Karaites of Egyptian descent (which make up the majority of the community in Israel and the United States) is that all fires are prohibited on Shabbat.

Fermented Foods on the Festival of Unleavened Bread ("Passover")

The Karaites of the Middle Ages had an internal debate regarding the permissibility of fermented foods during the seven days of the Festival of Unleavened Bread. At the center of the debate is the Torah's prohibition of *ḥametz* during the festival (Exodus 12:15). One group of Karaites believed that (as with the Rabbinic observance) the word *ḥametz* means "leavening," and accordingly only grains can become *ḥametz*.[28] It appears that this was the majority opinion of the Karaite sages in the Middle Ages. Another group of Karaites believed that *ḥametz* refers not only to leavened grains but to fermented foods as well. For example, vinegar is referred to in the Torah as *ḥometz yayin* (literally, "fermented wine") (Numbers 6:3). This latter interpretation is the majority opinion of Karaites today.[29]

The Separation of Milk and Meat

The Torah says three times, "Do not boil a kid (*gedi*) in its mother's milk." Rabbanites understand the verse to prohibit eating milk and meat together. The Karaites historically did not believe that the verse was intended to be an outright prohibition on eating milk and meat; rather, they believed that the prohibition applied strictly to the milk of the mother and the meat of the child.[30] However, some later Karaites such as Solomon ben Aaron (seventeenth century) believed that the verse prohibited consuming milk and meat;[31] whereas his contemporary, Mordecai ben Nisan, asserted that there was no such prohibition on milk and meat.[32]

The Shofar on Yom Teruah ("Rosh Hashanah")

On the first day of the Seventh Month, the Torah directs the Jewish people to observe a holiday called Yom Teruah (commonly referred to as "Rosh Hashanah"). According to Rabbinic law, the word "teruah" refers to the sound made from a shofar.[33] Karaites have long noticed that the verse in question does not make mention of a shofar. This is in contrast to Leviticus 25:9, which expressly commands the blowing of a shofar on Yom Kippur to announce the Jubilee year. As a result, Karaites almost universally held that there was no commandment to blow the shofar and, to this day, Karaite synagogues do not blow the shofar on Yom Teruah.[34]

Sukkot and the Four Species

There is also disagreement between the Karaites and the Rabbanites about what to do with the "four species" on Sukkot. In Leviticus 23:40, the Torah states, *"And you shall take on the first day [of the Holiday] the fruit of the goodly tree [or the goodly fruit tree], branches of palm-trees, and boughs of thick trees, and willows of the brook, and you shall rejoice before Adonai your God seven days."*

The reason for the dispute is that the Torah does not tell us what to do with these species. Similarly, the Torah does not expressly command the Israelites to build booths, only to dwell in them. According to Rabbinic law, the "four species" are to be used to form the *lulav* and *etrog*. The majority of Karaites assert that these items were to be used to build the sukkah, drawing from the example of the Jews living at the time of Ezra and Nehemiah (Nehemiah 8:15). A minority of Karaite sages believed that the "four species" were to be used to create edible bundles of fruits and greenery for consumption during the holiday.[35]

Tefillin/*Phylacteries*

Karaites do not believe that the Torah commands the use of phylacteries (*tefillin*). There are four passages that – according to Rabbinic law – serve as the underpinnings of the commandment to don phylacteries. In the first of those four passages (i.e., Exodus 13:9), the Torah uses the Hebrew word *ulzikkaron*, meaning "as a memorial." In the remaining three passages (i.e., Exodus 13:16; Deuteronomy 6:8–9; and Deuteronomy 11:18), the Torah uses the word *totafot*, which is often rendered in English as "frontlets." Reading these four verses together, Karaites asserted that the plain meaning of these verses is that one should remember Torah, *as if* it were between our eyes. In the words of the seventeenth-century Karaite Mordecai ben Nisan:

> And [the Karaite sages] say that [the seat of] understanding is in the head, [specifically] in the forehead, above the nostrils of the nose, between the eyes; therefore, the Torah commands that one should understand [the commandments] with understanding, and support them in one's memory, just as one would not forget something that is placed on one's forehead, between one's eyes. So, [when Scripture says:] *And thou shalt bind them for a sign upon thine hand, and they shall be as frontlets between thine eyes, and thou shalt write them upon the posts of thy house, and on thy gates*, the meaning is metaphorical, just as when King Solomon, peace be upon him, says in Proverbs 6: *Bind them continually upon thine heart*, and *tie them about thy neck* [Proverbs 6:21], and in chapter 7: *Bind them upon thy fingers, write them upon the table of thine heart* [Proverbs 7:3]; this is a metaphor, referring to the constancy with which one should eagerly study [the words of wisdom], and the joy and delight [that one should take] in them.[36]

These examples highlight several of the interpretations that came to signify Karaite theology and identity throughout history and even to this day.[37] These identities shifted in various eras and places with respect to how Karaites viewed themselves in light of the Rabbinic law as well as in relation to other interpretations of other Karaites.

Karaite Creeds

Throughout history, various Karaites have sought to encompass the movement's principles of faith. The most prominent Karaite expositor of a "principles of faith" is the twelfth-century Karaite Judah Hadassi, who lived in Byzantium. Judah Hadassi's ten principles of faith were set forth in his work *Eshkol ha-Kofer* (or *Cluster of Henna*) and were written about two decades prior to Maimonides' thirteen principles of faith.[38] The principles of faith taught most frequently in the Karaite community today, however, are based on those of Elijah Bashyachi (fifteenth century), which appear in his *Adderet Eliyahu* (or *Mantle of Elijah*):

(1) the entirety of the physical universe was created and has not forever existed;
(2) all things have an eternal Creator who was not Himself created;
(3) this Creator has no physical form and is single and unified in every sense;
(4) this Creator sent Moses;
(5) God gave His perfect Torah to Moses;
(6) Every believer should know the language and interpretations of the Torah;
(7) God sent the prophets other than Moses;
(8) God will resurrect men in the Day of Judgment;
(9) God gives to every man each according to his deeds and according to what he earns;
(10) God has not abandoned the Jewish people even though they are in their exile, and the Jewish people should yearn for salvation at the hands of the Messiah.[39]

Writing in Judeo-Arabic, the Karaite Israel Ha-ma'aravi (al-Maghribi) (fourteenth century)[40] set forth his own principles of faith, as follows:

(1) the belief in God;
(2) the belief in the messengership of Moses;
(3) the belief in the prophets of the *Tanakh*;
(4) the belief in the message of the Torah;
(5) the belief in the holy site of Jerusalem; and
(6) the belief in the day of judgment.[41]

Ha-ma'aravi's principles of faith contain no express acknowledgment of the coming of the Messiah.[42] This is in contrast to Hadassi's *Eshkol Ha-Kofer*,[43] Bashyachi's *Adderet Eliyahu*, and to the twelfth principle of Maimonides's thirteen principles of faith. This is also in contrast to the introduction to the Karaite prayer book by the thirteenth-century Karaite, Aaron ben Joseph: "There are some other things that one at prayer should have: ... And one should acknowledge the resurrection of the dead, for we all mention this in the prayers, and one should acknowledge the coming of the Messiah."[44]

Liturgy and Related Rituals

The Karaite conception of liturgy, prayer and the synagogue reflect the primacy that the movement places on its biblical roots. We briefly expound upon those concepts in this section.

Liturgy

The Karaite liturgy in its current form was composed by the aforementioned Karaite Aaron ben Joseph, author of *Sefer Ha-mivhar*. Karaites have two formal prayers daily, one at morning and one at evening (corresponding to the times of the daily sacrifice). Thematically, the Karaite prayer places a heavy emphasis on the sins of Israel, repentance, and the centrality of Jerusalem.

The Karaite Siddur consists mostly of biblical verses which have been woven together to form a new composition. For example, the traditional Karaite Shabbat service contains Psalms 90, A Prayer of Moses (*Tefilla le-moshe*). In the lead-up to this section, the prayer book weaves together two themes: (i) the fear or worship (Hebrew: *yira*) of God; and (ii) humility (Hebrew: *'anav*). These two themes are used to introduce verses about Moses himself, whom the Torah describes as humble (Numbers 12:3). All of this serves as an introduction to the recitation of Psalms 90.[45] In another example, the Karaite liturgy contains a composition commencing with *'Am zu yatzarti li* that weaves together themes of declaration (Hebrew: *safar*) and themes of praise (Hebrew: *halal*) collected from eight biblical sections.[46]

Karaite prayers are generally recited in five different ways:

(1) read solely by the cantor;
(2) read responsively by the cantor and the congregation;
(3) read responsively by a member of the congregation and the rest of the congregation;
(4) read by a member of the congregation and repeated by the entire congregation; and
(5) read by the congregation.

Most of the service is a dialogue between the cantor and the congregation; that is, it is a responsive reading that falls in category (ii) above. For example, in the aforementioned composition *'Am zu yatzarti li*, the cantor reads from the opening of Isaiah 43:21 through the *atnaḥ* (*'Am zu yatzarti li*) and the congregation responds with the final part of the verse (*tehilati yesapperu*). The cantor then reads the opening part of Psalms 96:3, which is the next verse in the composition, again stopping at the *atnaḥ* (*Saperu vagoyim kevodo*), and the congregation completes the verse (*bechol ha'amim nifle'otav*). In other responsive prayers, the cantor reads the entire sentence, and the congregation responds with the entirety of the next sentence.

According to the majority of Karaite sages, a proper prayer consists of five elements:

(1) Praise (*shevaḥ*): praising God for his many great deeds.
(2) Thanks (*hoda'ah*): thanking God for creating and maintaining the world.
(3) Confession (*vidui*): confessing one's sins.
(4) Request (*bakasha*): requesting forgiveness for one's sins with an emphasis on our own wrongdoings.
(5) Supplication (*techina*): begging God for forgiveness with an emphasis on God's abundant mercy.

A minority of Karaite sages add two more elements:

(6) Crying out (*tze'aka*): as in the verse, My voice will go out to God and I will cry out (Psalms 77:2).
(7) Calling out (*keria*): as in the verse, to you God, I will call out.[47]

The Tallit

Karaites wear *talitot* (prayer shawls) during all services (both morning and evening). The Karaite prayer shawl has cords (*gedilim*) with white and blue fringes interwoven on each corner, reflecting the commands in Numbers 15:38 (for a blue fringe) and Deuteronomy 22:12 (for cords). Karaites have ritualized this command in the form of the following blessing over the *tallit*: "Blessed are You, Adonai, our God, King of the universe, Who has sanctified us with His commandments, and commanded us to wear a four-cornered garment with fringes."[48] Karaites raise the four cords in front of their eyes during prayer when reciting the passages corresponding to Numbers 15:37–15:41, which reference looking upon the blue fringe to remember the commandments.

Many (and perhaps even most) of the earlier Karaite sages held that women were also obligated in the commandment to wear blue fringes. This is reflected in the writing of Jacob al-Qirqisani (tenth century), Levi ben Yefet (eleventh century) and Judah Hadassi (twelfth century). Later Karaite expositors, such as Aaron ben Elijah (fourteenth century), Elijah Bashyachi (fifteenth century), and Solomon ben Aaron deemed that the commandment is limited to men.[49]

Prayer Posture

Today, Karaites maintain many of the biblical prayer postures, from raising of the hands to prostrating with their heads to the ground. The Vilna Karaite Siddur contains an introduction written by Aaron ben Joseph, mentioning the postures found in the Torah:

> Therefore, you find [these prayer postures]: keeping the legs together, spreading out palms, lifting up and spreading out hands, lifting up eyes, bending the head, prostration, kneeling, bending the knees, and the other conditions that are indicated in the words of the prophets. All this is so that the general populace can see, and not stumble.[50]

Synagogue

Karaites remove their shoes before entering the sanctuary of the synagogue, reflecting the holiness of the location (see Exodus 3:5; Joshua 5:15). Women and men who are ritually impure do not enter the sanctuary.[51] This reflects a historical Karaite belief that the synagogue is analogous to the Temple with respect to purity laws.[52]

Karaites in Israel and Beyond

"It is often said that Karaites were the first Zionists."[53] This is due primarily to the zeal with which early Karaites, such as the aforementioned Daniel al-Kumisi (ninth century), advocated that Jews return to Jerusalem. Daniel al-Kumisi criticized his fellow Karaites for enriching themselves in the diaspora, while leaving Jerusalem a wasteland.[54] He exhorted them to return to Israel, but if they themselves would not return, he asked each community to send five individuals along with financial means to support themselves.[55] By the end of the tenth century, the Karaite Jewish community in Jerusalem came to an end, both due to internal factors and due to the Crusades.[56] The intellectual center of the community moved to Byzantium, giving rise to many of the sages we have mentioned earlier: Judah Hadassi (twelfth century), Aaron ben Joseph (thirteenth century), Aaron ben Elijah (fourteenth century) and Elijah Bashyachi (fifteenth century). In time, the impact of these Byzantium-based sages was felt throughout virtually every Karaite community, including the Polish-Lithuanian Commonwealth (such as the aforementioned Mordecai ben Nissan and Solomon ben Aaron), the Crimea, and twentieth-century Egypt.

Today, there is a very small Karaite community in Jerusalem. The community's Chief Hakham, Moshe Firrouz, lives in Be'er Sheva, the community's headquarters are in Ramle, and the largest population center has been in Ashdod. Despite all of this change, the centrality of Jerusalem in Karaite thought and liturgy is evident to this day.[57]

Conclusion

The sources of Karaite law are the written text, logical inference, and the burden of the inheritance. The fundamental tenet to search the Scripture well and not rely on others' opinions resulted in wide divergence in thought and interpretation between the early Karaites and the Rabbanites. In time, though, Karaites started adopting more and more Rabbinic views. Part of this rapprochement is undoubtedly due to the group's minority status, for minority groups tend to adopt the customs of the majority. One cannot fully discount, however, the role that the second part of the fundamental tenet ("do not rely on my opinion") played in this rapprochement, because Karaites did not view themselves as bound by their own sages, freeing them for a more rapid adoption of certain Rabbinic beliefs.

Notes

1 The historical rise of the Karaite movement is beyond the scope of this work, and there is a "paucity of evidence with which to reconstruct the early history of Karaism" (Cohen, 1978, 129). For now, it suffices to say that by the eighth century, we see the origins of what would become a unified Karaite Jewish movement. Certainly, by the end of the ninth century, Karaite Judaism existed as a formal movement (or "sect," in historical terms) independent from other Jewish movements.
2 For an English-language explanation of these concepts, see Tomer Mangoubi *Mikdash Me'at* (hereinafter, "Mangoubi") and Solomon ben Aaron's *Sefer Appiryon Asa' Lo,* translated in English under the title *The Palanquin*).
3 This is not to say that Karaites "reject" the Talmud outright. Indeed, we find the following statement in Elijah Bashyachi's introduction to his *Adderet Eliyahu*: "Moreover, the Sages have said that much of the Mishneh and the Talmud are words of our fathers" (Bashyachi 1835, folio 2a, right column).
4 We hope that the reader will also forgive us for painting in rather broad strokes regarding the Rabbinic tradition.
5 As an historical matter, however, 'Anan gave rise to a movement of Jews known as the Ananites. That movement eventually merged with what we now call the Karaites, and there is no doubt that the Karaite movement grafted 'Anan in as one of their own. See Lasker 2019, 100 et seq. For this reason, we cite some of 'Anan's opinions throughout.
6 In this section, adherents of Karaite Judaism are referred to as Karaites, and adherents of rabbinic Judaism are referred to as Rabbanites.
7 Lichaa 2015, *Comparing Purims*.
8 Harkavy 1903, 4–5.
9 Aaron ben Elijah, *Keter Torah* 1972, comment to Deuteronomy 22:10.
10 Solomon ben Aaron 2017, 33.
11 See Mangoubi, *Mikdash Me'at*, section 17. All of the earliest Karaite exegetes applied a rigorous set of rules when using logical inference on the laws of incest. This became a source of contention within the Karaite community, for these rules prohibited two brothers from marrying two sisters (in addition to several other types of relationships). See below on the 1910 Eupatoria conference, wherein the Crimean Karaites sought to reform these laws.
12 *See* Babylonian Talmud, Sanhedrin 76b.
13 Mordecai ben Nisan, *Royal Attire* 2017, 162 (cited in endnotes to this edition).
14 The examples concerning the new moon and ritual slaughter are excerpted from a series of questions and answers by the present author.
15 Karaite sources also advance a linguistic argument that the proper method of slaughter results from drawing a knife across the animal to be slaughtered. In Jeremiah 9:7, we find the phrase "their tongues have become a drawn arrow." The word drawn, *shachut*, is from the same root as *shechitah*, slaughter,

and conveys an arrow that has been pulled back across the bow. This verse does not necessitate, though, that the place of slaughter is the neck.

16 Applying this principle to the method of slaughter, both the Karaites and Rabbanites agree that slaughter is to be performed by slitting the neck, even if they disagree on the precise requirements. For more on this topic see Dascalu's edition of Ha-ma'aravi's *Karaite Creed & Discourse on Slaughter*, and Sardar's edition of Ha-kohen's *Ritual Slaughter*.

17 Bashyachi 1835, folio 2a, right column.

18 We note here that there is significant doubt as to how much of the maxim, and whether this part of the maxim in particular, was indeed set forth by 'Anan. E.g., Cohen 1978, 142. Regardless of its origin, "do not rely on my opinion" has become an integral part of the Karaite movement.

19 Apparently, the Karaites of Khurasan (in Persia) were pronouncing God's name in Kumisi's time, and those same Karaites believed that anyone replacing God's personal name with "Adonai" was a non-believer (Nemoy 1976, 51 fn. 6).

20 Nemoy 1976, 92 (translation mine).

21 Charlap 2013, 128–129.

22 I thank Michael Bernstein for alerting me to this source; I have adapted my translation here from the one he provided me. Bashyachi 1835, *Iggeret Gid Hanashe* (Introductory Letters page 2, right column).

23 Nemoy 1978, 265 (internal punctuation omitted).

24 I thank Tomer Mangoubi for providing this structure. These bullets were adapted from Lichaa 2017: "Women on the Fringes: Which Karaite Sages Got it Right?"

25 Kolatch 2007, 168. The fierce opposition to fires on Shabbat served as the basis for the polemical poem *Yerivai Ve'oyevai* by Israel Ha-Ma'aravi (al-Maghribi). The poem's core theme is that the author does not need the light of physical flames on the Sabbath eve, because God is his light (Weinberger 1990, 123–125).

26 Solomon ben Aaron 2017, 43.

27 Mordecai ben Nisan 2017, 41 fn. 32.

28 In addition to the five grains that Rabbanites believe become *chametz*, many Karaites believe that a sixth grain, millet, also becomes *chametz* (Babovich 2020, 47 fn. 50).

29 El-Kodsi 2007, 167 fn. 6 (describing the beliefs of the Karaites of Egypt, from whom most Karaites today descend).

30 Mangoubi, section 15.

31 Solomon ben Aaron 2017, 143.

32 Mordecai ben Nisan 2017, 49.

33 E.g., Babylonian Talmud, Rosh Hashana 15a.

34 Mordecai ben Nisan 2017, 81, 185 (endnotes, citing Daniel al-Kumisi as an example of a Karaite who advocated blowing the *Shofar*); Solomon ben Aaron 2017, 79.

35 Mordecai ben Nisan 2017, 85 fn. 53.

36 Mordecai ben Nisan 2017, 97 et seq.

37 Another example of an interpretation that goes to the essence of Karaism throughout the ages is the Karaite interpretation that the holiday of Shavuot ("Pentacost") should always fall on a Sunday.

38 Lasker 2019, 104.

39 Mangoubi, section 10.

40 For more on Israel Ha-ma'aravi in relation to fires on Shabbat, see fn. 25, *supra*.

41 Ha-ma'aravi 2017, 32–53.

42 For a slightly different formulation of the ten principles of faith by the seventeenth century Karaite, see Solomon ben Aaron, 2017, 103.

43 Lasker 2008, 58

44 Vilna Karaite Siddur (Volume 1) 1891, 3 (translation by Gabriel Wasserman).

45 In order, the verses included in this composition are: (i) Proverbs 16:6 (fear); (ii) Proverbs 15:33 (fear, humility); (iii) Proverbs 22:4 (humility, fear); (iv) Psalms 37:11 (humility); (v) Numbers 12:3 (Moses, humility); (vi) Numbers 12:8 (fear, Moses); (vii) Deuteronomy 34:10 (Moses). Technically, Numbers 12:8 uses the same root for fear as the other verses, but this verse does not refer to fearing or worshipping God. Rather, it refers to the fear of speaking to Moses. *Siddur* (Volume 1) 1891, 223. For simplicity, I have included the core meaning of the words (i.e., humility, fear), even though they are rendered differently in context.

46 The theme of this composition moves from being mostly about declaration toward being mostly about praise. In order, the verses included in this composition are: (i) Isaiah 43:21 (declare, praise); (ii) Psalms 96:3 (declare); (iii) Psalms 118:17 (declare); (iv) Psalms 102:22 (declare, praise); (v) Psalms 9:22 (declare); (vi) Psalms 145:6 (declare); (vii) Psalms 22:23–24 (declare, praise); (viii) Psalms 135:1–4 (praise). *Siddur* (Volume 1) 1891, 206. For simplicity, I have included the core meaning of the words (i.e., humility, fear), even though they are likely rendered differently in context.
47 These elements of prayer and their explanations are from Mangoubi, *Mikdash Me'at*, section 14.
48 *Baruch atta Adonai Elohenu melech ha'olam asher ḳiddeshanu bemitsvotav vetsivvanu lilbosh arba' kenafot betsitsit.* See Abbreviated Blessings Book, 60.
49 Solomon ben Aaron 2017, 115. Mordecai ben Nisan 2017, 187 (endnotes).
50 *Siddur* (Volume 1) 1891, 3 (translation by Gabriel Wasserman).
51 For these purposes, a non-exhaustive list of persons who are ritually impure include men who have had a seminal emission since nightfall; women during their period; or persons who have been under the same roof as a dead body within the previous week, etc.
52 Mangoubi, *Mikdash Me'at*, section 14.
53 Lasker 2019, 99.
54 Nemoy 1976, 78.
55 Nemoy 1976, 78.
56 Lasker 2019, 99.
57 Lasker 2019, 100.

References

Babovich, Toviyya. 2020. *The Chief Cornerstone*. Trans. Joel S. Davidi. Daly City, CA: Karaite Jews of America.
Bashyachi, Elijah. 1835. *Adderet Eliyahu*. Gozlow.
Charlap, Luba R. 2013. "The Interpretive Method of the Karaite Aaron ben Joseph: Uniqueness versus Conformity," *Revue des étude juives*, 172(1–2) (janvier–juin): 125–43.
Cohen, Martin A. 1978 "'Anan ben David and Karaite Origins," *JQR*, 68(3): 129–45.
El-Kodsi, Mourad. 2007. *The Karaite Jews of Egypt: 1882–1986* (Second Edition). Lyons, NY: np.
Ha-kohen, Shemuel. 2017. *Ritual Slaughter*. trans. Isaac Sardar. Daly City, CA: The Karaite Jews of America.
Ha-Ma'aravi (al-Maghribi), Israel. 2017. *The Karaite Creed & Discourse on Slaughter*. Trans. Raphael Dascalu. Daly City, CA: The Karaite Press.
Harkavy, Avraham. 1903. *Studien und Mittheilungen aus der Kaiserlichen Oeffentlichen Bibliothek zu St. Petersburg, VIII*. Öffentlichen: Sankt.
Kolatch, Albert. 2003. *The Jewish Book of Why*. New York: Penguin.
Lasker, Daniel J. 2008. *From Judah Hadassi to Eliyahu Bashyatchi: Studies in Late Medieval Karaite Philosophy*. Leiden & Boston: Brill.
———. 2019 "Karaites and Jerusalem: From 'Anan ben David to the Karaite Heritage Center in the Old City," in *Next Year in Jerusalem: Exile and Return in Jewish History*. Ed. Leonard J. Greenspoon. Studies in Jewish Civilization, vol. 30. West Lafayette, IN: Purdue University Press, 99–110.
Lichaa, Shawn. 2015. "Comparing Purims," The Torah.com, www.thetorah.com/article/comparing-purims (accessed 1 January 2021).
———. (undated) "How do we know how to properly slaughter an animal so that it is kosher for consumption, when the Torah does not describe slaughter in any detail?" www.karaites.org/questions--answers.html (accessed 1 January 2021).
———. (undated) "How do we know that the month starts with the sighting of the new moon, when the Torah does not expressly command us how to set our months?" www.karaites.org/questions--answers.html (accessed 1 January 2021).
———.2017. "Women on the Fringes: Which Karaite Sages got it right?" http://abluethread.com/2017/01/30/women-on-the-fringes-which-karaite-sages-got-it-right-reader-poll/ (accessed 1 January 2021).
Mangoubi, Tomer, *Mikdash Me'at*, available online at the Karaite Jews of America's Reading Room: www.karaites.org/reading-room.html (accessed 1 January 2021).

Mordecai ben Nisan. 2017. *Royal Attire*. Trans. Gabriel Wasserman. Daly City, CA: The Karaite Press.

Nemoy, Leon. 1976. "The Pseudo-Qumisian Sermon to the Karaites," *PAAJR* 43: 49–105.

———. 1978. "Two Controversial Points in the Karaite Law of Incest," *HUCP* 49: 247–65.

Solomon ben Aaron. 2017. *The Palanquin*. Trans. Esther Mangoubi. Daly City, CA: The Karaite Press.

Weinberger, Leon J. 1990. "Israel Dayyan's Zemer for the Sabbath," *JQR* 81:1–2, 119–25.

Liturgical Sources

Siddur Ha-tefillot Ke-minhag Ha-ḳaraim (Ḥeleḳ 1) (Vilna: 1891).

Abbreviated Blessings Book according to the Custom of the Karaite Jews (Second Edition). 2020. Daly City, CA: The Karaite Jews of America.

13
THE MODERN ORTHODOX IN AMERICA

Samuel Heilman

We begin with some basic social facts. According to the 2015 Pew Report on Orthodox Jews, Orthodox Jews as a group are, in contrast to the general American Jewish population, younger, more fertile, more religiously observant, more Republican, and socially conservative. The Pew report says they make up about 10% or 530,000 of American Jewry.[1] I suspect that figure is low by at least a third, since many in the *haredi* or so-called "ultra-Orthodox" population, who make up a large part of today's Orthodoxy, generally do not respond to surveys from those who are outsiders to their community (as the Pew researchers are) unless they believe they have something practical to gain from participation.

Orthodox Jews are, on average, younger than the rest of Jewry (likely because of their larger family size), with the bulk being under 25 years old, contrasting with the early twentieth-century image of Orthodox Jews as old and on the way to disappearing. That nearly all are raising their children as Jews is certain. While Orthodoxy in the past had a very high dropout rate, with about half becoming less observant as they reached adulthood, there can be no denying that in the past few generations, a majority (70% according to Pew) today who identify as Orthodox were raised as such. That is probably the result of the more than 80% that Pew claims send their children to day schools and yeshivas – compared to the tiny number (11%) of other Jews who do so. So far, all this is true for all types of Orthodox Jews. But what about the so-called "Modern Orthodox" who, according to Pew, are about 31% of the Orthodox, and are the focus of our interest here?

Definitions

Who are they? A precise definition of "Modern Orthodoxy" is elusive and even many of those who came to be associated with this worldview and its allied behaviors have become uncomfortable with the term, nor do they all agree on its parameters. After all, "modern" is a relative term, and constantly subject to change. Generally, the Modern Orthodox are those who identify themselves through their commitment to adhere faithfully to the beliefs, principles, and traditions of Jewish law and observance without being either remote from or untouched by life in the contemporary secular world and the spirit of free inquiry. As such, the Modern Orthodox Jew has been pulled in two directions. Those two directions are vaguely defined either as "not sufficiently religious" by those who tend toward the religious right, or "not modern enough," according to those who consider themselves more progressive on the religious left. In many ways, Modern Orthodoxy tries to hold on to these two opposites, having relationships of respect with non-Jews and embracing the larger surrounding open culture, while restraining their attachment to or assimilation by the general culture in line with the demands of Jewish practice and law. This may require a compartmentalization of different elements of their lives, even if this means holding onto contradictory values and practices. I have elsewhere called this the "contrapuntalist model," borrowing from musical language which refers to sound in counterpoint and with two or more independent melodic lines. Contrapuntalism is a kind of stabilized dualism in which the Modern Orthodox try to stand with their feet firmly in two very different worlds at once, allowing people to belong to multiple institutions and often competing cultures simultaneously. In a sense this is the essential element of "Modern Orthodoxy." In this contrapuntalist, pluralist model of Modern Orthodoxy, competing and often inharmonious loyalties to potentially rivalrous institutions and cultures that are in counterpoint are permitted, even encouraged. This is because the people involved believe that they have much to gain by living in what Peter Berger once called "plural life-worlds."[2] They generally believe optimistically that it is possible to be exposed to and even interact with and share in that general culture without necessarily succumbing to its assimilating tendencies – if one is vigilant and powerfully rooted in Jewish practice, and maintains social connections to an Orthodox community, and has received a good Orthodox Jewish education. But this also sometimes forces them to simply ignore (i.e. compartmentalize) the resulting internal conflicts in their religious lives.

In fact, contrapuntalism and compartmentalization grant the individual some modicum of autonomy in making, negotiating, and establishing competing and conflicting affiliations. This results in Modern Orthodox Jews often deciding for themselves, even on an ad hoc basis, how to handle their plural life worlds as well as the cultural and religious tensions emerging from them. At other times they turn, in line with traditional orthodox norms, to their rabbinic authorities for help in this task, although as the rabbis have become increasingly *haredi*, with the slide to the right of rabbinic training, they tend to be less prepared to guide contrapuntalism or compartmentalization.

Plural Life Worlds

What is the nature of these plural life worlds? One is made up of Jews who are affiliated with Orthodox institutions (synagogue, school, voluntary associations, summer camps, etc.), who observe Jewish dietary laws (keep kosher) and laws of "family purity" (in which wives use a *mikveh* or ritual bath after menstruation and before engaging in sexual relations), who religiously and rigorously observe the holy days and the Sabbath, engage in ongoing Torah study, and who have made some active public expression of a commitment to maintain Jewish values. In the another, is a commitment to secular learning, from primary school to university education. In the Pew 2020 survey sample, 20% of the Orthodox have post-graduate degrees, and an additional 17% have bachelor's degrees – leading to many of them having a higher income than other Orthodox Jews.[3] In Trencher's more focused 2019 study of the *Modern* Orthodox, over 60% of these Orthodox Jews have a post-graduate or professional degree, a remarkable fact considering on average between 3% and 4.5% of Americans do, and over 50% have post high school Jewish study.[4] A significant bulk of their financial resources are spent pursuing this learning, both Jewish and secular, which in the United States is not subsidized by the government and taxes as it is in Israel.

In addition to endorsing a liberal arts education and entry into mainstream general culture and affirming the idea of critical thinking, the Modern Orthodox maintain an active and regular involvement in and attachment to the outside world and its secular, pluralistic, *cosmopolitan* outlook. They encourage business pursuits, careers, and professional life. These have grown markedly during the last 60-odd years, a period which has also seen an increase in Orthodox day school and yeshiva education leading to intensified Orthodox parochial commitments. That is why I have also called these Jews "Cosmopolitan Parochials."[5]

Because of these joint commitments (particularly their strict observance of the ban of travel other than by foot on the Sabbath), these people also necessarily live together in Orthodox Jewish communities. As such, they remain "locals," bonded to a relatively uniform and parochial home community of like-minded individuals. Insofar as they identify with the beliefs and practices of that place, they confirm and maintain one another's Orthodox expression of Jewishness. For these Jews, the common mores and norms are the key to a sense of belonging – as such they constitute a specific religious culture that inhabits a special social space. Thus they remain parochial, relatively socially conservative, and committed to comparatively punctilious Jewish observance guided by a rabbinate that is generally slow to embrace change, and therefore these essentially Orthodox (i.e. social conservative) and parochial Jews engage with the outside secular culture guardedly. They are always careful not to be swept up by their cosmopolitan tendencies, even as they endeavor not to be totally insular like their more extreme and traditionalist fellow believers.

The latter are "the Ultra-Orthodox group [that] seeks to exclude" all that is different from it.[6] These more traditionalist Jews are commonly called *haredi* (anxious). They are generally quite conservative in their outlook, do not tend to diverge from group practices according to individual choices (strictly limiting personal autonomy), and do not share an optimistic attitude about the ability of the Orthodox to hold onto competing ways of life. They argue that even slight cultural contact is dangerous and will ultimately lead to a slippery slope toward perdition and especially the loss of its most suggestive members – generally the young – to assimilation by the majority and hence the demise of the Orthodox Jewish way of life. To avoid this, the latter have generally espoused a social stance of cultural insulation, leading to living in their own, socially sealed conformist communities and enclaves, strictly controlling the education of their young, and limiting anything beyond the most instrumental contact with those who do not share their ways of life and values. Wherever possible, they try to remain within their own institutions and tend to conform to the collective.

Thus, the two types of Orthodox are not completely distinct. One of the key concerns among *all* Orthodox Jews remains maintaining the continuity of their religious culture and protecting it from the erosion brought about by cultural contact with ways of life and people that they consider destructive. They all fear hostility from the outside world, and they are all worried about the risks of cultural assimilation. As a minority (even among Jews), they believe they must be vigilant in protecting themselves (and particularly the most vulnerable among them, their children) from what they view as the seductive and some of the base elements of popular Western democratic culture, with its permissiveness, openness, emphasis on individual independence or personal choice and autonomy as an ultimate value, and its implicit as well as sometimes explicit hostility to Jewish traditions and practices.

For the Modern Orthodox, contrapuntalism and its combination of competing attachments is not easy to maintain. In a 2019 study of a sample of people identifying as American Modern Orthodox Jews, Mark Trencher found that 88% of his sample reported "experiencing conflict" in their interaction with secular society and, when faced with this sort of tension, while 51% claimed to stand firm in their practices and beliefs, more than a third reported having to make compromises or being "flexible."[7] This suggests that some of the criticisms that the *haredim* make about Modern Orthodoxy may be true for at least this third.

On the other extreme, as I argued in 2006 in my *Sliding to the Right*,[8] there are significant segments of this Modern Orthodoxy that are hewing closer to *haredi* norms. This is partially because of the tendency of the Orthodox rabbinate to tend in this direction, since most Modern Orthodox have not pursued the rabbinate as a profession. In fact, as Trencher's data demonstrate, about 55–60% were bothered by the fact that their rabbis and leaders come "from more right-leaning segments of Orthodoxy."[9]

Yet for all the difficulty of compartmentalization and contrapuntalism, among these Orthodox Jews, the repeated patterns of religious life and the common patterns of engagement with the world outside as well as the regular retreats from it to their Orthodox enclaves – standing first on one foot, as it were, and then on the other – have taken on a kind of inertial character, so much so that these sort of shifting stances and involvements can go on almost automatically.

Center Versus the Extremes

A large segment of Modern Orthodox Jews calls the religious space they inhabit "the center," identifying themselves as "centrists," a category Cohen and I identified in our 1989 study. They mean that they embrace neither the insularity and religious extremism of those who choose to emphasize a set of practices that enforce separation from mainstream culture nor the possibly assimilative and religious flexibility of those whose lifestyle choice is subordinated to the desire to be firmly a part of mainstream general culture. In the 2019 Trencher study, about 42% identified with this label, which remains the single largest segment.[10] Others who still consider themselves as Modern Orthodox Jews, who feel more comfortable hewing closer to the *haredi* side of the spectrum, without fully embracing its desired insularity, tend toward seeing themselves as "traditionalist." They make up between a fifth to a quarter of this population according to Trencher's numbers. Finally, those who embrace a more liberal stance (about a third), including encouraging egalitarianism between men and women, tolerance of gay rights, and political progressivism, have recently begun referring to themselves as "Open Orthodox," explaining that, "while insisting on the foundational divinity of Torah and observance of *halakha*, this Orthodoxy is not rigid … [and] open to a wider spectrum."[11]

Affirming these divisions, a 2019 study of "Modern Orthodoxy" by Mark Trencher of Nishma Research, found that 85% of those self-identified Modern Orthodox Jews say that "Orthodox observance is an important part of their lives," but at least one third believe that "there is no longer a single, cohesive Modern Orthodox community. Modern Orthodoxy should acknowledge this and would perhaps be better off splitting into separate camps."[12]

There has been criticism from other Orthodox Jews of those calling themselves "Open Orthodox," claiming that they no longer represent a genuine Orthodox ideology or way of life. If Trencher's 2019 sample of those who view themselves on the "left" of Modern Orthodoxy – the place from where one might assume the "Open Orthodox" emerge – then there is some truth to this criticism. As he reports, these people claim they find Modern Orthodoxy "less spiritually inspiring" and "far less often see themselves as 'full-time Orthodox' and are far more willing to compromise in their interactions with secular society" as well as "far less comfortable with day-to-day Orthodox living."[13]

Which of these camps represents the mainstream of Modern Orthodoxy? Generally, one would assume the center does, given it is the largest segment. But of course, the center is a relative position, subject to change as the extremes move further apart. More recent data about Orthodox self-identification signals that contrapuntalist and cosmopolitan Orthodoxy, once the mainstream and dominant tendency of the movement, is now in decline if not in retreat. Not only is this decline demographic; the more cosmopolitan Modern Orthodox Jews simply have fewer children (as is characteristic of all Americans/Jews who have a lot of education and marry late) while those on the right wing (a number of whom probably have slid into the *haredi* camp) have increased their proportion of Orthodoxy through a far higher birthrate and an ability to hold onto their children's religious loyalties. As the majority seem to have slid to the right, therefore, so too has the center.

Reflecting this tendency, Trencher found that

> Modern Orthodox parents hope their children will be religiously observant. More than three fourths want their children to be typical Centrist Modern Orthodox Jews (58%) or more observant than that (18%). One in eight (13%) say their child's religious preferences are not so critical or relevant to them.

Looking more closely at these numbers, his study suggested that "there is a sense and there has been conjecture that Modern Orthodoxy as a whole has been shifting toward greater observance, i.e., 'moving to the right.'" Indeed, 39% of his respondents say they have become more observant and 23% say they have become less observant – a "net rightward shift" of +16%.[14]

Modern Orthodoxy is also in ideological retreat, with a growing insecurity about the moral superiority and sustainability of their way of being Orthodox. By this I mean there is a widespread feeling that only a more engaged and stringent Orthodoxy will survive in the contemporary social and cultural environment: a truism long argued by the *haredi* leadership. Part of this feeling is sustained by the fact that in the nearly universal parochial day school and yeshiva education of the Modern Orthodox, the religious and moral instruction to which the Orthodox have been increasingly exposed – from their rabbis and yeshiva or seminary teachers – comes from the *haredi* wing of Orthodoxy and not from the center or left. This is because the Modern Orthodox themselves generally did not choose to become rabbis and Jewish educators. Equipped with top-flight educations and university degrees, they have pursued other professions, and left Jewish education to their right-wing and far more insular counterparts. Those educators gradually instilled the idea in their students that *haredi* Orthodoxy only was the authentic way, and all else was in some way "*off the derech*," (OTD) a deviation from the Orthodox path.[15]

To be sure, there has been some push-back from the progressive quarters of Orthodoxy, where both ideologically and behaviorally there are people trying to compensate for and challenge the slide to the right. Among these are the efforts of those like the Open Orthodox who seek to empower women, such as those supporters and members of JOFA, the Jewish Orthodox Feminist Alliance and Matan, the Women's Institute for Torah Studies in Israel as well as the students and teachers in Yeshivat Chovevei Torah as well as Yeshivat Maharat and its supporters or the Shira Chadasha (in Jerusalem) and Darchei Noam (in Manhattan) as well as similar "partnership" congregations elsewhere. The fact that about a third of Modern Orthodoxy finds itself on the left extreme suggests that there is a population to whom these institutions and ideas potentially appeal. At the same time, many in the centrist and traditionalist Orthodox Jewish sectors dismiss them as marginal and not representing Orthodoxy.[16] Aspersions are cast on the rabbis from Chovevei Torah and Maharat, as seen in the refusal of the Rabbinical Council of America, the umbrella Orthodox organization, to allow its graduates to become members.[17]

Perhaps nothing has more vividly demonstrated Orthodoxy's slide to the right than its political behavior. In both Israel and the United States, the Orthodox vote is now firmly offered to parties that are right-wing and spurn the values of liberalism and progressivism. To be sure, those identified as Modern Orthodox vote more like the rest of American Jewry, supporting progressive or liberal candidates, but they are a shrinking proportion of the Orthodox vote, both in the United States and Israel. Thus, for example in the 2016 Presidential election, while American Jews overwhelmingly voted for the Democrat as they always do, the single largest group of Jews voting for the Republican Trump were the Orthodox.[18] That they should vote for the Republican candidate is not new; they have been doing this for the last four or five Presidential ballots. But this time, they voted for Trump in spite of his support by various anti-Semitic groups and notwithstanding his behavior and speech, which stands diametrically opposed to all that Orthodoxy would seem to stand for. Even American ex-pat Shlomo Riskin, once the poster rabbi for Modern Orthodoxy and now the municipal rabbi of the Efrat settlement and head of its Ohr Torah yeshiva, hailed Trump's election as a "victory for the Jewish people" and Israel.[19] Riskin, once an avatar of liberal Orthodoxy, and Rabbi Avrohom Levin, the head of the Telshe Yeshiva on the Orthodox right, both supported Trump: what could better symbolize the slide to the political right of Orthodoxy, both modern and *haredi*? Indeed, even the Rabbinical Council of America, the flagship organization of the Modern Orthodox rabbinate, published a full page ad in the *New York Times* with warm congratulations for President-elect Trump.

In 2020, as Mark Trencher of Nishma Research has found, the Orthodox again overwhelmingly voted in exactly the opposite direction to the rest of American Jewry, choosing Trump.[20] Indeed after seeing four years of a Trump presidency, 94% of those Orthodox Jews who voted for him in 2016 did so again in 2020. By contrast, 97% of those who voted for Hillary Clinton in 2016 stayed with the Democrats and voted for Biden. The divide in Orthodoxy remained essentially as it was four years earlier. Over 80% of those who voted for Trump in 2020 claimed that it was because of what they perceived as his strong support for Israel and a bit over 60% claimed it was because they believed he was better for "our nation's future." On the other hand, those of them who cared more about matters like science and health, voted overwhelmingly for Biden, with only 10% of those who claimed this concern choosing Trump.

Like the Christian evangelicals, Mormons, and white Catholics whose values appear to be far from those expressed by Donald Trump but who nevertheless voted for him, so too did all sorts of Orthodox Jews. One might argue that in their political behavior, the Orthodox act more like those right-wing Christians than they do like the rest of the Jews in America. On the other hand, in Israel, their nationalism and chauvinism appear pretty much in tune with the majority of Jewish Israelis.

Triumphalism

Yet another element of contemporary Orthodoxy has been its sense of triumphalism. The triumphalism comes from some remarkable successes of Orthodoxy beginning in the second half of the twentieth century. Among these is a powerful success in institution building. In the diaspora, and particularly America, this has been in building and maintaining synagogues. In the U.S. almost 40% of the synagogues are Orthodox, and in the New York metropolitan area, where Orthodox Jews are more than 20% of the Jewish population, that proportion rises to 57%. Wherever they are to be found, Orthodox Jews have been avid synagogue founders and builders. Moreover, in America are one third of those Jews who describe themselves as "regular synagogue goers." That pattern is undoubtedly repeated elsewhere in the diaspora and in Israel, where that proportion is probably twice that or more.

In America where intermarriage has been skyrocketing, about nine in ten of American Orthodox are married to Jews, and of that relative few who have intermarried, a quarter has spouses who converted to Judaism (and were the rabbis more open to conversion, that number would probably rise). In their family life the Orthodox maintain a high degree of stability, with a divorce rate that, although rising, remains far lower than the approximate 30% among other Jews and than much of the rest of America. What holds true for America is no less the case in the rest of the diaspora, and likely Israel as well.

The development and expansion of Jewish day schools and yeshivas that have become the institutions of first choice for the education of the Modern Orthodox young is a point of pride but also a source of concern. According to Trencher in 2017, 83% of those Modern Orthodox he surveyed had their children in grades 1 through 12 in such institutions.[21] These were schools that paid attention both to secular (91% of which encourage their students to attend college) and Jewish education and were key drivers of community building and continuity. To be sure, a whopping 89% of those Jews said the high cost of this education was the number one problem their community faced, and the question of how long this expense can be sustained represents a significant challenge to continuity. Moreover, there is not always a confidence that the teachers in these schools can teach what I have called contrapuntalist skills, or what Trencher calls the "how to resolve seeming contradictions between science and religion and comparative religion."[22] Indeed these concerns indicate that feelings of triumph about the day school and yeshiva growth may be less than all-embracing. As one respondent in the Trencher survey put it: "The cost of educating my children. The stress it causes us as parents takes away from whatever benefit they have going to a Jewish day school."[23]

The growing political influence of Orthodox individuals, both within the Jewish community and its organizational life (in some measure because non-Orthodox Jews increasingly focus their political concerns beyond the orbit of Jewish life) as well as in general society and politics (in America and Israel) has also contributed to a sense of triumphalism. Whether it was the yarmulke-wearing Modern Orthodox Ari Weiss, who was U.S. House Speaker Tip O'Neill's chief legislative aide in the decade between 1977 and 1987, Senator Joseph Lieberman running as the Democratic nominee for Vice-President, or Jacob Lew, Secretary of State in the George W. Bush administration, or the many Modern Orthodox leaders of such groups as the Council of Presidents of Major Jewish Organizations, the A.D.L. and others, these individuals who are unmistakably religiously observant and proudly Orthodox and modern have added to the sense of the movement of which they are part having become influential politically. This of course has long been true in Israel.

Yet another element in the powerful triumphalist attitude of Orthodoxy is its putative success in attracting new adherents, so-called "*baaley t'shuvah*," ("BTs") people who are currently Orthodox but were not raised as such. There is much evidence among these people that "they are trying to reclaim not just traditional Judaism, but the kinds of communal rhythms and obligations that are so often missing from contemporary American culture."[24] This sort of attraction has been a theme in many quarters of Orthodoxy, from the most insular to those we have called "Open Orthodox," and to some extent also accounts for Orthodox triumphalism, the attitude that many Orthodox Jews believe that "we have the answer for how Jewish life should be lived and preserved; that's why people are joining us." Trencher's 2017 study after all found BTs to be 42% of the Modern Orthodox. Moreover, in an analysis of the 2015 Pew data, Steven M. Cohen found that among younger so-called millennial Jews, three times as many are being attracted to Orthodoxy as among the baby boom generation. Trencher's figures confirm this: he found that 15% of Jews who identify as "observant Orthodox," the largest group, made that commitment between the ages of 18 and 24.[25]

But, is the triumphalism really in order? When comparing the BTs, people who might be called "the imports" into Orthodoxy, with those who were raised Orthodox but are no longer part of this community, those called OTD, the picture changes, leaving less room for triumphalism. Comparing just these two groups, even in the cohort with the most BTs, people between 30 and 49 years of age, while the BTs were about 47% of Orthodoxy, the OTDs numbered 53%. In fact, in every age group, the exports – those raised Orthodox but no longer considering themselves as Orthodox – outnumbered the imports. In 50–64-year-olds by 76% to 24% and among those 65 and older by a huge 96% to 4%. The Modern Orthodox are aware of this, as one can see in the fact that over 60% of them claim to be very concerned about people "leaving Orthodoxy" and nearly 70% feel that their community's leaders are "not adequately addressing" this problem.[26] Hence the triumphalism in the Orthodox world might not necessarily be based on the facts but merely an anecdotal perception of them.

Yet there is some room for a sense of satisfaction among those in the 30–49-year-old group, the one that represents in many ways the active leadership of the movement. Among them the imports and exports are very close in number, and it is quite possible that some of the BTs in this generation have moved to Israel and therefore do not appear in the American statistics. While other Jewish denominations have experienced large numbers of defections in this same generation, Orthodoxy clearly has been doing much better, as Cohen points out.[27] That fact alone does offer some sense of their triumph in the contest of continuity that constitutes perhaps the most important test for American Jewry. One must conclude that triumphalism that comes from the growth in Orthodox institutions, persistence (i.e. ability to offset losses from dropouts and grow demographically at the very least by its fertility, which even among the moderns is greater than among other Jews), its relatively stable marital patterns, and political influence has a basis in reality. But it is not the Modern Orthodox who are at the heart of this sense of triumph.

Why? The demographic data suggest that the three forces of BT, OTD, and fertility are – as far as can be determined – keeping the total Modern Orthodox community size flat. Couple that with the fact that many who were once ideologically attached to Modern Orthodox contrapuntalism have slid to the right and some to the left and one gets a sense that this segment of Orthodoxy is gradually being eclipsed by the *haredi* element, whose fertility is higher by far, whose ideological certainty is stronger, and whose triumphalism therefore seems to dominate Orthodoxy.

Relations with Others

Relations between the Orthodox and others has always been a fraught subject. For Modern Orthodox Jews who, as already noted, generally embrace the idea of their being engaged with mainstream culture, it is often jarring to discover that they are not always welcomed by the neighborhoods into which they seek to move. Increasingly, the Orthodox entry into a locality has been met with a backlash of resistance to Orthodox residence by others in places where they seek to enter. There are a variety of strategies of opposition, often from other Jews, from denying the establishment of *eruv*s in the diaspora to mass demonstrations against the presence of the Orthodox. There are a variety of examples, including the opposition in Tenafly, New Jersey, where for over a year in 2000–2001, the council would not agree to an *eruv* that would have made it easier for Orthodox Jews to move and observe the Sabbath in the area.[28] Opponents argued that allowing the symbolic fence to be built would "cause divisiveness in the town." Similarly, the planned expansion of a Modern Orthodox synagogue in the New York suburb of New Rochelle led to widespread objection from the local neighborhood, which claimed all sorts of dangers from this expansion. Perhaps the most transparent one however was the claim by some locals that they were in fear of "'Brooklynization' – a not-so-veiled reference to New Rochelle's rapidly growing Orthodox community."[29]

On the other hand, the Orthodox are aware that there are legitimate complaints about them. For example, as Trencher found in his 2017 study, over half see the fact that many of them treat other people "inappropriately" or are "dishonest in business" as significant problems for their group. They understand that contempt for the Orthodox is not always baseless. They know that loyalty to the tradition and attachment to Jewish observance does not always yield people with the highest moral standards or behavior, even though it is a principle of those who consider themselves "Torah-true Jews," a term once used as a meme for Orthodoxy, that because they answer to a "higher authority" they also are scrupulously moral and good neighbors to others.

Modern Orthodoxy is complex and by no means unitary. It is changing and will continue to change as indeed is the essence of anything that has "modern" as its first name. Whether it will continue to decline or reinvent itself remains to be seen.

Notes

1. www.pewforum.org/2015/08/26/a-portrait-of-american-orthodox-jews/, accessed March 18, 2020.
2. Peter Berger and Thomas Luckmann, *The Social Construction of Reality* (New York: Anchor Books, 1966).
3. See Pew Research Center 2015.
4. Mark Trencher 2019, p. 37. See also the U.S. Census: www.census.gov/library/stories/2019/02/number-of-people-with-masters-and-phd-degrees-double-since-2000.html, accessed April 1, 2020.
5. Samuel C. Heilman and Steven M. Cohen, *Cosmopolitans and Parochials: Modern Orthodox Jews in America* (Chicago, IL: University of Chicago Press, 1989).
6. Maxine Jacobson, *Modern Orthodoxy in American Judaism: The Era of Rabbi Leo Jung* (Boston, MA: Academic Studies Press, 2016).
7. Trencher 2019, p. 15.
8. Samuel Heilman, *Sliding to the Right: The Contest for the Future of American Orthodox Judaism* (Berkeley: University of California Press, 2006).
9. Trencher 2019, p. 12.
10. Trencher 2019, p. 10.
11. Avi Weiss, "Defining Open Orthodoxy," *Tablet* June 30, 2015: https://www.tabletmag.com/jewish-life-and-religion/191907/defining-open-orthodoxy, accessed March 27, 2020.
12. Trencher 2019.
13. Trencher 2019, p. 35.
14. Trencher, summary of key findings.
15. Judy Bolton-Fasman, "Off the Path Memoirs of Ex-Hasidic JewsShine Light on Faigy Mayer's World," *HaAretz* August 11, 2015: www.haaretz.com/jewish/features/1.670557
16. www.haaretz.com/misc/writers/elana-sztokman-1.472348
    www.haaretz.com/jewish/news/learning-talmud-without-asking-for-men-s-permission-1.455094
    www.haaretz.com/opinion/.premium-1.553902
    www.haaretz.com/israel-news/travel/religion-relics/.premium-1.664955
    www.haaretz.com/jewish/features/.premium-1.550190
    www.matan.org.il/en
17. David Berger, The Rabbinical Council of America and Yeshivat Chovevei Torah, *The Jewish Link*, July 9, 2015: www.jewishlinknj.com/op-eds/8820-the-rabbinical-council-of-america-and-yeshivat-chovevei-torah-a-response-to-rabbis-avi-weiss-and-asher-lopati
18. Samuel Heilman, "How Trump Split the Jewish Vote," www.haaretz.com/opinion/.premium-samuel-heilman-how-trump-split-the-jewish-vote-1.5459828
19. www.israelnationalnews.com/News/News.aspx/220038
20. Nishma Research 2020 Post-Election Survey, www.nishmaresearch.com/assets/pdf/Nishma%20Research%202020%20Post-Election%20Survey%2011-17-20.pdf
21. Trencher 2017, p. 14.
22. Trencher 2017, pp. 54, 57.
23. Trencher 2017, p. 74

24 Emma Green, "Why Orthodox Judaism Is Appealing to So Many Millenials," *The Atlantic*, March 31, 2016: www.theatlantic.com/politics/archive/2016/03/orthodox-judaism-millennials/476118/, accessed March 30, 2020.
25 Trencher 2019, accessed March 25, 2020.
26 Trencher 2019, p. 26.
27 Personal communication.
28 Eric Fetterman, "Orthodox Jews Not Welcome," *New York Post*, May 2, 2001: https://nypost.com/2001/05/02/orthodox-jews-not-welcome/, accessed March 30, 2020.
29 Jennifer Medina, "A Temple, 2 Graves and a Headache," *New York Times*, December 5, 2004: www.nytimes.com/2004/12/05/nyregion/a-temple-2-graves-and-a-headache.html, accessed March 30, 2020. See also Joseph Berger, "As a Synagogue Outgrows Its Space, Its Building Plans Draw Opposition," *New York Times*, Aug. 17, 2003: www.nytimes.com/2003/08/17/nyregion/as-a-synagogue-outgrows-its-space-its-building-plans-draw-opposition.html, accessed March 30, 2020.

References

Berger, David. 2015. "The Rabbinical Council of America and Yeshivat Chovevei Torah". *The Jewish Link*. July 9.
Berger, David and Thomas Luckmann. 1966. *The Social Construction of Reality*. New York: Anchor Books.
Bolton-Fasman, Judy. 2015. "Off the Path Memoirs of Ex-Hasidic Jews Shine Light on Faigy Mayer's World," *HaAretz* August 11. www.haaretz.com/jewish/memoirs-of-ex-hasidic-jews-shine-light-on-faigy-mayers-world-1.5385468
Fetterman, Eric. 2001. "Orthodox Jews Not Welcome," *New York Post*, May 2. https://nypost.com/2001/05/02/orthodox-jews-not-welcome/
Green, Emma. 2016. "Why Orthodox Judaism Is Appealing to So Many Millennials," *The Atlantic*, March 31. www.theatlantic.com/politics/archive/2016/03/orthodox-judaism-millennials/476118/
Heilman, Samuel. 2006. *Sliding to the Right: The Contest for the Future of American Orthodox Judaism*. Berkeley: University of California.
Heilman, Samuel. 2018. "How Trump Split the Jewish Vote," November 11, 2016 updated April 14, 2018. www.haaretz.com/opinion/.premium-samuel-heilman-how-trump-split-the-jewish-vote-1.5459828
Heilman, Samuel C. and Steven M. Cohen. 1989. *Cosmopolitans and Parochials: Modern Orthodox Jews in America*. Chicago, IL: University of Chicago Press.
Jacobson, Maxine. 2016. *Modern Orthodoxy in American Judaism: The Era of Rabbi Leo Jung*. Boston, MA: Academic Studies Press.
Medina, Jennifer. 2004. "A Temple, 2 Graves and a Headache," *New York Times*, December 5.
Pew Research Center. 2015. "A Portrait of American Orthodox Jews: A Further Analysis of the 2013 survey of U.S. Jews," www.pewforum.org/2015/08/26/a-portrait-of-american-orthodox-jews/
Trencher, Mark. 2017. "The Nishma Research Profile of American Modern Orthodox Jews," www.nishmaresearch.com/assets/pdf/Report%20-%20Nishma%20Research%20Profile%20of%20American%20Modern%20Orthodox%20Jews%2009-27-17.pdf
Trencher, Mark. 2019. "The Successes, Challenges, and Future of American Modern Orthodoxy," November 4: www.nishmaresearch.com/social-research.html
Trencher, Mark. 2020. "Priorities of Trump Voters vs. Biden Voters in the Orthodox Jewish Community: A Post-Election Analysis," (Nov.), Nishma Research.
Weiss, Avi. 2015. "Defining Open Orthodoxy," *Tablet*, June 30, 2015: www.tabletmag.com/jewish-life-and-religion/191907/defining-open-orthodoxy

14
HASKALAH
Jewish Practice and Romantic Religion

Olga Litvak

Jewish historiography typically credits the movement known as the "Jewish Enlightenment" (Heb. Haskalah) with initiating the programmatic reform of Jewish practice. Although few scholars would now be content to equate the *maskilic* project with the social process of secularization and the general relaxation of Jewish collective discipline, academic consensus still maintains that the movement aspired to liberate Judaism from the dead hand of rabbinic authority and the anachronism of popular custom. Sidelining the fact that the Haskalah was a literary movement driven as much by aesthetic means as by ideological ends, this highly partial view rests largely on a decontextualized and naive reproduction of polemical pronouncements aimed at contemporary Jewish behavior. It is true that *maskilim* often expressed frustration with the benighted condition of the Jewish masses; but it is equally true that they were just as frustrated, if not more so, with the attrition of Jewish practice among upwardly mobile elites. More importantly, within the *maskilic* literary system, Jewish practice occupied a privileged position as an object of representation, the emotional significance of which transcended the rationalist imperative of attaching philosophically tenable "reasons" to the commandments. While deliberate interventions to update and normalize Jewish practice almost always met with failure, *maskilic* literature proved much more successful in encouraging the creation of a modern Jewish sensibility ambivalent about the Enlightenment project that threatened to reduce Jewishness to an idea and strip Jewish memory of its social meaning. As an intellectual community, the Haskalah was committed to critical thought; but as Jewish writers, *maskilim* produced an impressive body of original literary work that shed light on the romantic side of familiar things. In this chapter, I argue that, as far as Jewish practice is concerned, it was in their discovery of the Jewish imagination rather than in their arguments on behalf of universal reason that *maskilim* made their singular contribution to Jewish intellectual history.

What does the Haskalah contribute to a history of Jewish practice? Any answer to this question depends on what sort of thing we are talking about, when we talk about the Haskalah. If the word "Haskalah" is the name we assign to a movement in Jewish history, what kind of movement is it? Despite the prodigious learning expended on trying to define the Haskalah ("intellectual revolution," "religious enlightenment," "cultural and social renewal"), much less attention has been paid to the outstanding fact that whatever the adherents of the Haskalah (Heb. *maskilim*, sing. *maskil*) may have meant by doing what they did, most of what they actually made should be classified primarily as literature in the modern sense of that word – i.e. texts that aspire to aesthetic value and that are made with the express purpose of achieving an aesthetic effect by appealing to the imagination of the individual reader. To say that the Haskalah was primarily a literary movement is also to say that its most salient effects on Jewish practice are indissolubly linked to the characteristic form of *maskilic* activity: the production of literature.

Bearing a strong family resemblance to contemporary Romantic intellectuals in late eighteenth- and early nineteenth-century Eastern Europe, *maskilim* attached singular importance to literary creativity and literary genius and elevated both the writing and the reading of imaginative literature to the status of culturally prestigious practices. It is fair to say that it was the Haskalah which first introduced the idea of a literary vocation into the Jewish lexicon. In doing so, the Haskalah also helped to form the consciousness of the modern Jewish reader, attuned to the sound as well as to the sense of words and prepared to entertain the distinction between telling lies and writing fiction. Thus, whatever pedagogic aim a particular writer pursued in any given work and whatever effect he hoped to have on Jewish society, it was primarily through the medium of literature that the *maskil* expressed his ideas and communicated them to the Jewish public. The medium was not, of course, incidental to the message; the translation of received ideas into the language of literature inevitably transformed their meaning. Not for the first time in Jewish history did a new way of writing radically alter the substance of what was being written – despite the explicit avowals of the writers themselves that they were only reproducing with greater clarity or accuracy a foundational knowledge of the world available, in principle if not always in fact, to any receptive rational being. Like the rabbinic movement, the Haskalah might be described as an unintended revolution in Jewish writing. The starting point of this essay is that their involvement in the production and consumption of imaginative literature shaped the way in which *maskilim* understood the practice of Judaism just as the semiotics of Talmudic discourse first shaped the practical demands of the system of practice that came to be known as *halakhah*.

Evidence for the "literariness" (Heb. *sifrut*) of the Haskalah may be found in virtually every sphere of *maskilic* activity. *Maskilim* not only wrote many books in every conceivable genre that falls under the scope of *belles-lettres*; they also created an infrastructure to support the public reception of literature. What we could call the *maskilic* literary system included the integration of new disciplines into the Jewish curriculum (philology, literary history, and criticism) and the introduction of new institutions (libraries, periodicals, literary societies) into the densely woven network of Jewish social life. The Haskalah can be credited with pioneering and original efforts in the highest registers of Hebrew verse as well as in the broadest vernacular of domestic comedy and every kind of artistic prose in-between, including the novel, the biography, the short story, and the *feuilleton*. *Maskilim* also enlarged the scope of Jewish literature through the work of translation or adaptation of contemporary European *belles-lettres*; Jewish Romantics turned Byron and Schiller into modern Hebrew poets and Sue's *Mystères de Paris* (1842–1843) into a bestselling Jewish novel. The first collective publishing venture of the Haskalah – a Hebrew monthly called *The Gatherer* (*Hameasef*, 1782–1811) – was essentially a literary review, as was practically every other *maskilic* periodical that followed in its footsteps. Whatever else they saw fit to print, all *maskilic* journals published poetry and scouted new literary talent, which is a good thing since the bibliography of virtually every *maskil* includes some attempt at original literary composition, literary history, or literary criticism. The *maskilic* connection to the emergence of modern Jewish literary culture is so intimate and obvious that the first authoritative scholarly history of "modern Hebrew literature" (in six hefty volumes!) is essentially a history of the Haskalah (Klausner 1952–1955).

Measurable and lasting achievements of the Haskalah are confined almost entirely to the arena of literature. Direct interventions aimed at reforming Jewish behavior were largely ineffective and counter-productive. In 1782, a Berlin *maskil* named N. H. Wessely (1725–1805) published a tract on educational reform called *Words of Peace and Truth*, which provoked a minor local scandal but had no discernible effect on the future of Jewish schooling (Feiner 2004, 87–104). In 1788, Wessely published *Songs of Praise* (Heb. *Shirei tiferet*) a six-volume Hebrew epic on the subject of the exodus from Egypt and arguably the first modern Hebrew poem. By 1900, *Shirei tiferet* had been reprinted thirteen times, making it one of the most impressive *maskilic* accomplishments of the century. In 1843, Isaac-Meir Dik (1807–1893), joined a group of like-minded *maskilim* in Vilna in petitioning the Russian deputy minister of education to pass an ordinance against "traditional Jewish attire on the grounds that it had no basis in Jewish law and was merely a custom that now served only to separate Jews from the gentiles" (Stanislawski 1983, 111). The intervention failed and, moreover, left in its wake a widespread public antipathy toward all *maskilic* social initiatives. Distaste for the ideas that he and his fellow *maskilim* supposedly stood for did not, however, keep Dik, a master story-teller, from the financial and psychological rewards of literary popularity: his books, he crowed in 1861, "were grabbed up in a hundred thousand copies and the booksellers receive new requests each day" (Roskies 1995, 68). Transplanting the delights of bourgeois melodrama into the register of Jewish domestic fiction, Dik, the writer, was able to trespass on intimate Jewish territory where Dik, the reformer, could not hope to tread.

There were, to be sure, important precedents for *maskilic* literariness. The post-biblical history of original Hebrew verse, both inside and outside the framework of liturgy, begins with the rabbinic period and continues uninterrupted thereafter; there were distinguished Hebrew poets in medieval Iberia and in Renaissance Italy whose substantial body of work remained a point of reference for their *maskilic* successors in Eastern Europe. But before the Haskalah, no explicitly literary composition intended to be read rather than studied – not even liturgical poetry or homiletic prose – encroached on the prestige and significance of *talmud torah* and its attendant genres of code and commentary. Even the vernacular book market, growing exponentially since the mid-seventeenth century, was dominated by instructional and exegetical texts (Baumgarten 2005). The tide turned in 1819, with the publication of the first original Jewish novel, *Revealer of Secrets* (Heb. *Megaleh-tmirin*) by the Galician *maskil* Joseph Perl (1773–1839); within a generation, reading modern Yiddish fiction, written entirely by *maskilim*, was a respectable middle-class occupation (Quint 2005). This is an impressive feat considering that *talmud torah* and European literature had, for most of Jewish history, represented antithetical values. The medieval Jewish philosopher Judah Halevi (1075–1141), himself a brilliant Hebrew poet, points out in his *Kuzari* (1140) – a work that could almost be described as a novel – that "the Bible removes itself from the normal sphere of poetry by placing the category of significance above that of harmony and beauty" (Fisch 1988, 1–2). In the age of print, the increasing popularity of "sweet words and poetic fictions" in the languages of the gentile nations represented a serious threat to the survival of Judaism. For Isaac Cardoso, a seventeenth-century Sephardic physician, the fact that Jews had no fine literature of their own was to their everlasting moral credit, to be counted among the *excelencias* of the Hebrew nation:

> Books of comedies and amorous novels, with their sweet words and poetic fictions are a strong indication of lasciviousness and a deceitful instrument of perdition, troublers of the soul, violators of purity in which time is wasted, teachers of vanities and vices. Comedies and tragedies were invented by profane nations, not by the holy people Israel, whom the Lord chose to sing His divine praises and not lascivious loves and

> vicious inventions. ... And it matters not if one says that they contain also many good things and moral judgments which can reform life and benefit customs, because there are asps hidden among the flowers. ... It is the sacred books which should be read, for in them is the true doctrine, the most sublime rhetoric and the most supreme delight.
>
> *Yerushalmi 1981, 375–376*

It was the *maskilic* domestication of literature which drove a wedge into these unexceptionable arguments; by the end of the nineteenth century, Jewish literature was a source of collective pride. Jewish readers now credited writers of Jewish "comedies and tragedies" with defending and preserving the glory of the "holy people Israel" rather than leading it to "perdition." By the early 1880s, Jewish educated society was celebrating the literary anniversaries of its most distinguished writers – self-identified *maskilim* – J. L. Gordon (1831–1892) and Sh. J. Abramovich (1835–1917) and congratulating them on twenty-five years of "selfless service for the good of [their] long-suffering people" (Litvak 2006, 131). Despite a chorus of complaints about their work being unappreciated and misunderstood, it was the "dissemination" of imaginative literature rather than the invention of new doctrine that placed *maskilim* in a position of moral authority as "agents of culture" (Gries 1996 and Reiner 2000). Thanks to the Haskalah, today's paradigmatic modern Jewish intellectual is not a rabbi, a doctor or a merchant, all professions with more longevity and a more solid Jewish pedigree, but the most unexpected thing of all – a mere inventor of "poetic fictions." Isaac Cardoso would have been shocked to see authors of "books of comedies and amorous novels" the likes of Philip Roth, Franz Kafka, and Isaac Babel included in any "Jewish canon" (Wisse 2001).

Cardoso objected precisely to the aspect of literature that distinguishes it from other kinds of writing: its imaginative appeal to the passions. Other kinds of texts may, of course, produce the aesthetic effect of literature incidentally but what we call literature is singular in being fabricated with this express purpose. To rehabilitate this tendency to "lasciviousness," *maskilim* had to show that the "supreme delight" they wished their readers to experience served the same "true doctrine" as the "sacred books." The *maskilic* pursuit of literature was hedged by Cardoso's suspicions. Wessely, sounding for all the world like Cardoso, warned the editors of *Hameasef*, against pandering to the profane desires of the romantic reader (Litvak 2012, 43). *Maskilim* insisted that Jewish literature ought to be Jewish, not merely written by Jews trying to imitate the nations. But how was the modern Jewish writer to "sing divine praises"? And, for that matter, why? In the face of the "sublime rhetoric" of Scripture, the prospects of a new Jewish literature might have seemed morally dim and practically uncertain. On-going debate about the status of modern Jewish literature in comparison with the biblical exemplar raised the stakes on literary creativity; the perceived urgency of the problem made *maskilim* write more, not less. Abraham Mapu (1808–1867), the author of the phenomenally successful *Love of Zion* (Heb. *Ahavat tsiyon*, 1853) became invested in writing fiction in stylized biblical Hebrew out of frustration with the popularity of "foreign" novels, "wheat gleaned in the fields of strangers" (Mapu 1970, 180). The language of the prophets would, he was sure, elevate alien subject matter to the transcendent status of "Jewish things," fashioned for the sake of heaven (Mapu 1970, 77 and 129–130). Against the pernicious influence of foreign exemplars, Jewish literature became a kind of *pharmakon*, an inoculating agent against "vanities and vices" by the same means as those foreign books which were inflaming Jewish desires and corrupting Jewish minds (Bitzan 2011).

These were risky educational claims, without the benefit of theological explanation or legal precedent. Doubtless it was in literature that "true doctrine" and Jewish "customs" found a more dynamic expression than the appeal to logical proof or scriptural proof-text; but its effects on the Jewish imagination, as Cardoso anticipated, were uncertain and possibly dangerous. Indeed, in turning to aesthetic means, the Haskalah dispensed with (or, in some cases, dodged) an entire discursive tradition that sanctified "justified law" (Halivni 1986), a process of devolution that began with Moses Mendelssohn, the founder of the Haskalah and the first to offer explicitly aesthetic arguments in defense of Jewish "ceremonial law" as a "living script," a kind of language (Litvak 2012, 34–45). Embedded in the structure of Talmudic legal exegesis, the tradition of "justified law" dedicated a discrete species of writing to formulating "reasons for the commandments" (Heinemann 2009); the Haskalah did not so much contest the possibility of finding such reasons as render the search academic – the object of learned discussion – and therefore irrelevant to performance. While their explicit ideological pronouncements upheld the universal virtue of reasonable arguments and deplored rabbinic exegesis for stifling the Jewish intellect (Harris 1995, 147–155), *maskilic* literary practice spoke more viscerally and more directly to the imagination and bypassed the intellect altogether. *Maskilic* literature might have done more to subvert the "rationalization" of Judaism and to preserve the sanctity of the Jewish tradition, especially in the eyes of a growing number of non-believers, than the opposition of any stubborn Jewish fanatic or religious enthusiast (Miron 2000).

In their poetry and prose, self-proclaimed Jewish "enlighteners" broadcast a Romantic theory of Jewish practice. To be more precise, theirs was an *anti-theory*, the strange fruit of a sustained, if mostly unacknowledged, literary campaign of attrition against the reduction of *halakhah* (Jewish conduct) to "reasons" or "systems." In the very act of representation, *maskilic* aesthetics fatally compromised the possibility of a future *maskilic* metaphysics. Embedded in the Romantic work of Jewish literature, the aesthetic brief against *Judaism*, the name we give to a modern religion with a philosophy, entailed an imaginative commitment to *Jewishness* as an "unjustified law" unto itself – an irrepressible and inevitable form of life, a *perpetuum mobile* of collective existence that was eternally self-renewing, a transcendent book without end (Krochmal 2010). One of the clearest examples of this tension between Judaism and Jewishness, symptomatic of *maskilic* literature and perhaps of Jewish literature as a whole, is "The Rabbi of Bacherach" by Heinrich Heine (1797–1856).

Whatever one makes of the relationship between Heine's Jewish commitments and his career as a German poet, "The Rabbi of Bacherach" (Heine 1994) belongs squarely within the context of *maskilic* literary practice. Heine began writing it in 1824, under the spell of his recent involvement with the Society for Culture and Knowledge of the Jews (*Verein für Kultur und Wissenschaft der Juden*), a typically short-lived *maskilic* literary club, founded in order to raise Jewish historical consciousness, elevate Jewish taste, and subject the "Jewish world" to "systematic, critical and comprehensive reflection." Impatient with this program and with the quality of the Society's publications – boring, abstruse, professorial – Heine conceived "The Rabbi of Bacherach" in a "state of revulsion." Against the "prevailing sentiments" of the Society, Heine saw its "emasculating philosophic Idealism" not as a spirited defense of the Jewish contribution to the universal progress of reason but as abject capitulation to Christian dictates about what a proper modern confession (Ger. *der Glaube*) was supposed to be. Disgusted by the prospect of his own complicity with the modernization of Jewish thought, Heine turned, instead, to the pathos of Jewish experience (Ger. *der grosse Judenschmerz*). "The Rabbi of Bacherach" started its life as a protest on behalf of the "crassest Rabbinism" against the "travesty of dismantling a venerable and proven religion down to a set of theological maxims." It was, to put it in Heine's own keen-edged idiom, a vindication of the Jewish "beard" against the Jewish "idea" (Schorsch 1994, 217–218).

Heine set his story in the Rhineland town of Bacharach during the fifteenth century. The protagonist, Rabbi Abraham, and his beautiful wife, Sara are a loving but childless couple. On the first night of Passover, during the celebration of the *seder* at the rabbi's home, strangers smuggle the corpse of a Christian infant into the house in order, presumably, to fabricate a blood libel against the rabbi and all the Jews of Bacharach. Fortunately, Rabbi Abraham realizes what is afoot and quickly makes his escape. Fleeing by boat up the Rhine, he and his wife travel to Frankfurt. During the journey, Sara is beset by a growing feeling of dread that in their absence, the remaining Jews of Bacharach, all of their family and friends, will have been massacred. This is the moment where the original narrative that Heine composed in 1824 stopped; in 1840, he returned to the story and added another two chapters, set in the Jewish community of Frankfurt, where the rabbi and his wife find refuge.

In the courtyard of the Frankfurt synagogue, Rabbi Abraham runs into an old school fellow, Don Isaac Abarbanel, a wholly fictional "nephew" of the fifteenth-century Iberian rabbi, philosopher, and statesman of the same name. Heine's "Don Isaac" is a smooth-talking Spanish cavalier and a convert to Christianity. At first, not knowing who she is, Don Isaac attempts to chat up the beautiful Sara; when the rabbi appears on the scene, the focus shifts to the conversation between these two long-lost friends about Don Isaac's apparent transformation into the character of a "Christian knight." Seeing that the rabbi's wife is languishing with hunger, Don Isaac promptly invites the couple to dine at the Jewish eating-house of the widow Elle Schnapper. Don Isaac professes to be an intimate friend of the widow and a great devotee of her cooking. As the threesome sit down to dinner, the story abruptly ends, returning neatly to its starting place – a Jewish meal, but this time blissfully free of the dark foreboding that hangs over the *seder* meal at the beginning.

With the company seated at the table waiting for the arrival of the steaming soup, Heine cuts off the narrative, not having resolved any of the questions posed by the plot. This is a dangerous gambit, which risks leaving the impression that "The Rabbi Bacherach" is an incomplete novel, an artistic feat that the poet – who made several passes at the novel form – somehow could not pull off (Sammons 1979, 95). Heine deepened the confusion by designating "Rabbi of Bacherach" as a "fragment" within the title of the tale, leaving the reader to puzzle out its significance; does the sub-title describe the unfinished state of the work or, more ambiguously, refer to its truncated character as a "unified" text, a "fragment" by definition (Rose 1976)? The ambiguity would not have been beyond the appreciation of Heine's contemporary audience; Romantic literary practice had transformed the "fragment" into an "acceptable and even fashionable form of text, recognized and appreciated by a reading public, and understood by writers and readers to develop a new and challenging form of eloquence in its very indeterminacy" (Bradshaw 2008, 74). Suggestively, the last word of the text of the story is *fehle*, which means "missing." And, to underscore the deliberate quality of an achieved effect, Heine added a final parenthetical note: "The conclusion of this and of the following chapters have gone missing but not from any fault of the author's" (Heine 1994, 145). The acknowledgment of loss is not to be taken as an alibi for authorial failure; what Heine is saying here is that the ostensible "fault" of the missing conclusion lies within the nature of the text itself. Heine's ironic disavowal highlights that the partial form of the "fragment" belongs not to the incompetence or whim of its author but to "The Rabbi of Bacherach" as a supremely finished work; the symbiosis between form and content is a sign of its perfection, its aesthetic integrity. In being broken off, "The Rabbi of Bacherach" is rendered complete. Why? Because "The Rabbi of Bacherach" is a Jewish text, which bears the weight of Jewish suspicion toward Christian happy endings. A Jewish anxiety traceable to the first Easter in history that such endings bode ill for Jews is already written into the first "Passover" chapter (compare Yuval 2006).

A self-consciously Jewish book, Heine's masterpiece is dead-set against the modern version of Christian "good news" delivered by nineteenth-century liberal reformers who, like the gospel writers, assumed the arrival of universal philosophical truth under the banner of Enlightenment. Fragmented, unfinished, deliberately archaic (like an archeological artifact, found broken), "The Rabbi of Bacherach" is Heine's Romantic act of Jewish dissent against modernity's Christological theory of progress. In 1840, Heine chose to locate himself within the sustained duration of the "Middle Ages," the Jewish past-continuous where he had begun back in 1824. By then, he seems to have concluded that what he started could not be finished, that no Jewish story could be ended except on Christian terms; the final comment, that the *fehle* is not his fault, is Heine's authorial bow to the inevitable, to the implications of his own text. An attentive Jewish reader, mindful of the counter-intuitive rabbinic injunction to prioritize that which is routine over that which is momentous (Heb. *tadir veshe'eino tadir, tadir kodem*), would not have been surprised to find that such a critical formal gesture involved a corresponding shift in scene, from the most apocalyptically charged meal of the Jewish year (Passover) which opens the story to the closing scene which evokes the recurrent miracle of *Freitagabend* (lit. "Sabbath eve," but even more literally, "Free-day eve"), a habitual celebration of freedom at the end of every working week, as if in recognition that ultimate redemption is always to be deferred to "next year in Jerusalem." The structure of "Rabbi of Bacherach" thus mirrors its central theme – the transcendence of ordinary Jewishness of the apocalyptic expectations of Passover, which is to say, the emancipation of Jewish practice from the philosophical demands of liberal Christian-inflected *Glaube*. To effect this emancipation is the province of Don Isaac. His function in the story (which is also the cultural function of Jewish literature) is to dispose of Jewish futurity and to expose the fallacy of enlightened assurances that the dark era of persecution known as the Middle Ages is actually over. Only a Christian convert, a kind of Jewish double-agent (whose uncle is a distinguished Jewish philosopher and a messianic prophet), is in a position to know how false such promises are; only a non-believing Jew, a Jewish renegade without the benefit of ideological commitments or providential expectations, can disenchant such hopes. But is Don Isaac really a convert? It is not so simple.

Here he is explaining to the pious Rabbi Abraham what a "Christian knight" is doing, hanging around the courtyard of a synagogue:

> "Well, then, [says Don Isaac] I shall take you to the best Jewish pastrycook [Ger. *der besten Garküche Israels*], my friend Schnapper-Elle, whose place is near here. I can already smell the delicious aroma from that kitchen! O, Abraham, if you only knew how that aroma speaks to me! It is that which has so often enticed me here, to the tents of Jacob, since I've been living in this city. It is not for love of intercourse with God's chosen people; truly, it is not to pray that I come to Jew Street, but to eat. ..."
>
> "You have never loved us, Don Isaac [says the rabbi]. ..."
>
> "Yes" – went on the Spaniard – "I like your cooking much better than your faith [Ger. *Glaube*], which lacks the right sauce. I never could digest it properly. Even in your best days, under my ancestor, when King David ruled over Judah and Israel, I never could have endured it. And I am sure that one fine morning I would have sprung from Mount Zion and emigrated to Phoenicia or Babylon, where the temples of the gods overflowed with an appetite for life [Ger. *die Lebenslust*]."
>
> "You blaspheme against God, Isaac," murmured the rabbi darkly, "you are worse than a Christian, you are a pagan, an idol-worshipper ..."

> "Yes, I am a pagan, and so I am equally revolted by the dry [Ger. *dürren*], joyless Hebrews as I am by dull [Ger. *trüben*], self-tormenting Nazarenes. May our dear lady of Sidon, holy Astarte, forgive me for kneeling before the all-sorrowing mother of the crucified one. Only my knees and my tongue worship death – my heart remains true to life."
>
> Heine 1994, 142

So far, Don Isaac has characterized only his own taste for Jewish food as "pagan." But as he continues, the conversation takes a strange turn.

> "But don't look so sour [Don Isaac reassures Rabbi Abraham]. My nose is no apostate. When once by chance I came into this street at dinner time and the well-known delightful odors of the Jewish kitchen ascended to my nose, I was seized with the same yearning [Ger. *Sehnsucht*] that our fathers felt for the fleshpots of Egypt – tasty memories of youth came back to me. I imagined once more the carp with brown raisin sauce, which my aunt prepared with such devotion for Sabbath eve; I saw once more the mutton stew with garlic and horseradish which might have raised the dead and the soup swarming-swimming [Ger. *schwärmerisch schwimmenden*] with dumplings – and my soul melted away like the notes of a nightingale in love. And ever since then, I have been eating at my friend's the lady Schnapper-Elle."
>
> Heine 1994, 143

Don Isaac's description of the transports of the Jewish table finally erases the line between Judaism and paganism. The Jewish table itself becomes a pagan temple, "overflowing with an appetite for life." Rabbi Abraham's modern hierarchy – being a pagan, an idol-worshipper is worse than being a Christian – implicitly locates Judaism alongside Christianity; but Don Isaac challenges this juxtaposition as a kind of category mistake. His Judaism is closer to paganism than to Christianity; what Don Isaac cannot stomach is *Glaube* – the elevation of credo above corpora. Heine's strong assonance of *dürren* and *trüben* (which I've tried, weakly, to reproduce in the alliteration of "dry" and "dull") blurs the difference between "Hebrews" and "Nazarenes." Whatever the doctrinal distinction between them, to Don Isaac's "ancestral" ears, they sound the same, insofar as they are both *Glauben*, modern confessions.

"Hebrews" and "Nazarenes" are suggestive terms – they belong not to the fifteenth century, when the story is set, but to the first half of the nineteenth, when the story was written. Heine is alluding, transparently, to his own contemporaries – to modern "believing" Jews and Christians who have jointly embraced *Glaube*, the enlightened idea of "confession" over cult, based ostensibly (but not really) on an original "Hebraic" or "Nazarene" idea of a primal, innocent, and most of all, dematerialized, spirituality. These terms had a powerful contemporary resonance for Heine's readers; the philosophical sophistication of modern piety rested, paradoxically, on what Ernest Gombrich describes as a Romantic "preference for the primitive" associated principally with the rejection of post-Renaissance "paganism" (Gombrich 2002, 87–176). In this scenario, "Christianity" and "Judaism" stood for the corrupt, degenerate versions of their authentic "Nazarene" and "Hebraic" former selves, a natural condition to which they needed to be restored. The object of Heine's satire is, precisely, the historically naive, dogmatic, and pretentious puritanism of a "reformed" Hebraism modeled on contemporary evangelical Christianity; for Heine, its unreconstructed "pagan" progenitor, ironically and conspicuously modern, is alive and well in the Jewish ghetto. In the voice of Don Isaac, Heine refers, with deliberate provocation, to the modern spiritual revival, both Jewish and Christian, as the "worship of death." Ten years before the publication of "Rabbi of Bacherach," he had called Peter Cornelius, one of the founders of the so-called "Nazarene" school of painting, a "dead creator" (Ger. *ein todter Schöpfer*); it was, he said, as if Cornelius' etiolated figures "did not have long to live and had all been born an hour before their death" (Heine 1986, 77–78). On the other side of this historical divide stands the archaic "kitchen of Israel," around the corner from the synagogue, whence it may be easily reached; the two institutions, prayer-house and eating-house, are contiguous. If the widow Schnapper is the Jewish incarnation of "holy Astarte" rather than a descendant of the all-sorrowing Jewish mother of the dead "Nazarene" then Don Isaac, the pagan, is a proper Jew after all. The Jewish body can neither be made nor destroyed by credal assertions.

What does Don Isaac mean by "my nose is no apostate"? Whatever his philosophy may be, his senses are Jewish. It is through the imaginative evocation – the memory – of physical presence that Don Isaac experiences Jewish sanctity. He does not recall his uncle, the famous Jewish philosopher and messianic prophet, but his aunt, the "devoted" Jewish cook. It is her stew, not his theology, that raises the dead; her fish, not his prayers, that constitutes divine service; her dumplings, not his doctrine, that are the source of "religious enthusiasm" (Ger. *Schwärmerei*), a word with a bad reputation among the religious "enlighteners" (La Vopa 1997) which Don Isaac's extravagant tribute to his aunt's elixir-like soup *schwärming* with matzah balls rehabilitates here. The memory of scent and taste produce desire and inspire "soul-melting" love. Eating is not the reflection but the source of religious conviction. The first principle of Judaism does not lie with philosophy but with performance: "Am Anfang," says Heine's Jewish Faust, "war die Tat." It is as if Don Isaac has to become a Christian in order to abjure his modern Jewish *Glauben*, reclaim his inner Jewish pagan and revert to his primal Jewish desire.

Of course, food is not just food; Don Isaac's unreconstructed and unreformed (circumcised and thus permanently marked) Jewish nose alludes to his irresistible sexual attraction to Sara, the rabbi's ravishing wife, whose presence likewise "speaks to" – appeals to (Ger. *anspricht*) – him in the same way as Jewish food, dispensed, likewise, by a Jewish beauty. When Don Isaac first sees Sara, she is just recovering from having fainted, the rabbi says, from hunger; but also from a surfeit of sad memories of her kin who are lost to her through Christian violence which she and the rabbi have escaped. Through the good offices of "the lady Schnapper" Sara's life – the life of the Jews – is resurrected by natural everyday means; her revival is a small ordinary miracle. Food is a restorative of both the individual and the collective body which promises a beginning. Barren at the beginning of the story, Sara is quite possibly pregnant by the end through some sort of vicarious intervention by the mysterious Don Isaac the master of love; is Don Isaac a Jewish parody of the angel Gabriel, the messenger of an immaculate conception, or is he one of the original biblical angels in Genesis 18 who comes to tell Sarah, wife of the patriarch Abraham, the good news that she will bear a son, a son to be *named Isaac* whose life assures the future of the Jewish people? (compare Goetschel 2019, 247–260). It is interesting that the scene in Genesis also involves a festive meal, linking feeding with fertility.

In a world governed by regular meals and eating rituals there are no big redemptive endings, only small interruptions that regularly punctuate the passage of time. The tiny, invisible (so small that he is only a glimmer in the reader's mind) Jewish infant, only just beginning to cook in his mother's womb interrupts the plot and reverses the sad course of Sara's memory, derailed at the start by the corpse of the Christian infant all-too-present under the rabbi's table. In the life of the Jewish corpus every life is the fragment of a greater whole, a macrocosm of which every individual is only (only!) a "fragment." The non-existent "conclusion" has to be lost, but not through the fault of the author. This is perhaps because the Jewish author is always already telling the same unfinished story, a story of which he is himself only a part. An ending does not exist because Don Isaac's unphilosophical Judaism without end precludes its existence. To attach any ending (even a happy ending) to this "history" is to transform Jewish life, full of ordinary, tiny miracles of survival and resilience into the great expectations of Jewish metaphysics which, to Don Isaac's nose, seemed somehow to smell of Christianity. An ending would defeat the hidden Jewish purpose of Don Isaac, the imaginary laughing nephew – even though it might comport with the program of that other Don Isaac, the actual philosophically and messianically minded uncle. The irony is vertiginous here; Don Isaac, the nephew who does not exist, stands for the empirical, sensual, biological reality of Jewish life; while the absent uncle, who was, at one time, a living historical person (although now he is, of course, a corpse) represents a kind of philosophical fiction that Heine ultimately sets aside as "indigestible."

Heine's intervention in nineteenth-century confessional politics is subtle and ingenious; but the aestheticization of Jewish practice at the expense of Jewish philosophy neither originated nor stopped with his work. It is a feature of Jewish literature that belongs to the Haskalah; the earliest example of Romantic irony directed at the philosophical project of Jewish Enlightenment can be found in Solomon Maimon's *Autobiography* (1792–1793) a text which Heine read and which quite possibly helped to inspire the creation of Don Isaac, the Sephardic free-thinker and alter ego of the modern Jewish poet. In *On the History of Religion and Philosophy in Germany* (1834), Heine cites Maimon's joke about Kantian apathy in the face of the *terribilitá* of the *shofar* while registering his own Romantic shudder at the memory of the same *shofar* being blown in Amsterdam's Spanish synagogue during the ritual excommunication of that "scorner of the Mosaic law, the Hidalgo Don Benedikt de Spinoza" (Heine 2007, 51).

Ostensibly realistic – which is to say aesthetically convincing – depictions of contemporary Jewish practice naturalized a living image of well-preserved tradition, sublime in its indifference to ideologically inflected historicist arguments that Judaism was a pathetic anachronism, urgently in need of reform. As an object of aesthetic contemplation, Jewish practice provided a rich moral resource, "rousing the mind and the heart, full of meaning, never ceasing […] to provide the occasion and opportunity for oral instruction" (Mendelssohn 1983, 102–103). In an age of scientific skepticism, fracturing rabbinic authority and increasing social mobility, the Jewish laughter of Don Isaac rose above the need for philosophical justification. To the extent that Jewish literature demanded imaginative assent to experience and capitalized on existing emotional attachments to Jewish life, effectively sidelining intellectual debate (who argues with one's nose?), the Romantic religion of the *maskilim* was conservative; but in privileging the immediacy of assent over precedent and argument, *maskilic* authors effectively acknowledged that in breaking the rabbinic monopoly on Jewish writing Jewish literature subverted the authority of Jewish law and undermined the primacy of *talmud torah*. This knowledge made *maskilim* slightly queasy; were they saving Judaism from becoming a corpse or officiating at its funeral? A nagging sense that, like Heine's Don Isaac, they had made a deal with the devil explains why *maskilic* literature so often strikes a dark elegiac note at odds, one might have thought, with a movement defined as the "Jewish enlightenment" (Miron 1981). The ambivalence might also explain the Romantic appeal of the idea of national sovereignty, Jewish politics being the only way to ensure the survival of Jewish practice under the name of culture.

References

Baumgarten, Jean. 2005. *Introduction to Old Yiddish Literature*. Ed. and trans. Jerold C. Frakes. Oxford: Oxford University Press.
Bitzan, Amos. 2011. "The Problem of Pleasure: Disciplining the German Jewish Reading Revolution, 1770–1870." PhD thesis. University of California, Berkeley.
Bradshaw, Michael. 2008. "Hedgehog Theory: How to Read a Romantic Fragment Poem." *Literature Compass* 5: 73–89.
Feiner, Shmuel. 2004. *The Jewish Enlightenment*. Trans. Chaya Naor. Philadelphia, PA: University of Pennsylvania Press.
Fisch, Harold. 1988. *Poetry with a Purpose: Biblical Poetics and Interpretation*. Bloomington, IN: Indiana University Press.
Goetschel, Willi. 2019. *Heine and Critical Theory*. London: Bloomsbury Academic.
Gombrich, E. H. 2002. *The Preference for the Primitive: Episodes in the History of Western Taste and Art*. London: Phaidon.
Gries, Zeev. 1996. "The Hasidic Managing Editor as an Agent of Culture," in *Hasidism Reappraised*. Ed. Ada Rapoport-Albert. Oxford: The Littman Library of Jewish Civilization, 141–155.
Halivni, David W. 1986. *Midrash, Mishnah and Gemara: The Jewish Predilection for Justified Law*. Cambridge, MA: Harvard University Press.
Harris, Jay M. 1995. *How Do We Know This? Midrash and the Fragmentation of Modern Judaism*. Albany, NY: State University of New York Press.
Heine, Heinrich. 1986. "Reisebilder III." Ed. Alfred Opitz. Volume 7/1 *Historisch-kritische Gesamtausgabe der Werke (Düsseldorfer Ausgabe)*. Ed. Manfred Windfuhr. Hamburg: Hoffmann und Campe, 9–152.
Heine, Heinrich. 1994. "Der Rabbi von Bacherach. (Ein Fragment)." Volume 5 *Historisch-kritische Gesamtausgabe der Werke (Düsseldorf Ausgabe)*. Ed. Manfred Windfuhr. Hamburg: Hoffmann und Campe, 107–147.
Heine, Heinrich. 2007. *On the History of Religion and Philosophy in Germany and Other Writings*. Ed. Terry Pinkard. Trans. Howard Pollack-Milgate. Cambridge: Cambridge University Press.
Heinemann, Isaac. 2009. *The Reasons for the Commandments in Jewish Thought: From the Bible to the Renaissance*. Trans. Leonard Levin. Boston, MA: Academic Studies Press.
Klausner, Joseph. 1952–1955. *Historiah shel hasifrut ha'ivrit hahadashah*. 6 vols. Jerusalem: Ahiasaf.
Krochmal, Nachman. 2010. *Moreh nevukhei hazeman*. Ed. Yehoyada Amir. Jerusalem: Karmel.
La Vopa, Anthony J. 1997. "The Philosopher and the *Schwärmer*: On the Career of a German Epithet from Luther to Kant." *Huntington Library Quarterly* 60: 85–115.
Litvak, Olga. 2006. *Conscription and the Search for Modern Russian Jewry*. Bloomington, IN: Indiana University Press.
Litvak, Olga. 2012. *Haskalah: The Romantic Movement in Judaism*. New Brunswick, NJ: Rutgers University Press.
Mapu, Abraham 1970. *Mikhtavei avraham mapu*. Ed. Ben-Zion Dinur. Jerusalem: Mossad Bialik.
Mendelsohn, Moses. 1983. *Jerusalem, or on Religious Power and Judaism*. Trans. Allan Arkush. Hanover NH and London: Brandeis University Press.
Miron, Dan. 1981. "Rediscovering Haskalah Poetry." *Prooftexts* 1: 292–305.
Miron, Dan. 2000. "Folklore and Antifolklore in the Yiddish Fiction of the Haskala." *The Image of the Shtetl and Other Studies of Modern Jewish Literary Imagination*. Syracuse, NY: Syracuse University Press, 49–80.
Quint, Alyssa. 2005. "'Yiddish Literature for the Masses'? A Reconsideration of Who Read What in Jewish Eastern Europe." *AJS Review* 29: 61–89.
Reiner, Elchanan. 2000. "A Biography of an Agent of Culture: Eleazar Altschul of Prague and His Literary Activity." *Schöpferische Momente des europäischen Judentums in der frühen Neuzeit*. Ed. Michael Graetz. Heidelberg: Universitätsverlag C. Winter, 229–247.
Rose, Margaret. 1976. "Über die strukturelle Einheit von Heines Fragment 'Der Rabbi von Bacherach.'" *Heine-Jahrbuch* 15: 38–51.
Roskies, David G. 1995. *A Bridge of Longing: The Lost Art of Yiddish Storytelling*. Cambridge, MA: Harvard University Press.
Sammons, Jeffrey L. 1979. *Heinrich Heine: A Modern Biography*. Princeton, NJ: Princeton University Press.
Schorsch, Ismar. 1994. "Breakthrough into the Past: The *Verein für Cultur und Wissenschaft der Juden*." *From Text to Context: The Turn to History in Modern Judaism*. Hanover NH and London: Brandeis University Press, 205–232.

Stanislawski, Michael F. 1983. *Tsar Nicholas I and the Jews: The Transformation of Jewish Society in Russia, 1825–1855*. Philadelphia, PA: The Jewish Publication Society.

Wisse, Ruth R. 2001. *The Modern Jewish Canon: A Journey Through Language and Culture*. New York: Free Press.

Yerushalmi, Yosef Hayim. 1981. *From Spanish Court to Italian Ghetto. Isaac Cardoso: A Study in Seventeenth-Century Marranism and Jewish Apologetics*. Seattle: University of Washington Press.

Yuval, Israel Jacob. 2006. "Rome or Jerusalem: The Foundations of Jewish-Christian Hostility." *Two Nations in Your Womb: Perceptions of Jews and Christians in Late Antiquity and the Middle Ages*. Trans. Barbara Harshav and Jonathan Chipman. Berkeley: University of California Press, 31–91.

15
RITUAL AND PRACTICE IN HASIDISM

Gadi Sagiv

Hasidic Jews in the twenty-first century can be recognized by their external practices. They are easily identifiable through men's distinctive clothing and hair-styling. One can often recognize long black suits, a wide belt, a circular fur-hat worn on Sabbath and festive occasions, long sidelocks, and knee-high socks. The more trained eye with greater familiarity can distinguish sub-groups within Hasidism.

Hasidism is often characterized as a Jewish pietistic movement that emerged in eighteenth-century Eastern Europe and developed into what seems to be the most prominent Jewish social religious movement worldwide in the last three hundred years. Hasidism emerged from circles of ascetic kabbalists, mystics, and magicians that were active in the southeastern areas of the eighteenth-century Polish-Lithuanian commonwealth, areas that today are primarily in Ukraine. The major figure of early Hasidism was a mystic and magician named Israel ben Eliezer, known as the *Baal Shem Tov*, or the *Besht* (1700–1760). As a religious movement, Hasidism is a mystical movement. Its theology is based on kabbalah, with an emphasis on the demand of mystical attachment with God.

Hasidism is discernible by its rituals even against the thick backdrop of the system of rituals of traditional Judaism, comprising both mandatory laws (*halakhah*) and customs (*minhag*). Namely, Jews have always behaved differently from their social surroundings, and Hasidic Jews, while easily recognizable as Jews, have always behaved somewhat differently from other Jews. Ritual features prominently in Hasidism as a mediator between theology and social reality. Many of the rituals are performed in the social realm, rooted in theological foundation. In fact, the name of the movement hints to practice: The word "Hasid" means "pious" in Hebrew, denoting a way of life that is believed to be more pious than others.

The importance of investigating ritual and practice in Hasidism is threefold: First, it helps understand how the Hasidic movement succeeded in attracting so many followers. Second, it is an example of the ways in which ritual and practice have played a role in a renewal process within Judaism. Third, it is a test case exemplifying the power of ritual to shape a religious social movement.

The exploration that follows focuses on rituals and practices commonly associated with Hasidism, although it bears mention that most are not Hasidic innovations. Rather, most of the rituals performed in Hasidism were performed or had their roots prior to the emergence of the

Hasidic movement in various historical contexts. The focus here is primarily Hasidism from its emergence in the eighteenth century until the Second World War. Namely, the period when Hasidism was still an Eastern European phenomenon. While Hasidism comprises sub-groups with differences in practice, the ensuing discussion does not address these internal differences; instead, it limits itself to common features.[1]

The discussion begins with a brief survey of some of these rituals and practices, followed by a brief examination of oppositions to these rituals, their interaction with the Jewish ritual system, and the role they played for those who practiced them. The survey is divided according to the social contexts of life and performance. Although there are several rituals that cross these boundaries, such as prayer that can be practiced at home alone or in a synagogue, the discussion maintains this division for the sake of clarity.

It bears mention from the outset that the following survey is very selective; it is virtually impossible to cover the entire system of ritual associated with Hasidism within the limits of such a brief chapter. In addition, the rituals presented here have never been a mandatory set of practices for all Hasidim. In contrast to the Jewish halakhah, laws that are basically mandatory, rituals in Hasidism were more like a repertoire from which every Hasid could select what suited his/her lifestyle. In that sense, they are more akin to Jewish custom. Notably, while women traditionally performed less of this repertoire, they did have rituals that were often associated with them more than men, such as storytelling.

Practicing Hasidism Individually

Although Hasidism was a social movement, several rituals associated with Hasidism could be performed by an individual Hasid in the private or domestic sphere, not requiring any contact with his fellow Hasidim.

Prayer was undoubtedly a prominent focal point for Hasidim; it was the focal point upon which a Hasid differed in ritual compared to his surroundings. In their guidelines for prayer, early Hasidic masters objected to the basic requirement of rabbinic Judaism, which called for reciting the prayer text with intention of the heart. Hasidic masters demanded more: They adopted mystical approaches to prayer, according to which prayer was a practice in which the performer had the opportunity to attach his soul to the divine (a mystical objective) followed by drawing influx from above to benefit the world (a magical objective).[2] Several Hasidic masters demanded that prayer be performed with intensive emotional arousal. That sort of demand, which accompanied mystical prayer, could also be understood as an aim in and of itself.

The emphasis on mystical contemplative prayer was not an innovation of Hasidism. Rather, it was emphasized among sixteenth-century kabbalists of Safed even more than by Hasidic masters. However, with an aim to reach broader audiences as compared to earlier kabbalists, Hasidic masters simplified mystical prayer, probably in order to make it more feasible for a wide circle of followers – great in number and diverse in education – rather than make it suited to limited circles of kabbalistic elite.

One manifestation of the importance afforded to prayer was the custom of using special prayer books that differed from non-Hasidim. While the text of the Jewish prayer is quite uniform across all branches of rabbinic Judaism, there are several versions of the printed text, with slight modifications, such as between Ashkenazic and Sepharadic versions. From the outset, Hasidim adopted existing versions of the prayer book and gradually named their versions 'Luria's Version' (*nusach ha-Ari*), after Isaac Luria, one of the celebrated figures in Safed. However, the Hasidic prayer book – or more accurately, prayer books, because there was no conformity – was not Luria's version. It was an amalgamation of various versions. Still, the nominal fact does bear weight: The title 'Luria's Version' actually connected Hasidim to the legendary mystical tradition of sixteenth-century Safed. Polemical texts against Hasidim banned those who used Luria's prayer book, opining that it should be limited to the elite. Opponents did not claim that the Hasidim's prayer book was not Luria's version. On the contrary; they accepted this as fact yet objected to the break from Ashkenazic custom, allowing it only to limited circles of kabbalists and not to wider circles.[3]

As we will see below, differences in Hasidim's prayer customs led to their voluntary social separation from the non-Hasidic community; Hasidim wanted to pray with other people who shared their versions of prayer. This separation constituted in itself a major point of opposition.

The importance afforded to contemplative prayer or prayer with emotional arousal generated practices that supported the tendency to elevate and deepen prayer, practices that often had inherent value. Examples of that sort of practice can be found in the emphasis on bodily purification such as emptying the bodily waste or ritual bathing in order to purify the body before prayer (more on this below). There were also spiritual and intellectual preparations, such as intensive study. One side-effect of those preparatory practices was Hasidim's delaying prayer as compared to non-Hasidim, taking the time beforehand to complete their preparations (one should know that there are halakhic boundaries to the time windows of the daily prayers). All of these practices were intended to generate the proper emotional state during prayer or pave the way for undisturbed contemplation.

During their prayers, Hasidim often adopted various practices intended to generate a proper state of mind or induce spiritual intent required for that sort of prayer, thereby removing obstacles that stood in its way, primarily alien thoughts. Namely, the intent was to ward off unwanted thought that arose in the worshipper's consciousness, contaminating the purity of the prayer. Thus, we find evidence about jumping, somersaulting, shouting, moving at a different pace and directions, but also standing still like freezing.

The practice of ritual bathing is particularly interesting. Ritual bathing is mandatory in Judaism for purification of certain formal states of purity. In the main, married women are obligated to bathe for purification after menstruation, but ritual bathing is not habitually mandatory for men. However, extensive ritual bathing was adopted by male Hasidim in accordance with a similar custom among some sixteenth-century kabbalists that used to immerse themselves on special days such as Sabbath and Festivals. Hasidim also renewed an ancient custom of ritual bathing after seminal emissions. In early Hasidism, ritual bathing did not only play a role in preparing for prayer, or a rite of passage; it gained importance in its own right as a moment of prayer and even mystical immersion inside the Godhead.[4]

The aforementioned Hasidic prayer books show not only the text of the Hasidic prayers; they also show the Hasidic masters' attempt to disseminate this text in print among wide circles of followers. The use of print for disseminating practice can also be seen in printed collections of brief recommendations for religious behavior – *hanhagot* in Hebrew – composed by eighteenth-century Hasidic masters who delivered these collections to their followers. Notably, these recommendations for pietistic behavior were not mandatory requirements. One ought to also keep in mind that written recommendations present a norm rather than a social reality. That is, we do not know to what extent these recommendations were actually performed. Still, the printing of these recommendations is important because it shows that early Hasidic masters sometimes attempted to regulate, or at least structure, the individual rituals a Hasid ought to practice. These written compilations of advice became an effective way for Hasidic leaders to disseminate their message: The written brief form without lengthy elaboration of ideas simplified distribution and made it acceptable to Hasidim who were not especially learned. Research into this rich conduct literature has shown that much of its content originated in sixteenth-century Safed and was adopted about two hundred years later by wide circles of Hasidim.[5]

Practicing Hasidism within the Hasidic Confraternity

From the second half of the eighteenth century, Hasidism can be described as comprising various groups of fellow Hasidim, each led by a mystic-magician who saw himself as following the ethos of the Besht. The leader of that sort of a group was called a *tsadik* (Hebrew for righteous). The prominent tsadikim (plural of tsadik) were not only local leaders but also leaders of groups of Hasidim residing in various places. To the term "Hasid" a new meaning was added: not only of a pious person, but also of a disciple of a certain tsadik. The tsadik often lived in a court to which Hasidim used to travel from disparate locations.

The Hasidim in a specific town that followed a particular tsadik constituted the basic social unit of Hasidim. These groups of local Hasidim used to gather in a space separate from the community's main synagogue.[6] This space, often called a *shtibl* (in Yiddish: a small house or a small room) or *kloyz* (a term for a study house), might have been the house of one of its members or a dedicated space. This social unit functioned like a confraternity, or a *chavura* or *chevra*, as it is called in Hebrew and Yiddish.[7] Those local confraternities played various social roles in the history of Hasidism, but in this chapter, we will limit our focus to the rituals and practices performed within those groups.

Hasidim who lived in the same place and followed the same tsadik used to meet in the *shtibl* for regular prayers or special occasions. Such festive occasions were not only holidays but also events related to the tsadik, such as marking the *yarhtzeit*, the anniversary of a celebrated tsadik's passing, or other significant dates in the history of their Hasidic group. Hasidim shared news about their tsadik and his family. They planned travel to the court or visits of personalities from the court.

During these gatherings Hasidim smoked, danced, and drank a lot of alcohol. These practices, which became symbols of Hasidic lifestyle, were crafted as rituals and imbued with esoteric meaning by the Hasidim themselves.[8]

One of the distinctive Hasidic practices among such confraternities of Hasidim, as well as in families of Hasidim, was storytelling about their masters and their admired character and deeds.[9] Hasidic sources attributed spiritual powers to the very act of telling such adulatory stories. For example, the Besht was known to have said that "when one tells stories in praise of the tsaddikim, it is as though he were engaged in *ma'aseh merkavah* (the mystical secret of the divine chariot)."[10] The spiritual power of stories was not only related to their content that expressed piety; there was also a belief that the story's text, the letters of the written text, had a metaphysical existence capable of influencing God. On a social level, when Hasidim told stories about their masters' supernatural qualities, they articulated and reinforced their belief in their master. The storytelling among the confraternity of Hasidim also bolstered their bonding, affording them a sense of pride as compared to other groups of Hasidim.

Compared to elitist discourses, whose understanding depended on rabbinic education, stories were more accessible to diverse populations. Hence, storytelling in Hasidism constituted an important practice through which women could express their Hasidic identity and affiliation. While expressing ethical values through Hasidic discourses was done primarily by men due to their rabbinic education, there are sources that indicate that women of the Hasidic elite told stories to both men and women, forming a unique form of spiritual leadership.[11]

Another example of practice that characterizes Hasidic confraternity within a community is the insistence on specially sharpened knives for the ritual slaughtering of animals (*shechitah*). Hasidim imbued the traditional ritual slaughtering with internal kabbalistic meanings. While these meanings were introduced hundreds of years prior to Hasidism, Hasidim made them into a social practice: They insisted on ritual slaughterers that knew these secrets and had their knives polished accordingly.[12] Consequently, Hasidim avoided using the services of non-Hasidic ritual slaughterers. The insistence on polished knives is another example of providing deeper spiritual meaning to existing rituals on the basis of kabbalistic traditions. In this case, the practice had a social aspect; the presence of Hasidic ritual slaughtering usually indicated the existence of a Hasidic community that insisted on that sort of slaughtering. As we will see below, this practice also had social implications that extended beyond the confines of the Hasidic fraternity.

The coexistence of several groups of Hasidim in the same local community, each affiliated with a different tsadik, became a source of tension and dispute. Quite often, controversies broke out between those groups. These fissures could be related to social disputes about nominations of religious functionaries that were often limited in number. But in numerous cases, these disputes revolved around religious practice, such as the exact text of the prayer a cantor should recite in synagogue where Hasidim of several groups used to pray.[13]

The coexistence of several groups of Hasidim in the same local community hints to a broader challenge of differentiation between Hasidic factions, not only in the confines of a single community.[14] Hasidim needed to explain to themselves and to others why there were numerous Hasidic groups despite the fact that they all saw themselves as the Besht's spiritual off-spring. The oft-given answer was that each tsadik had a different approach to religious practice. For example, the famous fur-hat, the *shtrayml*, is indeed a marker of Hasidism. But the specific styling of the *shtrayml* depends on the specific group to which the Hasid belongs.[15]

That urge to differentiate also manifested in adopting unique customs by particular Hasidic factions. Examples include loud prayer among Karlin Hasidim, a ritual of rectifying sins by reciting verses among Breslev Hasidim, and a blue thread on the tassels of clothing by Radzin Hasidim. The uniqueness displayed a unique Hasidic identity, which revealed the particular Hasidic identity in the local community.

Practicing Hasidism in the Local Community

Although Hasidim in a local community used to convene in separated prayer houses and often used Hasidim's services, such as in the case of slaughtering, rarely were Hasidim socially detached from the local non-Hasidic Jewish community. More likely, Hasidic masters provided services to the community.

This function began as early as the Besht, who filled the office of a professional kabbalist and magician of the town of Mezhibozh.[16] The Besht, a mystic and magician, was often asked to perform rituals for the entire community's well-being, such as warding off demons and evil forces, helping the infirm, and asking God to provide prosperity for communal members. Other Hasidic masters were given communal posts of rabbis and preachers, and conducted other practices for the community.[17]

Hasidim often attempted to actively increase their influence in a community and gain a stronghold of communal positions. The success in achieving such influence varied according to local circumstance. In communities with many Hasidim, they gained more influence. These attempts often engendered antagonism and opposition because the new institutions and posts they brought generated competition that could weaken former non-Hasidic institutions. Such was the case when Hasidim established their own prayer houses and stopped praying at communal synagogues, which was financially injurious to the community. Such was also the case when a Hasidic slaughterer came to town, and Hasidim, and perhaps others, too, began using his services, thereby decreasing the old slaughterer's clientele, and hence reducing the community's income from the *krupki* tax, imposed on all consumables, especially Kosher meat.

However, at times Hasidic institutions helped the local community, sometimes offering assistance that the community requested. As noted earlier, that sort of interaction existed as early as the times of the Besht. That interaction broadened in the nineteenth century during the gradual weakening of traditional Jewish communal institutions as part of the authorities' attempts to limit their power. At times, a Jewish community requested a tsadik to become its religious patron. The tsadik was expected to care for the community's spiritual welfare. He provided services such as paying regular visits to the community; intervening in times of epidemic or other kinds of distress; and nominating community functionaries, such as rabbis, cantors, and ritual slaughterers, thereby also strengthening the tsadik's position. The community, in turn, gave the tsadik some benefits, such as honorable titles, money, or franchises to community assets.

An example of a tsadik that gained responsibility for Jewish communities in the nineteenth century was Avraham Yehoshua Heschel of Apt (1748–1825). For example, this tsadik established a custom of ritual recitation of ancient rabbinic texts by members of a local community to protect that community from harm, particularly during epidemics. This Hasidic leader also recommended that Jewish communities join a public fast in 1824 to annul a decree issued by the Russian government forbidding Jews to dwell in rural areas.[18]

Another example of this sort of relationship in the realm of religious ritual and practices is a ceremony of inaugurating new grounds for cemeteries, often related to a spike in death due to epidemics. This ritual developed from older Ashkenazi rituals and was later attributed to the Besht, despite a lack of evidence. In some areas, only tsadikim were allowed to perform the inauguration because it required possessing concealed mystical knowledge that only they possessed.[19]

Practicing Hasidism at the Court of the Tsadik

While Hasidim spent most of their lives in their town of residence, it was visiting their leader, the tsadik, that constituted a social and religious highpoint. The tsadik's home was often surrounded by a court; for most Hasidim, traveling to the court was an exceptional event that they could not afford financially as part of their daily living. It is not surprising, then, that numerous sources present this travel as a pilgrimage to a holy place.[20]

Upon arrival at the court, a Hasid could partake in various rituals and ceremonies with the Tasdik, sometimes in private, sometimes as part of a group of Hasidim at the court at that time. Quite often, the Hasid arrived at the court with personal issues, requesting assistance from the tsadik. These could be family matters such as finding suitable matches to marry off their offspring, praying for family members who had health problems, and tackling financial difficulty. A Hasid believed that the tsadik could help because the tsadik was considered a mystic imbued with supernatural powers, a healer and wise counselor. In addition, Hasidim believed that the souls of the tsadik and his followers were connected in such a way that could facilitate the assistance of the specific tsadik to the specific Hasid.

Often ritualized was the private audience between Hasid and tsadik, a meeting that wasn't always available to the Hasid. The Hasid would write down his requests in advance on a note, called "*kvitl*" in Yiddish, and pay a sum of money that was called "*pidyon*"; that sum was not only a payment for the service provided but was also considered an offering with spiritual significance. Habitually, the Hasid poured his heart out to the tsadik. The tsadik would respond with a specific message, blessing, or promise to pray for the Hasid.

Private meetings with the tsadik generally took place during the weekdays. However, the tsadik appeared in public for several ceremonies on the Sabbath. Yosef Perl, a central proponent of the Jewish Enlightenment and fierce opponent of Hasidism, described in 1816 the prominence of the Sabbath third meal in the praxis of the Hasidim:

> Though the entire Sabbath is considered a time of special divine favor which is best spent in the rebbe's court, it is the period of the third meal which is thought to be the most desirable time for the bonding of the Hasid with his rebbe. On each and every Sabbath, following the afternoon prayers, the local Hasidim, along with visitors from other places, gather in the home of the rebbe; and when there is no rebbe present in the city, they gather in the home of a prominent Hasid, for the third meal. There they eat and drink a lot of wine, sing and dance. And it is during this time that the tsaddik delivers before the assembled his interpretations of the Torah and Talmud.[21]

The Hasidic sacramental meal, the so-called *Tish* (Table in Yiddish), might seem a complete novelty. Actually, it was a cluster of pre-existing Jewish practices such as the three sacramental meals in Sabbath and the sanctification of eating.[22]

However, one of the rituals comprising the *Tish* that does seem a novelty is symbolically distributing leftovers, *Shirayim* in Hebrew, to Hasidim attending the meal. Although Jewish traditional sources mention biblical laws of leaving parts of the corps for the poor as proof-texts for this custom, it resembles more closely Jewish ritual meals in which bread is distributed by the person leading the benediction ceremony, as well as the image of Jesus distributing wine and food in the last supper, and its reenactment in the catholic mass. Be the sources or parallels of this custom as they may, the custom of the Shirayim reifies and intensifies the social and spiritual bonding between the tsadik and his followers.

Another apex of the Hasidic Sabbath was the tasdik's delivery of a sermon to his followers, "interpretations of Torah and Talmud" mentioned in Yosef Perl's description quoted above. A famous example of a delivery of this sort of sermon is from philosopher Solomon Maimon's autobiography. Maimon visited the court of the Dov Ber of Mezerich (d. 1772), one of the most prominent Hasidic masters of the eighteenth century. He visited the court out of curiosity, just to leave it later, rejecting Hasidism as part of Jewish irrationalism. The following is part of his description:

> Finally, I arrived safely in M. After resting a while, I went to the leader's house, hoping to be introduced to him immediately. I was told that he couldn't speak with me just yet. But I was invited to share a meal with him on the Sabbath together with other guests, who had also come to visit him. I would then have the good fortune of speaking with the holy man in person and hearing the most exalted teachings directly from his mouth. In other words, our meeting would be open to others, but it would have individual parts meant just for me, and I should therefore consider it as a special audience.
>
> I arrived on the Sabbath for the festive meal and found that a large number of important men from all over the region had gathered for the occasion. The great man finally appeared, cutting an impressive figure, dressed as he was in a white Atlas robe.

Even his shoes and his tobacco container were white (among Kabbalists white is the color of grace). He gave each one of the arrivals a Schalam; that is, the great man greeted each of them.

We sat down to eat, and a solemn silence reigned during the meal. After we had finished, the leader sang a celebratory, spiritually uplifting melody. He held his hand in front of his forehead for a few moments, then began to call: "Z. from H.! M. from R.! S. M. from N.!"—the names and places of residence of all the new arrivals, something that astonished us more than a little. Each one of us was asked to recite a verse from the Holy Scripture. We did this. Thereupon the leader began to give a sermon, taking the verses we had recited as the text. Even though they were completely unconnected verses from different books of the Holy Scripture, he linked them together with such artistry that they seemed to form a single whole. Even more extraordinary was that each of us felt the part of the sermon dealing with his verse contained something referring directly to his own pressing personal concerns. Naturally, we were amazed.[23]

The sermon was presented to Maimon as an alternative for a personal meeting with the tsadik. Several striking characteristics ought to be noted in the practice of the sermon's delivery: First, the auditory and visual characteristics of the music as well as the white-colored garment and other objects. Second, the impression that the Maggid had a mystical-ecstatic experience prior to delivering the sermon. Third, the virtuoso sermon that tailored together all independent verses. And finally, the emphasis on personal reference to every attendant. Despite Maimon's later negative attitude toward Hasidism, one gathers the impression of an intense experience on the part of attendants.

Although not all Hasidic leaders used to deliver sermons, this practice was considered central among the rituals and practices associated with Hasidism. As the Hasidic movement grew and proliferated, various preaching styles surfaced and became part of the tsadikim's personal style. Some tsadikim delivered lengthy scholastic discourses whereas others presented brief aphorisms. Some based their talks on halakhah, others on kabbalah, with the majority focusing on general ethical subjects. Notably, in any of these focal points, interpretations of verses of the Hebrew Bible played a central role. Hasidic sermons were primarily homilies on verses of the weekly Torah portions (*Parashot*). The particular content of that homily varied according to the specific interest of the tsadik delivering the sermon.[24]

After this brief survey of rituals in Hasidism, let us now turn to a few general observations on rituals in Hasidism.

Tradition and Renewal in Hasidic Rituals

As noted above, most rituals associated with Hasidism were not Hasidic innovations. It would be more accurate to say that Hasidism renewed the Jewish ritual system on the basis of existing traditions. I call this process "ritualization" in a sense similar to Catherine Bell's (1992) definition of ritualization as a "way in which certain social actions strategically distinguish themselves in relation to other actions." The focus on ritualization allows for a more nuanced understanding of how Hasidim adapted the Jewish ritual system to differ from the existing one, and at the same time remain traditional.

Ritualization in Hasidism was done in more than one way. I will now introduce a few mechanisms of Hasidic ritualization. The following mechanisms of ritualization are not mutually exclusive; in many Hasidic rituals, it is possible to identify more than a single mechanism:

(1) *Popularization*: In many cases, ritualization occurred as a result of widening the circle of performers. Hasidic leaders encouraged their followers to perform rituals that were hitherto performed within smaller circles of a select few, rabbis and kabbalists. An example is popularizing ritual bathing by all Hasidim, a practice common prior to that time only in small circles of kabbalists. That sort of popularization was a major source of opposition toward early Hasidim.

(2) *Intensification or "pietization"*: Performing existing rituals with more devotion and possibly with new meaning. Examples are Hasidic prayer, which included mystical overtones in addition to simple meaning of the texts. Another example is Hasidic ritual slaughtering in which Hasidim expressed or performed piousness, insisting on the use of polished knives and emphasizing the practice's kabbalistic meaning.

(3) *Referring to the Jewish past*: Some of the new rituals introduced by Hasidic masters were taken from a glorious Jewish past. An example is the introduction of *Seder ma'amadot* by Avraham Yehoshu Heschel of Apt, a clear reference to the ancient times of the Jewish Temple.[25] Many other examples resonate with sixteenth-century Safed, such as the usage of *Nusah ha-'ari* in prayer.

(4) *Sanctification of daily practices*: Hasidim imbued non-religious activities with religious meaning, an approach known as "worship through corporeality" (*'avodah be-gashmiyut*).[26] Examples of those activities are smoking tobacco and dancing. Dancing was perceived to have magical powers.

(5) *Adoption and appropriation*: Hasidim adopted various rituals without any significant change in content. Nevertheless, they claimed that they were "Hasidic." Namely, that they were of Hasidic origin, or that they should be performed by Hasidic leaders. An example of this sort of ritualization is the ceremony of inaugurating cemeteries.

Hasidism can thus be seen an attempt to reform Jewish religious life by adapting the contemporaneous ritual system. However, Hasidism was not the only case of changes in the Jewish rituals system of Jews during this period of early modernity. Early Modern Judaism, the period in which Hasidism emerged, is characterized by intensive ritualization in Jewish culture in general.[27] The ritualization that characterizes Hasidism should thus be understood as part of a broader process of ritualization in Early Modern Judaism.

Opposition to Hasidic Ritual and Practice

In 1772, an organized campaign erupted against new Hasidim in several towns across the Polish-Lithuanian commonwealth. The opponents published polemical texts and eventually succeeded in banning the new Hasidim in a few places. In contemporaneous polemical texts, opponents often denounced Hasidic practices, generating an image that it was the religious practice, rather than theology or ideology, which spurred the opposition. Consider, for example, the following description of scandalous behavior on the part of Hasidim that was included in a 1772 polemical text:

> And always they would delay their prayer at least two hours at least until after the time of Kriyat Shema and after the time of prayer. And they waste their days in the smoke that flows from their mouths. And neither this nor that have they achieved for they

abandoned their Torah study and so too their prayer is a disgrace. For they say God forbid to intend the meaning of the words of the prayers, and should you [do that]—[it] is an alien thought. From them hang rings of rage like those of unclean Temple offerings. And they teach their children to behave like jesters during their prayer for they are a treacherous breed and they do somersaults in front of the holy ark as if thrown over by strangers and gentiles, their heads down, their feet up in the air. Has such turmoil ever before been seen or heard of? And their law is different from [that of] the Jewish people and they do not obey the law of the king, who is the Almighty, and they make to gather themselves into bunches who abandon the customs of the ancestors and they breached the border that our ancestors defined in their prayers. And everyone runs from the sound of their voice from the noise of their prayer and the city is rent asunder by the uproar. And they halt in the middle of the prayer, and they humiliate the students of the holy scripture, and are always engaged in laughter and merrymaking. All this is just the tip of their behavior.[28]

The authors of this text characterize Hasidim by their ritual and practice; perhaps that was because ritual and practice are more observable than ideas and theology. The quote describes disgraceful practices on the part of Hasidim: They delay their prayers and abandon Torah study, passing the time instead smoking; their prayers are noisy and include frenzied acts such as somersaulting inside the synagogue. The overall impression from this quote and the rest of this text is of antinomian tendencies among early Hasidim. Namely, Hasidim violate Jewish laws and customs maintained by rabbinic Jews for centuries. In addition, Hasidim were denounced because their separatism undermined the Jewish communities' cohesion, challenging the authorities of communal leaders and causing detriment to the income of the local communities.

While the authors of these texts indeed noted real Hasidic practices, the entire description is colored by exaggerated polemics. The authors portrayed a partial image of Hasidic practice, ignoring the context described above. Deferring the beginning of prayer, described by the authors as breaking the norms, was actually part of measures taken to ensure a more intentioned or purer prayer, without any alien thoughts. And their gathering into clusters seems to hint to the gathering of Hasidim in separate prayer houses to pray a Safedian-inspired prayer. It seems that the separate praying houses resulted in suspicions regarding rituals performed in secret.

The polemic against Hasidism, such as the aforementioned quote, generated an image of Hasidism as a movement with a lenient approach toward traditional Jewish practice, such as observing Jewish law and Torah study. This image was backed by the existence of a few sources that support that sort of lenient approach, as well as some evidence of rather anarchic behavior on the part of some groups of Hasidim.

However, Hasidic insistence on the inner meanings of practices, introducing extra stringencies (such as in ritual slaughtering) and introducing new customs, give an impression that the perception that the Hasidim were lenient with regard to halakhah should be reconsidered. Rather than the antinomian tendencies attributed to Hasidim, they actually expressed a hypernomian approach. In many cases they aimed to advance beyond regular norms, introducing and popularizing customs that were hitherto practiced by a select few. In fact, the term "Hasid" in Hebrew denotes a person that aspires to religious behavior above the norm. And these very aspirations contributed to the controversy against them.

From the early nineteenth century, the campaign of non-Hasidic Jews against Hasidim waned. In the final years of the eighteenth century and during many decades into the nineteenth century, the prominent opponents of the Hasidim were the *maskilim*, proponents of Jewish Enlightenment.

Consider, for example, an early maskilic text, published in 1797 by the Polish maskil Jacques Calmanson. This text describes the practice of the Besht:

> The sect, known in greater detail to Polish Jews only, emerged no more than twenty years ago. Międzybóż, a town in Podolia, is its cradle. It owes its nature to a rabbi steeped in fanaticism, who, taking advantage of the gullibility of those people who have always been immersed in a lack of learning, who have always craved novelty and been astonished by anything that resembles a miracle, was so adept that he was considered a prophet among them. He claimed that he had the power to cure all diseases through kabbalah. This particular novelty initially resulted in great adulation. The common people, attracted by one mere nothing and simultaneously repelled by another, eagerly ran to the fanatic's mud hut to regain their health, and although they could find only fault under his roof, the number of his followers nevertheless grew considerably.[29]

This text criticizes the kabbalistic ethos of the Besht as fanaticism, censuring him as taking advantage of the ignorance of simple Jews. The criticism of kabbalah here is not of its mystical nature but rather its magical aspect, on the basis of which the Besht presented himself as a healer.

While the eighteenth-century traditional opponents to Hasidim, the so-called *mitnagedim*, argued that Hasidim introduced a revolution with regard to traditional Judaism, maskilim argued against the religious conservatism of Hasidism. While *mitnagedim* saw the adoption of kabbalistic practices as pretentious, maskilim saw them as fanaticism.

What was the Effect of Hasidic Rituals?

What was the effect of the abovementioned rituals on the Hasidim who performed them or were in the audience? I will propose a few explanations that do not contradict each other.

(1) *Intensive religious experience*: While the Jewish ritual system facilitated intensive religious experience for all Jews, Hasidim were offered additional opportunities for intense religious experience. The mystical prayer recommended for Hasidim brought with it a promise for a more intimate and intense connection with God. From the tsadik's perspective, rituals are a language with which Hasidic leaders communicated the divine to their followers, affording them a sense of elevation and intimate connection. This function manifested primarily via rituals performed by the tsadik in front of his followers. In many of these rituals, the tsadik appeared as an embodiment of God, imbuing his community with a sense of close connection with God. Many Jews who attended those ceremonies admitted that the tsadik left a tremendous impression on them, as if they experienced a divine revelation.

(2) *A sense of renewal*: Ritual also provided Hasidim with a sense of renewal, in particular renewing the legendary Safedian culture. The mystical prayer, the prayer book attributed to Luria, collections of the *hanhagot*, ritual bathing, and the white Sabbath clothing of the tsadik, to mention but some of the rituals associated with Safed – are examples of connecting Safedian rituals to Hasidic culture. Hasidism was thus presented as a continuation

of Safedian pietism. These rituals provided Hasidim with the prestige of performing rituals that had hitherto been the exclusive domain of the kabbalistic elite.[30]

(3) *A sense of difference and superiority*: Ritual also provided Hasidim with a sense of difference as well as a sense of superiority, compared to others that did not perform those rituals – either non-Hasidic Jews, or Hasidim of other groups. As noted above, when Hasidim performed these sorts of rituals, they were accused of pretentiousness, ordinary people adopting practices that ought to be performed only by elitist circles. Hence, it is not improbable that Hasidim thought of themselves as more pious or religiously elevated than those who did *not* perform these rituals. Hasidic rituals, then, had an elitist image, perhaps because of the older kabbalistic prestige associated with many of these rituals. That sense of elitism did not require a Hasid to be learned. That's the power of ritual: It is a bodily action that seems to be performed in the same way whether performed by learned or unlearned Hasidim.

(4) *Increasing communal solidarity*: From a social perspective, it is possible to introduce the Durkheimian approach that rituals play a role in establishing in-group solidarity. The particular markers of specific groups displayed a unique and different Hasidic identity as compared to other groups at the local community level. That differentiation strengthened the bond between Hasidim of the same tsadik in a particular town. But it also displayed uniformity among Hasidim of that particular tsadik when they gathered from different places and met each other. This occurred when they arrived at the court, or when they visited other local communities. Either in their places of residence or when they met each other, common customs strengthened group solidarity.

(5) *Protection*: Many of the rituals performed by tsadikim had a protective role of apotropaic magic. This was evident in talismans tsadikim gave their followers. The protective role is also discernible in the rituals tsadikim performed at the communal level. Research has already shown that Hasidic leaders and their courts replaced various roles that these weakening institutions used to play, such as nominating slaughterers and rabbis, establishing cemeteries, negotiating with the non-Jewish authorities, and so on. I argue, however, that Hasidism did more than just replace a communal function with a Hasidic function; they replaced them with a "warranty." In addition to handling earthly communal matters, tsadikim, being mystics and magicians, also communicated with the upper realms on behalf of their community. They claimed to have evoked divine powers to protect members of the Jewish community. Hence, the social service they provided was "backed up" by a mystical-magical service.

Conclusion

From the nineteenth century, Hasidism became a major part of emerging orthodox Judaism. Although it ceased to exist as a separate movement, it did maintain many of the rituals described above. However, the orthodox observance of past customs may have weakened the sense of renewal that was significant when the rituals were performed in the eighteenth century. In the twentieth and twenty-first centuries, these rituals are considered by many to be part of mainstream Judaism. Moreover, for many non-Jews, the visibility of Hasidic rituals such as the dress codes, ritual meals, singing, and dancing – seem the representative features of Judaism in general.

Notes

1. For a discussion of internal differences and their significance: Sagiv 2021.
2. Jacobs 1972; Idel 1995, 149–170.
3. Jacobs 1972.
4. Kauffman 2012.
5. Gries 1989.
6. Wertheim 1992, 106–110.
7. Wodziński 2018, 32–36.
8. On smoking: Jacobs 1998; Goldman-Ida 2017, 279–305; on drinking alcohol: Dynner 2014, 35–45; on dancing: Biale et al. 2020, 216–220.
9. Biale et al. 2020, 220–221.
10. Ben-Amos and Mintz 1993, 1.
11. Kauffman 2019, 236–238.
12. Shmeruk 1955; Stampfer 2010, 342–355; Biale et al. 2020, 247–248.
13. Assaf 2010, 170–173.
14. Rapoport-Albert 1996, 135–136; Sagiv 2021.
15. Cooper 2021.
16. Rosman 1996, 125–126; 168–169; 173–186.
17. Biale et al. 2020, 105–110.
18. Sagiv 2021, 157–160.
19. Sagiv 2013.
20. Pedaya 1995; Gellman 2018, 105–121; Biale et al. 2020, 225–230.
21. Perl 1977, 111. Translated in Nadler 2005, 198.
22. Jacobs 1979; Nadler 2005.
23. Maimon 2019, 231–233.
24. Green 2013; Wiskind-Elper 2018; Sagiv 2019b.
25. Sagiv 2021, 157–160.
26. On the theology of "worship through corporeality" see Kauffman 2009.
27. Bar-Levav 2002. Notably Bar-Levav's usage of the term "ritualization" is somewhat different than the usage here.
28. Gellman 2019, 81–82.
29. Wodziński 2019, 101.
30. Sagiv 2019a.

References

Assaf, David. 2010. *Untold Tales of the Hasidim: Crisis & Discontent in the History of Hasidism*. Hanover and London: University Press of New England.
Bar-Levav, Avriel. 2002. "Ritualisation of Jewish Life and Death in the Early Modern Period." *The Leo Baeck Institute Yearbook* 47: 69–82.
Bell, Catherine. 1992. *Ritual Theory, Ritual Practice*. New York: Oxford University Press.
Ben-Amos, Dan, and Jerome R. Mintz, eds. 1993. *In Praise of Baal Shem Tov [Shivhei Ha-Besht]: The Earliest Collection of Legends About the Founder of Hasidism*. Northvale NJ and London: Jason Aronson.
Biale, David, David Assaf, Benjamin Brown, Uriel Gellman, Samuel Heilman, Moshe Rosman, Gadi Sagiv, and Marcin Wodziński. 2020. *Hasidism: A New History*. Princeton, NJ: Princeton University Press.
Cooper, Levi. 2021. "Shtrayml: An Ethnographic Tale of Law and Ritualization." *Polin: Studies in Polish Jewry* 33: 117–49.
Dynner, Glenn. 2014. *Yankel's Tavern: Jews, Liquor, and Life in the Kingdom of Poland*. New York: Oxford University Press.
Gellman, Uriel. 2018. *Ha-shvilim ha-yots'im me-lublin: tsmihata shel ha-hasidut be-polin*. Jerusalem: Shazar Center for Jewish History.
Gellman, Uriel. 2019. "Mitnagedim." In *Studying Hasidism: Sources, Methods, Perspectives*. Ed. Marcin Wodziński. New Brunswick, NJ: Rutgers University Press, 75–90.
Goldman-Ida, Batsheva. 2017. *Hasidic Art and the Kabbalah*. Leiden: Brill.

Green, Arthur. 2013. "The Hasidic Homily: Mystical Performance and Hermeneutical Process." In *As a Perennial Spring: A Festschrift Honoring Rabbi Dr. Norman Lamm*. Ed. B. Cohen. New York: Downhill Publishing, 237–65.

Gries, Zeev. 1989. *Sifrut Ha-Hanhagot: Toldoteha u-Mekomah Be-Hayei Hasidei R. Yisra'el Ba'al Shem-Tov*. Jerusalem: Mossad Bialik.

Idel, Moshe. 1995. *Hasidism: Between Ecstasy and Magic*. Albany: State University of New York Press.

Jacobs, Louis. 1972. *Hasidic Prayer*. London: Routledge & Kegan Paul.

Jacobs, Louis. 1979. "Eating as an Act of Worship in Hasidic Thought." In *Studies in Jewish Religious and Intellectual History, Presented to Alexander Altmann on the Occasion of His Seventieth Birthday*. Ed. Siegfried Stein and Raphael Loewe. Tuscaloosa, AL: University of Alabama Press, 157–66.

Jacobs, Louis. 1998 "Tobacco and the Hasidim." *Polin* 11: 25–30.

Kauffman, Tsippi. 2009. *Be-Khol Derakhekha Da'ehu: Tefisat Ha-Elohut Veha-'Avodah Be-Gashmiyut Be-Reshit Ha-Ḥasidut*. Ramat Gan: Bar-Ilan University Press.

Kauffman, Tsippi. 2012. "Ritual Immersion at the Beginning of Hasidism." *Tarbiz* 80: 409–25 (Hebrew).

Kauffman, Tsippi. 2019. "Hasidic Women: Beyond Egalitarianist Discourse." *Be-Ron Yaḥad: Studies in Jewish Thought and Theology in Honor of Nehemia Polen*. Ed. Ariel Evan-Mayse and Arthur Green. Boston, MA: Academic Studies Press, 223–57.

Maimon, Solomon. 2019. *The Autobiography of Solomon Maimon: The Complete Translation*. Ed. Yitzhak Y. Melamed and Abraham Socher, Trans. Paul Reitter. Princeton, NJ: Princeton University Press.

Nadler, Allan. 2005. "Holy Kugel: The Sanctification of Ashkenazic Ethnic Foods in Hasidism." In *Food and Judaism*. Ed. Leonard J. Greenspoon, Ronald A. Simkin, and Gerald Shapiro. Omaha, NE: Creighton University Press, 193–214.

Pedaya, Haviva. 1995. "On the Development of the Socio- religio-economic Model in Hasidism: The Pidyon, Havurah and Pilgrimage." In *Dat ve-Kalkala: Yahasei Gomlin*. Ed. Menachem Ben-Sasson. Jerusalem: Shazar Center, 311–73.

Perl, Yosef. 1977 *Ueber das Wesen der Sekte Chassidim*. Ed. Avraham Rubinstein. Jerusalem: Israel Academy of Sciences and Humanities.

Rapoport-Albert, Ada. 1996. "Hasidism after 1772: Structural Continuity and Change." In *Hasidism Reappraised*. Ed. Ada Rapoport-Albert. London: Littman Library of Jewish Civilization London, 76–140.

Rosman, Moshe. 1996. *Founder of Hasidism: A Quest for the Historical Ba'al Shem Tov*. Berkeley: University of California Press.

Sagiv, Gadi. 2013. "Hasidism and Cemetery Inauguration Ceremonies: Authority, Magic, and Performance of Charismatic Leadership." *The Jewish Quarterly Review* 103(3): 328–51.

Sagiv, Gadi. 2019a. "Ritualization as Religious Renewal in 18th-Century Hasidism." *Zutot* 16(1): 19–29.

Sagiv, Gadi. 2019b. "Homilies." In *Studying Hasidism: Sources, Methods, Perspectives*. Ed. Marcin Wodziński. New Brunswick, NJ: Rutgers University Press, 18–35.

Sagiv, Gadi. 2021. "The Narcissism of Small Differences? Rituals and Customs as Hasidic Identity-Markers." *Polin: Studies in Polish Jewry* 33: 151–71.

Shmeruk, Chone. 1955. "The Social Significance of Hasidic Shehitah." *Zion* 20: 42–72 (Hebrew).

Stampfer, Shaul. 2010. *Families, Rabbis and Education*. Oxford: Littman Library of Jewish Civilization.

Wertheim, Aaron. 1992. *Law and Custom in Hasidism*. Trans. Shmuel Himelstein. Hoboken, NJ: Ktav.

Wiskind-Elper, Ora. 2018. *Hasidic Commentary on the Torah*. London: Littman Library of Jewish Civilization.

Wodziński, Marcin. 2018. *Hasidism: Key Questions*. Oxford: Oxford University Press.

Wodziński, Marcin. 2019. "Maskilim." In *Studying Hasidism: Sources, Methods, Perspectives*. Ed. Marcin Wodziński. New Brunswick, NJ: Rutgers University Press, 91–107.

16
CONSERVATIVE JUDAISM

David Golinkin

Conservative Judaism, also known as Masorti Judaism, is one of the three principal modern Jewish religious denominations, emerging, along with Reform and Orthodoxy, in the 19th-century era of emancipation.

Seven Core Values of the Conservative Movement

Despite major sociological and halakhic changes from 1845 to 2020, the seven core values of the Conservative movement have remained more or less unchanged, from Zecharias Frankel in 1845 to The Historical School in the U.S., to Solomon Schechter in his inaugural address at the Jewish Theological Seminary of America (JTS) in 1902 and in his founding address of the United Synagogue in 1913, to Louis Finkelstein at the Rabbinical Assembly convention in 1927, to *Emet Ve-emunah* in 1988, to Ismar Schorsch in "The Sacred Cluster" in 1995, and to Arnold Eisen in 2015.

These leaders or groups of leaders stress all or most of the following basic values:

(1) the belief in God;
(2) the belief in Revelation and the centrality and authority of the Torah and Talmud to Judaism;
(3) the Torah and all of Judaism should be studied in an historical fashion using the tools developed by *Wissenschaft des Judenthums* ("The Science of Judaism") from Leopold Zunz until today;
(4) the authority of and commitment to halakhah and the observance of mitzvot such as Shabbat and kashrut, with a willingness to make changes within the framework of the traditional halakhic system;
(5) commitment to the Jewish people, *klal yisrael* (which Schechter called "Catholic Israel") – past, present and future;
(6) commitment to cultural Zionism such as that of Ahad Ha'am and/or the political Zionism of Herzl;
(7) commitment to Hebrew as the language of prayer and text study.

Nonetheless, as we shall see below, there were, and are, strong disagreements regarding some of these items, such as the conception of God, Revelation, biblical criticism, or the willingness to enact Takkanot (rabbinic enactments).

The Historical School

Reform Judaism arose in 1810 as an attempt to reformulate Judaism, no longer as a comprehensive way of life and national identity, but as a western-style religion, so as to accommodate the desire of Jews to acculturate into their host societies, while resisting total assimilation or conversion to Christianity. Radical and moderate wings of Reform emerged as its leaders debated the extent of changes from Jewish tradition, including the organ in the synagogue, abolition of circumcision, moving Shabbat to Sunday and the abolition of Hebrew from the prayer book.

Zecharias Frankel (1801–1875), Chief Rabbi of Saxony and of its capital Dresden, Germany, a proponent of moderate changes in Jewish practice, broke with his more radical colleagues at the Rabbinical Conference of Frankfurt (1845), over the issue of retaining Hebrew as the language of prayer. Frankel called for positive-historical Judaism, a phrase which has been the subject of great debate. Rivka Horwitz suggests on the basis of Frankel's writings that, as opposed to the written Canonical Law revealed when the Torah was given, Positive Law in the Talmud is the law which developed over the course of time in an organic fashion and which could have been influenced by the Greeks or Romans or Persians among whom the Jews lived. He apparently adopted this approach from Savigny (1779–1861) who called law which develops in an organic fashion among a people "positive law". Thus, in Frankel's opinion, the loyalties of generations of Jews to a particular practice, no less than a proof-text from an authoritative religious source, sanctified that practice.

In 1854, Frankel concretized his conservative yet flexible approach to Judaism in the Juedisch-Theologisches Seminar (Jewish Theological Seminary) of Breslau. Until destroyed by the Nazis in 1938, this rabbinical school trained approximately 250 rabbis and 480 teachers and served as the scholarly center for "Historical Judaism" in Central Europe. These graduates did not found a movement, but their approach to Jewish Studies and practice were definitely different from that of Orthodox and Reform rabbis in Germany and Europe.

In the United States, the rabbis and leaders who followed this approach in the 19th century called themselves "The Historical School". Like Zecharias Frankel in Germany, they initially tried to work together with the leaders of Reform Judaism, such as Rabbi Isaac Mayer Wise (1819–1900). When Wise founded Hebrew Union College (HUC) in Cincinnati in 1875, the rabbis of The Historical School such as Sabato Morais and Benjamin Szold supported that rabbinical seminary both in word and deed by raising funds for HUC.

The breaking point began with "the Trefa banquet" in July 1883 celebrating the first graduation of HUC at which a wide array of non-kosher food was served. It ended with the Pittsburgh Platform of November 1885 which, among other things, opposed "all such Mosaic and rabbinical laws which regulate diet, priestly purity and dress", and stated that "we consider ourselves no longer a nation, but a religious community, and therefore expect [no] return to Palestine" (Pittsburgh Platform, 1885). These two events led directly to the founding of the "Jewish Theological Seminary of New York" in January 1886 at Sheerith Israel Congregation by moderate rabbis and scholars, principally Sabato Morais, Henry Pereira Mendes, Alexander Kohut, and Cyrus Adler. The name was proposed by Kohut, a leading Talmudic scholar and one of the founders, as a way of following The Jewish Theological Seminary of Breslau. Kohut wanted the Seminary to serve all Jews, but that was not what transpired.

The 12 founders voted to found a seminary to train teachers and leaders for the coming generation in sympathy with the spirit of Conservative Judaism. The object of the Jewish Theological Association was the preservation in America of the knowledge and practice of historical Judaism. In March 1886, delegates from 60 congregations assembled at Sheerith Israel to complete the organization of the Association. Opening exercises were held in January 1887 when Kohut emphasized that the spirit at the Seminary will be that of Conservative Judaism and he stressed the necessity of observing the Law as well as studying it. It began with eight students and by March 1888 there were ten students aged 13–17 in the preparatory class taught by Rabbi Bernard Drachman and four aged 17–27 in the junior class taught by Dr Gustave Lieberman. They met from 3:30–5:30 pm five days a week. The first bi-annual report of March 1888 lists some 450 donors from New York, Philadelphia, Baltimore and other cities.

Leaders of the new seminary hoped that their school would become the unifying institution of all opponents of Reform. In addition to the moderate reformers of Sephardi or West European background, the Seminary's founders looked to secure the loyalty of the burgeoning East European Jewish population of New York. In this hope they were disappointed. In June 1898, 11 of the 13 founders of the Orthodox Jewish Congregational Union of America in New York were active members of the Seminary and The Historical School and the official languages were English and Hebrew. But by the second meeting of the Orthodox Union in 1900, it had been taken over by Eastern European rabbis and most of the speakers spoke in Yiddish.

Without significant congregational support, the Jewish Theological Seminary Association endured precarious finances during its first 15 years and was compelled to reorganize in 1902, but not before graduating 14 rabbis and three *hazzanim*, including Joseph H. Hertz, who became Chief Rabbi of the British Empire, and Mordecai M. Kaplan, preeminent theologian and founder of Reconstructionist Judaism.

Birth and Growth of the Conservative Movement in the United States and Canada (1902–1945)

Although the Seminary had not successfully engaged Orthodox Russian immigrants, a group of prominent Reform lay leaders envisioned that the school could yet serve to Americanize that group, and thus simultaneously preserve the Jewishness of the new arrivals and reduce the social tension occasioned by their "un-American" ways. After the death of Sabato Morais in 1897, Cyrus Adler mobilized Jacob Schiff, a supporter of the school since 1888, and his colleagues, including Louis Marshall, to reorganize JTS in 1902, to set the school on a firmer financial basis and thus produce the leadership for the successful acculturation of the children of the new immigrants.

Specifically, they raised the funds to engage Solomon Schechter (1847–1915) as President of the faculty of the new organization, the Jewish Theological Seminary of America (JTS). Born and raised in a Chabad Hasidic family in Focsani, Rumania, he learned *Wissenschaft des Judenthums* with Rabbis Isaac Hirsch Weiss and Meir Ish-Shalom for four years at the Bet Midrash in Vienna, followed by three years at the Hochschule and at the University in Berlin. Moving to London in 1882 and to Cambridge in 1890, Schechter attained fame as a reader in Rabbinics at Cambridge and as the discoverer of the Cairo Genizah. He was a first-rank rabbinic scholar with a gift for popularization, an orator equally at home in Jewish sources and in the classics of English rhetoric. In other words, Schechter personally exemplified the envisioned rabbinic graduate of JTS. Under his leadership, JTS was to fulfill its mission among American Jewry by producing religiously observant and intellectually open-minded rabbis.

In his inaugural address in 1902, Schechter maintained, like Kohut in 1887, that the Seminary should "create a theological center which should be all things to all men, reconciling all parties, and appealing to all sections of the community … this school should never become partisan ground or a hotbed of polemics". In other words, it appears that he wanted the Seminary to serve "Catholic Israel", a term he had coined in 1896 in place of "*klal yisrael*".

As it turned out, Schechter succeeded, after the fact, in making JTS the "fountainhead" of what would become a full-fledged denomination, Conservative Judaism. He engaged a faculty of leading scholars, including Louis Ginzberg, Alexander Marx, Israel Friedlaender and Israel Davidson and oversaw the creation of the preeminent Judaica library in America. He transformed JTS into a graduate-level program. "Schechter's Seminary", as it was widely known, graduated an increasing number of rabbis, then also teachers, after the 1909 organization of its Teachers' Institute under the leadership of Mordecai Kaplan.

Michael Cohen maintains that when Schechter and his disciples founded the United Synagogue in 1913, he vigorously opposed the creation of a third party, neither Orthodox nor Reform. This argument, however, is not supported by the facts. Since the Union of American Hebrew Congregations (UAHC) was founded in 1873 and the Orthodox Union in 1898 as described above, the founding of the United Synagogue by JTS and its alumni in 1913 was, by definition, the founding of a third movement. Second, Schechter was in word and deed a member of The Historical School as described above, which was very different in many respects from the other two camps. Third, Schechter wrote to Louis Marshall, the Chairman of the JTS Board in 1913, that when he received the call in Cambridge to head the Seminary, he understood that the purpose was to "create a Conservative School removed alike from both extremes, Radical-Reform and Hyper-Orthodoxy".

Finally, Schechter explicitly explains in his address at the founding convention of the United Synagogue exactly how the Conservative (or traditional or Orthodox or neo-Orthodox – he keeps switching his terminology) Union being founded is very different than both the Reform Movement and the new Orthodox immigrants from Russia. Even though he says that it was not his intention to feud with the existing parties and that his sympathies and convictions lay with the recent Orthodox immigrants, he clearly attacks both parties, especially the Orthodox. He attacks the Reform for their rejection of the Bible as the word of God, and of the Talmud and the Jewish Codes of law and of the traditional siddur, and for praying with uncovered heads. He attacks the recent Orthodox immigrants for their opposition to secular education and to the religious education of women and for the lack of decorum in their synagogues, organization, scientific methods of training rabbis, and proper pedagogical methods of teaching children. He says that the purpose of the new Union is not to create a new party but to consolidate an old one, the large number of Jews who are thoroughly American in habits of life and mode of thinking, have always maintained conservative principles and remained aloof from the Reform Movement. In short, Schechter founded the United Synagogue in order to provide a national synagogue organization for the many Americanized synagogues and Jews belonging to The Historical School who were positioned in the middle between the Reform Movement and the recent Orthodox immigrants. They, in turn, would support JTS, "the Conservative School", positioned in the middle between "Radical-Reform and Hyper-Orthodoxy".

Cyrus Adler who succeeded Schechter as President of JTS (1916–1940) was opposed to creating a third movement in American Judaism. He was, however, a good administrator and fundraiser. He systematized the school's administrative procedures and presided over the construction of its new campus which opened in 1930. While Adler was focused on JTS, a group of JTS faculty members and graduates built the infrastructure of the Conservative movement which Schechter had envisioned in 1913. There were 22 congregations at the founding convention of the United Synagogue in 1913; 220 in 1927; shrinking to 190 by 1945, probably because of World War II. They also built some of the main organizations of the Conservative movement. Prof. Louis Ginzberg (1873–1953) of JTS founded The Committee for the Interpretation of Jewish Law with five members to give halakhic guidance to the Conservative movement, which he ran single-handedly from 1917–1927. Mathilda Schechter, Solomon Schechter's widow, founded the Women's League as a subsidiary of the United Synagogue in 1918, while the Young People's League was founded in 1921, with 127 societies by 1927. In 1921, the United Synagogue began to publish *The United Synagogue Recorder* (1921–1929), which was later renamed.

The Alumni Association of JTS, founded in 1901, became The Rabbinical Assembly of the Jewish Theological Seminary (RA) in 1918 and the Rabbinical Assembly of America in 1940. The RA, in turn, founded the Committee on Jewish Law with ten members in 1927 to replace the previous committee. It also began to publish the *Proceedings of the Rabbinical Assembly* (1927–2004). In 1927, The United Synagogue published two versions of the *Festival Prayer Book* edited by five rabbis, including Alexander Marx and Louis Ginzberg from the traditional wing and Jacob Kohn from the liberal wing, one with the traditional Musaf and the other changing the sacrifices to the past tense. In 1929, the Federation of Men's Clubs was founded, while *Women's League Outlook* began to appear in 1930 (until 2007).

Not surprisingly, the growing movement had ideological "right" and "left" wings. The right wing consisted of Cyrus Adler at JTS while Louis Ginzberg ran The Committee for the Interpretation of Jewish Law. Ginzberg's more traditional disciples such as Louis Epstein, Boaz Cohen and Michael Higger led the RA Committee on Jewish Law from 1927–1948. Mordecai Kaplan was the leader of the movement's left wing, along with Jacob Kohn, Herman Rubenovitz, Solomon Goldman and Milton Steinberg. Kaplan's "Reconstructionist" definition of Judaism as an evolving religious civilization and his call to transform the modern synagogue into a comprehensive spiritual, intellectual and cultural Jewish center resonated even among Conservative rabbis who took issue with his rejection of supernaturalism. During the 1930s, Kaplan's *Judaism as a Civilization* and other publications spurred controversy among JTS faculty and in the broader movement, but the JTS administrative response, to assign Kaplan to teaching homiletics rather than Talmud, only increased his influence among generations of emerging rabbis along with the teachers he taught at The Teachers' Institute.

Rapid Growth and Expansion in the United States and Canada (1946–1990)

Conservative Judaism enjoyed its heyday during the 25 years following World War II, most of which corresponded with Prof. Louis Finkelstein's tenure as President and then Chancellor of JTS (1940–1972). Across the East, Midwest and Sunbelt regions of the country, returning veterans and their growing families, part of the "baby boom", moved to the newly expanding suburbs, creating hundreds of new synagogues. Between 1945 and 1949 and 1964 and 1971, The United Synagogue grew from 190 to 365 to 778 to 832 member congregations, comprising some 350,000 families with an estimated 1.5 million members. For the children of East European immigrants, the Conservative synagogue represented an attractive balance between tradition and change.

In his classic sociological study in 1955, Marshall Sklare described a typical suburban Conservative synagogue. It was a *Bet Tefillah* or house of prayer with an English-speaking rabbi, a cantor and a *shamash*; a *Bet Knesset* or house of assembly with a large range of social activities and an active sisterhood and men's club; and a Bet Midrash with a Sunday school, a Hebrew school which prepares the boys, and later on girls, for Bar/Bat Mitzvah, and adult education classes. The rabbi was in charge of all aspects of the synagogue.

This tremendous growth and expansion was expressed in every sphere of activity. Morris Silverman's *Sabbath and Festival Prayer Book* co-published by The Rabbinical Seminary and The United Synagogue in 1946 served perhaps as the most important unifier of the Conservative movement. This was followed later on by *The Weekday Prayer Book* edited by Gershon Hadas in 1961 and by the High Holiday Mahzor edited by Jules Harlow in 1972. The number of Conservative institutions and organizations founded in just 20 years from 1945 to 1965 is staggering: Robert Gordis founded *Conservative Judaism* magazine in 1945 (ceased publication in 2014), while Kaplan and JTS founded the Leaders Training Fellowship in 1946 in order to prepare young men and women to study at JTS.

Midwest Jewish leaders opened an educational summer camp, Camp Ramah Wisconsin, in 1947 and JTS became the camp's sponsor in 1948. The Ramah Camping Movement has since expanded to ten overnight and five day camps in North America and four Israel programs, with affiliated camps in South America, Israel and Ukraine. Its mission is to "inspire commitment to Jewish life and develop the next generation of Jewish leaders", which it has carried out with great success for over 70 years.

In 1947, Louis Finkelstein founded The Jewish Museum in New York. As America's West Coast was developing into a center of Jewish life, Mordecai Kaplan and Simon Greenberg of JTS opened the University of Judaism in Los Angeles in 1947; Greenberg continued to serve as President and then Chancellor (1948–1968). Later on, David Lieber (1956–1964 as Dean of Students and 1964–1993 as President) established its rabbinic program as a branch of JTS and its MBA program in non-profit management.

The year 1948 also saw the founding of The Cantors Assembly and The National Association of Synagogue Administrators and the reorganization and expansion of the Committee of Jewish Law and Standards (CJLS). In 1951, the United Synagogue created United Synagogue Youth which has brought hundreds of thousands of teenagers closer to Judaism through its chapters, *kinnusim*, camps, Israel and European pilgrimages and USY-on-Wheels. The Jewish Educators Assembly was also founded in 1951, while the JTS Cantorial School opened in 1952. The World Council of Synagogues (later renamed Masorti Olami) was founded in 1959; the Melton Center for Jewish Education at JTS in 1960; the Atid program for college students in 1961; and the Seminario Rabínico in Buenos Aires in 1962. In 1963, JTS opened Neve Schechter, its American Student Center in Jerusalem, where rabbinical students studied for one year. Finally, in 1965, Conservative day schools joined together to create the Solomon Schechter Day School Association.

As the movement expanded rapidly and faced the new conditions of Jewish life in suburbia, the tension between JTS and the Conservative movement increased. Under the leadership of Louis Finkelstein (1940–1972), who was also a prominent and prolific scholar of rabbinic Judaism, JTS continued to serve as the most important academic center of Jewish Studies in the world. Yet JTS also aspired to influence American society at large, both Jewish and Gentile, without identifying the school's prime task as the support of its denomination; rather, it saw the Conservative movement as its own support network. As a "bridge-builder", Finkelstein created ecumenical institutes such as The Institute for Religious and Social Studies and founded the award-winning "The Eternal Light" programs which were broadcast on 200 radio and 125 television stations. As a result, he was featured on the cover of *Time* magazine on October 15, 1951.

Conservative Judaism entered a more challenging era after 1970. The end of the postwar "baby boom" and the decay of urban and inner suburban neighborhoods hurt synagogue membership, and the number of United Synagogue member congregations dropped from its peak of 832 in 1971. Assimilation, including intermarriage, became more prevalent, and the social upheavals of the 1960s exacerbated the decline of the movement's appeal to young adults. Followers of Kaplan's Reconstructionist Judaism finally left the Conservative movement and opened their own rabbinical seminary in Philadelphia in 1968.

As a consequence of assimilation, the movement experienced a wide disparity between the high level of commitment to religious practice on the part of its rabbinic leadership and the lower degree observed by the majority of its laity. Moreover, some of the movement's minority of highly observant laity began to migrate to a revitalized Modern Orthodoxy. The resurgence of Orthodoxy, increasingly evident by 1970, both impressed and dismayed Conservative observers. Denominational leaders debated their response to the new conditions, traditionalists urging a reemphasis of commitment to *halakhah*, and liberals calling for outreach to the disaffected by means of bolder departures from tradition.

Beginning in the 1970s, Conservative Jews began to found *Chavurot* (small fellowship groups) as a result of the counter-culture and as a reaction to large, impersonal synagogue centers. At the same time, large synagogues began to open alternative services for specific groups such as egalitarian services, family services, learners' *minyanim*, and singles' services.

In 1963, Noah Golinkin developed the Hebrew Literacy Campaign which taught adults how to read the prayer book in 12 weeks. Adopted by the Federation of Jewish Men's Clubs in 1978, he wrote *Shalom Aleichem* (1978) followed by *Ayn Keloheynu* (1981) in order to implement the Campaign. In 1986, Golinkin published *While Standing on One Foot*, which teaches adults how to read Hebrew in one-day Hebrew Reading Marathons. By 2003 when he passed away, over 200,000 Conservative and Reform Jews had learned how to read the prayer book using these methods.

Since many Conservative Jews did not know how to perform basic Jewish rituals, Ron Wolfson of the University of Judaism developed the "Art of Jewish Living" series which teaches adults how to make Shabbat, run a Seder, celebrate Hanukkah, and mourn for relatives. All of these programs acknowledged that third- and fourth-generation American Jews did not receive a thorough Jewish education and must be taught basic Judaism using entirely new, user-friendly methods. Chancellor Gerson Cohen's years at JTS (1972–1986) were marked by the transition from European-born to American-born faculty. This transition was epitomized by the struggle over the ordination of women described below. Cohen also built and dedicated the new library in 1983 and founded the Seminary of Judaic Studies, later renamed the Schechter Institute, in Jerusalem in 1984.

Contraction in the United States (1990–2020)

Chancellor Ismar Schorsch (1986–2006), a prominent and prolific historian, was very successful in his role as Chancellor of JTS. He founded the William Davidson School of Education in 1996, which trains educators for day schools and afternoon schools, and he expanded the endowment of JTS while rebuilding and expanding the campus. He steered a centrist course between the left and right wings of the movement. He was an avid supporter of expanding the roles of women in Judaism, while opposing the ordination of avowed homosexuals and gay commitment ceremonies. During the tenure of Chancellor Arnold Eisen (2007–2020), an expert in Jewish thought and the sociology of American Judaism, JTS admitted and ordained gay rabbis and he initiated a Mitzvah Initiative which involved 75 congregations in studying the mitzvot in Judaism. He built a new and enlarged campus and library which was completed in 2020. Prof. Shuly Rubin Schwartz, an expert in American Jewish history, was appointed

Chancellor in mid-2020, at the height of the Covid-19 pandemic. She is the first woman to hold this prestigious position; only time will reveal her direction and priorities.

Meanwhile, the University of Judaism (UJ) under the leadership of President Robert Wexler (1992–2018), slowly separated itself from JTS. In 1996, it opened up its own Ziegler School of Rabbinic Studies, led since 1999 by Brad Artson, a prolific author and theologian, who also serves as Vice President of UJ. The leading professor at UJ is Elliot Dorff who has served for 50 years as Rector and Professor of Jewish Theology. UJ was renamed American Jewish University (AJU) in 2007 when it vastly expanded its adult education program via the acquisition of the Brandeis-Bardin Institute.

Despite the success of JTS and AJU, there has been a steady contraction in the Conservative movement in the United States since 1971. The United Synagogue of America (renamed The United Synagogue of Conservative Judaism in 1991), had 832 synagogues and 14 regional offices in 1971 vs. 572 synagogues and seven regions in 2020. Women's League had over 800 sisterhoods with 200,000 members in 1972 vs. 324 sisterhoods and 33,000 members in 2020. There were almost 400 Men's Clubs in 1977 vs. 250 in 2020. There were 25,000 children in USY in 1977 vs. 15,000 in 2020. According to Jack Wertheimer, membership in Conservative synagogues contracted from 915,000 in 1990 to 660,000 in 2000 to 500,000 in 2013.

This contraction was reflected in three major surveys. The National Jewish Population Surveys of 1990 and 2000 maintained that 33% of American Jews identified as Conservative. By the time of the Pew Report in 2013, Conservative Judaism seemed to have declined to only 18% of American Jews, with 970,000 people identifying as Conservative Jews. However, Alan Silverstein reanalyzed the Pew data in 2019, concluding that there are 1.2 million self-identified Conservative Jews in the United States, the same number as in the 2000 survey. Furthermore, if one restricts the Pew analysis to "Jews by Religion", 26% self-identify as Conservative Jews and 29% of American synagogue members are Conservative Jews, both numbers only slightly lower than the 2000 survey.

Some attribute the attrition since 1971 to the failure of the movement and its rabbis to teach their ideology and halakhic approach to the laypeople. David Golinkin points out that even though the Tosefta, Maimonides, Krochmal, Frankel and Schechter have praised "the middle way" in Judaism, the middle way in politics and religion frequently does not last. Similarly, Jonathan Sarna explains that the contraction was driven by American sociological trends. Most of the middle-of-the-road Protestant denominations such as Presbyterian, Episcopal, Lutheran and Methodist are also in decline. Finally, Jack Wertheimer saw room for optimism in 2018 as Conservative rabbis and synagogues emphasize inclusiveness, spirituality, musical creativity, shorter services, personalized attention and Judaism at home. Whether assimilatory or revival trends will predominate is the critical question facing American Conservative Judaism in the 21st century.

Birth and Growth of the Worldwide Masorti Movement (1959–2020)

While Conservative Judaism has been contracting in the United States since 1971, it has expanded rapidly worldwide: in Israel, Latin America, Europe and elsewhere.

The Masorti Movement in Israel

Unlike Reform and Orthodoxy, each of which has had non-Zionist and anti-Zionist wings, Conservative Judaism was a firm supporter of Zionism throughout the 20th century, beginning with Schechter's classic "Zionism: A Statement" in 1906. But most of its Zionism was cultural Zionism à la Ahad Ha'am. JTS opened Neve Schechter in Jerusalem in 1963 and USY and Ramah ran very successful summer programs in Israel, but there was no attempt to export Conservative Judaism to Israel. A few young dynamic Conservative rabbis including Moshe Cohen, Philip Spectre and Charles Segal made Aliyah in the 1960s and founded congregations in Haifa and Ashkelon. In 1972, six synagogues held the first national conference of the Conservative movement in Israel. More rabbis made Aliyah in the early 1970s after the Yom Kippur war.

In 1977, Conservative rabbis and laypeople launched a youth movement, *Noam* (*No'ar Masorti*) and in 1979, they created the *Masorti* ("Traditional") Movement. It has been led over the years by Michael Graetz, Moshe Tutnauer, Philip Spectre, Ehud Bandel, Yizhar Hess and Rakefet Ginsburg. The Foundation for Conservative (Masorti) Judaism in Israel (now called: Masorti Foundation) was founded in the U.S. in 1982 to help fund the Masorti Movement. The Masorti Movement led the Conservative movement as a whole to become part of the World Zionist Organization as *Mercaz Olami* in 1987. Camp Ramah-Noam was founded in 1988. The Masorti Movement has supported existing congregations and founded new ones and, by 2020, the movement had grown to over 80 *kehillot* (Congregations) and *havurot*; 26 are fully functioning communities and the rest hold their activities in schools and community centers. In addition, by 2017, Masorti rabbis were performing over 2,000 life-cycle events per year. Masorti also founded the Aderaba Center for children and young adults with special needs and *Al Mishmar Haknesset*, which serves as a watchdog regarding matters of religion and state.

Recent surveys summarized by Dan Feferman and Shmuel Rosner & Camile Fuchs indicate that 2–6% of Israelis identify with the Conservative/Masorti Movement, but only 7,500 adults actually belong to the Masorti Movement. There are various theories to explain this huge discrepancy, but it's very clear that more and more Israelis view Masorti (and Reform) as viable religious alternatives to the Orthodox establishment.

Since 1979, the Masorti Movement has led the struggle over "Who is a Jew?", so that the State of Israel would recognize Conservative/Masorti Conversions. Conversions performed abroad have been recognized by Israel's Ministry of Interior since the Shoshana Miller Supreme Court Case in 1988. The Rabbinical Assembly of Israel set up its own Bet Din for Conversion in 1991, headed over the years by Theodore Friedman, Reuven Hammer and Peretz Rodman, which converts 80–100 converts per year. In 2005, the Masorti and Reform movements filed a petition to Israel's Supreme Court to grant citizenship to Masorti and Reform converts who converted in Israel. In March 2021, the court finally ruled, by a vote of 8 to 1, to recognize these conversions for the purpose of citizenship. While hailed as a victory for religious pluralism, this ruling only affects some 30 to 40 converts per year. The State of Israel still does not recognize Masorti and Reform conversion of converts who are already citizens of Israel under the Law of Return.

In addition, the Masorti Movement cooperated with the Ne'eman Commission in 1997–1998 in order to find a national solution to conversion agreed upon by all the movements. Though the Israeli Chief Rabbinate rejected the commission's recommendations in 1998, 80 members of the Knesset approved them and the "Institute of Jewish Studies" was established by the Israeli government and the Jewish Agency. It is run by Orthodox, Conservative and Reform Jews, but the graduates are converted by a Modern Orthodox Bet Din. Even so, the Masorti Movement continues to marry and convert people and to demand that these marriages and conversions be recognized by the State of Israel.

Finally, the Masorti Movement has played a very active role since 1997 in making the Kotel accessible to Conservative and Reform Jews. The first agreement was reached in the year 2000 to use the area of Robinson's Arch for egalitarian prayer services. In 2013, the government built a large wooden platform for the Kotel Masorti/Azarat Yisrael. By 2015, over 50,000 people were attending services there every year. In January 2016, the government approved a new Kotel agreement worked out between the government and the Jewish Agency, but then froze the agreement in July 2016.

The Schechter Institute of Jewish Studies

The Seminary of Judaic Studies was founded in 1984 by JTS Chancellor Gerson Cohen, Reuven Hammer and the Masorti Movement for the purpose of training Masorti rabbis. That program – now called the Schechter Rabbinical Seminary, and headed by Rabbi Avi Novis-Deutsch (2015–) – runs the ordination, Mishlei and Ashira programs and hosts the overseas one-year rabbinical school programs of JTS and the Seminaro Rabínico. Lee Levine (Dean and then President, 1987–1994) expanded the mission and the programs. The Schechter Institute of Jewish Studies (1990), now headed by Doron Bar (2015–), runs a large Masters' program for 400 Israeli educators and communal leaders, with 1,850 graduates. The TALI Education Fund (1987), thanks to the dynamic leadership of Eitan Chikli (1994–2020), followed by Peri Sinclair (2020–), now provides enriched Jewish Studies to over 65,000 Israeli children at over 300 TALI public schools and pre-schools every year. Midreshet Yerushalayim, thanks to the dedication of Gila Katz (1991–2019), Reuven Stamov (2012–), and Irina Gritsevskaya (2019–), has been running a successful network of schools, synagogues and Ramah camps throughout Ukraine since 1991. Midreshet Schechter was run for many years by Yair Paz (1991–2014) as an outreach program for Russian immigrants; it is now run by Irina Gritsevskaya (2019–) as an outreach program for Israelis.

Benjamin Segal (1994–1999) renamed and restructured the institution, added research institutes and prizes, helped grow all of the programs, partnered with many institutions, and began to publish books and the *Nashim* journal. Alice Shalvi (1999–2000) secured funding for *Nashim* and for the Center for Women in Jewish Law. David Golinkin (2000–) achieved Israeli accreditation for the Schechter M.A. program (1996–2009), continued to grow all of the programs, founded research institutes, vastly expanded the library, and has published over 70 books in the fields of Halakhah, Midrash, Liturgy and other areas in Jewish Studies. He built a new campus in Jerusalem (2012); opened a new campus, the Neve Schechter Center for Jewish Culture in Tel Aviv (2012), which attracts 19,000 people every year to concerts, art exhibits and Bar/Bat mitzvah ceremonies; and opened a new campus in Kiev to house the Midreshet Yerushalayim synagogue center (2021). Thus, over the years, the Schechter Institutes have become the largest Conservative/Masorti organization in Israel, serving over 85,000 children and adults every year.

Latin America

Conservative Judaism has established a major presence in Latin America. The movement began to form in 1957 but really took off in 1959 when Marshall Meyer, a young JTS graduate, moved to Buenos Aires. He founded the first Ramah Camp in 1959, the journal *Majshavot* in 1961, the *Seminario Rabínico Latinoamericano* in 1962, the Bet El synagogue in 1963 and published a new siddur and machzor by the mid-1960s. Meyer served as Rector of the Seminario until 1983, assisted by Vice Rector Rabbi Mordechai Edery, originally from Spanish Morocco. Beginning in 1970, all Seminario students finished their rabbinical training in Israel under the tutelage of Theodore Friedman, Meyer's father-in-law. Beginning in 1985, the students finished their rabbinical training at Neve Schechter and since 1990 at the Schechter Rabbinical Seminary in Jerusalem.

Meyer returned to New York in 1984, but the Seminario continued to train rabbis and teachers for Latin America under the leadership of Richard Freund (Vice Rector, 1984–1986), Daniel Fainstein (Dean, 1986–1996), Abraham Skorka (Rector 1995–2017) and Ariel Stofenmacher (President, CEO, Rector 2011–). Over 100 rabbis have been ordained by the Seminario and in many Latin American countries Conservative Judaism is the dominant stream. Seminario graduates serve in some 60 synagogues in 16 countries, as well as in schools, summer camps, Hebrew sports clubs and cultural centers, adding a religious component to institutions that had previously been Jewish in a purely ethnic sense. Through the influence of the *Seminario*, Conservative Judaism has helped guide Latin American Jewry from an era of secular-Zionist, Socialist, Bundist, Yiddishist immigrant-created Jewish institutions to one in which native-born Jews express their distinctive religious identity.

Europe

As in Latin America, a single rabbinic pioneer, Louis Jacobs (1920–2006), was instrumental in founding Conservative/Masorti Judaism in England. Denied appointment as Principal of Jews College and his former pulpit at a London synagogue by the English Chief Rabbi in 1963 on account of his unorthodox theological writings, Jacobs and his followers left the Orthodox United Synagogue and opened the New London Synagogue. Members of that synagogue founded two kindred congregations closer to their north-west London homes, and in 1985, the three communities founded the Assembly of Masorti Synagogues. By 2020, Masorti UK included 14 synagogues with over 4,000 members, the Noam youth movement and Marom for 18–30-year-olds. Leading rabbis include Jonathan Wittenberg at New North London and Chaim Weiner, head of the European Masorti Bet Din for conversions.

Founded in 1989, the Conservative/Masorti Movement in France has been led by three graduates of the Schechter Rabbinical Seminary: Rivon Krygier at Adat Shalom, Paris since 1991; Yeshaya Delsace in Nice in 2000 and at Dor Vador in east Paris since 2009 and David Touboul in Nice since 2009. Four additional synagogues do not yet have a rabbi. Gesa Ederberg has been leading the Masorti Movement in Berlin since she was ordained by Schechter in 2003, while Reuven Stamov has been leading the Masorti Movement in Kiev since he was ordained by Schechter in 2012.

Masorti Olami (formerly The World Council of Synagogues) was founded in 1959 as the umbrella organization for all Conservative congregations outside of Israel and North America. Since moving to Jerusalem, it has been headed by Joseph Wernick, Tzvi Graetz and Maurico Balter. In supports a total of 135 Conservative/Masorti synagogues in Latin America, England, France, Germany, Sweden, Spain, Portugal, Prague, Poland, Africa, Australia and elsewhere. Rabbinic leadership in European Masorti institutions comes primarily from the Schechter Rabbinical Seminary in Jerusalem. In 2013, the Ziegler School of Rabbinic Studies founded the Zecharias Frankel College at the University of Potsdam in order to train Masorti rabbis for Europe; as of 2020, it had ordained three rabbis.

Ideological Debates

As noted above, even though one can discern seven core values of Conservative Judaism since 1845, there have been extensive debates regarding theological issues, such as the conception of God, Revelation and Biblical Criticism. As Schechter stressed, The Historical School did not offer a theological program of its own. There were two prominent JTS faculty members who broke this paradigm. Mordecai Kaplan (1881–1983) did not believe in God as a substantive, anthropomorphic entity. His naturalistic theology was influenced by his teacher John Dewey. Most Conservative rabbis and scholars rejected his approach, but he forced two generations of his students at JTS to work out their personal theology.

On the opposite end of the spectrum was Abraham Joshua Heschel (1907–1972) who taught at JTS from 1946 until his death. For Heschel, God was a living reality who takes a passionate interest in His creatures. "Faith is real only when it is not one-sided but reciprocal. Man can rely on God, if God can rely on Man. To have faith means to justify God's faith in man. Faith is awareness of divine mutuality and companionship, a form of communion between God and Man." Heschel's theology had a huge impact on his disciples, on the Conservative movement, and on non-Jews such as Martin Luther King Jr with whom he marched in Selma, Alabama.

Similarly, there were many different attitudes toward Revelation among Conservative rabbis which Elliot Dorff (1977, 110ff.) has divided into four approaches: (1) God dictated His will at Sinai and at other times but it was written down by human beings, hence the diverse traditions in the Bible; (2) human beings wrote the Torah at various times and places, but they were divinely inspired and therefore the Torah carries the insight and authority of God; (3) the Torah is the human record of the encounter between God and the Jewish people at Sinai; the Torah is the record of how human beings responded to God when they came into contact with Him; (4) Kaplan's approach: the Torah was written by human beings; Jewish law derives its authority as the "folkways", *minhag* of our people.

Halakhah

Law Committees: As mentioned above, The Committee on the Interpretation of Jewish Law (1917–1927) was run primarily by Prof. Louis Ginzberg. Beginning with the Committee on Jewish Law (1927–1948) which became the CJLS (1948–), the law committee became a meeting ground and a debating ground for the movement. The committee grew from 5 to 10 to 15 to 25 members. Beginning in 1927, they appointed rabbis from the right, left and center of the movement, and, later on, from the Rabbinical Assembly, JTS and the United Synagogue. Beginning in 1948, the CJLS issued majority and minority opinions. In more recent years, a *teshuvah* or responsum only became a valid opinion if it was supported by six members of the CJLS. Beginning in 1948, the CJLS and the RA developed the option of issuing "Standards of Rabbinic Practice" which are binding upon all members of the RA if approved by a two-thirds vote at the annual convention. To date, four Standards have been adopted. A Conservative rabbi may not: officiate at an intermarriage ceremony; perform a wedding if the woman was divorced without a *get*; perform a conversion without circumcision and immersion; or accept patrilineal descent.

In Israel, the Rabbinical Assembly of Israel founded the Va'ad Halakhah in 1985, chaired at first by Theodore Friedman and primarily by David Golinkin until 2005. It dealt with halakhic questions from Israel and Europe in Hebrew, following procedures similar to the CJLS. It has published six volumes of responsa thus far, dealing with Israeli issues such as the Sabbatical year, entering the Temple Mount, and army service for women and yeshivah students, along with general halakhic issues such as conversion, medical ethics and women in Judaism. It was revived in 2016 under the leadership of Shlomo Zacharov and Gil Nativ.

Responsa and Halakhic Guides

From 1917 to 1975, halakhic authorities such as Louis Ginzberg, Boaz Cohen, Michael Higger and Isaac Klein wrote hundreds of responsa both within the framework of the law committees and individually, but most of their responsa were never published. This changed drastically beginning in the 1970s as individual rabbis such as Isaac Klein, David Novak and David Golinkin began to publish their own responsa, along with the previously unknown responsa of Louis Ginzberg and six volumes of CJLS responsa covering the years 1927–2000. More recently, all of the responsa of the CJLS after 1980 and all of the responsa of the Va'ad Halakhah are available online.

Isaac Klein's *Guide to Jewish Religious Practice* appeared in 1979 shortly after he passed away; it has since become a standard code of law for Conservative Jews. In 2012, Martin Cohen and the RA published *The Observant Life* written by a group of Conservative rabbis. They dealt with many important, ethical issues that are not usually discussed in codes of Jewish law.

Halakhic Approaches

Not surprisingly, the different approaches to Revelation mentioned above have had an impact on the *poskim* (halakhic authorities) of the Conservative movement. As a rule, those who are more traditional theologically, such as Louis Ginzberg, Boaz Cohen, Isaac Klein, Joel Roth and David Golinkin, will only change something in Jewish law if they can find a textual basis for doing do within the Talmud and the poskim. Poskim with a more liberal theology, such as Philip Sigal, Seymour Siegel, Elliot Dorff and Gordon Tucker, are willing to change something in halakhah or make a Takkanah for ethical and/or theological reasons even if there is little or no textual support for the change being considered.

Halakhic Debates

From 1927, when the Committee on Jewish Law was founded, until today, there have been six major halakhic debates within the Conservative movement.

Agunot: The first (from 1930–1970) was the struggle to solve the plight of *agunot* or chained women who could not remarry because their husbands gave them a civil divorce but not a *get*. In the end, after a number of major attempts to cooperate with Orthodox rabbis in the 1930s and 1950s, the CJLS ended up using the Lieberman Ketubah (1953–1954), the pre-nuptial agreement (1968), and annulling the marriage when all else failed (1970).

Driving and electricity on Shabbat: The second major debate occurred in 1950 shortly after the Committee on Jewish Law was reorganized as the Committee on Jewish Law and Standards (CJLS) in 1948. This reorganization was a revolt against Louis Epstein, Boaz Cohen and the traditionalists. As a result, the majority ruled in 1950 that it's permissible to ride to the synagogue and use electric lights on Shabbat, while a minority opinion forbade these practices. This controversy resurfaced in 1990 when the Va'ad Halakhah ruled that it is forbidden to drive to synagogue on Shabbat in Israel.

Aliyot for women: In 1955, the CJLS adopted two responsa permitting aliyot for women. Ten members approved Sanders Tofield's responsum allowing aliyot for women on special occasions such as the *Aharon*; five approved Aaron Blumenthal's responsum allowing aliyot for women without restriction; and one voted against. These responsa paved the way for Bat Mitzvah girls having identical ceremonies to boys and, by 1995, 88% of Conservative synagogues allowed women to have aliyot.

Women in the minyan and the ordination of women: By the 1970s, feminism began to have a big impact on the Conservative movement. In 1972, a small group of feminists named "Ezrat Nashim" came to the Rabbinical Assembly convention, demanding a greater role for women in the synagogue. In 1973, the CJLS debated two responsa pro and con counting women in a minyan and finally approved a Takkanah to count women in the minyan. By 1988, 64% of Conservative synagogues counted women in the minyan.

Beginning in 1977, the Conservative movement and JTS fiercely debated the ordination of women as rabbis. This debate was only settled after Prof. Saul Lieberman, the leading Talmudist at JTS, passed away in 1983 and three of his major disciples left JTS shortly thereafter. As a result, Rabbi Amy Eilberg was ordained in 1985. Cohen's successor, Ismar Schorsch, completed this process by admitting women to the Cantorial School in 1987. By 2020, 20.5% of the RA members were women (327 out of 1,592 members).

As a reaction to that decision, some Conservative rabbis set up the Union for Traditional Conservative Judaism in 1979 which later split from the movement as the Union for Traditional Judaism (UTJ). It developed its own rabbinical association, law committee and rabbinical school, but by 2020 it had downsized to a virtual organization with an active website, social media and two staff members.

The attitude to women in Jewish law signaled a sea-change in the Conservative movement. It reflected the emergence of American-born, Conservative movement-educated faculty members as well as a greater degree of engagement between JTS and the Conservative movement.

Homosexuality: The next huge halakhic debate was about the ordination of homosexuals and commitment ceremonies. This battle raged in the CJLS in 1992 and again in 2006. In the end, the CJLS adopted two responsa in 2006, one opposed and one in favor. All of the Conservative rabbinical seminaries eventually began to ordain gay students as the result of huge public pressure regarding this issue.

Virtual minyanim: Finally, in 2020, the global pandemic forced the CJLS and the worldwide Conservative movement to grapple with the use of Zoom and Livestreaming on weekdays, Shabbat and festivals, with rabbis taking opposing positions. It is still too early to see how this issue will play out after the pandemic hopefully ends in the near future.

Liturgy

In addition to the four siddurim mentioned above, since the 1980s, the Conservative movement has published a series of new liturgical publications and a new *Humash*. Jules Harlow edited *Sim Shalom* in 1985. Leonard Cahan and Avram Reisner edited the new *Sim Shalom* in two volumes (1998–2002), followed by Reuven Hammer's *Or Hadash* commentary in two volumes (2003–2008). The Masorti Movement in Israel published *Siddur Va'ani Tefilati* in 1998, with a new best-selling edition in 2009. The Schechter Institute and the Rabbinical Assembly published *Megillot Hashoah*, The *Shoah* Scroll, a new liturgy for *Yom Hashoah*, in five languages beginning in 2003. *Mahzor Lev Shalem* edited by Ed Feld was published in 2010, followed by *Siddur Lev Shalem for Shabbat and Festivals* in 2016. These publications reflect a growing sensitivity to spirituality, participatory prayer, gender awareness and the level of knowledge of the average congregant.

The Rabbinical Assembly published *Moreh Derekh*, a new rabbi's manual edited by Perry Raphael Rank and Gordon Freeman in 1998. *Humash Etz Hayim* was published by the Conservative movement in 2001 in order to replace the outdated *Hertz Humash* of 1936. Edited by David Lieber and some of the leading rabbis and scholars of the Conservative movement, it aims to convey a synopsis of modern, critical scholarship along with the best of traditional midrash and homiletics.

Bibliography

General

Cardin, Nina Beth and David W. Silverman, eds. 1987. *The Seminary at 100*. New York: Jewish Theological Seminary of America and Rabbinical Assembly.

Dorff, Elliot. 1996. *Conservative Judaism: Our Ancestors to our Descendants* (second edition). New York: United Synagogue of America.

———. 2018. *Modern Conservative Judaism: Evolving Thought and Practice*. Lincoln: University of Nebraska Press.

Elazar, Daniel and Rela Mintz Gefen. 2000. *The Conservative Movement in Judaism*. Albany: State University of New York Press.

Ettenberg, Sylvia and Geraldine Rosenfield, eds. 1989. *The Ramah Experience: Community and Commitment*. New York: Jewish Theological Seminary of America.

Fierstein, Robert, ed. 2000. *The Rabbinical Assembly: A Century of Commitment*. New York: The Rabbinical Assembly.

Gillman, Neil and Joshua Gutoff. 1993. *Conservative Judaism: The New Century*. West Orange, NJ: Behrman House.

Golinkin, David and Michael Panitz. 2007. "Conservative Judaism", *The Encyclopaedia Judaica*, second edition, Vol. 5, 171–77.

Karp, Abraham. 1964. *A History of The United Synagogue of America 1913–1963*. New York: United Synagogue of America.

Nadell, Pamela. 1988. *Conservative Judaism in America: A Biographical Dictionary and Sourcebook*. New York, Westport, CT and London: Greenwood Press.

Parzen, Herbert. 1964. *Architects of Conservative Judaism*. New York: Jonathan David.

Rosenblum, Herbert. 1983. *Conservative Judaism: A Contemporary History*. New York: United Synagogue of America.

Sarna, Jonathan. 2019. *American Judaism: A History* (second edition). New Haven, CT and London: Yale University Press.

Schorsch, Ismar. 2004. *Polarities in Balance*. New York: The Jewish Theological Seminary.

Wertheimer, Jack, ed. 1997. *Tradition Renewed: A History of the Jewish Theological Seminary*. New York: The Jewish Theological Seminary of America.

Seven Core Values of Conservative Judaism

Finkelstein, Louis. 1927. "The Things that Unite Us", *Proceedings of the Rabbinical Assembly* 1, 42–53; reprint Waxman, Mordecai, ed. 1958. *Tradition and Change: The Development of Conservative Judaism*. New York: Rabbinical Assembly of America, 313–24.

Schorsch, Ismar. 1995. "The Sacred Cluster: The Core Values of Conservative Judaism", *Conservative Judaism* 47, no. 3: 3–12.

The Positive Historical School in Germany and The Historical School in the United States (1845–1902)

Davis, Moshe. 1963. *The Emergence of Conservative Judaism: The Historical School in 19th Century America*. Philadelphia, PA: The Jewish Publication Society of America.

Fierstein, Robert. 1990. *A Different Spirit: The Jewish Theological Seminary 1886–1902*. New York: The Jewish Theological Seminary of America.

Frankel, Zecharia. 1958. "On Changes in Judaism", in: Mordecai Waxman, ed., *Tradition and Change: The Development of Conservative Judaism*. New York: The Rabbinical Assembly of America, 43–50.

Ginzberg, Louis. 1928 *Students, Scholars and Saints*. Philadelphia, PA: The Jewish Publication Society of America, 195–216.

Horowitz, Rivka. 1984. *Zecharia Frankel and the Beginnings of Positive-Historical Judaism*. Jerusalem: Zalman Shazar Center (Hebrew).

Rabinowitz, Shaul Pinhass. 1898. *R. Zecharia Frankel*. Warsaw: Ahiassaf (Hebrew).

Birth and Growth of the Conservative Movement in the U.S. and Canada (1902–1945)

Adler, Cyrus. 1941. *I Have Considered the Days*. Philadelphia, PA: The Jewish Publication Society of America.
Bentwich, Norman. 1938. *Solomon Schechter: A Biography*. Philadelphia, PA: The Jewish Publication Society of America, and reprints.
Cohen, Michael. 2012. *The Birth of Conservative Judaism*. New York: Columbia University Press.
Fierstein, Robert, ed. 2002. *Solomon Schechter in America: A Centennial Tribute*. New York: no publisher stated.
Kaplan, Mordecai. 1934. *Judaism as a Civilization*. New York: Macmillan.
Schechter, Solomon. 1915. *Seminary Addresses and Other Papers*. Cincinnati, OH: Ark Publishing Company, and reprints.
Schorsch, Ismar. 2003. "Schechter's Seminary: Polarities in Balance", *Conservative Judaism* 55, no. 2: 3–23.
Scultn, Mel. 1993. *Judaism Faces the Twentieth Century: A Biography of Mordecai M. Kaplan*. Detroit, MI: Wayne State University Press.

Rapid Expansion in the U.S. and Canada (1945–1990)

Greenbaum, Michael. 2001. *Louis Finkelstein and the Conservative Movement: Conflict and Growth*. Binghamton, New York: Global Publications, Binghamton University.
Parzen, Herbert. 1964. *Architects of Conservative Judaism*. New York: Jonathan David, 207–18.
Sklare, Marshall. 1972. *Conservative Judaism: An American Religious Movement* (second edition). Glencoe, IL: Free Press.
Sklare, Marshall. 1972. "Recent Developments in Conservative Judaism", *Midstream* 18, no. 1: 3–19 and reactions in *Conservative Judaism* 27, no. 1 (Fall): 12–26; *Hadoar* 64, no. 30 (June 28, 1985): 481–89 (Hebrew).

Contraction in the U.S. (1990–2020)

Sarna, Jonathan. 2013. "Letter from Boston", *Hadassah Magazine*, January.
Sarna, Jonathan. 2014. "America's Religious Recession", *Mosaic*, November 13: https://mosaicmagazine.com/response/uncategorized/2014/11/americas-religious-recession/
Silverstein, Alan. 2019. "Conservative Judaism: Reassessing Numbers from 2013 Pew Survey", *Arizona Jewish Post*, February 22.
Wertheimer, Jack. 2018. *The New American Judaism*. Princeton, NJ and Oxford: Princeton University Press, 121–42.
Wertheimer, Jack, ed. 2000. *Jews in the Center: Conservative Synagogues and their Members*. New Brunswick, NJ and London: Rutgers University Press.
Wertheimer, Jack and Steven M. Cohen. 2014. "The Pew Survey Reanalyzed", *Mosaic*, November 2. https://mosaicmagazine.com/essay/uncategorized/2014/11/the-pew-survey-reanalyzed/
Wertheimer, Jack, Steven Bayme and Steven M. Cohen. 2015. "On Conservative Judaism: Why All the Talk about Failure?, *JTA*, October 12.

The Worldwide Masorti Movement

Israel

Feferman, Dan. 2018. *Rising Streams: Reform and Conservative Judaism in Israel*. Jerusalem: JPPI.
Hess, Yizhar and Einat Ramon. 2007. *The Reconstructionist* 71, no. 2: 42–65. *Conservative Judaism*. Spring-Summer 2011. 62, nos. 3–4.
Judaism. Fall 1982. 31, no. 4, 390–458.
The Masorti Movement: *Proceedings: First National Conference of the Conservative Movement in Israel*. Tu B'shevat 5732/1972 (Hebrew).
The Masorti Movement 10th Anniversary Year 5740-5750. November 1989;

Meirovich, Harvey. 1999. *The Shaping of Masorti Judaism in Israel*. New York: American Jewish Committee and the Argov Center of Bar Ilan University.

Rosner, Shmuel and Camile Fuchs. 2019. *Israeli Judaism: Portrait of a Cultural Revolution*. Jerusalem: JPPI.

Steinberg, Theodore. 2000 "A Brief History of the Rabbinical Assembly in Israel", in: Robert Fierstein, ed., *A Century of Commitment: One Hundred Years of the Rabbinical Assembly*. New York: The Rabbinical Assembly, 199–233.

Tabory, Ephraim. 2004. "The Israel Reform and Conservative Movements and the Market for Liberal Judaism", in: Uzi Rebhun and Chaim Waxman, eds., *Jews in Israel: Contemporary Social and Cultural Patterns*. Lebanon, NH: University Press of New England, 285–314.

The Schechter Institutes

Chikli, Eitan. 2004. *TALI Education: The Development and Realization of an Educational Idea*. DHL Dissertation, New York: Jewish Theological Seminary (Hebrew).

Golinkin, David. 2006. *Insight Israel: The View from Schechter*. Second series. Jerusalem: Schechter Institute of Jewish Studies, 229–69.

———. 2015. *From the Bet Midrash to the Schechter Institute… 1984–2015*. Jerusalem: Schechter Institute of Jewish Studies.

Latin America

Bronstein, Guillermo. 2002. *Judaísmo Masorti en Latinoamerica*. No place stated: The Rabbinical Assembly of Latin America.

Fainstein, Daniel and Theodore Friedman in: David Golinkin, ed. *Be'er Tuvia: From the Writings of Rabbi Theodore Friedman*, 1991. Jerusalem: The Masorti Movement. 23–26 (Spanish); 273–75 (English); 81–87 (Hebrew section).

Freund, Richard. 1992. "The Rabbinical Seminary of Latin America: The First Thirty Years", *Conservative Judaism* 44, no. 2: 67–78.

Freund, Richard. 2014. "Continuity and Change: The Fiftieth Anniversary of the Seminario and the Conservative Movement in Latin America", *Conservative Judaism* 65, no. 4: 72–89.

Meyer, Marshall. 1970. "A Decade of Conservative Judaism in Latin America", *Comunidades Judías de Latinoamerica*, Buenos Aires, 182–193 (Spanish).

Szteinhendler, Shmuel et al. 2000. "The Rabbinical Assembly in Latin America", in: Robert Fierstein, ed., *A Century of Commitment: One Hundred Years of the Rabbinical Assembly*. New York: The Rabbinical Assembly, 234–43.

Wolf, Isidoro. 1996. "The Beginning of the Seminario Rabínico Latinoamericano", *Eit La'asot* 4, 101–12 (Hebrew).

Ideological Debates

Dorff, Elliot. 1996. *Conservative Judaism: Our Ancestors to Our Descendants* (second edition). New York: United Synagogue of America.

Dorff, Elliot. 2018. *Modern Conservative Judaism: Evolving Thought and Practice*. Lincoln, NE: University of Nebraska Press.

Eisen, Arnold. 2015. *Conservative Judaism Today and Tomorrow*. New York: The Jewish Theological Seminary of America.

Eisen, Arnold and David Golinkin. 2014. "The Middle Way in Israel Today", in: David Golinkin, *Responsa in a Moment*, Volume 3. Jerusalem: Schechter Institute of Jewish Studies, 7–26.

Gordis, Robert. 1978. *Understanding Conservative Judaism*. New York: The Rabbinical Assembly.

Gordis, Robert, ed. 1988. *Emet Ve-emunah: Statement of Principles of Conservative Judaism*. New York: The Jewish Theological Seminary of America *et al*.

Siegel, Seymour and Elliot Gertel. 1985. *God in the Teachings of Conservative Judaism*. New York: The Rabbinical Assembly.

Waxman, Mordecai, ed. 1958. *Tradition and Change: The Development of Conservative Judaism*. New York: Rabbinical Assembly of America.

Halakhah

Law Committees

Abelson, Kassel. 2001. *Proceedings of the Committee on Jewish Law and Standards 1986–1990*. New York: The Rabbinical Assembly, i–v.

———. 2002. *Responsa 1991–2000*. New York: The Rabbinical Assembly, ix–xi.

Friedman, Tuvia. 1986. *Responsa of the Va'ad Halakah of the Rabbinical Assembly of Israel* 1, 1 (Hebrew).

Golinkin, David, ed. 1996. *The Responsa of Professor Louis Ginzberg*. New York and Jerusalem: The Jewish Theological Seminary of America, 25–27, 323.

——— ed. 1997. *Proceedings of the Committee on Jewish Law and Standards 1927–1970*. Jerusalem: The Rabbinical Assembly and the Schechter Institute of Jewish Studies, Vol. I, iii–xi.

Nadell, Pamela. 1988. *Conservative Judaism in America: A Biographical Dictionary and Sourcebook*. New York, Westport, CT and London: Greenwood Press, 1–18.

Responsa and Halakhic Guides

Allen, Wayne. 2009. *Perspectives on Jewish Law and Contemporary Issues*. Jerusalem: Schechter Institute of Jewish Studies.

———. 2011. *Further Perspectives on Jewish Law and Contemporary Issues*. No place stated: Trafford.

Cohen, Martin and Michael Katz, eds. 2012. *The Observant Life*. New York: The Rabbinical Assembly.

Golinkin, David, ed. 1986–1999. *Responsa of the Va'ad Halakah of the Rabbinical Assembly of Israel*, Vols. 1–6 (Hebrew).

———. 1992. *An Index of Conservative Responsa and Halakhic Studies 1917–1990*. New York: The Rabbinical Assembly.

———, ed. 1996. *The Responsa of Professor Louis Ginzberg*. New York and Jerusalem: The Jewish Theological Seminary of America.

———. 2000–2021. *Responsa in a Moment*. Vols 1–5. Jerusalem: Schechter Institute of Jewish Studies.

———. 2019. *Aseh Lekha Rav: She'elot Uteshuvot*. Jerusalem: Schechter Institute of Jewish Studies (Hebrew).

Golinkin, David, David Fine and Kassel Abelson *et al.* eds. 1985–2005. *Proceedings of the Committee on Jewish Law and Standards*, 1927–2000. 6 volumes (various titles and publishers).

Klein, Isaac. 1976. *A Time to Be Born, A Time to Die*. New York: The United Synagogue.

Klein, Isaac. 1979. *A Guide to Jewish Religious Practice*. New York: The Jewish Theological Seminary of America.

Klein, Isaac. 2005. *Responsa and Halakhic Studies* (second edition). Jerusalem: Schechter Institute of Jewish Studies.

Novak, David. 1974–1976. *Law and Theology in Judaism*. Vols. 1–2. New York: Ktav.

Siegel, Seymour and Elliot Gertel, eds. 1977. *Conservative Judaism and Jewish Law*. New York: The Rabbinical Assembly.

Susskind Goldberg, Monique and Diana Villa. 2010. *Ask the Rabbi: Women Rabbis Respond to Modern Halakhic Questions*. Jerusalem: Schechter Institute of Jewish Studies.

www.responsafortoday.com; www.rabbinicalassembly.org/jewish-law/committee-jewish-law-and-standards

Halakhic Approaches

Cohen, Boaz. 1959. *Law and Tradition in Judaism*. New York: The Jewish Theological Seminary of America, and reprints.

Dorff, Elliot. 2011. *The Unfolding Tradition: Philosophies of Jewish Law*. Revised edition. New York: Aviv Press.

Golinkin, David. 1991. *Halakhah for our Time: A Conservative Approach to Jewish Law*. New York: The United Synagogue of America.

———. 2000. "The Whys and Hows of Conservative Halakhah", in: *Responsa in a Moment*. Jerusalem: Schechter Institute of Jewish Studies, 11–21.

Roth, Joel. 1986. *The Halakhic Process: A Systemic Analysis*. New York: The Jewish Theological Seminary of America.

Siegel, Seymour and Elliot Gertel, eds. 1977. *Conservative Judaism and Jewish Law*. New York: The Rabbinical Assembly.

Women in Jewish Law

Berkowitz, Miriam. 2007, 2009². *Taking the Plunge: A Practical and Spiritual Guide to the Mikveh*. Jerusalem: Schechter Institute of Jewish Studies.

Golinkin, David. 2012. *The Status of Women in Jewish Law: Responsa*. Jerusalem: Schechter Institute of Jewish Studies.

Greenberg, Simon, ed. 1988. *The Ordination of Women as Rabbis: Studies and Responsa*. New York: The Jewish Theological Seminary of America.

Susskind Goldberg, Monique and Diana Villa. 2006. *Za'akat Dalot: Halakhic Solutions for the Agunot of Our Time*. Jerusalem: Schechter Institute of Jewish Studies (Hebrew).

17
REFORM

Oliver Leaman

Ritual is very much the key issue in the formation of Reform Judaism, as one would imagine. Any reform movement tries to change what people do or at least the way they do it. When Jews were largely excluded from civil society they had little option about changing their practices since they were expected to do things very differently from the general population. Remaining within the group meant absorbing and performing the group's acts, although no doubt levels of enthusiasm and knowledge varied from Jew to Jew. On the other hand, we should not ignore the ways in which even observant Jews were shaped by the environments in which they lived, sometimes antagonistically, with their gentile neighbors. There was a lively discussion in medieval times about how far Jews should adopt the customs of those around them. For example, what should be the rules about footwear when entering a synagogue? Some suggested removing the shoes in the Islamicate countries, since this is the local custom, and keeping them on in Christian Europe where this is the norm. The idea is not, of course, advocating doing what the majority do just because it is the majority, a principle that would quickly end Jewish distinctiveness. But when nothing legal hangs on it one might as well do what fits in with the prevailing culture. So adjusting to the hegemonic culture is by no means a recent phenomenon in Jewish life, but has always been a principle for any faith that survives turbulent changes over a long period.

The Reform movement in Judaism went at least one step further by criticizing the legal basis of Jewish ritual and practice. It started in a Germany that was itself starting to re-examine the intellectual basis of religion and sought to establish the study of religion on a scientific basis. This meant a number of things, but one of them was that the uncritical reception of tradition could no longer take place. The critical individual needs to carry out his or her religious tasks after having examined them and thought about them, and worked out whether they are really binding on him or her, and why. Seeing religion as a religious phenomenon means putting it within its historical context, and that could mean noting that some of what we are supposed to do today has very little basis in how the religion started. If we look at other forms of culture over time we might say that we do not follow the same medicine as our predecessors, since better ways of doing things have emerged, nor do we wear the same clothes. Practice has been reformed, and the same should apply in general to religion.

Enlightened Religion

Sometimes this was taken to be an attack on religion in general, and sometimes to particular religions, Judaism especially. Moses Mendelssohn was a prominent *Aufklärer* (Enlightener), translating the Jewish Bible into German, and was challenged to give up his religion and adopt Christianity, since the latter was seen as a more rational religion. He stoutly defended the rationality of Judaism and its rules. It was, though, a challenge to Jews who sought to enter normal society, there often remained civil penalties to being Jewish and in any case why not just do what everyone else was doing? If everyone was speaking German then Jews should speak German, and if most society was Christian then why not join the majority religion? The hegemonic culture always has a strong pull on those outside the norm, and Jews certainly felt it strongly during the modern period. One of the points of reforming religion was to make it more modern, so that it would fit in with the current ways of living a religious life, albeit within the framework of the original religion. Reform seeks to get rid of the superfluous features of religion and concentrate on the essence, and so ritual and practice can be expected to be cut along with anything else that seems to be merely traditional as opposed to rational.

It is worth referring here to the influence of Hegel as well as Kant here on the ways in which a religion could make itself look respectable. For Kant the key issue is rationality and Judaism seemed to suffer here due to its dependence on law and tradition. For Hegel, religions represent different degrees of human consciousness and rationality over time, and they improve. Christianity was seen by him as the ultimate aim of human civilization, while other religions merely represent earlier and inferior stages of the journey. This is a plausible view; after all, as time moves on things get in many ways better, we understand more of our environment and ourselves, and we often look condescendingly at the past and the customs of the past. Technology and science move on, and so should religion, the reformers suggested. Judaism is an unusual religion in some ways since typically people are born into it and do not adopt it as a result of examining its principles. We do not choose our parents, and to stick to a religion just because you were born in it seems rather like refusing to speak a language other than the one you were brought up to speak by your parents. The Christian narrative has for a very long time been that Judaism is a religion obsessed with senseless rules and rituals from which Jesus came to rescue the community. They stubbornly resisted and suffered the consequences accordingly. We should remember that this narrative also has a Protestant/Catholic dimension. In just the same way that the Church was reformed by the Protestant movement, Judaism needed a reform movement of its own, and got one eventually. (The same claim is often made today about Islam, ignoring the fact that reform movements in Islam are a frequent and recurrent event.) The reformed Christians remained Christians, but they did away with the hierarchy of the Roman Catholic Church and its antiquated ceremonies and rituals, or so the narrative went. The Reform movement in Judaism sought similarly to preserve the essence of the religion by purifying it and removing the accretion of ceremonial detritus that had built up over the centuries and millennia since Abraham set out on his journey from what is today Iraq.

Reform Jews did not want to be Protestants, but they often saw Protestant Christianity as the symbol of modernity and clarity in religion. There was then no reason why it should not be followed as a model, without of course the additional step of converting to that form of Christianity. One problem that did arise was that many Jews did convert after a stage as Reform Jews, perhaps because they did not see much difference between acting like Christians and being Christians. This dilemma was nicely described by Franz Rosenzweig who felt his family's form of religion was so lukewarm that it did not satisfy his spiritual enthusiasm, and he was seriously considering conversion until he came across an Orthodox service that inspired him to stay within the religion. Strange though that service was to him he could not help being impressed by its genuineness and it led him to believe that there must be more in Judaism than he had previously suspected. Interestingly, he did not return to a reformed style of Judaism but found within a form of orthodoxy an appropriate environment. The early Reform movement did closely resemble Protestant Christianity in its rituals and prayer services. Hebrew was largely or entirely eschewed, and the community and its ministers wore the same clothes as everyone else. Ministers resembled clerics, and services were decorous and short. The elaborate rules of kashrut were abandoned as was most of the rest of halakhah, being deemed superfluous. The vast system of commentary and jurisprudence found in the Talmud and Mishnah was largely set aside, although it could, like the Jewish Bible, be used as a source of inspiration. It was one source among others, and the idea that the Bible was the word of God was replaced with the idea that it was divinely inspired and needs to be treated carefully as a source of information and guidance.

Religion as Modern

When Jews moved in large numbers to America the Reform movement really took off. It was very difficult for many Jewish workers to obey the laws of Shabat, and some Reform synagogues, or temples as they were often known, held services instead on Friday night or Sunday, not on Saturday. Moving away from the traditional European context encouraged Jews to embrace what they saw as modernity and Reform Judaism encapsulated that better than orthodoxy, it seemed to many. The view was often that there was no point in moving to America if they carried on acting in the old ways, in religion along with other practices, and with Reform they could look like regular Americans, eat and worship like them, albeit in a Jewish environment. Religion need not encroach on their daily schedule very much, and that fitted in also to a country where there is lots to do and increasing wealth to pay for it. It is not surprising that Reform became the largest Jewish denomination in the United States. Assimilation and Reform seemed to go hand in hand; Reform Jews do not stick out in any way, they do not wear distinctive clothes or eat special food, they do not (usually) pray three times a day or say grace after meals, and so on.

It would be a mistake though to see Reform Jews as unenthusiastic about their religion, or their more Orthodox peers as being necessarily more enthusiastic. The latter can be pretty uninvolved in what they are doing, although they do a lot of things. They may just do it because they have been brought up to do it and have no particular commitment to it, in just the same way that I have no particular commitment now to writing this in English. It is a mistake to think that someone who looks distinctively Jewish is necessarily thinking about God or his or her religion all or even any of the time. They are certainly doing lots of things that most people do not do but that is all we can know about them. The reverse is also true, an individual may do very little to announce his or her religiosity yet it may be a very important, indeed the defining, part of their lives. In the Reform prayer book there are plenty of prayers to be said, although most of them never are, and of course the fact that the prayers are mainly in the vernacular language means that the person praying knows what he or she is saying. It is quite easy when one prays at speed in Hebrew to glide over what the words actually mean, especially if Hebrew is not one's native language. Some of the more radical movements in modern Judaism, such as Reconstructionism and Jewish Renewal, have been very successful at introducing into the prayer and communal schedule a whole range of new rituals and practices that many find very meaningful. They expand their spiritual lives and make them more committed to their religion and involved in it.

Reform fits in with the idea that over time modern societies become more secular. People were not seen as necessarily abandoning religion but certainly as placing it in a less central role in their lives. As society changes, the ways in which we behave tend to change also; religion, sport, education as well as everything else will be affected by this. Social practices that cannot adapt to change will die out and be replaced by versions of themselves that can adapt. Religions that have survived for millennia are rather good at adaptation, however, and in perverse ways the more things change the more some believers seek a form of religion that appears to be unchanging. We are familiar from the world of fashion how some clothes seem to go on and on even in an environment in which they are clearly unsuited. People often stay in relationships that are obviously not working for them, but they wish to continue to do what they have always done, or they are reluctant to change. So sometimes the more things change the more people want them to stay the same, and pretend that they have. This is as true of religion as it is of everything else. After all, if you do the same thing all the time whatever happens you may feel a sense of control over an increasingly unpredictable environment. Routine may have that effect and routine is, of course, a vital component of much religious ritual and practice.

Religion and Change

To continue with the contrast between the Reform and the more observant Jew, it is easy to see it as a contrast between a bad and a good Jew. Not morally bad of course, but deficient in the performance of his or her religious duties. On the other hand, one important contrast here is that the observant Jew knows largely at any point what his or her duties are, while the Reform Jew has to work them out on a case-by-case basis. There is no central form of authority that determines what is acceptable action and what should be avoided. There are certainly Reform rabbis and an institutional structure from which advice and directives appear, but not in the ways that a Beth Din, a legal court, issues rules. As one would expect, Reform communities have more autonomy to do what they find acceptable, and there is no fixed legislation that they have to obey. In many ways, then, the Reform Jew may have to do more thinking about his or her religion than an Orthodox Jew, since the solutions to problems do not come clearly delineated from some external legal source. In the COVID-19 pandemic in 2020, for example, the Haredi communities found it difficult to obey the general rules about not praying and attending funerals or studying in large groups until their religious leaders had acceded to them and declared that they were religiously valid. It was obvious to other denominations of Jews that large gatherings should be ended for the period of the pandemic, and they were. The Haredim see society as generally obstructive to them anyway and were suspicious of any instructions to break off from their traditional religious duties. Once their leaders told them what to do they obeyed, but not until then. Other Jews had to work it out for themselves, and it might be argued that this calls for more attention to what religion means to them, and why ritual and practice might be changed in particular situations. In some ways the Haredim had the easier task, they only had to obey what their leaders told them to do, while other Jews had to think about it and its ramifications.

What is at the heart of the issue is the fact that there are different ways that we can participate in an institution. Take being a fan of a sports team. Some people have all the gear, they have the insignia on their duvet and pillow cases, they wear the kit, they dress their children in the kit, they subscribe to the team's TV channel, they read about the team in their daily newspaper and so on. Other people occasionally pay attention to what "their" team is doing, and leave it at that. If their team loses they are not devastated, by comparison with the other sort of fan. Here clearly enthusiasm varies as does commitment. Yet it is not easy to say which is the good fan, and which is not. Perhaps the "bad" fan has other things going on in her life and so she is not that concerned about the performance of the team, and she is used to the fact that in sport there are successes and failures. Her attention is sporadic, but she is attentive. She needs to think about how much of her time and effort are going to be devoted to the team, and how much to other things. For the passionate fan this is not an issue at all, since she is totally committed to the team and everything connected to it. We might think that was an unbalanced way to behave, after all, as people say, it is only sport. The analogy with religion might seem to break down here, since we cannot say similarly, it is only religion. Our relationship with God and our religious community is an important factor in any life, and so someone who is only intermittently involved in it is lukewarm on issues on which they should have strong views and affiliations. Yet there are many things rightly important to us apart from religion, like our relationships with others, our ability to work and earn money, live an independent life, look after those dependent on us. Religions tend to validate these activities, but we may feel they are compelling regardless of this. We may do them because we feel we should do them, and not because we think our religion wants us to act in a certain way.

Religion and Enthusiasm

Is the person only occasionally involved in religion the Reform Jew, and the person entirely committed to it the Orthodox Jew? Not really, since the former may think much more about how to behave, what sorts of rituals to perform, than the latter who knows always what she ought to do. It is a bit like the contrast between two ways of being in love with someone. One person is passionately in love, brings flowers, sings at the bottom of balconies, writes poems, while another person is quite moderate in his behavior and does not really do much to display his feelings. Is the former like the Orthodox Jew and the latter like the Reform Jew? Not necessarily, since the person with little in the way of romantic behavior may nonetheless maintain his amorous attitude throughout his life, while the other person may move sporadically onto a different love object. That is a point worth noting about rituals, they can get in the way of a relationship becoming deep and constant. A ritual is often stylized and public, it has rules that need to be obeyed, although of course they are often adapted and change also. Someone who follows rituals can be full of performance and public behavior but remiss in really meaning it. It may even be the case that the ritual covers up real feelings, and these can flourish much more securely without the ritual. On the other hand, without the ritual or at least some kinds of public performance there is no evidence of those feelings in the first place. There is a difference, for example, between carrying out heart surgery and thinking about carrying out heart surgery, we need some evidence that something is going on that can be described in a certain way before we can credit someone with the right kind of feelings and ideas. We do have the notion of unrequited love, though, and love which does not announce itself for one reason or another, and it would be invidious to deny that love could exist in conditions like that.

This defense of the religiosity of Reform Jews does not acknowledge the fact that levels of religious behavior of such Jews is often far less frequent than it is for their Orthodox peers. They tend to pray less, attend synagogue less, and so on, and when they do Jewish things they tend to spend less time on them. They intermarry more and fewer of their children have a Jewish education of any significant type. The argument here has been that this does not necessarily make them any less serious as Jews, just Jews who follow different practices. It is worth counting here as different practices not doing what Orthodox Jews do. The recent fascination in Israel and elsewhere with Haredi Jewish life is a point at issue. Many movies and TV series such as *Shtisel* and *Unorthodox* concentrate on the lifestyle of the most distinctly Jewish denominations that exist today, and these films have proved remarkably popular among both Jews and gentiles. The latter perhaps enjoy them because they are all about what happens when tradition bumps up against modernity and raise issues about how to resolve that apparent conflict. This is a familiar issue for those coming from a wide variety of cultures, of course, and hence its grip on the public imagination. But for Jews it is about thinking about how their lives would be were they to follow those lifestyles, and thinking about them as possible options. They could have been brought up in communities like that, and most of them no doubt think how lucky they are that they were not. But the fact that they could have been is intriguing. It is a bit like looking at gruesome pictures of accidents that might have happened, and feeling glad that they did not, and yet compelled to think about what life would be like had they occurred.

The Reforming of Reform

It has been reported in recent decades that Reform has become more traditional, and there is some evidence for the use of more Hebrew and a generally more respectful reference among leaders of the denomination to traditional sources of authority. On the other hand, the ethical message of Reform has, if anything, become more radical. This was always important right from the start of the movement in Germany, the idea of monotheism implying an ethical universalism and bringing that idea very much for the first time into culture. It has developed in modern times into the elevation of *tikkun olam*, repairing the world, as a leading principle of the denomination. Of course, that could be interpreted in a variety of ways, but it is generally taken to mean relieving poverty, being kind, and siding with progressive ideas politically. On the other hand, the emphasis on a return to tradition should not be over-emphasized, since many congregations have incorporated radically new elements into their services, in an attempt at not losing members to more exotic denominations such as Jewish Renewal and Reconstructionism. Even more important than these competing groups are those tempted into some form of Jewish humanism, Christianity and Buddhism. It is not so much about trying to stop people leaving Judaism but about people wishing to stay within the religion in a weak sense but not actually being involved in it in any meaningful way. There also seems to be something of a move by young Jews to move into some form of orthodoxy. The changes to the prayer book, the use of different rituals and the emphasis on social action often look like desperate moves to try to look relevant to a skeptical audience.

Modern Reform is perhaps rather more disconnected from its past in terms of ritual than other Jewish denominations. Originally in Germany the idea was to follow the Karaite strategy of emphasizing the significance of the Bible and not of the oral law. The second day of religious holidays was abandoned since now we could determine the precise date and did not need to add a second day for safety. Services should be formal and organized, with starting and finishing times and the congregation should pray together rather than everyone doing their own thing. The concentration on the Bible as opposed to oral law has remained, but the Bible also has suffered at the hands of scientific discoveries and does not look as secure to many in the movement as in the past. It is seen as divinely inspired rather than divinely composed, and so the issue of which bits to accept and otherwise is firmly on the agenda. For one thing, many highly questionable things happen in the Bible and it is difficult to accept that that is how God wants us to behave, especially when it comes to working out rules for women and gay people. The egalitarian direction of Reform finds few echoes in the Bible. The Christian criticisms of Judaism as ritual-obsessed were taken to heart in early Reform and a type of Jewish ritual was developed which sought to show that the religion need be no more ritualistic than at least Protestant forms of Christianity themselves. Synagogue services could be as decorous as church services, rules about eating and drinking and wearing clothes could be similar to those of the Christian community. The calls in the liturgy for a return to the services of the Temple, or to Zion itself, could be jettisoned. Although in its later years the Reform movement became much more attracted to Zionism, recently this has been reversed and a far more critical attitude has emerged. This is hardly surprising since the entirely Orthodox Israeli official rabbinate would find it difficult to classify many Reform Jews as Jews at all, let alone Reform rabbis as real rabbis.

The trouble with looking for guidance to different religions is that it is like stealing scientific and trade secrets. In the latter case it means that you avoid the long work and expense on development and research but that by the time you establish the product everything has moved on. As religious actors have become more individualistic and independent, the Reform movement often continues to try to emulate the passivity of the traditional church attender. In any case, it is always difficult to foster a serious commitment to ritual when its sources seem so arbitrary. A written and oral law that are drawn on for our inspiration do often seem highly arbitrary. Although the oral law is not treated with the same respect as the Bible it is still often used for "guidance" and perhaps the idea is to find something Jewish that could be used in some way to motivate and inspire, while not really being treated as a whole as particularly relevant to anything. Midrash is similarly employed sometimes, and even Hasidic stories where they can be taken to make a useful point. The ritual framework within which those literatures are situated is completely ignored or rejected so one wonders how useful the snippets are. We often do this in religion, we pick at bits of it and use the parts we like, ignoring or rejecting everything else. That might work in a restaurant where we order merely what we want from the selection that is available, although it might not lead to a very balanced diet. Dana Evan Kaplan makes an interesting distinction between ritual and ceremony. He suggests that ritual is something we do because we think that God wants us to do it, and in a particular way, while ceremony is just something we do because it seems appropriate to us to do it in that way and on that occasion in response to what we have learned of religious ideas. He does not say this, but it may be that for Reform everything is ceremony not ritual. Certainly this captures the idea nicely that a vital aspect of religion is not just the letter of the law but how the law is interpreted, a dichotomy that runs right throughout this volume.

When it comes to the ordinary understanding of ritual, might it not be asked why the traditional forms of interpretation are no longer found to be relevant by Reform? After all, the oral law is all about interpretation and different rabbis have different takes on how to interpret particular texts and what they mean for practice. The Talmud is full of discussions like that and even the form of the Talmud reveals this, being a page of text surrounded by commentary, commentary on the commentary, as it were. Within the world of orthodoxy those are used of course as the source of yet more commentary, and the sifting through of different commentaries and their competing virtues and vices. There is a famous account of the stove of Akhnai in which the rabbis are in competition with God over a legal issue, they have one opinion and God has another (Bava Metzia 59a-b). They say that God has to agree with them since we are told that justice "is not in heaven" (Deut. 30:12) which they take to mean that the law is as they say it is, not what God thinks it is. Examining the biblical passage more closely it seems to be the point that people have no excuse for not doing what they ought to do since the information about how they should act is not in heaven, i.e. is not inaccessible to us. On the other hand, the idea that a legal issue has to resolved by legal authorities seems reasonable. This seems to be a good argument for what Reform legal authorities do, or even just a few Reform rabbis, or even just one individual. They have the freedom to decide what they ought to do in particular situations, and it seems that anything goes. Referring to Kaplan's distinction between ritual and ceremony, we need to decide what sort of religious behavior, if any, works for us and then we link it in some arbitrary way to something vaguely Jewish, perhaps Midrash or the Bible or whatever, and then we feel that our behavior is expressing where we are at. If it were a ritual we might be worried about whether it fits in with what God wants us to do, and we should remind ourselves here of the passage in the Bible where He kills the sons of Aaron not because they did not carry out the right ritual, but because they did not carry it out in completely the right way. That notion does not really exist in Reform, so the question about what we ought to do really focuses on us, not on God. It is worth contrasting this attitude with the Haredi Jewish population who, as their name suggests, are fearful of not behaving as God would want.

But, of course, in traditional Judaism anything does not go. There are ways of resolving legal disputes, and within different sects and denominations those ways are often different. Even within a group there will be disagreements about how to behave in particular situations, and that is acceptable since the parties to the dispute will all be working within something of a common framework of rhetorical techniques. For Reform it is not so easy to agree on a consensus of hermeneutic techniques. The principle of *tikkun olam*, which itself comes from the Kabbalah, is surely not strong enough to play much of a role here. In its original context, *tikkun olam* includes prayer and the rites and rituals of religion, but that presumably is because of the sense that those rituals are important and ought to be carried out, and so are doing what ought to be done. The idea that the rituals of the Jews have any special status offends against the universalist ethos of Reform, it harks back to the idea that Judaism is a particularistic religion that is only interested in its own community. This is a familiar claim of Christians and one that Reform tried to circumvent by stressing the universal message of Judaism in terms of some general ethical principles. Ritual is narrow while ethics is broad, or so it seems, and this does not provide much of a clue as to what our attitude to traditional rituals ought to be.

There is a problem with looking for a universal principle as the basis of what we do since whatever fills that slot will be very variable. It will be whatever is flavor of the month in terms of public concerns. It could be immigration rights, global warming, voter representation, equal opportunities for minorities, and so on. Not that there is anything wrong of course with those causes, but it is difficult to argue that they come close to encapsulating what a religion like Judaism is mainly about. This is a problem with all religious reform, you find some vague argument to link the religion with a major cause of some sort and then you say that the religion is all about that cause, but it patently is not. There may be plenty about the cause which is compatible with the religion, and no reason why people in the religion should not support the cause. To say that the religion is all about the cause is just wrong, though. There is also not enough in the cause to make the religion seem plausible as a religion, as opposed to merely being a container for a cause. We do not have to justify everything in universal terms. It is alright to be attached, for example, to a place and a culture. It is not equivalent to forcing others to share your views on this. Nor is it the same as saying that your views are the best and the only ones worth considering.

Once the oral law goes, it is difficult to know what to put in its place. Once the idea of the written law as being directly from heaven goes, a similar issue arises. The simulacrum of a liturgy always looks either too much or too little, since it is grounded in nothing except a tradition that no one in the movement accepts. Now for example more Hebrew is often used than in the past, head coverings are worn, prayer shawls also, but it is not clear why. A dynamic liturgy sounds like a good idea (Psalm 96:1 is often quoted: Bring to the Lord a new song …)

except when it changes for no apparent reason and fails in any case to have much resonance. Like the constantly changing parade of themes to be identified with Judaism and which fit in with what at particular times interests members of the community (or better, it is hoped by their ministers will interest them) the Reform movement in the USA looks very much like the Democratic Party at prayer. Not throwing out the baby with the bath water is always the aim of a successful reform movement, and it is difficult to establish clear criteria for success and failure.

What has been a big success in the various reform movements is keeping within the confines of a sort of Judaism a large number of people who would otherwise not fit at all into the religion. This might be because they are not halakhically Jewish or it could be because they have no interest in the rituals and practices that constitute traditional Judaism. It might be said that this is only temporary; their children, if they have any, are likely not to identify with the religion, or not be able to because of their parentage. In any case, the adherence to ritual is so minimal that it is not clear what is meant by saying that they are Jewish at all, it seems to make so little difference to them and to others. This is not the place to speculate on how religions may change and who are going to be winners and losers. On the other hand, a way of approaching religion that finds a place within it for those who are seeking a very different sort of connection to tradition is worth taking seriously. A connection, like a handshake, may be lukewarm and yet still significant.

Bibliography

Borowitz, Eugene B. 1983. *Reform Judaism Today*. New York: Behrman House.
Borowitz, Eugene. 1985. *Explaining Reform Judaism* (with Naomi Patz). New York: Behrman House.
Efron, John M. 2009. *The Jews: A History*. Upper Saddle River, NJ: Pearson Prentice Hall.
Ferziger, Adam S. 2009. "From Demonic Deviant to Drowning Brother: Reform Judaism in the Eyes of American Orthodoxy." *Jewish Studies* 15, 3: 56–88.
Frank, Daniel and Oliver Leaman. Eds. 1997. *The History of Jewish Philosophy*. London: Routledge.
Frank, Daniel, Oliver Leaman and Charles Manekin. Eds. 2002. *The Jewish Philosophy Reader*. London: Routledge.
Hoffman, Lawrence A. 2002. *The Journey Home: Discovering the Deep Spiritual Wisdom of the Jewish Tradition*. Boston, MA: Beacon Press.
Kaplan, Dana Evan. 2003. *American Reform Judaism: An Introduction*. New Brunswick, NJ: Rutgers University Press.
Kaplan, Dana Evan. 2013. *The New Reform Judaism: Challenges and Reflections*. Philadelphia, PA: Jewish Publication Society. https://digitalcommons.unl.edu/cgi/viewcontent.cgi?article=1218&context=unpresssamples
Meyer, Michael A. 1988. *Response to Modernity: A History of the Reform Movement in Judaism*. New York: Oxford University Press.
Meyer, Michael and W. Guenther Plaut. Eds. 2000. *The Reform Jewish Reader: North American Documents*. Cincinnati, OH: Union of Reform Judaism Press.
Romain, Jonathan. Ed. 2004. *Reform Judaism and Modernity: A Reader*. Norwich: SCM Press.
Washofsky, Mark. 1999. *Jewish Living: A Guide to Contemporary Reform Practice*. Cincinnati, OH: URJ Press.

18
JEWISH RITUAL AND SOCIAL JUSTICE IN AMERICA

Eric Caplan

Introduction

There is no universally accepted definition of the term "social justice." Generally speaking, social justice is associated with the belief that individuals have equal worth and possess an equal right to have their basic needs met (Finn and Jacobson, 2008). Societies must insure, therefore, that resources—including social, political and economic assets—are distributed fairly and equitably. For many contemporary thinkers, social justice also demands that we embrace diversity and confront, in Lee Anne Bell's formulation, "the ideological frameworks, historical legacies, and institutional patterns and practices that structure social relations unequally so that some groups are advantaged at the expense of other groups that are marginalized." All individuals and groups must have the "power to shape the institutions, policies, and processes that affect their lives" (Bell 2016). Whereas charity and direct service aim to alleviate hardship, social justice seeks to eradicate the root causes of suffering (Schindler and Seldin-Cohen 2018, 18–19).

The Hebrew Bible and Rabbinic tradition contain many passages that support—directly or indirectly—the participation of Jews in social justice efforts which are, by their very nature, focused beyond the Jewish community. The prophet Jeremiah, for example, informed the Jews exiled to Babylonia in the sixth century BCE of God's will that they "seek the welfare of the city to which I have exiled you and pray to the Lord in its behalf; for in its prosperity you shall prosper" (Jeremiah 29:7). God sends Jonah to prophesize to the people of Nineveh, a non-Jewish city, because He is concerned with the fate of all peoples (Jonah 1:1, 4:10–11). In the Book of Leviticus (19:34) the Israelites are commanded to treat the "stranger who resides with you" as a full citizen and to "love him as yourself, for you were strangers in the land of Egypt." And all of humanity, not just the Jews, are created in God's image (Genesis 1:26–28); a powerful assertion that renders the struggle for human rights into a religious obligation.

Turning briefly to the Babylonian Talmud, the rabbis claim that a Jew who has the ability to effectively protest the sinful conduct of anyone on earth and fails to do so, "is apprehended for the sins of the whole world" (Shabbat 54b–55a). Jews are instructed to support the non-Jewish poor along with the Jewish poor "in the interests of peace" (Gittin 61a). Much of the rabbinic tradition reads this phrase as meaning "to avoid the hatred of Gentiles that will ultimately jeopardize your security." Maimonides, however (Mishneh Torah, Kings and Wars, 10:12), connects this law to a verse in the Bible that asserts God's concern for "all of His works" (Psalms 145:9) and to one that sees the aim of Torah as being to foster "pleasant ways" and "peaceful paths" (Proverbs 3:17). Maimonides' message is clear: Jews do not cater to the needs of the non-Jewish poor out of fear but rather in imitation of God's own merciful ways.

In truth, passages such as the ones that I have cited occupy a very small space in the Jewish literary canon. Gerald J. Blidstein is undoubtedly correct when he concludes his survey of rabbinic sources pertaining to "responsibility for the welfare of general society," with the observation that this "is not the highest priority in our scheme of things. ... The people Israel seems called upon primarily to keep its house in order and to care for its own, to serve God and witness to Him." The rabbis do hope, however, that the Jews' "exemplary life" will become a model for other nations to imitate (Blidstein 1997, 55). Jonathan Sacks, like Blidstein in the continuation of his article, attributes Judaism's quietist approach to world betterment to the realities of pre-modern Jewish life.

> Jews had no civil rights. They had no vote. Until the nineteenth century, they were not admitted to universities, the professions, parliament, local government or offices of state. Even after emancipation, in the nineteenth and early twentieth centuries, they entered the public domain as citizens rather than as Jews. Public culture was either Christian or secular, and there was no point of entry for, or interest in, a Jewish voice.
>
> *Sacks 2005, 114–115*

The paucity of Jewish sources advocating for Jewish responsibility to the outside world is thus not surprising. But this lack, coupled with behavioral norms fostered through centuries of primarily looking inwards, makes it difficult to claim that Judaism is inexorably linked to social justice.

Such claims became prominent, nonetheless, in the writings of many nineteenth-century European Jews and were part of a larger intellectual phenomenon: the attempt, in the wake of the emancipation, to define the purpose and mode of Jewish life. In Western Europe, emancipation came with a clear expectation of acculturation and the majority of Jews responded by consuming European culture to an unprecedented extent. Many chose not to abandon their Judaism, creating instead forms of Jewish religious expression—Reform, Conservative (Positive-Historical), Orthodox—that suggested different approaches to balancing the demands of modernity and Judaism (Efron *et al.* 2018, 282, 321–331). It is within these circles that modern interpretations of the Jewish imperative to be "a light unto the nations" first arose.

In the East, Russia's five million Jews—the world's largest Jewish community at the time—lived in crippling poverty, and under a series of czars who were, for the most part, either hostile to them or indifferent to their plight. Beginning in 1881, the Russian state consciously sought to exclude Jews through the use of discriminatory laws and outright violence against them. By the 1880s, many Russian Jews concluded that only radical change could remedy their plight; Western-style religious reform would not be effective even if desired. Some Russian Jews embraced socialism, believing that the Jews, and other disadvantaged groups, could thrive within a new social order that discarded both cruel autocracy and oppressive capitalism. Others sought to protect Jews and to develop Jewish culture through the formation of self-governing communities that would exist alongside other autonomous national groups within European states that valued and protected this national diversity. Still others could see no future for Jews in Europe and became Zionists, sometimes mixing it with socialist commitments. Finally, a significant number of Russian Jews believed that both the security of the Jews and the ultimate betterment of society depended on their remaining faithful to the laws and ideals revealed by

God on Mt. Sinai and interpreted and enriched by rabbis throughout the ages (Efron et al. 2018, 351–367). Jews associated with each of these four responses believed that Jews had something important to contribute to the global fight for social justice.

Because, as Sacks indicates, Jews throughout Europe remained—albeit to varying degrees—at the margins of the intellectual and political life of the countries in which they lived, Jews in nineteenth- and early twentieth-century Europe still imagined that their primary contribution to the pursuit of social justice in their host societies would come from exemplifying, within their own Jewish communities, a standard of ethical living that their fellow citizens would wish to emulate. But their desire and sense of obligation to serve in that role became more pronounced than in any previous era of post-exilic Jewish life. Two examples will suffice. In the *Nineteen Letters* (1836), Samson Raphael Hirsch (1808–1888)—the leader of what became known as Neo-Orthodoxy—argued that God dispersed the Jews throughout the world so that they may teach, through their continued adherence to Jewish law, that humanity's ultimate purpose is not to amass wealth and power but rather to use these to create societies where love and righteousness prevail. "If only we were, or would become, that which we should be, if only our lives were a perfect reflection of our Law," says Hirsch, "what a mighty force we would constitute for steering mankind to the final goal of all human education!" (Hirsch 1969, 64–65).

In an essay written some 60 years later (1893), Achad Ha'am—the pen name of Asher Tzvi Ginsberg (1856–1927), a Russian Jew who founded the cultural Zionist school of thought—asserted that the Hebrew prophets' unwavering commitment to "the universal dominion of absolute justice" (Achad Ha'am 1912, 133) constitutes "the hallmark of the Hebrew national spirit" (p. 132); that the ultimate purpose of Jewish life is to proliferate righteousness throughout the world. Achad Ha'am, however, differs from Hirsch in two significant ways. First, unlike Hirsch, who sees God as the author of the Jewish moral mission, Achad Ha'am believes that the prophets themselves conceived of the Jewish people's unique role in history. Second, for Achad Ha'am, Jews cannot successfully model a just society in the diaspora.

> The ideal of the Prophets is to influence practical life in the direction of absolute Righteousness. … This influence, being practical and not theoretical, demands, as a necessary condition of its possibility… a union and concentration, at least partial, of all its forces, in the place where it will be possible for the nation to direct its life in accordance with its own character.
>
> *Achad Ha'am 1912, 137*

Only in the land of Israel can the Jews translate their moral commitments into concrete social and political institutions that other nations can emulate.

American Jewry's rich history of pursuing social justice as an expression of Jewish identity is unrivaled within modern Judaism and the focus of the remainder of this chapter. Between 1880 and 1920, the United States welcomed a large number of immigrants from Eastern Europe and the Jewish population grew from under 300,000 to 3.5 million (Sarna 2004, 375). Although a number of American Jews distinguished themselves as spokespersons for social causes prior to 1881, Jewish social justice activism did not become a significant phenomenon until the late nineteenth century when the Jewish community reached a critical mass. Like the work of their European contemporaries, the American Jewish social justice writings of this era emphasize the contributions that Jews can make to their host societies by exemplifying, within their own Jewish communities, a high standard of ethical living. While America's Jews did not face the same level of anti-Semitism that Europe's Jews often had to contend with, they still had limited power and political influence.

Jewish authors and activists for whom the pursuit of social justice was grounded in Jewish text, history and culture generally fell into one of three camps: socialists and labor organizers; upper-class American-born women affiliated with Jewish women's organizations founded in the 1880s and 1890s; and Reform rabbis. The genesis of these three Jewish camps should be seen as part of a broader social movement in the United States: The Progressive Era, which spans from the 1890s until the 1920s, and was a time of significant reform of the country's economic, social, political and cultural institutions (Martin 1954, 154). The following example gives a sense of the temper of much Progressive Era Jewish social justice thought.

In 1893, Minnie D. Louis (1841–1922)—an essayist and journalist most known for educational work within and outside the Jewish community—addressed the Jewish Women's Congress that convened in Chicago. Louis chides her listeners for worshipping "pomp and luxury" (America's "gods"). She sees the continued survival of the Jews while other nations have disappeared as an act of God that must serve a higher purpose. For Louis, God's plan for the Jews is set out in the writings of the prophet Isaiah (42:6–7):

> "I the LORD, in My grace, have summoned you, and I have grasped you by the hand. I created you, and appointed you a covenant people, a light of nations—opening eyes deprived of light, rescuing prisoners from confinement, from the dungeon those who sit in darkness".

Louis' understanding of the Jewish mission would clearly resonate with the European authors we have discussed. Interestingly, she believes that embracing this mission would also serve to diminish anti-Semitism.

> We imitate others, and we do not know what powers are in ourselves, and how we may still show mankind the way to happiness. Why shall we not now awe them, and weaken their hands, raised against us, by the overpowering glory of our righteousness, which we must derive from our Law?
>
> *Louis 1894, 184–185*

Anti-Semitism in the United States declined significantly in the aftermath of World War II. Restrictive barriers to Jews fell in colleges and in well-paying professional fields, facilitating the entrance of large numbers of Jews into the middle class (Sarna 2004, 276–77). Recent demographic studies underline the extent to which the large majority of America's Jews are solidly entrenched in the middle and upper classes. Whereas 8% of American adults report yearly household incomes over $150,000 and 10% have incomes between $100,000 and $149,000, 25% and 17% of the country's Jews, respectively, report these household incomes (Pew 2013, 42). A similar dynamic can be seen in levels of education. U.S. Jews are twice as likely to have an undergraduate degree than the national average (Pew 2013, 42; Steinhardt 2019, 3). Jews constitute, at most, 2.2% of the population of the U.S. (Steinhardt 2019, 1), yet 35% of *Forbes Magazine*'s 2009 list of 400 wealthiest Americans were either Jews or of Jewish origin and in 2014, approximately 30% of the 100 highest paid U.S. CEOs were Jewish (Weinfeld 2018, 96–100). After the 2020 U.S. midterm elections, Jews held 6.2% of seats in the House of Representatives and ten of the 100 seats in the Senate (Kampeas 2021).

Jews today participate in U.S. public life and discourse with confidence and authority. The rate of Jewish political engagement (voting turnout, campaign participation, lobbying), for example, is approximately 20% higher than the national average. Although this is only slightly higher than for other Americans with similar incomes and levels of education, this still places Jews among the most politically active sectors of U.S. society (Weisberg 2019, 99–104). Much of this political activity comes to support liberal policies. In fact, surveys show that Jews are among the most liberal groups in the United States, with 49% calling themselves liberal, vs. 21% of the general population who do so. Whereas 38% of Americans see themselves as Conservative, only 19% of Jews embrace this ideology (Pew 2013, 95–96). Liberalism is most closely associated with the Democratic party and, indeed, the Pew Research Center's study of America's Jews found that 70% "identify with or lean toward" that party (Pew 2013, 96) and exit polls of the 2020 Presidential election showed that approximately 70% of Jews voted for Joe Biden (American Enterprise Institute 2020). Conservatism, however, enjoys more support among the 10% of America's Jews who are Orthodox. Of Haredi (ultra-Orthodox) Jews, 65% self-define as "Republican/Conservative/Libertarian" as do 37% of Modern Orthodox Jews. Fifty-six percent of Haredim voted for Donald Trump in 2016 as did 29% of Modern Orthodox Jews (Nishmah 2020, 4–5). Preliminary data from the 2020 election indicates that up to 80% of Haredim might have voted for Trump but that he did not make similar gains among Modern Orthodox Jews (Magid 2020).

Beginning in the 1990s, a series of studies of American Jews have probed whether the majority take a liberal position on all issues and if their political stance is significantly different than Americans with similar levels of education and annual income. These papers have shown that Jews are uniquely—and in large numbers—liberal on a variety of cultural issues but that this rate of assent and distinctiveness does not extend to all economic questions. For example, data gathered for the American National Election Studies (1992–2012) and General Social Survey (1992–2016) indicate that whereas 81% of American Jews believe that abortion should be allowed "for any reason" and 70% say that same-sex sexual relations are not wrong, 41% and 36% of white[1] non-Jews, respectively, take these positions. Even after applying demographic controls to these findings, Jews come out as markedly liberal. Turning to economic policy, 52% of Jews favor governments providing more services vs. 36% of non-Jewish Whites who do so; but only 41% of Jews and 43% of non-Jewish Whites believe that governments should reduce income inequality. Controlling for education and income levels, Jews are slightly more liberal on the former issue than white Americans but identical to them on the latter policy concern. By way of contrast, data from the ANES studies of 1956–1968, show that Jews at that time were still decidedly on the liberal side of most economic issues (Weisberg 2019, 122–139).

Jewish social justice activists in today's America draw inspiration from the same biblical and rabbinic texts that spoke to Jews of the nineteenth and early twentieth centuries. But unlike their predecessors, they are addressing a largely affluent community. To these activists and writers, it is clear that the socio-economic position attained by American Jews brings with it an obligation to use their status and social capital to tackle America's collective ills more directly, aggressively and systematically than Minnie D. Louis could propose. This perspective is well-exemplified by Ruth Messinger and Aaron Dorfman in their contribution to the 2008 anthology, *Righteous Indignation: A Jewish Call for Justice*:

> We, as American Jews, have enormous power and political voice not just as individuals, but as a community. And with that power and voice comes equally great obligation. As the Babylonian Talmud explains, anticipating by thousands of years John F. Kennedy's admonition that "of those to whom much is given, much is required": "Whoever can prevent his household from committing a sin but does not, is responsible for the sins of his household; if he can prevent his fellow citizens, he is

responsible for the sins of his fellow citizens; if the whole world, he is responsible for the sins of the whole world."

Indeed, Messinger and Dorfman emphasize the universal dimension of this Talmudic passage, believing that telecommunications, the internet, international trade, tourism—among other engines of globalization—have made the international sphere and its many socio-economic challenges more immediate to us and thus part of the contemporary Jewish "universe of obligation" (Messinger and Dorfman 2008, 281–292). When this article was published, both authors held senior leadership positions in the American Jewish World Service (AJWS), the leading Jewish organization dedicated to ending poverty and promoting human rights in the developing world.

The vast majority of American Jewish social justice thought and activism today is spearheaded by non-Orthodox Jews. Shmuly Yanklowitz (1981–)—the founder and president of Uri L'Tzedek, the premier Orthodox social justice organization—suggests a number of reasons for Orthodox Jewry's lack of involvement. Orthodox Jews, especially Haredim, who constitute roughly two-thirds of the American Orthodox community, tend to be parochial and insular, a stance fostered by the memory of centuries of Jewish persecution and exclusion and by the real challenge of sustaining Jewish communal institutions while raising large families. Moreover, Orthodox Jews often value study over action, preserving the norms of the past— where outwardly focused social justice was not a central Jewish concern—over breaking new ground, and following the dictates of their religious leaders over exercising the autonomous critical thinking that defines social justice work (Yanklowitz 2014, 24–25). Because of the lack of Orthodox voices which, as we saw, tend to lean more toward Conservative positions, contemporary American Jewish social activism generally aligns with the center-left policies of the Democratic Party. *Righteous Indignation*, for example, includes articles advocating for the existence of a Jewish obligation to use renewable energy, provide universal health care, and protect reproductive rights, to support unions, liberal immigration policies, public schools and LGBTQ rights, and to seek justice for Palestinians. The 70 organizations that make up the Jewish Social Justice Roundtable—a "network … that strengthens and aligns the Jewish social justice field in order to make justice a core expression of Jewish life and help create an equitable world"—are largely focused on addressing the same issues explored in *Righteous Indignation* (www.jewishsocialjustice.org/affiliate-info).

Jewish Ritual and Social Justice

Jewish civilization is rich in religious ritual. There are holidays in all but one month of the Jewish calendar (Cheshvan); Shabbat comes weekly; prayers and blessings are recited at multiple times in the day; significant lifecycle events are marked in community; and laws regulate dietary and most other aspects of life. It is therefore not surprising that Jews who wish to engage the community on a variety of social justice issues have used Jewish ritual as a platform to convey and disseminate their message. This is true for all Jews, secular to Modern Orthodox. Integrating contemporary political concerns into ancient rituals can also, in the words of veteran Jewish activist-writer, Arthur Waskow, "carr[y] an enormous emotional charge [that is] far more explosive and far more productive of spiritual and social change than either religion-in-a-box or politics-in-a-box" (Waskow 1971, 23). The volume of social justice ritual resources increases each year, facilitated further in our day by the ease with which such materials can be formatted on a laptop and distributed at little cost via social media, websites and listservs.

Studies of North American Jews indicate that ritual observance is an important component of Jewish identity for both Orthodox and non-Orthodox Jews. In *The Jew Within*, a study of moderately affiliated American Jews, Steven M. Cohen and Arnold M. Eisen found that these Jews exhibit a "near-universal openness to ritual," and are especially drawn to practices that are situated in family and can be customized to express personal values (Cohen and Eisen 2000, 91–93, 96). A 2006 study of U.S. Jews aged 18–25, describes them as drawn to informal expressions of Jewishness such as "creating improvised seders or hosting dinners on Friday nights with their own versions of the traditional prayers" (Reboot 2006, 26). A more recent study of American Jews in their twenties and thirties found that they chose to imagine Judaism as a "tradition" because it allowed them to enjoy the benefits of ritual practice—the "occasions for gathering, and structures for socializing"—without the "prescriptive obligations or ... limitations on who can participate" that accompany seeing Judaism as a "religion" or "ethnicity." The question of "who can participate" is especially salient to the large number of non-Orthodox Jews today who have non-Jewish partners and close friends (Kelman *et al*. 2017, 160). The ritual materials circulated by social justice organizations help users customize ritual and make it more relevant to the Jews and non-Jews gathered around the table. These resources are thus well-suited to this particular moment in American liberal Jewish life.

Still, levels of ritual observance outside of Orthodox communities are relatively low. Whereas 76% of American Conservative Jews and 56% of Reform Jews fasted for all or part of Yom Kippur in 2012, far fewer lit Shabbat candles (34%/10%) or kept kosher in their homes (31%/7%). Of Conservative Jews, 52% attend synagogue seldom or a few times a year, as do 67% of Reform Jews (Pew 2013, 76–78). Liberal Jews, however, are more likely than Orthodox Jews to incorporate new readings and ritual forms into their practice. For this reason, most social justice organizations offer more resources for Hanukkah, Passover and Yom Kippur than for festivals and ritual observances which fewer liberal Jews observe. Materials for Passover are especially plentiful and reflect the full spectrum of social justice issues that concern American Jews. These resources are the focus of the discussion that follows.

In reconstructing ritual forms or creating readings to be incorporated into existing ritual, social justice thinkers and organizations act in the spirit of the mystics of Safed and the *paytanim* of the Middle Ages and earlier, who translated their religious beliefs into ritual and poetry that is now interspersed throughout liberal and Orthodox liturgy. That said, there is little historical precedent for enriching Jewish ritual and liturgy with materials that address economic or other social justice concerns.

Passover Haggadot

The Seder, a home service on the first or first and second evenings of Passover devoted to retelling the story of the Exodus from Egypt, is the central ritual observance of the festival. The basic framework of this retelling was first outlined in the Mishnah (200 BCE), and the texts and rituals of the Haggadah—the special liturgy used in the service—were canonized by the Geonim (750–1038 CE): "powerful religious authorities in Babylonia (Iraq), who recorded their own practice and dispatched it with expectations of its being followed elsewhere" (Hoffman 2008, 51).

The traditional Haggadah text asserts that "in each generation, every individual should feel as though he or she had actually been redeemed from Egypt" and that "whoever elaborates upon the story of the Exodus deserves praise." When juxtaposed, these passages suggest that the way to identify personally with the story is by adding something of relevance to you, something that is not included in the traditional telling. Over the last 125 years, doing so has often involved enriching the Seder with discussion about groups that need liberation, either from oppressive national forces or oppressive social institutions. Expansions of this sort "feel right" because the Bible repeatedly links the Jewish experience of slavery in Egypt with the command to care for the poor, the widow, the slave and the stranger. Moreover, the Exodus story celebrates a moment of radical change that has inspired activists and people in need of deliverance throughout the world, even if they doubt the historical accuracy of the Hebrew Bible's description of the event. The discussion of contemporary social issues around the Seder table is compelling and one of the reasons why the ritual is the most celebrated of all Jewish rituals today. Seventy percent of American Jews report that they attend a Seder (Pew 2013, 77).

The *Union Prayer Book* of 1892, the first official liturgy of American Reform Judaism, included a Haggadah text. This was updated and issued as a self-contained book in 1907 and revised again in 1923 (Balin 2008, 81–82). The Reform Haggadah created a template for modernizing the text that was followed by many subsequent non-Orthodox American Passover liturgies. Most notably, it replaced the *Maggid* section, which tells the Exodus story through a series of fairly complex rabbinic homilies, with a more straightforward narrative based on the Hebrew Bible. But its presentation of social justice concerns is markedly different than what we find in liberal Haggadot or in supplementary materials to be used at Seders of the last 70 years.

In the foreword to the 1923 edition, the editors note that the "Seder has thrilled [Jews] with an appreciation of the glories of their past, imbued them with an heroic power of endurance under the severest trials and persecutions, and *quickened within them the enthusiasm of high ideals of freedom*" (CCAR 1923, vii [emphasis mine]). What must Jews do, however, to act upon these "high ideals"? The core text of the Reform Haggadah is fairly silent on this. There are two main reasons for this silence. First, this Haggadah, like the traditional text, emphasizes the divine role in redemption over the human one. It instructs its readers, for example, that the matzah is "a symbol of divine help" and that the roasted shank-bone (*zero'a*) of the Seder plate reminds us that God "save[d] us in all kinds of distress." The latter passage concludes with a prayer that "[God] always shield the afflicted, and forever remove every trace of bondage from among the children of man" (CCAR 1923, 34–36). The service closes with a similar sentiment: "May He who broke Pharaoh's yoke shatter all fetters of oppression, and hasten the day when swords shall, at last, be broken and wars ended" (CCAR 1923, 78). This passive stance may, at least in part, reflect the limited political power and influence of Jews in the 1920s—including the middle- and upper middle-class Jews that still made up the majority of members of American Reform congregations. Second, as noted by Richard Sarason (2015, 68, 98–99), the 1923 Haggadah presents American Jewry as "a happy generation, [that] celebrate so calmly and safely and joyfully in our habitations" while "enjoying the liberty of this land" (CCAR 1923, 38–40). Unlike Jews of the 1960s and the present moment—or even the authors of the 1918 social justice platform of the Reform rabbinate—they seem to see few flaws in American society that need addressing.

The New Haggadah, edited by Rabbis Mordecai M. Kaplan, Eugene Kohn and Ira Eisenstein and published in 1941, approaches American and global realities more critically and places greater emphasis on the human role in bringing redemption. Kaplan (1881–1983) was the founder of Reconstructionist Judaism and is one of the most influential Jewish thinkers of the last century. Kohn and Eisenstein worked with him on all of the Reconstructionist liturgies of the 1940s and played pivotal roles in the dissemination of Reconstructionist thought. *The New Haggadah*'s break with the contented tone of the *Union Haggadah* is, in large part, a function of timing: the text was written in the aftermath of the Great Depression and in the midst of World War Two and the Nazi assault on the Jews. And its approach to redemption reflects Kaplan's understanding of God "as the Power or Process that makes for salvation"; a theological stance that rejects the supernatural understandings of God that form the basis of the Exodus story in the Hebrew Bible and in the traditional Haggadah. This is a theology that sees humans as largely responsible for their own deliverance and thus perceives appeals for divine intervention in the service of world betterment to be self-defeating.

Kaplan's view that participation in the Seder ritual should encourage Jews to combat all forms of injustice is readily apparent in the reading "Let My People Go," which appears toward the beginning of the service:

> We have dedicated this festival tonight to the dream and the hope of freedom, the dream and the hope that have filled the hearts of men from the time our Israelite ancestors went forth out of Egypt. People have suffered, nations have struggled to make this dream come true. Now we dedicate *ourselves* to the struggle for freedom. Though the sacrifice be great and the hardships many, we shall not rest until the chains that enslave all men be broken.
>
> But the freedom we strive for means more than broken chains. ... For men can be enslaved in more ways than one.
>
> Men can be enslaved to themselves. ... When laziness or cowardice keeps them from doing what they know to be the right ... they are slaves. ...
>
> Men can be enslaved by poverty and inequality. ... When the work men do enriches others, but leaves them in want of strong houses for shelter, nourishing food for themselves and for their children, and warm clothes to keep out the cold – they are slaves.
>
> Men can be enslaved by intolerance. When Jews ... must deny that they are Jews in order to get work – they are slaves. When they must live in constant fear of unwarranted hate and prejudice – they are slaves.
>
> How deeply these enslavements have scarred the world! The wars, the destruction, the suffering, the waste! Pesah calls us to be free. ... Pesah calls upon us to put an end to all slavery!
>
> *Kaplan et al. 1941, 11–13*

Kaplan and his co-editors use the Passover Seder to encourage social justice activism in multiple other ways. For example, to foster the faith that human activity can indeed improve the world, Moses' role in the redemption of the Israelites, largely absent from the traditional Haggadah, is added to the *Maggid* section under the heading "How Moses Freed Israel" (Kaplan *et al.* 1941, 41–50). Biblical verses stressing the need for Israel to act ethically, since it had experienced the pain of slavery, are also included (Kaplan et al. 1941, 53–57). And the authors present matzah as symbolizing Judaism's historical commitment to economic equality:

> In ancient times, the Israelites lived in the desert. Like all desert peoples, they lived simply. ... Even their bread was only an unleavened cake. ... Mazzah became the symbol of those early days when all people had little, but none had more—when equality prevailed among the Israelites. Let the mazzah be a symbol for us today. ... Luxuries when shared by all are good to have. ... But when the few have more than they need, and the many have not even life's necessities, then the plea of the Prophets [to return to the simple and modest ways of the desert] must be heard. Let us strive to bring about equality and justice for everyone.
>
> *Kaplan et al. 1941, 66–67*

The strong social justice messaging of the Reconstructionist Haggadah calls to mind the texts prepared by Histadrut/Labor Zionists and members of the socialist-Yiddishist Workmen's Circle for use in the "Third Seders" that their respective organizations held, beginning in the late 1920s. These were large public affairs celebrated on the Sunday before Passover or during the intermediate days of the festival. The first Haggadah printed and distributed by the Workmen's Circle national office did not appear, however, until 1950, followed a few years later by a Histadrut Haggadah. An English adaptation of the Workmen's Circle text was created in the early 1950s (Shuldiner 1999, 133–135). Two examples from it are sufficient to establish its temper. The Haggadah includes a Yiddish song (*Piramidn*/Pyramids) based on a poem by David Edelstadt (1866–1892) crediting Moses with the deliverance of the Israelites. "Who knows how long it would have continued/This bleak world of slavery/If in the land of pyramids/There would not have been a great hero/Who struggled for Jews/With his wisdom, with his sword" (Shuldiner 1999, 170). The traditional recitation of the ten plagues that God inflicted upon the Egyptians is replaced with a listing of contemporary "plagues"—aggressive war, communism, fascism, slave labor, genocide, disease, famine, human exploitation, religious bigotry and racial discrimination. Before the customary ritual of emptying a cup of wine of one drop for each plague, the following is read: "These are some of the evils that afflict modern society. None of these evils is insurmountable. Man, by the right exercise of his intelligence, can overcome all obstacles. To this task we rededicate ourselves at this Passover season" (Shuldiner 1999, 173). Lists of contemporary plagues have become common fixtures of social justice-themed Haggadot as has the emphasis on the transformative power of collective human action.

Arthur Waskow's *Freedom Seder* of 1969 took a more radical approach to formulating a Haggadah text that speaks to current social justice issues. The Haggadah was originally written to be used at a public Seder on April 4—the one-year anniversary of the murder of Martin Luther King Jr—which coincided with the third day of Passover. The Seder was held in a church basement in a predominantly African American neighborhood of Washington, with 800 Jews and non-Jewish Whites and Blacks in attendance, some also serving as service leaders. This first staging—supported and promoted by the nascent radical group, Jews for Urban Justice—received wide coverage in the media, Jewish and non-Jewish, and the published text sold tens of thousands of copies in the U.S. (Staub 2002, 163–164). Waskow's liturgy follows the structure of the traditional Haggadah but mainly focuses the conversation on the continued struggle of Blacks for equality and economic security in America. As Waskow writes in the Preface of the Haggadah, the Seder is a fitting context to honor King and explore the fate of America's Blacks because MLK drew inspiration from the story of the Israelite Exodus from Egypt. Participation in the Passover ritual should motivate us to free ourselves from the "Pharaohs" who enslave us. Accordingly, readers are invited to adapt the text as needed to best address the political concerns of changing times (Waskow 1970, v–vii).

The *Freedom Seder* is noteworthy in at least three ways. First, in its speaking equally to both Jews and non-Jews who gather together to jointly explore the meanings of the Exodus for twentieth-century Americans. Second, in its use of quotes from modern and contemporary Jewish *and* non-Jewish authors including Thomas Jefferson, Henry David Thoreau, MLK, Martin Buber, Eldridge Cleaver, Emmanuel Ringelblum, Mahatma Gandhi, Daniel Berrigan, Allen Ginsberg, George Orwell, Hannah Arendt—and in giving many of them Jewish honorific titles (Rabbi Thoreau, *Shofet* [biblical judge] Cleaver ...). In addition, modern songs of relevance to the themes of the Seder are sung, for instance, "We Shall Overcome," "Solidarity Forever" and "The Times They Are A-Changin'." Third, in the uniqueness of the subject matter itself. The *Freedom Seder* focuses on specific contemporary issues whereas, with very few exceptions, previous Haggadot took a more general approach. They spoke, for example, about injustice but did not deeply explore particular justice concerns. Many of the previously listed authors are referenced in the long discussion that follows the traditional enumeration of the Ten Plagues, about whether freedom can be won without violence. This was a pressing issue because of the growing number of Blacks who doubted that the non-violent posture of King could indeed uproot America's systemic racism. Both for tactical reasons and out of a sense of deep frustration, the Black struggle for civil rights had become more violent and Whites feared for their personal safety as never before.

Waskow introduces the topic by calling on participants to "remember the lesson of the plagues: the winning of freedom has not always been bloodless in the past." Blood was spilled in Egypt, in the American Revolution, in the Civil War that freed African Americans from slavery, and in the Warsaw Ghetto revolt of 1943. And "the struggle may not be bloodless during the next generation." Ultimately, however, the *Freedom Seder* does not endorse violence against people. "It is incumbent upon us," says Waskow, "not only to remember in tears the blood of the tyrants and the blood of the prophets and martyrs, but to end the letting of blood. To end it! To end it!"; a claim that leads into a quote from MLK on the power of non-violence (Waskow 1970, 14–21). Yet the Haggadah does sanction attacking the property of oppressors. It looks favorably, for example, at the damage done by the "D.C. Nine" to the offices of Dow Chemical on March 22, 1969 (Waskow 1970, 22–24). While few subsequent social justice-themed Haggadot explore the role of violence in movements of social change, many do include non-Jewish authors, contemporary music, and are focused, like the *Freedom Seder*, on specific socio-economic and political issues.

Feminist Haggadot first appeared in the mid-1970s and are, like the *Freedom Seder*, largely centered on a single issue. But their chosen focal point—the marginalization or outright absence of women's experience from core elements of Jewish religion and culture for centuries—is both broader in scope and more directly focused on Jewish life than Waskow's liturgy. The traditional Haggadah's recounting of the Jews' passage from slavery to freedom is a natural home for telling the story of women's struggles for equal rights and opportunity within society in general, and within Jewish religion and community, specifically. Moreover, the centrality of women to the Exodus story—Miriam, who watched over baby Moses and later led the women in song at the Sea of Reeds, and Shifra and Puah, the midwives who disobeyed Pharaoh's order to murder Jewish newborn males—rendered the Haggadah a fitting place to begin celebrating heroines that the tradition ignored or stigmatized and to thereby inspire contemporary Jewish women to insist that their own voices be heard and valued. Women's Seders took place, like the *Freedom Seder* and the Workmen's Circle Seder, during the intermediate days of Passover. Today, a number of the innovations they introduced are regularly incorporated into "mainstream" Haggadot.

The Women's Haggadah, by E. M. Broner and Naomi Nimrod, is perhaps the best-known feminist Passover text. Excerpts from it were published in *Lilith Magazine* in 1977, and a revised version appeared in 1993, prefaced with a rich account of how the Haggadah took form and was used over two decades. Important second-wave feminists, including Letty Cottin Pogrebin, Gloria Steinem and Bella Abzug, were regular attendees at the Seders in which *The Women's Haggadah* was first read (Zierler 2008, 71–72). Unlike traditional Haggadot where Miriam is absent, Broner and Nimrod place Miriam at the center of their liturgy. Their account of the Exodus story is told through Miriam's experience of it, beginning with Moses' birth and ending with the crossing of the sea. In addition, Miriam's exclusion from the telling of the story is presented as paradigmatic of Jewish women's historical plight. For example, the four daughters—a reworking of the four sons of the traditional Haggadah—ask, "How did it come about that Miriam was treated so badly?" The answer given traces her lot to the decision of the early rabbis to give greater religious weight to Genesis 2, where Adam is created before Eve and as his "fitting helper," than to Genesis 1, where God creates both at the same time, the two being equal and created in the Divine image (Broner and Nimrod

1993, 200–202). "The Lament of the Prophet Miriam" lists the many ways the Hebrew Bible sidelines or mistreats Miriam, and this is followed by stories of how the rabbinic tradition similarly mistreats Beruriah and other women of note in the Talmud (Broner and Nimrod 1993, 198–200, 204–207). In this Haggadah, the "Wicked Child" is not, as is customary, the one who distances himself from the retelling of the Exodus story; she is, rather, the child who "removes herself from the community of women" and breaks "the chain that links [her] to our heritage and the legacy of Miriam" (Broner and Nimrod 1993, 195). *The Women's Haggadah* concludes with "Miriam ha Neviah" (Miriam the Prophet) and omits the traditional invocation of the prophet Elijah who is symbolically invited into homes after the third cup of wine (Broner and Nimrod 1993, 216).

Whereas the deep emphasis placed on Miriam is a unique characteristic of Nimrod's and Broner's text, multiple contemporary liberal Haggadot now invoke Miriam, most commonly by suggesting that a "Miriam's Cup" be placed on the Seder table. The cup is filled with fresh water because of the rabbinic traditions that associate Miriam with finding water for the Israelites to drink in the desert and the Hebrew Bible's own association of Miriam with the crossing of the Sea of Reeds. In *The Open Door*, the Haggadah of American Reform Judaism, water from the cup is shared with those seated around the table at the start of the evening (Elwell 2002, 12–14). In the Reconstructionist Haggadah, *A Night of Questions*, attention is called to "Miriam's Cup" before blessing the first of four cups of wine, prior to singing *Dayyenu*, and within the section of ritual focused on Elijah (Levitt and Strassfeld 2000, 29, 63–65, 118–119). It is at the third point that the cup is passed so that all participants may drink from it.

The increasingly popular custom of adding an orange to the Seder plate has an interesting connection to feminist Seders. In the early 1980s, Susannah Heschel came across a feminist Haggadah edited by students at Oberlin College in which a crust of bread was placed on the Seder plate as an act of defiance against the statement of a wife of a rabbi that "there's as much room for a lesbian in Judaism as there is for a crust of bread on the seder plate." Heschel was moved by the students' sentiment but felt that it was an error to make this point through bread—a food that cannot be consumed or even be present in your house during Passover. The following year Heschel added, instead, an orange to her Seder plate "as a gesture of solidarity with Jewish lesbians, gay men, and others who are marginalized within the Jewish community (I mentioned widows in particular)." She chose an orange to symbolize "the fruitfulness for all Jews when lesbians and gay men are contributing and active members of Jewish life." In time, however, a story circulated that Heschel's addition to the Seder ritual came in response to a man who, in her presence, asserted angrily that "a woman belongs on the *bimah* [the raised platform in synagogues where the Torah is read] as much as an orange on the seder plate" (Heschel 2003, 209–210). This story, though incorrect, spread widely, and is sufficiently known to be referenced in the pages of the *New York Times* (Kristof 2018). Today, therefore, Jews who add an orange to their Seder plates often do so "as an affirmation of the significant contributions of women to Jewish life and to the entire Jewish community" (Cohen et al. 2003, 208–209). And this custom has led others to suggest different additions to the plate. For example, the social justice organization, T'ruah: The Rabbinic Call for Human Rights, has asked that a tomato be placed on the Seder plate as an act of solidarity with the difficult working conditions of Florida farmworkers. They provide ways to use this symbol that both educate Seder participants about the issues and encourage them to learn more (T'ruah 2019). A number of Haggadot place an olive on the Seder plate to facilitate conversation about the plight of Palestinians under Israeli occupation (Fishkoff 2011).

This section of the chapter has largely focused on ground-breaking social justice-themed Haggadot. Each year, however, many texts are circulated by social justice organizations for use within conventional Seders and a number of these groups and individual activists have also created full Haggadot. These are too numerous to probe here but a few titles are listed below to give a sense of the political issues of greatest interest to American Jews in the twenty-first century:

An Exodus in our Time: A Reflection on the Rohingya Crisis for the Passover Table (AJWS 2018)
Bread of Affliction: Matzah, Hunger and Race (Hazon 2017)
Next Year in a Just World: A Global Justice Haggadah (AJWS 2017)
Earth Justice Seder: The Passover Haggadah for Environmental Justice (RAC/COEJL 2016)
Racial Justice & Inclusivity Haggadah (Be'Chol Lashon 2020)
In Search of Freedom: A Passover Seder for Darfur (2008)
Immigrant Justice Freedom Seder (JCUA 2005)
The Other Side of the Sea: A Haggadah on Fighting Modern Day Slavery (T'ruah 2015; revised 2020)
The Human Rights Haggadah (Shlomo Levin, 2019)
Fifteen Steps to Freedom: A J Street [Israel-Palestine] Haggadah (2020)
The Promise of the Land: A Passover [environmental] Haggadah (Rabbi Ellen Bernstein, 2020)
Ma Nishtanah: A Gay, Lesbian, Bisexual, Transgender, Questioning, Ally Haggadah (2005)

Some activists have noted that Jewish ritual can support and motivate social justice activism even when it is not expressly crafted to do so. Jill Jacobs, Executive Director of T'ruah and an important writer of text-rich Jewish perspectives on socio-economic challenges, suggests three ways in which traditional ritual can support activism (Jacobs 2011, 164–167). First, Jewish prayer texts can move us to act. For example, the blessings recited in the morning service to thank God for creating us as free people or clothing the naked are also meant to "set an intention for our own contributions to the world. … We cannot thank God for giving us freedom without working to end the enslavement of others." Abraham Joshua Heschel stated this idea even more forcefully decades earlier when he wrote that "Prayer is a confrontation with Him who demands justice and compassion, with Him who despises flattery and abhors iniquity. … He brought us into being; He brought us out of slavery. And He demands" (Heschel 1970). Second, holidays such as Purim and Hanukkah celebrate wondrous transformations that have occurred in the life of the Jewish people and thus serve to remind us that change is indeed possible through sustained human effort. Finally, pausing to perform rituals can help activists avoid the burn out that is often the end result of months or years of non-stop organizing. Shabbat, for instance, "grants us a day to breathe, to spend time with family and friends, and to regain the energy to continue our work."

Critique

Drawing these types of connections between performing Jewish rituals and engaging in social justice work has proven much less controversial than efforts to integrate social justice concerns into Haggadot and other ritual forms. Many Jewish communal leaders and intellectuals, for example, were highly critical of the *Freedom Seder*. The temper of these critiques is well-exemplified by Robert Alter's piece on Waskow's Haggadah and Jewish radicalism in general (Alter 1971, 47–50). Alter sees Waskow and his colleagues on the Left as suffering from "a total incapacity to make significant distinctions about the meanings of words and of different political situations." The Statement of Principles of the National Jewish Organizing Project—included among the supplementary materials to be used at a *Freedom Seder*—names as Pharaohs members of the U.S. Congress and heads of auto companies for, respectively, "multiply[ing] the weapons that will someday burn us all to death" and "condemn[ing] the public to be mangled and die rather than spend their profits on a car that would protect its occupants." Such language, in Alter's view, both distorts the reality of Pharaoh's transgressions and provides no useful lens from which to analyze these current social realities. In addition, Waskow is criticized for misrepresenting Jewish religious ideas. The *Freedom Seder*'s Havdalah text, for instance, eliminates the hierarchies of holiness that are fundamental to the prayer and to Judaism itself. God is presented as making a distinction "between holy and equally holy … between the holiness of the Jewish people and the equal holiness of other peoples" and not "between sacred and profane … between Israel and the nations" as is customary. The previously discussed bestowing of Jewish titles on Gandhi, Arendt, Thoreau and others in the *Freedom Seder* strikes Alter as reflecting the author's "need to invest political stances with religious authority, and of his consequent assumption that views resembling his own have a self-evident religious validation." History has shown such certitude to be "a dangerous assumption," says Alter, and it ignores the fact that Jewish texts also contain ideas that conflict with Waskow's politics.

Alter is particularly troubled by the *Freedom Seder*'s references to "the *shofet* Eldridge Cleaver." Cleaver, a leader in the Black Panther Party, was a strong anti-Zionist at the time, expressing support for "Arab guerillas in the Middle East" and claiming that "Zionists, wherever they may be, are our enemies" (Dollinger 2018, 160–161). With tongue-in-cheek, Alter suggests that future editions of the Haggadah may feature "the appearance of the *shofet* Yassir Arafat." Although the text is "not explicitly anti-Zionist," Alter notes with disappointment that the words of the traditional Haggadah—"This year we celebrate here, but the next year we hope to celebrate in the land of Israel"—are immediately followed by the assertion that "where there is liberty, that is my country. That is my Israel." Whereas Waskow enthusiastically celebrates, for example, Black nationalism, in Alter's view, he sees the Jew as "obliged to be, first and last, a universalist" and shows little interest or empathy for the security challenges facing Israeli Jews. His primary concern is for "mankind." For this reason, Alter pronounces the *Freedom Seder* "a document of self-loathing and self-abasement masquerading as an expression of self-affirmation." This observation echoes the earlier critique of Jewish theologian and philosopher, Emil Fackenheim, who wondered why Waskow's concern for the world's oppressed does not include anxiety about the fate of Russian Jews or Jews still living in Iraq. According to Fackenheim, the *Freedom Seder* "denies to Jews alone in the name of Judaism the right to rise against their revilers and persecutors" (quoted in Staub 2002, 175).

Though separated by nearly 40 years, Hillel Halkin reaches similar conclusions about Jewish leftism in his review of the Jewish social justice anthology, *Righteous Indignation* (Halkin 2008). Like Alter, Halkin believes that the authors distort Jewish tradition, in this case by misrepresenting what the phrase "Tikkun Olam" (repairing the world) has meant historically; by arguing for the existence of a singular Jewish point of view on issues where the rabbinic tradition never put forth a coherent view (protecting the environment); or for pronouncing as Jewish, positions that outright contradict halakhah (on feminism, homosexuality). "Judaism has value to [leftist] Jews," says Halkin, "to the extent that it is useful, and it is useful to the extent that it can be made to conform to whatever beliefs and opinions they would have even if Judaism had never existed" (pp. 24–25). It would be more respectful and honest if the authors broke from the tradition rather than "coerce it into the service of contemporary causes" (p. 25). Moreover, like Alter's and Fackenheim's appraisal of Waskow's text, Halkin is troubled by the lack of focus on challenges particular to contemporary Jewish life.

> Just as the authors of these essays take almost no interest in the state of Israel, apart from chiding it for its various alleged faults ... so they take almost no interest in the American Jewish community except insofar as it is prepared to act outside of itself.
>
> *Halkin 2008, 26*

Although Halkin does not accuse the essayists of *Righteous Indignation* of "self-loathing and self-abasement" (p. 26) he does believe that their desire for "world repair now" reflects a dangerous Utopian view of human nature that ignores the complexity and cost of major societal change. A similar form of "messianic stance" (p. 26) among Jews, Halkin cautions, led to the destruction of the Second Temple in 70 CE and to the devastating Bar Kokhba Revolt of 65 years later.

Conclusion

The Jewish social justice writers and activists whose work I have presented here do not find such criticism convincing. First, as the editors of *Righteous Indignation* remark in their introduction to the book, the included authors are fully aware that Judaism is a multi-vocal tradition but believe that in emphasizing one perspective over another, they are acting in the spirit of the Jewish intellectual and rabbinic tradition (Rose *et al.* 2008, xv). Moreover, as Leonard Fein argued in the late 1980s, such interpretations of the tradition are essential to maintaining Judaism's relevance through time.

> It does not much matter, except to the curious, that when Rabbi Akiba, quoting Leviticus, said "Thou shalt love thy neighbor as thyself," he was almost surely referring exclusively to "thy Jewish neighbor." What matters is how we have chosen to understand the words. ... For our effort has been and must be to reach into our own souls, not into the minds of those who came before.
>
> *Fein 1988, 220–221*

Second, the majority of Jewish activists who engage Jewish tradition in their work are also, contrary to what Halkin implies, concerned about issues within the Jewish community. *Righteous Indignation* itself contains articles on the need to combat domestic violence within Jewish households, on the challenges facing multi-racial Jewish families, and on fighting anti-Semitism on the Left. These activists believe—again, in the words of the editors of *Righteous Indignation*—that "the American Jewish community has the creative, financial, and political resources to work on several fronts simultaneously" (Rose *et al.* 2008, xvi). It is only natural that one organization or individual might be more drawn to addressing universal issues, while another concentrates more time on particular concerns. And while the five articles on Israel-Palestine included in *Righteous Indignation* do contain significant criticisms of Israeli policy (and of other players in the region), they are written by people who are deeply engaged as Jews in the issues and active members of Jewish communities.

Halkin is undoubtedly correct that many of the policy positions of Jewish activists on the Left—and likely of those on the Right, as well—are ones they would have espoused "even if Judaism had never existed." But, as Michael E. Staub (2002, 7–8, 118) and David P. Shuldiner (1999, 77–78) have shown, Judaism, though not the impetus for Jewish social justice activism, plays a key role in justifying and sustaining political commitments by placing these in a rich narrative that transcends a particular moment but also speaks directly to it. This activism also serves to renew its participants' interest in Jewish text and ritual. Both the Jewish socialists of the first decades of the twentieth century that Shuldiner studies, and the activists of the 1960s that are the focus of Staub's work, were fairly alienated from the Jewish tradition until their activist path led them to look anew at the Hebrew Bible and to reconstruct rituals such as the Passover Seder. Liberal activists in both periods faced fierce opposition within certain sectors of the Jewish communal establishment and, specifically in the 1960s, found the "Jewishness" of their public policy positions questioned and branded as undermining the Jewish present and future. They responded to this critique by being even more emphatic in their assertions of personal Jewish identity and concern for the Jewish people, and they dug deeper into the Jewish tradition to find verses, rituals and historical moments that could support their political views. Like their predecessors, Jewish social justice activists will engage the Jewish tradition in their work in the coming years and in so doing will, as in the last decades, enrich the body of Jewish ritual.

Note

1 Weisberg compares Jews to white Americans because approximately 90% of America's Jews are white. See, in this regard, Ira M. Sheskin and Arnold Dashefsky, "An Open Letter to the Jewish Community: We Stand With Jews of Color," ejewishphilanthropy.com, May 26, 2020.

References

Achad Ha'am. 1912. "Priest and Prophet," *Selected Essays of Ahad Ha-Am*. Translated from the Hebrew, edited, and with an introduction by Leon Simon. Philadelphia: The Jewish Publication Society of America, 125–138.

Alter, Robert. 1971. "Revolutionism and the Jews: Appropriating the Religious Tradition," *Commentary* 51:2 (February): 47–54.

American Enterprise Institute (2020) "What We Know about Jews and the November Election," www.aei.org/politics-and-public-opinion/what-we-know-about-jews-and-the-november-election/ (accessed December 31, 2020).

Anisfeld, Sharon Cohen, Tara Mohr and Catherine Spector, eds. 2003. *The Women's Seder Sourcebook*. Woodstock, VT: Jewish Lights.

Balin, Carole B. 2008. "Moving Through the Movements: American Denominations and Their Haggadot," in *My People's Passover Haggadah Volume 1*, Lawrence A. Hoffman and David Arnow, eds. Woodstock, VT: Jewish Lights Publishing, 79–84.

Bell, Lee Anne. 2016. "Theoretical Foundations for Social Justice Education," in *Teaching for Diversity and Social Justice*, Maurianne Adams and Lee Anne Bell, eds. Taylor & Francis Group. *ProQuest Ebook Central*, https://ebookcentral.proquest.com/lib/mcgill/detail.action?docID=4355263 (accessed December 29, 2020).

Blidstein, Gerald J. 1997. "Tikkun Olam," in *Tikkun Olam: Social Responsibility in Jewish Thought and Law*, David Shatz, Chaim I. Waxman and Nathan J. Diament, eds. Northvale, NJ: Jason Aronson, Inc., 17–59.

Broner, E. M. and Naomi Nimrod. 1993. "The Women's Haggadah," in *The Telling*. San Francisco, CA: HarperCollins.

Central Conference of American Rabbis (CCAR). 1923. *The Union Haggadah: Home Service for Passover*.

Cohen, Steven M. and Arnold M. Eisen. 2000. *The Jew Within: Self, Family, and Community in America*. Bloomington & Indianapolis: Indiana University Press.

Dollinger, Marc. 2018. *Black Power, Jewish Politics: Reinventing the Alliance in the 1960s*. Boston, MA: Brandeis University Press.

Efron, John, Matthias Lehmann, and Steven Weitzman. 2018. *The Jews: A History*, Third Edition. New York: Routledge.

Elwell, Sue Levy ed. 2002. *The Open Door: A Passover Haggadah*. New York: Central Conference of American Rabbis.

Fein, Leonard. 1988. *Where Are We? The Inner Life of America's Jews*. New York: Harper & Row, Publishers.

Finn, Janet L. and Maxine Jacobson. 2008. "Social Justice," in *Encyclopedia of Social Work*, Oxford University Press. www-oxfordreference-com.proxy3.library.mcgill.ca/view/10.1093/acref/9780195306613.001.0001/acref-9780195306613-e-364 (accessed December 29, 2020).

Fishkoff, Sue. 2011. "From Oranges to Artichokes, Chocolate and Olives, Using Seder Plate as a Call to Action," www.jta.org/2011/04/12/lifestyle/from-oranges-to-artichokes-chocolate-and-olives-using-seder-plate-as-a-call-to-action (accessed January 13, 2021).

Halkin, Hillel. 2008. "How Not to Repair," *Commentary* (July/August), 21–27.

Heschel, Abraham Joshua. 1970. "On Prayer," in *Moral Grandeur and Spiritual Audacity: Essays*, Susannah Heschel, ed. (1996). New York: Farrar, Straus and Giroux, 261.

Heschel, Susannah. 2003."A Woman's Idea," in *The Women's Seder Sourcebook*, Sharon Cohen Anisfeld, Tara Mohr and Catherine Spector, eds. Woodstock, VT: Jewish Lights Publishing, 209–210.

Hirsch, Rabbi Samson Raphael. 1969. *The Nineteen Letters on Judaism*. New York and Jerusalem: Feldheim Publishers.

Hoffman, Lawrence A. 2008. "Peoplehood with Purpose: The American Seder and Changing Jewish Identity," in *My People's Passover Haggadah Volume 1*, Lawrence A. Hoffman and David Arnow, eds. Woodstock, VT: Jewish Lights Publishing, 47–69.

Jacobs, Jill. 2011. *Where Justice Dwells: A Hands-on Guide to Doing Social Justice in Your Jewish Community*. Woodstock, VT: Jewish Lights Publishing.

Kampeas, Ron. 2021. "Here are the 37 Jewish Members of Congress," Jewish Telegraph Agency, January 11, www.jta.org/2021/01/11/politics/here-are-the-36-jewish-members-of-congress?utm_source=JTA_Maropost&utm_campaign=JTA_DB&utm_medium=email&mpweb=1161-26400-34560 (accessed January 12, 2021).

Kaplan, Mordecai, Eugene Cohn and Ira Eisenstein, eds. 1941. *The New Haggadah*. New York: Behrman's Jewish Book House.

Kelman, Ari Y., Tobin Belzer, Ilana Horwitz, Ziva Hassenfeld and Matt Williams. 2017. "Traditional Judaism: The Conceptualization of Jewishness in the Lives of American Jewish Post-Boomers," *Jewish Social Studies* 23:1 (Fall): 134–167.

Kristof, Nicholas. 2018. "God and Her (Female) Clergy," *New York Times*, 31 March, www.nytimes.com/2018/03/31/opinion/sunday/easter-passover-god-women.html?rref=collection%2Fsectioncollection%2Fopinion-columnists&action=click&contentCollection=columnists&region=stream&module=stream_unit&version=latest&contentPlacement=5&pgtype=sectionfront (accessed January 13, 2021).

Levitt, Joy and Michael Strassfeld. 2000. *A Night of Questions: A Passover Haggadah*. Elkins Park, PA: The Reconstructionist Press.

Louis, Minnie D. 1894. "Mission-Work Among the Unenlightened Jews". *Papers of the Jewish Women's Congress*, Chicago September 4–7, 1893. Philadelphia: The Jewish Publication Society of America, 170–187.

Magid, Jacob. 2020. "Orthodox Jews Back Trump by Massive Margin, Poll Finds," *The Times of Israel*, October 15, www.timesofisrael.com/orthodox-jews-back-trump-by-massive-margin-poll-finds/ (accessed December 31, 2020).

Martin, Bernard. 1954. "The Social Philosophy of Emil G. Hirsch," *American Jewish Archives* (June): 151–165.

Messinger, Ruth and Aaron Dorfman. 2008."Am I My Brother's Keeper if My Brother Lives Halfway Around the Word?" in *Righteous Indignation: A Jewish Call for Justice*, Rabbi Or N. Rose, Jo Ellen Green Kaiser and Margie Klein, eds. Woodstock, VT: Jewish Lights Publishing, 281–292.

Nishmah Research. 2020. "A Political Survey of the American Orthodox Jewish Community," http://nishmaresearch.com/assets/pdf/Nishma%20Research%20Political%20Survey%20of%20the%20Orthodox%20Community%20Jan.%202020.pdf (accessed August 31, 2021).

Pew Research Center. 2013. "Portrait of Jewish Americans: Findings from a Pew Research Center Survey of U.S. Jews," www.pewforum.org/2013/10/01/jewish-american-beliefs-attitudes-culture-survey/ (accessed August 31, 2021).

Reboot. 2006. "'Grande Soy Vanilla Latte with Cinnamon, No Foam': Jewish Identity and Community in a Time of Unlimited Choices," www.bjpa.org/search-results/publication/329 (accessed August 31, 2021).

Rose, Rabbi Or N., Jo Ellen Green Kaiser and Margie Klein, eds. 2008. *Righteous Indignation: A Jewish Call for Justice*. Woodstock, VT: Jewish Lights Publishing.

Sacks, Jonathan. 2005. *To Heal a Fractured World: The Ethics of Responsibility*. Montreal: McGill-Queen's University Press.

Sarason, Richard S. 2015. "The Past as Paradigm: Enactments of the Exodus Motif in Jewish Liturgy," *Exodus in Jewish Experience: Echoes and Reverberations*, Pamela Barmesh and W. David Nelson, eds. Lanham, MD: Lexington Books, 53–110.

Sarna, Jonathan D. 2004. *American Judaism: A History*. New Haven, CT: Yale University Press.

Schindler, Judith and Judy Seldin-Cohen. 2018. *Recharging Judaism: How Civic Engagement Is Good for Synagogues, Jews, and America*. New York: Central Conference of American Rabbis.
Shuldiner, David P. 1999. *Of Moses and Marx: Folk Ideology and Folk History in the Jewish Labor Movement*. Westport, CT: Bergin & Garvey.
Staub, Michael E. 2002. *Torn at the Roots: The Crisis of Jewish Liberalism in Postwar America*. New York: Columbia University Press.
Steinhardt Social Research Institute, Brandeis University. 2019. "American Jewish Population Project: Summary and Highlights," https://ajpp.brandeis.edu/documents/2019/JewishPopulationDataBrief2019.pdf (accessed August 31, 2021).
T'ruah: The Rabbinic Call for Human Rights. 2019. "A Tomato on the Seder Plate," www.truah.org/wp-content/uploads/2019/04/Tomato-on-the-Seder-Plate-2019.pdf (accessed January 13, 2021).
Waskow, Arthur. 1970. *The Freedom Seder: A New Haggadah for Passover*. Washington, DC: The Micah Press.
Waskow, Arthur. 1971. *The Bush Is Burning*. New York: The Macmillan Company, 11–29.
Weinfeld, Morton. 2018. *Like Everyone Else but Different: The Paradoxical Success of Canadian Jews*. Second edition. Montreal: McGill-Queens University Press.
Weisberg, Herbert F. 2019. *The Politics of American Jews*. Ann Arbor, MI: University of Michigan Press.
Yanklowitz, Rabbi Dr. Shmuly. 2014. *The Soul of Jewish Social Justice*. Jerusalem and New York: Urim Publications, 21–27.
Zierler, Wendy I. 2008. "Where Have All the Women Gone? Feminist Questions About the Haggadah". *My People's Passover Haggadah Volume 1*, Lawrence A. Hoffman and David Arnow, eds. Woodstock, VT: Jewish Lights, 71–77.

19
THE AMERICAN JEWISH FAMILY

David C. Dollahite, Trevan G. Hatch, and Loren D. Marks

The authors are family scholars who study the nexus of religion and family relationships (Dollahite and Marks, 2020; Marks, Hatch, and Dollahite, 2018). We have conducted in-home, in-depth interviews (about two hours each) with 30 Jewish couples and families across several states. In this chapter we share many first-person quotations about ritual and practice in Jewish families from three major branches of Judaism: Conservative, Orthodox, and Reform. A unique aspect of these quotes is that a number are from observant Jewish children, youth, and young adults, a group that has been largely overlooked in studies of Jewish family life. The first and third authors have studied and published on American religious families, including Jewish families, for over 25 years. The authors are not Jewish, however, the first author spent a year studying prayer book Hebrew at a synagogue and six months studying Torah and Talmud with a Chabad rabbi. The second author has graduate training (master and doctoral level) in programs of Jewish studies at three Jewish institutions (Dollahite and Marks, 2018; Hatch and Marks, 2019; Marks and Dollahite, 2021; Marks et al., 2018).

Toward More Familial Judaism

Cohen and Eisen (2000) suggested that younger generations of Jews seem to be honoring their heritage and observing their religion in the home, with family. Jewish young adults, similar to young adults in general (Smith, 2009), appear to be moving away from the "organizations, institutions, and causes that used to anchor identity and shape behavior" for previous generations (Cohen and Eisen, 2000, p. 2). Goldscheider (2004) similarly acknowledged that Jews have generally become "less attached to religious activities and institutions" (p. 100). The family seems to be filling the vacuum. Goldscheider further argued that Judaism is not in decline as many have suggested, but that Judaism is in transition, or transformation.

This transformation has consisted of a movement away from communal institutions to the family, although in conjunction with communal institutions, and that the family has become "a central feature of Jewish continuity" (p. 127). Cohen (1999) similarly argued that Jewish identity has undertaken salient transformations. Jews in North America, he posited, now feel free to appropriate and incorporate into their individual lives only those aspects of Jewish culture and religion that are personally meaningful, which tend to be more relevant to the family and the home (Cohen and Eisen, 2000).

In the closing pages of his book, *Studying the Jewish Future*, one of the most notable sociologists of world Jewry, Calvin Goldscheider (2004), wrote the following:

> While family values and cohesion are central to the understanding of contemporary Jewish communities, few sociological studies have had a family focus. ... When we focus on family, we tend to measure only group processes of fertility and family structure, yet we have argued theoretically for the power of networks as a basis for continuity among ethnic populations. We need to refocus on the future of family networks. ...
>
> How do we conceptualize the Jewish family? Too often we start (and end) with indicators of family deterioration. We need to study how Jewish families strengthen their communities.
>
> Goldscheider, 2004, pp. 134–137

Need for In-depth Qualitative Exploration of Jewish Families

Scholars have discussed how to carry out family-centered research. Brodbar-Nemzer wrote in 1988 that the field of contemporary Jewish studies has been waiting for an "in-depth qualitative observational study of the American Jewish family" (p. 68). Understanding Jewish family processes, argued Brodbar-Nemzer (1988), "requires in-depth, largely qualitative approaches" (p. 72). Goldscheider (2002) acknowledged that a serious focus on Jewish families "has been conspicuously absent from our research agenda" (p. 207). "The top item on our research agenda for the next decade," he continued, "should be the systematic study of family relationships" (p. 208). Like Brodbar-Nemzer (1988), Goldscheider (2002, 2004) petitioned researchers to employ qualitative methods to examine the processes, meanings, and roles of Jewish families.

Steven Cohen, another leading sociologist of American Jewry, argued that new research questions and methods are required for studying the Jewish population. He suggested that this new approach must involve individuals and families using qualitative methods: "Quantitative methods alone cannot grasp the ways in which contemporary American Jews follow and depart from the attitudes, behaviors, and conflicts that they witnessed as children" (Cohen and Eisen, 2000, p. 3). Cohen and Eisen (2000) subsequently stressed the importance of studying contemporary American religion, and especially contemporary American Jewry, using "first-person narration" (p. 3).

Two monographs have been published since these scholars called for more in-depth, qualitative research on Jewish families more than 15 years ago. In the first monograph, published in 2013, Jonathan Boyarin provides, not a systematic social science treatment, an overview, or a history of Jewish family life, but

> explain[s] many of the underlying present-day concerns, both social and intellectual, that are shared by scholars in various disciplines as they try to understand, contrast, and compare the family patterns of Jews in many different times and places with their fellow Jews and with the non-Jewish populations among whom they live.
>
> Boyarin, 2013, p. xii

This resource is valuable for historians and scholars of Jewish studies in general, as it provides an array of historical snapshots, a "smorgasbord," of the Jewish family (p. xiv) that engages the usual issues such as identity, varieties of Jewish experience, and Jews' relation to the State of Israel.

The second volume, published in 2018, does explore the modern Jewish family from a social scientific perspective. Pomson and Schnoor (2018) conducted a ten-year longitudinal study with 16 diverse families (namely, single parents, intermarried couples, same-sex couples) from Toronto, Canada. They examined important issues such as family formation, various life-cycle experiences, Jewish day school, divorce, intermarriage, and home-based family ritual.

Our research complements the Pomson and Schnoor (2018) study. While we have not published a definitive monograph on Jewish families, we have conducted in-depth interviews with 30 observant Jewish families (60 spouses and 15 of their children) as part of our work in the American Families of Faith Project, which has produced a doctoral dissertation and six articles and book chapters to date (including the current chapter) exclusively on twenty-first-century Jewish families (Hatch, 2015; Hatch and Marks, 2014a; Hatch and Marks, 2014b; Hatch and Marks, 2019; Kelley et al., 2019; Marks and Dollahite, 2021; Marks, Hatch, and Dollahite, 2018) and more than 100 articles and two books that include in-depth study of Jewish families along with families from various other religious communities.

Jewish Families in the American Families of Faith Project

The American Families of Faith Project[1] is an ongoing two-decade national research project that involves in-depth interviews with nearly 300 families including 25–35 families each from the following 11 religious-ethnic communities: Asian American Christian, Black Christian, Catholic and Orthodox Christian, Evangelical Christian, Hispanic Christian, Jewish, Latter-day Saint, Mainline Protestant, Muslim, Interfaith, and Unaffiliated. Most of the more than 100 scholarly publications from the project include direct quotations from Jewish wives, husbands, and youth drawn from the 30 Jewish families we interviewed.

The rest of this chapter provides extensive quotations from Jewish women, men, and their adolescent or young adult children gathered in our interviews and published in various studies. Because of space constraints and because we highly value presenting the voices of those whom we interviewed, we will not provide in-depth introduction to or analyses of the quotations. Readers who wish to further place the words of our Jewish participants in richer context are invited to visit the studies from which the quotations are taken. In this chapter, we include brief discussion of the following topics: religious identity, balancing religious continuity and agency, religious exploration among youth, parent–youth religious conversations, religious sacrifices made by youth, sources of religious commitment, religious firmness and flexibility, how religion unites and divides families, relational reconciliation processes, relational struggles, relational benefits from religious ritual and tradition, regular family prayer, and Shabbat practices and family processes.

Religious Identity Issues

In a study on identity-centered religious being and action (Dollahite, Marks, Kear, et al., 2018) we discovered the importance that many religious parents place on being authentic in their parenting. Leah,[2] a Conservative Orthodox Jewish mother, said,

> I presented to [our children] an ever-expanding view of Judaism and that I was always honest about my angers with the religion, angers with the Rabbis, my own distress about the religion. [I wanted them to know] that whatever I chose to give them from the more Orthodox approach was something that I really believed in.

Eli, a Modern Jewish Orthodox father, similarly said that he wanted "to provide an … authentic … minimally-conflicted example of faith and behavior" for his children.

Parents described various ways they try to transmit their faith and sacred traditions to their children. A mother named Ariella explained the importance of teaching her children religious traditions:

> [I] try to pass on the traditions that are special and that are important. You know, how to make meals for the holidays. [Also, to] go to *shul*. My focus, I guess, is what happens at home. I mean we go to *shul* as a family. I go to *shul*, sometimes alone and sometimes the kids come with me. But in the house what I teach them is: This is how you set a *Shabbas* table, and these are the foods that you prepare for a traditional Sabbath meal, these are the foods that you prepare for a traditional Rosh Hashanah, which is [the] New Year's [celebration]. … I think teaching them how to make a Jewish home [is important], so that when they have a Jewish home, [they won't have] to look in a book.

Ron, a Conservative father, said,

> In terms of Judaism, [I want] to give [our children] a sense that this is a tradition that is worth preserving. To show them by example, and by instruction, that this is a tradition that commands respect, that deserves to be perpetuated, and that they have a responsibility to perpetuate it. But not out of … obligation, but that this is worth doing. That it'll be a positive influence in their lives. This is part of the self-definition that we embarked on [in our marriage] 22 years ago. We [want to] set something in front of them that they would *want* to take, to be a part of themselves. I think it is of paramount importance that this tradition continue, and it can only continue by positive example. So the children have to see something there that's worth doing.

Eli, a Modern Orthodox father, said that he likewise felt a duty "to transmit the tradition in as far as I understand it." In terms of teaching religious identity, a mother named Hannah reportedly wanted "to connect my children with Jewish history; [to] make them understand *their* part of it." She mentioned specifically her children's identity as pertaining to their religion. Saul, a father, similarly discussed the importance of his children's Jewish identity:

> The most important thing I would like to give my kids is the desire … to grow in their Jewish identity; the desire that they should grow in deeper interest in knowing who they are; the scripture of Torah and learning it; the desire to pursue it.

Balancing Religious Continuity and Agency

In a study on how religious families balance parents' desire for religious continuity with honoring their children's religious agency (Barrow, Dollahite, and Marks, 2020), we found that the importance religious parents placed on religious continuity often stemmed from a belief that religion was protective and might help children resolve challenges or make better life decisions.

Ephraim, a Conservative father, expressed his and his wife's desire to pass on their faith to future generations:

It's very important to us. What's tough is that we don't control [it]. I don't think there is anything … to the core of being Jewish, [that] we would want more than our children, God willing, our grandchildren, and their offspring, to be Jewish and have the same values.

Rachel, an Orthodox mother, and Levi, her 14-year-old son, described a process of balancing religious expectations with allowing children autonomy:

RACHEL: I think that, I think it's such a juggling act, that you want to …
LEVI: Balance it out.
RACHEL: Yeah, balance it out … Somebody once said to me …, "You have to have some … damage control, and at the same time, you want to also awaken in him the feelings for positive things." So, in other words … choose your battles. And each child, the Torah tells us that you have to educate the child according to his will. I think a major parenting tip there … you can have family rules, but you have to know that within the family, you're going to have so many individuals. And every rule has to be custom-made to the individual.

Caleb, a Reform father, expressed his view that it's important to let children learn for themselves by occasionally making mistakes. He said,

There's an expression that I try to keep with me, "the blessing of a skinned knee." The idea is that sometimes, the only way for a child to learn is for the child to do something and to fail at it. The old joke, "Doctor, it hurts when I do this." Then the doctor says, "Well, don't do that." The idea that sometimes you have to let your kids … experience pain to learn and to grow, and that we have to allow them … to experience pain.

Miriam, a Conservative mother, spoke with her daughter about the importance of allowing children to have different experiences and see different outcomes:

I think it's good to expose kids, sometimes, to the extremes and then let them see what that's like and then later in life they can choose what they want to do. But if they don't know what's out there, it's sometimes hard to know what your choices are.

Michael, a 14-year-old son, spoke of his parents' acceptance of his religious choices:

I think that you guys have brought us up in a way that I feel that I could choose to continue with Judaism or I could … really, I have the intentions of continuing Judaism, but I still have a long time so something could change. But I feel that you guys would be accepting of any choice that I would make.

Religious Exploration among Youth

In a study of religious exploration among highly religious American adolescents (Layton, Hardy, and Dollahite, 2012), a 12-year-old daughter spoke of the things she had learned in her Torah class about the story of Noah and the ark and how that stretched her to ask questions about things she had never considered before. She expressed that talking about and writing essays about the human aspects of Bible stories had broadened her mind about what she believed and how it applied to her life. A 14-year-old son said of his religious instruction and the exploration it has facilitated, "I've learned so much since I've been going to Chabad. I mean it's almost like trying to put your brain to think and understand what it's like to be a Jew."

A 20-year-old son reflecting back on his experience with religious exploration shared, "After the age of about 13–14, I did a bit of a teenage rebel thing and got less religious and went out to explore the world and see what there was."

Leaving home, generally for educational opportunities, was often a catalyst for religious exploration. Another 20-year-old son reflected on an experience earlier in his life about leaving home for religious education and exploring:

> Right after I turned 13, like two weeks after my bar mitzvah I convinced my parents to let me go down to a school in L.A. for Yeshiva, and so I spent a year living away from home for the first time in my life and … it was just getting away from home for the first time in my life. Also, when I got to Yeshiva coming from a community like this I had no idea what to expect. … I think that led to … a re-examination of things that wouldn't have happened had I been at home.

Adolescents and parents often don't agree, but that seems to be an important part of religious exploration. One 20-year-old son expressed that the difference of opinion and the related tensions in conversation were a normal part of his religious experience. He said, "You argue about it constantly, you try to figure out the real answer to various questions of what you should do about it. … It is of course, Judaism, and everyone disagrees about everything."

The experience of traveling to religious places often influenced developing faith. This was particularly true for Jewish youth. One 19-year-old son described, "Being in Israel definitely, it helped me. … [L]earning … why I was there. Reading a lot, it just, it helped me think that I want to be religious, I don't want to do anything else."

Because careful, sustained spiritual and religious exploration was typical for many Jewish youth, we include an extensive excerpt from Debra, a 17-year-old daughter. From the beginning of her interview she was very clear about her active exploration regarding her belief in God. She reported,

> I should probably say, just kind of in the beginning, that I'm still figuring out my definition of God, and that I do believe in some sort of higher faith, higher being, higher power. It would be very lonely, if it turned out there wasn't one. I'm not exactly sure what it is.

In spite of uncertainty, Debra was firmly committed in her faith tradition. Her interview revealed past exposure to and exploration of different branches of Judaism:

> We have relatives who are Modern Orthodox, we have friends who are Reformed. You know, I've been on the retreats. … I've been to Israel. I think if there's ever a lesson in diversity and getting along with people that are similar to you but not exactly the same, I would say Judaism has taught it to me more than anything and I think that goes with my parents for exposing me to so many different branches of Judaism.

Religious exploration occurs in different seasons for different youth, and commitment and confidence in the present moment may be the result of prior exposure and exploration. Debra continued and described her faith both in present and future terms by saying, "If I have kids, they're definitely being raised Jewish. … I feel that I'm secure enough in knowing that being Jewish is important to me."

She also reflected on her commitment to her traditions and rituals:

> I don't think that I could commit to spend the rest of my life with somebody who was just as devoted to raising their children a different faith. … People are like, "Oh, they could have a Christmas tree, and a Menorah." And I'm not really for that, I think that that's really confusing. … If I were to marry a non-Jewish spouse, it would have to be somebody who was either willing to convert, willing to attend things, even though if they didn't feel comfortable entirely, willing to attend things with me and support our children being raised [Jewish].

An interesting interface between the certainty of commitment and the insecurity of exploration is captured in Debra's discussion about her experience in visiting Israel,

> I just think that going to Israel … solidified me as being Jewish, at least for now, because I think I haven't really had my religious or spiritual … awakening or epiphany yet. I don't think that part has entirely clicked, 'cause like I said earlier, I'm just searching for what I think the higher power is, but I think Israel's come closer to that … it's my closest connection, right now.

Debra captured well a sense of peace with the dialectic of commitment and exploration that many youth, particularly Jewish ones, reported.

Parent–Youth Religious Conversations

In a study of parent–youth religious conversations (Dollahite and Thatcher, 2008), Rachel, an Orthodox mother, explained that even when they initially gave their children a chance to talk but then took over the conversation, the children did not always listen:

> We have relaxed conversation at the table, and then, we, either my husband or myself, after ten minutes we tell the kids to hold onto their chair, just try to listen. And they don't always listen as well as we'd like them to listen and they sometimes are like "blah, blah, blah."

Some families reported that when religious conversation was too restrictive for the adolescent children, it was a negative experience. Rachel, a 38-year-old Orthodox mother of seven learned that "If [they] have to sit rigidly—the children of all ages, and … you have this long lecture, it can actually be a very negative influence. The kids will feel restricted."

Rachel shared her discovery that, with their adolescent children, parents needed to listen more and talk less: "We find the older kids get, they have so much to say, and … after a whole day of school, they come home and they don't want to hear us talk, they want to talk."

Some Jewish families explained that openness and even constructively and warmly arguing were a welcomed and positive part of their culture. Ariella, a 42-year-old Conservative mother of two, said, "Jews are very open. They always tell it like it is. They're just open, they're out there. No one holds back anything." Esther, a 12-year-old Conservative girl explained, "Well, it's kind of a stereotypical thing that we [Jewish families] argue a lot, but it's true."

To borrow a phrase from the late Jewish scholar, Barbara Myerhoff, "We fight to keep warm" (1980, p. 153).

Religious Sacrifices Made by Youth

In a study of the types of sacrifices that religious youth reportedly made and the reasons they gave for making such sacrifices (Dollahite et al., 2009), we found that Jewish youth were passionate and articulate about the ways they sacrificed for their faith, often in the face of peer and cultural pressures. An 18-year-old Modern Orthodox young man:

> Like all the stuff we said before, we can't do on Shabbat. And I could, if I wasn't Jewish. And being at college where there's all people doing all this kind of stuff. And if I wasn't Jewish, I would … do it with them.

A 15-year-old Modern Orthodox boy:

> Not being able to watch TV on holidays and Shabbat, just like if I wasn't Jewish, I would. Like the sports games that are on Friday nights, Celtics games I don't watch, if they're on Friday night. But because I'm Jewish, and I'm observant, I didn't, even though I wanted to.

An 18-year-old Conservative young man:

> It's a net gain. … Yeah, of course you give up some things, but that doesn't mean … like what one gets in return, it more than compensates. It doesn't have to [just] be about religion, you know. Is it a sacrifice not to sleep around after you get married? Yeah, but it's definitely worth it. Right? Look what you get in return, it gives you a solid marriage and a lasting [marriage] … so really, that's a good deal.

One Jewish young woman remarked about the positive sense of identity and unity within her family that she feels is linked to the religious sacrifices she makes. She said, "Well, it's worth it because being Jewish is very special and we're different and I kind of like that a little bit. And I'm willing to make sacrifices so I can be Jewish."

Sources of Religious Commitment

In a study on the sources of religious commitment (Layton, Dollahite, and Hardy, 2011), Jewish parents and youth were among the more articulate in describing how various aspects of their faith tied them to Jewish tradition. This distinction was evident in how some youth spoke of traditional celebrations. For example, a ten-year-old girl named Leah explained the ritual celebrations that gave meaning to her experience of faith:

> Well, I like Rosh Hashanah because it's just, it's cool to be, well it's fun to be able to miss school and everybody says, "Well, where were you?" And you say, "I was celebrating New Year." And they say, "No, the New Year is in January," or something like that. Yom Kippur is fun because I get to see how far I can fast, and every year it

gets longer. ... Sukkah is fun because it's festive and it's on my birthday ... And I like Hanukkah ... it's just, it's fun to be able to light your own menorah, and to invite friends over to come do it with you ... and Purim is fun because you get to dress up, and Pesach is fun because the whole family's there.

Leah's descriptions of these events show that it is not only the religious meaning behind the celebrations that matters, but also the traditional and familial aspects of the celebrations. In particular, Leah focused on the "fun" experiences and the relational aspects of the traditions, such as being with "the whole family."

A 17-year-old son explained that his religious commitment has changed and he only attends for "high holy days." He said,

After bar mitzvah, I've only really gone, I've gone to temple not really that much. ... [I] stopped going to the classes. And I've only really been going on the high holy days and some bar mitzvahs. I mean if it's a bar mitzvah I'm invited to, then I go to their service. But after that, it's definitely dropped off after my bar mitzvah.

Others, however, were more deeply invested. An awareness of and commitment to the laws of his religion was described by a 20-year-old son:

Judaism is a very legal religion, and if you are dedicated to following [the laws] then it's, then there practically isn't any aspect of your life that isn't going to be affected. You can't separate the other things that you do from the religious things that you do. There really isn't any separation.

This commitment to the laws and the external behaviors associated with those laws was a salient part of the religious commitment for some youth. Other youth acknowledged the laws of the religious tradition even though they did not observe them.

When asked if his religious beliefs influenced his lifestyle, including food and media, a 17-year-old son stated, "Not really. We don't keep kosher." Conversely, a 12-year-old daughter explained why she is willing to sacrifice for her faith, "Well, it's worth it because being Jewish is very special and we're different. ... And I'm willing to make sacrifices so I can be Jewish, more Jewish than I can be if I don't do it."

A common way youth spoke of the commitment to their faith tradition or denomination was as a source of authority to guide or inform their choices. This is illustrated by a 20-year-old Orthodox son: "I go about my life and yet Judaism is always right there at this side of my mind, but it's not necessarily the guiding force so much as the informing force."

In relation to how parents anchored youth and young adults to the faith, a 20-year-old Orthodox son explained his father's commitment to the faith tradition and how that has influenced him:

He tells me that he very strongly felt ... I think he's someone who feels very much sensitive to the Holocaust and having lived right at that time, just after it, that he felt sort of the weight of all of the sacrifice that had been made for three thousand years, so that a father could pass to their son, [and] to their son, [and] to their son, the knowledge that we're Jewish and this is what it means.

Enjoying a sense of community and the feeling of family was the most common way youth experienced their commitment to the congregation. This was expressed by a 17-year-old

Orthodox daughter, whose commitment to having a strong community of believers influenced her decision regarding where she wanted to attend college:

> I visited the Chabad [Jewish Student Center] on campus. I went to a barbecue there, I met the rabbi. I really liked the family and that has really dictated why I'm going there. Just the religious community that surrounds it.

A 12-year-old daughter expressed that the fun and social aspects of Judaism influenced her commitment:

> I think it's really fun to have Shabbat with a lot of other families that are Jewish. And just meeting with them and … speaking about stuff. I'd also have to say things where there's a big quantity of people for me, [that] is most fun because I like it when everybody sings songs and stuff like that at Passover.

Fun was also important for a 14-year-old son who described the reason for his renewed commitment to religion:

> The first time when my parents took me to [synagogue], my Mom came downstairs and was dancing around the *bimah* [Torah podium]. … I was having a fun time. And so after *kiddushin* [prayer of sanctification] and everything else, after dinner I said to my Mom, 'Can we come back here again?' And so that's when I started getting more and more religious.

Religious Firmness and Flexibility

In a study on how parents balance religious firmness with religious flexibility (Dollahite, Marks, Babcock, et al., 2019), Abigail, a Reform mother, shared her family's flexibility with rituals:

> And because we're tired on Friday night, we don't get to synagogue as much as we want to. And, because of other time commitments, there's just never enough time to do as much as maybe we should for the Jewish community.

Ariella, a Conservative mother, shared a similar experience about her children's desire to perform their family sacred rituals. She said,

> We do the same rituals for our holidays and all our Sabbath activities and you know, a lot of times we have to nag them and pull them into things, but if we *don't* do something or if something is missed or if we say, "We are not going to do Shabbat," [then] they say, "What do you mean we're not doing it!?" [with animation] … They'll get mad that we don't do it. They're upset because it's not the way it usually is. They get upset if we don't hallow [the Sabbath]. It's very interesting. Sometimes they act like we are annoying them by dragging them through the ritual but if we don't have it there for them they get upset by it. … The religion provides a lot of strength and comfort and structure.

As was the case in most of the Jewish families we interviewed, children in Ariella's family made it clear that some degree of consistency and predictability in religious rituals is important.

Another mother, Miriam, shared her view about certain Jewish perspectives on gender in worship:

> I have a problem with gender roles [in] religion in general, so I ignore them. I don't abide by them or whatever. Like in Orthodox [Judaism], I'm often, not offended, but it's just that I don't agree with the idea of having women and men separated during ceremonies. Women are not allowed on the bimah [podium from which Torah is read] and you can't listen to a woman's solo voice and I just don't believe in that part of it.

A few participants, however, were not only less than fully reconciled to their faith's "institutional" beliefs, they were diametrically opposed to some beliefs and practices. One Orthodox father reported that, despite his connection to much of Jewish tradition, some aspects that he perceived as unnecessarily rigid were "anathema" to him. Elijah, another father, explained that in spite of his high level of both personal and synagogue-level involvement, "I profoundly disagree with institutional Judaism."

How Religion Unites and Divides Families

In a study of how religion can be both a unifying and divisive influence in families (Kelley, Marks, and Dollahite, 2019), Ziva, a no-longer-practicing Catholic who was raising her children Jewish, explained the concern her "very, very" Catholic father felt for her:

> [My father] thinks that I've given up something very big. … My father doesn't ever say anything about it, so it's not like it's an argument between us, but I know that he is concerned, because he is a very, very, deeply religious person.

As illustrated by the previous account, religion appeared to be a source of division for the father and the adult daughter.

A mother named Moriah similarly explained how her husband's non-religious parents struggled to understand their religious involvement and commitment. She stated, "[My husband's] parents, being non-religious, think [he has] given up a lot, because they don't understand what [he gets] out of … all the traditional things that we do. They don't see how it could possibly enrich [our lives]."

Our study identified gender-based practices as often having a unifying influence on parent–child relationships, as they appeared to provide important bonding between fathers and sons, or mothers and daughters. A mother named Basha said,

> When our kids were younger we did Shabbat dinners every Friday night and it was really fun for all of us I think. My daughter would run upstairs and put on her special Shabbat clothes and she and I would make *challah* [braided bread] together.

Whether it was a mother and daughter making *challah* together, or sons accompanying their fathers to pray, these gender-based religious practices often provided one-on-one time between fathers and sons and mothers and daughters.

A common conflict our sample dealt with were sports or other events that took place during Shabbat, their worship services, or other family practices. Dmisha, a mother, described how the activities her oldest daughter wanted to do with friends on Shabbat created conflict:

> We had a rule for the girls. The oldest one was old enough to date and go out and she wanted to go out on Fridays. I mean, she basically didn't want to come home on Friday. She wanted to go to the football games and date and do things and I said, "No. It's *Shabbat*. You come home. You have friends you want to be with? Invite them. We'll feed them too! And you will be with the family until 8 or 8:30 at night and then after that you can go out." And that was just looked upon as terribly restrictive.

Beyond feeling restricted by religious practices, children also expressed feelings of embarrassment and isolation from their peers, and these feelings often led to conflict with their parents. Sarah, a daughter, recalled why religious practices led her to struggle with her parents:

> It was a struggle. I don't want to go to services. None of my friends have to go to services on Saturdays, or … to … a boring Bar Mitzvah, I don't want to go. Nobody else I know has to go. … I think, the strongest sort of challenges … come from when you feel like being Jewish isolates you from your friends, or isolates you from the surrounding area, or that having any sort of strong faith isolates you.

The Jewish community can be a unifying influence for parents and children. One mother described how her religious community provided bonding time with her children by creating a shared social group:

> [Judaism] defines our social circle, … the majority of our friends are Jewish because we go there for Friday night dinners or they come here. We share holidays together, and so it defines again who we are, who our friends are, who our kids' friends are.

Efrem, a father, similarly described how his Jewish community helped him be more connected with his children and be more aware of their social life. In response to a question regarding how his involvement in religion had influenced his parenting, he said, "Being … an active part of a larger community just helps me see the connection between our kids and our family and the community and then thereby, our kids in the community."

Relational Reconciliation Processes

In a study of how religion can help families achieve relational reconciliation after conflict or distance (Dollahite, Marks, and Barrow, 2019), many reported that being able to see a bigger picture beyond the immediate conflict was a motivation for reconciliation. Saul, a husband, described how setting goals during Yom Kippur helped him and his wife Ruth desire to change and improve their relationship.

> Both of us always have something [in our Yom Kippur goals] about being a better spouse—stop yelling at each other or whatever we do. … There is some sense that a religious observance helps us to keep our focus on the big picture and reminds us of things we want to change. … If we didn't do that ritual, I don't think we would have the opportunity to say, "These are things I want to do better."

Bekah, a wife, described how her husband's ability to admit faults was an example to her and how his example benefited their marriage.

I think one of the strong points of Judaism is the sense of personal responsibility, and certainly in any conflict we've had, it's been really important to own up to whatever part we have in the conflict. And that's something that comes straight from Judaism, … [the] thought of "Did I do something wrong? And if so, I need to fix it, and apologize for it." As opposed to just, "Well, it'll go away, forget about it." And that's one of the things that I really admire about [my husband] Jerry is that he will always apologize. He will always say, "I'm wrong." I talk to a lot of friends who say, "My husband never says he's sorry. He'll do nice things, he'll go on from there, but he'll never say he's sorry." I think Jerry was raised with a sense of ownership for what he's done, and so I try to learn from him.

Relational Struggles

In a study of relational struggles in religious families (Dollahite, Marks, and Young, 2019), some participants felt that the religious teaching required of them was either unpleasant or difficult. Gabriella, a Conservative mother, said,

[One] challenge is that I have to teach our children about our history and [the] history of persecution. … That's not something that I look forward to. I have talked to them about the Holocaust and those discussions will go on for a lifetime at different levels.

Many couples stated that distance and disunity in the marriage occurred if a wife and husband had differing beliefs or levels of commitment. Hannah, speaking to her husband, Eli, stated,

But wasn't this actually, without our knowing it, all part of Hashem's [God's] plan? … You know, we didn't like it. We suffered, because we were unhappy, because we weren't on the same path, right? But obviously this was how it was intended to work itself out so that instead of you and me going divergent roads over it, we had to work together and find a place where we could be comfortable with each other and build a Jewish home together.

Participants reported relational struggles from differences in religious belief or practice. Seth, a husband, reported, "(Two of my brothers) married persons out of the faith and I don't think they'll have much religion of any sort now. … I mean, my parents love them very much but it *hurt* my parents." Seth later explained, "When we are all sitting around at the [ritual-filled] holidays. … There's a certain framework for life and marriage in Judaism … they [the non-Jewish family members] just don't get it."

Relational Benefits from Ritual and Tradition

In a study summarizing the relational benefits of Jewish ritual and tradition (Kelley et al., 2018), we found that specific Jewish practices and rituals influenced how couples and families interacted with each other. Jewish rituals and traditions enabled families to celebrate times of joy and to cope with difficulty, pain, and loss. A Reform youth named Caleb shared how ritual helped him cope with the violent death of his uncle:

I had an uncle who was murdered. … I found comfort [in] the ritual that's associated with death. [It] really helped me deal with the suddenness and the sadness of it. …

> The burial ritual, the funeral ritual, the *Shiva* ritual of staying at home [with family] for seven days … are things that helped me cope in the short term. And during the service … the *Kaddish* prayer … the prayer for memory [or] prayer for the dead, [was] very comforting for me. It's not that I necessarily believe that there is a G-d listening to my prayers. It's more that the comfort of doing something that I've done all of my life has made it comfortable and given me the space to deal with those kinds of trying situations.

Tevia, a Reform husband, explained how sharing Judaism had unified his marriage to Naomi:

> There's a lot of stuff I think we take for granted about our relationship in terms of knowing that we're on the same page with stuff. We don't even need to talk about it. … We're on the same page. … We just know that if [my wife] said, "I want to stay home this Saturday and just observe *Shabbat* [at home]," she knows I'm there. If she wanted to do something at the synagogue, we go.

The role of ritual and sacred "routine" was discussed by an Orthodox wife, Asha. In response to the question, "Are there ways that your religious beliefs or practices help you to avoid or reduce marital conflict?" Asha responded,

> The first thing that comes to mind is the routine. And another thing that I've come to understand and believe is that religious belief and truly religious moments don't just come from … nowhere. One has to be in the habit of religious practice and religious observance. … If you wait for the mood to hit you, it never will. But if you go, if you observe, if you practice, on a regular … basis, then you're open to G-d. … I think that our routine of going to synagogue every week, that it is something we do whether we really feel like it or not … it is what we chose to do. It's about the Sabbath. It's what you do on the Sabbath. It is such a calming experience, [even] when tensions are high, when frustration is high.

Uriel, a Conservative husband, explained how the Jewish teaching and aspiration of *shalom bayis* helped him and his wife resolve conflict:

> The Jewish version of domestic tranquility, of amity in the home, what Jews call *shalom bayis*, peace in the home, is a very big concept in Jewish thinking. It is not the notion of a compliant wife who will go along with everything a guy says, and therefore they have peace. … It's quite the opposite. They both know how to argue, they both hold their own. I think it's precisely because we can argue that we can do well. … That's the secret.

The observance of Shabbat reportedly facilitated peacefull parent–child relationships. Lila, a Reform mother, explained, "[Talking] about Jewish values as a family … Shabbat … pausing and coming together … [helps us] when conflict arises because we are all there … together as a family."

Pesha, a mother, reported feeling closer with her children during weekly parent–child blessings:

> Blessing the children on Friday night … is a special time when the parents bless the children. It is a beautifully wonderful and tender moment that we … do and our children have come to expect. [We don't just] put our hands on their heads and we bless

them ... we also each [say] something to each child about something that we're proud of that they've done this week. It's just a wonderful thing that ... we didn't make that up. ... [I]f we just look at what our tradition teaches us, it was already there. Jewish parents have been doing that for thousands of years.

Many participants, including parents and children, stated that in Judaism parent–child relational success is a shared responsibility. Benjamin, a 20-year-old Orthodox son; Deborah, his 17-year-old sister; Hannah, their mother; and Eli, their father, discussed this idea:

BENJAMIN (SON): [My family] argue[s] over little things all the time, of course, like anybody. But we've never had any serious, emotional arguments that disrupted general family life. I'm sure that Judaism has a lot to do with that ... because you have laws governing how you're supposed to act towards your parents and towards your children. And when you have a legal system, almost, [that prescribes] in what ways you can respond, you aren't so totally at sea, as many people are.
DEBORAH (DAUGHTER): On how to ... interact with your parents.
BENJAMIN (SON): And your children. It goes both ways.
HANNAH (MOTHER): [We have] mutual respect.
ELI (FATHER): We're very wise and loving parents. [kidding]
BENJAMIN (SON): Yeah. ... Having ... respect for your parents is something that is not generally a common trait in this society, but ... it's impossible to be Halakhically observant and not have respect for your parents.

A similar sense of responsibility and equity shared between parents and children seemed to be important to Alexandra, a Reform mother, who reflected,

One of the things that we do regularly ... when I'm wrong, [is that] I'm able to tell my daughter, "I've been wrong, and this is why I've been wrong." And to ask her forgiveness is a really important part of Judaism. ... If you have wronged another individual, you have to work out the relationship with the individual before you can get real forgiveness from G-d. [However], that's not why I do it. ... The real important part to me is that my daughter knows that I'm able to say "I'm wrong" when I'm wrong. ... I teach her that.

Regular Family Prayer

In a study of relational processes associated with regular family prayer (Chelladurai, Dollahite, and Marks, 2018), a Conservative mother named Gabriella said,

It is a chance to breathe, to relax. ... We've had a busy week and here's our time to be together and we always take a deep breath before we do this and let all the thoughts, craziness and worries, and everything slip away, and we say the blessing.

Gabriella and her husband Boaz, articulated this theme further:

BOAZ: We say prayers before dinner every night and that was actually a decision we made when my grandfather died. One of the memories I had of him was that he wouldn't sit down to a meal without saying a blessing, "Thanks for this bread." When he died, we decided, "Let's do that before each meal, that we'll remember him for eternity." And it really stuck. We started doing it right away and we have been doing it every day since his passing.

GABRIELLA: It's a chance for everyone to sit down and to breathe and think about these things before we get to eating and I think that is healthy for one thing, and it's nice that everyone isn't running off in their own direction. We all sit down and calm down and say the blessing and then start together. I mean there's so many benefits, there's a sense of ritual that I think kids love and we still love as adults; things that we do that have been done for generations and generations.

The ritual nature of family prayer sometimes involved meaningful physical touch. Abigail, a Jewish mother said, "I love the fact that when we sit down as a family ... that [we] say the *HaMotzi*, which is our blessing over the bread. And, that [we] hold hands, and that we look at each other."

Shabbat Practices and Family Processes[3]

In a study of how the rituals and practices of Shabbat influence family relationships (Marks, Hatch, and Dollahite, 2018), we referred to Shabbat as the weekly family ritual *par excellence*. This entire study focuses on Shabbat and we only have space here to excerpt a few of the quotes from young adults and couples (see Hatch and Marks, Chapter 26 this volume). Two of the most common purposes and benefits of Shabbat observance included family time and family unity, as illustrated by four adolescent/early adult sons and daughters from different families:

JOSIAH[4] (19-YEAR-OLD ORTHODOX SON): For me Shabbat is the pinnacle of everything. ... We all spend time together. We have three meals together. We play [games].

NATE (20-YEAR-OLD ORTHODOX SON): Well, Shabbat has the traditional role of being ... that time when families are generally together. ... I don't know if there's any particular practice ... that's ... more meaningful than [Shabbat] to me personally.

ZVI (20-YEAR-OLD ORTHODOX SON): At times in my life where I have not particularly been interested in aspects of Judaism for their own sake, Shabbat has always been the thing that I keep doing for the family's sake, because whether or not I care about it for religious purposes, it's such a big deal on a family level that that's not something you can cut out.

TOBI (17-YEAR-OLD ORTHODOX DAUGHTER): I think [Shabbat] is really nice because it's consistent. It's not changing at all ... and I kind of like that. ... [I] tell my friends [that] I'm eating at home tonight ... and I really like that consistency, that we all sit at the table together and say the prayers.

A Conservative couple reflected on a specific Shabbat-related "crisis" they faced:

JOSHUA: Early on when the kids were very young, we had a big crisis that we had to confront, and that was whether or not we would let the kids play soccer on Shabbat.
MELANIE: On Saturday morning.
JOSHUA: Yeah, because all of our [daughter's] friends were playing soccer, so we let her do it for a few weekends, and we hated it because it stole the family away from us. And

in the end we decided: "No, we weren't going to do [soccer on the Sabbath] ever again." And we've really held to that, not just with the children, but with ourselves as well, with very few exceptions. [Shabbat is] the one time we're all together.

An Orthodox couple, Alissa and Yigal, explained their Shabbat tradition of singing with their children:

> ALISSA: For sure, Shabbat observance [is meaningful to us]. ... We light Shabbat candles and we are not on the computer and we don't drive anywhere. [We] don't talk on the phone or go shopping or do weekly things, and that is very important personally and as a couple. ... [N]ow that our older daughter is bigger, we incorporated singing together on Shabbat. ... [R]ecently, we had friends over and we all started singing together, and they said, "We don't sing well." But all of us are tone deaf ... [the quality of the singing is not] the issue. It['s] ... the energy. Singing religious songs is really significant to me.
>
> YIGAL: Definitely singing together is important. ... Also another thing is kind of minor, but [it] is really beautiful. ... [O]n Friday night right after we light candles, we create a little dance with our kids and us. We dance for a minute or two while singing Shabbat songs. They love to do it and it's such a good thing. There are so many reasons why we love [our Shabbat dance]. Number one, we love it because we made it up. ... So that is why I love the dancing because it's something that we love doing and our children love doing. It injects our Judaism and our family with a sense of joy with the traditions.

A Reform couple discussed Shabbat blessings of their children in detail:

> SCOTT: Most Friday nights we do a blessing with the kids, and bless them, and whisper what they did good for the week in their ear, and they look forward to that.
>
> JULIE: In ... the Torah, there's a blessing where Jacob blesses Joseph's two sons, right before he dies. He's an elderly man, and he blesses Ephraim and Manasseh. ... It's a blessing in Hebrew, but it [says], "May God bless you and keep you. May his light shine upon you and be gracious unto you." It's the priestly benediction, so we say that blessing, and then we do whisper something [extra] in each of their ears.
>
> SCOTT: Now they look forward to it. I think if it was just a blessing, they wouldn't care.
>
> JULIE: So the [extra] thing that we whisper in their ear is not like, "Oh, I'm so glad you made an A on the spelling test," it's some kindness that [they] did. It's to [help them] ... always remember that the things that we told them that we were proud of them for were things that were acts that God would be proud of you [for]—how you acted to somebody else [with] kindness [and] honesty, things like that. So, you don't have to be a great athlete or a great student, it's [about] just being a good person. ... It's funny, because [one of our sons] is really serious about what we whisper in his ear, and if you whisper something vague [or] general, like "I'm really proud of how you were nice to your brother this week," then he'll say, "Like when?" ... You can't get away with [it] if you didn't pay attention that week to something. It really takes a lot of work to have something [specific to say]. So [you try to] ... catch them being really good.

Conclusion

As scholars of faith and family life in contemporary America, we have found the opportunity to conduct in-depth, sustained, and repeated study of Jewish families among the most interesting, meaningful, and professionally satisfying work we have done as social scientists. In this chapter, we have tried to fill the repeated call mentioned at the outset for vibrant qualitative insights into contemporary Jewish families. We have strived to do so in a unique way by highlighting the voices of those who generously shared their religious lives with us. We have appreciated the opportunity to learn from 30 diverse Jewish families via in-depth interviews in their own homes. It is their warmth and sharing of *shalom bayit* that has made it possible for us to share their voices and familial and relational insights with you.

Notes

1 See http://AmericanFamiliesofFaith.byu.edu for a detailed description of the project including sample, methods, and a listing of published works.
2 All names are pseudonyms.
3 See Chapter 26 on Shabbat by Hatch and Marks, this volume.
4 All participants' names are pseudonyms.

References

Barrow, Betsy H., David C. Dollahite, and Loren D. Marks. 2020. "How Parents Balance Desire for Religious Continuity with Honoring Children's Religious Agency," *Psychology of Religion and Spirituality*, 13: 222–34 https://doi.org/10.1037/rel0000307

Boyarin, Jonathan. 2013. *Jewish Families*. New Brunswick, NJ: Rutgers University Press.

Brodbar-Nemzer, Jay Y. 1988. "The Contemporary American Jewish Family," in Darwin L. Thomas (Ed.), *The Religion and Family Connection: Social Science Perspectives*. Provo, UT: BYU Religious Studies Center, 66–87.

Chelladurai, Joseph M., David C. Dollahite, and Loren D. Marks. 2018. "'The Family that Prays Together …': Relational Processes Associated with Regular Family Prayer," *Journal of Family Psychology*, 32, no. 7: 849–59. https://doi.org/10.1037/fam0000432

Cohen, Steven M. 1999. "Introduction," in Steven M. Cohen and Gabriel Horencyzk (Eds.), *National Variations in Jewish Identity: Implications for Jewish Education*. New York: State University of New York Press, 1–17.

Cohen, Steven M. 2012. "The demise of the 'Good Jew': Marshall Sklare award lecture," *Contemporary Jewry*, 32: 85–93.

Cohen, Steven M., and Arnold M. Eisen. 2000. *The Jew Within: Self, Family, and Community in America*. Bloomington, IN: Indiana University Press.

Dollahite, David C., and Loren D. Marks. 2018. "Introduction to the Special Issue: Exploring Strengths in American Families of Faith," *Marriage and Family Review*, 54, no. 7: 617–34. https://doi.org/10.1080/01494929.2018.1469569

Dollahite, David C., and Loren D. Marks. Eds. 2020. *Strengths in Diverse Families of Faith: Exploring Religious Differences*. New York: Routledge.

Dollahite, David C., and Jennifer Y. Thatcher. 2008. "Talking About Religion: How Religious Youth and Parents Discuss their Faith," *Journal of Adolescent Research*, 23, no. 5: 611–41. https://doi.org/10.1177/0743558408322141

Dollahite, David C., Loren D. Marks, and Betsy H. Barrow. 2019. "Exploring Relational Reconciliation Processes in Christian, Jewish, and Muslim Families," *Family Relations*, 68: 517–33. https://doi.org/10.111/fare.12371

Dollahite, David C., Loren D. Marks, and Kaity P. Young. 2019. "Relational Struggles and Experiential Immediacy in Religious American Families," *Psychology of Religion and Spirituality*, 11, no. 1: 9–21. http://dx.doi.org/10.1037/rel0000135

Dollahite, David C., Emily Layton, Howard M. Bahr, Anthony B. Walker, and Jennifer Y. Thatcher. 2009. "Giving Up Something Good for Something Better: Sacred Sacrifices Made by Religious Youth," *Journal of Adolescent Research*, 24, no. 6: 691–725. https://doi.org/10.1177/0743558409343463

Dollahite, David C., Loren D. Marks, Taleah M. Kear, Brittany M. Lewis, and Megan L. Stokes. 2018. "Beyond the Bucket List: Identity-centered Religious Calling, Being, and Action Among Parents," *Psychology of Religion and Spirituality*, 10, no. 1: 44–54. http://dx.doi.org/10.1037/rel0000130

Dollahite, David C., Loren D. Marks, Kate P. Babcock, Betsy H. Barrow, and Andrew H. Rose. 2019. "Beyond Religious Rigidities: Religious Firmness and Religious Flexibility as Complementary Loyalties in Faith Transmission," *Religions*, 10: 111. https://doi.org/10.3390/rel10020111

Goldscheider, Calvin. 2002. "The Marshall Sklare Memorial Lecture. 'Social Science and the Jews: A Research Agenda for the Next Generation'," *Contemporary Jewry*, 23: 196–219.

Goldscheider, Calvin. 2004. *Studying the Jewish Future*. Seattle: University of Washington Press.

Hatch, Trevan G. 2015. "Mishpacha in the American Diaspora: An Exploratory Study of Highly-Involved Jewish Families." PhD dissertation, Louisiana State University.

Hatch, Trevan, and Loren D. Marks. 2014a. "Bar Mitzvahs and Bat Mitzvahs," in Lawrence M. Ganong and Marilyn Coleman (Eds.), *The Social History of the American Family*. Thousand Oaks, CA: Sage, 104–5.

Hatch, Trevan G., and Loren D. Marks. 2014b. "Judaism and Orthodox Judaism," in Lawrence Ganong and Marilyn Coleman (Eds.), *The Social History of the American Family*. Thousand Oaks, CA: Sage, 781–4.

Hatch, Trevan G., and Loren D. Marks. 2019. "Judaism," in James J. Ponzetti, Jr., Maureen Blankemeyer, Sean M. Horan, Heidi Lyons, and Aya Shigeto (Eds.), *Macmillan Encyclopedia of Intimate and Family Relationships: An Interdisciplinary Approach*. New York: Macmillan/Gale/Cengage, 497–9.

Kelley, Heather H., Loren D. Marks, and David C. Dollahite. 2019. "Uniting and Dividing Influences of Religion in Marriage among Highly Religious Couples," *Psychology of Religion and Spirituality*, 12, no. 2: 167–77. http://dx.doi.org/10.1037/rel0000262

Kelley, Heather H., Ashley B. LeBaron, Lawrence J. Sussman, Jay Fagan, David C. Dollahite, and Loren D. Marks. 2018. "*Shalom bayit*—Peace of the Home: Ritual and Tradition in American Jewish Families," *Marriage and Family Review*, 54, no. 7: 706–18. https://doi.org/10.1080/01494929.2018.1478922

Layton, Emily, David C. Dollahite, and Sam A. Hardy. 2011. "Anchors of Religious Commitment in Adolescents," *Journal of Adolescent Research*, 26, no. 3: 381–413. https://doi.org/10.1177/0743558410391260

Layton, Emily, Sam A. Hardy, and David C. Dollahite. 2012. "Religious Exploration among Highly Religious American Adolescents," *Identity: An International Journal of Theory and Research*, 12, no. 2: 157–84.

Marks, Loren D., and David C. Dollahite. 2017. *Religion and Families: An Introduction*. New York: Routledge.

Marks, Loren D., and David C. Dollahite, 2021. "Approaching God: What Latter-day Saints Can Learn from Jewish Religious Experience," in Trevan G. Hatch and Leonard J. Greenspoon (Eds.), *"The Learning of the Jews": What Judaism can Teach Latter-day Saints*. Salt Lake City, UT: Greg Kofford Books.

Marks, Loren D., Trevan G. Hatch, and David C. Dollahite. 2018. "Sacred Practices and Family Processes in a Jewish Context: Shabbat as the Weekly Family Ritual *Par Excellence*," *Family Process*, 57, no. 2: 448–61. https://doi.org/10.1111/famp.12286

Myerhoff, Barbara. 1980. *Number Our Days*. New York: Touchstone.

Pomson, Alex, and Randal F. Schnoor. 2018. *Jewish Family: Identity and Self-formation at Home*. Bloomington, IN: Indiana University Press.

Smith, Christian. 2009. *Souls in Transition: The Religious and Spiritual Lives of Emerging Adults*. New York: Oxford.

20
A JEWISH FAMILY ON TV
Reflections on Ritual

Oliver Leaman

If we look at the statistics of the American Jewish population some trends are quite clear (Wertheimer (2018) provides a wealth of detail on this issue): a rapidly increasing rate of intermarriage, lack of identification with Israel and religious institutions among younger Jews, and growing lack of distinction between Jews and others. At the same time, of course, there has been a rapid growth of "traditional" Jewish ways of life by those who seek to emphasize the difference between Jews and others, and it may well be that eventually these will be the only Jews left in the world. Among this group also identification with the State of Israel may be weak or even totally rejected, while among other Jews there is now often more ambiguity in attitudes toward Zionism. The more assimilated part of the Jewish population might just completely disappear into the main population as today, for example, German Americans, once a majority of US citizens, have largely become invisible as an independent ethnic group. At the moment, though, modern Jews remain distinct to a degree not due to anything they do but because they are regarded as distinct by others. Traditional forms of anti-Semitism have persisted in remarkable ways and even countries with tiny or no Jewish population contain people with firm views on the evil power and influence of the Jewish community. Today Jews are often seen as harbingers of modernity and so enemies of those who are antagonistic to it.

This is not so different from the situation in the past, the role of Jews as rootless cosmopolitans at the forefront of social and technical change was one of the major complaints of anti-Semites and linked groups looking back nostalgically at a simpler past. That sort of clear labeling of who is taken to be the enemy is no longer so widespread but often circumlocution is employed to criticize groups such as bankers or Hollywood moguls. It is pretty clear who is meant by this sort of language, and when individual Jews are picked out for special criticism, the whole group is often implied although not stated. It is worth pointing out though that just as in the same way that we should no longer talk about just one form of Judaism or Jewish life, or one form of community or institution, so it is also the case that we should not think about just one form of anti-Semitism.

In the past there were often theological grounds for hostility to Jews, while today it is the hostility of many Jews in the United States to religion that makes them appear especially dangerous to those seeking to defend religion and what are taken to be traditional views. The characters in TV shows such as *Transparent* and *Schitts Creek* are a good example of this; their relationship with their religion, indeed, any religion is very far from traditional on any account of tradition. The characters in *Transparent* play around with Jewish ideas but ironically, in the same way that they produce the odd Yiddish phrase. They signal their membership of a group, but one they did not choose to join and yet find themselves in. In the past this might have been regarded as just destiny and one would have expected just to stay where you find yourself, but not today. As with moving from one sexual identity to another, this is no longer regarded as something fixed and irrevocable, but a personal feature that can be explored and interrogated. Jews have often played a liminal role in society, they were in a category difficult to define and understand, hence the complaints about them by those seeking to see the world in terms of clear and constant parameters. Nirenberg (2013) has identified the idea of anti-Judaism to describe a wider antagonism to Jews that is not necessarily based on racial difference. This can be used here to describe a very modern idea, albeit based on longstanding historical roots, of Jews as a target for those suspicious of modernity and what follows from it.

TV and Modernity

Modernity is often seen as disruptive. The Jews are accordingly often seen as disruptive, and the radical changes in the Jewish family as indicative of wider changes in American society. Society becomes more and more diverse, although of course it always was very diverse, the difference being that this diversity is now often officially celebrated and valued. The election of more progressive governments and the legislation increasing equal opportunities for those from previously marginalized groups is highly threatening to those who see social stability as being based on older forms of association, such as the institution of the traditional family. The question for conservatives is whether community is feasible in an era of changing and even collapsing institutions such as the "traditional" family. The Pfeffermans in *Transparent* are a good example of this; they appear to be very distant from a traditional family but are they? They are related to each other, they do get together with each other and often they discuss how they feel within their group. They expect help or at least sympathy when they discuss their troubles, and sometimes they even get it. On the whole, this is more a matter of finding someone to listen to them, and anything more might be regarded as an attack on their autonomy. They often seem to have little in common apart from the fact that they are part of the same family, and that is very modern too, we tend now to have far closer relations to non-family members. Paradoxically, despite this, like the Pfeffermans, people often end up spending time with their family and it does not always seem to be an enjoyable experience. The Roses also in *Schitts Creek* are often in each other's company, and they constantly bicker. On TV one often gets the impression that there is more warmth between the family members than is likely in real life. The exigencies of the show, of course, suggest the need for a nice tidy conclusion and a happy ending.

The Jewish question was the issue of the nineteenth century in Europe. It is often linked with the time of Napoleon's government that sought to regulate them with the principle that Jews can be citizens but then they cannot allow themselves to be dominated by a distinct culture. They cannot isolate themselves from the rest of society, speak their own languages, wear different clothes and seek to pursue an entirely alien lifestyle. If they want to do any of those things then they cannot be citizens. This pact with the Jews was enthusiastically grasped by most Jews, who quickly assimilated in European and then American society and threw off the old-time religion that had been such a mainstay for many centuries, indeed millennia. As with any such decision though, the exchange of one identity for another is not like changing clothes. All sorts of complicated issues arise, our relationships come to represent Venn diagram-like links with other people and institutions with the result that it is often not entirely clear who we are anymore. Add to this the fact that the precise nature of these links is constantly changing, if there ever were any precise links there at all in the first place, and we have the sort of very variegated Jewish family of today that is represented so well on TV and movies in general.

Attitudes to Jewish Rituals

Of course, some Jews rejected the pact and continued to practice a form of religion that really kept them out of the mainstream of society, but this was in the past a small minority that appeared to be rapidly shrinking. Now it has become much more significant as part of the Jewish community, due to low birth rates among more secular Jews, their high rates of intermarriage, and the contrasting high birth rates among the religious who rarely intermarried. This community is not surprised by anti-Jewish antagonism since it is seen as a part of Jewish history and culture, and reacts much more calmly than other groups to hostility. It is wrong to describe observant Jews as just one community, since they are divided in many ways. Some are very hostile to Zionism while others are ambivalent or enthusiastic about it, some regard themselves as modern orthodox while others seek to replicate the lifestyle of the past in Eastern Europe in a very specific way. It almost looks as though the variety that exists among more assimilated Jews is replicated by their more observant peers, although to the outside world this may not be noticeable.

It is rather like the custom on Purim to wear fancy dress, to celebrate the survival of the Jews in Persia from the anger of Haman, where orthodox Jews of one Hasidic community may wear the hats traditional among a different community. Only they know what is going on, to the rest of the world it is just one more orthodox Jew wearing a strange hat. The Pfeffermans in *Transparent* create their own rituals, as we all do, when Sarah goes to her former fiancé Tammy before Yom Kippur and apologizes for anything she may have done throughout the year to annoy her, like jilting her, for instance. In fact, most of the Jewish rituals we see in *Transparent* are suspect from any perspective that is not postmodern. That may appear to be equivalent to the virtual absence of ritual in reality, or it may be taken to be a serious attempt at behaving in accordance with the spirit of the ritual, with the Pfeffermans one never knows. Wedding is just a ritual, Rabbi Raquel suggests, typical of the ironic sophistication with which everything religious is regarded in the series, even by those who might be said to be in the ritual business. For the Roses in *Schitts Creek*, their Judaism seems to have left them when their money and status left, and now they have to play the role of the super-sophisticates down on their luck and out in the wilds.

We should not talk in terms of orthodox and other Jews, these labels are often very misleading, and yet they have a use. Many Jews are not religious and have varying commitment to their religion, or perhaps only identify as Jews as an ethnic group, with little in the way of doctrinal belief at all. Surveys of levels of religiosity tend to identify Jews as the least religious and also having the most positive views on the separation of religion and state. After all, Jews as a group have done well once that separation took place in the nineteenth century. Before, they were limited in what they could do and often even where they could live, what they could wear and so on. With emancipation came their participation in broader society, the professions, commerce and the arts, and they were often very successful in these areas. The community prospered as it integrated into society, and had few problems in casting off its previous ways of living. The connection with religion that remained was often tenuous. Those Jews who remained enthusiastic about their religion came to be regarded by the majority as faintly ridiculous and way behind the times. As Nietzsche pointed out in the nineteenth century, God was no longer someone who could be regarded as part of daily life. Traditional Jews are in many ways a parody of how most Jews want to live. As many Jews plunge headfirst into what they take modernity to be, those who are fearful do the reverse and seek to reject the modern. In fact, both groups have a fascination with modernity, the only difference is whether they view it positively or negatively and perhaps this is characteristic of marginal groups. They have less to hold onto than those who feel more fixed in a particular environment, but what they can hold onto is the *Zeitgeist*, and around that they can build a community. Of course, as we see with the Pfeffermans, what is constructed is often a variety of intersecting communities.

The idea behind the pact with the Jews was that if they behaved like ordinary citizens then they would be treated like ordinary citizens. Anti-Semitism would then disappear since the Jews themselves would disappear as a distinct group of people. One of the things that would make them ordinary would be having their own state. This is not what actually happened. Israel came to be seen not just as a state but as Jewish, and came to acquire all the negative features associated with Jews. The plan to change the ways in which Jews were perceived backfired, perhaps because the Jew has been such a recurrent symbol in culture that the creation of a state with different kinds of Jews in it did not resonate with the public for long. Suspicion fell on the local Jews for split loyalty and, despite their most fervent efforts to be ordinary in an ordinary state, it never actually worked. The attempt to be ordinary is often replaced with an exaggerated form of what is taken to be ordinary that is anything but, and surrounding that difference with a community that supports and creates new forms of association and living that are agreeable to the participants. Not an institution with its fixed parameters and rules, but a community where the rules have to be created as we go along. Maura's trip to Israel exemplifies this, it has touristy elements like the visit to the Western Wall (the women's section) and also its own unique flavor where she seems to be playing around with a role, rather than acting from that role. When her family joins her they seem to be bit players in her drama.

Judaism and Boundaries

Judaism is traditionally obsessed with boundaries. What is the difference between the Jew and the non-Jew, between kosher food and food that cannot be eaten, between the Shabat and the rest of the week? We are told to build a fence around the Torah at the start of *Mishnah Avot*. Shylock in the *Merchant of Venice* says that he can do business with the Christian merchants but cannot eat, drink or pray with them. These are all signs of the creation and reproduction of an institution, one in which people can live and find all the questions of what they are to do resolved for them. Gender and sexuality appear to many to be a very clear-cut institution, and in the recent political controversies in the United States about who can use public bathrooms, the reactions of conservatives have been revealing. The argument has been that there just are differences in gender, and so people should use the bathroom that fits with who they are. This is part of a whole series of debates and controversies; some people like the idea of there being clear and distinct borders between issues and some do not. It is a bit like the argument over national borders; some are enthusiastic on the preservation of clear border demarcations and some are not, and often the desire for clarity extends over a range of political and moral topics. For example, some countries have real problems with their citizens becoming citizens of other countries and remaining citizens of their original country. Some people have difficulty understanding how someone with one gender can change it since it is much simpler to think in terms of sticking with the gender that one had originally, like nationality.

To a degree, the debate is about how we are to react to change, and one can often hear in the puzzled voices of those trying to preserve the status quo how confused they are at the way in which their country and the communities within it are rapidly changing around them. Yet now, who we are is itself an open issue, and communities are arising where the rules of how to answer such questions are variable and different from how it was done in the past. To take a related example, some people have technology implanted in their bodies and describe themselves as transhuman. In a sense they are no longer entirely human, nor are they machines, but some sort of amalgam. Are they like the golem, a creature made from earth but without language, yet apart from that resembling a person and able to perform many human tasks? No, because transhumans can speak, and it might depend on how much of them is human. The law has to act with a broad brush to get the dividing line broadly right for most of us and many of our other distinctions are rather like that. The Pfeffermans are never happy to accept that the rules apply to them, although they appreciate that there are rules. For them the rules are the backdrop against which they work out their own rules. In this they represent the atmosphere of their time, they are not going to accede to general definitions of how to behave but will establish their own.

The aim of intersectionality is making things complex, so when Ali identifies with Palestinians in Ramallah she, at the same time, sympathizes with Jews in Israel, and struggles to find some way to reconcile them. That is the essence of non-binary existence; it is not rejecting one side and supporting another, it is remaining in a questioning and skeptical attitude toward both sides. This applies both to politics and to the personal of course. The discussion in the show of the ways in which language may need to change to reflect the non-binary is interesting in bringing out how integral to traditional language the binary is. Any change immediately looks awkward and unnecessary, until the implications of using the old language on trying to forge new ways of seeing relationships are considered. The attraction of the traditional runs deep, even Maura regrets that she was not told of earlier transgender members of her family, as though the existence of such predecessors would in some way validate her behavior, as though her behavior needed to be validated by anything.

Boundaries and Being Human

We often say of someone who is brain dead and being kept alive by a machine that they are like a vegetable. Sometimes the time comes to turn off the machines keeping them "alive", since there is little point in spending a lot of resources in looking after something with the status of a potato. They may have crossed the line from being a person to becoming something else, and modernity brings about many new such lines and distinctions as technical development creates novel situations and choices which never existed in the past. In many ways this was always the case. Athletes who are tested to determine whether they are men or women and so which sorts of competition they should go into often have rather ambiguous results. The issue should be fairly straightforward: a person is either a male (with an X and a Y chromosome) or a female (with two X chromosomes). But the reality is quite different, people develop in different ways and for some it is difficult to say precisely what their gender is. In some cases they look very much like they should be classified in one gender category and yet were such a decision to be taken they might be considered to be under an unfair advantage or disadvantage were they to compete in the other category. For example, a high production of testosterone would be helpful for some sporting events, and might be shared across the gender divide, but would not be advantageous for other events, and it just seems to be arbitrary to insist on a particular definition of gender.

In sport the central issue is what is fair. If someone is classified as a woman but comes close to being a man in some biological ways then that person may be taken to have an unfair advantage in some competitive events over women who have more recognizable female features. On the other hand, women do differ in their biological makeup and it would be surprising if a fairly narrow biological definition were to apply and rule out many potential competitors. Similarly with the Special Olympics that brings in the issue of what counts as a disability or what changes to bodies may actually be regarded as enhancements to sporting success. Physical and psychological problems clearly operate on a continuum, and perhaps everything does, so the search for clear answers to the issues that arise in dealing with social and personal identity needs to be a concern. Obviously there are sometimes clear answers but equally obviously sometimes not, and we should take both of these observations equally seriously. It is difficult not to conclude that definitions have limited value and they are constantly interrogated by the Pfeffermans. Both Shelly and Ali refuse to relax within an atmosphere of comfortable limits and definitions and even Shelly with her ironic use of Yiddish seems to operate within a social structure that she at the same time challenges. This is a powerful symbol of the sorts of change that the family in modern society is experiencing, where the old assumptions are no longer able to get the same grip on reality. This is how we arrive at the Yom Kippur breakfast and the escape from the bat mitzvah, both very different reactions to Jewish rituals and yet transgressional reactions that would make no sense if they were carried out by non-Jews.

Boundaries and Language

In the philosophy of language there is a theory called nominalism which urges suspicion of general concepts. All that really exists are names, hence the name of the theory, although it does have the problem of seeming to present a general argument itself. It would seem invidious to link this theory with a particular ethnic group, but there are reasons to think that Jews should be particularly close to it. In modern times Jews are often in the position of trying to define themselves by contrast with everyone else. They have to think about how kosher their food is going to be, if at all, who they are going to marry, what gender their partner should have, what synagogue they might join (probably none) and so on. This is the classic position of liminality, being between different worlds means there is often no clear answer. Of course, similar dilemmas occur to many in modern society but perhaps more so to the Jews, the traditional Other. The Nazis often claimed that the Jews were rootless cosmopolitans and while this entirely misrepresents the strong ties of patriotism that link many Jews to their countries of origin (Aberbach 2012), it is true that those links are often more complicated than is the case for many in other groups. This may be helpful in the sense that living on the edge gives one a view of both sides of something at the same time and stimulates creativity and mental flexibility, possibly achieved less readily by those whose roots are deep and simple.

There was a grim joke in the 1930s of a Jew holding up a poster saying "Down with dogs", and when someone asked him what was wrong with dogs, he asked what was wrong with Jews. The Nazis targeted different marginal groups whom they thought had a questionable status, something brought out in *Transparent* in the flashback to 1930's Germany. Is a disabled person really a person, or more of a vegetable, are people who practice "deviant" sex doing something wrong? Are Jews who as a community live all over the world really citizens of one country? People often have problems dealing with difference, and this brings us back to the rapidly changing and evolving Jewish family, the institution which is rapidly becoming more of a community and a symbol of the modern family itself. It is constantly disintegrating and yet seems to sort of survive. Kinship is losing its role as the source of identity and the erotic is disconnected from love, marriage and reproduction. The family in *Transparent* represents this diversity well, but then so would many other kinds of families. When institutions dissolve and change, communities often emerge to pick up the pieces in ways that preserve many of the significant aspects of the former institution.

In his attack on traditional attitudes to definition, Wittgenstein uses the concept of family resemblances to link "a complicated network of similarities overlapping and crisscrossing" (*Philosophical Investigations* I 66). The use of the idea of family is worth noting here, where the links between different family members are qualified in terms of resemblance rather than anything stronger. This is Wittgenstein's account of how the different uses of a word are linked to each other, not as aspects of some core meaning but something much looser and is far more accurate a description of how we actually treat meaning. We often think this cannot be right, that these different uses must have something in common with each other, but if we look and see how meaning actually operates, this essence is nowhere to be found. In other words, he replaces the idea of meaning as an institution with meaning as playing a role in an activity. Wittgenstein's philosophical point is represented nicely in modern culture where social roles are often ways in which people present themselves on particular occasions and have only notional rigidity.

It is important to recognize that this is a political issue as well as a semantic one. People who insist on a fixed and stable meaning at the center of language are those who value the idea of institutions with rigid rules and clear parameters. Those who accept that language is more of a community than an institution are able to work with looser connections between our ideas of how people ought to behave and link up with each other. Conservatives believe in the fragility of institutions and in the need to preserve them, even where the costs are high. It is for this reason, for example, that Confucius argues for the continuation of high expenditure on music and elaborate funerals, since they are appropriate for the marking of the rite of passage of parental death, and the family is the backbone of society. Once respect for hierarchy goes then everything goes, in his view, and it is no surprise that Confucius was also in favor of what he called the rectification of names, the return to what he saw as the original use of language. If people would only use language in the correct and traditional way, then that earlier form of stable society would return and everything would be alright.

Rituals and Change

Rituals do have this flavor of linking people with those in the past. I remember once being asked to help make up a *minyan* (quorum) for the recital of *kaddish* (prayer traditionally said to commemorate the anniversary of a death) on the *yahrzeit* (the anniversary) of someone whose daughter was firmly committed to the idea of the egalitarian *minyan* (one containing adult women as well as men) but wanted one only made up of men on this occasion because that is what her father, the deceased person being commemorated, would have wanted. Many secular people have cringed at a secular funeral, since no one really knows what to do, and much prefer the religious ceremony which at least has comprehensible roles for the participants, even though the beliefs that are being espoused are very far from what they actually believe (Lindsay 2006). Familiar words and practices often have more authenticity than alternatives that actually better represent what the participants believe. We often say and do things we do not believe in and not because we are being insincere but sometimes because we respect the ritual we are involved in and even admire many things about it. Like Maura Pfefferman at the Western Wall, and proudly in the women's section. What does she really believe about what she is doing? Like discovering she had transgender ancestors, connecting with the past should not be confused with trying to be traditional. We often do not believe in what tradition and its rituals say about Judaism, or we do not believe all of it.

We come, here, to see the complex role that ritual may have in modern lives, and yet its continuing significance despite or because of this. In my part of the United States people greet each other by asking how they are. This is the ritual, but it does not mean they are interested in how other people are, it is just a way of saying hello. It is so much easier to use an accepted form of greeting than to create one specifically for each occasion. Those who are religiously observant often remark that the advantage of their form of life is that they do not have to think about how to behave in many aspects of their lives since the religion tells them what to do. This is a point that Levinas makes, Jewish (and no doubt other forms of) ritual are designed to counter spontaneity, the feelings we might have toward the deity, by bringing in someone else, the Other. Ritual does this by inviting us to structure our worship by doing things with other people in one way or another (Levinas 1990). There is a danger of ritual making religion dry and automatic, unthinking in the worst sort of way where we undergo a performance and fail to feel anything throughout it all. This is why all religions stress the significance of balance and moderation, we have duties to God, to others, to ourselves and have to reconcile these all with each other in some way.

Groucho Marx is supposed to have said that marriage is a wonderful institution, but who, he asks, wants to live in an institution? Who wants to live within strict parameters and fixed rules? Well, many people do, living otherwise involves all sorts of problems and complications. Even within an institution there are many flexibilities and unanswered questions, as we can see from the to and fro of the discussions in the Talmud, which revolve around the corpus of Jewish law known as the Mishnah. Law looks like an institution, and it is, but even within that institution there are a lot of debates about what exactly the law is and how we should orient ourselves to it.

It has been argued here that the show *Transparent* is all about rough edges and readymade communities. The characters are intensely self-centered and yet compelling, and many people have emphasized how Jewish it is. The argument here is that it is often accurate on how Jewish families are changing and what implications this has for families as a whole. It is worth noting how important secrets are in the show. Jews are often seen historically as devious and secretive, and the characters in the series certainly play up to the stereotype. Culture depends on secrets, and *Transparent* certainly does. As Rabbi Raquel says to Josh Pfefferman, "Please don't do that to me – betray me and then tell me it is a gift" when he tries to put a positive spin on having broadcast the couple's secrets. The series is based on secrets, their revelation not necessarily making everything right again. Transparency can make everything less clear rather than the reverse. What rituals tend to do is cover things up; they allow us to approach God indirectly through the practice. This is far too subtle for TV with its desire to present feelings and emotions and bring everything to some sort of closure. On the other hand, television is often successful in presenting realistic aspects of the changing Jewish family and the latter's creative use of ritual in its sense of what it is to be Jewish in the contemporary world.

Bibliography

Aberbach, David. 2012. *The European Jews, Patriotism and the Liberal State, 1789–1939: A Study of Literature and Social Psychology*. New York: Routledge.
Bunzl, Matti. 2004. *Symptoms of Modernity: Jews and Queers in Late-Twentieth-Century Vienna*. Berkeley: University of California Press.
Cheyette, Bryan and Laura Marcus. eds. 1998. *Modernity, Culture and "The Jew"*, Oxford: Polity.
Katz, David. 1999. "Shylock's Gender: Jewish Male Menstruation in Early Modern England". *Review of English Studies*. 50, 440–62.
Leaman, Oliver. 2008. *Judaism*. London: I B Tauris.

Levinas, Emmanuel. 1990. "Religion for Adults", in *Difficult Freeedom*. Trans. S. Hand. London: Athlone, 14–17.
Lindsay, Keith. 2006. *And in the End: A Guide to the World's Weirdest Funerals*. London: Fusion.
Mendes-Flohr, Paul and Jehuda Reinharz. eds. 1995. *The Jew in the Modern World: A Documentary History*. Oxford: Oxford University Press.
Nirenberg, David. 2013. *Anti-Judaism: The Western Tradition*. New York: Norton.
Richmond, Michelle. 2017. *The Marriage Pact*. New York: Bantam.
Wertheimer, Jack. 2018. *The New American Judaism: How Jews Practice Their Religion Today*. Princeton, NJ: Princeton University Press.
Wittgenstein, Ludwig. 1958. *Philosophical Investigations*. Trans. G.E.M. Anscombe. Oxford: Blackwell.

PART IV
Practices

21
CIRCUMCISION

Oliver Leaman

Circumcision is often taken to be a defining ritual in Judaism. There are intense legal discussions about the status of Jewish males who have not been circumcised, but generally their status as members of the community is in doubt. For one thing the foreskin itself is often treated as something revolting and so its presence is problematic for someone performing a religious activity. It ritually contaminates the surroundings. On the other hand, since male circumcision is traditionally performed on the eighth day of life its absence can hardly be blamed on the individual himself, and so some legal views are more lenient. In recent times the practice has become more common since it is regarded as having health benefits, and yet an interesting discussion has arisen as to whether the practice might be regarded as child abuse. After all, it is for most children an unnecessary procedure, one with an element of risk and certainly a degree of pain, and removes a part of the body that someone might wish to retain. When it was rarer for the general community to be circumcised it was very much a mark of Jewish males, and proved to be an easy way to recognize them, and often came into derogatory language about Jews.

Now some Jews also question the procedure, and the traditional ways of performing it, and it falls within the category of religious ritual that offends some modern sensibilities, like Jewish forms of animal slaughter and the gender differentiation that takes place in some Jewish communities. This is not an issue that affects Jews alone, Muslims also are involved since they have similar rules of how to kill animals and circumcise, and include communities that see gender in ways at odds with the liberal sensibilities of modern Western society. It is easy for such religious communities to see the campaign against their basic practices as campaigns against them per se, and in the past this was no doubt the case. We may suspect the motives of those seeking to outlaw activities that are specific to particular religious groups, and in the past some legislatures have outlawed those activities while excluding the ban from religious groups. They have sought in this way to preserve the autonomy of those groups to practice their religion as they see fit. There are signs, in Europe at least, that those exclusions are coming to an end, and perhaps there are political reasons for this change. Nonetheless the main issue is surely a moral one, and if a practice or ritual is immoral then however significant it is to the religion it should not be allowed to continue.

Religious Diversity and Customs

We need to take the focus away from specific religions and look at what it is for a society to include diverse communities within it. Some of those communities are likely to have strange ideas about how to live and what to believe, and the general rule in liberal democracy is that provided what they do does not disrupt the general business of life they should be allowed to do whatever they like. If they want to do weird things, no problem, and it adds to the variety of lifestyles that are on offer to us all, what John Stuart Mill called experiments in living in *On Liberty*. We see what different people do and we wonder whether we would like to do that, and sometimes we try those practices and join those communities, and more often we just observe or sample them for a short time then return to what we normally do. One feature worth noticing here is that what communities do affects the young members of those communities in ways that are perhaps going to be long lasting and difficult to shake off later. On the other hand, the evidence suggests that people are capable of changing their attitudes to beliefs even, and indeed especially, those that have been inculcated in them from early childhood. It is difficult to think of their being indoctrinated in such a way that the beliefs become unchallengeable throughout their lives. It is worth saying also that being brought up within a religion involves not only accepting certain beliefs but also the rituals and practices that go along with them, and we need to experience this before we can really make an informed decision about our attitude to the religion. Mill would argue that since we do not know how we really ought to live then it is good to have available to us a wide variety of practices and we can observe and try them out and finally decide what suits us. This accords well with the ways in which many in consumer societies treat religion, as something you can pick up and put down at will, and where you can vary what you select and mix and match in accordance with individual likes and dislikes.

The thing about circumcision is that it is not something you can change your mind about later, although of course in the Hellenistic past Jews did try to alter the appearance of their genitals to fit in better with the general community. Even today there are groups in Israel and elsewhere opposed to circumcision for Jewish males, *Gonen al ha-yeled* (protect the child) and *Kahal*, a support group for uncircumcised boys. Then as now it was a sign, of some permanence, of basic difference, and always embarrassing for those who seek to avoid that difference. Spinoza settled on this physical issue as one permanently defining difference, and surely when the early Christians decided to insist merely on circumcision of the spirit they were on a winning ticket in the business of gaining adherents. Before then they could really only appeal to Jews, and afterwards there was no need for a painful rite of passage to be endured before a prospective convert could become a Christian. Of course, the circumcision of adults can be more of a symbolic event than anything very unpleasant, but it might not be so anodyne, and it takes place in a part of the body that has all sorts of serious physical and symbolic resonances. Spinoza in his *Theological Political Treatise* implies that it is a rather silly custom, despite its effectiveness in binding a community together and distinguishing it from other communities, but then Spinoza was not in favor of this sort of separatism. He liked the idea of reason defining what we do and slicing off bits of bodies for some ritual end does not fit in nicely with this idea. In any case his remarks on Judaism are rarely complimentary, by contrast with his apparent attitude to Christianity, hardly likely to endear him to the local Jewish community.

Similar issues arise over the slaughtering of animals. In 19th-century Europe there was a controversy about kashrut since it involves slitting the throat of animals in order to remove most blood, and the idea was that animals should be conscious when this is done to maximize the flow of blood. If the animal was stunned first then it looks like it is perhaps already dead without the appropriate slitting having taken place, and if it was stunned after the slitting of the throat then this might well impede the blood flow. At that time the controversy was about post-slitting stunning, since it was thought that this would be less painful for the animal than if its throat was just cut and it was allowed, or indeed encouraged, to bleed to death. Of course, advocates of religious forms of slaughter produce arguments that their methods are not cruel and a multitude of scriptural and other authoritative quotations advocating kindness to animals and in general. Similarly, advocates of male circumcision produce many scientific arguments about the value of the procedure for general health, and this is not the place to examine and evaluate such arguments. It is worth pointing out, though, that religions do not on the whole institute these sorts of rituals for health reasons, or at least not explicitly. In the very complex rules of what Jews can and cannot eat there is no mention of health, although God could be using his omniscience about the food properties of some things to encourage Jews not to eat them in order to help them be healthy. This seems unlikely or at least ineffective since there is no evidence that Jews live longer or are any healthier than any other community. Even those with a serious attitude to observing halakhic rules about what to eat and drink are not noticeably healthier than anyone else and even tend to suffer from some specific diseases that are widespread within that community.

Why ban certain foods that seem to be perfectly acceptable to eat from a health point of view? Anthropologists suggest that given the physical circumstances in which people live, some kinds of food become more efficient or suitable than others, and so the wrong type of food tends to be stigmatized (Harris 1985). In the Middle East, Christians used to keep pigs and they are very efficient converters of refuse into meat, albeit meat only available to Christians. Until fairly recently, Christians in Cairo used to operate a very efficient trash removal service that relied on pigs to deal with much of the refuse, until a panic over health, and no doubt a desire to be mean to the local Coptic population, led to a widespread culling of their source of livelihood, the pig. Certainly there are problems with eating some kinds of food, they may harbor diseases or be the product of undesirable practices, and yet it is presumably possible to take the food and prepare it in an acceptable manner from a health and social point of view. In that case some would argue that the ban on some foods should no longer be observed, since it is now fine to consume. Yet in the Bible it does not say do not eat pigs until you find a cure for the sorts of illnesses that you can catch from eating pigs, or that chewing the cud and dividing the hoof are signs of an animal that is tastier or healthier to eat than others. The prohibition is absolute, as is the avoidance of blood, yet many cuisines do employ blood in ways that do not appear to be bad for their consumers. Again, those who see religious laws as applicable at certain times and places, and not universally, would use this sort of argument to suggest that we vary our adherence to such rules and no longer slavishly follow them in very different circumstances. This would surely be Spinoza's view, he was not sympathetic to the idea of continuing with a ritual beyond the time when it has a point. The fact that God laid it down as a law would be a religious but not a rational motive to continue with the practice. If he had to make a choice between religion and reason, we know what decision he would make.

Reasons for Rules

Health is, of course, a relevant issue in deciding what we should do, but it is worth saying yet again that the Bible does not use this as its rationale for the restrictions on what Jews are supposed to eat and drink, nor for the practice of circumcision. In any case, if the method of slaughter is cruel, then that seems to provide an objection to carrying it out. It is possible to argue that of course the Bible does not advocate cruelty to animals, and there are many tender passages both there and in other authoritative Jewish texts about the significance of our duty toward other living things, presumably especially sentient things. Although early on we are told that the world and what is in it are there for our use, that does not mean we can do whatever we want with it. Some defenders of kashrut argue that there is evidence to suggest that having a throat cut without any stunning either before or after is the optimal way from an animal welfare point of view. This is not the place to examine such claims, but it seems implausible. I imagine most human beings who were facing a similar grim event would choose the stunning, were it available, in just the same way that we tend to be keen on anaesthesia before something unpleasant happens to our bodies. Even afterwards it would be better than nothing. The point of ritual slaughter is the removing of as much blood as possible, and it is far from clear how compatible that is with animal welfare.

Rav Kook used a Maimonidean form of argument here to suggest that the laws of kosher slaughter and food preparation are so onerous that God uses them to gradually wean us off our enthusiasm for eating animals. He realizes that if we were told to not eat them we would find this very difficult, and would probably disobey, but if he says we can eat them while making it harder and harder to do so while sticking to the rules, we may come to decide it is not worth the trouble. If you tell people that they can eat things which have blood in them but they should avoid the blood, a paradoxical situation is established. People will eventually appreciate that we should really avoid not only blood but also meat, since there is really no meat at all without blood to some degree, however thoroughly a carcass is cleaned. This is part of a gradual process and allows and encourages us to advance spiritually to a position where we avoid killing things in order to eat them, or eat things that have been killed, since we begin to see what is wrong with this process. Whether we agree with his position here is not that important, what is worth noting is the way he justifies a practice, and that is in terms of what he takes to be its ultimate aim and objective. This is a popular procedure and we can see why. If we know why a practice is legal or otherwise we can work out whether and how it might be varied while remaining faithful to its rationale. When it is under attack, we can defend it not just as the ritual carried out by a certain group of people but as having a higher purpose, one worth preserving and permitting.

There are problems with this strategy since it results in basing a ritual on a view of how things are in the world, and our understandings of that change. For example, the person who circumcises ritually in Jewish practice, the *mohel*, is usually very experienced and takes every care for the activity to be safe and as hygienic as possible. On the other hand, it is unlikely to be as safe to do it in a private home as it can be in hospital, and there are some practices surrounding it, like sucking the wound, that are definitely not safe. Like a lot of religious rituals, perhaps it is better now than how things were done in the past, but now we have more secure ways of carrying out the same task, and we might even question whether it should be carried out at all. When people are used to doing something in one way they may wish to carry on doing it whatever the consequences, as we saw with prayer in the Covid era. Some people refused to change their behavior since they always did things in a certain way and were going to carry on doing them in a certain way. This is to regard ritual not as a way of getting something done so much as a way of expressing oneself, as living a certain kind of life. The expression "whatever the consequences" is a useful one here since it reminds us of a basic dichotomy in ethics between those who act in order to bring about the best ends and those who adhere to general moral principles whatever the ends may happen to be. The consequentialist views the absolutist as uncompromising while the absolutist sees the consequentialist as too ready to chop and change.

Divine Laws

When it comes to religion the debate is really about authority. The rules that religion tells us to follow come from God and so they are taken to have a grounding in something really important and powerful. God would not establish rules that were dubious, and he might well expect us to follow those rules rigorously. It is worth noting that in the Pentateuch there are a lot of contraventions of the rules that attract at least formally capital punishment. On the other hand, we do not know how far those rules are supposed to be for every Jew everywhere and how far they are place or time limited, and we can of course interpret them in different ways. In the Jewish tradition there is a long-lasting system of commentary and debate so that the idea that there are a variety of ways of observing the rituals is quite acceptable, or at least the idea that there are a variety of ways of discussing such observance is quite acceptable. Judaism is not alone here; religions that have survived a long time tend to embody flexibility, which is not to say that all their adherents appreciate this.

It is often said that human laws, unlike divine laws, change but this is problematic since divine laws presumably also change as human beings and their circumstances change. For example, circumcising a child at home made sense when hospitals were not available and the local Jewish community had to make its own arrangements in any case for health care, but in modern conditions it is better to have the procedure carried out in a more sanitary environment, if it has to be carried out at all. But does it need to be carried out? What is the connection between a covenant made between human beings and God and a small bit of skin on the penis? How does what Abraham did in the past relate to us now? It is very different from making a commitment to obeying the law sent down by God at Sinai, here we are adhering to a set of principles, not chopping off a bit of skin. What is even more important here is that the choppers are not operating on themselves, they are carrying out what could easily be seen as an assault against someone defenseless and without his permission. The situation with animal slaughter is not that dissimilar, it is surely reasonable to think that animals would prefer not to be slaughtered, and if they were then to have this done in the most painless manner. This is not exactly a case calling out for informed consent, but it is not ridiculous to think of what animals would agree to were they given the choice.

The issue is about what the animals are there for. Are they for us, and so have no rights at all to be treated in a particular way, and even if they have no such rights should we not in any case treat them well? There is a familiar story (*Bava Metzia* 85a) about how the famous rabbi Yehuda ha-Nasi, the official author of the *Mishnah* was in synagogue and a calf escaped from the slaughter house and appealed to him to save it, and the rabbi said he should go to the fate for which he was designed. It is said that this heartlessness resulted in problems for the rabbi, and he was only relieved of them when a cat and its kittens were discovered in his house and he ordered that they not be killed. The problems were due to his lack of mercy and they came to an end when he displayed something of what God extends to all creation. It might be thought that his earlier heartlessness was unfairly dealt with, since he was right. According to many understandings of Judaism animals are there to be used. It is strange how in societies where animals are routinely killed for food and other reasons that escapees from the process are treated exceptionally well, perhaps the most incongruous event of this kind is the pardoning by the President of the United States of two turkeys on the eve of Thanksgiving, as though the killing of turkeys on the holiday was a result of something in general that the birds had done wrong! This brings out something of the peculiarity of what it is to justify a practice. Wittgenstein points out how justification comes to an end, epistemologically at least, at a certain stage. He uses the expression "the spade is turned" when we reach bedrock (Wittgenstein 1958, 217). He argues that activities have a certain autonomy, they are not attempts at doing something else, and so what the activity regards as an appropriate move within it is an appropriate move. We may criticize it for some other reason, but within the activity there are rules about what is done and if we change the rules then we are no longer involved in the same activity. This is why people who insisted on following their religious practices during the Covid epidemic were so oblivious to wider considerations. They were haredi Jews and their lives were built around communal prayer and study, and they would continue to act in the usual way. To ask them to do otherwise would go against their sense of who they are. Not that everyone in the group held such views, of course, but it is important to see that their strict adherence to rules is not a strategy to try to get to some end, it is just a part of who they are. The rituals and practices are constitutive of the religious identity of those performing them and cannot be cast off without risking that identity.

That is what impressed Spinoza about circumcision, the fact that it was a mark in the flesh and a rather permanent one at that. That is part of the moral problem also, the fact that something is done which cannot be changed and at a time when the person could not possibly give any form of consent, informed or otherwise. Similarly with animal slaughter, where living things are killed, and in a way that seems suboptimal from an animal welfare point of view, and once they are ritually slaughtered there is no going back. There are apparently easy alternatives. Jewish males don't have to be circumcised, Jews can eat things that have not been killed at all or that have been killed in what some argue is a more humane way. Nothing else would need to change about their other practices and beliefs. Something symbolic could be done, as for example the prayers on Yom Kippur that replicate to some degree the rituals that existed at the time of the Temple on that day. *Avodah* which is part of the additional service, *Musaf*, are not the same and of course the venue is not the same, but they represent the original and perform a similar function to the original rituals. There is a custom for a chicken to be killed and have its blood scattered around in connection with the Day of Atonement in a reference to the Temple sacrifices, something which is obviously potentially unpleasant for those present and presumably even more so for the chicken. The *kapporos* ceremony is obviously a bit similar to one carried out in Temple days, and the idea is that the chicken is a scapegoat for the individual over whom the blood is splattered. It is easy to imagine less gory alternatives, like giving money to charity which sometimes replaces it, and it might be argued that a general moral principle whereby a ritual that risks human or animal welfare should always be suspect and, if possible, replaced by something less dramatic and permanent.

Changing Divine Laws

This gets us to the very essence of rituals in religion. Should we expect them to fit in with ordinary life and its expectations, or should we expect them to shape our lives? Here, of course, taste comes in. Some people like their rituals to be demanding and all-encompassing, so that they know at every time what they are supposed to be doing, who with and how. The rituals do not rest on anything, they just express what it is to be Jewish for some groups of people. Other Jews want their rituals, if they employ any, to fit into their everyday lives and accord with certain principles such as being healthy, safe and convenient. It would be a mistake to see this latter group as being less serious about their religion than the former; it might be said that they need to think more about what rituals they are going to perform since they do not accept a readymade ensemble but have to make it up as they go along. If we look at the rituals from outside the system of which they are a part then other issues come into play, but we tend not to be anthropologists when considering our own repertoire of religious practices. We should be wary about the approach of those like Spinoza who criticize rituals for not being rational, since as Wittgenstein points out, from within the activity for which those rituals constitute the rules, they are rational. They are the principles of how to act, they are the rules of the game, as it were.

But games have all sorts of rules, some which never change and many which do. Every year the official bodies regulating sport change the latter. The peripheral rules change in order to preserve the effectiveness of the basic rules, it might be said, but of course it is not easy to know how to distinguish between these two categories. Maimonides distinguished between *hukkim* and *mishpatim*, he did not say that some were more important than others but the former are rules for which we can find no reason, unlike the latter. We can see why a rule against murder might be a good idea, but not mixing up different kinds of textiles in our clothing does not seem to have any point. Of course, the general point is to separate Jews from others, as Shylock suggests in the *Merchant of Venice* Act 1 Scene 3 when Bassanio invites him to eat with them and he replies that he can do business with them but not eat or drink with them. The distinction between axioms in a logical system and other forms of sentence are not difficult to establish, but it is much harder to do this with human activities. This was a familiar experience in the Covid pandemic for a religion to provide a different way for its adherents to do things, only to be met with the response that it was not the same. So participating in services via Zoom was not the same as being there in person, but who would have expected it to be? The complaint that it was not the same is true but banal, since it is obviously different given the change in the circumstances under which everyone is operating during a pandemic. The interesting question is whether the change in the ritual's delivery is so significant that it changes the meaning of the ritual as a whole, and here the answer is obviously not. The social aspect of prayer is important but surely not defining of what prayer basically is about, and those who confuse the social with the religious make a grave error here, one that is more due to a lack of imagination than anything else. It is often the case though that a peripheral aspect of an activity like religion takes on an enhanced meaning because of an emotional feature it possesses for individuals. A particular prayer that your father liked, a ceremony that someone close to you performed but complained about, a building where you remember going to religion classes, all these are quite minor aspects of the formal nature of religion but major sources of what makes religion important for us emotionally.

Basic Principles in Religion

Spinoza would hate this line of argument. It is not just that he wanted to emphasize the rational aspect of religion, but also the principles as he saw it that religions are based upon. Attaching ourselves to aspects that are not the principles is to take the wrong view of religions and what they are about. He does have a point here since it is difficult to justify someone adopting a peripheral feature of an activity and confusing it with something essential. On the other hand, the distinction between them is often quite difficult to establish and this is something that the Talmud talks about a lot. Some commentators seek to summarize the Torah in a neat and pithy sentence that expresses its essence. The most famous is Hillel who when asked to do this says, "Do to others what you would have them do to you", and then he says study, an addendum that is often conveniently forgotten. But others point to some obscure ritual, and suggest that is the essence of the religion. We may doubt the value of seeking the essence of any religion, of course, but the idea of summarizing something is important, since it enables us to think about what we see as the key words or concepts. The danger of such an approach is that it looks like we might think of that summary as representing what the religion is all about, and everything else linked with it is superfluous. Levinas sees ritual as something that makes it possible for us to be religious since it provides a structure for our lives and a discipline in accordance with which we can orient ourselves toward God and the rest of humanity. He is obviously impressed with a passage from the aggadic story found in *Ayn Yaakov*, which is a compilation of such stories, that he quotes (Levinas 1997, 19). It is about a debate among the major characters of the Mishnah as to what is the single most significant passage in the Torah. What is the one verse that seems to express the essence of Jewish life more than any other? There is a Baraita in *Torat Kohanim* (Chapter 4, Midrash 12) "Love your fellow man as yourself" (*Vayikra* 19;18). Rabbi Akiva said this is a great principle of the Torah. Ben Azai said, "This is the book of the generations of Adam – on the day that God created man, He made him in His Image" (*Bereshit* 5;1) is a greater principle than that. The Great Maharal of Prague (1525–1609) in his book *Netivot Olam* brings an addition to this Midrash, which was cited first by the author of *Ayn Yaakov* [Rabbi Ya'akov Ben Haviv (1460–1516) in his introduction to the book]. Ben Zoma says: We have found a more inclusive verse and it is "Shema Yisrael" (*Devarim* 6: 4). Ben Nanas says we have found a more inclusive verse than that and it is "Love your fellow man as yourself" (*Vayikra* 19;18). Shimon Ben Pazi says we have found a more inclusive verse than that and it is "The first lamb you shall sacrifice in the morning and the second lamb you shall sacrifice in the evening" (*Shemot* 29;39 and *Bamidbar* 28;4) [referring to the daily *Tamid* (perpetual) offering brought every morning and evening]. Rabbi Ploni stood up and said that the halacha is in accordance with Ben Pazi as it is written, "As all that I show you, the structure of the Mishkan and all its vessels: so shall you do" (*Shemot* 25;9). Yet the first three opinions look plausible as the fundamental teachings of the Torah. Ben Azai sees in the fact that all human beings are created in God's image the basic dignity of humanity value and existence. Rabbi Akiva and Ben Azai develop this point ethically by asking what its implications are for practice. We should love others as ourselves. As Hillel in the Talmud (*Masechet Shabbat* 31) puts it: "Do not do to others that which you would not like others to do to you." One cannot claim to respect the image of God in others if one does not act as though one loves them. Ben Zoma's teaching that "Shema Yisrael" is the most important teaching also makes sense. Jews are supposed to say this morning and night, it is all about our belief in God's absolute authority over us and our acceptance of His commandments. It is this commitment which Ben Zoma quite reasonably says lies at the heart of all of Judaism.

What seems rather perplexing is the teaching of Shimon Ben Pazi. How does his statement about the daily offering of a lamb brought morning and evening compare with the seemingly all-encompassing statements of the previous three sages? How can a Midrash state that the accepted view is that of Ben Pazi? After all, he talks about daily lambs and the others talk of fundamental principles. The Maharal suggests that the explanation of Ben Pazi, who stated that the verse "The one sheep you shall offer in the morning, …" is taken to be a greater teaching of the Torah as it emphasizes that a person should serve God regularly and carry out the orders that he has received. Ben Pazi believes the only way to transform our lives in a sustainable way is through such continual daily conduct. It has often been argued that Judaism is more about actions than abstract ideas and the daily carrying out of the rituals and practices of the religion mentioned by Ben Pazi is in line with this approach.

The passage about the *olat tamid*, the daily sacrifice, is legal or halakhic in direct and obvious ways, whereas the rather more abstract competing suggestions are not, so we should not be surprised that it wins the competition. Spinoza offers "To love God above all things and one's neighbor as oneself" (Spinoza 1925, 165). This is even worse in leading us further away from practical activities. Even if we focus on loving our neighbors we are left in perplexity, since what does it mean in terms of what we should do? But the daily ritual is easy to understand and doing something on a regular basis just because God has ordered it is a very tangible indication of our attitude toward Him. Similarly, we could move on from that in ways that Spinoza would dislike, to suggest that the rules of Judaism give their practitioners a way of expressing their love for God and those around them in tangible and comprehensible form.

Levinas takes up this idea when he notes that committing to the extraordinary in our everyday lives is that which ultimately transforms them and this is what he sees ritual doing. It is often mysterious why we are asked to do what we are in the Torah, something that might be confused with being irrational. It is certainly true that we are often told to do things that we do not understand. When Hugo Gryn worked as a rabbi in London he told the story of the ritual that his great aunt Julia insisted he follow whereby one does not throw away finger nails after cutting them but burns them (something he recounts in his book *Chasing Shadows*, 2001, 42). This for him was an important ritual from Jewish Ruthenia, and yet in itself it has no basis at all, not even any religious basis. Yet when recounting it he invariably had tears in his eyes. Presumably this was because it evoked the past, a past from which many of his relatives did not return, and the warmth of his childhood and the kindness of those in his community and family. Yet the ritual in itself is entirely empty of meaning; like many religious rituals, arbitrary and artificial. According to Levinas, rituals go against nature, and in this way let the divine into our everyday lives. This is what Reform gets wrong, he argues, the point is not to modernize rituals but to recognize the nature of acting religiously as a useful anachronism. We do not know how or why rituals have come about and we do not need to know. All we need to know is that the religion commends them to us.

Bibliography

Cohen, Shaye. 2005. *Why Aren't Jewish Women Circumcised? Gender and Covenant in Judaism*, Berkeley: University of California Press.
Greenspoon, Leonard Ed. 2010. *Rites of Passage: How Today's Jews Celebrate, Commemorate and Commiserate*. West Lafayette, IN: Purdue University Press.
Glick, Leonard. 2005. *Marked in Your Flesh: Circumcision from Ancient Judea to Modern America*. Oxford: Oxford University Press.
Gryn, Hugo. 2001. *Chasing Shadows*. Harmondsworth: Penguin.
Harris, Marvin. 1985. *Good to Eat: Riddles of Food and Culture*. New York: Simon and Schuster.
Hart, Mitchell. Ed. 2009. *Jewish Blood: Reality and Metaphor in History, Religion and Culture*. Abingdon: Routledge.
Levinas, Emmanuel. 1997. *Difficult Freedom: Essays on Judaism*. Trans. Seán Hand. Baltimore, MD: Johns Hopkins University Press.
Mill, John Stuart. *On Liberty*. www.econlib.org/library/Mill/mlLbty.html
Rosenblum, Jordan. 2010. *Food and Identity in Early Rabbinic Judaism*. Cambridge: Cambridge University Press.
Siegel, Sharon. 2014. *A Jewish Ceremony for Newborn Girls: The Torah's Covenant Affirmed*. Waltham, MA: Brandeis University Press.
Spinoza. 1925. *Tractatus Theologico-Politicus* XIII in *Opera*. Ed. Carl Gebhardt. Heidelberg: Carl Winter.
Spinoza. 2007. *Theological-Political Treatise*. Ed. Jonathan Israel. Trans. Michael Silverthorne and Jonathan Israel. Cambridge: Cambridge University Press.
Wittgenstein, Ludwig. 1958. *Philosophical Investigations*. Trans. G.E.M. Anscombe. Oxford: Blackwell.

22
BODY IMAGE AND JEWISH RITUALS AND PRACTICES

Jonathan E. Handelzalts and Shulamit Geller

The purpose of this chapter is to portray the possible associations between body image and Jewish rituals and practices. We will present a summary of definitions and cultural perspectives of body image in the literature, as well as general findings about the relationship between body image and religion. We will then explore findings regarding body image in Jewish rituals and practices, and specifically in the various denominations, and will suggest underlying mechanisms that may be relevant to issues of body image in Jewish ritual and practice. Finally, we will discuss the limitations of current studies and suggest directions for future research.

It should be noted that this chapter takes a social science perspective, studying body image in Jewish rituals and practices with quantitative as well as qualitative measures and summarizing available data on this subject. Further, as most of the studies were done with women, our conclusions and discussion pertain mainly to the body image of Jewish women. We will elaborate on future directions concerning research on Jewish men.

Body Image from a Sociocultural Perspective

The concept of *body image* refers to the multifaceted psychological experience of embodiment that encompasses one's body-related self-perceptions and self-attitudes, including thoughts, beliefs, feelings, and behaviors (Cash, 2004), both discrete positive and negative dimensions (Tylka, 2011). Characteristics emerging from positive body image include acceptance of one's body despite weight, body shape, and imperfections, and respect of one's body by attending to its needs and engaging in adaptive self-care behaviors (Avalos, Tylka and Wood-Barcalow, 2005). In contrast, body dissatisfaction, that is, the negative perceptions and feelings one has about one's body (Peat et al., 2008), may lead to inadequate self-care, in terms of health and protection, as well as to disordered eating (Cash et al., 2004).

Both dimensions, negative as well as positive body image, are thought to be rooted in cultural values and ideals, and develop from an early age within a sociocultural context (Ricciardelli et al., 2003). Sociocultural experiences are known to encourage appearance-related behaviors by inducing expectations regarding behavior, but also the ways in which individuals think and feel about their bodies (Thompson et al., 1999). Religion is one of the possible cultural variables that may affect body image. Thus, different cultural groups are thought to have different bodily experiences, and therefore much research in the field has focused on cross-cultural differences (e.g., McCabe et al., 2011, 2013; Swami et al., 2013).

Body Image and Religion

Religion is considered to be an agent through which an individual's attitudes and behavior and specifically in relation to his/her body are shaped (Christl et al., 2012; McCabe et al., 2011). It has been suggested that religion in general instills life with a sense of purpose and meaningfulness and may allow individuals to relate to their body more positively (Homan and Boyatzis, 2010; McCabe et al., 2011, 2013). Specifically, religiosity has been considered a potential buffer against eating disorders and body image dissatisfaction (Boyatzis and Quinlan, 2008; Homan and Boyatzis, 2010; Handelzalts et al., 2017; Jackson and Bergeman, 2011). It may influence well-being in different ways, such as by allowing individuals to construct meaning and set goals, increasing overall life satisfaction, offering social support, strengthening identity, restricting risky health behaviors, and promoting positive health behaviors (Kim, 2007).

As religiosity is a complex and multidimensional construct, ranging from general beliefs and attitudes to individuals' behaviors (Boyatzis et al., 2006) and may manifest itself differently across various religions and cultures, research on body image and religiosity is very heterogeneous in nature. Most research concerning religiosity and body image has focused mainly on the negative dimensions of body image, specifically, on body image dissatisfaction and disorders (Christl et al., 2012; Weinberger-Litman, 2007). However, religiosity has also been found to have positive impact on women's eating disorders, body dissatisfaction, and investment in their appearance (Goulet et al., 2017; Geller et al., 2018; Handelzalts et al., 2020; Sidi et al., 2020).

Although many studies report on the associations of religion-related variables and body image, most studies were conducted with Christian participants and overlooked other religious groups (Swami et al., 2014).

Body Image and Jewish Rituals and Practices

In this section, we describe studies associated with participants living in the USA and Israel. To the best of our knowledge, studies on this subject were only conducted with Jewish women; men were neglected in terms of the possible association between religiosity and body image. We will refer to this lacuna in the literature when suggesting topics for future research.

The Jewish population is a useful sample to research since it consists of distinct religious denominations with varying degrees of religious observance (Akrawi et al., 2015). Most studies refer to Ultra-Orthodox, Modern-Orthodox, and secular groups. However, it should be noted that many studies tend to overlook the fact that these groups are not homogeneous; for example, there are many different sects among Ultra-Orthodox Jews and a large variance within secular Jewish women. In addition, many studies tend not to take other distinct groups into account that may also be different, such as Reform Judaism and Reconstructionist Judaism.

Studies exploring the relationship between Jewish religion and women's bodies have mostly addressed eating disorders rather than body image, and have generally demonstrated the protective power of religiosity, although results were inconsistent. A study conducted in the USA that included 225 Jewish students belonging to either Ultra-Orthodox or secular groups showed that religiosity was associated with lower body dissatisfaction and less eating disorder symptomatology (Gluck and Geliebter, 2002). In another study conducted in the United States of 301 young Jewish women from heterogeneous denominations, mostly self-defining themselves as Orthodox or Modern-Orthodox, intrinsic religious orientation was associated with lower levels of body dissatisfaction and eating disorders (Weinberger-Litman et al., 2016). A study of 320 religious Modern-Orthodox adolescent Jewish Israeli girls found that a higher level of religiosity was associated with less eating-related psychopathology (Latzer et al., 2007).

On the other hand, in a study of 501 Jewish Israeli middle-aged women who comprised a broad range of religiosity, no significant differences were found in the frequency of serious eating disorders between the most and least religiously observant participants of the study. While traditional women had greater body dissatisfaction than the other participants, significant differences in body dissatisfaction were observed between Haredi and secular participants (Feinson and Meir, 2012; Feinson and Hornik-Lurie, 2016). Furthermore, in a study of 33 Ultra-Orthodox and 22 Modern-Orthodox Israeli women no difference in eating pathology was found between the Ultra-Orthodox and Modern-Orthodox women (Frenkel et al., 2018). Last, in a recent study of 580 Israeli Jewish women from Ultra-Orthodox, Modern-Orthodox, and secular denominations using both self-report measures of positive and negative body image attitudes, as well as the thin-ideal Implicit Association Test, findings demonstrated that while Ultra-Orthodox women report on more positive body image attitudes and fewer body image concerns, their implicit scores are similar to those of Modern-Orthodox and secular women, when taking their body-mass index (BMI) into account (Geller et al., 2021).

In a study of 230 women that compared Ultra-Orthodox, Modern-Orthodox, and secular Jewish women in Israel, we found that Ultra-Orthodox Jewish women had higher positive body image and lower negative body image; they also exhibited more positive attitudes regarding body care. Regarding body satisfaction, Modern-Orthodox women were significantly more satisfied with their bodies than the secular women. There thus seems to be continuum, ranging from secular, Modern-Orthodox, to Ultra-Orthodox women regarding body image (Handelzalts et al., 2017). These results were replicated in a subsequent study of 483 Jewish Israeli women belonging to the Ultra-Orthodox, Modern-Orthodox, and secular populations. Findings revealed that compared to secular Jewish women, Ultra-Orthodox Jewish women maintained more positive attitudes regarding their bodies, and reported lower levels of body image dissatisfaction (Geller et al., 2018).

As the literature review reveals, on the whole, women belonging to more Orthodox denominations tend to exhibit better body image as reflected in higher levels of positive body image, lower levels of negative body image, as well as fewer symptoms of eating disorders. What is also evident is that each study examined groups of women belonging to different denominations, sometimes with no clear differentiation between groups. We now turn to elaborate on the possible mediating mechanisms that may be involved in this suggested association between Jewish rituals and practices and body image.

What is it about Jewish rituals and practices that may help people to cope with body image concerns? Below we attempt to explain the effects of levels of religiosity by examining factors that may be present in varying degrees among members of different Jewish denominations.

Faith

Religious faith in general, that is, believing that one has a relationship with a Divine Being who loves one personally and unconditionally, may serve as a strong source of self-worth (Sherkat and Ellison, 1999), and thus may be beneficial in terms of body image. Accordingly, in a systematic review, strong and internalized religious beliefs coupled with a secure and satisfying relationship with God were found to be associated with lower levels of disordered eating, psychopathology, and concerns pertaining to body image (Akrawi et al., 2015). This review concluded that specific beliefs associated with positive body image consisted of the body having sacred qualities and being a manifestation of God. Although these findings were reported in the context of religion in general (studies of Christian and Jewish samples) and not Judaism in particular, these issues could be associated with elements of Jewish rituals and practices.

If so, what are the specific elements of Jewish faith that may be associated with body image? Religiously observant Jewish women may be less focused on appearance and more focused on moralistic or ritualistic pursuits (Mussap, 2009). In addition, they may be less likely to express dissatisfaction about their bodies because of the body's sacred status in Judaism. The Jewish concept of guarding the body (*sh'mirat haguf*), as emphasized by the *Halacha*, which is the Jewish code of conduct, is a value that exemplifies the message that individuals are beautiful just as they are. This value, which also stresses that each individual should take good care of their physical body and avoid excessive physical risks (Abramowitz and Silverman, 1997), may explain the correlation between body appreciation and body care that was found for Ultra-Orthodox and Modern-Orthodox women (Handelzalts et al., 2017) as well as the lower levels of eating disorders found in some studies of Orthodox women from various sects (Gluck and Geliebter, 2002; Latzer et al., 2007; Weinberger-Litman et al., 2018). In addition, in line with previous findings, the relationship between denomination and positive body image was fully mediated by strength of religious faith, demonstrating a significant relationship between strength of religious faith among Ultra-Orthodox women compared to Modern-Orthodox and secular women. Thus, strong and internalized religious beliefs manifested by religious observance and strong commitment, were associated with positive body image (Geller et al., 2018). In comparison, a greater level of extrinsic religious orientation (i.e., religious commitment motivated primarily by societal pressures or expectations) was found to be associated with greater disordered eating and body dissatisfaction, and a higher level of intrinsic religious orientation (i.e., religious commitment largely motivated from within) was found to be associated with lower levels of disordered eating and body dissatisfaction (Weinberger-Litman et al., 2016). These findings may shed light on the link between religiosity and body image (e.g., Homan and Boyatzis, 2010), suggesting that by focusing judgments of self-worth on moral and ritualistic pursuits relevant to the individual's religion rather than on appearance (Ferraro 1998), strong intrinsic faith may offer individuals the opportunity to select and work toward meaningful goals, and may serve as a basis for self-worth.

These findings could be explained by beliefs inferred from verses such as "So God created man in his own image, in the image of God created he him; male and female created he them" (Genesis 1:27). A person who believes in this notion might have a better positive body image and hold attitudes regarding a stronger need to take good care of one's body. This is in line with the Christian construct of sanctification regarding body image (the view of the body as having divine significance) that has been found to be positively correlated with body satisfaction (Jacobson et al., 2013). Thus, it is possible that the more these values are stressed, which in turn might be dependent on the strength of faith and belonging to a culture or denomination that stresses this notion, the better one's feelings toward one's body.

The notion that physical features and attractiveness may be less important than many other virtues is also exemplified in the verse "Favor is deceitful, and beauty is vain; but a woman who feareth the LORD, she shall be praised" (Proverbs 31:30, King James Bible). Here again, faith in God is stressed as opposed to any superficial feeling regarding one's appearance.

Modesty

Modesty is a concept found across different cultures and religions, such as Judaism, Christianity, and Islam (Andrews, 2011). Modesty indicates sexual purity and respectable womanhood

(Reagan 1997). It is a central value for Modern-Orthodox and Ultra-Orthodox Jewish women. In general, a modest dress code was found to be associated with lower objectification experiences (Fredrickson and Roberts, 1997), namely, allowing women's self-affirmation as human beings instead of as sexual objects (Holman, 2012). Thus, it was suggested that modesty is a buffering mechanism against cultural pressures pertaining to appearance (Mussap, 2009). Indeed, several studies exploring modesty among Muslim women, reported that dressing modestly was associated with less body dissatisfaction, with lower objectification experiences, less importance of appearance, and more positive body image (e.g., Demmrich et al., 2017; Kertechian and Swami, 2016; Swami et al., 2014; Wilhelm et al., 2019; Sidi et al., 2020).

While these associations between clothing restrictions (which may not be identical to modesty) and body image were obtained among Muslim women worldwide, for Jewish participants, to our knowledge, these associations were only reported in two unpublished manuscripts exploring modesty in Jewish samples in the United States and South Africa (Bachner-Melman and Zohar, 2019). This paucity of research and findings demonstrates the complicated association between modesty and body image (Bachner-Melman and Zohar, 2019), and could be attributed to the conflictual role that modesty may play for women, in view of the fact that this value applies only to women across religions.

In the Ultra-Orthodox community, modesty is a very important value (Longman, 2007). The Jewish concept of *tzeni'ut* (modesty) in contemporary Orthodox-*halakhic* discourse relates primarily to the responsibilities of women and girls, as a means of protecting men from earthly temptations (Elior, 2010). Women are required to observe the laws of modesty not for their own sake, but for the purpose of assimilating into the world of men (Nahary and Hartman, 2020). Modesty norms entail gender separation from a young age and strict standards of dress and behavior. Ultra-Orthodox girls and women are expected to dress, act, and speak modestly. They are instructed to cover most of their bodies, including elbows, knees, collarbones and toes, and after marriage they are required to cover their hair (Heilman, 1992). Clothing must be unobtrusive, so that white, black, grey, dark blue, and brown are common colors in the wardrobes of Ultra-Orthodox women and girls (Taragin-Zeller, 2014). Furthermore, the changes that the Jewish Ultra-Orthodox world has undergone in the twenty-first century, which have created options for participation in non-Orthodox arenas (such as work, leisure, academic studies, and the media) have given rise to the phenomenon of the *modesty tornado* in the form of stricter modesty requirements (e.g., requiring heavier tights for girls and sewing up slits in skirts) among Ultra-Orthodox women (Elor, 2017). These measures may also be interpreted as an attempt to protect the religious community from the negative effects of contemporary Western culture (Hartman, 2007), and maintaining the central essence of the Jewish people (Neriya-Ben Shahar, 2011).

On the one hand, modesty can be viewed as having positive attributes for women. This practice was reported to facilitate women's connection to their community, embracing them in a collective identity (Weiss, 2009), and helping them affirm their womanhood (Milligan, 2014). A qualitative study describing how the fashion of wearing capes evolved among some Ultra-Orthodox women showed that this practice may be perceived as a way for women to display a higher spiritual level, which might upgrade their own social status and roles in their communities (Block, 2011). An ethnographic research conducted at a Bais Yaakov seminary in Jerusalem by Taragin-Zeller (2014) demonstrated how female teachers and their pupils structure an ideology of modesty that expresses discontent with their limited religious roles as only wives and mothers. They thus transform modesty from a social-masculine obligation to a divine one, in which current ideals of modesty are seen as another realm in which Ultra-Orthodox women reconstruct their religious gender roles. After generations of connecting with God through their husbands and children, they currently use modesty to construct a way to connect directly with God (Taragin-Zeller, 2014).

From an opposite standpoint, it is argued that these acts of modesty serve as powerful tools of social control dominated by the male gaze in a similar way to other rituals, such as the Jewish marriage ceremony, and like the Jewish laws of divorce (Hartman, 2007). In this sense, a Jewish wife's hair covering demarcates the exclusive and unilateral property rights that her husband has to his wife's sexuality, and thus "keeps women in their place" (Weiss, 2009). Thus, when it comes to beauty, for example, wearing nice or tighter clothes or wearing makeup, the aforementioned female teachers and their pupils from Jerusalem structured their definition of beauty to be consistent with the traditional obligation, namely, that women should only exhibit their beauty to their husbands (Taragin-Zeller, 2015).

Although some subversive elements in the practice of modesty among Orthodox women are evident, it still primarily functions as a way to reinforce the community's traditional ideas, especially gendered religious roles. As a result, Orthodox women are in a state of constant negotiation with *halakhic* rules (Nahary and Hartman, 2020). This in turn may demonstrate the tension created by the opposing social and cultural forces encountered by Orthodox women (Taragin-Zeller, 2015). As various sub-denominations of Ultra-Orthodox and Modern-Orthodox women treat and exhibit modesty differently, future research in this conflictual arena should further investigate the ways modesty shapes self-perceptions in general and body image perceptions for Jewish women.

Media Exposure

According to the sociocultural perspective of body image (Tiggemann, 2011), the media plays a central role in exposing the public to unrealistic thin-ideal images, internalized by women of all ages (Fitzsimmons-Craft et al., 2016). Meta-analyses and studies that focused on visual media and included both correlational and experimental studies reported associations between various types of media exposure and women's dissatisfaction with their bodies, internalization of the thin-ideal, and disordered eating, behavior, and beliefs (Grabe et al., 2008; Eckler et al., 2017; Fardouly and Vartanian, 2016; Homan et al., 2012). Importantly, this general pattern of results attesting to media effects on body dissatisfaction has primarily emerged from research conducted in Westernized societies, including mainly white participants who share the same unrealistically thin "body perfect" ideal of female beauty (Bell and Dittmar, 2011; Fitzsimmons-Craft et al., 2016).

In recent decades, scholars have recognized the importance of studying associations between media, religion, and culture to understand religious communities' negotiation with modernity and globalization (Campbell and Golan, 2011), as may be reflected in the various associations between belonging to religions or specific denominations and media exposure. These associations may be highly relevant for various Jewish denominations, as these differ in their exposure to media. Regarding the media, two parallel processes have become evident in the Ultra-Orthodox community in recent years. On the one hand, the Ultra-Orthodox community stresses the need to preserve the community's unique character; it resents any external influence and therefore tends to isolate its members from the general public or the mass media (Livio and Tenenboim-Weinblatt, 2007). At the same time, the Ultra-Orthodox community favors a certain level of acceptance with some reservations, emphasizing the Internet as a useful tool that provides information and various services (Neriya-Ben Shahar and Lev-On, 2011).

Studies exploring the effect of the media on body images of young Jewish women belonging to different denominations have supported the premise that belonging to a certain religious denomination and religious identity may act as a factor protecting women from the negative effects of Western media images (Geller et al., 2018; Handelzalts et al., 2020). In particular, media exposure was found to be a mediator for the relationship between level of religiosity and concerns pertaining to body image for both positive and negative body image (Geller et al., 2018). Moreover, Ultra-Orthodox women were found to feel less pressured by the media than Modern-Orthodox women, who in turn were less pressured by the media than secular women in internalizing values pertaining to appearance (Handelzalts et al., 2020). These effects of the media (e.g., Grabe et al., 2008) demonstrate first and foremost the robust role media exposure plays in transmitting societal standards for female beauty (i.e., the desirability of thinness) and its consequent role in shaping both ideals of body image and negative perceptions of body image (e.g., Perloff, 2014) for all women—both directly and through internalization—regardless of denomination (Handelzalts et al., 2020).

These findings confirm the suggestion that religious identity may discourage body-centric media consumption (Mussap, 2009) among Ultra-Orthodox and Modern-Orthodox women as they simply consume no media at all or less media compared to secular women (Goldzak-Kunik and Leshem, 2017). However, the percentage of people using the Internet within various Jewish denominations (including Ultra-Orthodox Jews) has been reportedly growing in Israel and worldwide (Abramac, 2015; Campbell, 2015; Israel Internet Association, 2017; Neriya-Ben Shahar, 2019), revealing for example, that although applications like WhatsApp are condemned by Ultra-Orthodox leaders, its use is increasing in certain Ultra-Orthodox communities (Abramac, 2015). For example, in a sample of 150 Ultra-Orthodox women who work in high-tech hothouses designated exclusively for this population, which is indicative of the changes this community is undergoing, two-thirds of the respondents possessed a computer at home; half of these respondents had Internet access. About one-third of these women communicate through the Internet, mostly with other women (Neriya-Ben Shahar and Lev-On, 2011). Although this sample is not in any way representative of the Ultra-Orthodox community, it does reveal a trend and also exemplifies the heterogeneity of Ultra-Orthodox society.

In addition to the differences in the amount of media consumption, it may also be argued that the various religious groups differ in the quality of their media exposure. Specifically, in Israel, some parts of the Ultra-Orthodox population use the Internet through special means – usually through "kosher" Internet (Katz, 2012). Thus, although "everything is halakhic" within the Ultra-Orthodox community, including the media that they are exposed to, the everyday lives of religious people obviously include a combination of religious, non-religious, sacred, and secular discourses (Neriya-Ben Shahar, 2019).

Whether or not the use of media is actually greater than reported in surveys, Ultra-Orthodox women, as a whole, are thought to consume less media than secular and Modern-Orthodox women, and the content of the media that they do consume is either censored or restricted. It is therefore logical to assume that they are less pressured by the media than their secular counterparts. Neriya-Ben Shahar (2019) further argues that Ultra-Orthodox women who perceive themselves as agents of change utilize media only for what they consider appropriate purposes upon understanding both the advantages and the dangers inherent in the use of media, using religious terminology to reflect their attempts to control these hazards. They thereby connect the traditional with the modern and the sacred with the profane as a unique expression of their navigation between their simultaneous roles as both gatekeepers and agents of change.

These conclusions were somewhat supported and exemplified by a study conducted in Israel among 178 adolescent schoolgirls from three ethnically distinct communities in Israel: secular Jewish girls, Ultra-Orthodox girls, Christian Arab girls, and a group of 14 severely anorexic girls (Goldzak-Kunik and Leshem, 2017). Although Ultra-Orthodox adolescent girls' ideal body image was to be thinner, and their dissatisfaction with their body image was similar to secular, Christian, and anorexic girls, the correlation of BMI and ideal preference suggested that the thinner ideal of Ultra-Orthodox school girls was determined by their own body image, that is, each girl would like to be thinner in relation to her own body image. On the other hand, the thin-ideal of the other schoolgirls was unrelated to their body image, but to an externally determined ideal. It was assumed that this was an external, consensual ideal, influenced by exposure to the media. These results thus support the hypothesized buffering role of religion, along with media isolation, that promotes fewer eating disorders and less body image dissatisfaction in Ultra-Orthodox communities (Latzer et al., 2007, 2008, 2015; Gluck and Geliebter, 2002).

It is clear from the general literature that media exposure is an important variable in the study of body image. Further, studies have consistently shown that media exposure is a relevant mediator in the effect that Jewish faith and belonging to more Orthodox denominations have on body image. Future research should consider measuring not only the amount of media exposure but rather the content of the media to shed light on the relationship between religious rituals and practices and the effects of the media on body image.

Conclusions

This chapter has explored the associations between different variables of Jewish rituals and practices and variables related to body image. Generally, and in a broad perspective, several studies, using self-reports measures, have demonstrated this association for Jewish women, as was found for other religions and cultures around the world (e.g., Akrawi et al., 2015; Boyatzis and Quinlan, 2008; Homan and Boyatzis, 2010). The scientific evidence pertaining to the possible mechanisms associated with such links is less clear. Evidence was found for the possible mediating effect of faith and media exposure as explaining this connection (e.g., Geller et al., 2018; Handelzalts et al., 2020). Regarding modesty, although this variable may be highly relevant when studying Jewish rituals and practices and body image, no evidence was found for such an association (and no empirical studies have measured it). Most importantly, from a sociocultural perspective, modesty may be a highly multilayered concept, the influence of which over body image may be complex. Thus, future studies should employ modesty measures that could also reflect women's own subjective response to modesty values rather than simply how they adhere to extrinsic modesty rules dictated by society.

An anecdotal yet representative example of the immense stresses associated with both modesty and media exposure in Ultra-Orthodox communities in Israel in general, and specifically for Ultra-Orthodox women, may be reflected in some posters referring to the coronavirus during the second lockdown in one of the Ultra-Orthodox neighborhoods in Jerusalem (*Mea Shearim*). According to the posters, the pandemic had been caused by two main sources of infection—smartphones (one notice warned that "corona damages breathing, iPhone damages the soul"; the Hebrew words *neshima*, which denotes "breathing", and *neshama*, which denotes "soul" rhyme)—and of course, immodestly dressed women (Pfeffer, 2020).

Regarding the different mediators explored in this chapter, we would like to suggest that religious faith is of particular importance vis-à-vis body image. While modesty as well as media exposure are variables that are strongly associated with the individual's belonging to a certain denomination (for example, consuming less media and dressing modestly are part of what defines an Ultra-Orthodox woman), religious faith is a more general concept. The strength or essence of faith is not necessarily associated with belonging to a certain denomination (although sometimes it is). Thus, individuals who may not dress modestly or are exposed to the media may nevertheless hold views associated with the Jewish faith of the body as sacred or that inner qualities are more important than physical ones, thus promoting a positive body image. In this sense, the positive effect associated with Jewish faith may be a universal one that is not associated with any particular denomination.

Yet, findings from recent research using both implicit and explicit measures of body attitudes for the measurement of possible differences between women from three different Jewish religion denominations in Israel, revealed dissonance between explicit and implicit attitudes, such that when measuring thin-ideal internalization using an implicit measure, the difference obtained using self-report measures was eliminated (Geller et al., 2021). Moreover, the identification with the thin-ideal of Ultra-Orthodox women with higher BMI was more similar to the other groups than when asked directly using self-report measures, in which BMI had no effect. Such incongruence between Ultra-Orthodox women's explicit views and the implicit views can lead to experiencing cognitive dissonance, which can be damaging and even lead to poor mental health outcomes (Frenkel et al., 2018). These results, while implying a possible maladaptive effect for religiosity over body image, stress the importance of using both implicit and explicit measures of body image when assessing variables associated with religion.

Although the body of research associating Jewish rituals and practices and body image has been growing in recent years, research is still scarce. The major gap relates to the lack of studies on Jewish men and body image (Bachner-Melman and Zohar, 2019). This lack of studies is of course in line with the general lack of studies examining men's body image (Quittkat et al., 2019). Furthermore, following the lived religion theory that stresses the transition from studies about religion as institutions, beliefs, norms, and doctrines toward the daily practices of ordinary people (McGuire, 2008), who experience many different feelings in performing religious rituals and practices (Neriya-Ben Shahar, 2019), it is important to investigate the association between Jewish rituals and practices and body image among Jewish men and women in different cultural environments and settings and from various denominations (and not only in Israel and the USA). These studies should be conducted using the whole array of measures of body image, including both positive and negative aspects, implicit as well as explicit, as well as different conceptualizations of religion and religiousness.

All in all, the findings mentioned above stress the importance of offering women intervention programs that could help them to establish self-defined meaningful priorities while introducing aspects of religious commitment, regardless of their specific faith. Namely, applying principles advocated by most religions, such as focusing on serving others, actively engaging with one's community, and on inner strength rather than on appearance, may enable one to ignore the influence of external media that promote a thin-ideal body shape (Inman et al., 2014). For instance, clinicians implementing acceptance of the self and body and life's purpose rather than placing one's faith in false pursuit of extreme thinness have been successful in helping young Christian women with eating disorders (Richards et al., 2007).

Body image is an important factor related to the psychological well-being of people in modern times that results from the pressure of sociocultural forces. Since research has indicated that belonging to Ultra-Orthodox denomination may be associated with a more positive and less negative body image, research should aim to find the unique components associated with it in order to elucidate variables that could be implemented in therapy to help people cope with issues pertaining to body image. We have elaborated on the possible mechanisms of faith, modesty, and media exposure, but future research could pursue other directions. As religion in general, and Jewish rituals and practices in particular, influence people's sociocultural environment and are shaped by culture, this interdependent effect on people's body image should be of interest for researchers and clinicians.

References

Abramac, Gabi. 2015. "What's Up with WhatsApp in the Haredi World?" In *Conflict and Transformation*. Ed. Tadej Pirc. Ljubljana: A Priori, 153–70.

Abramowitz, Yosef I. & Silverman, Susan. 1997. *Jewish Family and Life: Traditions, holidays, and values for today's parents and children*. New York: Golden Books.

Akrawi, Daniel, Bartrop, Roger, Potter, Ursula, & Touyez, Stephan. 2015. "Religiosity, spirituality in relation to disordered eating and body image concerns: A systematic review." *Journal of Eating Disorders* 3: 29. https://doi.org/10.1186/s40337-015-0064-0

Andrews, Caryn S. 2011. "Defining and exploring modesty in Jewish American women." *Journal of Religion and Health* 50: 818–34. doi: 10.1007/s10943-010-9435

Avalos, Laura, Tracy L. Tylka, and Nichole Wood-Barcalow. 2005. "The body appreciation scale: Development and psychometric evaluation." *Body Image* 2, no. 3: 285–97.

Bachner-Melman, Rachel, & Zohar, Ada H. 2019. "Potential risk and protective factors for eating disorders in Haredi (Ultra-Orthodox) Jewish women." *Journal of Religion and Health* 58(6): 2161–74.

Bell, Beth T., & Dittmar, Helga. 2011. "Does media type matter? The role of identification in adolescent girls' media consumption and the impact of different thin-ideal media on body image." *Sex Roles* 65: 478–90. https://doi.org/10.1007/s11199-011-9964-x.

Block, Sima Z. 2011. "Shouldering the burden of redemption: How the 'fashion' of wearing capes developed in Ultra-Orthodox society." *Nashim: A Journal of Jewish Women's Studies & Gender Issue* (22): 32–55.

Boyatzis, Chris J., & Quinlan, Katherine B. 2008. "Women's body image, disordered eating and religion: A critical review of the literature." *Research in the Social Scientific Study of Religion* 19: 183–208.

Boyatzis, Chris J., Trevino, Kelly M., Manning, Alice E., & Quinlan, Katherine B. 2006. "The role of religion and spirituality in women's body image and eating behavior: Qualitative and quantitative approaches and clinical implications." *Counseling et Spiritualité* 25(2): 29–51.

Campbell, Heidi A. 2015. "Introduction: Studying Jewish Engagement with Digital Media and Culture." In *Digital Judaism*. Ed. Heidi A. Campbell. New York: Routledge, 1–15.

Campbell, Heidi A., & Golan, Oren. 2011. "Creating digital enclaves: Negotiation of the internet among bounded religious communities." *Media, Culture & Society* 33(5): 709–24. https://doi.org/10.1177/0163443711404464

Cash, Thomas F. 2004. "Body image: Past, present, and future." *Body Image* 1, no. 1: 1–5.

Cash, Thomas F., Phillips, Katherine A., Santos, Melanie T., & Hrabosky, Joshua I. 2004. "Measuring 'negative body image': validation of the body image disturbance questionnaire in a nonclinical population." *Body Image* 1(4): 363–72.

Christl, Taylor, Morgenthaler, Christoph, & Käppler, Christoph. 2012. "The role of gender and religiosity in positive body image development among adolescents in Germany." *Women's Studies* 41(6): 728–54.

Demmrich, Sarah, Atmaca, Sumeyya, & Dinç, Cuneyt. 2017. "Body image and religiosity among veiled and non-veiled Turkish women." *Journal of Empirical Theology* 30(2):127–47. doi:10.1163/15709256-12341359.

Eckler, Petya, Kalyango, Yusuf, & Paasch, Ellen. 2017. "Facebook use and negative body image among US college women." *Women & Health* 57(2): 249–67. doi:10.1080/03630242.2016.1159268.

Elior, Rachel. 2010. "'Present but Absent', 'Still Life', and 'A Pretty Maiden Who Has No Eyes'." *Studies in Spirituality* 20: 381–455.

Elor, Tamar. 2017. "The Winter of the Veiled Women in Israel." In *The Routledge International Handbook to Veils and Veiling*. Eds. Anna-Mari Almila and David Inglis. London: Routledge, 63–72.

Fardouly, Jasmine, & Vartanian, Lenny R. 2016. "Social media and body image concerns: Current research and future directions." *Current Opinion in Psychology* 9: 1–5. doi:10.1016/j.copsyc.2015.09.005.

Feinson, Marjorie C., & Hornik-Lurie, Tzipi. 2016. "Body dissatisfaction and the relevance of religiosity: A focus on ultra-orthodox Jews in a community study of adult women." *Clinical Social Work Journal* 44: 87–97. https://doi.org/10.1007/s10615-016-0574-5.

Feinson, Marjorie C., & Meir, Adi. 2012. "Disordered eating and religious observance: A focus on ultra-orthodox Jews in an adult community study." *International Journal of Eating Disorders* 45(1): 101–9. https://doi.org/10.1002/eat.20895.

Ferraro, Kenneth F. 1998. "Firm believers? Religion, body weight, and well-being." *Review of Religious Research* 39: 224–44.

Fitzsimmons-Craft, Ellen E., Bardone-Cone, Anna M., Crosby, Ross D., Engel, Scott G., Wonderlich, Stephan A., & Bulik, Cynthia M. 2016. "Mediators of the relationship between thin-ideal internalization and body dissatisfaction in the natural environment." *Body Image* 18: 113–22. doi:10.1016/j.bodyim.2016.06.006.

Fredrickson, Barbara L., & Roberts, Tomi-Ann. 1997. "Objectification theory: Toward understanding women's lived experiences and mental health risks." *Psychology of Women Quarterly* 21: 173–206. doi:10.1111/j.1471-6402.1997.tb00108.x.

Frenkel, Tlalit D., Latzer, Yael, & Lev-Wiesel, Rachel. 2018. "Relationship between the ideal woman model, self-figure drawing, and disordered eating among Jewish Ultra-Orthodox women and National Religious women." *Israel Journal of Psychiatry* 55(1): 73–81.

Geller, Shulamit, Handelzalts, Jonathan E., Gelfat, Rita, Arbel, Shirli, Sidi, Yael, & Levy, S. 2018. "Exploring body image, strength of faith, and media exposure among three denominations of Jewish women." *Current Psychology* 39: 1774–84. https://doi.org/10.1007/s12144-018-9876-9.

Geller, Shulamit, Sidi, Yael, Levy, Sigal, & Handelzalts, Jonathan E. 2021 (in press). "Body Image and Religion: Explicit and Implicit Attitudes among three denominations of Jewish women." *Psychology of Religion and Spirituality*. Advance online publication, http://dx.doi.org/10.1037/rel0000450

Gluck, Marci E., & Geliebter, Allan. 2002. "Body image and eating behaviors in Orthodox and Secular Jewish women." *The Journal of Gender-specific Medicine: JGSM: The Official Journal of the Partnership for Women's Health at Columbia* 5(1): 19–24.

Goldzak-Kunik, Galit, & Leshem, Micha. 2017. "Body image drawings dissociate ethnic differences and anorexia in adolescent girls." *Child and Adolescent Psychiatry and Mental Health* 11(1): 13.

Goulet, Carol, Henrie, James, & Szymanski, Lynda. 2017. "An exploration of the associations among multiple aspects of religiousness, body image, eating pathology, and appearance investment." *Journal of Religion and Health* 56(2): 493–506.

Grabe, Shelly, Ward, L. Monique, & Hyde, Janet S. 2008. "The role of the media in body image concerns among women: A meta-analysis of experimental and correlational studies." *Psychological Bulletin* 134(3): 460. doi:10.1037/0033-2909.134.3.460

Handelzalts, Jonathan E., Geller, Shulamit, Levy, Sigal, Vered, Tal, & Fisher, Shimrit. 2017. "Body image among three denominations of Jewish women in Israel." *International Journal of Culture and Mental Health* 10(2): 206–16. https://doi.org/10.1080/17542863.2017.1290126.

Handelzalts, Jonathan E., Geller, Shulamit, Sidi, Yael, & Levy, Sigal. 2020. "Religion and appearance investment: The mediating role of internalisation of socio-cultural pressures, in Jewish Israeli women." *Mental Health, Religion & Culture*, 23(1): 54–66. https://doi.org/10.1080/13674676.2019.1705777

Hartman, Tova. 2007. *Feminism Encounters Traditional Judaism: Resistance and Accommodation*. Waltham, MA: Brandeis University Press.

Heilman, Samuel C., 1992. *Defenders of the Faith: Inside Ultra Orthodox Jewry*. New York: Schocken Books.

Holman, Andrei. 2012. "Religion and the body: An overview of the insertions of religion in the empirical psycho-social research lines on the body." *European Journal of Science and Theology* 8(3): 127–34.

Homan, Kristin J., & Boyatzis, Chris J. 2010. "The protective role of attachment to God against eating disorder risk factors: Concurrent and prospective evidence." *Eating Disorders* 18(3): 239–58.

Homan, Kristin, McHugh, Erin, Wells, Daniel, Watson, Corrinne, & King, Carolyn. 2012. "The effect of viewing ultra-fit images on college women's body dissatisfaction." *Body Image* 9(1): 50–6. doi:10.1016/j.bodyim.2011.07.006.

Inman, Mary, Iceberg, Erica, & McKeel, Laura. 2014. "Do religious affirmations, religious commitments, or general commitments mitigate the negative effects of exposure to thin ideals?" *Journal for the Scientific Study of Religion* 53(1): 38–55. https://doi.org/10. 1111/jssr.12089.

Israel Internet Association. 2017 (January 11). "Hagolshim hacharedim [The ultra-Orthodox who are surfing the Internet]." Israel Internet Association. Retrieved from www.isoc.org.il/sts-data/the-yearbook-of-haredi-society-in-israel-2017

Jackson, Brenda R., & Bergeman, Cyndi S. 2011. "How does religiosity enhance well-being? The role of perceived control." *Psychology of Religion and Spirituality* 3: 149–61.

Jacobson, Heather L., Hall, M. Elizabeth L., & Anderson, Tamara L. 2013. "Theology and the body: Sanctification and bodily experiences." *Psychology of Religion and Spirituality* 5(1): 41–50.

Katz, Yaron. 2012. "Technology use in the religious communities in Israel: Combining traditional society and advanced communications." *Journal of Religion, Media & Digital Culture* 1: 1–30.

Kertechian, Sevag K., & Swami, Viren. 2016. "The hijab as a protective factor for body image and disordered eating: A replication in French Muslim women." *Mental Health, Religion & Culture* 19(10):1056–68. doi:10.1080/13674676.2017.1312322.

Kim, Karen H. 2007. "Religion, weight perception, and weight control behavior." *Eating Behaviors* 8: 121–131.

Latzer, Yael, Tzischinsky, Orna, & Gefen, Shira. 2007. "Level of religiosity and disordered eating psychopathology among modern-orthodox Jewish adolescent girls in Israel." *International Journal Adolescent Medicine and Health* 19: 511–21.

Latzer, Yael, Witztum, Eliezer, & Stein, Daniel. 2008. "Eating disorders and disordered eating in Israel: An updated review." *European Eating Disorders Review* 16(5): 361–74. https://doi.org/10.1002/erv.875.

Latzer, Yael, Weinberger-Litman, Sarah L., Gerson, Barbara, Rosch, Anna, Mischel, Rebecca, Hinden, Talia, Kilstein, Jeffrey, & Silver, Judith. 2015. "Negative religious coping predicts disordered eating pathology among Orthodox Jewish adolescent girls." *Journal of Religion and Health* 54(5): 1760–71.

Livio, Oren, & Tenenboim-Weinblatt, Keren. 2007. "Discursive legitimation of a controversial technology: Ultra-Orthodox Jewish women in Israel and the internet." *The Communication Review* 10(1): 29–56. dx.doi.org/10.1080/10714420601168467

Longman, Chia, 2007. "'Not us, but you have changed!' Discourses of difference and belonging among Haredi women." *Social Compass* 54(1): 77–95.

McCabe, Marita P., Mavoa, Helen, Ricciardelli, Lina A., Schultz, Jimaima T., Waqa, Gade, & Fotu, Kalesita. 2011. "Socio-cultural agents and their impact on body image and body change strategies among adolescents in Fiji, Tonga, Tongans in New Zealand and Australia." *Obesity Reviews* 12: 61–7.

McCabe, Marita P., Waqa, Gade, Dev, Anjileena, Cama, Tilema, & Swinburn, Boyd A. 2013. "The role of cultural values and religion on views of body size and eating practices among adolescents from Fiji, Tonga, and Australia." *British Journal of Health Psychology* 18(2): 383–94.

McGuire, Meredith B. 2008. *Lived Religion: Faith and Practice in Everyday Life.* Oxford: Oxford University Press.

Milligan, Amy K. 2014. *Hair, Headwear, and Orthodox Jewish Women: Kallah's Choice.* Lanham, MD: Lexington Books.

Mussap, Alexander J. 2009. "Strength of faith and body image in Muslim and non-Muslim women." *Mental Health, Religion and Culture* 12(2): 121–7. doi.org/10.1080/13674670802358190

Nahary, Gali, & Hartman, Tova. 2020. "Orthodox Jewish women's sexual subjectivity." *Sexual and Relationship Therapy* 1–19. doi:10.1080/14681994.2020.1743972

Neriya-Ben Shahar, Rivka. 2011. "Modesty Discourse in Female Haredi Newspapers 1960–1989." In *Gender in Israel.* Eds. Gideon Katz and Margalit Shilo. Sede-Boker: Ben-Gurion Research Institute for the Study of Israel and Zionism, 580–622 (Hebrew).

Neriya-Ben Shahar, Rivka. 2019. "'For we ascend in holiness and do not descend': Jewish ultra-Orthodox women's agency through their discourse about media." *Journal of Modern Jewish Studies* 18(2): 212–26.

Neriya-Ben Shahar, Rivka, & Lev-On, Azi. 2011. "Gender, religion and new media: Attitudes and behaviors related to the internet among Ultra-Orthodox women employed in computerized environments." *International Journal of Communication* 5: 875–95.

Peat, Christine M., Peyerl, Naomi L., & Muehlenkamp, Jennifer J. 2008. "Body image and eating disorders in older adults: A review." *The Journal of General Psychology* 135: 343–8.

Perloff, Richard M. 2014. "Social media effects on young women's body image concerns: Theoretical perspectives and an agenda for research." *Sex Roles* 71: 363–77.

Pfeffer, Anshil. 2020. "In ultra-Orthodox Jerusalem, Yom Kippur was stronger than the virus." www.haaretz.com/israel-news/.premium.MAGAZINE-in-ultra-orthodox-jerusalem-yom-kippur-stronger-than-virus-1.9193329.

Quittkat, Hannah L., Hartmann, Andrea S., Düsing, Rainer, Buhlmann, Ulrike, & Vocks, Silja. 2019. "Body dissatisfaction, importance of appearance and body appreciation in men and women over the lifespan." *Frontiers in Psychiatry* 10: 864.

Reagan, Leslie J. 1997. "Engendering the dread disease: Women, men, and cancer." *American Journal of Public Health* 87, no. 11: 1779–87.

Ricciardelli, Lina A., Marita P. McCabe, Kate E. Holt, and Jennifer Finemore. 2003. "A biopsychosocial model for understanding body image and body change strategies among children." *Journal of Applied Developmental Psychology* 24, no. 4: 475–95.

Richards, P. Scott, Hardman, Randy K., & Berrett, Michael E. 2007. "Spiritual approaches in the treatment of women with eating disorders." Washington, DC: American Psychological Association.

Sherkat, Darren E., & Ellison, Christopher G. 1999. "Recent developments and current controversies in the sociology of religion." *Annual Review of Sociology* 25: 363–94.

Sidi, Yael, Geller, Shulamit, Abu Sinni, Aline, Levy, Sigal, & Handelzalts, Jonathan E. 2020. "Body image among Muslim women in Israel: Exploring religion and sociocultural pressures." *Women & Health* 60(10): 1095–1108.

Swami, Viren, Miah, Jusnara, Noorani, Nazerine, & Taylor, Donna. 2014. "Is the hijab protective? An investigation of body image and related constructs among British Muslim women." *British Journal of Psychology* 105(3): 352–63. http://doi.org/10.1111/bjop.12045

Swami, V., Tovée, Martin, & Harris, Amy S. 2013. "An examination of ethnic differences in actual-ideal weight discrepancy and its correlates in a sample of Malaysian women." *International Journal of Culture and Mental Health* 6(2): 96–107.

Taragin-Zeller, Lea. 2014. "Modesty for heaven's sake: Authority and creativity among female Ultraorthodox teenagers in Israel." *Nashim: A Journal of Jewish Women's Studies & Gender Issues* 26: 75–96.

Taragin-Zeller, Lea. 2015. "Between Beauty and Modesty: Reinterpreting Female Piety in the Israeli Haredi Community." In *Love, Marriage, and Jewish Families Today: Paradoxes of the Gender Revolution*. Ed. Silvia B. Fishman. Lebanon, NH: Brandeis University Press, 308–26.

Thompson, J. Kevin, Leslie J. Heinberg, Madeline Altabe, and Stacey Tantleff-Dunn. 1999. *Exacting Beauty: Theory, Assessment, and Treatment of Body Image Disturbance*. New York: American Psychological Association.

Tiggemann, Marika. 2011. "Sociocultural Perspectives on Human Appearance and Body Image." In *Body Image: A Handbook of Science, Practice, and Prevention*. Eds. T. F. Cash & L. Smolak. New York: The Guilford Press, 12–19.

Tylka, Tracy L. 2011. "Positive Psychology Perspectives on Body Image." T. F. Cash & L. Smolak. eds. In *Body Image: A Handbook of Science, Practice, and Prevention*. Eds. T. F. Cash & L. Smolak. New York: Guilford Press, 56–64.

Weinberger-Litman, Sarah L. 2007. *The influence of religious orientation, spiritual well-being, educational setting, and social comparison on body image and eating disturbance in Jewish women*. Doctoral Dissertation, The City University of New York. Dissertation Abstracts International, 68(10-B), 7008.

Weinberger-Litman, Sarah L., Rabin, Laura A., Fogel, Joshua, Mensinger, Janell L., & Litman, Leib. 2016. "Psychosocial mediators of the relationship between religious orientation and eating disorder risk factors in young Jewish women." *Psychology of Religion and Spirituality* 8(4): 265.

Weinberger-Litman, Sarah L., Latzer, Yael, Litman, Lieb, & Ozick, Rachel. 2018. "Extrinsic religious orientation and disordered eating pathology among modern orthodox Israeli adolescents: The mediating role of adherence to the superwoman ideal and body dissatisfaction." *Journal of Religion and Health* 57(1): 209–22.

Weiss, Susan. 2009. "Under cover: Demystification of women's head covering in Jewish law." *Nashim: A Journal of Jewish Women's Studies & Gender Issues* 17(1): 89–115.

Wilhelm, Leonie, Hartmann, Andrea S., Becker, Julia C., Kisi, Melahat, Waldorf, Manuel, & Vocks, Silja. 2019. "Thin media images decrease women's body satisfaction: Comparisons between veiled Muslim women, Christian women and atheist women regarding state and trait body image." *Frontiers in Psychology* 10(1074): 1–14. doi:10.3389/fpsyg.2019.01074

23
HAIR

Amy K. Milligan

Introduction

Hair within Jewish thought takes on several unique personas. It exists at the intersection of insider and outsider, providing both community identity and being used by outsiders to stigmatize Jews. Just as there is not one monolithic Jewish experience, there also is not one type of Jewish hair, nor do Jews all encounter their hair in the same ways. Still, there are certain understandings of Jewish hair and of how it has traditionally been understood that offer a starting point for considering these multi-faceted experiences. There are several significant lifecycle events or age-specific experiences of hair within Judaism. It is prudent to note that these practices are most common within Orthodox Judaism, but that does not mean that they are not influential in shaping the thoughts and practices of non-Orthodox Jews. This chapter takes a chronological lifetime approach, beginning with childhood experiences of the first haircut, discussing the external hair marking choices of adult Orthodox Jews, and culminating with the role of hair in the mourning cycle and its care by the *Chevra Kadisha* (lit. sacred society) who tend to the deceased body. Finally, it offers a discussion of other specific instances of Jewish hair, including its role in the Holocaust, as well as the politics and stereotypes of Jewish hair, how hair has been used to celebrate Jewishness, how it has perpetuated false stereotypes both within and external to the community, and how hair is poised to be a conduit for navigating nuanced Jewish identity discussions.

Childhood

The first haircutting ritual of *upsherin* is commonly practiced among Orthodox Jewish communities, although in recent years it has become more common among Conservative and Reform Jews. *Upsherin* (Yiddish, lit. to shear off) marks the transitional shift between babyhood and childhood for a young boy. In the United States, the ritual includes two important rites of passage: the actual first haircut and an education initiation. Jewish haircutting rituals for young boys are traced to Palestinian Jewish practices in the Middle Ages. Although childhood haircutting rituals remained a largely Sephardic (Jews with Spanish and north-African roots) custom until the 1800s, they are now also commonly practiced among Ashkenazic Jews (Jews with German and Eastern European roots), especially those living in the United States and Israel.

In contrast, Ashkenazic communities began school or education initiations during the twelfth and thirteenth centuries; these practices later were blended with the Sephardic haircutting rituals as different diasporic communities converged and new rituals emerged (Pinson 2010; Milligan 2017).

Contemporary *upsherin* rituals begin with the haircutting ritual which usually takes place in the home or, less commonly, the synagogue. At the age of three, a young boy is considered ready to transition from baby/toddler to child and to begin learning responsibility for Jewish practice. His hair, which up until this point has not been cut, is often adorned with ribbons or pulled into a ponytail. For the first time, he wears a *yarmulke* (a skullcap) and *tzitzit* (knotted ritual fridges attached to a four-cornered garment) and is typically seated on his father's lap. His father, or sometimes a rabbi or *kohen* (a specific designation within Judaism that references descent from Aaron), will first snip the forelock, symbolizing where the boy will one day lay *tefillin* (leather boxes holding scripture that are bound to the forehead and left arm). This piece of hair is typically preserved, often pressed into a *Siddur* (prayer book). The rest of the boy's hair is then cut except for the front sides of the hairline, which will now form the boy's *payot* (sidelocks or sidecurls).

In the United States it is customary for the first haircut to be immediately followed by the alef-bet ritual. The boy is wrapped in his father's *tallit* (prayer shawl), placed on the lap of a male teacher or rabbi, and reads the Hebrew alef-bet off of a laminated card. The teacher will place a drop of honey on each letter and then reads each letter aloud with the child repeating. As the child reads each letter, he dips his finger into the honey and licks it off, symbolizing the sweetness of learning. In some communities, the child is also given a hardboiled egg with Torah verses decorated on it, honey cake, or other sweets. Pairing the physical transformation of the first haircut with a learning ritual symbolizes the new role of the child as a participatory member of the Jewish community.

There are numerous variations of the ritual. For example, at the end of the *upsherin*, some families shave the son's head, making his *payot* even more prominent. In other communities each person attending the *upsherin* will take a turn and cut a lock of hair. Sometimes the hair is collected and weighed and a donation is made in a corresponding amount to charity. Others will make a donation matching the total number of locks snipped, offering money to the child to place into a *tzedakah* (charitable giving) box that he holds on his lap. At the end of the ritual, the child is sometimes showered with candies representing sweetness raining down from the angels in Heaven. These treats are then given to guests in *pekalach* (small bags of sweets). In some Israeli communities it is common to wait until Lag Ba'Omer so that the son's hair can be cut at the tomb of Rabbi Shimon Bar-Yohai in Meron or at the Western Wall. Other variations include the practices of the Skver, Chernobyl, and Gur Hasidic communities, who perform *upsherin* at the age of two. This is based on Genesis 21:8 (Abraham prepares a great feast for Isaac's birthday) in comparison to the majority of practitioners who base their view on Leviticus 19:23 (it is forbidden to eat the fruit of a new tree for the first three years). Among some Sephardic communities, *upsherin* takes place at the age of five. This practice is referred to as *chalakah* (from the Arabic *lakya*, a haircut). This practice does not include a school initiation and reflects the practices of Musta'arabi Jews and Sephardic communities prior to Ashkenazic influence.

In the United States, a childhood haircutting practice for girls has also emerged among Jewish feminists. This practice, usually also referred to as *upsherin*, is different than egalitarian *upsherin* practices, in which a girl's hair is cut in the same way that a traditional *upsherin* is conducted except for the creation of *payot*. Egalitarian *upsherin* also affords the same role to the mother and the father in the ceremony (Cooper 2014; Gechter 2017). Feminist *upsherin*, in contrast, focuses on celebrating the role of Jewish women in the raising of Jewish girls. This ritual typically occurs with a woman-identified audience, focuses on empowering the girl as a Jewish learner, includes the speaking of intentions for the strength and future of the girl, and emphasizes the girl's personal spiritual connection with Judaism. Feminist *upsherin* often occurs when the girl is five or six years old, making her a much more active participant in the ritual. Although this practice is relatively uncommon, the women who practice it, as well as their daughters who have experienced it, identify feminist *upsherin* as a celebration of a community of women who will nurture and support both the daughter and her mother (Milligan 2019).

Adulthood

Men

Although beards are not required as part of Jewish law, they have customarily been associated with Jewish men, especially those who identify as Orthodox. Despite beards being relatively uncommon outside of Orthodoxy, they have a long-standing history as one of the most commonly utilized markers or stereotypes used when describing Jewish male bodies. In fact, beards were so synonymous with Jewishness that in 1408, Jews in Spain were prohibited from growing beards as a form of humiliation (Ginzberg 1903). Textual directives for beard wearing point to numerous sources, including the Talmudic lauding of the attractiveness of facial hair and the description of beards as *hadrat panim* (the splendor of one's face). The cultivation and maintenance of facial hair generally looks to Leviticus 19:27, which instructs, "You shall not round off the corners on your head or destroy the corners of your beards." This verse has been interpreted as the instruction for both the growth of a beard and the creation of *payot*. Historically, the prohibition against the full removal of facial hair was interpreted to mean shaving with a razor, such that when chemical depilatories became available in the nineteenth century, beard norms began to change. The electric shaver was eventually introduced, which enabled men to shave without actually taking a razor to their skin. This invention, coupled with the desire to culturally assimilate, prompted most Jewish men to begin shaving their faces (Horowitz 1994). Still, within Orthodox circles, especially among the ultra-Orthodox, many men choose to grow their beards as a sign of their piety or religious identity. Among Hasidic men, some choose to not even trim their beards. This practice is based on two factors: first, by not trimming their beards, they will not accidentally violate the prohibition against shaving; second, some kabbalists believe the beard to be holy. Kabbalist Rabbi Isaac Luria, also known as the Ari, encouraged men to not even touch their beards, lest some hairs fall loose.

There are instances when Jewish men are halakhically instructed not to shave, most notably during periods of mourning, including both personal mourning as well as communal mourning. In addition to mourning a close family member, men are directed not to shave during communal mourning during the counting of the Omer (the period between Passover and Shavuot when Jews mourn the deaths of the students of Rabbi Akiva) and the three weeks between the 17th of Tammuz and Tisha B'Av (when Jews mourn the destruction of the ancient temples in Jerusalem).

Payot (also referred to as *payos* or *payes*; lit. "corners") are the sidelocks or sidecurls grown by some Orthodox men. The way they are styled and worn varies between community, with some choosing to wear them untrimmed and prominently displayed and others tucked or even plucked. For example, Satmar Hasidim have prominent *payot*, typically tucked behind the ears in contrast to the Skver Hasidim, who twist their *payot* and wear them in front of the ears. Other variations include the Gerer Hasidim, who often tuck their *payot* under their *yarmulkes*, and the Belz Hasidim who wrap their *payot* around their ears. Most contemporary Jewish men choose not to grow *payot* at all, while some interpret the law to be fulfilled by having sideburns.

Women

Traditionally, Jewish women have covered their hair. Unlike other religious groups who begin covering hair at puberty or upon joining the religion, Jewish women traditionally begin hair covering after marriage. Historically, the practice was widespread, but it became less common during The Haskalah (Jewish Enlightenment, 1770–1880). This trajectory would continue as hair covering transitioned in the United States to being largely an Orthodox practice after the second wave of Jewish immigration (1880–1920) as Jews sought to assimilate into American culture. Daily hair covering is now most commonly practiced among Orthodox women, although some Conservative and Reform women choose to cover their hair during religious services. Although there are a number of external body markers for Orthodox Jewish men (*yarmulke*, *payot*, *kittel*, *tzitzit*, *tallit*), for many women, hair covering is the most prominent way she can externalize her religious identity. There are countless ways in which the hair can be covered, and the choice of hair covering method can also serve as an indication of the community to which a woman belongs. Options include *tichels* (scarves), hats and snoods, *sheitels* (wigs), and *shpitzels* (a head covering with a braid of hair across the front and covered by a scarf). All of these allow for a range of personal styling, including the hair color and style, the fabric and tie of the *tichel*, or the style of the hat. Although less common, some Hasidic women choose to shave their heads and wear wigs. There are several reasons for this choice, including: ease and comfort under a wig and wig cap; making it impossible that their natural hair would be seen protruding from under the wig; and the ability to be certain that they are fully submerged when using the *mikveh* (Schreiber 2006; Milligan 2014).

When visiting a *mikveh* (the bath used for ritual immersion), there are several rules about hair. First, the cutting, shaving, or waxing of hair should be done several days prior to immersion. When preparing for immersion, all false hair, including fake eyelashes, should be removed. The hair and scalp should be washed with shampoo but without conditioner, and the hair should be combed while still wet to remove all knots. Some communities allow the use of conditioner if the hair cannot be unknotted or combed. If a person chooses to wash prior to coming to the *mikveh*, the hair should be wet and recombed prior to immersion. All other bodily hair should also be washed; the pubic hair should be thoroughly washed and, if necessary, combed; and the underarm hair should also be carefully washed to rid it of deodorant or other residue. The *mikveh* attendant will check the whole body for loose hair. When immersing in the *mikveh*, the entire body must be submerged in the water at one time, including the hair. Women with long hair must be particularly attentive to ensure that all of their hair is submerged (Slonim 2006; Falk 2010).

End of Life

Hair takes on meaning at the end of life in two primary ways: for the deceased and for those who grieve. Death and bereavement are part of an extensive mourning practice within Judaism, a cycle of rituals that offer comfort to those who grieve and predictability for those facing death. Ultimately, these mourning rituals achieve two goals: *kavod ha-met* (showing respect for the deceased) and *nihum avelim* (comforting those who grieve) (Lamm 2000; Diamant 1999).

In traditional Jewish burial practices, the ways in which the body is handled are prescribed. Overseen by the *Chevra Kadisha* (lit. the holy society; a group of volunteers who care for the dead), the body is treated with the utmost respect. Among the many rituals associated with caring for the deceased body, the entire body is thoroughly cleaned before being wrapped in a plain linen garment. This action is called *taharah*. The body is washed from the top of the head to the feet, beginning with washing the hair as the first area of the body cleansed. The *Chevra Kadisha* washes both the hair and the scalp while ensuring that no water goes into the ears, mouth, or nose. Many communities use only water for *taharah*, but, less commonly, the hair is sometimes washed with vinegar or a mixture of egg and wine. After *taharah*, the entire body is dried. Some communities dry and comb the hair; however, in other communities the hair is left to dry on its own and is not combed. During the *halbashah* (the blessings said prior to dressing of the deceased body), an eggwhite and vinegar mixture is placed along the hairline, eyebrows, sideburns, and facial hair of men. This is done three times as *v'zarakti* (from Ezekial 36:25, "I will sprinkle clean water upon you and you shall be clean") is repeated. As the body is dressed for burial, a *mitznefet* (a headdress) is placed or draped over the hair of women. Women's hair is left loose and neat (combed only if necessary to achieve neatness). While the body is washed, it is customary for verses from *Shir haShirim* (Song of Songs) to be read aloud, including many verses that describe the perfection of the human body, including the hair. As the body is prepared for burial, any hair cut from the deceased postmortem must be included with the body at interment (Kelman, Fendel, and Goldstein 2013; Light 2013).

There are also rules and guidance about the hair of those who are grieving. Jewish mourning practices follow a cycle, broken down into several periods after the death of a close relative (usually a parent, sibling, spouse, or child). After the burial, mourners enter a period of mourning called *shiva*, which lasts for seven days. During that time, among other varying cultural practices like receiving guests while sitting on low stools, not wearing leather shoes, and covering mirrors in the home, mourners do not cut or shave their hair. In some communities, mourners also refrain from bathing and washing their hair if this will cause pleasure, only washing if it is necessary. Hair combing is permissible during *shiva*, as neatness is seen as honoring the dignity of the deceased and offering respect.

At the end of *shiva*, some communities extend the prohibition on haircutting for a full thirty days. The hair, in this case, is seen as an indication of the mourner being apart from society during her period of grief; however, this is not at the loss of personal hygiene or neatness. Individuals bathe and may comb and style their hair. For men, this also includes not shaving, allowing their facial hair to grow and serve as an indication of their mourning status. The hair, when cut, marks the rejoining of the individual with society after *Sheloshim*, the thirty-day period of the grief cycle. Less commonly, some individuals do not cut their hair for a full year, especially after the death of a parent. In this case, though, Talmudic law provides that if, after the thirty days of *Sheloshim*, the mourner is rebuked or criticized by friends and neighbors or if his hair is so long that he would appear to be "an eccentric," it is permissible for the mourner to cut his hair. Likewise, it is permissible to trim the moustache after *Sheloshim* if its growth interferes with eating (Zlotowitz 1991).

Holocaust

Hair color and texture played an important role in the Holocaust. Although the appearance of hair is not an accurate salient marker of Jewishness, stereotypes of "looking Jewish" were coupled with the Nazi propaganda-driven belief that Jews are genetically inferior. This undergirded a false supposition that Jews could be recognized by their dark eyes and hair. Numerous accounts of Holocaust survival exist in which the protagonist survives because she "did not look Jewish." Other examples include the role of the *kasharit* (a courier)—a young Jewish woman who brought information, goods, and even people between the Jewish ghettos and the outside world. These women were perceived to have Aryan features, and often dyed their hair blonde if it was not already naturally light colored.

During the Holocaust, one form of violence against Jewish prisoners was forced head shaving. By forcibly removing the hair of individuals, both identity and style were stripped from the person. Each prisoner was rendered theoretically indistinguishable from the others, having endured the humiliation of having their hair removed. This act was couched in the false pretense that this head shaving was for "sanitation." Indeed, Nazi propaganda falsely accused Jews as being dirty and for spreading lice. Upon arrival at concentration camps, Jews not only had their heads forcibly shaved and beards removed, but many also had their pubic hair clipped or shaved, all in the name of "delousing" or cleaning. This was also seen as a form of escape prevention. Other firsthand accounts detail how hair was forcibly removed from individuals before they were gassed in concentration camps, demonstrating that the hair removal was less about "cleanliness" than it was humiliation. The hair gathered was stored and later sold as industrial raw material. Longer hair, in particular, was packed and sold to make haircloth and felt. In camps where hair was not removed prior to gassing, like Auschwitz, hair was posthumously shaved from the dead bodies, disinfected, dried, and sold. As part of their permanent exhibit and memorial, the Auschwitz-Birkenau Memorial and Museum displays bales of haircloth and nearly two tons of human hair from over 40,000 individuals. Ironically, shaved heads would later go on to be associated with the neo-Nazi movement and its members (Auschwitz Museum 2021; Suedfeld, Paterson, Soriano, and Zuvic 2002).

Stereotypes and Cultural Pressures

One of the ways that Jewish bodies continue to be marginalized is through the stigmatization of Jewish hair. In addition to a number of other significant anti-Semitic body stereotypes, "Jewish hair" is often used as a marker, particularly in parody or caricature, of the undesirable or genetically inferior Jewish body. These harmful caricatures depict men with exaggerated *payot* and beards, excessive body hair, and/or large curly hair; women are shown with pronounced curly hair, often styled in larger-than-life coiffure.

These same stereotypes are used as a test of Jewishness, both within and outside of the community. For example, individuals can be told that they "don't look Jewish" based on their hair, which is a harmful statement rooted in Ashkenormativity and erasing the experiences of Jews of Color, converts, or Jews who simply do not have dark curly hair. Jewish hair, in this juxtaposition, demonstrates a tension experienced by Jews; if Judaism is an ethnoreligious identity and hair texture is genetic, is there such a thing as Jewish hair? And if there is, what does that mean for Jews who do not share the same hair type? Jewish hair both simultaneously exists and does not exist. The only logical conclusion is that Jewish hair is the hair of someone who identifies as Jewish, recognizing that there are many different types of hair that Jews may have, while simultaneously recognizing that stereotypes of certain types of Jewish hair have been used against Jews for centuries.

Many Jewish women who do have curly hair have long felt pressured to straighten their hair. There are various reasons for this choice, but recently some Jewish women have reclaimed their curls as an act of resistance to mainstream beauty culture. This "War of the Curls" is not the first time that Jewish hair has been used as political commentary. During the 1960s, Jewish men began wearing what they referred to as "Jewfros." This portmanteau of Jew and Afro (sometimes also called an "Isro" from Israel and Afro) became especially popular with Jewish athletes, as well as Jews who were engaged in the Civil Rights Movement. Although problematic in its appropriation of Black hair styling and terms, those who wore their hair styled this way saw their hair as a statement of Jewish pride, body liberation, or allyship.

Conclusion

Understandings of Jewish hair continue to shift as personal and communal relationships to Jewishness evolve. Contemporary Jews must make sense of both their contemporary understanding of their hair alongside of religious traditions with which they may not even engage; non-Orthodox Jews inherit the legacy of these traditional approaches to hair even if they do not ever personally participate with them unless they, for example, visit a *mikveh* or choose to be buried by a *Chevra Kadisha*. Still, understanding them can help Jews better understand each other and their own history.

Just as in the 1983 film adaptation of Isaac Bashevis Singer's play "Yentl," when Barbra Streisand dramatically cuts her hair to pose as a male student so that she can attend a *yeshiva*, hair is transformative for our identities. Contemporary Jewish practice is only just now beginning to grapple with what it means to have egalitarian and feminist haircutting rituals for children; how to include trans and gender nonconforming individuals in hair rituals or laws; or how to recognize that while stereotypes of Jewish hair exist, not all Jews have the same hair texture and by insinuating that they do, the experiences of Black Jews or other Jews with different hair types is erased.

In the end, hair is an entry point into the discussion of how Jewish bodies are treated and understood. It represents an ongoing relationship and wrestling with the Torah and Talmud; its changes follow the trajectory of a person's life; and it sits at the points of tension around gender, sexuality, and race that overlap with Jewish identity. In these ways, Jewish hair takes on deeply nuanced meanings for both the individual and the outsider, as one represents and cultivates her hair throughout her life.

References

Auschwitz Museum. 2021. *Hair*. http://70.auschwitz.org/index.php?option=com_content&view=article&id=299&Itemid=179&lang=en (accessed January 12, 2021).
Cooper, Alanna E. 2014. "A Little Girl's First Haircut." *Lilith*. http://lilith.org/articles/a-little-girls-first-haircut/ (accessed January 9, 2021).
Diamant, Anita. 1999. *Saying Kaddish: How to Comfort the Dying, Bury the Dead, and Mourn as a Jew*. New York: Schocken.
Falk, Pesach Eliyahu. 2010. *The Tznius Handbook: Educational Diagrams for Women and Girls*. New York: Feldheim.
Gechter, Elisha. 2017. "My Daughter Asked for an Upsherin." *My Jewish Learning: Jewish Orthodox Feminist Alliance*. www.myjewishlearning.com/the-torch/my-daughter-asked-for-an-upsherin/ (accessed January 9, 2021).
Ginzberg, Louis. 1903. "Beard." *The Jewish Encyclopedia*. New York and London: 611–15.
Horowitz, Elliott. 1994. "The Early Eighteenth Century Confronts the Beard: Kabbalah and Jewish Self-Fashioning." *Jewish History* 8(1–2): 95–115.
Kelman, Stuart, Dan Fendel, and Jessica W. Goldstein. 2013. *Chesed Shel Emet: The Truest Act of Kindness, Exploring the Meaning of Taharah*. New York: EKS Publishing.
Lamm, Maurice. 2000. *Jewish Way in Death and Mourning*. New York: Jonathan David Publishing.
Light, Richard A. 2013. *To Midwife a Soul: Guidelines for Performing Tahara*. New York: CreateSpace Independent Publishing Platform.
Milligan, Amy K. 2014. *Hair, Headwear, and Orthodox Jewish Women: Kallah's Choice*. Lanham, MD: Lexington Books.
Milligan, Amy K. 2017. "Hair Today, Gone Tomorrow: Upsherin, Alef-Bet, and the Childhood Navigation of Jewish Gender Identity Symbol Sets." *Children's Folklore Review* 38(1):7–25.

Milligan, Amy K. 2019. "Rebellious Hair: Jewish Feminist Reinterpretations of the Orthodox Jewish Ritual of Upsherin." In *Jewish Bodylore: Feminist and Queer Ethnographies of Folk Practices*. Lanham, MD: Lexington Books: 49–62.

Pinson, DovBer. 2010. *Upsherin: Exploring the Laws, Customs, and Meanings of a Boy's First Haircut*. New York: Iyyun Center for Jewish Spirituality.

Schreiber, Lynne. 2006. *Hide and Seek: Jewish Women and Hair Covering*. New York: Urim Publications.

Slonim, Rivka. 2006. *Total Immersion: A Mikvah Anthology*. New York: Urim Publications.

Suedfeld, P., H. Patterson, E. Soriano, and S. Zuvic. 2002. "Lethal Stereotypes: Hair and Eye Color as Survival Characteristics During the Holocaust." *Journal of Applied Psychology* 32(11): 2368–76.

Zlotowitz, Meir. 1991. *Mourning in Halachah*. New York: Mesorah Publishers.

24
CLOTHES

Oliver Leaman

There are rules connected to clothes and clothing in the Bible, although they are not extensive. Fringes are to be worn and they are described in a certain way, and there should be no mixture of wool and linen. The clothes of the priests are clearly described also, and although it is not human clothing, it is worth mentioning the extensive discussion of the clothing of the ark in the desert. Physical things have a significance and what surrounds them also is supposed to reflect that. It is not said why these clothing regulations are specified in such detail and to a degree presumably they are there to distinguish between one community and others. In recent years Jews have been very successful in a range of cultural activities, clothing of course being one of them, but there is no apparent connection between the modern designers, manufacturers, models, and retailers and the rituals surrounding clothing in the past or in the present among those Jews who still wear distinctive outfits.

Special Jewish Clothes

In the past Jews were sometimes stigmatized by having to wear clothing that distinguished them as different from everyone else, and this symbolized the legal and social penalties under which they lived. No doubt also they served to encourage conversion where this was available, since that would enable Jews to wear the same clothes as everyone else. It was one of the aims of emancipation for Jews to be able to live in society indistinguishable from everyone else, as citizens as well as Jews, and most seemed to welcome this opportunity. They cast off their distinctive clothing and blended in as well as they could with civil society, speaking the same languages as everyone else and engaging in the same occupations and cultural interests. They were so similar that in the twentieth century when fascist regimes decided to diminish their status they sometimes obliged them again to wear distinctive clothing, this time marked by a yellow Star of David or something similar. What is worth noting about this is that Jews were, on the whole, so well integrated that there was no way of discriminating against them unless they indicated their ethnic status in some deliberate way.

There always were Jews even under emancipation who wore stereotypically Jewish clothes, spoke in Jewish languages and oriented their lives around their religion in ways that directly distinguished them from everyone else. The clothes for both genders were modest in intention, hair styles were unusual and distinctive, and this is a group that showed no interest in assimilation into wider society. On the contrary, their clothes were part of their strategy of maintaining what they regarded as a traditional lifestyle with an orientation toward piety and a separation from the secular world, in so far as this is possible, of course. Clothes marked a link with a past in Eastern Europe, and many of these groups belonged to separate Hasidic communities named after a place where a distinguished rabbi and leader lived in the past. Although with the Holocaust the original places where the movement arose were no longer accessible or even desirable as places of regular habitation, they moved successfully to more welcoming environments in the United States and elsewhere. The United States and Israel are cultures that accept difference quite readily, and other parts of the world since the Holocaust have tolerated Jews with distinctive lifestyles. In a post-Holocaust world, it is difficult to justify being mean to a small Jewish citizen population. On the other hand, there are those in society whose dislike of Jews has led to this highly distinctive group being attacked since they are the only targets that can be easily distinguished from the general Jewish population. We normally wear clothes to blend in, to look normal, and there are costs to those who take a different strategy.

Orthodoxy and Modesty

One of the important principles of clothing for the Orthodox community is modesty, *tzniut*, and that generally means displaying only a limited amount of skin. Clothes encompass most of the body and hair, and in the case of married women sometimes all the hair is covered, either with a scarf or a wig. There is no general paradigm of modesty, each group has its own specific rules, hats for men will differ as do rules for women's hair, but in general the idea is to present a far more secluded physical presence than is the norm, especially when it is warm and most of the rest of the world is shedding clothes. Most Jews do not wear anything distinctive and would not be caught dead in the garb of the Orthodox, except perhaps on Halloween. Yet there is always a fascination with people who look different and unusual. Many years ago I wrote an introductory text on Judaism and spent most of the book saying how much like everyone else Jews were. I told the publishers to be careful about selecting a cover picture, and of course they nodded sagely and agreed. When the book emerged, on the cover was a Shabbat (or in the context I suppose it should be Shabbos) table richly furnished with challah and silver candlesticks and a family from the Orthodox community, dressed in their normal modest outfits and looking as though some substantial praying was in the offing. Actually, it is a good cover since anyone looking at it would think "Jews" and know what the book is about. But most of the book is actually about the kind of Jews who look like everyone else, who would not know what to do at a Shabbat table and whose idea of modesty is wearing socks (Leaman, 2010).

When I taught Jewish Studies my students, mainly gentile, would constantly talk about the warmth of the Jewish family, since their ideas often come from "Fiddler on the Roof." The clothes of the Orthodox do suggest stability, seriousness and a commitment to religion, but often what is going on underneath is very different. Violence, divorce, intimidation and so on are widespread in modern society, and the Orthodox community are not immune. They are certainly better at not washing their dirty linen in public, but they do have dirty linen. Clothes project a message and behind the message all sorts of things can be taking place that are at variance with the clothes. There is nothing unique to Judaism here, of course. The recent popularity of movies like *Shtisel* and *Unorthodox* actually come at the end of a relatively long period when the traditional communities in the Jewish world have been dramatized and wondered at.

These soap operas do exhibit how problematic such families can be, just like any other kind of family. They also bring out the variety of clothes that exist within these communities, since there are communities here and not just one community, and each group has its own rules about clothes, hair, hats and modesty.

Clothing and Subjectivity

One aspect of clothing that has been insufficiently studied in the world of the Orthodox is how the clothes feel to them. This is a bit surprising since for most of us clothes are about far more than just covering the body from the elements. There are clothes we really enjoy wearing, particular occasions call for particular clothes and we often define different stages of our lives in terms of clothes. Going out on a date, going to work, church or synagogue, gardening, going to bed, these all call for different outfits and we have all had the sensation of feeling uncomfortable because we are in what we take to be the wrong clothes. There is also a distinct feeling in being in the right clothes, where the clothes are right for what we want to do, for who we think we are. Sometimes, indeed quite often, we wear things that are not comfortable and yet they are the right things to wear on particular occasions. The tight bow tie, the shiny little-worn dress shoes, the starched shirt are all part of the uniform we wear on some formal occasions, they are not especially pleasant to wear in themselves and yet as harbingers of a special night to come, or an occasion, they are good to wear. There is a special sensation to wearing some clothes that we do not wear often, and presumably for those for whom those clothes are their normal garb, that sensation is missing. Then there is the sensation of wearing one's ordinary clothes, and that is itself a recognizable feeling and along with it go a range of emotions. Being dressed like everyone else around you, and distinct from most of the rest of the world, can be important. It might be said that there is a very special feeling in wearing what you think God wants you to wear, and that is certainly relevant, but we should not over-emphasize this point. There is a distinct feeling in wearing what you take to be the right clothes irrespective of how or why that notion of appropriacy is established.

What is taken to be the right clothes has little to do with what is comfortable. Fashion has nothing to do with the body really, it just happens to be displayed on the body. We often do unpleasant things to our bodies that we think will make us look good. For example, some people eat far less than they want to in order to shape their bodies in particular ways, or undergo rigorous exercise for the same reason, and that is not a lot of fun. People have tattoos, piercings, a variety of cosmetic surgery, wear high heels, heavy clothes in hot weather, light clothes in cold weather, and so on. None of these things is done for the body, quite the reverse, although they are done on the body. We tend to be suspicious of the motives of those wearing unusual clothes if we ourselves do not wear them; we often attribute it to a lack of freedom or a narrow upbringing yet this is far from the truth. It may be true in some cases but no more true than that we are all influenced to wear the clothes we wear by our upbringing and culture.

The Garden of Eden

The link between clothes and culture is hinted at early on in the Bible when Adam and Eve suddenly realize they are naked, something they had not noticed up to that time. They eat from the tree of knowledge and they start to think of themselves as separate from their environment, and their thinking turns to how they look. Why should we care how we look? Presumably the climate in Eden was pleasant enough all the time so they did not need clothes to survive or feel comfortable. The tree of knowledge made them aware of petty things, and their expulsion signaled the birth of society and its big and little rules. They started to make aesthetic judgments about how things looked, whereas earlier their thinking was directed to more serious and theoretical ideas, according to Maimonides.

Maimonides was dubious about material things, so when he suggests that they started thinking about material things he meant this as a criticism. For him the material side of religion was there for the majority of the community who could not think abstractly. We are material creatures and we like examples and ideas to be given a physical shape, otherwise we find them difficult to understand. Going further, we find it difficult to get excited by anything that is not material, and thinking about clothes is for him an excellent example of that. There is after all little that is more inconsequential than fashion. That is often how it seems with rituals in religion, there is the material aspect of religion and then the spiritual core or essence. It is not difficult to see which is more significant, or so it seems. What does it matter what people wear compared to what they are, how they think? It might be argued though that if the point of clothing is modesty, for a group of people, then it does matter, since it is not easy to be modest in immodest clothes. We could try but since we are material creatures the attempt is unlikely to succeed. If someone is in the presence of people dressed immodestly one might avert one's gaze but since we are material creatures that is unlikely to work for long. What Maimonides did not capture in his account of the issue of clothes in the Garden of Eden is that there is more to establishing a religious lifestyle than just thinking in the right way about abstract issues. He would accept this of course and claim that only a small elite can think of religion in non-materialistic terms, yet even they have bodies and need to think about how they are going to dress them. This brings in the fact that now they have acquired knowledge from the tree, however illicitly acquired, for the first time they have ideas that go beyond the entirely intellectual.

Adam and Eve are expelled from the Garden of Eden for having eaten the fruit of the tree of knowledge of good and evil, but before that God provided them with clothing: "And the Lord God made garments of skin for Adam and his wife and clothed them" (Gen 3:21). They were not completely naked in any case since right after their sin "they saw that they were naked and sewed together fig leaves, making themselves loincloths" (Gen 3:7). While in the Garden the *Zohar* suggests their clothes were really made of light to fit in with the perfection of the location. In Hebrew, the *Zohar* points out, the words for light and skin are pronounced the same, *or*, but spelled differently, light with an *alef* and skin with an *ayin*. Through their sin, Adam and Eve had to replace their garments of divine light with skin, a lower level of clothing (*Zohar*, II, 229a–b). These are taken to be the same sort of material as the special clothes worn by Aaron when tending the Tabernacle in the desert (Exodus 39:1, 41). Midrashic texts speculate on what happened to the clothes after their history in the Garden of Eden. *Pirkei de-Rabbi Eliezer* suggests the skin that God gave to Adam and Eve came from that sloughed off the serpent, and was then worn by Nimrod, Esau, and Jacob, ending up as Joseph's coat of many colors that was to lead to so many problems. *Midrash Tanchuma* suggests it was to become the High Priest's tunic in the future.

Embodiment, Symbolization and Gender

Ever since the writings of Mary Douglas we have got used to the idea of the body as something that symbolizes social norms and values. For one thing the body is a highly effective mechanism to represent social control and the hierarchy of power. It is also a means of resistance to those values and system of control, and agents may react in a whole range of different ways. When people are told to wear a certain outfit or cover up in a particular way this looks like an oppressive strategy, since otherwise surely people would just wear what everyone else wears. Of course, it is worth emphasizing that what everyone else wears is also just as much part of the same system of social values as anything else, just more invidious since it is less easy to notice. Let us look at the central rules about covering the head, which apply to both men and women, albeit in different ways. Young boys wear a kippah or yarmulke from an early age, and the principle this represents is that God is always above us. Girls do not have to do this, in the same way that in the Orthodox community girls have fewer obligatory rituals to perform, until they get married. Once married the principle of *tzniut* or modesty means that their hair, a potential source of sexual attraction to those not married to them, should be covered. Both men and women then have to cover their heads in some way, but the rationales are distinct. For men it represents an early statement of a developing relationship with God, for women it only arises after marriage, as though her hair has suddenly become an erotic factor about her that needs controlling. Its being covered represents her status as a married woman, linked to a certain man, and unavailable to anyone else.

In some ways the differences between these two types of head covering are not so different. Boys are often given yarmulkes or kippahs that fall off if they move quickly, and not given clips for them, and that of course discourages movement. Girls of the same age, by contrast, are able to run and jump and so on, although they may of course be discouraged from doing so. Boys will be encouraged to study holy texts and receive high status for doing so, while girls might be allowed more secular studies and so be better prepared for living in tandem with a secular society. The education the boys receive will only be useful within that community, girls may acquire transferable skills. With the growth of more egalitarian forms of Judaism some girls have taken to wearing kippot when praying. In communities stemming from Islamic countries Jewish girls also tend to value covering, even before marriage, and there are Mizrahi rabbinic authorities from an Orthodox perspective who advocate this. Even Maimonides did not rule it out. In interviews with girls and women a variety of views on head covering emerges, and the complexity and variety of responses ought to be carefully considered. Women know that what they are being asked to do is unusual and goes contrary to what most people do in society. They often discuss it, think about it, work out forms of accommodation that they find work for them, obey the law but disapprove of it, do not think that hair is really *erva* (naked), compare it to the laws of *niddah* (purity) which suggests that women are often impure and require cleansing (going to the *mikveh* or ritual bath). As a result they may query it, since they do not feel their hair is something dangerous. They may be following a tradition they do not want to do but think that God does want them to do it, so they will obey Him. The range of responses is vast and encompasses every possible reaction to the rules. Of course, many people just follow the rules without thinking about them at all, in just the same way that most mornings we just put our clothes on or say our prayers without really considering what we are doing or why we are doing it. It is just part of the daily routine, and we will probably keep on doing it for as long as we live and are able to do it. There is not time to question or think about everything, especially given the busy schedules of many in the traditional community.

Is there any essential difference between a married Jewish woman covering her hair, wearing a wig perhaps, or even shaving all her hair off and then covering her head and a secular woman starving herself to fit into fashionable clothes, or wearing uncomfortable shoes, or a corset of some kind to establish a fashionable physical contour? All these activities are to varying degrees uncomfortable, even painful, and far from what we might do if we were living "naturally", even if not in the Garden of Eden. We all do things which are perhaps surprising because of social and familial pressure, although the force of this should not be over-emphasized. We may do things because we want to, however surprising they seem. Some people working at home like to dress in business clothes when they do not need to. Magritte used to paint in a suit and tie, or so it was said, and there is nothing wrong with that, although most people would not make that choice. It might be argued that no one would do that unless they were forced to do it by subliminal pressures of one sort or another. That seems rather dogmatic; many things we do are unusual and represent perhaps how we want to express ourselves. We may feel comfortable in casual clothes but not comfortable working in them, there is no objective criterion of comfort. We may not of course expect nor even want to be comfortable when setting about certain tasks. The idea that we have been set a task and need to complete it is a common one. It might involve running long distances, pushing weights, or meditating, for example, all of which may not make us feel comfortable but which we could see as something we need to do.

Modesty Again

This might seem to be disingenuous since surely gender comes into the notion of fashion and ritual. *Tzniut* applies to women and their hair (and also of course their voice) in ways that do not apply to men. Men are seen as the active forces here, needing to be constrained against sexual predation especially on other men's wives, and as a result women are obliged to take unusual measures to remain safe. Some of these involve fashion, what to do with their hair and so on, and some to do with ritual purity and rules of *niddah* or purity. The rules dealing with blood have a disproportionately heavy effect on the lives of women, since they menstruate. Even at the height of the Covid-19 pandemic in New York City many Jewish women were prepared to use the *mikveh* so that they would be ritually pure after menstruation or other life events involving blood. Of course, rigorous cleaning operations took place at the *mikveh* but still one might have thought that it would have been better for people not to travel outside their homes to visit a bathing place that many others also visit to do something that could easily be done at home, albeit that would not have conferred ritual purity on the act. As with the rituals of what to do with hair this caused a good deal of discussion among Orthodox women, and some were prepared to forgo a visit given the emergency. Others noted that the rule actually originates in the Torah and so could not be avoided. Some no doubt just kept on going without even thinking about it, since it is just something they always do. Then something happens and perhaps they think about it for a bit, after which they resume what they were doing in the past or perhaps revise their future behavior. This variety of responses to rituals in unusual situations or emergencies makes it difficult to think of the participants as just submissive ciphers for social control.

Even in normal situations we cannot fail to notice a whole variety of strategies that women take to fashion and ritual. The same is true of course of men, and not enough research has been done really on how men feel about the restrictions that are imposed on them, or how they slightly vary what they do and wear to fit in with their own individual ideas. They are certainly in positions of authority in the Orthodox world and yet many of the rules that apply to them are not obviously a lot of fun. Much praying, studying and then the inability to earn a decent income due to a concentration on the praying and studying is combined with the heavy monotonous clothes that are perhaps better suited for an East European climate than many of the places that Orthodox Jewish men live nowadays. The uniform nature of the clothes should not be over-emphasized since the different groups have subtle differences in what people wear, how they wear their beards and sidecurls, *payot*, if they even have beards and *payot*. Those differences are not easy to observe to the outsider but are immediately noted by those within the community. On Purim it is a tradition for Jews to dress up in fancy costume to celebrate the survival of the Jews when they were threatened with massacre by Haman in Persia, a bit like a Jewish Halloween in so far as clothes are concerned. Of course, most of the fashion choices are far too immodest to be worn by the Orthodox but sometimes they swap hats with members of other Hasidic groups, so that someone who is really a Ger Hasid dresses as a Satmarer for the night, and so on, the joke only being accessible to a pretty limited audience, of course, but often offering great merriment to that audience.

It is often pointed out that in a relationship of inequality, both the master and the slave are affected. There are not necessarily winners and losers, just people with different and complementary roles. When it comes to clothes, some of the clothes that men wear are unusual and distinctive but not overly burdensome, like *tzitzit* or fringes for instance, or *kippot*, skullcaps. But the rest of the outfit is not especially suitable for the climate that many Orthodox men inhabit, white shirts are difficult to keep clean, and wearing lots of heavy clothes all day while others are in shorts and tee shirts is a demanding task. On the other hand, as with the women wearing what they think is appropriate but not necessarily particularly enjoyable, doing something you think you ought to do can be unpleasant, but the very unpleasantness magnifies the satisfaction in doing it. It is seen as a task and not all tasks are easy, or are supposed to be easy by those who select the task. Often rituals connected to being in a group are difficult and meant to be difficult, since the group only wants people in it who are capable of keeping up with a particular pattern of behavior. For example, Orthodox Jewish men are supposed to go to the synagogue frequently, pray a lot, study and have a large family, and not surprisingly their income levels tend to be low, since they are not educated or motivated to enter into the major professions or commercial activities in modern societies. That is a demanding lifestyle and a demanding costume regime fits in with that pattern, helping to emphasize the special nature of Orthodox life. An absence of normal cultural messages such as television, most music, secular newspapers and radio means that these communities are quite cut off from the other communities that are all around them. An important way of marking this separation, and maintaining it, is their clothes.

Uniforms and Uniformity

During the Covid-19 pandemic it was claimed that the haredi community found it difficult to stop doing their usual communal activities since they had few alternatives. The community suffered a great deal from the virus, they tend to live together in large groups, with both very old and very young in the same and contiguous households, and they are also often poor, and so like other ethnic minorities they suffered disproportionally in the pandemic. Jews tend to be older than other groups and so they were more vulnerable anyway. When orders to social distance came into the public arena in Europe, America and Israel the haredim were slow to react, and often just continued with their normal religious and social activities. It was not until their own leaders went along with the government orders that they started to obey, and the fact that there were, for them, no alternative activities due to their antipathy to television and so on did not make it harder for them to obey the instructions, since this is a group that is ready and willing to submit to authority. It has to be an authority that they accept and respect, of course, and the secular authorities do not on the whole fall under that description. This is a community that likes to be different, not only from secular gentile society but from the majority of other Jews also, and one aspect of that is how they dress. They purposely dress in a way to exclude others from their society, and to identify themselves as separate from the regular world. Their clothes hark back to a time when Jews were expected to dress differently from others, when they lived in their own communities and religion dominated their lives. They hark back to an even earlier time when Jews were forced to wear distinctive clothes and be identified as separate from everyone else, the idea being to stigmatize and exploit, and perhaps also to incentivize conversion and disappearance of the community. It is not surprising then that a haredi community which sees itself as very much linked with those earlier communities and their sufferings would stubbornly resist changing their regular activities just because they were told to do so by the government.

Yet we should not make the mistake of seeing everyone who wears a particular uniform as having necessarily uniform beliefs, even beliefs about what they are wearing. We often wear things we think are ridiculous or uncomfortable and put up with it, if the context is right. A good example in America is graduation of course, with the colors and tassels and mortar boards that have no purpose at all in themselves, but people are pleased to wear them and be photographed in them. A heavy suit on a hot day is perhaps not appropriate in itself but it does give the wearer the opportunity to practice virtues like obedience, patience, self-control and the ability to fit in with friends and companions. If one does something that is taken to please one's community and religious leaders, and perhaps the Almighty, then one has accomplished a worthwhile end. There is a Hasidic story that pokes fun at this idea called "Patchwork." Someone fasts from Shabat to Shabat, and at the end of the week he is waiting for the stars to appear so he can break his fast and feels understandably a frisson of pride at his ability to carry out the self-imposed task. As soon as he has that feeling he breaks his fast, since he realizes that the point of a ritual, even a self-imposed ritual, is not to make you feel pleased with yourself. The story is called patchwork for that reason; he has not integrated the different aspects of his life together properly, the point of religious rituals is to foster a sense of humility, and pride goes directly in contravention of this (Buber, 1947). On this point Maimonides disagreed with his hero Aristotle, since Aristotle thought that a level of pride in what one does is acceptable, even desirable in certain circumstances. Not according to Maimonides, there is no golden mean here, one has always to be as humble as possible by comparison with the Almighty, and that is what Judaism fosters (Frank, 1989).

Rituals and the Role of Clothes

There is always a problem in carrying out rituals; one may be happy at the way one is doing it, or even find concentrating on the ritual makes the practitioner forget why he is doing what he is doing, and that could obviate the point of the ritual. The point of the ritual is not to make us feel better. On the other hand, if we do feel better might this not help motivate us to continue with the ritual and make it part of our lives? There is a fine balance here between encouraging someone to do something because he or she enjoys doing it but not letting that enjoyment become what the action is all about. For example, it used to be a practice to put sweets in a book of Hebrew when a young child was starting to learn the language, presumably in the days when most Jewish children were not Israeli. The idea was that they associated learning the language and by extension Judaism with something sweet. On the other hand, if the child continued to think of Judaism as something that tastes nice and ought to taste nice, it might be difficult to continue since there are often events in religious life that are not especially enjoyable, nor even supposed to be. Yet there is a pleasure in doing what you think you are supposed to do, especially if it is quite difficult, and one assumes that for those who feel they are obliged to wear certain clothes or arrange their hair in a certain way, this sort of pleasure might be something they often feel.

This is always an issue with people who seek to establish a lifestyle for themselves which quite sharply distinguishes them from most people, even most people in their religion. To look back at the Hasidic story, many Jewish people enjoy special food and activities on the Shabat, but not many fast from Shabat to Shabat. Many Jews do different things from non-Jews on religious occasions, but not many study a good deal of Talmud or even Kabbalah. These are difficult and often puzzling texts, and require considerable preparation before tackling, they are completely inaccessible in their original languages to most Jews. Some Jews do occasionally pray, but others make sure they pray in a *minyan*, a quorum of ten adult Jewish men, three times a day and participate regularly in other religious activities. This is true of all religious communities, some members are much more committed to a wide range of activities, others are happy with a more semi-detached relationship. There is nothing specifically religious about this, it is true of many activities in life, some want to exercise at length and using all the right equipment, others are happy to do a few things and leave it at that.

Where religion is different is that in fully carrying out what one sees as one's duties, motivation is very important. It really does not matter if someone is a casual gardener or a very enthusiastic gardener, the state of the garden might reflect the difference but otherwise little hangs on it. One of the dangers of a busy religious life during which one accomplishes difficult tasks and carries out complex duties is that it can encourage a sense of being special and better than everyone else. That might of course be true, but it is not what a religious person ought to be thinking, and clothes might constitute a central aspect of this problem.

One of the things we concentrate too much on perhaps about clothes is how they look, not how they feel to wear. Of course these are related. When clothes are distinctive they have an effect on the wearer, they signal that he or she is different, and that is supposed to reflect on the wearer. Modest clothes are supposed to help you be modest, and wearing a kind of uniform is directed at making everyone in a group feel like they are in a group. Of course, everyone has their own feelings, and some people may be wearing the most modest of clothes and having the most immodest thoughts, and vice versa. A ritual can be self-defeating when it encourages the wrong sort of thinking from the point of view of the religion. With its emphasis on separation Judaism has often been accused of being too ritualistic and ending up with a concentration on rituals at the expense of more important religious objectives. The accusers have often included Jews of course who choose a different mode of Judaism from the Orthodox traditions of practice. It seems a bit unfair to criticize a ritual just because it is possible to carry it out without having the right mental accompaniments to it. That would provide a reason to criticize virtually any sort of practice where the subjective element could go awry. On the other hand, if the ritual was designed in such a way that it was likely to lead practitioners awry then it would be a suitable subject of criticism. How could we judge, what criteria could we employ to find out?

There was an extensive discussion in Chinese thought about this topic. Confucius and his followers advocated a close following of the rituals, since they argued that those rituals celebrated the links with the past and the social structure of the present, and symbolized respect for authority and persisting ethical values. Rituals were not just activities we perform on certain occasions; they solidify our grounding in a system of deference which is highly attractive. We defer to those who deserve that status, those older than us and those who represent the sort of tradition we want to extend into the present. By contrast, the Daoists argued that the important thing was to be natural, and ritual is not a natural reaction to events that we are experiencing. They represent a problematic social system and interfere with our ability to respond to the ways in which nature calls on us to respond when things change. Ritual is rigid while we should be flexible, ritual is objective while we should react subjectively to events, in accordance with how we feel at certain times and in particular places.

This sort of discussion occurs in one form or another in any culture that is organized in terms of rules; there are supporters of the rules and those who think they are arbitrary and stand in the way of how we ought to live. When it comes to clothes we can see how a Confucian would advocate wearing the clothes of the past, or at least those associated with the past, since in that way we are honoring earlier ways of doing things and those who did them. The fact that they might be expensive or inappropriate for modern conditions is irrelevant. What is more important is the link with the past, a past replete with significant events and religious leaders. We celebrate them in what we do today, in just the same way as when we celebrate religious festivals. We do not just think about freedom during Passover or the significance of repentance during the Day of Atonement. We follow a prescribed service of prayer and ritual that links us with the past and those in the past.

Our clothes may fit in with this attitude to what we do, they are not things we always choose but we are obliged to wear them since they are the right clothes, they fit into what we see as appropriate for a particular lifestyle. What is appropriate may be based on what we regard as tradition, or what our friends are wearing, what is comfortable to wear and so on. Similarly with our attitude to religious rituals, we may follow a traditional manner of carrying them out, or we may do something very different. Many, perhaps most, Jews do nothing. Thinking about what traditional Jews wear is useful in helping us consider the nature of embodiment in religion and culture. It is important to appreciate that although people may all be wearing similar clothes, they are far from all thinking in similar ways. It is a comforting illusion that dictators have when watching the serried ranks of their supporters in mass parades, but it is an illusion and should play no part in understanding the role of clothes in religion.

Bibliography

Buber, Martin. 1947. *Tales of the Hasidim: The Early Masters*. New York: Schocken.
Frank, Daniel. 1989. "Humility as a Virtue: A Maimonidean Critique of Aristotle's Ethics." In *Moses Maimonides and His Time*. Ed. Eric L. Ormsby. Washington, DC: Catholic University of America Press, 89–99.
Greenspon, Len. Ed. 2013. *Fashioning Jews: Clothing, Culture, and Commerce*. West Lafayette, IN: Purdue University Press.
Leaman, Oliver. 2010. *Judaism: An Introduction*. London: I. B. Tauris.
Maimonides. 1963. *Guide of the Perplexed*. Trans. S. Pines. Chicago, IL: University of Chicago Press.
Marzel, Shoshana-Rose. 2016. "The Jewish Wardrobe: From the Collection of the Israel Museum Jerusalem." *Fashion Theory*, 20(4): 495–497. doi: 10.1080/1362704X.2015.1102462
Silverman, Eric. 2013. *A Cultural History of Jewish Dress*. London: Bloomsbury Academic.
The Zohar: Translation and Commentary. 2004. 2 volumes. Pritzker edition. Trans. Daniel C. Matt. Stanford, CA: Stanford University Press.

25
FOOD

Maria Diemling

Introduction

Food plays a central part in Jewish ritual and practice. Dating back to biblical laws, prescriptions of what Jews are permitted and prohibited from eating have shaped Jewish observance and identity throughout Jewish history. Food has been used to draw boundaries between Jews and non-Jews but also between Jews with different levels of ritual observance or different interpretations of the requirements. Even the conscious rejection of Jewish dietary practice can at times be understood as an authentic expression of a Jewish spirit. Jason Rosenblum has described Jewish dietary practice as "bundled sets of social activities" that "construct, in part, a discrete identity" (Rosenblum, 2010, 5). Hasia Diner has suggested that the "connections between food and Judaism cannot be understood independent of the tectonic shifts in the social, political, and cultural histories that Jews lived through" with modernity exerting "a powerful and disruptive impact on the food-Judaism connection" (Diner, 2019, xv) that forced Jewish individuals and communities alike to consider their particular food choices. Aaron Gross goes so far as to claim that "no major historical development in Jewish life can be fully understood without reference to food" (2019, 9). Jonathan Brumberg-Kraus distinguishes between two types of works in Jewish Food Studies, text-centred studies of prescriptive and often idealised constructions of the meaning of (premodern) food and Jewish meals and sociological and anthropological studies of the (modern) "performance" of dietary choices. He concludes that the "major insight of all of these studies is the persistent connection between eating and Jewish identity in all its various manifestations. Jews are what they eat" (2012, 121).

In this chapter I will draw from both text-based and sociological studies to survey food ritual and practice in Jewish cultures. Following a broadly chronological structure, I will discuss the foundations of Jewish dietary laws as set out in the Torah and refined in rabbinic Judaism. In the Middle Ages, we find archaeological evidence of distinct Jewish food patterns but also opposition to rabbinic practice. In the early modern period, a rabbinic separation between crockery and cutlery used for meat and dairy indicates both changing patterns of eating in Europe and pious stringency among Ashkenazic Jews. "Eating as a Jew" was at times a subversive act, as the examples of Iberian Crypto-Jews and, much later, twentieth-century Soviet Jews demonstrate. In modernity, Reform Jews in Germany and the United States challenged and sometimes rejected traditional dietary laws while Jewish immigrants responded to the "exotic" food on offer in new environments by embracing the cosmopolitanism of Chinese food in New York or the local Levantine cuisine in Palestine. The pig industry in the State of Israel raises questions about the individual freedom to eat the most symbolic of all "treyf" (non-kosher) food in the Jewish State. More recently, contemporary concerns about the complex ethics of mass-produced food have led to a significant rise in veganism in Israel and elsewhere that challenges the traditional laws of kashrut by offering alternative ways of eating mindfully as Jews. The final section of this chapter discusses some economic aspects of kashrut, highlighting both the higher costs of a kosher diet but also the economic implications, particularly in regard to the non-Jewish world. While Jewish dietary laws are often seen as barrier between Jews and non-Jews, they have also offered economic opportunities across religious boundaries.

Biblical Times

The foundations for Jewish rituals and practices regarding dietary practices, food laws and Jewish identity are set out in the biblical dietary laws of the pre-exilic Book of Deuteronomy 14:3–21 and expanded in post-exilic Leviticus 11. Based on revelation, these laws are described as divinely decreed and almost never explicitly justified. They do not present a detailed food regimen but focus primarily on permitted and prohibited foods, mostly on animals and their treatment. They include rules about abstaining from eating certain animals that either belong to a certain category or are listed specifically, died a natural death or were killed by other animals. Other rules prohibit the consumption of blood and the sciatic nerve. A mother bird needs to be sent away from the nest before taking her eggs or chicks, a mother and her child must not be slaughtered on the same day and a kid must not be cooked in its mother's milk.

The food historian Jeffrey M. Pilcher has claimed that "more thought has been given to the origins of the ancient Hebrew dietary law than any other religion-related food topic" (2012, 417). Mary Douglas set out in her famous study *Purity and Danger* to examine the "hoary old puzzle" (2006, 51) of biblical food laws. Noting that the rules of Leviticus follow the same classification of three environments as in the creation myth in Genesis – land, water and air – Douglas argued that the prohibition of certain animals was a form of taboo on anomalous creatures that do not fit neatly into these distinctions and are contrary to holiness (2006, 69). She saw dietary rules as

> signs which at every turn inspired meditation on the oneness, purity and completeness of God. By rules of avoidance, holiness was given a physical expression in every encounter with the animal kingdom and at every meal. Observance of the dietary rules would thus have been a meaningful part of the great liturgical act of recognition and worship that culminated in the sacrifice in the Temple.
>
> *2006, 71*

The emphasis on dietary purity is a distinctive feature of religious observance in the Bible, with the purity of the Israelites depending on the purity of the animals they ate. Deuteronomy 14:2 describes the Israelites as holy people before listing the permitted animals who have cleft hoofs and chew their cud and excluding those who do not. The flesh of these prohibited animals must not be eaten and contact with their carcasses avoided. The first twenty verses of Leviticus 11 repeat the commandments of Deuteronomy 14, introducing the terms "pure" (*tahor*) and "impure" (*tame*) and add further specific categories of permitted and forbidden animals (Leviticus 11:29–31).

The blood taboo is a further ritual requirement. Deuteronomy 12:23 stipulates that "the blood is the life, and you must not eat the life with the meat". The Israelites are prohibited to consume the blood of animals, which is reserved for God. "It is offered to him on the altar and, by virtue of its exceptional potency, serves to expiate for sins committed inadvertently, thereby substituting for the lives of the worshipers" (Levine, 2013, 802).

An important difference between the rules in Deuteronomy 14 and Leviticus 11 is that the latter also addresses impurity caused by contact with forbidden animals, such as vessels used for cooking or storage. All food stored in vessels must be kept dry (Leviticus 11:32–34). Persons who come in contact with impure animals or their carcass must purify themselves. The concluding verses (Leviticus 11: 44–47) remind the Israelites that they are holy because God is holy, and of the distinction between the impure and the pure, between animals that can be eaten and those that cannot, demarcating clear boundaries between the Israelites and other nations. Biblical examples of this practice include Daniel and his friends opting for a vegetarian diet to avoid eating the impure palace food in Babylon (Daniel 1:8) and Jews choosing death over eating pork during the persecutions under the Seleucids (1 Maccabees 1:12–63).

The expanded rules of Leviticus 11 served as the baseline for later Jewish ritual and practice. Following the Babylonian Exile and the loss of the Temple, the concept of purity shifted from the public temple cult to the domestic household, a ritual development furthered by the innovations of rabbinic Judaism.

Rabbinic Judaism

Food played a crucial role in the transformation of Jewish practice between the beginning of rabbinic Judaism in the first century and the High Middle Ages nearly a millennium later (Kraemer, 2019, 59). While the actual diet of Jews living in the Mediterranean and the Near East did not change that much, ritual and practices underwent significant modifications and "eating itself came to be understood as potentially infused with holiness" (Kraemer, 2019, 78), an everyday activity promoting moral conduct (Avery-Peck, 2013, 809).

In the rabbinic period, biblical dietary laws were expanded and over the course of several centuries adopted beyond the small elite rabbinic circles. The rabbis clarified details of permitted animals and defined how permitted food should be prepared. A particular innovation in this new food regimen was the rabbinic interpretation of the biblical law not to boil a kid in its mother's milk (Exodus 23:19; Exodus 34:26; Deuteronomy 14:21), which ultimately led to a required separation of meat and dairy products that may neither be prepared together nor served in the same dish nor mixed with the same utensils. The consumption of milk after meat during the same meal was also prohibited (Avery-Peck, 2013, 809). A special category is the production and consumption of wine that is only permitted if prepared by an Israelite to avoid idolatrous practices. Rabbinic writings also made the procedures for slaughtering animals more explicit and stipulated that the animal's death must be quick and painless, the meat must be drained of all of its blood and the internal organs need to be checked for defects that would render it forbidden. Kosher meat also required a Jewish slaughterer (Avery-Peck, 2013, 809).

Jewish eating in the rabbinic era became more complicated and demanding. Commensality was a key focus of rabbinic interpretation of dietary laws, separating Jews from non-Jews and from Jews who had not yet adopted rabbinic practices (Rosenblum, 2010; Kraemer, 2019, 71).

Middle Ages

The different interpretation of biblical food laws was a major bone of contention between Jews following the rabbinic tradition and Karaites who rejected it. The Karaites were a prominent Jewish movement in the early Middle Ages in the Muslim world that at times posed a serious challenge to rabbinic authority. The rabbinic prohibition of mixing meat and dairy was, for Karaites, an inauthentic interpretation of the biblical commandment not to boil a kid in its mother's milk and this particular disagreement stood for the difference between Rabbanite and Karaite law. In practice, these differences seem more easily resolved as marriage contracts preserved in the Kairo Geniza indicate that "mixed couples" agreed in advance which rules applied to their own household. For example, Rabbanite Jews permitted birds like chicken and geese that are not mentioned in the Bible by deriving general characteristics of permitted fowl while Karaites only permitted birds explicitly allowed, such as turtledoves and pigeons. On the other hand, Rabbanites were more restrictive with cheese and accepted only rennet that derived from properly slaughtered kosher animals and bought cheese only when it was prepared by fellow Rabbanite Jews. Both groups also differed in what they regarded as acceptable regarding the ritual slaughter of animals, including the requirements from the "shohet" (ritual slaughterer) and the physical condition of the slaughtered animal (Freidenreich, 2014).

Recent archaeological excavations of Jewish quarters allow insights into the actual ritual practice and dietary habits of medieval Jews. A study of faunal assemblages from two fourteenth-century medieval sites in Catalonia, Tàrrega and Puigcerdà, showed consistent patterns of remains from kosher animals. Bones at both sites came primarily from sheep and goat, followed by fowl at Tàrrega and cattle at Puigcerdà, indicating different local conditions. The predominance of forelimb bones and a scarcity of pelvic remains indicate that Jews in these communities sold the hindquarters of animals to avoid the labour-intense purging of the sciatic nerve (Valenzuela-Lamas et al., 2014).

The analyses of bones and pottery in an excavation in central Oxford also clearly show the consistent level of observance of Jews living in the university town in the late twelfth and throughout the thirteenth century, with a complete absence of any pig bones and the dominance of kosher birds, domestic fowl and goose. The high proportion of bird bones (particularly goose) is exceptional, even in comparison with other medieval Jewish sites. Fish bones were limited but included herring but no (otherwise common) eel and only one fragment of marine shell. These findings are in marked contrast to the previous Saxon phase on the site where pig bones were present in quantity and bird bones were barely seen. The organic residue analysis of pottery shards showed that all vessels were used to process product from ruminant animals only, with no traces of non-kosher animals but no domestic fowl either, which may suggest that poultry were cooked by different means such as roasting in an oven. The researchers also noted the absence of dairy products found in the vessels but this applies to both excavated sites and all phases (not only the phase of evidenced Jewish settlement), which suggests that the vessels were not use to heat milk or produce dairy products and that in medieval Oxford milk products were either processed in wooden bowls or bought in (Dunne et al., 2021).

These archaeological findings demonstrate the consistent level of ritual observance of medieval Jews in their everyday food practice. But food rituals are also highly symbolic. Ivan Marcus has examined the initiation of young Jewish boys to systematic learning and the sweetness of Torah in the Middle Ages:

> The child is seated on the teacher's lap, the teacher shows him the writing tablet, honey cake, and egg on which the Hebrew alphabet or biblical verses have been

written. The two of them recite the texts, and the child licks honey off the tablet and eats the inscribed cakes and eggs.

Marcus, 1996, 77–78

Marcus has suggested that this is a "symbolic inversion" in which the child "enters the Torah (*nikhas la-torah*) by means of the Torah entering the child in the form of the special foods on which the verses of the Torah have been written" (Marcus, 1996, 78). He sees this practice as an "inward acculturation" of contemporary Christian eucharistic practice.

Early Modern Period

Lyndal Roper's (1991) concept of the "holy household" signifies the importance of the home for the (often very gendered) observance of religious rituals. In the Jewish home, not only the food but also the objects and cooking utensils were imbued with spiritual significance. While the lipid analysis of the archaeological findings in Oxford did not detect dairy residue in the pottery (for Jewish and non-Jewish sources alike), the practice of some separation between meat and dairy vessels was increasingly discussed by medieval rabbinic authorities but there were significant differences of opinion in law and practice (Kraemer, 2007, 102–107). From the sixteenth century onwards, changes in the eating habits in Western society and the increasing use of cutlery and individual dishes led to more stringency in Jewish law governing the separation of utensils used for meat and dairy. Joseph Caro's legal code *Shulhan Arukh* prohibits cutting cheese with a knife that is normally used for meat or eating cheese on a cloth used for meat although he permits keeping meat and dairy dishes in the same cupboard. R. Moses Isserles' gloss on Caro comments that

> all of Israel have already made it their custom to have two knives, and to mark one of them so that it will have a sign, and they are accustomed to marking the one used for dairy, and one should not change the custom of Israel.
>
> *Kraemer, 2007, 107–108*

David Kraemer has suggested that the "birth of the 'modern' Jewish kitchen" with a clear separation between meat and dairy dishes was first testified in the 1530 book of the Jewish convert Anthonius Margaritha who describes a more stringent domestic practice than the legal codes of the time indicate (Kraemer, 2007, 109–110). Kraemer argues that the domestic kitchen is where women were in control of the observance of kashrut and perform their own domestic piety, often to other women. Untrained in the fine details of halakhah that might allow more lenient solutions for infringements, pious women would err on the side of caution and choose a more stringent path that would prevent loss of time, food and resources. The emerging Hasidic movement in the eighteenth century insisted on pious stringency in public that distinguished them from the rest of the Jewish community. Hasidic shohatim used particularly well-honed knives for ritual slaughter, "a stringency that served to camouflage their real object, which was to avoid eating together with non-Hasidim" (Katz, 1993, 208), symbolising and effectuating the separation of the more observant (or differently observing) from the less observant (Kraemer, 2007, 118).

Another example of this tendency is the curious tale of the swordfish (*Xiphias gladius*) and its kosher status due to the particular nature of its scales. The renowned Sephardic scholar Rabbi Chaim ben Yisrael Benvenisti (1603–73) permitted the consumption of "the fish with the sword" but in the second half of the twentieth century the question if the swordfish is kosher led to a polemical debate between the Orthodox and Conservative rabbinate in the United States, and between American Orthodox rabbis and the Israeli rabbinate. Wittily paraphrasing a quote by the Marx Brothers, "the Password was Swordfish", Zivotofsky has suggested that the swordfish "has been the standard-bearer of the 'fish that is non-kosher because others had declared it kosher'. It was 'the password' that let everyone know that one was on the correct side of the law" (2008, 50).

Subversion and Resistance

Renée Levine Melammed has demonstrated the importance of ritual observance for crypto-Jews in fifteenth- and sixteenth-century Spain following the "largest mass conversion of Jews in history" (2002, 4). Her research focused on the domestic devotion of women who continued to observe dietary laws secretly to avoid being denounced to the Inquisition intent to root out heretic practices among these "New Christians". Ritual food practices included abstaining from eating or cooking with pork or pork products, eating foods that were forbidden by the Catholic Church on certain days (such as meat on Friday or during Lent), preparing food in advance before Friday evening or eating cold food on Friday nights and Saturdays and fasting on Jewish fast days. These and other ritual practices were carried out in "identification with the people of Israel and the hope of achieving salvation through the Law of Moses" (Levine Melammed, 2002, 167). At the same time, the domestic domain "became the center of judaizing", a "bastion of cultural and, even more so, religious resistance". This includes the private subversion of the Catholic faith they adhered to in public (2002, 170).

Centuries later, a different way of holding on to Jewish foodways emerged in the Soviet Union. Following the 1917 October Revolution, Jewish dietary laws were officially denounced as dangerous to public health and the national economy. Most Jews felt pressured into abandoning food observance. However, traces of Jewish dietary practices remained throughout the Soviet period. Traditional Jewish dishes were called "family recipes" and families kept eating Ashkenazic food such as gefilte fish, even if sometimes recipes were changed against the laws of kashrut and dairy butter replaced parve oil in a traditional meat dish as cookbooks from the time demonstrate. Despite the official disapproval of religious observance, some consciousness of kashrut procedures remained, although for many Soviet Jews "kosher" simply meant food prepared by a Jew or "with a Jewish soul". This could even include a recipe for "kosher pork" or knowledge of special butchers for pigs and rabbits, otherwise their meat would not be deemed "kosher". These examples indicate ritual awareness and the importance of preserving (adapted) family recipes as part of their Jewish self-understanding in an environment largely hostile to Jewish particularism (Shternshis, 2006).

Nineteenth-century Reform

In the nineteenth-century German Reform movement, dietary restrictions were seen as a "hindrance to the development of social relationships" (in the words of Abraham Geiger) and "a disturbing feature in the civic and social life of the Jews" as "these laws are particularly prone to continue the differences between them and other inhabitants" (Samuel Holdheim). These sentiments express the optimism of European Jews following the Enlightenment and the civic enfranchisement of Jews and the belief in the brotherhood of all humans (Kraemer, 2007, 138). "Excluding gentiles from table fellowship with Jews was an affront to universal human notions of brotherhood" (Zeller, 2014, 919).

In the US, the break with dietary practices was more radical but David Kraemer has made the important point that the changes in Jewish dietary observances in modernity are "affirmations of the Jewishness of those who assume them" (2007, 139). The Pittsburgh Platform (1885), a summary of key principles of the American Reform movement for nearly half a century, renounced the dietary laws in conjunction with a "statement of faith in the messianic quality of modernity":

> We hold that all such Mosaic and rabbinical laws as regulate diet, priestly purity and dress originated in ages and under the influence of ideas altogether foreign to our present mental and spiritual state. They fail to impress the modern Jew with a spirit of priestly holiness; their observance in our days is apt rather to obstruct than to further modern spiritual innovation.
>
> *Cited in Kraemer, 2007, 138–139*

The document asserts the belief in the essential unity of all peoples who come to recognise the enlightened truth and the hope that the divisions between humans are about to disappear. Abolishing the dietary restrictions is an act of affirmation of Jewish values and

> these rabbis, and those for whom they speak, are acting in what they believe to be a genuine Jewish spirit. For them, the identity of the modern Jew is best reflected in a thoroughly open dietary regimen. Though they are now eating as others, they are still eating as Jews.
>
> *Kraemer, 2007, 139*

Or, in Peter Knobel's words, they "did not desire to escape Judaism but to fulfil it" (cited in Balin, 2011, 9).

Chinese Food as 'Jewish Food'

An interesting twentieth-century phenomenon in the negotiation of Jewish food practice that indicates the creativity of Jewish ritual outside the confines of religiously motivated dietary laws is the long-standing affinity of Jews in New York with Chinese cuisine, dating back to the late nineteenth century. Tuchman and Levine have argued that as these Jews "declared their independence from traditional Jewish culture and affirmed their identity as sophisticated New Yorkers, they also forged a new, urban, Jewish culture". In their study based on over 100 interviews, they identified three themes: while Chinese food is not kosher and therefore non-Jewish, immigrant Jews and their families found the food more attractive and less threatening than other food because of the lack of dairy in Chinese food, familiar ingredients and the "disguised" chopped up and minced non-kosher ingredients a kind of "safe treyf". Second, Chinese restaurants were seen as cosmopolitan and sophisticated. Third, second- and third-generation Jewish immigrants perceived eating in a Chinese family as a "New York Jewish custom, a part of daily life and self-identity for millions of New York Jews", something that Jews did together (Tuchman and Levine, 1992, 385–386). For them Chinese food had become part of a "fondly remembered past". The popularity of Chinese food among American Jews is also indicated by the rise in kosher Chinese restaurants that use "imitation treyf" products, made from vegetarian kosher ingredients to replace pork, shellfish and eel on the menu, making Chinese food also popular with observant Jews (Plaut, 2012, 988).

A particular American Jewish tradition is eating Chinese on Christmas when other entertainment venues are closed. Plaut has observed that "Jews in America are celebrating a secular day in a highly charged popular ritual of eating Chinese and, more recently, other Asian ethnic foods" (2012, 964). Paired with popular Jewish comedy events across the United States, the practice of eating Chinese food and laughing with Jewish comedians, offers a positive affirmation of Jewish identity and "a new Jewish cultural reality whereby Christmas is not an isolating force" (2012, 1156).

Eating in Palestine/Israel

The immigration from Europe to Palestine and later Israel posed a different set of challenges. Food came to play a central role in the construction of a Jewish nation and the building of a Jewish national home in the Land of Israel. Cookbooks are "revealing artefacts of culture in the making" (Arjun Appadurai, cited in Raviv, 2015, 7) but the culture in the making was not a "kashrut nation" (to echo Laurence Roth's (2010) fine article on Jewish cookbooks in late twentieth-century North America) but one that embraced the land and its agricultural and commercial produce. Dr Erna Meyer's cookbook *How to Cook in Palestine*, published in 1936 in Tel Aviv on behalf of the WIZO (Women's International Zionist Organization) in German, Hebrew and English, was the first Jewish cookbook printed in Palestine during the British Mandate (Meyer, 1937?). Aimed primarily at middle-class immigrants from Nazi Germany, it urged bourgeois Jewish women to free their kitchen "from its Galuth-traditions" and "wholeheartedly adjust ourselves to healthy Palestine cooking" by using only locally produced products to support the national economy and for their health benefits. The cookbook is full of advertisements by local companies and their products are used in the recipes, "a perfect example of Zionism and capitalism going hand-in-hand" (Kessler, 2016). Meyer, an expert in domestic science, introduced readers to local vegetables such as eggplants, okra and marrow, suggested replacing butter by vegetable oil or *kokosin*, a local butter substitute, and using tomato ketchup to add spice and colour to simple dishes. Consuming and cooking is ideologised to help bewildered middle-class women to acclimatise "to our old-new homeland" and the kitchen becomes a place of change that aids the transition to a new Jewish identity in the spirit of Zionism (Rautenberg-Alianov, 2012).

By the 1960s, Israel had become self-sustaining through the agriculture of communal kibbutzim and the cooperative villages. The Israeli diet, drawing on many different influences, evolved into one similar to the historic Levantine and Middle Eastern Jewish diet (Raviv, 2015; Avieli, 2018) although only traditional Ashkenazic dishes such as gefilte fish, kugel or cholent are seen as particular "Jewish food", reflecting Ashkenazi cultural hegemony (Avieli, 2018, 221). Food served by government institutions, army and hospitals and the national airline El Al are under the supervision of Orthodox rabbis. Hotels, event halls and supermarkets, appealing to a broad clientele, offer typically only kosher food. In a 2009 survey, just under half of the Jewish population in Israel defined itself as "secular" (and either "anti-religious" or simply "non-religious") but 63–75% claim that they eat only kosher food and never eat pork (Myers, 2019, 125).

The Pig Industry in the State of Israel

While only a minority of Jewish Israelis eat pork, the Israeli pig industry has become a political issue about religious influence, cultural habits and individual liberty. It was widely debated after the foundation of the State of Israel, with many secular socialist Zionists rejecting national dietary laws or even arguing in favour of cheap pork meat to alleviate the meat shortage in the early years of the country, prompting the poet Nathan Alterman (1973) to comment, "[w]hen a Jewish nation makes a pig a *sine qua non*, its history shudders". Daphne Barak Erez has argued that in Israel the abhorrence of pig transcended its religious origins and, through the ideology of "statism" (2007, 36), became a quintessential symbol of a recently established "national identity inspired by a religious history but detached from religion as such" (2007, 37).

This was explicitly expressed in two anti-pig laws. The Local Authorities (Special Enablement) Law of 1956 authorises municipalities to limit the sale of pork products. The Pig Raising Prohibition Law of 1962 prohibited the breeding of pigs in the whole country, with the exception of Christian-populated areas in the Northern Galilee. Both laws were contested in Israeli courts in the 1950s and 1960s, mostly by Christian Arabs. In the 1980s, influential religious political parties used these laws to gain concessions before joining a coalition government. The large-scale immigration from the former Soviet Union in the 1990s provided additional challenges to these laws as both Jewish and non-Jewish immigrants sought out pork products. This went hand in hand with an increase of gourmet culture among secular, well-travelled Israelis who rejected any restrictions on what to eat. According to the Israeli Ministry of Agriculture, the volume of the pig industry has doubled in a decade and, at any given moment, about 120,000 pigs are kept in three Christian Arab breeding areas in the north, and in a unit at Kibbutz Lahav in the south. The number of regular pork consumers living in Israel is estimated as being between 500,000 to 700,000, including Christians and foreign workers, with an average of 200,000 slaughtered pigs a year that represent around 45–47% of total livestock slaughtered per year in Israel (data from Ben-Dov et al., 2014, 4). Israeli-bred pigs are also used for medical research (Shemer, 2017).

Barak Erez suggests that the legal discourse in Israel around pork marks a transition from an "identity discourse", based on symbolic legislation that appeals to a shared identity based on religious tradition, to a "rights discourse", in which personal freedoms compete with religious interests (2007, 113). Does to be a free Jew in a free Jewish country also mean the freedom to eat what you want?

Vegetarianism and Veganism

The first Ashkenazic Chief Rabbi of Palestine, Abraham Isaac Kook (1865–1935), expressed some of the strongest support for vegetarianism as a positive ideal in Torah literature. His teachings on ethical vegetarianism demonstrated deep feelings for animals as autonomous subjects and he "believed that vegetarianism is the diet most consistent with Jewish teachings" (Schwartz and Sears, 2019, 228). In Messianic times more spiritually evolved humans would understand that what they take from animals is theft or murder. Kook's interpretation of Genesis 9:3, that the permission to consume meat was a concession to human violence, is often cited as an orthodox voice in support of vegetarian or vegan diet. Kook was quite clear though that animal welfare is not the greatest moral concern in a world rife with conflict between humans. "Addressing himself to members of the vegetarian movement, Rabbi Kook remarks almost facetiously that one might surmise that all problems of human welfare have been resolved and the sole remaining area of concern is animal welfare" (Bleich, 1987, 85).

Many contemporary Israelis seem to disagree. In recent years vegetarianism and particularly veganism in Israel have become a mainstream phenomenon. In a 2018 survey, 5% of (mostly younger) Israelis defined themselves as vegans (Refael, 2018). This growing trend is even utilised by right-wing politicians and the IDF, the latter announcing in 2019 on Twitter that "with over 10,000 vegan soldiers (one in every eighteen soldiers) we are proud to be the most vegan army in the world", arguably trying to convey a superior moral stance (Avital, 2021, 82). Avital has observed that in the public discourse the battle for animal rights is presented as "the most important battle to be currently fought in the world" with a clearly identified villain and a clear solution. Unlike the acting forces in the complex Israeli-Palestinian conflict, animals have no agency and are seen as entirely innocent, helpful and mute and therefore need to be protected (Avital, 2021, 65).

This is not only a secular concern but increasingly popular with observant Israelis as well. "The garden of Eden, which was the ideal society, was a vegetarian society. Adam and Eve were vegans", said Rabbi David Rosen, one of a group of 75 rabbis from across the world and representing different strands of Judaism who in September 2018 signed a declaration in which they urged Jews to become vegans (Jewish Veg Rabbinic Statement). Asa Keisar, a religious scribe who grew up in a vegetarian Orthodox family, has become a figurehead for observant Jews embracing veganism in Israel. He argues that the world has changed and that, given the cruelty of the meat industry, "there is no kosher meat at all" (Holmes, 2018). He compares people who buy or eat animal products to those putting a stumbling block in front of the blind (Leviticus 19:14) as they are sinners who are also causing others working in the sector to sin. Keisar is also promoting a kosher and vegan certification, "Vegan Kosher", that certifies that a product is 100% vegan and kosher according to Jewish law. While similar and even more ambitious efforts in the US have failed to take off (Diemling, 2015a,189), this certification aims to make veganism "more accessible, convenient and acceptable" and aspires to "promote humanity to an existence where animals are no longer used by humans for food, clothing, entertainment or any other purpose" (Keisar, 2021).

Eco-Kashrut and Ethical Kashrut

Unlike Jewish vegetarianism or veganism, movements that consider the suffering caused to animals as unacceptable, the various forms of Eco-Kashrut have a much broader agenda. They are also concerned with food sustainability, environmentalism and the fair and just treatment of works in agriculture and the food industry. Introduced by R. Zalman Shacter-Shalomi (1924–2014), one of the founders of the American Jewish Renewal Movement, "Eco-Kashrut" is a contemporary form of ritual food observance that "focuses on the means of production far more than the material consumed" (Zeller, 2014, 922). Some Jews committed to Eco-Kashrut understand it as an alternative to or substitute for traditional Jewish dietary laws that do not sufficiently address contemporary concerns. For others, it is an evolution that combines the laws of kashrut with ecological principles. "What unites all of these forms of Jewish eating is the idea of intentionality, ethical eating, and a proclaimed continuity with tradition alongside innovation" (Zeller, 2014, 922).

These practices offer a contemporary interpretation of the ethical dimension of kashrut. The reasons for the biblical dietary laws have been debated by rabbinical authorities and biblical scholars alike and there is no consensus what ethical concerns, if any, motivate these laws. Increasingly, however, a specific Jewish food ethics that combines the centrality of food in the Jewish tradition with a thoughtful consideration of the ethical and moral obligations of living a consciously Jewish life, is emerging. The malpractice unearthed between 2000 and 2008 at the Agriprocessors meat processing plant in Iowa, run by a prominent Chabad Lubavitch family, shocked many American Jews. At its height, Agriprocessors supplied 60% of all kosher beef and 40% of kosher poultry in the US. The raid on the plant exposed the maltreatment of immigrant workers who were paid the lowest hourly wages of any abattoir in the US, regularly short-charged, given little or no safety instructions and trapped in exploitative rental agreements. About 800 of the workers were undocumented immigrant workers. Moses Pava has argued that the Rubashkin family "has brought shame not only to themselves but to the Jewish people, whom they profess to love with such abundance" and their behaviour toward vulnerable immigrant workers "demonstrates a profound moral myopia". He points out that "loving your neighbour" (Leviticus 19:18) is a "necessary ingredient to help build a just and caring food system and ultimately a just and caring society" (Pava, 2019, 326–327). Pava's comments highlight the human costs of the meat industry. The American Jewish author and apologist for vegetarianism, Jonathan Safran Foer, described these practices as "hillul ha-shem" (desecration of God's name) (Safran Foer, 2009, 69). Arguably this also reflects rabbinic discussion that the welfare of animals must not be put above the needs of humans but also that the killing of animals can affect human nature (Bleich, 1987, 84).

The Economics of Kashrut

The economics of kashrut are well demonstrated by Agriprocessors and their business practices. Its use of new efficient technology and packaging that kept meat fresh for longer, lowered the cost of kosher meat and made it more accessible and affordable, particularly for customers in small Jewish communities (Pava, 2019, 322), but it came at the price of human exploitation and cruelty to animals. Cheap meat means cutting corners on health and safety procedures because "humane treatment generally slows down a production line" (Renton, 2003).

The additional costs of kosher produce are not a modern phenomenon. The economic significance of a rabbinic seal of approval can be traced back to at least the first century CE, when a kosher fish broth, called garum castimoniale and made from fish with scales such as tuna, sardines, anchovies or mackerels, sold at higher prices than its non-kosher competitors (Kurlansky, 2003, 75).

Spending for Shabbat and holidays is a religious commandment. "Simchat Yom Tov", the commandment to "rejoice in your festivals" (Deuteronomy 16:4), has led to halakhic debate about what this rejoicing means. During the Second Temple period this was understood as men partaking of the flesh of the festival offering but after destruction of the Temple rabbis disputed if this requires the eating of ordinary meat. Maimonides interpreted this as a requirement to eat meat, drink wine, wear new clothes and give fruits and sweets to women and children. Other sages were equally clear that an effort needs to be made to enhance the joyfulness and festivity of the holiday in accordance with one's financial ability (Bleich, 1987, 87–89) although one should not be stingy with purchases for these occasions as the Talmud (Beitzah 16a) teaches that one's entire livelihood is allocated on Rosh Hashana, including expenditures for Shabbat and festivals.

The practice of having two separate sets of crockery and cutlery (even more if Passover provisions are included) has in recent decades extended in some strictly observant Jewish households to separate sinks, fridges and dishwashers. While these appliances may be one-off costs, there is no doubt that keeping kashrut adds significantly to food costs. An American survey from 2006 indicates that kosher consumers spend an average of $1,000 more on food annually (Fishkoff, 2010, 365). Kosher meat is significantly more expensive. One reason is the labour-intense and time-consuming removal of the sciatic nerve (porging or de-veining), based on the prohibition from eating the sinew that surrounds the sciatic nerve of the hind leg of domestic ruminants, the "sinew of Jacob" (Genesis 32:32, "gid hanasheh"). This has led throughout history to trading of meat with non-Jews. Agroprocessors sold a significant amount of the meat processed at their plants as non-kosher meat (Pava, 2019, 322) while, 600 years earlier, the absence of hind leg bones in the archaeozoological evidence from two

Jewish quarters in fourteenth-century Catalonia indicates that these parts of otherwise kosher animals were not consumed by Jews but sold on (at a lower price) to non-Jews outside the Jewish quarter. This practice recuperates some of the financial loss by forfeiting a significant part of an otherwise kosher animal. This practice was discussed among Christians and Muslims, with Islamic law usually permitting the meat butchered by People of the Book (Sura 5:5 in the Qur'an and confirmed by the vast majority of Sunnī jurists) and medieval Canon Law forbidding the practice. Shī'ī authorities, however, prohibited not only meat slaughtered by Jews but also most foodstuffs touched by Jews (Freidenreich, 2014, 191–196). The views of Christians authorities differed. Popular with Christians as the price of this meat was cheaper, it was also an intensely debated practice with accusations that Jews defiled this meat before selling it on (Diemling, 2015b, 127–132). In nineteenth-century Germany, "the large percentage of animals slaughtered by the Jewish method was problematic because it inferred that Jews profited from killing, a charge that played into extant stereotypes of Jews as economically shifty and driven by economic gain" (Judd, 2003, 126). When it was reported that the Germany army served "ritually slaughtered" beef, an animal rights movement in Berlin was outraged and one newspaper described it as a Jewish revenge plot on Germans (Judd, 2003, 127).

While ritually slaughtered meat has been regarded with suspicion, particularly in Europe where the practice is banned in several countries, the private kosher certification process and the kosher food industry in the US have been highly successful. The kosher certification is a private-sector regulation that reaches far beyond its core group of observant Jews. As suggested in an early and very successful advertisement for a kosher "Hot Dog" from the 1970s onwards, an industry that answers to "an even higher authority" (than the US government and its food regulations) implies trustworthiness, strict rules based on ancient laws, and divine approval (Fishkoff, 2010, 134). A kashrut inspector, overseeing the production of kosher food in China, acknowledged this implicitly when commenting that "food scandals are always good for the kosher business" (Marx, 2008).

In the United States, a network of over 300 private certifiers ensures the kosher status of food that generates more than $200 billion of the US's estimated $500 billion in annual food sales for a population of which less than 2% is Jewish and only a minority of them actually keep kosher. While a significant percentage of this food is "traditionally Jewish ethnic food", most certified kosher foods are mainstream products aimed at the general consumer and produced by the main international food manufacturers, but expensive upmarket products have also embraced this growing trend. Over 11.2 million Americans regularly buy kosher food but only 14% of these customers keep kashrut. Some customers, such as those who are vegetarians, lactose-intolerant, Muslims or Seventh-day Adventists, purchase it because they trust the label, however, the majority of American kosher food consumers buy kosher products because they think that these are of higher quality than non-kosher food (Fishkoff, 2010, 199). Described as a model of non-governmental registration, the kosher certification industry operates to uniform industry standards, requires professional training and has stringent control measures in place (Lytton, 2013).

Kosher business has become a truly global business phenomenon that reflects the contemporary capitalist system of production and distribution. China has the highest growth rate for the export of kosher food products. The adherence to dietary laws in Chinese production sites is overseen by a fleet of "mashgichim" (kashrut inspectors), "the foot soldiers of the kosher food industry" (Fishkoff, 2010, 228). In 1981, three rabbis worked on behalf of the Orthodox Union, one of the four agencies that certify the majority of kosher food sold in the US, in China. In 2009, more than 50 (seven on behalf of OU) travelled far and wide through China to visit food processing factories. Annually, China exports kosher ingredients and products, from tinned fruit to artificial flavouring and amino acids, worth $1.25 billion worldwide (Marx, 2008). In 2020, there were at least 1,270 certified kosher food factories in China (Tenorio, 2020).

As far as I can see, the ethics of producing kosher food products in Chinese factories have not yet been significantly challenged. The "mashgichim" only check the compliance to kashrut and not the working conditions of the employees. In contrast, the proposed new Israeli Vegan Kosher certification mentioned above indicates awareness of certain ethical standards and is aimed at customers who want more than a kosher seal of approval. It is advertised to producers as a potentially lucrative business opportunity because "the vegan consumer and the kosher consumer are both by nature discerning buyers" who will "not buy a product without a strict approval stamp" (Keisar, 2021). It has identified a market for ethical consumption among customers for whom a kosher seal of approval is not sufficient and may well appeal to non-Jewish customers as well.

The success of the global kosher food industry is a striking inversion of the historical mistrust of Jewish dietary practices (Freidenreich, 2011). The first commercial product that bore the Orthodox Union's discreet seal of approval was a tin of baked beans by the American company Heinz in 1923. "The minimalist symbol was created because Heinz executives, nervous that they might put off their Gentile customers, did not want packaging that looked manifestly Jewish" (Marx, 2008).

Conclusion

In his vegetarian manifesto, *Eating Animals*, Jonathan Safran Foer writes movingly about this grandmother who survived the Second World War and the Holocaust in Europe as a young woman. In her recollections of the suffering she went through, she mentions the severe starvation that forced her to eat from garbage bins. "If you helped yourself, you could survive. I took whatever I could find. I ate things I wouldn't tell you about." Toward the end of the war, a Russian farmer saw her condition, took pity and offered her a piece of meat from his house.

> "He saved your life."
> "I didn't eat it."
> "You didn't eat it?"
> "It was pork. I wouldn't eat pork."
> "Why?"
> "What do you mean why?"
> "What, because it wasn't kosher?"
> "Of course."
> "But not even to save your life?"
> "If nothing matters, there's nothing to save."
>
> Safran Foer, 2009, 16–17

Jewish food practices throughout history have always demonstrated that "it matters", that the ritual observance of dietary laws is not only a divine commandment but it matters to the community and to the individual, securing the survival of the Jewish people and of Judaism as a distinct ethno-religious culture. How this responsibility is interpreted has differed widely. As we have seen, the biblical dietary laws focus on the holiness and purity of the People of Israel. With the destruction of the Temple in Jerusalem, dietary purity moves to the domestic sphere with women playing a significant role in the "holy household" while male textual culture further defines how these rules are to be interpreted. The juxtaposition between the legal and the private aspects of food ritual and practices remains central to Jewish observance. It leads to differentiation and separation from others, from non-Jews, but also, often, from other Jews whose levels of ritual commitment are seen as less stringent. At times, when external circumstances threatened the survival of Jewish practice, secretly maintained domestic routines indicate a degree of resistance or even subversion. Even if the actual ritual practice bore little resemblance to prescriptive halakhah, the cultural memory of Jewish foodways affirmed Jewish heritage. Ethical considerations have led to negotiations of kashrut. Nineteenth-century Reform and its vision of universal brotherhood of all humanity challenged traditional dietary laws. More recently, concerns about factory farming, large-scale animal husbandry and the ensuing cruelty to animals, the treatment of workers in the meat industry and the environmental impact of meat consumption have questioned if food that is produced under these conditions can be kosher at all.

Zionist pioneers hoped to create a "new Jew" in the historical Land of Israel. Leaving behind the ways of old and embracing the produce of the Middle East was one way of adapting to the new old homeland. Migration of Jews from all over the world have influenced the foodways of Israeli Jews but this process has been politically fraught as the political debate about the Israeli pig industry has demonstrated. Finally, the economy of kashrut has been explored. Historically, the refusal of Jews to eat pigs, for example, has been regarded with suspicion in Europe and the non-kosher meat that was sold on by Jews was the subject of polemics. However, today a kosher certification is often seen as a shrewd business move that opens up new markets and kosher food has become a successful global business. As Fishkoff noted, "multinational corporations don't make kosher food to help Jews turn their bodies into holy vessels. They do it to make money" (2010, 370). The economic value of this lucrative industry is not to trivialise the importance that a significant number of Jews pay to food ritual and practices. As this survey has demonstrated, throughout Jewish history food has played an important role in how Jews perform religion, identity, community and belonging. To explore the relationship with food ritual and practice allows insights into key moments of the Jewish experience.

Bibliography

Alterman, Nathan. 1973. "Freedom of Religion and the Hooves", in *Seventh Column*, vol. 2. Tel Aviv: Hakibbutz Hameuhad. [Hebrew].

Avery-Peck, Alan J. 2013. "Dietary Laws: B. Rabbinic Judaism," in *Encyclopedia of the Bible and Its Reception* 6. Berlin-Boston: Walter de Gruyter, 807–809.

Avieli, Nir. 2018. *Food & Power: A Culinary Ethnography of Israel*. Oakland, CA: University of California Press.

Avital, Sharon. 2021. "Because We Care: Veganism and Politics in Israel," in *Veg(etari)an Arguments in Culture, History, and Practice*. Ed. Cristina Hanganu-Bresch and Kristin Kondrlik. The Palgrave Macmillan Animal Ethics Series. Cham: Palgrave Macmillan, 63–92.

Balin, Carole B. 2011. "Making Every Forkful Count": Reform Jews, Kashrut, and Mindful Eating, 1840–2010," in *The Sacred Table: Creating a Jewish Food Ethic*. Ed. Mary L. Zamore. New York: CCAR Press, 5–16.

Barak Erez, Daphne. 2007. *Outlawed Pigs: Law, Religion and Culture in Israel*. Madison, WI: University of Wisconsin Press.

Ben-Dov, D., Hadani, Y., Ben-Simchon, A. et al. 2014. "Guidelines for Pig Welfare in Israel," *Israel Journal of Veterinary Medicine* 69, no. 1: 4–15.

Bleich, J. David. 1987. "Survey of Recent Halakhic Periodical Literature: Vegetarianism and Judaism," *Tradition: A Journal of Orthodox Jewish Thought* 23, no. 1: 82–90.

Brumberg-Kraus, Jonathan. 2012. "'Bread from Heaven, Bread from the Earth': Recent Trends in Jewish Food History Writing," in *Writing Food History: A Global Perspective*. Eds. Kyri W. Claflin and Peter Scholliers. London-New York: Berg, 121–139.

Diemling, Maria. 2015a. "The Politics of Food: Kashrut, Food Choices and Social Justice (*tikkun olam*)," *Jewish Culture and History* 16, no. 2: 178–195.

Diemling, Maria. 2015b. "About Bakers, Butchers, Geese and Pigs: Negotiating the Boundaries of Jewish-Christian Relations in Schudt's *Merckwürdigkeiten*," *Frankfurter judaistische Beiträge* 40: 115–138.

Diner, Hasia. 2019. "Foreword," in *Feasting and Fasting: The History and Ethics of Jewish Food*. Eds. Aaron S. Gross, Jody Myers and Jordan R. Rosenblum. New York: New York University Press, xi–xvi.

Douglas, Mary. 2006. *Purity and Danger: An Analysis of Concept of Pollution and Taboo*. With a new preface by the author. London-New York: Routledge.

Dunne, J., Biddulph, E., Manix, P. et al. 2021. "Finding Oxford's medieval Jewry using organic residue analysis, faunal records and historical documents," *Archaeological and Anthropological Science* 13, no. 48 (February), 1–20.

Fishkoff, Susan. 2010. *Kosher Nation: Why More and More of America's Food Answers to a Higher Authority*. Kindle edition. New York: Schocken.

Freidenreich, David M. 2011. *Foreigners and their Food: Constructing Otherness in Jewish, Christian, and Islamic Law*. Berkeley: University of California Press.

Freidenreich, David. 2014. "Food and Drink – Medieval Period," in *Encyclopedia of Jews in the Islamic World Online*. Ed. Norman A. Stillman. https://referenceworks.brillonline.com/entries/encyclopedia-of-jews-in-the-islamic-world/food-and-drink-medieval-period-COM_000704 (accessed 28 February 2021).

Greenspoon, Leonard J., Simkins, Ronald A. and Shapiro, Gerald. Eds. 2005. *Food and Judaism*. Omaha, NE: Creighton University Press.

Gross, Aaron S. 2019. "Introduction," in *Feasting and Fasting: The History and Ethics of Jewish Food*. Eds. Aaron S. Gross, Jody Myers and Jordan R. Rosenblum. New York: New York University Press, 1–26.

Holmes, Oliver. 2018. "'There Is No Kosher Meat': The Israelis Full of Zeal for Going Vegan," *The Guardian*, 17 March 2018. www.theguardian.com/world/2018/mar/17/there-is-no-kosher-meat-the-israelis-full-of-zeal-for-going-vegan (accessed 28 February 2021).

Jewish Veg. 2017. "Jewish Veg Rabbinic Statement." www.jewishveg.org/rabbinic-statement (accessed 28 February 2021).

Judd, Robin. 2003. "The Politics of Beef: Animal Advocacy and the Kosher Butchering Debates in Germany," *Jewish Social Studies* 10, no. 1: 117–150.

Katz, Jacob. 1993. *Tradition and Crisis: Jewish Society at the End of the Middle Ages*. Translated and with an afterword by Bernard Dov Coperman. New York: Schocken.

Keisar, Asa. 2021. "Vegan Kosher Certification." https://asakeisar.com/en/vegan-kosher-certification/ (accessed 28 February 2021).

Kessler, Dana. 2016. "An Early Taste of Zionism'." *Tablet*, 31 August 2016. www.tabletmag.com/sections/food/articles/an-early-taste-of-zionism (accessed 28 February 2021).

Kraemer, David C. 2007. *Jewish Eating and Identity Through the Ages*. London-New York: Routledge.

Kraemer, David C. 2019. "Food in the Rabbinic Era," in *Feasting and Fasting: The History and Ethics of Jewish Food*. Ed. Aaron S. Gross, Jody Myers and Jordan R. Rosenblum. New York: New York University Press, 59–82.

Kurlansky, Mark. 2003. *Salt*. New York: Penguin.

Levine, Baruch. 2013. "Dietary Laws: I. Hebrew Bible/Old Testament," in *Encyclopedia of the Bible and Its Reception* 6. Berlin-Boston: Walter de Gruyter, 800–804.

Levine Melammed, Renée. 2002. *Heretics or Daughters of Israel? The Crypto-Jewish Women of Castile*. Oxford: Oxford University Press.

Lytton, Timothy D. 2013. *Kosher: Private Regulation in the Age of Industrial Food*. Cambridge, MA: Harvard University Press.

Marcus, Ivan G. 1996. *Rituals of Childhood: Jewish Acculturation in Medieval Europe*. New Haven, CT: Yale University Press.

Marx, Patricia. 2008. "Kosher Takeout." *The New Yorker*, 22 December 2008. www.newyorker.com/magazine/2009/01/05/kosher-takeout (accessed 28 February 2021).

Meyer, Erna. 1937? *How to Cook in Palestine*. Tel Aviv-Yafo: Wizo.

Myers, Jody. 2019. "Food in the Modern Era," in *Feasting and Fasting: The History and Ethics of Jewish Food*. Eds. Aaron S. Gross, Jody Myers and Jordan R. Rosenblum. New York: New York University Press, 110–139.

Pava, Moses. 2019. "Jewish Ethics, the Kosher Industry, and the Fall of Agroprocessors," in *Feasting and Fasting: The History and Ethics of Jewish Food*. Eds. Aaron S. Gross, Jody Myers and Jordan R. Rosenblum. New York: New York University Press, 317–329.

Pilcher, Jeffrey M. Ed. 2012. *Oxford Handbook of Food History*. Oxford: Oxford University Press.

Plaut, Joshua Eli. 2012. *A Kosher Christmas: 'Tis the Season to be Jewish*. New Brunswick, NJ: Rutgers University Press.

Rautenberg-Alianov, Viola. 2012. "'How to Cook in Palestine?' Guidebooks for German-Jewish Homemakers in Palestine in the 1930s and 40s." *UCLA: Center for the Study of Women*. https://escholarship.org/uc/item/1sx2m3bc (accessed: 28 February 2021).

Raviv, Yael. 2015. *Falafel Nation: Cuisine and the Making of National Identity in Israel*. Lincoln, NE: University of Nebraska Press.

Refael, Rina. 2018. "Will 400,000 Vegans Be Added in Israel in the Next Seven Years?" *Calcalist*, 4 April 2018. www.calcalist.co.il/articles/0,7340,L-3735187,00.html [in Hebrew] (accessed 28 February 2021).

Renton, Alex. 2003. *Planet Carnivore: Why Cheap Meat Costs the Earth (and How to Pay the Bill)*. Guardian Books. e-book.

Roper, Lyndal. 1991. *The Holy Household: Women and Morals in Reformation Augsburg*. Oxford: Oxford University Press.

Rosenblum, Jordan D. 2010. *Food and Identity in Early Rabbinic Judaism*. Cambridge: Cambridge University Press.

Roth, Laurence. 2010. "Toward a Kashrut Nation in American Jewish Cookbooks, 1990–2000," *Shofar* 28, no. 2: 65–91.

Safran Foer, Jonathan. 2009. *Eating Animals*. New York: Little, Brown and Company.

Schwartz, Richard H. and Sears, David. 2019. "The Vegetarian Teachings of Rav Kook," in *Jewish Veganism and Vegetarianism: Studies and New Directions*. Eds. Jacob Ari Labendz and Shmuly Yanklowitz. Albany, NY: State University of New York Press, 217–232.

Shemer, Simona. 2017. "Israeli Pigs Behind Much Leading Research on Diabetes, Cancer and Trauma Injuries." *No Camels: Israeli Innovation News*, 5 December 2017. https://tinyurl.com/Israeli-Pigs (accessed 28 February 2021).

Shternshis, Anna. 2006. *Soviet and Kosher: Jewish Popular Culture in the Soviet Union, 1923–1939*. Bloomington, IN: Indiana University Press.

Tenorio, Rich. 2020. "As Kosher Food Factories in China Fall Victim to COVID-19, Diaspora Feels Impact." *The Times of Israel*, 8 April 2020. www.timesofisrael.com/as-kosher-food-factories-in-china-fall-victim-to-covid-19-diaspora-feels-impact/ (accessed 28 February 2021).

Tuchman, Gaye and Levine, Harry G. 1992. "New York Jews and Chinese Food: The Social Construction of an Ethnic Pattern," *Contemporary Ethnography* 22, no. 3: 382–407.

Valenzuela-Lamas, Silvia, Valenzuela-Suau, Lua, Saula, Oriol *et al*. 2014. "*Shechita* and *Kashrut*: Identifying Jewish populations through zooarchaeology and taphonomy. Two examples from Medieval Catalonia (North-Eastern Spain)," *Quaternary International* 330: 109–117.

Zeller, Benjamin E. 2014. "Food Preparation, Cooking, and Ritual in Judaism," in *Encyclopedia of Food and Agricultural Ethics*. Eds. P.B. Thompson and D.M. Kaplan. Dordrecht: Springer, 916–923.

Zivotofsky, Ari Z. 2008. "The Turning of the Tide; The Kashrut Tale of the Swordfish," *BDD – Bekhol Derakekha Daehu (Journal of Torah and Scholarship)* 19: 5–53.

26
SANCTUARY IN TIME
Shabbat as the Soul of Modern Jewry and the Essence of "Doing" Judaism

Trevan G. Hatch and Loren D. Marks

Foundations of Shabbat

According to the Hebrew Scriptures, Shabbat was established from the foundations of the world. It was the climax of God's creation (Gen 1:1–2:3; Ex 20:11). God "hallowed" the seventh day "because on it, [He] rested from all the work that he had done in creation" (Gen 2:3, NRSV). Shabbat is also associated with the Exodus from Egypt (see Deut 5:12–15; cf. Ex 23:9–12). God commanded Israel to observe Shabbat as a remembrance that they "were slaves in the land of Egypt, and the Lord your God brought you out from there" (Deut 5:15, NRSV). After the Exodus, Moses received the Law. In the Decalogue (i.e., "Ten Commandments")—regarded as a summary of the entire Law—Shabbat is only one of two commandments of active observance (along with honoring one's parents), and is the only day of remembrance. The remaining eight commandments are prohibitions (see Ex 20:1–17).

On the holy day of Shabbat, all of Israel—including slaves, resident foreigners, and even livestock—rested from all labor (Ex 20:8–11, 23:12; Deut 5:12–15). Shabbat was a sign of God's covenant with Israel (Ex 31:13–17). The level of commitment to honor the covenant was reflected in the penalty for profaning it: death[1] (Ex 31:15, 35:2; Num 15:32–36).

Various temple rituals marked Shabbat as a day set apart from all other days, including special offerings (Num 28:9–10), twelve freshly baked loaves of bread for the sanctuary (Lev 24:8; 2 Chron 9:32), and songs (1 Chron 23:20–31; see, for example, Psalm 92, called "A Song for the Sabbath"). Several prophets warned that the fate of the nation, the building of the New Jerusalem in the messianic age, and the coming of the Messiah himself were all contingent on the nation properly observing Shabbat (Isa 56:2–6, 58:13–14; Jer 17:19–27; Ezek 20, 22:26; Neh 13:14–22).

Jews living many centuries after the destruction of the first temple (70 CE) and the exile to Babylon viewed Shabbat as an obligation to be observed with exactness, lest the nation suffer the same fate as their ancestors. Consequently, Shabbat became a prominent boundary marker for Jews during this time period (along with circumcision and dietary law observance), especially given that many of them lived in close proximity to non-Jews (e.g., Greeks and Romans). Just as earlier Israelite prophets expanded and reinterpreted Shabbat laws to adapt to changing contexts and needs of the people, so did Jews in the Greco-Roman period. For example, Jewish armies refused to fight on Shabbat and, consequently, suffered many lost lives and afflictions at the hands of Antiochus's Greek armies in the second century BCE. Pious Jewish leaders subsequently altered Shabbat laws to permit fighting for defense of life (1 Macc 2:31–41, 9:32, 43–46). Sages Shemaya and Abtalion also concluded that preserving life takes precedence over Shabbat observance after they found Hillel the Elder frozen in the snow on Shabbat (Babylonian Talmud, Yoma 35b). The weekly sacred day of remembrance also became a source of conflict between various Jewish groups. They were not unified in their interpretation of Shabbat laws. According to the New Testament Gospels, the Pharisees—Israel's legal and moral leaders—were unwavering in their loyalty to the expansions of the written and oral Law, a position that thrust them into debates with first-century followers of Jesus (Hatch, 2019). Indeed, the sages in the first few centuries CE debated Shabbat among themselves, perhaps more than any other legal issue (Collins, 2016).

After the temple's destruction in 70 CE, Shabbat observance became even more central for Jews, preserving the Jewish nation in the absence of its temple and sacrificial system. What was primarily a space-oriented system of approaching the divine before 70 CE was later transformed into a time-oriented system, with a particular focus on Shabbat. In fact, Shabbat was conceptualized as the new temple. The Rabbinic sages produced an entire tractate dedicated to Shabbat laws (*Mishnah Shabbat*). In this code of law (c. 200 CE), the rabbis listed thirty-nine Sabbath prohibitions, all relating to common labor work. At a glance, these prohibitions seem random but on closer inspection they are understood in light of the Tabernacle's construction laws in Exodus 31. In this section, the instructions on building the Tabernacle are abruptly interrupted with a command to "keep the Sabbath …; whoever does any work on it shall be cut off from the people" (Ex 31:14–15, NRSV). The rabbis deduced from this section that all types of labor required to build the Tabernacle were forbidden on Shabbat. Thus, their list of thirty-nine Shabbat prohibitions reflected the type of work mentioned in Exodus 31 (Ginsburg, 1989; Green, 1980). The takeaway is that the rabbinic Shabbat laws (time-oriented piety) were closely linked with Israel's previous tabernacle/temple laws (space-oriented piety). As Arthur Green (1980) explained in his essay, "Sabbath as Temple":

> The history of exile teaches Israel that a sacred day, unlike a sacred mountain or a sacred shrine, may be carried anywhere and remain safe from outward attack. The hidden lesson here learned also inevitably points to the idea that any place where that Sabbath is proclaimed holy comes to have just a touch of Jerusalem [i.e., the temple] residing within it.

p. 303

As generations passed, the rabbinic sages attached increased significance and reverence to Shabbat. The Babylonian Talmud preserves a tradition of Rabbi Hanina who on the eve of Shabbat, donned his best clothing and said, "Come, and let us go forth to welcome the Queen Sabbath" (119a). Rabbi Yannai also dressed in his best clothing and, addressing Shabbat as if she were a human, said, "Come, O bride, Come, O bride!" (119a). Wedding imagery of Shabbat as a bride is further illustrated in Pesikta Rabbati, a midrashic text of around the sixth century. In the parable, Shabbat lamented that she had no partner like the other days of the week. Shabbat, being the odd day out, asked God why she has no partner, to which God replied, "Israel is your partner" (117b, cited in Montefiore and Leowe, 1963, p. 195). Some rabbis believed that the messianic age would not come until all of Israel observed at least two consecutive Sabbaths (Babylonian Talmud, 118a). This is why some Israeli rabbis claimed in 2020 that this year was a likely time for the coming messiah, as COVID-19 would force everyone indoors and, as a result, Jews everywhere would observe Shabbat (Jones, 2020).

Theological and Mystical Expansions of Shabbat

Ginsburg (1989) explains the fundamental difference between the Shabbat conceptualizations of the rabbis in late antiquity and the mystics in medieval Europe: "For the Rabbis, the Sabbath was of heavenly origin, a gift *from* God. For most mystics, the Sabbath was even more sublime; it was an aspect *of* God" (p. 69). Just as Jerusalem is the center place of space, the navel of the universe, Shabbat was the Sacred Center, the navel of cosmic time. Time revolves around Shabbat. The mystics compared Shabbat to a central garden with a spring that overflows and nourishes all surrounding gardens—and referred to Shabbat as the middle stick on the menorah that provides light and energy to all other stems. Mystics also likened Shabbat to a wheel—the spokes representing the days of the week that are turned by the *central* components. Likewise, it was noted, Shabbat provided both light and lifeblood to the other six days of the week (Ginsburg, 1989).

Given this worldview, the mystics held Shabbat observance to be non-negotiable. If the Jewish people breached Shabbat, the well-being of the entire cosmos was threatened. The ripples from the Sacred Center (i.e., Shabbat) would explode outward, like the destructive waves of an atomic bomb, and demolish everything in its path. The mystics also intensified the earlier rabbinic imaging of Shabbat as a temple. Entering Shabbat became akin to entering the temple, and thereby raised the stakes for Jewish observance of the holy day. Shabbat observance held life and death implications for the mystics, undergirding their teaching that Shabbat must be protected at all costs: protection is ensured by proper observance.

How did these Shabbat conceptualizations translate to observance for many medieval mystics? Some mystics prepared for Shabbat by staying awake the entire night in sacred study on Shabbat Eve. They also immersed in the *mikvah* (ritual bath) on Friday afternoon. Rabbi Isaac Luria immersed twice, once to cleanse the body and soul to receive Shabbat, and again for the additional soul that is added to the observant Jew on Shabbat. After immersion, mystics would typically dress in their best clothing.[2]

The motif of Shabbat as a temple is revealed in many customs of the medieval mystics. The Shabbat meal table came to symbolize the altar of the temple. Washing hands before eating and the inclusion of twelve loaves of bread on the table (among others) reflected Israelite tabernacle/temple customs. Some mystics even folded the loaves to resemble the shewbread of the ancient temple. Some mystics were careful not to engage in idle talk or discuss business matters on Shabbat (Faierstein, 2013). They maintained that the forces of evil were restrained on Shabbat but that they were released after its conclusion. The freed demons would then attempt to stamp out the light that emanated from the Sacred Center:

> At the close of the Sabbath, during the transition from the sacred to the profane, from light to darkness ... the Holy One, blessed be He, and His *Shekhinah* [presence] take off the sacred garments of the Sabbath, and clothe themselves once more in secular garments. ... The fire of [the underworld] is rekindled and ... evil spirits burst from the hiding places to which they were consigned at the approach of the Sabbath. When the Sabbath departs, many hosts and companies fly through the world. ... They go out in haste, thinking to rule the world and the holy people. Demonic darkness and great terror fill the world, and at that moment the radiance of the additional soul disappears and man's soul is left naked, and when the Sabbath departs, the bond is broken, and the additional soul ascends, and soul and spirit remain separated, grief stricken.
>
> *Tishby, 1991, pp. 1236–1237*

These practices illustrate how Shabbat theology fostered a hyper-attentiveness of the mystics to sanctify Shabbat and to set it apart from all other days.

In more modern times, Jewish thinkers continued to articulate the significance of Shabbat with great zeal and respect. In the 1950s, Herman Wouk introduced Judaism to Christians and non-observant Jews in the first printing of the now classic volume, *This Is My God: The Jewish Way of Life*. He articulated that Shabbat is "a ceremony," a "dramatic" and "immemorial gesture" of celebration (Wouk, 1987, pp. 44, 49). A celebration of what? "All nations celebrate the day of their coming into being with a work stoppage and ceremonies. The Jews, who believe that God created the universe, celebrate its coming into being, and give thanks to its Maker, once a week" (Wouk, 1987, p. 49). For Wouk, Shabbat is not only a day of commemoration, but a foretaste of the messianic age.

Another influential thinker in the 1950s, Abraham Joshua Heschel, attempted to articulate the meaning of Shabbat for the modern Jew in his book, *The Sabbath*. He explained that Judaism conditions its adherents to cling to "holiness in time," not space. Judaism's "Sabbaths are our great cathedrals" and Jewish Shabbat ritual itself is *"architecture of time"* (Heschel, 1951, p. 8). For Heschel (1951), God gifted to the world through Judaism the idea that holiness is best associated with time; this is why "there is no mention of a sacred place in the Ten Commandments" (p. 79). He posited that just as the life of a Jew is a pilgrimage to the World to Come, so too is the week of a Jew a pilgrimage to Shabbat—a pilgrimage where one "seeks to displace the coveting of things in space for coveting the things in time—to covet the seventh day all days of the week" (pp. 90–91). Heschel further asks whether any institution is better positioned to improve the state of humanity than Shabbat:

> To set apart one day a week for freedom, a day on which we would not use the instruments which have been so easily turned into weapons of destruction, a day for being with ourselves, a day of detachment from the vulgar, of independence of external obligations, a day on which we stop worshipping the idols of technical civilization, a day on which we use no money, a day of armistice in the economic struggle with our fellow men and the forces of nature—is there any institution that holds out a greater hope for [humanity's] progress than the Sabbath?
>
> *p. 28*

The biblical and ancient near eastern origins, the classical rabbis' emphases, the medieval mystical expansions, and the modern theologians' articulations of Shabbat provide context for how Jews in the 21st century relate to this holy day in contemporary lived religious experience.

Shabbat in Lived Religious Experience

Social scientists who study modern Jewry have noticed in recent decades that Judaism has shifted to a home-based system. In their study of American Jewish identity, Cohen and Eisen (2000) posited that the institution of the home, as opposed to the community, is playing a greater role for young Jews in observing their cultural and religious traditions. They also observed that Jewish young adults seem to be distancing themselves from the "organizations, institutions, and causes that used to anchor identity and shape behavior" (p. 2). Goldscheider (2004) similarly acknowledged that Jews have become "less attached to ... institutions" (p. 100), and that home-based observance with family has become "a central feature of Jewish continuity" (p. 127).

The practice that has perhaps benefited most from this shift to home-based Judaism is Shabbat. One Pew survey (2013) revealed that nearly half of American Jews (45%) who have a

Jewish spouse reported that they *always or usually* light Sabbath candles. Had the survey included other Shabbat traditions, like sharing family meals, the percentage would likely have been higher. In lengthy interviews with thirty diverse American Jewish families, twenty-eight (93%) spontaneously mentioned Shabbat more than any other cultural or religious practice (Hatch, 2015; Marks, Hatch, & Dollahite, 2017). Further, when asked, *what practices or observances hold special meaning for you as a couple or family*, nineteen families (63%) mentioned Shabbat. Cohen and Eisen (2000) identified a similar emphasis on Shabbat in their study on American Jews. Throughout all of their interviews, they heard "exactly one disparaging remark about Sabbath observance," while most of their other participants placed high value on this day of commemoration (p. 86). Even many agnostic-atheist Jews observe Shabbat. One Conservative Jewish woman who was interviewed for the American Families of Faith Project (AFF)[3] explained: "I have a lot of friends who don't believe in God who celebrate Shabbat every Friday" (Hatch, 2015, p. 88).

Shabbat at Home: The Basics of Observance

Since its earliest days, Shabbat and its accompanying laws were ever expanding, so much so that even the sages in the second century acknowledged that the laws of Shabbat "are like mountains hanging by a string," meaning there is "little scriptural" support for the "many laws" (*Mishna Hagigah* 1:8, translation in Neusner, 1988, p. 130). This situation has presented challenges for the Jewish community. It is, perhaps, why for every "two Jews there are three opinions," as the popular saying goes. Nearly every aspect of Shabbat exists on a wide-ranging spectrum across branches and styles of observance.

On Friday morning, as Shabbat approaches, observant Jews are faced with many preparation tasks. Blu Greenberg (1983) in her book, *How to Run a Traditional Jewish Household*, allocated seventy pages to Shabbat alone. In traditional households, preparation begins with cleaning the home. The sweeping, vacuuming, dusting, laundering, snow shoveling, garden weeding, tomato picking, polishing of dinnerware, and organizing of any kind must be completed long before Shabbat begins at sunset on Friday evening. After the cleaning, the Shabbat meal must be either cooked or purchased (and retrieved or delivered). Grocery shopping, cooking, and even smaller tasks like chilling the wine, require careful planning and appropriately allotted time. Setting the Shabbat table with its specific items also requires attention (Greenberg, 1983). The preparation does not end there. The host turns off most appliances, unscrews lightbulbs to avoid inadvertently turning on lights after Shabbat begins, and sets timers on all necessary lights. If hosting a non-observant guest who might flick off the light switch in the bathroom, the host might tape the switch to the "on" position before guests arrive. Some Jews pre-tear facial tissues, bathroom toilet paper, and paper towels. Shabbat preparation also includes personal hygiene, such as pressing clothing, polishing shoes, and bathing (Greenberg, 1983).

Justification for these many tasks comes from Jewish law in antiquity that prohibits work, which includes starting or extinguishing fires, ripping or tearing materials, baking, and many other forms of work. Flicking a light or turning on a smartphone causes electron action that is equivalent to starting a fire. Some non-observant Jews, and many Christians have criticized some Orthodox Jews for missing the point. Greenberg (1983) responded to these common accusations:

> To one who is completely unfamiliar with the law, it almost seems petty and silly to go to such lengths over such a little thing as throwing a light switch. But this is one of the many basic steps in creating that special aura of Shabbat. ... Preparing paper in advance seems so remote from holy time. The objective outsider might say:

"This is pure legalism and highly ridiculous ... there's no work involved in tearing a piece of perforated toilet paper on the Sabbath." To which an insider might respond, "Look how clever the Rabbis were: even in as mundane a place as a bathroom, one is reminded of the uniqueness of the day."

Greenberg, 1983, pp. 39, 40

Shabbat is ushered in by a candle-lighting ceremony. Candles are lit several minutes before sunset. The prevalent custom is that two candles are lit, representing the two imperative verbs in the two versions of the Ten Commandments in "Remember" (Exodus 20:8) and "Observe" (Deut 5:12). Some light additional candles, one for each member of the family. Tradition stipulates that women light the candles and usher in Shabbat (Klein, 1992; Greenberg, 1983). The candle-lighting ceremony and subsequent rituals of the meal and family time are accompanied by special blessings—blessings of gratitude for Shabbat and family, and even special blessings on the children. After the Shabbat meal, both on Friday evening and after Synagogue service on Saturday morning and afternoon, the family typically engages in various quiet activities such as board games, napping, and Torah study (Greenberg, 1983). Many husbands and wives engage in sexual activity on Shabbat. Indeed, this is viewed as a commandment by some Jews. This practice is traced as far back as the twelfth century in the writings of Maimonides: "Sexual relations are considered a dimension of Sabbath pleasure. Therefore, Torah scholars [i.e., all observant men] who are healthy set aside Friday night as the night when they fulfill their conjugal duties" (Maimonides, *Mishneh Torah*, 30:14).

There are far too many practices and traditions to review here but, again, one must remember that these traditions vary widely from movement to movement (e.g., Ultra-Orthodox, Modern Orthodox, Conservative, Reform, Reconstructionist, etc.) and even from group to group within the same broader movement. Rabbi Isaac Klein details many of these same Shabbat traditions from the point of view of the Conservative Movement in his work, *A Guide to Jewish Religious Practice* (1992). Particulars of observance are in perennial flux. Since the 1980s and 1990s, the Jewish community has seen Ultra-Orthodox become more stringent on some matters while the more liberal movements have tended to become increasingly lenient or nuanced.

Shabbat at Home: Meaning Making, Identity, and Tradition

The previous section reviewed briefly some of the functions and rituals of Shabbat. But how are these functions and rituals conceptualized by those who actually perform them? And what social, cultural, or spiritual benefits do these practices reportedly yield? The common benefits revealed in various surveys and qualitative studies are related to identify formation, perpetuation of tradition, peace and relaxation, and family unity.

One woman in the Cohen and Eisen (2000) survey explained how she began lighting Shabbat candles. Her aging mother lamented that her candles—first owned by her mother—would not be used after she died because her daughter was non-observant. "Whereas in the past I might have felt guilty," she explained, "this time I sort of reacted with more sympathy about her feelings and her sense of self. This was important to her, and she wanted this part of her carried on. So I said, 'I'll light them'." Her husband welcomed the new practice because it was now infused with meaning and purpose: "It was about our relationship and it was even more wonderful because it was about my grandmother and because it was about the culture and being Jewish" (Cohen & Eisen, 2000, p. 81).

A middle-aged Conservative mother in the American Families of Faith survey also found deep meaning in lighting candles for tradition's sake: "[We light candles] because it's what [my] mother does and [my] grandmothers [did]. It is because all Jewish women that light candles on Friday night are saying blessings at the same time. … It's very special" (Hatch, 2015, p. 89). A Reform mother expressed a similar connection to the candle-lighting tradition. She used candlesticks that her grandmother and mother owned, and she planned to pass them on to her daughter: "Whether she uses them to light Shabbat candles or not, I don't know but that's really, really important to me" (Hatch, 2015, p. 89). A Conservative couple with two children commented on lighting candles in more detail:

> HUSBAND: I'm really affixed by the links we have with our early ancestors in Judaism. … When we celebrate Shabbat on Friday night, we are doing the same thing my relatives did thousands of years ago. That intrigues me. We light candles at my Mom's house that our family has been lighting for two hundred years. That's amazing. … I don't know that the Sabbath meal is a religious experience for most people but for me, it's the heart of religion.
>
> WIFE: We light candles every Friday night to welcome the Sabbath and I use two sets of candlesticks. One was given to us for our wedding and the other was my grandmother's that she used for I don't know how long. And then my husband's parents use a set of candlesticks that has been in my father-in-law's family for maybe two hundred years or so. And they've been passed down and polished, and my mother-in-law was saying that when they're gone the candlesticks will be passed down to us. The important thing is that in each generation, they are always passed down to the child who lights the candles every Friday night. Something like that, I think, is just incredible … the connection you feel with your family, with your people, and your history.
>
> *Hatch, 2015, p. 90*

Tradition and heritage are powerful for many Jews. They add meaning and salience to the traditions. Observant Jews also find practical and personal benefits of Shabbat. These include peace, serenity, and relaxation. A Modern Orthodox mother discussed how Sabbath is not just about doing or performing rituals, such as lighting candles or saying blessings, but is about avoiding stressful thoughts:

> It's funny, there's all this stressful air before Shabbat, getting ready and all this, and then you light the candles. Everything does change. And you know the laws about Shabbat, you're not even supposed to be thinking anything stressful, let alone talking about anything stressful. It's like you leave all the stresses of the rest of the week behind … and the kids are always very excited about it. They know that no one's going anywhere, no one's answering the phone, no one's driving anywhere, that we're just going to be here as a family.

A middle-aged Conservative father emphasized that Shabbat can help people reclaim their lives. Too many people "run everywhere and Shabbat is just one more day to run everywhere, and you know what? Your life is stolen from you." He explained that by having Shabbat, "We reclaim our lives, even if for a day, it's enough to get our bearings back and that is enough to sustain you throughout the week" (Hatch, 2015, p. 92).

Another benefit is that Shabbat protects family time. A twenty-year-old Orthodox man explained that observing Shabbat is non-negotiable, not because of Jewish law or "religious purposes," but for "the family's sake." He said, "It's such a big deal on a family level that that's not something you can cut out" (Marks, Hatch, & Dollahite, 2017, p. 6). A Conservative mother of three discussed her children's relationship to Shabbat:

> The kids know Friday night is Shabbat. They don't make plans. They know it's Shabbat. I'll pick them up from school [and] they'll be like "Tonight's Shabbat. Who's coming?" They're always asking. The older one said to me the other night, "I love Shabbat."
>
> Marks, Hatch, & Dollahite, 2017, pp. 7–8.

A Conservative mother explained what Shabbat means most to her as she sits across the table from her family:

> We've had a busy week and here's our time to be together and we always take a deep breath before we do this and let all the thoughts, craziness and worries, and everything slip away. … I think that when we take the time out, when we light the candles Friday night, that's a time that I feel really close to them. … When we sit across the table from each other, my husband and I, and the candles are lit, and you see the kids, there is something you get from that that is so deep. It's just a feeling that all is right in the world … it doesn't matter what else is going on. Right in that circle … it's awe-inspiring. That's what it means to me.
>
> Hatch, 2015, p. 93

Conclusion

The focus of this chapter has not solely been on the rituals and practices of Shabbat, but also on how Jews attach meaning to them and how these observances might foster strong Jewish identity. Jews ranging from agnostic-atheist to the most Ultra-Orthodox seem to have found some benefits from observing Shabbat at some level. Shabbat meaning-making across all forms of Jewry has, arguably, played a major role in preserving the Jewish people. Just as the temple and Torah preserved the Jewish nation in ancient times, Shabbat and Torah have preserved the Jewish nation since the Greco-Roman era. This fact reminds us of the famous dictum of the Hebrew poet and philosopher, Achad Ha'am: "More than Jews have kept Shabbat, Shabbat has kept the Jews" (Ha'am, n.d.)

A major question for social scientists who study the Jewish demographic centers on *how* Shabbat "keeps the Jews." Does ritual and habitual practice by itself foster Jewish identity, or must these rituals be meaningful? Sociologist and scholar of Jewish studies, Ellen LeVee, addresses this question about the meanings and functions of Shabbat by asking, "Can simply performing a ritual for the sake of family health, make the family healthy?" Responding to this question in connection with Shabbat ritual, she then wrote,

> I want to distinguish between meaning and function. The functions of the Sabbath … may or may not be its meaning. The more its meaning relies solely on these functions, the less able it is to perform them. … Shabbat, through its functions, may be satisfying, but it simply doesn't have enough authority of its own. It can be trumped by other personal desires. True meaning emerges when Shabbat is put in the context of what is ultimate in life. … Ultimacy gives Shabbat meaning, and thereby allows for it to fulfill the other functions.
>
> Marks, Hatch, & Dollahite, 2017, p. 12

Indeed, origins, history, tradition, function, and ultimacy all influence how and why Shabbat impacts Jewish families—and what Shabbat means to the Jewish people.

Notes

1 We note that this penalty was strictly conceptual, not reality; it was an explanation of later scribes who redacted the Hebrew Scriptures. The books of the Prophets, early Jewish literature, and records of medieval Jewish communities contain numerous examples of Jews profaning Shabbat with no punishment of death.
2 The mystics of Safed, a town in the Galilee, wore white garments, representing either the priestly temple garments, or the garments of light worn by Adam and Eve in Eden. The practice of wearing white garments on Shabbat began to fade in the late early modern period because opponents of mystical interpretations of Judaism viewed the practice as elitist and arrogant. The mystics also discouraged red or black clothing on Shabbat because these colors represented the forces of evil (Faierstein, 2013). These practices have since waned in western (i.e., Ashkenazi) Jewish communities as many Orthodox and Ultra-Orthodox Jews now wear black, even on Shabbat.
3 The American Families of Faith project (AFF) is a strengths-based approach to garner information regarding healthy processes. Specifically, the directors and scholars of the AFF project attended Jewish religious services, visited with rabbis, explained the project, and requested referrals for exemplar families. The total sample for this article was 30 families (N = 77 individuals; 30 wives/mothers, 30 husbands/fathers, and 17 adolescent children). Couples had been married for an average of slightly more than 20 years (range = 8–25 years) and identified as Orthodox (9), Conservative (5), Reform (14), with two unspecified. Families resided in five regions: New England (MA); Mid-Atlantic (DE, NJ); Pacific (CA); Mountain West (UT); and Gulf Coast (FL, LA). Wives' ages ranged from 35 to 59 (mean age = 46), husbands' ages ranged from 32 to 58 (mean age = 48), and ages of interviewed children ranged from 10 to 20 (mean age = 16). See https://americanfamiliesoffaith.byu.edu/.

References

Cohen, S. M., & Eisen, A. M. 2000. *The Jew within: Self, family, and community in America*. Bloomington, IN: Indiana University Press.
Collins, N. L. 2016. *Jesus, the Sabbath and the Jewish debate: Healing on the Sabbath in the 1st and 2nd centuries CE*. London: Bloomsbury T&T Clark.
Faierstein, M. M. 2013. *Jewish customs of Kabbalistic origin*. Boston, MA: Academic Studies Press.
Ginsburg, E. K. 1989. *The Sabbath in the classical Kabbalah*. Albany, NY: State University of New York Press.
Goldscheider, C. 2004. *Studying the Jewish future*. Seattle: University of Washington Press.
Green, A. 1980. Sabbath as temple: Some thoughts on space and time in Judaism. In S. Fishman and R. Jospe, eds. *Go and Study: Essays and Studies in Honor of A. Jospe*. Washington, DC: B'nai B'rith Hillel Foundations, 287–305.
Greenberg, B. 1983. *How to run a traditional Jewish household*. New York: Simon & Schuster.
Ha'am, A. (n.d.) *Al Parashat Derakhim*, Vol. 3, Ch. 30, cited in yivoencyclopedia.org, www.yivoencyclopedia.org/article.aspx/Sabbath.
Hatch, T. G. 2015. "Mishpacha in the American Diaspora: An Exploratory Study of Highly-Involved Jewish Families." PhD dissertation, Louisiana State University, Baton Rouge, LA.
Hatch, T. G. 2019. *A stranger in Jerusalem: Seeing Jesus as a Jew*. Eugene, OR: Wipf and Stock.
Heschel, A. J. 1951. *The Sabbath: Its meaning for modern man*. New York: Farrar, Straus, and Giroux.
Jones, R. 2020. "Top Rabbis Look at the Signs, Messiah is Coming!" *Israel Today*, August 3. www.israeltoday.co.il/read/top-rabbis-look-at-the-signs-messiah-is-coming/
Klein, I. 1992. *A guide to Jewish religious practice*. New York: Jewish Theological Seminary of America.
Maimonides, *Mishneh Torah*, 30:14. Translation by a Chabad organization, Chabad Ocean Drive. www.chabadoceandrive.com/library/article_cdo/aid/935256/jewish/Shabbat-Chapter-Thirty.htm#footnoteRef50a935256
Marks, L., Hatch, T., & Dollahite, D. 2017. Sacred practices and family processes in a Jewish context: Shabbat as the weekly family ritual par excellence. *Family Process*, 10: 1–14.
Montefiore, C. G., & Loewe, H. 1963. *A rabbinic anthology*. New York: Meridian.

Neusner, J. 1988. *The Mishnah: A new translation*. New Haven, CT: Yale University Press.
Pew. 2013. "A portrait of Jewish Americans." Pew Research Center, October 1. www.pewforum.org/2013/10/01/jewish-american-beliefs-attitudes-culture-survey/
Tishby, I. 1991. *The wisdom of the Zohar, vol. 3*. Oxford: Oxford University Press.
Wouk, H. 1987. *This is my God: The Jewish way of life*. Boston, MA: Little, Brown and Company.

27
SOMETIMES GOD SNEAKS BACK IN
Jewish Secular Rituals

Avner Dinur

[A]t the heart of such a language, in which we ceaselessly evoke God in a thousand ways, thus calling Him back into the reality of our life, he cannot keep silent […] those who endeavor to revive the Hebrew language did not truly believe in the Judgement to which their acts are summoning us.

Gershom Scholem, a letter to Franz Rosenzweig, Dec. 26, 1926

Tehilim on the big lawn
Shabbat eve, in summer: the dining room
floating like a ship, shining lights in its windows, children
are playing on the lawn. Parents in white shirts
chatting peacefully nearby.
The evening spreads its wings like a nesting bird
gathering its chick under her wing.
For me this is the most beautiful hour in the world, in the whole universe.
It was only yesterday that I played here (the dining room
was still a wooden shack with the smell of pepper and dripping resin)
today my son plays here and tomorrow
my grandson.

Eli Elon – Barefoot – Te'hiley Ein Shemer
(Shitim website, my translation)[1]

Every *Yom Kippur*, for more than ten years now, a crowd of hundreds gathers on a roof in Tel Aviv for a long and rich ceremony, arranged by the Secular *Yeshiva* of Bina. This event replaces for many, either the prayers in synagogue, or the meaningless wandering in the car-abandoned streets, or both.[2] The ceremony includes the following words, written by Muki Tzur:

To whom do we write these letters? To which address do we send our prayer? Who is writing them? Who receives them? […] does prayer bring to our consciousness responsibility or sensitivity to the other? Or is it directed inwards, to a place where we stand alone and ask redemption for ourselves only?

Bina, 2000, 2 (my translation)

A cynical atheist reading these questions will probably say that Tzur and his followers in this *Yeshiva* got it all wrong and that secular people do not need prayer, nor any other kind of ritual. What is the point in sending letters to a vacant address? One cannot identify as secular, the atheist might claim, if her life is filled with rituals that include clear religious markers.[3] Furthermore, these rituals can be seen as a sign of the weakness of secular Jews, they let God sneak into their lives because they are not strong enough in their (dis)belief. They are seeking some easy-to-get spirituality and therefore catch the baits that religious preachers scatter in their pool. This line of criticism is met by an expected attack on secular rituals that comes from the opposite direction. For orthodox, many traditional Jews, and for some reforms and conservatives, a secular *Yom Kippur* seems like a full break from tradition, of tradition.[4] The following chapter will consider this double-sided attack through a theological and textual reading of secular rituals. The analysis will show the ideas and values these rituals wish to manifest, the concept of God that is used in some of them, and, through this kind of reading, will consider their role in contemporary Jewish identity.

Most of the examples for Jewish secular rituals were found in the past in the Kibbutzim in Israel: holy day rituals, *Kabalot Shabbat*, weddings and funerals. In the last few decades, alongside the decline of the Kibbutzim, economically, socially, and ideologically, secular innovation moved to other loci, mainly to Jewish renewal organizations (Bina, Elul, Alma, Avichai, Kolot and others), and to the "blue" youth movements (movements oriented to the Israeli left). Many of these rituals are very impressive. They create rich, innovative, and well thought out ceremonies that bring change into some traditions which were fossilized for many generations, and which no longer represent the values that many Jews hold. On the other hand, they do not represent only change. They are well connected to Jewish tradition and they enable many Jews who no longer can find their place within religious rituals, to connect to their heritage. Despite all this cultural potential, secular rituals are practiced by very few people. The great majority of Jews in the world are not orthodox, but nonetheless most of them have never even heard about a non-religious (orthodox, reform, or conservative) ritual. The Jewish majority, in Israel at least, is composed of non-orthodox who do not know unorthodox ways to openly pronounce the values at the core of their Jewish identity.

The marginality of secular rituals within Jewish-Israeli contemporary culture is quite peculiar when looked at from the perspective of statistical surveys about self-definition. Many different studies in the last 40 years show that indeed there are secular Jews who are completely alien to any kind of tradition, but they are very few. Only 4–6% of the Jews in Israel define their identity as "anti-religious". The rest of secular and traditional Jews in Israel, 70% of the Jewish population or more, do not distance themselves from the practices of religion or tradition, but do not define themselves as "דתי" (religious, which is parallel in the Israeli context to orthodox). About 40–50% uses "חילוני" (secular) as the identity by which they define themselves, others use "מסורתי" (traditional). Most of the Jews in this majority do not find any contradiction between Jewish tradition and secular ways of thinking. This observation is relevant for different "religious" practices such as *Shabbat* and holiday traditions, and it also applies to questions of belief. Only 20% of the Jews in Israel claim in surveys that they do not believe in God.[5] These data testify to the gap between atheism and secular identity: Most of the Jews in Israel are non-religious Jews who do believe in God, and are committed to the continuity of Jewish tradition. We can expect that this soft and unorthodox attitude toward tradition will lead many Jews to construct for themselves secular (and not atheist) rituals, but as mentioned above, this is not what is happening.

Secular rituals, *Kabalot Shabbat*, holiday rituals, secular marriages, and funerals, have been studied by a few scholars. These studies examine the importance of secular rituals for understanding Israeli society. Although some of them present secular rituals in a very positive way, they are partly based on the assumptions of the above-mentioned imagined atheist, who criticized any attempt to construct a secular ritual. A few of these studies see secular rituals as a sign of a post-modern and post-secular approach, or as seeking for a spirituality based on the needs of the individual. On this view, secular rituals are, on the one hand, a consumable product, and on the other, they are a sign of a failure of secular ways of thinking, and a withdrawal from the ideas of secularism. Most of these studies were written from a sociological perspective, usually based on some classical studies (Durkheim, Turner and others) on the role of religion in modern societies.[6] They add a needed perspective on Israeli society because they challenge both the secularization thesis, and the secular–religious dichotomy.[7] They do not, however, examine secular rituals as a textual and theological phenomenon. Precisely because they see secular rituals as something in between, they fail to understand the secular ideology manifested in them. In this sense their perspective, just like the perspective of my imagined atheist, is unthinkably orthodox – they find in secular rituals an unfitting longing for something that was lost when modern society moved from the old world of religion to the new world of secularity. They use secular rituals to show how religious modern Jewish society is, but in doing so they miss some of the secular content located at the center of secular rituals. I would like to examine the same rituals from a different perspective. I see secular rituals, not as a withdrawal from secularity but exactly the opposite. They were established in order to emphasize the values of secular Judaism. They are a sign of richness, not of a lack. They are practiced by few, but they nonetheless represent the value system of most of the Jews in Israel, and partly also, in the world, and therefore they should be seen as essential markers of Jewish identity in the present. I suggest reading the texts of these rituals like any other text in Jewish heritage, a text we can compare to other texts, and explore the possibility that in the future, these texts will become canonical. At the moment this seems not very likely, but this is partly because of orthodox assumptions that this chapter wishes to challenge. Is it not like that for any text that was once new and seemed artificial and inauthentic, and now is part of tradition? A few examples will help justify this claim.

Secular Funerals, Passover and Shabbat

Weddings and funerals are more politically charged than other secular rituals. The reason for this might be financial – marriages are a good way for orthodox rabbis to earn secular money. Another, more deeply rooted reason, is the connection of marriages and funerals to a person's life cycle. These rituals serve rabbis in their wish to keep Jewish genealogy under orthodox surveillance, and to safeguard the ideology of the Jews as the chosen people. The demand of the orthodox to be involved in the personal life-cycle rituals of people who do not share a similar world view, is (outrageously) widely accepted in Israeli society and politically authorized by the Israeli state. Secular weddings are not recognized by the state and secular operated graveyards can be found almost solely in the Kibbutzim. This wide acceptance makes secular funerals and weddings quite a rare occasion. I will discuss here a very specific component of secular funerals – the *Kaddish*.[8]

From a secular perspective, the traditional *Kaddish* is the most problematic part of a Jewish funeral, for three reasons: the first is that most of the text is in Aramaic, a language that is foreign to almost all Jews in the present, so very little of the text is understood by the ones who say it. Secular Jews ask themselves, why should I say something that I totally do not understand at this difficult time? How can a funeral be authentic when this enigmatic text is read out loud? Moreover – we can presume that Aramaic was set as the language of the *Kaddish* in order for all listeners to understand the text in times when Hebrew, the holy language, was less understood, so in the present sticking to the same text actually subverts the original rationale of this cultural choice. The second reason is that secular Jews who do understand the text find the traditional *Kaddish* very unfitting. The text is not directed to the deceased in any way. It recites the glory of God, and it is not even clear what is the connection between these glories and a funeral. The third reason is that one possible connection between the traditional text and the event in which it is used is theodicy, justification of God's actions. It demands from the mourners, who in many cases find it difficult to accept the death of their beloved one, that they accept this reality as a heavenly creed and as an example of justice that we humans do not fully understand, a classical religious understanding that is foreign to many secular Jews. For these reasons it is hard or even unbearable for many secular Jews to say *Kaddish* in funerals, and still many do.

An interesting attempt to write a secular alternative can be found in a text by Shalom Samid from Kibbutz Negba. The opening words are of interest and can illustrate the tensions within many secular rituals: "יתגדל ויתקדש שם האדם, יתעלה פועל חייו, ויתברך בזיכרוננו על צרור מעלליו בימי חלדו..." (my rough translation: may the name of (this/the) human being be glorified and sanctified, may the fruits of his burden and the achievements of his life be blessed in our memory; Prashizky, 2014, 276). The text begins with two words that are an exact parallel to the traditional *Kaddish* (if there is such a thing as a "traditional" text, see note 4). This opening is the cornerstone of the text and a milestone that is supposed to put the listeners into the right orientation. The two words are very well known to many who are not familiar with the whole text, and they sign for the listeners that what we, secular Jews, do here is not just reading some text that we wrote, it is a *Kaddish*, and as such it takes part in a struggle over what should be considered as a Jewish funeral. In the next two words the content of the struggle becomes clear. Unlike the traditional *Kaddish*, it is not God who is glorified here. The word *Ha'adam* has a double meaning in this context, it can refer to the deeds of human beings in general, or to the memory of this specific individual that we should cherish in our hearts. This opening line can serve as an example of how polemical secular rituals are. It declares: There is a cultural struggle here and we, secular Jews, do not intend to let the orthodox determine the right interpretation (ortho = right, doxa = belief, understanding) of Judaism, our common culture and tradition. This way of phrasing is quite apologetic – it is used as a weapon in the struggle for recognition, both of the specific ritual, and of secular identity as a whole. The decision to begin a secular *Kaddish* in this way shows another thing, the need for religious traditional text alongside the new secular one. Samid relied on some basic knowledge of the tradition. If nobody will know the meaning and the context of the opening words, "יתגדל ויתקדש," the secular ritual as a whole will lose much of its meaning. We will see this also in the next rituals that will be examined.

The secular Passover will be discussed here as one prominent example of secular holy day rituals, many of which were structured in the Kibbutzim. It is not by coincidence that secular innovation manifested itself in this unique social structure. The founders of the Kibbutzim felt a need to renew Jewish holy days and to adjust them to the three revolutions in which they saw themselves as the avant-garde: (1) Secular revolution – changing Jewish traditional society and opening it to modernity, to the west, to the age of enlightenment, and narrowing the effects of religious understandings of this culture. (2) Autochthonic/native/agrarian revolution – changing the bourgeois Jew into a worker of the land, rooted in it. (3) Zionist-national revolution – to take the lead in creating a new nation and a new state. All three revolutions are present in the *Haggadot* of different Kibbutzim. Much of the traditional content of the *Haggadah* was put into the margins or even completely abandoned, and new content became central.

One example of a totally new content is a ritual for the beginning of the harvest that the Kibbutzim added to the *Haggadah* in the 1930s (Shoham, 2014, 42). This new ritual, usually involving young girls dancing and bringing to the stage the first sheaf of wheat that was harvested, represents all three revolutions: it includes agricultural content, it brings secular content to this holy day, content which replaces the glorification of God in the traditional *Haggadah*, and it is a revival of the main content of Passover in the time of the temple, as one of the *Regalim* – times for the nation to come together and bring their crops to Jerusalem. Matitiahu Shalem, who had a key role in shaping several Kibbutz holy day rituals, explained that one of the goals of the new *Seders* in the Kibbutzim was to reformulate the mass ceremonies that were held in the times of the temple (Feinstein, 2017, 285–6). By adding the ritual of the first harvest to Passover, to a ritual which included very different content throughout most generations of Jewish heritage, the members of the Kibbutzim were trying to "Passover" 2,000 years of Jewish continuity, and to bring Passover back to its biblical roots – Zionist negation of exile (שלילת הגלות) in its purest form.[9] The harvest ritual can be seen from the perspective of the present as a failure. In very few Kibbutzim is it still held today and very few people recognize Passover as a celebration of the beginning of harvest.

Another central change is the role of God in the Kibbutz *Haggadot*. The traditional *Haggadah* diminishes the role of human activity in the story of the exodus in order to emphasize the miraculous events. The great agent of this historical happening, Moses, is (almost) totally absent in the text, possibly because of the wish to stress the difference between Judaism and Christianity, a messenger-centered religion.[10] The *Haggadah* is very clear and explicit on this: "ויוציאנו ה' ממצרים, לא על ידי מלאך ולא על ידי שרף ולא על ידי שליח, אלא הקב"ה בכבודו ובעצמו". (God took us out of Egypt, not through an angel, not through a Saraph, and not through a messenger. The Holy One, blessed be he, did it in his glory by himself). In the secular *Haggadot*, by contrast, Moses reappears, and it is God's role that is diminished. In the *Haggadah* of Hashomer Hatzair, one of the Kibbutz movements and usually seen as more left and more secular in its orientation,[11] one can find that God was literally "kicked out" of the text, in a rather inelegant manner. For example, in the song "והיא שעמדה" (She who stood for us) it is the tradition to sing that in every generation different "villains" try to annihilate the Jewish people and God saves us from them, but in Hashomer Hatzair the text goes: "ואנו ניצלים מידם" (and we save ourselves from them). It is interesting to note that this subversive phrasing can be found in Hashomer Hatzair's *Haggadot* until sometime in the 1980s. In one later printing I found that the traditional phrasing comes back and (again) it is God who saves us. I could not find whether this return was intended and thought through. I can only speculate that the reason for the change is not (or not only) a weakening of secular ideology, but something quite banal – people were not used to singing the secular text and found it odd or forced. They therefore returned to the text they already knew and preferred it over the secular new one, although for many of them the traditional text was problematic and the new one closer to their worldview. Sometimes God finds his way into secular rituals because the tunes and the habits determine the practical result, more than any text, content or ideology. To conclude, we can say that human and divine action are in a struggle in the history of the Passover *Haggadah*. In traditional *Haggadot* it is clear who is the winner. In secular *Haggadot* it seems that the battle is not yet over.

Coming up with a whole new content to the holy day, like the beginning of harvest, or expelling God from the ceremony, are no doubt radical changes, but it seems that a much more radical change is the change in style and atmosphere of the event. The Seder was for many generations, and it still is for most Jews, a family event, sometimes the extended family, but almost always around one table and not more than 30 people. It is part of the family heritage, something that unites the family, a ritual in which one can find the special customs of every specific family, with all the specific foods, little habits, jokes, intrigues, loves and hates. This relatively intimate event was changed in the Kibbutzim into mass Seders, a gathering of the whole community, including hundreds of people, crowded in a dense dining hall, following from a distance a ceremony that was carried out on a distant stage. In some Kibbutzim the Seder included 2,000 people. This major change in what the Seder feels like was part of a wider phenomenon of mass Seders in Israel of the 1930s and 40s. It was probably a result of the need of many lonely, family-deprived people who immigrated to the newborn society (Shoham, 2014, 48–51). One challenge that comes with this change is the passivity of the people involved. It is hard to feel part of the event when you are one out of hundreds that are watching something happening on a stage (Feinstein, 2017, 282). Another challenge is the erasing of the nuclear family in this event and the producing of something that does not quite feel like one big family. It feels more like something that the poet, politician, and Holocaust survivor, Aba Kovner, called a (kabbalist) "breaking of the vessels":

> In this exodos (יציאת מצרים) of our time, we went out with no mother nor father. For years one could not see around the table of the Seder any grey hair, nor children who could ask the questions (קושיות). Ageless people, without sons, without fathers. But this cutoff was done for the sake of becoming a bridge, of making a revolution in a people, most of which was not ready for it. No other revolutionary movement, I believe, obliged itself for so much breaking of vessels (שבירת כלים).
>
> *Kovner 1965, my translation from Eran, 2018, 22*

Many Kibbutz members felt alienated from this kind of event. For people with a traditional background it was, and still is, seen as too far from tradition. For others, atheists or the anti-religious, it is too traditional and includes texts and ideas that are relics from religious ways of thinking: "Why should I say something I don't believe in?" Yet for others it is built on an ideology with a short life: "I don't see the Kibbutz as my big family", an ideology that was rejected by the second generation and other newcomers. All these examples show how hard it is for those who wish to renew traditions to overcome different barriers of estrangement. A ritual can be beautiful, thoughtful, deep, delicately designed to correlate both with tradition and with the "right" ideology, but this does not mean that it will be rooted in the heart and will actually become a tradition – a ritual that is practiced again and again.

In the mass Seders of the Kibbutzim one can hear different ideological calls which are directed outwards to three audiences – first, to the Jews in the diaspora, the Kibbutz Seder says: "This is what a real Jew looks like, a hard-working farmer with a new family, a new life style, and new holy days!" The second to the Israeli political right: "It is us, in the labor movement that are the real Zionists! We are renewing the times of the Bible, not the orthodox nor the settlers in the occupied territories". And third, to the Palestinians: "This is our land, and it always was!" The new ritual is shaped as if it is not new at all – it is a sign of long-lasting ownership of the land. All these calls are political, they are not motivated out of a secular need for spirituality. They show that secular rituals are far from being post-modern or post-secular.

Secular rituals change from one place to another and in many cases, in the same place, from time to time. In the rituals of the Sabbath, *Kabalot Shabbat*, this is more easily recognized since one can compare a ritual to what was practiced last week. Some leaders of secular rituals find a disadvantage in this, it is hard to include people in a ceremony that changes every week, and a ritual that is practiced only once is no ritual at all. Others see this as an advantage: secular Jews are not tied to one fixed formulation of the ritual so they can make their ceremonies much richer and more interesting. In secular *Shabbat* rituals, the tension between the need for change and the need for fixed content is usually answered by non-changing blessings that are accompanied with changing content, diverse songs or *Drasha* (sermon) on the weekly Torah Portion. And still, as we will now see, the question of continuity in *Kabbalot Shabbat* marks one of the great challenges of any secular ritual.

The example I am giving for the *Shabbat* ritual is somewhat personal, the *Kiddush*, secular Shabbat blessing for the wine, used in my community, Migvan, the urban Kibbutz in Sderot. I hope the reader will excuse the lack of objectivity and that the interesting content of the blessing will be enough to justify it. We can examine this secular *Kiddush* line by line:

	Migvan's Kiddush	*Translation (Migvan)*	*Traditional Kiddush*
1.	יום הששי ויכולו השמים והארץ וכל צבאם	the sixth day, the heaven and earth and all their host were completed	יוֹם הַשִּׁשִּׁי. וַיְכֻלּוּ הַשָּׁמַיִם וְהָאָרֶץ וְכָל צְבָאָם
2.	כי שבעה ימים סובבת ארץ על צירה ורק האדם עוצר לו את הזמן ומבדיל בין ימות החול לשבת קודשו	for seven days the earth rotates, and only humans stop their time and distinguish between the holy day of *Shabbat* and the days of the week	וַיְכַל אֱלֹהִים בַּיּוֹם הַשְּׁבִיעִי מְלַאכְתּוֹ אֲשֶׁר עָשָׂה. וַיִּשְׁבֹּת בַּיּוֹם הַשְּׁבִיעִי מִכָּל מְלַאכְתּוֹ אֲשֶׁר עָשָׂה:
3.	ויברך את יום השביעי ויקדש אותו כי בו שבת מכל מלאכתו	and he blessed the seventh day and sanctified it, because in it he rested from all his labor	וַיְבָרֶךְ אֱלֹהִים אֶת יוֹם הַשְּׁבִיעִי וַיְקַדֵּשׁ אֹתוֹ. כִּי בוֹ שָׁבַת מִכָּל מְלַאכְתּוֹ
4.	ואותו ייעד לשאר רוחו	and he designated it for his soul (or for his inspiration)	אֲשֶׁר בָּרָא אֱלֹהִים לַעֲשׂוֹת
5.	סברי חברי (הקהל עונה: לחיים!)	Hear me my friends, or: with the permission of my friends (the community answers: *Lehaim*!)	(סַבְרִי מָרָנָן (הקהל עונה: לחיים!
6.	ברוך בורא פרי הגפן, ברוכה את לנו השבת	Blessed is he who created the fruit of the Vine, blessed is the *Shabbat* for us.	בָּרוּךְ אַתָּה ה' אֱלֹהֵינוּ מֶלֶךְ הָעוֹלָם בּוֹרֵא פְּרִי הַגָּפֶן
7.			בָּרוּךְ אַתָּה ה' אֱלֹהֵינוּ מֶלֶךְ הָעוֹלָם. אֲשֶׁר קִדְּשָׁנוּ בְּמִצְוֹתָיו וְרָצָה בָנוּ. וְשַׁבַּת קָדְשׁוֹ בְּאַהֲבָה וּבְרָצוֹן הִנְחִילָנוּ. זִכָּרוֹן לְמַעֲשֵׂה בְרֵאשִׁית. תְּחִלָּה לְמִקְרָאֵי קֹדֶשׁ זֵכֶר לִיצִיאַת מִצְרָיִם. וְשַׁבַּת קָדְשְׁךָ בְּאַהֲבָה וּבְרָצוֹן הִנְחַלְתָּנוּ. בָּרוּךְ אַתָּה ה'. מְקַדֵּשׁ הַשַּׁבָּת

Source: Created by the author's community members. Unpublished.

The text begins with the exact words of the traditional *Kiddush*, in a similar way to what we saw earlier in the secular *Kaddish*. Then (2) comes a secular original and subversive text, according to which *Shabbat* is not something rooted in nature or in the way the world was created. It is a unique human ability to stop time and distinguish the holy from the simple and ordinary (ימות החול). The text here builds an argument against the author of Genesis – it is not true that on the sixth day the world was completed (1) and God rested and "invented" *Shabbat*. Even today we still build this world and we need the *Shabbat* to rest from our toil.

Line 3 goes back to the original text, but this text is inverted in line 4 to portray the meaning that a secular Jew can find in *Shabbat* – humans designate it for their inspiration, for their inner spirit (שאר רוחו). The traditional phrasing of line 3 clearly refers to God, blessing the *Shabbat*. In Migvan's secular *Kiddush* the same words are used, but they refer to humans. The combination of lines 2 and 4 claims that humans go through this unbelievable gesture of stopping time, not in memory of God's resting, but in order to make room in their lives for something that is hard to achieve through the week.

Line 5 and 6 are, at first glance, very similar to the traditional *Kiddush*, but on a closer look one can find significant differences. The original blessing that is very familiar to many, goes: ברוך אתה ה' אלוהינו מלך העולם, בורא פרי הגפן (Blessed are You, the Lord our God, King of the Universe, Creator of the fruit of the vine). Instead of this, in Migvan's *Kiddush* the word "God" was simply erased, and nothing replaces it: "ברוך בורא פרי הגפן". We can compare this erasing with another *Shabbat* blessing. In the blessing over the bread that follows ("המוציא לחם מן הארץ"), the text can allow erasing God and the blessing can still make literal sense. If God is not mentioned, the text can refer to the ones who bring bread from the earth, the farmer or the baker. In the *Kiddush*, the blessing for the wine, this option does not really work. Linguistically, the Hebrew words "בורא פרי הגפן" cannot apply to nature or to the process of evolution that created the fruit of the vine according to secular understanding. Nature is not an agent who can create things and who therefore should be blessed. It seems as though God was forcefully evacuated from line 6, and this can partly explain why later God comes back in. Line 7 from the traditional *Kiddush* is completely erased, mainly because of its racist connotations. The supremacy of the chosen people, and some of the other religious ideas captured in this line are foreign to the ideology of this community and therefore does not appear at all. It is possible that the wish to shorten the blessing is also part of the rationale here.

The *Kiddush* has been used in Migvan every week for more than 20 years. Only parts of the text were written by the members of the community. Other parts were used in other places in the past. The detailed history of how it came into being is not very clear. Different writers added to it and, as we will now see, it is still developing. The same rule applies to almost all the blessings in Jewish tradition. We do not know who wrote them, and usually have a very rough idea of when Jews began using them.[12] There is a further interesting development that happened to the *Kiddush* of Migvan. A few years after it came into use, one could notice that when a few of the members reach line 6, they put God back into the blessing and use (for this line only) the original and well-known blessing for God who created the fruit of the vine. This new combination is peculiar because the rest of the blessing stayed as it was, still clearly secular, filled with atheist rebellion and with a broad humanist message – it is human beings that are in focus, not God. And yet, a few of the members find it fitting to combine this ideology with the exact traditional text that the secular blessing was designed to negate. Furthermore – this development was not added to the written format of the blessing and therefore there is a gap now between what is written (כתיב) and what is read out loud (קרי). This kind of gap is well known from other Jewish traditional texts. It enables different readers to choose their preferred version, and it can also distinguish between the ones who know the ritual and realize they can put God back in the text, and the ones who do not know it and use the written version as it is.

We can learn from this gap something broader about secular rituals. The *Kiddush* of Migvan is a short-lived formulation that is a product of different vectors and forces in this community.

A few of the members think that the atheist message of the ritual should be clear and central. The very mentioning of God in the ritual of their community is quite offensive for them and they are not happy about others who let God sneak back in. For others, not mentioning God seems forced and bizarre, they want the *Kiddush* to be closer to the traditional one that they already know. So how can this community keep celebrating *Shabbat* together? There is a delicate balance and a mutual agreement that needs to be achieved and this agreement is even harder to reach when the participants feel free to reopen the agreement and change the ritual from time to time.

The children who participate in the ceremony are also an interesting factor in the acceptance of the new ritual, especially when we consider the possibility of it becoming canonical. For the second generation the new format of the ritual is the "גירסא דינקותא" the version that they experienced from an early age, and the only thing that they consider as *Kabalat Shabbat*. It seems natural for them that this is what Jews do on *Shabbat*. They soon realize, however, that in other places it works in different ways – in the houses of some of their friends and wider families *Shabbat* is not practiced at all, and in other homes, traditional and orthodox practices are used, even where the family itself is not orthodox. Secular children soon realize that what they experience as natural, traditional, part of the structure of the week, was actually invented by their parents, or somebody else from the last generation, and accordingly, they come to the conclusion that it is just as much their right to renew the ritual and to write their own new ceremony, which again, will not be considered a "real" ritual, because it will be practiced only a few times before it will be changed again.

This might be at the essence of what secularity means – freedom to establish your own way, but it also poses a great difficulty for secular Jews. The freedom to write your own text ruins the possibility that the ritual your parents wrote will become a real ritual – a new tradition. And again, this is not unique to the secular – every second generation of a new ritual or new text suffers from this difficulty.

The Return of God

How come God, who is supposed to be at the locus of secular criticism toward religion, finds his (or her) way back into the secular *Kiddush* of Migvan, the *Haggadah* of Hashomer Hatzair and Bina's *Yom Kippur* ceremony? I suggest that it was not God who was removed from the secular ritual in the first place, but a very specific and problematic theological worldview. The "return" of God to these rituals needs not be seen as a sign of weakness within secular (dis)belief, nor as a shift from the secular into the post-secular, but as a fearless unapologetic manifestation of secular values, which is rooted within the unique structure of Jewish identity as a whole. This statement is built, on the one hand, on a comparison between Jewish identity and other cultural or religious formulations, and on the other, on a secular theology inspired (among others) by Emanuel Levinas. In the framework of this chapter I will briefly examine these two ideas.

There are no secular-Christian rituals. When a German atheist, for example, puts a Christmas tree in his living room, it does not make him Christian, and the fact that this man sees himself as secular or atheist, does not make this practice a secular ritual. Why not? What is the difference between this tree and Migvan's secular *Kiddush*? Aren't they both a sign of the post-modern return to religion? Aren't they a post-secular search for spirituality in a materialistic age? The answer regarding the Christmas tree might indeed be affirmative. The examples discussed above show that regarding Jewish secular rituals, it is clearly negative. The Christmas tree in the German example does not symbolize a secular worldview. It is arranged for other purposes. It resembles a Jewish secular ritual only in being a sign of continuation of a cultural-religious tradition in a secular world and for secular people, but it is not designed to manifest a secular ideology. The decision of this German to decorate his house with a tree is not aimed at claiming his share in the Christian tradition and it does not threaten the church in any way. For him the tree is folklore. He might even recognize it as Christian folklore, but he knows that at the core of Christianity lies a belief system (*Credo*, Creed). If one does not believe in the main pillars of this system, he is not included in Christianity, no matter what his ethnic origins are or the folklore he takes part in.

The examples discussed above show how Jewish secular rituals do all these things that the Christmas tree does not: they claim an equal share in Jewish culture, they are a sign of a wide worldview that is represented in the details of the ritual, and they are threatening for the religious orthodox establishment because they challenge orthodox understandings of Jewish identity and common understandings of God. The reason for this difference lies within the uniqueness of Jewish identity – within an understanding, shared by all Jews to a certain degree, according to which Judaism is a tribal/national/ethnic/religious/family-like culture, and not a belief system. Almost all the Jews in the past and in the present define their culture, not as a universal creed that is expected to be shared by all humans, at least not for now, but as a culture in which the "ticket in" is one's maternal genealogical lineage. This is true even for Jews who sometimes claim that Judaism is a belief system, like many orthodox in the present. It is also true for great figures like Maimonides, who tried to establish a Jewish fixed creed. Maimonides insisted that all Jews should believe in the 13 pillars of faith, which he himself deduced from the tradition before his time. He very bluntly argued that those who do not believe in these truths should not be considered as Jews and they should be hated and destroyed in order to prevent them from harming the beliefs of "proper" Jews (Introduction to *Perek Helek*). It is however easy to show that even Maimonides was not following the full consequences of this assertion. Jews who claim that Judaism is built on a certain creed try to persuade other Jews to follow this creed and hardly make any effort to "market" their belief system to people out of the "tribe". *Giur*, conversion to Judaism is indeed possible, but unlike the missionary elements in Christianity or Islam, it never became a central feature of Jewish culture. In Judaism the missionary efforts were always directed only inwards. These efforts show that the orthodox concept of Jewish identity is not far from the secular understanding. They see secular Jews as Jews with the wrong system of beliefs, unlike the Christians who treat their heretics as non-Christians, and in the same way that secular Jews see the orthodox – Jews indeed, but with the wrong worldview.

The orthodox show in their inward-looking efforts that they are quite convinced by this seemingly unorthodox understanding: insisting on a fixed creed that everybody should believe in, is foreign to Judaism. A tribal-ethnic culture inherently builds within its boundaries cultural pluralism. Since a Jew is defined as such according to the ethnic identity of her/his mother, there will always be Jews who will not share the belief system that any establishment will try to enforce. In other words, the possibility to arrogantly devalue the belief system of the other and say "that's not what we believe in", is open for Christians and not for Jews. People of Christian background, who wake up one day and acknowledge that the Christian belief system is wrong, are not "secular Christians". Judaism is the only religion in which secular identity is part of the greater cultural-religious identity and in a place like Israel, it is not only part of Jewish identity – it is the identity of the great majority of Jews.

This cultural pluralism does not mean, of course, that only in Judaism can we find variations, or that tolerance to the other is a unique Jewish trait. It only means that every branch of the Christian religion will define its own understanding of the Christian creed as the only true Christian way, while Jews do not have this privilege, even if they are fundamental ultra-orthodox.

Jews accept the ethnic boundaries of this culture and that is why they fight other interpretations of this culture. They acknowledge that others are no less Jews than themselves.

This acknowledgment can be used to explain the appearance of God in secular rituals. As we saw, secular Jews, most of them at least, are not happy with an atheist alienation that is aimed toward their heritage, or toward the religious components of this heritage, including the belief in God. On the contrary, they use this tradition, including the theological content, and struggle against other Jewish streams with what they see as the right interpretation of this tradition. Secular Jews struggle not only as a demand to safeguard their own share of this tradition, but because they believe that the orthodox interpretation of this tradition is problematic and harmful. Mentioning God in secular rituals brings forward what secular Jews see as a misuse of this important cultural concept in orthodox rituals. This does not mean that they wish to annihilate orthodoxy, or that Jewish secular identity is intolerant to any other interpretation of Judaism or of who God is. Criticism of the other does not mean that there is no place in the world for this other.

Secular rituals are intended to represent secular values. These values are completely foreign to certain religious ideas and, as we will soon see, to certain concepts of God. However, they are not foreign to many values that are central in Jewish tradition, and which are represented in traditional rituals. Secular rituals were established in order to remind secular Jews how important secular-Jewish values are for them, to declare (in front of other secular and non-secular Jews) that secular Jews see themselves as part of this identity and this worldview, and of the actions that are obliged by it, including an obligation to encourage others to accept secular values. There is a certain, limited, missionary element in secular rituals. The use of God within these rituals is one way to represent this element and reclaim the secular ritual's share in Jewish tradition.

I have argued that secular rituals are very much needed in Jewish culture, and explained why they are absent from the two universal religions, Christianity and Islam. The question as to how can God be mentioned and used in these rituals, needs further attention. I suggested that God sneaks back into secular rituals because it was not him (her) who was rejected from them in the first place. So who was? Secular rituals find no place within them, first and foremost for the rabbis, the establishment, in other words the struggle is political. This statement is quite clear and obvious, but it does not capture the theological struggle one can find within secular rituals. A further theological observation would be that secularism and atheism are not synonyms, and that the God that is rejected in secular worldviews is a specific concept, central in orthodoxy – an ontological God. I am using here a differentiation between an ontological and an ethical understanding of God, which is taken from Emmanuel Levinas, and which will not be outlined here at length.[13] In the thought of Levinas, God is seen as an ethical demand, not as the ruler of the universe, and not even as a force which orders Jewish *Mitzvot* (commandments). For Levinas, God is the *Mitzvot* themselves. Following Levinas, I suggest that secular rituals reject God as an explanation for how the world was created or how it functions, but they need not reject God as an ethical demand.

Almost every line of traditional *Sidurim* (prayer books), orthodox, reform or conservative, is devoted to an ontological God. At the center of religious rituals, one finds the God of human history and of the natural world, praising and thanking God for the reality that he constructed for us, and asking him to make this reality a little more adjusted to what we wish to find in this life. I do not claim that all religious Jews are irrational people who believe that God will fix any reality that they want (Yeshayahu Leibowitz would be a good example for orthodox thinkers who do not accept the belief in an ontological God),[14] but even if many people who pray do not believe in the words that they say, that is the main content of their prayers, and one of the reasons that make secular Jews reject this kind of prayer. Orthodox blessings also portray the same picture. It is not the God of the commandments that is portrayed in orthodox rituals, it is clearly the ruler of the universe.

This specific image is far from being the only image that Jewish tradition composed. It is not even the central one. Jewish tradition is based on ritual and practice. Contrary to Christianity (and partly also to Islam), it deals with what people do, not with what they believe in. Accepting the Levinasian differentiation leads the secular Jew to stick to much of Jewish practice and ritual, and to negate the belief in the God of history that is so central to religious prayers and blessings.

There are many orthodox and many secular Jews who see secular identity as "Judaism without *Mitzvot*", and therefore as free from any obligation toward tradition or ritual. The secular identity that is constructed through the rituals examined above shows how misleading this view is. It is not the *Mitzvot* that secular ideology is rejecting, it is the concept of a governing God who controls the universe and unloads some of the responsibility that lays on human shoulders. I believe secular rituals need not be anti-theological, they can take part in a secular theology, based on the Levinasian differentiation between the ontological and the ethical, a theology which needs much further elaboration, beyond the scope of this chapter.

How can a secular Jew, who does not see God as responsible for the functioning of the world, bless the creator of the fruit of the vine, or ask God to make peace upon us (יעשה שלום עלינו)? A secular Jew does not believe that God will make peace upon us. Only an ontological God, the ruler of the universe, who stands at the center of religious belief and ritual, can do that. The secular understanding of the world insists on human responsibility toward the other, and toward the world as a whole. It does not look for any force beyond the world to which we should turn in order to promote the wish for peace. A secular Jew, however, finds in the traditional blessing for peace a way to phrase her values, her commitment to promote peace herself, without the help of God. The price she needs to pay, in saying something that she does not really believe in (that it is God who makes peace upon us), is not so great. The point in secular rituals which mentions God, is clearly not to call God back into the lives of secular Jews as Scholem feared (see above). It is not God but peace that they cherish and ask for when they say: העושה שלום במרומיו הוא יעשה שלום, עלינו ועל כל ישראל ועל כל יושבי תבל (the one who made peace in heaven, he will bring peace upon us, upon the whole of Israel, and upon the whole world; another Shabbat blessing in Migvan's secular version).

Jewish secular identity takes part in the present in the way most of the Jews in Israel understand not only their own identity but also what Judaism in general is all about. Therefore, although few people participate in secular rituals, they should not be seen as a weird decision of some eccentric rebels, but as a much wider identity marker.

Notes

1 I did not translate *Tehilim* to the common translation, Psalms, because the English/Latin originates from the musical character of the biblical book while Elon refers mostly to the literal Hebrew meaning – Glories. He is pointing at the glory of this moment, *Shabbat* eve, and the glory of his Kibbutz – Ein Shemer – and while doing so he also raises the question: what is glory for a secular Jew?
2 See more about Bina and read their full *Machzor* here: www.bina.org.il/ (accessed 24 Sept. 2020).
3 I will not suggest in this chapter definitions for terms like secular, religious or atheist. I try to use them in a common way that is shared by many in the Israeli context and beyond. Parts of my discussion challenge some common understandings of these terms. The terms are no doubt connected and even interdependent, but nonetheless, as the reader will soon realize, the discussion is partly built on a differentiation between atheists and secular Jews.

4 The term "tradition" or "traditional" that will be frequently used throughout the chapter should be read cautiously: I will make a few comparisons between the text used in secular rituals and the "traditional" version, but it's important to note that such a version doesn't exist. In almost every ritual, custom or text in the Jewish culture, one can find different and competing versions and every version has its own history. Every tradition was invented at some point, in many cases much later than is commonly thought (see Hobsbawm & Ranger, 1983). The idea that there is such a thing as "the traditional Jewish text" is a fiction that is marketed mainly by Orthodox Jews who wish to portray Judaism as a linear and non-pluralist culture. And still I cannot avoid this fiction because a few of the secular rituals are structured as a polemic against tradition, using this imagined tradition and subverting it in order to manifest secular values.
5 The statistical data used here are based on different surveys from a long period of time. The surveys are unfortunately inconsistent in their use of definitions like "religious", "traditional", "secular", or "atheist", but still, a rough picture of the identity of Israelis, as they define themselves, can be deduced from the surveys. See Arian & Keissar-Sugerman, 2011; Pew Research Center, 2016; Shafir & Yagur-Krol, 2018.
6 For sociological analysis of secular rituals see: Deshen, 1997; Sharaby, 2005; Azulay & Tabori, 2008; Prashizky, 2006, 2014; Shoham, 2014; Azulay, 2017; Marx, 2018. For an extensive discussion on secularity and the role of religion in our time see Taylor, 2007. For Israel as a post-secular society see Yonah & Goodman, 2004; Shenhav, 2008.
7 On the secularization thesis see, among many others: Habermas, 2008; Raz-Krakotzkin, 2017. In addition to the studies mentioned in note 6, and to other sociologists who challenge the secular–religious dichotomy, there are impressive works by philosophers and theologians who locate themselves in between the two "poles" and thus question the dichotomy. See: Buzaglo, 2008; Meir, 2012; Shilo, 2017.
8 See more on Jewish secular weddings in Prashizky, 2006.
9 On Zionist negation of exile see Raz-Krakotzkin 2013, 2017.
10 On the Christian influence on the Jewish Haggadah see Yuval, 1999. Moses is mentioned in the traditional *Haggadah* once, but not as an active agent in the story: "and the people believed in the Lord and in his Servant, Moses".
11 See more on the place of tradition and religion in Hashomer Hatzair in Elmaliach 2017.
12 See among many others: Mack, 2006.
13 This idea is very central in the works of Levinas and was discussed by many. For his short argument on this see Levinas 1990; for my own discussion on the ontological-ethical differentiation and secular theology in a wider sense, see Dinur 2014, 2015.
14 Leibowitz makes this point in numerous texts. See for example 1979, 340.

References

Arian, Asher & Ayala Keissar-Sugerman. 2011. *A Portrait of Israeli Jews: Beliefs, Observance, and Values of Israeli Jews, 2009* (Jerusalem: The Israel Democracy Institute and the Avi-Chai Israel Foundation). Also available online: www.idi.org.il/media/5032/%D7%93%D7%95%D7%97-%D7%90%D7%91%D7%99%D7%97%D7%99-%D7%94%D7%9E%D7%9C%D7%90.pdf (accessed 24 September 2020).
Azulay, Naama. 2017. "'Builders of 'Lighthouses in time': Virtual Ceremonies in Young Peoples' Communal Groups in the Israeli Secular Society". In Yuval Dror ed. *Kibbutz and Judaism*. Jerusalem: Bialik Institute and Yad Tabenkin, 162–208 (Hebrew).
Azulay, Naama & Ephraim Tabory. 2008. "'A House of Prayer for All Nations': Unorthodox Prayer Houses for Nonreligious Israeli Jews." *Sociological Papers* 13. Ramat Gan: Bar Ilan University, 22–41.
Bina. 2000. *Machzor le'Yom Hakipurim: Secular Yeshiva*. Tel Aviv: Bina (Hebrew).
Buzaglo, Meir. 2008. *A Language for the Faithful: Reflections on Tradition*. Jerusalem: Mandel (Hebrew).
Deshen, Slomo. 1997. "The Passover Celebrations of Secular Israelis", *Megamot* 38(4): 528–46 (Hebrew).
Dinur, Avner. 2014. "Secular Theology: A Critique of Israeli Secular Identity Using the Thought of Hans Jonas". In Gideon Kats, Shlalom Ratzabi & Yaacov Yadgar eds. *Beyond Halach: Secularism, Traditionalism and "New Age" Culture in Israel*. Sede Boker: Ben-Gurion University Press, 160–84 (Hebrew).
Dinur, Avner. 2015. "Secular Theology as a Challenge for Jewish Atheists", *Melilah* 12: 131–44.

Elmaliach, Tal. 2017. "To Restore the Exiled Divine Presence: The Relationship of HaShomer HaTzair to Religion and Jewish Tradition". In Yuval Dror ed. *Kibbutz and Judaism*. Jerusalem: Bialik Institute and Yad Tabenkin, 108–34 (Hebrew).

Elon, Eli "Barefoot – Psalms of Ein Shemer". *Shitim*. www.chagim.org.il/LITERATURE/%D7%AA%D7%94%D7%99%D7%9C%D7%99%D7%9D-%D7%A2%D7%9C-%D7%94%D7%93%D7%A9%D7%90-%D7%94%D7%92%D7%93%D7%95%D7%9C (accessed 10 September 2020, Hebrew).

Eran, Amira. 2018. "Correlations between Kibbutz Haggadot and Aba Kovner's 'Scroll of Testimony'", *Hachinuch Vesvivo* 40: 9–38 (Hebrew).

Feinstein, Nurith. 2017. "Dor Safra VeSaifa", *Ofakim Begeographia* 91–92: 270–98 (Hebrew)

Habermas, Jürgen. 2008. "Notes on Post-Secular Society", *New Perspectives Quarterly* 25(4): 17–29.

Hakibutz, Haartzi. 1988. *Passover Haggadah*. Drawings by Shmuel Katz. Tel Aviv: United Artists (Hebrew).

Hobsbawm, Eric & Terence Ranger eds. 1983. *The Invention of Tradition*. Cambridge: Cambridge University Press.

Leibowitz, Yeshayahu. 1979. *Judaism, Jewish People and the State of Israel*. Tel Aviv: Schoken (Hebrew).

Levinas, Emmanuel. 1990. "A Religion for Adults". In *Difficult Freedom: Essays on Judaism*. Trans. Sean Hand. Baltimore, MD: Johns Hopkins University Press, 11–23.

Mack, Hananel. 2006. *A Prayer and Prayers*. Jerusalem: Rubin Mass (Hebrew).

Marx, Dalia. 2018. "Welcoming the Sabbath in the Kibbutzim: Secular Religiosity", *Jerusalem Studies in Jewish Folklore* 31: 93–134 (Hebrew).

Meir, Moshe. 2012. *Two Together: A New Religious-Secular Philosophy*. Jerusalem: Magnes (Hebrew).

Pew Research Center. 2016. Israel's Religiously Divided Society. 8 March. www.pewforum.org/2016/03/08/israels-religiously-divided-society/ (accessed 24 September 2020).

Prashizky, Anna. 2006. *Wedding Rituals in Israeli Society: A Comparative Study of Ritualization and Performativity*. Ramat Gan: Bar Ilan University, Doctoral Dissertation (Hebrew).

Prashizky, Anna. 2014. "Inventing Jewish Rituals: Non-Orthodox Marriage and Funeral Rites in Israel". In Gideon Kats, Shlalom Ratzabi & Yaacov Yadgar eds. *Beyond Halachah: Secularism, Traditionalism and "New Age" Culture in Israel*. Sede Boker: Ben-Gurion University Press, 242–83 (Hebrew).

Raz Krakotzkin, Amnon. 2013. "Exile, History, and the Nationalization of Jewish Memory: Some Reflections on the Zionist Notion of History and Return", *Journal of Levantine Studies* 3: 2: 37–70.

Raz Krakotzkin, Amnon. 2017. "Exile Within Sovereignty: Critique of 'The Negation of Exile' in Israeli Culture". In Zvi Ben-Dor, Stefanos Geroulanos & Nicole Jerr eds. *The Scaffolding of Sovereignty*. New York: Columbia University Press, 393–420.

Scholem, Gershom. 1926, 1990. "On Our Language: A Confession" (letter to Franz Rosenzweig, 26 December 1926, trans. Ora Wiskind), *History and Memory* 2(2): 99.

Shafir, Moriel & Amit Yagur-Krol. 2018. "Press Announcement on Religion and Self-Definition of Extent Religiosity". Jerusalem: Central Bureau of Statistics. www.cbs.gov.il/he/mediarelease/DocLib/2018/195/32_18_195b.pdf (accessed 24 September 2020).

Sharaby, Rachel. 2005. "May Day Ceremonies in the State of Israel's First Decade: From a Sectorial to a National Holiday", *Megamot* 44(1): 106–36 (Hebrew).

Shenhav, Yehouda. 2008. "An Invitation to a Post-Secular Sociology of Israel", *Israeli Sociology* 10(1): 161–88 (Hebrew).

Shilo, Elchanan. 2017. *Existential Judaism*. Tel Aviv: Schoken (Hebrew).

Shoham, Hizky. 2014. *Let's Celebrate! Festivals and Civic Culture in Israel*. Jerusalem: Israel Democracy Institute (Hebrew).

Taylor, Charles. 2007. *A Secular Age*. Cambridge, MA: Harvard University Press.

Yonah, Yossi & Yehuda Goodman eds. 2004. *Maelstrom of Identities: A Critical Look at Religion and Secularity in Israel*. Tel Aviv: Van Leer & Hakibbutz Hameuchad, (Hebrew).

Yuval, Israel Jacob. 1999. "Easter and Passover as Early Jewish-Christian Dialogue". In Paul F. Bradshaw & Lawrence A Hoffman eds. *Passover and Easter: Origin and History to Modern Times*. Notre Dame, IL: University of Notre Dame Press, 98–124.

28
"FOR THE AMEN MEAL, YOU DON'T HAVE TO KEEP THE RELIGIOUS DUTIES"

Amen Meals as a New Age Phenomenon

Rivka Neriya-Ben Shahar

The beginning of the twenty-first century saw the emergence of a food-related ritual among Jewish women, known as the "Amen meal." This ritual, which first emerged in Israel's Ultra-Orthodox sector, rapidly spread to a broad spectrum of Jewish women, from Ultra-Orthodox to secular. Within a few years, the ritual also applied to the United States and Europe (Neriya-Ben Shahar 2015, 2018, 2019; Taylor-Guthartz 2016, 2021). This chapter's primary goals are to explore the Amen meal ritual, its characteristics, and components, demonstrate that this ritual is a part of the New Age phenomenon, and describe the social and cultural contexts that created and supported this ritual.

In the spring of 2011, I participated in 23 Amen meals celebrated by Jewish women in Israel. I also conducted 53 in-depth interviews with women who had experienced Amen rituals. Both methods, in-depth interviews and participant observations, are based on a qualitative-ethnographic-feminist study of attitudes (Reinharz 1992). The detection of the rituals and the participants was through my social-familial networks. Growing up in a National-Ultra-Orthodox community mean hundreds of family members and social frameworks, ranging from the Ultra-Orthodox to Modern Orthodox, traditional and secular people. Before and after the ritual, I asked the participants if they would agree to talk with me. Some of them wanted to have an informal talk before or after the ritual, and others decided to have a formal interview.

Although this snowball sample cannot be considered representative, I attempted, as much as possible, to collect representative data by carrying out the participant observations in various geographic and social settings. The women interviewed reflect multiple age groups, socio-economic backgrounds, geographic locations, religious observance levels, and ethnic origins. All the interviews and observations were taped and carefully transcribed. The data were analyzed in line with grounded theory (Strauss and Corbin 1990, 1994) and then with Mauthner and Doucet's (1998) voice-centered relational method, based on Brown and Gilligan's (1992) theory.

Amen Meal: The Ritual Characteristics and Components

Turner (1973) defined ritual as "[a] stereotyped sequence of activities involving gestures, words, and objects, performed in a sequestered place, and designed to influence preternatural entities or forces, on behalf of the actors' goals and interests" (p. 1100). The Amen meal is a new women's ritual, its primary goal is to recite the maximum number of amens, responding to the blessings over food. In Turner's terms, the activities and gestures are found in women's gatherings, as they sit in a circle and supply themselves with various types of food. The words are the women reciting the blessings in the order set by Jewish law (as reflected in the list below). Each woman recites a prayer in turn, and the others cry out Amen together; after reciting the blessing, each woman then tastes the specific food.

The actors' attempt to influence God is the *Yehi ratzon* prayer (may it be God's will that ...). The woman who goes last in the circle recites the *Yehi ratzon* – a prayer composed especially for this ceremony – out loud and the rest silently. Each section of the prayer has an associative link to the appropriate benediction: the blessing for baked goods is related to livelihood; for wine – marriage; for fruit – children and fertility; for vegetables – health; and for food and drinks outside the other categories –protection and success in all matters.

Names are inserted in the prayer, "especially for ... ." The woman then inserts the person's name to whom she is dedicating her prayer. In the end, all the women respond Amen and, after a moment of silence, the women begin to recite, in no particular order, the names of people who require help in that sphere, and the other women respond: "Amen!". In some groups, calling out names leads to a revelation of the person's story in question (a poor young widow; a sick friend). Sometimes, the woman telling her story cries and is supported by the group. The women then converse and eat together.

The Amen meal, as every ritual, is complex. Turner (1973) discusses the notion of a structure that combines various symbols. Every ritual symbol is based on actions, interactions, or ideas that could be perceived by the senses. The dominant symbol is the fixed point for a multivocal system, which included many dependent symbols of gestures, activities, objects, verbal behaviors, and social relationships between the ritual's actors.

The dominant symbol is the female gathering, and the presence of the various types of food that enables different blessings. The benedictions, a different one for each type of food, is uttered in a strictly prescribed Jewish halachic order (*Mezonot, Gefen, Etz, Adama, Shehakol*), which create the acronym MAGA ESH (in Hebrew, a touch of fire). According to Jewish folklore, reciting the blessings in the correct order is a good test of the piety of a groom. Since the ritual's goal is to say as many amens as possible, this order must be followed strictly.

Building on this dominant symbol, various dependent signs and multiple-choice activities are carried out by the ritual's actors: *Hafrashat Challah* (taking Challah), religious studies, recitation of psalms, singing spiritual songs, and candle lighting. Here is a short description of these symbolized activities.

The secondary food ritual held in many Amen rituals (and sometimes by itself) is the public *Hafrashat Challah* ceremony. This ordinary domestic halacha task, formerly an ancient practice carried out at home when baking bread, requires setting aside and burning a small part of the dough. With the founding of commercial bakeries, this ritual's performance declined. Recent years, however, have seen an upsurge in this practice and its movement into the public sphere (El-Or 2006).

Some of the ceremonies incorporate a study of Halachah (El-Or 1994) including the laws of Shabbat, kashrut, gossip, modesty (Targin-Zeller 2014), and so on. In some of the fixed, ongoing groups, the women study specific books and have a set program, progressing weekly/monthly through several halakhot (legal discussions) on chosen topics. Many ceremonies open with the reciting of the psalms (Sosis and Handwerker 2011). The women bring a loose-leaf version of the complete psalms and quietly recite them until the pages are finished. Late arrivals sit quietly and join in.

At some of the sessions, I saw the women sing Hasidic songs together, enjoying men's absence (in whose presence it is forbidden to sing). Candle lighting is usually accompanied by moving songs. Sered (1992) describes candle lighting in memory of the righteous as a women's ritual carried out mainly at holy gravesites. In many of the rituals that I observed, women lit candles in honor of Tzadikim (holy men).

The ritual's structure is usually an integration of primary and secondary ceremonies. For the most part, the women integrate one or two of the food-related rituals (Amen meal and "taking Challah"). In addition, intellectual-spiritual-experiential sub-rituals such as a study of Halakhah, recitation of psalms, communal singing, and candle lighting can be part of the ceremony as well.

Each symbol has multiple semantic meanings, their relationships connected as groups or oppositional binaries (Turner 1973). These symbols could be analyzed as connection points between the signifier, as perceived by the senses, the signified, the signified's conceptual aspect, and the connotative message, based on the culture's codes (Barthes 1968, 1977). The dominant symbol, the Amen meal itself, has five primary signifiers: baked goods, wine (mostly grape juice), fruits, vegetables, food, and drinks outside the other categories (mostly water or snacks). The women developed as part of the ritual's conceptual aspects themes such as livelihood, marriage, children and fertility, health, salvation, and anything else significant for them.

I would like to analyze the meanings involved here as based on Jewish, sometimes Israeli, culture. Baked goods, based on flour and water, are essential food for Jewish meals that enable – and demand – special blessing before and after the meal. They have an important place in religious meals such as on Shabbat and the holidays, weddings, and circumcisions. These characteristics connect them to the basic need for money and work. The wine is part of Shabbat and holiday Jewish rituals, which also have special blessings before and after. The reference to marriage is based on the Talmudic phrase (Talmud, Pesachim, 49a) "vine grapes and vine grapes," which means successful matchmaking and is used for engagement and wedding invitations. There is a Hebrew connection between the tree's fruits and fertility. The vegetables and health are connected to the Israeli culture of rich vegetables and salads in meals for regular and special events. The Hebrew word *Shehakol* means "everything," and there is a common term: "*Shehakol Kollel Hakol.*" This term means that the "other" category included the "everything" category, based on the legal ruling that when a person does not know what the right blessing is, *Shehakol* is the solution.

The secondary food ritual, *Hafrashat Challah* (taking Challah) ceremony, is linked to an existential fear of death. The Mishnah attributes this ritual's rationale to atonement for Eve's sin and mentions death in childbirth due to its neglect. "For three transgressions, women are punished and die during childbirth: for the fact that they are not careful in observing the laws of a menstruating woman, and in separating *Challah* from the dough, and in lighting the Shabbat lamp" (Mishnah, Shabat, 2, 6). Another meaningful connotation are the severing and separation processes, which are fundamental symbols in Jewish identity, represented mostly through the circumcision ceremony (Bilu 2003).

The sub-ritual's signifiers include halachic studies, Psalm recital, candle lighting, and religious singing. They signified communal Torah study, holy prayers, saints' memorial days, and community and personal connections. These meanings are like walking on a tightrope between male and female spaces in the Jewish Orthodox community (Neriya-Ben Shahar 2019). While the Torah study and synagogue prayers are male spheres, these women knowingly limit what they do, studying only practical halachic issues connected to their lives, and not attempting to gain a knowledge of wider issues (El-Or 1994). The reciting of psalms relates to women's prayers – mostly for sad events, without specific time and space. Therefore, women stay in a safe place of women-only traditional signs. Lighting candles is a traditional Jewish female ritual, connected to Shabbat and holidays and saints' tombs (Bilu 1998a, 1998b; Sered 1992). The religious songs are an integral part of the Jewish community, but the Ultra-Orthodox and some of the Orthodox would not sing when men are around. Therefore, the singing is both communal and personal, celebrating happiness and optimism and only possible in a male-free space.

There are binary oppositions between two relating symbols representing associative semantic opposition of the specific culture (Turner 1973). This binarity could be seen between the senses that accompanied the ritual. A strong multisensory experience imparts aesthetic-sensory energies to the participants. The shared meal is an enjoyable, fun-filled experience. The ceremonies appeal to multiple senses: smell, sight, taste, touch, and hearing. The essential binaries contrast the physical senses of eating and baking, compared to the spiritual senses of studying, praying, blessing, singing, and candle lighting. The women try to eliminate this oppositional binarity and create a new space of continuity and sharing (Neriya-Ben Shahar 2018). As I will show below, this inclusion includes various participants, but here it has different senses and a new connection between the nature–culture binary.

The multi-symbols are not only part of the ritual components. Still, they could be seen through the diversity of the ritual's setting: The timing and frequency, the framework, the heterogeneity and number of the participants, and the locations. This multiplicity and diversity are meaningful, especially when comparing it to the very strict and ordered regular Orthodox Jewish rituals.

Turner (1973) argued that ritual timing is connected to the season, part of the passage of other life cycle ceremonies, or response to a collective or personal crisis. The frequency of the Amen rituals is sometimes weekly or monthly. The rituals take place on the first day of the Hebrew month, traditionally a woman's holiday (Sered 1988). The passage or life cycle ceremonies are bat mitzvah, Simchat bat, housewarming, or engagement events. Others are around collective crises such as wars and terror, or personal turmoil such as the discovery of severe illness or dismissal from employment.

This ritual takes place in two main frameworks, casual and natural groups. In the first kind, the audience is not fixed and consists of previously unacquainted women who attend the ritual in response to public announcements. The ritual is held by a charismatic leader, a rebbetzin, who has been invited in advance. Taylor-Guthartz (2016, 2021) described a similar ritual in England, except there, the women include a man in the ritual, usually a rabbi. His is always the last blessing for each category (the most critical role). The second kind is natural groups, composed of women, such as extended family members or friends. They carry out the ritual independently, and their leaders come from within the group. The leader runs the ritual, and she is responsible for reminding each participant what to bring.

In the casual rituals, I mainly found an amalgamation of the Amen meals with some other sub-rituals and entertainment. At times, the two frameworks are integrated: natural groups of family members or friends invite a rebbetzin to run the ritual. Sometimes, these rebbetzins comprise the "artistic program" of other rituals, some of which are rites of passage, such as singles parties, housewarmings, and bat mitzvahs.

The participants are heterogeneous: differing in age, socioeconomic, religious, and ethnic backgrounds, representing varied geographical areas. I encountered the young and the elderly; women from Mizrahi and Ashkenazic backgrounds; women with diverse religious affiliations – secular, traditional, Modern Orthodox, and Ultra-Orthodox; from different walks of life – self-employed professionals, salaried workers, students, and homemakers; and from various locations – from the center and the periphery of Israel and from large cities and small communities. We can find a single secular woman at these ceremonies, a lawyer with a masters' degree, seated next to a married Ultra-Orthodox woman from the margins of society. In contrast, private ceremonies usually have a more homogeneous composition involving family members and friends, with several outside guests.

The number of participants in the ritual ranges from five to five hundred. The private rituals held in homes are smaller than the large, organized ones held in public settings. Yet, I attended rituals where the organizer invited scores of friends to her house and a rebbetzin (wife of a rabbi) to run the evening. Given that many of the rituals are unpublicized private ones, I could not arrive at a reliable estimate of the phenomenon's overall scope. Nonetheless, based on the fact that within two weeks, I identified three groups that met every month and four that met weekly, in addition to the public rituals orchestrated by rebbetzins, some of whom hold an average of three ceremonies per week, the number of women who have participated in these rituals since the year 2000 seems to be quite large.

The ceremonies are held in both the private sphere, women's homes, and in the public sphere such as halls, and synagogues. In general, the smaller groups gather in women's houses, each one hosting in turn. The large groups meet in public places. The location reflects a variety of environments, from luxury towers to an old broken tiny house in Mea Shearim. The same leaders could move in the same week from a hundred women, sitting in a small and hot crowded synagogue somewhere obscure, to a great new wedding hall in Tel Aviv, with the same number of participants, sitting around rich tables with waiters and other facilities.

The Amen ritual is based on an old ritual. Turner (1973) argued that rituals, like the societies that created them, are always changing. Therefore, most rituals are not a radical invention but a variant of an old ritual. This old-new creation is a hybrid combination of tradition and renewal elements (Werczberger 2017). The Amen ritual's traditional aspects are the recited benedictions, which is in keeping with the traditional order of recitation, the MAGA ESH.

Other parts of the ritual, such as reciting *Tehilim* and other prayers and candle lighting, are also traditional Jewish women's rituals (Sered 1991). "Mostly, I don't even have the time to pick up the siddur," confesses Libi (Ultra-Orthodox, 36, kindergarten teacher), "so an Amen meal is a perfect opportunity for prayer. My daily routine is hectic, and I can't pray enough, or recite *Tehilim* enough, so during every Amen meal, we recite the *Tehilim* together." In my observations, I found that many Amen meals begin with the reciting of *Tehilim*. The chapters are distributed among the participants, and with each woman repeating her portion, the entire book can be recited in about 15 minutes. "Women praying is much more powerful. Rebbe Pinchas said that women's power is prayer's power," said Rivka (Ultra-Orthodox, 28, full-time mother).

The first new aspect is the connections of different blessings to symbols. However, some of them are constructed from old traditions. The food as symbol is a Kabbalist traditional custom that can be seen, especially on the New Year of the Trees celebration rituals, in Tu Beshvat. And Yehi Ratzons are traditional Jewish (and sometimes women's) prayers. The second unique aspect is the women's ritual gathering and sharing, rare or even non-existent in many Jewish Orthodox groups. Most of the sharing rituals in Jewish Orthodox communities are for men only and usually need a minyan, ten men, and public spaces. The women's rituals are private, like *Challah* and Shabbat candles, and sometimes even secret, like a ritual bath. There is no Jewish formal religious ritual for women that needs a public space and a group.

At Amen meals, the ritual experiences are shared and based on sharing. The most important role is to be the last person to recite a blessing because that woman recites the *Yehi ratzon* prayer aloud and mentions the person in need of prayers. Sometimes she shares the reason behind her request, usually with tears. Then other women share their sad and exciting stories, problems, and struggles, and support each other. For the most part, the leader does not decide who will go last, and there is no need for an announcement, tension, competition, or conflict. The woman in question simply says, "I wish to go last for this blessing." From a structural perspective, the women usually sit in a circle and maintain eye contact. This seating arrangement makes it possible to notice when someone is experiencing difficulty, and the open space in the middle allows free access for a supportive touch.

The Amen rituals are circular, shared, and sharing, both structurally and essentially. This female space can be created because the women construct a safe female space for themselves, using inclusion and sharing as guidelines. Inclusion is reflected in the acceptance of every Jewish woman, without limitation or judgment. Women from all religious sectors participate in these rituals. They can be seen as reflecting "the entire people of Israel, as long as they possess a Jewish soul," explained Libi (Ultra-Orthodox, 36, kindergarten teacher). Religious and secular women from different sectors, countries of origin, and differing personal status participate. Even the fixed groups of women who hold Amen meals composed of friends or family members with a shared socioeconomic status invite outside acquaintances, enriching the women's circle. Women experience sharing, especially the integration of diverse types of women, as an essential feature of these rituals: "Ultra-Orthodox society doesn't accept the 'other.' But at Amen meals we get everyone! We have all kinds of women [...], and that's good," said Tamar (Ultra-Orthodox, 34, medical secretary).

In terms of the old-new ritual, I tried to find the origin of the Amen meal ritual. The participants directed me to Tovi Baron (Tzitlin), an Ultra-Orthodox Lithuanian woman from Bnei-Brak, Israel. When I interviewed her, she confirms that she invented the ritual, and it was her idea to connect the different blessings to the needs of those in the group. However, the *Yehi ratzon* prayer was created by anonymous women that she (and I) did not find. Baron, an event producer, requested one of the Bnei-Brak rabbis, rabbi Kesler, to help him reviving an old ritual called "Notrei Amenim" (the keepers of the Amens). Rabbi Kesler, who wrote a halachic book about blessings, wished to renew the old custom of collecting young, innocent children, giving them sweets, and encouraging them to study the right blessings – and also to respond "Amen." Baron created lovely kits for this small event, which was a great success. She then thought it could be a good idea for her next event for young girls in Ultra-Orthodox schools. The demand became greater and greater, especially when the girls told their mothers about the events, and she started to have an independent event for women.

The ritual itself, however, does not have any halachic origin. The blessings, and their order, requires only eating and drinking. There is a custom in the North-African Jewish communities to have memorial and mourning meals and devote the blessings and the amens to the dead person's soul. According to the Talmud (Menahot, 43, 2): "Rabbi Meir would say: A person is obligated to recite one hundred blessings every day" and this has been used to provide the ritual with a legal basis. They also said it was easy for men to get to a hundred quickly because they have three prayers a day. Women need to gather to get the same number. They also mentioned a Midrash about King David who stopped a pandemic by asking the Jewish people to make a hundred blessings a day (Bamidbar Raba, 18, 21). Therefore, the ritual could be seen as a variant of an old ritual, but it included many innovations that were started by women.

Turner (1973) suggested a paradoxical connection between the simplicity of ritual and its generalization. For example, the cross is simple, and therefore one of the most famous symbols for Christian believers. He said complicated rituals, with many different symbols, are mostly local, particular, and connected to a specific culture. As an Orthodox Jewish woman myself, I grew up within the multiple and complicated Jewish rituals relating to the Kosher and Niddah rules. The Shabbat and holidays were full of laws and customs. However, I found the complexity of the Amen ritual to be much higher than other Jewish rituals. There are no halachic rules for a new ritual, and there are no traditions of "my grandmother/grandfather used to do it this way." Therefore, the choices of how to perform the ritual are almost unlimited. Women have invented for themselves a complicated ritual that represents their specific local and particular culture. Their creativity enables them to (re-)develop for themselves a multivocal, modular, polysemic ritual. Based on the Amen meal's dominant symbol – food and connected blessing – they found a rich personal-communal system, which included many dependent characters, according to their tailor-made needs. The next part of the chapter will take the complexity of old and new symbols to the next step in the argument – that the Amen meal ritual is part of the New Age movement.

New Ritual/New Age

Tehila, the leader, is the most charismatic Rebbetzin I met in the Amen meal rituals. She looks much younger than her fifties and has the vitality of a very young woman. She is beautiful, short, and slim, with blue eyes and a cheerful face. She dressed in jeans, a short white t-shirt, and navy-blue jacket. There is a light blue headband on her long bright, organized hair. She holds many books but never opens them. She moved from subject to subject, from the Bible times to now. The main message is our power to change reality, the world. In her presence I feel that I forget all my academic feminist critical methodology. I just want to listen to this woman and do whatever she says.

The participants told me before we started that they admire her. Some of them come to her Bible studies weekly. Most of them come every month to this ritual. They use a mailing list to share her talks, which is transcribed during the lessons and ritual. The mailing list helps them share the food they bring to the ritual and then the recipes after the ritual. I count about 30 women, secular and religious, 15–60 years old, students and stay at home mothers, of all ethnic origins. Everyone is quiet when she talks.

We sit on a large porch of our host, one of the participants. There is a fantastic Jerusalem view from here. Some women enter the home to help the host organize the food for the Amen meal. The smell reminds me that because of the research for this study, my full-time job teaching, all the arrangements for traveling for a post-doc in the USA, my daughter's Bat Mitzvah organizations, and my three young kids, that I didn't eat enough today. I try to concentrate on the spiritual side of the ritual and forget the smell.

We stand in a circle, as Tehila asked us to give our hands to our neighbors and close our eyes. Tehila calls: "We are praying for the health of …", she recites name by name, from all the notes that the women gave her before. Some women added names spontaneously, and I join them, thinking about some of my relatives. Tehila continues: "I direct a long, long beam of light, from the Temple to every one of us. All of us are connecting now to each other and God." We sing together. Our eyes are still closing. She started a kind of meditation with us, calling us to connect to our inner point.

If somebody told me that I would take part in a ritual like this, holding hands with women that I don't know, trying to connect to myself, and simultaneously to the Temple and other women, I wouldn't believe it. However, as I felt in other Amen rituals, I slowly forget my critical academic and feminist perspective. The evidence is the tears that fall freely from my eyes. When I opened them, I saw tears on other women's faces. Something happened here, and it's hard to explain it in words. When we open our eyes, we see not only the tears, but nice small tables with fantastic food that the host and her helpers organized for us. The Amen meal started, and the sweets – fruit and homemade cookies and chocolate accompanied the salt from my tears

My research diary, June 2011

When I interviewed Tehila, she told me that she does not call herself "Orthodox" or "religious." She just has a direct connection to God. She uses this connection in her job as an alternative treatment. When I asked why she organized these Amen meals every Rosh Chodesh (the first day of the Jewish calendar month), she answered simply: "Why is it ideal to open the channels of plenty for the world at Rosh Chodesh? At this time, the sky is open, and we need to send it to all the world."

The unforgettable deep and meaningful experience with Tehila's group, led me to move from reading about rituals toward a broader framework. This group was unique, using the most mystic symbols, sending power through a long beam of light and the leader. The other leaders I met defined themselves on the spectrum between members of the strictest Ultra-Orthodox community to the most rigid Modern Orthodox community, while Tehila did not describe herself as religious. The participants could participate in the ritual dressed in jeans like secular women; not most of the leaders, who usually dressed more modestly than the other attendees. These components, and some minutes of meditation in the ritual, led me to study the New Age movement. In the second part of the chapter, the aim is to show that this ritual is part of the New Age phenomenon. It is based mostly on my interpretation of participant observations, accompanied by quotations from the interviewees representing the New Age characteristics, even without knowing what the movement is.

Hanegraaff (2000) reformulated Geertz's (1966) famous definition of religion as "Any symbolic system which influences human action by providing possibilities for ritually maintaining contact between the everyday world and a more general meta-empirical framework of meaning" (p. 295). Based on this definition, he argued that the New Age is a form of religion, with

> another symbolic system, in terms of which another ensemble of objects, words, images, sounds, actions, etc. carry another complex of meanings […] it enables [the believers …] to maintain contact between their everyday lives and the larger, more general framework of meaning.
>
> *p. 296*

The symbolic system, detailed in the first part of the chapter, is represented by Hanegraaff's (2002) insight about the New Age as a "spiritual supermarket" (p. 299). Other characteristics, also based on Hanegraaff (2002), are the individual choice to participate in the ritual, the contact between the participants' lives. The larger framework will be shown by the unmediated connection between the participants and God, the new relationship between the body and the soul, and a critical attitude toward the mainstream culture.

The New Age is "a manifestation *par excellence* of postmodern consumer society, the members of which use, recycle, combine and adapt existing religious ideas and practices as they see fit" (Hanegraaff 2002, 288). Therefore, the New Age is exemplified as a religious supermarket where the consumers have their spiritual shopping (Hanegraaff 1996, 2002). Ochs

(2007) argued that the new Jewish women's rituals allow improvisation, personalization, and choices, and enable creativity and spontaneity. She pointed out the simplicity of the rituals and the use of elementary materials that everyone can find at home such as candles and food. The Amen rituals are constructed and initiated at the request of the participants. The central ritual is carried out, but the ceremony integrates additional elements, such as the recitation of psalms, group study, candle lighting, and singing.

The various unlimited optional structures and combinations of the Amen rituals, detailed above reflect this eclectic private symbolic system. Some events included only a short Amen meal. In the old and small apartment in Mekor Baruch were five women who held the ritual every Wednesday. Small plates with tiny pieces of the necessary food for the blessings, a time period of twenty to thirty minutes, just the reciting of psalms and a quick Amen meal, and the ritual is done. There is a monthly event in the Har Nof neighborhood on the other side of the spectrum, which usually takes about three to four hours. During the meeting, every woman puts her handmade dish down and goes directly to the kitchen. All the women "play" with the dough together, preparing amazing rolls and *Challah*. When they arrive, they start the "*Challah* taking" ritual and put the rolls in the oven. Moving to the living room, they begin the Amen ritual with the baking smell all around. This group also functions in order to share and support each other, so every circle can take a long time. The meal itself, in the end, enables the creation of sub-groups and another round of sharing, from complaints about the university or job tasks to advice about children's education.

Other rituals started with the Amen meal, moved to the "*Challah* taking" ritual, and the women took the rolls for home baking. The candle lighting and the singing are at the end. Other rituals started with the reciting of psalms or halachic studies, moved to lighting candles and singing, and the Amen itself was at the end. Every group of women they invited decided for themselves, sometimes during the ritual, how to construct the order of the proceedings. Some are open to leave it to the women's choice every time. Other groups decided that the host has the right to organize the ritual structure as she wishes. Some groups, however, keep their order strictly "this is the way we do that," as they put it.

Following Berger (1967), Hanegraaff (2002) argued that contemporary Western religion is based on personal conscious choice. The privatization and individualism of their rituals characterize the religious and spiritual experiences of the New Age participants. The meaning framework builds on the movement from collective symbolism to manipulating eclectic private symbolic systems (Hanegraaff 1999). Indeed, a fundamental aspect of the spiritual market of symbols is the individual/private choice to conduct the Amen rituals. It is more than the questions of where, when, and with whom to share the spirituality and rituals. The choice itself is different from those in the usual religious systems.

> There is no real obligation. You don't have to come regularly. You go and try, and that's it. There is no criterion to get in. You don't have to go to your specific group, and there is a place for everyone. The widow wants to get married; the divorced woman wants to get married, and the single wants to get married […] all of them will come – women who wait for a baby and the bereaved mother. Everyone comes with the same sorrow she goes to sleep with at night. Everything reaches heaven. All wishes must be realized.
>
> *Tamar, Ultra-Orthodox, medical secretary*

Tali (secular, 50, white collar worker) addressed the choice aspect: "This is my choice. I feel connected to the mystical side, so I use any opportunity to take from the religion well. This is not a real religious ritual, so it's easy. Everything is not obligated here; it's easy-going". Shoshana (37, Orthodox, high school teacher) defined herself as strict Orthodox. She referred to the non-existence of religious obligations in the ritual:

> for the Amen meal you don't have to keep the religious duties. There is something nice, enabling about it. All of us have problems; we all have a hard time; all of us are human beings; we all have things to be thankful for and other things we are still waiting for. The ritual is in a particular place that doesn't cost anything, I do not have to do anything, just being here and now. It enables me to experience release, and at the same time, to feel something spiritual. There is something in the pleasure of spirituality that is higher than other nice things. Something higher, something that gives you power. I give to the creator, and the creator, with all of his good and plenty, enables me to feel connected to the origin, to him.

These ritual participants represent self-spirituality (Heelas 1996). The participants themselves are the ultimate sources of meaning and authority (Heelas & Woodhead 2005). The non-obligation Amen meal is a free choice. It is in marked contrast to the strict rituals of Jewish Orthodoxy, with its prayers and other practices, constructed by and authorized by men.

There is an attempt at an unmediated relationship between the Amen meal participants and God (Neriya-Ben Shahar 2015). This connection is a part of the New Age phenomenon, where Jewish individuals are looking for unmediated religious experience (Werczberger 2017). According to Ochs (2007), one of the tools for creating a new Jewish ritual is understanding the deep connection the Jewish people feel they have to God. After a long history of exclusion, the women also feel they need the link and a close relationship with God. Hodaya (Ultra-Orthodox, 25, and works at a photoshop) declared: "Women are connected to God […] Amen means to put a stamp on God's blessings. It's significant, especially for women, because we are very close to God." Tova (Modern Orthodox, 60, teacher) said: "Women are connected to Him, to our Father in heaven." "I think that God understands us. He understands that we like this thing [the ritual], he is waiting for it, and he is waiting for us, that we will hold and realize it. Because we are gentler, softer, we just need this thing [the ritual]," said Tamar (Ultra-Orthodox, 34, medical secretary). Shoshana (37, mother of eight, Orthodox, high school teacher) was one of the rare women who explicitly mentioned the New Age when she talked about God: "They call it the infinity … some of them call it the creator. All this culture of the New Age [… these rituals have] connection to the place of Good, place of plenty, place of God's blessings."

The importance of the connection is between women and God and between the women and their bodies. The Jewish religion governs the physical body by strict rules such as kosher food and the laws of purity (*niddah*). The food in the ritual is the reason for the blessings and the many Amen responses, and therefore it is necessary for the ritual. Usually, there is a differentiation between public prayer and Torah study spaces, they are mostly for men, without formal and ritual food, and the private spaces, where the family eat together on the holidays and Shabbat. In Amen meals, the female gathering itself is new, as is the women sharing food and talking after the formal ritual is completed.

The women's food sharing led to other levels of sharing. Ochs suggested that marking what was previously unmarked is one of the characteristics of women's rituals. These rituals "mark events linked to women's bodily experiences that previously have not evoked formal Jewish responses" (Ochs 2007, 48). The control of women's bodies is strict and includes rules of modesty and purity. For Orthodox Jewish women to talk about the body, and the connection between body and soul, is almost taboo. Miscarriages, fertility, and the monthly period are forbidden subjects in public conversation in many communities. While the formal ritual bath is mostly private and confidential, the Amen meal is an opportunity to share stories about fertility and other sensitive issues. Prayers and conversations related to the female body's functions became an integral part of some Amen rituals.

The most moving and meaningful Amen meals that I took part in were those that almost became a support group that enabled participants to talk about their most intimate, significant space, the female body. The New Age spirituality has a strong belief in cosmic and personal healing (Werczberger 2017), and many of the prayers were linked to maternal functions: fertility, healthy pregnancy, childbirth, children's health, the physical and emotional strength to care for children and partners, and cooking and housework. These topics are invested with great emotional energy, and tears accompany the women's prayers. Sarit (secular, 26, works for communication company) told me: "I got married a year ago, and I want to be pregnant (she used the biblical term: *Lehipaked*)." Like her friends, Sarit believes that women who take part in the Amen ritual and their prayers have expressive power.

Women talking about the body is often connected to the "taking Challah" ritual. Because taking Challah is a commandment for women, which is linked to birth and fertility, the women generally honor their friends in the ninth month of pregnancy with the dough's actual separation. Many women hold a familial/social taking Challah ceremony before birth. At times, however, women with fertility problems ask to have the ceremony, and they weep with their friends. It seems that women wish to appropriate for themselves a place that respects their bodies and allows them to pray for it without feeling rejected, and without purity/impurity issues (Douglas 1966).

However, this intimate discourse had substantial limitations. Even though their conversations about husbands, children, mothers-in-law, and so on risk being stigmatized as gossip, the women remain modest and respect the ritual and the privacy of the people they hear. Only a few women shared their marriage problems, and I heard no stories relating to sexual issues, even among the secular groups. Legitimation to talk, discuss, and pray about the female body regarding fertility and pregnancy problems created a safe place for these women, but not without boundaries.

Hanegraaff (1996) argued that the New Age ideology represents a "systematic counterreaction to existing cultural forms" (p. 514), which could be defined as "based on a common pattern of criticism directed against dominant cultural trends" (p. 515). This criticism reflects a fundamental dissatisfaction toward the culture (Hanegraaff 2000). I argue that the New Age aspects mentioned here represent the women's systematic dissatisfaction with Orthodox Judaism and culture. The creation of a new Amen meal ritual reflects a counterreaction to existing Jewish rituals. The individual choice and unique combination of the ritual components, the non-obligatory nature of the ritual, accompanied by body and soul sharing among the participants, are different from the normally strict, ordered, and compulsory rules that only apply to men in ordinary Jewish rituals.

Orthodox Judaism is constructed around strict halachic texts such as the *Shulchan Aruch*, and hundreds of halachic books derived from it, that control every moment of the Orthodox person's life, from waking up till sleeping (and including both of them also), in an annual cycle. The Amen meal is rich in details and symbols as well, some of them are traditional (lighting candles) or even halachic based (the order of the blessings and taking Challah). However, the personal choice of where, when, why, how, with whom to conduct the ritual is based on the women's wishes. They do not recite the blessings because they want to eat. They bless together because they want to get maximum amens for the ritual. They do not take Challah because they bake it for the family in their private kitchen. They choose to make it together to share the experience (and the hard work of the dough making). They are not obligated to do this ritual at all. They created the setting because they just want to do it. For a religion full of obligations and duties, this is new and different.

Orthodox Judaism enables a personal religious experience inside the community. Every man can hide in the *Tallit* and cry during the high holidays' prayers, but he must have a *minyan* (a group of ten men) to fulfill many obligations. The women, excluded from the community's experiences and mostly not included in the *minyan*, create for themselves an alternative women's society, where they can have the personal experience of being in a community.

There are invisible walls between communities in Israel, based on their attitudes toward strict halachic and also political rules. The "all Jewish women are invited" Amen meals are genuinely open to all. The Amen meal becomes like hospitals and health centers, places where everyone is the same. This might be one reason for men's opposition to this ritual (Neriya-Ben Shahar 2019). Like every mainstream religion and culture, Jewish actors, especially men, do not like a counterculture that takes a critical stance. They prefer not to have diversity that might limit their men-only religious power.

This counterculture criticism is one of the characteristics of the New Age movement: The spiritual market, the individual choices, the unmediated experience of connection between the participants and God, and the relationship between the body and the soul are all involved here. The detailed ritual description, accompanied by the argument that it is part of the New Age movement, leads to the last part of the chapter, figuring out why this ritual started here and now. The answer will position the Amen meal in its social and cultural context.

Amen Meal: Social and Cultural Context

The Amen meal is, like other New Age rituals, one of the responses to postmodernism and post-feminism. People felt they had lost their way and sought the solution in new ways of achieving spirituality.

Hanegraaff (2000) described the experiences of dissatisfaction with the mainstream culture. Daily reality does not include meaningful dimensions of personal and spiritual experiences. The grand narratives of science and rationality lose their credibility, leading to the rise of the New Age phenomenon (Hanegraaff 2002; Werczberger 2017). They cannot give meaning to human experiences, forcing New Age religiosity to take over. Western consumer culture based on individualism lost its grand narratives and created a new voluntary spiritual/religious.

In the Jewish/Israeli context, there is dissatisfaction with two narrative systems, religious and the secular. The connection between religion and state in Israel leads to a situation where faith and belief are always part of political struggle. The religious and ethnic gap and inequality in Israel are huge. The religious side's disappointment could be a part of the saturation of religious strictness that does not leave space for personal spirituality and experiences. Dissatisfaction with secular culture can stimulate a deep search for a spirituality that does not connect with traditional religious obligations. Another dissatisfaction is derived from the fact that Israeli Judaism has groups and classes where it is hard to change one's community, not only to become religious or change from Ultra-Orthodox or Modern Orthodox but also to move from specific Ultra-Orthodox groups to a different one or from Modern Orthodox to another community.

While the first context is connected to the ritual's religious side, the second context is post-feminism related to the gender side. The feminist norms and reality led the women to education and workplaces, promised them the public space's salvation. However, the decline of the women-circle, the individualistic life, left them without the support they enjoyed for many generations. The gap between the ideology and the reality, between the release of the feminist discourse, to the real life of women in Western workplaces, is enormous. The new superwomen were required to double their efforts, to do everything inside and outside the home. The second, sometimes the third job added to the traditional domestic and caring responsibilities (Gill 2016; Sperling and Owen 2018).

In Israel, the social norms for women created superwomen with large families and, simultaneously, full-time jobs. The homemade food and hosting other families for Shabbat and holidays built more muscles for these superwomen. The counterreaction is powerful, as Michal (Modern Orthodox, 50, architect) explained:

> These women want to return home, in its real meaning. The women are tired. They are tired of being perfect professional women and amazing mothers. Mothers with all the care that is simultaneously teaching and cooking and baking homemade food. My mother used to say that we are the generation that got all the work, from all directions. We need to do everything and then apologize. We don't have anything for ourselves, we don't give up on ourselves, and then we still feel the guilt. These women are tired, and these rituals can take them back, to home.

Therefore, I argue that the general dissatisfaction and specific disappointments led to a New Age ritual solution. The consequence is creating a women's space that enables a formulation of non-obligatory religious spirituality. At the same time, the ritual allows for a formulation of non-feminist womanhood. In the very divisive Israeli society (Goodman and Fischer 2004; Goodman and Yona 2004), women from all the socioeconomic classes, secular, traditional, Orthodox and Ultra-Orthodox, from all ethnic origins and geographic locations get together. They based a traditional ritual (Bilu 1998a, 1998b; Leon 2009, 2010; Yadgar 2015) to support their spiritual needs and overcome all other definitions and separations.

The Jewish women rewrote womanhood for themselves, created new and renewed female rituals. These rituals addressed traditional women's lives based on home, children, food, hugs, and women's support. The women's circle, the understanding of the women's body experiences, included fertility and birth, that tried to be hidden, is an essential part of the rituals.

The result is a popular ritual that functions as a vast and open spiritual shopping center. Women who need a traditional ritual get it; women who look for new experiences get those. If they want female empowerment or traditional female roles, they can find it there also. They invented a social-religious event, with fun and a good meal, and spiritual and emotional food. This ritual is connected to the old traditions but not inherent to the Jewish religion since "our mothers" did not do it. The ritual is also connected to womanhood but defiantly not intrinsic to femininity. While most Orthodox Jewish communities still separate women from many religious rituals, women created new and renewed rituals for themselves. These events invited secular career women and stay at home Ultra-Orthodox mothers of twelve to participate in the spiritual supermarket. For some hours they can enjoy participating in the circle of older women, with its consequent support and solidarity, without any awkwardness. The Amen rituals enable creating a new space that supplies women spiritual, feminine, and social gratifications and needs. A new powerful ritual for New Age powerful women.

References

Barthes, Roland. 1968. *Elements of Semiology*, trans. Annette Lavers and Colin Smith. New York: Hill and Lang.
Barthes, Roland. 1977. *Image, Music, Text*, trans. Stephen Heath. London: Fontana Press.
Berger, Peter L. 1967. *The Sacred Canopy: Elements of Sociological Theory of Religion*. New York: Doubleday.
Bilu, Yoram. 1998a. "Saints, cult, and pilgrimage as a universal phenomenon." In *To the Tombs of the Saints: Pilgrimages and Hillulot in Israel*. Ed. Rivka Gonen. Jerusalem: The Israel Museum, 11–26 (Hebrew).
Bilu, Yoram. 1998b. "Cult and Holy Place in Contemporary Israel." *Jerusalem Studies of Jewish Folklore* 19–20: 652–84 (Hebrew).
Bilu, Yoram. 2003. "From Milah (Circumcision) to Milah ("Word"): Male Identity and Rituals of Childhood in the Jewish Ultraorthodox Community." *Ethos* 31, no. 2: 172–203.
Brown. Lyn M. and Carol Gilligan. 1992. *Meeting at the Crossroad: Women's Psychology and Girls' Development*. Cambridge, MA: Harvard University Press.
Douglas, Mar. 1966. *Purity and Danger*. New York: Praeger.
El-Or, Tamar. 1994. *Educated and Ignorant: Ultraorthodox Jewish Women and their World*. Boulder, CO: Lynne Rienner.
El-Or, Tamar. 2006. *Reserved Seats: Religion, Gender, and Ethnicity in Contemporary Israel*. Tel Aviv: Am Oved. www.tamarelor.com/index.php/books/reserved-seats/.
Geertz, Clifford. 1966. "Religion as a Cultural System." In *Anthropological Approaches to the Study of Religion*. Ed. Michael Banton. ASA Monographs 3. London: Tavistock Publications, 1–46.
Gill, Rosalind. 2016. "Post-Postfeminism? New Feminist Visibilities in Postfeminist Times." *Feminist Media Studies* 16, no. 4: 610–30.
Goodman, Yehuda and Shlomo Fischer. 2004. "Toward an Understanding of Secularism and Religiosity in Israel: The Secularization Thesis and Possible Alternatives." In *Maelstrom of Identities: A Critical Look at Religion and Secularization in Israel*. Eds. Yehuda Goodman and Yossi Yonah. Jerusalem: Hakibutz Hameuhad and Van Leer, 346–90 (Hebrew).
Goodman, Yehuda and Yossi Yonah. 2004. "Introduction: Religiousness and Secularity in Israel: Possibilities for Alternative Views." In *Maelstrom of Identities: A Critical Look at Religion and Secularization in Israel*. Eds. Yehuda Goodman and Yossi Yonah. Jerusalem: Hakibutz Hameuhad and Van Leer, 3–37 (Hebrew).
Hanegraaff, Wouter J. 1996. *New Age Religion and Western Culture: Esotericism in the Mirror of Secular Thought*. New York: Brill.
Hanegraaff, Wouter J. 1999. "New Age Spiritualities as Secular Religion: A Historian's Perspective." *Social Compass* 46, no. 2: 145–60.
Hanegraaff, Wouter J. 2000. "New Age Religion and Secularization." *Numen* 47, no. 3: 288–312.
Hanegraaff, Wouter J. 2002 "New Age Religion." In *Religion in the Modern World: Traditions and Transformations*. Eds. Linda Woodhead, Christopher Partridge, and Hiroko Kawanami. London: Routledge, 249–63.
Heelas, Paul. 1996. *The New Age Movement: The Celebration of the Self and the Sacralization of Modernity*. Oxford: Blackwell.
Heelas, Paul and Linda Woodhead. 2005. *The Spiritual Revolution: Why Religion Is Giving Way to Spirituality*. Oxford: Blackwell.
Leon, Nissim. 2009. "Mizrahi Secularity (Soft Traditionalism from a Post-Orthodox Perspective)." *Pe'amim: Studies in Oriental Jewry* 122–123: 89–113 (Hebrew).
Leon, Nissim. 2010. *Soft Ultra-Orthodoxy: Religious Renewal in Oriental Jewry in Israel*. Jerusalem: Yad Ben Zvi (Hebrew).
Mauthner, Natasha and Andrea Doucet. 1998. "Reflections on a Voice-Centred Relational Method: Analyzing Maternal and Domestic Voices." In *Feminist Dilemmas in Qualitative Research: Public Knowledge and Private Lives*. Eds. Jane Ribbens and Rosalind Edward. London: Sage, 119–46.
Neriya-Ben Shahar, Rivka. 2015. "'At Amen Meals, it's Me and God'—Religion and Gender: A New Jewish Women's Ritual." *Contemporary Jewry* 35: 153–72.
Neriya-Ben Shahar, Rivka. 2018. "The Amen Meal: Jewish Women Experience Lived Religion through a New Ritual." *Nashim* 33: 160–78.
Neriya-Ben Shahar, Rivka. 2019. "'We Need to Worship Outside of Conventional Boundaries': Jewish Orthodox Women Negotiating Time, Space and Halachic Hegemony through New Ritual." *The Contemporary Jewry* 39, no. 3: 473–95.
Ochs, Vanessa L. 2007. *Inventing Jewish Ritual*. Philadelphia, PA: Jewish Publication Society.

Reinharz, Shulamit. 1992. *Feminist Methods in Social Research*. New York and Oxford: Oxford University Press.

Sered, Susan Starr. 1988. "The Domestication of Religion: The Spiritual Guardianship of Elderly Jewish Women." *Man* 23, no. 3: 506–21.

Sered, Susan Starr. 1991. "Conflict, Complement, and Control: Family and Religion among Middle Eastern Jewish Women in Jerusalem." *Gender & Society* 5: 10–29.

Sered, Susan Starr. 1992. *Women as Ritual Experts: The Religious Lives of Elderly Jewish Women in Jerusalem*. New York: Oxford University Press.

Sosis, Richard and W. Penn Handwerker. 2011. "Psalms and Coping with Uncertainty: Religious Israeli Women's Responses to the 2006 Lebanon War." *American Anthropologist* 113, no. 1: 40–55.

Sperling, Liz and Mairead Owen eds. 2018. *Women and Work: The Age of Postfeminism*. London: Routledge.

Strauss, Anselm and Juliet M. Corbin. 1990. *Basics of Qualitative Research*. Los Angeles, CA: Sage.

Strauss, Anselm and Juliet M. Corbin. 1994. "Grounded Theory Methodology." In *The Sage Handbook of Qualitative Research*. Eds. Norman K. Denzin and Yvonna S. Lincoln. Thousand Oaks, CA: Sage, 273–85.

Targin-Zeller, Lea. 2014. "Modesty for Heaven's Sake: Authority and Creativity among Female Ultra-Orthodox Teenagers in Israel." *Nashim* 26: 75–96.

Taylor-Guthartz, Lindsey. 2016. *Overlapping Worlds: The Religious Lives of Orthodox Jewish Women in Contemporary London*. Ph.D. diss. London: University College London.

Taylor-Guthartz, Lindsey. 2021. *Challenge and Conformity: The Religious Lives of Jewish Women*. Liverpool: Liverpool University Press.

Turner, Victor. 1973. "Symbols in African Ritual." *Science* 179, no. 4078: 1100–05.

Werczberger, Rachel. 2017. *Jews in the Age of Authenticity: Jewish Spiritual Renewal in Israel*. New York: Peter Lang.

Yadgar, Yaacov. 2006. "Gender, Religion, and Feminism: The Case of Jewish Israeli Traditionalists." *Journal for the Scientific Study of Religion* 45, no. 3: 353–70.

Yadgar, Yaacov. 2015. "Traditionalism." *Cogent Social Sciences* 1(1). https://doi.org/10.1080/23311886.2015.1061734

29
MODELS OF SEXUALITY (AND MARRIAGE) IN THE JEWISH TRADITION

Michael J. Broyde

Introduction

The Jewish tradition looks at its sexual law much like any standard religious or legal system does historically. Five common features are readily present within the classical Jewish legal tradition:

1. It prohibits incest.
2. It prohibits adultery.
3. It prohibits rape, and it prohibits marital rape – it does so much earlier than many other legal systems.
4. It recognizes that marriage serves both the purpose of companionship and reproduction.
5. Like other religious legal systems – and the common law – it prohibits bestiality, masturbation, and all other deviant sexual acts.

This chapter seeks to explain why the Jewish tradition until (relatively) recently did not mandate monogamy and comfortably endorsed non-marital sexuality. My argument will be counterintuitive to some. After all, Jews, like Christians, start with the creation story of Adam and Eve as set out in Genesis 2. Among the many basic lessons taught by the creation story is that God took but one rib from Adam and created but one Eve, who then partnered with Adam to create all humans.

The text in Genesis 2:24 seems to be as clear a theological endorsement of monogamy as one can find: "Thus, a man leaves his father and mother, and clings to his wife, and the two become one flesh." This verse is not speaking to Adam or Eve but to biblical readers generally to give them a sense of the divine imprimatur of monogamous marriage.[1] God could have taken two ribs from Adam – one from each side – and created Eve and Vivian, and the biblical story would have a different flavor (and would be harder to teach to children!). People should, this verse tells us, leave their parents and marry a single spouse to whom they must cling.

While incidents of polygamy – marriage by one man to two or more women – do recur in later stories within Genesis, a clear theme remains in the first book of the Torah that monogamy ought to be the biblical ideal. Abraham becomes a polygamist only after his wife Sarah appears to be barren, and this brings trouble to his household.[2] Jacob is tricked into polygamy and told that he cannot marry his true love Rachel unless he keeps Leah as a wife also.[3] There is no case of non-monarchical polygamy in the biblical tradition other than in cases of infertility or fraud in the creation of the marriage. The biblical Hebrew word for a co-wife in a polygamous relationship, *tzrah*, means literally "trouble." This is certainly a stinging indictment of polygamy.

Why then is exclusive monogamy not part of the Jewish tradition's contribution to modern marriage? Why is there no Talmudic exegesis noting that the verses in Genesis seem to mandate monogamy?[4] The answer is found in Jewish Law. The Bible itself – in the laws set out Exodus, Leviticus, and Deuteronomy – permits polygamy. And for the Jewish legal tradition, these explicit legal texts permitting polygamy supersede any inferences against polygamy that can be drawn from the stories found in Genesis. Consider the following verses from the biblical law:

> When a man has two wives, one beloved and one hated and both the loved and the hated wives both bear him children; however, the first born child is from the hated wife.[5]
> A king may not have too many wives, lest they lead his heart astray.[6]
> Do not marry a woman and then her sister to torment her as her rival.[7]
> If a man takes another wife, he may not diminish [this wife's] allowance, clothing or conjugal rights.[8]

Biblical Jewish Law permits polygamy, and Jewish Law thus permitted polygamy as well with little questioning.[9] There is almost nothing in the Talmudic literature that would cause one to question this.

While biblical law permits polygamy, it also prohibits various other sexual relationships and these prohibitions, too, entered Jewish Law. First, Jewish Law prohibits homosexual relationships based on a set of clear verses in Leviticus.[10] Second, Jewish Law prohibits polyandry – the marriage of one woman to multiple men – as a violation of the very nature of marriage which requires sexual exclusivity by the woman.[11] Third, Jewish Law prohibits sexual promiscuity. To most rabbis, random coupling without any ongoing relationship violated the biblical injunction against harlotry.[12] Other authorities limited this precise biblical violation to cases of sexual slavery and agreed that promiscuity was prohibited by an ancient rabbinic decree governing prostitution.[13] Three types of licit sexual association were left intact in the Hebrew Bible and in the Jewish legal tradition: (1) monogamous marriage; (2) polygamous marriage; and (3) non-marital but regular (rather than random) sexual companionship. These I shall take up in turn.

Sex and Marriage Laws

Marriage requires the mutual consent of both parties. Not only must this consent be unconditionally given, but as a matter of legal and religious theory, a person is under no ethical or religious duty to give that consent. Jewish Law allows a person to decline consent to marry for a number of reasons – for example, because the prospective spouse lacks financial resources or will not commit to a larger dowry or because the man or woman in question does not love the suitor, or loves someone else more. Marriage is a discretionary act in almost all cases. The more salient rules of marriage at Jewish Law are not the entrance rules, however, but the exit rules.[14] The Torah has only a few brief verses that incidentally mention divorce in the course of describing the remarriage of one's divorcee. Deuteronomy 24 states:

> When a man marries a woman and lives with her, and she does not find favor in his eyes, as he finds a sexual blemish on her part, and he gives her a bill of divorce, which he puts in her hand and sends her from the house. She leaves his house and goes to

the house of another. However, if the second husband hates her and writes her a bill of divorce, gives it to her and sends her from the house, or the second husband dies, the first husband, who sent her out, cannot remarry her.[15]

Talmudic authorities took these verses to mean that the husband has a unilateral right to divorce his wife without fault, but the wife has no reciprocal right to divorce her husband except in cases of hard fault.[16] Exit from marriage was thus drastically different from entry into marriage. It did not require the consent of both parties. The marriage could end when the husband alone wished to end it. Marriage was imbalanced in other ways as well. A man could be married to more than one wife, any of whom he could divorce at will, whereas a woman could be married to only one man at a time, and she had no clearly defined right of exit except on proof of her husband's serious fault.[17] Where the husband and wife no longer wished to live together, the husband could marry another and continue to support his first wife.

The Talmud mitigated these disparities between men and women by creating a minimum dower (*ketubah*) for all brides which was payable by the husband upon divorce. Payment of a minimum dower became, by rabbinic decree, a precondition to any marriage. A wife could, as a precondition to enter into marriage, insist on a dower higher than the minimum promulgated by the rabbis.[18] Thus, while the right to divorce remained unilateral with the husband with no right of consent by the wife, it was now restricted by a clear financial obligation imposed on the husband to compensate his wife if he exercised his right to engage in unilateral divorce absent judicially declared fault on her part. The Talmud even records views that if one cannot pay the financial obligation, then one is prohibited from being divorced.[19]

The Talmud also granted the wife the right to sue for divorce on proof of the husband's repugnancy, impotence, cruelty, and other grounds. In such a case, the husband was required to divorce his wife and often pay the dower too. The wife could divorce her husband who refused to have children by her,[20] and restrict his rights to divorce through a *ketubah* provision.[21] Soon after the close of the Talmudic period, the rabbis of that time (called *geonim*) greatly expanded the wife's right to sue for divorce. According to most opinions of the *geonim*, all the wife had to do was leave the household for a period of time, and she had an automatic right to divorce and claim at least a part of her dower.

These two changes in Talmudic law by the *geonim* were profound. These rabbis argued that marriage, like all partnerships, requires the perpetual consent of both parties to function properly. Thus, when either partner chooses to leave, the marriage should end. The *geonim* devised a mechanism to ensure that it did end – a form of annulment,[22] or coerced divorce that would be enforced even in the absence of proof of fault by the other party.[23] By the end of the *geonim* era (900 CE), the Jewish tradition had embraced a model of weak marriage which included few legal bonds that united the couple when love and friendship ended and gave either party a unilateral right to divorce.

Within two hundred years of the Jewish expulsion from Babylonia, the Jewish legal tradition largely spurned the *geonim*'s model of weak marriage in favor of three alternative models which came to exist concurrently.[24] The first was a model of strong marriage with limited and equal rights to divorce and no polygamy. This model came to prevail among European Jews led by Rabbenu Gershom. In Gershom's view, Jewish Law did not authorize the annulment of marriages. A better way to equalize the rights of the husband and wife to divorce was to restrict the rights of the husband and prohibit unilateral no-fault divorce by either husband or wife. Divorce was limited to cases of provable fault of either party or mutual consent by both parties. Fault was vastly redefined to exclude cases of soft fault such as repugnancy and, in only a few cases, could one spouse be forced to divorce the other.[25] And, as polygamy was prohibited, considerable pressure encouraged the man and woman in a troubled marriage to stay married. Absent fault, neither party could seek divorce without the consent of the other; unless divorce was in the best interest of both of them they would remain married.[26] Under this model, divorce became exceedingly rare.

A second model of slightly weaker marriage developed among other European Jews. Proponents of this model agreed that Jewish Law did not authorize the sweeping annulment power that the Babylonian rabbis had countenanced. They also agreed with Rabbenu Gershom that the best way to equalize the rights of husband and wife to divorce was to restrict the rights of the husband and prohibit unilateral no-fault divorce by either party. But these rabbis argued that desertion or abandonment was a proper ground for divorce. Thus, when the marital union had ceased to exist and the couple had de facto ended all marital relations, divorce could be compelled. Rabbenu Chaim Or Zarua was the authority who clearly elaborated on this approach.[27] Marriages, he said, could not be easily broken, but long-term abandonment was serious fault which entitled the abandoned party to sue for divorce.

A third model of weaker marriage emerged among Sefardi Jewry. This model effectively revived most of the Talmudic rules of divorce and polygamy. Proponents of this model, too, argued that Jewish Law did not authorize annulment. They also limited divorce to cases of hard fault – but only if the wife sued for divorce. Husbands could sue for divorce unilaterally and without proof of fault, provided they paid their dower. Under this model, a woman was expected to protect herself by insisting on her rights at the time of entry into marriage. If she wished to restrict her husband's entry and exit rights, she could do so by imposing a high dower payment. If she wished to curtail his right to take a second wife, she could insist on that right in the *ketubah*. She could use the waiver of her rights under the dower contract as an inducement to be given a unilateral divorce. In this model, marriage was a contractually regulated partnership, albeit one whose exit costs were contractually delineated but could be restricted.[28]

Even this brief historical summary of three thousand years of Jewish marriage and sex law underscores a few doctrines that are quite different from those that prevailed in the Christian West. First, in the Jewish tradition, marriage was never centrally constructed as monogamous, and monogamy was never constructed in its hard Catholic form of one husband with one wife for one lifetime. Second, divorce was always recognized as normative and permitted, albeit sometimes restricted, and mutual consent divorces were always permitted throughout Jewish history. Third, parties were free to construct the economic basis of their own marriage and could provide financial incentives to discourage or encourage divorce if they so wished. Fourth, Jewish Law maintained diverse models of divorce with no deep stigma associated with divorce.

Of course, this sexual diversity no longer exists. For the past two centuries, Jewish communities have slowly abandoned these early models. At a national rabbinic conference called in 1950 by the chief rabbis of Israel, Israeli Orthodox Jewry passed an enactment generally making monogamy and mutual consent divorce (with fault-based divorce possible) binding upon all Jews irrespective of their communal affiliations.[29] This decree reflected communal practices throughout Jewry with only very minor dissent from small Iranian Jewish communities. For the last fifty years, only one model of marriage is practiced among Jews, though a diversity of models and practices in marriage remains available in theory.[30]

Sexual Companionship and Jewish Law

Just as there were diverse models of marriage, there were diverse norms governing extramarital sexuality within the Jewish tradition. Consider the opening discussion in the classical sixteenth-century code of Jewish Law, *Shulchan Arukh*, in the section dealing with marriage law. Here, Rabbi Joseph Karo writes:

> A woman is not considered married until she has a valid wedding ceremony properly done; but if a man and a woman have a sexual relationship in a promiscuous way not for the sake of marriage, it is nothing. Even if they had a sexual relationship for the sake of marriage in secret, she is not his wife, even if she agreed to have sexual relations with no other, but rather we use judicial coercion to remove her from his house.

However, Rabbi Moses Isserles, writing the glosses that form the other half of this Jewish Law code, writes:

> [She must be removed from the house because] she will be embarrassed to immerse in a ritual bath as directed by Jewish Law and instead they will have sexual relations when such are prohibited.[31] *But, if a man has a steady faithful sexual relationship with a woman outside of marriage, and she immerses when mandated by Jewish law, there are those who say that this conduct is proper*, and this is the *pelegesh* [faithful sexual companion][32] mentioned in the Bible. There are those who say that such conduct is prohibited, and one violated the biblical commandment of not bringing a prostitute into the community through such conduct and flogging is proper.[33]

The classical Jewish Law code of the middle of the sixteenth century has no substantial agreement on the nature of extramarital sexuality. One view considers all extramarital sexuality as illicit; the other permits non-marital sexuality so long as it is not furtive or embarrassing.

This diversity of opinion is reflected in other classical literature on Jewish views of extramarital sexuality. The Bible is replete with stories of extramarital sexual activity by Abraham,[34] Jacob,[35] Judge Gideon,[36] King Saul,[37] King David,[38] King Solomon,[39] and many others. The Talmud, too, is replete with discussions of sexual companionship devoid of any clear indication that such conduct is wrong.[40]

Four main views of extramarital sexual activity have emerged in Jewish Law based, in part, on these biblical and classical sources. One view is that of Maimonides: this view reads the Jewish Law prohibition against harlotry to prohibit virtually all non-marital sexual relationships. Maimonides does recognize the single right of a king to sexual companionship outside of marriage,[41] but this exception has also been read as a limitation on the conduct of others. A comparable view is taken by Rabbi Solomon Aderet and Rabbi Joseph Karo. They posit that open sexual companionship was permitted by the natural law and was practiced in pre-biblical times but was prohibited by operation of normative Jewish Law once the Torah was given.[42]

A second view is that earlier Jewish Law permitted sexual companionship relationships, but later rabbinical decrees prohibited them. This view is explicitly noted by Rabbi Meir Abulafiya who posits that sexual companionship outside of marriage is generally permitted by the Torah, so long as it is does not lead to promiscuity.[43] At the time of the Torah, marriage was an institution that allowed and enforced certain values of financial support, long-term sexual fidelity, and the like. The Torah, however, in Abulafiya's view, allowed one to opt for a sexual relationship without these values and guarantees. The rabbis of the Talmud sensed that this model of faithful companionship was deeply unstable and easily led to promiscuity.[44] They thus prohibited even faithful sexual companionship as a necessary prophylactic rule against promiscuity.

A third view was adopted by Nachmanides, who saw no obligation either in the Torah nor the Talmud for parties to be married before entering a faithful sexual relationship. What was important was that the maternity and paternity of any children of such relationships be clearly established.[45] Nachmanides recognized the danger that such relationships might devolve into promiscuity. However, all he was prepared to do was to warn of the dangers but not prohibit the activity of extramarital sex. This was also the view of Rabbi Shlomo Luria, who refused to prohibit relationships of sexual companionship, although he thought them unwise.[46]

A fourth view was even more permissive. There is a clear tradition of authorities in the Jewish tradition who saw no problem with faithful sexual relationships outside of marriage. Consider, for example, a simple response of the Ran, Rabbi Nissim Gerona, who was a foremost authority of the fourteenth century. This question was before him: Does a woman who had been in a relationship of sexual companionship with one man, who now wished to marry another man, have to wait the 90 days mandated by Jewish Law for divorcees so as to allow paternity to be clearly known? Or was she exempted from this requirement, as women who engaged in promiscuous sexual relationships are? Rabbenu Nissim responded:

> The view of Judah, that she has to wait 90 days, is correct. Since she was known to be his sexual companion, this is not called promiscuity at all, since the sexual companion is faithful to a particular man, and thus not considered sexually promiscuous. The Jewish forefathers engaged in similar conduct, as it notes in the Talmud's discussion of wives and sexual companions, which is that wives had betrothal and financial rights, and sexual companions had neither. ... Thus, in this case, since she resided with him in a matter permitted by Jewish law, raised their son and he treated her like a sexual companion, she is not called promiscuous, and thus not exempt from the rules of waiting to establish paternity.[47]

Similar such observations and even proposals to welcome sexual companionship are clearly stated by Rabbi Abraham ben David of Posquires,[48] Rabbi Chasdai ben Sholom,[49] Rabbi David Kimchi,[50] and many others.[51] A classical responsa written by Rabbi Jacob Emdem (1697–1776) lauded the advantages of sexual companionship for both men and women,[52] compared to the many disadvantages that flow from tight monogamy.[53] He seriously contemplated – and indeed came very close to advocating for – the return to sexual companionship as a norm within the Jewish tradition.

Nearly every classical recounting of Jewish views to sexual companionship notes these four views and weighs them with seriousness. Consider, for example, the modern encyclopedia of Jewish family law, entitled *Otzar Haposkim*. *Otzar Haposkim* is an incomplete recapping of Jewish family law started in 1950 and is currently still less than half-way done. In its introduction to the issue of extramarital sexuality, this work states as follows:

"BUT IF ONE HAS A FAITHFUL SEXUAL COMPANION":

A. Summary of the views with regard to this matter. In this matter, Rabbi Isserles (Rama) recounts two views when one designates a faithful sexual companion, there are those who say such conduct is permitted and those who state such conduct is prohibited and liable for flogging as a violation of Jewish law. However, besides these two views, there are other views among the decisors, there are those who argue that this conduct is not a violation of the prohibition against promiscuity, but a violation of the positive obligation to marry; there are others who say that the prohibition is rabbinic and there are others who say that such conduct is permitted but it is improper to do so.[54]

The subheadings of this section underscore this diversity of views:

    B. Those who rule that a faithful sexual companion violates the prohibition against promiscuity.
    C. Those who say that a faithful sexual companion violates the positive obligation to marry.
    D. Those who say that a faithful sexual companion violates only a rabbinic prohibition.
    E. Those who say that a faithful sexual companion does not violate any prohibition, but such conduct is improper.
    F. Those who say that a faithful sexual companion is completely permitted.

The Jerusalem Talmud contemplates the possibility that a faithful sexual companion is actually fully and completely married but without any of the financial obligations or rights associated with a normal marriage.[55] This view is also taken by Rabbi Elijah of Vilna (Gra) in his commentary on the code of Jewish Law.[56] If this view is correct, it presents yet another model of marriage: the minimal marriage. All that is pledged in such a marriage is sexual fidelity by the woman and nothing else. There is no obligation to supply mutual support, conjugal relations, nurture, clothing, or any other normal marital obligation.[57]

Just as Jewish Law had diverse and weak doctrines of marriage, so too, it had diverse doctrines of extramarital sexuality. All authorities agreed that prostitution is prohibited. But a number of authorities posit that various types of sexual companionship outside of the framework of marriage are permissible.

Final Thoughts on the Development of Jewish Marital Ethics and Jewish Sexual Ethics

This chapter has documented two features of the Jewish tradition that are rarely discussed today among conservative religious commentators. First, monogamy is by no means the only model of marriage found even in the biblical tradition. Jewish Law put forward only weak and relatively modern prohibitions against polygamy and none against divorce or serial monogamy.[58] Several other models of marriage and divorce found a place in the Jewish tradition – ranging from polygamous, unilateral no-fault marriages to monogamous, hard-fault marriages with many types in between. Indeed, given their diversity, one is hard pressed to define any real historical model of Jewish "marriage and sexuality" as normative. Second, while the Jewish tradition did not countenance promiscuity or prostitution, it did countenance and protect faithful sexual companionship outside and alongside of marriage – ranging from simple companionate cohabitation without contemplation of marriage to a type of "minimal marriage" that demanded sexual fidelity of the couple to each other but little else.

Today, neither polygamy nor sexual companionship nor unilateral, no-fault divorce are permitted within the Jewish community. Monogamous marriage is now the norm, sexual companionship outside of marriage is prohibited, and divorce is allowed only on grounds of mutual consent or provable hard fault. This has become the norm everywhere.

I would like to consider why there has been this practical narrowing of options by examining a set of basic texts in Jewish marriage and divorce law from *Shulchan Arukh, Even Haezer*, which is the basic code of Jewish family law. The answer that I posit is that Jews found monogamous marriage with only mutual consent exit rights (or faulted exit) to be a very successful system that provides a stable platform for marital happiness, social growth, child development, and economic enhancement.[59] Jewish Law did not mandate this result; Jewish experience did.

As background for this examination, one needs to know that the *Shulchan Arukh* is a law code with two authors. The first is Rabbi Josef Karo (1488–1575) who lived in Tzefat, Israel and was a Sefardi Jewish Law scholar, a follower of the Maimonidean tradition. The second was Rabbi Moses Isserles (1530–1572) who lived in Cracow and was a European Jewish Law scholar, a follower of the Tosafot tradition. They did not jointly write this work. Rather, Rabbi Karo wrote the code, and Rabbi Isserles wrote extensive glosses on it while citing opinions and traditions left out by Rabbi Karo. It remains to this day the normative work of Jewish Law.

The first source is the opening discussion of marriage, found in *Shulchan Arukh, Even Haezer* 1:1, which states:

KARO: Every man must marry a woman in order to reproduce. Anyone who is not having children is, as if, they are killers, reducers of the place of people on this earth, and causing God to leave the Jewish people.

ISSERLES: Anyone who is without a wife, lives without blessing and without Torah and is not called a person. Once one marries a woman, all of one's sins are forgiven, as it states "one who finds a wife finds goodness, and seeks the will of God." Proverbs 18:22.

Rabbi Karo, because he has no Jewish Law doctrine permitting licit sexual conduct outside of marriage, notes simply that marriage is mandatory; as such, it is needed and necessary to have children, which is an obligation according to Jewish Law. Rabbi Isserles, who has the doctrine of faithful sexual companion as a rival to marriage, has to persuade people to marry. Thus, the virtues of marriage are noted, even in a law book where such notations are normally kept to the absolute minimum.

A similar exchange takes place two short paragraphs later, in *Even Haezer* 1:3, which states:

KARO: There is a duty upon every person to marry a woman when he is 18; one who marries earlier until the age of 13, has done a good deed, and before the age of 13, it is like promiscuity. Under no circumstances should a person wait past the age of 20 to marry. One who passes 20 years and does not want to marry, a Jewish court will force him to marry in order to fulfill the obligation to reproduce.

ISSERLES: Nowadays, our custom is not to compel people on this matter. So, too, one who has not fulfilled the obligation to have children, and comes to marry a woman who cannot have children, such as a sterile, or an elderly woman or a minor, since he loves her, or because she is wealthy; even if, according to Jewish law we should have protested this marriage, we have a custom going back for many generations, not to examine matters of marriage. Even if a man marries a woman and lives with her for ten years without children, our custom is not to divorce, even though they did not fulfill the obligation to procreate. The same is true for all other matters of marriage, except that one may not marry one who is forbidden to have a sexual relationship with [such as incest].

Again, Rabbi Karo not only posits marriage as the only model but posits that these marriages can be compelled – one who waits to marry beyond the prescribed age is beaten by a rabbinical court as an inducement to find a spouse. Rabbi Isserles, as a proponent of the legal possibility of faithful sexual companionship outside of marriage, posits that marriages must have more to them than a lawful way to have children. Indeed, he is prepared to contemplate as proper and permissible marital relationships that are non-procreative in nature or those for love or money. Marriage has values beyond reproduction that need to be considered according to this view. By engaging in a lengthy defense of the value of marriage outside of the technical framework of Jewish Law, Rabbi Isserles strengthened the institution of marriage and highlighted its benefits.

The same can be said with regard to divergent views of polygamy. Consider the basic exchange in the *Shulchan Arukh* with regard to polygamy. *Shulchan Arukh* 1:9–10 states:

> KARO: A man may marry many women, so long as he can support them all. ... Rabbi Gershom decreed that one may only marry one wife at a time ... but the decree was not accepted in all lands.
> ISSERLES: Only in a place where you know that it was not accepted, does it not apply, but normally, it applies everywhere.

If marriage is about reproduction, then polygamy is a normative option; indeed, in certain cases, it is even efficient, as is faithful sexual companionship. If, on the other hand, marriage is about love and companionship or other values that come from the relationship, polygamy is far from the ideal. Even as the Jewish tradition permitted polygamy, it did not treat such relationships as ideal; recall that the Hebrew word used to denote the co-wife was literally "trouble."

The same form of exchange occurs in the context of divorce in the *Shulchan Aruch* 1:8–10:

> KARO: A man should not divorce his first wife, unless he finds improper conduct on her part.
> ISSERLES: Except in cases of improper conduct, anyone who divorces his first wife, the heavenly altar cries tears. However, that was only in Talmudic times when divorce was against the will of the woman; but if divorce is with her consent, all is permitted.
> KARO: A man may divorce his wife without her consent.
> ISSERLES: All of this is according to technical Jewish law, but Rabbenu Gershom decreed that one may not divorce his wife without her consent, unless she has engaged in fault based activity.

Rabbi Karo contemplates marriage as a legal relationship where, at best, the only protections he can find for the wife, beyond her contractual rights, is that one's first wife should not be divorced – against her will – except for a good reason. Other than that, marriage has little value other than its reproductive value. Rabbi Isserles contemplates the central mutuality of marriage to make the parties happy, and when they are both unhappy, divorce is proper and normal. Just as he defends marriage as a source of happiness, Rabbi Isserles defends divorce in situations where the marriage does not make both parties happy. In order for marriage to be a valuable social institution, rather than a religious obligation, exit doctrines have to protect both parties and provide security to both parties also.

Unsurprisingly, this dispute becomes central to the question of marital sexuality as well. In *Shulchan Arukh, Even Haezer* 25:2, Rabbis Karo and Isserles have an important colloquy on sexuality within a marriage. This discussion focuses on how people should conduct themselves during marital sexuality:

KARO: One should not act in a light-headed manner with one's wife nor degrade one's speech with words of vanity, even privately. For scripture says, "[God] declares unto a person what is his [conversation]" (Amos 4:13). The sages of blessed memory taught: Even for the light conversation between husband and wife one will ultimately be held accountable. One should not converse with his wife during intercourse nor prior to it, in order that one's mind not wander to another woman, and if one conversed then immediately had marital relations, about this it is said, "[God] declares unto a person what is his [conversation]." But matters of marital relations one may discuss, in order to increase one's desire, or in order to calm and appease one's spouse if they had been quarreling. One should not be engaged in marital relations with such frequency that they are involved constantly, as this is degenerate, vulgar behavior. Rather, one should minimize intercourse as much as possible, so long as one does not neglect the conjugal obligations entirely without the consent of one's wife. Even when copulating to fulfill the conjugal obligations one should intend not for one's own pleasure, but as one repaying an obligation, as one is obligated in regular conjugal rights, and [with the intent] to fulfill the obligation from one's Creator to procreate, and that one have children who are involved in Torah and fulfill mitzvot among the Jewish people. One should only engage in intercourse with the consent of one's wife; if she is unwilling, one must sooth her until she is willing. One should behave very modestly during intercourse and not engage in relations in front of any type of person, even a minor, except for a baby who is unable to speak.

Rabbi Isserles writes a note between the sentence ending with the word "quarreling" and beginning with the word "One":

RAMA: *Couples may do privately as they please: have relations whenever they please, kiss any part of the body they please, and have ordinary and non-ordinary intercourse, even manual stimulation – only that they may not release semen in a non-procreative manner. Some are lenient and allow non-ordinary intercourse even if it leads to the release of semen in a non-procreative manner, provided that it not be done regularly [as a manner of birth-control]. And even though all these manners are permissible, anyone who sanctifies oneself with that which is absolutely permissible is considered holy.*

A close read of the note is clear: recreational – and not reproductive – sexuality is being defended within the Jewish rabbinic tradition. "The life of the law is not logic, but experience," Oliver Wendell Holmes, Jr. reminds us.[60] Jewish experience has concluded that monogamy with mutual consent or fault-based exit rights works and so does robust sexuality within a marriage. Jewish Law did not (and still has not) really reached that conclusion. Jewish life did.

Concluding Lessons

Jewish Law on sexuality is broader than traditional Jewish life in the year 2021. The faithful who obey Jewish Law see only monogamy and sexuality within marriage even as the texts aver to a variety of additional possibilities. It should be interesting to the modern mind to see that the Jewish tradition eventually settled on monogamy as the only model of sexuality or marriage that worked. The Jewish tradition has experimented with multiple models of sexuality and marriage – from polygamy, to faithful sexual companionship, to minimal marriages with no financial rights of one to the other, and to hard monogamy. Yet, the Jewish tradition ultimately chose the ho-hum model of monogamous sexuality.

Notes

1. Lemech is the first-recorded polygamist and is the subject of a great deal of speculation. Genesis 4:19–23.
2. Genesis 16:1–15.
3. Genesis 29:15–30. See more in my book, *Marriage, Divorce and the Abandoned Wife in Jewish Law: A Conceptual Approach to the Agunah Problems in America* (New York: Ktav, 2001), Appendix A on fraud in the creation of marriage.
4. A small number of medieval commentators derive the monogamous ideal from the verse in Genesis 2:24; see *Bal haTurim* and *Chizkuni* on it, and the notes in *Torah Shelama*, Genesis 2:24. However, there is only one Talmudic homily on the joys of monogamy; see note 9.
5. Deuteronomy 21:15. The verses continue and direct that the inheritance may not be diverted from the child of the hated wife.
6. Deuteronomy 17:17.
7. Leviticus 18:18.
8. Exodus 21:11. This particular verse deals with a slave who is then married by her master.
9. But see Avot Derabbai *Natan* (Proverbs of Rabbi Nathan) version 2, Chapter 2:1 (page 5a in the standard pagination) which states: "Rabbi Judah ben Betera states: Job would observe to himself that … if it had been proper for the first Adam to be given ten wives, it would have been done. But it was proper to give him only one wife, and I too need but one wife." This is the sole rabbinic homily about the theological basis for monogamy. See, for example, Abraham Naphtali Tzvi Roth, *The History of Polygamy Among the Jews* (Hebrew) *Mechakrim Bechachmat Yisrael Kezichrono shel Y.M Gutman*, 114–36 (Budapest: JTS, 1946) and Aaron Pinchek, *Polygamy in the Sources, Shanah Beshanah,* 320–358 (Jerusalem: Keren Kayamet Leyisrael, 1973).
10. Leviticus 19:13. Lesbian relationships were less violative of Jewish Law than male male homosexual ones, but were still prohibited. Maimonides maintained that such relationships were biblically prohibited. See *Commentary to Mishna Sanhedrin* 7:4. Whereas others thought the prohibition to be rabbinic. See R. Joshua Falk Cohen, commenting on *Tur, Even Haezer* 20:2. For more on this, see Angela Riccetti, "Lesbians and Jewish Law" (unpublished MA dissertation, Emory University).
11. See J. David Bleich, "*Annulment*," *Tradition* 33:1 (Fall 1998).
12. Denoted by the Hebrew word *kedasha* or the Hebrew word *zona*. See Deuteronomy 23:18 and Leviticus 19:29.
13. For more on this dispute, see Getsel Ellinson, *Nesuin Shelo Kedat Moshe Ve'Yisrael* (Jerusalem: Mossad Harav, 1973), 25–8. In addition, Jewish Law contained elaborate prohibitions against intermarriage, but these are different in type from our chapter, and thus are not discussed.
14. This proposition is spelled out and defended in some length in my book, *Marriage, Divorce and the Abandoned Wife in Jewish Law*.
15. Deuteronomy 24:1–4. Incidental mention of divorce is also found in Genesis 21:10, Leviticus 21:7, and Leviticus 22:13.
16. There was a three-sided dispute as to when divorce was proper. The School of *Shamai* recounted divorce was only proper in cases of fault. The school of *Hillel* recounted that divorce was proper for any displeasing conduct. Rabbi Akiva recounted that a man could divorce his wife simply because he wished to marry another and could not support both wives. See Talmud, Gitten 90a–b. As is always the rule in Jewish Law, the school of *Shamai* is rejected as incorrect.
17. Irving Breitowitz, *Between Civil and Religious Law: The Plight of the Agunah in American Society* (New York: Greenwood Press, 1993), 9.
18. For a discussion of the various issues raised by this document in modern Jewish Law, see Michael Broyde and Jonathan Reiss, "The Ketubah in America: Its Value in Dollars, its Significance in *Halacha* and its Enforceability in Secular Law," *Journal of Halacha and Contemporary Society* 47 (2004), 101–24.
19. This point is implicitly addressed in *Shulchan Aruch, Even Haezer* 117:11.
20. *Ta'anat b'eyna hutra l'yada*, see Yevamot 64a, *Shulchan Aruch, Even Haezer* 154:6–7, and *Aruch HaShulchan, Even Haezer* 154:52–53.

21 Yevamot 65a, but see also the view of Rav Ammi.
22 See Breitowitz, *Between Civil and Religious Law*, 62–65 for a discussion of the circumstances under which annulments were performed. There are five places in the Talmud where a marriage is declared terminated without the need for a *get* based on the concept that "all Jews who marry do so with the consent of the Sages, and the Sages nullified the marriage." These situations all revolve around marriages under duress or other cases where one of the parties acted improperly.
23 There is considerable evidence that the era of the *geonim* was the only one in which the annulment process (mentioned in very few cases in the Talmud and always either pre-consummation or involving bad faith marriages or divorces) was actually used with any consistency and scale by rabbinic authorities. Based on considerable evidence from the responsa literature, it appears that in cases where a divorce needed to be given by a husband who would not provide one, the *geonim* of that era annulled these marriages (under the *dina de'metivta* decree). It cannot be emphasized enough that whether the *geonim* used this power or not, regardless of rubric, such annulments remain a dead letter in modern Jewish Law. See Eliav Schochetman, "Annulment of Marriages," *Jewish Law Annual* 20: 349–97 (5757), for an extensive review of this issue. The broadest recasting of Jewish Law favoring annulments can be found in Menachem Elon, *Jewish Law: History, Sources and Principles* (Philadelphia: Jewish Publication Society, 1994), 641–42 and 856–77. Even Justice Elon concedes that in order even to contemplate the use of annulment, one needs a unified rabbinate, something that is far beyond the current contours of our community.
24 Only Maimonides maintained a form of this model, though even he denied any element of involuntary annulment. To Maimonides, marriage was a partnership; when either party wanted out, Jewish Law should allow him or her to leave. Maimonides disagreed with the *geonim* only as to the mechanism: he, and all the authorities who preceded him, ruled that annulments were not possible. Maimonides (Rambam) ruled that Jewish Law did not possess any annulment power but that the obligation upon a husband to divorce his wife for fault included her assertion (even if unproven) that "he was repugnant to her." In such a circumstance, the husband must divorce his wife, and a Jewish Law court should compel such a divorce under the threat of court sanction, including physical coercion, if the husband would not give the *get* of his own free will. Thus, according to Maimonides, both husband and wife had a unilateral right to divorce with no dower paid when the woman initiated divorce absent cause and dower paid when the husband initiated divorce without cause. Marriages could still be polygamous. This is a no-fault divorce system and remains to this day the normative rule of law in only small portions of the Jewish community (such as Yemen). This model, like the model of the *geonim*, achieved equality between the husband and the wife by granting to the woman the same right that the man had: the right to seek unilateral no-fault divorce.
25 This insight is generally ascribed to Rabbenu Tam in his view of *meus alay*. In fact, it flows logically from the view of Rabbenu Gershom, who not only had to prohibit polygamy and coerced divorce, but divorce for easy fault as Rambam's concept of repugnancy as a form of fault is the functional equivalent of no fault, identical in result to the *geonim*'s annulment procedure.
26 Absent the prohibition on polygamy, the decree restricting the right to divorce would not work as the husband who could not divorce would simply remarry and abandon his first wife. This prevented that conduct.
27 Rabbi Chaim Or Zarua, *Teshuva* 126. In modern times, this ruling resonates in the writings of Rabbi Yosef Eliyahu Henkin. Rabbi Henkin writes:

> If a husband and wife separate and he no longer desires to remain married to her and she desires to be divorced from him, in such a case divorce is a mitzvah [obligation] and commanded by Jewish law. ... One who withholds a Jewish divorce because he desires money for no just cause is a thief. Indeed, he is worse than a thief as his conduct violates a sub-prohibition (*abizrayu*) related to taking a human life.
>
> *Rabbi Joseph Elijah Henkin*, Adut le-Yisrael *143–44, reprinted in* Kol Kitvei ha-Rav Henkin *1:115a–b and Rabbi Moshe Feinstein*

Rabbi Feinstein writes:

> In the matter of a man and a woman who, for these past years, has not had peace in the house ... Since the *beit din* sees that it is impossible to make peace between them ... it is compelling that they should be divorced, and it is prohibited for either side to withhold a *get*, not the man to chain the woman to the marriage or the woman to chain the man to the marriage, and certainly not over financial matters.
>
> *Rabbi Moshe Feinstein*, Iggrot Moshe, YD *4:15*

28 *Shulchan Aruch* 1:3–5 and 119:1–4.
29 This rabbinic decree, however, does not render a second marriage invalid according to biblical law; therefore, if such a marriage does take place, it can be dissolved only by divorce. The criminal law of the state, however, renders it an offense on pain of imprisonment for a married person to contract another marriage without permission of a rabbinical court. Penal Law Amendment (Bigamy) Law, 5719-1959. Nevertheless, for Jewish citizens, no offense is committed if permission to marry a second wife was given by a final judgment of a rabbinical court and approved by the two chief rabbis of Israel. The latter's approval is accepted as conclusive proof that the permission was given according to the law. Special provisions relating to the grant of this permission are laid down in the *Takkanot ha-Diyyun be-Vattei ha-Din ha-Rabbaniyyim be-Yisrael*, 5720–1960. For the full text of this law, see Menachem Elon *Ha-Mishpat Ha-Ivri*, 1: 554–55 (Jerusalem: Magnes Press, 1988).
30 *Even Haezer* 26:1 (which is the first paragraph addressing marriage law). Why this is so will be discussed in the final sections.
31 Jewish Law dictates that, even in a marital relationship, there be periods of abstinence followed by ritual immersion in a bath, called a *mikva*. For more on this, see Norman Lamm, *A Hedge of Roses* (New York, 1974).
32 The Hebrew term *pelegesh* is generally translated as concubine, a term that I have declined to use, as the word "concubine" in modern English denotes some element of compulsion or slavery, and such elements are completely lacking from the Jewish Law use of the term. Instead, I use the term "sexual companion" or "faithful sexual companion," which is descriptive of what Jewish Law mandated. The modern term "mistress" seems lacking and "lover" denotes too emotional a relationship. Perhaps "paramour" is a better term, although its modern connotation is illicit. The modern IRS acronym, which is POSSLQ, – for "People of the Opposite Sex Sharing Living Quarters," – might be close also.
33 *Shulchan Aruch* EH 26:1 (emphasis added).
34 Genesis 25:1–6.
35 Genesis 35:22.
36 Judges 8:31.
37 2 Samuel 3:7.
38 2 Samuel 15:16.
39 1 Kings 11:3.
40 Although there are no cases of sexual companionship recorded in the Talmud involving Talmudic sages.
41 Laws of Kings 4:4.
42 *Rashba* 4:314. This is so, even as Rabbi Karo incessantly emphasizes the procreative basis of marriage, to the exclusion of any other model.
43 *Yad Ramah*, Sanhedrin 21a.
44 This criticism might parallel the Sunni/Shiite debate over temporary marriages which, perhaps, Abulafiya had encountered. For an example of this social phenomenon in modern times, see "Love Finds a Way in Iran: 'Temporary Marriage'," *The New York Times* (October 4, 2000), A3.
45 *Responsa Hameyucheset leRamban* 284.
46 *Yam Shel Shlomo Yevamot* 2:11.
47 *Responsa of the Ran* 68.
48 *RaVaD*, Commenting on *Ishut* 1:4
49 Quoted in *Rivash* 395 and 398.
50 Radak Samuel 2:12:11.
51 See *Otzar Haposkim* commentary on 26:1.
52 Such as the lack of a need for divorce, the absence of financial connections, and the ability to marry one's companion's relatives after the current relationship ends.
53 Prostitution and intermarriage as well as illicit sexuality within the marriage.
54 *Otzar Hapsokim* 26:1(5).
55 Jerusalem Talmud, *Sanhedren* 21:1. For more on this matter, *see* Getsel Ellinson, *Nisuin shel kedat Moshe Veysirael*, 40–47.
56 Commenting on *Even Haezer* 26:1.
57 Normative Jewish Law posits that fourteen different duties are regulated in the course of marriage. This stripped-down version has none. Even the obligation of sexual fidelity imposes no positive obligation but only a negative one.
58 Indeed, polygamy as a marriage model creates a divorce model as well. Although our secular society is deeply uncomfortable noting this, divorce produces an enormous amount of social and societal

turbulence for children and for the spouse (typically the wife) who did not seek divorce. Granting the right to end a marriage whenever either spouse wishes de-stabilized marriages. Polygamy was patterned on an alternative solution to that problem.

59 Or, to put it in a more modern form, Linda Waite and Maggie Gallagher are correct. Linda Waite and Maggie Gallagher *The Case for Marriage: Why Married People Are Happier, Healthier and Better Off Financially* (New York: Doubleday, 2000).

60 Holmes, Oliver Wendell Jr. *The Common Law*. Vol. I. (Boston, MA: Little, Brown and Company, 1881).

References

Breitowitz, Irving. 1993. *Between Civil and Religious Law: The Plight of the Agunah in American Society*. New York: Greenwood Press.

Broyde, Michael. 2001. *Marriage, Divorce and the Abandoned Wife in Jewish Law: A Conceptual Approach to the Agunah Problems in America*. New York: Ktav.

Ellinson, Getsel. 1973. *Nesuin Shelo Kedat Moshe Ve'Yisrael*. Jerusalem: Mossad Harav.

Elon, Menachem. 1988. *Ha-Mishpat Ha-Ivri*, 1: 554–55. Jerusalem: Magnes Press.

Elon, Menachem. 1994. *Jewish Law: History, Sources and Principles*. Philadelphia: Jewish Publication Society.

Feinstein, Moshe, 1996. Iggrot Moshe. Jerusalem: Frankel Publishing.

Henkin, Joseph Elijah. 1988. *Kol Kitvei ha-Rav Henkin*. New York: Balshon.

Holmes, Oliver Wendell Jr. 1881. *The Common Law*. Vol. I. Boston, MA: Little, Brown and Company.

Lamm, Norman. 1974. *A Hedge of Roses*. New York: Feldheim.

Pinchek, Aaron. 1973. *Polygamy in the Sources, Shanah Beshanah*. Jerusalem: Keren Kayamet Leyisrael.

Roth, Abraham Naphtali Tzvi. 1946. *The History of Polygamy Among the Jews, Mechakrim Bechachmat Yisrael Kezichrono shel Y.M Gutman*. Budapest: JTS Publications.

Takkanot ha-Diyyun be-Vattei ha-Din ha-Rabbaniyyim be-Yisrael, 5720–1960. Jerusalem: Government of Israel.

Waite, Linda and Gallagher, Maggie. 2000. *The Case for Marriage: Why Married People Are Happier, Healthier and Better Off Financially*. New York: Doubleday.

30
MUSIC AND THE EXPERIENCE OF JEWISH RITUAL AND PRACTICE

Gordon Dale

Music, scholars have long noted, is deeply entwined with ritual and practice. The nature of this relationship is complex: Not only is music often the vehicle for the articulation of liturgy in the enactment of rituals, but similar syntactic and temporal features are significant to both music and ritual. The scholarship on ritual is replete with references to music (important works include Jackson 1968; Blacking 1974; Staal 1989; Baranowski 1998; Barthelmes and Motte-Haber 1999; Howard 2006, as well as others), often in metaphoric terms in addition to ethnographic observations, to the extent that scholars have frequently turned to music as a useful comparative tool to explain the nature of ritual. In this chapter, I offer a view of the intersection of music, liturgy, and ritual in Jewish practice through three lenses: historical, phenomenological, and musico-theoretical. This exploration is not intended to be a comprehensive presentation of the repertoires, styles, or history of Jewish liturgical music. Rather, through this brief examination I intend to convey a sense of music's centrality to the experience of Jewish practice.

A Historical Sketch

A challenging element in the historical study of Jewish ritual is knowing where the story begins. Contemporary understandings of what constitutes Jewish ritual may prove anachronistic when analyzing ancient texts, as today's Jewish rituals are largely rooted in post-Temple rabbinic Judaism. Even so, it is valuable to note that the Hebrew Bible includes numerous references to music's involvement in praising God, with nine "songs" included in the TaNaKh, and a promise of a tenth song that will be sung at the time of the Messiah.[1] Jewish scribes write five of these songs in a form that deviates from the standard written format of the sacred text, emphasizing the structure of the song's form and setting aside these passages as special. Some suggest that there is a metatextual component to the patterns of these songs, as the formatting indicates whether those in the biblical narrative have successfully navigated the situation that they have been Divinely tasked with overcoming (Leibtag n.d.).

Music, the biblical text reveals, is a necessary ingredient for the successful execution of the Prophets' duties, as seen in the stories of David, Solomon, and Elisha. Similarly, music must be played by the Levites during the Temple service. Maimonides, based on Numbers 8:24, writes that, in addition to reaching physical maturation, the Levites trained for five years to perform their musical duties prior to beginning their service (*Mishneh Torah, Klei Hamikdash*, Ch. 3).

Those Levites who possessed a singing voice that was not deemed adequate were not permitted to sing in the Temple. We see, then, that the Bible believes the performance of music to be an important ritual that facilitates the Divine encounter.

Following the destruction of the second Temple, the synagogue took on a new importance. As a sign of mourning, the rabbis instituted a ban on music, though scholars debate the exact parameters of this ruling (Kahn 1986–1987). In the emerging model of the synagogue, musical instruments were not permitted on Shabat out of concern that the instrument might break and lead to repairing the instrument, which would be a violation of the Shabat laws (Maimonides, *Mishneh Torah, Shabbat* 23:4).

The post-Temple emphasis on synagogue-based worship, and the absence of musical instruments in ritual, led to a new soundscape for Jewish practice. While prayer was often an improvisational form of religious expression, the cantillation of the Torah emphasized a fixed text, with a musical system to match. Public cantillation of the Torah was instituted by Ezra the Scribe in approximately the fifth century BCE, and while weekday readings were done in the public square, the practice was moved to the synagogue as this new domain became a dominant space of worship. Around the 900s CE, the Tiberian Masoretes codified the system of musical notations used to indicate the proper melody for the recitation of the text. Earlier sources, however, make clear that musical practices were long associated with the recitation of the Torah. The Babylonian Talmud (*Nedarim* 37b), for example, records a debate over whether or not these melodies were given by God to Moses at Mount Sinai; a point that remains unresolved in the rabbis' dispute.

Trends in poetry also influenced Jewish liturgy, and in turn, its musical articulation. The liturgical poetry known as piyyutim became popular among Jewish communities between the third and sixth centuries, popularizing poetic forms that remain in Jewish liturgy to this day. As Abraham Zvi Idelsohn and Mark Slobin have suggested, the popularity of this poetry brought about a need for vocalists who could render the texts in melody with an appropriately high level of skill. Scholars suggest that this gave rise to the institution primarily associated with Jewish liturgical music—the cantorate—though more recent scholarship by ethnomusicologist Judah Cohen has questioned whether we might instead understand the cantorate as emerging in the nineteenth century but framed as an ancient institution in Jewish life, in much the same way that other social roles were similarly becoming professionalized at the time. In either case, synagogue music developed, and musical patterns known as *nusach* came to be associated with various liturgies. While little is known about the history of *nusach*, it is clear that the music systems of various Jewish communities around the world are deeply informed by local sounds.

As Mark Slobin (1989: 8) points out, cantors have long been looked at with skepticism by those in their communities. In *Sefer Tahkemoni*, Rabbi Judah al-Harizi records his impressions of a Baghdad synagogue that he visited in 1220 CE, in which the cantor, who at first appears to be a pious individual, sings boastfully but makes "more than 100 blatant errors," many of which were comical misreadings of the Hebrew prayers (Shiloah 1992: 68–69). Contemporary readers must assume that al-Harizi is being at least somewhat facetious in his presentation of the cantors' errors, but his distrust of the cantorate remains apparent, even if the piece is read as satire. The cantor is presented as self-indulgent rather than humble, performative rather than prayerful.

Halakhic writings, too, have sought to legislate who may serve as the cantor of a synagogue, partly out of a concern for a singer who is insincere and singing out of a love of his own voice rather than a love of God. According to the *Shulchan Arukh* (*Orach Chayim* 53:4), a cantor must be one who is "free of sin, never brought upon himself a bad reputation, even in his youth, who is liked by the nation, who has a pleasant voice, and who is used to reading Torah, Prophets, and Writings." This office is considered to be so important that if a community must decide between hiring a cantor and a rabbi, the cantor is given priority, assuming that the community has access to an authority who can answer halakhic questions (Appel 1979–80). It is clear that the musical aspects of the prayer rituals are considered by the halakhic authorities to be of very high importance, and that the musician who envoices the community's prayers must not only be technically proficient, but must also be of a high moral and spiritual character so as to be the best possible emissary for these prayers.

Jewish mystics have long been interested in this potential of music to facilitate communication with, and an experience of, the numinous. Mystics recognize the relationship between music and Divine connection in foundational Jewish texts, and give credence to their own experiences with music in the performance of Jewish rituals. Mystical teachings therefore seek to understand the supernal roots of song that give it such power (see Moshe Cordovero's *Pardes Rimonim*, Gate 23, Chapter 21:36, as well as Shiloah and Tenne 1977 and Idel 1997). The cantor, too, is a subject of kabbalistic inquiry, with the most famous exploration of this idea found in Rabbi Nachman of Breslov's teaching "Azamrah" (Likutei Moharan 282). In this teaching, Rabbi Nachman explains that the job of the cantor, also known as a *shaliach tzibur* ("emissary of the community") is to bring together "*nekudot tovot*" (lit. good points) found within each person, by recognizing the goodness within everyone in the prayer community and focusing on this while leading the prayer service. Here, Rabbi Nachman is drawing on the double meaning of the Hebrew word *nekudot*, which can mean both "points" as well as "musical notes." He explains that the bringing together of these *nekudot* is itself the very act of creating melodies, hence the relationship between music and representing the community in prayer. The text leaves ambiguity as to what it means when saying that one "creates melodies" through the act of bringing together the good points found within the members of the community. A follower of Rabbi Nachman who teaches within the Breslov community, suggested to me that perhaps the understanding of melody that we have in our corporeal world is actually just a metaphor for the real concept of melody that exists in the spiritual world. Thus, the cantor is one who, through leadership of the prayer ritual, delivers the community's prayers while consciously focusing on the merits of each person, to the spiritual realm.

A historical look at the synagogue soundscape makes clear that cantors, though, are not the only interpreters of liturgy through music. Composers, too, have often crafted the experience of Jewish ritual through the decisions made in the composition process. Synagogue music compositions should be understood as dictating more than the emotional content of the service, though this is certainly a central aspect of prayer that should not be minimized. Composers are often change-makers who implement a social-political vision for their religious community. When the Italian Renaissance composer Salomone Rossi's polyphonic vocal music introduced a dramatically different sound to the synagogue space, his rabbinic mentor, Rabbi Leon of Modena, wrote, "No longer will arrogant opponents utter bitter words about the Hebrew folk. They will see that it too possesses talent, the equal of the best endowed" (Jacobson 2008). Rossi's music utilized the conventions of the Italian motet as the basis for much of his composition, though it should be noted that he was careful to adjust his compositional practices to the needs of the Hebrew language so that the liturgy would be articulated accurately (Harrán 1987: 59). While Rossi struggled to find solid footing in his career as a composer throughout much of his life, he did enjoy the lifting of certain restrictions that other Jews faced, such as the wearing of the Star of David on his clothing. Thus, his uplifting of popular Italian music styles resulted in his own upward mobility in Mantuan society (ibid.).

The history of the Reform movement is another instructive example of liturgical music representing a vision for Jewish acceptance within the broader society. Beginning in the late eighteenth century, proponents of the Jewish Enlightenment (the *Haskalah*) began to view music as a useful tool within the ethos of *Bildung*, an educational model aimed at the refinement of one's character. Maskilic German Jews, particularly women, studied music as part of a broader education in the high culture of central European society (Cypess and Sinkoff 2018). This focus on music would soon become a central component of the nascent Reform movement, as Israel Jacobson made the organ a feature of his Westphalia synagogue. This was not the only musical component of Jacobson's vision for synagogue music; he created his own hymnal which based the music on the chorales of the Protestant Church. Equally significant is the manner in which he discarded certain musical traditions, as his service did not include a cantor, and instead Jacobson himself read, rather than chanted, the weekly portion of the Torah and the accompanying section of the book of Prophets known as the *haftarah* (Idelsohn 1929: 236). As Tina Frühauf (2009) has demonstrated, the organ soon became a symbol of modernity in German-Jewish life.

As the Reform movement developed, composers who were well trained in classical music wrote for the synagogue, creating a rich canon of grand music, the most significant figures of which were Salomon Sulzer and Louis Lewandowski. Sulzer, together with rabbinic partner Isaac Noah Mannheimer, sought to take a less radical approach to Reform than that of Jacobson, instead preferring to merge traditional Jewish liturgical music with popular hymns and classical music styles. Sulzer's music, and moreover his persona, became extraordinarily popular: "A mania spread among the *chazzanim* to sing *à la Sulzer*, to dress *à la Sulzer*, to wear their hair *à la Sulzer*, to cough *à la Sulzer*" (Idelsohn 1929: 256). Sulzer became so popular that in 1869 he was invited to the first Jewish synod, where he was asked to speak to the gathered rabbis about his views on the ways that Jewish prayer should look in liberal Jewish settings. Sulzer, we learn, was respected for more than just his voice, but also for his ideas about the future of Jewish practice and ritual. Lewandowski, too, was a moderate reformer, whose compositions shaped the form and atmosphere of the German synagogue. This was not only due to the music's beauty and subsequent popularity; following the publication of Lewandowski's monumental work, *Todah Wesimrah*, he was appointed chief choral master of all synagogues in Berlin, a role which allowed him to require the performance of his music in services. In this powerful position, Lewandowski was also able to move other talented composers from one congregation to another so that their music would not gain a foothold and challenge Lewandowski's own compositions. Thus, we see that music's expressivity is not the only shaper of synagogue sounds; structures of authority and power similarly impact the sounds of Jewish worship.

As Judah Cohen (2018) has argued, the nineteenth century was a time of professionalization of many knowledge areas, including that of the cantorate. By the 1880s professional organizations for European cantors began to form, and their newly organized members imagined themselves as heirs to all Jewish music of the past, and outlined the skills needed for one to be a cantor. These skills shifted away from communal responsibilities such as teaching and ritual slaughtering, and, following on the heels of Sulzer's success, emphasized instead the cantor's superior skill in the realm of musical prayer leadership. In addition, this professionalization and outlining of the cantor's attributes had another important outcome, as it made the cantorate an all-male domain. Women had, in fact, occupied important roles in synagogue worship until this time. The *sagerin* (or *firzogerin*) refers to a woman in the traditional Eastern European synagogue who, from their position in the women's section, led the women in singing, and assisted them in following the prayer service. While factors such as increased women's literacy may have had a role in the disappearance of the *sagerin* from synagogues (see

Taitz 2007), Cohen argues that the *sagerin* may also have been erased by the professionalization of the all-male institution of the cantor. Indeed the historiography of Jewish liturgical music has been dominated by male figures, though recent work challenges this paradigm (for example, see Adelstein 2013, and Ross 2016).

In the nineteenth century, synagogue music in the United States had parallel processes to their German counterparts. In Charleston, South Carolina's Kahal Kadosh Beth Elohim, debates during the early 1840s over the propriety of the organ, as well as other changes to the format of prayer, led to a major controversy, which has become known as the Charleston Organ Case. Opponents to the organ broke away and titled their new congregation Shearith Israel ("Remnants of Israel"), a clear sign that they believed their former prayer community had lost its way. The mid-1800s also saw the development of highly musical communities through the United States, with choirs becoming popular, and individual cantors hired to lead them. Sulzer's music was certainly an important factor in this trend, and his popularity (and in some cases his direct tutelage) also inspired American composers to write for the synagogue (Cohen 2018: 12). Furthermore, developments of new liturgies, such as the Union Hymnal, led to new music being brought into the synagogue, often changing the worship aesthetic (Schiller 1992).

The end of the nineteenth century saw a mass exodus from Eastern Europe, with approximately 2.5 million Jews leaving Europe between 1881 and 1924 (see the Library of Congress online exhibit "From Haven to Home: 350 Years of Jewish Life in America" for an overview of this time in Jewish immigration). This coincided with excitement about cantorial music, and many vocally gifted Jewish men tried their hand at the art. Opportunities for skilled cantors flourished in the early years of the twentieth century, as recording technology became increasingly available, and record players entered private homes. Early cantorial recordings from cantors such as Selmar Cerini and Gershon Sirota changed the way that cantorial music could be heard, as the sound of the Eastern European synagogue could now be consumed as entertainment in the home. Like Sulzer, the "star cantor" became a phenomenon, and synagogues gained prestige based on the quality of their cantor. Cantors immigrated to the United States to take jobs in American synagogues, and worshippers came to expect elongated services in which the cantor embellished the prayers with virtuosic vocal acrobatics within the conventions of *nusakh*. The Golden Age of cantorial music, as it came to be known, was a time that blurred the line between prayer and entertainment, as worshippers experienced services in new ways, and settings of liturgy were written that functioned as concert pieces rather than those that could be used in an actual prayer service. Several of these cantors, most famously Yossele Rosenblatt, came to be celebrities, and the figure of the cantor came to stand for an approach to life in America that was rooted in the traditions of Orthodoxy in Europe, as seen in the film *The Jazz Singer*.

While most Jews who left Eastern Europe during this time came to the shores of the United States, many participated in the "First Aliyah" (roughly 1882–1903) which brought 35,000 Jews to Mandatory Palestine. Similarly, as Zionism grew, music came to be an important component of defining national identity in pre-state Israel. A secular Jewish identity came to be formed among many early settlers, and their own rituals came to be important to these groups. The *kumzits*—a gathering of communal singing, often held around a campfire—has been described as "the favorite activity of the sabra" (Almog 2000). Religious music, too, thrived, as Jews from all over the world lived in close proximity to each other. Ethnomusicologist and cantor A.Z. Idelsohn's ten-volume thesaurus, in which he documents melodies collected in Jerusalem, is a testament to the diverse sounds that filled the soundscape.

In the United States, the performative aspect of prayer moved in creative directions, particularly in non-Orthodox Jewish synagogues. Composers such as Abraham Wolf Binder

(1895–1966) saw the synagogue as being in competition with entertainment opportunities such as Broadway shows and the rich nightlife of New York City, among upwardly mobile Jews. Binder sought a syncretic approach to synagogue music that would fuse the solo chanting of the cantor, great works of Classical Reform Judaism, and newly composed pieces of synagogue music. This marked not only a musical shift, but also an approach to synagogue life that fit twentieth-century life that became known as "Minhag America," in which "Reform congregations would give up their Teutonic coldness and the excess of rationalism they had imported from Germany while the Russians and Poles would cast off their inappropriate vestigial orthodoxy" (Kligman 2013). The underlying approach of hybridization Binder took to synagogue music has lasted, and remains central to the work of most progressive cantors, who see synergistic possibilities in the use of multiple genres of liturgical music.

A fundamental shift in the music of Jewish prayer came about in the United States in the 1960s and 70s, as the American folk revival became the vernacular music of the younger generation. Composers such as Debbie Friedman, Jeff Klepper, and Danny Freelander composed acoustic guitar-based music designed to facilitate communal singing in the Reform community. Simultaneously, Rabbi Shlomo Carlebach wrote new, folk-inspired melodies to the Orthodox liturgy in an attempt to reach out to non-Orthodox Jews and connect them to Orthodox practice. In both instances a desire to include those who were previously marginalized by dominant formats of prayer resulted in a shift toward participatory worship, facilitated by the music (Kligman 2001: 118). These folk-inspired liturgical repertoires and the emphasis on communal participation in prayer have been met with both embrace and opposition across the denominational spectrum. While some see this as a way to democratize the prayer experience and teach the liturgy to those who are unaccustomed to synagogue norms, others see this as a simplistic deviation from historically meaningful repertoires, whether they be *nusakh*, the compositions of Classical Reform, or more contemporary classical composers of Jewish liturgical music such as Ernest Bloch. The music of these folk-inspired liturgical musicians spread internationally through the recordings that they released, and crossed denominational boundaries in unexpected ways (for example, recent recordings of Hasidic men singing Friedman's melody for the Havdalah ceremony).

The push toward communal singing in prayer, particularly among North American progressive Jews, has led to the desire for other repertoires that can facilitate the experience of *communitas* in prayer. In the twenty-first-century, *nigunim*—both those from Hasidic communities and stylistically similar melodies composed by those who are not Hasidic—have become a popular vehicle for achieving this feeling in prayer services, as well as in paraliturgical singing events. Composer and prayer leader Joey Weisenberg has popularized the idea of "singing communities," which, through careful cultivation centralize *nigunim* in the creation of environments that are conducive to spiritually meaningful experiences. This ethos has spread internationally and has found a receptive audience among non-Orthodox congregations around the world.

Many Orthodox Jews, too, have taken steps to insert a renewed energy into their synagogues. In addition to the popularity of "Carlebach minyanim," synagogues draw on the melodies of contemporary Orthodox popular music to use in services. Many of the most popular songs in this genre use liturgical texts as their lyrics, but even those that do not can be sung as contrafact. Another trend has involved a look back to the Golden Age of cantorial music, as numerous Hasidic men have become expert practitioners of this music through close study of the recordings (Lockwood 2019). These Hasidic cantors have found employment in Modern Orthodox synagogues, and one such individual, Shulem Lemmer, signed with Universal Music Group and in 2019 released a record of both liturgical music and pop songs.

Technologies of music distribution, such as commercial recordings, sheet music collections, and internet-based platforms such as YouTube have been important ways in which Jewish liturgical music has traveled in recent decades. Given the easy access that contemporary Jews have to such diverse repertoires of liturgical music, contemporary prayer leaders have many repertoires from which to choose. Cantors combine diverse repertoires in order to create moods, and balance accessibility with artistry. This trend of combining repertoires, rather than choosing between them, may itself be emblematic of the current day, in which many individuals find meaning in sampling from the breadth of the internet's offerings.

The Experience of Jewish Music and Prayer

As the historical sketch above should make clear, it must be emphasized that music is not merely an accessory to prayer. For many, music is inextricably linked with the textual component of the prayer experience. While one who recites without melody the Kol Nidrei text has technically fulfilled this component of the Yom Kippur liturgy, nearly every congregation across the world would experience such a service as incomplete. Furthermore, many Jews today are unaware or ambivalent about the text's literal meaning (the renunciation of any vows taken that year), yet Kol Nidrei remains a part of the service precisely because its music is so important to Jews' *experience* of the prayer ritual. The centrality of music to prayer is even a halakhic matter: the *Shulchan Arukh* (Orach Chayim 51:9) explains that Psalm 100, a psalm of thanks, *must* be sung with a melody during the prayer service. In its deployment, the text is incomplete without melody.

Music also adds additional layers of meaning to the prayer service. *Nusakh*, for example, uses melodic motifs to mark the liturgical occasion, creating a unique ambiance for a text that might be used in many services. For example, the *nusakh* for the short, responsorial Bar'chu text is different for weekday, Sabbath, the three pilgrimage Festivals (Sukkot, Passover, and Shavuot), and High Holidays. In each case, one who regularly attends synagogue services and is accustomed to the semiotics of musical prayer will hear a sonic marking of the occasion, which creates a particular atmosphere through its sonic qualities and associations. In the examples listed below from Adolph Katchko,[2] the melody sung on Rosh Hashanah and Yom Kippur (Figure 30.1) imparts a feeling of grandeur and majesty that is appropriate to the theme of royalty that pervades the liturgy for these services. The dramatic opening of Bar'chu in the evening service of the three Festivals (Figure 30.2) marks the start of these special days on the calendar.

Figure 30.1 High Holiday Maariv
Source: Adolph Katchko, Volume 3

Figure 30.2 Shacharit Shalosh Regalim
Source: Adolph Katchko, Volume 2

Figure 30.3 Shabbat Maariv
Source: Adolph Katchko, Volume 1

Figure 30.4 Shabbat Schacharit
Source: Adolph Katchko, Volume 1

Contrastingly, the melodies used on Shabbat (Figures 30.3 and 30.4) are commensurate with their relative commonness, as they are fairly simple but still meaningful markers of the day.

The musical choices of prayer leaders, be they professional cantors or lay leaders, are designed to create particular experiences of prayer. For example, some progressive congregations have held themed services that feature the music of Disney films, The Beatles, Broadway shows, and more. Even prayer leaders in the most strictly observant communities make musical decisions about how prayer is to be experienced by those in the congregation. While the borrowing of music that is obviously from outside of Jewish contexts is frowned upon in these communities, the choice of one melody over another can frame the text in a way that signals an upcoming holiday, that honors an individual who recently passed away, or that frames the leader himself as belonging within one community or another. As ethnomusicologist Jeffrey A. Summit has shown in his analysis of a Simchat Torah service in Massachusetts, melody choice can have far-reaching connotations for identity politics, as it can imply a stance toward issues of nationalism, endogamy, assimilation, and more (Summit 1993).

The experience of ritual at home, as opposed to the synagogue, is shaped largely by musical considerations. In the home there is much greater opportunity for autonomy in the rituals that one chooses to perform, the texts that one recites or omits, and the mood that is to be the context for these rituals. Knowledge of a melody for a particular text makes it much more likely to be recited aloud in the home. An example is "Eishet Chayil," a selection from the book of Proverbs extolling the virtues of a "woman of valor," that is a component of the home liturgy for Friday night. Ben Zion Shenker, whose melody is sung around the world, reported that in his own community of Modzitzer Hasidim, the text was never sung aloud but rather recited in an undertone prior to his composing a melody for it (Dale 2017). Today, the melody has spread widely, and this text is sung aloud at Shabbat tables around the world, precisely because a well-loved melody has been transmitted. The melody is not significant only in its giving voice to the text—though this is certainly important—but also because it helps to create the experience of the Sabbath for so many Jews. Understanding ritual as experience, we reveal that music is an intrinsic component of the ritual.

A Musico-Theoretical Examination of Cantorial Evocation in Ritual

The musical decisions of prayer leaders exist in domains both large and small. By "large," I refer to the aforementioned themed services, as well as considerations of genre, instrumentation, and language choice. On a smaller, but no less impactful, level, cantors create musical phrases using the conventions of *nusakh* to bring to life the meaning of text. Familiar with the sounds of each service, cantors work to express and elevate the words through their musical choices. This is often done spontaneously, as the music system of *nusakh* frequently includes improvisation.

To make this point, I wish to call attention to several instances of this "text painting" within one *nusakh* setting, in this case the end of Psalm 97 for the Kabbalat Shabbat service held on Friday nights. To make these points I use the tools of music theory, but I wish to stress that the experience of prayer cultivated by the cantor through musical choices is not limited to those who can appreciate the technicalities of this musical complexity. Rather, anyone in attendance will be able to feel the emotions evoked through the cantor's choices, and those with an understanding of the text's meaning will be able to understand more deeply the ways that the cantor expresses and explains the liturgy through music. Thus, for those who are deeply familiar with the words of the siddur, *nusakh* is not only an emotional experience, but also an intellectual one. The following setting by Adolph Katchko, found in Volume Three of his "Otzar Hachazzanut," is a rich example.[3]

In this setting, Cantor Katchko largely adheres to the conventions of Ashkenazi chazzanut practices, though he at times deliberately breaks the listeners' expectations in order to highlight the meaning of the text. In Ashkenazi worship, the Kabbalat Shabbat service is traditionally sung in the mode known as "Hashem Malach," characterized by a major third in the main part of the octave, a flat seventh, and a minor third above the octave. True to convention, Katchko begins his *nusakh* with a major triad, establishing the fifth scale degree as a recitation tone before

Figure 30.5 Sha'm'a V'Tismach Tzion
Source: Adolph Katchko, Volume 3

Figure 30.5 Continued

a short, but more elaborate, phrase that emphasizes the word "*Tzion.*" The major tonality here matches the rejoicing of Zion, but there is a bit of a switch in mood as the music jumps to the high F and reaches the A♭, emphasizing the minor tonality characteristic of the higher register of the mode. This switch adds a new dimension to the text, perhaps emphasizing a certain darkness in the daughters of Zion celebrating God's judgement of the nations of the world. This darkness carries through "*l'ma'an mishpatecha,*" ["because of your judgements"], with "*l'ma'an*" stated twice, and "*mishpatecha*" stated three times for emphasis. The phrase concludes with a descending major phrase on "*Adonoy,*" which seems to be a reassurance that God is indeed just. This is reinforced through a series of ascending triad phrases on "*Ki Ato Adonoy elyon,*" which clearly represent God's transcendence. Katchko reinforces this sense of majesty by ending the phrase on an A natural, the major third, rather than the A♭ found earlier that indicated a minor tonality. The phrase dips down on the word "*ho'oretz*" [the land], then jumps back up to reinforce God's exaltedness among all false gods, who are represented in lower pitches than the previous phrases that indicate God's loftiness.

There is a distinct switch on the words "*Ohavei Adonoy*" ["Those who love God"] as Katchko introduces a minor triad in the lower end of the mode, leading to a recitation tone on the fifth degree. This mirrors the opening phrase of the setting, but this time, rather than the bright major triad, we have a dark minor triad that contrasts with the text. The meaning of the minor tonality is revealed as the text continues to "*sinu ra*" ["hate evil"], which is sung with a dissonant raised fourth scale degree.[4] This dissonance continues through the syntactic phrase, with the word "*miyad*" ["from the hand"] repeated three times, stressing the urgency of the situation of the holy people who are being rescued by God. When we reach the word "*or*" ["light"], we have another abrupt change, but this time Katchko's note choices seem to mirror the introduction of light into the darkness we have just experienced. On "*or*" he sings a B♭, which contrasts with the B natural we have heard in the preceding phrases, and quickly moves to a held D natural at the end of the word "*Tzadik*" [righteous], hinting at a modulation to the IV chord, emphasizing the shift that the text has brought forth. The phrase ends on a held G at the end of "*simcho*" ["happiness"], which hints at a C major chord, the dominant of the original key, and pulls the ear toward the tonic of F, implying that a conclusion is near. Katchko hints at a harmonic resolution as he sings the major third and fifth of the I chord, but avoids the tonic until he sings a sustained high F on "*badonoy,*" emphasizing the importance and grandeur of God's name. He sings extended dramatic runs on *v'hodu l'zecher kod'sho* (and give thanks to

His holy name), which end in a climactic way, and seem to be an offering of thanks in the most profound and beautiful way.

Through these musical choices, Katchko breathes life into the text. Not only is the liturgy far more dramatic than if merely read, but here the cantor offers interpretations of the text as he chooses when to showcase minor or major tonalities, dissonance and consonance, higher and lower registers. All of this contributes to the experience of the liturgy in ritual. Through this one example we see the manner in which music is an active force in the creation of the embodied ritual experience.

Conclusion

Centralizing music in our conceptions of Jewish practice enables us to move toward an understanding of ritual as embodied and experienced. As shown in this brief overview, Jewish liturgical musicians have long understood the ability of music to elevate the prayers of the Jewish people, and the leaders who have shaped Jewish tradition could not help but agree. Yet, a thread has run throughout Jewish history that sees musicians as a threat, precisely because of music's power. An egotistical musician could easily turn the sacred ritual into a performance, diverting attention toward oneself rather than toward God. Similarly, musicians have the potential to uncouple the liturgy from ritual, and repurpose the text for entertainment or political ideology. Indeed, this has been a common occurrence, as liturgical music is invoked in diverse situations toward various ends. Despite these potential pitfalls, music remains a crucial component of Jewish ritual and practice, at times superseding the liturgical text itself.

Notes

1 Midrash Tanchuma, Beshalach 10 describes the following as the nine songs of Tanakh: Is. 30:29, Ex. 15, Num. 21, Deut. 32:1–52, Josh. 10:12–13, Jud. 5, 1 Sam. 2, 2 Sam. 22, Song of Songs. The tenth song is alluded to in Ps. 98:1.
2 Adolph Katchko (1888–1958) was a significant figure of the Golden Age of cantorial music, who served for more than two decades as the cantor at Congregation Anshe Chesed in Manhattan. Katchko's three-volume *Otzar Ha'hazzanut* remains a primary text for teaching *chazzanut* to cantorial students in the Debbie Friedman School of Sacred Music of Hebrew Union College-Jewish Institute of Religion. While there are numerous *nusakh* volumes in existence, I feature his *nusakh* here because it is widely respected and commonly used by cantors. *Nusakh* differs both on the geographic level and by the individual cantor, and my point here is not to explore these differences. Rather, I seek to compare the ways that one cantor sang the same text on different calendrical occasions, and thus a comparison of Katchko's *nusakh* is a helpful illustration. One should note that Katchko's volumes generally do not repeat a bit of *nusakh* that is consistent from one service to another. My titles for these transcriptions indicate the manner in which the *nusakh* is listed in the volumes, but it is possible that, for example, he would sing the same Bar'chu for both the morning and evening service during the three pilgrimage festivals, even though the volume only indicates it in the morning service.
3 This setting can be heard sung by Cantor Deborah Katchko Gray, the granddaughter of Adolph Katchko, on her record "Three Generations of Cantorial Art."
4 This phrase uses the Ukrainian Dorian mode, characterized by a minor third and a raised fourth, creating an augmented second between the third and fourth scale degrees.

References

Adelstein, Rachel. 2013. "Braided Voices: Women Cantors in Non-Orthodox Judaism." Ph.D. diss. University of Chicago.
Almog, Oz. 2000. *The Sabra: The Creation of the New Jew*. Berkeley: University of California.

Appel, Gersion. 1979–1980. "The Sheliah Tzibbur in Halakhah and Jewish Tradition." *Journal of Jewish Music and Liturgy* 3(1): 2–9.

Baranowski, Ann. 1998. "A Psychological Comparison of Ritual and Musical Meaning," *Method & Theory in the Study of Religion* 10: 3–29.

Barthelmes, Barbara & Helga de la Motte-Haber (eds). 1999. *Musik und Ritual. Veröffentlichungen des Instituts für Neue Musik und Musikerziehungen*. Darmstadt 39. Mainz: Schott.

Blacking, John. 1974. *How Musical Is Man?* Seattle: University of Washington Press.

Cohen, Judah M. 2018. "Professionalizing the Cantorate—and Masculinizing It? The Female Prayer Leader and Her Erasure from Jewish Musical Tradition?" *The Musical Quarterly* 101(4): 455–81.

Cypess, Rebecca and Nancy Sinkoff. 2018. *Sara Levy's World: Gender, Judaism, and the Bach Tradition in Enlightenment Berlin*. Rochester, NY: University of Rochester Press.

Dale, Gordon. 2017. "Music in Haredi Jewish Life: Liquid Modernity and the Negotiation of Boundaries in Greater New York." Ph.D. diss. The Graduate Center, CUNY.

Frühauf, Tina. 2009. *The Organ and its Music in German-Jewish Culture*. New York: Oxford University Press.

Harrán, Don. 1987. "Salomone Rossi, Jewish Musician in Renaissance Italy," *Acta Musicologica* 59(1): 46–64.

Howard, Keith (ed.). 2006. *Music and Ritual*. Netherlands: Semar Publishers.

Idel, Moshe. 1997. "Conceptualizations of Music in Jewish Mysticism," in *Enchanting Powers: Music in the World's Religions*, ed. Lawrence E. Sullivan. Cambridge, MA: Harvard University Press, 159–88.

Idelsohn, Abraham Zvi. 1929. *Jewish Music in its Historical Development*. New York: Henry Holt and Company.

Jackson, Anthony. 1968. "Sound and Ritual," *Man* 3: 293–99.

Jacobson, Joshua. 2008. "Defending Salamone Rossi: The Transformation and Justification of Jewish Music in Renaissance Italy," *Colloquium Journal* (5): 85–92.

Kahn, Aharon. 1986–1987. "Music in Halachic Perspective," *Journal of Jewish Music and Liturgy* 9 (1986–87): 55–72; 10 (1987–88): 32–49; 11 (1988–89): 65–75.

Kligman, Mark. 2001. "Contemporary Jewish Music in America," *The American Jewish Year Book* 101: 88–141.

Kligman, Mark. 2013. "Reestablishing a 'Jewish Spirit' in American Synagogue Music: The Music of A. W. Binder," in *The Art of Being Jewish in Modern Times*, eds. Barbara Kirshenblatt-Gimblett and Jonathan Karp. Philadelphia: University of Pennsylvania Press, 270–87.

Leibtag, Menachem. N.d. "Ha'azinu: The Five Songs in Tanach." https://outorah.org/p/37745/

Library of Congress. N.d. "From Haven to Home: 350 Years of Jewish Life in America." www.loc.gov/exhibits/haventohome/haven-home.html (accessed December 20, 2020).

Lockwood, Jeremiah. 2019. "A Cantorial Lesson: The Lineage of a Learning Encounter." *Studies in American Jewish Literature, Special Issue, American Jews and Music*. www.academia.edu/40580083/A_Cantorial_Lesson_The_Lineage_of_a_Learning_Encounter

Ross, Sarah M. 2016. *A Season of Singing: Creating Feminist Jewish Music in the United States*. Waltham, MA: Brandeis University Press.

Schiller, Benjie Ellen. 1992. "The Hymnal as an Index of Musical Change in Reform Synagogues," in *Sacred Sound and Social Change: Liturgical Music in Jewish and Christian Experience*, eds. Lawrence A. Hoffman and Janet R. Walton. Notre Dame, IL: University of Notre Dame Press, 187–212.

Shiloah, Amnon. 1992. *Jewish Musical Traditions*. Detroit, MI: Wayne State University Press.

Shiloah, Amnon and Ruth Tenne. 1977. *Music Subjects in the Zohar: Texts and Indices*. Jerusalem: The Magnes Press, The Hebrew University (Hebrew).

Slobin, Mark. 1989. *Chosen Voices: The Story of the American Cantorate*. Urbana: University of Illinois Press.

Staal, Frits. 1989. *Rules Without Meaning: Ritual, Mantras, and the Human Sciences* (Toronto Studies in Religion 4). New York: Peter Lang.

Summit, Jeffrey A. 1993. "'I'm a Yankee Doodle Dandy?': Identity and Melody at an American Simḥat Torah Celebration." *Ethnomusicology* 37(1): 41–62.

Taitz, Emily. 2007. "Firzogerin," in *Encyclopaedia Judaica* (second edition), eds. Fred Skolnik and Michael Berenbaum. Detroit, MI: Macmillan Reference USA, Vol. 7, 50–51.

31
THE THEOLOGICAL IMPLICATIONS OF THE STATE OF ISRAEL

Vernon H. Kurtz

The birth of the State of Israel in 1948 created a new reality for the Jewish people and the religious community which is part of it. For almost 2,000 years Jews around the world offered prayers for the return to Zion and, in particular, to Jerusalem. Now it was a reality. How should the Jewish world, and especially the religious part of it, contend with this new reality? Was the birth of the state simply a factor of world geopolitics or was there true religious meaning attached to the event? Did it signal the beginning of a new era in human history and Jewish existence therein? Did it symbolize the coming of the Messianic age, or at least an advancement toward it?

There was considerable debate about these issues in the religious community at that time and various solutions were proposed then and have been embellished upon over the years. It is my intention to study the original prayer written for the welfare of the State of Israel, look at a number of its variants, establish who recites it and who does not, and then see the implications of those opinions as they manifest themselves in the celebration of a new significant day on the Jewish calendar – *Yom Ha'Atzmaut* – Israel Independence Day.

In August 1948, a few months after the declaration of the state, a Prayer for the Welfare of the State of Israel was written for congregations to recite during their Shabbat services, expressing gratitude to God for the establishment of the state, asking God to bless its leaders and to bring back to Israel those members of the Jewish people who remain in exile. It was published in newspapers of that time.[1] There has been considerable scholarly discussion as to who was the author of this prayer. After extensive research by Dr. Joel Rappel it has been proven that the prayer was written by the Ashkenazic Chief Rabbi Isaac A. Herzog and that the writer Shai Agnon commented on it and corrected a number of points.[2] The prayer received the endorsement of the Chief Sephardic Rabbi Ben Zion Uziel as well.

Ever since that time there are those in the religious communities who recite the very same prayer on every Shabbat and Festival in their synagogues. There are others who are uncomfortable with some of the language used in the prayer and, though they do recite a prayer for the welfare of the state, they change some of the verbiage of the prayer, some with extensive changes and others with minor but significant ones. There are others who are totally opposed to reciting any such prayer and are rather adamant in their opposition. And there are still others for whom any kind of prayer is not necessary. It will be my task to delve into each of these positions, examine the history, theology and sociology behind them, and see how the various groups then implement these positions in their ritual calendar.

The Zionist Movement which was established by Theodor Herzl at the first Zionist Congress in 1897 to a large extent received much of its backing and support from those who might be termed as secular, that is, not religiously observant, in the common sense of the term. While there were some in the religious community who supported the vision of a Jewish state, the religious community, to a large extent, remained quite suspicious of this Movement. Some felt that it was not their province to return to Zion and create an independent Jewish reality there on their own as that should be left to God and the advent of the Messianic age. Others were not as dogmatic but still could not see themselves following in the footsteps of those who envisioned a state which, at least to the visionary and those who followed him in leadership, would be established upon secular norms of law and practice.

While some of these arguments continued over time, historical events, including and especially the Holocaust, changed some minds on the project. While there were some who still felt that returning to Zion was dependent upon God and the coming of the Messiah, there was a considerably large group who felt that here was an opportunity to assist God in the bringing of the Messianic age and anything they could do to help in that endeavor would be a holy undertaking. Still others were ambivalent and while they were willing to help in the establishment and the securing of the state they felt less comfortable in identifying the religious context in which it was created and in which it endured.[3]

Let us examine the prayer itself and see how these views manifest themselves both in the language of the prayer and in the fact that only some in the religious community recite these words exactly as they were first written. First of all, we must state that to the majority of the historical Zionist Movement and the current population of the State of Israel this discussion is either just academic or, in fact, not necessary at all. To most Israelis and Jews around the world who might call themselves secular, the existence of the Jewish state has no theological significance at all. To secular Zionists the state was simply a geopolitical undertaking aimed at saving the Jewish people from the dangers of anti-Semitism and annihilation and an opportunity to actualize Jewish national aspirations of returning to its ancient homeland. It hoped to gain official recognition from the international community and join other nation states in the global community. Once the state was established it was seen to be a normal secular state and a society based along European and American lines.[4] This point of view continues among secular Jews throughout the world who see the state as a geopolitical fact that has many challenges, ranging from security to economic to social issues, like any other country. For many of them the state has not lived up to its great potential as a "model society" as envisioned by Zionist thinkers and it is the role of government and civil society to work toward that goal. For them, the State of Israel is like any other country with major accomplishments and major flaws but in no way does the creation and the existence of the state symbolize a new era of human history and they give no religious significance to the state, its organs and its purpose.

The prayer that is recited in most modern Orthodox and Conservative synagogues around the Jewish world, composed by Rabbi Herzog, contains a number of elements. According to Dalia Marx,[5] "the prayer begins in a lofty and poetic style before reverting to less flowery prose dependent on proof-texting from biblical verses." She summarizes its contents as encompassing a number of requests: Peace and protection for the state; wisdom for its leaders; the victory and safety of Israel's soldiers and defenders; ingathering of diaspora Jews; success in Israel for the religious mandates of tradition; redemption and the coming of the Messiah; acceptance of God by all the inhabitants of the world.

The key phrase of the prayer which adds a theological imprint to it occurs in the first major request. It asks God to bless the State of Israel *reishit tz'michat g'ulateinu*. This phrase has been translated in various ways. The most common translation is "the beginning of the flowering of our redemption." Rabbi Herzog seems to be the originator of this phrase as it does not appear in rabbinic literature. When asked about it, Herzog cited a passage from the Babylonian Talmud in the tractate Sanhedrin, making clear that messianic associations were precisely what he intended.[6] This theology follows that promoted by Rabbi Abraham Isaac Kook, the first Ashkenazi Chief Rabbi of Palestine during the British mandate, who saw in Zionism and the return to the land a spiritual renewal of the Jewish people. While he himself never used the phrase, "Kook saw a divine process revealing itself as historical events around him unfolded."[7]

This phrase adds possible messianic impact to the establishment of the secular State of Israel and gives religious meaning to the state and the way it enacts its legislation and promotes the welfare of its citizens. Though as Jacob J. Schacter writes:

> the incipient state surely was not recognized as "our redemption"; it was even understood as representing neither "the beginning of our redemption" nor "the flowering of our redemption", the best that can be asserted is that it is "beginning of the flowering of our redemption", once again two steps removed from redemption.[8]

The state is seen in a religious messianic light. As Menachem Friedman writes, "the term which bears intense religious-historical significance yet is non-binding from a religious point of view, was then found appropriate by various religious factions."[9] Reciting this prayer with this significant phrase and its theological meaning can only impress upon the worshippers that the State of Israel in its modern manifestations is unlike any other nation state in the world. It bears with it a theological meaning which implies we are on our way to the redemption itself, however slowly, and the establishment of the State of Israel and its wellbeing is a significant marker on that journey.

Religious Zionists who hold these views see the state in religious terms, one which should reflect attachment to tradition and *Halakhah*. For them the Land of Israel as promised to the people of Israel by God is now actualized in the modern State of Israel. Thus, the activities of the state, its leaders and organs are seen in that light. The prayer composed by Rabbi Herzog and recited in the synagogue gives light to that view and position. This stance, as we shall see, has a significant impact upon how those who take this phrase in its literal sense view the celebration of Israel Independence Day.

There are others who see in the establishment of the State of Israel some religious import but they are not willing to be as literal in their understanding of the state as the bearer of even the beginnings of the messianic journey. To them attributing full theological import to the state and its organs is troublesome. Some of the more liberal denominations are willing to recognize the new historical reality created by the establishment of the state but are unwilling to go as far as both Rabbi Kook and Rabbi Herzog did in giving it a definitive redemptive quality. Some of this is seen in the translation of the above-mentioned phrase in the prayer and other times it is seen in its absence. For instance, in the Conservative Movement in the United States the two most recent Prayer Book publications of the Movement look at the phrase, in one case in translation and in another case both in Hebrew and in its translation, as aspirational rather than as factual. *Siddur Sim Shalom* uses the exact same Hebrew phrase but translates it as "with its promise of redemption."[10] This translation looks to the state as a promise of redemption but not as "the beginning of the flowering" of said redemption. Clearly the translator was uncomfortable conveying the fact that the State of Israel represented even the beginning of the journey to the Messianic age.

In the newest Prayer Book edition of the Conservative Movement, *Siddur Lev Shalem*, the editors see the phrase as even more aspirational. While the phrase is present in the Hebrew it is preceded by the word *tehay* in square brackets leaving it to those who are reciting the prayer to add the word if they so wish. This is translated in the English as "[that it may be] the beginning of our redemption."[11] Clearly an aspirational wish and not a definitive fact, the editors of the Prayer Book wanted to leave it up to the rabbi, cantor and the parishioners to decide how to look at this phrase and, through it, the entire enterprise of the establishment of the state. In a note on the side of the page the editors state that the "Hebrew word *tehay* was added by the Chief Rabbi of England, Immanuel Jakobovits, turning the phrase 'the beginning of the redemption' into an expression of hope, rather than a statement of fact." It is interesting to note that the editors, by creating the bracketed words, have also allowed those who recite the prayer to see the state as "the beginning of our redemption" should they decide not to recite the prayer with the bracketed words included. On the margins of the Prayer Book in smaller print is added an alternative prayer to the one commonly used in which the phrase does not occur at all.

The latest Prayer Book published by the Masorti Movement (the Conservative Movement in Israel), *Va'ani Tefillati*, suggests an entirely new prayer for the state which does not include the phrase at all and then in the margin states that the well-known prayer which we have been discussing can be found in its entirety in the back of the book, thus enabling the worshippers to decide which prayer they wish to recite, one with its messianic implications or one without.[12]

Dalia Marx in her article surveys modern Reform prayer books and their liturgy in Israel, Europe and the United States as it pertains to the prayer for the State of Israel. She finds some commonalities but also some very important differences among the various editions. While the 1982 Israeli Reform Prayer Book, *Ha'Avodah Shebalev*, includes the phrase from the original prayer it also "provides significant variations and an altogether different theology and ideology" as the prayer is taken as a whole.[13] This includes viewing the diaspora as a legitimate choice of habitation and "instead of petitions for the coming of the messiah, we get an emphasis on understanding and fellowship among all the inhabitants of the land."[14]

She continues in analyzing other prayers found in Reform liturgy and states:

> Relating to the State of Israel as "the first sprouting of our redemption" has proved especially problematic over the years. Many have been troubled by its messianic pretensions, holding that the State of Israel does not merit the title. Seeing the state as already redemptive, moreover, has led some extremists to demand a post-historical morality that permits violence toward Arabs.[15]

In looking at the other prayer books of the Movement in different geographical locations she notes that the phrase denoting the messianic component of the State of Israel rarely appears and if it does it is aspirational rather than declarative. She writes that in examining a German Reform text, the 2009 *T'filot l'khol hashanah: Jüdisches Gebetbuch*, and the American "Gates of Prayer" she finds that

> rather than have it refer to the past, as if Israel has already entered messianic times, it projects the phrase into the future: "So that it may be the first sprouting of our

redemption." It is hard to read this emendation of the English as anything less than a critique of traditionalists who see Israel as necessarily conferring messianic status on the present. In concept, it is reminiscent of the Gates of Prayer, which, as we saw, preferred praying that "the promise of her [Israel's] beginning may ripen into fulfillment."[16]

In fact, Joel Rappel who has written widely on the history and meaning of the original prayer has stated that there are over 200 versions of the prayer from different communities around the world housed in the archives of Bar Ilan University.[17] As we will see these ideological issues play themselves out in how Yom Ha'Atzmaut is celebrated by the liberal movements.

There is a third view concerning the religious impact of the establishment of the State of Israel. This is mostly held by those who are called or call themselves Haredi (ultra-Orthodox) Jews. While the overarching motive behind Haredi opposition to the establishment of the state stems from a historical animosity and rivalry between orthodox observant Jews and secular progressive forces throughout Jewish Exile history,[18] there are members of the group who are not willing to see in the establishment of the State of Israel messianic implications and, in fact, some of them see the establishment of the state and its existence almost as blasphemy. They did not recognize, and continue to ignore, the religious symbolism of the establishment of the state. As Aviezer Ravitzky writes:

> from the Haredi point of view, the State of Israel is a religiously neutral entity, part of the secular realm still belonging to the age of exile. The state's conception and birth were neither holy nor profane; it represents neither a messianic awakening nor an anti-Semitic eruption. Rather, it should be judged like any other historical phenomenon: according to its concrete relationship to Torah, and according to the attitude of its leaders and adherents to the precepts of *Halakhah*.[19]

Joseph Dan adds, "although Haredim generally acknowledge that they and their yeshivot have derived great benefit from the existence of a Jewish state, many still view it as an affront to divine providence, deserving of harsh punishment from God."[20]

Those who hold this point of view and base it on theological principles find their proof in a Talmudic passage appearing in the Babylonian Talmud tractate Ketubot 110b–111a (the text also appears in *Midrash Tanhuma Deuteronomy 4* and *Song of Songs Rabbah 2:7* with some variations). In the context of a discussion which attempts to defend Rabbi Zeira's desire to leave Babylon and go to the Land of Israel, the text states that God adjured three oaths upon the world. Two of the oaths pertain to the people of Israel and one oath to the other nations of the world:

> What are the three oaths? One that Israel not ascend the wall; one, that the Holy One, Blessed be He, adjured Israel not to rebel against the nations of the world; and one, that the Holy One, Blessed be He, adjured the idolaters not to oppress Israel overly much.

The accepted understanding of these texts is that the Jews were sworn not to forcefully reclaim the Land of Israel and not to rebel against the other nations, and the other nations in their turn were sworn not to subjugate the Jews excessively. Most Haredi Jews see these oaths as still in place. Thus the establishment of the State of Israel and of its acknowledgment as a move toward the Messianic age is out of place and, for some, even heresy. To be sure, modern Orthodox

Jews also take these Talmudic sources seriously but they suggest that these oaths are no longer relevant.[21] However, the ultra-Orthodox, who have an ambivalent view of the State of Israel, insist that these oaths and their interpretation that only God will bring the Messianic age are still in place and they present a serious challenge to the enterprise of the state being seen as part of even "the beginning of the flowering of our redemption."

Thus, since for ultra-Orthodox Haredi Jews the state has no messianic implications, none of the prayers mentioned above will find themselves in their prayer books and they will not be recited in synagogue services. Seeing this theological premise as central to ultra-Orthodoxy's view of the state, it will stand to reason that any religious celebration of Israel Independence Day will be looked down upon and even be seen as inappropriate and out of place.

Finally, there is another group which frankly comprises most of Israeli Jewry and diaspora Jewry as well. They are termed secular Jews, but this may be a misnomer. It is difficult to bunch them together as their views of Jewish life may be different but, for our purposes, they uphold a common view and that is that the establishment of the State of Israel does not have messianic implications. For them the state is like any other. Truth be told, they see it as a Jewish state which should live up to its potential as a democratic state based on appropriate Jewish values and communal ethics. For them the prayer does not have significant import and "is often accompanied by a dismissive attitude towards traditional Judaism and its 'diaspora mentality,' and an express wish that Israel become a 'normal' society – that is, a secular society along European and American lines."[22] For them the celebration of Israel Independence Day will look different than for those who see the State of Israel as part of the journey to the Messianic age. It will be a cause for great celebration but without religious and messianic implications.

Let us now look at the celebration of Yom Ha'Atzmaut, Israel Independence Day, as an example of where these groups differ in their ideology, theology and commemoration of the establishment of an independent State of Israel in the ancient homeland after almost 2,000 years of exile.

It is interesting to note that Israel has a unique way of preparing for the day. The previous day to Independence Day (from nightfall to nightfall, following the Jewish calendar in its definition of a day) is Yom Hazikaron, Remembrance Day for Israel's fallen soldiers and victims of terrorism. The entire day is devoted to memorializing those who gave their lives in defense of the state and by law all places of entertainment are closed and broadcasting and educational bodies note the solemnity of the date. A siren is heard throughout the country to begin the day (in the evening), is sounded again in the morning, with everyone stopping for a minute of silence. The day very often is spent visiting military cemeteries as almost every family in Israel has been touched by the loss of someone. The day, thus, has become ritualized memory observed by all segments of Israeli society, with the possible exception of some extreme Haredi groups for the reasons mentioned above.

As Yom Hazikaron ends at nightfall Yom Ha'Atzmaut begins. There is a public ceremony at Mt. Herzl in Jerusalem and the celebrations commence. For most Israelis, and, in fact, most Jews around the world, Israel Independence Day is a day of great rejoicing and celebration. Those who see in the State of Israel theological implications give voice to that opinion in a number of ways. The Religious Zionist movement sees the day as a time for thanksgiving and gratitude to God for the privilege of living at a time when there is an independent state which once more sits in its ancient homeland. Thus, while in some ways the religious character of the day is still in the process of formation, a number of ritual and liturgical choices give the day religious character. Services in the evening and in the morning are celebratory and prayers are added that are also added on other holidays throughout the Jewish calendar year, such as special psalms, the *Hallel* prayer, in some cases a special Torah reading, and a Haftorah reading. There is still some discussion whether the *Hallel* should be recited with the opening blessing, but even for those who are not willing to recite it, the fact that these Psalms of Praise are recited demonstrates the religious nature of the day.[23] There is also present in some prayer books a version of the *Al Hanisim* prayer that is also recited on Purim and Hanukkah. There are even special prayer books and liturgies that have been created both in Israel and in the diaspora for the day. Very often the day at home is recognized with a celebratory meal in the same fashion as other holidays are commemorated.

The liberal movements, too, see in the day a cause for celebration and many, though not all, give it religious significance. Both the Conservative and the Reform Movements in Israel and in the diaspora add many of the same prayers to their daily services to signify the religious connotation of the historical event. There are also new prayers specifically written for Israel Independence Day which have become part of the liturgies of the day. In an article in the periodical *Conservative Judaism*,[24] I analyzed many of the *Al Hanisim* prayers present in Conservative Movement prayer books and found a number of differing liturgies dependent upon the date, location and religious views of the authors and editors. Whatever the slant of the prayer, again, the fact that it appears in the liturgy recognizes the miraculous nature of the event and signifies the religious import given to the state and the celebration of its independence day.

For most Haredi Jews, with their ambivalence and sometimes even animosity toward the state, Israel Independence Day is not celebrated at all. There are no changes in the daily prayers, there is no festivity on that date, and some of the most extreme of the group even fast on this day and recite prayers for fast days.[25] While the latter do not encompass a large number, it is consistent with their view of the non-acceptance of the State of Israel as a Jewish state.

For most Israeli and diaspora Jews Yom Ha'Atzmaut is celebrated like any other nation's independence day. To be sure, many religious Israelis once they have concluded their religious services follow the same pattern. It is typical to celebrate the day with family and friends. There are celebrations in the streets of most Israeli cities and towns, hikes in nature, BBQs, visits to national parks, picnics, house parties, visits to army bases, air shows, and a general spirit of rejoicing throughout the land. It is popular to watch on television the major ceremony at Mt. Herzl signifying the beginning of the day, and very often on the day itself the International Bible Contest and the Israel Prize ceremony both take place in Jerusalem. In short, the day is celebrated much as anyone in any country around the world would celebrate their independence day, of course, with the flavor of Israel. For diaspora Jews the celebration of the day from afar has been a way to express solidarity with the State of Israel and to strengthen their alliance with it.

Thus, from this short schematic description of the celebration of Israel Independence Day we can see that each group approaches the day consistent with its views of the implications of the establishment of the state and its possible theological imprint. As the State of Israel plays a major role in Jewish history, ideology, theology and practice, this should not surprise us. The citizens of the State of Israel and world Jewry are still attempting to process what it means after 2,000 years to return to its ancient homeland and establish a modern state there. There are various points of view present even more than 70 years after the establishment of the state. The recitation, or non-recitation, of The Prayer for the Welfare of the State of Israel in its various forms and the celebration, or non-celebration, of Yom Ha'Atzmaut, Israel Independence Day, are but two examples of modern Jewry's attempt to deal with this new reality.

Notes

1 Steinberg (2012) 31 and note 4
2 Rappel (2019) JPPI Podcast; and Steinberg (2012) note 5
3 Dan (2004) 123
4 Ibid.
5 Marx (2014) 56
6 Gold (2018) 67
7 Gold (2018) 67–68
8 Schacter (2015) 96
9 Friedman (1988) 189
10 *Siddur Sim Shalom* (1989) 417
11 *Siddur Lev Shalem* (2016) 178–179
12 *Va'Ani Tefilati* (2009) 133 and 285
13 Marx (2014) 59
14 Marx (2014) 60
15 Ibid. and note 22
16 Ibid. 64 and note 22
17 Rappel (2019) JPPI Podcast
18 Haredim and Zionism, Wikipedia
19 Ravitzky (1996) 145
20 Dan (2004) 123
21 Ravitzky (1996) 208; and Three Oaths, Wikipedia
22 Dan (2004) 123
23 Diamond (2020)
24 Kurtz (2003)
25 Independence Day, Wikipedia

Bibliography

Dan, Joseph. 2004. "Jewish Sovereignty as a Theological Problem," *Azure* no. 16 (Winter): 123–139.
Diamond, Eliezer. 2020. "Beyond the Flag: The Religious Dimensions of Yom Ha"Atzma'ut." Online lecture April 27, 2020. www.youtube.com/watch?v=kTk70W-UlBc (accessed August 10, 2021).
Friedman, Menachem. 1988. "The State of Israel as a Theological Dilemma," in *Israel State and Society: Boundaries and Frontiers.* Edited by Baruch Kimmerling. Albany: State of New York Press, 165–215.
Gold, Neal. 2018. "Reishit Tz'michat G'ulateinu: Theological Challenges of the Prayer for Israel in Liberal Prayer Books," *CCAR Journal: The Reform Jewish Quarterly* (Spring): 61–81.
Haredim and Zionism, Wikipedia, https://en.wikipedia.org/wiki/Haredim_and_Zionism (accessed April 13, 2020).
Independence Day (Israel), Wikipedia, https://en.wikipedia.org/wiki/Independence_Day_(Israel)#Religious_customs (accessed April 13, 2020).
Kurtz, Vernon. 2003. "Liturgy as Ideology," *Conservative Judaism* Vol. 55, no. 3 (Spring): 30–37.
Marx, Dalia. 2014. "The Prayer for the State of Israel: Universalism and Particularism," in *All the World: Universalism, Particularism and the High Holy Days.* Ed. Lawrence Hoffman. Woodstock: Jewish Lights Publishing, 49–76.
Rappel, Joel. 2019. "Is the Israeli Independence day a religious holiday?" Jewish Journal/JPPI Podcast, The Jewish People Policy Institute, Second Series, www.jppi.org.il (accessed March 12, 2020).
Ravitzky, Aviezer. 1996. *Messianism, Zionism and Jewish Religious Radicalism.* Trans. Michael Swirsky and Jonathan Chapman. Chicago, IL: University of Chicago Press.
Savia, Nadav. 2019. "10 Ways Jewish Israelis Will Celebrate Yom HaAtzmaut This Year", www.reformjudaism.org/jewishholidays/yom-hazikaron-yom-haazmaut-10-ways-jewish-israelis-will-celebrate-yom-haatzmaut May 3, 2019 (accessed April 17, 2020).
Schacter, Jacob J. 2015. "The Beginning of the Flowering of Our Redemption," in *The Koren Mahzor for Yom HaAtzmaut and Yom Yershalayim.* Jerusalem: Koren Publishers, 93–100.
Siddur Lev Shalom. 2016. Ed. Edward Feld. New York: The Rabbinical Assembly, Inc.

Siddur Sim Shalom. 1989. Ed. Jules Harlow. New York: The Rabbinical Assembly of America.
Steinberg, Avraham. 2012. *Prayers for the Welfare of the State and for the Welfare of the State of Israel*. Jerusalem: Yad Harav Herzog.
Three Oaths, Wikipedia, https://en.wikipedia.org/wiki/Three_Oaths (accessed April 1, 2020).
Va'ani Tefilati. 2009. Ed. Zev Keinan. Tel Aviv: Miskal – Yedioth Ahronoth Books and Chemed Books.
Yom Ha'atzmaut – Israeli Independence Day, Jewish Virtual Library, www.jewishvirtuallibrary.org/yom-haatzmaut-israeli-independence-day (accessed April 13, 2020).

32
DEATH AND DYING

Simcha Paull Raphael

Introduction

Over the course of millennia Judaism developed an extensive system of rituals designed to meet the needs of the dying and bereaved and their families. While some of these rituals have a textual basis in the Hebrew Bible, most Jewish death practices reached a classical form during the Middle Ages, and then developed further shaped by modernity.

Goses, *Vidui* and Traditional Deathbed Practices

The book of Ecclesiastes reminds us of the organicity of the human life cycle. Given that we are mortal human beings, "there is a time for being born and a time for dying" (Ecc. 3:2). Jewish tradition recognizes the immediacy of the dying experience and provides specific guidelines for companioning those leaving behind physical embodied life.

According to the Code of Jewish Law, *Shulchan Arukh*—the medieval legalistic guide for Jewish practice—one who is dying is referred to as a *goses*. A *goses* is a person in a state of "active dying", that is, in a sacred nether realm, between life and death, between this world and the world beyond. Further, the *Shulchan Arukh* asserts "a dying person is to be considered as a living being in all matters" (*Yoreh Deah*, 339). The primary task for those present at the deathbed is to offer complete respect and dignity for one who is dying.

As one approaches death, ritual guidelines are never to leave them alone, even for a moment. Psychologically, one is to be present for a dying person providing compassionate companionship and helping calm fears. Spiritually, traditional understanding is that since the process of the soul separating from the body can be confusing, being present at the death moment helps assist the soul in its departure. To offer comfort as death approaches Judaism prescribes recitation of Psalms. In particular, Psalm 23 is perhaps best known of all the Psalms. Although usually associated with funerals, it is frequently chanted at the deathbed. Additionally Psalm 30, Psalm 121, and Psalm 150 are also appropriate choices, as is Psalm 119, which is an acrostic. It is traditional to choose verses whose opening letters spell out the individual's Hebrew name.

Another practice at this time is recitation of the *vidui*, the deathbed confessional. There are two different types of *vidui* prayers. One version assumes the person approaching death is conscious enough to recite the prayer for themselves, peacefully preparing for death. The second version is recited on behalf of one who is dying, within range of their hearing. It is said that for dying patients hearing is the last sense to go; even if in an unconscious coma, people can still hear words of those around them. Central to the *vidui*, is this understanding: "May my death be an atonement for my sins" (*Yoreh Deah* 338). In the contemporary world, this theology of death, that in dying one dies needing atonement from sin, is often problematic. In liberal Jewish communities, newer versions of the *vidui* assert a profoundly different theology: "For all those I may have hurt, I ask forgiveness. Upon all who have hurt me, I bestow forgiveness" (Shapiro 1993, 22).

With the rich resources of the internet, and contemporary liturgical improvisation, today there are numerous versions of these prayers available, spawning the re-emergence of the deathbed *vidui* in Jewish life.

Deathbed Visions

According to Rabbinic tradition, the moment of death itself is said to be a painless departure of the soul. It is described in the Talmud as being like "taking a hair out of milk" (Ber. 8a). Additionally, in mystical texts there are descriptions of deathbed visions that parallel contemporary near-death experiences. For example, the so-called life-review vision is described as follows: "when God desires to take back a person's spirit, all the days they have lived in this world pass in review" (*Zohar* I, 221b). And further, replicating the stories told of dying individuals seeing deceased loved ones appear, we find in the Zohar:

> At the hour of a person's departure from the world, their father or mother and other relatives gather round, and they see them and recognize them, and likewise all with whom they had associated in this world, and they accompany their soul to the place where it is to abide.
>
> *Zohar I, 218a*

These are but a few of the traditional teachings that demonstrate the inherent Jewish understanding that death is a transition from one realm of being to another, from embodied consciousness to what Nahmanides calls *olam haneshamot*, the world of souls.

Between Death and Burial: *Aninut*

At the moment of death, or when one first hears news of a death, it is traditional to recite the formula "*baruch dayan ha-emet*", literally "blessed be the true judge". The theological implication of this is recognition that human beings do not have control over the destiny of life and death; in the face of life's finality, death is ultimately in the hands of God. Once death has occurred, Judaism sets in place an entirely different ritual framework. The immediate tasks now are to support the bereaved as they begin to cope with death and start preparation for the funeral.

Jewish tradition speaks of the mourner, at this point, as being in a state of *aninut*. Technically, *aninut* is the short period between death and burial. It is a time of raw, hyper-acute grief when mourners are confused, disoriented, in shock, especially when death has been sudden or violent. During *aninut*, mourners are exempt from all religious obligations, *mitzvoth*, in order to focus exclusively on funeral preparations. (To clarify: one is exempt from *mitzvoth t'aseh*, positive commandments, but *mitzvoth lo t'aseh*, the negative commandments, ethical moral prohibitions, remain in place.)

Death is a normal life cycle event, and what transpires at this point for individuals and families occurs within the context of community—at least for those who affiliate with a community. Depending upon a family's communal involvement, a rabbi; Hevra Kaddisha, i.e. Jewish burial society; funeral director; as well as friends and family can all be involved in providing functional and emotional support for bereaved family members.

Preparation for Burial: Hevra Kaddisha

Hevra Kaddisha, literally "Fellowship of the Holy," is the Jewish burial society, a communal organization within Jewish life responsible for the care, ritual preparation and burial of dead bodies. Depending upon the size and structure of a Jewish community, the Hevra Kaddisha may be affiliated with one individual synagogue; a trans-denominational organization serving the entire community; or employees of a funeral home, particularly in larger urban areas. Traditionally, male Hevra Kaddisha members care for the ritual preparation of men; female Hevra Kaddisha members care for women.

Common to all Hevra Kaddisha practice is a sacred process of guarding, washing, purifying and dressing the body of the deceased—referred to as the *met*—in preparation for burial. The sequence of rituals is carried out at a funeral home, although in pre-modern times, and in some older communities this would be done in a building on the cemetery grounds.

The Hevra Kaddisha ritual processes are as follows: S*hmira*, literally "guarding", consists of watching over the body of the deceased and reciting Psalms. As a container of the soul, the body of a deceased person is sacred, and never to be left alone. It has to be protected from death until burial, safeguarded from animals, rodents and insects—certainly that was the case before modernity and the creation of refrigeration in funeral homes. A *shomer*, or guard, remains in close proximity to the body, reciting Psalms, preferably in Hebrew, though in the vernacular if necessary. This prayerful vigilance takes place, before, during and after the body is ritually cleansed. Even once the body is placed in a coffin, *shmira* continues until start of the funeral.

Next, is the process known as *rehitza*, washing the *met* to remove any dirt, foreign matter or extraneous substances, such as bandages, medical apparatus, etc. This is followed by a sacred process called *tahara*, literally "purification", a water ritual consisting of cascading twenty-four quarts of water over the body, in a continuous flow. Together *rehitza*, washing, and *tahara*, purification, function as a way of cleansing the body of earthly defilements, washing away the suffering of a lifetime. These ritual practices are both functional and spiritual. On one hand they provide gentle, compassionate care tending to the lifeless body of a deceased person; on the other hand, they offer conscious comfort for the disembodied soul, as it transitions from this world to the world beyond.

Following this, the *met* is dried and clothed in burial shrouds, white linen garments known as *tachrichim*. Fashioned after the sacred garb worn by the High Priest in the Jerusalem Temple on Yom Kippur, the *tachrichim* are hand-sewn, with no knots—that could hinder the departure of the soul—and no pockets—because whether rich or poor, in death we take no possessions with us. Next a large white sheet is draped inside the casket, traditionally a plain pine box, unadorned and without nails, and the *met* is placed in the coffin and wrapped cocoon-like in the white sheet. A prayer shawl is placed around the *met*—for men in Orthodox communities, and for men and women (who would have worn a prayer shawl in her lifetime) in liberal communities. Next a sachet of earth from the Mount of Olives in Jerusalem is sprinkled within the casket, with some placed over the heart, eyes and genitals of the *met*. The Jerusalem earth is a symbol of the ultimate resurrection of the dead which, according to Rabbinic tradition will begin on the Mount of Olives, a symbol of God's ultimate triumph over death.

As these ritual acts are being carried out, members of the Hevra Kaddisha recite ancient liturgies created specifically for preparing a body for burial. The first comprehensive Jewish burial manual was *Maavor Yabok*, by Rabbi Aaron Berechiah of Modena, published in Mantua, Italy in 1626. In the very last prayer of the *tahara* process, members of the Hevra Kaddisha surround the casket and speak directly to the *met*, assuring the soul that everything was performed according to custom, and asking for forgiveness for any indiscretion or errors. In essence these Hevra Kaddisha practices and liturgies are designed to prepare the soul of the deceased to be welcomed into the transcendent realms of the world beyond.

The Jewish Funeral

Jewish funeral rituals have existed as long as Jews have lived and died. In Genesis 23:17 we read how Abraham bought the Cave of Makhpelah in Hebron to bury his wife Sarah; subsequently, he and his descendants were buried there. This inaugural story of Sarah's burial is the archetypal paradigm of Jewish burial, demonstrating the responsibility one holds for respectful burial of the dead.

In traditional terms, this next stage of ritual practice is called *halvayat hamet*, "accompanying the deceased". For the deceased, the Jewish funeral respectfully disposes of the physical body in the earth; and honorably remembers their life and legacy. For surviving family members, the funeral provides opportunity to say goodbye to a loved one, express emotions of grief and loss, and experience compassionate support of family, friends and community.

Traditionally, the Jewish funeral is designed to be very simple. There is no fanfare, flowers, embalming, open casket, or glorification of a dead body. This simplicity, although often eroded in contemporary times, is the traditional way of Jewish burial. On first hearing news of a death, one would rip their clothing across the heart, a cathartic expression of grief. Today a ritual known as *kriah*—rending of the garments, takes place prior to the funeral service. Instead of tearing one's clothing, some mourners choose a variant on the traditional custom, and wear a symbolic black ribbon. As the ribbon is cut one recites "*baruch dayan ha-emet*", "blessed be the true judge". The psychological function of *kriah* is a catharsis of emotions: tearing one's garment expresses an angry outburst at human powerlessness in the encounter with death. In a symbolic sense, the torn ribbon is a visual representation of the torn heart one experiences at the death of a loved one.

Jewish funeral liturgy is intentionally simple. At the funeral home (or in some cases, the synagogue) the officiating clergy recites Psalm 23, and—although there are many variations based upon the denominational orientation—Psalm 16 and Psalm 90. This is followed by the *Adonai Mah Adam* prayer asserting the existential reality of life and death: "A human being is like a momentary passing breeze; a person's days are but a transient shadow; at dawn, life blossoms and renews itself; at dusk it withers and dries up." *El Maleh Rachamim* is then chanted in a dirgeful melody, petitioning God that the deceased "find rest under the wings of the Divine Presence (Shechinah) … [and] in the heavenly Garden of Eden".

In addition a eulogy, or *hesped* is presented honoring the life of the deceased. Usually delivered by officiating clergy, today it is common for friends or family to also share stories and memories of the deceased. Overall, the eulogy, like the act of *kriah*, facilitates a process of emotional discharge for mourners. And finally the funeral service concludes with mourners saying the Mourners' Kaddish.

Burial Ritual

From the funeral home, mourners are transported to the cemetery. Walking toward the grave escorting the coffin, Psalm 91 is recited. It is traditional to stop seven times along the way, the folk level understanding of this is that it is designed to ward off evil spirits. Additional graveside liturgy includes the *Tz'adduk Ha-Din* prayer, which asserts that God is "The Sheltering Rock; His work is perfect for all His ways are justice." In essence this prayer is an antidote to the sometimes seeming meaninglessness of death, affirming a divine source of justice in the world.

Next is the pinnacle moment of Jewish burial. After the casket is lowered into the earth, mourners and accompanying family and friends shovel earth into the grave. There is a stark realism as sounds of earth hitting the wooden box echo for all to hear, as the deceased is being returned to the earth—"from dust to dust". There may be additional Psalms or prayers recited, followed by the Burial Kaddish which begins with the declaration "Magnified and sanctified be the great name of God" and upholds a belief in resurrection, referring to "that world which He is to create anew, and to revive the dead and to raise them to an everlasting life". In the raw poignancy of death, Jewish burial liturgy affirms a vision of hope and aspiration for total redemption.

A *minyan*, a quorum of ten people, is required for recitation of Kaddish, reminding us that the Jewish funeral is a communal ritual, with friends and family present to support the bereaved and say goodbye to the deceased. Similarly, the collective nature of the burial is most apparent as the graveside service concludes. Walking away from the graveside, immediate family members pass through two parallel rows formed by those present who say: "May God comfort you among the mourners of Zion and Jerusalem". This ritual act indicates to the family: "We are with you in your time of loss, you are not alone in your suffering".

Jewish funeral rituals serve a definite psychological function assisting the bereaved family in accepting the reality of death; providing a ritual context for beginning the process of mourning; and offering communal support for bereaved family members. Caring for the bereaved is a Jewish communal value. This is central to Jewish understanding, in both death and life.

Cremation: The Non-Traditional Alternative

According to traditional Jewish practice, cremation is prohibited. However, historically there is not a clear-cut prohibition against cremation in the Talmud. In ancient Palestine and Babylonia, the underlying assumption was that cremation was not practiced. Given the desert climate of the Middle East, in-ground and cave burial were the standard operating procedures. And in Mishnaic times, cremation was to be avoided simply because it was an idolatrous Roman practice. Both Talmud (Sanhedrin 46b) and Maimonides (*Sefer HaMitzvot* 231, 536) emphasize the practice of in-ground burial; and in *Shulchan Arukh*, and other classical codes there is no overt condemnation of cremation. The campaign against cremation started when the Reform movement began advocating for the permissibility of cremation in the closing decades of the 19th century. This in turn provoked a vociferous Orthodox backlash, and only then did cremation come to be seen as a denial of the resurrection (*Kol Bo Al Aveilut*, 54ff). This persists to this day.

The doctrine of resurrection of the dead, *techiyat hametim*, is a central Rabbinic tenet: the belief is that at the end of time, God will intervene in the human realm, the socio-political order will be divinized, there will be a messianic transformation, and all the dead will be brought back to life. If one is cremated, so goes the traditional rationalization, one cannot participate in the resurrection. Hence the prohibition. However, liberal Jewish practice holds a flexible attitude toward cremation. As early as 1892 the Central Conference of American Rabbis began to permit officiation following cremation. With urban mobility and spiraling costs of burial, today many Jews are choosing to be cremated. This trend will undoubtedly continue to grow in the future.

Shivah: Seven Days of Communal Mourning

Returning from the cemetery, mourners wash their hands outside of the home (usually of the deceased or immediate family member) and upon entering, the seven-day period of mourning—"sitting *shivah*"—begins. During this time, the bereaved suspend worldly activities and devote full attention to remembering and mourning their beloved one. Family members and friends visit the *shivah* house to offer condolences and support.

The institution of *shivah* is very old in Jewish tradition. Earliest mention of a seven-day period of mourning occurs in Genesis where it indicates Joseph observed seven days of mourning after the death of his father Jacob (Gen. 50:10). According to the Talmud, at the time of Noah and the Flood, God "mourned seven days for the destruction of the world" (San. 108b). *Shivah* commences on the day of burial and concludes on the morning of the seventh day. During the Sabbath, there is a temporary cessation in the observance of mourning.

According to Jewish law, *shivah* is observed for parents, a spouse, sibling or child. In the case of an infant of less than thirty days, there is no *shivah* observance, traditionally. However, in recent years there is an acknowledgment of the intensity of grief in the case of infant loss and miscarriage, and people are now creating observing mourning rituals in such cases. The *shivah* begins with a traditional meal for mourners called *seudat havra'ah*, "the meal of consolation". Provided by friends and family this meal traditionally consists of foods which are round, symbolic of the cyclical nature of life. Traditionally this has been lentils and hard-boiled eggs. Although the symbolism is sometimes lost, the purpose in eating these foods is to remind the mourner that life is cyclical and continues even in the face of death.

Throughout the *shivah*, mourners sit on low stools (hence the term "sitting *shivah*"), indicative of their bereaved state. They are also prohibited from wearing leather, bathing, engaging in marital relations and even studying Torah, regarded as a pleasurable activity to be avoided during mourning. In the *shivah* house, it is customary to cover all mirrors, so mourners will avoid looking at themselves, and instead reflect upon the meaning of life and death. Another reason for this practice, according to medieval Jewish understanding, was that the spirit of the departed could remain in the house as an image hidden in the mirror.

Each day during *shivah*, traditional morning, afternoon and evening prayers are recited. During these services mourners recite the Kaddish prayer. For the complete seven-day period a candle flame burns continuously in remembrance of the departed. According to Proverbs 20:27: "The candle of God, is the soul of the person." The glowing candle is seen, symbolically, as a divine guide for the soul, or a remembrance of the soul's divine nature.

Shivah concludes with mourners walking around the block. This serves the function of beginning re-entry into life, after the intensive week of mourning during *shivah*. Interestingly, according to the Zohar it is said that "for seven days the soul goes to and fro from one's house to one's grave, from one's grave to one's house, mourning for the body" (*Zohar* I, 218b). According to mystical understanding, this suggests that the soul of the deceased remains in proximity to the world of the living in the immediate days following death. Psychologically, walking around the block is a re-emergence into daily life; but spiritually, in a symbolic sense, this ritual act is seen as a way of escorting the soul on its journey.

Shivah is an ancient Jewish ritual designed to give mourners emotional support and time for emotional discharge during this acute phase of mourning. When practiced with dignity and respect as prescribed by Jewish tradition, this ritual has a powerful psychological efficacy in assisting the process of bereavement and healing.

Shloshim: Thirty Days of Transition

Judaism, in its wisdom, prescribes an ongoing and gradated process of mourning. The first thirty days after a death, referred to as *shloshim* (meaning thirty), is a transitional period designed to carry one from the initial impact of death and burial toward a gradual reestablishment of the daily rhythms of life.

As with *shivah*, traditionally there are a series of *halakhic* prohibitions, though less restrictive, including no haircutting, shaving, wearing new clothes, getting married, attending parties, listening to music, etc. Traditionally during this time, mourners say the Kaddish daily in synagogue. For those mourning a child, spouse or sibling, according to traditional Jewish practice, thirty days constitutes the full time of mourning. However, in the case of death of a parent, the formal process of mourning continues for one year.

Psychologically, the function of *shloshim* is to act as a transitional phase in which the mourner slowly integrates the reality of death and its impact. In the first days and weeks after a death, mourners can be disoriented, exhausted from the visceral impact of grief, feeling numb, disconnected. Over the course of *shloshim*, mourners slowly resume active life, moving from shock and disorientation toward gradual acceptance of death.

At the end of *shloshim*, it is traditional for mourners to gather friends and family and study in honor of the deceased. The merit of this study is said to have a beneficent effect on the state of the soul. At every juncture along the way, traditional Jewish practices provide moments for connection between the living and the dead.

Kaddish: Historical Background, Traditional and Psychological Perspectives

For those who have lost a parent, the mourning process continues for a full year. Traditionally, the ritual highlight of this period is the daily recitation of the Kaddish prayer. A mourner "says Kaddish" for eleven months as a way of remembering, honoring and memorializing the deceased. The word "kaddish" is derived from a Hebrew root, *l'kadesh*—"to make holy". An ancient Aramaic prayer dating from Geonic times, c. 7th century C.E. Kaddish was recited at the conclusion of Talmudic study in ancient Babylonia. Later this prayer was integrated into synagogue liturgy. The earliest reference to Kaddish as a memorial prayer was made in 13th-century Rhineland by Rabbi Isaac ben Moses of Vienna (c. 1180–1250) in a book *Or Zarua* (Shabbat, 50) (Wieseltier 1988, 46ff.). Following the devastation of Jewish life after the First (1096–1099) and Second (1147–1149) Crusades, saying Kaddish emerged as way for bereaved orphans to honor their deceased parents.

By the late 16th century, we find in Rabbi Moses Isserles' gloss to the *Shulchan Arukh* (*Yoreh Deah* 376:4) that recitation of Mourner's Kaddish had become accepted practice in both Ashkenazic and Sephardic communities.

Recitation of Kaddish is a public act, said during morning and evening prayer services in the presence of a minyan, or quorum of ten worshippers. Originally, mourners recited Kaddish for an entire year. However, since the maximum length of time in Gehenna, the postmortem realm of purgation, is said to be twelve months, in the mid-16th century Rabbi Moshe Isserles limited recitation of Kaddish to eleven months (*Yoreh Deah*, 376.4 *Rema*). Out of filial respect, one would not assume one's parent had merited maximum punishment in Gehenna. Although the process of mourning continues until the end of the first year, a mourner completes saying Kaddish thirty days before the first anniversary of the death.

Besides being a liturgical prayer, Kaddish is a process for healing grief. Publicly reciting Kaddish for eleven months is the method Judaism prescribes for recovery from loss and bereavement. And since the act of saying Kaddish is a communal one, it also forces mourners to interact with other people in the synagogue environment. This serves an important function, breaking the social isolation of mourning. Saying Kaddish also helps a mourner remember the deceased, appreciating the legacy that person left behind. Since many people are not necessarily involved in organized religious life, it is helpful to think of Kaddish as *both* a specific ritual act one performs in synagogue as well an internal process of working through the nature of one's relationship with the person who has died.

Yahrzeit: *Traditional Perspectives*

Yahrzeit is the traditional term for the anniversary of a person's death. Derived from a Yiddish word meaning "year's time", *Yahrzeit* is a time for commemorating the death of a family member; for remembering their life and legacy; and for honoring their memory through a number of specifically prescribed Jewish rituals. *Yahrzeit* is observed on the anniversary date of a person's death, according to the Hebrew calendar. If the exact date of death is unknown, a person may choose an approximate date and observe that annually as the time of *Yahrzeit*. In Sephardic tradition, observance of the anniversary of a death is called *Yom Hillula*.

The custom of observing the anniversary of a death is an ancient one. The first reference to a *Yahrzeit* is found in the Book of Judges: "And it was a custom in Israel, that the daughters of Israel went yearly to lament the daughter of Yiftach the Gileadite, four days in a year" (Judges 11:40). In Talmudic times, *Yahrzeit* was observed regularly; individuals would fast upon the anniversary of a parent's death.

Yahrzeit is observed through a very few simple customs. The most common observance associated with *Yahrzeit* is the lighting of a memorial candle, which burns for a twenty-four-hour period. Like the *shivah* candle, the *Yahrzeit* lamp is linked to the passage of Proverbs 20:27 "A person's spirit is the lamp of the Lord".

Traditionally, there is no formal prayer for kindling the *Yahrzeit* lamp. However, it is common to offer personal prayers on behalf of the departed, and to silently connect with one's own private thoughts and feelings about the person whose *Yahrzeit* is being commemorated. It is also traditional to attend synagogue services and recite a Kaddish in honor of one's *Yahrzeit*.

Another traditional custom some practice is fasting on the *Yahrzeit* for one's parents, although today this is not a widely followed custom. Instead, people contribute to charity, do charitable deeds, or sponsor a synagogue Kiddush in honor of the deceased. It is also a traditional practice to spend some time in study specifically to honor a departed one.

Psychologically, *Yahrzeit* provides a time for the living to remember the dead and the legacy they left behind. This is especially important as time passes on and the memory of a person fades. By observing *Yahrzeit* people are able to reconnect with feelings and memories about the deceased, and to note the passing of the cycles of time.

Yizkor: *Traditional Perspectives*

Yizkor is a Hebrew word which means "remembrance". It refers to memorial services held four times each year in honor of those who have died. Traditionally *Yizkor* prayers are offered during morning synagogue services on Yom Kippur, Shemini Atzeret, and the last days of Passover and Shavuot.

The practice of remembering the dead was an entirely new liturgical innovation developed progressively in the Middle Ages. Given the cultural trauma of major anti-Jewish outbreaks—first during the Crusades and later at the time of the Black Death—a need arose to memorialize and honor deceased martyrs (I. Marcus 2002, 463). Over time the Yizkor prayer services evolved and emerged as a "communal family liturgical memorial", in which all deceased family members were honored (Freehof 1965, 185). During the 16th–18th centuries, days for remembering the dead became established on the liturgical calendar: first Yom Kippur (*Tanhuma*, on Deut. 3:21) and then, additionally, only in the 1800s, at the time of the three pilgrimage festivals.

It is customary to recite *Yizkor* for a deceased parent, child, sibling or spouse. It has also become common practice to recite *Yizkor* prayers on behalf of the six million Jewish martyrs of the Holocaust. While the general practice is to recite *Yizkor* in a synagogue, it is not uncommon for a person to recite private *Yizkor* prayers in one's home. In addition to reciting prayers on *Yizkor*, there are two other specific customs associated with *Yizkor*. As with *Yahrzeit*, it is common at the time of *Yizkor* to contribute to *tzedakah* in memory of the departed, and to kindle a memorial lamp on the sundown of the festival when *Yizkor* is recited.

Psychologically, *Yizkor* provides a special and sacred time to remember and honor those who have died. During the regular ongoing cycle of life, it is easy to be pre-occupied with the demands of daily living and often difficult to take the time to remember people who once were part of our life. *Yizkor* is a time for the remembrance of souls. It offers opportunity to connect with our memories about one who has died, and to reflect on their life and their legacy.

Through the saying of the *Yizkor*, the spiritual bond between the living and the soul of the departed is developed and strengthened. It is this spiritual bond which links the past to the present and allows us to prepare for the future with hope and with a sense of feeling connected to those whom we have known and loved.

From deathbed through to burial, from *shivah* through to the cyclical remembrance of loved ones at *Yizkor*, Judaism provides ritual forms that offer comfort and help us find meaning and communal connection in the face of the fragility of life. When practiced with an awareness of the inherent psychological and spiritual wisdom of Jewish death traditions, these practices help individuals and families navigate the vicissitudes and changes of the cycles of life and death.

Bibliography

Berman, Rochel U. 2005. *Dignity Beyond Death: The Jewish Preparation for Burial*. New York: Urim Publications.

Brener, Anne. 2018. *Mourning and Mitzvah: A Guided Journal for Walking the Mourner's Path Through Grief to Healing*, 25th anniversary edition. Woodstock, VT: Jewish Lights Publishing.

Cardin, Nina Beth. 2007. *Tears of Sorrow, Seeds of Hope: A Jewish Spiritual Companion for Infertility and Pregnancy Loss*, 2nd edition. Woodstock, VT: Jewish Lights Publishing.

Caro, Joseph. 1954. *Code of Hebrew Law: Shuhan Aruk Yoreh De'ah*, trans. Chaim Denburg. Montreal, QC: Jurisprudence Press.

Diamant, Anita. 2019. *Saying Kaddish: How to Comfort the Dying, Bury the Dead and Mourn as a Jew*, revised edition. New York: Schocken Books.

Freehof, Solomon B. 1965. "Hazkarath Neshamoth", *Hebrew Union College Annual*, Vol. 36: 179–89.

Friedman, Dayle A., David Levin and Simcha Paull Raphael. Eds. 2021. *Jewish End-of-Life Care in a Virtual Age*. Boulder, CO: Albion-Andalus Books.

Goldberg, Sylvie-Anne. 1996. *Crossing the Jabbok: Illness and Death in Ashkenazi Judaism in Sixteenth through Nineteenth Century Prague*, trans. Carol Cossman. Berkeley: University of California Press.

Goldin, Hyman E. 1956. "Laws Concerning a Dying Person, and the Care to Be Taken of the Dead Body". In *HaMadrikh: The Rabbi's Guide*. New York: Hebrew Publishing Co., 107.

Greenwald, Yekutiel (n.d.) *Kol Bo Al Aveilut*. New York: Philipp Feldheim, Inc.

Hallote, Rachel S. 2001. *Death, Burial, and Afterlife in the Biblical World*. Chicago, IL: Ivan R. Dee.

Heilman, Samuel C. 2001. *When a Jew Dies*. Los Angeles: University of California Press.

Kornbluth, Doron. 2012. *Cremation or Burial: A Jewish View*. Monsey, NY: Mosaica Press.

Marcus, Jacob R. 1947. *Communal Sick-Care in the German Ghetto*. Cincinnati, OH: Hebrew Union College Press.

Marcus, Ivan. 2002. "A Jewish-Christian Symbiosis: The Culture of Early Ashkenaz", in *Cultures of the Jews: A New History*. Ed. David Biale, vol. 2. New York: Schocken.

Marx, Dalia. 2014. "From the Rhine Valley to Jezreel Valley: Innovative Versions of the Mourners Kaddish in the Kibbutz Movement", in *Between Tradition and Modernity: Rethinking Old Opposition, Essays in Honor of David Ellenson*. Eds. Michael Meyer and David A. Myers. Detroit, MI: Wayne State University Press.

Nahmanides. 1983. *The Gate of Reward*. Trans. Charles B. Chavel. New York: Shilo Publishing House.

Raphael, Simcha Paull. 2015. *The Grief Journey and the Afterlife: Jewish Pastoral Care for Bereavement*. Boulder, CO: Albion-Andalus Books.

Raphael, Simcha Paull. 2016. *May the Angels Carry You: Jewish Prayers and Meditations for the Deathbed*. Boulder, CO: Albion-Andalus Books.

Raphael, Simcha Paull. 2019. *Jewish Views of the Afterlife*, 25th anniversary edition, 3rd edition. Lanham, MD: Rowman and Littlefield.

Raphael, Simcha Paull. 2021. "Transformation of Jewish Death Rituals in Times of Crisis, Pandemic and Cultural Dislocation", in *Jewish End-of-Life Care in a Virtual Age: Our Traditions Reimagined*. Eds. Dayle A. Friedman, David Levin and Simcha Paull Raphael. Boulder, CO: Albion-Andalus Books.

Shapiro, Rami. 1993. *Last Breaths: A Guide to Easing Another's Dying*. Miami, FL: Temple Beth Or.

Weiss, Abner. 1991. *Death and Bereavement: A Halakhic Guide*. Hoboken, NJ: Ktav Publishing.

Wieseltier, Leon. 1988. *Kaddish*. New York: Alfred A. Knopf.

33
BETWEEN TRADITION AND INNOVATION
Alternative Funeral Rites in Israel

Anna Prashizky

Introduction

Alongside the control over life cycle rituals such as weddings and funerals among Israeli Jews maintained by the Orthodox rabbinical establishment, secular Israelis are increasingly adopting various non-Orthodox rites, and a growing number of secular bodies and entrepreneurs are engaged in shaping, conducting and directing such rituals. One may even assert that these "alternative rituals," as they are commonly known, are evolving into a new and widely accepted fashion among middle- and upper-class secular Israelis. For our present purpose, I define as "alternative" any ritual that differs from the Orthodox pattern and is not recognized by the rabbinate and the Ministry of the Interior (with regard to weddings), or a funeral rite that is not conducted by the Chevra Kadisha (the official Orthodox burial society). In other words, I mean any ritual that offers an alternative and/or undermines the Orthodox ritual, but at the same time refers to it, criticizes and amends it. The liturgical Jewish tradition constitutes an important point of reference for the new non-Orthodox rituals, which in various ways draw upon the bank of traditional Jewish symbols and rituals, and quite often recognize them as part of the cultural heritage of the Jewish people.

The alternative ritual in Israel is an extremely multi-faceted phenomenon that draws on and merges at least six different intellectual sources: liberal Judaism, as manifested in the Reform movement; secular Israelis' reclaiming the so-called "Jewish library" (a collection of canonic texts in Jewish religion, history and culture) also termed Jewish Renewal; the revitalized kibbutz movement; the "civil trend," manifested, for example, in civil marriage ceremonies; the assorted New Age movements with various types of spiritual and mystic rituals; and the sexual minorities (LGBT) movement. It is worth noting that the new ritualism is deeply rooted in Israel's kibbutz traditions and in European and American liberal Judaism; one of the main arenas for secular ritual activity has been the kibbutz movement (Zeira, 2002). Over the last 30 years, mass migration to Israel with the economic and demographic changes it entailed has also influenced alternative ways of burial. Specifically, FSU immigrants not recognized by the Orthodox authorities as Jews had problems with burials, because only Jews can be buried on the Jewish cemeteries. Additionally, more and more secular Israelis rejected Orthodox burial service. The alternatives created by secular entrepreneurs motivated by ideology, profit or their combination provided a variety of new burial services (Ben-Porat, 2013). The emergence of a novel cultural system of ritual serving as a symbolic foundation for secular Israelis at major turning points in their lives can teach us a great deal about the transformations that the Israeli society is currently undergoing. The chapter explores how secular Israelis who reject the Orthodox ritual mark the burial of their loved ones. One of the central questions is, how are these new rituals linked to the Orthodox Jewish ritual and to what extent do they represent new burial forms and repertoires?

This chapter makes two central claims. First, I trace the major components of non-Orthodox funeral rites in Israel. I propose to view them as a novel type of post-secular and post-modern ritual that combines components associated with the meta-categories of religion and secularism, rather than exchanging one set for another. I argue that the new alternative ritual in Israel is characterized by a varied hybridization of canonic religious prayers and appeals to God with components devoid of religious connotation and even perceived to convey an unequivocally anti-religious message, such as poems and songs of secular Israeli and world poets and singers. The second claim is that in the frame of alternative rituals, the canonic and more static repertoire of the Jewish Orthodox funeral is replaced by the new, more flexible repertoire of literary creativity exemplified by modern Hebrew and world poetry. Officials at alternative funerals propose to the family the selection of famous poems and different versions of secular prayers instead of the Orthodox blessings. In this way, a new repertoire of alternative (non-Orthodox) funeral is being created that can be seen as a part of the process of new canonization.

Theoretical Background: A New Paradigm for the Analysis of Ritual

The parallel existence of official and individual rituals in contemporary society has inspired an alternative set of concepts to frame the new reality, a new paradigm of ritual that constitutes the theoretical foundation of this chapter. The basic premise of this approach is that we find numerous instances of ritual in modern or post-modern industrial society, and that they play no less significant a role than did those in traditional society (Bocock, 1974). In other words, ritualism has not declined in contemporary society, but has merely changed its forms. Religious rituals have been replaced by civil, political, sporting, aesthetic and individual rituals denoted together by the term secular ritual (Moore and Myerhoff, 1977). These scholars defined secular ritual as associated with ideology, possessing immanent meaning, obeying the logic of this world alone, and which is operationally effective as shown by empirical results. Another term coined by scholars in the context of the new ritualism is ceremony of definition or individual defining ceremony, which refers to unofficial, unique events conducted by invisible or marginal social groups seeking to define their identity in a dramatic way and display it in public, thereby gaining visibility and recognition (Myerhoff, 1987).

Giddens (1991) has likewise addressed the transformations undergone by ritual at the personal level. He maintains that modern society differs from its traditional counterpart because the same ritual transitions are accompanied by a reflexive path of self-realization. Present-day ritual constitutes largely a means of self-searching and self-expression that entails a proliferation of newly designed and invented personal and alternative rituals. A further important development is found in the domain of the new spirituality practiced beyond the boundaries of established religion (Wuthnow, 1998). It is characterized by negotiation and search associated with defining one's identity and is manifested most clearly in New Age ritualism merged with consumer culture. Adherents of the New Age search for spiritual meaning and choose novel ritual practices through consumption (Alfred, 2000; Tavori, 2007).

Another expression of the new ritualism is the invention of rituals and an active approach toward them. This phenomenon is acquiring a growing legitimacy: people invent rituals and are aware of this. Scholars, too, suggest that people ignore various ritual "experts" and take the initiative designing rituals that meet their own needs, thus becoming the creators of their life story (Grimes, 2000; Ochs, 2007). In most current cases that involve the invention or reinterpretation of ritual, a new paradigm is gradually replacing assumptions that have been in place for years. In the new model, ritual constitutes primarily a means toward self-expression, a novel type of language (Bell, 1997). Finally, one of the major and most immediate developments within the new ritualism can be attributed to the impact of feminism. This manifests in the entry of women to rituals customarily led and controlled by men; the active resistance of women in conservative religions; the creation of rituals for women; and elevation of women's status in various rituals (Koren, 2011; Marx, 2009; Roll *et al.*, 2001).

All the above-mentioned scholars assert that a novel type of ritual has emerged in contemporary society. This is a form of ritual that is not necessarily religious in the traditional sense, but rather possesses a secular sanctity expressed in the context of a secular nation state, or a spirituality that breaks out of the confines of established religion. It is a personal form of ritual that constitutes an arena and a platform for defining the individual's identity and is part of a process of self-realization. It is, furthermore, an initiatory form of ritual that enables freedom of choice and action with regard to ritual, as people invent their own ritual and conduct ritual activity on their own accord. And finally, this is a more female-oriented ritual that enables women to play an active role in the arena of ritual and addresses experiences that are unique to women.

The creation of alternative life cycle rituals is not confined to the Israeli society but is observed in many Western countries, accompanied by the dissemination of popular and scholarly guides encouraging ritual-oriented activism (Eichenwald, 2007). Adopting this new paradigm of ritual analysis, this chapter examines the components of the new ritual, focusing on non-Orthodox funeral rites conducted in present-day Israel. The aim is to analyze them from post-secular and post-modern perspectives, trying to establish their links with and divergence from Orthodox Jewish ritual (Rose, 1996; Gurevich, 1998; Shenhav, 2008).

The Post-Secular Perspective

In recent decades, the post-secular perspective has gained ascendance in the social sciences, as scholars began to question the basic premises of the secularization thesis that asserted a linear process of distancing from religion (Casanova, 1994; McLennan, 2007). The post-secular perspective maintains that religion and secularization are closely linked and interdependent, and that complex hybrids of religiosity and secularity have emerged, rather than a process of replacement. A post-secular outlook for the study of Israeli society has recently been proposed, focusing on the new phenomena in the Israeli society, such as secular houses of prayer and study, the Israeli New Age, and the Jewish Renewal Movement (Shenhav, 2008; Neeman, 2011; Klein Oron and Ruah-Midbar, 2010; Ruah-Midbar, 2014). These studies question the ostensibly clear-cut distinction between secular and religious people and highlight the complexity of these categories that are intimately linked (Yona and Goodman, 2010; Yedger, 2010), as well as the appearance of a new religious identity, so-called religious secularity.

This chapter seeks to examine the new ritual practices conducted by secular Israelis at funerals from a post-secular perspective, thereby contributing to the critical discourse on religious and secular people in Israel. While the thesis of secularization asserts that secular rituals have replaced religious ones through a process of secularization in modern society, this discussion argues that post-secular and post-modern rituals are replacing religious rituals (as part of the secular public chooses to create new rituals to replace the Orthodox ones). I further assert that within pluralistic Israeli society these new rituals coexist with the canonic religious ones, while secular public can practice both types at different moments of life cycle stages. While the religious public typically adheres to the Orthodox rituals, even in this sector of Israelis we observe some deviations, for example avoidance of Orthodox weddings for feminist reasons.

Methodology

This ethnography investigates the various forms of non-Orthodox funeral rituals performed by secular Israelis recognized as Jews by the state institutions. By contrast to the Orthodox funeral canon, there is no established pattern of alternative rituals; they display great diversity of form and content, shaped by the officiating figure and the wishes of the mourners burying a loved one.

The present study offers an anthropological, qualitative-interpretational analysis based on participant observation at dozens of such alternative events in Israel, as well as interviews with key figures at these events, such as officials and family members. The observations were conducted over the past ten years at secular kibbutz cemeteries (in the Jerusalem area and in northern Israel) and a variety of alternative funerals conducted by Reform and secular rabbis. I interviewed ten organizers/officials of alternative funerals and received additional information from the Havaya institute on the variety of funerals, complemented by the questionnaires collected at a Kibbutz Movement Symposium on Rituals of Mourning (Tel Aviv, February 2009) for funeral homes' personnel. Additionally, I analyzed the guidebook for creating new life cycle rituals in Israel (Eichenwald, 2007) and articles about alternative funerals in the two central Israeli cites (www.english.tkasim.org.il/, www.havaya.info/havaya-english/).

In analyzing this material, I employed a qualitative-interpretational approach focusing on the symbolic meaning of the various rituals. On the assumption that a ritual event tells a certain story and provides a version of social order that "presents the world" within a frame defined by time and place (Geertz, 1990), my core question is: what alternative type of social order do non-Orthodox funeral rites suggest? Furthermore, according to the qualitative paradigm, people arrange their concepts of the world through stories (Shkedi, 2004). There is a good deal to be gained from interpreting the life stories that people recounted in the interviews.

Jewish Burial Rites

Orthodox burial rites are not a monolith and embrace differences between the customs of Mizrahi and Ashkenazi Jews. Orthodox religious burials and treatment of the dead are controlled and conducted by the Ministry of Religion and the Burial Society (Hevra Kadisha). The key rites of the Orthodox funeral rite (with some ethnic variations) include presenting and burying the body wrapped in a white shroud (rather than placed in a coffin), the rending of a garment by the next of kin, the eulogy, *Kaddish* prayer, proceeding on foot to the grave while bearing the deceased, the *Tsiduk ha-din* (justification of divine judgment) prayer, the *El malei rachamim* prayer, and an appeal for forgiveness. Funeral motions are accompanied by reading or chanting the excerpts from canonical Jewish sources, such as the Mishnah, the psalms, and various prayers.

Most alternative rituals examined in this study included traditional elements of the Orthodox burial, albeit to varying degrees and in different ways. Some key elements appear in the alternative events in their traditional version, others with some new components, and yet others are called by their traditional name but are infused with a novel content. Although Orthodox Jewish tradition bans cremation, Israelis can also choose to be cremated through the recently established Aley Shalechet company[1] that offers an officiating service and designs a private ritual in line with the wishes of the deceased and their family.[2] In Judaism the mourning period begins at the moment of death and extends for several months after the funeral (Rubin, 1997).

Let me now focus on a funeral conducted at Kibbutz Ma'aleh Ha-Hamisha, of a woman named Miriam who died in her nineties. Thus, let us examine one specific case, with additions from other cases of alternative funerals. The Ma'aleh Ha-Hamisha cemetery is located in a rural area that affords a wide view of the Judean hills. It is surrounded by numerous pine trees and the graves and their environs are adorned with colorful flowers and greenery. Miriam's family chose a non-Orthodox funeral led by a female Reform rabbi in a plot that they had purchased in the kibbutz cemetery. They define themselves as secular people not belonging to the Reform (or any other) community. They were referred to the rabbi by a cemetery employee and chose her for her openness and willingness to shape the rite according to their views. In an interview, the deceased woman's daughter, who lived in Jerusalem, explained why she had wished to bury her mother in a kibbutz cemetery and choose a secular form of burial. They oppose Orthodoxy and religious coercion and dislike Orthodox cemeteries, which they regard as harsh and alienating places devoid of greenery and flowers, unwelcoming to visit and remember the deceased. These words imply the dislike of the Orthodox dictate and a wish to rebel against it, thus matching the anthropological findings on secular Israelis' attitudes toward the Orthodox funeral. Scholars found a sense of unease and discomfort among secular mourners and pointed to the discord between the religious rites and secular values, serving as a point of friction in the ongoing tensions between Orthodox and secular Jews (Abramovitz, 1993; Ashkenazi, 1993).

Another reason mentioned in the interview was the desire to choose a funeral rite appropriate to the participants' worldview, designed according to their wishes and not dictated by religion. In other words, they wished to have a free hand in deciding how the ritual should be conducted. One should not view the preference for a non-Orthodox rite as an expression of outright secularity, but rather the one that respects Jewish values. The interviewee stressed that they were spiritual but not religious people; Jewish but not Orthodox, who sought a ritual that would faithfully express their identity and was not dictated by the religious authorities. The incorporation of traditional Jewish elements in the ritual reflected a compromise, or as she put it, allowing everyone, including the religious mourners, to feel comfortable with the ritual. In other words, the desire to preserve the thread that connected them with traditional Judaism and its representatives and not to sever this link altogether. Members of Miriam's family washed and dressed her body themselves prior to burial. It was placed in a casket and not covered in shrouds as is customary in Chevra Kadisha funerals. The use of a casket is one of the major differences between the Orthodox and other burial rites. However, some families who opt for an alternative funeral conducted in a civil cemetery do turn to a religious society to purify the body according to the procedures of Orthodox Judaism.

The funeral began with some introductory remarks about the deceased by the female Reform rabbi, which she delivered facing the coffin at the entrance to the cemetery. She then invited people to carry the coffin to the grave. Following the burial of the casket, eulogies were delivered alongside the grave, in the following order. (1) Shmuel, Miriam's brother-in-law, recited a poem that he himself composed. He had, in fact, intended to read a poem by the Welsh poet Dylan Thomas, but instead recited his own, dedicated to the deceased. He moved the Dylan Thomas poem to the next memorial occasion: the thirtieth day after Miriam's death. (2) A personal piece written by the deceased's eldest granddaughter Bat Ami. (3) A reading of four passages beginning with the letters n-sh-m-a (spelling the Hebrew word soul) written specially by her youngest granddaughter Yael. (4) A eulogy delivered by the Reform rabbi, in which she reviewed the deceased's life and character. (5) A musical interlude – the Song of the Birds. This was followed by a recitation of the traditional *El malei rachamim* prayer by the female rabbi. The ritual concluded with a reading of a secular version of the *Kaddish* prayer recited by Ariela, the deceased's niece, who was very close to her and was therefore chosen for this role. We shall now address all the parts of the funeral in turn.

Rending (*keri'ah*)

It is customary to make a tear in a garment worn by mourners at the cemetery before accompanying the deceased to their grave. There are various customs associated with rending, and in some cases this is done at the point of death or upon hearing of the death. Generally, a Chevra Kadisha functionary makes a tear in a garment worn on the upper part of the body by the deceased's close relatives. The mourner stands, and the functionary makes a tear with a knife and the mourner then recites the blessing: "Blessed are you, lord our God, king of the universe, the judge of truth." The mourner then extends the cut by pulling on the garment. Rending is one of the key symbols of a Jewish funeral, equivalent to the breaking of a glass at weddings. The two customs share the same symbolism. As Rubin (1997) explains, customs of rending, breaking and removing have a special meaning in Judaism. The individual who passes from one life stage to another partakes in a ritual at which the rending or the removal indicate the changes he/she is undergoing. Examples include circumcision (removal of the foreskin), breaking a glass at a wedding, and rending at a funeral. These are irreversible processes that mark a change of status that cannot be undone. According to Rubin, rending possesses further significance as a means of expressing and releasing emotions of anger at the death of the loved one on the part of the mourner. Rubin furthermore explains that rending is a formal ritual act governed by clear-cut rules (the halakha determines the size of the tear and its precise location on the garment, and stipulates which relatives of the deceased are obliged to undergo *keri'ah*). Rending is done while standing and marks a special expression of respect and acceptance of authority manifested in the *Barukh dayan emet* prayer. This prayer constitutes a public declaration of belief in God and in the justice of His deeds. How is the *keri'ah* performed in non-Orthodox funeral rituals? My observations suggest that there is no single rule here. At some alternative funerals the custom is maintained, while at others it is not. At Miriam's funeral no rending was performed since the family did not wish to observe the practice.

Eulogies

By eulogy we refer to "everything said about the deceased in public" (Rubin, 1997). The eulogy forms an integral part of the Orthodox funeral. My observations at alternative funerals and conversations with the functionaries who officiated at them indicate that personal memories generated by eulogies constitute the salient and ever-expanding element of these new rituals. At Miriam's funeral, eulogies served to paint an ideal portrait of the deceased, to describe her life story and character. Her relatives and friends added observations from their own perspectives. Thus, at alternative funeral rituals the individual biographic memory of the deceased is placed at the center of the public ritual stage, providing opportunities for story-sharing. The primary theme of alternative funerals is therefore the personal portrait of the deceased person rather than symbolic ritual actions. Such personalization and individualization of post-mortem rituals is a typical tendency in contemporary Western societies (Ramshaw, 2009), reflective of a broad post-modernism shift that entails an equation of meaningful with personal. When people are not embedded in a traditional community, the private world becomes the locus of meaning-making. A new ritual is likely to be meaningful to the extent that it is personally designed and expresses personal experiences and memories.

Music and Poetry

At Miriam's funeral, the family eulogies ended with the playing of the Song of the Birds. Playing recorded music that the deceased loved or that highlights her character, as well as live music played on a violin, guitar or flute beside the fresh grave are commonplace at alternative funerals. At another kibbutz funeral, for example, a friend of the deceased played on a flute (that he had received as a gift from him) the Blessed Spirits piece from Gluck's *Orpheus in the Underworld*. At this funeral, contemporary Israeli poems were recited, along with the traditional *El malei rachamim* and *Kaddish* prayers. One of the deceased's sons played a guitar and sang a Frank Sinatra song in English. The Hebrew poets such as Tchernichovsky, Bialik, Alterman, Amihai and Rabikovich are often recited at alternative funerals, as well as poems in other languages if the deceased and/or the family originated in another country. Sometimes poems written by the deceased themselves or verses composed about them by family and friends are recited, as was the case at Miriam's funeral. At the funeral of a renowned Israeli writer held at the same kibbutz, a poem by the Russian poet Anna Ahmatova was read, along with a poem by the deceased, and then a close friend of his read the excerpts from his diary. At this funeral, a secular *Kaddish* was recited as well as the traditional *El malei rachamim*. At another funeral that I visited recently (2016) in a northern kibbutz, the family sang together the man's favorite song by the late Israeli singer Aric Einstein "Fly Away, Little Bird."

Music, literature and poetry are the means of elevating human spirit and reaching the sublime. One may thus view them as spiritual and even religious elements. Music enables people to share strong feelings, helping mourners to express their grief and to imbue them with beauty and a possibility of joy. In a sense, poetry serves as an equivalent of religious blessings, which likewise entail the divine sublimity and spirituality. In this spirit, secular rabbi and the poet Coby Viner has published an article titled "Hebrew Poetry as Secular Prayer," where he describes the significance of the contemporary Hebrew poetry that is likely to replace the traditional Jewish blessings and prayers (www.tkasim.org.il).

This tendency is enhanced by the influence of European non-Jewish funeral rites, both religious and secular, at which it is customary to play instruments and sing. It is worth noting that playing flute music was a customary part of Jewish funerals during the Talmud era. Rubin (1997) suggested that this custom may have been discontinued as part of the attempt by sages to ban song and music altogether. Thus, despite the common current view, singing and playing music were by no means foreign to the spirit of the Jewish funeral. This demonstrates that art plays a major role in the new rituals that enhance one's spiritual and holy experience. As Abramowitz (1993) notes in his article on the secular Israelis' attitudes toward the Orthodox funeral rites, many of them are offended by the lack of aesthetic variety in the burials conducted by the Chevra Kadisha. Investing in the aesthetic aspects of the new rituals meets the need felt by secular Israelis sharing Western values. At alternative funerals this influence is manifested in several aspects, such as burying the deceased in a coffin rather than in shrouds; placing wreaths and flowers on the grave instead of or alongside the Jewish custom of placing stones; arranging chairs at the cemetery, installing shading on hot summer days, and distributing bottles of water to the attendees; use of loudspeakers and a microphone to enable all the participants to hear the eulogies clearly; and distributing leaflets communicating the order of the ritual and showing a photograph of the deceased.

Tsiduk ha-din (Justification of Divine Judgment)

Following the burial and closure of the grave, the mourners recite the *Tsiduk ha-din* prayer. As its name suggests, this prayer deals with justification and acceptance of divine judgment. Its first line well demonstrates the central idea of the entire prayer: "His work is perfect, for all His ways are justice; a God of faithfulness and without iniquity, righteous and just is He."

The *Tsiduk ha-din* prayer was not recited at the funeral rituals examined in this study. Following is an explanation offered by Ya'ir Rotkovitch, who officiates at funerals conducted by Sha'ar Orkhei Teqasim Hiloni'im, of the irrelevance of this prayer to the secular ritual:

> In *Tsiduk ha-din* one says: "God, you are just, we have sinned". This assuages the sense of injustice. It symbolizes reliance on a divine justice concealed from human sight ... its lack of understanding of matters of life and death. I find this bizarre. Because why should one justify the judgment, especially at funerals of young people! It is natural to recite *Tsiduk ha-din* at the funeral of someone who died at the age of ninety. But it is unnatural [to do so] at the funeral of a young woman who died prematurely. It is neither sensible nor humane to justify the judgment. I suggest reciting a different poem that expresses the sense of loss. The family is suffering. If you feel that God is unjust then perhaps we should leave God alone for now. This has nothing to do with atheism or with a lack of faith in God. It just doesn't have anything to do with God. Let us speak about people because this is a secular humanistic funeral. It is mankind that stands at the center, and not God.

Rotkowitch suggests replacing justification of the judgment, which is directed at God, with a song that underscores that we are a single living human fabric, a poem written and put to music by Moty Hammer and performed by Hava Alberstein. This is one of the many examples of how canonic elements of the institutionalized ritual are replaced by the contemporary rites derived from poetry and art.

El Malei Rachamim

The *El malei rachamim* and the *Kaddish* are probably the two prayers most closely associated with Jewish rites of bereavement. They are also recited at official rituals marking Israel's Remembrance Day. The *El malei rachamim* prayer rests upon the belief that the soul lives on after death. The mourners appeal to God and beg him to receive the soul of the deceased and to grant it eternal life and perfect rest in paradise.

The shaping and conduct of non-Orthodox ritual are rather flexible, reflecting the tastes and needs of its participants. For example, at many funerals at Kibbutz Ma'ale Ha-Hamisha conducted by Meir Wilansky, ordained by a secular rabbinate as a burial master, he sings the *El malei rachamim* in his strong voice in the traditional style of Ashkenazi religious song. His desire to adhere to this tradition, subject to the agreement of the deceased's family, has influenced the way in which many funerals are conducted. The Reform female rabbi at Miriam's funeral likewise recited the *El malei rachamim* prayer. She clearly served as an agent of the Jewish tradition, albeit in a progressive rendition. She recited all the religious blessings and included components and customs of the traditional Jewish funeral, explaining their meaning to the mourners. Implementing this principle, the guide book for Jewish Israeli alternative rituals *Life's Cycles* (Eichenwald, 2007) offers on each page the traditional component of the Orthodox ritual and then, next to it, the alternatives and possible additions. Thus, next to the *El malei rachamim* prayer one can find the poem by the famous poet Abba Kovner called "The Master of Dreams."

Kaddish

Kaddish is one of the most famous and powerful Jewish symbols; one can hardly imagine a prayer that evokes stronger emotional responses (Marx, 2014). *Kaddish* is recited in the Aramaic language: it evolved in Babylon where Aramaic was at that time the spoken language, and has been preserved in the same form to this day. It is not confined to the rite of bereavement and is recited at various occasions in public prayer. Originally *Kaddish* had no connection to death customs; rather, it concluded prayers after a sermon or a Torah study session. The *Kaddish* became the mourners' prayer after the Crusader persecutions and cruel pogroms at the end of the eleventh century in Ashkenaz (Marx, 2014).

Different versions of the Orthodox *Kaddish* exist, and one finds variations among the versions used by the different ethnic groups. As Rabbi Steinsaltz (1994) notes, the *Kaddish* is a laudatory prayer, honoring God in this world. The traditional *Kaddish* is intended to glorify the name of God and requests that his honor and glory be spread throughout the world. It is a type of hymn in praise of God and a request for future redemption. Its famous opening is: "Magnified sanctified be His Great Name, In the world that He created according to His will. And may He establish His kingdom." It is customary to recite a full *Kaddish*, with the reciter facing Jerusalem, and if he is in Jerusalem, facing the temple mount. Thus, the small earthly place attains a sacred meaning. The chronotope of the *Kaddish* is the holy chronotope of eternity, transcending time, place and words.

The origins of Israel's alternative ritualism are to be found in the rural settlements of the 1920s in Palestine, whose members spent considerable time deliberating the relevance of traditional Jewish rituals associated with the individual's life cycle, and in particular the reciting of *Kaddish* at funerals. At funerals held in the kibbutzim at that time it was apparently commonplace to maintain silence during the proceedings, and to refrain from reciting *Kaddish* and from following other traditional Jewish customs and rituals (Rubin, 1988; Zeira, 2002). Sometime later, various versions of a secular *Kaddish*, which are still in use in some kibbutzim, were composed, alongside alternative versions of other blessings and elements of the funeral. A survey of bereavement customs prevalent in kibbutzim conducted by the Havaya institute in 2008 found that in some kibbutzim it is customary to recite the traditional *Kaddish*, while in others different versions of the secular *Kaddish* are used, generally in line with the family's preference. There is thus nowadays no standard procedure for reciting *Kaddish* at kibbutz funerals. Similarly, Marx (2014) outlined that there were three distinct stages of the uses of *Kaddish* in the kibbutz movement: spontaneity and silence; creative adaptations of the prayer; and retreat to tradition. According to her, the number of kibbutzim in which the traditional prayer is recited is the same as those in which a special kibbutz secular prayer is in use. My research shows that this literary creativity is continuing until today, finding its way into alternative funerals of secular Israelis.

At Miriam's funeral a secular *Kaddish* composed by Shalom Smid, a member of Kibbutz Negba, was recited:

> May the name of man grow exalted and sanctified
> May his life's work rise up
> And be blessed in our memory with all his deeds during his life on earth
> And with the work that he failed to complete
> The dreams that were woven and faded away
> And precious qualities, as well as human weaknesses, that have vanished
>   Through the misty veil of time…
>
> *Jaffe, 2006*

Exactly like other new versions, this secular *Kaddish* begins with a paraphrasing of the first line of the traditional prayer. This and other versions, such as *Ma'ayan Kaddish* by Ali Alon (Eichenwald, 2007), are frequently used by officials at various types of non-Orthodox, Reform, and kibbutz funerals. The principal difference between the traditional and the secular *Kaddish* cited above is to be found in the object of the prayer. God is completely taken out of the picture and replaced by man, his deeds, and his works. The new *Kaddish* glorifies mankind. One may view the secular *Kaddish* as presenting the antithesis of, and a challenge to, the traditional belief in God and His worship. Belief in the continuing life of the soul after death is likewise suspended, and replaced by the concept of the memory that the deceased leaves to posterity in the form of his children and his life achievements, a memory that endures across generations. The new *Kaddish* also underscores mankind's affinity with nature.

In this way, the transcendentalism of nature replaces that of God. Whether one adheres to the traditional *Kaddish* or abandons it depends on the circumstances of the particular ritual. Like the decision about whether to retain the traditional *El malei rachamim* prayer, this is up to the discretion of the burial leader and the family. The debate over the relevance of the traditional *Kaddish* at secular funerals continues to this day. Some would replace it with a secular *Kaddish*, others favor a Hebrew translation, and yet others wish to retain the canonic Aramaic version of the prayer.

Constructing the Alternative Ritual

How does the alternative ritual differ from the Orthodox rite? Below is an excerpt from my interview with Yair Rotkovitch, who presides over life cycle rituals and is a member of Tkasim – Sha'ar Orkhei Teqasim Hiloni'im in Israel (www.english.tkasim.org.il/):

> The secular ritual is more intimate, closer to the person. There is no established, predetermined protocol here that tells us what to do. Although some fixed order makes sense, because at the time of sorrow a person needs to be told what to do. … At the rending I hand them knives and invite them to tear the garment. I involve them. As to the eulogies – I do them in one set, but the order is flexible. Things can move forward or backward. And sometimes I change plans because it's not appropriate or because there's no time. Say some relative unexpectedly wishes to speak and that takes time, so I discard something I'd planned before. I prefer things being natural and spontaneous to a protocol. This is one supreme rule of a secular ritual: nothing is mandatory. The primary obligation is to listen to the family. Whatever the family wants must be done. My job is to direct this … the ritual must express the person. The ritual serves the mourners. And so I always tell the family – whatever you want, I'm with you, just as you want it.

Improvisation, custom design of the ritual from a broad set of possible elements, the lack of a canonical template or protocol, intimacy, spontaneity, flexibility and dynamism are the images and notions commonly associated with the new rituals. Some of these are articulated by those who preside over non-Orthodox rituals, who portray their creation as an evolving process. This is a bricolage-like activity, a major attribute of post-modernism. As Gurevich (1998) notes:

> The post-modern person prefers the role of *bricoleur* or inventor, who improvises and combines different things, the inventor who does not discover transcendental truth but develops combinatory possibilities, with which he is comfortable and which fit in

with the tradition and the habits of the community to which he belongs. The position of the leader who creates the new ritual is characterized by activity, implementation and performance. This is a subject who invents himself.

This self-invention takes place in the ritual arena of the alternative funeral in a way appropriate to a post-modern subject. Components of one's own identity, self-expression and self-searching lie at the center of this arena. The evolution of the new ritual and its adaptation to the individual taste of the performer (a custom-made suit, as one interviewee put it) is closely linked to consumption. In this respect, the conductors of these rituals function also as providers of a service to their customers, who choose and order a product in line with their views and tastes.

As described above, at Miriam's funeral we witnessed a secular Israeli family from Jerusalem that approached a Reform female rabbi to preside over her funeral at a kibbutz cemetery. Of particular note at this event is the intimate merging of the religious *El malei rahamim* prayer with a secular *Kaddish*, which may be regarded as a clearly anti-religious declaration. All this tells us something about the complex and hybrid nature of this and similar non-Orthodox funerals. Another example is the recitation of the traditional *Kaddish* at civil funeral rituals at which the ashes of the deceased are scattered following cremation by the Aley Shalechet company. To differing degrees, the eclectic, non-systematic and selective use of Jewish symbols and customs characterizes all the new rituals. At these events, religious Jewish elements, such as prayers, blessings, supplication to God, and belief in the after-life of the soul, frequently appear alongside erasure of the name of God and rejection of his existence. They form rather organic hybrids with secular tropes derived from Hebrew and world poetry and performances of recorded or live music, both classical and popular.

Concluding Discussion

This chapter tries to portray the non-Orthodox funeral rituals conducted in Israel as a new form of ritualism that casts doubt on the distinction commonly made in the social sciences between the religious and secular ritual. I assert that these new alternative rituals are postmodern and post-secular, fitting neatly into these two interrelated concepts. They are postmodern in the sense that they lack a canonical format, are hybrid by nature, and encompass processes of improvisation, change, invention and combination, containing elements of free choice on the part of those who conduct them. They are post-secular because they typically involve processes of integration and merging of the meta-categories of religiosity and secularism. In other words, the new ritualism practiced by the secular Jewish public of Israel is a fluid, flexible, dynamic phenomenon that is constantly evolving. It can be branded as personal ritualism that marks the individual's reflexive quest for self-realization, but is also tied to the weight of traditional Judaism, with which it conducts a dialog through the various ritual elements. Alternative burials display a blurring and erasure of boundaries between the trends toward individualism and its ties to collective identity; between religiosity, spirituality and secularization; the link to the Reform movement or to New Age fashions; Orthodox, liberal and secular Judaisms; and last but not least, between the Israeli and global Western culture. They furthermore embody an amalgamation of these diverse elements to form novel combinations.

From the interviews with officials and performers of the rituals, we learn that these new performances are generally created by studying, interpreting or referring to Orthodox Jewish rituals, in some cases by way of negation. While this reference may purport to be secular, as in new rituals that are explicitly defined as such (by, for example, Makhon Ha-teqasim Hahiloni'im, Havaya, etc.), it challenges the distinction between religiosity and secularization and establishes itself as a hybrid form of ritualism that incorporates various combinations of both. The paraphrasing of holy language and the introduction of common canonical expressions to new blessings and texts, as in a secular *Kaddish* or alternative personalized blessings, all bear a clearly discernible religious significance. The use of traditional concepts which acquire an alternative meaning, as well as the secular *Kaddish* and a personalized version of the n-sh-m-a letters at funerals, indicate the link to the Orthodox ritual.

In her book on the invention of Jewish rituals in the USA, Ochs (2007) arrived at similar findings. According to her, as they go about inventing rituals, the performers employ a Jewish toolkit that contains the essential components of texts, rituals and customs, and Jewish beliefs and concepts. The new texts include elements of the traditional Jewish toolkit and thus appear familiar and "Jewish" to the participants, despite the changes introduced to them. Thus, the traditional components of the Orthodox rituals function as key symbols of the new rituals.

Viewing alternative funeral rituals in Israel from the broader theoretical perspective of the role that ritual plays in contemporary society, one can conclude that ritual is changing. It now engages more with the personal identity of those who preside over the ritual and the generation of individual memory. It focuses more on intimate social relationships, and has become more reflexive and self-oriented. Yet the new ritual is still largely concerned with the divine and with transcendental entities, which are not entirely replaced by people and their relationships. The new ritualism rather incorporates both religious and secular elements, combining personal identity with collective Jewish identity. The new ritual arena of non-Orthodox funerals constitutes one of the sites that illustrate the complexity of religiosity and secularity in Israel and blurs the dichotomous distinction between them.

Another major feature of the new non-Orthodox ritualism is the active participation of women, including women's assumption of the role of ritual officials in their capacity as Reform and secular rabbis. Finally, art plays an important role in the new rituals. The reading of poetry and the playing of instruments and of recorded music (banned by the Orthodox canon) characterizes these events, forming an integral part of the rituals and turning them into an enhanced esthetic experience.

These transformations in funeral rituals reflect the broader ideational changes occurring in the Israeli society: the post-modern and post-secular turn, feminism and the improved status of women; and the growing individualism reflecting the increased presence of Western ideas and lifestyles in Israel. The large immigration from the former Soviet Union, economic growth in the context of globalization, a neoliberal economic order, a consumer society and new demands for recognition by non-Orthodox groups – all have enabled the emergence of dramatic changes in the area of alternative funerals. Other simultaneous shifts included alternative weddings and legal struggles around civil marriage, the sales of pork and commerce on the Sabbath (Ben-Porat, 2013), which are beyond the scope of this chapter.

Notes

1 According to the explanation provided on the organization's website: www.aleyshalechet.co.il
2 In some cases, individuals approach Aley Shalechet or a similar organization and sign a will stipulating that their body be cremated after their death.

References

Abramovitz, H. 1993. "Funeral in Jerusalem: An Anthropological Perspective," in R. Malkinson, S. Rubin and E. Viztum, eds. *Loss and Bereavement in Israeli Society*. Jerusalem: Kena, 181–96.
Alfred, L. 2000. "Plastic Shamans and Astroturf Sun Dances," *American Indian Quarterly* 24(3): 329–52.

Ashkenazi, M. 1993. "What Is the Custom? Funeral Rites and Confusion among Middle Class Israelis," *Israel Social Science Research* 8(2): 1–22 (Hebrew).
Bell, Catherine. 1997. *Ritual: Perspectives and Dimensions*. New York: Oxford University Press.
Ben-Porat, G. 2013. *Between State and Synagogue: The Secularization of Contemporary Israel*. Cambridge: Cambridge University Press.
Bocock, R. 1974. *Ritual in Industrial Society: A Sociological Analysis of Ritualism in Modern England*. London: Allen and Unwin.
Casanova, J. 1994. *Public Religions in the Modern World*. Chicago, IL: University of Chicago Press.
Eichenwald, D. ed. 2007. *Life's Cycles: Ceremonies of Jewish Life*. Tel Aviv: Mishkal (Hebrew).
Geertz, C. 1990. *Interpretation of Cultures*. Jerusalem: Keter (Hebrew).
Giddens, A. 1991. *Modernity and Self-Identity*. Stanford, CA: Stanford University Press.
Grimes, R. 2000. *Deeply into the Bone: Re-Inventing Rites of Passage*. Berkeley: University of California Press.
Gurevich, D. 1998. *Post-modernism: Culture and Literature in the Late 20th Century*. Tel-Aviv: Dvir Publishing House (Hebrew).
Jaffe, A. 2006. "The Kaddish in Jewish Tradition – Religion Versus Modernity," *Mifneh* 50: 61–64 (Hebrew).
Klein Oren, A. and M. Ruah-Midbar. 2010. "Secular in Theory, Religious in Practice: The Israeli New Age's Attitude Toward Halakha," *Israeli Sociology* 12(1): 57–80 (Hebrew).
Koren, I. 2011. *You Are Hereby Renewed to Me: Gender, Religion and Power Relations in the Jewish Wedding Ritual*. Jerusalem: Magnes Press (Hebrew).
Marx, D. 2009. "Influences of the Feminist Movement on Jewish Liturgy: The Case of Israeli Reform Prayer," *Sociological Papers* 14: 67–81.
Marx, D. 2014. "From the Rhine Valley to Jerusalem Valley: Innovative Versions of the Mourners' Kaddish in the Kibbutz movement," in Michael Meyer and David Myers, eds. *Between Jewish Traditions and Modernity: Rethinking an Old Opposition. Essays in Honor of Ellenson David*. Detroit, MI: Wayne State University Press, 123–141.
McLennan, G. 2007. "Towards Postsecular Sociology," *Sociology* 41(5): 857–70.
Moore, S. and B. Myerhoff. 1977. *Secular Ritual*. Assen and Amsterdam: Van Gorcum.
Myerhoff, B. 1987. "Life, Not Death in Venice: Its Second Life," in H. Goldberg, ed. *Judaism Viewed from Within and Without*. New York: State University of New York press, 143–69.
Neeman, R. 2011. "Tel Aviv Prayer: An Israeli Prayer House in Tel Aviv," *Israeli Sociology* 12(2): 413–31 (Hebrew).
Ochs, V. 2007. *Inventing Jewish Rituals*. Philadelphia, PA: The Jewish Publication Society.
Ramshaw, E. 2009. "The Personalization of Post-modern Post-mortem Rituals," *Pastoral Psychology* 59(2): 171–78.
Roll, S., A. Esser and B. Enzner-Probst, with C. Methuen and A. Berlis, eds. 2001. *Women, Ritual and Liturgy*. Leuven: Peters.
Rose, M. 1996. *The Post-Modern and the Post-Industrial*. Cambridge: Cambridge University Press.
Ruah-Midbar, M. 2014. "A Channeler, A Healer and A Shaman Meet at Rabbi's. Beyond Halacha: Secularism, Traditionalism and New Age Culture in Israel," *Iyunim Bitkumat Israel*, 7: 498–528 (Hebrew).
Rubin, N. 1988. "Bereavement on the Non-religious Kibbutz: The Use of Holy Symbols in Secular Society," *Megamot* 31: 53–64 (Hebrew).
Rubin, N. 1997. *The End of Life: Rituals of Burial and Bereavement in the Sources of Hazal*. Tel-Aviv: Ha-kibbutz ha-me'uhad (Hebrew).
Shenhav, J. 2008. "An Invitation to a Post-secular Outline for the Study of Israeli Society," *Israeli Sociology* 10(1): 161–88 (Hebrew).
Shkedi, A. 2004. *Words of Meaning: Qualitative Research – Theory and Practice*. Tel-Aviv: Ramot (Hebrew).
Steinsaltz, A. 1994. *The Sidur and Prayer – A Dictionary of Concepts and Related Material. Part II*, Tel Aviv: Yediot Aharonot, Hemed Books (Hebrew).
Tavori, I. 2007. *Dancing in a Field of Thorns*. Tel Aviv: Ha-kibbutz ha-me'uhad (Hebrew).
Wuthnow, R. 1998. *After Heaven: Spirituality in America since the 1950s*. Berkeley: University of California Press.

Yedger, Y. 2010. *Traditionalists in Israel: Modernism Devoid of Secularization.* Jerusalem: Keter (Hebrew).
Yona, Y. and Y. Goodman. 2010. *A Whirlpool of Identities: A Critical Discussion of Israeli Religiosity and Secularity.* Jerusalem:Van-Leer Institute (Hebrew).
Zeira, M. 2002. *Rural Collective Settlement and Jewish Culture in Eretz Israel during the 1920s.* Jerusalem: Yad Ben-Zvi Press (Hebrew).

PART V
Languages

34
THE HEBREW LANGUAGE AS A SOURCE OF RITUAL AND PRACTICE

Stefan Reif

A widely recognized phenomenon in the history of religious behavior is the manner in which ritual has chosen to express itself from the earliest times. Art, movement, cult, symbolism and gesture have often played central roles in their different ways during a variety of periods, but an almost ubiquitous method of expressing ritual and its objectives has been by way of language. Just as thought and language have exercised mutually powerful influences, so language has been employed to give shape to ritual and practice but has at the same time also left its mark on aspects of such religious structures (Bell 1997, part 1, section 3). Hebrew language and Jewish religious expression are often regarded by scholars, as well as by practitioners, as inseparably linked in the history of the people who gave the world not only the Bible but also early forms of Judaism that impacted on the emergence of Christianity and Islam, as well as on much of modern thought. As Solomon Schechter put it "the disappearance of the Hebrew language was always followed by assimilation … and the disappearance of Judaism" (Bentwich 1938, 291–92). When and where was this link forged, and for how long and in what manner has it existed? Was Hebrew's role in Jewish ritual a unique and unchallenged one and did the characteristics of the language remain uniform in this religious context? Any attempt to answer these and related questions necessitates an historical assessment of how Hebrew has been employed in Jewish ritual and practice from biblical, through Talmudic and medieval times, into the modern period.

That Hebrew was an integral part of the life of those who were the earliest known ancestors of what became the Jewish people is clear from biblical and extra-biblical sources. The oldest texts preserved in the Hebrew Bible, including the poems of Genesis 49, Deuteronomy 33 and Judges 5, were composed and transmitted in Hebrew, although the script was the ancient Canaanite one and not the Aramaic one that was adopted after the Babylonian Exile of the early sixth century BCE. That same script, or a variation on it, was used in inscriptions from the Holy Land known as the Gezer Calendar, the Moabite Stone and the Siloam Inscription, as well as on smaller and more recently discovered artefacts. These sources range from around 1150 until the seventh century BCE (Sáenz-Badillos 1993, 50–75). Given that those who wrote and transmitted the earliest biblical teachings knew Hebrew and utilized the language in their daily lives, one may justifiably inquire whether such a utilization may also be identified in their rituals and religious practices during those centuries. The historical reply is necessarily somewhat complex. The earliest Hebrew psalms, prayers, blessings and oaths may certainly be said to have had some form of ritual application, even if its precise nature is a matter of some controversy. Their style was not only poetic and liturgical but may also at times have had elements of the legal, formulaic and personal on the one hand, and the historical and educational on the other.

The former three areas such as are represented by the appeals and prayers recorded in the names of Abraham (Gen 18:22–32), Jacob (Gen 28:16–22) and Moses (Num 12:13) do not appear to have an obvious ritual association and may therefore merely be noted without expansion (Reif 1993, 32–37). The two latter areas, concerning education and history, do, however, warrant closer attention. Even in its earliest forms, as for example in parts of Exodus 12, the Passover rituals were closely associated with the tale of the exodus from Egypt and the demand was made of the Israelites that they should explain to their children the nature of that association. Not only was a paschal lamb to be offered in the Temple but a domestic ritual was also to be performed at which such an explanation could be offered. The Hebrew for that offering, and for one of the names of the Passover festival, was based on the root *psḥ* which naturally formed the basis for, and stood at the center of, the domestic ritual. Links were thus being made between language, ritual, history and education (Safrai and Safrai 2009, 2–8). The association of another pilgrim festival, namely, Sukkot (Tabernacles), with education is made in a later, but probably essentially still a pre-exilic tradition recorded in Deut 31:10–13. The acts of reading, listening and learning the sacred text (whatever it precisely contained at its earliest stage) was to be done as a public ritual and the transmission was presumably in the language of the community, again demonstrating a connection between Hebrew, exegesis and religious practice (Tigay 1996, 498–500).

There was undoubtedly a more formal – perhaps even national – cult too, in what has traditionally been seen as the First Jerusalem Temple, destroyed in 586 BCE, and/or in other sacred sites in the kingdoms of Israel and Judah. Even for those who take a more minimalist position and deny the existence of such a Temple before the Exile, there was undoubtedly some form of cultic activity that was the basis for later developments in the Second Temple period beginning in the late sixth century. That being the case, and in the light of the evidence cited above, it seems reasonable to postulate that the language of that cult must also have been Hebrew. Remarkably, the biblical texts do not specifically testify to any extensive use of that language, or indeed any language in the formal cultic sphere. In the matter of the actual sacrificial offerings themselves, the only reference to any recitation is the mention of the requirement to make a confession (as in Lev 5:5, 16:21) but no text, nor even any brief formula, is suggested for this. More concrete documentation about formulas is to be found in the case of the priestly blessing recorded in Num 6:24–26 (beginning "May the Lord bless you and keep you") and the farmer's declaration prescribed in Deut 26:5–10 (beginning "My father was a migrant from Aram"). The first of these formulas, of which there is inscriptional evidence from the sixth pre-Christian century in the form of a silver amulet from the wider Jerusalem area, not far from the cultic centre, was used in an apotropaic or liturgical fashion and therefore had a ritual purpose. It either derived from, or was incorporated into, the cultic service but its precise function is not attested until the latter part of the Second Temple period. Whether it originated as a popular blessing and was at some point linked with the priesthood, or was from the outset a cultic formula, is unclear. It is poetically structured in sets of three, five and seven words of blessing that are invoked from the deity and the vocabulary is that of simple classical Hebrew (Barkay *et al.* 2004, 44–52).

The second formula, for use in the ceremony of offering the first fruits in the temple, was by its very definition linked with the cultic ritual, although from what actual date is not clear. It is not only the gift to the temple of the agricultural produce vouchsafed to the donor by God that is the theme but also the people's origins and their divine rescue from the Egyptian bondage, which effectively becomes the central element. Tigay has expressed the liturgical importance of this in very perceptive and succinct terms:

> This shift of the focus of a religious ceremony from exclusive attention to the role of God in nature to an emphasis on his role in history is one of the most important and original features of the Bible. Its effect on liturgy is this type of prescribed prayer, which leads the worshipper from the immediate experience to an understanding of the larger picture. This kind of prayer is an important one in Jewish liturgy.
>
> Tigay 1996, 238

The language is again simple classical Hebrew with something of a lyrical flavor and the reference to Aramean origins would seem to indicate an early date for at least the introduction, if not for much of the formulation (Tigay 1996, 237–40). Isaiah's famous trishagion (6:1–7), in the context of a description of a theophany and a recognition of the holiness and glory of God, also smacks of a well-rehearsed formula theophany.

If the early biblical traditions laid strong foundations for the subsequent development of Hebrew and early Judaism, the languages and rituals of the Jews underwent a process of major construction in the Second Temple period. It was during those centuries that a strong national identity and a state that was at times fairly powerful were created by the Jews who were called upon to interact with the Persian, Greek and Roman empires that by and large dwarfed them. In the area of language, the Aramaic script replaced the ancient Hebrew one; Aramaic and Greek became competitors of Hebrew; and the more extensive and popular form of Hebrew that gradually developed into Mishnaic Hebrew emerged not only as a vernacular but also as the language of the newer literature such as the book of Ben Sira (Segal 1958, 53–69). Hurvitz has identified the differences between the pre-exilic and the post-exilic forms of Hebrew, noted the attendant changes in priestly language, and distinguished genuine archaic language from later archaizing tendencies. Linguistic developments were matched by those in the realm of ritual (Hurvitz 1972, 2017). Personal and communal liturgy began to merge, the established Temple and the parvenu synagogue effectively functioned side by side, and seeds were sown that later blossomed into the pietistic rituals recorded at Qumran and among the scholastic forerunners of the rabbis, and into the fixed prayers proposed and championed by Rabban Gamaliel and some of his contemporaries (Elbogen 1993, 187–95).

These complex trends had practical and significant consequences that were no less complex. There was a growing awareness of, and even a degree of sympathy for, multilingualism. Rabbi Jonathan of Eleutheropolis (Bet Guvrin) in third-century Roman Palestine claimed that, while Hebrew was the language of revelation, Greek was best for lyrical use, Latin for military purposes and Aramaic for funerals (y. Meg. 1.11(9); 71b). That last-mentioned language was employed for authoritative renderings and interpretations of the Hebrew Bible (*targumim*) which even acquired a ritual status. The language of greetings, requests and law found its way into the earliest formulations of early rabbinic benedictions and prayers and there was a distinct contrast between the linguistic preferences of Qumran and tannaitic worshippers. The former was more committed to the forms that were more reminiscent of biblical style while the latter opted for modes of expression that were more independent of that register. After the destruction of the Temple there was considerable controversy for some two or three centuries about the degree to which the formal system of worship could legitimately move into the synagogue. As it gradually did precisely that, so the practice of Jewish rituals, many of which were essentially of biblical origin, were given fresh form, content and authority by the rabbis and Mishnaic Hebrew was utilized in their formulation (Reif 2006, 33–69).

Rabban Gamaliel and his followers in the second century may have had a clear agenda about standardizing Jewish ritual and its linguistic expression but the story of the subsequent four centuries does not bear out the theory that such an agenda was comprehensively and universally adopted (Langer 1999, 2000; Fleischer 2000). A truly scientific analysis reveals a welter of trends and tensions. For some of the Talmudic teachers, the most important theological principle was the study of Torah, while for others it was ethical behavior or statutory worship. The daily application of the principle was by means of a ritualization of its practical manifestation. What this meant was that such religious behavior was the substitute for, or even the replacement of, the temple cult. Similarly, scriptural readings were not simply exercises in adult education but attracted to themselves rules and regulations that transformed them into frequent forms of worship. The *shema'* and the *'amidah* were totally ritualized and the domestic ways of marking the arrival and departure of Sabbaths and festivals that were centered on meal-times received similar treatment (Reif 1993, 88–121; 128–29). The *seder* at the festive meal on the first evening of Passover was given over to the message that the Jews, who had lost their state, their capital city, their temple and their freedom, were still nevertheless the chosen people who were free to make that meal no less noble, intellectual and educational than the formal meals of the Greeks and Romans (Safrai and Safrai 2009, 16–56; Tabory 2008, 6–16). The Grace after meals was altered from its original character of gratitude for food to a declaration of the rabbinic theology concerning the land of Israel and Jerusalem, as well as a mini-tract on theodicy (Idelsohn 1967, 122–25).

There is no doubt that the Talmudic rabbis preferred Hebrew as the language of prayers, benedictions and rituals, but Greek was used even for such a central prayer as the *'amidah* in some Hellenized communities (van der Horst and Newman 2008) and Aramaic was the medium used for many aspects of the religious life of the communities in Roman Palestine and Babylonia (Smelik 2013, 100–38). The Jews in the latter centers also demonstrated their independence from their coreligionists in Roman Palestine in many ways, including the reading of the Torah in one year and not three and a half, the recitation of the priestly benediction by the prayer-leader and not necessarily the priests, and the preference for their own formulations for the concluding eulogy in various doxological formulations (Reif 1993, 157–61, 182–83). That said, there was nevertheless an agreement that the language of the rituals should be Mishnaic Hebrew as they knew and utilized it, and not the Hebrew that was characteristic of the sacred scriptures. This created some linguistic anomalies. The *shema'* was recited as it occurred in the Hebrew Bible but the *'amidah* was couched in the language of Mishnaic Hebrew. The first verse of the *shema'* was even interrupted with the phrase "Blessed be his honored name and his sovereignty for evermore" which was a doctored version of an earlier phrase adjusted to insert a reference to royalty and divinity that were decidedly not those of the Hellenized rulers or Roman Caesars. To cite another example of Hebrew ritual language that expressed innovative theology, God had been metaphorized as Father or as King in earlier Hebrew sources but it was only in Rabbinic Hebrew that he was liturgically invoked as "our Father, our King" (Reif 2006, 123–24; Reif 2017, 314–33). There was also a specific rejection (y. Ber. 1.8 (3d)) of the use of biblical verses within the daily statutory prayers that was only gradually relaxed over the centuries. The language of mystics such as that of those who were engaged in celestial speculations (*Hekhalot*) was also slowly incorporated into the prayers, as in the case of the *qedushah* which, once given authority by the Babylonian leaders, quickly became widely standard among the various Jewish communities (Elbogen 1993, 54–61). Even more linguistically significant is the fact that the most important prayer created and given a prominent liturgical status in the post-Talmudic period was the *qaddish*, the well-known version of which is in Aramaic and not Hebrew. Since there are some Genizah texts in which it is also recorded in Hebrew, the question arises whether it was composed in the Aramaic of Babylonia and translated in the homeland or other parts of the diaspora, or composed there in Hebrew and translated into Aramaic in the eastern communities (Lehnardt 2002).

One of the most remarkable achievements of the leaders ("Geonim") of the Babylonian centers of rabbinic scholarship in the post-Talmudic period from about the seventh until the eleventh century was to centralize, authorize and standardize most aspects of the Jewish religious practice that they inherited and to present this process as one that had enjoyed the stamp of approval of the tannaim and amoraim who preceded them. Some historians still labor under this misapprehension, failing to appreciate adequately that the Talmud is not a finalized legal code with a commentary and categorical halakhic instruction and that it was only the work of the Geonim that metamorphosed it into such. As a result of their efforts, rituals were organized and made consistent, greater stress was placed on the community and the synagogue than on the individual and the home, the oral nature of the prayers was exchanged for the first structured prayer books, and authoritative liturgical practice was accepted as an essential component of the Jewish religious life. Where the Talmud had made a suggestion, recorded a view or offered a midrashic interpretation, the Geonim took everything Talmudic as mandatory and harmonized dissident views as often and as powerfully as they could. If Rabbi Meir had proposed that one should aim to recite a hundred blessings each day (b. Menaḥ. 43b), this was, for the Geonim, not his way of stating the general importance of thanking God for his bounty but a specific requirement that necessitated a list of items from one to 100. Above all, the Babylonian rites were regarded as the correct ones and those of the land of Israel were denigrated as ignorant, misguided and inferior (Brody 1998).

The linguistic impact was no less than the halakhic one. When in the ninth century Amram ben Sheshna of Sura provided the Spanish communities with a precise text of blessings and prayers for the whole year he defined it as being divinely sanctioned and laid out "in accordance with the traditions we have inherited and with what has been formulated by the Tannaim and Amoraim" (Hedegård 1951, 4 (English), 2 (Hebrew)). The irony is that his text was so widely used that it was corrupted by local copyists while the prayer book composed by one of his successors in Sura, Sa'adya ben Joseph, was perhaps too recondite for the average Jewish congregant and remained fairly unspoilt and almost pristine. He justified the content, language and phraseology of his text by stating that he "had felt the need to collect and record the prayers and blessings that are recited in our age … because they are neglected, expanded and contracted." Any variant of custom or formulation was clearly being regarded by him as simply wrong or illicitly altered. The Geonic principle was to follow the statement of the second-century tanna R. Yose that it was forbidden to depart from any liturgical formulation laid down by the sages (b. Ber. 40b) but it was they who defined which formulation that was to be. The relatively new Hebrew prayers for the divine gift of good life in the new year that were suggested for inclusion in various parts of the *'amidah* during the Ten Days of Repentance were close in literary and linguistic style to the liturgical poetry that had captured the imagination of the worshippers from at least the sixth century and they had virtually no Talmudic pedigree. Nonetheless, Sa'adya cites them as the custom of "some folk" and includes them in his prayer book. On the other hand, with regard to the addition to the *qiddush* on the first evening of Passover of a Hebrew benediction in praise of wine, he is decidedly less enthusiastic. It seems that this was a fairly widespread custom and may have been a Jewish version of an ode to Bacchus and Sa'adya would have none of it. He ruled that "this addition is forbidden and its recitation invalidates the whole religious procedure [of Passover eve at the *seder*]" (Davidson, Joel and Assaf 1963, 10–12, 141, 220).

The liturgical poetry (or *piyyuṭ* in Hebrew) just mentioned is also of singular importance for this discussion. The genre may well have been inspired, or at least influenced, by the hymnology of Byzantine Eastern Christianity, which composed music, hymns and poems for church ceremonies and festivals on biblical, homiletical and theological themes. These compositions, which used Greek as their language, were already flourishing when the earliest known Jewish poets came on the scene in the land of Israel in about the sixth century. These Jewish poets used Hebrew as their language, the synagogal readings, prayers and ceremonies as their basic texts, and rabbinic Judaism, especially as expressed in the targumic and midrashic materials, as their theology. The poets and cantors innovated and improvised in a most extensive fashion and produced a vast variety of new forms of language, as well as structured poetry. Unprecedented verbal and nominal forms were coined, and cryptic and allusive Hebrew phrases were employed to add to the lyrical quality. The novel genre invaded almost every aspect of Jewish liturgical expression, establishing its presence and threatening to dominate the whole environment of ritual and worship. Eventually, the codifiers of rabbinic law, many of whom bewailed the growing power of *piyyuṭ*, succeeded in exercising control over it and compromised by permitting it a limited role within the standard prayers. As far as the innovative poetic Hebrew was concerned, its influence became a permanent feature of the language and contributed in no small degree to the development of the language and its ability to cope with the fresh demands of the Jewish medieval world (Weinberger 1998, 1–18; Sáenz-Badillos, 1993, 209–14).

The dominance of the rabbinic centers in Babylonia and in the land of Israel had come to an end by the beginning of the twelfth century and the control of Jewish ritual and its linguistic medium then moved to the newly expanding communities of Italy, Spain, North Africa, Franco-Germany and Yemen. While maintaining much of what they had inherited from the Geonic period, the Jews in each of these geographical areas made their own special contributions to such developments, so that the formulation of benedictions, prayers and other rituals took on the fresh flavors of the Italian, Sefardi, Maghrebi, Ashkenazi and Temani rites. One of the major, and most controversial, linguistic issues from that period onwards was the nature of the Hebrew to be used in Jewish religious practices. The Masoretes dominated the field of Biblical Hebrew and virtually codified the systems to be used for the reading and writing of the scriptural texts. Their systems inspired the creation of treatises on Hebrew grammar and philology and led to the notion that this form of the language was the authoritative and conventional one. The vocalization system of Ben Asher of Tiberias also ultimately became the standard by which to measure all others. Meanwhile, however, the language of ritual in all its manifestations had accrued to itself characteristics that did not tally with these notions of Biblical Hebrew, such as Mishnaic grammar, syntax and vocabulary, Aramaic and broader Semitic influences or remnants, and what are today known as non-standard vocalizations. What was to be the "correct" language of Jewish ritual? The halakhic authorities of the high Middle Ages were divided between those who saw Biblical Hebrew as the linguistic yardstick for ritual and others who pressed for the retention of what they knew as *leshon ḥazal*, "the language of our departed rabbis". The former pressed for the language of revelation to be the language of ritual while the latter argued that liturgy was formulated authoritatively by the rabbis and their predecessors. It is a moot point which of the groups is to be defined as the more linguistically conservative (Sáenz-Badillos 1993, 245–54). Is the word for "your truth" *amitakh* or *amitekha*? Should one say with regard to the institution of the Sabbath *tiqqanta* or *tikkanta*? If the singular for a limb is *ever* should the plural not be *avarim* rather than *evarim*? May one mark the Hebrew plural with a final *nun* rather than a final *mem* as in the word *mamlikhim* for declaring God as King?

The Jewish mystical movements of the Middle Ages also interacted powerfully with the Hebrew language when they prescribed how to conduct various religious practices. The Ashkenazi pietists of the twelfth and thirteenth centuries regarded prayer not only as the fulfillment of a halakhic duty but also as a means of engaging with the essence of God. To that end, they were anxious to maintain what they regarded as the authenticity of every liturgical item and one means of achieving this was by counting the precise numbers of Hebrew letters and words in each case and adhering to these. Sometimes, this meant a sacrifice of the conventional grammar as in the phrase *befeh 'amo* ("in the mouth of his people") for the standard *befi 'amo* in the *barukh sheamar* prayer. The Spanish mystics of the thirteenth century employed and popularized such Hebrew terms as the *Eyn Sof*, *Aṣilut* and *Sefirot* to refer to God and the emanations from the divinity to the material world. Their ideas and their vocabulary were championed by Moses de Leon, incorporated into the Zohar, and promoted and extended by Isaac Luria and the Safed kabbalists of the sixteenth century. It was the latter group that inserted all manner of special formulas into the prayers and, despite the objections of some, these gradually found their way into the standard liturgies especially by way of the Hasidic movement of Eastern Europe. Special formulas were composed for recitation before the performance of a ritual and these included biblical and Rabbinic Hebrew, Aramaic and mystical terminology. Notions of magic, as in the use of amulets, also demanded the use of special Hebrew words, numbers and formulations (Goetschel 1987, 43–64, 17–57, 179–86; Dan and Talmage 1982, 85–120; Dan 2007, 25–36; Schiffman and Swartz 1992).

As the Jewish presence in medieval and early modern Europe expanded and interacted with dominant Christianity, it became politic for the copyists of prayer books to omit or alter some Hebrew terms that might offend Christians, especially those who had been converted from Judaism and had come to occupy influential offices in the Church. *Goy* and *'arel* ("uncircumcised") as terms for the non-Jew were replaced by *nokhri* ("heathen") or *akum* ("idolater") or *kuti* ("Samaritan"). This tendency became more pronounced after the Counter Reformation and the invention of printing (Popper 1969). The novelty and popularity of the latter medium, as well as of the growing role of the ḥazan in the synagogue, not only led to the swift and wide dissemination of alternative Hebrew terms but also of erroneous Hebrew and faulty vocalization. The "great grammarian" Shabbethai (Ha-)Sofer of Przemysl in Poland (c.1635–c.1640) wrote an extensive commentary of the Ashkenazi prayer book in which he stressed the need for what he defined as correct Hebrew. He criticized both printers and cantors for their sloppiness, ignorance and inconsistency in this linguistic area and blamed them for prayers going unanswered and the delay in the messianic redemption. The Mishnaic Hebrew *va-ho* should be corrected to the Biblical Hebrew *ve-hu* and the Mishnaic use of *samekh* for *sin* was also erroneous (Reif 1979, 26, 37).

This controversy about the language of the ritual continued into modern times and is well represented in the differences of grammatical outlook of Jacob Emden, who defended traditional liturgical Hebrew, and Solomon Hanau who was a purist and opted for using only the biblical form (Sáenz-Badillos 1993, 268; Reif 1993, 49–50, 262–67). When preparing their editions of the Hebrew prayers, benedictions and rituals, the German scholars Wolf Heidenheim and Seligmann Baer did more than their fair share of "correction". Their ideas were not only a continuation of the earlier "correctors" such as Shabbethai but also owed much to the broader Jewish Enlightenment that had begun in the eighteenth century and to its academic offshoot the *Wissenschaft des Judentums* (championed by Leopold Zunz and Moritz Steinschneider) which sought to examine Judaism historically, to identify what were seen as its most authentic elements, and to promote a Jewish history, language and literature of which modernists could be proud. In this connection they extolled the beauty of the Hebrew prayers and lamented the fact that, in their view, the purity of their language had been sullied over the centuries by departures from the pristine language of the Hebrew Bible. Any language used in Jewish rituals had to be decorous, rational and systematic and changes were made to that end, at times without clear indication and at others with scholarly arguments that were historically unjustified. Mystical language attracted scholarly derision (Zunz 1859, 24). Ismar Elbogen, in his scientific study of the history of Jewish worship which was outstanding in its day, in the first third of the twentieth century, had little time for a whole range of linguistic novelty dating from the post-Talmudic and early medieval periods. Indeed, he argued that liturgical creativity "failed at the end of the talmudic period and was followed by a slack time, when further development was hindered by severe persecution" (Elbogen 1993, 213).

If Elbogen was in favor of mildly reforming the language and content of the rituals, there had already been others in the nineteenth century who had been more radical and even iconoclastic about the use of Hebrew and the notion of Zion within Jewish ritual. The whole issue of the language, content and style of the rituals was a burning one for nineteenth-century Jewry in central and western Europe, and three main movements, namely, the Neo-Orthodox, the Positive-Historical and the Reform or Neologue, each responded to the challenge in its own way. All these communities made linguistic changes in the rituals and used the vernacular (mainly German, French or English), while omitting or adjusting the notions of Zion and the messianic redemption. Even Modern Orthodoxy, as represented by Samson Raphael Hirsch in Frankfurt, and by Hermann Adler and Simeon Singer in London, opted for some degree of adjustment or even omission. Only the communities of the Islamic world and of Eastern Europe continued to be largely committed to their traditional prayer books. Such a state of affairs was maintained to a greater or lesser degree until the middle of the twentieth century when the Holocaust and the establishment of the State of Israel brought major changes. The progressive movements revived an interest in the use of Hebrew and the inclusion of aspects of Jewish national freedom within Jewish ritual, while some of the more rigidly Orthodox movements attempted to restore what they saw as the more traditional linguistic and contextual elements of the liturgy that had been dominant in the Islamic world and in Eastern Europe. The Israeli pronunciation of Hebrew and the inclusion of prayers concerning the State of Israel were two of the topics on which the Ultra-Orthodox and the Modern Orthodox differed (Reif 2014, final two sections). Those who settled in Turkish and British Palestine before the establishment of the Jewish State in 1948 brought with them an acquaintance with the traditional Hebrew sources, including the prayers. This sound Jewish knowledge made an impact on the contemporary Hebrew language and its development, sometimes positively, as with the incorporation of words and phrases from such a knowledge, and at other times negatively when forms that were too closely associated with ritual were adjusted. To conclude anecdotally, if you said to such early 'olim, even if secular, that someone thought he was the wise son of the *mah nishtanah* (Passover *seder*), or that a text was as large as the letters of the *qiddush levanah* (ritual of blessing the moon), they would have known exactly what you meant. On the other hand, they perhaps tended at the stage to avoid using *leshev* to sit because it was reminiscent of sitting in the sukkah and of rabbinic usage, and *shuv* because of its religious sense of repentance.

References

Barkay, Gabriel, Marilyn Lundberg, Andrew Vaughn and Bruce Zuckerman. 2004. "The Amulets from Ketef Hinnom: A New Edition and Evaluation", *BASOR* 334: 41–71.
Bell, Catherine. 1997. *Ritual: Perspectives and Dimensions*. New York: Oxford University Press.
Bentwich, Norman. 1938. *Solomon Schechter*. Philadelphia, PA: Jewish Publication Society of America.

Brody, Robert. 1998. *The Geonim of Babylonia and the Shaping of Medieval Jewish Culture*. New Haven, CT: Yale University Press.
Dan, Joseph. 2007. *Kabbalah: A Very Short Introduction*. Oxford: Oxford University Press.
Dan, Joseph and Frank Talmage. 1982. *Studies in Jewish Mysticism*. Cambridge, MA: Association for Jewish Studies.
Davidson, Israel, B. I. Joel, and S. Assaf, eds. 1963. *Siddur R. Saadya Gaon*. Jerusalem: Reuven Mass for Mekize Nirdamim.
Elbogen, Ismar. 1993. *Jewish Liturgy: A Comprehensive History*, trans. Raymond P. Scheindlin. Philadelphia, PA: Jewish Publication Society.
Fleischer, Ezra. 2000. "Controversy, On the Origins of the 'Amidah: Response to Ruth Langer", *Prooftexts* 20: 380–84.
Goetschel, Roland, ed. 1987. *Prière, Mystique et Judaïsme*. Paris: Presses Universitaires de France.
Hedegård, David. 1951. *Seder R. Amram Gaon*. Lund: Lindstedts.
Hurvitz, Avi. 1972. *The Transition Period: A Study in Post-Exilic Hebrew and its Implications for the Dating of Psalms*. Jerusalem: Bialik Institute (Hebrew).
Hurvitz, Avi. 2017. *From Genesis to Chronicles: Chapters in the Linguistic History of Biblical Hebrew*. Jerusalem: Bialik Institute.
Idelsohn, A. Z. 1967. *Jewish Liturgy and Its Development*. New York: Schocken.
Langer, Ruth. 1999. "Revisiting Early Rabbinic Liturgy: The Recent Contributions of Ezra Fleischer", *Prooftexts* 19: 79–94.
Langer, Ruth. 2000. "Controversy, Considerations of Method: A Response to Ezra Fleischer", *Prooftexts* 20: 384–87.
Lehnardt, Andreas. 2002. *Qaddish: Untersuchungen zur Enstehung und Rezeption eines rabbinischen Gebetes*. Tübingen: Mohr Siebeck.
Popper, William. 1969. *The Censorship of Hebrew Books*, ed. M. Carmilly-Weinberger. New York: Ktav.
Reif, Stefan C. 1979. *Shabbethai Sofer and his Prayer Book*. Cambridge: Cambridge University Press.
Reif, Stefan C. 1993. *Judaism and Hebrew Prayer*. Cambridge: Cambridge University Press.
Reif, Stefan C. 2006. *Problems with Prayers: Studies in the Textual History of Early Rabbinic Liturgy*. Berlin: de Gruyter.
Reif, Stefan C. 2014. "Jewish Prayer and Liturgy", *Oxford Bibliography Online*. Available from: www.oxfordbibliographies.com/view/document/obo-9780199840731/obo-9780199840731-0086.xml
Reif, Stefan C. 2017. *Jews, Bible and Prayer: Essays on Jewish Biblical Exegesis and Liturgical Notions*. Berlin: de Gruyter.
Sáenz-Badillos, Angel. 1993. *A History of the Hebrew Language*, trans. John Elwolde. Cambridge: Cambridge University Press.
Safrai, Shemuel and Ze'ev Safrai. 2009. *Haggadah of the Sages*. Jerusalem: Carta.
Schiffman, Lawrence and Michael D. Swartz. 1992. *Hebrew and Aramaic Incantation Texts from the Cairo Genizah*. Sheffield: JSOT Press.
Segal, Moshe Zvi. 1958. *Sefer Ben Sira Ha-Shalem*. Jerusalem: Bialik Institute.
Smelik, Willem F. 2013. *Rabbis, Language and Translation in Late Antiquity*. Cambridge: Cambridge University Press.
Tabory, Joseph. 2008. *JPS Commentary on the Haggadah*. Philadelphia, PA: Jewish Publication Society.
Tigay, Jeffrey H. 1996. *The JPS Torah Commentary. Deuteronomy*. Philadelphia, PA: The Jewish Publication Society.
Van der Horst, Pieter and Judith H. Newman. 2008. *Early Jewish Prayers in Greek*. Berlin: de Gruyter.
Weinberger, Leon J. 1998. *Jewish Hymnography: A Literary History*. London: Littman.
Zunz, Leopold. 1859. *Die Ritus des synagogalen Gottesdienstes geschichtlich entwickelt*. Berlin: Springer.

35
THE ROLE OF JUDEZMO/LADINO IN 'OTTOMAN SEPHARDIC' JEWISH RELIGIOUS RITUAL AND PRACTICE

David M. Bunis

Zahud̲ de shabad̲ pishkad̲o, prasifuchi i pastel,
I el guevo haminad̲o, kon salero i pimyentel.
Komer en purim ojuelas i en hanuká bimuelos,
Pésaḥ oyas i kasuelas, ansí vimos de los aguelos,
Tomar demazyad̲a prasa, asad̲ura i molejas.
Shevod̲ koza de masa, i tishá beav lentejas.
En kipur kalsetas blankas i dos poyos kon fid̲eos,
I yenos asta las trankas de mod̲os de echos feos.
En purim mod̲os de vinos es koza ke muncho enporta,
I brindar kon los vizinos i dizir ke se la porta.[1]
  Ḥayyim Yom Ṭov Magula, Ṭova tokaḥat Megulla
      (Izmir, 1756 [1739]), 2b

The Judezmo/Ladino Language of the Ottoman Sephardim[2] and their Descendants

In the earliest stages of Judaism, the primary texts, regulations and prayers standing at the core of Jewish religious ritual and practice were formulated, canonized, studied and debated in the two earliest languages used by Jews: Hebrew, and then additionally, Aramaic. But these two classic Jewish languages were not the only ones which played a role in the transmission and practice of Judaism. The dispersion of the Jews from their historic homeland in the Land of Israel to the myriad parts of the diaspora in which, by expulsion or choice, they re-settled and interacted intensively with diverse local peoples led to the rise of new *Jewish languages*—distinctive Jewish variants of the local languages used by the peoples with whom the Jews came into contact.

One such language is that which originated among the Jews of medieval Christian Iberia—or *Sefarad*,[3] as this geographic area has come to be known traditionally among Jews. The language arose among the descendants of Iberian Jews many of whom, in earlier Iberia under Islam, seem primarily to have used Jewish varieties of Ibero-Arabic as their main spoken and partly written language. In Christian Iberia the Jews came to use somewhat distinctive varieties of Ibero-Romance (among them Castilian, Aragonese, Catalan, Portuguese); with their expulsions from Aragon and Castile (1492), and Portugal (1497) the Jewish emigrants brought these varieties to the Ottoman Empire, parts of North Africa, and parts of Western and Central Europe. Early on after the expulsions, in the Ottoman regions and its successor states—such as Turkey, Greece, Bosnia, Serbia, Macedonia, Bulgaria, Romania, Israel—and in parts of the Austro-Hungarian Empire, on the one hand, and in North Africa, on the other hand, evolving forms of these varieties, mostly reflecting popular medieval Jewish Castilian, began to coalesce into local regional varieties of primarily two post-expulsion Sephardic Jewish languages. In the Ottoman regions the varieties came to be known among the Jews and their neighbors as the 'Jewish language' (*djuḏezmo* and *djuḏyó/djiḏyó* among the Jews; *Yahudice/Musevice* and its variants among the Turks, etc.), as well as *laḏino*, *levantino*, *espanyol* and *djudeo-espanyol*; and in Northern Morocco, as *ḥakitía* (probably 'language of recounting,' from Arabic *ḥ-k-y*). Sharing three of the main general features which came to characterize the Jewish diaspora languages as a sociolinguistically defined language group, these language varieties of the Sephardic Jews were: (a) traditionally written in diverse adaptations of the Hebrew alphabet (e.g., ג׳וד׳יזמו, representing *djuḏezmo* 'Judezmo; Judaism'); (b) they contained a linguistic component deriving from Hebrew and Aramaic, often in structural fusion with elements deriving from other components of the languages (e.g., *mazalozo* 'lucky' < Hebrew מזל/*mazzal* + -*ozo*, cf. Old Spanish -*oso*); and (c) they preserved elements from the Jewish languages spoken previously by the ancestors of the speech group (e.g., *alḥaḏ* 'Sunday,' from [Jewish] Ibero-Arabic *al-ḥadd*; *meldar* 'to read, study [especially Jewish texts],' from Jewish Latin *meletare* < Jewish Greek *meletáō*).

The present chapter will focus on the role played by the traditional Iberian-origin Jewish language of the Ottoman Sephardim and their descendants (henceforth to be referred to as Judezmo) in their observance of Jewish religious ritual and practice and its transmission over the generations, *De la fasha asta la mortaja* ('From [the time the baby wore] swaddling clothes until [the aged person was wrapped in a] shroud,' i.e., from the cradle to the grave). Throughout the discussion Judezmo sources will be cited, with translations; the sources originally appeared in the traditional Hebrew-letter Judezmo orthography, but to aid the reader unfamiliar with that orthography they will be transcribed in a slightly modified version of the Romanization promoted by the Israel National Authority for Ladino and Its Culture and the Ladino Academy of Israel, on which orthography see Bunis (2019) and Schwarzwald (2021).

Judezmo Speakers as a Tradition-bound Jewish Society that Underwent Modernization

Until the early twentieth century the Judezmo-speaking Sephardim were, in large measure, a tradition-bound society, observing Orthodox Jewish traditions in the variants accepted by the group. There were divergences from one community to another, and also divergences within communities between men as a group, especially traditionally more educated men and women and, to an extent, children. Following World War I, and especially after World War II, a significant portion of the Judezmo speech community throughout the language's traditional speech region gradually distanced itself from many of the traditional religious and cultural practices observed by earlier generations and moved toward a more modern, secular,

Europeanized lifestyle. The following discussion will focus primarily on the habits and customs of those Judezmo speakers, especially those of the society's modern period (which began around the end of the eighteenth century), who led a more traditional life with respect to Judaism as a religion, and some of the reactions of the more secularized modern Judezmo speakers to those habits and customs (see also Dobrinsky 2001). Especially rich sources of information in Judezmo on the traditional religious life of this speech group in the Ottoman and Austro-Hungarian empires and their successor states is the significant popular rabbinical literature created in the language for the sake of those of its members who could not read rabbinical works in Hebrew,[4] and the Judezmo press and modern-style literature which flourished in the language from the middle of the nineteenth century.[5] Among Judezmo speakers, Judezmo has played a central role in ritual observance, both of Jewish calendar and life cycle highpoints, and Jewish spiritual life in general. In this connection it should be noted that Islamic religious literature in vernaculars other than Arabic, such as Persian and Turkish, had begun to develop centuries before the arrival of the Sephardim in the empire (Peacock 2019); the widespread popularity of that literature in the Ottoman regions perhaps helped motivate and strengthen the use of analogous traditions among the Sephardim of the empire. The question of Jewish prayer in a language other than Hebrew had already been raised in the Mishna (e.g., Sota 32a); this, and the ensuing discussion in rabbinical literature over the centuries, established a basis for the validity of prayer and religion-oriented texts in Jewish diaspora languages.

Jewish Calendric Cycle

Like some other Jewish groups of the Levant and Middle East, and unlike the Ashkenazim, Judezmo speakers often used non-Hebrew-origin names, sometimes alternating with Hebrew-origin names, for some of the festivals of the Jewish calendar: e.g., *frutas* or *frutikas* '(little) fruits' for Tu Bishvat. Even some of the Hebrew-origin terms used in connection with the calendric cycle diverged from those used by other Jewish speech communities, and frequently had Hispanic-origin synonyms (Corré 1984); e.g., *tefilá* not only meant Jewish prayer but also specifically *šaḥarit* or 'the morning prayer,' with Hispanic-origin *orasyón* also used in modern Judezmo for 'prayer'; *zemirod* for the initial morning prayers known among Ashkenazim as *pesuqe de-zimra*; *kipur* for 'Yom Kippur,' and *moed*, or *fyesta*, for 'Jewish holiday' in general, while both *taní(d)* and *ayuno* were used for a 'fast day.' Some of the functionaries in charge of the prayers and other ritual tasks in the community were known in some areas by distinctive names, e.g., *haham* 'religious scholar, rabbi,' *hahamesa* (or *rubisa*) 'rabbi's wife' (Romance fem. *-esa*, *-isa*), *hahamlik* 'rabbi's office' (*-lik* denoting a profession, etc., from Turkish), *hahambashí* 'chief rabbi' (Tk. *başı* 'its head'), *rubí* 'elementary religious school teacher,' *rubisa* 'school teacher's wife.' To demonstrate respect, the titles of the functionaries were traditionally preceded by *sinyor* 'sir, master,' e.g., *sinyor haham*, and so too were historical heroes such as those mentioned in biblical texts, e.g., *el sinyor de Avram Avinu* 'master Abraham Our Forefather.' The everyday congregants, too, were known as *los sinyores yahidim*, from Hebrew *yaḥid* 'individual.' The synagogue and its parts, and the names given to other objects and institutions central to religious life, were sometimes called by distinctive names, some of Hebrew and Arabic origin, e.g., *kal* or *keilá* 'synagogue,' *tevá* 'prayer platform,' *ehal* 'Torah ark,' *karraya de shabad* 'Sabbath lamp,' *talega*/ *korracha* 'bag for carrying prayer articles,' *harachín(a)* or *takyá* 'skullcap.' Rabbinic scholars wore special hats (*bonete* or *mema*) and long, wide-sleeved robes (*anterí*), and these are still used in some communities (e.g., Istanbul).[6]

Daily and Holiday Prayers

The early-morning cry of *A tefilá! A tefilá!* 'To the morning prayer! To the morning prayer!' by the synagogue beadle making his rounds in the Jewish quarters awoke the congregants and hastened them to morning prayers. Afternoon and evening prayers (*minhá i arvid*) might be said in the synagogue, a place of business or even a café or the open air.

Characteristic of the formal prayer services in the synagogue in general, the prayers were traditionally recited in Hebrew or, according to the particular text, Aramaic (e.g., *kadish* 'memorial prayer'). However, from the earliest period of Jewish letter-press printing, instructions for the recitation of prayers, holiday uses and customs and so on were printed in some prayer books in Judezmo; a prayer book printed in Naples in 1490 is perhaps the earliest printed Jewish prayer book with some Judezmo instructions (regarding the Passover seder) (Cohen 2020a). Women, to the extent that they prayed, often prayed in the vernacular; in mid-sixteenth-century Salonika a Judezmo (only) prayer book was published for women, whose prayers in the *azará* or *eznoga* 'women's section of the synagogue' might be presided over or assisted by particularly learned women or by a *hazán de las mujeres* ([Benveniste] 1712 [1568], 4a; for an edition see Schwarzwald 2012).

In Constantinople in 1739, the prolific Judezmo writer and translator Rabbi Avraham Asa published a Judezmo translation of the entire daily prayer book to accompany the Hebrew text, making it possible for men to follow the meaning of the prayers, and potentially even to pray (as individuals) in the vernacular. (As will be seen, the Judezmo translation of some individual prayers were already included with their Hebrew texts in prayer books for the Ottoman Sephardim published from the seventeenth century on; in the nineteenth century several more Hebrew prayer books were published with complete Judezmo translations, e.g., Alsheh and Alsheh (1865). Around 1925 an edition was published in Sarajevo with Judezmo in Romanization.) Also in 1739, Asa began to publish a Judezmo translation of the entire Hebrew Bible (Asa 1739b), enabling participants in the Sabbath and holiday prayer service to follow the relevant Torah portions read, and also to test their sons' knowledge of the weekly Torah portion, as learned in the religious elementary school (*meldar* or *havrá*) recalled in children's songs such as *"La Torá, la Torá, el ijiko a la havrá"* (and other variants) 'The Torah, the Torah, the little boy to school.'[7] The Hebrew letters were taught with the help of mnemonic devices such as *la álef* (א)—*alas* 'wings,' *la bed* (ב)—*boka* 'mouth'; from the Square alphabet letters and vowels, the Rashí font and the *soletreo* cursive script, boys progressed to the study of portions of the Pentateuch and Prophets, their translation into Judezmo (*ladinar*) and interpretation (*perush*), to other sacred texts. Rabbi Ya'aqov Hulí (1730, 74a), in the first volume, on Genesis, of the highly popular and frequently reprinted Judezmo exegetical work, *Me-'am lo'ez* which he initiated in Constantinople in 1730, instructed each father to *"sea mishtadel ke no salga su ijo am aares ... Es ehréah ke se anbeze a meldar, a lo manko ke sepa el ladino del Arbá veesrim entero para ke lo pueda meldar"* 'strive so that his son does not turn out an ignoramus in traditional Jewish learning ... It is necessary for him to learn to read/study, at least so that he knows the Ladino translation of the entire Hebrew Bible so he can study it.' The *modaá* or prayer of declaration of faith was recited in Judezmo once in a week or a month or at least twice a year, before ten males; a version was printed in Constantinople (Toledo 1732, end) and also elsewhere.

Judezmo rabbinic works from the sixteenth century and later echoed earlier rabbinic pronouncements that Jewish religion-oriented texts and various prayers could and should be phrased in a language understood by the student and worshipper. In the Hebrew and vernacular introductions to his Judezmo translation of parts of the *Šulḥan 'aruk* published in Salonika, 1568 Ma'ir [Benveniste] grappled (f. 3a) with the question of religion-oriented texts in the vernacular; he stated that his book was printed *"en ladino de letra entera kon puntos para ke todos se puedan aprovechar de eyo, afilú el ke no konose mas ke las letras i los puntos i save el soletreo"* 'in Judezmo [rather than Hebrew] in Square letters with vowels so that all can make use of it, even one who knows no more than the letters and vowels and how to join them to write Judezmo.' Benveniste argued that people should understand the *ladino* 'vernacular translation from the Hebrew' of the basic prayers and benedictions (f. 56b).

In 1733, in the second volume, on Exodus, of *Me'am lo'ez* (part one) Ya'aqov Hulí approved of the use of Judezmo, for those unfamiliar with Hebrew, for reciting the *'eruv* prayer establishing an enclosure for Sabbaths and holidays (Hulí 1733, 137b), the *qidduš* 'Sabbath and holiday sanctification prayer' (196a), the *birkat ha-mazon* 'grace after meals' (195b), and the *havdalah* 'separation from the Sabbath and festivals' (199b). Concerning the Passover Haggadah, Avraham Asa (1749, 234b) recommended that the master of the house *"dirá 'A lahmá anyá' asta 'Ma nishtaná' ... en lashón ke entyenden las mujeres i los chikos i les deklarará toda la agadá en ladino"* 'say "Ha laḥma 'anya" until "Maništana" ... in a language that the women and children understand and that he explain to them the entire Haggadah in Ladino.' Various simplified, non-canonic prayers, such as the child's prayer before going to sleep (beginning *"A la kama me va echar"* 'I will lie down in bed'), and prayers by groups of young pupils taken out of school by their teachers to pray for rain in times of drought were also recited in Judezmo.

The highest level rabbinic literature produced among the Ottoman Sephardim was composed in Hebrew. But to provide insights into the meaning, laws and observances connected with the daily prayer cycle, and the Sabbath and Jewish festivals, for the majority of Judezmo speakers, who were not completely familiar with Hebrew, an extensive literature was produced by the Ottoman rabbis in Judezmo, in diverse prose and poetic genres which greatly enriched the holiday experience. Printed in Italy and in cities once constituting part of the Ottoman Empire such as Jerusalem, Constantinople, Salonika, Izmir, Belgrade and Sarajevo, as well as Vienna, New York, Seattle, Buenos Aires and elsewhere, these works shed interesting light on Sabbath and other holiday and ritual customs once practiced among the Jews of the empire and its successor states (for synthetic overviews, see Zimmels 1976; Dobrinsky 2001). Particularly enlightening are the writings of the rabbis Yosef Karo (b. Toledo, 1488–d. Safed, 1575; e.g., 1550–1559; on the Judezmo adaptation see Cohen 2015; on Judezmo halakhic works in general see Cohen, forthcoming), Ḥayyim Benveniste (1603–1673) of Constantinople (e.g., 1657–1734, 1671–1717), Yosef Molho (1692–1768) of Salonika (e.g., 1756), Ḥayyim Yosef David Azulay (1724–1806) of Eretz Israel and Livorno (e.g.1786), Eli'ezer ben Šem Ṭov Papo (d. 1898) of Sarajevo (e.g., 1862), Izmir chief rabbis Ḥayyim Palachi (1788–1868; e.g., 1873) and Avraham Palachi (c.1809–1898; e.g., 1853), Šem Ṭov Gaguine (1884–1953) of Jerusalem and Manchester (e.g., 1934–1960), and in more recent years, Nisim Behar (1913–1990) of Istanbul and Bat Yam (e.g., 1959). For example, in the Judezmo-language *Sefer mešeq beti* of Rabbi Eli'ezer ben Šem Ṭov Papo of Sarajevo, the Sabbath rituals and religious practices observed by the Sephardim of his native city are documented in rich detail (Šmid 2012). Rabbis in other areas recorded local customs with which they were familiar; e.g., in his Judezmo moralistic work *We-hokiaḥ Avraham* (1877 [1853], 205a–205b), Avraham Palachi remarked:

> *Me plazyó muncho el minag de Tekyir Dagí, ya[gén] a[lea] E[loim], ke entran sin sapatos a el bed akenésed, i afilú agora, ke rov aolam yevan chapín, se akavidan en esto.*

> (I very much liked the custom of Tekirdağ [Turkey], may God protect it, where they enter the synagogue without shoes, and even now, when most everyone wears patent leather shoes, they still take care to observe this.)

Sabbath (*el shabaḏ* or *sabá*)

In some communities (e.g., Salonika) in the late afternoon on Fridays the synagogue beadles roamed around the Jewish neighborhoods proclaiming *"Asendeḏ/Asendyendo ke ya es taḏre!"* 'Light Sabbath candles, because it's late already!' Paralleling the Hebrew structure *lel šabbat* 'night of Sabbath,' Friday night is called *noche de shabaḏ*. As in other communities, the Friday night synagogue service was conducted in Hebrew; but some men read the Song of Songs to themselves in Judezmo (a version is printed in a maḥzor from Venice, 1736 and in other prayer books as well as in editions of the Five Megilloth, e.g., Constantinople 1744). Among men, the traditional Sabbath greeting is Hebrew *Shabaḏ shalom!* and its reply, *Shabaḏ shalom mevorah!*; women might instead use more Hispanized *Buen shabaḏ!* 'Good Sabbath,' the reply being *Salud i viḏa!* 'Health and life!' Special Sabbath foods included the minced meat pie, *pastel*, and various other fish or meat delicacies (Bunis 1984). The *kidúsh* 'sanctification prayer' might be made over wine or *rakí* 'anise or other brandy,' and both drinks, as well as *kavé* 'Turkish-style black coffee' and *dulses* 'sweets,' jellied or baked, played a major role in all celebrations.[8] The Sabbath blessing over bread might be pronounced over twelve *pitikas* 'little pitas.' A Judezmo version of the grace after meals, *"Ya komimos i bevimos"* 'We have eaten and drunk' is added to the Hebrew version. Today, some Ottoman Sephardim have adopted the hymn *"Bendigamos al Altísimo"* 'Let us bless the Most High' from the Spanish-Portuguese tradition, but it was not part of the original Ottoman Sephardic paraliturgy. Most table hymns sung by Ottoman Sephardim were in Hebrew, but some were in the vernacular. The poem collection *Zemirot Yisrael* of Yisrael Najara (1587) (Safed) illustrates how religious poetry, both canonized pieces and new creations, were sung contrafactum, to the tunes of pre-existing vernacular songs in Judezmo, Turkish, Greek, Arabic and other languages used in the Ottoman Empire.

On the Sabbath day, too, the formal prayers were chanted in Hebrew; but the auctioning off of the synagogue honors such as taking out the Torah from the ark and putting on its adornments, the haham's *derashá* 'sermon,' as well as all other interactions between the synagogue leadership and the congregants were conducted in Judezmo; after removing the Torah scroll from the ark a Judezmo version of the *Beriḵ šemeh* prayer (*"Bindicho Su Nombre"* 'Blessed Be His Name') was chanted by the congregation instead of the original Aramaic text, which very few could understand. At the end of the morning service a Judezmo version (*"Non komo muestro Dyo"*) was added to the singing of *"En kelohenu"* in Hebrew, the two languages used in alternation for each stanza. After the morning service, a special *dezayuno* 'breakfast' was served, including *guevos haminaḏos* 'hardboiled eggs,' *borrekas*, *bulemas* and other filled pastries, cheese, vegetables and *rakí* 'anise brandy.' At home *qidduš* was recited and the mid-day meal served. In addition to the traditional Hebrew and Aramaic table hymns sung by followers of the 'Sephardic rite,' hymns might be sung in Judezmo (e.g., *"Enveluntó Aḏonay"* 'God Desired') or Hebrew and Judezmo (e.g., Yisrael Najara's Aramaic *"Ya Ribbon 'Alam,"* rendered into Judezmo as *"Ya Sinyor del Mundo"*), part of *"Yom Ha-šabbat en kamohu," "Elaw mi hiqša."* Before and after religious study sessions a passage might be said in Judezmo.

At home, on the Sabbath as on all holidays and special occasions, during a gesture known as *la bezamano* 'kissing the hand,' young people approached their elders, took their hand, said something to the order of *"Daká le bezaré la mano"* 'Give me your hand and I'll kiss it,' and having kissed it, they brought it to their forehead and received the elders' blessings. Avraham Asa (1729, part 2, 10a) alluded to the custom in rhymed verse: *"Shabaḏ noche i día beza la mano, a paḏre i maḏre i grande ermano, i a vyejo i kano"* 'On the Sabbath, in the evening and during the day, kiss the hand of your father and mother and older brother, and elder and one whose hair is gray.'[9] Boys might recite—*en lashón i en laḏino* 'in Hebrew and literal Judezmo translation'—the weekly Torah portion they had learned in school, or other texts relevant to the season, such as the Book of Job before Tish'a Be-av, Esther before Purim, Ruth before Shavuoth. In the religious study halls, schools and small study groups Hebrew and Aramaic texts were focused on; but Judezmo was the language of instruction. When less educated people met on the Sabbath to study the *Me-'am lo'ez* with a learned scholar, the language of the text studied as well as the accompanying discourse was Judezmo. Notices in the synagogue and other communal centers giving religious-oriented information meant for the whole community were printed in that language. In the Jewish courts as well, testimony and supporting documents were often presented and recorded in Judezmo; some of these documents were later published in collections of *še'elot u-tšuvot* 'rabbinical responsa.'[10]

The filled *pitas* 'flat pastries' specially made for the Sabbath are called *pitas/pitikas de shabad*, and the traditional Sabbath stew, kept warm overnight in a local baker's oven, is known as *hamín*; the large vessel used to cook it and keep it warm, the *haminero* (cf. Sp. *-ero* denoting a vessel); the plate or bowl used to serve an individual portion of *hamín*, the *haminiko*; the act of baking (e.g., an egg) in the *hamín*, *enhaminar* (cf. Sp. verbalizers *en- -ar*); the traditional egg hardboiled in the *hamín*, the *guevo (en)haminado* (cf. Sp. *huevo en- -ado*). Metaphorically, something small and of little value might be called *una haminada* (cf. Sp. *-ada*); an extortionist, a *hamindjí* (cf. Tk. *-ci* [*-djí*] 'practitioner of a trade'), the act of giving him a bribe, *dar hamín* 'giving *hamín*,' and of his accepting it, *komer hamín* 'eating *hamín*.' Various types of *hamín* were served during the course of the year, depending upon the season and upon particular occasions celebrated at the time, e.g., *hamín de Beshalah* or *de ashuré* 'special dish eaten on Tu Bišvat' (cf. the Torah portion *Be-sallaḥ*, Ex. 13:17–17:16), and in the cold season meat *hamín* (*"azen enel e[n]vyerno hamín de pachás"* 'during the winter they make *hamín* with trotters' (Magriso 1746, 91a)).

As in the case of numerous other holidays, the Sabbath and its symbols are alluded to in various folk tales, folk proverbs and sayings (recent treatments include Alexander-Frizer 2008; Bornes-Varol *c.* 2010). For example, the uniqueness of the Sabbath—and by extension, of anything one wants to single out—may be expressed by the saying *"No kada día es shabad"* 'Not every day is the Sabbath.' Instead of telling a housewife to mind her own business directly she might be told *"Tu mira tu hamín!"* 'You watch your own *hamín*!'; the chancy outcome of any particular ḥamín, like that of a new son-in-law in the family, is expressed by the saying *"Yerno i hamín, komo te salen"* 'A son-in-law and the Sabbath stew, as they happen to turn out for you'; and a discreet way of telling a man his fly is open is *"La butika avyerta en día de shabad!"* 'Your shop is open on the Sabbath day!' Children born on the Sabbath might be named *Shabatula* (cf. Gk. hypocoristic feminine *-oúla*), reducing to *Setula*, if a girl, or *Shabad*, *Shabetay* or *Shabatulo*, if a boy.

In a Judezmo adaptation of Ḥayyim Yosef David Azulay's Hebrew-language halakhic work *More ba-'ešba'* (1786), Yehuda Konfino (1893, 61a), who was born in Tekirdağ (Turkey), related how the Saturday-night *avdalá* or 'separation from the Sabbath' ritual should be practiced, as taught by his father and by his teacher and rabbi, Nissim Moshe Fins:

> *Ke se akavide en la avdalá de tener siryo de sera ensendido delantre de el la ora de avdalá. I vidi ke mi si[nyor] padre, zé[her] sa[dik] li[vrahá], uzava ke kuando eskapava la avdalá matava dito siryo ke dishimos kon un pokitiko del vino ke sovra de el vazo de la avdalá, i el fumiko ke salía lo golía, i se abokava para golerlo byen. I me dizía ke era segulá buena para hohmá, i por no olvidar lo ke melda. I ke diga las berahod de la avdalá komo su razón. I después en su punto ke diga los pesukim de 'Vayitén lehá Aeloim,' ke es segulá para tener berahá i azlahá. I después ke diga las syen i trenta vezes de 'Eliyau' asigún está kopyado en los livros, ke es segulá buena. I vidi a mi si[nyor] padre i a mi si[nyor] haham, hari[bí] Nesim Moshé Fins, zé[her] sa[dik]*

li[vrahá], de Tekírdagí, ya[gén] a[lea] E[loim], en estos syen i trenta 'Eliyau' … aprisipyo dizían syen i trenta vezes 'Ashem U Aeloim,' apuntando kon el dedo enriva de eyos, i después dizían las syen i trenta vezes 'Eliyau,' i después dizían los dos pesukim ke están detrás.

(One should take care in the havdalah ceremony to have a wax candle burning before him at the time of the havdala. And I saw that my father, the memory of a righteous man for a blessing, was accustomed, when he finished the havdalah, to extinguish this candle that we mentioned with a little wine that was left over from the havdalah glass, and he used to smell the bit of smoke that rose up, and he would bend down in order to smell it well. And he told me it was a good charm for acquiring wisdom, and for not forgetting what one studied. And one should say the blessings as required. And then immediately after he should say the verse *"Wa-yitten leka Ha-Elohim"* ['So God give thee,' Gen. 27:28] which is a good charm for having bounty and success. And afterward one should say *"Eliyyahu"* 130 times as printed in the prayer books, which is another good charm. And I saw my father and my honored rabbi, Nissim Moshe Fins, the memory of righteous men for a blessing, of Tekirdağ, may God watch over it, in these 130 recitations of "Eliyyahu" at the beginning they said *"Ha-Shem Hu Ha-Elohim"* ['The Lord, He is God,' I Kings 18:39] 130 times, pointing with their index finger above them, and then they said *"Eliyyahu"* 130 times, and then they said the two verses that follow them.)

Following the Hebrew havdalah service, Judezmo hymns such as *"El Dyo Alto kon Su Grasya"* 'Most High God in His Mercy,' *"Buenas semanas vemos vinir"* 'Let's see good weeks coming,' *"Buenas semanas mos de el Dyo"* 'May God give us good weeks' were sung. Making the transition on Saturday night from the Sabbath back to the regular work week, people greeted their fellow Jews with Hebrew *Shavua tov mevorah!* 'A good, blessed week!' to which the reply was *Alenu vealah!* 'Upon us and upon you!'; and also with Judezmo expressions such as *Buenas semanas!* 'Good weeks!' and replies such as *Semanada buena (i klara)!* '[Have a] good (and bright/clear) week!' and *Esta i munchas!* 'This [week] and many more!'

Elul Observances

On *Rosh Hodesh Elul*, the eve of the last month of the Jewish calendar, which was followed by *Rosh Ashaná* '(Jewish) New Year,' a *mishmará* or obligatory 'nocturnal vigil' was organized, the men spending the entire night deep in sacred study. Before dawn during all of Elul, in response to the invitation in Judezmo of the synagogue attendants who passed by their homes to wake them, men traditionally rose and made their way to the synagogue to chant *selihod* 'penitential prayers' in Hebrew and Aramaic, with a few read by some in Judezmo, e.g., Yehuda Ibn Bal'am's *"Bezokri 'al miškavi"* 'On thinking of my eternal rest,' *"Im afes"* 'If there is no more [hope],' and *"Marana de-višmaya/Muestro Sinyor ke en los syelos"* ('Our Lord in the Heavens'), *"Ija mía, mi kerida"* 'My daughter, my beloved.' These encouraged people to *tornar en teshuvá* 'do penitence.' On the first day of each new Hebrew month women traditionally did not work, bringing upon themselves the epithet *ros·hoderas* 'observers of Rosh Hodesh.' A report on the Jewish community of Kastoria (Greece) appearing in the 30 September 1897 issue of *El Tyempo* of Constantinople noted, with some ridicule, that: *"Un día antes de rosh hódesh, las mujeres se renden al talmud torá por enformarsen del melamed a ke ora tyene lugar el molad porke, en sus kreensa, no deven lavar las ropas en·el momento del molad"* ('A day before the New Hebrew Month the women go to the Talmud Torah to learn from the teacher at precisely what time the new moon will appear because, in their belief, they should not wash clothes at that moment') (Anon. 1897).

Rosh Hashanah (Roshashaná) '(Jewish) New Year'

Before Rosh Hashanah, also known as *Kapo de anyo* 'Head of the year'—or, in contrast to the *roshashaná trefá* 'non-kosher [or non-Jewish] New Year,' *roshashaná kašer* 'the kosher Rosh Hashana'—it was the custom to visit the graves of deceased relatives and saintly men of the local community, who were asked to intercede on behalf of the living (*traer a los muertos* 'bringing the dead'). Some members made the *ziara* (from Arabic *ziyāra*) or 'ritual pilgrimage' to Jerusalem and other holy cities in the Land of Israel. At holy sites such as the Western Wall and the graves of sainted scholars some men read various prayers in Hebrew, Judezmo or both. Upon their return they were honored with the title *hadjí* 'pilgrim to the Land of Israel,' and their wives, feminine *hadjía*; some people, especially the elderly, remained in the Land until their demise (see below).

The first evening meal of the holiday began with the ceremony called *los yeirasones* 'recitations of the *Yehi rason* (or "may it be Your will") prayer,' Hebrew blessings over symbolic foods meant to give a positive start to the year. Such foods included delicacies such as *kalavasa amaría* 'yellow pumpkin,' *borrekitas de bofe* and *de kalavasa* 'lung- and pumpkin-filled pastries,' and *fritadikas de puero* 'fried leek-balls.' In the synagogue most of the holiday prayers were recited in Hebrew; but from the late nineteenth century some prayer books contained Judezmo translations, and in the early twentieth century, and especially between the world wars, an increasing number of holiday hymns began to be recited, or at least read silently by individual congregants, in Judezmo, e.g., the poetic composition *"Aḥot qetana"* 'Little sister,' by sixteenth-century rabbi Abraham Hazan, and *"ʿEt šaʿare raṣon"* 'Time of the gate of [divine] will,' by Yehuda Ibn ʿAbbas of twelfth-century Fez, intoned on the first night of the holiday. Adapted from Ashkenazi maḥzorim in connection with the prayer *"U-ntanne toqef"* 'Let us proclaim the awesomeness' of uncertain authorship, which began to be recited in some Sephardic synagogues in the nineteenth century, the legend of Rabbi Amnon of Mayence in Judezmo translation was added to the holiday maḥzor used by Judezmo speakers (e.g., Maḥzor Vienna, 1887a, 67ff). That maḥzor also has translations of other holiday hymns such as *"Yede rašim"* 'Hands of the poor' of Yehuda Halevy, and *"Šofeṭ kol ha-areṣ"* 'Judge of all the earth' of Šelomo Ibn Gevirol. In some synagogues other prayers, e.g., *"Ya šimka aromimka"* 'God I shall extoll Your name' and *"Ha-yom harat ʿolam"* 'Today the world is born,' were also sung in Judezmo. From the early twentieth century, Judezmo translations of the special High Holiday hymns used in the Ottoman Sephardic liturgy also began to be published in Latin characters (e.g., Israel 1910); from the modern period a tradition of singing some of these hymns in Judezmo was established, and in some congregations it continues to this day.

The traditional holiday greetings were Hebrew *"Tizku le-šanim rabbot (neʿimot we-ṭovot)!"* 'May you merit many (pleasant and good) years!' to which was replied *"Tizku we-tihyu we-taʾariḵu yamim!"* 'May you have merit and live and be worthy of many days,' or Judezmo *"Para munchos anyos!"* 'For many years!', *"Anyada buena (i klara)!"* 'A good (and bright) year!', *"Vidas largas ke me tengas!"* 'May you have a long life!', to which varied and sometimes lengthy blessings were added such as *"Anyada buena, gurlía i byen estrenada!"* 'A good, successful, well-begun year!' or *"Anyada buena i gansyoza kon parnasá buena i mezonod buenos i el Šem Iḏbarah ke te akontente en todo lo ke demandas!"* 'A good and prosperous year with a good livelihood and good sustenance and may the Name Blessed Be He satisfy you in all that you ask!'

To help Judezmo speakers keep up with the progression of the Jewish year, Judezmo calendars and almanacs (*lúaḥ*, *halilá*, later also *kalendaryo*; e.g., Mordoh 1848) were widely distributed.

Fast Days (*Tanides/Taaniyod*); Excommunication (*Hérem*)

Ṣom Gedalya, the minor fast day observed on the day following Rosh Hashanah, is also known as *Kipur chiko* 'Little [Yom] Kippur'; and Šiv'a 'Asar be-Tamuz is called *Tesabeav chiko* 'Little Ninth of Av.' The prayers for the 'minor' fast days (i.e., all except Yom Kippur) were incorporated in a prayer book called *Seder arba'* [or ḥameš/ḥamišša, including the Fast of Esther] *ta'aniyyot* 'Order of the four [or five] fasts' (see also Tisha be-Av below).

Fasts were also proclaimed during times of communal calamity and danger; for example, in Salonika in 1842 *"a·la okazyón de la viruela apregonaron tanid i tanyeron shofar"* 'during the time of the outbreak of smallpox they declared a fast and blew the shofar.'[11] But the popular belief held that after a day of fasting the Jews replenished themselves well enough, as expressed in the proverb *"Un día de taní (taanid), syete días de mal para el pan"* 'One day of fasting, seven days of sorrow for the bread loaves.'[12]

Throughout the Jewish world, certain instances of extreme religious or social misbehavior of individual community members as perceived by the local religious authorities might result in the excommunication of the guilty parties, if living, or their exorcism, if deceased; fasting might be a part of the religious acts performed in this connection. Of the Spanish-Portuguese Jews, Yosef Kaplan wrote "In no other Jewish communities have we found such widespread use of the punishment of excommunication as in the Sephardic communities of Amsterdam and Hamburg."[13] Excommunication was also practiced, if rarely, among the Ottoman Sephardim as well. An intriguing modern-day example in the Jewish community of Izmir, categorized by the incident's westernized newspaper reporter as evidence of a kind of communal dementia, was related in the 23 April 1896 issue of *El Tyempo*.[14] The community's more progressive, liberal sector was said to be determined to replace the older, more traditional and conservative communal administrators and institutions with more progressive ones, while the existing religious establishment was vehemently opposed to such change. The religious leadership argued that they had found among the progressives, anonymous papers demanding administrative changes by means of threats. Unable to determine who the guilty progressive individuals were, the religious leaders decided to excommunicate them, unnamed, in the synagogue, using an extreme form of the ceremony, the *ḥerem kolbo* 'all inclusive excommunication, constituting a kind of moral death sentence' (also known as *ḥérem del nahash/kulevro* 'excommunication of the "snake"' – Hebrew *naḥaš* 'snake,' ordinarily called *kulevro* in Judezmo, here used as an acronym of **n**idduy, **ḥ**erem, **š**emata, three types of excommunication). As reported in *El Tyempo*:

> [T]uvo lugar la prononsyasyón de esta sentensya de muerte moral en·el Ka[l] Ka[dosh] Algazi, kon una solemnidad ekstraordinarya. El templo era yeno de todos los myembros del kuerpo rabíniko i de algunos mansevos kuryozos de ver esta esena esmovyente i sin eshemplo en las anales de·la komunidad ... La seremonia se empesó a·las oras dos i medya a·la turka i eya duró kaje una ora entera.
>
> Después de aver resitado algunos salmos, dyeron lektura del salmo 190 envokando las maldisyones del Syelo sovre el akuzado deskonosido. El rabino Yis·hak Palachi avryó después el ehal akódesh. Dos otros rabinos ke observavan el ayuno desde el día de antes se prezentaron delante los sifré torá i dyeron uno entre las manos de un rabino. Resitaron alora penitensyas i konfesyones (selihod i viduyim) i tanyeron kuatro vezes kon un shofar. Después de esto, prononsyaron la eks[ko]mulgasyón mayor o hérem de Yeoshua Bin Nun. Personas ke asistyeron a esta estranya seremonia no pudyeron remetersen fasilmente de·la empresyón ke eyos sintyeron. Era un aspekto ke enspirava oror i terror."

(The pronouncement of this moral death sentence took place in the Holy Congregation Algazi with extraordinary solemnity. The temple was full of all the members of the rabbinical corps as well as some young men curious to see this moving scene, unprecedented in the annals of the community … The ceremony began at 2:30 Ottoman time [i.e., two and a half hours after sunset] and lasted practically a whole hour.

After having recited various other Psalms, they gave a reading of Psalm 190, invoking the curses of Heaven upon the unknown accused. Rabbi Yiṣḥaq Palachi then opened the Torah Ark. Two other rabbis who were fasting since the day before approached the Torah scrolls and put one of them into the hands of one of the rabbis. They then recited penitential and confessional prayers (seliḥot and widduyim) and sounded a shofar four times. After this, they pronounced the great excommunication or Excommunication of Joshua Bin Nun [cf. Joshua 6:26]. The people who attended this strange ceremony could not easily recover from the impression it had made upon them. It was an act that inspired horror and terror.)

Kippur

The formal prayers during this day of fasting and penitence were recited in Hebrew according to the Sephardic rite, including that known among Judezmo speakers as *"Kal niḏré"* 'All vows.' Judezmo passages appear in maḥzorim in connection with *"U-ntanne toqef"* 'Let us proclaim the awesomeness' and other prayers (e.g., Maḥzor 1887c, 65, which also has a translation of the *"Widduy"* 'Confession,' and other holiday hymns such as *"Keter malḵut"* 'Royal crown' of Šelomo Ibn Geviról and the *"Qeduša"* 'Sanctification' of Avraham Ibn 'Ezra). Typical Judezmo blessings, with some calques of parallel Hebrew blessings, were *"Eskritos i siyaḏos en livros de viḏas largas, de parnasá buena, de pas i de repozo"* '[May you be] written and sealed in the book of long life, of a good livelihood, of peace and tranquility!' and, calquing the prayer *"Tiḵle šana we-qileloteha, taḥel šana u-virkoteha"* by Avraham Ḥazzan Gerondi of thirteenth-century Girona (Catalonia), *"Se ateme el anyo kon sus maldisyones, empese el anyo kon sus bindisyones!"* 'May the old year and its curses end, may the new year and its blessings begin!'[15]

Sukkot (Sukoḏ)

Also known by its loan-translation *Kavanyas* 'Booths,' Sukkot was a time of family and community celebration inside and outside the synagogue. During *Simḥat Tora* in some communities such as Salonika, the Torah scrolls were joyously paraded in the street; Hebrew *piyutim* 'hymns' were sung, some with literal Judezmo translations, verse by verse, for example, *"Mi-pi El / De boka del Dyo"* 'From the mouth of God.' As during the other *shalosh regalim* 'three pilgrimages to Jerusalem' holidays, the traditional greeting was Hebrew *"Mo'adim le-simḥa!"* 'Seasons for happiness,' and its reply, *"Ḥaggim u-zmanim le-sason!"* 'Holidays and times for joy,' or in Judezmo, *"Buen moeḏ!"* 'Good holiday.' Most of the prayer service was recited in Hebrew, but in the modern era, with a decline in Hebrew studies in the increasingly secular-oriented Jewish schools, and the growing number of Jewish children studying in non-Jewish schools, prayer selections were increasingly recited in Judezmo. Some of the more conservative members of the community objected to the trend; for example, journalist Alexandre Benghiat of Izmir complained that in 1919: *"Myentres los tres moaḏim en las orasyones, los piyutim serán kantaḏos en djuḏezmo, en lugar ke syempre, asta agora, lo fueron i lo deven ser en lashón akóḏesh"* ('On the Three

Festivals during the prayer services, the hymns will be sung in Judezmo, instead of, as until now, they always were—and should be—sung, in the Holy Tongue.'[16])

Sukkot is alluded to in various folk proverbs and sayings; for example, *"Ken lo metyó a Djohá en mi suká?"* 'Who put [the Turkish folklore hero, based on a real-life Muslim religious leader] Djohá [cf. Tk. Nasrettin Hoca] in my sukkah?' used to express surprise and dismay at an unexpected and unpleasant turn of events (for Djohá tales with English translations, see Koen-Sarano 2003). The flowers used to decorate the sukkah were known as *flores de suká* 'Sukkah flowers/roses.'

Hanukkah

The oil or candle lamp lit in honor of Hanukkah is known as a *hanukía* (cf. Hebrew *ḥanukka* + Judezmo *-ia*, from Hispanic *-illa* or *-ía*), which evidently provided the inspiration for Israeli Hebrew *ḥanukkiyyá*; and the gift given during the holiday is called a *hanukalik* (cf. Tk. *-lik*, object connected to whatever the base of the word indicates). Traditionally, as observed by Rabbi Eli'ezer ben Šem Ṭov Papo (1862, 62b), *"Uzan las mujeres de·no azer melahá todo tyenpo ke adren las kandelas (hanukías)"* 'The women do not do any work while the Hanukkah lights are burning.' Yiṣḥaq Magriso (1764, 45a) of eighteenth-century Constantinople in his *Sefer Me-'am lo'ez* on Numbers noted another holiday custom: *"Uzaron de komer en hanuká kozas de kezo i leche por zéher de la leche ke le dyo a bever ... Yeudid a el rey Aliforni ke kon esto lo enborachó i lo mató"* 'They are used to eating dairy foods and milk [during Hanukkah] in remembrance of the milk that Judith gave King Holofernes by means of which she caused him to go into a stupor and she killed him.'

Celebrating the one-day supply of oil that lasted eight days in the rededicated temple in Jerusalem, foods prepared with oil such as *bimuelos* 'fritters' and *keftés de espinaka* 'spinach patties' (cf. Sp. *buñuelos*, Tk. *köfte*) are also central. Hanukkah is referred to in holiday rhymed ditties such as *"Hanukía, bayla mi tía, Hanuká, bayla mi vavá"* 'Hanukkah lamp, dance my aunt, Hanukkah dance my grandma.' In the nineteenth century, *komplas* 'rhymed couplets' (Sp. *coplas*) recounting the Hanukkah story began to appear (e.g., Yeni 1880; see Heredia 1981).[17] In honor of Purim and other religious holidays, biblical stories were reenacted by schoolboys, sometimes from printed plays; e.g., Moše Šemuel Ko[n]fino's *Pyesa de Yaakov Avinu kon sus ermanos* (Bucharest, 1862; text in Bunis 1995). Among Judezmo speakers *Hanuká* served as both a feminine personal name (the affectionate form is *Hanukita*, cf. Šabbetay 1651, no. 6) and a surname.

Tu (or Ḥamisha 'Asar) Bishvat

As noted above, this holiday is often referred to as *Frutas* or *Frutikas* '(Little) Fruits' because of the fruits (and produce) from the Holy Land eaten in its honor ceremonially at the *Séder tu bishvat* celebration held in the home or a public place. The holiday was also known as *La ashuré*, reminiscent of the name of a sweet pudding made of harvest products such as cereals, sugar, raisins, etc.[18] During the holiday it was said that the trees embraced. The service in the holiday booklet, called *"Peri 'eṣ hadar"* 'Fruit of the Citrus Tree' (1762), adapted from the anonymous *Ḥemdat yamim* (Izmir, c.1731) follows the order of the service established in the sixteenth century in the Land of Israel by the kabbalist Isaac Luria and his associates, constituting something of a parallel to the Passover seder. In editions of the booklet (known in Salonika as a *gemareka*, from *gemará* 'Talmud tractate'), in Hebrew, used for the ceremony, some Judezmo instructions are given and a number of the symbolic fruits and other natural foods are referred to by their Judezmo names (e.g., *níshpolas* 'medlars,' cf. Sp. *níspero* + Tk. *muşmula*, Gk. *moúsmoulo*, etc.). Some of the editions (e.g., Izmir, 1876) include couplets in honor of the holiday such as the *"Kantiga de las rozas"* 'Song of the flowers,' and *"Konplas de Tu Bishvat"* 'Tu Bishvat couplets' or *"Kantiga de las frutas"* 'Song of the fruits.'[19]

Purim

According to discussion in the rabbinical responsa of pre-expulsion Iberia, Megillat Esther was read to women in the vernacular in various medieval Iberian communities; although some rabbis objected to the practice it continued in Sephardic communities of the Ottoman Empire and Austro-Hungary into the twentieth century (Bunis 2004). As in other communities, during the reading noise was made at the mention of Haman's name (*dar/aharvar Amán* 'giving/beating Haman') with an *amaniko* 'noise-maker.' However, as some members of the community became 'civilized' they complained vociferously against what they called *"esta fea i atrazada seremonya ke kedó aínda en los djudyós de Turkía de harvar el Amán en purim ... la kavza de azernos kayer en bokas de las umod"* 'this ugly and backward ceremony that has remained amongst the Jews of Turkey of beating Haman on Purim ... the cause of our being slandered among the Gentiles.'[20]

As noted above, Judezmo rhymed couplets focusing on the Purim story and the foods and beverages served in honor of the holiday are known from the early eighteenth century.[21] The couplets also encouraged Jews to give charity to all during the holiday, despite the sometimes hostile environment: Ḥayyim Yom Ṭov Magula (1756 [1739], 14a) wrote: *"Aspros dad kon las dos manos, a proves guestros ermanos, i a turkos i krisyanos, aún ke no mos pueden ver"* 'Give coins with both hands, to your poor [Jewish] brothers, and to Muslims and Christians, although the latter cannot stand to see us.'

In the mid-nineteenth century Saʻadi Halevi Aškenazi, a prolific author and editor of Judezmo books and newspapers created and published additional Purim *komplas* (1858). A special Judezmo Purim collection by Yosef Šabbetay Farḥi of Jerusalem called *Sefer Alegría de Purim* (Book of the Joy of Purim) was first published in Livorno in 1875; it contained poetic texts and parodic marriage contracts alluding to the heroes and villains of the Purim story. The gifts of food required by halakha to be given on the holiday are often known as *platos* or *platikos* '(little) plates,' while additional holiday gifts are called *purimlikes* (cf. Tk. -*lik*). Among the special foods featured during Purim are the *folar*, a hardboiled egg encased in a pastry scaffold representing that used to hang Haman and his sons (thus the special Sabbath associated with Purim is called *shabad de folares*), the *orejas de Amán* 'Haman's ears,' and the *roskitas* 'round filled dough bracelets.' The Sabbath preceding the festival was popularly known as *el shabad de la kopeta* (Sabbath of the almond nougat), deriving from a characteristic sweet treat served in its honor, as well as *shabad de las novyas* (Sabbath of the brides), so named because of the many bride dolls given as gifts during the holiday. Under Greek influence, in some communities (e.g., Salonika) a Purim *karnavalya* 'carnival' was held. Toward Purim it was customary to say *"Purim, purim lanu, pésah en la mano"* 'We have Purim, Purim, Passover is at hand'; while traditional holiday greetings include *"Buen purim!"* 'Good Purim!' to which is sometimes added *"Buenos anyos!"* 'Good years!', *"Purim alegre!"* 'Happy Purim!' (perhaps under recent Ashkenazi or Israeli influence), and Hebrew *"Purim tov mevorah!"* 'A good, blessed Purim!' Children born on Purim often received a name connected with the holiday, e.g., *Mordohay* (or *Modrohay*) or *Ester*.

Passover

A saying reminding Judezmo speakers that Passover follows on the heels of Purim is *"Purim es haver de pésah"* 'Purim is the friend of Passover.' The many costs incurred during Passover are symbolized by the ironic interpretation of the holiday name, *Pésah*, as an acronym representing *parás sin hazbón* 'money without keeping an account' (cf. Tk. *para* 'money,' Sp. *sin* 'without,' Hb. *ḥešbon* 'account'). After the long and strenuous period of house preparation by the community's wives and daughters, and the search for the *ḥameṣ* remaining in the house, called among Judezmo speakers *kal hamirá*, and getting rid of it, or *des·hamesear* (cf. Jud./Sp. *des- -ear*, Hb. *ḥameṣ*), in the evening the Passover seder was celebrated joyously in the home or courtyard. Manuscript haggadot with Judezmo instructions are known from the fourteenth to fifteenth centuries (Cohen 2020a), and from at least the early sixteenth century (e.g., Anon., Venice 1524) Judezmo instructions for conducting the seder were printed as part of the haggadah; from the seventeenth century (e.g., Venice, 1609) practically the entire text was translated into Judezmo and chanted, in alternation with the Hebrew text, as part of the seder service. In the modern era parts or all of the haggadah with Judezmo were printed in the maḥzor for the Shalosh Regalim 'Three Festivals' (e.g., 1887b). For those assimilated community members no longer familiar with the Hebrew alphabet, both the Hebrew text and the Judezmo text began to be printed in Cyrillic characters in Bulgaria (Anon. 1927; see Studemund-Halevy 2021; Schwarzwald forthcoming; on their lexicons, see Schwarzwald 2008)) and in Modern Turkish Romanization in the Turkish Republic (Meṣulam *c.*1930; see also Azose 1995 for a recent Romanization). The haggadah translation also served as a basis for numerous parodies (Papo 2012).

Considerable discussion in Ottoman Sephardic Hebrew and Judezmo rabbinic works focused on the foods permitted and forbidden during Passover. Matzot and derived unleavened dough foods are often known as *boyos*; Sephardic cookbooks today offer an idea of the rich traditional Passover menu (Weingarten 2016). Some Sephardim took particular care in the observance of the Passover dietary laws. In his *Me-'am lo'ez* on Exodus Ya'aqov Hulí (1733, 54a) wrote:

Tengo visto en Kostandina en un gevir ke es temerozo del Dyo i kazó a su ijo en shabaḏ agaḏol ke era érev pésah i izo toḏa la fyesta kon masá, ke dezde noche de vyernes no entró pan en su kaza.

(I saw in Constantinople a wealthy man who was God-fearing and he married off his son on Shabbat Ha-gadol [the Great Sabbath, preceding Passover] and he made all of the festive foods with matzah, because from Thursday night no bread entered his home.)

Adopting a ruling mentioned in Ḥayyim Benveniste's Hebrew-language *Kenesset ha-gedola* (1657–1734), Avraham Asa in his Judezmo work *Sefer šulḥan ha-melek* (1749, 230a) noted that: *"En Kostandina uzan isur por friir peshes kon masá majaḏa, porke no se yeren i los frían kon arina, lo kual azer bimuelos de masá es mutar"* 'In Constantinople there is a custom to forbid the frying of fish in ground matzah, so that they don't mistakenly fry them with regular flour, but *bimuelos* (fritters) made with matzah flour are allowed.'

After the festive meal, at the end of the seder service traditional Hebrew and Aramaic hymns were sung, with some Judezmo adaptations: *"Ken supyense i entendyense"* 'Who knows and understands' and *"Un kavritiko"* 'One kid' (cf. *"Eḥad mi yodea'"* and *"Ḥad gadya"*). In 1776 a collection of *"Konplas de Pésah"* were published in Salonika, and throughout the Judezmo speech communities, diverse popular songs concerning the holiday were sung (e.g., in Salonika, one beginning *"A Moshé, A Moshé, azme este mandaḏo"* 'Moses, Moses, perform this commandment for me'). *Pésah* and *Pesaha* were used as personal names, and *Pésah* also as a surname. Holiday gifts were known as *pesahlikes*.

From Passover to Shavuoth the Mishna tract *Pirqe Avot* (Ethics of the Fathers) was traditionally chanted in the synagogue in Hebrew and calque Judezmo, in alternating paragraphs: e.g., Heb. *"Kol Yisrael yeš lahem ḥeleq la-'olam ha-ba"* / Jud. *"Toḏo Israel ay a eyos parte a el mundo el vinyén"* ('All of Israel has a part in the World to Come'); a Judezmo printed edition first appeared in Salonika *c*.1570 (Cohen 2020b). Like many outstanding phrases in sanctified texts like the Bible and Mishnah, the calque phrase *"a el anyo el vinyén,"* calquing Hebrew *"la-šana ha-ba'a,"* 'next year' (literally, 'to the year the coming') in the Passover seder was borrowed into everyday speech, in this case used in the sense of 'at some far off, unspecified time—and perhaps never.'

Lag La-'omer (18 Iyar)

Falling on the thirty-third day of the counting of the *'omer* from Passover, this holiday is also known among Judezmo speakers as *La Baryohá* or *La Nochaḏa del Sinyor* 'the Evening of the Master,' allusions to Šim'on Bar Yoḥay, the Mishnaic sage of the second century CE, the anniversary of whose death is commemorated on this date. It is celebrated with a festive meal. A booklet by David Arditi (1889) contains a Judezmo prayer to be recited over the grave of Bar Yoḥay in Miron.

Shavuot

Often called *Shevóḏ/Sevó*, the holiday is honored with a night-long religious study session known as the *meldado, mishmará* or *limuḏ* 'reading session.' Unique to Judezmo speakers is the chanting of a Judezmo translation of the book of Ruth, Šelomo Ibn Gevirol's *Azharot* 'Warnings' (a versification of the Torah), and the original Judezmo paraliturgical composition *"La ketubá de la ley"* 'Marriage Contract of the Law,' by Yehuda León Kala'i of eighteenth-century Salonika, appearing, among others, in Šemuel Modiliano's *Renanat mizmor* (Salonika, 1753). It is based on motifs in the poem *"Dodi yarad le-ganno"* 'My beloved went down to his garden,' by the sixteenth-century Sephardic poet Yisrael Nadjara of Damascus. In the latter, Israel is compared to a bride, and the Torah to her marriage contract. Various Judezmo rhymed verses in honor of the holiday were also published, e.g., those beginning *"Aḏonay Dyo Poḏerozo"* 'Lord God Most Powerful' (a versification of the Decalogue), *"El Alto Sinyor mos dyo una ley"* 'The Most-High Lord gave us a Torah' and *"Bindicho sea muestro Dyo"* 'Blessed be Our God,' and the *"Kantika de las rozas"* 'Song of the flowers,' having the refrain *"Es de alavar a el Sur Hay Olamim"* 'One must praise the Eternal Rock of the World.'

The holiday is celebrated with dairy foods. Basing himself on local tradition, Alexandre Benghiat, a Judezmo journalist cum grocer in Izmir offered the following explanation for the custom:

Nozotros tambyén, djuḏyós de Ezmir, estamos uzaḏos a azer algunas komiḏas dulses en shevoḏ, i en estas komiḏas entra en la mas parte poko muncho de leche, tal ke zerdé, sutlach, arrós kon leche, echétera, afuera ke primer i sigundo día de shevoḏ nos plaze bever tambyén leche. Kontan a este sujeto la lejenda ke sigye:	We too, the Jews of Izmir, are used to making some sweet foods on Shavuot, and in these foods there is mostly milk, such as *zerdé* (saffron rice), *sutlach* (rice baked with milk), rice cooked with milk, etc., in addition to our also liking to drink milk on the first and second days of Shavuot. On this subject they recount the following legend:

Moshé Rabenu nasyó en el syete Adar i tuvo seído guadrado eskondido en kaza de su madre myentres tres mezes, asta el sesh siván. En este día Yohéved, madre de Moshé, muncho espantada por los órdenes de Paró, ke ovligava a todo presyo ke todos los ijikos nasidos djudyós devían ser echados al río, mete i eya tambyén al chiko Moshé en el río, adyentro de un sestiko, i lo rekomenda a la proteksyón del Dyo. La ija de Paró ve el sestiko, lo kita del río i bushka alechadera para el chiko de adyentro. Tenyendo la nevuá ke sus lavyos ivan un día avlar kon el Dyo, no los kere auzar a mamar del pecho de una non djudía. Yohéved es echa vinir, grasyas a la ezveltés de Miryam, i el chiko Moshé empesa a mamar del pecho ke el ya estuvo savoreando tres mezes. Es en suvenir de este fato, ke se tendría pasado en el sesh siván—ke fue en la séguita primer día de shevod—ke nozotros bevemos leche en este día, sigún tuvo bevido Moshé el mezmo.	Moses Our Master was born on the seventh of Adar and was kept hidden in the home of his mother for three months, until the sixth of Sivan. On this day Yocheved, Moses' mother, very frightened by Pharoah's orders, requiring that all Jewish boys be thrown into the river, also puts little Moses in the river, in a small basket, and commends him to God's protection. Pharoah's daughter sees the little basket, takes it out of the river and looks for a nursemaid to nurse the little boy inside. Prophesizing that his lips would one day speak with God, she did not want to accustom them to nurse from the breast of a non-Jewish woman. Yocheved is summoned, thanks to the swiftness of Miriam, and little Moses begins to nurse from the breast that he was already used to savoring for three months. It is in memory of this occurrence, which would have taken place on the sixth of Sivan— following which would be the first day of Shavuot—that we drink milk on this day, just as Moses himself had drunk.

(Created by the author)

The holiday greetings are those of the Three Festivals (*"Moʻadim le-simḥa!"*; *"Ḥaggim u-zmanim le-sason!"*) or simply *"Buen shevod!"* 'Good Shavuoth.' A warning against dropping one's guard when the weather begins to get warm during this changeable season is the saying *"Si no vyene sevó no te kites la samara"* 'If Shavuot has not yet come don't put away your fur-lined winter coat.'

Tišʻa be-Av (*Tesabeá*)

On this fast day commemorating the destruction of the first and second Temples and other major Jewish disasters, Hebrew *qinot* and mournful Judezmo *endechas* 'dirges,' *romansas* 'ballads' and elegies such as that relating the story of Hannah and her seven sons are intoned. Some of the latter are known in fragments probably from the sixteenth century (Corré 1968; Gutwirth 1993; Díaz-Mas 2011). During the morning service, traditionally recited in Hebrew, the Haftara (Jeremiah 8:13–9:23) was recited in Hebrew; in the prayer books for the Four Fasts (or the version for the Five Fasts) various variants of a prose text in Judezmo adapted from Jeremiah are printed in between the paragraphs of the Haftara text (e.g., in that from Venice, 1624). The 'bitter exile from Sefarad' (*mar golat Sefarad*) is also recalled in the Tisha be-Av dirges (*qinot*) (e.g., *Seder Arbaʻ Taʻaniyot*, Venice. 1624, ff. 69b, 82b). An edition of the *Seder Arbaʻ Taʻaniyot ke-minhag Qa[hal] Qa[doš] Sefaradim* 'Order of the Four Fasts according to the custom of the Holy Congregation of Sephardim' published in Venice, 1755 (f. 7a) contains a penitential prayer for Tisha be-Av incorporating the following alternating Judezmo and Hebrew verses recalling the expulsions from Iberia:

Desterrados de vila en vila [or viya en viya], / Por Aragón i Kasti(l)ya /
Por ke la siya / de el reyno la an deshado.
(Expelled from one village and another, / Throughout Aragon and Castile /
Because the Seat / of the Kingdom has left it.)
Mi-kefar el kefar nitpazarnu, / Be-ʿir Kastilya Aragona, /
Kisse malkutenu lo nakona, / Lule A[donay] kullanu avadnu.
(From village after village we were dispersed, / In the cities of Castile and Aragon, /
The Seat of our Kingdom was not ready, / Without God we would all have been lost.)

The edition of *Seder Arbaʿ Taʿaniyot* (order of fasts) published in Salonika in 1798 contains a Judezmo version of the *"Qina ʿal ʿasara haruge ha-malkut"* 'Dirge for the ten martyrs of the kingdom'; and *Seder Arbaʿ taʿaniyot* edited in Vienna, 1811 by Yisrael Bekar Ḥayyim of Belgrade and Vienna (ff. 54a–54b), has a Judezmo translation of *"Bore ʿad ana"* 'Creator, whither?', intoned on the Sabbath before Tisha be-Av (*Šabbat Eka*). The collections of Tisha be-Av dirges in many fast day prayer books include two recalling the expulsions from Iberia (in Bekar Ḥayyim's edition, ff. 94b–96a): *"Avinu ha-gemul ha-ze qiwwinu"* 'Our Father We Awaited This Retaliation' contains the verse:

Yaṣeʾu aḥekem gerušim / Mi-Šereṣ u-mi-Sevilya /
Raʾiti ki ʿorpehem qašim / Heveti geruš Kastilya /
We-Siṣilya Aragon / Granada ʿolalay /
(Your brethren went forth expelled / From Jerez and from Sevilla /
I saw that they were stiff-necked / I brought the expulsion from Castilla /
And Sicily, Aragon, / Granada, my babes.)

"Mi ha-av yeyasser beno" 'Who is the Father Who Would Torment His Son?' includes a variant of the same verse.[22]

In the synagogue the number of years since the destruction of the Temples and the expulsions of the Jews from Spain and other countries was proclaimed in Judezmo from the prayer platform. This day of sad commemoration and all associated with it symbolize national mourning: thus a forlorn-looking person is said to have a *Kara de tesabeav* 'Tisha be-Av face.'

Change of Season

It was widely believed that during the *tekufá* (Heb. *tequfa*) or *dulse* 'change of the season of the year' a vein of blood passed through the drinking water. Anyone who drank water during that time would risk swelling up. The calamity could be neutralized by spilling out any standing water or adding to the water some brandy, a piece of iron, or especially something sweet (*dulse* 'sweet').

Life Cycle

The many halakhic works produced by the Judezmo-speaking rabbis of the Ottoman Empire and its successors offer much information on the community's daily and holiday religious life, from the time of the arrival of the expellees from Iberia in the late fifteenth century into modern times. For example, from Hulí's *Me-ʿam loʿez* on Genesis (1730, 49b) readers are reminded that an observant Jew *"syempre deve de ir kuvijada la kavesa"* 'must always have his head covered.' Because their surroundings were not always encouraging, the Jews refrained from certain practices in public places. For example, Asa wrote in rhymed verse in his *Sorke ṣibbur* (1733, 9a): *"Agora, bavonod, pezgado el kativeryo, i salir delantre los goyim kon taled i tefilín no ay remedyo, enperó ken mora serka el kal no se vede de eyo"* ('Now, for our sins, the exile is heavy, and going out [of one's home] before the Gentiles wearing a prayer shawl and phylacteries is impossible, but one who lives close to the synagogue should not avoid doing it.')

Nonetheless, the Jews, especially the males, interacted intensively with their Ottoman neighbors, learning much about their beliefs and practices and to an extent being influenced by them, but always synthesizing those beliefs and practices with elements drawn from traditional Judaism. For example, Rabbi Yiṣḥaq Molho of eighteenth-century Salonika reported having heard about a *kará kondjó* or 'black bogey (a demon invoked to frighten naughty children [compare Turkish *karakoncolos*, the latter element apparently from Greek])

> from a Turk who used to sleep in a Christian inn, and there were Christians in the inn and a demon called Kará Kondjó used to enter the inn and harm the Christians, and the Jew used to cover himself with his fringed prayer shawl and the demon did not touch him.
>
> Molho 1769, 132a

Some customs and habits were characteristic of particular communities. For example, Yehuda Konfino remarked in his *Me-'am lo'ez ḥadaš* (1893, 51b): *"Tanto bueno es este minag de la djente de Estanbul ... de enfrente se konose la peá de el de Estanbul"* 'The custom of the people of Istanbul is very good; from the front one recognizes the sidelocks of a man from Istanbul.' In some places, for example Salonika, the Jews wore clothes which distinguished them somewhat from the non-Jews, and the costume of married and unmarried Jewish women also differed (Judah Magnes Museum 1989, Juhasz and Russo-Katz 1990). Ottoman Sephardic dress and halakhically related issues already began to be addressed in the earliest rabbinic works; e.g., in his *Bet Yosef* (1550–1559, Oraḥ ḥayyim 10, 12), Yosef Karo discussed whether the *feradjé* coat (cf. Tk. *ferace*), having four corners, needed ritual fringes. Many of the observations offered by the rabbis in their works concerned the major events of the Jewish life cycle; some of these will be noted in the following paragraphs.

Birth, Circumcision, Child-naming, Bar Mitsva

As in the case of many of the calendar cycle traditions, following modernization and, for many Judezmo speakers, partial or complete secularization, especially following the world wars, many of the life cycle observances which had been practiced for centuries are today no longer kept up, and men and women tend to mingle freely. But during the long period that the community maintained its traditions, the celebration of high points in the life cycle tended to be observed separately by men and women. For example, before the availability of modern medicine in the community, when labor and childbirth were fraught with danger, women maintained certain observances of their own; in this connection Chief Rabbi Avraham Palachi of nineteenth-century Izmir wrote (Palachi 1877, 13a): *"Vidi kuantas mujeres ke, la ora de el parir, toman néder ke si el Shem Yidbarah las eskapa i tyenen parto bueno i kolay de azer Meza de Eliau Anaví"* 'I have seen many women who, during childbirth, take an oath that if God grants them a good, easy delivery, they will make a festive meal [for rabbinical scholars and the poor] in honor of Elijah the Prophet [believed to assist those in trouble].'

Upon the birth of a child the mother's female relatives and friends visited her and entertained her with songs (*kantikas*) in Judezmo (e.g., *"Kantika de la parida"* 'Song of the New Mother,'

"Oh, ke mueve mezes" 'Oh, what nine months'). They were sung to one of the *makames* or 'musical modes' of Ottoman music—understood by Judezmo speakers as the modes in which both religious and secular Jewish music were set—sometimes to the accompaniment of a *pandero* 'tambourine'. The father was regaled in a separate gathering of males with songs in Hebrew and Judezmo, e.g., *"Kuando el rey Nimroḏ"* 'When King Nimrod,' comparing the father of the boy undergoing circumcision to Avram Avinu 'Abraham Our Forefather.' There was a gender distinction in the choice of the blessing used to announce a birth: if a boy, it was *Besimán tov!* 'For a good sign!'; if a girl, *Bemazal tov!* 'May she have a good fortune!' (the word *mazal* also denoting, in this case, a good husband).

The cloth in which the newborn was wrapped (*fasha*) was prepared during the women's *kortar fashaḏura* ceremony. Amulets and talismans (*kameoḏ*) were placed to ward off the *ojo malo* or *aynarah* or *nazar* 'evil eye' (the terms being from Spanish, Hebrew and Turkish, respectively). Compliments were always preceded by expressions such as *Aynarah no!* or *Mashallá!* or *G̱uaḏraḏo de nazar!* 'No evil eye!' On the night before a circumcision (*el birkaḏ milá*) a *viola* or *shemirá* 'night of religious study to protect the boy' was held (on protective ceremonies see Lévy and Lévy Zumwalt *c.* 2002); various Hebrew and Judezmo *kantikas de shemirá* were sung, e.g., one popular in Edirne beginning *"Empesar kero una farsa, ke vos sea por membransa"* 'I want to begin a tale, so that you remember the event.' Later a modest party and name-stating ceremony was held (*el faḏamyento*); the naming of a girl was also celebrated in a ceremony called by some *zéveḏ abaḏ* (Hb. *zeved ha-bat* 'gift for the daughter'), during which some Judezmo religious songs were sung (e.g., *"Mi palomba"* 'My dove' and *"Una eya"* 'She is one'). Before the modern era some fathers were known to be disappointed over the birth of a girl, in no small measure because, in order for her to marry, her family would have to provide a dowry—a hard obstacle for the more modest families. Nonetheless, the Ottoman rabbis taught that parents should rejoice over a girl as over a boy. Yiṣḥaq Yehuda Abba (1890, 106b) of Izmir recalled a festivity, celebrated with 'seven candles,' at which newly born girls received their names:

Mire i se alegre [el paḏre], ke esta ija le será bee[zraḏ] A[el] de mazal alto i bueno i pueḏe alkansar i tomar un yerno savyo, riko i famozo por toḏo el mundo, i nunka se le pyeḏre su fama, ke se nombra "Este si[nyor] es yerno de Fulano," ki al ken aeṣ́á nehoná es ke aga la nochaḏa de faḏa sigún su poḏer kon gosto i alegría i kombide a sus kerovim i a sus amigos i yame al hazán de su keilá o a su si[nyor] haham konosiḏo i atakane syete siryos sigún el uzo ke yamamos Syete Kandelas por mostrar ke esta ija va tener bee[zraḏ] A[el] mazal klaro i va tener su paḏre i toḏos muncha azlahá i berahá i la va kazar kon muncho aḏalet sin tener menester de dinguno, amén.

(Upon the birth of a daughter [the father] should look and rejoice, for with God's help this girl will bring him great good fortune and may enable him to take as his son-in-law a wise scholar, rich and famous throughout the world, and his reputation will never be lost because people will say "This gentleman is So-and-so's son-in-law." Therefore, he would be correctly advised to make the night of naming the girl as joyous and happy as he can afford, and invite his relatives and friends and call the cantor from his synagogue or his well known rabbi, and prepare seven tapers, in accordance with the ceremony we call "Seven Candles," to show that, with God's help, this girl will have good luck, and her father and others will have much success and blessing, and he will marry her off with great pomp, and without having to ask anyone for help, amen.)

The first-born boy and girl in a family were traditionally named after the grandfathers and grandmothers, even if still alive; because of the special honor accruing to the first-born they were generally nicknamed *Bohor* 'primogenitor,' if a boy, or *Bohora*, if a girl (from Hebrew *bekor*). Before the modern era boys usually received biblical-origin Hebrew names, while girls might just as well receive names of Hispanic, Turkish or Balkan origin carrying positive connotations (Schwarzwald 2010); thus a girl whose parents saw her as queenly might called her *Malká*, from Hebrew, *Reyna* or *Rena*, from Spanish, or *Sultana*, from Turkish (from Arabic). Children who were believed to be in danger because their older siblings had died were as if purchased by neighbors and their names were changed to masculine *Merkado* or feminine *Merkada* 'Purchased' to mislead the Angel of Death.

Individuals who experienced illness or misfortune might have their names changed, or an extra name such as *Hayim* 'Life' added, through the ceremony known as *meṣalaín*. To further protect themselves they might order amulets (*kameod*) or magical remedies (*segulod*), in Hebrew or Judezmo, from a religious scholar specializing in their preparation; Gentile neighbors too requested magic Hebrew-letter charms from these specialists, some of them written in the special 'letters of the angels.' Some Ottoman Sephardim believed themselves to have suffered from *espanto* 'spiritual fright' or the 'evil eye,' which could cause all kinds of mishaps, including that mentioned in the rhyming verse collection *"Koplas nuevas"* (1778, 19a): *"Tanto fue el nazar, ke no ayegó a kazar"* 'The effect of the evil eye [cast on him] was so great, that he could not find a mate.' To counteract them people might have special incantations known as *prekantes* recited for them, and *endulkos* or 'appeasement ceremonies' performed by female specialists called *endulkaderas* (Alexander and Papo 2011). The rabbis often turned a blind eye to such practices so long as they were accompanied by formal prayer to God. With modernization and a growing attraction to all things Western European, these beliefs fell into decline, and children began to receive, or in adulthood to change their original traditional names to French or Italian ones; e.g., little *Avramiko* (from *Avram*) might became adult *Alberto*, and *Mazaltika* (from *Mazal Tov*), *Matilda*. At the age of thirteen a boy was said to *kumplir minyán* '(be able to) complete the prayer quorum of ten males'; he then learned to wear *tefilín* 'phylacteries' wound and tied in the distinctive Sephardic way.

All personal celebrations were accompanied by festive meals, with scholars and the poorer members of the community often participating. Some of the more conservative and ascetic members of the religious community refrained from such meals; one of them was the father of Ya'aqov Hulí. Hulí noted in *Me-'am lo'ez* on Genesis (1730, 93b):

"*Mi sinyor padre, … syendo el rov de los días aziya tanid, kuando aviya alguna seudá de misvá, se tomava de la meza un biskocho kon alguna fruta i kon akeyo kortava tanid la noche.*"

(My honored father, … since he fasted on most days, when there was some festive meal accompanying a religious celebration, he would take from the festive table a cookie with some fruit and with them he broke the fast in the evening.)

Marriage

Throughout the traditional period, marriages were arranged through *kazamenteros* 'matchmakers.' Once the match was decided upon, the remaining steps included the *kinyán* or 'religious engagement ceremony' performed in the presence of a *haham* 'rabbi,' followed in some places (e.g., Salonika) by: the *lavadura de la lana* 'washing of the wool' to be used in the future couple's bedding, with the participants, all females, singing love songs such as *"I las almadrakes de la lana fina"* 'And the mattresses of fine wool'; a family gathering to celebrate the displaying of the bride's *ashuar* 'trousseau' and its assessment by the *maarihim* 'assessors'; a gathering on a

Saturday night preceding the wedding to rejoice with the bride at an *almosama* feast; and as the wedding day approached, the bride's visit to the *banyo* (or *hamam* or *mikvé*) 'ritual bath' for her premarital immersion, accompanied by an entourage of relatives, friends and *chalgidjís* 'traditional musicians,' with the singing of bridal songs (*Kantikas de novya*) such as *"Ya salyó de la mar la galana"* 'The lady emerged from the sea.' The traditional *kombidadero* 'wedding inviter' strolled through the Jewish neighborhoods shouting an invitation, and some wealthier community members printed Judezmo invitations for private distribution or had them printed in the Judezmo press.

In some communities it was the custom for a bridegroom to wear a woman's adornment during the marriage ceremony; Yehuda Papo, in his Judezmo adaptation of *Pele yo'eṣ*, by his father, Eli'ezer ben Yiṣḥaq Papo of Silistra, expressed his objection (Papo 1870, 302):

Se topa en algunos lugares una regla negra ke la noche de la hupá le meten en la kavesa del novyo un afeyte de mujer i es koza muy manka ... en el día ke le pedronan los pekados, azer sefté kon azerlo pasar un pekado de la ley.

(One finds in a few places a bad custom that on the night of a wedding they put on the groom's head a woman's adornment and it is a very unworthy thing ... on the day when his sins are forgiven to start things off by committing a sin of the Torah.)

On the wedding night the bride and groom were led under the *hupá* or *talamó* 'wedding canopy' and the *kidushim* 'marriage ceremony' was performed by the *haham*. Although the *ketubá* 'wedding contract' is usually in Aramaic, at the turn of the twentieth century a contract was printed in New York in both Aramaic and Judezmo. As its name, *ocho días de la hupá* or *ocho dias de la seva* indicates, the wedding festivities lasted for a week, and during the traditional era men and women were segregated. On the last day fish was symbolically served and the bride was praised in songs such as *"El novyo le dize a la novya"* 'The groom says to the bride.' At this and other religious celebrations of the life cycle male *pizmondjís* 'hymn singers' (from Hebrew *pizmon* 'hymn' and Turkish *-cî*) entertained; in the women's section the females sang love songs in Judezmo and engaged in *baylar a la turka* 'Ottoman-style dances.' Extemporaneously composed Judezmo *komplas* praising the bride and groom might be recited and *shakás* 'jokes' told by *shakadjís* 'comedians.'

Demise

Elderly people made sure to *kortar mortaja* 'cut their shroud' in anticipation of their death; sometimes this was performed ceremoniously in a group (on death and mourning customs see Rafael and Bachar 2012; Scharhon and Scharhon 2013). Upon a person's demise the male *rohasim* (Heb. *roḥaṣim*) and female *rohesas* 'washers of the body' performed the *rehisá* 'ritual cleansing' and *albashá* 'clothing' of the body. *Shomerim* 'guards' oversaw the body over night while reading Psalms and Hebrew prayers. The body was brought through the streets to the *bedahé* (Heb. *bet ha-ḥayyim* 'house of the living') 'Jewish cemetery' with an entourage, with a *hazán* 'cantor' intoning memorial prayers and shopkeepers on the streets passed temporarily closing their shops in honor of the deceased. At the cemetery the service was conducted in Hebrew. Men blessed the mourners with Hebrew *"Lo tosifu le-da'ava 'od"* 'May there be no more sorrows' and women with Judezmo *"Mas de ninguno no!"* 'May there be no other [losses]'; a typical reply was *"Tu ke bivas!"* 'May you live!' The deaths of more outstanding individuals were announced in the local Judezmo press; necrologies (*nekrolojías*) ended with impromptu blessings in Judezmo but obligatory Hebrew *"Tehe nišmato/a ṣerura bi-ṣror ha-ḥayyim"* 'May his/her soul be bound up with the bundle of life.' At the *kortadura de anyo* 'end of the mourning year' and thereafter, each year, on the *nochada del padre* or *la madre* 'evening [marking the death] of the father' or 'mother'—among some also known as *la petirá* or *el yarsáy(t)* (from Yiddish *yórtsayt* 'year's memorial')—the family held a *meldado* (or *limud* or *midrash*), i.e., a memorial study and prayer service with refreshments such as *rakí*, *kavé* and *dulses* 'sweets.' Thus the memory of the deceased, who had helped transmit the Jewish traditions in Sephardic style to the younger generations, would remain alive and revered.

As noted, members of the community traditionally made pilgrimages to the Holy Land, which until the end of World War I was a part of the Ottoman Empire, in honor of the major festivals; some immigrated outright. Ya'aqov Hulí, who himself had been born in Eretz Israel, wrote in his *Me-'am lo'ez* on Genesis (1730, 151b): *"Syendo la morada de Eres Israel es muy valutada, deve el ben adam de prekurar muncho kon sus vente unyas a no salir de akeya tyera santa"* ('Since dwelling in the Land of Israel is very valuable [religiously], a person should try with all his might [literally, with his ten nails] to not leave that holy land.')

The eighteenth-century poet Ḥayyim Magula (1756 [1739], 11a–b) expressed the communal yearning for the Messiah and the return to the Land: *"Mos yeve a nuestra tyera del modo ke dezeamos, sin espada i sin gera, venga ya i lo veamos"* 'May He bring us to our land in the way we desire, without swords and without war, may He come already and may we see Him.' During the same century Ya'aqov Berav II composed a series of songs, some in Judezmo, praising the re-establishment of the city of Tiberias. Judezmo songs were also composed in honor of Jerusalem and other places in the Holy Land and the saints buried in them.

Elderly people immigrated to the Land in order to lead lives of spirituality and end their days there. On this Rabbi Hulí (1730, 219b) wrote:

Todo ken tyene zahud ke es niftar en Eres Israel su maalá es muy grande, i luego ke muere se va la alma en Mearad Amahpelá i de ayí se va a su lugar; i todo ke se entera en Eres Israel komo si estuvyera enterado debasho del mizbéah, ke es tanto kuanto si estuvyera enterado debasho del Kisé Akavod.

(Everyone who has the merit to pass away in the Land of Israel, its value is very great; and as soon as the person dies the soul goes to the Me'arat Ha-Makpela [in Hebron] and from there it goes to its final destination; and everyone who is buried in the Land of Israel it is as if the person were buried under the ancient altar, which is exactly as if he were buried under the Seat of Honor.)

Rabbi Raḥamim Menaḥem Mitrani of nineteenth-century Edirne immigrated to Jerusalem; in his *Me-'am lo'ez* on Joshua (Mitrani 1870, 180b) he reported on an observance he witnessed, which is maintained in Israel to this day:

Akí en ir akódesh Yerusháláyim, ti[bané] ve[tikonén] bi[merá] be[yamenu] a[mén], vidi minag bindicho ke akojen minyán en la kaza de el niftar i aí dizen tefilá i minhá i arvid i siduk adín i eshkavá i entre los syete días de el avelud vyenen la djente a kaza del niftar i meldan un poko i se van; i este minag es muy bueno, si para el niftar i si por mizvod nehum avelim, i ansí uzan afilú kuando no tyene ninguno ke los guadren los syete días de el avelud.

(Here in the Holy City of Jerusalem, may it be rebuilt and reconstituted speedily and in our days, amen, I saw a blessed custom according to which they gather in the house of the deceased and there they say the morning and afternoon and evening prayers and the Ṣidduq ha-din and memorial prayers for the deceased and during the seven [initial] days of mourning people come to the home of the deceased and they [pray and] study a little and leave; and this custom is very good, both for the deceased and for upholding the commandments of comforting those in mourning, and they do this even when the deceased has no one to observe the seven days of mourning.)

Traditional Customs and Lifestyle in Decline

Following the long traditional era, and especially following World War I, the Ottoman Empire and the new nation-states which emerged from its dismemberment experienced a gradual Westernization, modernization and secularization. At first the Ottoman Jews tended to resist such changes. But with time many came to shift their orientation from Ottoman Jewish religious and cultural traditionalism to Western European liberal humanism, and with this change many of the traditional religion-centered habits and customs declined; among the more extremely westernized Sephardim, they fell entirely into disuse. Some of those who viewed them through new, Western Europeanized eyes were happy to see the old practices go. Even the younger rabbis tended to change their thought patterns regarding the traditional ways and habits. One Judezmo journalist saw a contrast between the modern rabbis and the local Muslim and Christian spiritual leaders; with a touch of irony he wrote *"Los ombres de la ley turka i krisyana ... están daínda a la vyeja i no saven od ahad shebatorá lo ke kere dezir modas mata sanos"* 'The Muslim and Christian men of religious law are still old-fashioned and do not even understand one letter of the Torah [i.e., they are completely unfamiliar] when it comes to deadly, new-fangled ways.'[23] As in some synagogues today, the newly-acquired modern liberalism did not prevent the men from complaining that the ladies were the ones making noise in the synagogue, as expressed by a journalist in Salonika: *"Antes de empesar la tefilá paresería kol demamá daká si no eran las toses, los sarnudos ... de las mujeres"* 'Before the start of the morning prayer it would have been extremely quiet, if not for the coughs and sneezes of the women.'[24] In the Istanbul community, widespread superstitious beliefs were attributed to the women; journalist Eliyya R. Karmona listed a number of such beliefs—*"las kreansas vanas de algunas mujeres, ke kreen en munchas bavajadas ke nozotros yamamos akí en Estambul Simanim del Séfer Rahel"* 'the superstitious beliefs of some women, who believe in a lot of nonsense which we here in Istanbul call "Signs of the Book of Rachel".'[25] A decline in religious practice on the part of both men and women was alluded to by Karmona in a list of *"Unos kuantos byervos antika"* ('A few words [and presumably practices] now antiquated'): they included, *en las mujeres* (among women): *tevilá* 'ritual immersion'; and *en los ombres* (among men): *kadísh* 'memorial prayer for a close relative,' *avdalá* 'separation from the Sabbath ceremony,' *zimún* 'ritual summoning of a halakhically minimum number of men for the grace after meals,' *birkada[le]vaná* 'blessing over the new moon,' *netilá* 'ritual hand washing before eating bread.'[26]

Members of the community who began to revel in a secular-oriented lifestyle were pleased to see the old ways decline and disappear. But for others, the disappearance of the traditional religious rituals and practices once so central to communal life evoked a sense of nostalgia and longing. On the eve of World War II, during which the vast majority of the Jews of Macedonia, Bosnia and Serbia were killed in the Holocaust, Alberto Molho, a Judezmo journalist in Salonika who used the pseudonym 'Napolitán,' wrote in his weekly *Aksyón* Judezmo newspaper column *Por dezbafar* ('To unburden the heart'):

Muchos de mis amigos me se van burlando por la manya ke tengo de estar de syempre avlando en estas kolonas los uzos de shaná-tra-katraka. Ma mil ke se burlen, iné non me van a empiḏir a mi de estarme akoḏrando de las gostozas tradisyones del empesijo de este syékolo.[27]

(Many of my friends keep laughing at me for my habit of always writing in this column about our customs of long ago. But, much as they may laugh, they will not dissuade me from recalling our savory traditions at the turn of this [20th] century.)

Despite the decline in many of the traditional rituals and other religious practices involving the use of Judezmo, in some families and communities certain traditions survive and have even become stronger. At the Passover seder, for example, some passages are recited in Judezmo, and the preparation of traditional foods, and the use of their Judezmo names, continue. In some synagogues, such as those in Seattle, Washington, Los Angeles, Salonika and Istanbul, Judezmo versions of prayers such as *"Berik̠ šemeh"* / *"Bindicho Tu santo nombre"* and *"En kelohenu"* / *"Non komo muestro Dyo"* are still sung, and recordings and prayer books published for the Seattle community by Hazzan Isaac Azose (1995, 1999, 2007, 2011, 2012a, 2012b, 2014) incorporate a significant amount of Judezmo material, including translations of long texts such as the Passover Haggadah, Pirqe Avot, Megillat Rut and the *"Ketubá de la ley."* Increasing interest in Judezmo in many parts of the world, both at the grass roots and higher educational levels, have encouraged the creation of new online and offline language courses, new holiday-centered songs, such as Flora Jagody's *"Ocho kandelikas"* 'Eight little candles,' for Hanukkah, and even new holiday and life cycle traditions proposed by members of the Ladinokomunita Internet social network (Bunis 2020). Who knows but that the Judezmo language and culture revival may yet bring about a revival of old, long-abandoned Sephardic religious traditions as well.

Notes

1 The special merit of the Sabbath is fish, spinach and cheese pie, and minced meat pie, / and the egg hardboiled in the Sabbath stew, with salt and pepper. / On Purim eat filled dough pockets and on Hanukkah dough fritters, / On Passover filled pans and casseroles, that's what we saw from our grandparents, / take lots of leeks, roast and gizzards. / On Shavuot foods made with dough, and lentils on Tish'a Be-Av. / On Yom Kippur white stockings and two chickens with noodles / And full to the gills with all kinds of ugly stuff. / On Purim all sorts of wines is something of great import, / And make toasts with one's neighbors.

Judezmo exists in numerous and divergent regional forms; the pronunciation in this chapter reflects that of Salonika, which hosted one of the largest Ottoman Sephardic communities, most of whose members perished in the Holocaust. Note the values of the Roman-letter symbols used in the present chapter (as advocated by the Israel National Authority for Ladino and Its Culture and the National Ladino Academy of Israel, with a few innovations) to transcribe Judezmo words in Romanization: ch = Eng. 'chop,' d = Eng. 'bandana,' ḏ = Eng. 'bother' (or at the end of a word, 'ether'), dj = 'judge,' g = Eng. 'guard,' g̠ = Mod. Gk. 'gamma,' h = Ger. 'auch,' j = 'rouge,' s = Eng. 'boss' (or at the end of a word, before a voiced sound, 'rose'), sh = Eng. 'shop' (or at the end of a word, before a voiced sound, 'rouge'); the other symbols are pronounced more or less as in English (for more on Judezmo orthography, see Bunis 2019; Schwarzwald 2021). Words ending in a vowel, or in the consonant symbols -n or -s are ordinarily stressed on the next to last syllable; those ending in the others, on the last syllable. Irregular stress is indicated here by an acute accent on the stressed syllable. Unless another source is indicated, sources for the words of Hebrew and Aramaic origin cited may be found in Bunis 1993a; numerous references to proverbs and sayings incorporating the words will also be found there. This research was supported by The Israel Science Foundation (grant no. 1930/17). Warm thanks to Hazzan Isaac Azose for details on the Judezmo passages appearing in his prayer books and for answers to many questions; on Azose as an active tradition bearer see Jackson 2015). Cordial thanks to Mr. Jacky Benmayor for answering questions about the Salonika tradition. Sincere appreciation is also expressed to the HebrewBooks.Org, Ryzman Edition site (https://hebrewbooks.org/home.aspx) for making so many important Jewish books accessible to one and all.

2 From at least the period following the Ottoman Tanzimat Reforms (1839–1876) the Sephardim of the Ottoman Empire distinguished themselves from other Jewish groups by calling themselves in Judezmo *los djudyós otomanos* or *los djudyós osmanlís* 'Ottoman Jews' (e.g., *El Tyempo* vol. 5, no. 927 [Constantinople, 1877], 4; *La Amérika* 7, 332 [New York, 1917], 2), and their Jewry, *el djudaízmo otomano* (*La Époka* 27, 1342 [Salonika, 1902], 1). An early example of 'Ottoman Jewry' in English with particular reference to the Ottoman Sephardim as a group of interest to Spanish intellectuals at the turn of the twentieth century is:

> Of late years a movement has been set on foot in influential circles in Spain to bring about the repatriation of the descendants of the [Jewish] exiles [from Iberia], and for this purpose a society known as the 'Alianza Hispano-Israelita' has recently been formed. ... But the enthusiasm aroused among Ottoman Jewry by the dawn of a new era in Turkey [i.e., the Second Constitutional era, 1908–1920] is likely to prove a serious barrier to the success of the 'back-to-Spain' movement. And apart from that, before Spain could expect the re-entry of any considerable number of Jews certain restrictions on the exercise of the Jewish religion which are still in force would have to be removed; for instance, even to-day [i.e., in 1909] Jews are not allowed to hold religious services in a public building.
>
> *Quex, 1909*

Cf. also French 'les Sephardims ottomans' and 'les Israélites ottomans' (B[erl]. 1922, 3). The Ottoman Sephardim perceive of themselves as being a subgroup of the more encompassing *djudaízmo sefaradí* 'Sephardic Judaism/Jewry' (e.g., *La Amérika* 9, 421 [New York, 1919], 2).

3 Originally a biblical toponym of uncertain location mentioned in Obadiah 1:20, from at least the time of the composition of the Aramaic Targum Yonatan (probably second century CE) it had come to denote Spain.
4 On this literature, see Romero 1992b; Lehmann 2005.
5 On the language of the earliest surviving Judezmo periodical see Bunis 1993b.
6 Mézan 1925 and Moskona 1970 offer sketches of the calendar and life cycle habits and customs of Sephardim of Bulgaria; Molho 1950 gives rich details about those of Salonika and Bunis 1999 demonstrates how the latter are depicted in Judezmo fiction; Estrugo 1958 describes religious customs of the Jews of Izmir; and Levy 1987 discusses those of the Island of Rhodes.
7 The religious-oriented Judezmo song repertoire is extensive; space limitations will allow mention of only a few representative pieces. One of the richer inventories is Levy 1965–1980; for discussion by genre, see Weich-Shahak 2006.
8 Traditional Sephardic Sabbath and holiday recipes are available in many cookbooks; recent ones include Sendowski 2015 and Weingarten 2016; on Sabbath customs see Šmid 2012.
9 The custom had a parallel among Turkish Muslims (cf. T. *[babanın] elini öp-*).
10 For a rich collection from the sixteenth and seventeenth centuries, see Benaim 2011.
11 *La Époka* (Salonika, 14 September 1883), 384.
12 *La Époka* 27, 1318 (Salonika, 13 December 1901), 5.
13 Kaplan 2019.
14 "Una kriza estranya en la komunidad djudía de Esmirna," *El Tyempo* 24, 57 (Constantinople, 1896), 623–624.
15 E.g., *La America* 2, 60 (11 September 1912), 1.
16 *El Meseret* 23, 67 (Izmir, 1919), 3.
17 For a bibliography of the *komplas* see Romero 1992a; for a selection, Romero 1988.
18 It should be noted that a similar dish, called *Aşure*, is traditionally eaten by Turks on the Muslim holiday called by them by that name, celebrated on the tenth of Muharrem.
19 On Tu Bisvhat *komplas*, see Armistead and Silverman 1968; Romero 1976.
20 *El Tyempo* 9, 1351 (Constantinople, 1881), 3.
21 The bibliography on the subject is extensive, e.g., Romero 2008; the late Iacob M. Hassán was a pioneer in the study of the Judezmo *komplas* (e.g. Hassán 1987).
22 On these as well as on unpublished Tišʻa be-Av prayers mentioning the expulsions from Iberia see David 1992.
23 *La Boz de la Verdad* 175 (Andrianople, 1911), 4.

24 *Aksyón* 4, 972 (Salonika, 1932), 2.
25 *El Djugetón* 5, 27 (Constantinople, 1913), 7.
26 *El Djugetón* 20, 47 (Constantinople, 1928), 3.
27 *Aksyón* 10, 2742 (Salonika, 1938), 2.

Bibliography

Abba, Yiṣḥaq Yehuda. 1890 [1888]. *Sefer leḥem Ye'uda*. Izmir [Salonika]. (References are to the second (1890) edition.)
Alexander, Tamar, and Eliezer Papo. 2011. "El enkanto de la majia: Sephardic Magic: History, Trends and Topics," *El Prezente* 5: 9–31.
Alexander-Frizer, Tamar. c. 2008. *The Heart Is a Mirror: The Sephardic Folktale*, trans. Jacqueline S. Teitelbaum. Detroit, MI: Wayne State University Press.
Alsheh, Ya'aqov, and Yosef Yiṣḥaq Alsheh. 1865. *Tefillat kol pe … 'im targum ladino*. Vienna: Yosef Yiṣḥaq Alsheh.
Andjel, Yosef, ed. 1929–1940. *Aksyón*. Daily. Salonika.
Anon. 1524. *Temunot, teḥinnot, tefillot Sefarad*. Venice.
Anon. 1798. *Seder arba' ta'aniyot*. Salonika.
Anon. 1897. "La komunidad djudía de Kastoría," *El Tyempo* (Constantinople) vol. 26, no. 1, 4–5.
Anon. 1927. *La Agada de Pesakh, trezladado libero i klaro*. Sofia: Itskhak Perets Liberiia Sinai.
Arditi, David, ed. 1889. *Sefer šivḥe ribbi Šim'on ben Yoḥay*. Salonika.
Armistead, Samuel G., and Joseph H. Silverman. 1968. "*Las Complas de las Flores* y la poesía popular de los Balcanes," *Sefarad* 28: 395–438.
Asa, Avraham. 1729. *Letras de ribí Akivá … tanbyén al kavo unos kuantos dinim*. Constantinople.
Asa, Avraham. 1733. *Sefer ṣorḵe ṣibbur: Dinim*. Constantinople.
Asa, Avraham. 1739a. *Ḥamišša ḥumše tora 'im la'az*. Constantinople.
Asa, Avraham. 1739b. *Bet tefilla en librán i en ladino*. Constantinople.
Asa, Avraham. 1749. *Sefer šulḥan ha-meleḵ … kopyado en ladino*. Constantinople.
Azose, Isaac. 1995. *Passover Agada, Hebrew, Ladino and English*. Seattle, WA: n.p.
Azose, Isaac. 1999. *The Liturgy of Ezra Bessaroth* [2 compact discs]. Seattle, WA: Ezra Bessaroth Synagogue.
Azose, Isaac. 2007. *Zihron Rahel for Pesah, Shavuot and Sukkot* according to the Rhodes and Turkish traditions. Seattle, WA: Sephardic Traditions Foundation.
Azose, Isaac. 2011. *Tefila LeDavid for Rosh Hashana, Rhodes Tradition*. Seattle, WA: Sephardic Traditions Foundation.
Azose, Isaac. 2012a [2002]. *Siddur Zehut Yosef Daily and Sabbath Siddur* according to the Rhodes and Turkish traditions (as practiced in Seattle, Washington, USA). Seattle, WA: Sephardic Traditions Foundation.
Azose, Isaac. 2012b. *Tefila LeMoshe, Order of the Five Fasts, Rhodes Tradition*. Seattle, WA: Sephardic Traditions Foundation.
Azose, Isaac. 2014. *Kol Yaakov Yom Kippur Mahzor, Rhodes Tradition*. Seattle, WA: Sephardic Traditions Foundation.
Azulay, Ḥayyim Yosef David. 1774. *Sefer birke Yosef*. Livorno.
Azulay, Ḥayyim Yosef David. 1786. *More ba-eṣba'*. Livorno.
Baris·hak, Yosef, ed. 1911–1922. *La Boz de la Verdad*. Bi-weekly. Edirne.
Behar, Nisim. 1959. *El gid para el pratikante*. Istanbul: n.p.
Benaim, Annette. 2011. *Sixteenth-Century Judeo-Spanish Testimonies*. Leiden: Brill.
Benveniste, Ḥayyim. 1657–1734. *Kenesset ha-gedola*. Livorno–Izmir–Constantinople–Izmir.
Benveniste, Ḥayyim. 1671–1717. *Sheyare kenesset ha-gedola*. Izmir–Constantinople.
[Benveniste], Ma'ir. 1712 [1568]. *Sefer šulḥan ha-panim/Meza de el alma*. Venice [Salonika].
B[erl], A[lfred]. 1922. "Les Israélites Ottomans et le Sionisme," *Paix et Droit* 2, 4: 2–3.
Bornes-Varol, Marie-Christine, and Flore Guerón Yeschua. c.2010. *Le proverbier glosé: judéo-espagnol-Bulgarie*. Paris: Geuthner.
Bunis, David M. 1984. "Food Terms and Culinary Customs in Rabbi Eliezer ben Šem Ṭov Papo's *Sefer Dammeseq 'Eli'ezer*: Judezmo Rabbinical Literature as a Folkloristic and Linguistic Resource," *Jerusalem Studies in Jewish Folklore* 5–6: 151–195 (in Hebrew).
Bunis, David M. 1993a. *A Lexicon of the Hebrew and Aramaic Elements in Modern Judezmo*. Jerusalem: Magnes Press.

Bunis, David M. 1993b. "The Earliest Judezmo Newspapers: Sociolinguistic Reflections," *Mediterranean Language Review* 6–7: 5–66. Reprinted 2016 in *Jewish Journalism and Press in the Ottoman Empire and Turkey*, ed. Rifat N. Bali. Istanbul: Libra, 145–230.

Bunis, David M. 1995. "*Pyesa di Yaakov Avinu kun sus ijus* (Bucharest, 1862): The First Judezmo Play?" *Revue des Études Juives* CLIV, 3–4: 387–428.

Bunis, David M. 1999. *Voices from Jewish Salonika*. Jerusalem–Thessaloniki: Misgav Yerushalayim–Ets Haim.

Bunis, David M. 2004. "Distinctive Characteristics of Jewish Ibero-Romance, Circa 1492," *Hispania Judaica Bulletin* 4: 105–137.

Bunis, David M. 2019. "La ortografia de *Aki Yerushalayim*: Un pinakolo de la estoria de la romanizasion del djudezmo (djudeo-espanyol)," *Aki Yerushalayim* 101: 8–24.

Bunis, David M. 2020 "Sephardic Customs as a Discourse Topic in the Ladinokomunita Internet Correspondence Circle," in *Minhagim: Custom and Practice in Jewish Life*, eds. Joseph Isaac Lifshitz, Naomi Feuchtwanger-Sarig, Simha Goldin, Jean Baumgarten and Hasia Diner. Berlin: De Gruyter, 161–197.

Cohen, Dov. 2015. "Who Is the Author of the Ladino *Shulhan ha-Panim* (Salonika 1568)?" *Hispania Judaica Bulletin* 11, 2: 33–61 (in Hebrew).

Cohen, Dov. 2018. "New Sources in Portuguese Aljamiado: A Collection of Letters Concerning the Commercial Activities of Sephardic Jews in the Ottoman Empire," in *Portuguese Jews, New Christians and "New Jews"*, eds. Claude B. Stuczynski and Bruno Feitler. Leiden-Boston: Brill, 73–101.

Cohen, Dov. 2020a. "Missing Treasures: Tracking Lost Ladino Books," *Zutot* 17: 58–73.

Cohen, Dov. 2020b. "The Discovery of the First Printed Translation into Ladino of Pirkey Avot (Thessaloniki, ca. 1570)," *Sefarad* 80, 1: 117–136.

Cohen, Dov. Forthcoming. "A Panoramic Survey of Judeo-Spanish Halakhic Books," in *Rabbinical Writing in Judezmo/Ladino and Yiddish*, ed. Katja Šmid, David M. Bunis and Chava Turniansky.

Corré, Alan D. 1968. "Una elegía judeo-española para el nueve de 'Ab'," *Sefarad* 28: 399–402.

Corré, Alan D. 1984. "A Comparative Sephardic Lexicon," in *Hispania Judaica*, Vol. 3, eds. M. Sola-Solé, Samuel G. Armistead and Joseph H. Silverman. Barcelona: Puvill, 37–60.

David, Avraham. 1992. "An Unknown Dirge on the Expulsion from Spain," *Pe'amim* 49, 24–31 (in Hebrew).

Díaz-Mas, Paloma. 2011. "Sephardic Songs of Mourning and Dirges," *European Judaism* 44, 1: 84–97.

Dobrinsky, Herbert C. 2001 [1986]. *A Treasury of Sephardic Laws and Customs*. Hoboken, NJ: Ktav; New York: Yeshiva University Press.

Estrugo, José M. 1958. *Los sefardíes*. Habana: Editorial Lex.

Farḥi, Yosef Šabbetai. 1875. *Sefer Alegría de Purim*. Livorno.

Fresco, David et al. 1872–1930. *El Tyempo*. Istanbul.

Gaguine, Shemtob. 1934–1960. *Keter Shem Tob: The Rites and Ceremonies and Liturgical Variants of the Sephardim of the East and West and of the Ashkenazim, Their Origin and Significance*, 7 vols. Kaidan–London–Jerusalem.

Gutwirth, Eleazar. 1993. "A Judeo-Spanish *Endecha* from the Cairo Genizah," *Mediterranean Language Review* 6–7: 113–120.

Haggada šel pesaḥ. 1609. Venice.

Halevy Aškenazi, Sa'adi. 1858. *Komplas muevas de purim*. Salonika.

Hassán, Iacob M. 1987. "Un género castizo sefardí: las coplas," in *Los sefardíes: cultura y literatura*, ed. Paloma Díaz-Mas. San Sebastián: Universidad del País Vasco, 103–123.

Ḥayyim, Yisrael Beḵar, ed. 1811. *Seder Arba' ta'aniyot*. Vienna.

Ḥemdat yamim. c.1731. Izmir.

Heredia, M. Martín. 1981. "Las coplas de Hanuká," in *Actas de las jornadas de Estudios Sefardíes*, ed. Antonio Viudas Camarasa. Cáceres: Universidad de Extremadura, 115–122.

Hulí, Ya'aqov. 1730. *Sefer me-'am lo'ez: Berešit*. Constantinople.

Hulí, Ya'aqov. 1733. *Sefer me-'am lo'ez: Šemot*, Vol. 1. Constantinople.

Israel, Reuben Eliau. 1910. *Traducion libera de las poezias ebraicas de Roş Aşana i Kipur*. Craiova: I. Samitca şi D. Baraş.

Jackson, Maureen. 2015. "Reaching Beyond the Local: The Itineraries of an Ottoman-Sephardic-American 'Minhag'," *Contemporary Jewry* 35, 1: 89–105.

Judah Magnes Museum. 1989. *Embellished Lives: Customs and Costumes of the Jewish Communities of Turkey*, ed. Michael L. Chyet. Berkeley, CA: Judah L. Magnes Memorial Museum.

Juhasz, Esther, and Miriam Russo-Katz. 1990. *Sephardi Jews in the Ottoman Empire, Aspects of Material Culture*. Jerusalem: Israel Museum.
Kaplan, Yosef. ed. 2019. "Preface," in *Religious Changes and Cultural Transformations in the Early Modern Western Sephardic Communities*. Brill: Leiden.
Karmona, Eliyya R. 1908–1931. *El Djugetón*. Istanbul.
Karo, Yosef. 1550–1559. *Bet Yosef*, 4 volumes. Venice-Sabbioneta.
Koén-Sarano, Matilda. 2003. *Folktales of Joha, Jewish Trickster*. Philadelphia, PA: Jewish Publication Society.
Ko[n]fino, Moše Šemuel. 1862. *Pyesa de Yaakov Avinu kon sus ermanos*. Bucharest.
Konfino, Yehuda. 1893. *Me-'am lo'ez ḥadaš*. Jerusalem: Lilienthal.
Konplas de Pésah. 1776. Salonika.
Koplas nuevas [de purim]. 1778. Constantinople.
Lehmann, Mattias B. 2005. *Ladino Rabbinic Literature and Ottoman Sephardic Culture*. Bloomington: Indiana University Press.
Levy, Isaac. 1965–1980. *Antología de liturgia judeo-española*, 10 volumes. Jerusalem: Israel Ministry of Education and Culture.
Lévy, Isaac Jack, and Rosemary Lévy Zumwalt. c.2002. *Ritual Medical Lore of Sephardic Women*. Urbana, IL: University of Illinois Press.
Levy, Rebecca Amato. 1987. *I Remember Rhodes*. New York: Sepher-Hermon Press for Sephardic House at Congregation Shearith Israel.
Magriso, Yiṣḥaq. 1746. *Sefer me-'am lo'ez: Šemot*, Vol. 2. Constantinople.
Magriso, Yiṣḥaq. 1764. *Sefer me-'am lo'ez: Be-midbar*. Constantinople.
Magula, Ḥayyim Yom Ṭov. 1756 [1739]. *Ṭova tokaḥat Megulla*. Izmir.
Maḥzor … kefi minhag qa[hal] qa[doš] sefaradim, Vol. 1. 1736. Venice.
Maḥzor le-roš ha-šana minhag Sefarad. 1887a. Vienna: Schlesinger.
Maḥzor le-šaloš regalim minhag Sefarad. 1887b. Vienna: Schlesinger.
Maḥzor le-yom ha-kippurim minhag Sefarad. 1887c. Vienna: Schlesinger.
Medina, Šemu'el de. 1597. *Še'elot u-tšuvot […] me-ha-ḥakam […] Šemu'el de Medina*, part three: Ḥošen ha-mišpaṭ. Salonika.
Meşulam, David, ed. c.1930. *La agad'a de pesah, kon karakteres latinos, ebreo i lad'ino*. Istanbul: Sebat Matbaası.
Mézan, Saul. 1925. *Les Juifs espagnols en Bulgarie*. Sofia: Ha-Mishpat.
Mitrani, Moše. 1629. *Sefer še'elot u-tšuvot*. Venice.
Mitrani, Raḥamim Menaḥem. 1870. *Me-'am lo'ez: Yehošua'*, Vol. 2. Izmir.
Modiliano, Šemuel. 1753. *Renanat mizmor*. Salonika.
Molho, Michael. 1950. *Usos y costumbres de los sefardíes de Salónica*. Madrid: Arias Montano. (*Traditions and Customs of the Sephardic Jews of Salonica*. trans. Alfred A. Zara, ed. Robert Bedford. 2006. New York: Foundation for the Advancement of Sephardic Studies and Culture.)
Molho, Yiṣḥaq. 1769. *Orḥot ṣaddiqim*. Salonika.
Molho, Yosef. 1756. *Šulḥan gavoah*. Salonika.
Mordoh, Daniel. 1848. *Ḥemdat Daniel*. Salonika.
Moskona, Isak. 1970. "Material and Spiritual Life of the Bulgarian Jews," *Annual* (Sofia) 5: 103–147.
Naar, Devin. 2016. *Jewish Salonica*. Stanford, CA: Stanford University Press.
Najara, Yisrael. 1587. *Zemirot Yisrael*. Safed.
Palachi, Avraham. 1877 [1853]. *Sefer we-hokiaḥ Avraham*. Izmir [Salonika]. (References are to the second, 1877, edition.)
Palachi, Ḥayyim. 1873. *Ḥayyim ba-yad*. Izmir: Roditi.
Papo, Eli'ezer ben Šem Ṭov. 1862. *Sefer Dammeseq Eli'ezer*, Vol. 1. Belgrade.
Papo, Eli'ezer ben Yiṣḥaq. 1870. *Pele yo'eṣ … en ladino*, trans. Yehuda Papo, Vol. 1. Vienna.
Papo, Eliezer. 2012. *We-hitalta le-vinka ba-yom ha-hu*, 2 vols. Jerusalem.
Peacock, A.C.S. 2019. "Vernacular Religious Literature," in *Islam, Literature and Society in Mongol Anatolia*, Vol. 2. Cambridge: Cambridge University Press, 188–217.
Peri 'eṣ hadar. 1876. Izmir.
Quex. 1909. "From Foreign Lands," *The Reform Advocate* (Chicago) 37, 3: 76–77.
Rafael Vivante, Shmuel, with Moshe Elisha Bachar. 2012. *Beit hachaim—Final Resting Place: Laws and Customs of Mourning among the Judeo-Spanish (Ladino) Speaking Communities*. Ramat Gan: Merkaz Salti (in Hebrew and Judezmo).

Romero, Elena. 1976. "Complas de Tu-bišbat," in *Poesía: Reunión de Málaga de 1974*, ed. Manuel Alvar, Vol. 1. Málaga: Diputación Provincial, 279–311.
Romero, Elena. 1988. *Coplas sefardíes: Primera selección*. Córdoba: El Almendro.
Romero, Elena. 1992a. *Bibliografía analítica de ediciones de Coplas Sefardíes*. Madrid: CSIC.
Romero, Elena. 1992b. *La creación literaria en lengua sefardí*. Madrid: Mapfre.
Romero, Elena. 2008. *Y hubo luz y no fue tan buena: Las coplas sefardíes de Purim y los tiempos modernos*. Tirocinio: Barcelona.
Šabbetay, Ḥayyim. 1651. *Sefer še'elot u-tšuvot ha-šayyakot le-Ṭur 'Even Ha-'ezer*, 2 volumes. Salonika.
Scharhon, Morris, and Alan Scharhon, eds. 2013. *A Time to Weep: A Guide to Bereavement Based on the Customs of the Seattle Sephardic Community*. Seattle: Sephardic Ezra Bessaroth Synagogue and Sephardic Bikur Holim Synagogue.
Schwarzwald (Rodrigue), Ora. 1989. *Targume ha-ladino le-Firké Avot*. Jerusalem: Mif'al massorot ha-lašon šel 'edot Yisra'el.
Schwarzwald, (Rodrigue), Ora. 2008. *Millon ha-haggadot šel pesaḥ be-ladino*. Jerusalem: Magnes Press.
Schwarzwald (Rodrigue), Ora. 2010. "First Names in Sephardi Communities," in *Pleasant Are Their Names: Jewish Names in the Sephardi Diaspora*, ed. Aaron Demsky. Bethesda, MD: University Press of Maryland, 191–207.
Schwarzwald (Rodrigue), Ora. 2012. *Sidur para mujeres en ladino, Salónica, siglo XVI*. Jerusalem: Ben-Zvi Institute.
Schwarzwald (Rodrigue), Ora, ed. 2021. *Las Ortografias del Ladino*. Jerusalem: La Akademia Nasionala del Ladino en Israel.
Schwarzwald, Ora. Forthcoming. "Ladino in Cyrillic letters: Uniqueness of the Sofia 1935 Haggadah," *Massorot* 21 (in Hebrew).
Seder arba' ta'aniyyot. 1624. Venice.
Sendowski, Linda Capeloto. 2015. *Sephardic Baking from Nona and More Favorites: A Collection of Recipes for Baking Desayuno and More*. Beverly Hills, CA: Self-published.
Sephardic Studies Program, University of Washington at Seattle. http://jewishstudies.washington.edu/omeka/exhibits/show/sephardic-life-cycles/meldado-memorial-sacred-space
Šmid, Katja. 2012. *El Séfer Méšec betí, de Eliézer Papo: Ritos y costumbres sabáticas de los sefardíes de Bosnia*. Madrid: CSIC.
Studemund-Halevy, Michael. 2021. "From Rashi to Cyrillic: Bulgarian Judeo-Spanish (Judezmo) Texts in Cyrillic," in *The Romance-Speaking Balkans*, ed. Annemarie Sorescu-Marinković, Mihai Dragnea, Kahl Thede, Blagovest Njaguloz, Donald L. Dyer and Angelo Costanzo. Leiden: Brill, 12–37.
Toledo, Avraham 1732. *Koplas de Yosef Aṣadik*. Constantinople.
Weich-Shahak, Susana. 2006. *En buen siman* [book and compact disc]. Haifa: Pardes (in Hebrew).
Weingarten, Marcia Israel. 2016. *Sephardic Heritage Cookbook*. Los Angeles: Sephardic Temple Or Hadash Sisterhood.
Yeni, Šelomo Aharon (brought to the press by). 1880. *Nes wa-fele*. Salonika.
Zimmels, H. J. 1976. *Ashkenazim and Sephardim: Their Relations, Differences, and Problems as Reflected in the Rabbinical Response*. London: Marla.

36
YIDDISH

Jan Schwarz

Yiddish language, literature, and culture contain a wellspring of Jewish ritual and practice. This is reflected in the structure and vocabulary of the Yiddish language itself. It is also filtered through a variety of literary genres and cultural forms, beginning in the pre-modern period and continuing through the present day. The reader of a Yiddish short story by Scholem Aleichem and I.B. Singer encounters words, concepts, narrative forms and stylistic devices that are informed by religious and/or secularized versions of Jewish rituals and practice. In some cases, the essential point of the Yiddish is related to specific Jewish laws and rituals. Without knowledge of these, it is impossible to appreciate the story's literary qualities.

The following survey of examples from Yiddish language, literature and culture demonstrates how they each employ Jewish rituals and practices. They represent but a tiny sample of the vast Yiddish literary and cultural sources that have contributed to the ways in which Jews have practiced the sabbath and other holidays, life cycle events, *mitzvot* (sacred obligations), and aspects of daily living.

The Language of the Way of the SHaS

In the *History of the Yiddish Language* (1973, republished in 2008), the Yiddish linguist Max Weinreich (1899–1973) describes Yiddish as 'The Language of the Way of the SHaS.' The Hebrew acronym SHaS initially referred to the six orders of the Mishna, but it became a colloquial name for the entire Talmud. Weinreich's depiction indicates that the Yiddish language itself is steeped in the decrees and instructions of *halakha* (Jewish law) as well as diverse Jewish customs and lore. As Weinreich demonstrates, Yiddish is deeply rooted in the religious way of life prescribed in the Talmud. The language has contributed to *yidishkeyt* (Jewishness) in everything from daily practices and rituals to synagogue worship to life cycle events from cradle to grave.

The Yiddish view of Jewish life begins with words that make a distinction between Jews and non-Jews, *lehavdl loshen* (differentiation language). This discrepancy is vital to certain aspects of Jewish law and, as a result, Yiddish consists of distinctions between *yidishkeyt* and *goyishkeyt*, (non-Jewishness). The word *goy* simply means 'nation' or 'people' in biblical Hebrew, but *goy* refers in Yiddish to a 'non-Jew.' *Goy* has a slightly derogative meaning in Yiddish, and there are also the words *sheygets* and *shikse* (non-Jewish man and woman) which are actually pejorative.

Another example of *lehavdl loshen* is the Yiddish designation for a Christian house of prayer, *tifle*, originating with Jeremiah (23:13) and Job (1:22 and 24:12) in the meaning of 'unseemliness.' A Jewish house of prayer, in contrast, is a *shtibl* (little prayer house), *shul* (synagogue) or *besmedresh* (house of study) indicating the intimacy of Jewish study, devotion, and prayer. These examples demonstrate that Yiddish and Hebrew are closely intertwined in what Weinreich calls 'the internal bilingualism' of Yiddish.

Pre-modern Literature and Prayer

In the late Middle Ages, Yiddish literary works were prefaced by the formulaic address to 'women or men who are like women;' that is, women and men with little knowledge of Hebrew, the holy tongue. Glikl of Hamil's *Memoirs*, written 1699–1719 in a Western Yiddish dialect in response to her husband's sudden death, in order to 'forget her sorrows during the long nights,' remained in her family's possession until it was published almost two hundred years later. The memoir employs some of the genres of pre-modern Yiddish literature: the *mayse* (story) book, Yiddish adaptations of the Bible such as the popular *Tsenerene*, 'the women's Bible', and *tkhines*, Yiddish prayers. The creation of a library of pre-modern books that were both moralistic and entertaining reflected and contributed to Jewish ritual and practice.

Glikl's memoirs exemplifies the *musar*, or morality books published in the early eighteenth century that served as a guide to Jewish ritual and practice in the home, particularly with regard to the role of women. A distinct characteristic of pre-modern Yiddish literature for and sometimes by women (such as the Yiddish prayers by Sarah bas Tovim), is the use of a specific typography known as '*vaybertayts*,' or women's Yiddish. This was used by Jewish publishers only for books in Yiddish, in stark contrast to the font used for Hebrew books (Baumgarten, 2005, 62–63.) Another feature of Yiddish books from this period is that the majority of Yiddish books were published in a small format, indicating that they were intended to be read in the home, as opposed to the synagogue or study hall.

The *tkhines*, special Yiddish prayers to be recited by women, became very popular in the seventeenth and eighteenth centuries. They initiated a new realm of private prayer in the home and the synagogue. Several collections of *tkhines* were published as booklets aimed at a female readership. They included prayers pertaining to Jewish women's experience, such as baking challah (a ritual aspect to bread baking for shabbat and holidays), immersion in the *mikve*, or the ritual bath, and pregnancy and childbirth. While these collections do indicate that this period saw an increased focus on the role of Jewish women in the religious worship, they had no impact on the gender division in Jewish society. Women remained excluded from the high-status activity of studying the Hebrew and Aramaic scriptural texts and being counted in a *minyan* (prayer quorum); these activities continued to be entirely a male domain (Niger, 1913).

Modern Literature

The rise of the *haskole*, the Jewish Enlightenment in the late eighteenth century, saw the emergence of a modern Yiddish literature. It served as an ideological tool in the struggle for Jewish emancipation from the rabbinical authorities. Jewish ritual and practice became the conceptual battleground in the evolution of traditional Jewish society that took place first in Western Europe and then, beginning in the early nineteenth century, in Central and Eastern Europe. Yiddish fiction and theater exposed the backwardness of Jewish ritual and practice through satires and caricatures, demolishing their sanctity. This literature's intended readership was the majority of traditionally observant Jews, but it primarily reached a small elite of male *maskilim* (proponents of the Enlightenment).

With the appearance of Sholem Yankev Abramovitsh's novels in the 1860s and 1870s narrated by the folksy narrator Mendele the Bookseller (*moykher sforim*), modern Yiddish literature became increasingly popular among a Jewish mass readership. His entertaining Yiddish novels displayed Jewish rituals and practice in their mocking depictions of holiday celebrations, religious worship, and dietary laws.

I.L. Peretz's story collections *Khsidish* (Hasidic stories) and *Folkstimlekhe geshikhtes* (Stories in the Folk Manner) feature Jewish rituals and practice in non-normative ways, highlighting their humanist and universal aspects. Peretz' Hasidic story, 'If Not Higher' (1893) depicts the practice of *slikhes* (penitential prayers) in the weeks prior to the Jewish new year. The protagonist, a Litvak, follows a Hasidic *rebbe* on the night of *slikhes*. Jews originating in the area of *Lite* (Baltic states, eastern Poland and White Russia are stereotypically characterized by rationality and dry humor.) When the *rebbe* disguises himself as a Russian peasant and knocks on the door of a poor non-Jewish woman, the astonished Litvak watches how the *rebbe* split woods with an ax. Then, he starts heating her hut, while he recites the penitential prayers. The story imagines the *rebbe* as a combination of a *narodniki* – a Russian revolutionary who lives among poor people – and a Hasidic holy man. At the end, the Litvak becomes the *rebbe*'s disciple, and the story a hagiography to his master.

Scholem Aleichem's novel *Tevye the Dairyman* (first serialized in Yiddish journal between 1895 and 1914) provides examples of Jewish rituals and practice conveyed through Tevye's colloquial monologues, Bible quotations, and narrative twist and turns. In each chapter, Tevye is confronted by one of his five daughters, each of whom wants to escape their retrograde Jewish village. Tevye produces and sells dairy products to the rich Jews of Yehupets (a fictional city modeled on Kiev) who summer in their nearby dachas. The high season for Tevye's business is during the Jewish holiday of *shvues* (Shavuot) in early summer. A common practice among Ashkenazi Jews is to eschew meat and eat dairy meals such as cheese blintzes on the holiday. The encounters between Tevye's daughters and their future male partners take place during the *shvues* season and their love stories start around a table with tasty *blintses*. When Tevye's daughter Chave elopes with a Ukrainian lad and then converts to Russian orthodoxy, Tevye follows the custom of sitting *shive* (observing the traditionally Jewish seven-day mourning period) over a converted child as if she had actually died.

Ashkenazi Literary Worlds

In the works of two of the most important Yiddish prose writers after 1945, I.B. Singer and Chaim Grade, Jewish ritual and practice are represented on a spectrum from conventional to radical subversion. In Grade and Singer's literary recreation of a world that is no more, they chart a mythological Yiddish-land in Central and Eastern Europe. Grade portrays Vilna, the Jerusalem of Lithuania, during the interwar period in novels whose titles indicate their origins in traditional Jewish life: *Der shulhoyf* (the Vilna Courtyard), the cluster of Jewish prayer houses and synagogues in central Vilna; *Di agune* (the abandoned wife forbidden to remarry according to Jewish religious law); *Di mames shabosim* (My mother's sabbath days), a memoir that describes the life of Grade's mother, a Vilna market vendor of apples, and ends with the author's return from the Soviet Union to a destroyed Vilna in 1944. Like his first work, *Musernikes* (1939) about the students in the Muser yeshiva, Grade's themes and styles replicate the voices and mind sets of Vilna Jews who live according to Orthodox Jewish law. These literary works derive their dynamic tension from the intermingling of traditional Jewish ritual and practice with the secular Jews who challenge them in defiance and rejection.

In Singer's first novel, *Satan in Goray* (1996 [1935]), a mid-seventeenth century Jewish *shtetl* is depicted in the aftermath of the Cossack pogroms in the grips of the Sabbatai Zevi messianic movement. Based on historical chronicles, the novel creates a rich catalogue of conventional and transgressive Jewish religious practices. In Singer's childhood memoir, *In My Father's Rabbinical Court* (1956; see Singer, 1991), the impoverished Jews in the Warsaw neighborhood Krochmalne Street prior to World War I are petitioning the author's father about Jewish law and rituals in his religious court (*beth din*).

Singer's book about his father's rabbinical court provides a catalogue of the conflicts between Jewishness and modernity that shapes the Jewish petitioners' lives. This is a vivid example of how Singer drew his literary creativity from the subversion of traditional Jewish practice. In a *feuilleton* in *Forverts*, Yitskhok Varshavski (one of Singer's journalistic pseudonyms) characterizes the *besdn-shtub* (the rabbinical court):

> In no other institution among Jews was the surrounding way of life reflected more accurately than in the religious court of a rabbi or an unauthorized rabbi. The ritual questions, the religious judgements based on the Torah, the divorces, the weddings that were litigated in the rabbinical court gave a picture of Jewish life in all its specificity and strangeness.
>
> Singer, Forverts, *August 13, 1944, Section 2, p. 2*

Yiddish life-writing is a particularly rich source of Jewish rituals and practice in works such as Yekhezkel Kotik's 'My Memoirs' (2002 [1913]), I.J. Singer's, *Of a World That Is No More* (1946; see Singer, 1970) and Y.Y. Trunk's, *Poland: Memoirs and Pictures* (7 vols, 1944–1953; see Trunk, 2007). Similarly, in fictionalized memoirs such as Scholem Aleichem's *From the Fair* (1913–1916) and Joseph Buloff's *From the Old Marketplace* (1992), the fashioning of the protagonist's identity is deeply interwoven with the rituals and practice in the Jewish family and community.

Cinema and TV Series

The representations of Jewish life in the Yiddish cinema are also the result of the fictional imagination in the form of narrative plots, characterization, and stylistic and thematic features. The Yiddish cinema borrows frequently from the choreography, stylistic effects, and props from the Yiddish theater. From its inception in the late nineteenth century, the Yiddish theater derived its specificity from the creative and subversive use of Jewish rituals and practice.

The silent movie *Ost und West* (1923) depicts the religious worship and fasting during Yom Kippur in a European *shtetl*. Visiting the *shtetl* with her father from the US, a young Jewish girl (played by Molly Picon) breaks the fast on Yom Kippur, the holiest day of the Jewish year. In a hilarious scene, she is stuffing herself with food meant for the break the fast meal. In another scene, the 'American *shikse*' teaches the yeshiva *bokhers* to shimmy while she leads them in dancing. The mixed dancing of a woman and religious men crystalizes the film's subversive portrayal of Jewish life in a farcical manner. The film seeks to 'explain East to West, making East seem more comprehensible. To this end, the film features a number of didactic tableaux that "document" various Jewish rituals – the *shabes* meal, the Yom Kippur service, a traditional wedding – with suitable dignity' (Hoberman, 1991, 66).

In the 1939 feature film *Tevye*, directed by Maurice Schwartz who stars in the title role, a series of Jewish rituals are presented in intimate detail. They include the *havdole* ritual marking the end of the Sabbath, Tevye's teaching psalms in Ashkenazic Hebrew to his grandchild, and blessings before and after family meals. The inclusion of synagogue worship in the films *Der dybbuk* (1936) and *Der vilner shtot khazn* (The Vilna City Cantor, 1940) situated in the Jewish *shtetl* and city exemplifies the cinematographic representation of religious practice. The films' nostalgic view of the traditional Jewish life that is regulated 24/7 by rituals and practice, spoke intimately to a secularized Jewish American audience longing for the lost world of their childhood and youth in the old country.

The exorcism of *dybbuks* documented by Jewish anthropologists such as Sh. Ansky prior to World War I vividly documented traditional Jewish beliefs in the supernatural. In the film version of Ansky's play, *Der dybbuk*, the exorcism is enacted in a series of esoteric rituals such as the burning of black candles, Hebrew incantations, and mystical prayers underscored by a haunting musical soundtrack. The choreography of the stunning dance of death is based on literary and anthropological accounts of wedding dances (Gollance, 2019). A recurrent figure in the Yiddish cinema, the *badkhn*, or wedding jester, recites rhymed stanzas in *Der dybbuk* and *Yidl mitn fidl* (1936) with great dramatic force, that can be viewed as authentic expressions of a ritual that has remained a staple of the traditional Jewish wedding to this day.

In the TV series *Unorthodox* (2020) and *Shtisel* (2017–2020), contemporary Ultra-Orthodox Jewish communities in New York and Jerusalem are the settings for family dramas centered around arranged marriages both as a repressive and a sustaining social practice. In the mini-series *Unorthodox*, a young married woman flees her Yiddish-speaking community of Satmar Hasidim in New York and starts a new life as a modern, secular woman in Berlin. The narrative trajectory is similar to Enlightenment narratives about a protagonist's rebellion against the narrowness of a religiously regulated Jewish life that she eventually leaves.

Shtisel, which is primarily in Hebrew with conversations in Yiddish and some Yiddish phrases inserted into Hebrew dialogues, depicts a more romanticized view of arranged marriages, sabbath celebration, and burial rituals. These provide the backdrop for a gallery of characters struggling to find fulfilment within the boundaries of a Haredi community. In the final episode of *Shtisel*'s third season (the last so far), the patriarch of the family, Shulem Shtisel, sits with his brother and son at the dinner table. Suddenly they are surrounded by many of their deceased relatives who begin to talk with one another. Shulem mentions a book by a Yiddish author that he once read while in the bathroom, where the reading of holy books is forbidden. The name of the author is I.B. Singer, and the scene is reminiscent of the supernatural mixing of the living and the dead characteristic of his literary work. As in *Der dybbuk*, the blurring of life and death magically infuses this scene about a Haredi family deeply rooted in the rituals and practice of the way of the SHaS.

Contemporary Ritual and Practice

In the twenty-first century, Yiddish remains the colloquial language of many Haredi communities. Outside of that world, however, Yiddish language and culture worlds are primarily employed in connection with Holocaust commemorations. The partisan hymn *Zog nisht keyn mol* has become a regular feature at Holocaust memorial events organized by Jewish *landsmanshaftn* (societies organized according to their families' home towns in Europe) in connection with the annual commemoration of the Warsaw Ghetto Uprising and also at the sites of concentration camps, ghettos, and in (former) Jewish communities in Eastern Europe and in the US. Typically, Holocaust memorial events close with the singing of the partisan hymn in Yiddish, with the audience rising as for a national anthem. It is also a common practice at Holocaust memorial events to read Yiddish poems and excerpts from war testimonies. The inclusion of Yiddish language and culture creates a highly emotional identification with the destroyed Central and Eastern European communities.

In the secular celebration of Passover at a 'Third Seder,' a variety of Yiddish *hagodes* (Passover Haggadah) have been published under the auspices of Yiddishist groups such as the Workmen's Circle (Arbeter ring) and Bund and used instead of a traditional Haggadah. They include material derived from Yiddish literature and songs, often with an explicit ideological socialist bend, as well as the traditional text of the four questions in Yiddish.

Contemporary *siddurim* and *makhzorim* (prayer books) created by the Reconstructionist, Conservative, and Reform movements in North America, include Yiddish poetry of all types, as well as Holocaust poems in the *yizkor* sections of holiday services. A popular *tkhine*, 'Got fun avrom,' recited prior to the Havdalah ritual, is included in many of these prayer books as well as some Orthodox versions.

The Yiddish summer programs, starting with the Uriel Weinreich summer program in New York in 1968, have mushroomed in recent years throughout Europe and Israel. In addition to the regular language and literature instruction similar to other intensive language programs, the Yiddish summer programs have created their own set of rituals and practices. They typically take the students on excursions to Jewish cemeteries and memorial sites, and teach a core repertoire of Yiddish literature and song practiced by the students in recitations and communal singing. In the contemporary Haredi communities, where Yiddish language and culture always play a prominent role, they are particularly visible in the Purim *shpiels* that continue the practice of comedy and satire that began in the European Jewish *shtetl* of the Middle Ages.

To follow the role of Yiddish in Jewish ritual and practice is to understand both continuity and change in the language and culture of Ashkenazi Jews the world over.

Bibliography

Abramovitsh, Sholem Yankev. 1986. *Of Bygone Days: In A Shtetl and Other Yiddish Novellas*. Ed. Ruth R. Wisse. Detroit, MI: Wayne University Press.

Ansky, S. 2002. *The Dybbuk and Other Writings*. Ed. David Roskies. Trans. Golda Werman. New Haven, CT: Yale University Press.

Baumgarten, Jean. 2005. *Introduction to Old Yiddish Literature*. Ed. and trans. Jerold C. Frakes. Oxford: Oxford University Press.

Buloff, Joseph. 1992. *From the Old Marketplace*. Cambridge, MA: Harvard University Press.

Glikl of Hamil. 1896. *Memoirs*. In *Zikhroynes mares Glikl Hamil: mi-shnas. Die Memoiren der Glückel von Hameln, 1645-1719*. Ed. David Kaufmann. Pressburg Bratislava: A. Alkalay; Frankfurt a. M.: J. Kaufmann.

Gollance, Sonia. 2019. "Gesture, Repertoire, and Emotion: Yiddish Dance Practice in German and Yiddish Literature." *Jewish Social Studies: History, Culture, Society*, vol. 25, no. 1: 101–127.

Grade, Chaim. www.yiddishbookcenter.org/language-literature-culture/yiddish-literature/focus-chaim-grade

Grade, Chaim. 1978. *The Agunah*. New York: Menorah Publishing Company.

Grade, Chaim. 1997. *My Mother's Sabbath Days: A Memoir*. Oxford: Jason Aronson.

Hoberman, Jim. 1991. *Bridge of Longing: Yiddish Film Between Two Worlds*. New York: Schocken Books.

Kotik, Yekhezkel. 2002 [1913]. 'My Memoirs,' in *Journey to a Nineteenth-Century Shtetl: The Memoirs of Yekhezkel Kotik*. Ed. David Assaf. Detroit, MI: Wayne State University Press.

Niger, Shmuel. 1913. "*Di yidishe literatur un di lezerin*" (Yiddish Literature and the Female Reader) *Der pinkes* 1. Vilna.

Peretz, Yitskhok Leibush. 1989. *The I.L. Peretz Reader*. Ed. Ruth R. Wisse. Schocken Books.

Scholem Aleichem https://yivoencyclopedia.org/article.aspx/sholem_aleichem

Scholem Aleichem. 1985. *From the Fair*. Trans. C. Leviant. New York: Viking.

Scholem Aleichem. 1987 *Tevye the Dairyman and the Railroad Stories*. Trans. Hillel Halkin. New York: Schocken Books.

Singer, I.B. 1996. *Satan in Goray*. Trans. Jacob Sloan with an introduction by Ruth Wisse. New York: Farrar, Straus and Giroux.
Singer, I.B. 1991. *In My Father's Court*. New York: Farrar, Straus and Giroux.
Singer, I.J. 1970. *Of a World That Is No More*. Trans. J. Singer. New York: Viking.
Trunk, Yehiel Yeshaia. 2007. *Poyln: My Life within Jewish Life in Poland: Sketches and Images*. Trans Anna Clarke. Eds. Piotr Wróbel and Robert M. Shapiro. Toronto: University of Toronto Press.
Weinreich, Uriel. 2008. *History of the Yiddish Language*. Yale: Yale University Press/YIVO.

PART VI

Others

37
JEWISH MAGICAL PRACTICES

Ortal-Paz Saar

Introduction

If one were to rely on the passages in the Hebrew Bible concerning magic, this chapter would seem unnecessary. As the book of Deuteronomy emphatically states, magical practices are prohibited to the Children of Israel, so that they do not resemble the surrounding nations. From the succinct "You shall not permit a witch (*mekhashefah*) to live" (Exodus 22:18) to the detailed yet obscure "There shall not be found among you anyone who makes his son or his daughter pass through the fire, or one who practices witchcraft, or a soothsayer, or one who interprets omens, or a sorcerer" (Deuteronomy 18:10), the Torah's attitude to the practice of magic is unequivocal: it is forbidden. Yet when one attempts to understand the nature of the forbidden practices one runs into a wall of fuzziness. What precisely was considered *kishuf*, and in what practices did a *mekhashefah* engage? Incidentally, the same sort of terminological difficulties continue when modern scholars try to define magic, and these endeavours have generated a wealth of literature.[1]

Despite the original prohibitions on magic, practices that seem to fit the above description do appear in biblical stories. One of the most famous incidents revolves around the Woman of Endor (1 Samuel 28:3–25). King Saul, after disposing of all the "mediums and spiritists" (*ovot ve-yidʿonim*) in the country, wishes to seek the advice of prophet Samuel, who is no longer alive. He addresses his men with the request "Find me a woman who is a medium (*baʿalat ov*), so I may go and inquire of her". He is then taken, disguised as a common man, to a woman in Endor, who summons up the spirit of the dead prophet. The biblical verses do not describe the actions performed by the woman, just the end result, when she pronounces, "I see gods coming out of the ground", and then moves on to describe a man who, in King Saul's eyes, fits the description of Samuel. The passage implies that the woman saw an apparition and was able to allow the king to converse with it, though how precisely this took place remains unclear. The Hebrew Bible contains other instances that might resemble magical acts, such as curses or healings, but these are usually performed by men whose power has been religiously endorsed: they act in the name of God and presumably through His power.[2] Consequently, their actions are not regarded by the biblical narrators as magical, even if a modern reader might identify them as such.

This trend continues more fiercely in later periods. The rabbinic literature redacted in the first five centuries of the Common Era (Mishnah, Tosefta, Talmud) contains descriptions of respectable rabbis who engage in magic and discuss the permissibility of related actions. From these narratives one can glimpse a good typology of magical practices. First, according to form: practices can be oral (uttering specific phrases or incantations), they can be written (for instance, inscribing a text and carrying it as an amulet), or they can involve a manipulation of materials (such as carrying around plants or minerals that function as amulets). Some practices, like the one meant to heal the bite of a rabid dog in BT Yoma 84a (below), involve a combination of forms. Second, practices differ according to their aim: magic for protection and healing, harmful magic, or practices for divining the future and obtaining knowledge of hidden facts. From sources outside the rabbinic literature one can learn about the existence of additional aims: sowing love and hate, obtaining success in business, winning in a court of law, finding hidden treasure, and many more.

The aim of this chapter is to present a brief overview of magical practices employed by Jews in accordance with the main categories listed above, ranging across time and space, but focused primarily on Late Antiquity and the medieval periods.[3] In most cases these practices can be identified as Jewish due to the languages employed or the context in which they were found, and not because of their content. Often, there was nothing specifically "Jewish" about Jewish magic, and its practices and associated products closely resembled those of non-Jews. Nonetheless, in some instances one can observe distinctive Jewish features among the practices.

Protective (Apotropaic) and Healing Magic

This category of practices is attested through biblical and rabbinic texts as well as objects that go back as far as the early sixth century BCE. This is not surprising, given the perennial human demand for improving one's health, ensuring fecundity and an easy child delivery, preventing harm and disease, and keeping away natural and supernatural enemies, such as wild animals, robbers, and demons. Apotropaic and healing magic could consist of oral rituals as well as the inscribing of a text, or a manipulation of materials considered to have a beneficial effect. This section will provide some examples of each.

Oral Magical Practices

These are attested among Jewish practices for protection and healing, although not always on a positive note. For instance, Rabbi Akiva opposed an oral ritual for healing, when he counted among the people who have no share in the World-to-Come also: "one who whispers over a wound and says 'Every illness that I placed upon Egypt I will not place upon you, for I am the Lord your healer' (Exodus 15:26)" (Mishnah Sanhedrin 10:1).[4] Possibly, some rabbis combatted this practice because they regarded it as disrespectful (sometimes these "whispers" would be accompanied by spitting over the wound), or as resembling non-Jewish customs. Regardless, we can learn from the words attributed to Rabbi Akiva about some of the incantations that were uttered during these oral rituals. It seems that at times these were merely biblical verses related to healing. However, when uttered outside of a religiously sanctioned context, they were considered by some to be inappropriately used.

Other rabbinic passages shed additional light on the use of oral magic. One of them is the list of aims described in PT Shabbat 14:3, which states that it is allowed to "whisper for the eye and the intestines and snakes and scorpions" during the day of Shabbat.[5] The "eye" here might refer to the harm caused by the evil eye, and not to the organ. It seems that these instances were considered particularly dangerous, so as to deserve the uttering of incantations even during Shabbat. Other rabbis, however, would prohibit them nevertheless: "One should not read a verse over a wound on Shabbat" (PT Shabbat 6:2). What precisely was whispered or read in each case remains unknown. Such magical "whispers" could also be uttered in negative contexts, as will be shown further below.

Oral magic for protection and healing is also attested outside the rabbinic literature, for instance in *Sefer ha-Razim* (*The Book of Secrets*), one of the earliest surviving Jewish handbooks of magic, composed around the third or fourth century CE.[6] The book's first recipe is designated "If you wish to perform an act of healing", and it advises to:[7]

> arise in the first or second hour of the night and take with you myrrh and frankincense. This (is to be) put on burning coals in the name of the angel who rules over the first encampment, who is called 'WRPNY'L, and say the names of the seventy-two angels who serve before him seven times, and say as follows: l, N son of N, beseech you that you will give me success in healing N son of N.

This relatively simple practice involves both uttering an incantation composed of angelic names as well as a manipulation of materials with supposed purificatory properties. The immediate aim is not to heal a patient, but to succeed later, when the healing practice is to be performed.

Another source for oral magic is *Ḥarba de-Moshe* (*The Sword of Moses*), composed in Aramaic and Hebrew in the second half of the first millennium CE.[8] This manual begins with a long list of names of supernatural beings, that are then used in magical recipes for various aims. For a particular aim, one must utter or write a particular sequence of names. For example, *The Sword of Moses* includes instructions such as: "For an (ear?)ache, recite in his ear on the painful side from 'WNṬW until HWTMY'S",[9] or "For an earache, say in his left ear from ŠDY until 'HYH backward".[10] Most recipes, however, consist of uttering a formula combined with a manipulation of materials, for instance: "For a woman that miscarries, say over a cup of wine or over *shekhar* (an alcoholic beverage) or water from TWSY until ŠQBS and she should drink (it) for seven days".[11]

Protective and healing practices of oral magic continue to be attested in later periods. Medieval handbooks of magic, such as those that survive in European manuscripts or in the Cairo Genizah, contain recipes that indicate Jews kept "whispering" over wounds or uttering incantations as part of their rituals for protection. Such practices also survive in early-modern and modern Jewish magic.

Textual Practices and Written Amulets

The Talmud mentions both textual amulets and those made of plants: "Our Rabbis taught: What is an expert's amulet? One that has healed (once), a second time and a third time; whether it is an amulet in writing or an amulet of roots" (BT Shabbat 61a). Inscribed magical objects used for protection and healing indeed were (and sometimes still are) common among Jews. The rabbinic literature mentions that written amulets—while containing holy names just like the phylacteries and the *mezuzah*—need not be saved from a fire during Shabbat, thus shedding some light on the content of their text (Mishnah Shabbat 8:3). One also learns about the manner in which such amulets were employed: for instance, some were carried around in a bracelet, a ring, or small tube (*silona*) (PT Shabbat 6.2). These latter tubular metal containers are attested in the archaeological record; some contained rolled textual amulets (discussed below), and others probably held various natural materials (the "roots" mentioned above).[12]

A special class of Jewish inscribed amulets are made of metal. An impressive number of thin metal strips (*lamellae*) on which a text was incised with a sharp instrument was uncovered throughout the area of ancient Palestine, as well as in other places where Jews resided, such as Egypt or Georgia.[13] The earliest artefacts in this group are two silver *lamellae* that date to the early sixth century BCE and were uncovered in Ketef Hinnom in Jerusalem.[14] Each of them was inscribed in paleo-Hebrew letters and contained the text of the Priestly Benediction found in Numbers 6:24–26. The silver strips were rolled up and it is very likely they were meant to be carried on a person's body and used as amulets. Their specific function is not mentioned in the text.

In Late Antiquity many more metal amulets are attested in Jewish contexts. Occasionally, the names of the amulets' users are mentioned, turning them into personalized magical objects. The users are almost always designated by their matronym (X son/daughter of Y-female name), as opposed to the common way of referring to people in everyday life by their patronym.[15] The names indicate that these amulets were worn by Jewish men and women, and sometimes produced by Jewish magical practitioners for non-Jewish clients. The amulets' aims are sometimes explicitly noted, and thus we know that they were used against fevers, migraines, to facilitate child delivery or more generally to expel the demons that haunt one's limbs. The following is an example of such a metal amulet, meant to protect a person named Esther from a variety of evil entities (Figure 37.1).[16] The amulet text contains both Aramaic and Hebrew, for example: *'eyn biša* and *'ayn ra'a*, meaning "evil eye". The last lines, that survived only in part, are a direct quotation from Exodus 15:26, the same verse mentioned above as having been used in oral magic for healing (and harshly opposed by some rabbis).

> A proper amulet for Esther
> daughter of Ṭ'ṬYS,
> to save her from evil tormentors,
> from an evil eye,
> from a spirit, from a demon,
> from a shadow-spirit, from all evil tormentors,
> from an evil eye, from
> … from an impure spirit
> … "If you diligently
> heed the voice of the Lord
> your God and do what is
> right in His sight,
> give ear
> to His commandments
> and keep all His statutes,
> Every illness that I placed upon Egypt
> I will not place upon you,
> for I am the Lord your healer."

Similar metal amulets were used by non-Jews throughout Late Antiquity, invoking a variety of supernatural entities, from Graeco-Roman or Egyptian deities to Jesus.[17] When written in Greek, which was the *lingua franca* in many regions, it is sometimes hard to determine the religious affiliation of the amulet producers (let alone its users): the adjured entities fit well in a Jewish, Christian, or polytheistic context, and appeals to *Adonaie*, *Sabaoth*, *Iao* or Michael and Ouriel became common in different religious milieus, not just the Jewish one.[18]

Jewish Magical Practices

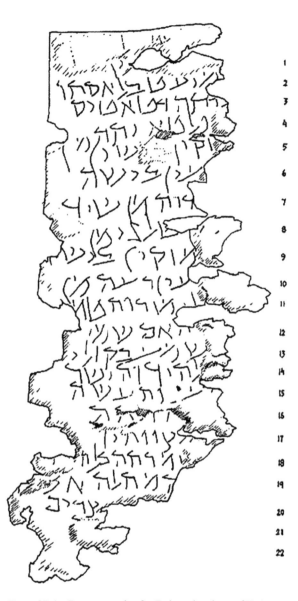

Figure 37.1 Bronze amulet for Esther, daughter of Tatis
Source: After Naveh and Shaked 1985, 100

Another special class of textual practices for protection and healing, which were not mentioned in the rabbinic sources but were widely used by Jews in Late Antiquity, are the Mesopotamian incantation bowls (or magic bowls).[19] These are small clay objects, usually the size of a modern cereal bowl, on which a text has been inscribed with ink. The text is generally found on the inner surface of the bowl, written in a spiral from the centre outwards, although other styles exist, such as concentric circles or "rays" of words radiating from the centre. The magic bowls were written in three dialects of the Aramaic language, each with

Figure 37.2 An incantation bowl in Jewish Aramaic, for the protection of ʾUmmu-l-ḥubāb.
Source: Vorderasiatisches Museum collection VA.3854. © Staatliche Museen zu Berlin –
Vorderasiatisches Museum, photograph: Olaf M. Teßmer.

its own alphabet: Jewish Aramaic (written with the square "Hebrew" letters still used today), Syriac, and Mandaic. These last two were typically employed by Christians and Mandaeans, respectively. The inscribed text was usually an apotropaic one, meant to keep away negative supernatural entities as well as diseases and, occasionally, human enemies. Rarely, other aims are listed on the bowls, such as obtaining love and favour or success in business. A small number of magic bowls are aggressive in nature, and they will be described further below.

The inscribed bowls would usually be buried upside down in the four corners of a dwelling or under the threshold. Some of them are even labelled, e.g., "of the inner room, of the hall", designating their intended location. More rarely, bowls may have been found in other locations, such as a cemetery. Most of the bowls were not uncovered in controlled archaeological excavations, but derive from the antiquities market. Hence, without a context, the knowledge about their method of use remains limited.

Incantation bowls were a very popular phenomenon yet surprisingly restricted in time and place: they appear around the fourth or fifth century CE, cease to exist around the eighth century, and are found exclusively in the area of present-day Iraq and, in small numbers, west Iran. To date, no magic bowls have been found in other regions where Jews lived, such as Syria-Palestine, as if their use only found favour with Babylonian Jews (and other religious groups in that area). It is also interesting to note that the Babylonian Talmud, which was redacted around the same time and place where the bowls flourished, does not mention them at all, despite the fact that it refers to many magical practices.[20]

A typical incantation on such a bowl (see Figure 37.2) requests:[21]

> That there may be healing from Heaven for ʾUmmu-l-bāb (ʾUmmu-l-ḥubāb) daughter of Rummāna, and may she be healed by the mercy of Heaven from fever and from shivering and from the evil eye and from the evil blast-spirit and from the evil satan and from the evil spirit and from the evil educator-spirit and from the evil (female) companion-spirit and from the evil lilith, male and female, and from all evil spirits,

blast-spirits and noxious spirits, whether their name has been mentioned or whether their name has not been mentioned. All of you, you are bound and sealed from her by the signet-ring of El Shaddai, and by the signet-ring of Solomon son of David, king of Israel, by which are sealed three hundred and sixty six demons, (by) which Adam sealed his son Seth.

Non-textual Amulets

In addition to written amulets, such as the metal *lamellae* and the incantation bowls, Jews also used non-textual protective and healing magic. One of the most impressive examples derives from the second century CE, during Bar Kochba's revolt, and was uncovered in a cave that probably served as a hiding place from the Romans (known in modern times as the "Cave of Letters"). It is a child's shirt made of linen, the margins of which had been tied by a caring hand into small bundles containing different materials: a seashell, some salt crystals, iron slag, asphalt, wax, and seeds (Figure 37.3).[22] The excavator, Yigael Yadin, interpreted these bundles as representing a phenomenon mentioned in a rabbinic discussion about amulets and permission to carry them during the Sabbath: "Boys (common children) go out with knots (*qesharim*) and princes (royal or wealthy children) with bells" (Mishna Shabbat 6:9).[23] The Babylonian Talmud elaborates on the potential uses of knots: "Abbaye said: 'Mother told me: Three (knots) stop (the illness), five heal, seven are effective even against witchcraft'" (BT Shabbat 66b). The "knots" seem to be a likely description of the little bundles on the child shirt from the Cave of Letters. They were probably meant to protect him or her from dangers such as diseases or the evil eye, keeping harm away.

This artefact has survived thanks to the dry climatic conditions in the Judean Desert. Mostly, organic magical objects have not reached us, and even if they had, archaeologists would likely have difficulties identifying them as such. The rabbinic literature provides examples of the types of non-textual amulets that were used by Jews in antiquity: roots, grasshoppers eggs, foxes' teeth, nails from a crucifixion (Mishnah Shabbat 6:10).[24] Evidently, unless found in a specific archaeological context, an animal tooth or an iron nail would not be regarded as magical artefacts.

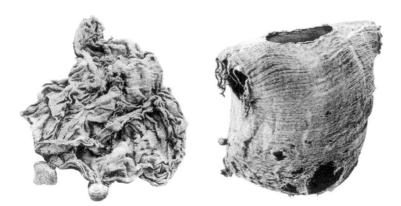

Figure 37.3 Child's linen shirt with "knots" on the margins, before and after unfolding. Judean Desert, "Cave of Letters".

Source: From Yadin 1963, plate 89. Courtesy of the Israel Exploration Society.

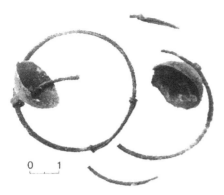

Figure 37.4 Bronze bracelets with bells from a tomb in Beit Shemesh, Israel.
Source: From Seligman, Zias, and Stark 1996, 54. Courtesy of the Israel Antiquities Authority.

Other non-textual amulets that were used by Jews in antiquity were more durable. They include metal jewellery, gems, and glass amulets. The former was already mentioned in the Mishnaic dictum about "princes go out with bells". The purpose of such bells probably was to repel evil entities through the sound they constantly made when moving, or avert the evil eye by attracting attention to their sound rather than the wearer.[25] Miniature bells meant to be worn on the body were indeed found in archaeological excavation in modern Israel. Occasionally, they were still attached to the wearer's body, as in the case of a pair of bronze bracelets with bells, uncovered on the wrists of a girl's skeleton (Figure 37.4). The girl died at 13–15 years of age, probably during childbirth – her skeleton also contained the bones of her unborn child. They were interred in a burial cave dated to the fourth or fifth century CE, in present-day Beit Shemesh, Israel.[26] While the religious identity of the persons buried in this cave could not be established, it is clear that such metal amuletic jewellery was in use by Jews and non-Jews alike.

Another example of metal jewellery with a magical purpose are metal rings, glass pendants, and gems bearing the figure of a lion. Sometimes the lion is accompanied by a star/sun and moon, or by a short inscription in Greek, such as IAO or THEOS. This motif was found among different religious groups, not only Jews, given the universal connotation of the lion as a powerful and majestic figure. Figure 37.5 shows one example, discovered in a tomb in Sajur, Israel, and dated to Late Antiquity.[27] The religious identity of the buried persons is uncertain, but there is a high probability that they were Jews.[28] Interestingly, one of the recipes in the Jewish magic manual *Sefer ha-Razim* recommends the use of a signet ring bearing a lion's image, as part of a practice "for preventing sleep from your enemies": "And write thus and put (the writing) in the mouth of a dog's head, and place wax on its mouth, and seal it with a ring that has a lion (engraved) upon it".[29]

Manipulation of Materials

Most Jewish practices for protection and healing involve writing or uttering a text, and practices relying exclusively on a manipulation of materials are rare. Often they would be hard to distinguish from a perceived medicinal use of these materials, and it is our "external" interpretation of these practices that labels them as magical. As mentioned above, the rabbinic literature refers to an "amulet of roots" (*qami'a shel 'ykarin*) (Tosefta Shabbat 5.9; BT Shabbat 61a) or "an amulet

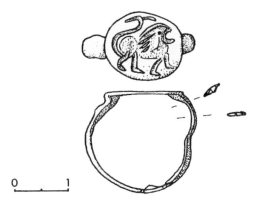

Figure 37.5 Bronze ring with roaring lion from a tomb in Sajur, Israel.
Source: From Braun, Dauphin, and Hadas 1994, 112. Courtesy of the Israel Antiquities Authority.

of herbs" (*qami'a shel 'asabim*) (PT Shabbat 6.2), which are allowed to be carried around during the day of Shabbat. Other materials mentioned are minerals, such as "a preserving stone" (*even tequma*), which was meant to prevent abortions (BT Shabbat 66b).[30] These amulets are clearly perceived as healing devices, sometimes even preventive ones; for instance, the Tosefta permits carrying such amulets not only for persons suffering from epilepsy, who already had an attack, but also for one who wishes to prevent having an attack. Similarly, the Babylonian Talmud permits carrying the "preserving stone" not only for women who are currently pregnant, but also for those who might become pregnant and consequently fear an abortion.

Ancient science often regarded the qualities of plants and minerals, even when used externally, as medicinal, not magical. Scientists and physicians such as Pliny the Elder and Galen counted them among medical remedies, and thus one should be careful when categorizing the above-mentioned amulets as magical: they may have been perceived as wholly natural therapies. Other manipulation practices, however, have a more magical tone, such as that attributed to Rav Huna and described in BT Shabbat 67a:

> For tertian fever, let one bring seven thorns from seven palm trees, and seven slivers from seven beams, and seven pegs from seven bridges, and seven (measures of) ashes from seven ovens, and seven (measures of) dust from seven door sockets, and seven (measures of) tar from seven boats, and seven cumin seeds, and seven hairs from the beard of an old dog, and let him bind it to the opening of the neckline (of his garment) with a thread of hair.

The reiteration of the typological number seven, as well as the nature of the materials, reflect a type of practice different from the more medically oriented ones described above. Other healing practices that involve a manipulation of materials also include writing or speaking, and they, too, are clearly magical in nature. One instance is a ritual described in the Babylonian Talmud Yoma 84a, when the rabbis discuss methods for healing a person bitten by a rabid dog:[31]

> What is the cure? Abaye said: Let him take the hide of a male hyena and write upon it: 'I, N son of N, am writing on you, hide of a male hyena, *knty knty qlyrws* – and some say, *qndy qndy qlwrws* – YH YH YHWH Sabaot Amen Amen Selah', and take

his clothes off and bury them in a cemetery for twelve months, and take them out and burn them in an oven, and spread the ashes on a crossroads. And throughout these twelve months, when he drinks water he should drink it only through a bronze tube, lest he see the reflection of the demon and be endangered.

This passage describes an elaborate procedure for what was perceived as a potentially deadly situation. The person who was bitten by the rabid dog should write a spell on a specific material, including their name, and then perform a multi-stage practice with the material. The locations specified (cemetery, crossroads) are known as liminal places, particularly suited for engaging in magical actions.

Harmful and Aggressive Magic

Not all the magical practices described in Jewish sources had a positive end in view. Some were meant to cause harm, infertility, separation between lovers, and even death to perceived enemies or, occasionally, to seemingly undeserving people. As before, one can distinguish between oral aggressive practices, written ones, and a manipulation of materials with or without the addition of words. Perhaps not surprisingly, there is less tangible evidence for aggressive magic than for positive practices, no matter what period is examined. One reason for this is that the products of negative magic were often destroyed by the very people who employed them, as part of the magical practice: through burying or burning, for example. Additionally, Jewish aggressive magic often called for non-durable products, such as eggs or bones on which a text had been written. In antiquity this tendency stood in sheer opposition to the pervasive Graeco-Roman curse tablets, that were usually inscribed on lead and thousands of which survive.[32]

Oral Practices

The ability of certain people to harm through their words is described already in the Hebrew Bible, for instance in the story of prophet Elisha who is taunted by a group of young boys, shouting at him: "Up you go, baldy". Elisha curses the boys in the name of the Lord, "and two female bears came out of the forest and mangled forty-two of these children" (2 Kings 2:23–24). The curse and subsequent punishment appear disproportionate to the action that caused them, and seem to reflect a negative trait of the up-to-here positive Elisha. Nonetheless, it seems that the author of the story incorporated the curse together with other miraculous abilities of the same man, which were performed in the name of God or through His power. The message appears to be that holy men are powerful, and they can choose to use their power for good or bad ends.[33]

The same notion surfaces in later rabbinic sources, when the rabbis are described as harming other people, sometimes even their own colleagues. A rather extreme example occurs after the death of Rabbi Adda bar Abba, when five other sages state that they are responsible for his death, one explicitly through curses: "Rav Yosef said: I punished him, as I cursed him" (BT Bava Batra 22a). A more concrete aggressive procedure from the rabbinic world is described in BT Moʿed Qatan 17a. When a rabbinic scholar is harassed by a violent man, he goes to seek the advice of Rav Yosef. The latter, after initially suggesting that the violent man be placed under a ritual ban, modifies his advice: "Take [the ban] and place it in a jug, and set it down in a cemetery, and blow on it a thousand *shofar* blasts over forty days. [The rabbinic scholar] went and did this. The jug burst and the violent man died." Interestingly, it is not the ban that kills the tormenter, but the action of manipulating a specific object (a jug) in a specific setting (a cemetery).

The power of aggressive magic might also be alluded to in a passage about courts of law: "When they who engaged in whispering in judgment multiplied, fierceness of (the divine) anger increased against Israel and the *Shechinah* departed" (Tosefta Sotah 14:1; BT Sotah 47b). The "whispering in judgement" could be a reference to oral magic meant to silence legal opponents or to manipulate the opinion of judges, which is attested in Jewish magic manuals like *Sefer ha-Razim* and *Ḥarba de-Moshe*, as well as in later recipes and even products of Jewish magic.[34]

Outside the rabbinic sources, many magic manuals include recipes for aggressive magic. A good example can be found in *Sefer ha-Razim*, which provides instructions for sending some "angels of wrath and fury" to perform different destructive tasks, such as capsizing a ship, exiling one's enemy, or making him bedridden:[35]

> Take water from seven springs on the seventh day of the month, in the seventh hour of the day, in seven unfired pottery vessels, and do not mix them with one another. Expose them beneath the stars for seven nights; and on the seventh night take a glass vial, on the name of your enemies, and pour the water into it, and break the pottery vessels and throw them to the four winds of the sky, and say thus to the four directions: HHGRYT who dwells in the east, SRWKYT who dwells in the north 'WLPH who dwells in the west, KRDY who dwells in the south, accept from my hand at this time that which I throw to you, to affect N son of N, to break his bones, crush all his limbs, and shatter his conceited power, as these pottery vessels are broken. And may there be no recovery for them just as there is no repair for these pottery vessels.

This oral practice is accompanied by a detailed manipulation of materials, focused around the number seven. The practitioner performs an act of sympathetic magic, in which the shattering of the clay vessels is supposed to trigger the shattering of the enemy's bones and power.

Ḥarba de-Moshe, too, suggests what to do "[i]f you wish to kill a person":[36]

> take mud from the two banks of the river and make a figure and write his name on it. And take seven thorns from a withered date palm and make a bow of *ḥuskaniata* wood and strands of horse hair and put the figure in a cloth bag and stretch the bow over it and shoot it and say over every thorn (the supernatural names) from 'QTDS until PRSWSY, may N son of N be injured. And he will be removed from you.

Textual Practices

The Jewish magical literature, from *Sefer ha-Razim* through *Ḥarba de-Moshe*, and up to medieval and modern sources, provides a wealth of recipes for harming others through the inscribing of a text. The latter, for instance, suggests what to do if you wish "to send a dream against someone":[37]

> write on a silver plate from 'BNSNS until QYRYW'S and place (it) in the mouth of a cock and slaughter it while it is placed in its mouth and turn its mouth around and place it between its thighs and bury (it) at the bottom part of a wall. And put your heel

on its place and say thus: in the name of [ ] may the swift messenger go and torment N son of N in his dreams until my will is fulfilled.

Whereas if your wish is merely "to impose your terror over all people",[38] "write on a lead plate from QBZQY'L until GTHWTY'L and bury (it) in a synagogue on the western side".[39]

Only rarely, however, do products of written aggressive magic survive. An interesting case in point are several Mesopotamian magic bowls that were meant to hurt rather than protect. As mentioned earlier, these are exceptions to the rule that most bowls were designated for apotropaic and healing purposes. The following quotation is from the beginning of such a bowl.[40] It derives from a private collection and there is no secure information about its original context, but presumably it was buried in the vicinity of Judah's home, workplace, or in a liminal location fitting for aggressive magic, such as a cemetery.

> Seized, clasped and bound and crooked are his luck and his angels and his stars and his planets. And all the vomit and spittle of Judah son of Nanay, that his tongue may dry up in his mouth, that his spittle may dissolve in his throat, that his hind legs may dry, that sulphur and fire may burn in him, that his body may be struck by scalding, that he may be choked, become estranged, become disturbed to the eyes of all those who see him, and that he may be banned, broken, lost, finished, vanquished, and that he may die, and that a flame may come upon him from heaven, and shiver seize him, and a fracture catch him, and a rebuke burn in him.

The bowl text then seeks to apply to Judah son of Nanay several biblical verses, all of which deal with destruction and harm, for example: Psalm 69:24, 26, Exodus 22:23, Deuteronomy 28:22. The writer combined a knowledge of magic with a close familiarity with the biblical text, from which he quotes extensively (a rather unusual occurrence in the bowls).

Another exceptional product of aggressive magic derives from a later period, and was discovered among the fragments of the Cairo Genizah. It is a text written in Hebrew, Aramaic, and Judaeo-Arabic on a narrow, rectangular piece of paper, intended to harm Ali son of Nuḥ the Ishmaelite. It would seem that Ali unlawfully took a house from the person who commissioned the spell, and the latter sought to expel him from that house and punish him for his wrongdoings. The following is an excerpt from this curse:[41]

> This writing is appointed for Ali the Ishmaelite. May he be cursed and wander from place to place, and there should be no standing for this Ali, and he should have no comfort in this dwelling, which he has taken, and the place which he has taken by robbery, until they (Ali and his relatives?) go and fall to bed, in illness, all the days of their lives, when he sits in the place which he has robbed, with the 248 limbs that are in the body of this Ali.[42]

Manipulation of Materials

As could be seen above, some of the recipes for aggressive magic comprise a manipulation of materials. Just as with protective magic, most of these also include writing or uttering a text. Practices consisting of a sheer manipulation of materials are rare, and it seems that they were less favoured by Jews in the periods discussed here.[43] It also is possible that, given their relative simplicity, such practices were transmitted orally rather than in writing, and hence less information about them survives.

Summary

This chapter sought to briefly describe Jewish practices of magic from a broad perspective. It was shown that, despite the original biblical prohibitions on practicing magic (however that may be understood), some Jews in all periods, places, and from all walks of life did engage in actions that could be labelled as "magical". From the various sources mentioned above one can glimpse a wide array of aims for which magic was employed by Jews. Protection and harm are the two broadest categories, but many others exist. One of the most frequent ones is love magic, meant to install attraction, social "grace and favour" and, conversely, hate and separation between individuals.[44] Another interesting aim is that of enhancing one's memory in order to succeed in Torah study. Through spells adjuring various angels, including *Sar Torah* (the Prince of Torah), some Jews sought to magically improve their scholarly abilities.[45] While spells for memory are also found in non-Jewish magical traditions, those aimed specifically for Torah study are of course peculiar to Judaism. Other magical practices were meant to win at sports or gambling, obtain success in business or in a court of law, detect thieves, interpret dreams, divine the future, and many other aims, covering almost every conceivable field of human endeavours. It appears that what scholars tend to label "magic" was (and still is) accepted by many Jews, including those pertaining to the religious establishment. Sometimes, these practices even included passages from the Hebrew Bible and Jewish "holy names", or appeals to the Jewish God, thus treading on the thin threshold separating magic from religion.

Notes

1. For general theories on magic and their application in different cultures, see the encyclopaedia articles under "Magic" in Jones 2005; Harari 2017, 15–67. For definitions of magic within Judaism, see Harari 2017, 159–203.
2. Bohak 2008, 13–35.
3. For detailed studies of ancient and medieval Jewish magic, see Bohak 2008, Harari 2017, and Trachtenberg 2004 [1939]. The latter, although outdated, still provides a good picture. For Jewish magic in later periods, see Bohak 2019 and the references there. Primary sources of Jewish magic, such as recipes for specific aims, amulets, and curses can be found in a variety of editions. Good starting places are Naveh and Shaked 1985, Naveh and Shaked 1993, and Schiffman and Swartz 1992. For a rich bibliography on Jewish magic from all periods, see Bohak 2009.
4. See also BT Sanhedrin 101a.
5. See also Tosefta Shabbat 7:23 (8:11).
6. The most recent and elaborate edition of *Sefer ha-Razim* is Rebiger and Schäfer 2009. For an English translation, see Morgan 1983.
7. *Sefer ha-Razim*, First Heaven, First Firmament (Morgan 1983, 23–24).
8. Harari 2012.
9. Harari 2012, 83.
10. Harari 2012, 84.
11. Harari 2012, 86.
12. For more references, see Bohak 2008, 373–374.
13. For metal amulets, see Naveh and Shaked 1985, Naveh and Shaked 1993, and Eshel and Leiman 2010.
14. Barkay *et al.* 2004.
15. The practice of using matronyms in magic is pervasive and also attested outside of Judaism, for instance in Graeco-Roman curse tablets (*defixiones*). Matronyms are also used in Jewish institutionalized religious rituals, such as prayers for a specific person (Golinkin 2002). This probably stemmed from the desire to achieve precision ("*mater certa, pater semper incertum*"). For additional references, see Bohak 2008, 286 n. 166; Harari 2017, 219, n. 29.
16. Naveh and Shaked 1985, 98–101 (Amulet 13). This bronze amulet was uncovered in archaeological excavations of the ancient synagogue in Ma'on, near kibbutz Nirim in southern Israel. It was part of

a cache of 19 bronze amulets, all rolled up, which was found in the apse of the synagogue (Naveh and Shaked 1985, 90; Bohak 2008, 315–318).
17 Kotansky 1994.
18 Kotansky 1994, 105–106.
19 The literature on magic bowls in different dialects is vast. Thousands of such objects exist and many hundreds of them have been published. The two volumes of Naveh and Shaked 1985 and 1993 are good starting places. For more recent references, see the bibliography in Bhayro et al. 2018.
20 A single possible reference to the bowls might be found in BT Bava Metzia 29b: "Rabbi Yoḥanan said: A cup of sorcerers (or sorcery) and not a cup of lukewarm water", the meaning being, presumably, that lukewarm water could be more dangerous to the body than the former. Some scholars interpret the sentence differently, and translate in the second part "sorcery-dissolvers" instead of "lukewarm water" (Bohak 2008, 390–391). Regardless of which translation is the right one, the possibility of the "cup of sorcerers" referring to the (harmful) incantation bowls is not very likely.
21 Bhayro et al. 2018, 16–23 (Bowl VA.3854)
22 Yadin 1963, 256–258, and plates 89–90. Together with the child shirt another piece of linen cloth was found. It, too, contained small bundles ("sacs") tied around with string, containing the same sort of materials as those in the shirt bundles. The excavator suggested it was meant to be hung around the neck, or used as a bandage, perhaps with apotropaic properties.
23 Some later rabbis attempt to interpret the term "knots" as garlands of a particular plant (*puʾah*, perhaps the madder plant) (BT Shabbat 66b).
24 The Mishnaic passage indicates that some rabbis permitted the use of such amulets, while others opposed them "because of the Ways of the Amorites", meaning magical practices and beliefs common among non-Jews.
25 Numerous examples of miniature bells (*tintinnabula*) survive from the Graeco-Roman world, sometimes in connection to amulets shaped in phallic forms (*fascina*). The latter were meant to avert the evil eye.
26 Seligman, Zias, and Stark 1996, 54–55.
27 Incidentally, the tomb also contained bronze bracelets and tiny bells.
28 Braun, Dauphin, and Hadas 1994, 107–108.
29 *Sefer ha-Razim*, Second Heaven, Fourth Firmament (Morgan 1983, 49).
30 This stone might have been identical to the *aetites*, a hollow geode in which a smaller crystal can be found. The stone and its anti-abortive properties were mentioned by several Graeco-Roman sources, such as Pliny (*Natural History* 36.39).
31 For a discussion of this passage, see Bohak 2008, 417–419.
32 For a discussion of Jewish attitudes to cursing and the absence of Jewish curse tablets, see Saar 2021.
33 See also Bohak 2008, 20–27.
34 See, for example, Saar 2017, 174 (a recipe for favour in front of a judge). The Cairo Genizah has even preserved an amulet meant to bestow favour on its bearer in the eyes of a judge (Saar 2017, 165).
35 *Sefer ha-Razim*, First Heaven, Second Firmament (Morgan 1983, 26).
36 Harari 2012, 89.
37 Harari 2012, 89.
38 Harari 2012, 93.
39 For a discussion of such products of magic, see Saar 2017, 94–95; Saar 2021.
40 Naveh and Shaked 1985, 174–179 (Bowl 9); republished in Levene 2013, 126–127.
41 Schiffman and Swartz 1992, 83–92; Naveh and Shaked 1993, 164–166 (Geniza 12).
42 Jewish sources ascribe the number 248 to the limbs in the human body (Mishnah Ohalot 1:8).
43 For some self-standing manipulation practices in the field of love magic, see Saar 2017, 134–143.
44 Saar 2017.
45 Swartz 1996.

References

Barkay, Gabriel, Marilyn J. Lundberg, Andrew G. Vaughn, and Bruce Zuckerman. 2004. "The Amulets from Ketef Hinnom: A New Edition and Evaluation," *Bulletin of the American Schools of Oriental Research* 334: 41–71.

Bhayro, Siam, James Nathan Ford, Dan Levene, and Ortal-Paz Saar. 2018. *Aramaic Magic Bowls in the Vorderasiatisches Museum in* Berlin. Leiden: Brill.

Bohak, Gideon. 2008. *Ancient Jewish Magic: A History*. Cambridge and New York: Cambridge University Press.
Bohak, Gideon. 2009. "Prolegomena to the Study of the Jewish Magical Tradition," *Currents in Biblical Research* 8: 107–150.
Bohak, Gideon. 2019. "How Jewish Magic Survived the Disenchantment of the World," *Aries* 19: 7–37.
Braun, Eliot, Claudine Dauphin, and Gideon Hadas. 1994. "A Rock-Cut Tomb at Sajur," *Atiqot* 25: 103–115.
Eshel, Hanan and Rivka Leiman. 2010. "Jewish Amulets Written on Metal Scrolls," *Journal of Ancient Judaism* 1: 189–199.
Golinkin, David. 2002. "The Use of Matronymics in Prayers for the Sick," in Aharon Demsky ed. *These Are the Names: Studies in Jewish Onomastics*, vol. III. Ramat-Gan: Bar-Ilan University Press, 59–72.
Harari, Yuval. 2012. "The Sword of Moses (Ḥarba de-Moshe): A New Translation and Introduction," *Magic, Ritual, and Witchcraft* 7: 58–98.
Harari, Yuval. 2017. *Jewish Magic before the Rise of Kabbalah*. Detroit, MI: Wayne State University Press.
Jones, Lindsay (ed.). 2005. *Encyclopedia of Religion*, 2nd Edition. Detroit, MI: Thomson Gale.
Kotansky, Roy. 1994. *Greek Magical Amulets: The Inscribed Gold, Silver, Copper, and Bronze* lamellae. Part I: *Published Texts of Known Provenance*. Köln: Westdeutscher Verlag.
Levene, Dan. 2013. *Jewish Aramaic Curse Texts from Late-Antique Mesopotamia: "May These Curses Go Out and Flee"*. Leiden: Brill.
Morgan, Michael A., trans. 1983. *Sepher ha-Razim: The Book of the Mysteries*. Chico, CA: Scholars Press.
Naveh, Joseph and Shaul Shaked. 1985. *Amulets and Magic Bowls: Aramaic Incantations of Late Antiquity*. Jerusalem: Magnes Press.
Naveh, Joseph and Shaul Shaked. 1993. *Magic Spells and Formulae: Aramaic Incantations of Late Antiquity*. Jerusalem: Magnes Press.
Rebiger, Bill and Peter Schäfer. 2009. *Sefer ha-Razim I und II: Das Buch der Geheimnisse I und II*. 2 vols. Tübingen: Mohr Siebeck.
Saar, Ortal-Paz. 2017. *Jewish Love Magic: From Late Antiquity to the Middle Ages*. Leiden: Brill.
Saar, Ortal-Paz. 2021. "Jewish Curse Tablets?," *Religion in the Roman Empire* 7: 149–166.
Schiffman, Lawrence H. and Michael D. Swartz. 1992. *Hebrew and Aramaic Incantation Texts from the Cairo Genizah: Selected Texts from Taylor-Schechter Box k1*. Sheffield: Sheffield Academic Press.
Seligman Jon, Joe Zias, and Harley Stark. 1996. "Late Hellenistic and Byzantine Burial Caves at Giv'at Sharet, Bet Shemesh," *Atiqot* 29: 43–62.
Swartz, Michael D. 1996. *Scholastic Magic: Ritual and Revelation in Early Jewish Mysticism*. Princeton, NJ: Princeton University Press.
Trachtenberg, Joshua. 1939 (reprinted 2004). *Jewish Magic and Superstition: A Study in Folk Religion*. Jerusalem: Sefer Ve Sefel Publishing.
Yadin, Yigael. 1963. *The Finds from the Bar Kokhba Period in the Cave of Letters*. Jerusalem: Israel Exploration Society.

38
DISABILITIES AND INCLUSION

Abigail Uhrman

This discussion deals with individuals with disabilities and their families. While there are numerous examples of successful accommodations in the area of Jewish ritual and practice, a discussion limited to these exemplars would inaccurately and inauthentically reflect the challenges and opportunities of disabilities inclusion in the Jewish community. More than a particular program or intervention, inclusion is a mindset; it is about how to hold diversity and equity as core values and ensure their expression in all aspects of communal life. In that spirit, the chapter explicates the hallmarks of a Jewish inclusive ethos and practice. Included is a discussion of its roots in biblical and rabbinic texts and theology, its form and function in contemporary Jewish life, and examples of successful initiatives.

A Jewish Moral Imperative

The Bible is replete with stories of individuals with disabilities: In his later years, Isaac was blind; Jacob developed a limp after his famed encounter with the "*ish;*" and Moses, the most celebrated leader in the Torah, had a stutter. The list continues (Prouser, 2012). In some instances, the narrative explicitly remarks on these figures' disabilities (Astor, 1985; Prouser, 2012). In others, the disability is merely intimated or suggested by the characters' words and/or behaviors. Regardless, ability does not—at least in biblical times—bar a person from participation and communal leadership. In this way, the Tanakh powerfully models inclusive practice. It also reinforces the benefits of inclusion for the *entire* people, able-bodied and disabled, alike. In renowned disability activist, Shelly Christensen's (2018) retelling of the story of Abraham and the three strangers, she remarks not only on Abraham and Sarah's hospitality toward the unknown "others" but on the news the hosts would have failed to receive had they not welcomed their mysterious guests. What gifts might we miss if we do not open our doors and bring people in? How our lives—individually and collectively—are enriched when we broaden our tents and embrace the "strangers" in our midst. Similarly, when Miriam is separated after contracting leprosy, the Israelites await her return before moving forward in their journey. The camp cannot go on unless all are present, Christensen explains. When even "one member of our community is left behind, we are not whole" (pp. 1–2).

In addition to these biblical heroes and heroines, there are oft-cited biblical phrases and passages that offer further support for disabilities inclusion. God's creation of people in God's image, *b'tzelem Elohim* (Genesis 1:27), is regularly referenced. *All* people, so the text suggests, are fashioned in God's likeness; *all* are infinitely holy and uniquely valuable. Despite later rabbinic discussions that obscure the thrust of this message (discussions of humans' distinguishing features that might exclude some individuals with disabilities from full participation in Jewish ritual life), the *b'tzelem Elohim* precept is, by wide margins, invoked to reinforce the godliness of all humankind and promote the inclusion of marginalized "others."

Later, in Leviticus 19:14, more specific directives are given: "Do not insult the deaf, and do not put a stumbling block before the blind; you shall fear your God. I am the Lord." Beyond the theoretical dictum of *b'tzelem Elohim*, here the community is, in practical terms, obligated to protect the vulnerable.

As the Israelites are on the edge of the Promised Land, Moses again reiterates this sentiment and responsibility.

> You stand on this day, all of you, before the Lord your God … to enter into covenant of the Lord your God … I make this covenant … not with you alone, but with those who are standing here … and with those who are not with us here this day.
> *Deuteronomy 29:9–14*

"All of you," *kulchem*, Moses declares, are part of the covenant. It is not only reserved for the wise, powerful, or connected; it belongs to *every* member of the community, then and now.

The portrait of disabilities in rabbinic literature is somewhat more complex. At various points, the rabbis debated whether people with disabilities could participate in certain rituals and practices and fulfill certain *halachic*, legal, requirements (Belser, 2016). Still, despite these legalistic, rabbinic discussions, a clear and powerful inclusive ethos can be found. The famous Talmudic principle *kol Yisrael arevim zeh lazeh*, all of Israel is responsible for each other (Shevuot 39a), is an apt example. There are no limitations on what this responsibility looks like and to whom it applies; presumably, every person in Israel qualifies. This requirement suggests the interdependence of the community and demands that the needs of all are considered (Uhrman, Holtz, & Kress, 2018). There is even, in Maimonides's Mishneh Torah in *Hilchot Brachot*, a blessing praising difference in the world: "Thank you, God … *mishaneh ha'briyot*, for creating diversity."

In the vast corpus of rabbinic literature, there are numerous other examples of teachings and stories that honor the dignity, inherent worth, and equality of each person. In full recognition of the more troubling biblical and rabbinic texts, there is a strong and compelling case to be made for acceptance and inclusion. The overwhelming, guiding principle is, "supportive of vulnerable people and … seeks to empower the disempowered" (Jones, 2006, p. 8). As noted speaker, educator, consultant, and disabilities activist, Matan Koch, explains, "the single most overriding ethical imperative to all Jews … is that society should not treat people with disabilities as anything other than equal" (Koch, n.d.).

In addition to the clear Jewish imperative, the sheer number of individuals with disabilities lends further support for Jewish inclusion. The data from the 2010 United States Census reveals that over 56.7 million Americans have a disability. This includes: 8% of children under 15; 21% of people 15 and older; 17% of people 21 to 65; and 50% of adults 65 and older (United States Census Bureau, 2012). Similarly, according to the World Health Organization, nearly 200 million people around the world live with disabilities, and the prevalence of disabilities is on the rise (World Health Organization, 2011). If, as is assumed, the Jewish community mirrors the general population, the proportion of Jews with disabilities is significant. As Bill Gaventa (2018), renowned expert in disabilities and faith communities, contends, "The plain facts about the prevalence of disabilities are evidence that people with disabilities and their families are among us. If they are not in your synagogue," he continues, "then that says more about us than it does about them" (p. 18).

Defining Terms

Disabilities is a catch-all term for a number of different conditions. According to the Center for Disease Control, a disability is, "any condition of the body or mind (impairment) that makes it more difficult for the person with the condition to do certain activities (activity limitation) and interact with the world around them (participation restrictions)" (Center for Disease Control, n.d.). A disability can affect a person's movement, thinking, remembering, vision, hearing, learning, communicating, social relationships, and/or mental health. "Although 'people with disabilities' sometimes refers to a single population," it continues, "this is actually a diverse group with a wide range of needs. Two people with the same disability can be affected in different ways. Some disabilities may be hidden or not easy to see." The Center for Disease Control's definition cites the World Health Organization's three dimensions of disability:

1. Impairment in a person's body structure or function, or mental functioning; examples of impairments include loss of a limb, loss of vision or memory loss.
2. Activity limitation, such as difficulty seeing, hearing, walking, or problem solving.
3. Participation restrictions in normal daily activities, such as working, engaging in social and recreational activities, and obtaining health care and preventive services.

Center for Disease Control, n.d.

While the above definition includes mental health conditions, the focus of this chapter is on the other categories of disability. The purpose is not to ignore individuals with mental health conditions; rather, given the array of physical and cognitive impairments that are already subsumed under the disabilities umbrella, and the potentially unique needs of those with psychiatric disabilities and mental health conditions, the hope is that this somewhat more limited discussion will offer a more cohesive and useful overview of Jewish inclusion efforts. That said, many of the best practices identified will have wide application.

An additional point of clarification: Inclusion is a contested term and used to describe a variety of practices (Baglieri et al., 2011; Hicks-Monroe, 2011). For the purposes of this discussion, Shelly Christensen's (2018) definition will be used:

Inclusion extends beyond an open door, a ramp, or special services and activities for people with disabilities. Inclusion means that obstacles to belonging are eliminated. Inclusion makes it possible for all people to participate, rejoice, worship, learn, find comfort and solace in times of need, and contribute to the community.

p. 45

This definition is necessarily broad, with attention on both the "structure of the inclusion," the practices and policies that move a community forward, and the "spirit of belonging," the support, collaboration, and imagination necessary to build communities where all can find a home. This understanding of inclusion encompasses a "continuum" of forms (Schleien et al., 2017). While inclusion can look many different ways, the expressed goal of communal participation, engagement, and belonging is consistent (Chistensen, 2018). Certainly "inclusion," as defined above, is not limited to a specific dimension of diversity; the focus here, however, is on individuals with disabilities and their families.

The Jewish Community: Experiences, Obstacles, and Opportunities

In recent years, the topic of inclusion has taken on greater urgency and is receiving growing attention. There has been a rise in the number of programs and initiatives; in the Reform, Conservative, and Orthodox movements, entire departments have been established and/or expanded to develop resources, supports, and services to meet the needs of individuals with disabilities and their families. An area of particular note is Jewish education. While there remains work to be done, there has been a notable increase in the field's understanding of and responsiveness to diverse learners (Pomson, 2017). Jewish summer camp is often hailed as particularly successful in this regard. Inclusion programs at day and overnight camps have proliferated and the range of participants served broadened (Shefter et al., 2017).

At the same time, there is, both in the "structure of inclusion" as well as the "spirit of belonging," much room to grow. With regard to the former, existing offerings and accommodations for individuals with disabilities and their families remain limited in number and scope. This includes physical barriers to inclusion (i.e. inaccessible spaces that bar or hamper participation of those with limited mobility), communication obstacles (i.e. large print prayer books, Braille prayer books, sign language interpreters, assistive hearing devices, etc.), and insufficient program accommodations (i.e. religious school classes for diverse learners, accessible adult education opportunities, etc.). Although many communities are making significant strides, the progress is regrettably slow. Parents, specifically, have expressed frustration at the pace of change and the inadequate support they and their child/ren receive (Uhrman, 2017). Here, there appear to be notable denominational differences: For less religiously observant parents, many would like their child involved in the Jewish community but have little energy to invest given their other parenting responsibilities. The dearth of opportunities and lack of guidance from the organized Jewish community is discouraging and, as a result, parents are often resigned to minimal Jewish engagement. Few have the wherewithal to explore options beyond those with which they are already familiar and/or that would require additional research and personal and financial investment. Some more observant families express similar disappointment; for this group, however, Jewish involvement is non-negotiable. They are committed to finding ways in for their child and family despite the challenges it might pose (Uhrman, 2017).

Another significant issue vis-à-vis the "structure of instruction" are the supports offered for individuals with disabilities and their families across the lifespan. While the Jewish community has done much to increase and improve the offerings for children with disabilities, there are too few opportunities for these individuals once they "age out" of the community's existing programs (Blas et al., 2015). This is true for the general population, as well; there is a distinct and pressing need to better support individuals into adulthood and throughout their adult lives (Carter, 2016). Here, again, the Jewish camping movement has been at the forefront of work in this area. In addition to the increase in camper-age programs, there has been an effort to provide vocational training for young adults with disabilities (Blas, 2010; Olson, 2017). These initiatives are still limited, but the strides in this area signal a gradual and meaningful shift in the understanding of, and responsiveness to, issues of disabilities inclusion in adulthood.

In addition to the "structure of inclusion," growth is, as mentioned, also needed in the area of the "spirit of belonging." The experiences of individuals with disabilities and their families in the Jewish community are highly uneven. While there are many stories of acceptance, belonging, and support, there is also a

> tough side ... ongoing experiences that have been as hurtful and wounding as the others have been healing and empowering. One inevitably hears from individuals and parents who gave up ... because their requests and efforts led nowhere. Even worse, their experiences conveyed, "You are not welcome here."
>
> *Gaventa, 2018, p. 16*

With little institutional support, these families can feel alone, shunned, and/or marginalized; parents struggle to determine the nature of their families' Jewish lives and find a comfortable, accepting religious and spiritual home (Uhrman, 2017).

These barriers to inclusion can be attributed to a number of misconceptions and attitudinal obstacles. Some common misconceptions include the belief that inclusion is too expensive and there aren't enough funds and/or resources to do this work; there aren't many people with disabilities in their community; the community is already inclusive; people with disabilities might be disruptive during worship; etc. (Christensen, 2018). Attitudinal obstacles similarly impede change. Fostered by individual and cultural biases and misinformation about disabilities, these factors create powerful resistance to change. It also foments the stigma with which individuals with disabilities and their families contend (Christensen, 2018).

Despite these challenges, in most instances, Jewish institutions desire to be inclusive, but they are unaware of their limitations and/or do not yet know how to appropriately welcome those with differing needs into their communities (Christensen, 2018). Many parents, for example, find that inattention to disability issues is more a result of lack of awareness and "benign neglect" than "malicious intent" (Uhrman, 2017). An area of note, here, is clergy: Although interactions with Jewish professionals is mixed, most found that rabbis and cantors—when prodded—were receptive and helpful, welcoming advice and guidance to best meet the needs of their congregants. Seminaries have, in recent years, made a concerted effort to raise the profile of these issues in their training programs, and albeit gradual, the needle seems to slowly be moving (Christensen, 2017).

The complexity of the portrait notwithstanding, there is growing empirical support for the importance of this work and its continued progress. Numerous studies

> affirm the significance of faith and congregational connections in the lives of people with disabilities and their families ... Yet the inclusion of people with ... disabilities in faith communities across the United States remains uneven, and many ... still struggle to envision what it might look like to welcome this segment of their community well.
>
> *Carter, 2016, p. 168*

The "sense of connection and membership that might emerge," however, meaningfully "contribute[s] to their own flourishing in faith and life" (Carter, 2016, p. 179).

Beyond benefits to the individual, inclusion can benefit the entire family unit, as well. As family systems theory suggests, the family is the primary and, possibly, most powerful system to which a person belongs. The unique relationships and interactions within the family have deep, lasting implications for the development and adjustment of *all* family members (Turnbull et al., 2006). Engagement in Jewish life is no exception, and Jewish educational decisions are an apropos case in point: Parents' religious educational decisions are about more than just the child—they involve parents' beliefs about their children, their worldview, their relationships to others, and reflect the ways in which families envision their Jewishness and Jewish identity (Bulman, 2004; Goldring & Phillips, 2008; Pomson, 2007; Pomson & Schnoor, 2008; Smrekar & Goldring, 1999). Parents' experiences with their child's Jewish education, then, have far-reaching implications for parents' own lives and their family's Jewish connections.

This understanding is further supported by the work of psychologist Urie Bronfenbrenner (1979) and his Ecological Systems Theory. In his research, Bronfenbrenner describes four nested systems and the ways in which they interact to influence human development: the microsystem—the people and settings in which an individual has direct contact, such a family members and peers; the mesosystem—the relationships between various parts of the microsystem, such as the interaction between the family and the religious institutions with which they are affiliated; the exosystem—the systems in which the individual does not directly participate but, nonetheless, have implications for development such as a family member's workplace; and the macrosystem—the broader cultural and social milieu in which a person lives and operates and the societal norms, beliefs, expectations, and assumptions that shape an individual's experience and development. Although Bronfenbrenner's (1979) research concluded here, a fifth system, the chronosystem, was later added to his theory. Accordingly, individuals are not only influenced by their immediate settings and relationships, but past experiences have developmental impact and resonance for the current moment as well as future developmental potential. A parent's own religious experiences, for example, may have long-term influence on their parenting decisions.

Per both Family Systems and Bronfenbrenner's theories, development is deeply influenced by myriad factors including a range of settings, relationships, and interactions. Whether directly or indirectly connected to the individual, the various systems and their dynamic interactions all shape a person's perspectives, beliefs, and behaviors. The connections are infinitely complex, and despite the ever-present messiness of these interactions, the influence that an individual with a disability can have on the religious lives and engagement of their family is clear. The need for inclusion, then, has expansive implications in the lives of Jewish families.

Research also supports the positive impact that inclusion efforts have on the broader community (Blas, 2010; Kopelowitz, 2013). In interacting with individuals with disabilities, neurotypical individuals report greater comfort with individuals with disabilities and more awareness of disability issues (Kopelowitz, 2013; Singfer, Kress, & Uhrman, 2018). There is also a strong sense that religious institutions are "incomplete without the gifts and faith of people with disabilities. When purposeful and person-centered," there is much to gain from enabling a diversity of people to, "flourish in community together" (Carter, 2016, p. 168). There are many impediments, but there is much support for sustaining a commitment to realizing a more inclusive Jewish future.

Building Blocks of Successful Inclusion

There are numerous examples of Jewish organizational, educational, and spiritual leaders who have prepared their staff, anticipated roadblocks and push-back, and creatively addressed multiple needs with limited resources. In reviewing these institutions, a number of common themes emerge (Kress & Uhrman, 2018).

Power of (Outside) Partnerships

By and large, most institutions do not go it alone. The journey toward inclusion involves both external expertise (often in the form of local or national organizations) and additional funding. As sites' experience with inclusion grows, leaders consider how much of these external resources could be internalized and what functions are best filled through an ongoing external relationship.

One of the most striking examples is the work of the Ruderman Family Foundation and their many collaborations and contributions to Jewish organizational life. The foundation's mission is to "advocate for and advance the inclusion of people with disabilities throughout our society" (Ruderman Family Foundation, n.d.) and, until recently, they have devoted significant resources to furthering this work in the Jewish community.

One of Ruderman's many projects was with USCJ, the umbrella organization for Conservative movement-affiliated congregations. In 2015, the USCJ Ruderman Inclusion Action Community was formed. This program provided cohorts of synagogues expert consultation on inclusive practices and assisted congregations in developing cohesive visions and action plans (USCJ, n.d.). The initiative had broad aims to:

> foster inclusivity within all aspects of congregational community from the entryway to the *bima* (platform) …; from educational programs to prayer services; from social activities to the perceptions and attitudes of congregants and leaders … to ensure that people with disabilities and their families fully and comfortably participate in congregational life.
>
> *USCJ, n.d.*

As a result of this partnership, inclusion, especially in the area of ritual and practice, became an area of real priority for many Conservative congregations. Professional and lay leaders worked in tandem to create and/or expand their inclusion committees, write or revise their inclusion mission statement, conduct a congregational needs assessment, and develop a robust action plan. As a result, many synagogues were able to offer greater accommodations. These included a wide array of improvements ranging from architectural remodels to expanded resources and materials. Most significantly, it changed the inclusion conversation; by raising the profile of inclusion, the initiative ignited meaningful discussions about individuals with disabilities and their families in synagogue policies, practices, and all other aspects of religious life.

Persistent Parents

In many cases, parents push an institution to provide the services needed for their child/ren (Novick & Glanz, 2011). Inclusion takes on a face; it is no longer an abstract idea. Concrete planning can occur, moving the discussion beyond "what if?" worries about roadblocks. The efforts that are most successful purposely work toward getting buy-in from a wide range of stakeholders. This ensures that inclusion isn't just championed by the parent that spearheaded the effort, but it is something for which a number of people advocate.

The experiences of families with school-age children best illustrate this trend. As has historically been the case, many Jewish educational programs operate under a "one-size-fits-all" model: Designed to accommodate a limited spectrum of neurotypical children's needs, with minimal variation on either side, parents can choose to opt-in to the existing program or not. There are countless stories, however, of parents with a child with a disability who have pushed back. To ensure that their child be afforded these Jewish educational opportunities, they have worked with the institutions to find ways to accommodate their child's unique needs. These persistent parents have helped spawn a number of new initiatives: Camps have included a wider diversity of campers; schools have broadened their reach; and b'nei mitzvah ceremonies have been retooled for greater flexibility. The concern here is the longevity and sustainability of these efforts. The centrality of individual parents in driving the process raises questions about what needs to happen in order to continue these programs and initiatives beyond the individual child and family.

Integration

While inclusion might begin with a single learner, best practice suggests that inclusion not be treated in isolation. Rather, inclusion must be linked holistically and authentically both to the central values articulated by a site and into the ongoing administrative structure. As Jewish institutions embark on their process, inclusion is most successful when organically and intentionally incorporated into their mission and vision. In these cases, diversity is understood as a value-added to their program, helping them further achieve their religious, spiritual, social, and programmatic goals. Add-ons are at risk for being cut off; integration is crucial for success. Connection to core priorities is an ongoing process; leaders need to maintain their focus on inclusion over time and in the face of other initiatives and demands on resources.

There are a number of powerful examples of integration across Jewish organizational life. Mission statements with inclusion at their core are but one hallmark of organizations that embody this stance. When inclusion is central to the institution's foundational ethos, there is far greater potential that it continually be considered. Some possible extensions of this integrated vision might include: membership applications and information that boldly communicate the institution's inclusive vision; an active inclusion committee in which members serve in a range of other leadership roles throughout the organization; specified budget lines to fund needed building improvements, materials, resources, and personnel to further the institution's inclusion mission; etc. (Christensen, 2018).

Powerful Leadership

The site leadership plays a crucial role in ensuring that inclusion remains a priority. These leaders often have a personal passion for or connection to disability and are able to provide a narrative that integrates work in this area with the core priorities of the institution. The trust that they inspire in their constituents helps maintain momentum even when inevitable bumps in the road are encountered. Leaders mobilize allies among both staff and lay leadership.

Although there remains much work to be done in this area, changes in rabbinical and cantorial training programs reflect the value of powerful leadership. In recent years, seminaries have instituted new courses and seminars devoted to issues of inclusion. For example, Yeshivat Chovevei Torah, a Modern Orthodox rabbinical school, requires a "weeklong, immersive, and multi-dimensional program" with the expressed goal of developing "activists in the area of disabilities" (Yeshivat Chovevei Torah, n.d.). Other schools have similar initiatives of varying intensity.

There are also a number of rabbis in the field who are working to champion this cause. This includes rabbis, cantors, and educators across the denominational spectrum and many of whom have disabilities themselves. These individuals have been outspoken about the need for greater awareness, sensitivity, and accommodations and have advocated for meaningful change in their immediate communities and in the Jewish world more broadly. But one example is Ruti Regan, a Conservative rabbi and disabled disability advocate. "We have something important to offer the world," she explains. "Our Torah is worth celebrating … If we embrace accessibility as a sacred practice … barriers need not be insurmountable. Accessibility is not optional, and our people with disabilities are not disposable" (*The New York Jewish Week*, 2019).

Range of Models to Meet Varied Needs

"Inclusion" manifests at these sites in multiple ways; the realities of meeting the needs of a range of individuals preclude a one-size-fits-all approach, or doctrinaire adherence to a particular theory of inclusion. In fact, multiple modes are often implemented even within the same site, and the person with disabilities and their family dictate the evolution of the accommodation or program.

Here, too, there are countless examples in the Jewish community. Howard Blas's work on b'nei mitzvah is an especially apt model of this theme at work. Over the years, Blas has trained numerous children with disabilities for their b'nei mitzvah ceremonies. As he frequently reminds families, one "becomes" a bar/bat mitzvah; one doesn't "have" a bar/bat mitzvah or "get" bar/bat mitzvah-ed, allowing them latitude to reimagine this rite of passage. In conversation with the child and parents, Blas offers a range of options to explore: non-Saturday ceremonies, different venues, creative events, etc. Nothing is off the table. His only qualification is that the bar not be set either too high or too low; understanding that these young people have many gifts, he wants to ensure that the program is tailored to their unique needs, skills, and talents. Some examples of Blas-guided b'nei mitzvah have included: a PowerPoint bat mitzvah, an art exhibit celebration, a service in Israel, and a ceremony at summer camp (H. Blas, personal communication, January 2021).

Patience and Organizational Learning

The above themes emerge from the stories of inclusive Jewish institutions (Kress & Uhrman, 2018). At the same time that these elements promote action in the sites, they pose challenges. Where will resources come from? If we are meeting the needs of the children of persistent parents, what about the needs of families that might have a harder time making their voices heard? How can inclusion stay pinned to the list of high priorities in the face of never-ending demands for other institutional changes?

Inclusion is a pressing concern, but those looking for a quick fix will inevitably be disappointed. The most successful sites take a long view, learning as they go and being willing to experiment. "Getting it right" is an oversimplification; the answer to the question of the "right" approach for a setting evolves over time. Challenges and setbacks are a part of the process. The questions in the previous paragraph need to be asked, to suggest that their answer requires an ongoing process of learning within an organization.

Bright Spots

As alluded to throughout, there is some wonderful work being done vis-à-vis Jewish ritual and practice for individuals with disabilities and their families. Due to the wide range of individual and family needs, many different efforts and initiatives reflect progress in this area. Below, broad categories of accommodations are discussed with specific examples in each.

Structural and Architectural Improvements

The Americans with Disabilities Act (ADA), signed into law in 1990, is considered the most comprehensive federal civil rights legislations for people with disabilities (ADA National

Network, n.d.). Title III of the ADA discusses the accessibility of public spaces. Although religious organizations are exempt from this provision, many Jewish institutions have invested in structural and architectural improvements.

Some improvements have been extensive: Entire remodels of synagogues' sanctuary and classroom spaces, elevators added for full building access, bathroom renovations to allow for wheelchair accessibility, etc. In some cases, sensory rooms have been created. Sensory rooms are therapeutic spaces with an array of equipment that provide individuals with disabilities personalized sensory input; they are used to help children focus and calm themselves so that they are better prepared for prayer, learning, and social interaction. Items included in a sensory room can vary; they may include yoga balls, manipulatives, mirror walls, light walls, body socks, and swings (Ray, 2017). Sensory rooms can range in size and scope; some congregations use a shared space, and others have built entirely new areas for this expressed purpose.

Other renovations have been more limited in reach, requiring fewer resources and/or funding. These include building ramps or installing lifts to ensure full access to the *bima* (the raised platform from where services are led), creating accessible *amuds* (the podium used for leading prayers and chanting Torah) that can be raised and lowered, and designating cut-out seating areas in various locations throughout a prayer room or program area for wheelchair users.

To be sure, the list of structural and architectural changes is far more expansive; above are but a few of the many accommodations that have made the buildings and physical spaces of Jewish organizations more accessible and inclusive.

Prayer

The accommodations in the area of prayer are extensive. The responses of different communities vary depending on a number of factors, including the particular institutions' *halachic* considerations. That said, by wide margins, clergy and educators across the religious and denominational spectrum have met the challenge of inclusion with care, attention, and creativity.

Before even entering the prayer space, congregations have considered their inclusive practices. Many have trained greeters at the door, welcoming people and serving as a resource as needed. A number have also created accessibility carts (J. Gendel, personal communication, January 2021). On these carts, placed outside the entrance to the chapel or sanctuary, are a number of items and resources to encourage the full participation of a range of members in the prayer service. Items might include reading glasses, fidget toys, social stories, noise-canceling headphones, directions to a quiet or sensory room and accessible bathrooms, books and games for young children, etc. The goal is to not only provide resources for individuals with disabilities and their families but also to promote institutions' inclusive stance; this is but one way that communities signal the importance of inclusion to their constituents and visitors.

Synagogues often offer large print *siddurim* (prayer books) for those who need them. Some also have a Braille *siddur* available, although given their expense and size, this is a rarer find (L. Tuchman, personal communication, January 2021). In some cases, new *siddurim* have been written and designed to meet the needs of people with disabilities: For example, an online *siddur* for children with learning disabilities was created (Frazer, 2020). Using text and pictures, this *siddur* is more user-friendly and inviting. Camps have also invested in making accessible *siddurim*. While the content and format vary, all provide multiple points of entry for their campers with disabilities (H. Blas, personal communication, January 2021).

To engage the deaf and hard of hearing in the prayer experience, synagogues have responded with a range of accommodations: hearing devices, captioning services, sign language interpreters, hearing loops, etc. (J. Gendel, personal communication, January 2021).

Some synagogues have also refined and/or recommunicated their policies vis-à-vis noise and food in the sanctuary or chapel. Many have official statements expressing their open acceptance of what may otherwise be seen as vocal disturbances or distractions and their allowance of snacks and drinks, as necessary. For younger children (including neurotypical children), communities have created designated "prayground" spaces, play space areas in the adult prayer service with chairs, toys, and books so that parents can participate while watching and helping their children.

Daily and Lifecycle Rituals

Here, too, the accommodations are vast. An example of an adaptation of a daily ritual is lowering the height of *mezuzot*, the cases and scrolls affixed to the doorposts of a house or building and the entryways to each room. It is customary to touch a *mezuzah* and kiss the fingers that touched it upon entering a space. They often, however, are placed higher up on the doorpost, making access difficult for some members of the community. In recent years, there have been a number of initiatives to move the *mezuzah* down so that more people can participate in and fulfill this *mitzvah*, religious commandment or obligation.

Stories of adapted lifecycle ceremonies abound. As discussed earlier, b'nei mitzvah are the most apt example; there are myriad ways in which b'nei mitzvah have been reimagined to meet a wider spectrum of needs (Blas, 2010; Vogel & Reiter, 2003). The same is true for other lifecycle events, although these efforts are seemingly less extensive and, like many other examples of successful accommodations, highly individualized.

Future Directions

There has been marked progress in the inclusion of individuals with disabilities and their families in the Jewish community in recent years. There remains, however, ample room for growth. Although not an exhaustive list, this includes expanding services to meet the needs of individuals across the lifespan, systemic coordination of inclusion efforts, greater integration of the value inclusion into all aspects of organizational life, a more robust research agenda, and, finally, further emphasis on the "spirit of belonging" within Jewish institutions.

The primary emphasis in many Jewish institutions is school-age children and their families. Even in these instances efforts often fall short. Still, there is an accepted understanding of the need to include this constituent group. There is relatively little attention, however, to the experiences of adults with disabilities in the Jewish community (Blas et al., 2015). Despite the examples above, there are few larger scale religious and educational programs for people of different ages and stages of life. A concerted attempt to address this gap in services would go a long way in welcoming in and benefitting from the participation of this considerable group.

As mentioned, many initiatives are the result of work and dedication of a single person. While these initiatives can yield meaningful results, it is critical that organizations consider how they might encourage systemic, rather than merely episodic, change. This requires that institutions reaffirm their inclusion commitments: In order for inclusion to permeate an organization and transform institutional culture and practice, it must be prioritized in the mission and on the communal agenda. It also requires coordination among various groups and arms of the Jewish community. Such coordination will not only elevate the importance of inclusion in all areas of Jewish life, but it will also allow for the sharing and leveraging of communal resources.

Research is yet another area ripe for growth. Existing scholarship is extremely limited; there are few studies that explore issues of disability inclusion in organized Jewish life. A comprehensive research agenda might include a widescale needs assessment, helping to identify what services, programs, and resources are currently available and what might be needed for inclusion to meaningfully take root. Documentation, documenting the stories of individuals with disabilities and their families and chronicling their experiences systematically across the population, could also be instructive. Not only could such work build awareness about disability issues, but it could also serve to mobilize the community to change. Finally, the Jewish community could benefit from further engagement with non-Jewish faith communities vis-à-vis these issues. While there are some attempts to foster inter-religious connections, there are many more opportunities to do so. In particular, the research literature on disabilities in these other religious traditions is far more developed; a closer look at the findings might surface some meaningful insights.

Last, as has been the theme throughout, there is room for improvement in further engendering a "spirit of belonging" in Jewish communal life. An area of particular note is listening to the voices of individuals with disabilities in the Jewish community. As Lauren Tuchman, believed to be the first blind rabbi, relates:

> Inclusion work is often challenging. We must always encounter the work with a sense of holy responsibility and deep humility, being willing to partner with Jews with disabilities, who are the experts on their own lives and asking them what it is they want from Jewish life. Too often we look at a person with a disability and assume that it would be too expensive, burdensome or resource-heavy to include them. What we fail to ask is, what message are we sending about Jewish communal belonging when we exclude?

Tuchman recognizes the "increasing number of synagogues engaged wholeheartedly in access and inclusion … both on the individual level and as part of larger cohorts of communities within each movement of Judaism. Nevertheless," she explains, "the work is far from done" (*The New York Jewish Week*, 2019).

Conclusion

For the entire Jewish community, the potential benefits of engaging in the work of inclusion are immeasurable, and the religious and moral imperative is widely evident. Gaventa's (2018) reflections are instructive here:

> In a world determined to highlight differences and division, to prove that some are in, and others are out, people of faith have the opportunity and capacity to say and show, "That's not what God's people are about. Here, everyone's in, if they want to be, because God created each of us."
>
> p. 18

Inclusion has powerful roots in Jewish history and consciousness, and the Jewish community today must continue to work to fully realize this vision. The Jewish community has an obligation to heed Gaventa's words.

As it says in Pirkei Avot 2:21, "*Lo alecha hamlacha ligmor, v'lo ata ben chorim l'hibatil mimena.*" "You are not expected to complete the task, but neither are you free to avoid it." Yes, the task is great and goals ambitious, but the possibilities are endless and infinitely sustaining.

References

ADA National Network. n.d. *Religious entities under the Americans With Disabilities Act.* https://adata.org/factsheet/religious-entities-under-americans-disabilities-act

Astor, C. 1985. *Who Makes People Different: Jewish Perspectives on the Disabled.* New York: United Synagogue of America.

Baglieri, S., Valle, J. W., Connor, D. J., & Gallagher, D. J. 2011. "Disability studies in education: The need for a plurality of perspectives on disability." *Remedial and Special Education* 32(4): 267–78.

Belser, J. 2016. "Judaism and Disability." In D. Y. Schumm & M. Stoltzfus, Eds., *Disability and World Religions: An Introduction.* Waco, TX: Baylor University Press, 93–114.

Blas, H. I. 2010. "Campers with Developmental Disabilities: The Tikvah Program." In M. Cohen & J. S. Kress, Eds. *Ramah at 60: Impact and Innovation.* New York: Jewish Theological Seminary, 209–27.

Blas, H., Kirshner, D. F., Remz, A., Ruskay-Kidd, I., & Uhrman, A. 2015. *Disabilities, Inclusion, and Jewish Education.* New York.

Bronfenbrenner, U. 1979. *The Ecology of Human Development: Experiments by Nature and Design.* Cambridge, MA: Harvard University Press.

Bulman, R. C. 2004. "School choice stories: The role of culture." *Sociological Inquiry* 74: 492–519.

Carter, E. W. 2016. "A place of belonging: Research at the intersection of faith and disability." *Review and Expositor* 113(2): 167–80.

Center for Disease Control. n.d. *Disability and Health Overview.* www.cdc.gov/ncbddd/disabilityandhealth/disability.html

Christensen, S. 2018. *From Longing to Belonging.* Inclusion Innovations.

Frazer, J. 2020. "Groundbreaking siddur for people with learning disabilities and autism launched." *The New York Jewish Week.* December 20. https://jewishnews.timesofisrael.com/groundbreaking-siddur-for-people-with-learning-disabilities-and-autism-launched

Gaventa, B. 2018. "Foreword." In S. Christensen, *From Longing to Belonging.* Inclusion Innovations, 15–19.

Goldring, E. & Phillips, K. 2008. "Parental preferences and parent choices: The public-private decision about school choice." *Journal of Educational Policy* 23: 209–30.

Hicks-Monroe, S. L. 2011. "A review of research on the educational benefits of the inclusive model of education for special education students." *Journal of the American Academy of Special Education Professionals* 61–69.

Jones, M. 2006. "Judaism, theology & the human rights of people with disabilities." *Journal of Religion, Disability & Health* 1–60.

Koch, M. n.d. *Igniting a fire for universal inclusion.* www.matankoch.com

Kopelowitz, E. 2013. *The Impact of Ramah programs for children, teens, and young adults with disabilities.* www.campramah.org/pdf/final_report_research_ramah_special_needs_programs_web.pdf

Kress, J. & Uhrman, A. 2018. *Profiles of Diversity.* New York: William Davidson Graduate School of Education, Jewish Theological Seminary.

Novick, R. M. & Glanz, J. 2011. "Special Education: 'And You Shall Do That Which Is Right and Good …'." In H. Miller, L. Grant, & A. Pomson, Eds. *International Handbook of Jewish Education.* Dordrecht: Springer, 959–80.

Olson, D. 2017. "It's off to work we go: Attitude toward disability at vocational training programs at Jewish summer camps." *Journal of Jewish Education* 83(1): 27–48.

Pomson, A. 2007. "Schools for Parents: What Parents Want and What they Get from Their Children's Jewish Education." In J. Wertheimer, Ed. *Family Matters: Jewish Education in an Age of Choice.* Waltham, MA: Brandeis University Press, 101–43.

Pomson, A. 2017. "Special needs in Jewish education: Making a start, after 80 years." *Journal of Jewish Education* 83(1): 1–3.

Pomson, A. & Schnoor, R. F. 2008. *Back to School: Jewish Day School in the Lives of Adult Jews.* Detroit, MI: Wayne State University Press.

Prouser, O. H. 2012. *Esau's Blessing: How the Bible Embraces Those with Special Needs.* Ben Yehuda Press.

Ray, B. 2017. "Sensory Room 101." *Edutopia,* June 28. www.edutopia.org/article/sensory-room-101-betty-ray

Ruderman Family Foundation. n.d. *Our Story.* https://rudermanfoundation.org/about-us/our-story/

Schleien, S. J., Miller, K. D., Walton, G., Roth, C., & Tobin, L. 2017. "Inclusive camp: Making summer camp a joyful place for everyone." *Camping Magazine* 90(5): 22–4.

Shefter, L., Uhrman, A. L., Tobin, L., & Kress, J. S. 2017. "Inclusion coordinators at Jewish summer camps: Roles and challenges." *Journal of Jewish Education* 83(1): 69–84.

Singfer, D., Kress, J. S., & Uhrman, A. L. 2018. *Staffing Tikvah: Results of a Survey of Past Tikvah Staff.* New York: William Davidson Graduate School of Jewish Education – JTS.

Smrekar, C. & Goldring, E. 1999. *School Choice in Urban America: Magnet Schools and the Pursuit of Equity.* Williston, VT: Teachers College Press.

The New York Jewish Week. 2019. "Eight Jews with Disabilities Explain How Communities Fall Short on Inclusion." February 17. https://jewishweek.timesofisrael.com/8-jews-with-disabilities-explain-how-communities-fall-short-on-inclusion/

Turnbull, A., Turnbull, R., Erwin, E. J. & Soodak, L. C. 2006. *Families, Professionals, and Exceptionalities: Positive Outcomes through Partnerships and Trust* (5th ed.). Columbus, OH: Merrill Prentice Hall.

Uhrman, A. L. 2017. "The parent perspective: Disability and Jewish day schools." *Journal of Jewish Education* 83(1): 4–26.

Uhrman, A., Holtz, B., & Kress, J. 2018. "Embracing diversity while building Jewish community: An imperative." *Gleanings* 5(3): 4–6.

United States Census Bureau. 2012. "Nearly 1 in 5 people have a disability in the U.S., Census Bureau reports." www.census.gov/newsroom/releases/archives/miscellaneous/cb12-134.html

USCJ. n.d. *Disability Inclusion.* https://uscj.org/leadership/ruderman-inclusion-action-community

Vogel, G. & Reiter, S. 2003. "Spiritual dimensions of bar/bat mitzvah ceremonies for Jewish children with developmental disabilities." *Education and Training in Developmental Disabilities* 38(3): 314–22.

World Health Organization. 2001. *World Report on Disability.* www.who.int/disabilities/world_report/2011/report.pdf

Yeshivat Chovevei Torah. *Mission and Major Achievements.* www.yctorah.org/about/mission-and-major-accomplishments

39

THE EARLY CHRISTIAN RECEPTION OF JEWISH RITUALS DURING THE "PARTING OF THE WAYS"

Paul A. Hartog

In academic discourse, the "parting of the ways" refers to the process of earliest Christianity becoming a distinct movement, differentiated from its Jewish roots.[1] This process affected rituals, as early Christians both adapted existing Jewish rituals and formed their own distinctive rituals. This two-fold nature of development (reception and differentiation) is reflected in numerous early Christian texts, but this essay will focus upon examples found in the Book of Acts, as further illustrated by materials in the so-called "Apostolic Fathers."

The Book of Acts does not represent a comprehensive history of earliest Christianity, but rather serves as a highly selective rendition of the growth of the early Jesus movement (from roughly 30 to the early 60s CE).[2] In particular, Acts focuses upon the ministries of the Apostle Peter and the Apostle Paul. Peter was viewed as "the apostle to the circumcised" (Jews), and Paul as "the apostle to the uncircumcised" (Gentiles).[3] Initially, the disciples only proclaimed the Christian message to fellow Jews (Acts 11:19).[4] Early on, both Jews and Gentiles conceived of the Jesus movement as a sectarian development within Judaism, and its adherents were known as followers of "the Way" and as "the sect of the Nazarenes" (Acts 9:2; 19:9, 23; 24:5, 14, 22; 28:22).[5] Yet the Book of Acts also reflects tensions between the Jesus movement and its early Jewish framework.

This dual nature of rooted reception and identity differentiation affected the adaptation of Jewish ritual traditions. On the one hand, the early Jesus movement inherited customs and rituals from its Jewish roots (Acts 28:17).[6] On the other hand, the movement increasingly sought to distinguish itself from that received inheritance (Acts 15:1, 5).[7] The proto-martyr Stephen was accused of changing "the customs that Moses delivered to us" (Acts 6:14), and Paul was accused of teaching "all the Jews who are among the Gentiles to forsake Moses, telling them not to circumcise their children or walk according to our customs" (Acts 21:21, 28). Paul was also accused of "teaching everyone everywhere against the people [the Jews] and the law and this place [the Temple]" (Acts 21:28), which he denied (Acts 28:17).[8]

A key turning point was the so-called "Jerusalem Council" (or "Jerusalem Assembly") of 49 CE, which concluded that circumcision was not required of Gentile converts (Acts 15). Historians also point to the destruction of Jerusalem and its Temple (70 CE) and to the Bar Kochba revolt (132–135 CE) as other key impetuses in "the parting of the ways."[9] In general, the ritualistic differentiation between Christianity and Judaism became more pronounced as early Christianity progressed through the second century. Many (though not all) of the works included among the so-called "Apostolic Fathers" were written within the second century, and this essay will further illustrate trajectories using examples from that collection.[10] Ignatius of Antioch, who is classed among the Apostolic Fathers, resolutely contrasted the specific terms of "Christianity" and "Judaism" (Ign. *Magn.* 10.1–3; Ign. *Phld.* 6.1).[11]

Prayer and Temple Worship

Acts records that the earliest disciples "were devoting themselves to prayer" (1:14), undoubtedly a continuation of the Jewish practice of *tefillah*.[12] In Jewish tradition, the Jerusalem Temple served as a locus of worshipful prayer (Isa. 56:7; cf. 1 Macc. 12:11; Josephus, *C. Ap.* 2.193–98), and this tradition continued in Acts (22:17).[13] As a specific example, the apostles Peter and John "were going to the temple at the hour of prayer, the ninth hour" (Acts 3:1; cf. Josephus, *A.J.* 14.65). According to Acts 6: 4, the apostles devoted themselves "to prayer and to the ministry of the word." The centurion Cornelius, a Godfearer, "prayed continually to God" (Acts 10:2).[14] Like the apostles, Cornelius purposefully prayed "at the ninth hour" (Acts 10:30). The twelfth chapter of Acts recounts a specific prayer meeting, held in a Jerusalem home (Acts 12:12). While imprisoned in Philippi, Paul and Silas spent the night "praying and singing hymns to God" (Acts 16:25). Later in Acts, Paul "knelt down and prayed" with the elders of the Ephesian church (Acts 20:36). The Book of Acts thus reflects not only a general continuation of the Jewish practice of prayer, but also the perpetuation of some particulars, such as set times of intentional prayer (Acts 3:1; 10:30; cf. Dan. 9:21; Jdt. 9:1).[15]

According to Acts, some early Christians continued to visit the Jerusalem Temple, even while also meeting together in their homes: "day by day, attending the temple together and breaking bread in their homes" (Acts 2:46–47).[16] Acts 3 relates that the apostles Peter and John attended the Temple, and the crowd that subsequently gathered made its way to Solomon's Portico (Acts 3:11).[17] Two chapters later, the apostles reappear in the Temple in Solomon's Portico (Acts 5:12), teaching the people (5:25).

At the same time, the Book of Acts represents a reorientation of worship, as the early Christians moved away from Temple-centrality.[18] To buttress this change of orientation, Stephen tapped into echoes from the Hebrew Scriptures regarding God's transcendence, as he insisted that "the Most High does not dwell in houses made by hands" (Acts 7:48; Cf. 1 Kings 8:27; Isa. 66:1–2). Paul similarly declared to the Athenians that "The God who made the world and everything in it, being Lord of heaven and earth, does not live in temples made by man" (Acts 17:24).

The Temple is not a locus of Christian worship within the Apostolic Fathers.[19] In Ignatius, Jesus himself is metaphorically depicted as both Temple and high priest.[20] Nevertheless, the common theme of prayer naturally reappears throughout the Apostolic Fathers.[21] Peter Tomson has argued that the "Lord's Prayer" (as reflected in Matthew, Luke, and the *Didache*) became "a Christian boundary marker at the rupture that occurred between Jews and Christians," as did the rabbinic prayer of eighteen benedictions.[22] *Didache* 8.2–3 recommends praying the "Lord's Prayer" three times daily.

Sabbaths

The Book of Acts mentions the observance of Jewish festivals, including the Day of Atonement, the days of Unleavened Bread, Passover, and Pentecost (Acts 12:2–4; 20:6–7, 16; 27:9). In Acts

20, Paul hastened from the coast of Asia Minor to Jerusalem, in order to arrive by Pentecost (Acts 20:16). According to Acts 2, the earliest Jesus followers were gathered in an upper room on Pentecost (Acts 2:1) when they experienced the "baptism by the Holy Spirit." They then preached to a crowd of Jews and proselytes gathered at Jerusalem for the festival (Acts 2:11). In the Christian accounting (later reflected in the Christian liturgical calendar), Pentecost became the celebration of the giving of the Holy Spirit and the foundation of the Church as a Spirit-filled community.

Acts also interacts with traditions and practices of the Jewish Sabbath (cf. Acts 1:12). Barnabas and Paul visited the synagogue of Pisidian Antioch "on the Sabbath day" (Acts 13:14). After the customary reading of the Law and the prophets, the synagogue rulers invited the visitors to share "any word of encouragement" (Acts 13:15). Some of the hearers urged them to return the next Sabbath (Acts 13:42–43), and a large crowd gathered the following Sabbath (Acts 13:44). In Acts 16, Paul and Timothy went to the riverside outside the city gates of Philippi on the Sabbath, where they found a group of women worshiping God (Acts 16:13–14). Based upon this narrative, many biblical scholars assume that the Roman colony of Philippi did not have a functioning synagogue at the time.[23] In Thessalonica, Paul attended synagogue services over the course of three Sabbaths (Acts 17:2), and in Corinth "he reasoned in the synagogue every Sabbath" (Acts 18:4).

Nevertheless, with the "parting of the ways" between the early Jesus movement and its Jewish roots, Christians generally moved toward Sunday worship rather than Sabbath observance. Such First Day observance appears briefly in Acts. Chapter 20 mentions a Christian gathering "on the first day of the week," in which the attendees assembled "to break bread" and to listen to Paul's teaching (Acts 20:7). A few other New Testament texts (1 Cor. 16:2; Rev. 1:10) reflect Sunday worship, but the shift becomes even clearer in the Apostolic Fathers (Ign. *Magn.* 9.1; *Did.* 14.1; *Barn.* 15.6–8). Justin Martyr explained,

> But Sunday is the day on which we all hold our common assembly, because it is the first day on which God, having wrought a change in the darkness and matter, made the world; and Jesus Christ our Saviour on the same day rose from the dead.
> *Justin, 1 Apol. 67; cf. Justin, 2 Apol. 41*[24]

While the Pauline Epistles seem to frame Sabbath observance vs. non-observance as a non-issue (Col. 2:16; cf. Rom. 14:5–6), some Apostolic Fathers portrayed Sabbath keeping in a very negative tenor (*Barn.* 2.5; 15.8; *Diogn.* 4.1–3; cf. Aristides, *Apol.* 14).

Liturgy and Scripture Reading

A summary of early Christian worship appears in Acts 2:42: "And they devoted themselves to the apostles' teaching and the fellowship, to the breaking of bread and the prayers." Undoubtedly, facets of this early Christian worship (such as teaching from the Scriptures) would have been inherited from Jewish worship practices.[25] The earliest Christians would have been familiar with the worship practices of the Jewish synagogue.[26] Whenever the converted Paul came to a new city in his missionary travels, his *modus operandi* was to visit the local synagogue, seeking opportunity to proclaim "the word of God" through the lens of his new faith in Jesus of Nazareth (Acts 9:20; 13:5; 14:1; 17:10; 19:8). His "preaching boldly in the name of the Lord" naturally led to tension and even conflict (Acts 9:28). Yet Paul's familiarity with synagogue worship was not peculiar. Apollos was also "competent in the Scriptures," and he addressed synagogue assemblies as well (Acts 18:24–26).

While Acts does not provide a comprehensive description of an early church service, the liturgical core seems to have included prayer, teaching from the Scriptures, and the "breaking of bread" (probably a reference to a celebration of the "Lord's Supper," perhaps integrated with a full communal meal) (Acts 2:42; 20:7).[27] The "breaking of bread" as a formative rite (the "Eucharist") is accentuated in the Apostolic Fathers (*Did.* 9–10).[28] The *Didache* portrays participation in the Eucharistic meal through the lens of ritual purity, exhorting its readers not to give that which is holy to "the dogs."[29] The *Didache* insists upon baptism as a prerequisite for Eucharistic participation (*Did.* 10), as well as the regular confession of transgressions in order to ensure a "pure sacrifice" (*Did.* 14).[30] Ignatius of Antioch recurrently emphasized the importance of the Lord's Supper celebration (Ign. *Eph.* 20.2; Ign. *Phld.* 4.1; Ign. *Smyrn.* 6.2; 8.1).[31] Later in the second century, Justin provided a fuller description of early Christian liturgy.[32] According to him, Sunday services included the reading of the prophets or the "memoirs of the apostles," a time of instruction, prayer, the Lord's Supper, and a collection of offerings (Justin, *1 Apol.* 67).[33] Pliny the Younger relates that early Christian corporate worship also included singing hymns to Jesus Christ and the making of solemn vows to live uprightly (*Epistle* 10.96).[34] Therefore, Jewish worship practices had been supplemented with new and distinctively Christian practices like apostolic readings, the Lord's Supper, and hymns directed to Jesus.

Another divergence from previous Jewish practice was reflected in the use of the Hebrew Scriptures.[35] On the one hand, the Book of Acts directly quotes from the prophets (Acts 2:16–21; 3:18; 13:47; 28:25–27) and the Psalms (Acts 1:16–17; 2:25–28). Stephen's speech in Acts 7 provides a summary review of biblical redemptive history. On the other hand, the Hebrew Scriptures were now interpreted through the particular lens of the life and ministry of Jesus of Nazareth, thus adopting a focused "Christological" interpretation. In the Christian perspective, "the utterances of the prophets, which are read every Sabbath" were fulfilled in Jesus (Acts 13:28; cf. 17:11; 18:5). Therefore, when the Apostle Paul attended the synagogue in Thessalonica, he reasoned from the Scriptures that the Messiah was to suffer and rise from the dead (Acts 17:2–3).[36] Perhaps the most famous episode of a Christian reading of the Hebrew Scriptures transpires in Acts 8. An Ethiopian eunuch was perusing the book of Isaiah, and Philip joined him and shared a Christian interpretation of Isaiah 53. "Then Philip opened his mouth, and beginning with this Scripture he told him the good news about Jesus" (Acts 8:35; cf. Luke 24:44–46). In the early second century, Ignatius of Antioch had already insisted that the Hebrew Scriptures should be interpreted through the particular prism of the gospel of Jesus' death and resurrection (Ign. *Phld.* 8.2).[37] Within later second-century literature, Justin's *Dialogue with Trypho, A Jew* elaborates upon the resulting tensions between Jewish and Christian interpretations of the Hebrew Scriptures.[38]

Baptism and Ritual Washing

The Apostle Peter's sermon at Pentecost called upon his hearers to "be baptized every one of you in the name of Jesus Christ for the forgiveness of sins" (Acts 2:38). His sermon achieved its aim in some of his listeners, as "those who received his word were baptized" (Acts 2:41). This rite of baptism was extended to Samaritans in chapter 8, as some believed the "good news" and then "were baptized, both men and women" (Acts 8:12). The household of the God-fearing Cornelius, a Gentile centurion "well spoken of by the whole Jewish nation" (Acts 10:22), was "baptized in the name of Jesus Christ" (10:48), and Paul was baptized in Damascus upon his conversion (9:18; 22:16). Paul's church planting ministry led to more baptisms, as many "believed and were baptized" (Acts 16:15, 33; 18:80). Acts emphasizes not only water baptism but also a baptism with the Holy Spirit (Acts 1:4–5; 11:15–16; 19:1–6).[39] The converts who had received John the Baptist's "baptism of repentance" but had not heard of the Holy Spirit were therefore re-baptized (Acts 19:5).

Scholars have linked the rite of Christian baptism with Jewish purification rituals, by way of both comparison and contrast.[40] *Tevilah b'mayim* was the immersion of an individual in water for ritual purification purposes.[41] On the Day of Atonement, the high priest immersed himself five times before putting on the high priestly garments (*Yoma* 3.3–4). Jews who had become ritually defiled (by touching a human corpse or the carcass of an unclean animal, or through an unclean emission from the body, etc.), were to be immersed in a *mikveh* (water pool) before being allowed entry into the Temple.[42] Excavations have uncovered over 150 *mikvaoth* from the first century CE in Jerusalem alone.[43] Within Second Temple Judaism, Gentile converts to Judaism were ritually immersed—the three requirements for male proselytes were circumcision, immersion (*tevilah*), and sacrifice (*b. Kerithoth* 8b–9a), although the details seem to have fluctuated still in the late first century CE (*b. Yebamoth* 46a; 47a).[44] Scholars agree, however, that John the Baptist's ministry preceded the development of Christian baptism (cf. Acts 1:5, 22; 10:37; 11:16; 13:24; 18:25; 19:3–4).[45] Moreover, the Qumran community already practiced an initiatory ritual of the bathing of the body in water.[46]

Justin Martyr contrasted Christian baptism and Jewish proselyte baptism (Justin, *Dial.* 14.1; 19.2; 29.1; 46.1).[47] Historians note that Jewish proselyte baptism was self-administered (in the presence of at least two or three male witnesses), while Christian baptism was administered by another. As a general rule, Jewish ritual immersion could be repeated, while Christians normally viewed baptism as a singular and non-repeatable event.[48] In fact, Hegesippus (a second-century Christian author) referred to the "Hemerobaptists" ("Daily Baptizers") among the Jewish sects (Eusebius, *Hist. eccl.* 4.22.7).[49] Moreover, Jewish as well as Gentile converts to Christianity were initiated by baptism (Acts 2:38; 10:45–48), manifesting an equal need for such initiation but also an equality of unity within the church (Gal. 3:27–28).[50] A more fundamental distinction was the particular practice of Christian baptism "in the name of the Lord Jesus" (Acts 2:38; 8:16; 10:48; 19:5; *Did.* 9.5) or in the triadic name of "the Father, Son, and Holy Spirit" (Matt. 28:19; *Did.* 7.1–3).[51] Nevertheless, continuities of reception are also apparent, as the *Didache*'s treatment of baptism in running vs. still water and cold vs. warm water reflects similar Jewish discussions related to ritual immersions.[52]

Casting of Lots

In the ancient world, a variety of objects served as lots to cast, including wood pieces, stones, and ostraca. The "casting" of lots normally involved throwing the objects upon the ground (sometimes from the hand, but often from a container used for shaking, whether a cloth bag, urn, or other vessel), in order to be "read." An example of the casting of lots appears in the first chapter of Acts. Attempting to replace Judas Iscariot, the early Jesus followers cast lots to select a twelfth disciple. They narrowed down the alternatives to either Matthias or Joseph (also called Barsabbas or Justus). "And they cast lots for them, and the lot fell on Matthias, and he was numbered with the eleven apostles" (Acts 1:26).[53] The election of Matthias illustrates the beginning of a status transformation of the disciples from followers to leaders.[54]

The casting of lots was a ritualistic form of decision making employed within the Jewish tradition. According to Prov. 16:33, "The lot is cast into the lap, but its every decision is from the LORD." Proverbs later explains, "The lot puts an end to quarrels and decides between powerful contenders" (Prov. 18:18). Joshua mentions lots being cast "before the LORD" (Josh. 18:6; 19:51). According to the Torah, the casting of lots was employed to designate a goat for the Lord and a goat for Azazel (Lev. 16:8–10). The casting of lots was employed in the distribution of land or residency (Num. 26:55; 33:54; 34:13; 36.2; Josh. 14–19; 21:4–12; 1 Chron. 6:61–65; Neh. 11:1; Isa. 34:17; Joel 4:3; Obad. 11) and the distribution of bounty (Ps. 22:19; Isa. 17:14; Nah. 3:10). Lots were also employed in the attribution of guilt (Josh. 7:14–18; 1 Sam. 14:42), the selection of military roles (Judg. 20:9), the selection of leadership (1 Sam. 10:20), and the assignment of religious duties (1 Chron. 24:5, 7, 31; 25:8; 26:12–14; Neh. 10:34).[55] The results of the casting of lots could be equated with God himself speaking (Judg. 20:9, 18). On the other hand, the casting of lots was not an exclusively Jewish practice (Esth. 3:7–8; 9:24; Jonah 1:7; Matt. 27:35; John 19:24).[56]

The *Book of Jubilees* claims that Noah assigned land to his three children by casting lots (*Jub.* 8:10–11). The Qumran community employed the use of lots in decision making (1 QS 5.2–3; 6.16; 1 QM 1.5; 11.7). Josephus shares a few narratives in which lots were used to decide outcomes (Josephus, *A.J.* 6.62; Josephus, *B.J.* 3.387–391; 4.155; 7.396). Both the Mishnah and the Talmud reflect the continuing use of the casting of lots. The Talmud discusses some specific facets of the practice, including the use of an urn to shake the lots, the types of wood used in forming lots, and the use of black and white stones in other cases.[57]

Almsgiving and Charity

The apostles Peter and John encountered a mendicant "who sat at the Beautiful Gate of the temple, asking for alms" (Acts 3:9). In this specific case, they declined to give to the beggar, declaring that they had neither silver nor gold (Acts 3:6). But Acts praises almsgiving elsewhere, depicting such charity as "a holistic participation in God's ways."[58] In the city of Joppa, the female disciple Tabitha (also called Dorcas) became famous for her "good works and acts of charity" (Acts 9:36). The centurion Cornelius was "a devout man who feared God with all his household," and he "gave alms generously to the people" (Acts 10:2).[59] His alms, along with his prayers, "ascended as a memorial before God" (Acts 10:4).[60] Christians outside of Judea sent relief support to Judean believers, who suffered under a great famine during the reign of Claudius (Acts 11:27–30). Paul labored with his own hands (as a tentmaker or leatherworker), partly in order to "help the weak" (Acts 20:35).[61] He personally made the trip to Jerusalem to bring alms and to present offerings (Acts 24:17). In support of such charity, Paul quoted a dominical saying: "It is more blessed to give than to receive" (Acts 20:35).

Of course, such almsgiving had roots in the Jewish tradition. When Polycarp, the Christian leader of the church of Smyrna, encouraged almsgiving in an early second-century letter, he declared, "When you are able to do good, do not put it off, because charity [almsgiving] delivers one from death" (Pol. *Phil.* 10.2).[62] The final phrase echoes Tobit 4:10–11, 29.[63] Of course, the ministry of Jesus of Nazareth served as a bridge toward early Christian developments. The *Didache* exhorted, "As for your prayers and acts of charity and all your actions, do them all just as you find it in the Gospel of our Lord" (*Did.* 15.4).

Moreover, Acts and the New Testament epistles particularly highlight the care of widows (Acts 6:1; James 1:27; 1 Tim. 5:3–16), a concern underscored within the Torah (Ex. 22:22–24; Deut. 10:18; 14:28–29) and Nevi'im (Isa. 1:17, 23; Jer. 22:3; Zech. 7:10). Among the Apostolic Fathers, Ignatius encouraged compassion for widows, orphans, prisoners, the oppressed, the hungry, and the thirsty (Ign. *Smyrn.*6.2; cf. *1 Clem.* 8.4; *Barn.* 20.2). Ignatius exhorted Polycarp, "Do not let the widows be neglected" (Ign. *Pol.* 4.1). Polycarp insisted that church elders "must be compassionate, merciful to all, turning back those who have gone astray, visiting all the sick, not neglecting a widow, orphan, or poor person" (Pol. *Phil.* 6.1). The *Shepherd of Hermas* recommended taking the food saved in fasting and donating it to "a widow or an orphan or someone in need" (*Herm.* 56.7; cf. 38.10; 50.8; 104.2).[64] The early Christian care for the poor primarily focused upon the needy within the Christian community (Gal. 6:10).[65]

Burial

When Tabitha (Dorcas) fell ill and died, her friends washed her and laid her in an upper room (Acts 9:37). When the Apostle Peter arrived upon the scene, "All the widows stood beside him weeping and showing tunics and other garments that Dorcas made while she was with them" (Acts 9:39). Earlier in Acts, when Sapphira passed away shortly after her spouse Ananias died and was buried (Acts 5:6), "they carried her out and buried her beside her husband" (Acts 5:9–10). According to Acts 8:2, "Devout men buried Stephen and made great lamentation over him."

The Book of Acts itself recognizes the precedent of Jewish burial.[66] The Apostle Peter's sermon at Pentecost recognized that "the patriarch David ... both died and was buried, and the tomb is with us to this day" (Acts 2:29). Jesus of Nazareth himself had been buried in a tomb (Acts 2:29). As portrayed elsewhere in the New Testament, some of his followers took his body "and wound it in linen clothes with the spices, as the manner of the Jews is to bury" (John 19:49).

In the Hebrew Scriptures, being left unburied represented being cursed for covenant unfaithfulness (Deut. 28:26). A common desire was to be buried with one's ancestors (Gen. 49:29–33; 50:25–26; 2 Sam. 19:38; 1 Kings 11:23).[67] The Torah expressed concern with being defiled by contact with the deceased (Num. 19:16; Deut. 21:22–23), but it did not stipulate how soon after death proper burial was to follow. Although the Jewish obligation for burial primarily rested upon one's heirs (Gen. 23:3; 25:9), within early Christianity the believing community often took up the responsibility (Aristides, *Apol.* 15; *Mart. Pol.* 18.2). Acts mentions the mourning that accompanied death (Acts 9:39), even as Jewish tradition called for ritual lament.[68] Josephus counseled, "All who pass while a burial is proceeding must join the procession and share the mourning of the family" (Josephus, *C. Ap.* 2.205).[69]

Laying On of Hands

A ritualistic "laying on of hands" occurs several times within the Book of Acts.[70] After the first deacons were chosen by the Jerusalem church, they were placed before the apostles, who "prayed and laid their hands on them" (Acts 6:6). In chapter 8, the apostles Peter and John visited a band of new Samaritan believers, then "they laid their hands on them and they received the Holy Spirit" (Acts 8:17). A chapter later, Ananias of Damascus laid his hands upon the newly converted Saul (Acts 9:12), an action affiliated with both his reception of the Holy Spirit and physical healing (Acts 9:17). The believers in Antioch "laid their hands" on Barnabas and Paul, and after the symbolic commissioning they sent them off to missionary work (Acts 13:3). In Ephesus, Paul "laid his hands" on disciples of John the Baptist, so that the Holy Spirit might come upon them (Acts 19:6). Paul also prayed over and laid his hands on Publius (a leading figure on the island of Malta), as a ritual of healing (Acts 28:8).

Such ritualistic laying on of hands had roots in the Jewish tradition.[71] In the Hebrew Scriptures, the laying on of hands could represent a consignment to condemnation (Lev. 24:14) or the transference of sin or guilt within the sacrificial system (Ex. 29:10, 15, 19; Lev. 1:4; 3:20; 4:15; 8:14, 18, 22; 16:21–22; Num. 8:12; 2 Chron. 29:23). But the action commonly represented a conveyance of blessing (Gen. 48:12–20), an investment of authority (Num. 27:20; Deut. 34:9), or a commissioning to leadership (Num. 8:10; 27:22–23; Deut. 34:9).[72] The laying on of hands was considered an elemental practice within early Christianity (Heb. 6:1–2), where it sometimes represented an ordination to leadership (1 Tim. 5:22).[73] In both the Hebrew Scriptures and early Christianity, a basic representation of the laying on of hands was the bestowal of a gift from God (1 Tim. 4:14; 2 Tim. 1:6).

The figure of Jesus seems to have represented a mediating influence in the passing of the ritual tradition, as his laying on of hands pictured the conveyance of blessing (Matt. 19:15; Mark 10:16; Luke 4:40; 13:13; 18:15–16) but especially the provision of healing (cf. Matt. 9:18, 25; Mark 5:23; 6:5; 7:32; 8:23, 25; 16:18; Luke 4:40; 13:13). The notion of healing by the laying on of hands continues into Acts (Acts 5:12; 9:17; 14:3; 19:11; 28:8).[74] But a new and recurring emphasis within Acts falls upon the bestowal of the gift of the Spirit (Acts 8:17; 19:6), which may find an earlier precedent in the affiliation between the Spirit or "the spirit of wisdom" and the laying on of hands in the Hebrew Scriptures (Deut. 34:9; Num. 27:18; cf. Acts 6:3, 5–6, 10).

Kashrut

An episode in the tenth chapter of Acts vividly illustrates a shift away from kosher food regulations. The Apostle Peter relates a visionary experience, in which he sees a large sheet descend from heaven, filled with a menagerie of mammals and reptiles and birds. The narrative explains,

> And there came a voice to him: "Rise, Peter, kill and eat." But Peter said, "By no means, Lord; for I have never eaten anything that is common or unclean." And the voice came to him again a second time, "What God has made clean, do not call common." This happened three times, and the thing was taken up at once to heaven.
> *Acts 10:13–16*[75]

Although directly addressing *kashrut* regulations, the import of the scenario led to another application.[76] As Clinton Wahlen notes, "Peter's vision in Acts 10 focuses on food, while the surrounding narrative applies the vision to people."[77] When Peter was invited by the Gentile, God-fearing Cornelius into his home, the apostle responded, "You yourselves know how unlawful it is for a Jew to associate with or to visit anyone of another nation, but God has shown me that I should not call any person common or unclean" (Acts 10:28).[78] Upon his return to Jerusalem, Peter was criticized for eating with the uncircumcised, but he defended his actions (Acts 11:2–4). Evidently, however, Peter was not always consistent in his table-fellowship practices (Gal. 2:11–16).[79]

The Apostolic Fathers reflect varying tactics concerning the non-reception of *kashrut* dietary regulations. The *Didache* does repeat a prohibition against food sacrificed to idols (*Did.* 6.3), as paralleled in the letter of the "Jerusalem Council" of Acts 15 (cf. Rev. 2:14, 20). In his Corinthian correspondence, the Apostle Paul himself developed a multi-faceted response to the question of food sacrificed to idols (1 Cor. 8–10; cf. Rom. 14:13–23).[80] One rationale was his insistence that demons lie behind idol worship (1 Cor. 10:19–20), a view appearing in the Hebrew Scriptures (Deut. 32:16–17; Ps. 106:37; cf. Baruch 4.7; *Jub.* 22:17).

The *Epistle of Barnabas* includes a lengthy section that spiritualizes away the kosher food laws found in the Torah (*Barn.* 10)—they are interpreted as prohibitions against associating with pig-like people, crow-like people, hyena-like people, weasel-like people, etc.[81] Ignatius of Antioch metaphorically employed acceptable and unacceptable "food" in another direction, applied to acceptable and heretical instruction: "Partake only of Christian food, and keep away from every strange plant, which is heresy" (Ign. *Trall.* 6.1).

Fasting

The Christian believers in Antioch "were worshiping the Lord and fasting" when they set apart Barnabas and Paul for missionary work (Acts 13:2). Barnabas and Paul appointed elders "in every church, with prayer and fasting," and "they committed them to the Lord in whom they had believed" (Acts 14:23). The ritual practice of fasting has roots in the Jewish tradition, as recognized by the Apostolic Fathers themselves (*1 Clem.* 53.2; 55.6; *Barn.* 6.7; 14.2).[82] In the Hebrew Scriptures, fasting was often summoned during times of peril (Judg. 20:26; 1 Sam. 7:6; 14:24; 2 Chron. 20:3; Neh. 9:1; Esth. 4:3, 16; Jer. 36:3, 9; Joel 1:14; 2:12–15; Jonah 3:5), and it was sometimes associated with the ritual wearing of torn clothing, sackcloth, and ashes (1 Kings 21:27; Neh. 9:1; Ps. 35:13; Isa. 58:5; Joel 2:13; Jdt. 4:10; 8:5; cf. *Jos. Asen.* 10). At other times, Jewish fasting could function as a regular spiritual practice (Jdt. 8:6). Fasts could vary in length of time (1 Sam. 31:13; 2 Sam. 1:12). The Hebrew Scriptures sometimes describe fasting as occurring "before the Lord," and fasting could be accompanied by penitential prayer (2 Sam. 12:16–17; Jer. 36:9; Joel 1:14; 2:15–17). Such fasting was "a ritual expression of remorse, submission, and supplication."[83]

One can draw direct lines of influence from the Jewish traditions through Tertullian's *On Fasting*.[84] Among the Apostolic Fathers (who mention fasting far more than Acts does), Polycarp exhorted, "Let us be self-controlled with respect to prayer and persevere in fasting" (Pol. *Phil.* 7.2). *2 Clement* provided this comparison between prayer, fasting, and almsgiving: "Charitable giving, therefore, is good, as is repentance from sin. Fasting is better than prayer, while charitable giving is better than both" (*2 Clem.* 16.4). The *Shepherd of Hermas* relates the author's personal practice of fasting (*Herm.* 6.1; 9.2).[85] The *Shepherd* counseled, "Every request requires humility. Fast, therefore, and you will receive what you request from the Lord" (*Herm.* 18.6). The *Shepherd* went on to describe fasting as an opportunity to share excess food with others (*Herm.* 55.9). The *Shepherd* directed,

> You must taste nothing except bread and water on that day on which you fast. Then you must estimate the cost of the food you would have eaten on that day on which you intend to fast, and give it to a widow or an orphan or someone in need.
>
> *Herm.* 56.7

Yet the Apostolic Fathers also reflect a desire to stand distinct from Jewish practices of fasting. The *Didache* counsels its readers to fast on Wednesdays and Fridays, in direct contrast to the Monday and Thursday observances in Jewish fasting (*Did.* 8.1; cf. *m. Ta'an* 1.6; *m. Meg.* 3.6).[86] The *Didache* also insists that converts fast one or two days prior to receiving baptism (*Did.* 7.4).[87] Moreover, the Apostolic Fathers reflect a tendency to reframe "true fasting" as abstinence from evil and obedience to God's commands. The *Shepherd* explained,

> Commit no evil in your life, and serve the Lord with a clean heart; keep his commandments and walk in his ordinances, and do not permit any evil desire to enter you heart, and believe in God. And if you do these things, you will complete a fast that is great and acceptable to God.
>
> *Herm.* 54.5

Shaking Off Dust

When Paul and Barnabas faced opposition in Pisidia, they were forced out of the district. In response to this rejection, they turned to a customary Jewish ritual, as they "shook off the dust from their feet" against the Pisidians and left for Iconium (Acts 13:51). Craig Keener explains, "Many scholars argue that Jewish travelers normally shook dust from their feet when leaving a pagan town, so that [Paul's] action treats Jewish communities … as if they were pagan."[88] Keener adds, "Whether or not Jewish people practiced this gesture customarily, they would have grasped this symbolism easily enough" (cf. Neh. 5:13).[89] In Corinth, when Paul again faced opposition, "he shook out his garments" as a sign that he was moving toward a Gentile focus, declaring, "From now on I will go to the Gentiles" (Acts 18:6; cf. the instructions of Hillel in *t. Sukkah* 4:3).[90] As with other cases of ritual reception, Jesus of Nazareth served as a bridge, by instructing his disciples to enact the symbolism of shaking the dust off their feet (Matt. 10:14; Luke 9:5; 10:5–10).[91]

Circumcision

A debate concerning the necessity of circumcision became the focal topic of the so-called "Jerusalem Council" in Acts 15. Some individuals from Judea had come to Antioch, teaching that "Unless you are circumcised according to the custom of Moses, you cannot be saved" (Acts 15:1). When representatives from Antioch came to Jerusalem to discuss the matter, "some believers who belonged to the party of the Pharisees" reiterated, "It is necessary to circumcise them and to order them to keep the law of Moses" (Acts 15:5). After hearing from several church leaders, the assembly concluded that "we will be saved through the grace of the Lord Jesus" (Acts 15:11), and thus circumcision should not be required of Gentiles.[92] Nevertheless, the Jerusalem church did compose a letter to the Antioch church, with some further counsel.

> For it has seemed good to the Holy Spirit and to us to lay on you no greater burden than these requirements: that you abstain from what has been sacrificed to idols, and from blood, and from what has been strangled, and from sexual immorality.
> *Acts 15:28–29; cf. Acts 21:25*

Commentators have proposed Jewish backgrounds to these injunctions, sometimes suggesting the regulations for aliens (*gerim*) in Leviticus 17–18 or the "Noahide Laws" applicable to Gentiles.[93] Interestingly, the next pericope in Acts relates the circumcision of Timothy, whose mother was a Jew but whose father was a Gentile (Acts 16:1–3).[94] Paul then took Timothy with him on further missionary travels, and they shared the "Jerusalem Council" decisions with others (Acts 15:4). In his own letters, Paul counseled Gentile believers in Jesus not to become circumcised (1 Cor. 7:18; Gal. 5:2). In a declaration that would have alarmed his opponents, Paul reasoned, "For neither circumcision counts for anything nor uncircumcision, but keeping the commandments of God" (1 Cor. 7:19; cf. Gal. 6:15).

Among the Apostolic Fathers, Ignatius opposed the imposition of circumcision (Ign. *Phld.* 6.1). The *Epistle of Barnabas* declared that circumcision had been abolished, while a circumcision of the ears (a willingness to hear) remained, "In order that when we hear the word we might believe" (*Barn.* 9.4).[95] Barnabas' further emphasis upon a circumcision of the heart (*Barn.* 9.5) reflected conceptual models not only in New Testament documents (Rom. 2:28–29; Col. 2:11) but also in the Hebrew Scriptures (Deut. 10:16; 30:6; Jer. 4:4).[96] In the Book of Acts itself,

Stephen underscored a "circumcision" of the heart and ears—characterized by an openness to the apostolic proclamation of a Jesus-centered gospel (Acts 7:51). *Barnabas* concludes, "He circumcised our ears and hearts for this very purpose, so that we might understand these things" (*Barn.* 10.12).[97] Justin portrayed circumcision as "a type of the true circumcision, by which we are circumcised from deceit and iniquity" (Justin, *2 Apol.* 41).[98]

Vowing and Head Shaving

The Apostle Paul took a vow, and he cut his hair as a ritual sign of commitment (Acts 18:18).[99] When Paul purified himself (along with some acquaintances), he paid for their expenses and the shaving of their heads (Acts 21:24; cf. Josephus, *A.J.* 19.294). "Then Paul took the men, and the next day he purified himself along with them and went into the temple, giving notice when the days of purification would be fulfilled and the offering presented for each one of them" (Acts 21:26).[100] Among the Apostolic Fathers, *1 Clement* exhorts, "Sacrifice to God a sacrifice of praise, and pay your vows to the Most High" (52.3).

Solemn vows appear in the Hebrew Scriptures (Gen. 28:20; Num. 21:2; Judg. 11:30–31; 1 Sam. 1:11), and Numbers 30:1–16 conveyed the laws of vowing. Ecclesiastes 5:4–5 declares, "When you vow a vow to God, do not delay paying it, for he has no pleasure in fools. Pay what you vow. It is better that you should not vow than that you should vow and not pay." This text led to differing responses within the rabbinic tradition. R. Judah stated, "Better than both is he who vows and pays," while R. Meir declared, "Better than both is he who does not vow at all."[101] An entire tractate of the Talmud was dedicated to vows (*Nedarim*).[102]

In journeying to Jerusalem to fulfill his vow, the Apostle Paul was following Jewish custom (cf. Josephus, *B.J.* 2.31.3). As the Midrash declares, "He who vows and pays his vow will be vouchsafed to pay his vow in Jerusalem" (Lev. R. 37:4).[103] The rabbinic tradition spoke of shaving at the door of the sanctuary (*B. Yoma* 16a; *Naz.* 45a). The closest parallel to Paul's actions may involve the Nazirite vow (Num. 6:1–21; cf. Judg. 13:4–7; 1 Sam. 1:11; Ezek. 44:20; Amos 2:12). Nazirites were to let their hair grow during the period of their vow (Num. 6:5), and then were to shave their hair in the sanctuary and offer it to God (Num. 6:18). Some interpreters have called Paul's action "a Nazirite-like private vow," perhaps modified by diaspora practice or personal adaptation.[104]

Conclusion

Among the Apostolic Fathers, the *Epistle to Diognetus* expressed a polarizing rhetoric regarding Jewish rituals:

> But with regard to their qualms about meats, and superstition concerning the Sabbath, and pride in circumcision, and hypocrisy about fasting and new moons, I doubt that you need to learn from me that they are ridiculous and not worth discussing.
>
> *Diogn.* 4.1[105]

Nevertheless, some early Christian authors were more measured in their approach to differentiation. Jewish traditions affected early Christian rituals, even though the nature and extent of influence were not always acknowledged by Christians themselves. The "parting of the ways" between Christianity and Judaism was complex and multi-faceted. In the case of rituals, the process involved both the reception of previous Jewish traditions and the adaptation and even rejection of traditions, as reflected in the Book of Acts and the Apostolic Fathers.

Notes

1. For recent studies of this complex topic, see Standhartinger 2020; Vogel 2020. For a seminal introduction, see Cohen 1954. Of course, both earliest Christianity and contemporaneous Judaism reflected diversity in belief and practice.
2. On the relationship of Acts to history, see Hemer 1989.
3. Gal. 2:7–8.
4. Cf. Matt. 10:5–6; 15:24.
5. English translations of scriptural texts come from the English Standard Version (ESV).
6. Cf. Acts 26:3.
7. Reverse adaptation could also occur, as reflected in Acts 19:11–13.
8. See Marguerat 2009, 101, 114.
9. On the complexities of the question, see Nicklas 2014.
10. For example, *1 Clement* is commonly dated to the mid-90s, and the *Didache* is sometimes dated as early as 70. Some have dated the *Martyrdom of Polycarp* and the *Epistle to Diognetus* into the third century.
11. See Robinson 2009, 204; Boyarin 2018; Donahue 1978.
12. Cf. Paul's adaption of the *Shema* in 1 Cor. 8:4–6.
13. "Prayer" 1971, 980. Cf. Falk 1995, 267–301.
14. For a comparison between Godfearers and proselytes (as found in Acts) see Ferguson 2003, 546–51. Cornelius probably attended the synagogue and would have had at least a basic understanding of Jewish purity regulations (Wahlen 2005, 509).
15. See Keener 2015, vol. 2, 1044–47; early Christians may have modified the placement of exact times, while keeping the tenor of structured prayer; see Falk 1995, 293–98.
16. See Elliott 1991.
17. Solomon's Portico was a colonnade located on the eastern side of the Outer Court of the Temple (John 10:23; Acts 5:12).
18. Regev 2014, 118–38.
19. Although the Temple itself is mentioned (e.g., *1 Clem.* 23.5). See Simon 1985.
20. Lookadoo 2018. In Pauline letters, Christians are described as "the temple of the Holy Spirit" (1 Cor. 3:16–17; 6:19; 2 Cor. 6:16; Eph. 2:21).
21. Maschke 1992; Schwiebert 2015. A lengthy personal example appears in *Mart. Pol.* 7.2–8.1 cf. 14.1–3.
22. Tomson 2015. A peculiar early Christian practice was addressing God as *Abba* (Rom. 8:15; Gal. 4:6), a custom rooted in Jesus' ministry (Mark 14:36).
23. Bruce 1988, 310–11; Keener 2015, vol. 3, 2384.
24. English translation from the ANF.
25. Sigal 1984; Leithart 2002.
26. Such influence went beyond liturgy, as reflected in the leadership of "elders" within churches (cf. Acts 20:17). See Burtchaell 2004.
27. Ign. *Smyrn.* 8.1–2 mentions both the Eucharist and a "love feast."
28. Schwiebert 2008; Clabeaux 2015; Bobertz 2010; Wolmarans 2005.
29. Cf. Matt. 7:6; 15:26–27; van de Sandt 2002. On the theme of purity in the *Didache*, see Repschinski 2008.
30. van de Sandt 2015; Draper 2008.
31. Stefanut 2013.
32. See Ferguson 1994.
33. On the Gospel texts as the "memoirs of the Apostles," see Cirafesi 2016; Hill 2007.
34. Cf. 1 Cor. 14:26; Eph. 5:19; Col. 3:16; Löhr 2014, 167.
35. See Blowers and Martens 2019.
36. Kavanagh 1983.
37. See Hartog 2017.
38. Skarsaune 2007; Hengel 1999.
39. McCollough 2017.
40. Lichtenberger 1999; Ferguson 2009, 60–82.
41. The Mishnah (*Mikvaoth* 1.1–8) describes six gradations of water purification rituals. See Ferguson 2009, 63–65.
42. "Mikveh" 1971, 1534–44.
43. Ferguson 2009, 64.
44. Rouwhorst 2019, 169; Rouwhorst 2009, 108–11; Cohen 1999, 218–25.

45 Smith 1982, 13–32.
46 Sutcliffe 1960; Lichtenberger 2000; Ferguson 2009, 68–71; Gnilka 1961; Robinson 1957.
47 Cf. *POxy* 840, lines 8–45.
48 A central debate in the *Shepherd of Hermas* concerns post-baptismal sins. Cf. Hartman 1994, 127–43.
49 The topic of "Hemerobaptists" was picked up by Epiphanius and the *Apostolic Constitutions* (see Ferguson 2009, 72).
50 Cf. Draper 1997.
51 Ferguson 2009, 132–38, 201–06; Stewart-Sykes 2008, 351.
52 Ascough 1994; Mitchell 1995; Rordorf 1996.
53 See Brug 1998. David Peterson emphasizes that this casting of lots took place prior to the reception of the Spirit at Pentecost. See Peterson 2009, 128–29.
54 Estrada 2004, 1–45.
55 Cf. Luke 1:9.
56 See Pervo 2009, 56 n.65; Keener 2015, vol. 1, 776–79.
57 "Lots" 1971, 512.
58 Reardon 2016, 477.
59 Reardon 2016.
60 Marguerat 2009, 105.
61 See Hock 2007.
62 English translations of the Apostolic Fathers come from Holmes 2007. On almsgiving in Polycarp, see Downs and Rogan 2016, 628–36.
63 Hartog 2013, 140. Cf. Garrison 1993; Downs 2018; Gal. 6:6–10.
64 The *Shepherd of Hermas* castigated deacons who misused their position and "plundered the livelihood of widows and orphans, and profited themselves from the ministry that they received to carry out" (*Herm.* 103.2).
65 "Needy" was a relative term, of course. See Buell 2008.
66 The practice of burial is assumed in *1 Clem.* 16.10.
67 Cf. Neh. 2:5.
68 "Burial" 1971, 1518.
69 English translation from Thackeray 1997, 375.
70 See Coppens 1979.
71 Hruby 1970; Hoffman 1979.
72 See also *Jub.* 25:14; *Jos. Asen.* 8:9; 16:6.
73 See Dowd 2002; Creech 2002.
74 Cf. Flusser 1957.
75 On "common or unclean" or "common and unclean," see Wahlen 2005; Parsons 2000; 1 Macc. 1:62–63; 4 Macc. 7:6.
76 Djomhoué 2005; Parsons 2000.
77 Wahlen 2005, 505.
78 Staples 2019; Nguyen 2012. Peter had already stayed at the house of Simon of Joppa, a tanner (Acts 10:8–9, 32). Cf. Oliver 2013.
79 For Jewish disapproval of eating with Gentiles, see *Jub.* 22.16; *Jos. Asen.* 7.1; cf. Tob. 1:10–12. Cf. Neyrey 1991.
80 See Fotopoulos 2019.
81 On the intersection of biblical interpretation and social identity in the *Epistle of Barnabas*, see Yuh 2019.
82 As recognized by *1 Clem.* 53.2; 55.6.
83 "Fasting and Fast Days" 1971, 1190.
84 "Fasting and Fast Days" 1971, 1192.
85 Hauck 1993.
86 See Wilhite 2019, 173.
87 Draper 2000, 135–36.
88 Keener 2015, vol. 2, 2106.
89 Keener 2015, vol. 2, 2106. On the accompanying "blood guilt" in Acts 18:6, see Josh. 2:19; Judg. 9:14; 2 Sam. 1:16; 1 Kings 2:33, 37; Ezek. 33:4–6.
90 Paul's Jewish opponents threw off their cloaks and flung dust into the air, to express their disapproval of Paul's Gentile mission (Acts 22:22–23).
91 "Shaking off dust" from the feet may depict an antithesis to hospitality (Keener 2015, vol. 2, 2105).

92 Wahlen 2005, 517.
93 Keener 2015, vol. 3, 2260–69; Steffek 2009; Callan 1993; Perrot 1981. See, however, Butticaz 2009, 124–29; Witherington 1998, 464–67; Klinghardt 1988, 185–86; Wilson 1984, 84–102.
94 Marguerat 2009, 113. Contrast the case of Titus in Gal. 3:3.
95 Paget 1991. On the "parting of the ways" in the *Epistle of Barnabas*, see Horbury 1999.
96 See also Justin, *Dial*. 29.1; 38.4–39.1; 41.4; 43.2–4; 113.6–7; 114.4.
97 Tomson 2019.
98 English translation from the ANF.
99 In Acts, Paul's Jewish opponents bound themselves by their own vow of opposition (Acts 23:12, 21).
100 David Aune has argued that the purification entailed ritual immersion in one of the *mikvaoth* near the Temple Mount (Aune 2011, 309–10).
101 "Vows and Vowing" 1971, 227.
102 "Vows and Vowing" 1971, 227.
103 "Vows and Vowing" 1971, 228.
104 Haenchen 1971, 545–46; Barrett 1998, vol. 2, 877–78.
105 Cf. Justin, *Dial*. 18.

References

Ascough, Richard S. 1994. "An Analysis of the Baptismal Ritual of the *Didache*," *Studia Liturgica* 24, no. 2: 201–13.

Aune, David E. 2011. "Paul, Ritual Purity, and the Ritual Baths South of the Temple Mount (Acts 21:15–28)," in *Celebrating Paul*, Catholic Biblical Quarterly Monograph Series 48. Ed. Peter Spitaler. Washington, DC: Catholic Biblical Association of America, 287–320.

Barrett, C. K. 1998. *A Critical and Exegetical Commentary on the Acts of the Apostles*, 2 vols, ICC. London: T&T Clark.

Blowers, Paul M., and Peter W. Martens. 2019. *The Oxford Handbook of Early Christian Biblical Interpretation*. Oxford: Oxford University Press.

Bobertz, Charles A. 2010. "Ritual Eucharist within Narrative: A Comparison of *Didache* 9–10 with Mark 6:31–44; 8:1–9," *Studia Patristica* 45: 93–99.

Boyarin, Daniel. 2018. "Why Ignatius Invented Judaism," in *The Ways that Often Parted*, Early Christianity and Its Literature 24. Eds. Lori Baron, Jill Hicks-Keeton, and Matthew Thiessen. Atlanta, GA: SBL, 309–24.

Bruce, F. F. 1988. *The Book of the Acts*. Rev. ed. New International Commentary on the New Testament. Grand Rapids, MI: Eerdmans.

Brug, John F. 1998. "Acts 1:26—Lottery or Election?" *Wisconsin Lutheran Quarterly* 95, no. 3 (Summer): 212–14.

Buell, Denise Kimber. 2008. "'Be Not One Who Stretches out Hands to Receive but Shuts Them When it Comes to Giving': Envisioning Christian Charity When Both Donors and Recipients Are Poor," *Wealth and Poverty in Early Church and Society*, Holy Cross Studies in Patristic Theology and History. Ed. Susan R. Holman. Grand Rapids, MI: Baker Academic, 37–47.

"Burial." *Encyclopaedia of Judaica*, vol. 4. New York: Macmillan: 1515–23.

Burtchaell, James Tunstead. 2004. *From Synagogue to Church*. Cambridge: Cambridge University Press.

Butticaz, Simon. 2009. "Acts 15 or the 'Return of the Repressed'? The Church and the Law in Acts," in *The Torah in the New Testament*. Library of New Testament Studies 401. Eds. Michael Tait and Peter Oakes. London: T&T Clark, 118–32.

Callan, Terrance. 1993. "The Background of the Apostolic Decree (Acts 15:20, 29, 21:25)," *Catholic Biblical Quarterly* 55, no. 2 (April): 284–97.

Cirafesi, Wally V. 2016. "Justin's ἀπομνημονεύματα and Ancient Greco-Roman Memoirs," *Early Christianity* 7, no. 2 (June): 186–212.

Clabeaux, John J. 2015. "The Ritual Meal in *Didache* 9–10: Progress in Understanding," in *The Didache: A Missing Piece of the Puzzle in Early Christianity*. Eds. Jonathan A. Draper and Clayton N. Jefford. Atlanta, GA: SBL: 209–30.

Cohen, Abraham. 1954. *The Parting of the Ways: Judaism and the Rise of Christianity*. London: Lincolns-Prager.

Cohen, Shaye. 1999. *The Beginning of Jewishness: Boundaries, Varieties, Uncertainties*. Berkeley: University of California Press.

Coppens, Joseph. 1979. "L'imposition des mains dans les Actes des apôtres," in *Les Actes des apôtres: Traditions, redaction, théologie*. Bibliotheca Ephemeridum Theologicarum Lovaniensium 48. Ed. Jacob Kremer. Leuven: Leuven University Press: 404–38.

Creech, Robert R. 2002. "A Response to 'Ordination' in Acts and the Pastoral Epistles," *Perspectives in Religious Studies* 29, no. 2 (Summer): 219–21.

Djomhoué, Priscille. 2005. "Une histoire de rapprochement: Actes 10-11, 18," *Foi et vie* 104, no. 4 (August): 71–82.

Donahue, Paul J. 1978. "Jewish Christianity in the Letters of Ignatius of Antioch," *Vigiliae Christianae* 32, no. 2 (June): 81–93.

Dowd, Sharyn. 2002. "Ordination in Acts and the Pastoral Epistles," *Perspectives in Religious Studies* 29, no. 2 (Summer): 205–17.

Downs, David J. 2018. "Almsgiving and Competing Soteriologies in Second-Century Christianity," *Religions* 9, no. 7 (July): 1–13.

Downs, David J., and Wil Rogan. 2016. "'Let Us Teach Ourselves First to Follow the Commandment of the Lord' (Pol *Phil* 4.1): An Additional Note on 'The Commandment' as Almsgiving," *New Testament Studies* 62, no. 4: 628–36.

Draper, Jonathan A. 1997. "The Role of Ritual in the Alternation of Social Universe: Jewish-Christian Initiation of Gentiles in the *Didache*," *Listening* 32 (Winter): 48–67.

Draper, Jonathan A. 2000. "Ritual Process and Ritual Symbol in *Didache* 7–10," *Vigiliae Christianae* 54, no. 2: 121–58.

Draper, Jonathan A. 2008. "Pure Sacrifice in *Didache* 14 as Jewish Christian Exegesis," *Neotestamentica* 42, no. 2: 223–52.

Elliott, John H. 1991. "Temple versus Household in Luke-Acts," in *The Social World of Luke-Acts: Models of Interpretation*. Ed. Jerome H. Neyrey. Peabody, MA: Hendrickson, 211–40.

Estrada, Nelson P. 2004. *From Followers to Leaders: The Apostles in the Ritual of Status Transformation in Acts 1–2*. Journal for the Study of the New Testament Supplement Series 255. London: T&T Clark.

Falk, Daniel K. 1995. "Jewish Prayer Literature and the Jerusalem Church in Acts," in *The Book of Acts in Its Palestinian Setting*, vol. 4. Ed. Richard Bauckham. Grand Rapids, MI: Eerdmans, 267–301.

"Fasting and Fast Days." 1971. *Encyclopaedia of Judaica*, vol. 6. New York: Macmillan: 1189–96.

Ferguson, Everett. 1994. "Justin Martyr and the Liturgy," *Restoration Quarterly* 36, no. 4: 267–78.

Ferguson, Everett. 2003. *Backgrounds of Early Christianity*, 3rd. ed. Grand Rapids, MI: Eerdmans.

Ferguson, Everett. 2009. *Baptism in the Early Church: History, Theology, and Liturgy in the First Five Centuries*. Grand Rapids, MI: Eerdmans.

Flusser, David. 1957. "Healing through the Laying on of Hands in a Dead Sea Scroll," *Israel Exploration Journal* 7, no. 2: 107–08.

Fotopoulos, John. 2019. *Food Offered to Idols in Roman Corinth: A Social-Rhetorical Reconsideration of 1 Corinthians 8:1-11:1*. Wissenschaftliche Untersuchungen zum Neuen Testament 151. Tübingen: Mohr Siebeck.

Garrison, Roman. 1993. *Redemptive Almsgiving in Early Christianity*. Journal for the Study of the New Testament Supplement Series 77. Sheffield: JSOT.

Gnilka, Joachim. 1961. "Die essenischen Tauchbäder und die Johannestaufe," *Revue de Qumran* 3, no. 2 (May): 185–207.

Haenchen, Ernst. 1971. *The Acts of the Apostles: A Commentary*. Philadelphia, PA: Westminster.

Hartman, Lars. 1994. "Obligatory Baptism—But Why? On Baptism in the *Didache* and in the *Shepherd of Hermas*," *Svensk exegetisk årsbok* 59: 127–43.

Hartog, Paul. 2013. *Polycarp's Epistle to the Philippians and the Martyrdom of Polycarp*, Oxford Apostolic Fathers Series. Oxford: Oxford University Press.

Hartog, Paul. 2017. "The Good News in Old Texts? The 'Gospel' and the 'Archives' in Ign. *Phld.* 8.2," *Studia Patristica* 93, no. 19: 105–21.

Hauck, Robert J. 1993. "The Great Fast: Christology in the *Shepherd of Hermas*," *Anglican Theological Review* 75, no. 2 (Spring): 187–98.

Hemer, Colin J. 1989. *The Book of Acts in the Setting of Hellenistic History*. Wissenschaftliche Untersuchungen zum Neuen Testament 49. Tübingen: Mohr Siebeck.

Hengel, Martin. 1999. "The Septuagint as a Collection of Writings Claimed by Christians: Justin and the Church Fathers before Origen," in *Jews and Christians: The Parting of the Ways, A.D. 70 to 135*. Ed. James D. G. Dunn. Grand Rapids, MI: Eerdmans: 39–84.

Hill, Charles E. 2007. "Was John's Gospel among Justin's 'Apostolic Memoirs'?" in *Justin Martyr and His Worlds*. Eds. Sara Parvis and Paul Foster. Minneapolis, MN: Fortress Press, 88–94, 191–93.

Hock, Ronald F. 2007. *The Social Context of Paul's Ministry: Tentmaking and Apostleship*. Minneapolis, MN: Fortress.

Hoffman, Lawrence A. 1979. "L'ordination juive à la veille du christianisme," *La Maison-Dieu* 138 (June): 7–47.

Holmes, Michael W. 2007. *The Apostolic Fathers: Greek Texts and English Translations*, 3rd ed. Grand Rapids, MI: Baker Academic.

Horbury, William. 1999. "Jewish-Christian Relations in *Barnabas* and Justin Martyr," in *Jews and Christians: The Parting of the Ways, A.D. 70 to 135*. Ed. James D. G. Dunn. Grand Rapids, MI: Eerdmans, 315–46.

Hruby, Kurt. 1970. "La notion d'ordination dans la tradition juive," *La Maison-Dieu* 102 (April): 30–56.

Kavanagh, Aidan. 1983. "Scripture and Worship in Synagogue and Church," *Michigan Quarterly Review* 22, no. 3 (Summer): 480–94.

Keener, Craig S. 2015. *Acts: An Exegetical Commentary*, 4 vols. Grand Rapids, MI: Baker Academic.

Klinghardt, Matthias. 1988. *Gesetz und Volk Gottes: Das lukanische Verständnis des Gesetzes nach Herkunft, Funktion und seinem Ort in der Geschichte des Urchristentums*. Wissenschaftliche Untersuchungen zum Neuen Testament 32. Tübingen: Mohr Siebeck.

Leithart, Peter J. 2002. "Synagogue or Temple? Models for the Christian Worship," *Westminster Theological Journal* 64, no. 1 (Spring): 119–33.

Lichtenberger, Hermann. 1999. "Syncretistic Features in Jewish and Jewish-Christian Baptism Movements," in *Jews and Christians: The Parting of the Ways, A.D. 70 to 135*. Ed. James D. G. Dunn. Grand Rapids, MI: Eerdmans: 85–98.

Lichtenberger, Hermann. 2000. "Baths and Baptism," in *Encyclopedia of the Dead Sea Scrolls*. Eds. Lawrence H. Schiffman and James C. Vanderkam. Oxford: Oxford University Press, 85–89.

Löhr, Hermut. 2014. "What Can We Know about the Beginnings of Christian Hymnody?" in *Literature or Liturgy? Early Christian Hymns and Prayers in their Literary and Liturgical Context in Antiquity*. Wissenschaftliche Untersuchungen zum Neuen Testament 363. Eds. Clemens Leonhard and Hermut Löhr. Tübingen: Mohr Siebeck, 157–74.

Lookadoo, Jonathon. 2018. *The High Priest and the Temple: Metaphorical Depictions of Jesus in the Letters of Ignatius of Antioch*. Wissenschattlide Untersuchungen zum Neuen Testament 473. Tübingen: Mohr Siebeck.

"Lots." 1971. *Encyclopaedia Judaica*, vol. 11. New York: Macmillan, 510–13.

Marguerat, Daniel. 2009. "Paul and the Torah in the Acts of the Apostles," in *The Torah in the New Testament*. Library of New Testament Studies 401. Eds. Michael Tate and Peter Oakes. London: T&T Clark, 98–117.

Maschke, Timothy. 1992. "Prayer in the Apostolic Fathers," *Second Century* 9, no. 2 (Summer): 103–18.

McCollough, David J. 2017. *Ritual Water, Ritual Spirit: An Analysis of the Timing, Mechanism, and Manifestation of Spirit-Reception in Luke-Acts*. Milton Keynes: Paternoster.

"Mikveh." 1971. *Encyclopaedia Judaica*, vol. 11. New York: Macmillan, 1534–44.

Mitchell, Nathan. 1995. "Baptism in the Didache," in *The Didache in Context: Essays on Its Text, History, and Transmission*. Ed. Clayton N. Jefford. Leiden: Brill, 226–55.

Neyrey, Jerome H. 1991. "Ceremonies in Luke-Acts: The Case of Meals and Table-Fellowship," in *The Social World of Luke-Acts: Models of Interpretation*. Ed. Jerome H. Neyrey. Peabody, MA: Hendrickson, 361–87.

Nguyen, VanThanh. 2012. "Dismantling Cultural Boundaries: Missiological Implications of Acts 10:1–11:18," *Missiology* 40, no. 4 (October): 455–66.

Nicklas, Tobias. 2014. *Jews and Christians? Second-Century "Christian" Perspectives on the "Parting of the Ways."* Tübingen: Mohr Siebeck.

Oliver, Isaac W. 2013. "Simon Peter Meets Simon the Tanner: The Ritual Insignificance of Tanning in Ancient Judaism," *New Testament Studies* 59, no. 1 (January): 50–60.

Paget, James Carleton. 1991. "*Barnabas* 9.4: A Peculiar Verse on Circumcision," *Vigiliae Christianae* 45, no. 3 (September): 242–54.

Parsons, Mikeal C. 2000. "'Nothing Defiled AND Unclean': The Conjunction's Function in Acts 10:14," *Perspectives in Religious Studies* 27, no. 3 (Fall): 263–74.

Perrot, Charles. 1981. "Les décisions de l'Assemblée de Jérusalem," *Recherches de science religieuse* 69, no. 2 (April–June): 195–208.

Pervo, Richard I. 2009. *Acts: A Commentary*, Hermeneia. Minneapolis: Fortress.
Peterson, David G. 2009. *The Acts of the Apostles*. Pillar New Testament Commentary. Grand Rapids, MI: Eerdmans.
"Prayer." 1971. *Encyclopaedia Judaica*, vol. 13. New York: Macmillan, 978–84.
Reardon, Timothy W. 2016. "Cleansing through Almsgiving in Luke-Acts: Purity, Cornelius, and the Translation of Acts 15:9," *Catholic Biblical Quarterly* 78, no. 3 (July): 463–82.
Regev, Eyal. 2014. "Prayer Within and Without the Temple: From Ancient Judaism to Early Christianity," *Henoch* 36, no. 1: 118–38.
Repschinski, Boris. 2008. "Purity in Matthew, James and the *Didache*," in *Matthew, James, and Didache: Three Related Documents in Their Jewish and Christian Settings*. Society of Biblical Literature Symposium Series 45. Eds. Huub van de Sandt and Jürgen K. Zangenberg. Atlanta, GA: SBL 379–95.
Robinson, John A. T. 1957. "The Baptism of John and the Qumran Community," *Harvard Theological Review* 50, no. 3 (July): 175–92.
Robinson, Thomas A. 2009. *Ignatius of Antioch and the Parting of the Ways: Early Jewish-Christian Relations*. Peabody, MA: Hendrickson.
Rordorf, Willy. 1996. "Baptism According to the Didache," in *The Didache in Modern Research*, Arbeiten zur Geschichte des antiken Judentums und des Urchristentums 37. Ed. Jonathan A. Draper. Leiden: Brill, 212–22.
Rouwhorst, Gerard. 2009. "A Remarkable Case of Religious Interaction: Water Baptisms in Judaism and Christianity," in *Interactions between Judaism and Christianity in History, Religion, Art and Literature*, Jewish and Christian Perspectives 17. Eds. Marcel Poorthuis, Joshua Schwartz, and Joseph Turner. Leiden: Brill: 103–26.
Rouwhorst, Gerard. 2019. "Initiation by Circumcision and Water Baptism in Early Judaism and Early Christianity," in *Ritual Dynamics in Jewish and Christian Contexts: Between Bible and Liturgy*, Jewish and Christian Perspectives 34. Eds. Claudia D. Bergmann and Benedikt Kranemann. Leiden: Brill, 165–89.
Schwiebert, Jonathan. 2008. *Knowledge and the Coming Kingdom: The Didache's Meal Ritual and Its Place in Early Christianity*. Library of New Testament Studies 373. London: T&T Clark.
Schwiebert, Jonathan. 2015. "Pray 'In This Way': Formalized Speech in *Didache* 9–10," in *The Didache: A Missing Piece of the Puzzle in Early Christianity*. Eds. Jonathan A. Draper and Clayton N. Jefford. Atlanta, GA: SBL, 189–207.
Sigal, Phillip. 1984. "Early Christian and Rabbinic Liturgical Affinities: Exploring Liturgical Acculturation," *New Testament Studies* 30, no. 1: 63–90.
Simon, Marcel. 1985. "*L'Épître de Barnabé* et le Temple," in *Les Juifs au regard de l'histoire*. Ed. Gilbert Dahan. Paris: Picard, 31–36.
Skarsaune, Oskar. 2007. "Justin and His Bible," in *Justin Martyr and His Worlds*. Eds. Sara Parvis and Paul Foster. Minneapolis, MN: Fortress, 53–76, 179–87.
Smith, Derwood C. 1982. "Jewish Proselyte Baptism and the Baptism of John," *Restoration Quarterly* 25, no. 1: 13–32.
Standhartinger, Angela. 2020. "'Parting of the Ways': Stationen einer Debatte," *Evangelische Theologie* 80, no. 6: 406–17.
Staples, Jason A. 2019. "'Rise, Kill, and Eat': Animals as Nations in Early Jewish Visionary Literature and Acts 10," *Journal for the Study of the New Testament* 42, no. 1 (September): 3–17.
Stefanut, Romulus D. 2013. "Eucharistic Theology in the Martyrdom of Ignatius of Antioch," *Studia Patristica* 45, no. 13: 39–47.
Steffek, Emmanuelle. 2009. "Some Observations on the Apostolic Decree in Acts 15.20, 29 (and 21.25)," in *The Torah in the New Testament*. Library of New Testament Studies 401. Eds. Michael Tait and Peter Oakes. London: T&T Clark, 133–40.
Stewart-Sykes, Alistair. 2008. "Ἀποκύησις λόγῳ ἀληθείας: Paraenesis and Baptism in Matthew, James, and the *Didache*," in *Matthew, James, and Didache: Three Related Documents in Their Jewish and Christian Settings*, Society of Biblical Literature Symposium Series 45. Eds. Huub van de Sandt and Jürgen K. Zangenberg. Atlanta, GA: SBL, 341–59.
Sutcliffe, Edmund F. 1960. "Baptism and Baptismal Rites at Qumran?" *Heythrop Journal* 1, no. 3: 179–88.
Thackeray, H. St. J. 1997. *Josephus: The Life against Apion*, Loeb Classical Library. Cambridge, MA: Harvard University Press.

Tomson, Peter J. 2015 "The Lord's Prayer (*Didache* 8) at the Faultline of Judaism and Christianity," in *The Didache: A Missing Piece of the Puzzle in Early Christianity*. Eds. Jonathan A. Draper and Clayton N. Jefford. Atlanta, GA: SBL 165–87.

Tomson, Peter J. 2019. "The *Didache*, Matthew, and *Barnabas* as Sources for Jewish and Christian History," in *Studies on Jews and Christians in the First and Second Centuries*, Wissenschaftliche Untersuchungen zum Neuen Testament 418. Tübingen: Mohr Siebeck, 501–32.

van de Sandt, Huub. 2002. "'Do not Give What Is Holy to the Dogs' (*Did*. 9:5d and Matt 7:6a): The Eucharistic Food of the *Didache* in Its Jewish Purity Setting," *Vigiliae Christianae* 56, no. 3: 223–46.

van de Sandt, Huub. 2015. "Baptism and Holiness: Two Requirements Authorizing Participation in the *Didache*'s Eucharist," in *The Didache: A Missing Piece of the Puzzle in Early Christianity*. Eds. Jonathan A. Draper and Clayton N. Jefford. Atlanta, GA: SBL, 139–64.

Vogel, Manuel. 2020. "Jüdisch versus christliche: 'Parting of the Ways' als Problem der Terminologie in Quellen- und Beschreibungssprache," *Evangelische Theologie* 80, no. 6: 418–31.

"Vows and Vowing." 1971. *Encylopaedia Judaica*, vol. 16. New York: Macmillan, 227–28.

Wahlen, Clinton L. 2005. "Peter's Vision and Conflicting Definitions of Purity," *New Testament Studies* 51, no. 4 (October): 505–18.

Wilhite, Shawn J. 2019. *The Didache: A Commentary*, Apostolic Fathers Commentary Series. Eugene, OR: Cascade.

Wilson, Stephen G. 1984. *Luke and the Law*, SNTS Monograph Series 50. Cambridge: Cambridge University Press.

Witherington III, Ben. 1998. *The Acts of the Apostles: A Socio-Rhetorical Commentary*. Grand Rapids, MI: Eerdmans.

Wolmarans, J. L. P. 2005. "The Semiotics of the Ritual Meal in the *Didache*," *Acta Patristica et Byzantina* 16, no. 1: 308–24.

Yuh, Jason N. 2019. "Do As I Say, Not As They Do: Social Construction in the *Epistle of Barnabas* through Canonical Interpretation and Ritual," *Harvard Theological Review* 112, no. 3 (July): 273–95.

40
CHRISTIANITY

Ruth Langer

One of the best ways to learn about one's own culture is to decenter it. Exploring the practices of others, seeking to understand them from the inside, leads one to identify and name elements of one's own practices that one otherwise takes for granted, presuming them simply "normal" or "human" when they are loaded with culturally specific meanings. For example, I am one of a handful of Jewish liturgists who attends an annual meeting of several hundred Christian liturgists. This community is very welcoming; its opening and closing liturgies seek full inclusivity. Planning such a service, though, proves to be complex. The organizers usually presume that the grammar of a Christian worship service is universal; the liturgy need only avoid naming Jesus. However, Jewish worship operates with a different grammar, and many beloved hymns (like "Amazing Grace") express explicitly Christian theology without naming Jesus. Naming these issues brings them to the surface. It has allowed us to think creatively about how to structure a truly shared experience, and in the process to identify what is essential and what is extraneous to our communities' self-understanding and ritual expression (Langer, 2015).

These differences operate at a number of intertwining levels. Christianity grew from Judaism but then, until recently, repudiated these roots and rejected Judaism's ongoing legitimacy. This caused it to differentiate itself sharply from Jewish ritual practice. However, many Jews lived as a minority in Christian lands, inevitably influenced by Christian ritual modes. The interplay between Jewish and Christian rituals and practices is therefore ever shifting and complex. This essay will highlight various themes arising from this interaction over two millennia, looking at questions of influence, imitation, and deliberate differentiation.

Worship and its Contexts

As the New Testament testifies, the first Christians were ethnically and culturally Jews. They lived according to the teachings of Torah; their primary official worship of God was the sacrifices offered on behalf of all Israel by the hereditary priesthood of the Jerusalem Temple. This they did both vicariously, rarely actually witnessing these rituals, and occasionally in Jerusalem, presenting personal offerings as needed. They also attended local synagogues, both inside and outside the Land of Israel, gathering with the local Jewish communities to read and study Scripture. There is no evidence for communal verbal worship in synagogues in this period, though. Early Jesus-followers also gathered for ritualized meals, structured by consumption of wine and bread.

Discontinuities with Jewish practices began within decades. As increasing numbers of gentiles joined the Jesus movement without first becoming Jews, they introduced non-Jewish cultural elements, reshaping the community's practices, and further differentiating emerging Christianity from other forms of Judaism. The Jewish revolt against Rome (66–70 CE)—and especially its failure—was a significant element in exacerbating this differentiation. Many Judean Jesus-followers did not participate in the revolt, marking themselves as non-participants in the Jewish messianic hope for renewed political independence. The Roman destruction of the Temple ended the biblically decreed Jewish mode of worship in which these Jesus-believers had participated. We do not know how many Judean sub-communities offered solutions to the religious void created by the loss of the Temple, but we do know that the two surviving responses, of the Jesus-believers and the rabbis, evolved into today's Christianity and Judaism, respectively. These two communities both compensated for the loss of the Jerusalem liturgical center by constructing new matrices of ritual practices around the surviving pre-existing elements and concepts. However, Jews and Christians imbued these shared elements with different meanings and emphases and combined them differently, creating different ritual "grammars."

Thus, the fundamental building blocks of rabbinic liturgy came to be:

1. The recitation of Sh'ma (Dt 6:4–9, 11:13–21 and Nu 15:37–41) preceded by two paragraph-length blessings on God's work as Creator and Revealer of Torah, and followed by one on God as Redeemer and, in the evening, one on God as Protector. This element is recited every morning and evening and probably originated as a home ritual tied to sleeping and awaking. Dt 6:4 becomes important as a declaration of God's absolute unity.
2. The Prayer (Tefillah or Amidah), consisting of eighteen blessings (later nineteen) on weekdays, morning, afternoon, and evening, but seven on Sabbaths and most holidays when an additional recitation is added. The first three blessings of praise and the last three of thanksgiving appear in every service; the intermediate petitionary blessings are replaced by a single "sanctification of the day" on holy days. A brief penitential liturgy begins the weekday petitions, but the petitions culminate in requests for the messianic restoration of the Jewish state. This complex element emerges after the destruction of the Temple and fulfills many worship functions of its sacrifices. This is most evident in the times decreed for the services and in the inclusion of biblical passages about that day's special Temple offerings in the additional service on holy days.
3. The reading of Scripture, the function of the pre-rabbinic synagogue. The primary, longest lection is on the Sabbath morning, drawn from a seriatim reading of every word in the Torah, accompanied by a short prophetic lection that connects thematically. Short readings from the beginning of the week's Torah portion punctuate the week on the Sabbath afternoon, Monday and Thursday mornings.
4. The Grace after Meals, also a series of blessings, probably emerging from communal meals, but required after any proper meal (defined by its including bread).

By the third century, the rabbinic worship service, ideally located in the synagogue, consisted of the first three elements, in that order. Ritual meals (4) continued to exist, even accompanied by study of Torah, but neither integrated with the rest of this liturgy nor associated with the synagogue. By the High Middle Ages, various recitations of Psalms, supplicatory prayers, and more prefaced and followed this core, especially in the morning. Preaching or teaching Torah could also be included, but was not necessarily combined with worship.

The basic pattern of the Christian communal worship service combines and interprets differently its received elements from these same contexts of Temple, synagogue, and home/table:

A. the Liturgy of the Word, i.e., the reading of Scripture. The New Testament narrates that Jesus and Paul visited synagogues (cf. Luke 4:16–28, Acts 13:15), where they read and then interpreted Scripture, and this, introduced and followed by various other texts, early formed the core of virtually every Christian liturgy. Contemporary standardized lectionaries retrieve the pattern of the early church, with readings from the Old Testament, an Epistle, and then a Gospel. The Gospel reading is sequential over the year, and the Old Testament echoes its theme in a clearly secondary role, analogous to the prophetic reading in rabbinic practice. Preaching follows the reading and interprets it. (White, 1990, 142–156).
B. Eucharist, an elaborated ritual meal of wine and bread remembering the Last Supper and Jesus' own sacrifice as a sin offering. Thus, it combines elements derived from a home-based ritual meal with themes of Temple sacrifice. It takes place on an altar, i.e., a place of sacrifice, that functions now as a table, the locus of a meal. For churches who understand the bread and wine to re-present (rather than recall) Jesus' sacrifice, becoming by the ritual his body and blood, performance of the liturgy on a sanctified altar in the dedicated space of the church is very important.

Thus, Christians developed their church-based liturgical framework by merging the three discrete ritual contexts of Second Temple-era Jewish ritual life. Rabbinic practice also found continuity in discontinuity by preserving these contexts, but differently. To the Second Temple-era synagogue Torah reading, they prefaced new elements (1 and 2). Recollection of the Temple and expectation of its restoration is particularly prominent in (2) and the later introductory readings, but rabbinic worship includes no symbolic sacrifice. (1) may indeed be imported to public prayer from the home context. Meals themselves (4), though, remain discrete from public worship. Consequently, only the reading of Scripture is a direct cognate between Christian and Jewish liturgy, but is very different in its content and liturgical context. It should be added that Christian monastic liturgies came to focus on the Psalter, a shared text, but daily rabbinic Jewish recitation of Psalms emerges late enough that it is hard to claim continuity with the Second Temple contexts (Langer, forthcoming).

Calendar

Most of this difference reflects the fundamentally different sacred narratives that Jews and Christians live by and that shape their perceptions of time. Before turning to these differences, though, it is critical to recognize that these conceptions fit within a shared metanarrative. Both traditions conceive of time as linear. Time begins with God's creation of an ideal world (Gen 1–2). Human disobedience led to expulsion from this paradise (Gen 3) and life in the blemished reality that we ourselves know. Time will end with the return, perhaps just of the righteous, to paradise. Jews and Christians differ, though, in their understandings of this intermediate time between the expulsion from Eden and regaining it. In Jesus' time, many Jews hoped that God would send a Messiah to initiate this transformation. Just as God had saved Israel in the past, bringing it home from exile in Egypt (and later Babylonia) to independent life in the Land of Israel, so too, God would again save this people, instituting an age of peace, prosperity, political independence, and universal worship of God. This messianic age would precede the end of time, the "world to come." In the perception of most Jews, neither Jesus nor anyone else has yet fulfilled these messianic roles. Jesus' followers indeed recognized that the prophetic visions of peace and prosperity were yet unrealized, but they understood his messianic role differently. Ritual participation by baptism in Jesus' sacrificial death enables forgiveness of the human sinfulness that (in Christian but not in rabbinic Jewish understanding) prevents God's salvation of individuals and of humanity collectively. His crucifixion and resurrection irretrievably initiated the messianic age. Jesus will, in the future, return to complete the Messiah's earthly tasks and initiate the end times, the eschaton. These different understandings of the era of human history in which we are living shape the stage on which these communities' ritual dramas play.

The most important example of this difference is in the narrative underlying Jews' and Christians' calendars. Although Jesus' crucifixion and resurrection took place during the season of the biblical Jewish Passover, Christianity deeply transformed that spring festival's meaning. The Jewish Passover celebrates and relives the Exodus from Egypt, God's first, paradigmatic, and dramatic saving of Israel. In biblical times, this celebration began with the Temple sacrifice and ritual consumption of a lamb, recalling the protective rituals performed in Egypt to survive the plague of the first born. The Roman destruction of the Jerusalem Temple in 70 CE ended this and all Jewish sacrificial rituals. Over several generations, the home-based Seder celebrated today emerged. This elaborate study of the biblical Exodus narrative is performed in the context of a ritual meal. This meal contains foods like unleavened bread and bitter herbs, themselves symbolic of the Exodus, but no lamb. This ritual remembers and celebrates God's past saving acts, and concludes by anticipating the future messianic redemption. The Seder thus firmly locates its participants in pre-messianic times.

This narrative, extended, also shapes the rabbinic interpretation of all the biblical pilgrimage festivals. Exactly fifty days after the Exodus, the biblical Israelites received the Torah at Mt. Sinai (Ex 19–20). In rabbinic understanding, the Feast of Weeks (Shavuot, i.e., Pentecost) commemorates this central event of the desert wandering. The booths of the fall harvest festival (Sukkot) similarly come to symbolize the fragile temporary desert homes of the Israelites during the forty years in the wilderness.

The cycle of Torah readings reinforces this narrative arc. The rabbis decreed that every word of the Pentateuch be proclaimed in order from a handwritten, error-free scroll. This deliberately archaic form of the book symbolizes a direct connection to the text God dictated to Moses at Sinai. Through this, the gathered community symbolically stands again at Sinai and relives the events from God's creation of the world to their ancestors' standing on the brink of their full salvation and entering the land at the end of Deuteronomy (Langer, 1998, 51–52). Gradually over the first millennium CE, this crystallized into an annual "journey." On Simchat Torah, the final day of the fall cluster of holidays, Jews conclude Deuteronomy and only "enter" the land with the prophetic reading from Joshua 1. Before doing this, though, they return immediately to begin Genesis again, reinforcing the unredeemed state of our world. Many Jews mark time by this cycle, naming each week according to its Torah portion. Thus, God's saving the Israelites from Egypt, in expanded form, marks Jewish time throughout the year.

This annual cycle corresponds to the natural solar year, with an extra lunar month intercalated as necessary to ensure that Passover always falls at the time of the spring barley harvest. However, the Bible teaches that a seven-day cycle, not evident from nature, was built into creation from the beginning. The Bible connects this six-day work week followed by a seventh day of complete rest not only with the seven days of creation (Ex 20:11, cf. Gen 1–2:3), but with God's saving the Israelites from the drudgery of Egypt (Dt 5:15). Thus, consciousness of the Exodus permeates even the weekly cycle of time.

Contrast this with the Christian cycle. Living in messianic times, Christians layered a new, Christ-centered set of meanings onto this received calendar. Within a century of the crucifixion, some Christian leaders, at least in Syria and Asia Minor, favored celebrating the weekly Sunday anniversary of Christ's resurrection and rejected Jewish Sabbath observance. Others continued to observe the Saturday Sabbath for centuries. Beginning in the Constantinian era, though, Christians began to apply Sabbath themes and practices to the Sunday Lord's Day, eventually fully merging the two (Bradshaw and Johnson, 2011, 3–28). Thus, Christians came to associate the weekly day of rest, not with God's first act of salvation, the Exodus, but with God's ultimate act of salvation and initiation of messianic times, Jesus' resurrection.

Similarly, Christians transformed the Jewish annual cycle to recall this new narrative of salvation. Passover and Pentecost remained central dates but now as the dates of the crucifixion/resurrection and then the Holy Spirit's coming down upon the community fifty days later (Acts 2). Indeed, the most common names for the celebration of the resurrection derive from "*Pascha*," the Aramaic for Passover, the Germanic "Easter" being a major exception. This annual celebration of Jesus' death and resurrection seems to have emerged by the second century in two forms, one a celebration tied to the Jewish date of Passover and the other on the following Sunday. The Council of Nicaea in 325, concerned about the need to consult with Jews to determine the feast's date, ruled that only the Sunday observance was permitted, determined by the first full moon after the spring equinox. Thus, Easter remained roughly in the Passover season, calculated also by a combination of lunar and solar factors, but was no longer strictly tied to the Jewish calendar (Bradshaw and Johnson, 2011, 39–59). Pentecost still follows fifty days later, also on a Sunday. In contrast to rabbinic Judaism where the weeks between the festivals became a season of semi-mourning, this "Easter Season," from its earliest attestation in the late second century, was usually a season of rejoicing (Bradshaw and Johnson, 2011, 69–74). Other elements of the Christian calendar developed with no specific historical relationship to Jewish practices.

Imitation and Differentiation: Examples of Intersections

By the late first century, Christians found themselves competing with Jews for their very survival. Only Jews were exempted from the Roman civic cults, understood to invoke divine protection for the state. Rome began persecuting non-Jewish Christians for failure to participate in this worship. Christians began to present themselves as the new and only true Israel, heirs to Israel's relationship to God. The failure of the revolt and destruction of the Temple were God's punishment to Jews for rejecting Christ. One consequence of this move was a turn to anti-Jewish rhetoric among church leaders and a deliberate further differentiation of Christians from their Jewish roots. Christians following Jewish practices were increasingly labeled as "Judaizers" and the practices of Jewish Christians were increasingly labeled heretical. Thus, especially after Christianity became licit, and then the formal and majority religion of the Roman Empire from the fourth century, Christians had little reason, occasion, or incentive to learn from Jewish practices (Kessler, 2010, ch. 3).

There are some exceptions to this, though. The contents of Christian polemics against Jews occasionally reflect actual interactions over ritual matters. Most detailed (if still vague) are St. John Chrysostom's fulminations in 386–387, over eight sermons, against members of his Antioch church who Judaized by attending synagogue services. Apparently, the entertainment value and perceived efficacy of the ancient synagogue ritual, as well as the sanctity of the Torah scrolls, attracted local attention (Wilken, 1983, ch. 3). There is no evidence, though, that the Antioch synagogue offered a rabbinic-style liturgy. Its language was also apparently Greek and accessible to outsiders. With time, though, Christians were forbidden to enter synagogues and the rabbinic style made little use of vernaculars. Detailed Christian knowledge about Jews in the medieval and early modern periods came mostly from baptized Jews, and was frequently polemical (Deutsch, 2012, ch. 5).

Changes to this rejection of Judaism came mostly from the post-Holocaust search for positive relations. The Catholic 1965 *Nostra Aetate* (para. 4) encourages joint study and friendly visiting, leading to real outreach for understanding in both directions. Study of Jesus' world has led to retrievals of early practices, albeit sometimes, like church Seders, of dubious historicity. Questions arise too over when retrieval becomes appropriation, denying Judaism its uniqueness. Jews, as a minority culture, were always (until modern Israel) much more influenced by their neighbors than the reverse. This is evident in the choices made in synagogue architecture, that frequently dialogue with the esthetic of local sacred architecture. Thus, in Christian lands, we find synagogues built like churches, but often with subtle differentiation. The thirteenth-century Altneuschul in Prague supports its roof with gothic arches, but with a fifth rib, perhaps to avoid a cross shape. In the nineteenth century, Jews in Savannah, Georgia, built a fully gothic structure minus a transept, while Cincinnati Jews even included a transept in their Plum Street Temple. They, however, decorated this building in the elaborate "Moorish" style, that, popular then also in Europe, consciously sought to recreate the so-called "Golden Age" of co-existence of Jews, Muslims, and Christians in medieval Spain. However, as the cathedral across the street constructed its steeples, the bell-less "minarets" on this synagogue's façade supposedly grew taller too. Another synagogue in Brookhaven, Mississippi looks, inside and out, like a simple Baptist church. Stained glass also marks synagogues, like churches, as religious structures, most often, but not always (e.g., Pittsburgh's Rodef Shalom Congregation), without depicting human figures (Folberg, 1995, 85, 144–145; Gruber, 1999, 34–35, 86–88, 104; "History of Plum Street Temple").

We hear this influence of the majority culture in the musical aesthetics employed as well. Musical modes echo current and local preferences. Sometimes Jews borrow common melodies, sometimes even drinking or marching songs, now "sanctified" into liturgical usage. The best known of these is the common melody for the Hanukkah hymn, *Ma'oz Tzur* (Rock of Ages) (Bayer, 2007). Among liberal Jews, choices of instrumentation fit this same mold. Traditional Jews consider instrumental music inappropriate on Sabbaths and holy days, restricting its ritual use mostly to weddings. One of the first reforms of the modern synagogue, beginning already in the eighteenth century, was the introduction of the organ, first for use only before the Sabbath, but eventually for full liturgical practice (Ellenson, 1995). From the 1960s on, as in churches, other instrumentation, including that inspired by popular music, became common. Traditional Jews also objected to hearing women's voices, so choirs, where they existed, consisted of men and boys. Liberal Jews in the nineteenth century added women's voices. This organ and choir, sometimes replacing the cantor entirely, performed music that was esthetically often indistinguishable from that of the church down the street (Goldberg, 1992–93). A perusal of the early twentieth-century American *Union Hymnal* will find mostly English hymns, some barely adapted from their Christian originals (e.g., #4, #103). The burgeoning of Israeli culture, including especially the rebirth of Hebrew as a spoken language, has banished most of these in recent decades, though, and given Jewish liturgical music a more distinctive voice.

The language of prayer is another place where we find imitation and differentiation. The official language of rabbinic prayer was Hebrew from the beginning, with a few exceptions in Aramaic, the most common vernacular. The rabbis did permit vernacular prayer for the less educated (m. Sotah 7:1–2, t. Sotah 7:7; see Langer, 1998a, 22–23). Some Jewish prayers in Greek have survived from late antiquity, but there is little evidence that they were rabbinic (van der Horst and Newman, 2008). From the early modern period, we have evidence of written vernacular prayers, mostly for women, both in Yiddish and in Iberian languages. There is little or no evidence for communal vernacular prayer among Jews before the nineteenth century, except, perhaps, among *conversos* reverting to Judaism in seventeenth-century Amsterdam (Langer, 2012, 245–246).

Christians, in contrast, seem to have placed a greater emphasis originally on vernacular translations of the Bible and corresponding prayer. With time, these became frozen into the archaic liturgical languages of regional churches, even as the vernaculars evolved. The Western church, for instance, retained the Vulgate Bible and its Latin as the language of liturgy and learning even as it spread to lands speaking unrelated languages. Thus, there are analogies between the roles of Latin, Hebrew, and other church languages such as Old Slavonic. The Protestant Reformation retrieved vernacular prayer and Bible translation. The turn to vernacular ritual had little impact on Jewish practice for several centuries. However, movements to reform Judaism follow this linguistic model. In the late eighteenth century, Moses Mendelsohn translated the Bible into German; several German translations of the liturgy followed. Through the nineteenth century, as the Reform Movement organized in Western Europe and America, vernacular liturgy became increasingly important, to the point that Rabbi David Einhorn's *Olath Tamid* contained only occasional key lines in Hebrew (Petuchowski, 1968; Friedland, 1997, ch. 1). English vernacular prayer imitated Christian liturgical English, with its deliberately archaic pseudo-Elizabethan mode, understood to communicate sanctity. Vernacular prayer, of course, made Jewish liturgy accessible to non-Jews. Awareness of this shaped a reformulation of any concepts that sounded strange to Christians. Among both Christians and Jews, the 1960s' revolutions led to a rejection of this anachronistic linguistic register in favor of an updated, if still formally proper and sometimes poetic English. Again, though, the revival of Hebrew as a living vernacular in Israel, the introduction of transliterations into liberal prayer books, and musical retrieval and innovation have, in recent decades, sent the pendulum swinging back toward increased Hebrew prayer.

Christians had long been aware of Jewish festivals, especially Purim and Simchat Torah whose noise penetrated to the streets. The Passover season itself presented severe tensions, exacerbated when differences in calendation led Jews to celebrate their carnival-like Purim just as Christians mourned Christ crucified at Jewish hands. But the more common Easter–Passover overlap led to the blood libel and its false but enduring accusation that Jews required Christian blood to produce *matzah*, thus ritually crucifying Christ again (Teter, 2020). *Matzah* production from flour and water never changed, but as reforming nineteenth-century Jews sought to make their rituals acceptable to their Christian neighbors, they sought to calm or abolish the rowdy celebrations, along with all other elements that distinguished behavior in the synagogue from that of the (Protestant) church. They, and sometimes the local government, published rules of decorum for Jewish worship, banning raucous activities like the blotting out of Haman's name on Purim or dancing on Simchat Torah, as well as chatting and moving about during the service, actively venerating the Torah, bringing small children, and anything that detracted from the dignity of the synagogue (Petuchowski, 1968, ch. 6). However, as Jews became more integrated into Western society and the world became more comfortable with cultural diversity after World War II, synagogue decorum often relaxed. Many of the features banned in the nineteenth century re-emerged; a decorous, church-like synagogue is increasingly rare.

This interaction with the majority Christian culture had several other specific impacts on Jewish ritual life. The role of the rabbi changed dramatically in modernity, from teacher, halakhic decisor, and only occasional preacher, to ritual officiant and pastor, modeled on the social and religious roles of the Christian priest and pastor. While Judaism has no sacraments entrusted specifically to ordained ministers, the equivalents of Christian sacraments moved increasingly onto the rabbinic task list. Indeed, underlying this was a very different concept of the role of the sacred than in traditional Judaism. Fundamentally, Judaism never fully distinguished between sacred and profane areas of life. It does indeed differentiate between the heightened sacredness of the Sabbath and holy days and the lesser sacredness of the workaday world. However, because every moment of life is lived before God, guided by Torah, even the most mundane act is inherently sacred. For instance, urine and feces are themselves not sacred, but rabbinic tradition teaches Jews to praise God for creating our bodies with working orifices by which to eliminate them (b. Ber. 60b). Thus, the rabbinic aspiration is to guide the entire community into a life informed by Torah at all times, to ritualize and sanctify every aspect of life. The elevation of clergy in imitation of Christianity often encourages the formation of a secularized laity that feels less personal responsibility for deep Jewish education and consciously living a life guided by Torah.

Similarly, Christian influence heightens the distinction between synagogue and home as ritual realms, with the synagogue more sanctified and the home more secularized. Yes, the synagogue is the holiest place because of the presence of the Torah scroll (m. Megillah 3:1), but a *minyan* (prayer quorum) gathered elsewhere is still sacred. Though a synagogue usually has an elevated platform from which Torah is read (the *bimah*), this is primarily functional. It is not a sanctified altar, a place whose access is restricted to consecrated clergy and the rituals they alone may perform. Altar rails demarcating this sacred space, once common in Catholic churches and still present as elaborate tall *iconostases* in orthodox ones, have no parallel in most synagogues. They appear in some archaeological remains from Byzantine Palestine, where they may indeed have been a symbolic transfer of the Jerusalem Temple's barrier separating the priestly and Israelite areas (Fine, 1998). Railings on a *bimah* otherwise serve merely to prevent falls.

A modern result of thinking of the synagogue in the image of a church is the movement of more lifecycle ceremonies into this space. Circumcisions and baby namings had long been performed among the community gathered for prayer there, and Jewish adulthood (*bar mitzvah* and today also for girls, *bat mitzvah*) was marked by taking an adult role in the service. Confirmation, a modern borrowing from churches for older teens, is often integrated into *Shavuot* services. However, Jewish funerals and weddings often take place elsewhere. While many Christian traditions integrate marriages and funerals into a full Eucharistic liturgy, necessitating their location in a church, parallel Jewish observances call for different contexts. Traditional Jews maintain the biblical tradition that a human corpse is a significant source of ritual impurity (Nu 19:11–22). Torah requires that *kohanim*, men of priestly descent, avoid contact with death except for close relatives (Lev 21:1–4). As this contact includes being in an enclosed space, Jews perform funerals either outdoors or in dedicated structures, today often funeral homes, that the priests could avoid entering. Liberal Jews today do not share this concern, but funerals in synagogues are still rare. The Jewish funeral itself also does not generate a regular prayer context. Instead, it begins a period of formal mourning (*shiva*) in which weekday communal prayer gatherings meet in the home of the mourner. Influences from Christian practices appear mostly in actual burial practices, such as delayed funerals, elaborate coffins, mausoleums, or cremation.

Weddings, in contrast, often take place in the large communal space of synagogues, but they need not be located there. A Jewish wedding's location is marked by the *ḥuppah*, the canopy symbolizing the couple's new home. When this *ḥuppah* functioned, literally or symbolically, as the bridal chamber in which a marriage would be consummated, it was deemed inappropriate to locate it directly by the Torah ark. However, this function has been largely dissociated from the structure today, resulting in many weddings located in synagogue sanctuaries. The Christian model that the church is the appropriate place for a wedding may have encouraged this trend.

Some Jews prefer to locate the ḥuppah outdoors at night, invoking God's blessing to Abraham that his descendants be numerous as the stars (Gen 15:5, 22:17; Lamm, 1991, 183–185). No matter where the wedding ceremony is located, its prayers are recited over cups of wine, on the model of a home liturgy, and separate from the daily communal prayer structure. At the party and for the entire following week, the wedding blessings are repeated at communal meals.

Conclusion

Although the early church learned much from Jewish ritual practice, over time the impact of Christian ritual on Judaism has been much more significant, both because of Christian concerns about Judaizing, and because Jews were the minority. In recent years, though, this situation has shifted. The post-Holocaust rapprochement between Christians and Jews generated Christian interest in Jewish ritual practice, both for their own sake and as part of retrieving the Jewish Jesus. Simultaneously, the State of Israel has nurtured a flourishing majority Jewish culture, encouraging Jews worldwide to celebrate their own distinctiveness. This culture also influences the practices of Israel's Christian minority. Thus, the millennia-old dance between Jewish and Christian syncretism, imitation, and distinctiveness continues in ever shifting dimensions.

References

Bayer, Bathja. 2007. "Ma'oz Ẓur." In *Encyclopaedia Judaica*, ed. Michael Berenbaum and Fred Skolnik, 2nd ed., vol. 13. Detroit, MI: Macmillan Reference USA, 496–97. *eBooks*: link.gale.com/apps/doc/CX2587513215/GVRL?u=mlin_m_bostcoll&sid=GVRL&xid=dd82bd94 [accessed 30 Jan. 2021].

Bradshaw, Paul F., and Maxwell E. Johnson. 2011. *The Origins of Feasts, Fasts, and Seasons in Early Christianity*. Collegeville, MN: Liturgical Press.

Deutsch, Yaacov. 2012. *Judaism in Christian Eyes: Ethnographic Descriptions of Jews and Judaism in Early Modern Europe*. Trans. Avi Aronsky. Oxford University Press.

Ellenson, David. 1995. "A Disputed Precedent: The Prague Organ in Nineteenth Century Central European Legal Literature and Polemics." *Leo Baeck Yearbook* 40: 251–64.

Fine, Steven. 1998. "'Chancel' Screens in Late Antique Palestinian Synagogues: A Source from the Cairo Geniza." In *Religious and Ethnic Communities in Later Roman Palestine*, ed. Hayim Lapin. Studies and Texts in Jewish History and Culture 5. Bethesda: University Press Maryland, 67–85.

Folberg, Neil. 1995. *And I Shall Dwell Among Them: Historic Synagogues of the World*. New York: Aperture Foundation, Inc.

Friedland, Eric L. 1997. *"Were Our Mouths Filled with Song": Studies in Liberal Jewish Liturgy*. Cincinnati, OH: Hebrew Union College Press.

Goldberg, Joseph, trans. 1992–93. "Maharam Mintz: On the Conduct of the Hazzan." *Journal of Jewish Music and Liturgy* 15: 37–47.

Gruber, Samuel D. 1999. *Synagogues*. New York: MetroBooks.

"History of Plum Street Temple." https://www.wisetemple.org/about/our-history/history-of-plum-street-temple/ [accessed January 30, 2021].

Kessler, Edward. 2010. *An Introduction to Jewish-Christian Relations*. Cambridge: Cambridge University Press.

Lamm, Maurice. 1991. *The Jewish Way in Love and Marriage*. Middle Village, NY: Jonathan David Publishers, Inc.

Langer, Ruth. 1998. "From Study of Scripture to a Reenactment of Sinai." *Worship* 72, no. 1: 43–65.

Langer, Ruth. 1998a. *To Worship God Properly: Tensions Between Liturgical Custom and Halakhah in Judaism*. Cincinnati, OH: Hebrew Union College Press.

Langer, Ruth. 2012. *Cursing the Christians? A History of the Birkat HaMinim*. New York: Oxford University Press.

Langer, Ruth. 2015. "The Blessings and Challenges of Interreligious Prayer." *Proceedings of the North American Academy of Liturgy*: 27–35.

Langer, Ruth. Forthcoming. "The Early Medieval Emergence of Jewish Daily Morning Psalms Recitation, *Pesuqei D'zimra*." In *The Psalms in Jewish Liturgy, Ritual and Community Formation from Antiquity to the Middle Ages: Biblical Texts in Dynamic, Pluralistic Contexts*, eds. Claudia Bergmann, Tessa Rajak, Benedikt Kranemann, and Rebecca Sebbagh. Leiden: Brill.

Petuchowski, Jakob J. 1968. *Prayerbook Reform in Europe: The Liturgy of European Liberal and Reform Judaism.* New York: World Union for Progressive Judaism.

Teter, Magda. 2020. *Blood Libel: On the Trail of an Antisemitic Myth.* Cambridge, MA: Harvard University Press.

Union Hymnal: Songs and Prayers for Jewish Worship. 1932. Third Edition. New York: Central Conference of American Rabbis.

van der Horst, Pieter W., and Judith H. Newman. 2008. *Early Jewish Prayers in Greek.* Commentaries on Early Jewish Literature. Berlin/New York: Walter de Gruyter.

White, James F. 1990. *Introduction to Christian Worship, Revised Edition.* Nashville, TN: Abingdon Press.

Wilken, Robert L. 1983. *John Chrysostom and the Jews: Rhetoric and Reality in the Late 4th Century.* Berkeley/Los Angeles/London: University of California Press.

41
SAMARITANS

Reinhard Pummer

Samaritans are a branch of Yhwh worshiping Israelites. Modern scholarly opinion is nearly unanimous in dating their birth as an independent community in the time shortly before the turn of the eras, more precisely in the late second century BCE.[1] It is now generally accepted among scholars that the Samaritans are not a sect of Judaism that broke away from its mother religion late in the history of Israel.[2] Rather, they constitute a branch of the religion of Israel that eventually went its own way, developing its own traditions and customs. Notwithstanding the scholarly consensus, many Jews – and some Christians – still see the Samaritans as syncretists as intimated by a certain reading of 2 Kings 17:29. According to the Samaritans' own beliefs, they are the original Israelites who have lived in the land of the Bible for more than 3,000 years (127 consecutive generations) and have kept the revelation received by Moses undiluted. They see themselves, therefore, as the שמרים "guardians (of the Torah and the ancient Israelite tradition)" and in modern parlance they prefer the name "Israelite Samaritans" (הישראלים השומרונים), i.e., Israelites who are settled in Samaria.

Samaritans differ from the Jews in the following major points: their sacred center is Mount Gerizim in the vicinity of ancient Shechem (today Tel Balāṭa) and modern Nablus (ancient Neapolis), not Mount Zion; their sacred scripture consists of the Pentateuch alone without the Ketubim and Nebi'im of the Jewish canon; and they have a functioning priesthood, the high priest being the head of the community; the institution of the rabbinate does not exist among them; they celebrate the Feast of Passover as it is prescribed in Exodus 12, i.e., they slaughter, roast and eat a certain number of sheep as opposed to celebrating the Seder of the Jews; and they perform three times a year a pilgrimage to the top of Mt. Gerizim – on Matzot, Shavout and Sukkot; no pilgrimages are performed by the Jews ever since the Second Temple was destroyed in 70 CE.

Today, the Samaritans live primarily in two locations – Kiryat Luza on Mt. Gerizim and Ḥolon, a southern suburb of Tel Aviv. They number approximately 860 individuals and worship in two synagogues on Mt. Gerizim and two synagogues in Ḥolon. Despite the testimony of literary and epigraphic sources, archaeological evidence and the scholarly consensus that the Samaritans had a sanctuary on the main summit of Mt. Gerizim from the fifth to the second century BCE, the Samaritans deny that they ever had a temple on the mountain.[3]

The chief rituals and customs of the Samaritans are based on the Pentateuch. Apart from expansions and orthographic details, the Samaritan Pentateuch is in essence the same as the

Jewish Pentateuch.[4] The main differences are the added Tenth Commandment after Exod 20:17 and Deut 5:18 that puts the emphasis on Mt. Gerizim with the help of a number of passages from other verses;[5] the change in the law of the altar in Deut 27:4 (Gerizim instead of Ebal); and the use of the perfect instead of the imperfect in the formula of the place chosen by Yhwh for worship in all twenty-one passages in Deuteronomy, i.e., whereas the Samaritan Pentateuch reads, "the place that the Lord your God *has* chosen," the Jewish Pentateuch reads, "the place that the Lord your God *will* choose."[6] These changes in the common Israelite Pentateuch were made in all likelihood in the Hellenistic period.[7]

Since Samaritanism is a branch of Yahwism, there are of course similarities between Samaritan and Jewish rituals and practices, as will be seen below. Moreover, the estrangement between the two religions did not mean that there were no further contacts between them. On the contrary, they remained close to each other throughout their histories, even if their relationship had its ups and downs. Cultural contacts are identifiable in literature, architecture, art and customs throughout late antiquity, the Middle Ages and beyond. In the following discussion of Samaritan rituals and customs, it will be seen that the influences of the societies among which they lived and live are undeniable even if they do not affect the core beliefs of Samaritanism.[8] Examples are the use of Jewish terminology for certain aspects of their tradition and the participation in folkloristic customs connected with such Jewish festivals as Purim and Hanukkah.[9] There are of course also influences from Arab culture, ranging from certain naming customs in Nablus to marriage practices and the terms for a variety of traditions and institutions.

The Samaritans did not create the kind of literature that corresponds to the body of rabbinic writings, such as Mishna, Tosefta and the Talmud. Apart from exegetical and liturgical texts, they do have a voluminous halakhic literature, mostly in Arabic and largely unedited and untranslated into European languages, but it does not have the same standing as the rabbinic literature in Judaism. Neither individual halakhic treatises written by distinguished Samaritan scholars nor collections of questions and answers are decisive in assessing and deciding concrete cases or situations. Rather, it is the oral tradition that is crucial in everyday life.[10] Since religion is at the foundation of the Samaritans' identity, tradition determines all aspects of their life, including of course rituals and practices.

Given the small size of the community – presently there are approximately 860 Samaritans in all, a substantial increase from the 163 individuals in 1922[11] – there are no Samaritan sects, although in antiquity one or more sects did exist. But very little is known about them and they have long ceased to exist.[12] This is not to say that disputes among the contemporary Samaritans about halakhic issues do not occur, but when they do, they do not lead to the formation of factions that separate themselves from the main body of the community.

In all their publications about their community they underline in one form or another the major principles that they see as constitutive of their identity: "1. Perpetual residence in the Holy Land. 2. Obligatory participation in the Sacrifice on Mount Gerizim at Passover. 3. Celebration of the Sabbath as written in the Torah. 4. Adherence to the laws of purity and impurity as prescribed in the Torah." In addition, they underline the four principles of faith: "1. One God, who is the God of Israel; 2. One prophet, Moses son of Amram; 3. One holy book, the Pentateuch: the Torah handed down by Moses; 4. One holy place, Mount Gerizim." The last principle has a short appendix: "To these is added belief in the Taheb, son of Joseph, the 'Prophet like Moses' who will appear on the Day of Wrath and Judgment in the latter times."[13] However, today this belief plays virtually no role in the lived religion.[14]

The following outlines the most important Samaritan rituals and practices and points out some of the similarities to and differences from Jewish usage. It is through the traditions and rituals described here – learned and practiced by every Samaritan from childhood on – that the Samaritans have preserved their identity throughout many centuries.

Prayer

Community prayer is said, or chanted, in the synagogue twice a day on weekdays – once in the morning and once in the evening. On Sabbaths, a third service is added at noon or in the afternoon. Prayer is preceded by the ritual washing of hands, mouth, nose, face, ears and legs while reciting appropriate prayers and biblical verses, namely Lev 15:31; Deut 28:8; Gen 2:7; Exod 15:26 and 40:31–32. Since Samaritans no longer have *miqva'ot*, as they did in antiquity, they perform the ritual at home. Before entering the synagogue, shoes are removed and left at the entrance.

Genital discharge (Lev 15:13–16) makes men and women ritually impure. For men, this means that after intercourse or nocturnal emissions they are impure for one day and at the prayers in the synagogue they must stand in a specified area in the back and are not allowed to participate aloud in the prayers. All worshipers must wear a head covering during the service, be it a tarboosh or any other kind of head-wear.[15] Samaritans do not wear *tefillin* as do the Jews. They interpret the passages Exod 13:9,16; Deut 6:8 and 11:18 in a spiritual sense – it is their duty to remember God's commands. Part of the prayer ritual are prostrations similar to Islamic gestures. The concept of *minyan*, a quorum of ten adult men, is unknown to the Samaritans. Some of the gestures performed during prayer are reminiscent of Muslim prayer gestures, such as the holding of the hands as if the praying person were reading, the stroking with one hand over the face, and the prostration. This is not to say that these gestures were adopted from the Muslims.[16]

Synagogues

Both Jews and Samaritans say their communal prayers in synagogues. The oldest Jewish synagogues go back to the time around the turn of the eras. For the Samaritans we have indications that in the diaspora, on the Greek island of Delos, there probably existed a synagogue in the second century BCE. As to Palestine, the oldest Samaritan synagogues for which we have archaeological evidence date from the third/fourth century CE. Architecture, furnishings and mosaic art show many similarities between the two traditions. Different from Jewish synagogues, in today's Samaritan synagogues there are no benches but the worshipers pray on carpets – shoes are therefore left on the outside – and their prayer movements are reminiscent of prayers in mosques.[17] Antique synagogues of both Samaritans and Jews were furnished with stone benches, usually along the walls, although worshipers may also have been standing or sitting on wooden benches or mats.[18]

In the front of the synagogue is the Torah shrine or Holy Ark (ארון הקודש), closed off with an embroidered curtain. During the service the Torah scroll is displayed, opened always on the same passage – the blessing of Aaron in Lev 9:22 on the top of the column to Lev 11:39 at the bottom of it. The scroll is used to bless the congregation but not to read from. The Torah is read on Sabbath morning in the houses of the community members. During the synagogue service so-called *qeṭafim* (singular *qaṭaf*) are recited. They are a collection of abbreviated Torah verses.[19]

The worshipers in Samaritan synagogues are only men. Women pray at home; only on Yom Kippur do they attend the synagogue. Contemporary Samaritans reason that the laws of ritual purity and impurity (see below) make this necessary. As mentioned, any discharge from the genitals makes men and women ritually impure. Women are therefore ritually impure during menstruation and after childbirth. However, because they may have unforeseen bleeding at other times, too, it is safer for them not to attend regular synagogue services.

Today, as well as the four Samaritan synagogues in use, two on Mt. Gerizim and two in Ḥolon, there is another synagogue in Nablus but since the Samaritans moved their dwellings to the top of the mountain it is unused.

Sabbath

As for the Jews, the Sabbath is a special day for the Samaritans. Apart from abstention from all work, there is a special dress for men – as noted, women do not pray in the synagogue – and special prayers are said. The men's Sabbath dress is a long, usually striped robe, and over it they wear a prayer shawl (*ṭallīt*) in the form of a long white robe.[20] An additional *ṭallīt* is worn by the priest who holds the Torah scroll. The head must be covered as always during prayer; priests wear white turbans instead of the red ones on weekdays. As noted already, in addition to the two daily prayer services, there is a third service held in the afternoon. The Sabbath service consists therefore of the following parts: eve of the Sabbath, Sabbath morning, Sabbath afternoon, and termination of the Sabbath. There are no sermons. After the morning service the weekly portion of the Torah is read by men and women in their homes.

No fire or electricity is used on Sabbath; even refrigerators are unplugged and the food is eaten cold or kept in thermos bottles. The lights are left on in the kitchen and in the main room of the house for reasons of safety.[21]

Circumcision

As in Judaism, in Samaritanism circumcision of a male child is to be performed on the eighth day after birth. In Gen 17:14, which in the Masoretic text reads: "Any uncircumcised male who is not circumcised in the flesh of his foreskin shall be cut off from his people; he has broken my covenant," the Samaritan Pentateuch, following Gen 17:12, inserts the words "on the eighth day" as does the Septuagint. The Samaritans never postpone circumcision beyond the eighth day. If it has to be postponed for health reasons, they find a way to justify their action.[22] The circumcision is now performed by a Jewish circumciser (*mōhel*) rather than by a Samaritan priest as was the case in the past.[23] The ceremony takes place in a community hall and the boy is held by a female relative. After the completion of the ritual, the boy receives his name and a celebration by the community follows. Neither *perī'ah* (uncovering of the *glans penis*) nor *meṣīṣa* (sucking of the blood from the wound) are carried out. These procedures are not mentioned in the Bible but were instituted by the rabbis (see *M. Shabbat* 19:2). They may have been a response to the attempt by some Jews to obliterate their circumcision through epispasm to better fit in with the Greco-Roman society.[24] In antiquity as today, the Samaritans were and are well known for being faithful in carrying out circumcision.[25]

Redemption of the First Born

According to Exod 13:13–15 and Num 18:15–16 every first-born son must be redeemed (פדיון הבן), i.e., every first-born son was destined to become a priest unless he was "redeemed" by a sacrifice. Today, the Samaritans present the high priest with a sum of money that depends on the financial situation of the family. The custom was not always observed.[26]

Completion of the Torah

There is no Bar Mitzvah in the Samaritan tradition but a ceremony that celebrates a child's completion of the reading of the Torah. Children, boys as well as girls, begin to read the Torah when they are five or six years old and gradually read the whole book. When they have finished reading all of it, they then must memorize the final verses of the Scripture and recite them in front of the congregation. This ceremony is called *ḥatīmat tōrah*. It takes place at different times in the life of the children, depending on when he or she finishes the task. Usually it occurs between seven and ten years of age. Although it is not the same as the Jewish Bar Mitzva, Israeli Samaritans call the ceremony by that name and, like the Jewish Bar Mitzva, the ceremony now is followed by an opulent party.[27]

The Laws of Purity and Impurity

Ritual purity and impurity are extremely important aspects of the life of the Samaritans and are observed with great strictness.[28] Their observance is often enumerated among the principles that identify someone as a member of the community.[29] Today, they are primarily connected with sexual matters. As mentioned in connection with the prayer in the synagogue, men become ritually impure for one day after sexual intercourse and nocturnal emission. In such cases a man – and his wife after intercourse – has to wash and is unclean until the evening (Lev 15:16–18).[30]

Ritual impurity is much more important in the case of women. Women are impure for seven days during menstruation, forty days after the birth of a boy, and eighty days after that of a girl (Lev 12:2–5; 15:19–28). During this time – called נדה *niddah* as in Judaism[31] – everybody and everything they touch becomes also impure. They are therefore isolated during this time in order not to contaminate others, with all the consequences this has for the family. At the end of their days of impurity they are to bathe in the bathtub with running water since there are today no Samaritan *miqva'ot*, as mentioned above.[32] The strict adherence to these rules of purity and impurity sets the Samaritans apart from other communities and many women value it for this reason, although some are less than happy about it.

Marriage

Traditionally, three successive acts lead to marriage: proposal (*kiddūshīn*), betrothal (*'erūsīn*) and wedding (*nissū'īn*).[33] The official proposal is supposed to obtain the girl's agreement to the marriage, although in fact it confirms the acceptance of the prior negotiations between the two families. The groom is absent from the ceremony. In the house of her parents and in the presence of male relatives, a priest and two witnesses, the girl is asked for her consent. When she has given it, the priest recites the "Hear, oh Israel" and with this the engagement is concluded. Since it still can be dissolved, sexual contact is not permitted. At the betrothal ceremony the groom and the bride are present, although the latter may be represented by a guardian. The groom asks the bride or her guardian for her hand and hands over the *mohar*, a symbolic sum of money.[34] From now on, divorce is necessary if the couple wants to separate, and all financial transactions must be reversed. The next stage is the wedding which today is performed together with the betrothal. In the course of the wedding, the marriage contract, called *ketubbah*, is read by a priest and handed over to the father of the bride. Besides the date of the marriage, the names of the groom and the bride, it lists the names of their fathers, grandfathers and those of the witnesses as well as the *mohar*. It is introduced with a religious poem (*piyyūṭ*).[35] The festivities of the wedding last a week and include elements of Arabic folklore, both in Nablus and in Ḥolon.[36]

Since the Samaritans follow the patrilinear principle rather than the matrilinear one as the Jews do, it was not permitted in the past for women to marry non-Samaritans, whereas Samaritan men could marry Jewish women already in the nineteenth century if the women agreed to live according to the Samaritan tradition. The small numbers of the Samaritans made this necessary. Today, however, women and men of any or no religion are possible marriage candidates as long as they are willing to lead a Samaritan life. So far, a number of Samaritan men have entered into marriages with women from such countries as the Ukraine and Russia.[37]

Pilgrimage

As laid down in Deut 16:16; Exod 23:14–17; and 34:18–23, three times a year – on Matzot, Shavout and Sukkot – the Samaritans, men and women, make a pilgrimage to the top of Mt. Gerizim. The prayers begin in the synagogue at 1:00 or 2:00 a.m. The pilgrimage as such starts around four o'clock in the morning when the congregation leaves the synagogue in Kiryat Luzah, all the while singing and praying. In the course of the pilgrimage they stop at several stations or "altars" which commemorate specific events in the biblical history. They are: the Twelve Stones of Joshua (Deut 27:4 SP); the altar of Adam and his son Seth; the Eternal Hill on the very top of the Mountain (Gen 49:26 SP; Deut 33:15 SP), the longest of the stops; "God will provide" (Gen 22:8); the Altar of Isaac; the Altar of Noah; and again the Eternal Hill which is circumambulated by the pilgrims two and a half times while they recite a prayer seven times. The recital of the blessing is the high point of the pilgrimage. Beginning with Aaron's and Moses' blessings of Israel (Lev 9:22–23), all Pentateuchal passages which speak of blessing are then said in sequence in the *qaṭaf* form.[38] The pilgrimage ends here at around 9:00 a.m. The participants embrace and kiss one another and wish each other peace.[39]

Pesach (Passover) and Matzot (Festival of Unleavened Bread)

For the calculation of the feast days the Samaritans have their own calendar which is a combination of the lunar and solar systems.[40] Its basis is the Bible but it includes also elements from the Julian calendar and the Arab astronomical tables. Unlike the Jewish calendar, it is not based on the observation of the moon but on calculation. Today, the computer is used for this purpose. There are no months-names but the months are numbered from the first to the twelfth. The "First Month" corresponds to Nisan in the Jewish calendar and to April/May in the Gregorian calendar. To make sure the seasons always occur in the same months, an additional month is inserted when needed. In some years Samaritan and Jewish feasts are therefore celebrated one month apart.

The most important Samaritan feast and at the same time the best known to outsiders is Passover. Unlike the Jews, the Samaritans celebrate it as prescribed in Exodus 12, i.e., one-year-old lambs are slaughtered, roasted and eaten. The celebration takes place on Mt. Gerizim on the fifteenth of the First Month. The number of the lambs sacrificed depends on the size of the community (cf. Exod 12:3–4). After having been fleeced and inspected for possible blemishes, they are put on skewers and lowered into "ovens" called *tannūrīm*, i.e., stone-lined pits in the ground, and roasted. After about four hours they are taken out and eaten. The ceremony is accompanied by readings from the Bible and by prayers.[41]

Matzot, the Feast of Unleavened Bread, is a feast separate from Passover and celebrated on the twenty-first day of the First Month. It is on this day that the Samaritans undertake the first pilgrimage of the religious year.

Shavuot (Pentecost)

Fifty days after Matzot, the Feast of Weeks or Shavuot is celebrated as prescribed in Lev 23:15–16. But whereas the majority of the Jews understands the "Sabbath" in Lev 23:15 as "feast day" and equates it with the first day of Passover from which seven weeks must be counted before the celebration of Shavuot, the Samaritans understand it as the first day (Sunday) of the eighth week.

The Wednesday before Shavuot is called יום מקרתה "Day of Scripture," or יום מעמד על הר סיני "Day of Standing on Mt. Sinai." The feast commemorates the giving of the Law. The special service lasts from Tuesday midnight to 6:00 p.m. on Wednesday. During the recitation of the Ten Commandments, the Torah scroll is lifted up at each Commandment.

On Shavuot the second pilgrimage of the year takes place.

The Festival of the Seventh Month

The festival of the Seventh Month (מועד החדש השביעי) (Lev 23:23–25) corresponds to the first of the month of Tishri in the Jewish religious calendar, the Jewish Near Year. However, the Samaritans do not celebrate it as their New Year's Day. They do observe the custom of blowing the Shofar today, but there were times when it was said that the Shofar was blown only when the temple built by Joshua was still in existence.[42] The day is above all the first of the ten Days of Penitence and begins the preparation for the Day of Atonement.

Yom Kippur (The Day of Atonement)

The tenth day of the First Month is the Day of Atonement (Lev 23:26–32). The Samaritans – men, women and children – fast for twenty-four hours, abstain from work and pray in the synagogue. It is the only day in the year on which women pray with the men in the synagogue.

Fasting is understood as abstaining from food and drink for the whole twenty-four hours by every member of the community over the age of one year. The prayers also last twenty-four hours, but not every individual must spend the whole time in the synagogue; periods of rest are allowed.

Yom Kippur is now the second day on which the Shofar is blown – once at the beginning and once at the conclusion. In the Mt. Gerizim synagogue, the Abisha Scroll, the most revered Torah scroll of the Samaritans, is taken out of the safe and the congregation is blessed with it.

The day concludes with a festive meal, and on the next morning the preparations for Sukkot begin.

Sukkot (Tabernacles)

The festival is celebrated on the fifteenth day of the Seventh Month (Lev 23:33–36, 23:39–44). In preparation for it, the Samaritans gather in the preceding week decorative fruits that are used to build the sukkah. The latter differs, however, from that of the Jews in several respects. One is that the sukkah is built *inside* the houses of each family, something which would make a Jewish sukkah invalid. The reason for this practice is now said to be the persecutions by

Byzantines or Muslims in the past which did not permit the erection of the sukkah outdoors. It is, however, possible that the custom is much more recent; unfortunately, we do not have any sources that contain information on it. The second difference from Jewish sukkot is that the Samaritan sukkot have no side walls, only a roof. Today, in most houses a metal grid is hung from the ceiling of the living room (or supported by metal posts) and the fruits are fastened on it, arranged in colorful patterns. This is how the Samaritans interpret Lev 23:40a: "On the first day [of the feast] you shall take the fruit of majestic[43] trees (פרי עץ הדר), branches of palm trees (כפת תמירים), boughs of leafy trees (ענף עץ־עבת) and willows of the brook (ערבי־נחל)." The Torah does not specify what is to be done with these fruits. Only in Neh 8:14–18 instructions are given about the use of the fruits and plants collected by the people for the feast, namely to make booths: and the people made the booths

> on the roofs of their houses, and in their courts, and in the court of the house of God, and in the square at the Water Gate and in the square at the Gate of Ephraim. And all the assembly of those who had returned from the captivity made booths and lived in them.
>
> *Neh 8:15–16*

The Jews use them to make the *lūlav*, i.e., a bouquet made with these plants and named after the largest branch in it, the palm leaf; the bundle was to be held in the hand and waved at certain moments in the prayer. Together with the *'etrōg*, a citrus fruit, they are called in the rabbinic tradition the Four Species (ארבעה מינים).[44] On Sukkot, i.e., on the first day of the Seven Days Festival, the third pilgrimage of the year to the peak of Mt. Gerizim takes place.

On the twenty-second day of the Seventh Month, the last festival of the liturgical year, *shemini atseret*, שמיני עצרת (Eighth [day] of the Assembly) is celebrated (Lev 23:36; Num 29:35). At the conclusion of the service, a Torah scroll is carried around the inside of the synagogue while the worshipers clap their hands.

After the completion of the last festival of the liturgical cycle, the sukkot are dismantled, the fruits are processed and the dry branches are burned.[45]

Conclusion

By conscientiously observing their traditional rituals and customs the Samaritans keep their identity intact. Even if from time to time they make modifications to some parts of the traditional observances, the fundamental elements remain unchanged. Especially through their Passover celebration and their pilgrimages to Mt. Gerizim three times a year they emphasize again and again their identity as an independent form of Israelite Yahwism.

Notes

1 For a recent comprehensive overview of the various facets of Samaritanism see Pummer 2016b. For the Samaritan rituals and practices see Pummer 1987 (with illustrations); Pummer 1989.
2 On this question see Pummer 2010.
3 The temple on the lower peak, Tell er-Ras, north of the main summit, was once considered by some archaeologists to have been the Samaritan temple. However, new excavations have shown that it was a Roman temple dedicated to Zeus and built in the second century CE. For a thorough description of the remains of this building see Magen 2009, 236–56. On the temple built by Joshua see below and Pummer 2016a, 10–11.
4 For a discussion of the present scholarly views see Pummer 2016b, 195–213.

5 The Samaritan tradition counts the Jewish first commandment as preamble. The additional text is composed primarily of passages from Deuteronomy, namely. Exod. 13:11a, Deut. 11:29a; 27:2b–3a.4–7; 11:30.
6 The passages are: Deut 12:5, 11, 14, 18, 21, 26; 14:23, 24, 25; 15:20; 16:2, 6, 7, 11, 15, 16; 17:8, 10; 18:6; 26:2; 31:11.
7 This is the view accepted by most recent biblical scholars. For a detailed analysis see Heckl 2017.
8 For discussions of Samaritan rituals and customs see also Pummer 1987, 1989, 2016b, 257–88; Schreiber 2014, 87–135.
9 Since Samaritan children go to state schools, they participate in the custom of dressing up for Purim and eating jam-filled doughnuts on Hanukkah as their fellow students do.
10 For an overview of Samaritan halakha see Pummer 2016b, 231–39 with further references. Rothschild 2005, 104★ characterizes this type of halakhic reasoning as "un sentiment halakhique collectif" to be studied with "une sorte d'ethno-sociologie juridique."
11 See a list of numbers from 1806 to 1931 in Schur 1992, 152–53 and the population figures from 1954 to 2013 in www.israelite-samaritans.com.
12 The only modern monograph is Isser 1976. See also Fossum 1989 and Isser 1999.
13 All three preceding quotes are from Tsedaka 2017, 14. Similar declarations are to be found on the websites www.israelite-samaritans.com and www.the-samaritans.net.
14 And in fact, one Samaritan website states that "The Day of Vengeance and Recompense is a fundamental Samaritan belief" but it "is not deemed a Principle of Faith" (www.israelite-samaritans.com in the section "Principles of Faith"). For the concept of the Taheb see Dexinger 1986 and 1998.
15 On tarboosh and turban see Pummer 1987, 17.
16 For a discussion see Pummer 1987, 15–16 and the references cited there.
17 See the illustrations in Pummer 1987, Plates XXI–XXIII, and the discussion of the prayer gestures on pp. 15–16. See also the online gallery of pictures by the Israeli photographer Ori Orhof: https://orhof.smugmug.com/SamaritanHolidays/. Elderly and frail men pray now on chairs.
18 For the Jewish synagogues see Levine 2005, 337–40.
19 On the *qeṭafim see* Pummer 1989, 674–75.
20 For illustrations of the Sabbath dress and the prayer shawl see Plates XXII and XXIII in Pummer 1987.
21 See Tsedaka 2017, 19.
22 For a famous example of such a rationalization see Pummer 2016b, 270.
23 In Nablus, a Muslim doctor or male nurse may be called upon (Schreiber 2014, 107).
24 See 1 Macc 1:14–15 and 1 Corinthians 7:18.
25 See Pummer 2005, 31.
26 See, e.g., Mills 1864, 191–92.
27 See the description in Schreiber 2014, 109.
28 On the details of the implications of ritual purity and impurity for contemporary Samaritans see Schreiber 2014, 125–35. The importance of the purity and impurity rules becomes clear also from the large amount of space dedicated to them in the halakhic works of the eleventh century, namely the Kitāb al-Ṭabbāḫ and the Kitāb al-Kāfī. For the texts and translations see Wedel 1987, 112–21 (Kitāb al-Ṭabbāḫ, transl.); 'Abd al-'Al 1957, 502–72 (Kitāb al-Kāfī, transl.); Noja 1970, 65–73 (Kitāb al-Kāfī, transl.). 'Abd al-'Al 1957, 163–240 compares the two works with each other on their teachings about the subject, and the Samaritan halakha on impurity with the Jewish halakhic traditions. For a monograph on the subject see Bóid 1989.
29 Up until recently, this was the case on the website www.israelite-samaritans.com, but it is now (25.6.2020) replaced with "Principles of Faith" that do not include purity and impurity. However, another Samaritan website enumerates it among the identifying characteristics of Samaritans, a subcategory of the Five Principles of Faith: www.the-samaritans.net (accessed June 25, 2020).
30 The Torah specifies also the consequences of discharge from the genitals at other times: Lev 15:2–15 for men and Lev 15:25–28 for women.
31 The Samaritans use also the term *imsammad* of unclear derivation (see the discussion in Schreiber 2014, 126–27).
32 The recently published introduction to Samaritanism by the Samaritan journalist, scholar, and community leader, Benyamim Tsedaka devotes a long section to these rules (Tsedaka 2017, 32–34).
33 For details see Schreiber 2014, 109–18.
34 For the actual cost of a marriage to the families involved see Schreiber 2014, 113–14.

35 See Pummer 1993 and 1997; Florentin 2005, 77–87.
36 Schreiber 2014, 115.
37 On the question of inter-marriage between Samaritans and non-Samaritans see Corinaldi 2005 and Schreiber 2018.
38 For the concept of the *qaṭaf* see above.
39 For details see Pummer 1987, 23–25.
40 For the main modern work on the Samaritan calendar see Powels 1977, and for her account in English, Powels 1989.
41 For photos and videos see the Samaritan websites: www.israelite-samaritans.com and www.the-samaritans.net, as well as the website of the Israeli photographer Ori Orhof: http://orhof.smugmug.com/SamaritanHolidays/.
42 On the building of the temple by Joshua see Stenhouse 1985, 33. For details on the use of the Shofar see Pummer 1989, 686.
43 The exact meaning of הדד is uncertain.
44 Note that 2 Macc 10:6–7 compares the celebration of Hanukkah with that of Sukkot.
45 For a discussion of the question of the origin and meaning of this custom see Pummer 2018, 60–61.

References

'Abd al-'Al, Dorreya Mohammed. 1957. "A Comparative Study of the Unedited Work of Abu 'l-Ḥasan al Ṣūrī and Yūsuf ibn Salamah." Ph.D. dissertation. Leeds: Leeds University.

Bóid, Iain Ruairidh Mac Mhanainn. 1989. *Principles of Samaritan Halachah*. Studies in Judaism in Late Antiquity 38. Leiden: E.J. Brill.

Corinaldi, Michael. 2005. "The Problem of the Patrilineal or Matrilineal Descent and Inter-Marriage According to the Samaritan and Rabbinic Halakhah," *Proceedings of the Fifth International Congress of the Société d'Études Samaritaines, Helsinki, August 1–4, 2000*. Edited by Haseeb Shehadeh, Habib Tawa, and Reinhard Pummer. Paris: Librairie Orientaliste Paul Geuthner, 171–81.

Dexinger, Ferdinand. 1986. *Der Taheb. Ein "messianischer" Heilsbringer der Samaritaner*. Kairos – Religionswissenschaftliche Studien 3. Salzburg: Otto Müller.

Dexinger, Ferdinand. 1998. "Reflections on the Relationship Between Qumran and Samaritan Messianology," in *Qumran Messianism: Studies on the Messianic Expectations in the Dead Sea Scrolls*. Edited by James H. Charlesworth, Hermann Lichtenberger, and Gerberm S. Oegema. Tübingen: Mohr Siebeck, 83–99.

Florentin, Moshe. 2005. *Late Samaritan Hebrew: A Linguistic Analysis of Its Different Types*. Studies in Semitic Languages and Linguistics 43. Leiden; Boston, MA: Brill.

Fossum, Jarl E. 1989. "Sects and Movements," in *The Samaritans*. Edited by Alan D. Crown. Tübingen: J.C.B. Mohr Siebeck, 293–389.

Heckl, Raik. 2017. "Überlegungen zu Form und Funktion der Zentralisationsformel im Konzept des samaritanischen Pentateuchs, zugleich ein Plädoyer für die Ursprünglichkeit der masoretischen Lesart," *Zeitschrift für Altorientalische und Biblische Rechtsgeschichte* 23, 191–208.

Isser, Stanley Jerome. 1976. *The Dositheans: A Samaritan Sect in Late Antiquity*. Studies in Judaism in Late Antiquity 17. Leiden: E.J. Brill.

Isser, Stanley Jerome. 1999. "The Samaritans and Their Sects," in *Cambridge History of Judaism. Vol. 3: The Early Roman Period*. Edited by William Horbury, William David Davies and John Sturdy. Cambridge: Cambridge University Press, 569–95.

Levine, Lee I. 2005. *The Ancient Synagogue: The First Thousand Years*. 2nd Edition. New Haven, CT: Yale University Press.

Magen, Yitzhak. 2009. *Flavia Neapolis: Shechem in the Roman Period*, Volume 1. Judea & Samaria Publications 11. Jerusalem: Staff Officer of Archaeology – Civil Administration of Judea and Samaria; Israel Antiquities Authority.

Mills, John. 1864. *Three Months' Residence at Nablus and an Account of the Modern Samaritans*. London: John Murray.

Noja, Sergio. 2005. *Il Kitāb al-Kāfī dei Samaritani*. Istituto Orientale di Napoli. Pubblicazioni del Seminario di Semitistica. Ricerche 7. Naples.

Powels, Sylvia. 1977. *Der Kalender der Samaritaner anhand des Kitāb ḥisāb as-sinīn und anderer Handschriften*. Studia Samaritana 3. Berlin and New York: Walter de Gruyter.

Powels, Sylvia. 1989. "The Samaritan Calendar and the Roots of Samaritan Chronology," in *The Samaritans*. Edited by Alan D. Crown. Tübingen: J.C.B. Mohr Siebeck, 691–742.

Pummer, Reinhard. 1987. *The Samaritans*. Iconography of Religions 23.5. Leiden: E.J. Brill.

Pummer, Reinhard. 1989. "Samaritan Rituals and Customs," in *The Samaritans*. Edited by Alan D. Crown. Tübingen: J.C.B. Mohr Siebeck, 650–90.

Pummer, Reinhard. 1993 and 1997. *Samaritan Marriage Contracts and Deeds of Divorce*. 2 vols. Wiesbaden: Otto Harrassowitz.

Pummer, Reinhard. 2005. "The Rabbis and Samaritan Circumcision," in *Feasts and Fasts: A Festschrift in Honour of Alan David Crown*. Edited by Marianne Dacy, Jennifer Dowling and Suzanne Faigan. Mandelbaum Studies in Judaica 11. Sydney: Mandelbaum Publishing, 31–40.

Pummer, Reinhard. 2010. "Samaritanism: A Jewish Sect or an Independent Form of Yahwism?" in *Samaritans: Past and Present: Current Studies*. Edited by Menachem Mor and Friedrich V. Reiterer. Studia Judaica 53, Studia Samaritana 5. Berlin; New York: De Gruyter, 1–24.

Pummer, Reinhard. 2016a. "Was There an Altar or a Temple in the Sacred Precinct on Mt. Gerizim?" *Journal for the Study of Judaism* 47: 1–21.

Pummer, Reinhard. 2016b. *The Samaritans: A Profile*. Grand Rapids, MI: William B. Eerdmans.

Pummer, Reinhard. 2018. "Synagogues – Samaritan and Jewish: A New Look at Their Differentiating Characteristics," in *The Samaritans in Historical, Cultural and Linguistic Perspectives*. Edited by Jan Dušek. Studia Judaica 110, Studia Samaritana 11. Berlin: De Gruyter, 51–74.

Rothschild, Jean-Pierre. 2005. "État et perspectives de la recherche sur la halakha samaritaine," in *Samaritan, Hebrew and Aramaic Studies: Presented to Professor Abraham Tal*. Edited by Moshe Bar-Asher and Moshe Florentin. Jerusalem: The Bialik Institute, 77★–104★.

Schreiber, Monika. 2014. *The Comfort of Kin: Samaritan Community, Kinship, and Marriage*. Brill's Series in Jewish Studies 51. Leiden; Boston, MA: Brill.

Schreiber, Monika. 2018. "The Arab, the Jewish, and the Ukrainian Marriage: Picking Spouses in the Samaritan Community," in *The Samaritans in Historical, Cultural and Linguistic Perspectives*. Edited by Jan Dušek. Studia Judaica 110, Studia Samaritana 11. Berlin: De Gruyter, 267–98.

Schur, Nathan. 1992. *History of the Samaritans: 2nd Revised and Enlarged Edition*. Beiträge zur Erforschung des Alten Testamentes und des antiken Judentums 18. Frankfurt am Main; Bern; New York; Paris: Peter Lang.

Stenhouse, Paul. 1985. *The Kitāb al-Tarīkh of Abū 'l-Fatḥ: Translated into English with Notes*. Studies in Judaica 1. Sydney: Mandelbaum Trust, University of Sydney.

Tsedaka, Benyamim. 2017. *Understanding the Israelite-Samaritans from Ancient to Modern: An Introductory Atlas*. Jerusalem: Carta Jerusalem.

Wedel, Gerhard. 1987. "Kitāb aṭ-Ṭabbāḥ des Samaritaners Abū l-Ḥasan aṣ-Ṣūrī. Kritische Edition und kommentierte Übersetzung des ersten Teils." Ph.D. dissertation. Freie Universität Berlin.

42
INTERFAITH RITUALS

Jonathan Romain

If there is one major social phenomenon that has characterised religious life in recent times, it has been the sharp rise in interfaith marriage. It has affected all faith groups, but especially the Jewish community which, apart from an ultra-Orthodox wing, has largely become very integrated in whichever country it has settled.[1]

However, it was not unknown in much earlier periods and occurred even in the Bible, with Joseph marrying an Egyptian and Moses taking a Midianite wife. They typified the scenario of Jews who were living as a minority outside the land of Israel. However, as relations between Jews and their non-Jewish neighbours soured over the centuries, owing to both religious discrimination and political persecution, interfaith relations became much more limited. In a hostile environment where there was no secular middle ground and only competing religious cultures, such unions were seen as a betrayal of Judaism and labelled as 'marrying out'. Those involved were ostracised by their families and shunned by the Jewish community.

From the 19th century onwards, though, the ghetto walls – both physical and psychological – crumbled and Jews re-entered wider society after a long absence. Working together, studying together, sharing leisure pursuits together inevitably led to personal relationships developing. The prize of integration involved the cost of intermarriage.

Rabbis of all denominations initially voiced dire warnings against this development, either relying on fiery sermons or initiating programmes such as youth groups and summer camps to encourage Jewish-Jewish marriages. They worried about the continuing observance of the individuals concerned, the potential loss of the next generation and the overall impact on the Jewish community.

Despite both strategies – the condemnations and the attempts to encourage Jewish social opportunities – intermarriage has become commonplace. In the United States it is estimated that the rate among newlyweds is 58%, while that in England is 26%.[2] As a result, most synagogue groups have had to come to terms with the fact that many of their members now live in mixed-faith households. This is not the case among orthodoxy, but is certainly true of Reform congregations, who have accepted that they must deal with Jewish life as it is, not as they might wish it to be.

A key component in this acceptance is the realisation that Jews who marry non-Jews are not doing so as a deliberate rejection of their Judaism. They would have been just as willing to marry someone Jewish, but circumstances determined otherwise. They see no contradiction

DOI: 10.4324/9781003032823-48

between loving their non-Jewish partner and valuing their Jewish heritage. Crucially, they wish their partner to be able to share that heritage, and for their children to have access to it along with the faith, if any, to which their partner is attached. They also wish their partner and children to be made to feel welcome in their synagogue and participate in communal life if they so wish. This has led to a burst of creative religious energy, both by interfaith families and by congregations in developing ways of harmonising rituals for dual-faith households or where the other partner has no religious affiliation.

It should be noted, though, that even within this broad spectrum of acceptance, there are significant variations. Some rabbis will accept non-Jewish partners into the community, but do not wish to alter traditional Jewish cycle of life ceremonies to accommodate them. A personal welcome, but little change to Jewish lifestyle. Other rabbis feel that the former cannot happen properly without the latter, and so various forms of ritual inclusion need to be introduced, in order to make them feel welcome rather than tolerated. Yet others, especially in the USA, consider that the dramatically high number of mixed-faith couples means it is now time to embrace them with responses that are innovative and creative.

The shift to this much more radical approach can be seen in the decision of the organisation previously known as Interfaith Family to change its name to 18Doors in early 2020 with the tagline of 'Unlocking Jewish' (with 18 being the numerical value of the Hebrew word *chai*, meaning 'life'). It reflects the fact that many such families are not made up of two partners, each with their own faith. Instead, there might just be one partner with faith, or neither having an active faith in terms of belief system, but still having very different religio-cultural backgrounds and seeking to understand each other's heritage in ways that were previously barred.

This process starts with the path to marriage itself. Many Jews who realise that their relationship with a non-Jew is becoming increasingly serious wish to introduce them to Jewish life. At first this tends to be family ceremonies at home – such as a Sabbath evening meal or candelabra-lighting at *Hanukkah*. Some parents will be only too delighted to share such rituals, but others might feel they are thereby giving the go-ahead to the relationship when they are not happy with someone non-Jewish becoming part of the family.

In the latter instance, they may well consult their rabbi. An Orthodox minister will usually reinforce the parents' reservations and encourage them to try to split up the couple. By contrast, Reform rabbis generally advise them that they have to accept their offspring's choice and that being antagonistic is more likely to ensure that, if the marriage goes ahead, the couple will be less inclined to pursue a Jewish life and may even break off contact with the parents. Conversely, if they show Jewish life to be warm and welcoming, then the non-Jewish partner is more likely to want to adopt it, or at least support the son/daughter in honouring their Jewish roots. To put it more bluntly, at a time when the Jewish 'children' are no longer living at home but are grown adults, living elsewhere and financially independent, the parents no longer have the power or authority, as they did in previous generations, to determine their child's choice of partner. Their options are keeping the channels of communication open or endangering family links. The more positive their response to the non-Jewish partner, the more likely the couple are to maintain Jewish life.

Meanwhile, policies among rabbis are changing. Some will simply make the couple welcome as and when they come to a service or social event. Others will be more pro-active and offer to set up a meeting with them to discuss the possibilities on offer. This will include conversion for those who want to adopt Judaism for themselves, in which case, once the process is completed, they will no longer be an interfaith family but a Jewish one. All branches of Judaism accept that once a person has converted they are fully equal to a born-Jew and not to be treated differently in any way. They will, of course, still have non-Jewish family of their own, and care will need to be taken to ensure they do not feel estranged, or that the person converting does not feel guilty at leaving the faith of their childhood. Gaining a Jewish family should not be at the expense of losing one's existing family.

It may be that the non-Jewish partner does not want to convert – either because they have a faith of their own or because they are not interested in matters of faith – but still wants to acquire a deeper knowledge of the religious culture into which they are marrying. The result has been that many synagogues now offer 'Introduction to Judaism' or 'Judaism 101' courses for such couples. These cover basic knowledge of Judaism – home life, festivals, history, ethics – from an adult perspective. It is usually expected that the Jewish partner will attend too, partly to be supportive, but also to enrich their own Jewish understanding, as many of them will have ceased formal Jewish education around the period of *bar/batmitzvah* and have a fairly limited knowledge. Joint attendance also helps introduce the couple to others in the same situation, begin to establish a social niche within the synagogue and make them feel that they belong. The classes are conducted purely on an information basis, not for the purposes of conversion. In some cases, however, that knowledge can lead to individuals deciding that, contrary to their own expectations, they do wish to become Jewish and enrol in a formal conversion process.

The actual wedding ceremony for interfaith couples has been subject to huge variations. In earlier decades, rabbis of all groupings refused outright to officiate as a sign of their disapproval. Even when rabbis were prepared to meet with and accept the couples, there was an attitude of 'We can help counsel you and be involved in the rest of your life, but not be involved in the act of outmarriage itself'. This was not so much out of a desire to punish the couples, but from the fear that to do so would be taken as endorsing such unions. However, the rising numbers, and the realisation that the Jewish partner still valued their Jewishness, has led to a change of heart among Reform rabbis. It has been recognised that if the couple want a Jewish element to one of the most important days of their life, then it achieves nothing to deny it; instead, it should be taken as an opportunity to show that Jewish practices can be a beneficial thread that runs throughout their marriage. It can also be an opportunity to ask the couple to attend a basic course on Judaism as preparation for their life together. Some rabbis will require them to commit to creating a Jewish home and bringing up any children exclusively as Jewish. Others will require that Judaism is the primary religion, allowing the non-Jewish partners to express their faith at home, and share it with the rest of the family, but with Judaism still being the main identity.

Practices vary enormously. In Britain, for instance, there has been a desire among most rabbis to make a differentiation between a Jewish-Jewish wedding and an interfaith one. Services for the latter may take place in synagogue and be led by a rabbi, but it will not include a *huppah*, the seven blessings, exchange of rings or a *ketubah*. It is also forbidden to have a minister of another faith co-officiate or participate in the ceremony.[3] Despite the list of restrictions, this is seen as a major concession, allowing a previously forbidden ceremony to now take place, and – rather than be limited to the couple's home or some other venue – to do so in front of the Ark. However, many couples take a very contrasting view and regard it as highly limiting, banning many of the key elements that make a Jewish wedding so memorable. While some are grateful that they have now been 'brought in from the cold', others feel short-changed by the regulations. It should be noted that the ceremony at best is only a blessing, not a marriage, as British law states that a rabbi is only permitted to marry a couple where both partners profess the Jewish faith. As a result, the couple have to undergo a Register Office marriage to make their union recognised legally before the religious ceremony can take place.

In the United States, though, a very different situation is in place. Rabbis, like most ministers of religion, are empowered to marry a mixed-faith couple legally. Moreover, they have much more freedom to tailor the ceremony to the couple's religious inclinations and preferences. Unless the non-Jewish partner objects for some reason, most Jews want the service to be 'the real thing', be it in a synagogue or a neutral venue. This is from a triple motive. First, there is a genuine to desire to make it as meaningful as possible for themselves; second, to reassure the Jewish family that they still wish to honour their Jewish lineage; and third, to share the best of Jewish practice with the non-Jewish family. A *huppah*, or some similar canopy, is the norm, being one of the best-known visual aspects of the day. To omit the exchange of rings would be equally unthinkable, so that everyone can witness the actual moment of marriage and the public declaration of vows. It may be that the formula of 'By this ring you are married to me in holiness according to the law of Moses and Israel' is changed, either because it is considered inappropriate or because wording that is more personal is substituted. One example is:

BRIDE: By this ring I take you to be my husband. In front of all our friends and family, I promise to love you and to care for you, to be by your side and to spend the rest of my life with you.

GROOM: By this ring, I take you to be my wife. I promise to grow old with you, to be your companion through life, and to share with you all the joys and difficulties it may bring.

Another example is:

GROOM: For me, this is about you being my partner for life and me affirming it in public

BRIDE: For me, this is the expression of the love we have had for many years and will continue to flourish.

In the case of other traditional elements, there is often a similar tendency to keep the structure, but alter the content. Thus the format of *sheva berachot*, the seven blessings can be maintained, but instead of using the existing ones, updated versions are used, or ones composed by the couple themselves to reflect the nature of their relationship. In reality, it means they are often more relevant than the original ones, as talk of 'the sound of happiness and rejoicing being heard in the towns of Judah and the streets of Jerusalem' do not necessarily carry much resonance in New York or Boston. An example of the modern compose-it-yourself blessings is the rabbi declaring:

1. May your marriage enrich your lives.
2. May you work together to build a relationship of substance and quality.
3. May the honesty of your communication build a foundation of understanding, connection and trust.
4. May you respect each other's individual personality and philosophy, and give each other room to grow and fulfill each other's dreams.
5. May your sense of humour and playful spirit continue to enliven your relationship.
6. May you understand that neither of you is perfect: you are both subject to human frailties: and may your love strengthen when you fall short of each other's expectations.
7. May you be best friends, better together than either of you are apart.

Alternatively, seven individuals, be it family or friends of the couple, are asked to say the blessings, or even write their own versions. In the following examples they have chosen to focus on seven particular qualities and build the blessings around them:

1. Love
May you be blessed with love. May your admiration, appreciation and understanding of each other foster a love that is passionate, tranquil and real. May this love between you be strong and enduring, and bring peace into your lives.

2. A loving home
May you be blessed with a loving home filled with warmth, humour and compassion. May you create a family together that honours traditions old and new. May you teach your children to have equal respect for themselves and others, and instil in them the value of learning and making the world a better place.

3. Humour and play
May you be best friends and work together to build a relationship of substance and quality. May your sense of humour and playful spirit continue to enliven your relationship. May you respect each other's individual personality and perspective, and give each other room to grow in fulfilling your dreams.

4. Wisdom
May you be blessed with wisdom. May you continually learn from one another and from the world. Together, may you grow, deepening your knowledge and understanding of each other and of your journey through life.

5. Health
May you be blessed with health. May life bring you wholeness of mind, body and spirit. May you keep each other well-balanced and grounded, and live long that you may share many happy years together

6. Art, beauty, creativity
May your life be blessed with the art and beauty of this world. May your creative aspirations and experiences find expression, inspire you and bring you joy and fulfilment. May you find happiness together in adventures big and small, and something to celebrate each day of your lives.

7. Community
May you be blessed with community. May you always be blessed with the awareness that you are an essential part of a circle of family and friends. May there always be within this group love, trust, support and laughter, and may there be many future occasions for rejoicing in their company.

A similar transformation will often take place with the wedding document, which is also subject to enormous variations. In cases where the rabbi permits, a full *ketubah* is used, although it can also have individual touches, as in the case of a marriage in which one partner was Chinese, where the text was also in mandarin and the document printed on silk. In other instances, there will not be a traditional *ketubah* and instead the couple will have a more innovative document, perhaps referred to as a 'Covenant of Love'. It might just be in English, although with some Hebrew calligraphy to give it a 'Jewish flavour'. The wording will often be that chosen by the couple and reflect a text they find significant. An example of this is:

On Sunday the 28th October 2019 in Burford, Andrew Collins and Melanie Levi entered into a covenant to celebrate their marriage.

It is a covenant of promise and hope. It is a covenant of different traditions coming together in mutual loving-kindness. It is a covenant of new beginnings and new opportunities. It is a covenant of companionship and love.

TO THIS COVENANT WE AFFIX OUR SIGNATURES:

_____   &   _____
Groom   *Bride*

_____   &   _____
Witness   *Witness*

The breaking of the glass will almost always end the ceremony, being such an iconic moment that has become well known outside Jewish circles. However, in keeping with the egalitarian spirit of many modern couples, groom and bride sometimes each smash a glass. (It also puts an end to the lame joke of old that 'this is the last chance the groom has to put his foot down'.) In keeping with the inter-faith nature of the occasion, the rabbi will often give a more modern explanation for the glass smashing, no longer linking it to mourning for the Temple and the destruction of Jerusalem in the first century. Instead, the rabbis may say something like: 'Every marriage has the sound of stamping feet and arguments, alongside the joys. But a good marriage is where the arguments are resolved and the joys are shared.'

This is typical of the wider role of the rabbi throughout the ceremony, acting not only as officiant, but as Master of Ceremonies, with the task of explaining rituals that may not be familiar to non-Jewish family and guests. The rabbi's running commentary (e.g., 'We are standing underneath a canopy which represents …' or 'Now comes the moment when …') will be designed to make everything feel as inclusive as possible. He or she is also likely to introduce the proceedings by acknowledging the interfaith nature of the wedding and remarking that it represents not only the union of two individuals, but also that of two traditions. Some might even comment that whereas, in the past, the relationship between the two faiths was marked by rivalry and conflict, now it is being replaced by love. It may also be that if the non-Jewish partner has a faith background, their minister will also participate, be it jointly with the rabbi or for a particular section in the service. While some rabbis are resistant to this, others welcome the opportunity to show that the respect shown by the non-Jewish family for Jewish life is reciprocated for their tradition, and would consider anything less than a shared role as one-sided.

As well as the inclusion or exclusion of traditional Jewish rituals, an interfaith ceremony will often be characterised by additional material not normally found in a purely Jewish one. This might be passages relevant to the other partner's faith, such as the exquisite passage on love in Paul's First Letter to the Corinthians (13. 3–13). It is often the case, though, that the material may come from many other sources. This is because while a Jewish only (or Christian only) ceremony will usually follow the service laid down in the Prayer Book, an interfaith one lacks any official text and the couple are free to be much more creative in their choice of readings. It can be a very fruitful exercise, involving the couple delving into their respective traditions, deciding which aspects are critical for them and which they wish to share with their new family.

The couple may also request readings that are not necessarily from either faith, but which resonate with their relationship and reflect their hopes. This will also apply if the other person does not have a faith background, but wishes to have secular passages to which they can relate.

There can also be ritual additions that acknowledge the non-Jewish person's heritage in other ways, especially in marriage that are not just interfaith but interracial too. In the case of a Jewish-Sino union, the glass that was to be stamped upon was not wrapped in the usual white cloth, but a red one, as the color is a symbol of good luck in Chinese culture. In another instance, the couple not only smashed the glass together but then jumped over a broomstick that had been laid next to it, as 'jumping the broom' was a long-standing rite for the non-Jewish family.

Alternatively, some couples have two ceremonies, one in synagogue and one in the place of worship of the other person's faith background, with one being the official marriage and the other being a blessing. These instances usually occur if both partners are strongly attached to a particular place of worship (or their family is) and they have always envisaged getting married there. It could also be that they want a level of faith content that one minister cannot sanction and the only way to accommodate this is by holding separate services. David and Sukrana, for instance, had separate Jewish and Hindu ceremonies, as they felt they wished to enjoy each of them fully and not compromise the integrity of either one by curtailing any elements.[4]

The actual home life of an interfaith couple will be subject to various negotiations, so that both will feel comfortable with the domestic atmosphere they are creating. To a limited extent, this mirrors the same process as might happen with a Jewish couple, who often have different traditions that need harmonizing. Questions might include: will there be a *mezuzah* on the front door and internal ones? Will they light candles on a Friday night and make *kiddush*? Keeping *kosher* will also need to be discussed, with a variety of different compromises adopted: from not observing it at all, to avoiding pork or some other specifically forbidden foods, to keeping some degree of positive *kashrut*, to distinguishing between what is consumed at home and what is eaten when outside it, to observing a greater degree of *kashrut* at special occasions, such as Yom Kippur or Pesach.

Similar variations are evident in the celebration of festivals. Some families will observe the festivals of both faiths with gusto – be it for religious reasons or cultural ones – with Easter egg hunts following a *seder*, and a Christmas tree alongside a *hanukkiah*. Others decide that this mix is either religiously incompatible or confusing for the children, and will opt for just one set of them. Others find it easier to keep the home a religion-free zone and for any such observances to occur outside, in the church, synagogue or mosque. In this respect, they are emulating, albeit for different reasons, what many Jewish-Jewish families have done, i.e. outsourcing domestic Jewish observances to the place of worship. This has been responsible for the rise of the communal *seder*, the synagogue *sukkah* and Friday night meals – all once exclusively celebrated at home, but now commonplace in synagogues instead.

These early discussions, and the manner in which they are conducted, can be very important in setting the tone for the more complex decisions regarding children. Whereas the couple can often reach easy compromises between themselves – such as one will go to synagogue and the other go shopping, and they meet for lunch afterwards – when children appear, with whom will they go? This in turn begs the wider question of how the children will be brought up – in one faith, both faiths or neither? Closely linked is the question of how the children see themselves, as identity and education are not the same. Thus a child may consider themselves Jewish, but be brought up with a knowledge of both the faiths in the marriage. A third element is status – how the Jewish community views them. Whereas Orthodox synagogues adhere to the matrilineal line and will only recognize the child of a Jewish mother as Jewish, Reform will regard a child with one Jewish parent as Jewish, whether it be their mother or father.[5] It means that, in Orthodox circles, there is more angst when a Jewish man marries a non-Jewish partner, whereas in Reform communities there is just as much chance of the children having Jewish status whatever is the gender of the Jewish partner. The role of the rabbi, or an interfaith counsellor attached to the congregation, can be important in helping a couple to explore a variety of options, respecting the integrity of each partner and reaching a conclusion that works best for them.

The advice usually given is to discuss everything in advance – before the marriage takes place – so that any difficulties can be ironed out, red lines acknowledged and both partners know what is and is not going to happen. This applies especially to the birth of a child, when quick decisions have to be made at a time when parents are sleep-deprived, while subterranean memories of their own childhoods may unexpectedly seem much more important than before. If it is a boy, will they circumcise him, baptise him, do both or neither? Whereas Jews are used to millennia of conditioning for a circumcision to take place, it may be totally alien to the non-Jewish partner. Having just given birth to a baby boy, and feeling highly protective toward the fragile new creation, the last thing they may wish to do is subject him to any incisions and cuts. The words 'barbaric' and 'mutilation' are sometimes used. The role of the rabbi can be crucial in explaining the significance of the circumcision and reassuring the couple of the absence of any long-term physical or psychological harm. Even if the non-Jewish partner is happy to have it done, they may still think it odd that a medical procedure takes place on the dining room table rather than in an operating theatre. A common compromise in such cases is that the latter will agree to it, but prefer it to be performed by a doctor in the surgery rather than by a *mohel* at home. In reality, the procedure is no safer, but it can feel more clinical, while the practical result is the same. The blessings can still be said, wherever the circumcision takes place, although some families will dispense with them. Another scenario is to have a hospital circumcision to satisfy the physical requirement, which is then followed by an eclectic naming ceremony at home which both sets of families attend. In such cases, an increasingly favored ritual is for the baby to be handed along a line of grandparents (and aunts and uncles) to welcome the child into the extended family. If, however, the couple decide not to have their son circumcised, that does not affect his Jewish status. Both for the Orthodox and Reform, a Jewish child who is uncircumcised is an uncircumcised Jew.

For girls being brought up as Jewish, be it exclusively or alongside another faith, there can be a baby blessing ceremony – done at home by the rabbi or in synagogue in front of the Ark. It is normally the case that both parents participate, reading passages that each of them can say in good conscience. The prayers give thanks for the arrival of the child and express the hope that it will be blessed with health and happiness. Other lines will indicate a commitment to Jewish involvement, though these can be re-worded if they prove too contentious:

> God be with me and my family; may our love for our child draw us even more closely together in helpfulness and in trust. Teach us to carry on through our child the heritage of Israel, so that its tradition of wisdom and holiness may never cease.

There are some families who will also have a baptism for their child, especially if the non-Jewish partner is attached to the Church, or feels that it is important to their family. Although it can be seen as a quid pro quo, strictly speaking it is not a direct balancing, as baptism confers a Christian identity, whereas a circumcision or baby blessing does not. The same use of dual initiation can apply to the rites of any other faith to which the non-Jewish partner belongs. Families' reactions can vary greatly, with some joyously attending both events, while in other cases, each side only attends their own faith ceremony. There might also be many a rabbi who feels that this religious double-act is theologically unacceptable. However, others will permit it as a way of honouring both faiths, as well as being aware that birth rites do not by themselves determine subsequent religious upbringing.

If the child's Jewish life does become the dominant one, then a *barmitzvah* will take place at 13 years old for boys and a *batmitzvah* for girls. It should be noted that whereas Orthodox synagogue do the latter at 12, Reform synagogues – to which a mixed-faith couple is much more likely to belong – hold them at the same age as for boys. One question that arises is to what extent the non-Jewish parent and their family can participate in the service. Custom varies enormously from synagogue to synagogue. Some will permit the non-Jewish parent onto the *bimah* to stand by their child, but not permit them to have any active role. The thinking is that only Jews can take part in the service itself. Others will encourage the non-Jewish partner to be as involved as a Jewish parent might be, by reading a prayer or performing one of the *mitzvot*, such as opening the Ark. In this case, the thinking is that the *bar/batmitzvah* could not happen without the non-Jewish parent's tacit acceptance, or active support, and appreciation should be expressed for that. In addition, there is a desire not to discriminate between different members of the family, which would be both divisive and unethical. Here, too, there are different practices: some synagogues will limit participation to the non-Jewish parent, others to the grandparents, while others will extend it to all non-Jewish members of the family or even close friends.

The subject of interfaith marriage is often thought to raise issues primarily about the wedding and children, but it can be equally applicable to time of death. This has always been the case, but has become much more evident in recent decades, as the big rise in interfaith marriages occurred from the 1950s onwards, and many of those couples have been approaching the end of their lives. One concern is where the couple can be buried. Until recently, it was either assumed, or laid down in local deeds of trust, that only Jews could be buried in a Jewish cemetery. Some couples simply accepted this and were buried in separate places. Other couples wished to be together and so opted for non-denominational cemeteries. This went against the traditional expectation that a Jew – however observant or lapsed – would be buried in a Jewish cemetery. But this tended to carry less weight for those who had already broken the tradition of marrying within the faith, while it was over-ridden by the desire to be buried side-by-side. Another option was to choose to be cremated, with the ashes being scattered in the rose garden that was often nearby, buried in a non-denominational cemetery or placed in a columbarium. Cremation is prohibited by Orthodox Judaism but is permitted within Reform circles.

Two factors have led to a major change in this area. First the number of interfaith couples passing away began to grow, and second there was a much greater acceptance by the Jewish community that interfaith couples should be accommodated within Jewish life rather than being shunned. As was mentioned above, many of the Jewish partners still valued Jewish tradition, and if the non-Jewish partner was content to be buried in a Jewish cemetery there were an increasing number of requests for that to be possible. This was accompanied by a feeling among many rabbis that it would be wrong to separate a couple in death who had been together in life. It would also be upsetting for any children to have to visit their parents in separate venues. Reform synagogues therefore began to permit mixed-faith burials in their cemeteries. This was initially done in a cautious way, as there was concern that the families of those already buried there might object. The solution was to create a separate area within the Jewish cemetery where interfaith burials could take place. Others opened new cemeteries that were open to those of all faiths. Others permitted them within the Jewish cemetery but on condition that the couple be buried in a single in-depth grave (rather than two graves next to each other), so that it could be said that, as each plot contained someone Jewish, the Jewish integrity of the cemetery had still been maintained. The increasing prevalence of Jews with non-Jewish partners not only being members of synagogues, but involved in their leadership, has led to a further change in attitude by which cemeteries previously limited to Jews now accept interfaith couples in their main section.

In the case of a funeral of a Jew with a non-Jewish partner, the service is exactly the same as that of any other funeral service, although there may be a higher percentage of prayers in English to make non-Jewish members of the family feel included. In Reform communities, the non-Jewish partner and any children will be treated as mourners and extended all the usual courtesies. If they wish, for instance, to hold a *shivah* or any other mourning rituals, that will be permitted, although they will not be obligated to do so if it is not in accord with their wishes. In the case of the funeral of the non-Jewish partner, different cemeteries have different rules. Some will insist that only a rabbi may officiate, although the rabbi will make the service as inclusive as possible and tailor it to the particular needs of the family. This tends to happen if the deceased did not have a strong faith of their own, if at all, or if they had become involved in synagogue life and knew the rabbi better than their own minister. However, if the non-Jewish partner did have a strong religious identity, then the service could be taken, for instance, in a church and led by their priest with a full Christian service, then followed by burial at the Jewish cemetery. That way, the person's faith can be honoured, while avoiding non-Jewish prayers at the cemetery. Many Jewish cemeteries will prohibit any symbols or quotations associated with another faith being engraved on the tombstone. Instead, there may be a line from a common source, such as the Psalms, or a more personalized inscription.

In those instances where a funeral takes place in a non-Jewish cemetery, most Reform rabbis will still officiate for the Jewish partner, while there are some who are also called upon to do so for the non-Jewish partner too. This might be because the non-Jewish partner felt more comfortable in Jewish life than elsewhere, or because the Jewish partner wants their rabbi to be the one leading the prayers. It begs the question of whether it is more appropriate to have the minister of the person who died taking the service, or the minister of the person who survived. The answer will vary from family to family, but what is key is that rabbis are now willing to assist in whatever way best helps the mourners.

This change in attitude is symptomatic of the massive policy-shift toward interfaith couples that has occurred within Jewish life – from condemnation to acknowledgement to acceptance to engagement. Not only have they been welcomed into communities, but Jewish practices and cycle of life rituals have been expanded to accommodate them. The cry of Tevye in *Fiddler on the Roof*: 'A fish and a bird can fall in love, but where will they build a home?' was an authentic expression of a previous generation's attitude – not just hostile, but genuinely puzzled as to how such relationships could possibly succeed. Now, though, whereas objections remain in some quarters, many parts of the Jewish world have created a space for interfaith couples to feel at home within it.

Notes

1 I am grateful to Rabbi Danny Burkeman of Temple Shir Tikva, Wayland, Massachusetts, and to Rabbi Malcolm Cohen of Temple Sinai, Las Vegas, Nevada – both of whom gave comments on my final text.

2 Graham, David. 2016. *Jews in couples: Marriage, intermarriage, cohabitation and divorce in Britain.* London: Institute for Jewish Policy Research, 16.
3 *Ceremonies of Celebration after a Mixed-Faith Wedding* Assembly of Reform Rabbis UK July 2012.
4 For more examples, see the website of 18Doors, which is highly recommended: https://18doors.org
5 The date of this change varies. In the United States, this was the result of decisions taken by the Reform Movement in 1983. In Britain, it occurred in 2015. Reform in Israel has not accepted it, nor do communities in Europe.

INDEX

Aaron 3–4, 8–9, 13, 94, 255, 328, 338, 570, 573
Abraham: blessing children 353: burying Sarah in Machpelah cave 439; circumcising Isaac 75, 309; hospitality 526; polygamist, 400, 404; prays 463: prepares feast for Isaac 328; traveling 249; outdoors wedding 566
Abraham the son of Maimonides 127, 163
Abram 3
Abramovich, S. 206
Abulafiya, Meir 404
Achad ha-Am 229, 237, 259
Adam 9, 13–14, 267, 312, 337–8, 354, 369, 400, 410, 517, 573
Adam and Eve 9, 337–8; and the snake's skin 354, 369
Adelman, P. 21
Adelman, R. 14
Aderet, Solomon 404
Adler, Cyrus 232
Adler, Hermann 470
'afiqoman 109, 111–12, 114, 119; *see also* Passover
Aggadic 16, 18, 51, 98, 171, 311
Agnon, S. 427
agunah 241, 410
Akiba/Akiva 14, 39, 271, 312, 329, 512
Aleichem, Shalom 501, 503–4
Alexander, E. 25
Alfasi, Isaac 165
Alkabetz, Shlomo 137
almemor 73
Alter, R. 269–70
alternative funerals in Israel *see* funerals, alternative
Amen meal ritual 385–99
amidah 38, 42, 96, 168–9, 466–7, 559
Amora 26–7, 31–43, 48, 467
Amos 8, 409, 550
Amram ben Sheshna Gaon 172

amulets 464, 512–15, 518, 523
aninut 437
Anisfeld, R. 17–18
Anti-Semitism 152–3, 155–6, 175, 198, 260, 271, 294–6, 332, 428, 431, 444
'aqbiyya 130
Arabic 127, 132, 139, 146, 164, 186, 328, 473, 474, 480, 491, 522, 569, 573
Aramaic 17, 95, 373, 374, 442, 454, 463, 465–9, 472, 473, 475, 477, 478–9, 485, 492, 496, 502, 513–16, 522, 562–3
archaeology 59–70
Arie, Malachi Beit 126
ark 4, 73, 80, 84, 150–1, 224, 279, 335, 474, 477, 482, 565, 570, 581, 586–7
arka'ot shel goyim see gentile courts
art, ritual for the synagogue 72–74
Ashkenaz 18, 72–82, 97, 98, 101–3, 105, 107, 109, 112, 115, 117, 120–21, 140, 146, 151, 154, 163–78, 216–17, 220, 327–8, 345, 350, 352–3, 369, 388, 422, 427, 429, 442, 449, 453–4, 468–9, 474, 480, 484, 503, 505–6; *see also* Sefardi, Yiddish
atarah 74
Atonement, Day of 310, 344, 482, 541, 544 *see* fasting, Yom Kippur
atzei hayyim 73
avodah 310–11
Azulai, Hayyim 175

Baal 17
ba'al ha-brit 102
Baal Shem Tov 7, 215, 218–20, 225
ba'alat ha-brit 75, 102
bais Yaakov 318
Balberg, M. 12
Bar Kochba 164

Index

bar mitzvah 75, 280, 283, 286, 572
Bar-Yochai, Shimon 140, 145, 328
Barthes, Roland 129
bat mitzvah 234, 238, 241, 299, 388, 391, 534, 565
bathing 33–4, 62–3, 217, 331, 340, 365, 441, 544 *see mikveh*
Beit Yosef 49–50
Bell, C. 13–14, 222, 257, 463
Benvenisti, Chaim ben Israel 349, 475–6
betrothal 27–8, 30–1, 76, 405, 496, 572
Ben Bag Bag 3, 21
Ben Eliezer. Israel 215 *see* Baal Shem Tov
Ben Gamliel, Shimon 15, 167
Ben Yechiel, Asher 165
Ben Zimrah, David 142
Berger, Peter 194
Berkovitz, J. 49
Besht *see* Baal Shem Tov
beth/bet din 237, 239, 251, 504
bet ha-hayyim 492
bet midrash 140, 170, 231, 233
bet ha-mikdash 168–9
bimah 20, 73, 118, 268, 284–5, 565, 587
Binder, A. 418–19
birkat hamazon 41, 170–1
birkat Kohanim 169–71, 476
bitter herbs 36, 561 *see maror*
Blas, Howard 534
Blidstein, G. 258
Bloch, E. 419
b'nei mitzvah 238, 533–4, 536
body image 314–26; *see also* modesty, orthodox
book culture 93–136
bowls 65, 67, 79, 108, 109, 112–15, 348, 515, 516, 522, 525
Boyarin, J. 276
bread 14, 21, 42, 78–9, 81, 107, 118, 128, 150, 170, 184, 221, 265, 268–9, 285, 290, 361, 378, 386, 420, 477, 481, 485, 494, 502, 541–3, 548, 559–61, 573–4
brit milah 13 *see* circumcision
Bronfenbrenner, U. 531
Brumberg-Kraus, J. 345
Buber, M. 266, 342
Byzantine 59, 65, 126–7, 134, 140, 142, 468, 565, 575
b'zelem Elohim 527

Caesarea 61
Calmanson, Jacques 225
candles: Amen ritual 395; black 505; female ritual 388; Hanukah 495; to honor *tzadikim* 387; Karaites 183–4; magic 150; naming ceremonies 499; Passover 79, 153; Sefardim 173; Shabat 16, 77, 117, 263, 291, 336, 365–8, 389, 477, 483, 585; with *shofar* 118; simplicity of 393; *see also* Amen ritual, Hanukah, Judezmo, Shabat

calendar 17, 34, 36–8, 78, 156, 262, 392, 420, 427–8, 432, 443–4, 463, 474, 479, 489, 561, 573, 574
cantor 96, 128, 174, 187, 219, 220, 233, 234, 242, 414–26, 430, 468, 469, 490, 492, 505, 530, 533, 563 *see hazan*
Cardoso, Isaac 205–7
Carlebach, Shlomo 419
Caro *see* Karo
ceremonial objects/calendar 78–84
ceremonial objects/ life cycle 74–78
Chabad 354
Chair of Elijah 13, 75, 85
challah 285, 336, 386, 387, 389, 393, 395, 396, 502
chavurah/havurah 137, 218
chevra/hevra 218
chevra kadisha 327, 330, 331, 333, 438
Chinese food 346, 351–2, 356–7
Chinese philosophy 343
Chouraqi, André 175
Christensen, Sally 526
Christian libels 121
Christianity 14, 32, 52, 66, 67, 73, 93, 102, 105, 121, 126, 129, 134, 139, 145, 147, 151, 163–4, 168–9, 175, 194, 198, 207–12, 230, 248–50, 253–5, 277, 297, 306–7, 315, 317, 320–22, 348, 350, 353, 356, 364–5, 375, 379–82, 390, 400, 403, 463, 464, 468–9, 472–3, 484, 489, 494, 502, 514, 516, 539–67, 568, 584, 586, 588
circumcision: Chair of Elijah 13; Conservatives 240; differentiation 361; gentile converts to Christianity 540; gentile converts to Judaism 544, 586; innovation 451; Jerusalem Council 549–5O1; and Judaism 305–13; Judezmo culture 489–90; pictures of 93, 102–4, 121; rabbinic discussion 26–7, 30; Reform 230; Roman hostility 14; Samaritans 571; symbolic 387; in synagogues 565; swaddling clothes 74–5, 151
clothes: body image 319; burial 545; death 77; distinctive 489; festivals 355; and freedom 265; Islamic world 129–31; Jewish Question 295; and Judaism 335–44; magic 520; mourning 442; Reform 248, 250–1, 254; sexuality 145; Shabat 285; social identity 7, 9; washing 34, 130, 479; *see also* body image, modesty
Cohen, Aryeh 34
Cohen, Gerson 235
Cohen, Judah 417
Cohen, Michael 232
Cohen, Shaye 26
Cohen, Steven 199, 276
Conservatives 229–47
contract 28, 50, 53, 76, 156, 167, 348, 403, 408, 412, 484, 486, 492, 572; *see also ketubah*
Cordovero, Moses 138, 141, 416
Cover, R. 21–2, 47–8

Covid 5, 236, 251, 308, 310–11, 340–1, 362
cremation 32, 440–1, 449, 452, 565, 587
crown 76, 482; *see also atarah*

dairy 347–51, 348, 483, 486, 506
dayyan 131
damages 48
David 3, 61, 209, 390, 404, 414, 517, 546
Davis, E, 21
Dead Sea Scrolls 59
death and dying 436–45; *see also* funerals, secular rituals
desert 4, 6, 7, 9, 10, 64, 125, 265, 268, 335, 338, 440, 517, 561
devekut 146
diaspora 36, 48, 60, 65, 138–40, 144, 151, 154–5, 163, 182, 188, 198–200, 259, 328, 376, 428, 430, 432–3, 467, 472–4, 550, 570
dina d'malchuta dina 48
Diner, H. 345
disability *see* inclusion
divorce 28–9, 48–50, 154, 199, 277, 319, 336, 393, 401–3, 405–8, 504, 572; *see also get*
doresh 16
Douglas, M. 14, 346, 338, 395
Dov Ber of Mezerich 221
dowry 130, 401, 490
Dura Europos 17, 66, 94–5, 99
Durkheim, E. 13, 226, 373

Eden *see* garden
Eisen, Arnold 275
Eisenstadt, Yaakov 167
Eisenstein, J. 174
El malei rahamin 453
Elbogen, I. 470
Elijah 13, 17, 154, 268, 489
Elisha 414, 520
Emden, Jacob 469
Enlightenment 138, 150–1, 203, 207, 209–12, 221, 225, 249, 330, 350–1, 374, 417, 468, 502, 503, 505 *see* Haskalah
enthusiasm 3, 6, 127, 131, 207, 211, 248, 250, 252, 264, 270, 295, 297, 308, 343, 467, 495
erev rav 8
erusin 27, 166–7, 543; *see also* marriage, wedding
Esau 338
Essenes 64–5
Esther 39, 82, 478, 481, 484 *see* Purim
etrog 185
eucharist 560, 565
eulogies 32, 451
excommunication 212, 481–2

Falk, Ze'ev 168
family 275–301

fashion 9, 76, 82, 99–100, 251, 318, 337–40, 438
see clothes
fasting: early Christians save food for poor 545–6, 548, 550; fast days 350; Judezmo 482–3; plague 481; as remembrance 443; Samaritans 574; *shtetl* movies 504; Tisha B'Av communal 40; Yom Kippur 38, 482
Feinstein, Moses 164, 172, 411
feminism 21, 241, 270, 396, 398, 448, 457
Finkelstein, Louis 233
fish 348
Five Books 3, 6, 8–9, 568
Foer, Jonathan 357
food 345–60; *see also kashrut*
footwear 33–4, 38, 130, 156–7, 188, 222, 248, 331, 337, 339, 365, 476, 570
four species 36, 184–5, 575
Frankel, Zecharias 229–30, 236
Friedman, D. 20
Friedman, M. 429
funerals 31–3, 77, 212, 288, 565, 588 *see* alternative funerals, death and dying, hair, secular rituals
funerals, alternative in Israel 446–59
Fustat 128

Gafney, W. 21
garden 21, 131–3, 343, 354, 363, 365, 486, 587; of Eden 167, 337–9, 439
Gedalya 481
gedilim 187
Geiger, A. 350
gender 25, 39, 77, 102–3, 121, 151–2, 156, 219, 242, 285, 297–300, 305, 318–19, 333, 335, 338, 340, 349, 397, 490, 502, 537, 586; *see also Transparent*
gentile courts 48–50
Gemara 13, 172
Geniza 125–7, 129, 130, 131–4, 522
Geonic/Gaonic 14, 18, 54, 96, 141, 164, 171, 442, 467–8
ghilala 130
Gerizim, Mount 568–9, 573–5
get 49, 240–1
gevurah 175
gezerah shavah 13
ghilala 130
Giddens, A. 447
Ginsburg, E. 363
Ginzberg, Louis 233
Goitein, S. 129
Golden Calf 6, 13, 27
Goldish, M. 49
Goldscheider, C. 275–6, 364
Golinkin, Noah 235
Gombiner, Avraham 173
Gonen al ha-yeled 306

Gordon, J. 206
goses 436
grace after meals 559; *see also birkat ha mazon*
Grade, C. 503
Greek 62, 74, 134, 163–5, 230, 361–2, 465–6, 514, 518, 562, 563, 570
Green, A. 262
Greenberg, B. 365
grief 32, 77, 331, 363, 437, 439, 441–3, 452; *see also kaddish*
Grimes, R. 14
Gross, A. 345
Gryn, H. 313
Guide of the Perplexed 165

haggadah 16, 74, 76, 79, 82–3, 107–22, 263–70, 375; Christian influence 383; Judezmo 476, 495; progressive 379; third seder 506 *see haggadot*, Passover
haggadot 16, 71, 76, 79, 82–3, 89, 107–10, 114–15, 263–4, 266–9, 375
hadas/Besamimbüchse 79 *see havdalah*
hafokh 21
hakhnasat ha-kallah 29 *see* weddings
hair 34, 82, 157, 214, 318–19, 327–34, 336–7, 339–40, 342, 376, 391, 442, 477, 519, 521, 550
halakhah 12, 15, 21, 59, 67, 74, 77, 137–8, 141–3, 146, 164–5, 166–9, 170, 175, 196, 204, 207, 215–6, 222, 224, 229, 234, 235, 240–1, 250, 270, 349, 358, 387, 429, 431, 451, 484, 501
Halevi 52, 132, 205
Halevy, Haim David 164
Halivni, D. 13, 207
Halkin H.. 270–1
Haman 39, 82, 87, 296, 340, 484, 564
hametz 184
Hanau, Solomon 469
hanhagot 217
Hanukkah/ Hanukah 39, 78, 81–2, 150, 153–4, 235, 263, 269, 283, 433, 483, 495, 563, 569, 577, 580
Hanukkiah 585
haredi 262, 431–2 *see* Israel, prayers for, orthodox, ultra
Hashomer Hatzair 375, 379
Hasidism 215–28
Haskalah 203–14, 331, 417, 502
Hatam Sofer 172
hatzi kaddish 172
havdalah 13–14, 35, 79, 117, 270, 418, 476, 479, 506
hazan 96, 98, 174–5, 469 *see* cantor
Hebrew 463–71
Hegel 249
headcover 130
Heine, H. *see The Rabbi of Bacherach*
Herman, G. 39

Herod 59–61
Herzl, T. 428
Herzog, I. 427, 429
Heschel A. J. 164, 175, 176, 240, 269, 364
Heschel of Apt, Avraham Yehoshua 220, 223
Heschel, Susannah 268
hesped 31–2
Hillel 270, 311–12, 362
Hirsch, Samson Raphael 470
Hoffman, L. 26
Holdheim, S. 350
Holocaust 156–7, 175, 283, 287, 331–2, 336, 357, 376, 428, 444, 470, 494, 496, 505–6, 563, 566
Hoshen Mishpat 47
house *see* Islam
Huli, Ya'qov 476, 488
ḥulla 130
huppah 28, 29–31, 76, 107, 581–82
Hymes, D. 18–19

Idel, Moshe 140
inclusion 526–39
initiation 30, 83, 94, 101, 104–7, 328, 348, 544, 562, 587
interfaith rituals 579–89
Iron Age 59
Isaac 526
Isaiah 3, 127, 187, 191, 260, 465, 543
Islam, medieval world of: books 125–9; clothing 129–31; the house 131–4
Israel, prayers for the State of 427–35
Isserles 165, 349, 404–5, 407–9, 442

Jacob 3, 15, 34, 35, 36, 37, 38, 74, 291, 338, 355, 400, 404, 441, 464, 526
Joseph 338, 569, 579
Jacobsen, I. 417
al-Jahiz 126
Jakobovits, I. 430
Jellinek, A. 18
Jeremiah 3, 189, 257, 487, 502
Jerusalem 35, 40, 60, 62, 64–8, 73, 81, 82, 153, 168, 170, 182, 186, 188–9, 197, 209, 234–5, 237–8, 239, 318–19, 321, 329, 357, 361–3, 375, 391, 418, 427, 432–3, 438, 440, 449–50, 454, 456, 464, 466, 476, 480, 482–4, 493, 503, 505, 514, 540–2, 544–7, 549–50, 558–9, 561, 565, 582, 584
Jewish Renewal 154, 250, 253, 354, 446, 448
Jonah 3–4, 257, 545, 548
Josephus 38, 59, 62, 63, 65, 541, 545–6, 550
Joshua 482
jubba 130
Judaizers 31, 562, 566
Judea/n 14, 61–4, 125, 450, 517, 545, 549, 559
Judezmo 472–500
jukanniyya 130

Kabbalah 137–8, 141–6, 222, 225, 255, 343
kaddish 171–2, 288, 300, 373–4, 377, 438–43, 449, 451–7, 475
kahal 306
kal vahomer 13
kalal 64
kallot 18
Kanarek, J. 13
Kant, I. 212, 249
Kaplan D. 254–5
Kaplan, M. 231–5, 239–40, 264–5
kapporet 73
Karaites 179–92
Karo, Joseph 47–8, 49, 54, 136–7, 142–3, 146, 163, 165, 169–71, 349, 403–4, 407, 408–9, 476, 490; *see also* Shulchan Arukh
kashrut/kosher 13, 15–16, 62, 73, 101, 128, 181, 194, 220, 229–30, 250, 263, 283, 297, 299, 306, 308, 320, 346–52, 354–8, 386, 390, 480, 547, 585; *see also* food
Katchko, A. 420
kavod ha-met 330
keri'ah/kriah 77, 439, 451; *see also* death and dying
ketubah 28, 153–4, 167, 241, 402–3, 410, 581, 583
kibbutz 352–3, 373, 375–7, 446, 449–50, 452–5
kiddushin 27, 166, 284
al-Kindi, Abd al-Masih 126
kittel 168, 175, 330
klal ufrat 13
klal yisrael 229
Klein, I. 366
kloyz 218
kohanim 62, 170, 565; *see also* birkat kohanim, priests
kochim 65
kol nidrei 420, 482
kollelim 175
Kook, I. 308, 353, 429
kosher *see* kashrut
Kraemer, D. 40–3, 347, 349–51
kvitl 220

Lag B'omer 145, 328, 486
Langer, R. 40
law 46–55
Leontopolis 60
Levinas 311–13
Levites 27, 52, 414
likutim 168
Lords Prayer 541
lulav 17, 67, 81, 169, 185
Luria, I. 329

ma'aseh goyim 166
ma'aseh haroqeah 101, 106

ma'aseh merkaveh 218
Maccabees 39
magic 223, 511–25
Maharal of Prague 312
mahzor 73, 76, 80, 96, 97, 99–100, 101–2, 104, 106, 107, 115, 121–2, 234, 242
Maimon, Solomon 221
Maimonides: on Ashkenazi practices 174; ban on the study of his philosophy 164; on burial 440; clothes 338; codifier 165–6; covering women's hair 339; decoration of his works 82, 127; gentile courts 48; harlotry 404; hukkim vs. mishpatim 311; on imitation of divine mercy 257–8; life 163; marriage 411; the middle way 236; music 414–15; on pride 342; principles of faith 13, 185–6, 380; property law 132; reasons for commandments 16; sex on shabat 366; spending on food for shabat 355; rules on blessings 172–3; Talmud 54; women and *mitsvot* 169
majlis 133
malḥafa 130
Mapu, Abraham 206
Marks, S. 28
maror 118 *see* bitter herbs
marriage 27–31, 49, 76, 107, 140, 153–4, 166–9, 198, 235, 240, 277, 294, 286, 237, 241, 278, 282, 286–8, 299, 301, 318–19, 330, 339, 348, 373, 386–7, 395, 400–13, 446, 457, 484, 486, 491–2, 505, 565, 569, 572–3, 579, 581–9; *see also* dowry, gender, sex
Marx, Dalia 428, 430
Maskilim 203–204, 225 *see* Haskalah
material culture: early modern period 137–49; Islamic world 125–36; images in medieval books 93–124
matsah 109–12, 114, 116, 118
matzah 36, 40, 118, 211, 264, 265, 285, 564; *see also* matsah, Passover
mayse 502
meat 347, 353–8 *see* kashrut
mekhashefah 511
Megillah 39, 82, 565; *see also* Esther, Purim
Melammed, R. 350
menorah 67, 154, 281, 283, 363
menstruation 51, 63, 167, 194, 217, 340, 387, 571–2
Merchant of Venice 311
Messiah 186, 361–2, 414, 428, 430, 493, 543, 560–1
met 438
mezuzah 154, 157–8, 513, 536, 585
Midrash 12–24, 98–9, 100, 154, 238, 242, 254–5, 312, 338, 362, 390, 431, 467–8, 550
mikveh 27, 62, 63, 65, 68, 77, 170, 173, 194, 330, 333, 339, 340, 363, 389, 396, 404, 492, 502, 544
Mill, J.S, 306

minhag 96, 104, 116, 120, 143, 164–6, 215, 240, 419, 487
minyan 5, 170–1, 241–2, 300, 326, 343, 389, 396, 419, 440, 442, 502, 565, 572
miracle 7, 37, 39, 81, 209, 211–12, 226
Miriam 16, 21, 154, 267–8, 487, 526
mishkan 167, 312
Mishnah: apodictic nature of 13; and *Birkat HaMazon* 170; on boundaries 297; casting of lots 545; and challah 387; daily prayers 42; food blessings 40; and funerals 449; *hesped* 31–2; and Kabbalah 143, 146; and law 301; and Levinas 312; and magic 512–13, 517; Passover 16, 263, 486; *pidyon ha-ben* 27; pilgrimage festivals 35–6; Purim 39; Reform 250; on Shabat 173, 362; Siclian synagogues 73; *talit* 99; and Talmud 25, 43; and Yehuda ha-Nasi 309; on *Yeridat HaDorot* 138; water purification 551; weddings 30, 76
Mishneh Torah 16, 48, 54, 82, 165, 167, 169, 172–4, 257, 366, 414, 416, 527
Mitnagdim 225
mitzvah/mitzvot 3, 15–16, 21, 138, 141, 166, 169, 229, 235, 381–2, 409, 437, 501, 587
Mizrahi 176, 339, 388, 450
modernity 20, 116, 209, 223, 249–50, 253, 258, 294–5, 297–8, 319, 345, 351, 374, 417, 436, 438, 504, 564
modesty 317–19; *see also* clothes, *tzniut*
mohel 308
Mordechai 39, 82 *see* Purim
Moses: and Aaron 9; illustrated 76; blessing Israel 579; changing customs 540; hero in mahzorim 83, 138; his inclusivity 527; in the Judezmo seder 485–7; law at Sinai 250, 361, 561; in magic 513; marrying a Midianite 579; his mother Miriam 16; and music 415; his prayers 464; punished 4; seat of 67; Samaritans following his law 568–9; in secular haaggadot 375, 383; his stutter 526: warns the community 6; in wedding service 582; wedding Zipporah 197
Musar 502
music 414–26

Nachman of Bratzlav/Breslov 416
Nahmanides 163, 169, 171, 404, 437
naming girls 27, 490, 565, 586
ner tamid 67
New Age *see* Amen ritual
Newman, J. 53
Nicaea Counil of 562
niddah 339–40, 390, 394, 572
Najara, Israel 146
niggun 419
Nimrod 338
nusakh 422, 418–19, 420, 425; *see also* cantors

Obadiah of Bertinaro 75
Ochs. V. 154, 394, 457
olat tamid 312
onen 31
Orach Hayyim 163, 170
Orthodox, modern 193–202
Orthodox, ultra 176–7, 193, 196, 315–22, 366, 388, 368, 380, 384, 431–3, 470, 505, 579; *see also* haredi
Ottoman 137–40, 142, 145–6, 472–99
over le asiyatan 173–3
Ozar Masaot 174

Palestinian Arabs 20, 61, 262, 268, 298, 354, 376
parokhet 73
payot 328–30, 332, 340
Passover: blood libel 208; Christianity 541, 561–2, 564; exodus 464; freedom 209, 263–7, 269, 344; images 71, 76, 78–9, 82–3, 87, 93–4, 101–2, 107–9, 111, 117–18, 122; Judezmo 475–6, 483–6, 495; Karaites 184; kashrut 355; midrash 16, 18, 20; music 420; remembrance 444; ritual objects 150, 154; Samaritans 568–9, 573–5; secular 373–5; seder 464, 467, 470; talmud 35–6, 40; temple 60, 62; *see also* Pesach
Peleg-Barkat, O 61
Pentateuch 3–4, 6, 8–10, 171, 568
Pentecost: *Acts* 541–2; Emendation 137; Peter 543, 546; Samaritans 574; tikkun 144; Torah cycle 561–2 *see* Shavuot
Perl, Yosef 221
Pesach; *Acts* 541; cleaning pictured 94, 107–9; explaining to children 464; family 283–4; food 355–6; interfaith 585; Jewish vs. Christian view of 561–2, 564; Judezmo 475–6, 483–6, 495; Miriam's cup 16; music 420; and remembrance 444; Sa'adya 467–8; Samaritans 573–4, 568–9; secular observance 373–6; Yiddish haggadah 506; *see also* haggadah, Passover, seder
peshat 183
Pesiqta de rav kahana 17–18, 51, 54
pidyon 220–1
pidyon ha-ben see redemption of the first born; ietists, Ashkenazi 98, 100, 138, 144–5, 217, 465
Pilcher, J. 346
pilgrimage 34, 59–60, 62, 68, 81, 131, 145, 220, 234, 364, 420, 425, 444, 480, 482, 493, 561, 568, 573–4
Pirqe de Rabbi Eliezer 13–14
Pitzele, P. 19
piyyut 80, 83, 98, 100–1, 107, 121, 468
Plaskow, J. 20–1
poskei halakhah 142
power 4, 6, 10, 13–15, 17, 19, 21, 47, 49, 98, 128, 132, 138, 140, 146–7, 155, 179, 194, 197–9, 215–16, 223, 225–6, 257, 259–61, 263–4, 266–7, 276, 280–1, 294, 299, 309, 315,

319, 329, 338, 345, 367, 389, 39–2, 394–7, 403, 411, 416–17, 425, 439, 442, 454, 463, 465–9, 486, 511, 518, 520–1, 526–7, 530–1, 533–4, 537, 544, 580–1
priest/priestly 3, 7–10, 9–10, 17, 21, 27, 62, 65, 67, 74, 94–5, 169, 230, 291, 335, 338, 351, 369, 438, 464–6, 514, 541, 544, 558, 564–5, 568, 571–2, 588
Promised Land 4, 527
Protestant 138, 236, 249, 250–1, 254, 417, 564
puberty 171, 330
purification 217
purity, laws of 50–3, 63–5, 68, 146, 188, 194, 205, 217, 230, 317, 339
Purim; book of Esther 39; clothes 340; and Christians 564, 569; family 283, 296; *al ha-nisim* prayer 433; Judezmo 472, 478, 483–5, 495–6; justice 260; Karaites 180; purim play 505–6; Samaritan children 576; Talmud 81–2, 87; *see also* Esther
purity 27, 32, 50–3, 63–5, 68, 146, 194, 205, 217, 230, 317, 339–40, 346, 347, 351, 357, 394–5, 470, 543, 565, 569, 570, 572, 576; *see also mikveh, niddah, tzniut*

qedushta 17
qiddush 467, 470 *see kiddush*
Qumran 64–5, 68, 465, 544–5

The Rabbi of Bacherach 207–12
Rabbanites 180 *see* Karaites
Rambam *see* Maimonides
Ramban *see* Nahmanides
Red heifer 52–3
Ramah 50
Reconstructionist Judaism 235
Redemption of the first born 26, 27, 75, 571
Reform 8, 16, 20, 138, 164, 203, 205–6, 209–12, 223, 229–32, 235–7, 240, 248–56, 258, 260, 263–4, 268, 275, 279, 280, 284, 287, 288–9, 291, 313, 315, 327, 330, 345, 350–1, 358, 366–7, 372, 375, 381, 417, 419, 430, 433, 440, 446, 449, 450, 453, 455–7, 470, 506, 529, 563–4, 579–80, 586, 587–8
Regan, Ruti 533–4
rehitza 438
Rabins, A. 20
Rema 171
revelation 36, 40, 139, 225, 229, 231, 239–41, 301, 346, 386, 465, 468, 569
Rif 171
ring 76–7, 107–8, 166, 513, 518–19, 582
Riskin, Shlomo 198
Roman 14, 25, 32, 35, 52, 54, 59, 72–4, 76, 96, 126, 134, 230, 361, 368, 440, 465–6, 514, 517, 520, 523, 542, 559, 562, 571, 575, 562, 571, 575

Roper, L. 349
Rosenblum, Jason 345
Rosh Chodesh 21, 392
Rosh Hashanah 17, 37–9, 67, 80, 98, 168, 171, 174–5, 184, 278, 282, 355, 420, 479–80
Rubin, N. 26

Sa'adya Gaon 96, 163
Sabbath 13–14, 16–18, 26, 34–5, 62, 78–80, 101, 109, 144, 150, 154, 183–4, 194–5, 209–10, 215, 217, 221, 225, 234, 278, 284, 288, 291, 361–70, 371–2, 376, 376, 420, 422, 441, 457, 466, 468, 474, 476–9, 484–5, 488, 494, 501, 503, 505, 517, 541–3, 574, 550, 559, 562, 570–1; *see also* Shabat
Sabbatian 138, 147
Sacks, J. 258
sacrifice 571
sagerin 417
Salonica 138, 542–3 *see* Judezmo
Samaritans 568–78
Samuel 511
sandeket 75
Satmar 329, 341, 505
Satlow, M. 28–31
Saul 511
Schechner, R. 19
Schechter, Solomon 229, 231–3
Schechter, Mathilda 233
Schlanger, Judith 128
Schitts Creek 294–5
Schneerson, Levi 168
Schorsch, Ismar 235
Schwartz, Shuly 235–6
scroll 39, 60, 67, 73, 74, 95, 100, 118, 126–7, 150–1, 242, 477, 482, 536, 561, 562, 565, 570, 571, 574–5
seat of Moses 67
secular rituals 371–84; *see also* funerals, alternative
seder 16, 20, 35, 39, 79, 83, 94, 101, 107, 109–15, 118, 122, 150, 154, 208, 223, 235, 263–72, 375–6, 466, 468, 470, 475, 481, 483, 485–8, 495, 506, 563, 568, 585; *see also* Passover
Sefardi/Sephardi/Sepharadim 17, 71, 77, 140, 163–78, 205, 212, 231, 327–8, 403, 407, 427, 442, 443, 468, 472–500
Sefer ha-Razim 521
seudat havra'ah 441
sex 15, 21, 28–30, 34, 35, 38, 63, 130, 145, 168–9, 194, 211, 295, 297, 299, 317–18, 333, 339–40, 340, 366, 395, 400–13, 446, 549, 572
Shabat; boundaries 297; balance 342; candles 173, 263; Conservatives 229, 235, 241–2, 284; fires and Karaites 183; food 355; gender 285–6; justice 262, 269; Karaite liturgy 186; music 415; naming children 478; modern Orthodox 281; family 288, 290–1; images 336; Reform 250;

secular kabbalat shabbat 372; *see also* candles, family, Sabbath, material culture, secular rituals
Shabbethai Ha-Sofer of Przemysl 469
Shacter- Shalomi, Z. 354
shaliach/sheliach tsibur 97–8, 416
Shas 176
ShaS 501, 505
shaving 34, 329, 550, 329–32, 339, 342
Shavuot 18, 36, 60, 78, 83, 100, 105–16, 137, 329, 420, 444, 478, 486–7, 496, 503, 561, 565, 574; *see also* Pentecost
shechinah 137, 144–6, 171, 363, 439, 531
shehecheyanu 168
Sheiltot de Rav Aha 18
shema/ sh'ma 15, 40, 42–3, 96, 223, 312, 362, 466, 559
Shenker, Ben zion 422
shevut 34
Shimon ben Gamliel 15, 42, 167
shiva 77, 288, 331, 333, 441–4, 493–4, 565, 588 see death and dying
shloshim 331, 442
shmira 438
shmirat ha-guf 317
shoes *see* footwear
shofar 17, 37, 67, 80, 117–18, 120, 153, 184, 212, 481–2, 520, 574
shomer 438, 568
shtibl 218, 502
Shuldiner, D. 271
Shulchan Arukh 48, 50, 54, 143, 165, 169, 170–1, 173–4, 349, 395, 404, 406–8, 415, 420, 436, 440, 442; *see also* Isserles, Karo
siddur 79, 96, 144, 176, 186, 188, 190, 232, 238, 242, 328, 389, 422, 429–30, 434, 506, 535
sifrei minhagim 143
Simchat Torah 6, 36, 40, 83, 100, 166, 240, 259, 309, 415, 482, 561, 574
Sinai, Mount 6, 36, 40, 83, 100, 166, 240, 259, 309, 425, 561, 574
Singer I B 333, 501, 503–5
Singer I J 504
Singer, Simeon 470
skin 63, 73, 81, 183, 279, 305, 309, 329, 336, 338, 451, 571
Sklare, Marshall 233
slavery 16, 264–7, 269, 401, 412
social justice 257–74
Solomon 185, 405, 414, 518, 541, 551
Spinoza 212, 306, 312
Star of David 154–5, 157, 335, 416
Staub, M. 271
Steiner, G. 19
Steinsalz, A. 454
strange fire 4
strangers 4, 206, 208, 224, 257, 526
Streisand, Barbra 333

sukkah 17, 35–6, 39, 81–2, 169, 185, 283, 470, 483, 574–5, 585
Sukkot 15, 35–6, 40, 60, 67, 81, 184–5, 464, 482–3, 561, 568, 574–5; *see also sukkah*
Summit, J. 422
sword of Moses 513
swordfish kosher controversy 249–50
synagogue 17–18, 33, 42, 59, 63, 65–8, 71–5, 79–80, 82–7, 94–103, 117, 120, 122, 130, 133, 144–6, 150–2, 155–6, 158, 166, 170, 174, 184, 186, 188, 194, 198, 200, 208, 209, 211–12, 216, 218–20, 224, 229–30, 232–42, 248, 250, 252, 254, 263, 268, 275, 284–5, 299, 309, 328, 337, 341, 366, 371, 387, 389, 415–21, 427–9, 431, 438–9, 441–4, 465, 467, 469, 474–82, 486, 488–9, 494–5, 501–3, 505, 528, 532, 535–7, 542–3, 558–60, 562–5, 568, 570–5, 580–2, 585–8

ta'amei hamitzvot 16 *see* reasons
tachrichin 438
takkanot ha-kahal 49
tallit/talit 80, 96–7, 99–100, 107, 118, 131, 167–8, 187, 328, 330, 396
Talmud: Adam 13; *amida* 173; basic principles 311; calendrical rituals 34; and casting of lots 545; comforting the mourner 32–4; Conservatives 229, 241; and cremation 440; daily prayer 42–3; on death 437; divorce 410, 411; dowry 402; feast and blessings 30–1; food blessings 40–2; Frankel 230; funeral and disposal 31–2; and the Geonim 467; hair 333; high holidays 37–8; Hillel 312, 362; *huppah* 29–30; on impurity 51; as institution 301; and justice 257, 261; kaddish 172; Kaplan 233; Karaites 179, 189; knowledge of 343; and magic 512–13, 516–17, 519; and Maimonides 54; marriage 167–8; matchmaking 387; minor festivals 38–40; and Moses 138; mourning meal 390; and music 415, 452; and Noah 441; Pilgrimage festivals 34–7; Reform 250, 254; and Rosh Hashana 355; Sabbath 34–5; Samaritans 569; Schechter 232; and ShaS 501; Song at the Sea 17; State of Israel 429, 431; study of 107; at the Tish 221; Tu B'shvat 483; and vows 550; reciting the blessings 169–71; sex 404–6; wedding procession 29; wedding feast and blessings 30–31; women 268; and Zohar 142–3
Talmud torah 205, 212, 479
Tanakh 180, 526
Tanna 19, 25–8, 30–3, 35–42, 465, 467
Targum 17–19, 95, 465, 468, 496
techiyat ha-metim 440
tefilin 168, 171, 185, 328, 491, 570
Temples 4, 8, 10, 17, 35–6, 38, 40–2, 50–1, 59–63, 65–8, 81, 83, 94–5, 147, 168–9, 188,

209, 223–4, 254, 310, 329, 346–7, 357, 361, 363, 368–9, 375, 391, 414–15, 438, 464, 466, 482–3, 488, 540–1, 544–5, 558, 560–3, 565, 568, 574–5, 584; Second 125–6, 164, 271, 355, 362, 465, 487, 559; Third 60, 94
Temple Mount 240, 454
Temple of Peace 62
Ten Commandments 17, 34, 100, 361, 366, 574
tena'im 167
thawb 130
Tigay, J. 465
tikkun 154, 253, 255, 270
tikkun leil shavuto see Pentecost Emendation
Tish 221
Tisha b'Av 329, 481, 487–8; *see also* fasting
tkhines 502
Tosafot 169, 407
Transparent 294–302
Trencher, Mark 196, 199
Trivellato, F. 49
tsadik/tzaddik/tzadik 146, 218, 424
tzedakah 328
Tu b'shvat 147, 389, 474, 483–4
Tur 50
Turner, V. 21, 373, 385–90
Twersky, I. 54
tziduk ha-din 452
tzitzit 328, 330, 341
tzniut 155, 318, 336, 339–40
Tzum Gedalya 481

ultra orthodox *see* orthodox, ultra
upsherin 327–9
Uziel, Benzion 175, 427

Veganism 353–4
vidui 38, 436–7, 168, 187
Vilna Gaon 170

Waskow 262, 266–7, 269–70
water 4, 16, 18, 51, 60, 62–3, 82–3, 102, 106, 118, 131, 133, 154, 173, 256, 268, 330–1, 346, 387, 438, 452, 488, 513, 520–1, 524, 543–4, 548, 551, 564, 572, 575

wedding 28–31, 33, 41, 76–7, 107–8 (Moses, 153–4, 166–9 Ash vs. Sef, 240, 296, 362, 367, 372–3, 387, 389, 404, 446, 449, 451, 457, 492, 504–5, 563, 565–6, 572–3, 581, 583, 587
Weinreich, Max 501
Weisenberg, J. 419
Wessely M. 205
Western Wall 59, 94–5, 297, 300, 328, 480
wine 16, 26, 30, 33, 35–6, 39, 41, 76, 78–9, 81, 107, 118, 128, 150, 154, 156, 167, 184, 221, 266, 268, 347, 355, 365, 377–8, 386–7, 467, 477, 479, 496, 513, 559–60, 566
Wise, Isaac 230
Wissenschaft des Judentums 229, 469
Wittgenstein 300, 309
Wouk, H. 364
Wimpel 75

yahrzeit 218, 443
yarmulke 199, 328–30, 339
Yehuda Ha-Nasi 309
yeridat ha-dorot 138
yeshiva 18, 139–40, 175–6, 193, 195, 197–9, 240, 280, 333, 371–2, 431, 503–4, 533
Yiddish 104, 116–17, 120, 141, 153–4, 175, 205, 218, 220–1, 231, 239, 265, 266, 295, 299, 327, 443, 492, 501–7, 564
yizkor 443–4; Yiddish additions 506
Yochanan 52
Yom ha'atzmaut 432
Yom hazikaron 432
Yom Kippur 37–8, 40, 80–1, 97, 150, 168, 174–5, 184, 237, 263, 282, 286, 296, 299, 310, 371–2, 379, 428, 438, 444, 474, 481–2, 504, 574, 585
Yosef, Ovadia 168

zimun 171
Zionist 156, 188, 229, 236–7, 239, 254, 258–9, 265, 294–5, 352, 358, 374–6, 418, 428–9, 432
Zohar 137–49, 338, 437, 441, 469
Zoroastrian 32
Zvi, Sabbatai 147 *see* Sabbatian

Milton Keynes UK
Ingram Content Group UK Ltd.
UKHW021829180324
439528UK00006B/40